Fundamentals of
Corporate Finance

THE McGRAW-HILL/IRWIN SERIES IN FINANCE, INSURANCE AND REAL ESTATE

Stephen A. Ross Franco Modigliani Professor of Finance and Economics
Sloan School of Management Massachusetts Institute of Technology Consulting Editor

Financial Management

Block, Hirt, and Danielsen
Foundations of Financial Management
Fourteenth Edition

Brealey, Myers, and Allen
Principles of Corporate Finance
Tenth Edition

Brealey, Myers, and Allen
Principles of Corporate Finance, Concise
Second Edition

Brealey, Myers, and Marcus
Fundamentals of Corporate Finance
Seventh Edition

Brooks
FinGame Online 5.0

Bruner
Case Studies in Finance: Managing for
Corporate Value Creation
Sixth Edition

Cornett, Adair, and Nofsinger
Finance: Applications and Theory
Second Edition

Cornett, Adair, and Nofsinger
M: Finance
First Edition

DeMello
Cases in Finance
Second Edition

Grinblatt (editor)
Stephen A. Ross, Mentor: Influence through
Generations

Grinblatt and Titman
Financial Markets and Corporate Strategy
Second Edition

Higgins
Analysis for Financial Management
Tenth Edition

Kellison
Theory of Interest
Third Edition

Ross, Westerfield, and Jaffe
Corporate Finance
Ninth Edition

Ross, Westerfield, Jaffe, and Jordan
Corporate Finance: Core Principles and
Applications
Third Edition

Ross, Westerfield and Jordan
Essentials of Corporate Finance
Seventh Edition

Ross, Westerfield, and Jordan
Fundamentals of Corporate Finance
Ninth Edition

Shefrin
Behavioral Corporate Finance: Decisions that
Create Value
First Edition

White
Financial Analysis with an Electronic
Calculator
Sixth Edition

Investments

Bodie, Kane, and Marcus
Essentials of Investments
Eighth Edition

Bodie, Kane, and Marcus
Investments
Ninth Edition

Hirt and Block
Fundamentals of Investment Management
Tenth Edition

Hirschey and Nofsinger
Investments: Analysis and Behavior
Second Edition

Jordan and Miller
Fundamentals of Investments: Valuation and
Management
Sixth Edition

Stewart, Piros, and Heisler
Running Money: Professional Portfolio
Management
First Edition

Sundaram and Das
Derivatives: Principles and Practice
First edition

Financial Institutions and Markets

Rose and Hudgins
Bank Management and Financial Services
Eighth Edition

Rose and Marquis
Financial Institutions and Markets
Eleventh Edition

Saunders and Cornett
Financial Institutions Management: A Risk
Management Approach
Seventh Edition

Saunders and Cornett
Financial Markets and Institutions
Fifth Edition

International Finance

Eun and Resnick
International Financial Management
Sixth Edition

Robin
International Corporate Finance
First Edition

Real Estate

Brueggeman and Fisher
Real Estate Finance and Investments
Fourteenth Edition

Ling and Archer
Real Estate Principles: A Value Approach
Third Edition

Financial Planning and Insurance

Allen, Melone, Rosenbloom, and Mahoney
Retirement Plans: 401(k)s, IRAs, and Other
Deferred Compensation Approaches
Tenth Edition

Altfest
Personal Financial Planning
First Edition

Harrington and Niehaus
Risk Management and Insurance
Second Edition

Kapoor, Dlabay, and Hughes
Focus on Personal Finance: An active
approach to help you develop successful
financial skills
Third Edition

Kapoor, Dlabay, and Hughes
Personal Finance
Tenth Edition

SEVENTH EDITION

Fundamentals of
Corporate Finance

Richard A. Brealey
London Business School

Stewart C. Myers
Sloan School of Management
Massachusetts Institute
of Technology

Alan J. Marcus
Carroll School of
Management
Boston College

**McGraw-Hill
Irwin**

FUNDAMENTALS OF CORPORATE FINANCE

Published by McGraw-Hill/Irwin, a business unit of The McGraw-Hill Companies, Inc., 1221 Avenue of the Americas, New York, NY, 10020.

Some ancillaries, including electronic and print components, may not be available to customers outside the United States.

This book is printed on acid-free paper.

2 3 4 5 6 7 8 9 0 QVS/QVS 1 0 9 8 7 6 5 4 3

ISBN 978-0-07-131474-9
MHID 0-07-131474-1

To Our Wives

About the Authors

Richard A. Brealey

Professor of Finance at the London Business School. He is the former president of the European Finance Association and a former director of the American Finance Association. He is a fellow of the British Academy and has served as a special adviser to the Governor of the Bank of England and as director of a number of financial institutions. Professor Brealey is also the author (with Professor Myers and Franklin Allen) of this book's sister text, *Principles of Corporate Finance*.

Stewart C. Myers

Gordon Y Billard Professor of Finance at MIT's Sloan School of Management. He is past president of the American Finance Association and a research associate of the National Bureau of Economic Research. His research has focused on financing decisions, valuation methods, the cost of capital, and financial aspects of government regulation of business. Dr. Myers is a director of The Brattle Group, Inc., and is active as a financial consultant. He is also the author (with Professor Brealey and Franklin Allen) of this book's sister text, *Principles of Corporate Finance*.

Alan J. Marcus

Mario Gabelli Professor of Finance in the Carroll School of Management at Boston College. His main research interests are in derivatives and securities markets. He is co-author (with Zvi Bodie and Alex Kane) of the texts *Investments* and *Essentials of Investments*. Professor Marcus has served as a research fellow at the National Bureau of Economic Research. Professor Marcus also spent 2 years at Freddie Mac, where he helped to develop mortgage pricing and credit risk models. He currently serves on the Research Foundation Advisory Board of the CFA Institute.

Preface

This book is about corporate finance. It focuses on how companies invest in real assets, how they raise the money to pay for these investments, and how those assets ultimately affect the value of the firm. It also provides a broad introduction to the financial landscape, discussing, for example, the major players in financial markets, the role of financial institutions in the economy, and how securities are traded and valued by investors. The book offers a framework for systematically thinking about most of the important financial problems that both firms and individuals are likely to confront.

Financial management is important, interesting, and challenging. It is *important* because today's capital investment decisions may determine the businesses that the firm is in 10, 20, or more years ahead. Also, a firm's success or failure depends in large part on its ability to find the capital that it needs.

Finance is *interesting* for several reasons. Financial decisions often involve huge sums of money. Large investment projects or acquisitions may involve billions of dollars. Also, the financial community is international and fast-moving, with colorful heroes and a sprinkling of unpleasant villains.

Finance is *challenging*. Financial decisions are rarely cut and dried, and the financial markets in which companies operate are changing rapidly. Good managers can cope with routine problems, but only the best managers can respond to change. To handle new problems, you need more than rules of thumb; you need to understand why companies and financial markets behave as they do and when common practice may not be best practice. Once you have a consistent framework for making financial decisions, complex problems become more manageable.

This book provides that framework. It is not an encyclopedia of finance. It focuses instead on setting out the basic *principles* of financial management and applying them to the main decisions faced by the financial manager. It explains why the firm's owners would like the manager to increase firm value and shows how managers choose between investments that may pay off at different points of time or have different degrees of risk. It also describes the main features of financial markets and discusses why companies may prefer a particular source of finance.

We organize the book around the key concepts of modern finance. These concepts, properly explained, simplify the subject. They are also practical. The tools of financial management are easier to grasp and use effectively when presented in a consistent conceptual framework. This text provides that framework.

Modern financial management is not "rocket science." It is a set of ideas that can be made clear by words, graphs, and numerical examples. The ideas provide the "why" behind the tools that good financial managers use to make investment and financing decisions.

We wrote this book to make financial management clear, useful, interesting, and fun for the beginning student. We set out to show that modern finance and good financial practice go together, even for the financial novice.

Fundamentals and Principles of Corporate Finance

This book is derived in part from its sister text *Principles of Corporate Finance*. The spirit of the two books is similar. Both apply modern finance to give students a working ability to make financial decisions. However, there are also substantial differences between the two books.

First, we provide much more detailed discussion of the principles and mechanics of the time value of money. This material underlies almost all of this text, and we spend a lengthy chapter providing extensive practice with this key concept.

Second, we use numerical examples in this text to a greater degree than in *Principles*. Each chapter presents several detailed numerical examples to help the reader become familiar and comfortable with the material.

Third, we have streamlined the treatment of most topics. Whereas *Principles* has 34 chapters, *Fundamentals* has only 25. The relative brevity of *Fundamentals* necessitates a broader-brush coverage of some topics, but we feel that this is an advantage for a beginning audience.

Fourth, we assume little in the way of background knowledge. While most users will have had an introductory accounting course, we review the concepts of accounting that are important to the financial manager in Chapter 3.

Principles is known for its relaxed and informal writing style, and we continue this tradition in *Fundamentals*. In addition, we use as little mathematical notation as possible. Even when we present an equation, we usually write it in words rather than symbols. This approach has two advantages. It is less intimidating, and it focuses attention on the underlying concept rather than the formula.

Organizational Design
Fundamentals is organized in eight parts.

Part 1 (Introduction)   provides essential background material. In the first chapter we discuss how businesses are organized, the role of the financial manager, and the financial markets in which the manager operates. We explain how shareholders want managers to take actions that increase the value of their investment, and we introduce the concept of the opportunity cost of capital and the trade-off that the firm needs to make when assessing investment proposals. We also describe some of the mechanisms that help to align the interests of managers and shareholders. Of course, the task of increasing shareholder value does not justify corrupt and unscrupulous behavior. We therefore discuss some of the ethical issues that confront managers.

Chapter 2 surveys and sets out the functions of financial markets and institutions. This chapter also reviews the crisis of 2007–2009. The events of those years illustrate clearly why and how financial markets and institutions matter.

A large corporation is a team effort, and so the firm produces financial statements to help the players monitor its progress. Chapter 3 provides a brief overview of these financial statements and introduces two key distinctions—between market and book values and between cash flows and profits. This chapter also discusses some of the shortcomings in accounting practice. The chapter concludes with a summary of federal taxes.

Chapter 4 provides an overview of financial statement analysis. In contrast to most introductions to this topic, our discussion is motivated by considerations of valuation and the insight that financial ratios can provide about how management has added to the firm's value.

Part 2 (Value)   is concerned with valuation. In Chapter 5 we introduce the concept of the time value of money, and, since most readers will be more familiar with their own financial affairs than with the big leagues of finance, we motivate our discussion by looking first at some personal financial decisions. We show how to value long-lived streams of cash flows and work through the valuation of perpetuities and annuities. Chapter 5 also contains a short concluding section on inflation and the distinction between real and nominal returns.

Chapters 6 and 7 introduce the basic features of bonds and stocks and give students a chance to apply the ideas of Chapter 5 to the valuation of these securities. We show how to find the value of a bond given its yield, and we show how prices of bonds fluctuate as interest rates change. We look at what determines stock prices and how stock valuation formulas can be used to infer the return that investors expect. Finally, we see how investment opportunities are reflected in the stock price and why analysts focus on the price-earnings multiple. Chapter 7 also introduces the concept of market efficiency. This concept is crucial to interpreting a stock's valuation; it also provides a framework for the later treatment of the issues that arise when firms issue securities or make decisions concerning dividends or capital structure.

The remaining chapters of Part 2 are concerned with the company's investment decision. In Chapter 8 we introduce the concept of net present value and show how to calculate the NPV of a simple investment project. We then consider more complex investment proposals, including choices between alternative projects, machine replacement decisions, and decisions of when to invest. We also look at other measures of an investment's attractiveness—its internal rate of return, payback period, and profitability index. We show how the profitability index can be used to choose between investment projects when capital is scarce. The appendix to Chapter 8 shows how to sidestep some of the pitfalls of the IRR rule.

The first step in any NPV calculation is to decide what to discount. Therefore, in Chapter 9 we work through a realistic example of a capital budgeting analysis, showing how the manager needs to recognize the investment in working capital and how taxes and depreciation affect cash flows.

We start Chapter 10 by looking at how companies organize the investment process and ensure everyone works toward a common goal. We then go on to look at various techniques to help managers identify the key assumptions in their estimates, such as sensitivity analysis, scenario analysis, and break-even analysis. We explain the distinction between accounting break-even and NPV break-even. We conclude the chapter by describing how managers try to build future flexibility into projects so that they can capitalize on good luck and mitigate the consequences of bad luck.

Part 3 (Risk) is concerned with the cost of capital. Chapter 11 starts with a historical survey of returns on bonds and stocks and goes on to distinguish between the specific risk and market risk of individual stocks. Chapter 12 shows how to measure market risk and discusses the relationship between risk and expected return. Chapter 13 introduces the weighted-average cost of capital and provides a practical illustration of how to estimate it.

Part 4 (Financing) begins our discussion of the financing decision. Chapter 14 provides an overview of the securities that firms issue and their relative importance as sources of finance. In Chapter 15 we look at how firms issue securities, and we follow a firm from its first need for venture capital, through its initial public offering, to its continuing need to raise debt or equity.

Part 5 (Debt and Payout Policy) focuses on the two classic long-term financing decisions. In Chapter 16 we ask how much the firm should borrow and we summarize bankruptcy procedures that occur when firms can't pay their debts. In Chapter 17 we study how firms should set dividend and payout policy. In each case we start with Modigliani and Miller's (MM's) observation that in well-functioning markets the decision should not matter, but we use this observation to help the reader understand why financial managers in practice *do* pay attention to these decisions.

Part 6 (Financial Analysis and Planning) starts with long-term financial planning in Chapter 18, where we look at how the financial manager considers the combined effects of investment and financing decisions on the firm as a whole. We also show how measures of internal and sustainable growth help managers check that the firm's planned growth is consistent with its financing plans. Chapter 19 is an introduction to short-term financial planning. It shows how managers ensure that the firm will have enough cash to pay its bills over the coming year, and describes the principal sources of short-term borrowing. Chapter 20 addresses working capital management. It describes the basic steps of credit management, the principles of inventory management, and how firms handle payments efficiently and put cash to work as quickly as possible.

Part 7 (Special Topics) covers several important but somewhat more advanced topics—mergers (Chapter 21), international financial management (Chapter 22), options (Chapter 23), and risk management (Chapter 24). Some of these topics are touched on in earlier chapters. For example, we introduce the idea of options in Chapter 10, when we show how companies build flexibility into capital projects. However, Chapter 23 generalizes this material, explains at an elementary level how options are valued, and provides some examples of why the financial manager needs to be concerned about options. International finance is also not confined to Chapter 22. As one might expect from a book that is written by an international group of authors, examples from different countries and financial systems are scattered throughout the book. However, Chapter 22 tackles the specific problems that arise when a corporation is confronted by different currencies.

Part 8 (Conclusion)   contains a concluding chapter (Chapter 25), in which we review the most important ideas covered in the text. We also introduce some interesting questions that either were unanswered in the text or are still puzzles to the finance profession. Thus the last chapter is an introduction to future finance courses as well as a conclusion to this one.

Routes through the Book

There are about as many effective ways to organize a course in corporate finance as there are teachers. For this reason, we have ensured that the text is modular, so that topics can be introduced in different sequences.

We like to discuss the principles of valuation before plunging into financial planning. Nevertheless, we recognize that many instructors will prefer to move directly from Chapter 4 (Measuring Corporate Performance) to Chapter 18 (Long-Term Financial Planning) in order to provide a gentler transition from the typical prerequisite accounting course. We have made sure that Part 6 (Financial Analysis and Planning) can easily follow Part 1.

Similarly, we like to discuss working capital after the student is familiar with the basic principles of valuation and financing, but we recognize that here also many instructors prefer to reverse our order. There should be no difficulty in taking Chapter 20 out of order.

When we discuss project valuation in Part 2, we stress that the opportunity cost of capital depends on project risk. But we do not discuss how to measure risk or how return and risk are linked until Part 3. This ordering can easily be modified. For example, the chapters on risk and return can be introduced before, after, or midway through the material on project valuation.

Changes in the Seventh Edition

Users of previous editions of this book will not find dramatic changes in either the material or the ordering of topics. But throughout we have tried to make the book more up to date and easier to read. Here are some of the ways that we have done this.

Improving the Flow   A major part of our effort in revising this text was spent on improving the flow. Sometimes this has meant a word change here or a redrawn diagram there, but in several instances we have made more substantial changes. For example, we now introduce the concept of the investment trade-off and the cost of capital in Chapter 1. We think it fits more naturally there. Look also at the start of Chapter 4 (Measuring Corporate Performance). We emphasize here that financial ratios serve to show how much value management has added and what the sources of that value are. Figure 4.1 signposts the questions that managers need to ask and some of the financial ratios that help to answer them. We think that this introduction serves to prevent the chapter from becoming a tedious list of ratios. Similarly, in Chapter 8, we have reworked the discussion of the internal rate of return and its pitfalls and believe that the discussion of IRR now flows more easily.

Updating   Of course, in each new edition we try to ensure that any statistics are as up to date as possible. For example, since the previous edition we have available an extra 3 years of data on security returns. These show up in the figures in Chapter 11 of the long-run returns on stocks, bonds, and bills. Measures of EVA, data on security ownership, bond yields, and dividend and repurchase payouts are just a few of the other cases where data have been brought up to date.

Recent Events Not surprisingly, there are plenty of references in this edition to the crisis of 2007–2009 and its impact on financial managers. But there are also many less dramatic examples of recent changes in the financial landscape. For example, as you might expect, in our discussion of ethical issues, Bernard Madoff steps briefly on stage. Another example is Chapter 3 (Accounting and Finance), where you will find a discussion of SOX, of mark-to-market accounting, and of recent developments in international accounting standards.

Concepts Agency theory and behavioral finance are not new ideas, but the dot-com boom and bust and the financial crisis have focused increased attention on them. That is reflected in several places throughout the book. The material on efficient markets in Chapter 7 now includes a section on price bubbles as well as a discussion of behavioral biases. Other topics that have received increasing emphasis include company valuation, real options, and stock repurchases.

New Illustrative Boxes The text contains a number of boxes with illustrative real-world examples. Many of these are new. Look, for example, at the box in Chapter 1 that discusses the difficult ethical issues raised by Goldman Sachs' sale of a package of low-grade mortgages during the financial crisis, the box in Chapter 6 that introduces credit default swaps, or the box in Chapter 17 that describes the dividend cut by JPMorgan.

More Worked Examples We have added more worked examples in the text, many of them taken from real companies. For instance, when we discuss company valuation in Chapter 7, we show how the constant-growth model can be used to value Aqua America.

New Calculator and Spreadsheet Boxes We have reworked the explanations of how to use calculators or spreadsheets to solve financial problems. For example, we have shown how use of the function key can guide users through spreadsheet functions. We believe that this is much simpler than remembering the formula for each function. As in past editions, every spreadsheet in the text is available on the text Web site at **www.mhhe.com/bmm7e.** We have also written many new Web exercises, several of which require the student to download data into a spreadsheet for analysis.

Assurance of Learning
Assurance of learning is an important element of many accreditation standards. *Fundamentals of Corporate Finance, Seventh Edition,* is designed specifically to support your assurance-of-learning initiatives. Each chapter in the book begins with a list of numbered learning objectives, which are referred to in the end-of-chapter problems and exercises. Every test bank question is also linked to one of these objectives, in addition to level of difficulty, topic area, Bloom's Taxonomy level, and AACSB skill area. *Connect,* McGraw-Hill's online homework solution, and *EZ Test,* McGraw-Hill's easy-to-use test bank software, can search the test bank by these and other categories, providing an engine for targeted assurance-of-learning analysis and assessment.

AACSB Statement
The McGraw-Hill Companies is a proud corporate member of AACSB International. Understanding the importance and value of AACSB accreditation, *Fundamentals of Corporate Finance, Seventh Edition,* has sought to recognize the curricula guidelines detailed in the AACSB standards for business accreditation by connecting selected questions in the test bank to the general knowledge and skill guidelines found in the AACSB standards.

The statements contained in *Fundamentals of Corporate Finance, Seventh Edition,* are provided only as a guide for the users of this text. The AACSB leaves content coverage and assessment within the purview of individual schools, the mission of the school, and the faculty. While *Fundamentals of Corporate Finance, Seventh Edition,* and the teaching package make no claim of any specific AACSB qualification or evaluation, we have, within the test bank, labeled selected questions according to the six general knowledge and skills areas.

ORGANIZATION

New and Enhanced Pedagogy
A great deal of effort has gone into expanding and enhancing the features in **Fundamentals of Corporate Finance.**

Brealey / Myers / Marcus
Your guide through the challenging landscape of corporate finance.

Chapter Opener

Each chapter begins with a chapter narrative to help set the tone for the material that follows. Learning Objectives are also included to provide a quick introduction to the material students will learn and should understand fully before moving to the next chapter.

CHAPTER 5

The Time Value of Money

Key Terms in the Margin

Key terms are presented in bold and defined in the margin as they are introduced. A glossary is also available at the back of the book.

5.4 Level Cash Flows: Perpetuities and Annuities

Frequently, you may need to value a stream of equal cash flows. For example, a home mortgage might require the homeowner to make equal monthly payments for the life of the loan. For a 30-year loan, this would result in 360 equal payments. A 4-year car loan might require 48 equal monthly payments. Any such sequence of equally spaced, level cash flows is called an **annuity.** If the payment stream lasts forever, it is called a **perpetuity.**

annuity
Equally spaced level stream of cash flows, with a finite maturity.

perpetuity
Stream of level cash payments that never ends.

How to Value Perpetuities

Some time ago the British government borrowed by issuing loans known as consols. Consols are perpetuities. In other words, instead of repaying these loans, the British government pays the investors a fixed annual payment in perpetuity (forever).

How might we value such a security? Suppose that you could invest $100 at an interest rate of 10%. You would earn annual interest of $.10 \times \$100 = \$10$ per year and

Numbered Examples

Numbered and titled examples are integrated in each chapter. Students can learn how to solve specific problems step-by-step as well as gain insight into general principles by seeing how they are applied to answer concrete questions and scenarios.

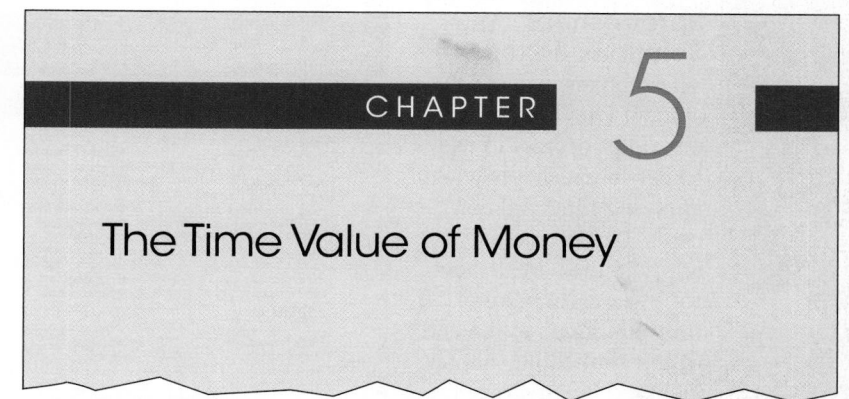

EXAMPLE 5.8 ▶ Winning Big at the Lottery

In August 2006 eight lucky meatpackers from Nebraska pooled their money to buy Powerball lottery tickets and won a record $365 million. We suspect that the winners received unsolicited congratulations, good wishes, and requests for money from dozens of more or less worthy charities, relations, and newly devoted friends. In response, they could fairly point out that the prize wasn't really worth $365 million. That sum was to be paid in 30 equal annual installments of $12.167 million each. Assuming that the first payment occurred at the end of 1 year, what was the present value of the prize? The interest rate at the time was about 6%.

The present value of these payments is simply the sum of the present values of each annual payment. But rather than valuing the payments separately, it is much easier to treat them as a 30-year annuity. To value this annuity, we simply multiply $12.167 million by the 30-year annuity factor:

$$PV = 12.167 \times \text{30-year annuity factor}$$

$$= 12.167 \times \left[\frac{1}{r} - \frac{1}{r(1 + r)^{30}}\right]$$

At an interest rate of 6%, the annuity factor is

$$\left[\frac{1}{.06} - \frac{1}{.06(1.06)^{30}}\right] = 13.7648$$

(We could also look up the annuity factor in Table A.3.) The present value of the cash payments is $12.167 × 13.7648 = $167.5 million, much less than the much-

What makes Brealey/Myers/Marcus such a powerful learning tool?

PEDAGOGY

Spreadsheet Solutions Boxes

These boxes provide the student with detailed examples of how to use Excel spreadsheets when applying financial concepts. Questions that apply to the spreadsheet follow and their solutions are given at the end of the applicable chapter. Denoted by an icon, these spreadsheets are available on the book Web site at **www.mhhe.com/bmm7e.**

SPREADSHEET SOLUTIONS

Multiple Cash Flows

While uneven cash-flow problems are conceptually straightforward, they rapidly become tedious and prone to errors from "typos," even if you use a financial calculator. It really helps to use spreadsheets. The following figure is a spreadsheet solution of Example 5.7.

The spreadsheet lists the time until each payment in column A. This value is used for the number of periods (nper) in the PV formula in column C. The values for the cash flow in each future period are entered as negative numbers in the PV formula. The present values (column C) therefore appear as positive numbers. Column E shows an alternative to the use of the PV function, where we calculate present values directly.

An interactive version of this spreadsheet can be found at www.mhhe.com/bmm7e.

Spreadsheet Questions

5.1 Find the present value of the three payments at interest rates of 5% and 11%. Explain why the values change as they do.

5.2 Total payments over the 3 years are $16,000. What is the present value if the three payments are instead $6,000, $5,000, $5,000? Why does the present value fall? (Use an interest rate of 8%.)

eXcel

You can find this spreadsheet at www.mhhe.com/bmm7e.

	A	B	C	D	E
1	Finding the present value of multiple cash flows using a spreadsheet				
2					
3	Time until CF	Cash flow	Present value	Formula in Col C	Alternative formula for Col C

Excel Exhibits

Selected exhibits are set as Excel spreadsheets. They are also available on the book Web site at **www.mhhe.com/bmm7e.**

SPREADSHEET 19.1 Dynamic Mattress's cash budget for 2010 (figures in millions of dollars)

	A	B	C	D	E
	Quarter:	First	Second	Third	Fourth
1					
2					
3	A. Accounts Receivable				
4	Receivables (beginning of period)	30.0	32.5	30.7	38.2
5	Sales	87.5	78.5	116.0	131.0
6	Collections				
7	On sales in current period (80%)	70.0	62.8	92.8	104.8
8	On sales in previous period (20%)[a]	15.0	17.5	15.7	23.2
9	Total collections	85.0	80.3	108.5	128.0
10	Receivables (end of period) = Rows 4+5-9	32.5	30.7	38.2	41.2
11					
12	B. Cash Budget				
13	Sources of cash				
14	Collections of accounts receivable (row 9)	85.0	80.3	108.5	128.0
15	Other	1.5	0.0	12.5	0.0
16	Total collections	86.5	80.3	121.0	128.0
17	Uses of cash				
18	Payments of accounts payable	65.0	60.0	55.0	50.0
19	Labor & other expenses	30.0	30.0	30.0	30.0
20	Capital expenses	32.5	1.3	5.5	8.0

eXcel

You can find this spreadsheet at www.mhhe.com/bmm7e.

Finance in Practice Boxes

These are excerpts that appear in most chapters, usually from the financial press, providing real-life illustrations of the chapter's topics, such as ethical choices in finance, disputes about stock valuation, financial planning, and credit analysis.

FINANCE IN PRACTICE

The Hazards of Secured Bank Lending

The National Safety Council of Australia's Victoria Division had been a sleepy outfit until John Friedrich took over. Under its new management, NSC members trained like commandos and were prepared to go anywhere and do anything. They saved people from drowning, fought fires, found lost bushwalkers, and went down mines. Their lavish equipment included 22 helicopters, 8 aircraft, and a mini-submarine. Soon the NSC began selling its services internationally.

Unfortunately the NSC's paramilitary outfit cost millions of dollars to run—far more than it earned in revenue. Friedrich bridged the gap by borrowing $A236 million of debt. The banks were happy to lend because the NSC's debt appeared well secured. At one point the company showed $A107 mil-

suspicious banker would ask to inspect a particular container. Friedrich would then explain that it was away on exercise, fly the banker across the country in a light plane, and point to a container well out in the bush. The container would of course be empty, but the banker had no way to know that.

Six years after Friedrich was appointed CEO, his massive fraud was uncovered. But a few days before a warrant could be issued, Friedrich disappeared. Although he was eventually caught and arrested, he shot himself before he could come to trial. Investigations revealed that Friedrich was operating under an assumed name, having fled from his native Germany, where he was wanted by the police. Many rumors continued to circulate about Friedrich. He was variously

Calculator Boxes and Exercises

In a continued effort to help students grasp the critical concept of the time value of money, many pedagogical tools have been added throughout the first section of the text. Financial Calculator boxes provide examples for solving a variety of problems, with directions for the three most popular financial calculators.

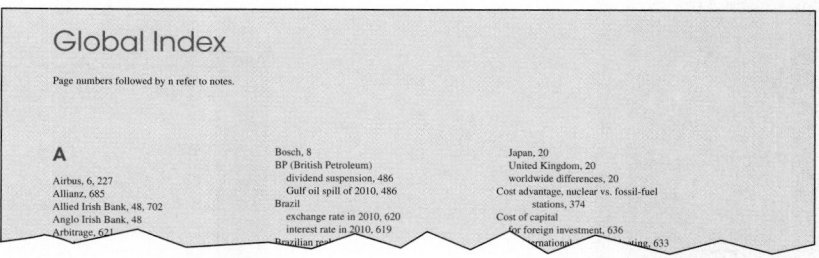

FINANCIAL CALCULATOR

An Introduction to Financial Calculators

The basic financial calculator uses five keys that correspond to the inputs for common problems involving the time value of money:

| n | i | PV | PMT | FV |

Each key represents the following input:

the number of periods. (We have been using t t...

"compute" key, which may be labeled *CPT* or *COMP*, and then press *FV*. Your calculator should show a value of −$177.16 trillion, which, except for the minus sign, is the future value of $24.

Why does the minus sign appear? Most calculators treat cash flows as either inflows (shown as positive numbers) or outflows (negative numbers). For example, if you borrow $100 today at an interest rate of 12%, you receive money now (a *positive* cash flow), but you will have to pay back $112 in a year, a *negative* cash flow at that time. Therefore, the calculator displays *FV* as a negative number. The following time line of cash flows shows the reasoning employed. The final negative cash flow of $112 has the same present value...

Self-Test Questions

Provided in each chapter, these helpful questions enable students to check their understanding as they read. Answers are worked out at the end of each chapter.

If you start with the present value of $15,133.06 in the bank, you could make the first $8,000 payment and be left with $7,133.06. After 1 year, your savings account would receive an interest payment of $7,133.06 × .08 = $570.64, bringing your account to $7,703.70. Similarly, you would make the second $4,000 payment and be left with $3,703.70. This sum left in the bank would grow with interest to $4,000, just enough to make the last payment.

The present value of a stream of future cash flows is the amount you need to invest today to generate that stream.

Self-Test 5.5

In order to avoid estate taxes, your rich aunt Frederica will pay you $10,000 per year for 4 years, starting 1 year from now. What is the present value of your benefactor's planned gifts? The interest rate is 7%. How much will you have 4 years from now if you invest each gift at 7%?

Global Index

The Global Index appears at the end of the text for easy reference to international material.

Global Index

Page numbers followed by n refer to notes.

A

Airbus, 6, 227
Allianz, 685
Allied Irish Bank, 48, 702
Anglo Irish Bank, 48
Arbitrage, 621

Bosch, 8
BP (British Petroleum)
  dividend suspension, 486
  Gulf oil spill of 2010, 486
Brazil
  exchange rate in 2010, 620
  interest rate in 2010, 619
Brazilian re... ...ting, 633

Japan, 20
  United Kingdom, 20
  worldwide differences, 20
Cost advantage, nuclear vs. fossil-fuel
  stations, 374
Cost of capital
  for foreign investment, 636

Summary
This feature helps review the key points and learning objectives to help provide closure to the chapter.

SUMMARY

What are the differences between the bond's coupon rate, current yield, and yield to maturity? (*LO1*)

A bond is a long-term debt of a government or corporation. When you own a bond, you receive a fixed interest payment each year until the bond matures. This payment is known as the coupon. The **coupon rate** is the annual coupon payment expressed as a fraction of the bond's **face value.** At maturity the bond's face value is repaid. In the United States most bonds have a face value of $1,000. The **current yield** is the annual coupon payment expressed as a percentage of the bond price. The **yield to maturity** measures the average rate of return to an investor who purchases the bond and holds it until maturity, accounting for coupon income as well as the difference between purchase price and face value.

How can one find the market price of a bond given its yield to maturity or find a bond's yield given its

Bonds are valued by discounting the coupon payments and the final repayment by the yield to maturity on comparable bonds. The bond payments discounted at the bond's yield to maturity equal the bond price. You may also start with the bond price and ask what interest rate the bond offers. the interest   that equ   he present val   of bond payments to

Quiz, Practice, and Challenge Problems
New end-of-chapter problems are included for even more hands-on practice. Each question is labeled by topic, and learning objective, and questions are separated by level of difficulty. Answers to selected problems are provided at the back of the book.

QUESTIONS

connect
FINANCE

QUIZ

1. **Risk Management.** Large businesses spend millions of dollars annually on insurance. Why? Should they insure against all risks or does insurance make more sense for some risks than others? (*LO1*)

2. **Hedging.** (*LO2*)
   a. An investor currently holding $1 million in long-term Treasury bonds becomes concerned about increasing volatility in interest rates. She decides to hedge her risk by using Treasury bond futures contracts. Should she buy or sell such contracts?
   b. The treasurer of a corporation that will be issuing bonds in 3 months also is concerned about interest rate volatility and wants to lock in the price at which he could sell 8% coupon bonds. How would he use Treasury bond futures contracts to hedge his firm's position?

3. **Commodity Futures.** What commodity futures are traded on futures exchanges? Who do you think could usefully reduce risk by buying each of these contracts? Who do you think might

PRACTICE PROBLEMS

7. **Hedging with Futures versus Puts.** A gold-mining firm is concerned about short-term volatility in its revenues. Gold currently sells for $1,200 an ounce, but the price is volatile and could fall as low as $1,000 or rise as high as $1,400 in the next month. The company will bring 1,000 ounces to the market next month. (*LO2*)
   a. What will be total revenues if the firm remains unhedged for gold prices of $1,000, $1,200, and $1,400 an ounce?
   b. The futures price of gold for 1-month-ahead delivery is $1,080. What will be the firm's total revenues at each gold price if the firm enters a 1-month futures contract to deliver 1,000 ounces of gold?
   c. What will total revenues be if the firm buys a 1-month put option to sell gold for $1,080 an ounce? The puts cost $12 per ounce.

CHALLENGE PROBLEMS

26. **Option Portfolios.** Repeat the three parts of Practice Problem 9 except that now the problem is to devise a package of investments with the payoffs shown in Figure 23.9. This package of investments is known as a "butterfly." (*LO1*)

27. **Option Pricing.** Look again at the Google call option that we valued in Section 23.2. Suppose that by the end of January 2011 the price of Google stock could double to $920 or halve to $230. Everything else is unchanged from our example. (*LO2*)
   a. What would be the value of the Google call in January 2011 if the stock price is $920? If it is $230?
   b. Show that a strategy of buying three calls provides exactly the same payoffs as borrowing the present value of $460 from the bank and buying two shares.
   c. What is the net cash flow in July 2010 from the policy of borrowing PV($460) and buying two shares?
   d. What does thi   tell you abou   value of the   option?

Excel Problems

Most chapters contain problems, denoted by an icon, specifically linked to Excel templates that are available on the book Web site at **www.mhhe.com/bmm7e**.

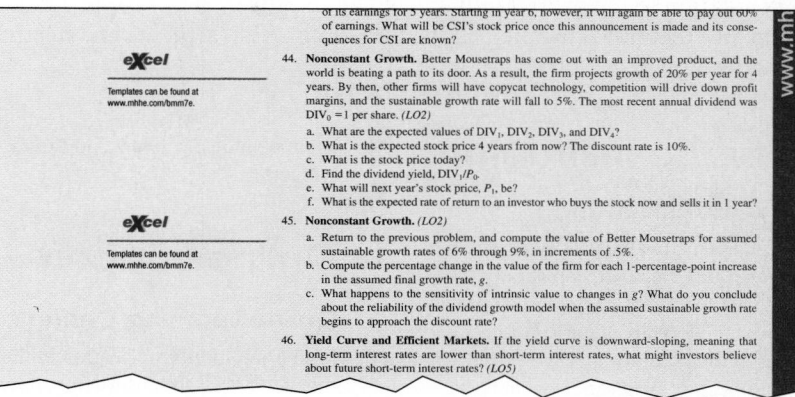

of its earnings for 5 years. Starting in year 6, however, it will again be able to pay out 60% of earnings. What will be CSI's stock price once this announcement is made and its consequences for CSI are known?

44. **Nonconstant Growth.** Better Mousetraps has come out with an improved product, and the world is beating a path to its door. As a result, the firm projects growth of 20% per year for 4 years. By then, other firms will have copycat technology, competition will drive down profit margins, and the sustainable growth rate will fall to 5%. The most recent annual dividend was $DIV_0 = 1$ per share. *(LO2)*
   a. What are the expected values of DIV_1, DIV_2, DIV_3, and DIV_4?
   b. What is the expected stock price 4 years from now? The discount rate is 10%.
   c. What is the stock price today?
   d. Find the dividend yield, DIV_1/P_0.
   e. What will next year's stock price, P_1, be?
   f. What is the expected rate of return to an investor who buys the stock now and sells it in 1 year?

45. **Nonconstant Growth.** *(LO2)*
   a. Return to the previous problem, and compute the value of Better Mousetraps for assumed sustainable growth rates of 6% through 9%, in increments of .5%.
   b. Compute the percentage change in the value of the firm for each 1-percentage-point increase in the assumed final growth rate, g.
   c. What happens to the sensitivity of intrinsic value to changes in g? What do you conclude about the reliability of the dividend growth model when the assumed sustainable growth rate begins to approach the discount rate?

46. **Yield Curve and Efficient Markets.** If the yield curve is downward-sloping, meaning that long-term interest rates are lower than short-term interest rates, what might investors believe about future short-term interest rates? *(LO5)*

Web Exercises

New to this edition! Most chapters have Web Exercises that allow students to utilize the Internet to apply their knowledge and skills with real world companies.

   c. What happens to the sensitivity of intrinsic value to changes in g? What do you conclude about the reliability of the dividend growth model when the assumed sustainable growth rate begins to approach the discount rate?

46. **Yield Curve and Efficient Markets.** If the yield curve is downward-sloping, meaning that long-term interest rates are lower than short-term interest rates, what might investors believe about future short-term interest rates? *(LO5)*

WEB EXERCISES

1. Review Table 7.2, which lists the market values of several firms. Update the table. Which company's value has changed by the greatest percentage since 2010, when the table was created? (*Hint:* Look for the price per share and the number of shares outstanding. The product of the two is total market capitalization.) Now calculate book value per share. Have the book values for any firm changed? Which seems to be more stable, book or market value? Why?

2. From finance.yahoo.com, obtain the price-earnings ratios of Adobe Systems (ADBE) and American Electric Power (AEP). Which of these two firms seems to be more of a "growth stock"? Now obtain a forecast of each firm's expected earnings per share in the coming year. You can find earnings forecasts on yahoo.com under "Analysts Estimates." What is the present value of growth opportunities for each firm as a fraction of the stock price? (Assume, for simplicity, that the required rate of return on the stocks is $r = 8\%$.) Are the relative values you obtain for PVGO consistent with the P/E ratios?

Minicases

Integrative minicases allow students to apply their knowledge to relatively complex, practical problems and typical real-world scenarios.

MINICASE

Terence Breezeway, the CEO of Prairie Home Stores, wondered what retirement would be like. It was almost 20 years to the day since his uncle Jacob Breezeway, Prairie Home's founder, had asked him to take responsibility for managing the company. Now it was time to spend more time riding and fishing on the old Lazy Beta Ranch.

Under Mr. Breezeway's leadership Prairie Home had grown slowly but steadily and was solidly profitable. (Table 7.6 shows earnings, dividends, and book asset values for the last 5 years.) Most of the company's supermarkets had been modernized and its brand name was well known.

Mr. Breezeway was proud of this record, although he wished that Prairie Home could have grown more rapidly. He had passed up several opportunities to build new stores in adjacent counties. Prairie Home was still just a family company. Its common stock was distributed among 15 grandchildren and nephews of Jacob Breezeway, most of whom had come to depend on generous regular dividends. The commitment to high dividend payout[16] had

Prairie Home's value depended not just on its current book value or earnings but on its future prospects, which were good. One financial projection (shown in the top panel of Table 7.7) called for growth in earnings of over 100% by 2022. Unfortunately, this plan would require reinvestment of all of Prairie Home's earnings from 2016 to 2019. After that the company could resume its normal dividend payout and growth rate. Mr. Breezeway believed this plan was feasible.

He was determined to step aside for the next generation of top management. But before retiring, he had to decide whether to recommend that Prairie Home Stores "go public"—and before that decision he had to know what the company was worth.

The next morning he rode thoughtfully to work. He left his horse at the south corral and ambled down the dusty street to Mike Gordon's Saloon, where Francine Firewater, the company's CFO, was having her usual steak-and-beans breakfast. He asked Ms. Firewater to prepare a formal report to Prairie Home stockholders, valuing the company on the assumption that its shares were publicly traded.

Supplements

In addition to the overall refinement and improvement of the text material, considerable effort was put into developing an exceptional supplement package to provide students and instructors with an abundance of teaching and learning resources.

For the Instructor

Instructor's Manual

Updated and enhanced by Peter Crabb, Northwest Nazarene University, this supplement includes a descriptive preface containing alternative course formats and case teaching methods, a chapter overview and outline, key terms and concepts, a description of the PowerPoint slides, video teaching notes, related Web links, and pedagogical ideas.

PowerPoint Presentation System

Prepared by Nicholas Racculia, Saint Vincent College and Thomas McLaughlin, these visually stimulating slides have been fully updated with colorful graphs, charts, and lists. The slides can be edited or manipulated to fit the needs of a particular course.

Print and Online Test Bank

Nicholas Racculia, Saint Vincent College, with help from Thomas McLaughlin, has revised and added new questions and problems. Over 2,000 true/false, multiple-choice, and discussion questions/problems are available to the instructor at varying levels of difficulty and comprehension. All questions are tagged by learning objective, topic, AACSB category, and Bloom's Taxonomy level. Complete answers are provided for all test questions and problems, and creating computerized tests is easy with EZ Test Online!

Solutions Manual

Peter Crabb, Northwest Nazarene University, has prepared this resource containing solutions to all the end-of-chapter problems. This can also be made available to your students or packaged with the text at a discount. Please contact your McGraw-Hill/Irwin representative for more details.

DVD

ISBN 13: 9780073363653
ISBN 10: 0073363650
Our professionally produced videos showcase key topics in corporate finance, such as time value of money and capital budgeting.

Online Support

Online Learning Center

Find a wealth of information online! At this book Web site, instructors have access to teaching supports such as electronic files of the ancillary materials and solutions templates for the Excel problems. Students have access to study materials created specifically for this text as well as the Excel spreadsheets, which have been denoted by an icon in the text. A link to the following support material, as described below, is also included.

McGraw-Hill *Connect*™ Finance

Less Managing. More Teaching. Greater Learning.

McGraw-Hill *Connect*™ Finance is an online assignment and assessment solution that connects students with the tools and resources they'll need to achieve success.

McGraw-Hill *Connect*™ Finance helps prepare students for their future by enabling faster learning, more efficient studying, and higher retention of knowledge.

McGraw-Hill *Connect*™ Finance Features

Connect™ Finance offers a number of powerful tools and features to make managing assignments easier, so faculty can spend more time teaching. With *Connect*™ Finance, students can engage with their coursework anytime and anywhere, making the learning process more accessible and efficient.

Simple Assignment Management With *Connect*™ Finance, creating assignments is easier than ever, so you can spend more time teaching and less time managing. The assignment management function enables you to:

- Create and deliver assignments easily with selectable end-of-chapter questions and test bank items.
- Streamline lesson planning, student progress reporting, and assignment grading to make classroom management more efficient than ever.
- Go paperless with the eBook and online submission and grading of student assignments.

Smart Grading When it comes to studying, time is precious. *Connect*™ Finance helps students learn more efficiently by providing feedback and practice material when they need it, where they need it. When it comes to teaching, your time also is precious. The grading function enables you to:

- Have assignments scored automatically, giving students immediate feedback on their work and side-by-side comparisons with correct answers.
- Access and review each response and manually change grades or leave comments for students to review.
- Reinforce classroom concepts with practice tests and instant quizzes.

Self-Quiz and Study The Self-Quiz and Study (SQS) connects each student to the learning resources needed for success in the course. For each chapter, students:

- Take a practice test to initiate the Self-Quiz and Study.
- Immediately upon completing the practice test, see how their performance compares to chapter learning objectives.
- Receive SQS recommendations for specific readings from the text,

supplemental study material, and practice work that will improve their understanding and mastery of each learning objective.

Student Progress Tracking *Connect™ Finance* keeps instructors informed about how each student, section, and class is performing, allowing for more productive use of lecture and office hours. The progress-tracking function enables you to:

• View scored work immediately and track individual or group performance with assignment and grade reports.
• Access an instant view of student or class performance relative to learning objectives.
• Collect data and generate reports required by many accreditation organizations, such as AACSB and AICPA.

McGraw-Hill *Connect™ Plus Finance* McGraw-Hill reinvents the textbook learning experience for the modern student with *Connect™ Plus Finance*. A seamless integration of an eBook and *Connect™ Finance*, *Connect™ Plus Finance* provides all of the *Connect™ Finance* features plus the following:

• An integrated eBook, allowing for anytime, anywhere access to the textbook.
• Dynamic links between the problems or questions you assign to your students and the location in the eBook where that problem or question is covered.
• A powerful search function to pinpoint and connect key concepts in a snap.

In short, *Connect™ Finance* offers you and your students powerful tools and features that optimize your time and energies, enabling you to focus on course content, teaching, and student learning. *Connect™ Finance* also offers a wealth of content resources for both instructors and students. This state-of-the-art, thoroughly tested system supports you in preparing students for the world that awaits.

For more information about Connect™, go to **www.mcgrawhillconnect.com**, or

contact your local McGraw-Hill sales representative.

Tegrity Campus: Lectures 24/7

Tegrity Campus is a service that makes class time available 24/7 by automatically capturing every lecture in a searchable format for students to review when they study and complete assignments. With a simple one-click, start-and-stop process, you capture all computer screens and corresponding audio. Students can replay any part of any class with easy-to-use, browser-based viewing on a PC or Mac.

Educators know that the more students can see, hear, and experience class resources, the better they learn. In fact, studies prove it. With Tegrity Campus, students quickly recall key moments by using Tegrity Campus's unique search feature. This search helps students efficiently find what they need, when they need it, across an entire semester of class recordings. Help turn all your students' study time into learning moments immediately supported by your lecture.

To learn more about Tegrity, watch a 2-minute Flash demo at **http://tegritycampus.mhhe.com**.

McGraw-Hill Customer Care Contact Information

At McGraw-Hill, we understand that getting the most from new technology can be challenging. That's why our services don't stop after you purchase our products. You can e-mail our product specialists 24 hours a day to get product training online. Or you can search our knowledge bank of frequently asked questions on our support Web site. For customer support, call **800-331-5094**, e-mail **hmsupport@ mcgraw-hill.com**, or visit **www.mhhe.**

com/support. One of our technical support analysts will be able to assist you in a timely fashion.

McGraw-Hill Higher Education and Blackboard have teamed up. What does this mean for you?

1. **Your life, simplified.** Now you and your students can access McGraw-Hill's Connect™ and Create™ right from within your Blackboard course – all with one single sign-on. Say goodbye to the days of logging in to multiple applications.
2. **Deep integration of content and tools.** Not only do you get single sign-on with Connect™ and Create™, you also get deep integration of McGraw-Hill content and content engines right in Blackboard. Whether you're choosing a book for your course or building Connect™ assignments, all the tools you need are right where you want them – inside of Blackboard.
3. **Seamless Gradebooks.** Are you tired of keeping multiple gradebooks and manually synchronizing grades into Blackboard? We thought so. When a student completes an integrated Connect™ assignment, the grade for that assignment automatically (and instantly) feeds your Blackboard grade center.
4. **A solution for everyone.** Whether your institution is already using Blackboard or you just want to try Blackboard on your own, we have a solution for you. McGraw-Hill and Blackboard can now offer you easy access to industry leading technology and content, whether your campus hosts it, or we do. Be sure to ask your local McGraw-Hill representative for details.

Blackboard

Do More

Acknowledgments

We take this opportunity to thank all of the individuals who helped us prepare this seventh edition. We want to express our appreciation to those instructors whose insightful comments and suggestions were invaluable to us during this revision.

Marlena Akhbari
Wright State University

Timothy Alzheimer
Montana State University

Tom Arnold
University of Richmond

Chenchu Bathala
Cleveland State University

Robert Balik
Western Michigan University

Richard Bauer
Saint Mary's University

LaDoris Baugh
Athens State University

Anindam Bandopadhyaya
*University of
Massachusetts–Boston*

John R. Becker Blease
*Washington State
University–Vancouver*

Edward Boyer
Temple University

Stephen Borde
*University of Central
Florida*

Stephen Buell
Lehigh University

Deanne Butchey
*Florida International
University*

Shelley Canterbury
George Mason University

Michael Casey
*University of Central
Arkansas*

Fan Chen
University of Mississippi

Nicole Choi
*Washington State
University–Pullman*

Bruce Costa
University of Montana

Morris Danielson
St. Joe's University

Kenneth Daniels
*Virginia Commonwealth
University*

Natalya Delcoure
Sam Houston State University

Alan D. Eastman
*Indiana University of
Pennsylvania*

Richard Elliot
*University of Utah-
Salt Lake City*

Mike Evans
Winthrop University

James Falter
Franklin University

John Fay
Santa Clara University

Michael Ferguson
University of Cincinnati

Richard Fedler
Georgia State University

Sharon Garrison
University of Arizona

Ashley Geisewite
*Southwest Tennessee
Community College*

Homaifar Ghassem
*Middle Tennesee State
University*

Phillip Giles
Columbia University

Gary Gray
*Penn State University-
University Park*

Mahfuzul Haque
Indiana State University

James J. Hopper
*Mississippi State
University*

Larry Holland
*University of
Arkansas–Little Rock*

Jian "Emily" Huang
*Washington State
University–Pullman*

Stoyu Ivanov
San Jose State University

Bharat Jain
Towson University

Raymond Jackson
*University of
Massachusetts–Dartmouth*

Keith Jacob
University of Montana

Benjamas Jirasakuldech
*Slippery Rock University of
Pennsylvania*

Daniel Jubinski
Saint Joseph's University

Alan Jung
*San Francisco State
University*

Ayala Kayhan
Louisiana State University

Marvin Keene
Coastal Carolina University

Eric Kelley
University of Arizona

Dong Man Kim
*California State University–
San Bernardino*

Ladd Kochman
Kennesaw State University

Mark Lane
*Hawaii Pacific
University-Honolulu*

Linda Lange
Regis University

Doug Letsch
Walden University

Scott W. Lowe
James Madison University

Yuming Li
*California State
University–Fullerton*

Sheen Liu
*Washington State
University–Vancouver*

Wilson Liu
James Madison University

Qianqiu Liu
University of Hawaii-Manoa

Yulong Ma
*California State University–
Long Beach*

Brian Maris
*Northern Arizona
University*

Jose Mercardo
*University of Central
Missouri*

Derek Mohr
*State University of New York
at Buffalo*

Tammie Mosley
*California State University–
East Bay*

Vivian Nazar
Ferris State University

Bonnie Van Ness
University of Mississippi

Srinivas Nippani
*Texas A&M University–
Commerce*

Prasad Padmanabhan
Saint Mary's University

Ohaness Paskelian
University of Houston-Downtown

Richard Ponarul
California State University-Chico

Gary Porter
John Carroll University

Eric Powers
University of South Carolina

Ronald Prange
Western Michigan University

Robert Puelz
Southern Methodist University

Nicholas Racculia
Saint Vincent College

Sunder Raghavan
Embry-Riddle University

Ganas K. Rakes
Ohio University

Thomas Rhee
California State University– Long Beach

Jong Rhim
University of Southern Indiana

Joe Riotto
New Jersey City University

Mukunthan Santhanakrishnan
Idaho State University

Maria Schutte
Michigan Technological University

Adam Schwartz
Washington & Lee University

John Settle
Portland State University

Henry Silverman
Roosevelt University

Tammie Simmons-Mosely
California State University East Bay

Michael G. Sher
Metropolitan State University

Ron Spicer
Colorado Tech University

Jan Strockis
Santa Clara University

Roberto Stein
Tulane University

Tom Strickland
Middle Tennessee State University

Joseph Tanimura
San Diego State University

Steve Tokar
University of Indianapolis

Damir Tokic
University of Houston-Downtown

Michael Toyne
Northeastern State University

James Turner
Weber State Universtiy

Joe Walker
University of Alabama–Birmingham

Kenneth Washer
Texas A&M University– Commerce

K. Matthew Wong
St. John's University

David Yamoah
Kean University

Fred Yeager
St. Louis University

Kevin Yost
Auburn University

Emilio R. Zarruk
Florida Atlantic University

Shaorong Zhang
Marshall University

Yilei Zhang
University of North Dakota

Zhong-Guo Zhou
California State University-Northridge

In addition, we would like to thank our supplement authors, Peter Crabb and Nicholas Racculia, with assistance from Thomas McLaughlin. Their efforts are much appreciated as they will help both students and instructors. We also appreciate help from Aleijda de Cazenove Balsan and Malcolm Taylor.

We are also grateful to the talented staff at McGraw-Hill/Irwin, especially Michele Janicek, Executive Editor; Karen Fisher, Development Editor II; Dana Pauley, Senior Project Manager; Matthew Diamond, Senior Designer; Melissa Caughlin, Marketing Manager; Jennifer Jelinski, Marketing Specialist; Keri Johnson, Photo Researcher; Debra Sylvester, Buyer II; and Susan Lombardi, Senior Media Project Manager and Ron Nelms, Media Project Manager.

Finally, as was the case with the last six editions, we cannot overstate the thanks due to our wives, Diana, Maureen, and Sheryl.

Richard A. Brealey
Stewart C. Myers
Alan J. Marcus

Contents in Brief

Part One
Introduction

1   Goals and Governance of the Corporation   2
2   Financial Markets and Institutions   30
3   Accounting and Finance   52
4   Measuring Corporate Performance   78

Part Two
Value

5   The Time Value of Money   112
6   Valuing Bonds   158
7   Valuing Stocks   184
8   Net Present Value and Other Investment Criteria   226
9   Using Discounted Cash-Flow Analysis to Make Investment Decisions   262
10   Project Analysis   290

Part Three
Risk

11   Introduction to Risk, Return, and the Opportunity Cost of Capital   316
12   Risk, Return, and Capital Budgeting   344
13   The Weighted-Average Cost of Capital and Company Valuation   370

Part Four
Financing

14   Introduction to Corporate Financing   398
15   How Corporations Raise Venture Capital and Issue Securities   422

Part Five
Debt and Payout Policy

16   Debt Policy   444
17   Payout Policy   478

Part Six
Financial Analysis and Planning

18   Long-Term Financial Planning   502
19   Short-Term Financial Planning   526
20   Working Capital Management   558

Part Seven
Special Topics

21   Mergers, Acquisitions, and Corporate Control   590
22   International Financial Management   618
23   Options   644
24   Risk Management   670

Part Eight
Conclusion

25   What We Do and Do Not Know about Finance   690

Appendix A   A-1
Appendix B   B
Glossary   G
Credits   C-1
Global Index   IND
Index   IND-5

Contents

Part One   Introduction

Chapter 1
Goals and Governance of the Corporation   2

1.1   **Investment and Financing Decisions**   **4**
The Investment (Capital Budgeting) Decision   6
The Financing Decision   6

1.2   **What Is a Corporation?**   **8**
Other Forms of Business Organization   9

1.3   **Who Is the Financial Manager?**   **10**

1.4   **Goals of the Corporation**   **11**
Shareholders Want Managers to Maximize Market Value   11
The Ethics of Maximizing Value   14
Do Managers Really Maximize Value?   16
Corporate Governance   19

1.5   **Careers in Finance**   **20**

1.6   **Topics Covered in This Book**   **23**
Snippets of History   23

Summary   **25**
Questions   26

Chapter 2
Financial Markets and Institutions   30

2.1   **The Importance of Financial Markets and Institutions**   **32**

2.2   **The Flow of Savings to Corporations**   **33**
The Stock Market   35
Other Financial Markets   36
Financial Intermediaries   38
Financial Institutions   40
Total Financing of U.S. Corporations   42

2.3   **Functions of Financial Markets and Intermediaries**   **43**
Transporting Cash across Time   43
Risk Transfer and Diversification   43
Liquidity   44
The Payment Mechanism   45
Information Provided by Financial Markets   45

2.4   **The Crisis of 2007–2009**   **47**

Summary   **48**
Questions   49

Chapter 3
Accounting and Finance   52

3.1   **The Balance Sheet**   **54**
Book Values and Market Values   57

3.2   **The Income Statement**   **59**
Profits versus Cash Flow   60

3.3   **The Statement of Cash Flows**   **63**
Free Cash Flow   65

3.4   **Accounting Practice and Malpractice**   **66**

3.5   **Taxes**   **68**
Corporate Tax   68
Personal Tax   69

Summary   **71**
Questions   71

Chapter 4
Measuring Corporate Performance   78

4.1   **Value and Value Added**   **80**
How Financial Ratios Help to Understand Value Added   80

4.2   **Measuring Market Value and Market Value Added**   **81**

4.3   **Economic Value Added and Accounting Rates of Return**   **84**
Accounting Rates of Return   86
Problems with EVA and Accounting Rates of Return   87

4.4   **Measuring Efficiency**   **88**

4.5   **Analyzing the Return on Assets: The Du Pont System**   **90**
The Du Pont System   90

4.6   **Measuring Financial Leverage**   **92**
Leverage and the Return on Equity   94

4.7   **Measuring Liquidity**   **95**

4.8   **Calculating Sustainable Growth**   **97**

4.9   **Interpreting Financial Ratios**   **98**

4.10 **The Role of Financial Ratios—and a Final Note on Transparency**   **101**
Transparency   103

Summary   **103**
Questions   105
Minicase   **110**

Part Two   Value

Chapter 5
The Time Value of Money   112

5.1   Future Values and Compound Interest   114

5.2   Present Values   117
Finding the Interest Rate   123

5.3   Multiple Cash Flows   124
Future Value of Multiple Cash Flows   124
Present Value of Multiple Cash Flows   126

5.4   Level Cash Flows: Perpetuities and Annuities   127
How to Value Perpetuities   127
How to Value Annuities   129
Future Value of an Annuity   133

5.5   Annuities Due   136

5.6   Effective Annual Interest Rates   138

5.7   Inflation and the Time Value of Money   139
Real versus Nominal Cash Flows   139
Inflation and Interest Rates   141
Valuing Real Cash Payments   143
Real or Nominal?   144

Summary   144
Questions   145
Minicase   156

Chapter 6
Valuing Bonds   158

6.1   The Bond Market   160
Bond Characteristics   160

6.2   Interest Rates and Bond Prices   161
How Bond Prices Vary with Interest Rates   163
Interest Rate Risk   165

6.3   Yield to Maturity   166

6.4   Bond Rates of Return   168

6.5   The Yield Curve   171
Nominal and Real Rates of Interest   172

6.6   Corporate Bonds and the Risk of Default   174
Variations in Corporate Bonds   177

Summary   178
Questions   178

Chapter 7
Valuing Stocks   184

7.1   Stocks and the Stock Market   186
Reading Stock Market Listings   187

7.2   Market Values, Book Values, and Liquidation Values   189

7.3   Valuing Common Stocks   191
Valuation by Comparables   191
Price and Intrinsic Value   192
The Dividend Discount Model   194

7.4   Simplifying the Dividend Discount Model   197
The Dividend Discount Model with No Growth   197
The Constant-Growth Dividend Discount Model   197
Estimating Expected Rates of Return   199
Nonconstant Growth   200

7.5   Growth Stocks and Income Stocks   202
Valuing Growth Stocks   205
Market-Value Balance Sheets   205

7.6   There Are No Free Lunches on Wall Street   206
Method 1: Technical Analysis   206
Method 2: Fundamental Analysis   210
A Theory to Fit the Facts   211

7.7   Market Anomalies and Behavioral Finance   212
Market Anomalies   212
Bubbles and Market Efficiency   213
Behavioral Finance   214

Summary   215
Questions   217
Minicase   223

Chapter 8
Net Present Value and Other Investment Criteria   226

8.1   Net Present Value   228
A Comment on Risk and Present Value   229
Valuing Long-Lived Projects   230

8.2   Using the NPV Rule to Choose among Projects   234
Problem 1: The Investment Timing Decision   235
Problem 2: The Choice between Long- and Short-Lived Equipment   236
Problem 3: When to Replace an Old Machine   238

8.3   The Payback Rule   239
Discounted Payback   240

8.4   The Internal Rate of Return Rule   240
A Closer Look at the Rate of Return Rule   241
Calculating the Rate of Return for Long-Lived Projects   241

A Word of Caution 243
Some Pitfalls with the Internal Rate of Return Rule 243

8.5 The Profitability Index 248
Capital Rationing 249
Soft Rationing 249
Hard Rationing 249
Pitfalls of the Profitability Index 249

8.6 A Last Look 250

Summary 251
Questions 252
Minicase 258
Appendix: More on the IRR Rule 259
Using the IRR Rule to Choose between Mutually
Exclusive Projects 259
Using the Modified Internal Rate of Return when there
are Multiple IRRs 260

Chapter 9
Using Discounted Cash-Flow Analysis to Make Investment Decisions 262

9.1 Identifying Cash Flows 264
Discount Cash Flows, Not Profits 264
Discount *Incremental* Cash Flows 266
Discount Nominal Cash Flows by the
Nominal Cost of Capital 269
Separate Investment and Financing Decisions 270

9.2 Calculating Cash Flow 271
Capital Investment 271
Operating Cash Flow 271
Changes in Working Capital 273

9.3 An Example: Blooper Industries 274
Cash-Flow Analysis 274

Calculating the NPV of Blooper's Project 276
Further Notes and Wrinkles Arising
from Blooper's Project 277

Summary 281
Questions 282
Minicase 287

Chapter 10
Project Analysis 290

10.1 How Firms Organize the Investment Process 292
Stage 1: The Capital Budget 292
Stage 2: Project Authorizations 292
Problems and Some Solutions 293

10.2 Some "What-If" Questions 294
Sensitivity Analysis 295
Scenario Analysis 297

10.3 Break-Even Analysis 298
Accounting Break-Even Analysis 298
NPV Break-Even Analysis 300
Operating Leverage 303

10.4 Real Options and the Value of Flexibility 305
The Option to Expand 305
A Second Real Option: The Option to Abandon 307
A Third Real Option: The Timing Option 307
A Fourth Real Option: Flexible Production
Facilities 308

Summary 308
Questions 309
Minicase 315

Part Three   Risk

Chapter 11
Introduction to Risk, Return, and the Opportunity Cost of Capital 316

11.1 Rates of Return: A Review 318

11.2 A Century of Capital Market History 319
Market Indexes 319
The Historical Record 319
Using Historical Evidence to Estimate
Today's Cost of Capital 322

11.3 Measuring Risk 324
Variance and Standard Deviation 324
A Note on Calculating Variance 327
Measuring the Variation in Stock Returns 327

11.4 Risk and Diversification 329
Diversification 329
Asset versus Portfolio Risk 330
Market Risk versus Specific Risk 333

11.5 Thinking about Risk 334
Message 1: Some Risks Look Big and Dangerous
but Really Are Diversifiable 335
Message 2: Market Risks Are Macro Risks 336
Message 3: Risk Can Be Measured 336

Summary 337
Questions 338

Chapter 12
Risk, Return, and Capital Budgeting 344

12.1 Measuring Market Risk 346

Measuring Beta 346

Betas for Dow Chemical and Consolidated Edison 348

Total Risk and Market Risk 350

Portfolio Betas 350

12.2 Risk and Return 352

Why the CAPM Makes Sense 354

The Security Market Line 355

How Well Does the CAPM Work? 356

Using the CAPM to Estimate Expected Returns 359

12.3 Capital Budgeting and Project Risk 359

Company versus Project Risk 359

Determinants of Project Risk 361

Don't Add Fudge Factors to Discount Rates 362

Summary 362

Questions 363

Chapter 13
The Weighted-Average Cost of Capital and Company Valuation 370

13.1 Geothermal's Cost of Capital 372

13.2 The Weighted-Average Cost of Capital 373

Calculating Company Cost of Capital as a Weighted Average 374

Use Market Weights, Not Book Weights 376

Taxes and the Weighted-Average Cost of Capital 377

What If There Are Three (or More) Sources of Financing? 378

Wrapping Up Geothermal 379

Checking Our Logic 379

13.3 Measuring Capital Structure 380

13.4 Calculating the Weighted-Average Cost of Capital 382

The Expected Return on Bonds 382

The Expected Return on Common Stock 382

The Expected Return on Preferred Stock 383

Adding It All Up 384

Real-Company WACCs 384

13.5 Interpreting the Weighted-Average Cost of Capital 384

When You Can and Can't Use WACC 384

Some Common Mistakes 385

How Changing Capital Structure Affects Expected Returns 386

What Happens When the Corporate Tax Rate Is Not Zero 387

13.6 Valuing Entire Businesses 387

Calculating the Value of the Concatenator Business 388

Summary 389

Questions 390

Minicase 394

Part Four   Financing

Chapter 14
Introduction to Corporate Financing 398

14.1 Creating Value with Financing Decisions 400

14.2 Patterns of Corporate Financing 400

Do Firms Rely Too Heavily on Internal Funds? 403

Are Firms Issuing Too Much Debt? 403

14.3 Common Stock 404

Ownership of the Corporation 406

Voting Procedures 407

Classes of Stock 407

14.4 Preferred Stock 407

14.5 Corporate Debt 409

Debt Comes in Many Forms 409

Innovation in the Debt Market 414

14.6 Convertible Securities 415

Summary 416

Questions 417

Chapter 15
How Corporations Raise Venture Capital and Issue Securities 422

15.1 Venture Capital 424
Venture Capital Companies 425

15.2 The Initial Public Offering 426
Arranging a Public Issue 427
Other New-Issue Procedures 430
The Underwriters 431

15.3 General Cash Offers by Public Companies 431
General Cash Offers and Shelf Registration 432
Costs of the General Cash Offer 433
Market Reaction to Stock Issues 433

15.4 The Private Placement 434

Summary 435
Questions 436
Minicase 439
Appendix: Hotch Pot's New-Issue Prospectus 440

Part Five   Debt and Payout Policy

Chapter 16
Debt Policy 444

16.1 How Borrowing Affects Value in a Tax-Free Economy 446
MM's Argument 447
How Borrowing Affects Earnings per Share 448
How Borrowing Affects Risk and Return 450
Debt and the Cost of Equity 451

16.2 Capital Structure and Corporate Taxes 454
Debt and Taxes at River Cruises 454
How Interest Tax Shields Contribute to the Value of Stockholders' Equity 456
Corporate Taxes and the Weighted-Average Cost of Capital 456
The Implications of Corporate Taxes for Capital Structure 458

16.3 Costs of Financial Distress 458
Bankruptcy Costs 459
Costs of Bankruptcy Vary with Type of Asset 461
Financial Distress without Bankruptcy 461

16.4 Explaining Financing Choices 463
The Trade-Off Theory 463
A Pecking Order Theory 464
The Two Faces of Financial Slack 465

Summary 467
Questions 468
Minicase 474
Appendix: Bankruptcy Procedures 475

Chapter 17
Payout Policy 478

17.1 How Corporations Pay Out Cash to Shareholders 480
Paying Dividends 480
Limitations on Dividends 481
Stock Dividends and Stock Splits 481

17.2 Stock Repurchases 482
Why Repurchases Are Like Dividends 483
Repurchases and Share Valuation 484

17.3 How Do Corporations Decide How Much to Pay Out? 485
The Information Content of Dividends and Repurchases 486

17.4 The Payout Controversy 487
Why Dividends Are Irrelevant in Perfect and Efficient Capital Markets 488
The Assumptions behind Dividend Irrelevance 490

17.5 Why Dividends May Increase Value 491

17.6 Why Dividends May Reduce Value 492
Taxation of Dividends and Capital Gains under Current Tax Law 493

Summary 494
Questions 494
Minicase 499

Part Six   Financial Analysis And Planning

Chapter 18
Long-Term Financial Planning   502

18.1 What Is Financial Planning?   504
Financial Planning Focuses on the Big Picture   504
Why Build Financial Plans?   505

18.2 Financial Planning Models   506
Components of a Financial Planning Model   506
Percentage of Sales Models   507
An Improved Model   508

18.3 Planners Beware   512
Pitfalls in Model Design   512
The Assumption in Percentage of Sales Models   513
The Role of Financial Planning Models   514

18.4 External Financing and Growth   515

Summary   519
Questions   520
Minicase   525

Chapter 19
Short-Term Financial Planning   526

19.1 Links between Long-Term and Short-Term Financing   528

19.2 Working Capital   531
The Components of Working Capital   531
Working Capital and the Cash Conversion Cycle   533
The Working Capital Trade-Off   536

19.3 Tracing Changes in Cash and Working Capital   537

19.4 Cash Budgeting   539
Forecast Sources of Cash   539
Forecast Uses of Cash   541
The Cash Balance   541

19.5 A Short-Term Financing Plan   543
Dynamic Mattress's Financing Plan   543
Evaluating the Plan   544

19.6 Sources of Short-Term Financing   545
Bank Loans   545
Secured Loans   547
Commercial Paper   548

Summary   549
Questions   550
Minicase   556

Chapter 20
Working Capital Management   558

20.1 Accounts Receivable and Credit Policy   560
Terms of Sale   560
Credit Agreements   562
Credit Analysis   562
The Credit Decision   565
Collection Policy   569

20.2 Inventory Management   571

20.3 Cash Management   573
Check Handling and Float   574
Other Payment Systems   575
Electronic Funds Transfer   576
International Cash Management   578

20.4 Investing Idle Cash: The Money Market   578
Yields on Money Market Investments   580
The International Money Market   580

Summary   581
Questions   582
Minicase   588

Part Seven   Special Topics

Chapter 21
Mergers, Acquisitions, and Corporate Control   590

21.1 Sensible Motives for Mergers   592
Economies of Scale   594

Economies of Vertical Integration   594
Combining Complementary Resources   595
Mergers as a Use for Surplus Funds   595
Eliminating Inefficiencies   595

21.2 **Dubious Reasons for Mergers 596**
Diversification 596
The Bootstrap Game 596

21.3 **The Mechanics of a Merger 598**
The Form of Acquisition 598
Mergers, Antitrust Law, and Popular Opposition 598

21.4 **Evaluating Mergers 599**
Mergers Financed by Cash 599
Mergers Financed by Stock 601
A Warning 602
Another Warning 602

21.5 **The Market for Corporate Control 602**

21.6 **Method 1: Proxy Contests 603**

21.7 **Method 2: Takeovers 604**

21.8 **Method 3: Leveraged Buyouts 607**
Barbarians at the Gate? 608

21.9 **Method 4: Divestitures,
Spin-Offs, and Carve-Outs 610**

21.10 **The Benefits and Costs of Mergers 610**

Summary 612
Questions 613
Minicase 616

Chapter 22
International Financial Management 618

22.1 **Foreign Exchange Markets 620**
Spot Exchange Rates 620
Forward Exchange Rates 622

22.2 **Some Basic Relationships 623**
Exchange Rates and Inflation 624
Real and Nominal Exchange Rates 626
Inflation and Interest Rates 626
The Forward Exchange Rate and
the Expected Spot Rate 629
Interest Rates and Exchange Rates 630

22.3 **Hedging Exchange Rate Risk 631**
Transaction Risk 631
Economic Risk 632

22.4 **International Capital Budgeting 633**
Net Present Values for Foreign Investments 633
Political Risk 635

The Cost of Capital for Foreign Investment 636
Avoiding Fudge Factors 636

Summary 637
Questions 638
Minicase 642

Chapter 23
Options 644

23.1 **Calls and Puts 646**
Selling Calls and Puts 647
Payoff Diagrams Are Not Profit Diagrams 649
Financial Alchemy with Options 650
Some More Option Magic 650

23.2 **What Determines Option Values? 652**
Upper and Lower Limits on Option Values 652
The Determinants of Option Value 652
Option-Valuation Models 655

23.3 **Spotting the Option 657**
Options on Real Assets 657
Options on Financial Assets 659

Summary 662
Questions 662

Chapter 24
Risk Management 670

24.1 **Why Hedge? 672**
The Evidence on Risk Management 673

24.2 **Reducing Risk with Options 674**

24.3 **Futures Contracts 676**
The Mechanics of Futures Trading 677
Commodity and Financial Futures 679

24.4 **Forward Contracts 680**

24.5 **Swaps 681**

24.6 **Innovation in the Derivatives Market 683**

24.7 **Is "Derivative" a Four-Letter Word? 684**

Summary 685
Questions 686

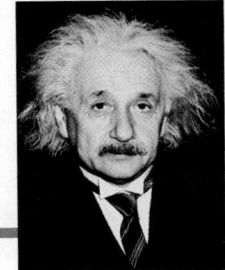

Part Eight   Conclusion

Chapter 25
What We Do and Do Not Know about Finance   690

25.1 What We Do Know: The Six Most Important Ideas in Finance   692

Net Present Value (Chapter 5)   692

Risk and Return (Chapters 11 and 12)   692

Efficient Capital Markets (Chapter 7)   692

MM's Irrelevance Propositions (Chapters 16 and 17)   693

Option Theory (Chapter 23)   693

Agency Theory   694

25.2 What We Do Not Know: Nine Unsolved Problems in Finance   694

What Determines Project Risk and Present Value?   694

Risk and Return—Have We Missed Something?   695

Are There Important Exceptions to the Efficient-Market Theory?   696

Is Management an Off-Balance-Sheet Liability?   696

How Can We Explain Capital Structure?   697

How Can We Resolve the Payout Controversy?   697

How Can We Explain Merger Waves?   697

What Is the Value of Liquidity?   698

Why Are Financial Systems Prone to Crisis?   698

25.3 A Final Word   699

Questions   699

Appendix A   A-1

Appendix B   B

Glossary   G

Credits   C-1

Global Index   IND

Index   IND-5

CHAPTER 1

Goals and Governance of the Corporation

LEARNING OBJECTIVES

After studying this chapter, you should be able to:

(1) Give examples of the investment and financing decisions that financial managers make.

(2) Distinguish between real and financial assets.

(3) Cite some of the advantages and disadvantages of organizing a business as a corporation.

(4) Describe the responsibilities of the CFO, treasurer, and controller.

(5) Explain why maximizing market value is the logical financial goal of the corporation.

(6) Explain why value maximization is not inconsistent with ethical behavior.

(7) Explain how corporations mitigate conflicts and encourage cooperative behavior.

RELATED WEB SITES FOR THIS CHAPTER CAN BE FOUND AT WWW.MHHE.COM/BMM7E.

To grow from small beginnings to a major corporation, FedEx needed to make good investment and financing decisions.

To carry on business, a corporation needs an almost endless variety of assets. Some are tangible assets such as plant and machinery, office buildings, and vehicles; others are intangible assets such as brand names and patents. Corporations finance these assets by borrowing, by reinvesting profits back into the firm, and by selling additional shares to the firm's shareholders. Therefore, the firm's financial managers face two broad questions: First, what investments should the corporation make? Second, how should it pay for those investments? The *investment decision* involves spending money; the *financing decision* involves raising it.

We start this chapter with examples of recent investment and financing decisions by major U.S. and foreign corporations. We review what a corporation is and describe the roles of its top financial managers. We then turn to the financial goal of the corporation, which is usually expressed as *maximizing value,* or at least adding value. Financial managers add value whenever the corporation can invest to earn a higher return than its shareholders can earn for themselves.

But is maximizing value really a sound and realistic goal? If a corporation maximizes value for its shareholders, can it also be a good corporate citizen? If we ask managers to increase firm value, won't they be tempted to cut corners and try dishonest tricks? Will the managers really focus on increasing value, or will they pursue their own narrow, selfish interests? We consider the conflicts of interest that arise in large corporations and the mechanisms that help to align the interests of managers and stockholders.

Finally, we look ahead to the rest of this book and look back to some entertaining snippets of financial history.

1.1   Investment and Financing Decisions

Fred Smith is best known today as the founder of FedEx. But in 1965 he was still a sophomore at Yale, where he wrote an economics term paper arguing that delivery systems were not keeping up with increasing needs for speed and dependability.[1] After leaving the Marine Corps in 1969, he joined his stepfather at a struggling equipment and maintenance firm for air carriers. He observed firsthand the difficulties of shipping spare parts on short notice. He saw the need for an integrated air and ground delivery system with a central hub that could connect a large number of points more efficiently than a point-to-point delivery system. In 1971, at the age of 27, Smith founded Federal Express.

Like many start-up firms, Federal Express flirted again and again with failure. Smith and his family had an inheritance of a few million dollars, but this was far from enough. The young company needed to purchase and retrofit a small fleet of aging Dassault Falcon jets, build a central-hub facility, and hire and train pilots, delivery, and office staff. The initial source of capital was short-term bank loans. Because of the company's shaky financial position, the bank demanded that the planes be used as collateral and that Smith personally guarantee the loan with his own money.

In April 1973 the company went live with a fleet of 14 jets, servicing 25 U.S. cities out of its Memphis hub. By then, the company had spent $25 million and was effectively flat broke, without enough funds to pay for its weekly delivery of jet fuel. In desperation, it managed to acquire a bank loan for $23.7 million. This loan had to be backed by a guarantee from General Dynamics, which in return acquired an option to buy the company. (Today, General Dynamics must regret that it never exercised this option.)

In November of that year, the company finally achieved some financial stability when it raised $24.5 million from venture capitalists, investment firms that provide funds and advice to young companies in return for a partial ownership share. Eventually, venture capitalists invested about $90 million in Federal Express.

In 1977 air cargo deregulation allowed private firms to compete with the Postal Service in package delivery. Federal Express responded by expanding its operations. It acquired seven Boeing 727s, each with about seven times the capacity of the Falcon jets. To pay for these new investments Federal Express raised about $19 million by selling shares of stock to the general public in an *initial public offering (IPO)*. The new stockholders became part-owners of the company in proportion to the number of shares they purchased.

From this point on, success followed success, and the company invested heavily to expand its air fleet as well as its supporting infrastructure. It introduced an automated shipping system and a bar-coded tracking system. In 1994, it launched its fedex.com Web site for online package tracking. It opened several new hubs across the United States as well as in Canada, France, the Philippines, and China. In 2007 FedEx (as the company was now called) became the world's largest airline measured by number of planes. FedEx also invested in other companies, capped by the acquisition of Kinko's for $2.4 billion in 2004. By 2010, FedEx had about 270,000 employees, annual revenue of $35 billion, and a stock market value of $28 billion. Its name had become a verb—to "FedEx a package" was to ship it overnight.

Even in retrospect, FedEx's success was hardly a sure thing. Fred Smith's idea was inspired, but its implementation was complex and difficult. FedEx had to make *good investment decisions.* In the beginning, these decisions were constrained by lack of funds. For example, used Falcon jets were the only option, given the young company's precarious financial position. At first it could service only a short list of the major cities. As the company grew, its investment decisions became more complex. Which type of planes should it buy? When should it expand coverage to Europe and Asia? How many operations hubs should it build? What computer and tracking systems were

---

[1] Legend has it that Smith received a grade of C on this paper. In fact, he doesn't remember the grade.

necessary to keep up with the increasing package volume and geographic coverage? Which companies should it acquire as it expanded its range of services?

FedEx also needed to make *good financing decisions.* For example, how should it raise the money it needed for investment? In the beginning, these choices were limited to family money and bank loans. As the company grew, its range of choices expanded. Eventually it was able to attract funding from venture capitalists, but this posed new questions. How much cash did the firm need to raise from the venture capitalists? How big a share in the firm would the venture capitalists demand in return? The initial public offering of stock prompted similar questions. How many shares should the company try to sell? At what price? As the company grew, it raised more funds by borrowing money from its banks and by selling publicly traded bonds to investors. At each point, it needed to decide on the proper form and terms of financing as well as the amounts to be raised.

In short, FedEx needed to be *good at finance.* It had a long head start over potential competitors, but a series of bad financial decisions would have sunk the company. The particulars of any company's history may differ, but, like FedEx, all successful companies must make good investment and financing decisions. And, as with FedEx, those decisions range from prosaic and obvious to difficult, complicated, and strategically crucial.

Let's widen our discussion. Table 1.1 gives an example of a recent investment and financing decision for each of nine corporations. Five are U.S. corporations. Four are foreign: GlaxoSmithKline's headquarters are in London, LVMH's in Paris,[2] Santander's in Madrid, and Honda's in Tokyo. We have chosen very large public corporations that

TABLE 1.1 Examples of recent investment and financing decisions by major public corporations

Company (revenue in billions, 2010)	Recent Investment Decisions	Recent Financing Decisions
GlaxoSmithKline (£28 billion)	Spent £3.7 billion in 2009 on research and development of new drugs.	Financed R&D expenditures with reinvested cash flow generated by sales of pharmaceutical products.
Boeing ($64 billion)	Completed testing of its 787 Dreamliner aircraft, developed at a cost of more than $10 billion.	Bolstered its cash position by borrowing nearly $6 billion.
Walmart ($405 billion)	Planned in 2011 to open more than 150 stores in the U.S. and more than 600 overseas.	Repaid over $6 billion of long-term debt, bought back $7 billion of its shares, and paid a dividend to shareholders of $4 billion.
Union Pacific ($17 billion)	Acquired 127 new locomotives in 2009 at a cost of $287 million.	Financed many of the new locomotives by long-term leases.
Banco Santander (€42 billion)	Acquired Sovereign Bank for $1.9 billion.	Financed the acquisition by an exchange of shares.
Ford Motor Company ($121 billion)	Announced $2.3 billion investment in U.K. manufacturing facilities over the next 5 years to support production of low-carbon emission vehicles.	Paid off $7 billion in automotive debt in the second quarter of 2010.
LVMH (€20 billion)	Engaged in capital expenditures of €729 million, including new store openings for Louis Vuitton and new production facilities for Christian Dior, Hennessy, and Veuve Clicquot.	Issued a 3-year bond in 2008, raising 200 million Swiss francs.
Honda (¥10,011 billion)	Invested ¥90 billion to develop new motorcycle models and modernize production facilities.	Issued $1 billion of debt maturing in 3 and 5 years.
Chevron ($171 billion)	Announced plans to invest with its partners in the Gorgon liquefied natural gas project in western Australia. The total cost of the project is forecast at more than A$40 billion.	Arranged credit facilities with various banks that would allow it to borrow $5.1 billion.

---

[2] LVMH (Moët Hennessy Louis Vuitton) markets perfumes and cosmetics, wines and spirits, leather goods, watches, and other luxury products. And, yes, we know what you are thinking, but "LVMH" really is short for "Moët Hennessy Louis Vuitton."

you are likely to be familiar with. You have probably traveled on a Boeing jet, shopped at Walmart, or driven a Ford, for example.

Take a look at the decisions now. We think you will agree that they appear sensible—at least there is nothing obviously wrong with them. But if you are new to finance, it may be difficult to think about *why* these companies made these decisions and not others.

The Investment (Capital Budgeting) Decision

capital budgeting or **capital expenditure (CAPEX) decision**
Decision to invest in tangible or intangible assets.

Investment decisions, such as those shown in Table 1.1, are often called **capital budgeting** or **capital expenditure (CAPEX) decisions.** Some of the investments in the table, such as Walmart's new stores or Union Pacific's new locomotives, involve tangible assets—assets that you can touch and kick. Others involve intangible assets, such as research and development (R&D), advertising, and the design of computer software. For example, GlaxoSmithKline and other major pharmaceutical manufacturers invest billions every year on R&D for new drugs. LVMH is estimated to spend some $600 million a year promoting its luxury brands.

Most of the investments in Table 1.1 have long-term consequences. For example, Boeing's Dreamliner may produce returns over 30 years or more. Other investments may pay off in only a few months. For example, with the approach of the Christmas holidays, Walmart spends nearly $40 billion to stock up its warehouses and retail stores. As the goods are sold over the following months, the company recovers its investment in these inventories.

The world of business can be intensely competitive, and corporations survive and prosper only if they can keep launching new products or services. In some cases the costs and risks of doing so are amazingly large. Boeing has invested more than $10 billion to develop the new 787 Dreamliner series of aircraft. At the same time its European archrival, Airbus, has invested more than $12 billion in the new A380 superjumbo aircraft. Each firm has "bet the company" on the success of these investments. But do not think of companies as making billion-dollar investments on a daily basis. Most investment decisions are smaller, such as the purchase of a truck, machine tool, or computer system. Corporations make thousands of such investments each year. The cumulative amount of these small expenditures can be just as large as the occasional jumbo investments shown in Table 1.1.

Not all capital investments succeed. The Iridium communications satellite system, which offered its users instant telephone connections worldwide, soaked up $5 billion in investment before it started operations in 1998. It needed 400,000 subscribers to break even but attracted only a small fraction of that target number. Iridium defaulted on its debt and filed for bankruptcy in 1999. The Iridium system was sold a year later for just $25 million.

Although the investment in Iridium was clearly disastrous, it may have been rational given what was known in the early 1990s when the go-ahead decision was made. It may have been a good decision thwarted by bad luck. The Iridium system may have been launched too soon and too ambitiously. (The system survived bankruptcy and is operating profitably today.[3])

There are no free guarantees in finance. But you can tilt the odds in your favor if you learn the tools of investment analysis and apply them intelligently. We will cover these tools in detail later in this book.

The Financing Decision

financing decision
The form and amount of financing of a firm's investments.

The financial manager's second main responsibility is to raise the money that the firm requires for its investments and operations. This is the **financing decision.** When a company needs to raise money, it can invite investors to put up cash in exchange for a share of future profits or it can promise to pay back the investors' cash plus a fixed rate

---

[3] The private investors who took over the system concentrated on aviation, maritime, and defense markets rather than on retail customers. In 2008 prospects were sufficiently encouraging for the company to go public again. By 2010, the company was solidly profitable and planning upgrade and replacement of its communications satellite system.

of interest. In the first case, the investors receive shares of stock and become share-holders, part-owners of the corporation. The investors in this case are referred to as *equity investors,* who contribute *equity financing.* In the second case, the investors are lenders, that is, *debt investors,* who one day must be repaid. The choice between debt and equity financing is often called the *capital structure decision.* Here "capital" refers to the firm's sources of long-term financing. A firm that is seeking to raise long-term financing is said to be "raising capital."

real assets
Assets used to produce goods and services.

financial assets
Financial claims to the income generated by the firm's real assets.

Notice the essential difference between the investment and financing decisions. When the firm invests, it acquires **real assets,** which are then used to produce the firm's prod-ucts and services. The firm finances its investment in real assets by issuing **financial assets** to investors. A share of stock is a financial asset, which has value as a claim on the firm's real assets and on the income that those assets will produce. A bank loan is a finan-cial asset also. It gives the bank the right to get its money back plus interest. If the firm's operations can't generate enough income to pay what the bank is owed, the bank can force the firm into bankruptcy and stake a claim on its real assets. Shares of stock and other financial assets that can be purchased and traded by investors are called *securities.*

The firm can issue an almost endless variety of financial assets. Suppose it decides to borrow. It can issue debt to investors, or it can borrow from a bank. It can borrow for 1 year or 20 years. If it borrows for 20 years, it can reserve the right to pay off the debt early if interest rates fall. It can borrow in Paris, receiving and promising to repay euros, or it can borrow dollars in New York. (As Table 1.1 shows, LVMH chose to bor-row Swiss francs, but it could have borrowed euros or dollars instead.)

Self-Test 1.1

Are the following capital budgeting or financing decisions? (*Hint:* In one case the answer is "both.")

a. Intel decides to spend $1 billion to develop a new microprocessor.
b. Volkswagen borrows 350 million euros (€350 million) from Deutsche Bank.
c. Royal Dutch Shell constructs a pipeline to bring natural gas onshore from a production platform in Australia.
d. Avon spends €200 million to launch a new range of cosmetics in European markets.
e. Pfizer issues new shares to buy a small biotech company.

The financial manager is involved in many other day-to-day activities that are essen-tial to the smooth operation of the firm, but not dramatic enough to show up in Table 1.1. For example, if the firm sells goods or services on credit, the firm has to make sure that its customers pay their bills on time. Corporations that operate internationally must constantly transfer cash from one currency to another. Manufacturing companies must decide how much to invest in inventories of raw materials and finished goods.

Self-Test 1.2

Which of the following are financial assets, and which are real assets?

a. A patent.
b. A share of stock issued by Bank of New York.
c. A blast furnace in a steel-making factory.
d. A mortgage loan taken out to help pay for a new home.
e. After a successful advertising campaign, potential customers trust FedEx to deliver packages promptly and reliably.
f. An IOU ("I owe you") from your brother-in-law.

1.2 What Is a Corporation?

corporation
A business organized as a separate legal entity owned by stockholders.

We have been referring to "corporations." But before going too far or too fast, we need to offer some basic definitions.

A **corporation** is a distinct, permanent legal entity. Suppose you decide to create a new corporation.[4] You would work with a lawyer to prepare *articles of incorporation,* which set out the purpose of the business and how it is to be financed, managed, and governed. These articles must conform to the laws of the state in which the business is incorporated. For many purposes, the corporation is considered a resident of its state. For example, it can enter into contracts, borrow or lend money, and sue or be sued. It pays its own taxes (but it cannot vote!).

A corporation's owners are called *shareholders* or *stockholders.*[5] The shareholders do not directly own the business's real assets (factories, oil wells, stores, etc.). Instead they have indirect ownership via financial assets (the shares of the corporation).

limited liability
The owners of a corporation are not personally liable for its obligations.

A corporation is legally distinct from the shareholders. Therefore, the shareholders have **limited liability** and cannot be held personally responsible for the corporation's debts. When the U.S. financial corporation Lehman Brothers failed in 2008, no one demanded that its stockholders put up more money to cover Lehman's massive debts. Shareholders can lose their entire investment in a corporation, but no more.

EXAMPLE 1.1   ▶   Business Organization

Suppose you buy a building and open a restaurant. You have invested in the building itself, kitchen equipment, dining-room furnishings, plus various other assets. If you do not incorporate, you own these assets personally, as the *sole proprietor* of the business. If you have borrowed money from a bank to start the business, then you are personally responsible for this debt. If the business loses money and cannot pay the bank, then the bank can demand that you raise cash by selling other assets—your car or house, for example—in order to repay the loan. But if you incorporate the restaurant business, and then the corporation borrows from the bank, your other assets are shielded from the restaurant's debts. Of course, incorporation also means that the bank will be more cautious in lending, because the bank will have no recourse to your other assets.[6]

Notice that if you incorporate your business, you exchange direct ownership of its real assets (the building, kitchen equipment, etc.) for indirect ownership via financial assets (the shares of the new corporation).

When a corporation is first established, its shares may be privately owned by a small group of investors, perhaps the company's managers and a few backers. In this case the shares are not publicly traded and the company is *closely held.* Eventually, when the firm grows and new shares are issued to raise additional capital, its shares are traded in public markets such as the New York Stock Exchange. Such corporations are known as *public companies.* Most well-known corporations in the United States are public companies with widely dispersed shareholdings. In other countries, it is more common for large corporations to remain in private hands, and many public companies

---

[4] In the United States, corporations are identified by the label "Corporation," "Incorporated," or "Inc.," as in *US Airways Group, Inc.* The United Kingdom identifies public corporations by "plc" (short for "Public Limited Corporation"). French corporations have the suffix "SA" ("Société Anonyme"). The corresponding labels in Germany are "GmbH" ("Gesellschaft mit beschränkter Haftung") and "AG" ("Aktiengesellschaft").

[5] "Shareholder" and "stockholder" mean exactly the same thing and are used interchangeably.

[6] The bank may ask you to put up personal assets as collateral for the loan to your restaurant corporation. But it has to ask and get your agreement. It doesn't have to ask if your business is a sole proprietorship.

may be controlled by just a handful of investors. The latter category includes such well-known names as Fiat, Porsche, Benetton, Bosch, IKEA, and the Swatch Group.

A large public corporation may have hundreds of thousands of shareholders, who together own the business. An individual may have 100 shares, receive 100 votes, and be entitled to a tiny fraction of the firm's income and value. On the other hand, a pension fund or insurance company may own millions of shares, receive millions of votes, and have a correspondingly large stake in the firm's performance.

Public shareholders cannot possibly manage or control the corporation directly. Instead, they elect a *board of directors,* who in turn appoint the top managers and monitor their performance. This *separation of ownership and control* gives corporations permanence. Even if managers quit or are dismissed, the corporation survives. Today's stockholders can sell all their shares to new investors without disrupting the operations of the business. Corporations can, in principle, live forever, and in practice they may survive many human lifetimes. One of the oldest corporations is the Hudson's Bay Company, which was formed in 1670 to profit from the fur trade between northern Canada and England. The company still operates as one of Canada's leading retail chains.

The separation of corporate ownership and control can also have a downside, for it can open the door for managers and directors to act in their own interests rather than in the stockholders' interest. We return to this problem later in the chapter.

There are other disadvantages to being a corporation. One is the cost, in both time and money, of managing the corporation's legal machinery. These costs are particularly burdensome for small businesses.

There is also an important tax drawback to corporations in the United States. Because the corporation is a separate legal entity, it is taxed separately. So corporations pay tax on their profits, and shareholders are taxed again when they receive dividends from the company or sell their shares at a profit. By contrast, income generated by businesses that are not incorporated is taxed just once as personal income.[7]

Other Forms of Business Organization

Corporations do not have to be prominent, multinational businesses such as those listed in Table 1.1. You can organize a local plumbing contractor or barber shop as a corporation if you want to take the trouble. But most corporations are larger businesses or businesses that aspire to grow. Small "mom-and-pop" businesses are usually organized as sole proprietorships.

What about the middle ground? What about businesses that grow too large for sole proprietorships but don't want to reorganize as corporations? For example, suppose you wish to pool money and expertise with some friends or business associates. You can form a *partnership* and enter into a partnership agreement that sets out how decisions are to be made and how profits are to be split up. Partners, like sole proprietors, face unlimited liability. If the business runs into difficulties, each partner can be held responsible for *all* the business's debts.

Partnerships have a tax advantage. Partnerships, unlike corporations, do not have to pay income taxes. The partners simply pay personal income taxes on their shares of the profits.

Some businesses are hybrids that combine the tax advantage of a partnership with the limited liability advantage of a corporation. In a *limited partnership,* partners are classified as general or limited. General partners manage the business and have unlimited personal liability for its debts. Limited partners are liable only for the money they invest and do not participate in management.

Many states allow *limited liability partnerships (LLPs)* or, equivalently, *limited liability companies (LLCs).* These are partnerships in which all partners have limited

---

[7] The U.S. tax system is unusual in this respect. To avoid taxing the same income twice, many other countries give shareholders at least some credit for the taxes that the corporation has already paid.

liability. Another variation on the theme is the *professional corporation (PC),* which is commonly used by doctors, lawyers, and accountants. In this case, the business has limited liability, but the professionals can still be sued personally, for example, for malpractice.

Most large investment banks such as Morgan Stanley and Goldman Sachs started life as partnerships. But eventually these companies and their financing requirements grew too large for them to continue as partnerships, and they reorganized as corporations. The partnership form of organization does not work well when ownership is widespread and separation of ownership and management is essential.

1.3 Who Is the Financial Manager?

chief financial officer (CFO)
Sets overall financial strategy.

treasurer
Responsible for financing, cash management, and relationships with banks and other financial institutions.

controller
Responsible for budgeting, accounting, and taxes.

What do financial managers do for a living? That simple question can be answered in several ways. We can start with financial managers' job titles. Most large corporations have a **chief financial officer (CFO),** who oversees the work of all financial staff. As you can see from Figure 1.1, the CFO is deeply involved in financial policy and financial planning and is in constant contact with the chief executive officer (CEO) and other top management. The CFO is the most important financial voice of the corporation and explains earnings results and forecasts to investors and the media.

Below the CFO are usually a **treasurer** and a **controller.** The treasurer looks after the firm's cash, raises new capital, and maintains relationships with banks and other investors that hold the firm's securities. The controller prepares the financial statements, manages the firm's internal budgets and accounting, and looks after its tax affairs. Thus the treasurer's main function is to obtain and manage the firm's capital, whereas the controller ensures that the money is used efficiently.

Self-Test 1.3

Fritz and Frieda went to business school together 10 years ago. They have just been hired by a midsized corporation that wants to bring in new financial managers. Fritz studied finance, with an emphasis on financial markets and institutions. Frieda majored in accounting and became a CPA 5 years ago. Who is more suited to be treasurer and who controller? Briefly explain.

In large corporations, financial managers are responsible for organizing and supervising the capital budgeting process. However, major capital investment projects are so closely tied to plans for product development, production, and marketing that managers from these other areas are inevitably drawn into planning and analyzing the projects. If the firm has staff members specializing in corporate planning, they are naturally involved in capital budgeting too. For this reason we will use the term *financial*

FIGURE 1.1 Financial managers in large corporations.

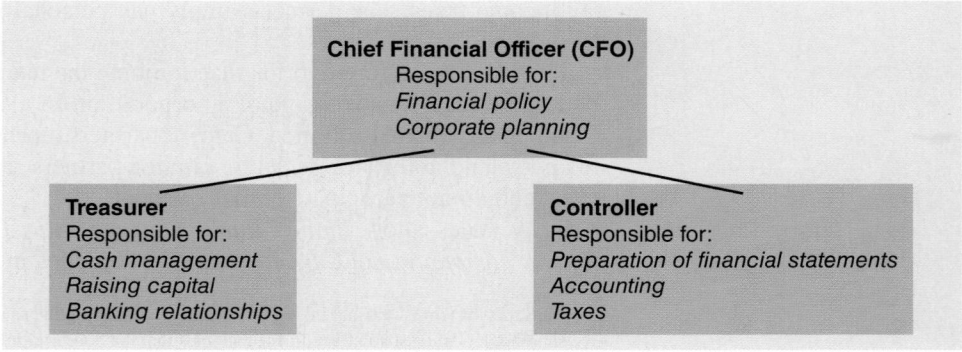

Chief Financial Officer (CFO)
Responsible for:
Financial policy
Corporate planning

Treasurer
Responsible for:
Cash management
Raising capital
Banking relationships

Controller
Responsible for:
Preparation of financial statements
Accounting
Taxes

FIGURE 1.2 Flow of cash between investors and the firm's operations. Key: (1) Cash raised by selling financial assets to investors; (2) cash invested in the firm's operations; (3) cash generated by the firm's operations; (4a) cash reinvested; (4b) cash returned to investors.

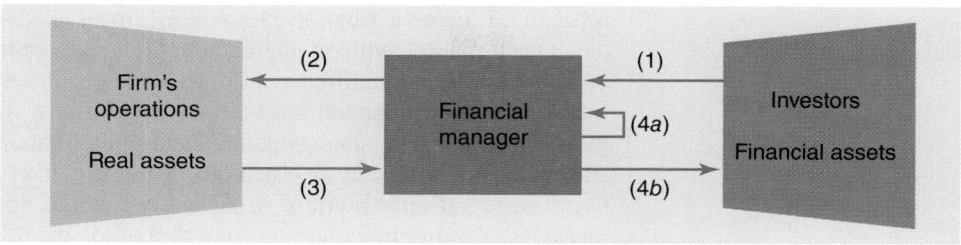

manager to refer to anyone responsible for an investment or financing decision. Often we will use the term collectively for all the managers drawn into such decisions.

Because of the importance of many financial issues, ultimate decisions often rest by law or by custom with the board of directors. For example, only the board has the legal power to declare a dividend or to sanction a public issue of securities. Boards usually delegate decision-making authority for small- or medium-sized investment outlays, but the authority to approve large investments is almost never delegated.

Now let's go beyond job titles. What is the essential role of the financial manager? Figure 1.2 gives one answer. The figure traces how money flows from investors to the corporation and back again to investors. The flow starts when cash is raised from investors (arrow 1 in the figure). The cash could come from banks or from securities sold to investors in financial markets. The cash is then used to pay for the real assets (investment projects) needed for the corporation's business (arrow 2). Later, as the business operates, the assets generate cash inflows (arrow 3). That cash is either reinvested (arrow 4a) or returned to the investors who furnished the money in the first place (arrow 4b). Of course, the choice between arrows 4a and 4b is constrained by the promises made when cash was raised at arrow 1. For example, if the firm borrows money from a bank at arrow 1, it must repay this money plus interest at arrow 4b.

You can see examples of arrows 4a and 4b in Table 1.1. GlaxoSmithKline financed its drug research and development by reinvesting earnings (arrow 4a). Walmart decided to return cash to shareholders by buying back its stock (arrow 4b). It could have chosen instead to pay the money out as additional cash dividends.

Notice how the financial manager stands between the firm and outside investors. On the one hand, the financial manager is involved in the firm's operations, particularly by helping to make good investment decisions. On the other hand, he or she deals with financial institutions and other investors and with financial markets such as the New York Stock Exchange. We will say more about these financial institutions and markets in the next chapter.

1.4 Goals of the Corporation

Shareholders Want Managers to Maximize Market Value

For small corporations, shareholders and management may be one and the same. But for large corporations, separation of ownership and management is a practical necessity. For example, Walmart has over 300,000 shareholders. There is no way that these shareholders can be actively involved in management; it would be like trying to run New York City by town meetings. Authority has to be delegated.

How can shareholders effectively delegate decision making when they all have different tastes, wealth, time horizons, personal opportunities, and tolerance for risk? Delegation can work only if the shareholders have a common goal. Fortunately there is a natural financial objective on which almost all shareholders can agree: Maximize the current market value of shareholders' investment in the firm.

This simple, unqualified goal makes sense when the shareholders have access to well-functioning financial markets and institutions. Access gives them the flexibility to manage their own savings and consumption plans, leaving the corporation's financial managers with only one task, to increase market value. For example, a corporation's roster of shareholders will usually include both risk-averse and risk-tolerant investors. You might expect the risk-averse to say, "Sure, maximize value, but don't touch too many high-risk projects." Instead, they say, "Risky projects are okay, provided that expected profits are more than enough to offset the risks. If this firm ends up too risky for my taste, I'll adjust my investment portfolio to make it safer." For example, the risk-averse shareholder can shift more of his or her portfolio to safe assets, such as U.S. government bonds. Shareholders can also just say good-bye, selling off shares of the risky firm and buying shares in a safer one. If the risky investments increase market value, the departing shareholders are better off than they would be if the risky investments were turned down.

EXAMPLE 1.2 ▶   Value Maximization

Fast-Track Wireless shares trade for $20. It has just announced a "bet the company" investment in a high-risk, but potentially revolutionary, WhyFi technology. Investors note the risk of failure but are even more impressed with the technology's upside. They conclude that the possibility of very high future profits justifies a higher share price. The price goes up to $23.

Caspar Milquetoast, a thoughtful but timid shareholder, notes the downside risks and decides that it's time for a change. He sells out to more risk-tolerant investors. But he sells at $23 per share, not $20. Thus he captures the value added by the WhyFi project without having to bear the project's risks. Those risks are transferred to other investors, who are more risk-tolerant or more optimistic.

In a well-functioning stock market, there is always a pool of investors ready to bear downside risks if the upside potential is sufficiently attractive. We know that the upside potential was sufficient in this case, because Fast-Track stock attracted investors willing to pay $23 per share.

The same principles apply to the timing of a corporation's cash flows, as the following self-test illustrates.

Self-Test 1.4

Rhonda and Reggie Hotspur are working hard to save for their childrens' college education. They don't need more cash for current consumption but will face big tuition bills in 2020. Should they therefore avoid investing in stocks that pay generous current cash dividends? Explain briefly.

Sometimes you hear managers speak as if the corporation has other goals. For example, they may say that their job is to "maximize profits." That sounds reasonable. After all, don't shareholders want their company to be profitable? But taken literally, profit maximization is not a well-defined corporate objective. Here are two reasons:

1. Maximize profits? Which year's profits? A corporation may be able to increase current profits by cutting back on outlays for maintenance or staff training, but that will not add value unless the outlays were wasteful in the first place. Shareholders will not welcome higher short-term profits if long-term profits are damaged.

2. A company may be able to increase future profits by cutting this year's dividend and investing the freed-up cash in the firm. That is not in the shareholders' best interest if the company earns only a very low rate of return on the extra investment.

In a free economy a firm is unlikely to survive if it pursues goals that reduce the firm's value. Suppose, for example, that a firm's only goal is to increase its market share. It aggressively reduces prices to capture new customers, even when this leads to continuing losses. What would happen to such a firm? As losses mount, it will find it more and more difficult to borrow money, and it may not even have sufficient profits to repay existing debts. Sooner or later, however, outside investors would see an opportunity for easy money. They could buy the firm from its current shareholders, toss out existing management, and increase the firm's value by changing its policies. They would profit by the difference between the price paid for the firm and the higher value it would have under new management. Managers who pursue goals that destroy value often land in early retirement. **The natural financial objective of the corporation is to maximize market value.**

The Investment Trade-Off   Okay, let's take the objective as maximizing market value, or at least adding market value. But why do some investments increase market value, while others reduce it? The answer is given by Figure 1.3, which sets out the fundamental trade-off for corporate investment decisions. The corporation has a proposed investment project (the purchase of a real asset). Suppose it has sufficient cash on hand to finance the project. The financial manager is trying to decide whether to go ahead. If he or she decides not to invest, the corporation can pay out the cash to shareholders, say as an extra dividend. (The investment and dividend arrows in Figure 1.3 are arrows 2 and 4*b* in Figure 1.2.)

Assume that the financial manager is acting in the interests of the corporation's owners, its stockholders. What do these stockholders want the financial manager to do? The answer depends on the rate of return on the investment project and on the rate of return that stockholders can earn by investing in financial markets. If the return offered by the investment project is higher than the rate of return that shareholders can get by investing on their own, then the shareholders would vote for the investment project. If the investment project offers a lower return than shareholders can achieve on their own, the shareholders would vote to cancel the project and take the cash instead.

Figure 1.3 could apply to Union Pacific's decisions to invest in new locomotives. Suppose Union Pacific has cash set aside to buy 20 new locomotives. It could go ahead with the purchase, or it could choose to cancel the investment project and instead pay the cash out to its stockholders. If it pays out the cash, the stockholders could then invest for themselves.

Suppose that Union Pacific's new-locomotives project is just about as risky as the U.S. stock market and that investment in the stock market offers a 10% expected rate

FIGURE 1.3 The firm can either keep and reinvest cash or return it to investors. (Arrows represent possible cash flows or transfers.) If cash is reinvested, the opportunity cost is the expected rate of return that shareholders could have obtained by investing in financial assets.

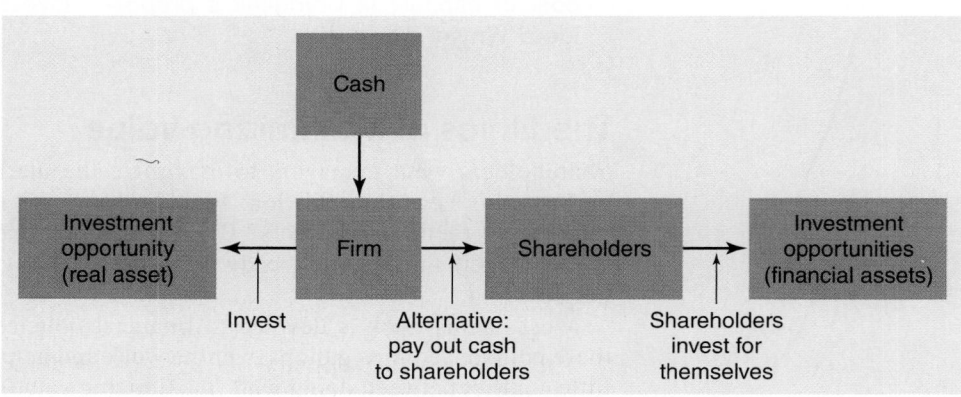

of return. If the new locomotives offer a superior rate of return, say 20%, then Union Pacific's stockholders would be happy to let the company keep the cash and invest it in the new locomotives. If the new locomotives offer only a 5% return, then the stockholders are better off with the cash and without the new project; in that case, the financial manager should turn the project down.

As long as a corporation's proposed investments offer higher rates of return than its shareholders can earn for themselves in the stock market (or in other financial markets), its shareholders will applaud the investments and the market value of the firm will increase. But if the company earns an inferior return, shareholders boo, market value falls, and stockholders clamor to get their money back so that they can invest on their own.

In our example, the minimum acceptable rate of return on Union Pacific's new locomotives is 10%. This minimum rate of return is called the *hurdle rate* or **opportunity cost of capital.** It is called an *opportunity cost* of capital, because it depends on the alternative investment *opportunities* available to investors in financial markets. Whenever a corporation invests cash in a new project, its shareholders lose the opportunity to invest the cash on their own. Corporations increase value by accepting all investment projects that earn more than the opportunity cost of capital.

Notice that the opportunity cost of capital depends on the risk of the proposed investment project. Why? It's not just because shareholders are risk-averse. It's also because shareholders have to trade off risk against return when they invest on their own. The safest investments, such as U.S. government debt, offer low rates of return. Investments with higher expected rates of return—the stock market, for example—are riskier and sometimes deliver painful losses. (The U.S. stock market fell 38% in 2008, for example.) Other investments are riskier still. For example, high-tech growth stocks offer the prospect of higher rates of return but are even more volatile than the stock market overall.

Managers look to the financial markets to measure the opportunity cost of capital for the firm's investment projects. They can observe the opportunity cost of capital for safe investments by looking up current interest rates on safe debt securities. For risky investments, the opportunity cost of capital has to be estimated. We start to tackle this task in Chapter 11.

Opportunity cost of capital
Minimum acceptable rate of return on capital investment.

> ## Self-Test 1.5
>
> Investing $100,000 in additional raw materials, mostly palladium, should allow Cryogenic Concepts to increase production and earn an additional $112,000 next year. This payoff could cover the investment, plus a 12% return. Palladium is traded in commodity markets. The CFO has studied the history of returns from investments in palladium and believes that investors in the precious metal can reasonably expect a 15% return. What is the opportunity cost of capital? Is Cryogenic's proposed investment in palladium a good idea? Why or why not?

The Ethics of Maximizing Value

Shareholders want managers to maximize the market value of their shares. But perhaps this begs the question. Is it *desirable* for managers to act in the selfish interests of their shareholders? Does a focus on enriching the shareholders mean that managers must act as greedy mercenaries riding roughshod over the weak and helpless?

Most of this book is devoted to financial policies that increase value. None of these policies requires gallops over the weak and helpless. In most instances, there is little conflict between doing well (maximizing value) and doing good. The first step in doing well is doing good by your customers. Here is how Adam Smith put the case in 1776:

> It is not from the benevolence of the butcher, the brewer, or the baker, that we expect our dinner, but from their regard to their own interest. We address ourselves, not to their humanity but to their self-love, and never talk to them of our own necessities but of their advantages.[8]

Profitable firms are those with satisfied customers and loyal employees; firms with dissatisfied customers and a disgruntled workforce will probably end up with declining profits and a low stock price. Most established corporations can add value by building long-term relationships.

Of course, ethical issues do arise in business as in other walks of life. When the stakes are high, it is often tempting for managers to cut corners. Laws and regulations seek to prevent managers from undertaking dishonest actions. But written rules and laws can help only so much. In business, as in other day-to-day affairs, there are also unwritten rules of behavior. These work because everyone knows that such rules are in the general interest. But they are reinforced because good managers know that their firm's reputation is one of its most important assets and therefore playing fair and keeping one's word are simply good business practices. Thus huge financial deals are regularly completed on a handshake, and each side knows that the other will not renege later if things turn sour.

Reputation is particularly important in finance. If you buy a well-known brand in a supermarket, you can be fairly sure of what you are getting. But in financial transactions the other party often has more information than you, and it is less easy to be sure of the quality of what you are buying. Therefore, honest financial firms seek to build long-term relationships with their customers and to establish a name for fair dealing and financial integrity. Major banks and securities firms protect their reputations. When something happens to undermine reputations, the costs can be enormous.

Of course, trust is sometimes misplaced. Charlatans and swindlers are often able to hide behind booming markets, for it is only "when the tide goes out that you learn who's been swimming naked."[9] The tide went out in 2008 and a number of frauds were exposed. One notorious example was the Ponzi scheme run by the disgraced financier Bernard Madoff.[10] Individuals and institutions invested around $20 billion with Madoff and were told that their investments had grown to $65 billion. That figure turned out to be completely fictitious. (It's not clear what Madoff did with all this money, but much of it was apparently paid out to early investors in the scheme to create an impression of superior investment performance.) With hindsight, the investors should not have trusted Madoff or the financial advisers who steered money to him.

Madoff's Ponzi scheme was (we hope) a once-in-a-lifetime event. (Ponzi schemes pop up frequently, but none has approached the scope and duration of Madoff's.) It was astonishingly unethical, illegal, and bound to end in tears. More complex ethical issues were raised by the banking crisis of 2007–2009. Look, for example, at the nearby box that describes a deal involving the investment bank Goldman Sachs. Some observers believed that Goldman's actions reflected all that is worst on Wall Street. Others see them as simply an example of an investment bank performing one of its main functions as an intermediary between willing buyers and sellers.

---

[8] Adam Smith, *An Inquiry into the Nature and Causes of the Wealth of Nations* (New York: Random House, 1937; first published 1776), p. 14.

[9] The quotation is from Warren Buffett's annual letter to the shareholders of Berkshire Hathaway, March 2008.

[10] Ponzi schemes are named after Charles Ponzi, who founded an investment company in 1920 that promised investors unbelievably high returns. He was soon deluged with funds from investors in New England, taking in $1 million during one 3-hour period. Ponzi invested only about $30 of the money that he raised. But he used part of the cash provided by later investors to pay generous dividends to the original investors, thus promoting the illusion of high profits and quick payoffs. Within months the scheme collapsed and Ponzi started a 5-year prison sentence.

Goldman Sachs Causes a Rumpus

In 2006 the investment bank Goldman Sachs was approached by a major hedge fund that was pessimistic about the outlook for house prices. Goldman helped the fund to construct a complicated deal that would pay off if a $2 billion package of low-grade residential mortgages declined in value. Goldman then approached some banks that it knew were optimistic about the prospect for house prices and who might therefore be prepared to take the other side of the bargain.

In the event, house prices slumped, many of the owners defaulted on their mortgages, and the hedge fund made a profit of around $1 billion. The banks on the other side of the transaction lost heavily. Goldman's role in the transaction subsequently came in for heavy criticism. One criticism centered on the fact that Goldman shared the hedge fund's concerns about the housing market and in 2007 had circulated internal warning memos to its traders. Some therefore questioned whether it was ethical for Goldman to take a pessimistic view on housing in its own trading positions and at the same time continue to sell what it regarded as overvalued securities to its customers. There were also questions about what Goldman was legally and ethically obliged to reveal. Although one of the banks was heavily involved in choosing the package of mortgages and rejected many of the suggested contents of the package, none of them was aware that the mortgages had originally been proposed by the hedge fund manager and therefore could be particularly toxic.

A senate subcommittee that investigated the deal lambasted Goldman for "unbridled greed" and suggested that the firm had operated with "less oversight than a pit boss in Las Vegas." When the SEC announced that it was charging Goldman with fraud and material omissions and misrepresentations, the market value of the bank's stock declined by about $10 billion, far more than any penalty that Goldman might be expected to pay. Investors, it seemed, believed that the damage to Goldman's reputation was much more important than any fine. Three months later the bank admitted that the marketing material linked to the package of subprime mortgages was "incomplete" and agreed to pay a $550 million fine.

The event raised several difficult ethical questions. When an investment bank is employed to give advice on a new issue or a merger, it is essential that the client can trust the bank to give an honest and impartial view. But the situation becomes less clear-cut when the bank is acting as a middleman or trading securities. Much of the debate on the Goldman deal therefore centered on whether the bank was simply an intermediary between sophisticated traders or whether it had deeper responsibilities.*

* These issues are discussed in the context of the Goldman deal in S. M. Davidson, A. D. Morrison, and W. J. Wilhelm, Jr., "Computerization and the ABACUS: Reputation, Trust, and Fiduciary Responsibility in Investment Banking," January 2011, available at SSRN: **http://ssrn.com/abstract=1747647**.

It is not always easy to know what is ethical behavior, and there can be many gray areas. For example, should the firm be prepared to do business with a corrupt or repressive government? Should it employ child labor in countries where that is the norm? A nearby box presents several simple situations that call for an ethically based decision, along with survey responses to the proper course of action in each circumstance. Compare your decisions with those of the general public.

Self-Test 1.6

Without knowing anything about the personal ethics of the owners, which company would you better trust to keep its word in a business deal?

a. Harry's Hardware has been in business for 50 years. Harry's grandchildren, now almost adults, plan to take over and operate the business. Successful hardware stores depend on long-term loyal customers.

b. Victor's Videos just opened for business. It rents a storefront in a strip mall and has financed its inventory with a bank loan. Victor has little of his own money invested in the business. Video shops usually command little customer loyalty.

Do Managers Really Maximize Value?

Owner-managers have no conflicts of interest in their management of the business. They work for themselves, reaping the rewards of good work and suffering the penalties of bad work. Their *personal* well-being is tied to the value of the firm.

In most large corporations the managers are not the owners, and so managers may be tempted to act in ways that are not in the best interests of shareholders. For example, they might buy luxurious corporate jets or overindulge in expense-account dinners.

Things Are Not Always Fair in Love or Economics

What constitutes fair behavior by companies? One survey asked a number of individuals to state whether they regarded a particular action as acceptable or unfair. Before we tell you how they responded, think how you would rate each of the following actions:

1a. A small photocopying shop has one employee who has worked in the shop for 6 months and earns $9 per hour. Business continues to be satisfactory, but a factory in the area has closed and unemployment has increased. Other small shops in the area have now hired reliable workers at $7 an hour to perform jobs similar to those done by the photocopying shop employee. The owner of the photocopying shop reduces the employee's wage to $7.

1b. Now suppose that the shop does not reduce the employee's wage but he or she leaves. The owner decides to pay a replacement $7 an hour.

2. A house painter employs two assistants and pays them $9 per hour. The painter decides to quit house painting and go into the business of providing landscape services, where the going wage is lower. He reduces the workers' wages to $7 per hour for the landscaping work.

3a. A small company employs several workers and has been paying them average wages. There is severe unemployment in the area, and the company could easily replace its current employees with good workers at a lower wage. The company has been making money. The owners reduce the current workers' wages by 5%.

3b. Now suppose instead that the company has been losing money and the owners reduce wages by 5%.

4. A grocery store has several months' supply of peanut butter in stock on shelves in the storeroom. The owner hears that the wholesale price of peanut butter has increased and immediately raises the price on the current stock of peanut butter.

5. A hardware store has been selling snow shovels for $15. The morning after a large snowstorm, the store raises the price to $20.

6. A store has been sold out of the popular Beanie Baby dolls for a month. A week before Christmas a single doll is discovered in a storeroom. The managers know that many customers would like to buy the doll. They announce over the store's public address system that the doll will be sold by auction to the customer who offers to pay the most.

Now compare your responses with the responses of a random sample of individuals:

| | Percent Rating the Action As: | |
Action	Acceptable	Unfair
1a	17	83
1b	73	27
2	63	37
3a	23	77
3b	68	32
4	21	79
5	18	82
6	26	74

Source: Adapted from Daniel Kahneman, Jack L. Knetsch, and Richard Thaler, "Fairness as a Constraint on Profit Seeking: Entitlements in the Market," *American Economic Review* 76 (September 1986), pp. 728–741. Reprinted by permission of American Economic Association and the authors.

They might shy away from attractive but risky projects because they are worried more about the safety of their jobs than the potential for superior profits. They might engage in empire-building, adding unnecessary capacity or employees. Such problems can arise because the managers of the firm, who are hired as *agents* of the owners, may have their own axes to grind and nests to feather. Therefore they are called **agency problems.**

These agency problems can sometimes lead to outrageous behavior. For example, when Dennis Kozlowski, the CEO of Tyco, threw a $2 million 40th birthday bash for his wife, he charged half of the cost to the company. Conrad Black, the boss of Hollinger International, used the company jet for a trip with his wife to Bora Bora. These of course were extreme examples. The agency problems encountered in the normal course of business are less blatant. But agency problems do arise whenever managers think just a little less hard about spending money that is not their own.

Think of the company's net revenue as a pie that is divided among a number of claimants. These include the management and the workforce as well as the lenders and shareholders who put up the money to establish and maintain the business. The government is a claimant, too, since it gets to tax the profits of the enterprise. It is common to hear these claimants called **stakeholders** in the firm. Each has a stake in the firm, but their interests may not coincide.

All the stakeholders are bound together in a complex web of contracts and understandings. For example, when banks lend money to the firm, they insist on a formal contract stating the rate of interest and repayment dates, perhaps placing restrictions on dividends or additional borrowing. Similarly, large companies have carefully worked

agency problems
Managers are agents for stockholders, but the managers may act in their own interests rather than maximizing value.

stakeholder
Anyone with a financial interest in the firm.

out personnel policies that establish employees' rights and responsibilities. But you can't devise written rules to cover every possible future event. So the written contracts are supplemented by understandings. For example, managers understand that in return for a fat salary they are expected to work hard and not spend the firm's money on unwarranted personal luxuries.

What enforces these understandings? Is it realistic to expect managers always to act on behalf of the shareholders? The shareholders can't spend their lives watching through binoculars to check that managers are not shirking or dissipating company funds on the latest executive jet.

A closer look reveals several arrangements that help to ensure that the shareholders and managers are working toward common goals.

Legal and Regulatory Requirements CEOs and financial managers have a legal duty to act responsibly and in the interests of investors. For example, the Securities and Exchange Commission (SEC) sets accounting and reporting standards for public companies in order to ensure consistency and transparency.

Board of Directors Boards of directors have often been portrayed as passive supporters of top management. But the balance has tipped toward greater board independence. In response to Enron, WorldCom, and other corporate scandals, Congress passed the Sarbanes-Oxley Act, known widely as SOX. SOX requires corporations to place more independent directors on the board, that is, more directors who are not managers or are not affiliated with management. More than half of all directors are now independent. Boards also now meet in sessions without the CEO present. In addition to its restrictions on board activities, SOX requires each CFO to sign off personally on the corporation's accounting procedures and results.

Blockholders Although U.S. corporations typically have thousands of individual shareholders, they often also have *blockholders,* that is, individual investors that hold 5%, 10%, or more of the corporation's shares. The blockholders may include wealthy individuals and families—for example descendants of a founder—other corporations, institutional investors, pension funds, or foundations. When a 5% blockholder calls the CFO, the CFO answers.[11]

Institutional shareholders, particularly pension funds and hedge funds, have become more active in monitoring firm performance and proposing changes to corporate governance. More chief executives have been forced out in recent years, among them the CEOs of GM, Starbucks, AIG, Fannie Mae, and Freddie Mac. Boards outside the United States, which traditionally have been more management-friendly, have also become more willing to replace underperforming managers. The list of departures includes the heads of Royal Bank of Scotland, Peugeot Citroen, Lenovo, Swiss Re, and Versace.

Specialist Monitoring Managers are subject to the scrutiny of specialists. Their actions are monitored by the security analysts who advise investors to buy, hold, or sell the company's shares. They are also reviewed by banks, which keep an eagle eye on the progress of firms receiving their loans.

Compensation Plans Managers are spurred on by incentive schemes that produce big returns if shareholders gain but little or nothing if they do not. For example, Larry Ellison, CEO of the business software giant Oracle Corporation, received total compensation of $68.6 million for 2010. Only a tiny fraction ($250,000) of that amount was salary. The lion's share was in the form of stock and option grants.

[11] A large block of shares may give effective control even when there is no majority owner. For example, Larry Ellison's billion-plus shares in Oracle Corporation give him a 23% stake in the company. Barring some extreme catastrophe, this holding means that he can run the company pretty much as he wants to and as long as he wants to.

Those options will be worthless if Oracle's share price falls from its 2010 level but will be highly valuable if the price rises. Moreover, as founder of Oracle, Ellison holds shares in the firm worth $38 billion. No one can say for certain how hard Ellison would have worked with a different compensation package. But one thing is clear: He has a huge personal stake in the success of the firm—and in increasing its market value.

Well-designed compensation schemes encourage management to maximize shareholder wealth. But some schemes are not well designed, and in these cases poorly performing managers may receive large windfall gains. For example, during Robert Nardelli's roughly 6-year tenure as CEO of Home Depot, the stock price fell by more than 20% while shares of its rival, Lowe's, more than doubled. When Nardelli was ousted in January 2007, he received a farewell compensation package of about $210 million. Needless to say, shareholders were not impressed by the board's generosity.

Takeovers   Poorly performing companies are more likely to be taken over by another firm. The further a company's stock price falls, the easier it is for another company to buy up a majority of its shares. The old management team is then likely to find itself out on the street. We discuss takeovers in Chapter 21.

Shareholder Pressure   If shareholders believe that the corporation is underperforming and the board of directors is not sufficiently aggressive in holding managers to task, they can try to replace the board in the next election. The dissident shareholders will attempt to convince the other shareholders to vote for their slate of candidates to the board. If they succeed, a new board will be elected and it can replace the current management team. For example, in 2008 billionaire shareholder Carl Icahn felt that the directors of Yahoo! were not acting in shareholders' interest when they rejected a bid from Microsoft. He therefore invested $67 million in Yahoo! stock and muscled himself and two like-minded friends onto the Yahoo! board.

Disgruntled stockholders also take the "Wall Street Walk" by selling out and moving on to other investments. The Wall Street Walk can send a powerful message. If enough shareholders bail out, the stock price tumbles. This damages top management's reputation and compensation. A large part of top managers' paychecks comes from stock options, which pay off if the stock price rises but are worthless if the price falls below a stated threshold.

We do not want to leave the impression that corporate life is a series of squabbles and endless micromanagement. It isn't, because practical corporate finance has evolved to reconcile personal and corporate interests—to keep everyone working together to increase the value of the whole pie, not merely the size of each person's slice.

Agency problems are mitigated in practice in several ways: legal and regulatory standards; compensation plans that tie the fortunes of the managers to the fortunes of the firm; monitoring by lenders, stock market analysts, and investors, and ultimately the threat that poorly performing managers will be fired.

Self-Test 1.7

What is an agency problem? Give two or three examples of decisions by managers that lead to agency costs.

Corporate Governance

Financial markets and institutions are supposed to direct financing to all firms that can invest at superior rates of return. But financing moves from investors to firms only if investors are protected. This creates the need for a system of *corporate governance* so that money can flow to the right firms at the right times. Governance includes well-designed incentives for managers, standards for accounting and disclosure to investors, requirements for boards of directors, and legal sanctions for fraud or self-dealing by management. When scandals happen, we say that corporate governance has broken down. When corporations compete effectively and ethically to deliver value to shareholders, we are comforted that corporate governance is working properly.

Think, for example, of the financial history of FedEx, which we reviewed at the start of the chapter. FedEx survived and grew because it had access to financing from outside investors. That financing was forthcoming because investors trusted the company to invest wisely. In other words, they had faith in the U.S. system of corporate governance, and they trusted the directors and managers of FedEx to try to increase shareholder value.

Chapter 1 is not the right place for a worldwide tour of corporate governance. But be aware that governance laws, regulations, and practice vary. The differences are more dramatic in continental Europe and Japan than in Canada, the United Kingdom, Australia, and other English-speaking companies. In Germany, for example, banks often own or control large blocks of stock and can push hard for changes in the management or strategy of poorly performing companies. (Banks in the United States are prohibited from large or permanent holdings of the stock of nonfinancial corporations.) Large German firms also have two boards of directors: the supervisory board *(Aufsichtsrat)* and the management board *(Vorstand).* Half of the supervisory board's members are elected by employees. Some French firms also have two boards, one including employee representatives.

1.5 Careers in Finance

Well over 1 million people work in the financial services industry in the United States, and many others work as financial managers in corporations. We can't tell you what each one does all day, but we can give you some idea of the variety of careers in finance. The nearby box summarizes the experience of a small sample of recent graduates.[12]

We explained earlier that corporations face two principal financial decisions: the investment decision and the financing decision. Therefore, as a newly recruited financial analyst, you may help to analyze a major new investment project. Or you may instead help to raise the money to pay for it, perhaps by negotiating a bank loan or by arranging to lease the plant and equipment. Other financial analysts work on short-term finance, managing collection and investment of the company's cash or checking whether customers are likely to pay their bills. Financial analysts are also involved in monitoring and controlling risk. For example, they may help to arrange insurance for the firm's plant and equipment, or they may assist with the purchase and sale of options, futures, and other exotic tools for managing risk.

Instead of working in the finance department of a corporation, you may join a financial institution. The largest employers are banks. Banks collect deposits and relend the cash to corporations and individuals. If you join a bank, you may start in a branch office, where individuals and small businesses come to deposit cash or to seek a loan. You could also work in the head office, helping to analyze a $500 million loan to a large corporation.

Banks do many things in addition to lending money, and they probably provide a greater variety of jobs than other financial institutions. For example, if you work in the cash management department of a large bank, you may help companies to transfer huge sums of money electronically as wages, taxes, and payments to suppliers. Banks

---

[12] The careers are fictitious but based on the actual experiences of several of the authors' students.

Working in Finance

Susan Webb, Research Analyst, Mutual Fund Group

After majoring in biochemistry, I joined the research department of a large mutual fund group. Because of my background, I was assigned to work with the senior pharmaceuticals analyst. I start the day by reading *The Wall Street Journal* and reviewing the analyses that come in each day from stockbroking firms. Sometimes we need to revise our earnings forecasts and meet with the portfolio managers to discuss possible trades. The remainder of my day is spent mainly in analyzing companies and developing forecasts of revenues and earnings. I meet frequently with pharmaceutical analysts in stockbroking firms, and we regularly visit company management. In the evenings I study for the Chartered Financial Analyst (CFA) exam. Since I did not study finance at college, this is quite challenging. I hope eventually to move from a research role to become a portfolio manager.

Richard Gradley, Project Finance, Large Energy Company

After leaving college, I joined the finance department of a large energy company. I spent my first year helping to analyze capital investment proposals. I then moved to the project finance group, which is responsible for analyzing independent power projects around the world. Recently, I have been involved in a proposal to set up a company that would build and operate a large new electricity plant in southeast Asia. We built a spreadsheet model of the project to make sure that it was viable. We had to check that the contracts with the builders, operators, suppliers, and so on, were all in place before we could arrange bank financing for the project.

Albert Rodriguez, European Markets Group, Major New York Bank

I joined the bank after majoring in finance. I spent the first 6 months in the bank's training program, rotating between departments. I was assigned to the European markets team just before the 2010 Greek crisis, when worries about a possible default caused interest rates on Greek government debt to jump to more than 4% above the rate on comparable German government debt. There was a lot of activity, with everyone trying to figure out whether Greece might be forced to abandon the euro and how this would affect our business. My job is largely concerned with analyzing economies and assessing the prospects for bank business. There are plenty of opportunities to work abroad, and I hope to spend some time in Madrid or one of our other European offices.

Sherry Solera, Branch Manager, Regional Bank

I took basic finance courses in college, but nothing specific for banking. I started here as a teller. I was able to learn about banking through the bank's training program and also by evening courses at a local college. Last year I was promoted to branch manager. I oversee the branch's operations and help customers with a wide variety of problems. I'm also spending more time on credit analysis of business loan applications. I want to expand the branch's business customers, but not by making loans to shaky companies.

---

also buy and sell foreign exchange, so you could find yourself working in front of one of those computer screens in a foreign exchange trading room. Another glamorous bank job is in the derivatives group, which helps companies to manage their risk by buying and selling options, futures, and so on. This is where the mathematicians and the computer buffs thrive.

Investment banks, such as Goldman Sachs or Morgan Stanley, help companies sell their securities to investors. They also have large corporate finance departments that assist firms in mergers and acquisitions. When firms issue securities or try to take over another firm, a lot of money is at stake and the firms may need to move fast. Thus, working for an investment bank can be a high-pressure activity with long hours. It can also pay very well.

The insurance industry is another large employer. Much of the insurance industry is involved in designing and selling insurance policies on people's lives and property, but businesses are also major customers. So, if you work for an insurance company or a large insurance broker, you could find yourself arranging insurance on a Boeing 787 in the United States or an oil rig in Indonesia.

Life insurance companies are major lenders to corporations and to investors in commercial real estate. (Life insurance companies deploy the insurance premiums received from policyholders into medium- or long-term loans; banks specialize in shorter-term financing.) So you could end up negotiating a $50 million loan for construction of a new shopping center or investigating the creditworthiness of a family-owned manufacturing company that has applied for a loan to expand production.

Then there is the business of "managing money," that is, deciding which companies' shares to invest in or how to balance investment in shares with safer securities, such as the bonds (debt securities) issued by the U.S. Treasury.

Take mutual funds, for example. A mutual fund collects money from individuals and invests in a portfolio of stocks or bonds. A financial analyst in a mutual fund analyzes the prospects for the securities and works with the investment manager to decide which should be bought and sold. Many other financial institutions also contain investment management departments. For example, you might work as a financial analyst in the investment department of an insurance company. (Insurance companies also invest in traded securities.) Or you could be a financial analyst in the trust department of a bank that manages money for retirement funds, universities, and charities.

Stockbroking firms help investment management companies and private individuals to invest in securities. They employ sales staff and dealers who make the trades. They also employ financial analysts to analyze the securities and help customers to decide which to buy or sell.

Investment banks and stockbroking firms are largely headquartered in New York, as are many of the large commercial banks. Insurance companies and investment management companies tend to be more scattered. For example, some of the largest insurance companies are headquartered in Hartford, Connecticut, and many investment management companies are located in Boston. Of course, some U.S. financial institutions have large businesses outside the United States. Finance is a global business. So you may spend some time working in a branch overseas or making the occasional trip to one of the other major financial centers, such as London, Tokyo, Hong Kong, or Singapore.

Finance professionals tend to be well paid. Starting salaries for new graduates are in the region of $45,000, rather more in a major New York investment bank and somewhat less in a small regional bank. But let us look ahead a little: Table 1.2 gives you an idea of the compensation that you can look forward to when you become a senior financial manager.

If you would like to learn more about careers in finance, we suggest you start by logging on to **www.careers-in-finance.com**. This site describes jobs in commercial banking, corporate finance, financial planning, insurance, investment banking, money management, and real estate. For each area the site describes the types of jobs available, the skills and talents needed, salary ranges, and so on. We have listed several other useful job Web sites on our book Web site at **www.mhhe.com/bmm7e**.

TABLE 1.2 Representative compensation for jobs in finance

Career	Annual Compensation
Commercial Banking	
Loan officer	$100,000
Financial analyst	$58,000
Corporate Finance	
Financial analyst	$63–81,000
Assistant treasurer	$88–113,000
Chief financial officer	$260–390,000
Major Investment Banks	
First-year analyst	$90,000
Vice president	$500,000
Managing director/partner	$800,000
Department head	$2 million
Money Management	
Portfolio manager	$500,000+
Bank trust department	$90–180,000
Hedge fund head	$1.3 million

Source: Careers-in-Business, LLC.; **www.careers-in-finance.com**, **www.salary.com**.

1.6 Topics Covered in This Book

This book covers investment decisions, then financing decisions, and then a variety of planning issues that require an understanding of both investment and financing. But first there are three further introductory chapters that should be helpful to readers making a first acquaintance with financial management. Chapter 2 is an overview of financial markets and institutions. Chapter 3 reviews the basic concepts of accounting, and Chapter 4 demonstrates the techniques of financial statement analysis.

In Parts 2 and 3 we look at different aspects of the investment decision. The first is the problem of how to value assets, and the second is the link between risk and value. Our discussion of these topics occupies Chapters 5 through 13.

Nine chapters devoted to the simple problem of finding real assets that are worth more than they cost may seem excessive, but that problem is not so simple in practice. We will require a theory of how long-lived, risky assets are valued, and that requirement will lead us to basic questions about financial markets. For example:

- How are corporate bonds and stocks valued in capital markets?
- What risks are borne by investors in corporate securities? How can these risks be measured?
- What compensation do investors demand for bearing risk?
- What rate of return can investors in common stocks reasonably expect to receive?
- Do stock prices accurately reflect the underlying value of the firm?

Intelligent capital budgeting and financing decisions require answers to these and other questions about how capital markets work.

Financing decisions occupy Parts 4 and 5. The two chapters in Part 4 describe the kinds of securities corporations use to raise money and explain how and when these securities are issued. Part 5 covers debt policy and dividend policy. We will also describe what happens when firms find themselves in financial distress because of poor operating performance, excessive borrowing, or both.

Part 6 covers financial analysis and planning. We cover long- and short-term financial planning and the management of working capital. *Working capital* refers to short-term assets (such as cash, inventories, and money due from customers), net of short-term liabilities (such as the money that the firm has promised to pay to suppliers, banks, or other short-term lenders).

Part 7 covers three important problems that require decisions about both investment and financing. First we look at mergers and acquisitions. Then we consider international financial management. All the financial problems of doing business at home are present overseas, but the international financial manager faces the additional complications created by multiple currencies, different tax systems, and special regulations imposed by foreign institutions and governments. Finally, we look at risk management and the specialized securities, including futures and options, that managers can use to hedge or lay off risks.

Part 8 is our conclusion. It also discusses some of the things that we don't know about finance. If you can be the first to solve any of these puzzles, you will be justifiably famous.

Snippets of History

Now let's lighten up a little. In this book we are going to describe how financial decisions are made today. But financial markets also have an interesting history. Look at the nearby box, which lays out bits of this history, starting in prehistoric times, when the growth of bacteria anticipated the mathematics of compound interest, and continuing nearly to the present. We have keyed each of these episodes to the chapter of the book that discusses its topic.

Finance through the Ages

Date unknown *Compound Growth.* Bacteria start to propagate by subdividing. They thereby demonstrate the power of compound growth. *(Chapter 5)*

c. 1800 B.C. *Interest Rates.* In Babylonia, Hammurabi's Code established maximum interest rates on loans. Borrowers often mortgaged their property and sometimes their spouses, but lenders were obliged to return spouses in good condition within 3 years. *(Chapter 6)*

c. 1000 B.C. *Options.* One of the earliest recorded options is described by Aristotle. The philosopher Thales knew by the stars that there would be a great olive harvest, so, having a little money, he bought options for the use of olive presses. When the harvest came, Thales was able to rent the presses at great profit. Today financial managers need to be able to evaluate options to buy or sell a wide variety of assets. *(Chapter 23)*

15th century *International Banking.* Modern international banking had its origins in the great Florentine banking houses. But the entire European network of the Medici empire employed only 57 people in eight offices. Today the London-based bank HSBC has around 300,000 employees in 88 different countries. *(Chapter 14)*

1650 *Futures.* Futures markets allow companies to protect themselves against fluctuations in commodity prices. During the Tokugawa era in Japan, feudal lords collected rents in the form of rice, but often they wished to trade their future rice deliveries. Rice futures therefore came to be traded on what was later known as the Dojima Rice Market. Rice futures are still traded, but now companies can also trade in futures on a range of items from pork bellies to stock market indexes. *(Chapter 24)*

17th century *Joint Stock Corporations.* Although investors have for a long time combined together as joint owners of an enterprise, the modern corporation with a large number of stockholders originated with the formation in England of trading firms like the East India Company (est. 1599). *(Chapter 15)*

17th century *Money.* America has been in the forefront in the development of new types of money. Early settlers often used a shell known as wampum. For example, Peter Stuyvesant raised a loan in wampum, and in Massachusetts it was legal tender. Unfortunately, the enterprising settlers found that with a little dye the relatively common white wampum shells could be converted profitably into the more valuable black ones, which confirmed Gresham's law that bad money drives out good. The first issue of paper money in America (and almost in the world) was by the Massachusetts Bay Colony in 1690, and other colonies soon set their printing presses to producing money. In 1862 Congress agreed to an issue of paper money that would be legal tender. These notes, printed in green ink, immediately became known as "greenbacks." *(Chapters 19, 20)*

1720 *New-Issue Speculation.* From time to time investors have been tempted by speculative new issues. During the South Sea Bubble in England one company was launched to develop perpetual motion. Another enterprising individual announced a company "for carrying on an undertaking of great advantage but nobody to know what it is." Within 5 hours he had raised £2,000; within 6 hours he was on his way out of the country. Readers nearly two centuries later could only wonder at the naïve or foolhardy investors in these ventures—that is, until they had a chance to participate in the follies unearthed by the financial crisis of 2008–2009. *(Chapter 2)*

1792 *Formation of the New York Stock Exchange.* The New York Stock Exchange (NYSE) was founded in 1792 when a group of brokers met under a buttonwood tree* and arranged to trade shares with one another at agreed rates of commission. Today the NYSE is the largest stock exchange in the world, trading on average about 2 billion shares a day. *(Chapter 7)*

1929 *Stock Market Crashes.* Common stocks are risky investments. In September 1929 stock prices in the United States reached an all-time high, and the economist Irving Fisher forecast that they were at "a permanently high plateau." Some 3 years later stock prices were almost 90% lower, and it was to be a quarter of a century before the prices of September 1929 were seen again. Eighty years later, history came close to repeating itself. After stock prices peaked in July 2007, they slumped over the next 20 months by 54%. *(Chapter 11)*

1960s *Eurodollar Market.* In the 1950s the Soviet Union transferred its dollar holdings from the United States to a Russian-owned bank in Paris. This bank was best known by its telex address, eurobank, and consequently dollars held outside the United States came to be known as eurodollars. In the 1960s U.S. taxes and regulation made it much cheaper to borrow and lend dollars in Europe than in the United States, and a huge market in eurodollars arose. *(Chapter 14)*

1971 *Corporate Bankruptcies.* Every generation of investors is shocked and surprised by a major corporate bankruptcy. In 1971 the Penn Central Railroad, a pillar of American industry, suddenly collapsed. Penn Central showed assets of $4.6 billion, about $21 billion in today's dollars. At that time it was the largest corporate bankruptcy in history. In 2008 the investment bank Lehman Brothers smashed Penn Central's record. *(Chapter 16)*

1972 *Financial Futures.* Financial futures allow companies to protect themselves against fluctuations in interest rates, exchange rates, and so on. It is said that they originated from a remark by the economist Milton Friedman that he was unable to profit from his view that sterling (the U.K. currency) was overpriced. The Chicago Mercantile Exchange founded the first financial futures market. Today futures exchanges trade 1.9 billion contracts a year of financial futures. *(Chapter 24)*

1986 *Capital Investment Decisions.* The largest investment project undertaken by a private company was the construction of the tunnel under the English Channel. This started in 1986 and was completed in 1994 at a total cost of $15 billion. The cost of the proposed natural gas pipeline from the North Slope of Alaska to Alberta, Canada, is estimated at over $30 billion. *(Chapters 8, 9)*

1988 *Mergers.* The 1980s saw a wave of takeovers culminating in the $25 billion takeover of RJR Nabisco. Over a period of 6 weeks three groups battled for control of the company. As one of the contestants put it, "We were charging through the rice paddies, not stopping for anything and taking no prisoners." The takeover was the largest in history and generated almost $1 billion in fees for the banks and advisers. *(Chapter 21)*

1993 *Inflation.* Financial managers need to recognize the effect of inflation on interest rates and on the profitability of the firm's investments. In the United States inflation has been relatively modest, but some countries have suffered from hyperinflation. In Hungary after World War II the government issued banknotes worth 1,000 trillion pengoes. In Yugoslavia in October 1993 prices rose by nearly 2,000% and a dollar bought 105 million dinars. *(Chapter 5)*

1780 and 1997 *Inflation-Indexed Debt.* In 1780, Massachusetts paid Revolutionary War soldiers with interest-bearing notes rather than its rapidly eroding currency. Interest and principal payments on the notes were tied to the rate of subsequent inflation. After a 217-year hiatus, the U.S. Treasury issued inflation-indexed notes called TIPS (Treasury Inflation Protected Securities). Many other countries, including Britain and Israel, had done so previously. *(Chapter 6)*

1993 *Controlling Risk.* When a company fails to keep close tabs on the risks being taken by its employees, it can get into serious trouble. This was the fate of Barings, a 220-year-old British bank that numbered the queen among its clients. In 1993 it discovered that Nick Leeson, a trader in its Singapore office, had hidden losses of $1.3 billion (£869 million) from unauthorized bets on the Japanese equity market. The losses wiped out Barings and landed Leeson in jail, with a 6-year sentence. In 2008 a rogue trader at the French bank Societé Generale established a new record by losing $7 billion on unauthorized deals. *(Chapter 24)*

1999 *The Euro.* Large corporations do business in many currencies. In 1999 a new currency came into existence when 11 European countries adopted the euro in place of their separate currencies. They have since been joined by six other countries. This is not the first time that different countries have agreed on a common currency. In 1865 France, Belgium, Switzerland, and Italy came together in the Latin Monetary Union, and they were joined by Greece and Romania the following year. Members of the European Monetary Union (EMU) hope that the euro will be a longer-lasting success than this earlier experiment. As we write this in 2010, the euro is facing its first major test as EMU members attempt to bail out the Greek and Irish governments to prevent them from defaulting on their debt. *(Chapter 23)*

2002 *Financial Scandals.* A seemingly endless series of financial and accounting scandals climaxed in this year. Resulting bankruptcies included the icons Enron (and its accounting firm, Arthur Andersen), WorldCom, and the Italian food company Parmalat. Congress passed the Sarbanes-Oxley Act to increase the accountability of corporations and executives. *(Chapters 1, 14)*

2007–2009 *Subprime Mortgages.* Subprime mortgages are housing loans made to homeowners with shaky credit standing. After a decade in which housing prices had consistently gone up, lenders became complacent about the risks of these home loans and progressively loosened lending standards. When housing prices stalled and interest rates increased in 2007, many of these loans went bad. Some large banks such as Lehman Brothers went to the wall, while others such as Wachovia and Merrill Lynch were rescued with the aid of government money. *(Chapters 2, 14)*

---

* The American sycamore, *Planatus occidentalis.*

SUMMARY

What are the two major decisions made by financial managers? *(LO1)*

Financial management can be broken down into (1) the **investment,** or **capital budgeting,** decision and (2) the **financing** decision. The firm has to decide (1) which real assets to invest in, and (2) how to raise the funds necessary to pay for those investments.

What does "real asset" mean? *(LO2)*

Real assets include all assets used in the production or sale of the firms' products or services. They can be tangible (plant and equipment, for example) or intangible (patents or trademarks, for example). In contrast, **financial assets** (such as stocks or bonds) are claims on the income generated by real assets.

What are the advantages and disadvantages of forming a corporation? *(LO3)*

Corporations are distinct, permanent legal entities. They allow for separation of ownership and control, and they can continue operating without disruption even as ownership changes. They provide **limited liability** to their owners. On the other hand, managing the corporation's legal machinery is costly. Also, corporations are subject to double taxation, because they pay taxes on their profits and the shareholders are taxed again when they receive dividends or sell their shares at a profit.

Who are the principal financial managers in a corporation? (*LO4*)

Almost all managers are involved to some degree in investment decisions, but some managers specialize in finance, for example, the treasurer, controller, and CFO. The **treasurer** is most directly responsible for raising capital and maintaining relationships with banks and investors that hold the firm's securities. The **controller** is responsible for preparing financial statements and managing budgets. In large firms, a **chief financial officer** oversees both the treasurer and the controller and is involved in financial policymaking and corporate planning.

Why does it make sense for corporations to maximize shareholder wealth? (*LO5*)

Value maximization is the natural financial goal of the firm. Shareholders can invest or consume the increased wealth as they wish, provided that they have access to well-functioning financial markets.

What is the fundamental trade-off in investment decisions? (*LO6*)

Companies either can invest in real assets or can return the cash to shareholders, who can invest it for themselves. The return that shareholders can earn for themselves is called the **opportunity cost of capital.** Companies increase shareholder wealth whenever they can earn a higher return on their investments than the opportunity cost of capital.

Is value maximization ethical? (*LO7*)

Shareholders do not want the maximum possible stock price; they want the maximum honest price. But there need be no conflict between value maximization and ethical behavior. The surest route to maximum value starts with products and services that satisfy customers. A good reputation with customers, employees, and other stakeholders is important for the firm's long-run profitability and value.

How do corporations ensure that managers act in the interest of stockholders? (*LO8*)

Conflicts of interest between managers and stockholders can lead to **agency problems.** These problems are kept in check by compensation plans that link the well-being of employees to that of the firm; by monitoring of management by the board of directors, security analysts, and creditors; and by the threat of takeover.

QUESTIONS

QUIZ

1. **Financial Decisions.** Give several examples of (a) investment decisions and (b) financing decisions. (*LO1*)

2. **Corporations.** What are the key differences between a corporation and a sole proprietorship? What is the difference between a public and a private corporation? (*LO3*)

3. **Corporations.** What is the key advantage of separating ownership and management in large corporations? (*LO3*)

4. **Limited Liability.** What is limited liability, and who benefits from it? (*LO3*)

5. **Corporations.** What do we mean when we say that corporate income is subject to *double taxation*? (*LO3*)

6. **Real versus Financial Assets.** Which of the following are real assets, and which are financial? (*LO2*)

   a. A share of stock.
   b. A personal IOU.
   c. A trademark.
   d. A truck.
   e. Undeveloped land.
   f. The balance in the firm's checking account.
   g. An experienced and hardworking sales force.
   h. A bank loan agreement.

7. **Financial Managers.** Which of the following statements more accurately describes the treasurer than the controller? (*LO4*)

   a. Monitors capital expenditures to make sure that they are not misappropriated.
   b. Responsible for investing the firm's spare cash.

c. Responsible for arranging any issue of common stock.
d. Responsible for the company's tax affairs.

8. **Value Maximization.** The objective of value maximization makes sense when stockholders have access to modern financial markets and institutions. Briefly explain why. *(LO5)*

9. **Value Maximization.** Give an example of an action that might increase short-run profits but at the same time reduce stock price and the market value of the firm. *(LO5)*

10. **Cost of Capital.** Why do financial managers refer to the *opportunity* cost of capital? How would you find the opportunity cost of capital for a safe investment? *(LO5)*

11. **Agency Costs.** What are agency costs? List some ways by which agency costs are mitigated. *(LO7)*

PRACTICE PROBLEMS

12. **Agency Problems.** Many firms have devised defenses that make it much more costly or difficult for other firms to take them over. How might such takeover defenses affect the firm's agency problems? Are managers of firms with formidable takeover defenses more or less likely to act in the firm's interest rather than their own? *(LO7)*

13. **Financial Decisions.** What is the difference between capital budgeting decisions and capital structure decisions? *(LO1)*

14. **Financial Assets.** Why is a bank loan a financial asset? *(LO2)*

15. **Real Assets.** Explain how investment in an R&D program creates a real asset. *(LO2)*

16. **Financial Managers.** Explain the differences between the CFO's responsibilities and the treasurer's and controller's responsibilities. *(LO4)*

17. **Limited Liability.** Is limited liability always an advantage for a corporation and its shareholders? *Hint:* Could limited liability reduce a corporation's access to financing? *(LO3)*

18. **Goals of the Firm.** You may have heard big business criticized for focusing on short-term performance at the expense of long-term results. Explain why a firm that strives to maximize stock price should be *less* subject to an overemphasis on short-term results than one that simply maximizes profits. *(LO5)*

19. **Value Maximization.** Fritz is risk-averse and is content with a relatively low but safe return on his investments. Frieda is risk-tolerant and seeks a very high rate of return on her invested savings. Yet both shareholders will applaud a low-risk capital investment that offers a superior rate of return. Why? What is meant by "superior"? *(LO5)*

20. **Goals of the Firm.** We claim that the goal of the firm is to maximize current market value. Could the following actions be consistent with that goal? *(LO5)*

a. The firm adds a cost-of-living adjustment to the pensions of its retired employees.
b. The firm reduces its dividend payment, choosing to reinvest more of earnings in the business.
c. The firm buys a corporate jet for its executives.
d. The firm drills for oil in a remote jungle. The chance of finding oil is only 1 in 5.

21. **Goals of the Firm.** Explain why each of the following may not be appropriate corporate goals: *(LO5)*

a. Increase market share.
b. Minimize costs.
c. Underprice any competitors.
d. Expand profits.

22. **Agency Issues.** Sometimes lawyers work on a contingency basis. They collect a percentage of their clients' settlements instead of receiving fixed fees. Why might clients prefer this arrangement? Would the arrangement mitigate an agency problem? *(LO7)*

23. **Reputation.** As you drive down a deserted highway, you are overcome with a sudden desire for a hamburger. Fortunately, just ahead are two hamburger outlets; one is owned by a national

brand, the other appears to be owned by "Joe." Which outlet has the greater incentive to serve you catmeat? Why? *(LO6)*

24. **Agency Issues.** One of the "Finance through the Ages" episodes that we cited is the 1993 collapse of Barings Bank, when one of its traders lost $1.3 billion. Traders are compensated in large part according to their trading profits. How might this practice have contributed to an agency problem? *(LO7)*

25. **Cost of Capital.** British Quince comes across an average-risk investment project that offers a rate of return of 9.5%. This is less than the company's normal rate of return, but one of Quince's directors notes that the company can easily borrow the required investment at 7%. "It's simple," he says. "If the bank lends us money at 7%, then our cost of capital must be 7%. The project's return is higher than the cost of capital, so let's move ahead." How would you respond? *(LO5)*

26. **Cost of Capital.** In a stroke of good luck, your company has uncovered an opportunity to invest for 10 years at a guaranteed 6% rate of return. How would you determine the opportunity cost of capital for this investment? *(LO5)*

27. **Cost of Capital.** Pollution Busters, Inc., is considering purchase of 10 additional carbon sequesters for $100,000 apiece. The sequesters last for only 1 year before becoming saturated. Then the carbon is sold to the government.

    a. Suppose the government guarantees the price of carbon. At this price, the payoff after 1 year is $115,000 for sure. How would you determine the opportunity cost of capital for this investment? *(LO5)*
    b. Suppose instead that the sequestered carbon has to be sold on the London Carbon Exchange. Carbon prices have been extremely volatile, but Pollution Busters' CFO learns that average rates of return from investments on that exchange have been about 20%. She thinks this is a reasonable forecast for the future. What is the opportunity cost of capital in this case? Is purchase of additional sequesters a worthwhile capital investment? *(LO5)*.

28. **Agency Issues.** Discuss which of the following forms of compensation is most likely to align the interests of managers and shareholders: *(LO7)*

    a. A fixed salary.
    b. A salary linked to company profits.
    c. A salary that is paid partly in the form of the company's shares.

29. **Agency Issues.** When a company's stock is widely held, it may not pay an individual shareholder to spend time monitoring managers' performance and trying to replace poor performers. Explain why. Do you think that a bank that has made a large loan to the company is in a different position? *(LO7)*

30. **Corporate Governance.** How do clear and comprehensive financial reports promote effective corporate governance? *(LO7)*

31. **Corporate Governance.** Some commentators have claimed that the U.S. system of corporate governance is "broken" and needs thorough reform. What do you think? Do you see systematic failures in corporate governance or just a few "bad apples"? *(LO7)*

32. **Ethics.** In some countries, such as Japan and Germany, corporations develop close long-term relationships with one bank and rely on that bank for a large part of their financing needs. In the United States companies are more likely to shop around for the best deal. Do you think that this practice is more or less likely to encourage ethical behavior on the part of the corporation? *(LO6)*

33. **Ethics.** Is there a conflict between "doing well" and "doing good?" In other words, are policies that increase the value of the firm (doing well) necessarily at odds with socially responsible policies (doing good)? When there are conflicts, how might government regulations or laws tilt the firm toward doing good? For example, how do taxes or fees charged on pollutants affect the firm's decision to pollute? Can you cite other examples of "incentives" used by governments to align private interests with public ones? *(LO6)*

34. **Ethics.** The following report appeared in the *Financial Times* (October 28, 1999, p. 1): "Coca-Cola is testing a vending machine that automatically raises the price of the world's favorite soft drink when the temperature increases . . . The new machine, believed to have been tested in Japan, may well create controversy by using hot weather to charge extra. One rival said the idea of charging more when temperatures rose was 'incredible.'" Discuss. *(LO6)*

SOLUTIONS TO SELF-TEST QUESTIONS

1.1   a. The development of a microprocessor is a capital budgeting decision. The investment of $1 billion will purchase a real asset, the microprocessor design and production facilities.

       b. The bank loan is a financing decision. This is how Volkswagen will raise money for its investment.

       c. Capital budgeting.

       d. Capital budgeting. The marketing campaign should generate a real, though intangible, asset.

       e. Both. The acquisition is an investment decision. The decision to issue shares is a financing decision.

1.2   a. A real asset. Real assets can be intangible assets.

       b. Financial.

       c. Real.

       d. Financial.

       e. Real.

       f. Financial.

1.3   Fritz would more likely be the treasurer and Frieda the controller. The treasurer raises money from the financial markets and requires a background in financial institutions. The controller requires a background in accounting.

1.4   There is no reason for the Hotspurs to avoid high-dividend stocks, even if they wish to invest for tuition bills in the distant future. Their concern should be with only the risk and expected return of the shares. If a particular stock pays a generous cash dividend, they always have the option of reinvesting the dividend in that stock or, for that matter, in other securities. The dividend payout does not affect their ability to redirect current investment income to their future needs as they plan for their anticipated tuition bills.

1.5   Because investors can reasonably expect a 15% return in other investments in palladium, the firm should take this as the opportunity cost of capital for its proposed investment. Although the project is expected to show an accounting profit, its expected return is only 12%. Therefore, the firm should reject the project: its expected return is less than the 15% expected return offered by equivalent-risk investments.

1.6   Harry's has a far bigger stake in the reputation of its business than Victor's. The store has been in business for a long time. The owners have spent years establishing customer loyalty. In contrast, Victor's has just been established. The owner has little of his own money tied up in the firm, and so has little to lose if the business fails. In addition, the nature of the business results in little customer loyalty. Harry's is probably more reliable.

1.7   Agency problems arise when managers and shareholders have different objectives. Managers may empire-build with excessive investment and growth. Managers may be unduly risk-averse, or they may try to take excessive salaries or perquisites.

CHAPTER 2

Financial Markets and Institutions

LEARNING OBJECTIVES

After studying this chapter, you should be able to:

(1) Understand how financial markets and institutions channel savings to corporate investment.

(2) Understand the basic structure of mutual funds, pension funds, banks, and insurance companies.

(3) Explain the functions of financial markets and institutions.

(4) Understand the main events behind the financial crisis of 2007–2009.

RELATED WEB SITES FOR THIS CHAPTER CAN BE FOUND AT WWW.MHHE.COM/BMM7E.

The façade of the New York Stock Exchange is imposing. But financial managers need a deeper understanding of how financial markets work.

If a corporation needs to issue more shares of stock, then its financial manager had better understand how the stock market works. If it wants to take out a bank loan, the financial manager had better understand how banks and other financial institutions work. If the firm wants to commit to a capital investment, for example, a factory expansion or a new product launch, the financial manager needs to think clearly about the cost of the capital that the firm raises from outside investors. As we pointed out in Chapter 1, the opportunity cost of capital for the firm is the rate of return that its stockholders could expect to get by investing on their own in financial markets. This means that the financial manager needs to understand how prices are determined in the financial markets in order to make wise investment decisions.

Financial markets and institutions are the firm's financial environment. You don't have to understand everything about that environment to begin the study of financial management, but a general understanding provides useful context for the work ahead. For example, it will help you to understand why you are calculating the yield to maturity of a bond in Chapter 6, the net present value of a capital investment in Chapter 9, or the weighted-average cost of capital for a company in Chapter 13.

This chapter does three things. First, it surveys financial markets and institutions. We will cover the stock and bond markets, mutual and pension funds, and banks and insurance companies. Second, we will set out the functions of financial markets and institutions and look at how they help corporations and the economy. Third, we will discuss the financial crisis of 2007–2009. An understanding of what happens when financial markets do *not* function well is important for understanding why and how financial markets and institutions matter.

2.1 The Importance of Financial Markets and Institutions

In the previous chapter we explained why corporations have to be good at finance in order to survive and prosper. All corporations face important investment and financing decisions. But of course those decisions are not made in a vacuum. They are made in a financial environment. That environment has two main segments: financial markets and financial institutions.

Large corporations have to go to financial markets and institutions for the financing they need to grow. When they have a surplus of cash, and no need for immediate financing, they have to invest the cash, for example, in bank accounts or in securities. Let's take Apple Computer, Inc., as an example.

Table 2.1 presents a timeline for Apple and examples of the sources of financing tapped by Apple from its start-up in a California garage in 1976 to its cash-rich status in 2010. The initial investment in Apple stock was $250,000. Apple was also able to get short-term financing from parts suppliers who did not demand immediate payment. Apple was able to get the parts, assemble and sell the computers, and then pay off its accounts payable to the suppliers. (We discuss accounts payable in Chapter 19.) Then, as Apple grew, it was able to obtain several rounds of financing by selling Apple shares to private venture capital investors. (We discuss venture capital in Chapter 15.)

TABLE 2.1 Examples of financing decisions by Apple Computer

April 1976: Apple Computer, Inc., founded	Mike Makkula, Apple's first chairman, invests $250,000 in Apple shares.
1976: First 200 computers sold	Parts suppliers give Apple 30 days to pay. (Financing from accounts payable.)
1978–79	Apple raises $3.5 million from venture capital investors.
December 1980: Initial public offering	Apple raises $91 million, after fees and expenses, by selling shares to public investors.
May 1981	Apple sells 2.6 million additional shares at $31.25 per share.
April 1987	Apple pays its first dividend at an annual rate of $.12 per share
Early 1990s	Apple carries out several share repurchase programs.
1994	Apple issues $300 million of debt at an interest rate of 6.5%.
1996–97: Apple reports a $740 million loss in the second quarter of 1996. Lays off 2,700 employees in 1997.	Dividend is suspended in February 1996. Apple sells $661 million of debt to private investors in June 1996. The borrowing provides "sufficient liquidity" to execute Apple's strategic plans and to "return the company to profitability."
September 1997: Acquires assets of Power Computing Corp.	Acquisition is financed with $100 million of Apple stock.
2004: Apple is healthy and profitable, thanks to iMac, iPod, and other products.	Apple pays off the $300 million in long-term debt issued in 1994, leaving the company with no long-term debt outstanding.
2005–10	Apple's profits grow rapidly, but it pays no cash dividends. Instead it invests in short-term marketable securities, which accumulate to $25.6 billion by 2010.
From start-up to 2010	Apple stockholders reinvest $37.2 billion of earnings. Thus Apple's 2010 balance sheet shows cumulative retained earnings of $37.2 billion.

In December 1980, it raised $91 million in an initial public offering (IPO) of its shares to public investors. There was also a follow-up share issue in May 1981.[1]

Once Apple was a public company, it could raise financing from many sources, and it was able to pay for acquisitions by issuing more shares. We show a few examples in Table 2.1.

Apple started paying cash dividends to shareholders in 1987, and it also distributed cash to investors by stock repurchases in the early 1990s. But Apple hit a rough patch in 1996 and 1997, and regular dividends were eliminated. The company had to borrow $660 million from a group of private investors in order to cover its losses and finance its recovery plan. Apple was generally profitable, despite the rough years, and it financed growth by plowing back earnings into its operations. These retained earnings had cumulated to $37.2 billion by 2010.

Apple is well known for its product innovations, including the Macintosh computer, the iPod, and the iPad. Apple is not special because of financing. In fact, the story of its financing is not too different from that of many other successful companies. But access to financing was vital to Apple's growth and profitability. Would we have iMac computers, iPods, or iPads if Apple had been forced to operate in a country with a primitive financial system? Definitely not.

A modern financial system offers financing in many different forms, depending on the company's age, its growth rate, and the nature of its business. For example, Apple relied on venture capital financing in its early years and only later floated its shares in public stock markets. Still later, as the company matured, it turned to other forms of financing, including the examples given in Table 2.1. But the table does not begin to cover the range of financing channels open to modern corporations. We will encounter many other channels later in the book, and new channels are opening up regularly. The nearby box describes one recent financial innovation, micro-lending funds that make small loans to businesspeople in the poorer parts of the world.

2.2 The Flow of Savings to Corporations

The money that corporations invest in real assets comes ultimately from savings by investors. But there can be many stops on the road between savings and corporate investment. The road can pass through financial markets, financial intermediaries, or both.

Let's start with the simplest case of a small, closely held corporation, like Apple in its earliest years. The orange arrows in Figure 2.1 show the flow of savings from shareholders in this simple setting. There are two possible paths: The firm can sell new shares, or it can reinvest cash back into the firm's operations. Reinvestment means additional savings by existing shareholders. The reinvested cash could have been paid out to those shareholders and spent by them on personal consumption. By *not* taking and spending the cash, shareholders have reinvested their savings in the corporation. **Cash retained and reinvested in the firm's operations is cash saved and invested on behalf of the firm's shareholders.**

Of course, this small corporation has other financing choices. It could take out a bank loan, for example. The bank in turn may have raised money by attracting savings accounts. In this case investors' savings flow through the bank to the firm.

Now consider a large, public corporation, for example, Apple Computer in 2010. What's different? Scale, for one thing: Apple's annual revenues in 2010 were $65 billion, and its balance sheet showed total assets of $75 billion. The scope of Apple's activities

---

[1] Many of the shares sold in the 1981 issue were previously held by Apple employees. Sale of these shares allowed the employees to cash out and diversify some of their Apple holdings but did not raise additional financing for Apple.

Micro Loans

A few years ago, Chheang Leang and her husband were earning just 25 cents a day from rice farming and palm juice production in her Cambodian village. But then she took out a loan for $25 to buy fertilizer for the rice fields and to improve palm oil production. The following year, she borrowed $125 to buy a motorcycle and cart to sell ice cream and fruit juice. Next she took out a loan of $200 to buy six piglets. She used additional loans of $125 and $200 over the next two years to buy supplies for her ice cream and juice business. The investment in livestock and in the ice cream and fruit juice business allowed Chheang Leang to increase her income tenfold.

Five thousand miles to the west in a village in Malawi, Funny Mbewe opened a grocery store to supplement the family income. However, with almost no money to buy stock, she struggled to make the venture pay. The breakthrough came when Funny was able to borrow $70 to buy

new stock. The grocery store is now the biggest in the area, selling everything from food and stationery to pain medication.

Micro loans, such as those to Chheang Leang and Funny Mbewe, are made by microfinance institutions that specialize in lending small amounts of money to help poor people launch small enterprises. Some of these microfinance companies are run as businesses and some as charities. They raise capital from individual and institutional investors, vet would-be borrowers, offer management assistance, and administer the loans. Most of the loans are for small amounts and are short-term. The borrowers who take out these micro loans pay relatively high rates of interest because the loans are generally made in countries with weak currencies, and the administrative cost is relatively large. Even so, these loans can extend a lifeline to people who may not otherwise be able to gain credit.

has also expanded: It now has dozens of products and operates worldwide. Because of this scale and scope, Apple attracts investors' savings by a variety of different routes. It can do so because it is a large, profitable, public firm.

The flow of savings to large public corporations is shown in Figure 2.2. Notice two key differences from Figure 2.1. First, public corporations can draw savings from investors worldwide. Second, the savings flow through financial markets, financial intermediaries,

FIGURE 2.1 Flow of savings to investment in a closely held corporation. Investors use savings to buy additional shares. Investors also save when the corporation reinvests on their behalf.

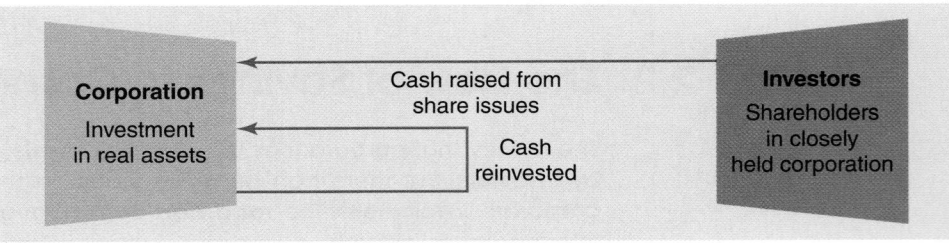

FIGURE 2.2 Flow of savings to investment for a large, public corporation. Savings come from investors worldwide. The savings may flow through financial markets or financial intermediaries. The corporation also reinvests on shareholders' behalf.

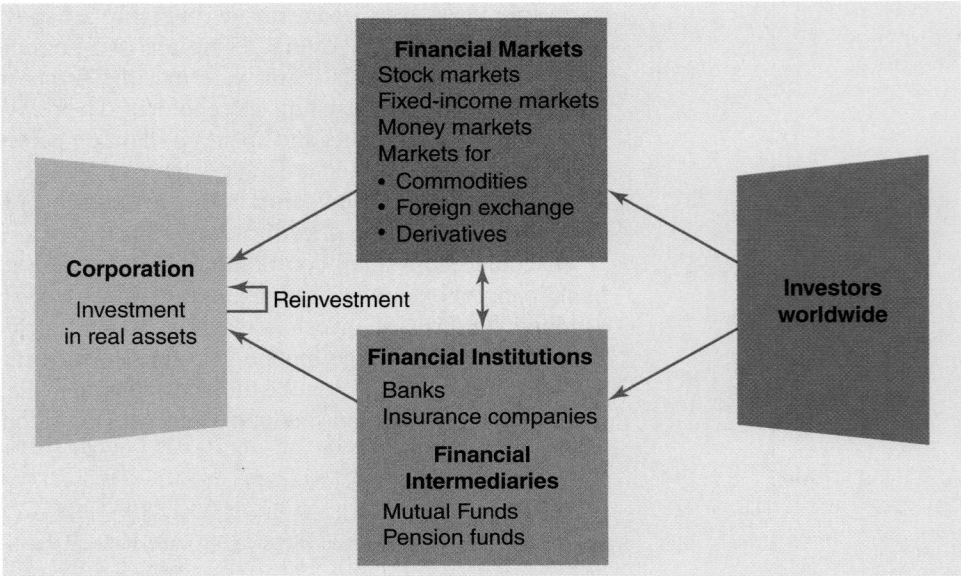

It's Not Your Grandfather's NYSE

The business of trading stocks has changed fundamentally in the last decade. In the old days, most trading was done on the crowded floor of the New York Stock Exchange (NYSE) or on the much smaller American Stock Exchange (AMEX). But by the turn of this century, most trades were routed through the NYSE's computer systems or through NASDAQ, a competing system that ties together a network of security dealers.

The trend toward electronic trading, plus rapid expansion in trading volumes, set off a wave of takeovers and consolidation. The NYSE, which used to be owned by a "club" of NYSE members, changed to a for-profit corporation and merged with Archipelago, which had developed an efficient electronic trading system. In 2006 the NYSE bought the European trading system Euronext, beating out the rival bidder Deutsche Börse, the German exchange. In 2008 NYSE Euronext took over AMEX.

Other exchanges joined the party. The London Stock Exchange was a perennial target of (unsuccessful) bids by the Swedish exchange OMX, Euronext (before it was acquired by the NYSE), Deutsche Börse, Macquarie Bank from Australia, and NASDAQ. NASDAQ later purchased OMX (Sweden).

"There's an obvious advantage of centralizing exchanges," says Wharton Finance Professor Richard J. Herring. Bigger exchanges have lower trading costs, which attracts more traders and listing companies. As trading volume increases, liquidity improves.

Consolidation is not limited to stock markets. Euronext was attractive to the NYSE partly because of its markets for options and commodities. The two largest Chicago commodities exchanges, the Chicago Mercantile Exchange and the Chicago Board of Trade, merged in 2007 as the CME Group. In March 2008, the CME Group announced that it would acquire the New York Mercantile Exchange in a deal to join the two largest U.S. futures exchanges.

Source: Hal Weitzman and Anuj Gangahar, "CME casts its eye in Nymex's direction," *Financial Times*, January 28, 2008. Used with permission of *Financial Times*.

or both. Suppose, for example, that Bank of America raises $300 million by a new issue of shares. An Italian investor buys 4,000 of the new shares for $15 per share. Now Bank of America takes that $60,000, along with money raised by the rest of the issue, and makes a $300 million loan to Apple. The Italian investor's savings end up flowing through financial markets (the stock market), to a financial intermediary (Bank of America), and finally to Apple.

Of course our Italian friend's $60,000 doesn't literally arrive at Apple in an envelope marked "From L. DaVinci." Investments by the purchasers of the Bank of America's stock issue are pooled, not segregated. Sr. DaVinci would own a share of all of Bank of America's assets, not just one loan to Apple. Nevertheless, investors' savings are flowing through the financial markets and the bank to finance Apple's capital investments.

The Stock Market

financial market
Market where securities are issued and traded.

A **financial market** is a market where securities are issued and traded. A security is just a traded financial asset, such as a share of stock. For a corporation, the stock market is probably the most important financial market.

As corporations grow, their requirements for outside capital can expand dramatically. At some point the firm will decide to "go public" by issuing shares on an organized exchange such as the New York Stock Exchange (NYSE); that first issue is called an *initial public offering* or *IPO*. The buyers of the IPO are helping to finance the firm's investment in real assets. In return, the buyers become part-owners of the firm and share in its future success or failure. (Most investors in the Internet IPOs of 1999 and 2000 are by now sorely disappointed, but many IPOs pay off handsomely. If only we had bought Apple shares on their IPO day in 1980 . . .) Of course a corporation's IPO is not its last chance to issue shares. For example, Bank of America went public in the 1930s, but it could make a new issue of shares tomorrow.

primary market
Market for the sale of new securities by corporations.

A new issue of shares increases both the amount of cash held by the company and the number of shares held by the public. Such an issue is known as a *primary issue,* and it is sold in the **primary market.** But in addition to helping companies raise new cash, financial markets also allow investors to trade securities among themselves. For example, Smith might decide to raise some cash by selling her Apple stock at the same time that Jones invests his spare cash in Apple. The result is simply a transfer

secondary market
Market in which previously issued securities are traded among investors.

of ownership from Smith to Jones, which has no effect on the company itself. Such purchases and sales of existing securities are known as *secondary transactions,* and they take place in the **secondary market.** Notice that Smith and Jones are happy for Apple to raise new capital and invest in long-term projects, as long as they can sell their stock in the secondary market when they need the cash.

Stock markets are also called *equity markets,* since stockholders are said to own the common equity of the firm. You will hear financial managers refer to the capital structure decision as "the choice between debt and equity financing."

Most trading in the shares of U.S. corporations takes place on the NYSE and on NASDAQ, which tends to attract listings from smaller, high-tech companies. The business of trading is changing rapidly, however, as the box on page 35 explains.

Now may be a good time to stress that the financial manager plays on a global stage and needs to be familiar with markets around the world. For example, Apple's stock is traded on the NASDAQ market and also in Germany on the Deutsche Börse. China Telecom, Deutsche Bank, Nokia, Novartis, Petrobras (Brazil), Sony, Toyota, Unilever, and over 400 other overseas firms have listed their shares on the NYSE. We return to the trading and pricing of shares in Chapter 7.

Other Financial Markets

Debt securities as well as equities are traded in financial markets. The Apple bond issue in 1994 was a public issue (see Table 2.1). Table 1.1 in the previous chapter also gives examples, including the debt issues by Honda and LVMH.

A few corporate debt securities are traded on the NYSE and other exchanges, but most corporate debt securities are traded *over the counter,* through a network of banks and securities dealers. Government debt is also traded over the counter.

A bond is a more complex security than a share of stock. A share is just a proportional ownership claim on the firm, with no definite maturity. Bonds and other debt securities can vary in maturity, in the degree of protection or collateral offered by the issuer, and in the level and timing of interest payments. Some bonds make "floating" interest payments tied to the future level of interest rates. Many can be "called" (repurchased and retired) by the issuing company before the bonds' stated maturity date. Some bonds can be converted into other securities, usually the stock of the issuing company. You don't need to master these distinctions now; just be aware that the debt or **fixed-income market** is a complicated and challenging place. A corporation must not only decide between debt and equity finance. It must also consider the design of debt. We return to the trading and pricing of debt securities in Chapter 6.

The markets for *long-term* debt and equity are called **capital markets.** A firm's *capital* is its long-run financing. Short-term securities are traded in the **money markets.** "Short term" means less than 1 year. For example, large, creditworthy corporations raise short-term financing by issues of *commercial paper,* which are debt issues with maturities of at most 270 days. Commercial paper is issued in the money market.

fixed-income market
Market for debt securities.

capital market
Market for long-term financing.

money market
Market for short-term financing (less than 1 year).

Self-Test 2.1

Do you understand the following distinctions? Briefly explain in each case.

a. Primary market vs. secondary market.
b. Capital market vs. money market.
c. Stock market vs. fixed-income market.

Prediction Markets

Stock markets allow investors to bet on their favorite stocks. Prediction markets allow them to bet on almost anything else. These markets reveal the collective guess of traders on issues as diverse as New York City snowfall, an avian flu outbreak, and the occurrence of a major earthquake.

Prediction markets are conducted on the major futures exchanges and on a number of smaller online exchanges such as Intrade (www.intrade.com) and Iowa Electronic Markets (www.biz.uiowa.edu/iem). Take the 2008 presidential race as an example. On the Iowa Electronic Markets you could have bet that Barack Obama would win by buying one of his contracts. Each Obama contract promised to pay $1 if he won the presidency and nothing if he lost. If you thought that the probability of an Obama victory was 55% (say), you would have been prepared to pay up to $.55 for his contract. Someone who was relatively pessimistic about Obama's chances would have been happy to *sell* you such a contract, for that sale would turn a profit if Obama were to lose. With many participants buying and selling, the market price of a contract revealed the collective wisdom of the crowd.

Take a look at the accompanying figure from the Iowa Electronic Markets. It shows the contract prices for the two contenders for the White House between June and November 2008. Following the Republican convention at the start of September, the price of a McCain contract reached a maximum of $.47. From then on the market suggested a steady fall in the probability of a McCain victory.

Participants in prediction markets are putting their money where their mouth is. So the forecasting accuracy of these markets compares favorably with that of major polls. Some businesses have formed internal prediction markets to survey the views of their staff. For example, Google operates an internal market to forecast product launch dates, the number of Gmail users, and other strategic questions.*

---

* Google's experience is analyzed in B. Cowgill, J. Wolfers, and E. Zitzewitz, "Using Prediction Markets to Track Information Flows: Evidence from Google," working paper, Dartmouth College, January 2009.

Presidential futures prices, 2008 election

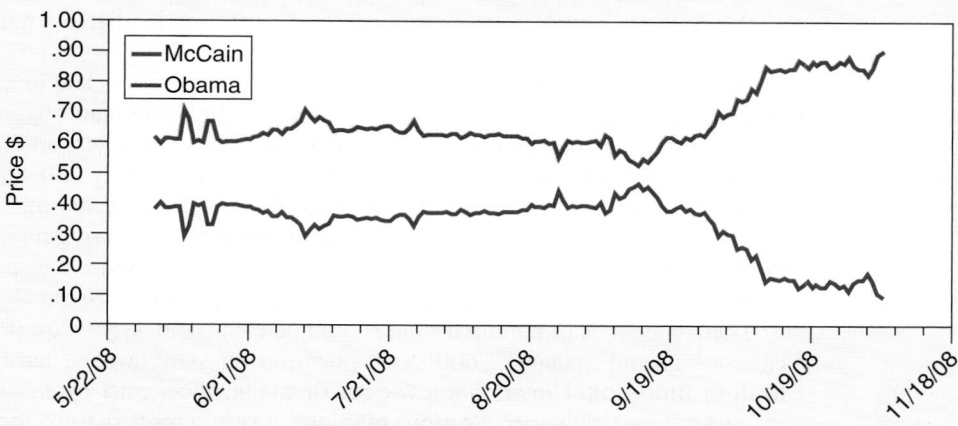

Source: Iowa Electronic Markets, **www.biz.uiowa.edu/iem**

The financial manager regularly encounters other financial markets. Here are three examples, with references to the chapters where they are discussed:

- *Foreign-exchange markets* (Chapter 22). Any corporation engaged in international trade must be able to transfer money back and forth between dollars and other currencies. Foreign exchange is traded over the counter through a network of the largest international banks.
- *Commodities markets* (Chapter 24). Dozens of commodities are traded on organized exchanges, such as the New York Mercantile Exchange or the Chicago Board of Trade. You can buy or sell corn, wheat, cotton, fuel oil, natural gas, copper, silver, platinum, and so on.
- *Markets for options and other derivatives* (Chapters 23 and 24). Derivatives are securities whose payoffs depend on the prices of other securities or commodities. For example, you can buy an option to purchase IBM shares at a fixed price on a fixed future date. The option's payoff depends on the price of IBM shares on that date. Commodities can be traded by a different kind of derivative security called a futures contract.

Commodity and derivative markets are not sources of financing but markets where the financial manager can adjust the firm's exposure to various business risks. For example, an electric generating company may wish to lock in the future price of natural gas or fuel coal by trading in commodity markets, thus eliminating the risk of a sudden jump in the price of its raw materials.

Wherever there is uncertainty, investors may be interested in trading, either to speculate or to lay off their risks, and a market may arise to meet that trading demand. In recent years several new markets have been created that allow punters to bet on a single event. The nearby box discusses how prices in these markets can reveal people's predictions about the future.

Financial Intermediaries

financial intermediary
An organization that raises money from investors and provides financing for individuals, corporations, or other organizations.

A **financial intermediary** is an organization that raises money from investors and provides financing for individuals, companies, and other organizations. For corporations, intermediaries are important sources of financing. Intermediaries are a stop on the road between savings and real investment.

Why is a financial intermediary different from a manufacturing corporation? First, it may raise money in different ways, for example, by taking deposits or selling insurance policies. Second, it invests that money in *financial* assets, for example, in stocks, bonds, or loans to businesses or individuals. In contrast, a manufacturing company's main investments are in plant, equipment, or other *real* assets.

We will start with two important classes of intermediaries, mutual funds and pension funds.

mutual fund
An investment company that pools the savings of many investors and invests in a portfolio of securities.

Mutual funds raise money by selling shares to investors. The investors' money is pooled and invested in a portfolio of securities. Investors can buy or sell shares in mutual funds as they please, and initial investments are often $3,000 or less. Vanguard's Explorer Fund, for example, held a portfolio of nearly 600 stocks with a market value of $10 billion at the end of 2010. An investor in Explorer can increase her stake in the fund's portfolio by buying additional shares, and so gain a higher share of the portfolio's subsequent dividends and price appreciation.[2] She can also sell her shares back to the fund if she decides to cash out of her investment.[3]

The advantages of a mutual fund should be clear: Unless you are very wealthy, you cannot buy and manage a 600-stock portfolio on your own, at least not efficiently. **Mutual funds offer investors low-cost diversification and professional management. For most investors, it's more efficient to buy a mutual fund than to assemble a diversified portfolio of stocks and bonds.**

Mutual fund managers also try their best to "beat the market," that is, to generate superior performance by finding the stocks with better-than-average returns. Whether they can pick winners consistently is another question, which we will address in Chapter 7.

In exchange for their services, the fund's managers take out a management fee. There are also the expenses of running the fund. For Explorer, fees and expenses absorb about .5% of portfolio value each year. This seems reasonable, but watch out: The typical mutual fund charges more than Explorer does. In some cases fees and expenses add up to 2% per year. That's a big bite out of your investment return.

---

[2] Mutual funds are not corporations but investment companies. They pay no tax, providing that all income from dividends and price appreciation is passed on to the funds' shareholders. The shareholders pay personal tax on this income.

[3] Explorer, like most mutual funds, is an *open-end* fund. It stands ready to issue shares to new investors in the fund and to buy back existing shares when its shareholders decide to cash out. The purchase and sale prices depend on the fund's net asset value (NAV) on the day of purchase or redemption. *Closed-end* funds have a fixed number of shares traded on an exchange. If you want to invest in a closed-end fund, you must buy shares from another stockholder in the fund.

Mutual funds are a stop on the road from savings to corporate investment. Suppose Explorer purchases part of the new issue of shares by Bank of America. Again we show the flow of savings to investment by orange arrows:

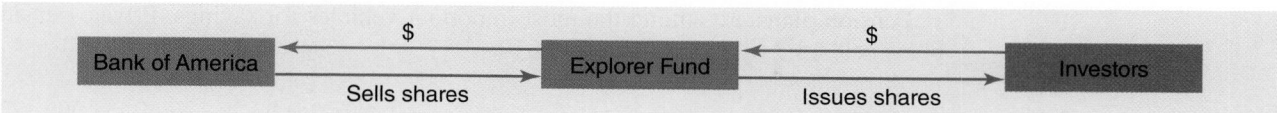

There are 7,600 mutual funds in the United States. In fact there are more mutual funds than public companies! The funds pursue a wide variety of investment strategies. Some funds specialize in safe stocks with generous dividend payouts. Some specialize in high-tech growth stocks. Some "balanced" funds offer mixtures of stocks and bonds. Some specialize in particular countries or regions. For example, the Fidelity Investments mutual fund group sponsors funds for Canada, Japan, China, Europe, and Latin America.

hedge fund
A private investment pool, open to wealthy or institutional investors, that is only lightly regulated and therefore can pursue more speculative policies than mutual funds.

Like mutual funds, **hedge funds** also pool the savings of different investors and invest on their behalf. But they differ from mutual funds in at least two ways. First, because hedge funds usually follow complex, high-risk investment strategies, access is restricted to knowledgeable investors such as pension funds, endowment funds, and wealthy individuals. Don't try to send a check for $3,000 or $5,000 to a hedge fund; most hedge funds are not in the "retail" investment business. Second, hedge funds try to attract the most talented managers by compensating them with potentially lucrative, performance-related fees.[4] In contrast, mutual funds usually charge a fixed percentage of assets under management.

Hedge funds follow many different investment strategies. Some try to make a profit by identifying *over*valued stocks or markets and selling short. (We will not go into procedures for short-selling here. Just remember that short sellers profit when prices *fall*.)[5] "Vulture funds" specialize in the securities of distressed corporations. Some hedge funds take bets on firms involved in merger negotiations, others look for mispricing of convertible bonds, and some take positions in currencies and interest rates. Hedge funds manage less money than mutual funds, but they sometimes take very big positions and have a large impact on the market.

pension fund
Fund set up by an employer to provide for employees' retirement.

There are other ways of pooling and investing savings. Consider a pension plan set up by a corporation or other organization on behalf of its employees. There are several types of pension plan. The most common type of plan is the *defined-contribution* plan. In this case, a percentage of the employee's monthly paycheck is contributed to a **pension fund**. (The employer and employee may each contribute 5%, for example.) Contributions from all participating employees are pooled and invested in securities or mutual funds. (Usually the employees can choose from a menu of funds with different investment strategies.) Each employee's balance in the plan grows over the years as contributions continue and investment income accumulates. The balance in the plan can be used to finance living expenses after retirement. The amount available for retirement depends on the accumulated contributions and on the rate of return earned on the investments.[6]

---

[4] Sometimes these fees can be very large indeed. For example, *The Wall Street Journal* estimated that hedge fund manager John Paulson earned $1 billion in fees in 2010.

[5] A short seller borrows a security from another investor and sells it. Of course, the seller must sooner or later buy the security back and return it to its original owner. The short seller earns a profit if the security can be bought back at a lower price than it was sold for.

[6] In a *defined-benefit* plan, the employer promises a certain level of retirement benefits (set by a formula) and the *employer* invests in the pension plan. The plan's accumulated investment value has to be large enough to cover the promised benefits. If not, the employer must put in more money. Defined-benefit plans are gradually giving way to defined-contribution plans.

Pension funds are designed for long-run investment. They provide professional management and diversification. They also have an important tax advantage: Contributions are tax-deductible, and investment returns inside the plan are not taxed until cash is finally withdrawn.[7]

Pension plans are among the most important vehicles for savings. Private pension plans held $5.7 trillion in assets in 2010.

Self-Test 2.2

Individual investors can buy bonds and stocks directly, or they can put their money in a mutual fund or a defined-contribution pension fund. What are the advantages of the second strategy?

Financial Institutions

financial institution
A bank, insurance company, or similar financial intermediary.

Banks and insurance companies are **financial institutions.**[8] A financial institution is an intermediary that does more than just pool and invest savings. Institutions raise financing in special ways, for example, by accepting deposits or selling insurance policies, and they provide additional financial services. Unlike a mutual fund, they not only invest in securities but also loan money directly to individuals, businesses, or other organizations.

Commercial Banks   There are nearly 7,000 commercial banks in the United States. They vary from giants such as JPMorgan Chase with $1.7 trillion of assets to midgets like the Tightwad Bank with some $20 million.

Commercial banks are major sources of loans for corporations. (In the United States, they are generally not allowed to make equity investments in corporations, although banks in most other countries can do so.) Suppose that a local forest products company negotiates a 9-month bank loan for $2.5 million. The flow of savings is:

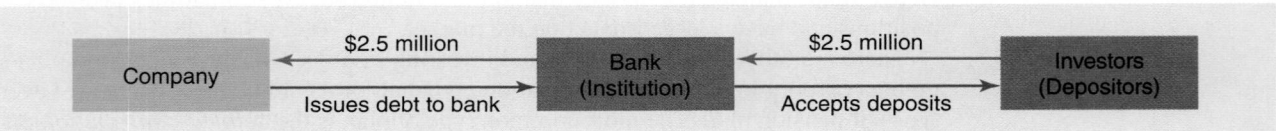

The bank provides debt financing for the company and, at the same time, provides a place for depositors to park their money safely and withdraw it as needed.

Investment Banks   We have discussed commercial banks, which raise money from depositors and other investors and then make loans to businesses and individuals. *Investment banks* are different.[9] Investment banks do not take deposits, and they do not

---

[7] Defined-benefit pension plans share these same advantages, except that the employer invests rather than the employees. In a defined-benefit plan, the advantage of tax deferral on investment income accrues to the employer. This deferral reduces the cost of funding the plan.

[8] We may be drawing too fine a distinction between financial intermediaries and institutions. A mutual fund could be considered a financial institution. But "financial institution" usually suggests a more complicated intermediary, such as a bank.

[9] Banks that accept deposits and provide financing to businesses are called *commercial* banks. *Savings* banks accept deposits and savings accounts and loan the money out mostly to individuals, for example, as mortgage loans to home buyers. Investment banks do not take deposits and do not loan money to businesses or individuals, except as *bridge loans* made as temporary financing for takeovers or other transactions. Investment banks are sometimes called *merchant banks.*

usually make loans to companies. Instead, they advise and assist companies in raising financing. For example, investment banks *underwrite* stock offerings by purchasing the new shares from the issuing company at a negotiated price and reselling the shares to investors. Thus the issuing company gets a fixed price for the new shares, and the investment bank takes responsibility for distributing the shares to thousands of investors. We discuss share issues in more detail in Chapter 15.

Investment banks also advise on takeovers, mergers, and acquisitions. They offer investment advice and manage investment portfolios for individual and institutional investors. They run trading desks for foreign exchange, commodities, bonds, options, and derivatives.

Investment banks can invest their own money in start-ups and other ventures. For example, the Australian Macquarie Bank has invested in airports, toll highways, electric transmission and generation, and other infrastructure projects around the world.

The largest investment banks are financial powerhouses. They include Goldman Sachs, Morgan Stanley, Lazard, Nomura (Japan), and Macquarie Bank. In addition, the major commercial banks, including Bank of America and Citigroup, all have investment banking operations.[10]

Insurance Companies   Insurance companies are more important than banks for the *long-term* financing of business. They are massive investors in corporate stocks and bonds, and they often make long-term loans directly to corporations.

Suppose a company needs a loan of $2.5 million for 9 years, not 9 months. It could issue a bond directly to investors, or it could negotiate a 9-year loan with an insurance company:

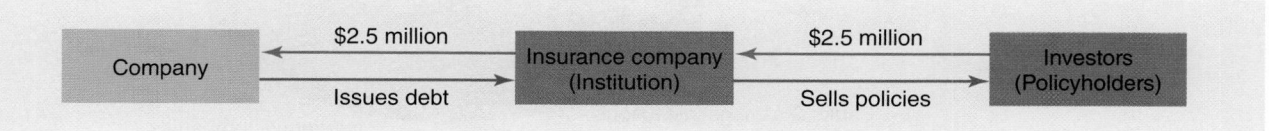

The money to make the loan comes mainly from the sale of insurance policies. Say you buy a fire insurance policy on your home. You pay cash to the insurance company and get a financial asset (the policy) in exchange. You receive no interest payments on this financial asset, but if a fire does strike, the company is obliged to cover the damages up to the policy limit. This is the return on your investment. (Of course, a fire is a sad and dangerous event that you hope to avoid. But if a fire does occur, you are better off getting a return on your investment in insurance than not having insurance at all.)

The company will issue not just one policy but thousands. Normally the incidence of fires "averages out," leaving the company with a predictable obligation to its policyholders as a group. Of course the insurance company must charge enough for its policies to cover selling and administrative costs, pay policyholders' claims, and generate a profit for its stockholders.

Self-Test 2.3

What are the key differences between a mutual fund and a bank or an insurance company?

---

[10] Bank of America owns Merrill Lynch, one of the largest investment banks. Merrill was rescued by Bank of America in 2009 after making huge losses from mortgage-related investments.

Total Financing of U.S. Corporations

The pie chart in Figure 2.3 shows the investors in bonds and other debt securities. Notice the importance of institutional investors—mutual funds, pension funds, insurance companies, and banks. Households (individual investors) hold less than 20% of the debt pie. The other slices represent the rest of the world (investors from outside the United States) and various other categories.

The pie chart in Figure 2.4 shows holdings of the shares issued by U.S. corporations. Here households and nonprofit organizations make a stronger showing, with 36.5% of the total. Pension funds, insurance companies, and mutual funds add up to 48.5% of the total. Remember, banks in the United States do not usually hold stock in other companies. The rest-of-the-world slice is 13.3%.

The aggregate amounts represented in these figures are enormous. There is $11.4 trillion of debt behind Figure 2.3 and $21 trillion of equity behind Figure 2.4 ($21,000,000,000,000).[11]

Chapter 14 reviews corporate financing patterns in more detail.

FIGURE 2.3 Holdings of corporate and foreign bonds, third quarter 2010. The total amount is $11.4 trillion.

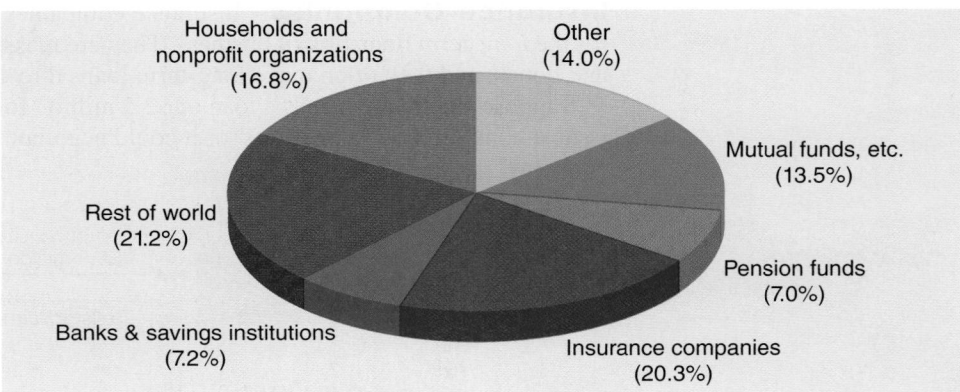

Source: Board of Governors of the Federal Reserve System, Division of Research and Statistics, *Flow of Funds Accounts,* Table L.212 (**www.federalreserve.gov**).

FIGURE 2.4 Holdings of corporate equities, third quarter 2010. The total amount is $21.0 trillion.

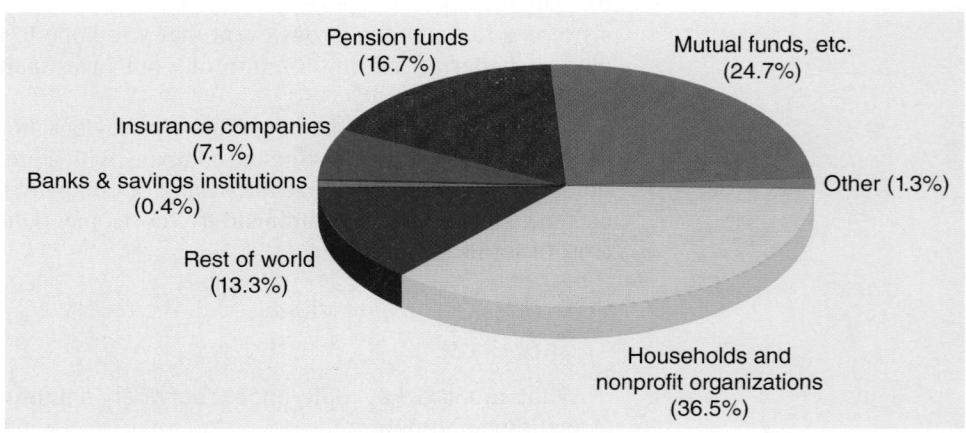

Source: Board of Governors of the Federal Reserve System, Division of Research and Statistics, *Flow of Funds Accounts,* Table L.213 (**www.federalreserve.gov**).

[11] The total market value of shares issued by U.S. *nonfinancial* corporations is $12.9 trillion. "Nonfinancial" excludes financial institutions, such as banks and insurance companies.

2.3 Functions of Financial Markets and Intermediaries

Financial markets and intermediaries provide financing for business. They channel savings to real investment. That much should be loud and clear from Sections 2.1 and 2.2 of this chapter. But there are other functions that may not be quite so obvious.

Transporting Cash across Time

Individuals need to transport expenditures in time. If you have money now that you wish to save for a rainy day, you can (for example) put the money in a savings account at a bank and withdraw it with interest later. If you don't have money today, say to buy a car, you can borrow money from the bank and pay off the loan later. Modern finance provides a kind of time machine. Lenders transport money forward in time; borrowers transport it back. Both are happier than if they were forced to spend income as it arrives. Of course, individuals are not alone in needing to raise cash from time to time. Firms with good investment opportunities, but a shortage of internally generated cash, raise cash by borrowing or selling new shares. Many governments run deficits and finance current outlays by issuing debt.

Young people saving for retirement may transport their current earnings 30 or 40 years into the future by means of a pension fund. They may even transport income to their heirs by purchase of a life insurance policy.

In principle, individuals or firms with cash surpluses could take out newspaper advertisements or surf the Web looking for counterparties with cash shortages. But it is usually cheaper and more convenient to use financial markets and intermediaries. It is not just a matter of avoiding the cost of searching for the right counterparty. Follow-up is needed. For example, banks don't just loan money and walk away. They monitor the borrower to make sure that the loan is used for its intended purpose and that the borrower's credit stays solid.

Risk Transfer and Diversification

Financial markets and intermediaries allow investors and businesses to reduce and reallocate risk. Insurance companies are an obvious example. When you buy homeowner's insurance, you greatly reduce the risk of loss from fire, theft, or accidents. But your policy is not a very risky bet for the insurance company. It diversifies by issuing thousands of policies, and it expects losses to average out over the policies.[12] The insurance company allows you to pool risk with thousands of other homeowners.

Investors should diversify too. For example, you can buy shares in a mutual fund that holds hundreds of stocks. In fact, you can buy *index funds* that invest in all the stocks in the popular market indexes. For example, the Vanguard 500 Index fund holds the stocks in the Standard & Poor's Composite stock market index. (The "S&P 500" tracks the performance of the largest U.S. stocks. It is the index most used by professional investors.) If you buy this fund, you are insulated from the company-specific risks of the 500 companies in the index. These risks are averaged out by diversification. Of course you are still left with the risk that the level of the stock market as a whole will fall. In fact, we will see in Chapter 11 that investors are mostly concerned with *market risk,* not the specific risks of individual companies.

Index mutual funds are one way to invest in widely diversified portfolios at low cost. Another route is provided by exchange traded funds (ETFs), which are portfolios of stocks that can be bought or sold in a single trade. These include Standard & Poor's

---

[12] Unfortunately for insurance companies, the losses don't always average out. Hurricanes and earthquakes can damage thousands of homes at once. The potential losses are so great that property insurance companies buy *reinsurance* against such catastrophes.

Depository Receipts (SPDRs, or "spiders"), which are portfolios matching Standard & Poor's stock market indexes. The total amount invested in the spider tracking the benchmark S&P 500 index was about $94 billion by early-2011. You can also buy DIAMONDS, which track the Dow Jones Industrial Average; QUBES or QQQs, which track the NASDAQ 100 index; and Vanguard ETFs that track the Vanguard Total Stock Market index, which is a basket of almost all the stocks traded in the United States. You can also buy ETFs that track foreign stock markets, bonds, or commodities.

ETFs are in some ways more efficient than mutual funds. To buy or sell an ETF, you simply make a trade, just as if you bought or sold shares of stock.[13] To invest in an open-ended mutual fund, you have to send money to the fund in exchange for newly issued shares. If you want to withdraw the investment, you have to notify the fund, which redeems your shares and sends you a check or credits your account with the fund. Also, many of the larger ETFs charge lower fees than mutual funds. Vanguard's fee for managing its Total Stock Market ETF is .07% per year. For a $100,000 investment, the fee is only .0007 × 100,000 = $70.

Financial markets provide other mechanisms for sharing risks. For example, a wheat farmer and a baking company are each exposed to fluctuations in the price of wheat after the harvest. The farmer worries about low prices, the baker about high prices. They can both rest easier if the baker can agree with the farmer to buy wheat in the future at a fixed price. Of course, it would be difficult, to say the least, if the baker and the farmer had to contact an Internet dating service to get together to make a deal. Fortunately no dating service is needed: Each can trade in commodity markets, the farmer as a seller and the baker as a buyer.

Liquidity

liquidity
The ability to sell an asset on short notice at close to the market price.

Markets and intermediaries also provide **liquidity,** that is, the ability to turn an investment back into cash when needed. Suppose you deposit $5,000 in a savings bank on February 1. During that month, the bank uses your deposit and other new deposits to make a 6-month construction loan to a real estate developer. On March 1, you realize that you need your $5,000 back. The bank can give it to you. Because the bank has thousands of depositors, and other sources of financing if necessary, it can make an illiquid loan to the developer financed by liquid deposits made by you and other customers. If you lend out your money for 6 months directly to the real estate developer, you will have a hard time retrieving it 1 month later.[14]

The shares of public companies are liquid because they are traded more or less continuously in the stock market. An Italian investor who puts $60,000 into Bank of America shares can recover that money on short notice. (A $60,000 sell order is a drop in the bucket, compared with the normal trading volume of Bank of America shares.) Mutual funds can redeem their shares for cash on short notice because the funds invest in traded securities, which can be sold as necessary.

Of course, liquidity is a matter of degree. Foreign exchange markets for major currencies are exceptionally liquid. Bank of America or Deutsche Bank could buy $200 million worth of yen or euros in the blink of an eye, with hardly any effect on foreign exchange rates. U.S. Treasury securities are also very liquid, and the shares of the largest companies on the major international stock exchanges are only slightly less so.

---

[13] ETFs are in this respect like closed-end mutual funds (see footnote 3 above). But ETFs do not have managers with the discretion to try to "pick winners." ETF portfolios are tied down to indexes or fixed baskets of securities. ETF issuers make sure that the ETF price tracks the price of the underlying index or basket.

[14] Of course, the bank can't repay all depositors simultaneously. To do so, it would have to sell off its loans to the real estate developer and other borrowers. These loans are *not* liquid. This raises the specter of bank runs, where doubts about a bank's ability to pay off its depositors cause a rush of withdrawals, with each depositor trying to get his or her money out first. Bank runs are rare, because bank deposits are backed up by the U.S. Federal Deposit Insurance Corporation, which insures bank accounts up to $250,000 per account.

Liquidity is most important when you're in a hurry. If you try to sell $500,000 worth of the shares of a small, thinly traded company all at once, you will probably knock down the price to some extent. If you're patient and don't surprise other investors with a large, sudden sell order, you may be able to unload your shares on better terms. It's the same problem you may face in selling real estate. A house or condominium is not a liquid asset in a panic sale. If you're determined to sell in an afternoon, you're not going to get full value.

The Payment Mechanism

Think how inconvenient life would be if you had to pay for every purchase in cash or if Boeing had to ship truckloads of hundred-dollar bills around the country to pay its suppliers. Checking accounts, credit cards, and electronic transfers allow individuals and firms to send and receive payments quickly and safely over long distances. Banks are the obvious providers of payment services, but they are not alone. For example, if you buy shares in a money market mutual fund, your money is pooled with that of other investors and used to buy safe, short-term securities. You can then write checks on this mutual fund investment, just as if you had a bank deposit.

Information Provided by Financial Markets

In well-functioning financial markets, you can *see* what securities and commodities are worth, and you can see—or at least estimate—the rates of return that investors can expect on their savings. The information provided by financial markets is often essential to a financial manager's job. Here are three examples of how this information can be used.

Commodity Prices   Catalytic converters are used in the exhaust systems of cars and light trucks to reduce pollution. The catalysts include platinum, which is traded on the New York Mercantile Exchange.

In February a manufacturer of catalytic converters is planning production for July. How much per ounce should the company budget for purchases of platinum in that month? Easy: The company's CFO looks up the market price of platinum on the New York Mercantile Exchange—$1,795 per ounce for delivery in July (This was the closing price for platinum in late February 2011, for delivery in July.) The CFO can lock in that price if she wishes. The details of such a trade are covered in Chapter 24.

Interest Rates   The CFO of Catalytic Concepts has to raise $400 million in new financing. She considers an issue of 30-year bonds. What will the interest rate on the bonds be? To find out, the CFO looks up interest rates on existing bonds traded in financial markets.

The results are shown in Table 2.2. Notice how the interest rate climbs as credit quality deteriorates: The largest, safest companies, which are rated Aaa ("triple-A"), can raise long-term debt at a 5.11% interest rate. The interest rates for Aa, A, and Baa climb to 5.70%, 5.98%, and 6.32%, respectively. Baa companies are still regarded as *investment grade,* that is, good quality, but the next step down takes the investor into

TABLE 2.2 Interest rates on long-term corporate bonds, May 2010. The interest rate is lowest for top-quality (Aaa) issuers. The rate rises as credit quality declines.

Credit Rating	Interest Rate
Aaa	5.11%
Aa	5.70
A	5.98
Baa	6.32
Ba	7.34
B	8.49

Source: Barclays corporate bond indexes.

junk bond territory. The interest rate for Ba debt climbs to 7.34%. Single-B companies are riskier still, so investors demand 8.49%.

There will be more on bond ratings and interest rates in Chapter 6. But you can see how a financial manager can use information from fixed-income markets to forecast the interest rate on new debt financing. For example, if Catalytic Concepts can qualify as a Baa-rated company, and interest rates are as shown in Table 2.2, it should be able to raise new debt financing for approximately 6.3%.

Company Values   How much was Alaska Air Group worth in February 2011? How about Bob Evans Farms, Callaway Golf, Estée Lauder, or GE? Table 2.3 shows the answers. We simply multiply the number of shares outstanding by the price per share in the stock market. Investors valued Alaska Air Group at $2,155 million, GE at $222 *billion.*

Stock prices and company values summarize investors' collective assessment of how well a company is doing, both its current performance and its future prospects. Thus an increase in stock price sends a positive signal from investors to managers.[15] That is why top management's compensation is linked to stock prices. A manager who owns shares in his or her company will be motivated to increase the company's market value. This reduces agency costs by aligning the interests of managers and stockholders.

This is one important advantage of going public. A private company can't use its stock price as a measure of performance. It can still compensate managers with shares, but the shares will not be valued in a financial market.

Cost of Capital   Financial managers look to financial markets to measure, or at least estimate, the **cost of capital** for the firm's investment projects. The cost of capital is the minimal acceptable rate of return on the project. Investment projects offering rates of return higher than their cost of capital are worthwhile, because they add value; they make both the firm and its shareholders better off financially. Projects offering rates of return less than the cost of capital subtract value and should not be undertaken.[16]

Thus the hurdle rate for investments inside the corporation is actually set outside the corporation. The expected rate of return on investments in financial markets determines the cost of capital.

The opportunity cost of capital is generally *not* the interest rate that the firm pays on a loan from a bank or insurance company. If the company is making a risky

cost of capital
Minimum acceptable rate of return on capital investment.

TABLE 2.3 Calculating the total market values of Alaska Air Group and other companies in February 2011. (Shares and market values in millions. Ticker symbols in parentheses.)

	Number of Shares	× Stock Price	= Market Value
Alaska Air Group (ALK)	35.92	× $60	= $2,155
Bob Evans Farms (BOBE)	30.24	× $31.39	= $949
Callaway Golf (ELY)	64.11	× $7.80	= $500
Estée Lauder (EL)	197.43	× $90.86	= $17,938
General Electric (GE)	10,640	× $20.82	= $221,525

Source: Yahoo! Finance, **finance.yahoo.com**

---

[15] We can't claim that investors' assessments of value are always correct. Finance can be a risky and dangerous business—dangerous for your wealth, that is. With hindsight we see horrible mistakes by investors, for example the gross overvaluation of Internet and telecom companies in 2000. On average, however, it appears that financial markets collect and assess information quickly and accurately. We'll discuss this issue again in Chapter 7.

[16] Of course, the firm may invest for other reasons. For example, it may invest in pollution control equipment for a factory. The equipment may not generate a cash return, but may still be worth investing in to meet legal and ethical obligations.

investment, the opportunity cost of capital is the expected rate of return that investors can achieve in financial markets at the same level of risk. The expected rate of return on risky securities is normally well above the interest rate on corporate borrowing.

We introduced the cost of capital in Chapter 1, but this brief reminder may help to fix the idea. We cover the cost of capital in detail in Chapters 11 and 12.

Self-Test 2.4

Which of the functions described in this section require financial markets? Explain briefly.

2.4 The Crisis of 2007–2009

The financial crisis of 2007–2009 raised many questions, but it settled one question conclusively: Yes, *financial markets and institutions are important.* When financial markets and institutions ceased to operate properly, the world was pushed into a global recession.

The financial crisis had its roots in the easy-money policies that were pursued by the U.S. Federal Reserve and other central banks following the collapse of the Internet and telecom stock bubble in 2000. At the same time, large balance-of-payments surpluses in Asian economies were invested back into U.S. debt securities. This also helped to push down interest rates and contribute to the lax credit.

Banks took advantage of this cheap money to expand the supply of *subprime mortgages* to low-income borrowers. Many banks tempted would-be homeowners with low initial payments, offset by significantly higher payments later.[17] (Some home buyers were betting on escalating housing prices so that they could resell or refinance before the higher payments kicked in.) One lender is even said to have advertised what it dubbed its "NINJA" loan—*NINJA* standing for "No Income, No Job and No Assets." Most subprime mortgages were then packaged together into *mortgage-backed securities* that could be resold. But, instead of selling these securities to investors who could best bear the risk, many banks kept large quantities of the loans on their own books or sold them to other banks.

The widespread availability of mortgage finance fueled a dramatic increase in house prices, which doubled in the 5 years ending June 2006. At that point prices started to slide and homeowners began to default on their mortgages. A year later Bear Stearns, a large investment bank, announced huge losses on the mortgage investments that were held in two of its hedge funds. By the spring of 2008 Bear Stearns was on the verge of bankruptcy, and the U.S. Federal Reserve arranged for it to be acquired by JPMorgan Chase.

The crisis peaked in September 2008, when the U.S. government was obliged to take over the giant federal mortgage agencies Fannie Mae and Freddie Mac, both of which had invested several hundred billion dollars in subprime mortgage-backed securities. Over the next few days the financial system started to melt down. Both Merrill Lynch and Lehman Brothers were in danger of failing. On September 14, the government arranged for Bank of America to take over Merrill in return for financial guarantees. However, it did nothing to rescue Lehman Brothers, which filed for bankruptcy protection the next day. Two days later the government reluctantly lent $85 billion to the giant insurance company AIG, which had insured huge volumes of mortgage-backed

---

[17] With a so-called *option ARM loan* the minimum mortgage payment was often not even sufficient to cover that month's interest on the loan. The unpaid interest was then added to the amount of the mortgage, so the homeowner was burdened by an ever-increasing mortgage that one day would need to be paid off.

securities and other bonds against default. The following day, the Treasury unveiled its first proposal to spend $700 billion to purchase "toxic" mortgage-backed securities.

Uncertainty about which domino would be next to fall made banks reluctant to lend to one another, and the interest rate that they charged for such loans rose to 4.6% above the rate on U.S. Treasury debt. (Normally this spread above Treasuries is less than .5%.) This had an immediate knock-on effect on the supply of credit to industry, and the economy suffered one of its worst setbacks since the Great Depression. Unemployment rose rapidly, and business bankruptcies tripled.

Few developed economies escaped the crisis. As well as suffering from a collapse in their own housing markets, many foreign banks had made large investments in U.S. subprime mortgages. A roll call of all the banks that had to be bailed out by their governments would fill several pages, but here are just a few members of that unhappy band: the Royal Bank of Scotland in the United Kingdom, UBS in Switzerland, Allied Irish Bank in Ireland, Fortis in Belgium, ING in Holland, Hypo Group in Austria, and West Lb in Germany.

Who was responsible for the financial crisis? In part, the U.S. Federal Reserve for its policy of easy money. The U.S. government also must take some of the blame for encouraging banks to expand credit for low-income housing. The rating agencies were at fault for providing triple-A ratings for many mortgage bonds that shortly afterward went into default. Last but not least, the bankers themselves were guilty of promoting and reselling the subprime mortgages. As we suggested in the last chapter, managers were probably aware that a strategy of originating massive amounts of subprime debt was likely to end badly. Perhaps they were trying to squeeze in one more fat bonus before the game ended. That is why we described the mess as largely an *agency* problem—a failure to incentivize managers to act in shareholders' interests.

The banking crisis and subsequent recession left many governments with huge mountains of debt. By 2010 investors were becoming increasingly concerned about the position of Greece, where for many years government spending had been running well ahead of revenues. Greece's position was complicated by its membership in the single-currency euro club. Although much of the country's borrowing was in euros, the government had no control over its currency and could not simply print more euros to service its debt. Investors began to contemplate the possibility of a Greek government default and became increasingly reluctant to lend to the country. As we write this, Greece is still afloat, thanks partly to a rescue package from the International Monetary Fund, the European Commission, and the European Central Bank. Attention has shifted to Ireland, where in the midst of a brutal recession, the government put up 34 billion euros to take over the Anglo Irish bank.

SUMMARY

Where does the financing for corporations come from? *(LO1)*

The ultimate source of financing is individuals' savings. The savings may flow through **financial markets** and **intermediaries.** The intermediaries include mutual funds, pension funds, and financial institutions, such as banks and insurance companies.

Why do nonfinancial corporations need modern financial markets and institutions? *(LO1)*

It's simple: Corporations need access to financing in order to innovate and grow. A modern financial system offers different types of financing, depending on a corporation's age and the nature of its business. A high-tech start-up will seek venture capital financing, for example. A mature firm will rely more on bond markets.

What if a corporation finances investment by retaining and reinvesting cash generated from its operations? *(LO1)*	In that case the corporation is saving on behalf of its shareholders.
What are the key advantages of mutual funds and pension funds? *(LO2)*	**Mutual** and **pension funds** allow investors to diversify in professionally managed portfolios. Pension funds offer an additional tax advantage, because the returns on pension investments are not taxed until withdrawn from the plan.
What are the functions of financial markets? *(LO3)*	**Financial markets** help channel savings to corporate investment, and they help match up borrowers and lenders. They provide **liquidity** and diversification opportunities for investors. Trading in financial markets provides a wealth of useful information for the financial manager.
Do financial institutions have different functions? *(LO3)*	**Financial institutions** carry out a number of similar functions but in different ways. They channel savings to corporate investment, and they serve as **intermediaries** between borrowers and lenders. Banks also provide liquidity for depositors and, of course, play a special role in the economy's payment systems. Insurance companies allow policyholders to pool risks.
What happens when financial markets and institutions no longer function well? *(LO3)*	The financial crisis of 2007–2009 provided a dramatic illustration. The huge expansion in subprime mortgage lending in the United States led to a collapse of the banking system. The government was forced into a costly bailout of banks and other financial institutions. As the credit markets seized up, the country suffered a deep recession.

QUESTIONS

QUIZ

1. **Corporate Financing.** How can a small, private firm finance its capital investments? Give two or three examples of financing sources. *(LO1)*

2. **Corporate Financing.** Is it possible for an individual to save and invest in a corporation without lending money to it or purchasing additional shares? Explain. *(LO1)*

3. **Corporations.** What is meant by the separation of ownership and control for public corporations? What potential problems does this separation create? *(LO1)*

4. **Financial Markets.** The stock and bond markets are not the only financial markets. Give two or three additional examples. *(LO1)*

5. **Financial Intermediaries.** You are a beginning investor with only $5,000 in savings. How can you achieve a widely diversified portfolio at reasonable cost? *(LO2)*

6. **Financial Intermediaries.** What are the key advantages of a defined-contribution pension plan as a vehicle for retirement savings? *(LO2)*

7. **Financial Intermediaries.** Is an insurance company also a financial intermediary? How does the insurance company channel savings to corporate investment? *(LO2)*

8. **Corporate Financing.** What are the largest institutional investors in bonds? In shares? *(LO2)*

9. **Financial Markets and Institutions.** List the major functions of financial markets and institutions in a modern financial system. *(LO3)*

10. **Financial Markets.** On a mountain trek, you discover a 6-ounce gold nugget. A friend offers to pay you $2,500 for it. How do you check whether this is a fair price? *(LO3)*

11. **Financial Markets.** What kinds of useful information can a financial manager obtain from financial markets? Give examples. *(LO3)*

12. **The Financial Crisis.** True or False? (*LO4*)
   a. The financial crisis was largely caused by banks taking large positions in the options and futures markets.
   b. The prime cause of the financial crisis was an expansion in bank lending for the overheated commercial real estate market.
   c. Many subprime mortgages were packaged together by banks for resale.
   d. The crisis could have been much more serious if the government had not stepped in to rescue Merrill Lynch and Lehman Brothers.

PRACTICE PROBLEMS

13. **True or False?** (*LO1*)
   a. Financing for public corporations must flow through financial markets.
   b. Financing for private corporations must flow through financial intermediaries.
   c. The sale of policies is a source of financing for insurance companies.
   d. Almost all foreign exchange trading occurs on the floors of the FOREX exchanges in New York and London.
   e. The opportunity cost of capital is the capital outlay required to undertake a real investment opportunity.
   f. The cost of capital is the interest rate paid on borrowing from a bank or other financial institution.

14. **Liquidity.** Securities traded in active financial markets are liquid assets. Explain why liquidity is important to individual investors and to mutual funds. (*LO2*)

15. **Liquidity.** Bank deposits are liquid; you can withdraw money on demand. How can the bank provide this liquidity and at the same time make illiquid loans to businesses? (*LO2*)

16. **Corporate Financing.** Financial markets and intermediaries channel savings from investors to corporate investment. The savings make this journey by many different routes. Give a specific example for each of the following routes: (*LO1*)
   a. Investor to financial intermediary, to financial markets, and to the corporation.
   b. Investor to financial markets, to a financial intermediary, and to the corporation.
   c. Investor to financial markets, to a financial intermediary, back to financial markets, and to the corporation.

17. **Financial Institutions.** Summarize the differences between a commercial and an investment bank. (*LO2*)

18. **Mutual Funds.** Why are mutual funds called financial intermediaries? Why does it make sense for an individual to invest her savings in a mutual fund rather than directly in financial markets? (*LO2*)

19. **The Financial Crisis.** What were the causes of the financial crisis? We mentioned several. Can you suggest others that we have not identified? (*LO4*)

WEB EXERCISES

1. Log on to finance.yahoo.com and use the Web site to update Table 2.3. How have market values of these companies changed?

2. Find the Web sites for the Vanguard Group, Fidelity Investments, and Putnam Investments. Pick three or four funds from these sites and compare their investment objectives, risks, past returns, fund fees, and so on. Read the prospectuses for each fund. Who do you think should, or should not, invest in each fund?

3. Morningstar provides data on mutual fund performance. Log on to its Web site. Which category of funds has performed unusually well or badly?

SOLUTIONS TO SELF-TEST QUESTIONS

2.1   a. Corporations sell securities in the primary market. The securities are later traded in the secondary market.

        b. The capital market is for long-term financing; the money market for short-term financing.

        c. The market for stocks versus the market for bonds and other debt securities.

2.2   Efficient diversification and professional management. Pension funds offer an additional advantage, because investment returns are not taxed until withdrawn from the fund.

2.3   Mutual funds pool investor savings and invest in portfolios of traded securities. Financial institutions such as banks or insurance companies raise money in special ways, for example, by accepting deposits or selling insurance policies. They not only invest in securities but also lend directly to businesses. They provide various other financial services.

2.4   Liquidity, risk reduction by investment in diversified portfolios of securities (through a mutual fund, for example), information provided by trading.

CHAPTER 3

Accounting and Finance

LEARNING OBJECTIVES

After studying this chapter, you should be able to:

(1) Interpret the information contained in the balance sheet, income statement, and statement of cash flows.

(2) Distinguish between market and book values.

(3) Explain why income differs from cash flow.

(4) Understand the essential features of the taxation of corporate and personal income.

RELATED WEB SITES FOR THIS CHAPTER CAN BE FOUND AT WWW.MHHE.COM/BMM7E.

Accounting and finance are not the same, but accounting basics are necessary to understand finance.

In Chapter 1 we pointed out that a large corporation is a team effort. All the players—the shareholders, lenders, directors, management, and employees—have a stake in the company's success, and all therefore need to monitor its progress. For this reason the company prepares regular financial accounts and arranges for an independent firm of auditors to certify that these accounts present a "true and fair view."

Until the mid-nineteenth century most businesses were owner-managed and seldom required outside capital beyond personal loans to the proprietor. When businesses were small and there were few outside stakeholders in the firm, accounting could be less formal. But with the industrial revolution and the creation of large railroad and canal companies, the shareholders and bankers demanded information that would help them gauge a firm's financial strength. That was when the accounting profession began to come of age.

We don't want to get lost in the details of accounting practice. But because we will be referring to financial statements throughout this book, it may be useful to review briefly their main features. In this chapter we introduce the major financial statements: the balance sheet, the income statement, and the statement of cash flows. We discuss the important differences between income and cash flow and between book values and market values. We also discuss the federal tax system.

This chapter is our first look at financial statements and is meant primarily to serve as a brief review of your accounting class. It will be far from our last look. For example, we will see in the next chapter how managers use financial statements to analyze a firm's performance and assess its financial strength.

3.1 The Balance Sheet

balance sheet
Financial statement that
shows the firm's assets
and liabilities at a
particular time.

Public companies are obliged to file their financial statements with the SEC each quarter. These quarterly reports (or 10Qs) provide the investor with information about the company's earnings during the quarter and its assets and liabilities at the end of the quarter. In addition, companies need to file annual financial statements (or 10Ks) that provide rather more detailed information about the outcome for the entire year.

The financial statements show the firm's balance sheet, the income statement, and a statement of cash flows. We will review each in turn.[1]

Firms need to raise cash to pay for the many assets used in their businesses. In the process of raising that cash, they also acquire liabilities to those who provide funding. The **balance sheet** presents a snapshot of the firm's assets and liabilities at one particular moment. The assets—representing the uses of the funds raised—are listed on the left-hand side of the balance sheet. The liabilities—representing the sources of that funding—are listed on the right.

Some assets can be turned more easily into cash than others; these are known as *liquid* assets. The accountant puts the most liquid assets at the top of the list and works down to the least liquid. Look, for example, at Table 3.1, which shows the consolidated balance sheet for Home Depot (HD), at the end of 2009.[2] ("Consolidated" simply means that the balance sheet shows the position of Home Depot and any companies it owns.) You can see that Home Depot had $1,421 million of cash and marketable securities. In addition, it had sold goods worth $964 million but had not yet received payment. These payments are due soon and therefore the balance sheet shows the unpaid bills or *accounts receivable* (or simply *receivables*) as a current asset. The next asset consists of inventories. These may be (1) raw materials and ingredients that the firm bought from suppliers, (2) work in process, and (3) finished products waiting to be shipped from the warehouse. For Home Depot, inventories consist largely of goods in the warehouse or on the store shelves; for manufacturing companies, inventories would be more skewed toward raw materials and work in progress. Of course, there are always some items that don't fit into neat categories. So there is a fourth entry, *other current assets*.

Up to this point all the assets in Home Depot's balance sheet are likely to be used or turned into cash in the near future. They are therefore described as *current assets*. The next assets listed in the balance sheet are longer-lived or *fixed assets* and include items such as buildings, equipment, and vehicles.

The balance sheet shows that the gross value of Home Depot's property, plant, and equipment is $37,345 million. This is what the assets originally cost. But they are unlikely to be worth that now. For example, suppose the company bought a delivery van 2 years ago; that van may be worth far less now than Home Depot paid for it. It might in principle be possible for the accountant to estimate separately the value today of the van, but this would be costly and somewhat subjective. Accountants rely instead on rules of thumb to estimate the *depreciation* in the value of assets, and with rare exceptions they stick to these rules. For example, in the case of that delivery van the accountant may deduct a third of the original cost each year to reflect its declining value. So if Home Depot bought the van 2 years ago for $15,000, the balance sheet would show that accumulated depreciation is $2 \times \$5,000 = \$10,000$. Net of depreciation the value is only $5,000. Table 3.1 shows that Home Depot's total accumulated depreciation on fixed assets is $11,795 million. So while the assets cost $37,345 million, their net value in the accounts is only $37,345 - \$11,795 = \$25,550$ million.

---

[1] In addition, the company provides a statement of the shareholders' equity, which shows how much of the firm's earnings has been retained in the business rather than paid out as dividends and how much money has been raised by issuing new shares or spent by repurchasing stock. We will not review in detail the statement of shareholders' equity.

[2] We have simplified and eliminated some of the detail in Home Depot's published financial statements.

TABLE 3.1

BALANCE SHEET OF HOME DEPOT (Figures in $ milions)					
Assets	**2009**	**2008**	**Liabilities and Shareholders' Equity**	**2009**	**2008**
Current assets			Current liabilities		
Cash and marketable securities	1,421	519	Debt due for repayment	1,020	1,767
Receivables	964	972	Accounts payable	8,185	8,221
Inventories	10,188	10,673	Other current liabilities	1,158	1,165
Other current assets	1,327	1,198	Total current liabilities	10,363	11,153
Total current assets	13,900	13,362			
Fixed Assets			Long-term debt	8,662	9,667
Tangible fixed assets			Deferred income taxes	319	369
Property, plant, and equipment	37,345	36,223	Other long-term liabilities	2,140	2,198
Less accumulated depreciation	11,795	9,989			
Net tangible fixed assets	25,550	26,234	Total liabilities	21,484	23,387
Intangible asset (goodwill)	1,171	1,134	Shareholders' equity:		
Long-term investments	33	36	Common stock and other paid-in capital	6,390	6,133
Other assets	223	398	Retained earnings	13,588	12,452
			Treasury stock	$ (585)	(808)
Total Assets	40,877	41,164	Total shareholders' equity	19,393	17,777
			Total liabilities and shareholders' equity	40,877	41,164

Note: Column sums subject to rounding error.
Source: Derived from Home Depot annual reports.

In addition to its tangible assets, Home Depot also has valuable intangible assets, such as its brand name, skilled management, and a well-trained labor force. Accountants are generally reluctant to record these intangible assets in the balance sheet unless they can be readily identified and valued.

There is, however, one important exception. When Home Depot has acquired other businesses in the past, it has paid more for their assets than the value shown in the firms' accounts. This difference is shown in Home Depot's balance sheet as "goodwill." Most of the intangible assets on Home Depot's balance sheet consist of goodwill.

Now look at the right-hand portion of Home Depot's balance sheet, which shows where the money to buy its assets came from. The accountant starts by looking at the company's liabilities—that is, the money owed by the company. First come those liabilities that are likely to be paid off most rapidly. For example, Home Depot has borrowed $1,020 million, due to be repaid shortly. It also owes its suppliers $8,185 million for goods that have been delivered but not yet paid for. These unpaid bills are shown as *accounts payable* (or *payables*). Both the borrowings and the payables are debts that Home Depot must repay within the year. They are therefore classified as *current liabilities.*

Home Depot's current assets total $13,900 million; its current liabilities amount to $10,363 million. Therefore the difference between the value of Home Depot's current assets and its current liabilities is $13,900 − $10,363 = $3,537 million. This figure is known as Home Depot's *net current assets* or *net working capital.* It roughly measures the company's potential reservoir of cash.

Below the current liabilities Home Depot's accountants have listed the firm's long-term liabilities—that is, debts that come due after the end of a year. You can see that banks and other investors have made long-term loans to Home Depot of $8,662 million.

Home Depot's liabilities are financial obligations to various parties. For example, when Home Depot buys goods from its suppliers, it has a liability to pay for them; when it borrows from the bank, it has a liability to repay the loan. Thus the suppliers and the bank have first claim on the firm's assets. What is left over after the liabilities have been paid off belongs to the shareholders. This figure is known as the shareholders' *equity.* For Home Depot the total value of shareholders' equity amounts to $19,393 million. Table 3.1 shows that Home Depot's equity is made up of three parts. One portion, $6,390 million, has resulted from the occasional sale of new shares to investors. A much larger amount, $13,588 million, has come from earnings that Home Depot has retained and reinvested in the business on the shareholders' behalf.[3] Finally, treasury stock is a large negative number, −$585 million. This represents the amount that Home Depot has spent on buying back its shares. The money to repurchase them has gone out of the firm and reduced shareholders' equity.

Figure 3.1 shows how the separate items in the balance sheet link together. There are two classes of assets—current assets, which will soon be used or turned into cash, and long-term or "fixed" assets, which may be either tangible or intangible. There are also two classes of liability—current liabilities, which are due for payment shortly, and long-term liabilities.

The difference between the assets and the liabilities represents the amount of the shareholders' equity. This is the basic balance sheet identity. Shareholders are sometimes called "residual claimants" on the firm. We mean by this that shareholders' equity is what is left over when the liabilities of the firm are subtracted from its assets:

$$\text{Shareholders' equity} = \text{total assets} - \text{total liabilities} \qquad (3.1)$$

Self-Test 3.1

Suppose that Home Depot borrows $500 million by issuing new long-term bonds. It places $100 million of the proceeds in the bank and uses $400 million to buy new machinery. What items of the balance sheet would change? Would shareholders' equity change?

common-size balance sheet
All items in the balance sheet are expressed as a percentage of total assets.

When comparing financial statements, analysts often calculate a **common-size balance sheet,** which reexpresses all items as a percentage of total assets. Table 3.2 is Home Depot's common-size balance sheet. The financial manager might look at this common-size balance sheet and notice right away that in 2009 cash and marketable securities accounted for a higher proportion of the firm's assets than they did in the previous year. There may be good reasons for this, but the manager might wish to check that control of working capital has not become lax.

By the way, it is easy to obtain the financial statements of almost any publicly traded firm. Most firms make their annual reports available on the Web. You also can find key financial statements of most firms at Yahoo! Finance. (finance.yahoo.com) or Google Finance (finance.google.com).

FIGURE 3.1

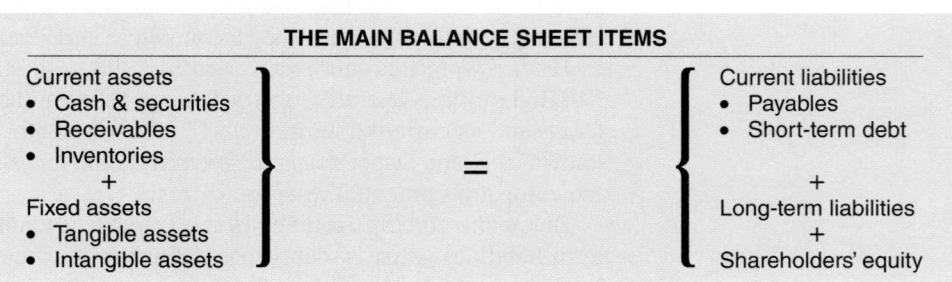

THE MAIN BALANCE SHEET ITEMS

---

[3] Here is an occasional source of confusion. You may be tempted to think of retained earnings as a pile of cash that the company has built up from its past operations. But there is absolutely no link between retained earnings and cash balances. The earnings that Home Depot has kept in the business may have been used to buy new equipment, trucks, warehouses, and so on. Typically only a small proportion will be kept in the bank. Notice that Home Depot's balance sheet lists $13,588 in retained earnings but only $1,421 in cash and marketable securities.

TABLE 3.2

COMMON-SIZE BALANCE SHEET OF HOME DEPOT (All items expressed as percentage of total assets)					
Assets	**2009**	**2008**	**Liabilities and Shareholders' Equity**	**2009**	**2008**
Current assets			Current liabilities		
Cash and marketable securities	3.5%	1.3%	Debt due for repayment	2.5%	4.3%
Receivables	2.4%	2.4%	Accounts payable	20.0%	20.0%
Inventories	24.9%	25.9%	Other current liabilities	2.8%	2.8%
Other current assets	3.2%	2.9%	Total current liabilities	25.4%	27.1%
Total current assets	34.0%	32.5%			
Fixed Assets			Long-term debt	21.2%	23.5%
Tangible fixed assets			Deferred income taxes	0.8%	0.9%
Property, plant, and equipment	91.4%	88.0%	Other long-term liabilities	5.2%	5.3%
Less accumulated depreciation	28.9%	24.3%			
Net tangible fixed assets	62.5%	63.7%	Total liabilities	52.6%	56.8%
Intangible asset (goodwill)	2.9%	2.8%	Shareholders' equity:		
Long-term investments	0.1%	0.1%	Common stock and other paid-in capital	15.6%	14.9%
Other assets	0.5%	1.0%	Retained earnings	33.2%	30.2%
			Treasury stock	−1.4%	−2.0%
Total Assets	100.0%	100.0%	Total shareholders' equity	47.4%	43.2%
			Total liabilities and shareholders' equity	100.0%	100.0%

Note: Column sums subject to rounding error.
Source: Home Depot annual report, 2009.

Book Values and Market Values

Throughout this book we will frequently make a distinction between the book values of the assets shown in the balance sheet and their market values.

generally accepted accounting principles (GAAP)
Procedures for preparing financial statements.

book value
Value of assets or liabilities according to the balance sheet.

Items in the balance sheet are valued according to **generally accepted accounting principles,** commonly called **GAAP.** These state that assets must be shown in the balance sheet at their *historical cost* adjusted for depreciation. **Book values** are therefore "backward-looking" measures of value. They are based on the past cost of the asset, not its current market price or value to the firm. For example, suppose that 2 years ago Home Depot built an office building for $30 million and that in today's market the building would sell for $40 million. The book value of the building would be less than its market value, and the balance sheet would understate the value of Home Depot's asset.

Or consider a specialized plant that Intel develops for producing special-purpose computer chips at a cost of $800 million. The book value of the plant is $800 million less depreciation. But suppose that shortly after the plant is constructed, a new chip makes the existing one obsolete. The market value of Intel's new plant could fall by 50% or more. In this case market value would be less than book value.

The difference between book value and market value is greater for some assets than for others. It is zero in the case of cash but potentially very large for fixed assets where the accountant starts with initial cost and then depreciates that figure according to a prespecified schedule. The purpose of depreciation is to allocate the original cost of the asset over its life, and the rules governing the depreciation of asset values do not reflect actual loss of market value. The market value of fixed assets usually is much higher than the book value, but sometimes it is less.

The same goes for the right-hand side of the balance sheet. In the case of liabilities the accountant simply records the amount of money that you have promised to pay. For short-term liabilities this figure is generally close to the market value of that promise. For example, if you owe the bank $1 million tomorrow, the accounts show a book liability of $1 million. As long as you are not bankrupt, that $1 million is also roughly the value to the bank of your promise. But now suppose that $1 million is not due to be repaid for several years. The accounts still show a liability of $1 million, but how much your debt is worth depends on what happens to interest rates. If interest rates rise after you have issued the debt, lenders may not be prepared to pay as much as $1 million for your debt; if interest rates fall, they may be prepared to pay more than $1 million.[4] Thus the market value of a long-term liability may be higher or lower than the book value. **Market values of assets and liabilities do not generally equal their book values. Book values are based on historical or** *original* **values. Market values measure** *current* **values of assets and liabilities.**

The difference between book value and market value is likely to be greatest for shareholders' equity. The book value of equity measures the cash that shareholders have contributed in the past plus the cash that the company has retained and reinvested in the business on their behalf. But this often bears little resemblance to the total market value that investors place on the shares.

If the market price of the firm's shares falls through the floor, don't try telling the shareholders that the book value is satisfactory—they won't want to hear. Shareholders are concerned with the market value of their shares; market value, not book value, is the price at which they can sell their shares. Managers who wish to keep their shareholders happy will focus on market values.

We will often find it useful to think about the firm in terms of a *market-value balance sheet*. Like a conventional balance sheet, a market-value balance sheet lists the firm's assets, but it records each asset at its current market value rather than at historical cost less depreciation. Similarly, each liability is shown at its market value. **The difference between the market values of assets and liabilities is the market value of the shareholders' equity claim. The stock price is simply the market value of shareholders' equity divided by the number of outstanding shares.**

EXAMPLE 3.1 ▶ Market- versus Book-Value Balance Sheets

Jupiter has developed a revolutionary auto production process that enables it to produce cars 20% more efficiently than any rival. It has invested $10 billion in producing its new plant. To finance the investment, Jupiter borrowed $4 billion and raised the remaining funds by selling new shares of stock in the firm. There are currently 100 million shares of stock outstanding. Investors are very excited about Jupiter's prospects. They believe that the flow of profits from the new plant justifies a stock price of $75.

If these are Jupiter's only assets, the book-value balance sheet immediately after it has made the investment is as follows:

BOOK-VALUE BALANCE SHEET FOR JUPITER MOTORS (Figures in billions of dollars)			
Assets		**Liabilities and Shareholders' Equity**	
Auto Plant	$10	Debt	$4
		Shareholders' equity	6

Investors are placing a *market value* on Jupiter's equity of $7.5 billion ($75 per share times 100 million shares). We assume that the debt outstanding is worth $4 billion.[5] Therefore, if you owned all Jupiter's shares and all its debt, the value of your investment would be $7.5 + $4 = $11.5 billion. In this case you would own the company lock, stock, and barrel and would be entitled to all its cash flows.

---

[4] We will show you how changing interest rates affect the market value of debt in Chapter 6.

[5] Jupiter has borrowed $4 billion to finance its investment, but if the interest rate has changed in the meantime, the debt could be worth more or less than $4 billion.

Because you can buy the entire company for $11.5 billion, the total value of Jupiter's assets must also be $11.5 billion. In other words, the market value of the assets must be equal to the market value of the liabilities plus the market value of the shareholders' equity.

We can now draw up the market-value balance sheet as follows:

MARKET-VALUE BALANCE SHEET FOR JUPITER MOTORS			
(Figures in billions of dollars)			
Assets		**Liabilities and Shareholders' Equity**	
Auto Plant	$11.5	Debt	$4
		Shareholders' equity	7.5

Notice that the market value of Jupiter's plant is $1.5 billion more than the plant cost to build. The difference is due to the superior profits that investors expect the plant to earn. **Thus, in contrast to the balance sheet shown in the company's books, the market-value balance sheet is forward-looking. It depends on the profits that investors expect the assets to provide.**

Is it surprising that market value generally exceeds book value? It shouldn't be. Firms find it attractive to raise money to invest in various projects because they believe the projects will be worth more than they cost. Otherwise, why bother? You will usually find that shares of stock sell for more than the value shown in the company's books.

Self-Test 3.2

a. What would be Jupiter's price per share if the auto plant had a market value of $14 billion?
b. How would you reassess the value of the auto plant if the value of outstanding stock were $8 billion?

3.2 The Income Statement

income statement
Financial statement that shows the revenues, expenses, and net income of a firm over a period of time.

If Home Depot's balance sheet resembles a snapshot of the firm at a particular time, its **income statement** is like a video. It shows how profitable the firm has been during the past year.

Look at the summary income statement in Table 3.3. You can see that during 2009 Home Depot sold goods worth $66,176 million and that the total expenses of acquiring and selling these goods were $43,764 + $15,907 = $59,671 million. The largest expense item, amounting to $43,764 million, consisted of the cost of goods sold, which included the acquisition cost of its products, the wages of its employees, and other expenses incurred to obtain and sell its wares. Almost all the remaining expenses were administrative expenses such as head office costs, advertising, and distribution.

In addition to these out-of-pocket expenses, Home Depot also made a deduction for the value of the plant and equipment used up in producing the goods. In 2009 this charge for depreciation was $1,806 million. Thus Home Depot's *earnings before interest and taxes (EBIT)* were

$$\text{EBIT} = \text{total revenues} - \text{costs} - \text{depreciation}$$
$$= 66,176 - 59,671 - 1,806$$
$$= \$4,699 \text{ million}$$

TABLE 3.3

INCOME STATEMENT OF HOME DEPOT, 2009		
	$ million	**% of sales**
Net sales	66,176	100.0
Cost of goods sold	43,764	66.1
Selling, general & admininstrative expenses	15,907	24.0
Depreciation	1,806	2.7
Earnings before interest and income taxes	4,699	7.1
Interest expense	676	1.0
Taxable income	4,023	6.1
Taxes	1,362	2.1
Net income	2,661	4.0
Allocation of net income		
Dividends	1,525	2.3
Addition to retained earnings	1,136	1.7

Source: Derived from Home Depot annual report, 2009.

The remainder of the income statement shows where these earnings went. As we saw earlier, Home Depot has partly financed its investment in plant and equipment by borrowing. In 2009 it paid $676 million of interest on this borrowing. A further slice of the profit went to the government in the form of taxes. This amounted to $1,362 million. The $2,661 million that was left over after paying interest and taxes belonged to the shareholders. Of this sum Home Depot paid out $1,525 million in dividends and reinvested the remaining $1,136 million in the business. Presumably, these reinvested funds made the company more valuable.

The $1,136 of earnings that Home Depot retained, or reinvested, in the firm show up on its balance sheet as an increase in retained earnings. Notice that retained earnings in Table 3.1 increased by $1,136 million in 2009, from $12,452 million to $13,588 million. However, shareholders' equity increased by more than this amount, primarily because Home Depot sold some of its treasury stock during the year.

Just as it is sometimes useful to prepare a common-size balance sheet, we can also prepare a **common-size income statement.** In this case, all items are expressed as a percentage of revenues. The last column of Table 3.3 is Home Depot's common-size income statement. You can see, for example, that the cost of goods sold consumes 66.1% of revenues and that selling, general, and administrative expenses absorb a further 24.0%.

common-size income statement
All items on the income statement are expressed as a percentage of revenues.

Profits versus Cash Flow

It is important to distinguish between Home Depot's profits and the cash that the company generates. Here are two reasons why profits and cash are not the same:

1. *Depreciation.* When Home Depot's accountants prepare the income statement, they do not simply count the cash coming in and the cash going out. Instead, the accountant starts with the cash payments but then divides these payments into two groups—current expenditures (such as wages) and capital expenditures (such as the purchase of new machinery). Current expenditures are deducted from current profits. However, rather than deducting the cost of machinery in the year it is purchased, the accountant makes an annual charge for depreciation. Thus the cost of machinery is spread over its forecast life.

   When calculating profits, the accountant does *not* deduct the expenditure on new equipment that year, even though cash is paid out. However, the accountant *does* deduct depreciation on assets previously purchased, even though no cash is currently paid out. For example, suppose a $100,000 investment is depreciated by $10,000 a year.[6] This depreciation is treated as an annual expense, although the cash actually went out of the door when the asset was first purchased. For this reason, the deduction for depreciation is classified as a *noncash* expense.

To calculate the cash produced by the business, it is necessary to *add* back the depreciation charge (which is not a cash payment) and to *subtract* the expenditure on new capital equipment (which is a cash payment).

2. *Cash versus accrual accounting.* Consider a manufacturer that spends $60 to produce goods in period 1. In period 2 it sells these goods for $100, but its customers do not pay their bills until period 3. The following diagram shows the firm's cash flows. In period 1 there is a cash *outflow* of $60. Then, when customers pay their bills in period 3, there is an *inflow* of $100.

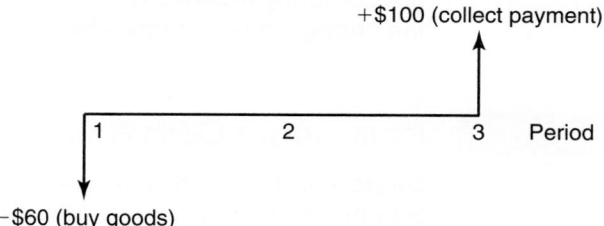

It would be misleading to say that the firm was running at a loss in period 1 (when cash flow was negative) or that it was extremely profitable in period 3 (when cash flow was positive). Therefore, to construct the income statement, the accountant looks at when the sale was made (period 2 in our example) and gathers together all the revenues and expenses associated with that sale. For our company the income statement would show:

Revenue	$100
less Cost of goods sold	60
Profit	$ 40

This practice of matching revenues and expenses is known as *accrual accounting.*

Of course, the accountant cannot ignore the actual timing of the cash expenditures and payments. So the cash outlay in the first period will be treated not as an expense but as an *investment* in inventories. Subsequently, in period 2, when the goods are taken out of inventory and sold, the accountant shows a *reduction* in inventories.

To go from the cost of goods sold in the income statement to the cash outflows, we need to subtract the investment in inventories that is shown in the balance sheet:

Period:	1	2
Cost of goods sold (income statement)	0	60
+ Investment in inventories (balance sheet)	60	(60)
= Cash paid out	60	0

The accountant also does not ignore the fact that the firm has to wait until period 3 to collect its bills. When the sale is made in period 2, the figure for accounts receivable in the balance sheet is increased to show that the company's customers owe an extra $100 in unpaid bills. Later, when the customers pay those bills in period 3, accounts receivable are reduced by $100. Therefore, to go from the

---

[6] We discuss depreciation rules in Chapter 9.

revenues shown in the income statement to the cash inflows, we need to subtract the investment in receivables:

Period:	2	3
Sales (income statement)	100	0
− Investment in receivables (balance sheet)	100	(100)
= Cash received	0	+100

We will return to these issues in more detail in Chapter 9, but for now we summarize the key points as follows: **Cash *outflow* is equal to the cost of goods sold, which is shown in the income statement, *plus* the change in inventories. The cash that the company *receives* is equal to the sales shown in the income statement *less* the change in uncollected bills.**

EXAMPLE 3.2 ▶ Profits versus Cash Flows

Suppose our manufacturer spends a further $80 to produce goods in period 2. It sells these goods in period 3 for $120, but customers do not pay their bills until period 4.

The cash flows from these transactions are now as follows:

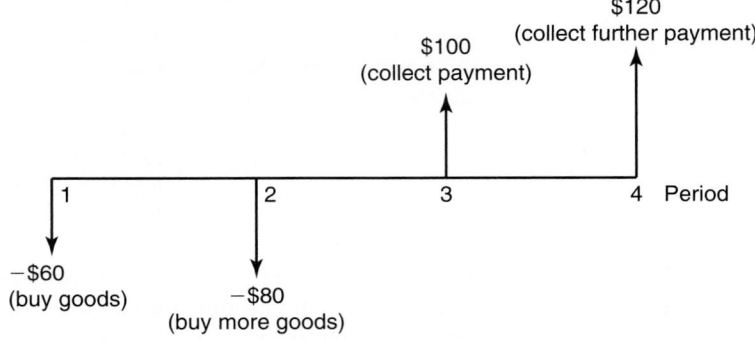

How do the new transactions affect the income statement and the balance sheet? The income statement will match costs with revenues and record the cost of goods sold when the sales are made in periods 1 and 2. The difference between the costs shown in the income statement and the cash flows is recorded as an investment (and later, disinvestment) in inventories. Thus, in period 1 the accountant shows an investment in inventories of $60 just as before. In period 2 these goods are taken out of inventory and sold, but the firm also produces a further $80 of goods. Thus there is a net increase in inventories of $20. As these goods in turn are sold in period 3, inventories are reduced by $80. The following table confirms that the cash outflow in each period is equal to the cost of goods sold that is shown in the income statement plus the change in inventories.

Period:	1	2	3
Cost of goods sold (income statement)	0	60	80
+ Investment in inventories (balance sheet)	60	−60 + 80 = 20	−80
= Cash paid out	60	80	0

The following table provides a similar reconciliation of the difference between the revenues shown in the income statement and the cash inflow:

Period:	2	3	4
Sales (income statement)	100	120	0
− Investment in receivables (balance sheet)	100	−100 + 120 = 20	−120
= Cash received	0	+100	+120

In the income statement the accountant records sales of $100 in period 1 and $120 in period 2. The fact that the firm has to wait for payment is recognized in the balance sheet as an investment in receivables. The cash that the company *receives* is equal to the sales shown in the income statement *less* the investment in receivables.

Self-Test 3.3

Consider a firm that spends $200 to produce goods in period 1. In period 2 it sells half of those goods for $150, but it doesn't collect payment until one period later. In period 3 it sells the other half of the goods for $150, and it collects payment on these sales in period 4. Calculate the profits and the cash flows for this firm in periods 1 to 4.

3.3 The Statement of Cash Flows

The firm requires *cash* when it buys new plant and machinery or when it pays interest to the bank and dividends to the shareholders. Therefore, the financial manager needs to keep track of the cash that is coming in and going out.

We have seen that the firm's cash flow can be quite different from its net income. These differences can arise for at least two reasons:

1. The income statement does not recognize capital expenditures as expenses in the year that the capital goods are paid for. Instead, it spreads those expenses over time in the form of an annual deduction for depreciation.
2. The income statement uses the accrual method of accounting, which means that revenues and expenses are recognized when sales are made, rather than when the cash is received or paid out.

statement of cash flows
Financial statement that shows the firm's cash receipts and cash payments over a period of time.

The **statement of cash flows** shows the firm's cash inflows and outflows from operations as well as from its investments and financing activities. Table 3.4 is the cash-flow statement for Home Depot. It contains three sections. The first shows the cash flow from operations. This is the cash generated from Home Depot's normal business activities. Next comes the cash that Home Depot has invested in plant and equipment or in the acquisition of new businesses. The final section reports cash flows from financing activities such as the sale of new debt or stock. We will look at these sections in turn.

The first section, cash flow from operations, starts with net income but adjusts that figure for those parts of the income statement that do not involve cash coming in or going out. Therefore, it adds back the allowance for depreciation because depreciation is not a cash outflow, even though it is treated as an expense in the income statement.

Any additions to current assets need to be *subtracted* from net income, since these absorb cash but do not show up in the income statement. Conversely, any additions to current liabilities need to be *added* to net income because these release cash. For example, you can see that the decrease of $8 million in accounts receivable is added to income, because the collection of payment on previous sales is a source of cash to the firm. In addition, Home Depot decreased inventories by $485 million. The decrease in inventory levels freed up cash. Thus the $485 million decrease in inventories must be added to calculate the cash flow from operations. On the other hand, Home Depot does

TABLE 3.4

STATEMENT OF CASH FLOWS OF HOME DEPOT, 2009 (Figures in $ millions)	
Cash provided by operations	
Net income	2,661
Noncash expenses	
Depreciation and amortization	1,806
Changes in working capital	
Decrease (increase) in accounts receivable	8
Decrease (increase) in inventories	485
Increase (decrease) in accounts payable	−36
Decrease (increase) in other current assets	−129
Increase (decrease) in other current liabilities	−7
Total decrease (increase) in working capital	321
Cash provided by operations	4,788
Cash flows from investments	
Cash provided by (used for) disposal of (additions to) property, plant, and equipment	−1,122
Sales (acquisitions) of other investments	141
Cash provided by (used for) investments	−981
Cash provided by (used for) financing activities	
Additions to (reduction in) short-term debt	−747
Additions to (reduction in) long-term debt	−1,005
Dividends paid	−1,525
Net issues (repurchases) of stock	480
Other	−108
Cash provided by (used for) financing activities	−2,905
Net increase (decrease) in cash and cash equivalents	902

Source: Calculated from data in Tables 3.1 and 3.3.

not pay all its bills immediately. These delayed payments show up as payables. In 2009 Home Depot had fewer bills outstanding: accounts payable *decreased* by $36 million. Paying off those bills resulted in a reduction in cash.

We have pointed out that depreciation is not a cash payment; it is simply the accountant's allocation to the current year of the original cost of the capital equipment. However, cash does flow out the door when the firm actually buys and pays for new capital equipment. Therefore, these capital expenditures are set out in the second section of the cash-flow statement. You can see that Home Depot spent $1,122 million on new capital equipment. Notice that (gross) property, plant, and equipment on Home Depot's balance sheet increased by precisely this amount. On the other hand, Home Depot freed up $141 million by selling off other investments (this amount shows up as the change in the sum of intangible fixed assets plus other assets). Total cash used by investments was $981 million.

Finally, the third section of the cash-flow statement shows the cash from financing activities. Home Depot used 747+1,005 = $1,752 million to retire debt and $1,525 million to pay dividends to its stockholders, but it raised $480 million of cash through stock sales.[7]

To summarize, the cash-flow statement tells us that Home Depot generated $4,788 million from operations, spent $981 million on new investments, and used $2,905 million in financing activities. Home Depot earned and raised more cash than it spent. Therefore, its cash balance increased by $902 million. To calculate this change in cash balance, we subtract the uses of cash from the sources:

---

[7] You might think that interest payments also ought to be listed in this section. However, it is usual to include interest in the first section with cash flow from operations. This is because, unlike dividends, interest payments are not discretionary. The firm must pay interest when a payment comes due, so these payments are treated as a business expense rather than as a financing decision.

	In Millions
Cash flow from operations	$4,788
− Cash flow for new investment	− 981
+ Cash provided by new financing	−2,905
= Change in cash balance	+ 902

Look back at Table 3.1 and you will see that cash accounts on the balance sheet did indeed increase by this amount in 2009.

Self-Test 3.4

Would the following activities increase or decrease the firm's cash balance?

a. Inventories are increased.
b. The firm reduces its accounts payable.
c. The firm issues additional common stock.
d. The firm buys new equipment.

Free Cash Flow

The statement of cash flows tracks the cash flows from all the firm's activities. It shows how much cash has come from the firm's day-to-day operations and how much has come from the issue of new stock or debt. It also shows whether this cash was paid out to investors or reinvested in new plant and equipment or working capital. Often, however, you may want to know how much cash the company has available for distribution to investors after it has paid for any new capital investment or additions to working capital. This is called the firm's **free cash flow.**

Free cash flow has three parts. First, the cash that the firm generates from its ongoing operations is equal to

free cash flow
Cash available for distribution to investors after firm pays for new investments or additions to working capital.

$$\text{Earnings before interest and tax (EBIT)} - \text{taxes} + \text{depreciation}$$

Not all of this cash is available to the firm's investors, however. As we've discussed, net investments in working capital, such as inventory or receivables, soak up cash. So we must subtract the change in net working capital excluding cash. In addition, the firm needs to invest in fixed assets, and these investments also use cash. Thus,

$$\begin{aligned}\text{Free cash flow} = \ &\text{EBIT} - \text{taxes} + \text{depreciation}\\ &- \text{change in net working capital}\\ &- \text{capital expenditures}\end{aligned}$$

EXAMPLE 3.3 ▶ Free Cash Flow for Home Depot

We use both the income statement and the statement of cash flows to compute Home Depot's free cash flow. From the 2009 income statement, EBIT was $4,699 million, taxes were $1,362 million, and depreciation expense was $1,806 million. From the statement of cash flows (Table 3.4), the change in working capital was −$321 million (representing a net disinvestment in working capital that released cash), and net capital expenditures were $981 million. Therefore, Home Depot's free cash flow was

Free cash flow = $4,699 − $1,362 + $1,806 − (−$321) − $981 = $4,483 million

Some of this money was paid out to Home Depot's investors as interest or dividends. The remainder was used to buy back stock or repay debt.

3.4 Accounting Practice and Malpractice

Managers of public companies face constant scrutiny. Much of that scrutiny focuses on earnings. Security analysts forecast earnings per share, and investors wait to see whether the company can meet or beat the forecasts. A shortfall, even if it is only a cent or two, can be a big disappointment. Investors might judge that if you could not find that extra cent or two of earnings, the firm must be in a really bad way.

Managers complain about this pressure, but do they do anything about it? Unfortunately, the answer appears to be yes, according to Graham, Harvey and Rajgopal, who surveyed about 400 senior managers.[8] Most of the managers said that accounting earnings were the single most important number reported to investors. Most admitted to adjusting their firms' operations and investments to produce the earnings that investors were looking for. For example, 80% were prepared to decrease discretionary spending in R&D, advertising, or maintenance to meet earnings targets.

Of course, managers may not need to adjust the firm's operations if they can instead adjust their accounting methods. U.S. accounting rules are spelled out by the Financial Accounting Standards Board (FASB) and its generally accepted accounting principles (GAAP). Yet, inevitably, rules and principles leave room for discretion, and managers under pressure to perform are tempted to take advantage of this leeway to satisfy investors. In more extreme cases, managers may simply break the rules.

Here are some examples of gray areas that demand judgment calls and may tempt those who wish to conceal unflattering information to misuse any leeway in accounting rules:

- *Revenue recognition.* As we saw above, firms record a sale when it is made, not when the customer actually pays. But the date of sale is not always obvious. For example, suppose that you sell goods today but you give the customer the right to return them "if not fully satisfied." Have you made the sale when the goods are delivered or only when you can be sure that they will not be returned? Some companies have used this ambiguity to deliberately inflate their profits. For example, in 1997 the head of Sunbeam, "Chainsaw" Al Dunlap, allegedly moved millions of dollars of appliances to distributors and retailers to produce record profits. This process is termed *channel stuffing.* Between 1997 and 2001 Xerox also took an overly optimistic view of its revenues. Whenever a customer signed a long-term lease of a copy machine, Xerox booked the entire stream of future rental payments in the period that the lease contract was signed instead of spreading them over the life of the contract. In so doing, it inflated profits by around $3 billion.
- *Cookie-jar reserves.* The giant mortgage-pass-through firm Freddie Mac earned the Wall Street nickname "Steady Freddie" for its unusually smooth and predictable pattern of earnings growth, at least until 2008 when it suddenly collapsed in the wake of the meltdown in subprime mortgages. Unfortunately, it emerged in 2003 that Freddie achieved this predictability in part by misusing its reserve accounts. Normally, such accounts are intended to allow for the likely impact of events that might reduce earnings, such as the failure of customers to pay their bills. But Freddie seemed to "overreserve" against such contingencies so that it could "release" those reserves and bolster income in a bad year. Its steady growth was largely a matter of earnings management.
- *Off–balance sheet assets and liabilities.* Before its bankruptcy, Enron became infamous for its special-purpose vehicles, which allowed it to hide large potential liabilities from the public. Enron had also guaranteed the outstanding debt of other companies in which it had an ownership stake. To present a fair view of the firm, Enron should have recognized these potential liabilities on its balance sheet. But

---

[8] J. R. Graham, C. R. Harvey, and S. Rajgopal, "The Economic Implications of Corporate Financial Reporting," *Journal of Accounting and Economics* 40 (2005), pp. 3–73.

the firm created and placed paper firms—the special-purpose vehicles—in the middle of its transactions. The ambiguity of ownership resulting from these technically independent entities led Enron to exclude these liabilities from its own financial statements.

- *Mark-to-market accounting.* Many assets and liabilities, such as buildings, employee pension benefits, and even some infrequently traded securities, do not have easily observable prices. Common practice has been to value these at historic cost. But advocates of mark-to-market accounting believe that financial statements would give a truer picture of the firm if they reflected the current market value of assets and liabilities. Critics respond that when markets are faltering, market prices may be unreliable. If assets can be sold only at fire-sale prices, then those prices may no longer be indicative of fundamental value. This was a contentious issue in 2008, when banks resisted calls to revalue their holdings of subprime mortgages at market prices. In the end, they were allowed to put off write-downs on assets deemed to be only "temporarily impaired." But this practice certainly makes it harder to discern the true condition of the firm.

EXAMPLE 3.4 ▶ Lehman Brothers' Repurchase Agreements

As the financial crisis of 2007–2009 worsened, Lehman Brothers desperately looked for a way to improve its apparent financial health. It did so using an arcane accounting trick that removed about $50 billion from its balance sheet. The trick was called Repo 105. Lehman sold $50 billion of bonds to several other investment banks with an agreement that it would repurchase those bonds at a slightly higher price within a week or so. This arrangement is thus called a repurchase or "repo" agreement. Everyone knows that a repurchase agreement is not really a sale of the bonds—it is for all intents and purposes a loan, with the higher repurchase price the implicit interest payment. The bonds serve only as collateral—if Lehman defaults on the promised repurchase, it will not get its bonds back. Repurchase agreements are thus commonly, and properly, treated in U.S. law as loans. But in this case Lehman entered into the transaction through its European office, and pledged bonds worth more than 105% of the cash it received. This loophole allowed it to obtain an opinion from a British law firm that the repo could qualify under English law as a true sale of assets. Lehman's plan was to use the money it received from selling the bonds to pay off some of its other debts. Then, *after* it had filed its quarterly financial reports, it would borrow the funds necessary to repurchase the bonds. But until that time it would look less indebted than it actually was. The firm (barely) followed the letter of the law but used the discretion allowed to it under accounting practice to paint a misleading picture of its actual condition. By the way, Lehman was not alone in using "window dressing" to pretty up its balance sheet around a quarterly financial report. For example, Bank of America admitted to similar (though far smaller) transactions at the end of several fiscal quarters between 2007 and 2009.

Investors worry about the fact that some companies seem particularly prone to inflate their earnings by playing fast and loose with accounting practice. They refer to such companies as having "low-quality" earnings, and they place a correspondingly lower value on the firms' stock.

The years between 2000 and 2003 were filled with a seemingly unending series of accounting scandals. Firms such as Global Crossing, Qwest Communications, World-Com, and Fannie Mae misstated profits by billions of dollars. And this was not exclusively a U.S. phenomenon. Parmalat, an Italian dairy company, was dubbed "Europe's Enron" after it falsified the existence of a bank account to the tune of $5.5 billion and

Accounting Convergence?

While the United States still uses generally accepted accounting principles, or GAAP, the European Union has adopted International Financial Reporting Standards (IFRS). IFRS rely more on general principles and judgment than on thousands of pages of specific rules tailored to every conceivable situation. Although IFRS offer more apparent leeway than is provided by the U.S. system, critics of the U.S. approach argue that once firms find a loophole in GAAP, they are not legally bound to obey even the spirit of the rules. In contrast, despite the greater flexibility offered by the European system, firms still must be able to defend their accounting choices as consistent with the broad principles of IFRS. IFRS seem on the way to becoming a global standard, even outside the European Union. By 2009, over 100 countries had adopted them.

IFRS are making inroads even in the United States. In 2007, the SEC began allowing foreign firms to issue securities in the United States if their financial statements are prepared using IFRS. Previously, listing in the United States required that statements be prepared in accordance with GAAP rules. In 2008, the SEC went even further when it proposed allowing large U.S. multinational firms to report earnings using IFRS rather than GAAP starting in 2010, with all U.S. firms to follow by 2014. Further convergence toward uniform global accounting standards would enhance the consistency and comparability of cross-border financial statements, which, according to the SEC, was precisely the goal of its new ruling.

---

eventually entered bankruptcy. The French media and entertainment firm Vivendi Universal nearly ended up in bankruptcy after it was accused of accounting fraud.

In response to these and other scandals, in 2002 Congress passed the Sarbanes-Oxley Act, widely known as SOX. The act attempts to ensure that a firm's financial reports accurately represent its financial condition. SOX created the Public Accounting Oversight Board to oversee the auditing of public companies, and it requires that CEOs and CFOs personally sign off on the firm's financial statements.

But managers and investors worry that these reforms have gone too far. The costs of SOX and the burden of meeting detailed, inflexible regulations are pushing some corporations to return from public to private ownership. Some blame SOX and onerous regulation in the United States for the fact that an increasing number of foreign companies have chosen to list their shares in London rather than New York.

There is also a vigorous debate over "rules-based" versus "principles-based" approaches to accounting standards. The United States follows a rules-based approach, with hundreds of pages of rules governing virtually every circumstance that possibly can be anticipated. In contrast, the European Union takes a principles-based approach to accounting. Its International Financial Reporting Standards set out general approaches that financial statements should take to valuing assets. Europe and the United States have been engaged for years in attempts to coordinate their systems, and many in the United States have lobbied for the greater simplicity that principles-based accounting standards might offer. The nearby box reports on those efforts.

3.5 Taxes

Taxes often have a major effect on financial decisions. Therefore, we should explain how corporations and investors are taxed.

Corporate Tax

Companies pay tax on their income. Table 3.5 shows that there are special low rates of corporate tax for small companies, but for large companies (those with income over $18.33 million) the corporate tax rate is 35%.[9] Thus for every $100 that the firm earns it pays $35 in corporate tax.

When firms calculate taxable income they are allowed to deduct expenses. These expenses include an allowance for depreciation. However, the Internal Revenue Service (IRS) specifies the rates of depreciation that the company can use for different

---

[9] In addition, corporations pay state income taxes, which we ignore here for simplicity.

TABLE 3.5 Corporate tax rates, 2011

Taxable Income, $	Tax Rate, %
0–50,000	15
50,001–75,000	25
75,001–100,000	34
100,001–18,333,333	Varies between 39 and 34
Over 18,333,333	35

TABLE 3.6 Firms A and B both have earnings before interest and taxes (EBIT) of $100 million, but A pays out part of its profits as debt interest. This reduces the corporate tax paid by A.

	Firm A	Firm B
EBIT	100	100
Interest	40	0
Pretax income	60	100
Tax (35% of pretax income)	21	35
Net income	39	65

Note: Figures in millions of dollars.

types of equipment. The rates of depreciation used to calculate taxes are not the same as the rates used when the firm reports its profits to shareholders.[10]

The company is also allowed to deduct interest paid to debtholders when calculating its taxable income, but dividends paid to shareholders are not deductible. These dividends are therefore paid out of after-tax income. Table 3.6 provides an example of how interest payments reduce corporate taxes.

The bad news about taxes is that each extra dollar of revenues increases taxable income by $1 and results in 35 cents of extra taxes. The good news is that each extra dollar of expense *reduces* taxable income by $1 and therefore reduces taxes by 35 cents. For example, if the firm borrows money, every dollar of interest it pays on the loan reduces taxes by 35 cents. Therefore, after-tax income is reduced by only 65 cents.

Self-Test 3.5

Recalculate the figures in Table 3.6 assuming that firm A now has to make interest payments of $60 million. What happens to taxes paid? Does net income fall by the additional $20 million interest payment compared with the case considered in Table 3.6, where interest expense was only $40 million?

When firms make profits, they pay 35% of the profits to the Internal Revenue Service. But the process doesn't work in reverse; if the firm suffers a loss, the IRS does not simply send it a check for 35% of the loss. However, the firm can carry the losses back, deduct them from taxable income in earlier years, and claim a refund of past taxes. Losses can also be carried forward and deducted from taxable income in the future.[11]

Personal Tax

Table 3.7 shows the U.S. rates of personal tax. Notice that as income increases, the tax rate also increases. Notice also that the top personal tax rate is higher than the top corporate rate.

---

[10] If the company assumes a slower rate of depreciation in its income statement than the Internal Revenue Service assumes, the tax charge shown in the income statement will be higher in the early years of a project's life than the actual tax payment. This difference is recorded in the balance sheet as a liability for deferred tax. We will tell you more about depreciation allowances in Chapter 9.

[11] Losses can be carried back for a maximum of 3 years and forward for up to 15 years.

TABLE 3.7 Personal tax rates, 2011

Taxable Income (dollars)		Tax Rate, %
Single Taxpayers	**Married Taxpayers Filling Joint Returns**	
0–8,500	0–17,000	10
8,500–34,500	17,000–69,000	15
34,500–83,600	69,000–139,350	25
83,600–174,400	139,350–212,300	28
174,400–379,150	212,300–379,150	33
379,150 and above	379,150 and above	35

marginal tax rate
Additional taxes owed per dollar of additional income.

The tax rates presented in Table 3.7 are **marginal tax rates.** The marginal tax rate is the tax that the individual pays on each *extra* dollar of income. For example, as a single taxpayer, you would pay 10 cents of tax on each extra dollar you earn when your income is below $8,500, but once income exceeds $8,500, you would pay 15 cents of tax on each extra dollar of income up to an income of $34,500. If your total income is $40,000, your tax bill is 10% of the first $8,500 of income, 15% of the next $26,000 (ie., 34,500 − 8,500), and 25% of the remaining $5,500:

$$\text{Tax} = (.10 \times \$8,500) + (.15 \times \$26,000) + (.25 \times \$5,500) = \$6,125$$

average tax rate
Total taxes owed divided by total income.

The **average tax rate** is simply the total tax bill divided by total income. In this example it is $6,125/$40,000 = .153 = 15.3%. Notice that the average rate is below the marginal rate. This is because of the lower rates on the first $34,500.

Self-Test 3.6

What are the average and marginal tax rates for a single taxpayer with a taxable income of $70,000? What are the average and marginal tax rates for married taxpayers filing joint returns if their joint taxable income is also $70,000?

The tax rates in Table 3.7 apply to "ordinary income," primarily income earned as salary or wages. Interest earnings also are treated as ordinary income.

The treatment of dividend income in the United States leads to what is commonly dubbed the "double taxation" of corporate earnings. Each dollar the company earns is taxed at the corporate rate. Then, if the company pays a dividend out of this after-tax income, the shareholder pays personal income taxes on the distribution. The original earnings are taxed first as corporate income and again as dividend income. Suppose instead that the company earns a dollar which is paid out as interest. The dollar escapes corporate tax because the interest payment is considered a business expense that reduces the firm's taxable income.

Capital gains are also taxed, but only when the gains are realized. Suppose that you bought Bio-technics stock when it was selling for 10 cents a share. Its market price today is $1 a share. As long as you hold on to your stock, there is no tax to pay on your gain. But if you sell, the 90 cents of capital gain is taxed. The marginal tax rate on capital gains for most shareholders is 15%.

Financial managers need to worry about the tax treatment of investment income because tax policy will affect the prices individuals are willing to pay for the company's stock or bonds. We will return to these issues in Part 5 of the text.

The tax rates in Table 3.7 apply to individuals. But financial institutions are major investors in corporate securities. These institutions often have special tax provisions. For example, pension funds are not taxed on interest or dividend income or on capital gains.

www.mhhe.com/bmm7e

SUMMARY

What information is contained in the balance sheet, income statement, and statement of cash flows? *(LO1)*

Investors and other stakeholders in the firm need regular financial information to help them monitor the firm's progress. Accountants summarize this information in a balance sheet, income statement, and statement of cash flows.

The **balance sheet** provides a snapshot of the firm's assets and liabilities. The assets consist of current assets that can be rapidly turned into cash and fixed assets such as plant and machinery. The liabilities consist of current liabilities that are due for payment within a year and long-term debts. The difference between the assets and the liabilities represents the amount of the shareholders' equity.

The **income statement** measures the profitability of the company during the year. It shows the difference between revenues and expenses.

The **statement of cash flows** measures the sources and uses of cash during the year. The change in the company's cash balance is the difference between sources and uses.

What is the difference between market and book value? *(LO2)*

It is important to distinguish between the book values that are shown in the company accounts and the market values of the assets and liabilities. **Book values** are historical measures based on the original cost of an asset. For example, the assets in the balance sheet are shown at their historical cost less an allowance for depreciation. Similarly, the figure for shareholders' equity measures the cash that shareholders have contributed in the past or that the company has reinvested on their behalf. In contrast, **market value** is the current price of an asset or liability.

Why does accounting income differ from cash flow? *(LO3)*

Income is not the same as cash flow. There are two reasons for this: (1) Investment in fixed assets is not deducted immediately from income but is instead spread (as charges for depreciation) over the expected life of the equipment, and (2) the accountant records revenues when the sale is made, rather than when the customer actually pays the bill, and at the same time deducts the production costs even though those costs may have been incurred earlier.

What are the essential features of the taxation of corporate and personal income? *(LO4)*

For large companies the **marginal rate of tax** on income is 35%. In calculating taxable income the company deducts an allowance for depreciation and interest payments. It cannot deduct dividend payments to the shareholders.

Individuals are also taxed on their income, which includes dividends and interest on their investments. Capital gains are taxed, but only when the investment is sold and the gain realized.

LISTING OF EQUATIONS

3.1   Shareholders' equity = total assets − total liabilities

QUESTIONS

|FINANCE

QUIZ

1.   **Balance Sheet.** Construct a balance sheet for Sophie's Sofas given the following data. What is shareholders' equity? *(LO1)*

   Cash balances = $10,000

   Inventory of sofas = $200,000

   Store and property = $100,000

   Accounts receivable = $22,000

   Accounts payable = $17,000

   Long-term debt = $170,000

2. **Financial Statements.** Earlier in the chapter, we characterized the balance sheet as providing a snapshot of the firm at one point in time and the income statement as providing a video. What did we mean by this? Is the statement of cash flow more like a snapshot or a video? *(LO1)*

3. **Income versus Cash Flow.** Explain why accounting income generally will differ from a firm's cash inflows. *(LO3)*

4. **Working Capital.** QuickGrow is in an expanding market, and its sales are increasing by 25% per year. Would you expect its net working capital to be increasing or decreasing? *(LO3)*

5. **Tax Rates.** Using Table 3.7, calculate the marginal and average tax rates for a single taxpayer with the following incomes: *(LO4)*
   a. $20,000
   b. $50,000
   c. $300,000
   d. $3,000,000

6. **Tax Rates.** What would be the marginal and average tax rates for a *corporation* with an income level of $100,000? *(LO4)*

7. **Taxes.** A married couple earned $95,000 in 2011. How much did they pay in taxes? What were their marginal and average tax brackets? *(LO4)*

8. **Cash Flows.** What impact will the following actions have on the firm's cash balance? *(LO3)*
   a. The firm sells some goods from inventory.
   b. The firm sells some machinery to a bank and leases it back for a period of 20 years.
   c. The firm buys back 1 million shares of stock from existing shareholders.

PRACTICE PROBLEMS

9. **Profits versus Cash Flow.** Start-up firms typically have negative net cash flows for several years. *(LO3)*
   a. Does this mean that they are failing?
   b. Accounting profits for these firms are also commonly negative. How would you interpret this pattern? Is there a shortcoming in our accounting rules?

10. **Book versus Market Values.** *(LO2)*
   a. In early 2010, the market values of the shares of many banks (e.g., Bank of America or Citigroup) were less than book value per share. How would you interpret this pattern?
   b. At the same time, Google's market value per share was more than four times its book value. Is this consistent with your analysis in part (a)?

11. **Profits versus Cash Flow.** Value Added Inc. buys $1 million of sow's ears at the beginning of January but doesn't pay immediately. Instead, it agrees to pay the bill in March. It processes the ears into silk purses, which it sells for $2 million in February. However, it will not collect payment on the sales until April. *(LO3)*
   a. Prepare a table showing the firm's net income and investment in net working capital for each month between January and April. In what month will sales revenue and production cost be recognized?
   b. What is the firm's cash flow in each month between January and April?
   c. Does your answer to (b) make sense to you? In which months is cash being exchanged?

12. **Balance Sheet/Income Statement.** The year-end 2010 balance sheet of Brandex Inc. listed common stock and other paid-in capital at $1,100,000 and retained earnings at $3,400,000. The next year, retained earnings were listed at $3,700,000. The firm's net income in 2011 was $900,000. There were no stock repurchases during the year. What were the dividends paid by the firm in 2011? *(LO1)*

13. **Taxes.** You have set up your tax preparation firm as an incorporated business. You took $70,000 from the firm as your salary. The firm's taxable income for the year (net of your salary) was $30,000. How much taxes must be paid to the federal government, including both your personal taxes and the firm's taxes? Assume you pay personal taxes as an unmarried taxpayer. By how much will you reduce the total tax bill by reducing your salary to $50,000, thereby leaving the firm with taxable income of $50,000? Use the tax rates presented in Tables 3.5 and 3.7. *(LO4)*

14. **Market versus Book Values.** The founder of Alchemy Products, Inc., discovered a way to turn lead into gold and patented this new technology. He then formed a corporation and invested $200,000 in setting up a production plant. He believes that he could sell his patent for $50 million. *(LO2)*

    a. What are the book value and market value of the firm?

    b. If there are 2 million shares of stock in the new corporation, what would be the price per share and the book value per share?

15. **Income Statement.** Sheryl's Shipping had sales last year of $10,000. The cost of goods sold was $6,500, general and administrative expenses were $1,000, interest expenses were $500, and depreciation was $1,000. The firm's tax rate is 35%. *(LO1)*

    a. What are earnings before interest and taxes?

    b. What is net income?

    c. What is cash flow from operations?

16. **Cash Flow.** Can cash flow from operations be positive if net income is negative? Can it be negative if net income is positive? Give examples. *(LO3)*

Templates can be found at
www.mhhe.com/bmm7e.

17. **Cash Flows.** Ponzi Products produced 100 chain letter kits this quarter, resulting in a total cash outlay of $10 per unit. It will sell 50 of the kits next quarter at a price of $11, and the other 50 kits in two quarters at a price of $12. It takes a full quarter for it to collect its bills from its customers. (Ignore possible sales in earlier or later quarters.)

    a. Prepare an income statement for Ponzi for today and for each of the next three quarters. Ignore taxes. *(LO1)*

    b. What are the cash flows for the company today and in each of the next three quarters? *(LO3)*

    c. What is Ponzi's net working capital in each quarter? *(LO1)*

18. **Profits versus Cash Flow.** During the last year of operations, accounts receivable increased by $10,000, accounts payable increased by $5,000, and inventories decreased by $2,000. What is the total impact of these changes on the difference between profits and cash flow? *(LO3)*

19. **Income Statement.** A firm's income statement included the following data. The firm's average tax rate was 20%. *(LO1)*

Cost of goods sold	$8,000
Income taxes paid	2,000
Administrative expenses	3,000
Interest expense	1,000
Depreciation	1,000

    a. What was the firm's net income?

    b. What must have been the firm's revenues?

    c. What was EBIT?

20. **Profits versus Cash Flow.** Butterfly Tractors had $14 million in sales last year. Cost of goods sold was $8 million, depreciation expense was $2 million, interest payment on outstanding debt was $1 million, and the firm's tax rate was 35%. *(LO3)*

    a. What was the firm's net income and net cash flow?

    b. What would happen to net income and cash flow if depreciation were increased by $1 million? How do you explain the differing impact of depreciation on income versus cash flow?

    c. Would you expect the change in income and cash flow to have a positive or negative impact on the firm's stock price?

    d. Now consider the impact on net income and cash flow if the firm's interest expense were $1 million higher. Why is this case different from part (b)?

21. **Cash Flow.** Candy Canes, Inc., spends $100,000 to buy sugar and peppermint in April. It produces its candy and sells it to distributors in May for $150,000, but it does not receive payment until June. For each month, find the firm's sales, net income, and net cash flow. *(LO3)*

22. **Financial Statements.** Here are the 2010 and 2011 (incomplete) balance sheets for Nobel Oil Corp. *(LO1)*

NOBEL OIL CORP. BALANCE SHEET, AS OF END OF YEAR					
Assets	2010	2011	Liabilities and Owners' Equity	2010	2011
Current assets	$ 310	$ 420	Current liabilities	$210	$240
Net fixed assets	1,200	1,420	Long-term debt	830	920

www.mhhe.com/bmm7e

a. What was owners' equity at the end of 2010 and 2011?

b. If Nobel paid dividends of $100 in 2011, and made no stock issues, what must have been net income during the year?

c. If Nobel purchased $300 in fixed assets during the year, what must have been the depreciation charge on the income statement?

d. What was the change in net working capital between 2010 and 2011?

e. If Nobel issued $200 of new long-term debt, how much debt must have been paid off during the year?

23. **Financial Statements.** South Sea Baubles has the following (incomplete) balance sheet and income statement.

BALANCE SHEET, AS OF END OF YEAR (Figures in millions of dollars)					
Assets	2010	2011	Liabilities and Shareholders' Equity	2010	2011
Current assets	$ 90	$ 140	Current liabilities	$ 50	$ 60
Net fixed assets	800	900	Long-term debt	600	750

INCOME STATEMENT, 2011 (Figures in millions of dollars)	
Revenue	$1,950
Cost of goods sold	1,030
Depreciation	350
Interest expense	240

a. What is shareholders' equity in 2010 and 2011? *(LO1)*

b. What is net working capital in 2010 and 2011? *(LO1)*

c. What are taxable income and taxes paid in 2011? Assume the firm pays taxes equal to 35% of taxable income. *(LO4)*

d. What is cash provided by operations during 2011? Pay attention to changes in net working capital, using Table 3.4 as a guide. *(LO3)*

e. Net fixed assets increased from $800 million to $900 million during 2011. What must have been South Sea's *gross* investment in fixed assets during 2011? *(LO1)*

f. If South Sea reduced its outstanding accounts payable by $35 million during the year, what must have happened to its other current liabilities? *(LO1)*

The table below contains data on Fincorp, Inc., that you should use for Practice Problems 24–31. The balance sheet items correspond to values at year-end of 2010 and 2011, while the income statement items correspond to revenues or expenses during the year ending in either 2010 or 2011. All values are in thousands of dollars.

24. **Balance Sheet.** Construct a balance sheet for Fincorp for 2010 and 2011. What is shareholders' equity? *(LO1)*

25. **Working Capital.** What happened to net working capital during the year? *(LO1)*

26. **Income Statement.** Construct an income statement for Fincorp for 2010 and 2011. What were reinvested earnings for 2011? How does that compare with the increase in shareholders' equity between the two years? *(LO1)*

27. **Earnings per Share.** Suppose that Fincorp has 500,000 shares outstanding. What were earnings per share? *(LO1)*

28. **Taxes.** What was the firm's average tax bracket for each year? Do you have enough information to determine the marginal tax bracket? *(LO4)*

29. **Balance Sheet.** Examine the values for depreciation in 2011 and net fixed assets in 2010 and 2011. What was Fincorp's gross investment in plant and equipment during 2011? *(LO1)*

30. **Cash Flows.** Construct a statement of cash flows for Fincorp for 2011. *(LO1)*

	2010	2011
Revenue	$4,000	$4,100
Cost of goods sold	1,600	1,700
Depreciation	500	520
Inventories	300	350
Administrative expenses	500	550
Interest expense	150	150
Federal and state taxes*	400	420
Accounts payable	300	350
Accounts receivable	400	450
Net fixed assets†	5,000	5,800
Long-term debt	2,000	2,400
Notes payable	1,000	600
Dividends paid	410	410
Cash and marketable securities	800	300

*Taxes are paid in their entirety in the year that the tax obligation is incurred.
† Net fixed assets are fixed assets net of accumulated depreciation since the asset was installed.

31. **Book versus Market Value.** Now suppose that the market value (in thousands of dollars) of Fincorp's fixed assets in 2011 is $6,000 and that the value of its long-term debt is only $2,200. In addition, the consensus among investors is that Fincorp's past investments in developing the skills of its employees are worth $2,900. This investment of course does not show up on the balance sheet. What will be the price per share of Fincorp stock? *(LO2)*

Templates can be found at www.mhhe.com/bmm7e.

32. **Taxes.** Turn back to Table 3.7, which shows marginal personal tax rates. Make a table in Excel that calculates taxes due for income levels ranging from $10,000 to $10 million. *(LO4)*

a. For each income, calculate the *average* tax rate of a single taxpayer. Plot the average tax rate as a function of income.

b. What happens to the difference between the average and top marginal tax rates as income becomes very large?

c. Explain why, when analyzing very large firms, we may be content simply treating the corporate tax rate as 35% without worrying about tax brackets at relatively low income levels.

CHALLENGE PROBLEM

33. **Taxes.** Reconsider the data in Practice Problem 13 which imply that you have $100,000 of total pretax income to allocate between your salary and your firm's profits. What allocation will minimize the total tax bill? *Hint:* Think about marginal tax rates and the ability to shift income from a higher marginal bracket to a lower one.

WEB EXERCISES

1. Find Microsoft (MFST) and Ford (F) on finance.yahoo.com, and examine the financial statements of each. Which firm uses more debt finance? Which firm has higher cash as a percentage of total assets? Which has higher EBIT per dollar of total assets? Which has higher profits per dollar of shareholders' equity?

2. Now choose two highly profitable technology firms, such as Intel (INTC) and Microsoft (MSFT), and two electric utilities, such as American Electric Power (AEP) and Duke Energy (DUK). Which firms have the higher ratio of market value to book value of equity? Does this make sense to you? Which firms pay out a higher fraction of their profits as dividends to shareholders? Does this make sense?

3. Log on to the Web site of a large nonfinancial company and find its latest financial statements. Draw up a simplified balance sheet, income statement, and statement of cash flows as in Tables 3.1, 3.3, and 3.4. Some companies' financial statements can be extremely complex; try to find a relatively straightforward business. Also, as far as possible, use the same headings as in these tables, and don't hesitate to group some items as "other current assets," "other expenses," and so on. Look first at your simplified balance sheet. How much was the company owed by its customers in the form of unpaid bills? What liabilities does the company need to meet within a year? What was the original cost of the company's fixed assets? Now look at the income statement. What were the company's earnings before interest and taxes (EBIT)? Finally, turn to the cash-flow statement. Did changes in working capital add to cash or use it up?

4. The schedule of tax rates for individuals changes frequently. Check the latest schedules on either www.irs.gov or moneycentral.msn.com. What is your marginal tax rate if you are single with a taxable income of $70,000? What is your average tax rate?

SOLUTIONS TO SELF-TEST QUESTIONS

3.1 Cash and equivalents would increase by $100 million. Property, plant, and equipment would increase by $400 million. Long-term debt would increase by $500 million. Shareholders' equity would not increase: Assets and liabilities have increased equally, leaving shareholders' equity unchanged.

3.2 a. If the auto plant were worth $14 billion, the equity in the firm would be worth $14 − $4 = $10 billion. With 100 million shares outstanding, each share would be worth $100.
   b. If the outstanding stock were worth $8 billion, we would infer that the market values the auto plant at $8 + $4 = $12 billion.

3.3 The profits for the firm are recognized in periods 2 and 3 when the sales take place. In both of those periods, profits are $150 − $100 = $50. Cash flows are derived as follows.

Period:	1	2	3	4
Sales	0	150	150	0
− Change in accounts receivable	0	150	0	(150)
− Cost of goods sold	0	100	100	0
− Change in inventories	200	(100)	(100)	0
= Net cash flow	−200	0	+150	+150

In period 2, half the units are sold for $150 but no cash is collected, so the entire $150 is treated as an increase in accounts receivable. Half the $200 cost of production is recognized, and a like amount is taken out of inventory. In period 3, the firm sells another $150 of product but collects $150 from its previous sales, so there is no change in outstanding accounts receivable. Net cash flow is the $150 collected in this period on the sale that occurred in period 2. In period 4, cash flow is again $150, as the accounts receivable from the sale in period 3 are collected.

3.4 a. An increase in inventories uses cash, reducing the firm's net cash balance.
   b. A reduction in accounts payable uses cash, reducing the firm's net cash balance.
   c. An issue of common stock is a source of cash.
   d. The purchase of new equipment is a use of cash, and it reduces the firm's net cash balance.

3.5

	Firm A	Firm B
EBIT	100	100
Interest	60	0
Pretax income	40	100
Tax (35% of pretax income)	14	35
Net income	26	65

Note: Figures in millions of dollars.

Taxes owed by Firm A fall from $21 million to $14 million. The reduction in taxes is 35% of the extra $20 million of interest income. Net income does not fall by the full $20 million of extra interest expense. It instead falls by interest expense less the reduction in taxes, or $20 million − $7 million = $13 million.

3.6   For a single taxpayer with taxable income of $70,000, total taxes paid are

$$.10 \times 8,500 + [.15 \times (34,500 - 8,500)] + [.25 \times (70,000 - 34,500)] = \$13,625$$

The marginal tax rate is 25%, but the average tax rate is only 13,625/70,000 = .195, or 19.5%. For the married taxpayers filing jointly with taxable income of $70,000, total taxes paid are

$$(.10 \times 17,000) + .15(69,000 - 17,000) + .25(70,000 - 69,000) = \$9,750$$

The marginal tax rate is 25%, and the average tax rate is 9,750/70,000 = .139, or 13.9%.

Measuring Corporate Performance

LEARNING OBJECTIVES

After studying this chapter, you should be able to:

1. Calculate and interpret the market value and market value added of a public corporation.

2. Calculate and interpret key measures of financial performance, including economic value added (EVA) and rates of return on capital, assets, and equity.

3. Calculate and interpret key measures of operating efficiency, leverage, and liquidity.

4. Show how profitability depends on the efficient use of assets and on profits as a fraction of sales.

5. Understand how a company's sustainable growth depends on both its payout policy and its return to equity.

6. Compare a company's financial standing with its competitors and its own position in previous years.

RELATED WEB SITES FOR THIS CHAPTER CAN BE FOUND AT WWW.MHHE.COM/BMM7E.

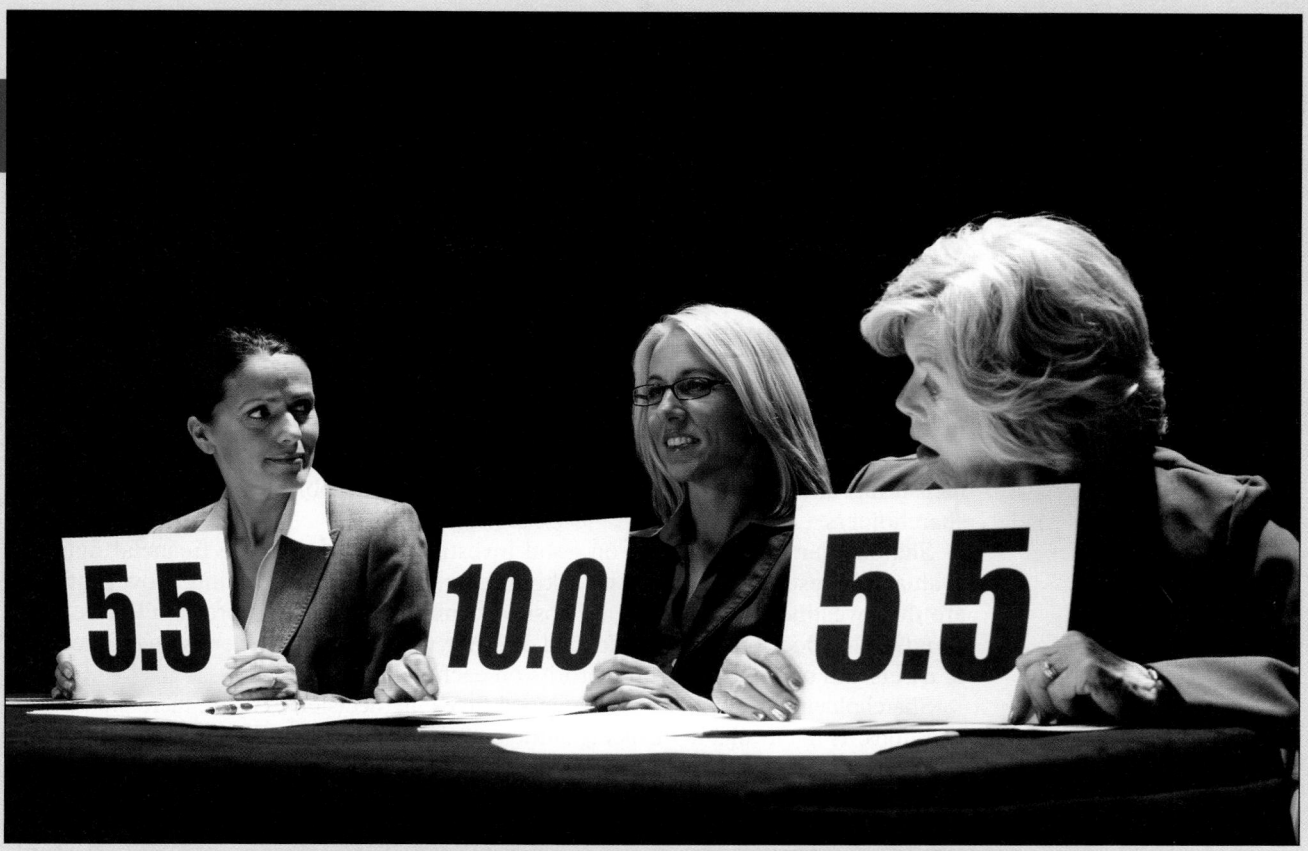

When managers need to judge a firm's performance, they start with some key financial ratios.

In Chapter 1 we introduced the basic objective of corporate finance: Maximize the current *value* of shareholders' investment in the firm. For public corporations, this value is set in the stock market. It equals market price per share multiplied by the number of shares outstanding. Of course, the fluctuations in market value partly reflect events that are outside the financial manager's control. Nevertheless, good financial managers always strive to *add value* by superior investment and financing decisions.

How can we judge whether managers are doing a good job at adding value or where there may be scope for improvement? We need measures of value added. We also need measures that help explain where the value added comes from. For example, value added depends on profitability, so we need measures of profitability. Profitability depends in turn on profit margins and on how efficiently the firm uses its assets. We will describe the standard measures of profitability and efficiency in this chapter.

Value also depends on sound financing. Value is destroyed if the firm is financed recklessly and can't pay its debts. Value is also destroyed if the firm does not maintain adequate liquidity and therefore has difficulty finding the cash to pay its bills. Therefore, we will describe the measures that financial managers and investors use to assess debt policy and liquidity.

These financial measures are mostly *financial ratios* calculated from the firm's income statement and balance sheet. Therefore, we will have to take care to remember the limitations of these accounting data.

You have probably heard stories of whizzes who can take a company's accounts apart in minutes, calculate a list of financial ratios, and divine the company's future. Such people are like abominable snowmen: often spoken of but never truly seen. Financial ratios are no substitute for a crystal ball. They are just a convenient way to summarize financial data and to assess and compare financial performance. The ratios help you to ask the right questions, but they seldom answer them.

4.1 Value and Value Added

How Financial Ratios Help to Understand Value Added

The good news about financial ratios is that they are usually easy to calculate. The bad news is that there are so many of them. To make it worse, the ratios are often presented in long lists that seem to require memorization first and understanding maybe later.

We can mitigate the bad news by taking a moment to preview what the ratios are measuring and how the ratios connect to the ultimate objective of value added for shareholders.

Shareholder value depends on good investment decisions. The financial manager evaluates investment decisions by asking several questions, including: How profitable are the investments relative to the cost of capital? How should profitability be measured? What does profitability depend on? (We will see that it depends on efficient use of assets and on the bottom-line profits on each dollar of sales.)

Shareholder value also depends on good financing decisions. Again, there are obvious questions: Is the available financing sufficient? The firm cannot grow unless financing is available. Is the financing strategy prudent? The financial manager should not put the firm's assets and operations at risk by operating at a dangerously high debt ratio, for example. Does the firm have sufficient liquidity (a cushion of cash or assets that can be readily sold for cash)? The firm has to be able to pay its bills and respond to unexpected setbacks.

Figure 4.1 summarizes these questions in somewhat more detail. The boxes on the left are for investment, the boxes on the right for financing. In each box we have posed a question and given examples of financial ratios or other measures that the financial manager can use to answer the question. For example, the bottom box on the far left of Figure 4.1 asks about efficient use of assets. Three financial ratios that measure asset efficiency are turnover ratios for assets, inventory, and accounts receivable.

FIGURE 4.1 An organization chart for financial ratios. The figure shows how common financial ratios and other measures relate to shareholder value.

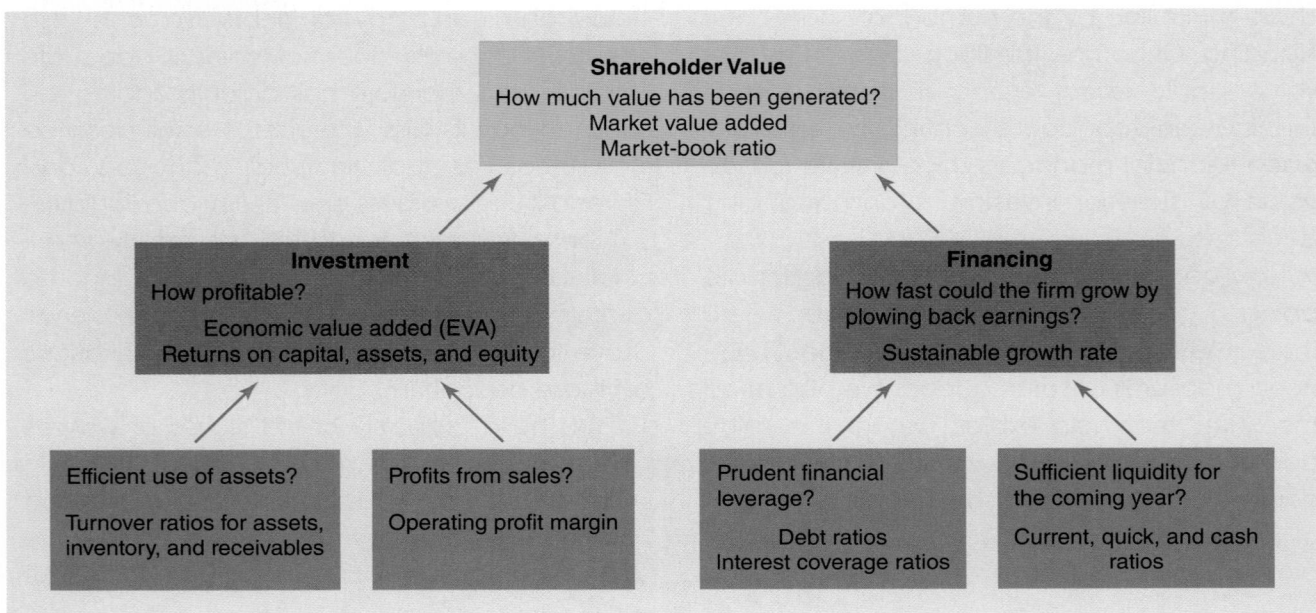

The two bottom boxes on the right ask whether financial leverage (the amount of debt financing) is prudent and whether the firm has enough liquidity for the coming year. The ratios for tracking financial leverage include debt ratios, such as the ratio of debt to equity, and interest coverage ratios. The ratios for liquidity are the current, quick, and cash ratios.

We will explain how to calculate and interpret these and the other ratios in Figure 4.1. For now you can read the figure as an organization chart that locates some important financial ratios and shows how they relate to the objective of shareholder value.

Now we start at the top of the figure. Our first task is to measure value. We will explain market capitalization, market value added, and the market-to-book ratio.

4.2 Measuring Market Value and Market Value Added

Twenty years have passed since your introductory finance class. You are well into your career, and Home Depot is on your mind. Perhaps you are a mutual-fund manager trying to decide whether to allocate $25 million of new money to Home Depot stock. Perhaps you are a major shareholder pondering a sellout. You could be an investment banker seeking business from Home Depot or a bondholder concerned with Home Depot's credit standing. You could be the treasurer or CFO of Home Depot or of one of its competitors. You want to understand Home Depot's value and financial performance. How would you start?

market capitalization
Total market value of equity, equal to share price times number of shares outstanding.

Home Depot's common stock closed 2009 at a price of $28.72 per share. There were 1,693 million shares outstanding, so Home Depot's **market capitalization** or "market cap" was $28.72 × 1,693 = $48,623 million, or nearly $50 billion. This is a big number, of course, but Home Depot is a big company. Home Depot's shareholders have, over the years, invested billions in the company. Therefore, you decide to compare Home Depot's market capitalization to the book value of Home Depot's equity. The book value measures shareholders' cumulative investment in the firm.

market value added
Market capitalization minus book value of equity.

You turn to Home Depot's income statement and balance sheet, which are reproduced in Tables 4.1 and 4.2.[1] At the end of 2009, the book value of Home Depot's equity was $19,393 million. Therefore, Home Depot's **market value added,** the difference between the market value of the firm's shares and the amount of money that shareholders have invested in the firm, was $48,623 − $19,393 = $29,230 million.

TABLE 4.1 Income statement for Home Depot, 2009

Net sales	66,176
Cost of goods sold	43,764
Selling, general, & administrative expenses	15,907
Depreciation	1,806
Earnings before interest and income taxes	4,699
Net interest expense	676
Taxable income	4,023
Taxes	1,362
Net income	2,661
Allocation of net income	
Dividends	1,525
Addition to retained earnings	1,136

Source: Home Depot annual report, 2009.

---

[1] For convenience the statements are repeated from Chapter 3. We are pretending that you actually had these statements on January 1, 2010. They were not published until March.

TABLE 4.2 Home Depot's Balance Sheet (millions of dollars)

Assets	2009	2008
Current assets		
Cash and cash equivalents	1,421	519
Receivables	964	972
Inventories	10,188	10,673
Other current assets	1,327	1,198
Total current assets	13,900	13,362
Fixed Assets		
Net tangible fixed assets	25,550	26,234
Total intangible fixed assets	1,171	1,134
Total fixed assets	26,721	27,368
Other assets	256	434
Total assets	40,877	41,164

Liabilities and Shareholders' Equity	2009	2008
Current liabilities		
Debt due for repayment	1,020	1,767
Accounts payable	8,185	8,221
Other current liabilities	1,158	1,165
Total current liabilities	10,363	11,153
Long-term debt	8,662	9,667
Other long-term liabilities	2,459	2,567
Total liabilities	21,484	23,387
Shareholders' equity:		
Common stock and other paid-in capital	6,390	6,133
Retained earnings	13,588	12,452
Treasury stock	$ (585)	(808)
Total shareholders' equity	19,393	17,777
Total liabilities and shareholders' equity	40,877	41,164

Source: Home Depot annual reports.

In other words, Home Depot shareholders have contributed about $19 billion and ended up with shares worth almost $49 billion. They have accumulated nearly $30 billion in market value added.

The consultancy firm EVA Dimensions calculates market value added for a large sample of U.S. companies. Table 4.3 shows a few of the firms from EVA's list. ExxonMobil heads the group. It has created $148.5 billion of wealth for its shareholders. Xerox is near the bottom of the class: The market value of its shares is $9.1 billion *less* than the amount of shareholders' money invested in the firm.

TABLE 4.3 Stock-market measures of company performance, July 2010. Companies are ranked by market value added (dollar values in millions).

	Market Value Added	Market-to-Book Ratio		Market Value Added	Market-to-Book Ratio
ExxonMobil	148,502	1.81	Home Depot	26,941	1.78
Walmart	121,364	1.94	Lowe's	9,702	1.37
Google	110,566	7.71	FedEx	9,231	1.51
Coca-Cola	93,745	3.63	Dow Chemical	3,382	1.06
Johnson & Johnson	83,997	2.14	JCPenney	−4,653	0.62
AT&T	27,080	1.11	Xerox	−9,128	0.57

Source: We are grateful to EVA Dimensions for providing these statistics.

Exxon is a large firm. Its managers have lots of assets to work with. A small firm could not hope to create so much extra value. Therefore, financial managers and analysts also like to calculate how much value has been added *for each dollar that shareholders have invested*. To do this, they compute the *ratio* of market value to book value. For example, Home Depot's **market-to-book ratio** at the end of 2009 was[2]

market-to-book ratio
Ratio of market value of equity to book value of equity.

$$\text{Market-to-book ratio} = \frac{\text{market value of equity}}{\text{book value of equity}} = \frac{\$48,623}{\$19,393} = 2.5$$

In other words, Home Depot has multiplied the value of its shareholders' investment 2.5 times.

Table 4.3 also shows market-to-book ratios for mid-2010. Notice that Google has a much higher market-to-book ratio than Exxon. But Exxon's market value added is higher because of its larger scale.

Self-Test 4.1

Shares of Notung Cutlery Corp. closed 2010 at $75 per share. Notung had 14.5 million shares outstanding. The book value of equity was $610 million. Compute Notung's market capitalization, market value added, and market-to-book ratio.

The market-value performance measures in Table 4.3 have three drawbacks. First, the market value of the company's shares reflects investors' expectations about *future* performance. Investors pay attention to current profits and investment, of course, but they also avidly forecast investment and growth. Second, market values fluctuate because of many risks and events that are outside the financial manager's control. Thus, market values are noisy measures of how well the corporation's management is performing. Third, you can't look up the market value of privately owned companies whose shares are not traded. Nor can you observe the market value of divisions or plants that are parts of larger companies. You may use market values to satisfy yourself that Home Depot as a whole has performed well, but you can't use them to drill down to compare the performance of the lumber and home

---

[2] The market-to-book ratio can also be calculated by dividing stock price by book value per share.

improvement divisions. To do this, you need accounting measures of profitability. We start with economic value added (EVA).

4.3 Economic Value Added and Accounting Rates of Return

When accountants draw up an income statement, they start with revenues and then deduct operating and other costs. But one important cost is *not* included: the cost of the capital the firm employs. Therefore, to see whether the firm has truly created value, we need to measure whether it has earned a profit after deducting *all* costs, including the cost of its capital.

Recall from Chapters 1 and 2 that the cost of capital is the minimum acceptable rate of return on capital investment. It is an *opportunity* cost of capital, because it equals the expected rate of return on opportunities open to investors in financial markets. The firm creates value only if it can earn more than its cost of capital, that is, more than its investors can earn by investing on their own.

The profit after deducting all costs, *including the cost of capital,* is called the company's **economic value added** or **EVA.** The term "EVA" was coined by Stern Stewart & Co., which did much to develop and promote the concept. EVA is also called *residual income.*

In calculating EVA, it's customary to take account of all the long-term capital contributed by investors in the corporation. That means including bonds and other long-term debt as well as equity capital. Total long-term capital, usually called *total capitalization,* is the sum of long-term debt and shareholders' equity.

At the end of 2008 Home Depot's total capitalization amounted to $27,444, the sum of $9,667 of long-term debt and $17,777 of shareholders' equity. This was the cumulative amount that had been invested by Home Depot's debt and equity investors. Home Depot's cost of capital was about 7.5%.[3] So we can convert the cost of capital into dollars by multiplying total capitalization by 7.5%: $.075 \times \$27,444$ million $= \$2,058$ million. To satisfy its debt and equity investors, Home Depot needed to earn total income of $2,058 million.

Now we can compare this figure with the income that Home Depot actually generated for its debt and equity investors. In 2009 debt investors received interest income

> **economic value added (EVA)**
> After-tax operating income minus a charge for the cost of capital employed. Also called *residual income.*

TABLE 4.4 EVA and ROC, July 2010. Companies are ranked by EVA (dollar values in millions)

	1. Operating income*	2. Cost of Capital, %	3. Total Capitalization	4. EVA = 1 − (2 × 3)	ROC, %, = 1 ÷ 3
ExxonMobil	28,641	5.8	182,424	17,586	15.7
Walmart	15,396	5.2	129,374	8,639	11.9
Johnson & Johnson	11,952	7.1	73,778	6,638	16.2
Coca-Cola	7,093	5.5	35,643	4,943	19.9
Google	6,577	12.0	16,483	4,788	39.9
FedEx	952	6.4	17,954	−241	5.3
JCPenney	465	6.5	12,234	−330	3.8
Dow Chemical	2,638	5.7	56,129	−526	4.7
Xerox	712	9.6	21,326	−1,091	3.3
AT&T	16,779	8.2	250,440	−3,760	6.7

*Net income plus after-tax interest.
Note: EVAs do not compute exactly because of rounding in the cost of capital.
Source: We are grateful to EVA Dimensions for providing these statistics.

---

[3] This is an after-tax weighted-average cost of capital, or WACC. A company's WACC depends on the risk of its business. The WACC is almost the same as the opportunity cost of capital, but with the cost of debt calculated after tax. We will explain WACC and how to calculate it in Chapter 13.

of \$676 million. The after-tax equivalent, using Home Depot's 35% tax rate, is $(1 - .35) \times 676 = \$439$ million.[4] Net income to shareholders was \$2,661 million. Therefore, Home Depot's after-tax interest and net income totaled $\$439 + 2,661 = \$3,100$ million. If you deduct the dollar cost of capital from this figure, you can see that the company earned $\$3,100 - 2,058 = \$1,042$ million *more* than investors required. This was Home Depot's EVA or residual income:

$$\text{EVA} = \text{after-tax interest} + \text{net income} - (\text{cost of capital} \times \text{total capitalization})$$
$$= 439 + 2,661 - 2,058 = \$1,042 \text{ million}$$

The sum of Home Depot's net income and after-tax interest is its after-tax *operating income.* This is what Home Depot would earn if it had no debt and could not take interest as a tax-deductible expense. After-tax operating income is what the company would earn if it were all-equity financed. In that case it would have no (after-tax) interest expense and all operating income would go to shareholders.

Thus EVA also equals:

$$\text{EVA} = \text{after-tax operating income} - (\text{cost of capital} \times \text{total capitalization})$$
$$= 3,100 - 2,058 = \$1,042 \text{ million}$$

Of course Home Depot and its competitors do use debt financing. Nevertheless, EVA comparisons are more useful if focused on operating income, which is not affected by interest tax deductions.

Table 4.4 shows estimates of EVA for our sample of large companies. ExxonMobil again heads the list. It earned over \$17 billion more than was needed to cover its cost of capital. By contrast, AT&T was a laggard. Although it earned an accounting profit of over \$16 billion, this figure was calculated *before* deducting the cost of capital. *After* deducting the cost of capital, AT&T made an EVA loss of about \$3.8 billion.

Notice how the cost of capital differs across the 10 firms in Table 4.4. The variation is due to differences in business risk. Relatively safe companies like Walmart and Coca-Cola tend to have low costs of capital. Riskier companies like Xerox and especially Google have high costs of capital.

EVA, or residual income, is a better measure of a company's performance than is accounting income. Accounting income is calculated after deducting all costs *except* the cost of capital. By contrast, EVA recognizes that companies need to cover their opportunity costs before they add value.

EVA makes the cost of capital *visible* to operating managers. There is a clear target: Earn *at least* the cost of capital on assets employed. A plant or divisional manager can improve EVA by reducing assets. Evaluating performance by EVA pushes managers to flush out and dispose of underutilized assets. Therefore, a growing number of firms now calculate EVA and tie managers' compensation to it.

Self-Test 4.2

Roman Holidays, Inc., had operating income of \$30 million on a start-of-year total capitalization of \$188 million. Its cost of capital was 11.5%. What was its EVA?

---

[4] Why do we take interest after tax? Remember from Chapter 3 that when a firm pays interest, it reduces its taxable income and therefore its tax bill. This tax saving, or *tax shield,* will vary across firms depending on the amounts of debt financing. But we want to focus here on operating results. To put all firms on a common basis, we subtract the interest tax shield from reported income, or, equivalently, we look at after-tax interest payments. By ignoring the tax shield, we calculate each firm's income as if it had no debt outstanding and shareholders got the (pretax) interest. To be consistent, the cost of capital is defined as an after-tax weighted-average cost of capital (WACC). We will have more to say about these issues in Chapters 13 and 16.

Accounting Rates of Return

EVA measures how many dollars a business is earning after deducting the cost of capital. Other things equal, the more assets the manager has to work with, the greater the opportunity to generate a large EVA. The manager of a small division may be highly competent, but if that division has few assets, she is unlikely to rank high in the EVA stakes. Therefore, when comparing managers, it can be helpful to measure the firm's profits *per dollar of assets.* Three common measures are the return on capital (ROC), the return on equity (ROE), and the return on assets (ROA). These are called *book rates of return,* because they are based on accounting information.

Return on Capital (ROC)   The return on capital is equal to after-tax operating income divided by total capitalization. In 2009 Home Depot's operating income was $3,100 million. It started the year with total capitalization (long-term debt plus shareholders' equity) of $27,444 million. Therefore its **return on capital (ROC)** was[5]

$$\text{ROC} = \frac{\text{after-tax operating income}}{\text{total capitalization}} = \frac{3,100}{27,444} = .113, \text{ or } 11.3\%$$

ROC is one prominent accounting or book rate of return. A book rate of return can be computed in different ways. For example, when we divided Home Depot's operating income by its total capitalization at the start of 2009, we ignored the company's additional financing and investment during that year. If the additional investment contributed a significant part of the year's operating income, it's better to divide by the average of the total capitalization at the beginning and end of the year.[6] Home Depot's ROC for 2009 would decrease slightly to

$$\text{ROC} = \frac{\text{after-tax operating income}}{\text{average total capitalization}} = \frac{3,100}{(27,444 + 28,055)/2} = .112, \text{ or } 11.2\%$$

As we noted earlier, Home Depot's cost of capital was about 7.5%. This was the return that investors could have expected to earn at the start of 2009 if they invested their money in other companies or securities with the same risk as Home Depot's business. So in 2009 the company earned $11.2 - 7.5 = 3.7\%$ more than investors required.

Think again about how Home Depot creates value for its shareholders. It can either invest in new assets or pay out cash to the shareholders, who can then invest the money for themselves in financial markets. When Home Depot invests in a new store or warehouse, it deprives shareholders of the opportunity to invest on their own. The return that shareholders are giving up by keeping their money in the company is the opportunity cost of capital. If Home Depot earns more than the cost of capital, it makes its shareholders better off: It is earning a higher return than they could obtain for themselves. If it earns less than the cost of capital, it makes its investors worse off: They could earn a higher return simply by investing on their own in financial markets. So shareholders want the company to invest only in projects for which the return on capital is at least as great as the cost of capital.

The last column in Table 4.4 shows ROC for our sample of well-known companies. Notice that Google's return on capital was 39.9%, nearly 28 percentage points above its cost of capital. Although Google had a higher return on capital than ExxonMobil, it had a lower EVA. This was partly because it was more risky than Exxon and so had a higher cost of capital, but also because it had far fewer dollars invested than Exxon.

return on capital (ROC)
After-tax operating income as a percentage of long-term capital.

---

[5] The numerator of Home Depot's ROC is again its after-tax operating income, calculated by adding back after-tax interest to net income. More often than not, financial analysts forget that interest is tax-deductible and use pretax interest to calculate operating income. This complicates comparisons of ROC for companies that use different fractions of debt financing. It also muddies comparisons of ROC with the after-tax weighted-average cost of capital (WACC). We cover WACC in Chapter 13.

[6] Averages are used when a flow figure that builds up over the course of the year (here, income) is compared with a snapshot figure of assets or liabilities (here, capital). Sometimes it's convenient to use a snapshot figure at the end of the year, although this procedure is not strictly correct.

The five companies in Table 4.4 with negative EVAs all have ROCs less than their cost of capital. The spread between ROC and the cost of capital is really the same thing as EVA but expressed as a percentage return rather than in dollars.

return on assets (ROA)
After-tax operating income as a percentage of total assets.

Return on Assets (ROA)   **Return on assets (ROA)** measures after-tax operating income as a fraction of the firm's *total* assets. Total assets (which equal total liabilities plus shareholders' equity) are greater than total capitalization because total capitalization does not include current liabilities. For Home Depot, ROA was

$$\text{Return on assets} = \frac{\text{after-tax operating income}}{\text{total assets}} = \frac{3,100}{41,164} = .075, \text{ or } 7.5\%$$

Using average total assets, ROA was slightly higher at 7.6%:

$$\text{ROA} = \frac{\text{after-tax operating income}}{\text{average total assets}} = \frac{3,100}{(41,164 + 40,877)/2} = .076, \text{ or } 7.6\%$$

For both ROA and ROC, we use after-tax operating income, which is calculated by adding after-tax interest to net income. We are again asking how profitable the company would have been if it were all-equity financed. This what-if calculation is helpful when comparing the profitability of firms with different capital structures. The tax deduction for interest is often ignored, however, and operating income is calculated using pretax interest. Some financial analysts take *no* account of interest payments and measure ROA as net income for shareholders divided by total assets. This calculation is *really*—we were about to say "stupid," but don't want to offend anyone. This calculation ignores entirely the income that the firm's assets have generated for debt investors.

Self-Test 4.3

What is the difference between after-tax operating income and net income to shareholders? How is after-tax operating income calculated? Why is it useful in calculating EVA, ROC, and ROA?

return on equity (ROE)
Net income as a percentage of shareholders' equity.

Return on Equity (ROE)   We measure the **return on equity (ROE)** as the income to shareholders per dollar that they have invested. Home Depot had net income of $2,661 million in 2009 and shareholders' equity of $17,777 million at the start of the year. So Home Depot's ROE was

$$\text{Return on equity} = \text{ROE} = \frac{\text{net income}}{\text{equity}} = \frac{2,661}{17,777} = .150, \text{ or } 15.0\%$$

Using average equity, ROE was

$$\text{ROE} = \frac{\text{net income}}{\text{average equity}} = \frac{2,661}{(17,777 + 19,393)/2} = .143, \text{ or } 14.3\%$$

Self-Test 4.4

Explain the *differences* between ROE, ROC, and ROA.

Problems with EVA and Accounting Rates of Return

Rates of return and economic value added have some obvious attractions as measures of performance. Unlike market-value-based measures, they show current performance and are not affected by all the other things that move stock market prices. Also, they can be calculated for an entire company or for a particular plant or division. However, remember that both EVA and accounting rates of return are based on book (balance sheet) values for assets. Debt and equity are also book values. As we noted in the last chapter, accountants do not show every asset on the balance sheet, yet our calculations take accounting data at face value. For example, we ignored the fact that Home Depot has invested large sums in marketing in order to establish its brand name. This brand name is an important asset, but its value is not shown on the balance sheet. If it were shown, the book values of assets, capital, and equity would increase, and Home Depot would not appear to earn such high returns.

EVA Dimensions, which produced the figures in Tables 4.3 and 4.4, does make a number of adjustments to the accounting data. However, it is impossible to include the value of all assets or to judge how rapidly they depreciate. For example, did Google really earn a return on capital of 39.9%? It's difficult to say, because its investment over the years in search engines and other software is not shown in the balance sheet and cannot be measured exactly.

Remember also that the balance sheet does not show the current market values of the firm's assets. The assets in a company's books are valued at their original cost less any depreciation. Older assets may be grossly undervalued in today's market conditions and prices. So a high return on assets indicates that the business has performed well by making profitable investments in the past, but it does not necessarily mean that you could buy the same assets today at their reported book values. Conversely a low return suggests some poor decisions in the past, but it does not always mean that today the assets could be employed better elsewhere.

4.4 Measuring Efficiency

We began our analysis of Home Depot by calculating how much value that company has added for its shareholders and how much profit the company is earning after deducting the cost of the capital that it employs. We examined its rates of return on equity, capital, and total assets, which were all impressively high. Our next task is to probe a little deeper to understand the reasons for Home Depot's success. What factors contribute to this firm's overall profitability? One is the efficiency with which it uses its many types of assets.

Asset Turnover Ratio   The asset turnover, or sales-to-assets, ratio shows how much sales are generated by each dollar of total assets, and therefore it measures how hard the firm's assets are working. For Home Depot, each dollar of assets produced $1.608 of sales:

$$\text{Asset turnover} = \frac{\text{sales}}{\text{total assets at start of year}} = \frac{66{,}176}{41{,}164} = 1.608$$

Like some of our profitability ratios, the sales-to-assets ratio compares a flow measure (sales over the entire year) to a snapshot measure (assets on one day). Therefore, financial managers and analysts often calculate the ratio of sales over the entire year to the *average* level of assets over the same period. In this case,

$$\text{Asset turnover} = \frac{\text{sales}}{\text{average total assets}} = \frac{66{,}176}{(40{,}877 + 41{,}164)/2} = 1.613$$

The asset turnover ratio measures how efficiently the business is using its entire asset base. But you also might be interested in how hard *particular types* of assets are being put to use. Below are a couple of examples.

Inventory Turnover   Efficient firms don't tie up more capital than they need in raw materials and finished goods. They hold only a relatively small level of inventories of raw materials and finished goods, and they turn over those inventories rapidly.

The balance sheet shows the cost of inventories rather than the amount that the finished goods will eventually sell for. So it is usual to compare the level of inventories with the cost of goods sold rather than with sales. In Home Depot's case,

$$\text{Inventory turnover} = \frac{\text{cost of goods sold}}{\text{inventory at start of year}} = \frac{43,764}{10,673} = 4.1$$

Another way to express this measure is to look at how many days of output are represented by inventories. This is equal to the level of inventories divided by the daily cost of goods sold:

$$\text{Average days in inventory} = \frac{\text{inventory at start of year}}{\text{daily cost of goods sold}} = \frac{10,673}{43,764/365} = 89 \text{ days}$$

You could say that on average Home Depot has sufficient inventories to maintain operations for 89 days.

In Chapter 20 we will see that many firms have managed to increase their inventory turnover in recent years. Toyota has been the pioneer in this endeavor. Its *just-in-time* inventory system ensures that auto parts are delivered exactly when they are needed. Toyota now keeps only about one month's supply of parts and finished cars in inventory and turns over its inventory about 12 times a year.

Receivables Turnover   Receivables are sales for which you have not yet been paid. The receivables turnover ratio measures the firm's sales as a multiple of its receivables. For Home Depot,

$$\text{Receivables turnover} = \frac{\text{sales}}{\text{receivables at start of year}} = \frac{66,176}{972} = 68$$

If customers are quick to pay, unpaid bills will be a relatively small proportion of sales and the receivables turnover will be high. Therefore, a high ratio often indicates an efficient credit department that is quick to follow up on late payers. Sometimes, however, a high ratio may indicate that the firm has an unduly restrictive credit policy and offers credit only to customers who can be relied on to pay promptly.[7]

Another way to measure the efficiency of the credit operation is by calculating the average length of time for customers to pay their bills. The faster the firm turns over its receivables, the shorter the collection period. Home Depot's customers pay their bills in about 5.4 days:

$$\text{Average collection period} = \frac{\text{receivables at start of year}}{\text{average daily sales}} = \frac{972}{66,176/365} = 5.4 \text{ days}$$

Self-Test 4.5

The average collection period measures the number of days it takes Home Depot to collect its bills. But Home Depot also delays paying its own bills. Use the information in Tables 4.1 and 4.2 to calculate the average number of days that it takes Home Depot to pay its bills.

The receivables turnover ratio and the inventory turnover ratio may help to highlight particular areas of inefficiency, but they are not the only possible indicators. For example, a retail chain might compare its sales per square foot with those of its competitors, an airline might look at revenues per passenger-mile, and a law firm might

---

[7] Where possible, it makes sense to look only at *credit* sales. Otherwise, a high receivables turnover ratio (or, equivalently, a low average collection period) might simply indicate that a small proportion of sales are made on credit. For example, if a retail customer pays cash for a purchase at Home Depot, that transaction will have a collection period of zero, regardless of any policies of the firm's credit department.

look at revenues per partner. A little thought and common sense should suggest which measures are likely to produce the most helpful insights into your company's efficiency.

4.5 Analyzing the Return on Assets: The Du Pont System

We have seen that every dollar of Home Depot's assets generates $1.61 of sales. But Home Depot's success depends not only on the efficiency with which it uses its assets to generate sales but also on how profitable those sales are. This is measured by Home Depot's profit margin.

Profit Margin   The profit margin measures the proportion of sales that finds its way into profits. It is sometimes defined as

$$\text{Profit margin} = \frac{\text{net income}}{\text{sales}} = \frac{2,661}{66,176} = .040, \text{ or } 4.0\%$$

This definition can be misleading. When companies are partly financed by debt, a portion of the revenue produced by sales must be paid as interest to the firm's lenders. So profits from the firm's operations are divided between the debtholders and the shareholders. We would not want to say that a firm is less profitable than its rivals simply because it employs debt finance and pays out part of its income as interest. Therefore, when we are calculating the profit margin, it makes sense to add back the after-tax debt interest to net income. This leads us again to after-tax operating income and to the **operating profit margin:**

operating profit margin
After-tax operating income as a percentage of sales.

$$\text{Operating profit margin} = \frac{\text{after-tax operating income}}{\text{sales}}$$
$$= \frac{2,661 + (1 - .35) \times 676}{66,176} = .047, \text{ or } 4.7\%$$

The Du Pont System

We calculated earlier that Home Depot has earned a return of 7.5% on its assets. The following equation shows that this return depends on two factors—the sales that Home Depot generates from its assets (asset turnover) and the profit that it earns on each dollar of sales (operating profit margin):

$$\text{Return on assets} = \frac{\text{after-tax operating income}}{\text{assets}} \tag{4.1}$$

$$= \underbrace{\frac{\text{sales}}{\text{assets}}}_{\text{asset turnover}} \times \underbrace{\frac{\text{after-tax operating income}}{\text{sales}}}_{\text{operating profit margin}}$$

Du Pont formula
ROA equals the product of asset turnover and operating profit margin.

This breakdown of ROA into the product of turnover and margin is often called the **Du Pont formula,** after the chemical company that popularized the procedure. In Home Depot's case the formula gives the following breakdown of ROA:

$$\text{ROA} = \text{asset turnover} \times \text{operating profit margin}$$
$$= 1.61 \times .047 = .075$$

The Du Pont formula is a useful way to think about a company's strategy. For example, a retailer may strive for high turnover at the expense of a low profit margin (a "Walmart strategy"), or it may seek a high profit margin even if that results in low turnover (a "Bloomingdales strategy"). You would naturally prefer both high profit margin and high turnover, but life isn't that easy. A high-price and high-margin strategy will typically result in lower sales per dollar of assets, so firms must make trade-offs between these goals. The Du Pont formula can help sort out which strategy the firm is pursuing.

All firms would like to earn a higher return on their assets, but their ability to do so is limited by competition. The Du Pont formula helps to identify the constraints that firms face. Fast-food chains, which have high asset turnover, tend to operate on low margins. Classy hotels have relatively low turnover ratios but tend to compensate with higher margins.

EXAMPLE 4.1 ▶	Turnover versus Margin

Firms often seek to improve their profit margins by acquiring a supplier. The idea is to capture the supplier's profit as well as their own. Unfortunately, unless they have some special skill in running the new business, they are likely to find that any gain in profit margin is offset by a decline in asset turnover.

A few numbers may help to illustrate this point. Table 4.5 shows the sales, profits, and assets of Admiral Motors and its components supplier, Diana Corporation. Both earn a 10% return on assets, though Admiral has a lower operating profit margin (20% versus Diana's 25%). Since all of Diana's output goes to Admiral, Admiral's management reasons that it would be better to merge the two companies. That way, the merged company would capture the profit margin on both the auto components and the assembled car.

The bottom row of the following table shows the effect of the merger. The merged firm does indeed earn the combined profits. Total sales remain at $20 million, however, because all the components produced by Diana are used within the company. With higher profits and unchanged sales, the profit margin increases. Unfortunately, the asset turnover is *reduced* by the merger since the merged firm has more assets. This exactly offsets the benefit of the higher profit margin. The return on assets is unchanged.

Figure 4.2 shows evidence of the trade-off between turnover and profit margin. You can see that industries with high average turnover ratios, for example, grocery stores, tend to have lower average profit margins. Conversely, high margins are typically associated with low turnover. The classic examples here are electric or water utilities, which have enormous capital requirements and therefore low asset turnover ratios. However, they have extremely low marginal costs for each unit of additional output and therefore earn high markups. The two curved lines in the figure trace out the combinations of profit margin and turnover that result in an ROA of either 3% or 6%. Despite the enormous dispersion across industries in both margin and turnover, that variation tends to be offsetting, so for most industries the return on assets lies between 3% and 6%.

TABLE 4.5 Merging with suppliers or customers will generally increase the profit margin, but this will be offset by a reduction in asset turnover.

	Millions of Dollars					
	Sales	Profits	Assets	Asset Turnover	Profit Margin	ROA
Admiral Motors	$20	$4	$40	.50	20%	10%
Diana Corp.	8	2	20	.40	25	10
Diana Motors (the merged firm)	20	6	60	.33	30	10

FIGURE 4.2 **Median ROA, profit margin, and asset turnover for 23 industries, 1990–2004**

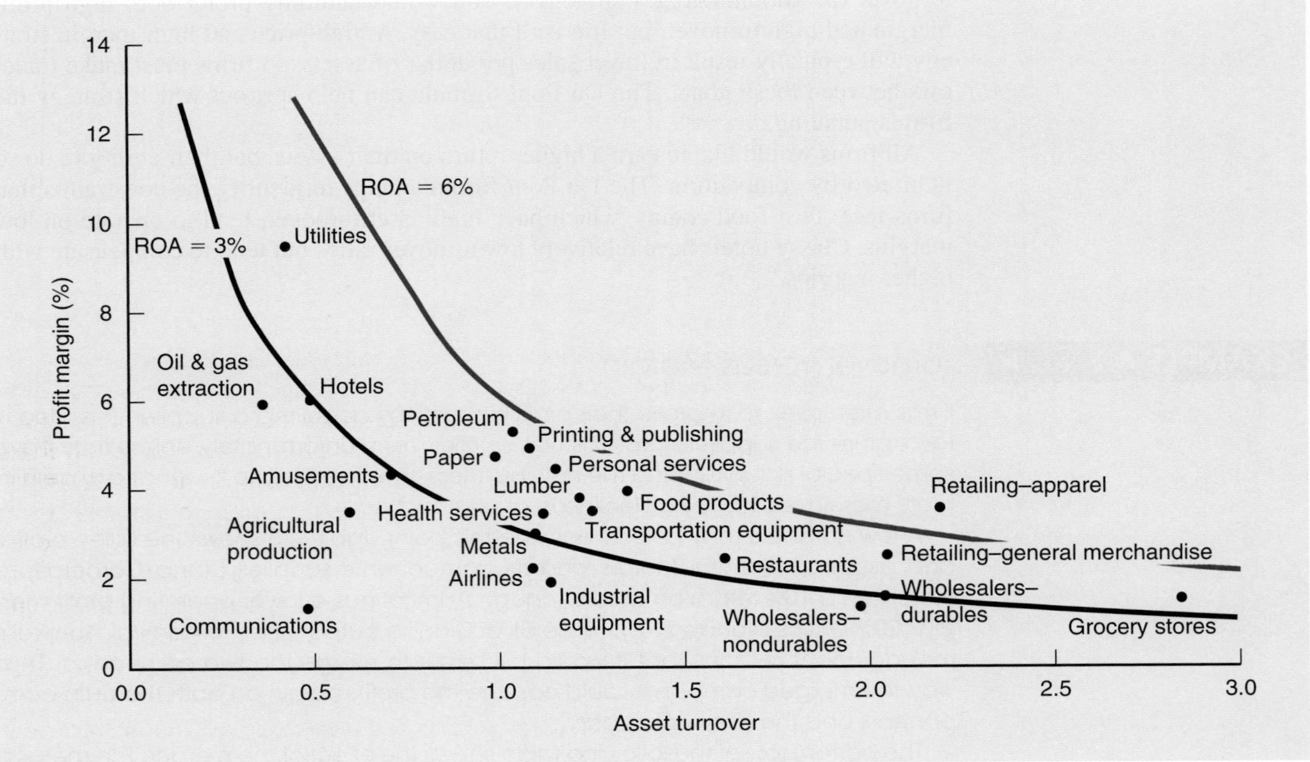

Source: Thomas I. Selling and Clyde P. Stickney, "The Effects of Business Environments and Strategy on a Firm's Rate of Return on Assets." Copyright 1989, CFA Institute. Reproduced and republished from *Financial Analysts Journal*, January–February 1989, pp. 43–52, with permission from the CFA Institute. All rights reserved. Updates courtesy of Professors James Wahlen, Stephen Baginski and Mark Bradshaw.

Self-Test 4.6

The Du Pont formula (Equation 4.1) seems to suggest that companies with higher asset turnover ratios generally will have high ROAs. Why may this not be so?

4.6 Measuring Financial Leverage

As Figure 4.1 indicates, shareholder value depends not only on good investment decisions and profitable operations but also on sound financing decisions. We look first at measures of financial leverage and then at measures of liquidity.

When a firm borrows money, it promises to make a series of interest payments and then to repay the amount that it has borrowed. If profits rise, the debtholders continue to receive only the fixed interest payment, so all the gains go to the shareholders. Of course, the reverse happens if profits fall. In this case shareholders bear most of the pain. If times are sufficiently hard, a firm that has borrowed heavily may not be able to pay its debts. The firm is then bankrupt, and shareholders lose most or all of their entire investment.

Because debt increases returns to shareholders in good times and reduces them in bad times, it is said to create *financial leverage.* Leverage ratios measure how much financial leverage the firm has taken on. CFOs keep an eye on leverage ratios to ensure that lenders are happy to continue to take on the firm's debt.

Debt Ratio Financial leverage is usually measured by the ratio of long-term debt to total long-term capital (that is, to total capitalization). Here long-term debt should include not just bonds or other borrowing but also financing from long-term leases.[8] For Home Depot,

$$\text{Long-term debt ratio} = \frac{\text{long-term debt}}{\text{long-term debt} + \text{equity}} = \frac{8{,}662}{8{,}662 + 19{,}393} = .31, \text{ or } 31\%$$

This means that 31 cents of every dollar of long-term capital is in the form of debt.

Leverage may also be measured by the debt-equity ratio. For Home Depot,

$$\text{Long-term debt-equity ratio} = \frac{\text{long-term debt}}{\text{equity}} = \frac{8{,}662}{19{,}393} = .45, \text{ or } 45\%$$

The difference between these two ratios is moderate for Home Depot, 31% versus 45%. But the debt-equity ratio climbs dramatically for highly leveraged companies. A company financed two-thirds with debt and one-third with equity has a long-term debt ratio of 67% (2/3) and a debt-equity ratio of 2. Sometimes you see projects such as oil pipelines financed with 90% debt and 10% equity. In that case the debt-equity ratio is 90/10 = 9.

The long-term debt ratio for the average U.S. manufacturing company is about 30%, but some companies deliberately operate at much higher debt levels. For example, in Chapter 21 we will look at leveraged buyouts (LBOs). Firms that are acquired in a leveraged buyout usually issue large amounts of debt. When LBOs first became popular in the 1990s, these companies had average debt ratios of about 90%. Many of them flourished and paid back their debtholders in full; others were not so fortunate.

Notice that debt ratios make use of book (accounting) values rather than market values.[9] In principle, lenders should be more interested in the *market value* of the company, which reflects the actual value of the company's assets and the actual cash flows those assets will produce. If the market value of the company covers its debts, then lenders should get their money back. Thus you would expect to see the debt ratio computed using the market values of debt and equity. Yet book debt ratios are used almost universally.

Does use of book rather than market leverage ratios matter much? Perhaps not; after all, the market value of the firm includes the value of intangible assets generated by research and development, advertising, staff training, and so on. These assets are not easy to sell, and if the company falls on hard times, their value may disappear altogether. Thus, when banks demand that a borrower keep within a maximum debt ratio, they usually define that ratio in terms of book values and they ignore the intangible assets that are not shown on the balance sheet.

Notice also that these measures of leverage ignore short-term debt. That probably makes sense if the short-term debt is temporary or is matched by similar holdings of cash, but if the company is a regular short-term borrower, it may be preferable to widen the definition of debt to include all liabilities. In this case,

$$\text{Total debt ratio} = \frac{\text{total liabilities}}{\text{total assets}} = \frac{21{,}484}{40{,}877} = .53, \text{ or } 53\%$$

Therefore, Home Depot is financed 53% with long- and short-term debt and 47% with equity.[10] We could also say that its ratio of total debt to equity is 21,484/19,393 = 1.11.

Managers sometimes refer loosely to a company's debt ratio, but we have just seen that the debt ratio may be measured in several different ways. For example, Home Depot has a debt ratio of .31 (the long-term debt ratio) and also .53 (the total debt

---

[8] A finance lease is a long-term rental agreement that commits the firm to make regular payments. This commitment is just like the obligation to make payments on an outstanding loan.

[9] In the case of leased assets, accountants estimate the value of the lease commitments. In the case of long-term debt, they simply show the face value, which can be very different from market value.

[10] In this case, the 53% of debt includes other liabilities, including accounts payable and other current liabilities.

ratio). This is not the first time we have come across several ways to define a financial ratio. There is no law stating how a ratio should be defined. So be warned: Do not use a ratio without understanding how it has been calculated.

Times Interest Earned Ratio   Another measure of financial leverage is the extent to which interest obligations are covered by earnings. Banks prefer to lend to firms with earnings that cover interest payments with room to spare. *Interest coverage* is measured by the ratio of earnings before interest and taxes (EBIT) to interest payments. For Home Depot,

$$\text{Times interest earned} = \frac{\text{EBIT}}{\text{interest payments}} = \frac{4,699}{676} = 7.0$$

By this measure, Home Depot is conservatively financed. Sometimes lenders are content with coverage ratios as low as 2 or 3.

The regular interest payment is a hurdle that companies must keep jumping if they are to avoid default. The coverage ratio measures how much clear air there is between hurdle and hurdler. The ratio is only part of the story, however. For example, it doesn't tell us whether Home Depot is generating enough cash to repay its debt as it becomes due.

Cash Coverage Ratio   As we explained in Chapter 3, depreciation is not a cash expense. Depreciation is deducted when calculating the firm's earnings, even though no cash goes out the door. Suppose we add back depreciation to EBIT in order to calculate operating cash flow. We then calculate a *cash* coverage ratio.[11] For Home Depot,

$$\text{Cash coverage ratio} = \frac{\text{EBIT} + \text{depreciation}}{\text{interest payments}} = \frac{4,699 + 1,806}{676} = 9.6$$

Self-Test 4.7

A firm repays $10 million face value of outstanding debt and issues $10 million of new debt with a lower rate of interest. What happens to its long-term debt ratio? What happens to its times interest earned and cash coverage ratios?

Leverage and the Return on Equity

When the firm raises cash by borrowing, it must make interest payments to its lenders. This reduces net profits. On the other hand, if a firm borrows instead of issuing equity, it has fewer equityholders to share the remaining profits. Which effect dominates? An extended version of the Du Pont formula helps us answer this question. It breaks down the return on equity (ROE) into four parts:

$$\text{ROE} = \frac{\text{net income}}{\text{equity}} = \underset{\substack{\uparrow \\ \text{leverage} \\ \text{ratio}}}{\frac{\text{assets}}{\text{equity}}} \times \underset{\substack{\uparrow \\ \text{asset} \\ \text{turnover}}}{\frac{\text{sales}}{\text{assets}}} \times \underset{\substack{\uparrow \\ \text{operating} \\ \text{profit margin}}}{\frac{\text{after-tax operating income}}{\text{sales}}} \times \underset{\substack{\uparrow \\ \text{"debt burden"}}}{\frac{\text{net income}}{\text{after-tax operating income}}}$$

(4.2)

---

[11] Depreciation of intangible assets is called *amortization* and is therefore also added back to EBIT. This gives EBIT + depreciation + amortization = EBITDA. EBITDA coverage ratios are common. You may also encounter still other ratios, in addition to the standard ratios covered here. You will see some examples in Table 4.8 on page 101.

Notice that the product of the two middle terms in Equation 4.2 is the return on assets. It depends on the firm's production and marketing skills and is unaffected by the firm's financing mix.[12] However, the first and fourth terms do depend on the debt-equity mix. The first term, assets/equity, which we call the *leverage ratio,* can be expressed as (equity + liabilities)/equity, which equals 1 + total-debt-to-equity ratio. The last term, which we call the "debt burden," measures the proportion by which interest expense reduces profits.

Suppose that the firm is financed entirely by equity. In this case, both the leverage ratio and the debt burden are equal to 1, and the return on equity is identical to the return on assets. If the firm borrows, however, the leverage ratio is greater than 1 (assets are greater than equity) and the debt burden is less than 1 (part of the profits is absorbed by interest). Thus leverage can either increase or reduce return on equity. In fact, we will see in Chapter 16 that leverage increases ROE when the firm's return on assets is higher than the interest rate it pays on its debt. Since Home Depot's return on capital exceeds the interest rate on its debt, return on equity is higher than return on capital.

Self-Test 4.8

a. Sappy Syrup has a profit margin below the industry average, but its ROA equals the industry average. How is this possible?
b. Sappy Syrup's ROA equals the industry average, but its ROE exceeds the industry average. How is this possible?

4.7 Measuring Liquidity

liquidity
Access to cash or assets that can be turned into cash on short notice.

If you are extending credit to a customer or making a short-term bank loan, you are interested in more than the borrower's financial leverage. You want to know whether the company can lay its hands on the cash to repay you. That is why credit analysts and bankers look at several measures of **liquidity.** Liquid assets can be converted into cash quickly and cheaply.

Think, for example, what you would do to meet a large unexpected bill. You might have some money in the bank or some investments that are easily sold, but you would not find it so easy to turn your old sweaters into cash. Companies, likewise, own assets with different degrees of liquidity. For example, accounts receivable and inventories of finished goods are generally quite liquid. As inventories are sold off and customers pay their bills, money flows into the firm. At the other extreme, real estate may be quite *illiquid.* It can be hard to find a buyer, negotiate a fair price, and close a deal at short notice.

Managers have another reason to focus on liquid assets: Their book (balance sheet) values are usually reliable. The book value of a catalytic cracker may be a poor guide to its true value, but at least you know what cash in the bank is worth.

Liquidity ratios also have some *less* desirable characteristics. Because short-term assets and liabilities are easily changed, measures of liquidity can rapidly become outdated. You might not know what the catalytic cracker is worth, but you can be fairly sure that it won't disappear overnight. Cash in the bank can disappear in seconds.

Also, assets that seem liquid sometimes have a nasty habit of becoming illiquid. This happened during the subprime mortgage crisis in 2008. Some financial institutions had set up funds known as *structured investment vehicles (SIVs)* that issued short-term debt backed by residential mortgages. As mortgage default rates began to climb, the market in this debt dried up and dealers became very reluctant to quote a price.

---

[12] Again, we use after-tax operating income, which is the sum of net income and after-tax interest.

Bankers and other short-term lenders applaud firms that have plenty of liquid assets. They know that when they are due to be repaid, the firm will be able to get its hands on the cash. But more liquidity is not always a good thing. For example, efficient firms do not leave excess cash in their bank accounts. They don't allow customers to postpone paying their bills, and they don't leave stocks of raw materials and finished goods littering the warehouse floor. In other words, high levels of liquidity may indicate sloppy use of capital. Here, EVA can highlight the problem, because it penalizes managers who keep more liquid assets than they really need.

Net Working Capital to Total Assets Ratio   Current assets include cash, marketable securities, inventories, and accounts receivable. Current assets are mostly liquid. The difference between current assets and current liabilities is known as *net working capital*. It roughly measures the company's potential net reservoir of cash. Since current assets usually exceed current liabilities, net working capital is usually positive. For Home Depot,

$$\text{Net working capital} = 13{,}900 - 10{,}363 = \$3{,}537 \text{ million}$$

Home Depot's net working capital was 9% of total assets:

$$\frac{\text{Net working capital}}{\text{Total assets}} = \frac{3{,}537}{40{,}877} = .09, \text{ or } 9\%$$

Current Ratio   The current ratio is just the ratio of current assets to current liabilities:

$$\text{Current ratio} = \frac{\text{current assets}}{\text{current liabilities}} = \frac{13{,}900}{10{,}363} = 1.34$$

Home Depot has $1.34 in current assets for every dollar in current liabilities.

Changes in the current ratio can be misleading. For example, suppose that a company borrows a large sum from the bank and invests it in marketable securities. Current liabilities rise and so do current assets. If nothing else changes, net working capital is unaffected but the current ratio changes. For this reason it is sometimes preferable to net short-term investments against short-term debt when calculating the current ratio.

Quick (Acid-Test) Ratio   Some current assets are closer to cash than others. If trouble comes, inventory may not sell at anything above fire-sale prices. (Trouble typically comes *because* the firm can't sell its inventory of finished products for more than production cost.) Thus managers often exclude inventories and other less liquid components of current assets when comparing current assets to current liabilities. They focus instead on cash, marketable securities, and bills that customers have not yet paid. This results in the quick ratio:

$$\text{Quick ratio} = \frac{\text{cash} + \text{marketable securities} + \text{receivables}}{\text{current liabilities}} = \frac{1{,}421 + 964}{10{,}363} = .23$$

Cash Ratio   A company's most liquid assets are its holdings of cash and marketable securities. That is why analysts also look at the cash ratio:

$$\text{Cash ratio} = \frac{\text{cash} + \text{marketable securities}}{\text{current liabilities}} = \frac{1{,}421}{10{,}363} = .14$$

A low cash ratio may not matter if the firm can borrow on short notice. Who cares whether the firm has actually borrowed from the bank or whether it has a guaranteed line of credit that lets it borrow whenever it chooses? None of the standard measures of liquidity takes the firm's "reserve borrowing power" into account.

> *Self-Test 4.9*
>
> **a.** A firm has $1.2 million in current assets and $1 million in current liabilities. If it uses $.5 million of cash to pay off some of its accounts payable, what will happen to the current ratio? What happens to net working capital?
> **b.** A firm uses cash on hand to pay for additional inventories. What will happen to the current ratio? To the quick ratio?

4.8 Calculating Sustainable Growth

Home Depot's leverage and liquidity ratios are checks on whether its financing policies are safe and sound. But what about the *amount* of financing that is available for investment and growth? To put it another way, how fast could Home Depot grow? Would its growth be limited by the availability of financing?

The answer to the last question is in principle no. In well-functioning financial markets, a company's growth is limited not by financing opportunities but by limits to good investment opportunities and by limits to other resources, including trained management and staff. If the company has investment projects that add value, it should be able to issue stock, if necessary, to finance them.

But the window to issue stock may not always be open. For example, a financial manager who believes that investors are unduly pessimistic will be reluctant to issue stock at what he or she sees as a depressed price. Therefore, financial managers and analysts are interested in knowing how fast the firm can grow if it relies only on internal financing, keeping the long-term debt ratio constant. They calculate the firm's *sustainable growth rate.*

Mature companies grow mainly by reinvesting earnings. How rapidly they grow depends on the proportion of earnings that is kept in the business and the profits that the company can earn on the new capital.

In 2009 Home Depot earned $2,661 and paid $1,525 in dividends. The proportion of earnings paid out as dividends was, therefore,

$$\text{Payout ratio} = \frac{1{,}525}{2{,}661} = .57, \text{ or } 57\%$$

The remaining 43% of earnings was reinvested and "plowed back" into the business and added to the firm's equity capital.[13] Thus,

$$\text{Plowback ratio} = 1 - \text{payout ratio} = 1 - .57 = .43$$

Home Depot's return on equity (ROE) was 15%. If it continues to reinvest 43% of its earnings and to earn 15% on this money, both its earnings and its book equity will increase by $.43 \times .15 = .065$, or 6.5% a year:

$$\text{Sustainable growth rate} = \frac{\text{earnings} - \text{dividends}}{\text{equity}}$$
$$= \frac{\text{earnings} - \text{dividends}}{\text{earnings}} \times \frac{\text{earnings}}{\text{equity}}$$
$$= \text{plowback ratio} \times \text{ROE}$$
$$= .43 \times .15 = .065, \text{ or } 6.5\%$$

---

[13] We assume that payout to shareholders comes as cash dividends only. Companies also pay out cash by repurchasing stock. Strictly speaking, the payout ratio should be defined as the ratio of dividends and repurchases to net income. We discuss repurchases in Chapter 17.

This measure is often known as the **sustainable rate of growth.**

The sustainable growth rate assumes that the firm's long-term debt ratio is held constant. Home Depot could grow its assets at a faster rate by borrowing more and more, but that growth strategy would not be sustainable in the long run.

Home Depot's sustainable growth rate is moderate. But sometimes the formula for sustainable growth will result in crazy values, for example, sustainable growth rates above 30% or even 40%. No company could expect to maintain growth rates like these forever. Often, in such cases, firms are selling products at an early stage of their life-cycle. Competition in these new markets is scarce, return on equity is high, and, with ample opportunities for profitable reinvestment, firms respond with very high plowback ratios. For example, the ROE for computer software firms in 2010 was more than double that of electric utilities. And most software companies paid no dividends at all, but instead plowed *all* their earnings back into the firm.[14] But eventually, as the industry matures, price competition will increase, ROE will decline, and with fewer profitable opportunities for reinvestment, firms will plow back less of their earnings. As ROE and the plowback ratio both decline, growth also must slow.

4.9 Interpreting Financial Ratios

We have shown how to calculate some common summary measures of Home Depot's performance and financial condition. These are summarized in Table 4.6.[15]

Now that you have calculated these measures, you need some way to judge whether they are high or low. In some cases there may be a natural benchmark. For example, if a firm has negative value added or a return on capital less than the cost of that capital, it is not creating wealth for its shareholders.

But what about some of our other measures? There is no right level for, say, the asset turnover or profit margin, and if there were, it would almost certainly vary from industry to industry and company to company. For example, you would not expect a soft-drink manufacturer to have the same profit margin as a jeweller or the same leverage as a finance company. All financial ratios must be interpreted in the context of industry norms.

Table 4.7 presents some financial ratios for a sample of industry groups. Notice the large variation across industries. Some of these differences, particularly in profitability measures, may arise from chance; in 2009 the sun shone more kindly on some industries than others. But other differences may reflect more fundamental factors. For example, notice the comparatively high debt ratios of food product companies. In comparison, computer and electronic companies tend to borrow far less, and these differences are true in both good times and bad. We pointed out earlier that some businesses are able to generate a high level of sales from relatively few assets. Differences in turnover ratios also tend to be relatively stable. For example, you can see that the asset turnover ratio for beverage and tobacco firms is more than double that for food product companies. But competition ensures that beverage and tobacco firms earn a correspondingly lower margin on their sales. The net effect is that the return on assets in the two industries is broadly similar.

[14] These data are based on the firms in the Value Line Investment Survey industry group.

[15] If you would like to see how we calculated these ratios or to calculate your own, you can use the live Excel spreadsheet available on our Web site at **www.mhhe.com/bmm7e**.

TABLE 4.6 Summary of Home Depot's performance measures

Performance Measures		
Market value added ($ millions)	market value of equity − book value of equity	29,230
Market-to-book ratio	market value of equity ÷ book value of equity	2.5
Profitability Measures		
Return on assets (ROA)	after-tax operating income/total assets	7.5%
Return on capital (ROC)	after-tax operating income/(long-term debt + equity)	11.3%
Return on equity (ROE)	net income/equity	15.0%
EVA* ($ millions)	after-tax operating income − cost of capital × capital	1,042
Efficiency Measures		
Operating profit margin	after-tax operating income/sales	4.7%
Asset turnover	sales/total assets at start of year	1.61
Fixed-asset turnover	sales/fixed assets at start of year	2.42
Receivables turnover	sales/receivables at start of year	68.1
Average collection period (days)	receivables at start of year/daily sales	5.36
Inventory turnover	cost of goods sold/inventory at start of year	4.10
Days in inventory	inventories at start of year/daily cost of goods sold	89.0
Leverage Measures		
Long-term debt ratio	long-term debt/(long-term debt + equity)	30.9%
Long-term debt-equity ratio	long-term debt/equity	44.7%
Total debt ratio	total liabilities/total assets	52.6%
Times interest earned	EBIT/interest payments	6.95
Cash coverage ratio	(EBIT + depreciation)/interest payments	9.62
Liquidity Measures		
Net working capital to assets	net working capital/total assets	0.09
Current ratio	current assets/current liabilities	1.34
Quick ratio	(cash + marketable securities + receivables)/current liabilities	0.23
Cash ratio	(cash + marketable securities)/current liabilities	0.14
Growth Measures		
Payout ratio	dividends/earnings	0.57
Sustainable growth	(1 − payout ratio) × ROE	6.5%

*Authors' calculation.

You can find this spreadsheet at
www.mhhe.com/bmm7e.

TABLE 4.7 Financial ratios for major industry groups, 2009

	LT Debt Assets	Interest Coverage	Current Ratio	Quick Ratio	Asset Turnover	Profit Margin (%)	Return on Assets (%)	Return on Equity (%)	Payout Ratio
All Manufacturing	0.22	2.58	1.43	1.03	0.77	5.19	4.02	12.94	0.43
Food Products	0.28	3.74	1.40	0.84	1.19	7.99	9.52	18.09	0.47
Clothing	0.21	9.60	1.39	0.54	2.01	6.99	14.04	22.48	0.09
Beverage & Tobacco	0.27	3.95	1.15	0.52	2.82	3.20	9.04	−4.43	−0.54
Chemicals	0.26	2.62	1.36	1.04	0.48	9.04	4.34	22.12	0.36
Drugs	0.24	3.19	1.56	1.28	0.38	11.00	4.20	26.08	0.29
Machinery	0.18	2.83	1.32	0.90	0.70	6.15	4.33	8.55	0.66
Electrical	0.12	4.30	1.10	0.72	0.59	8.02	4.75	9.55	0.54
Motor Vehicles	0.20	−0.24	0.99	0.77	0.98	−0.42	−0.41	−25.25	−0.24
Computer and Electronic	0.16	3.26	1.94	1.64	0.59	4.92	2.91	16.29	0.08
Paper	0.32	2.68	1.27	0.90	0.89	7.96	7.09	13.38	0.47

Source: Authors' calculations using data from U.S. Department of *Commerce, Quarterly Financial Report for Manufacturing, Mining and Trade Corporations,* March 2010. Available at **http://www.census.gov/econ/qfr/current/qfr_pub.pdf**.

Self-Test 4.10

Even within an industry, there can be a considerable difference in the type of business that companies do, and this shows up in their financial ratios. Here are some data on assets, sales, and income for two companies. Calculate for each company the asset turnover, the operating profit margin, and the return on assets. In each case the values are expressed as a percentage of sales. One of these two companies is Walmart. The other is Tiffany. Which one is which? Explain.

	Company A	Company B
Sales	100	100
Assets	40.0	87.3
Net income + after-tax interest	4.0	11.1

When looking for benchmarks to evaluate performance, it usually makes sense to limit the comparison to the firm's major competitors. Table 4.8 sets out some key performance measures for Home Depot and Lowe's. The two companies are similar in many respects. For example, their liquidity measures are nearly identical. However, Home Depot's ROA is higher, due to its slightly higher asset turnover ratio as well as its better operating profit margin. Home Depot relies far more heavily on debt than Lowe's. This shows up in both its higher leverage ratios as well as its lower coverage ratios. This greater indebtedness could be a problem in an economic downturn. Despite its higher ROA and ROE, Home Depot actually has a lower sustainable growth rate than Lowe's. This is because it pays out a far larger share of earnings as dividends. This means more dividends today, but with lower reinvestment in the firm, future earnings and dividends may grow more slowly.[16]

It may also be helpful to compare Home Depot's financial ratios with its own equivalent figures in earlier years. For example, you can see in Figure 4.3 that Home Depot's return on assets declined from nearly 16% in 2005 to below 10% in 2008

FIGURE 4.3 Home Depot financial ratios over time

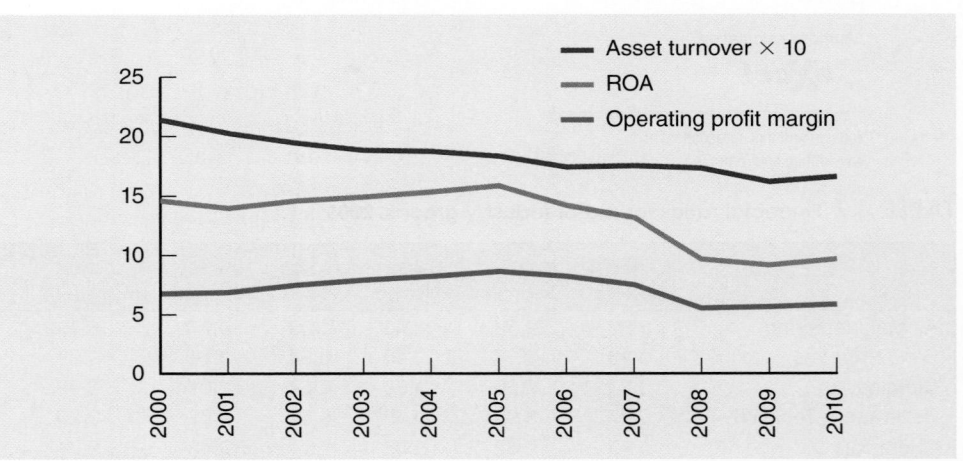

Note: We pointed out earlier in the chapter that there is more than one way to calculate several ratios. Value Line's figures do not precisely match the values in Table 4.6.
Source: Value Line Investment Survey, April 2, 2010.

---

[16] One apparently large and puzzling discrepancy between the two firms is in receivables turnover or, equivalently, average collection period. With its dramatically higher receivables turnover and lower collection period, Lowe's appears to be far more efficient in collecting its bills. But this is actually an illusion. Lowe's tends to sell its accounts receivable to other parties, and thus maintains lower receivables on its balance sheet. The lesson? Ratios can tip us off to differences in strategy as well as to emerging business strengths or problems, but you will generally have to probe further to fully understand the implications of the numbers.

TABLE 4.8 Selected financial measures for Home Depot and Lowe's, 2009

	Home Depot	Lowe's
Performance Measures		
Market value added ($ millions)	29,230	16,181
Market-to-book ratio	2.5	1.85
Profitability Measures		
Return on assets (ROA)	7.5%	6.0%
Return on capital (ROC)	11.3%	8.5%
Return on equity (ROE)	15.0%	9.9%
EVA* ($ millions)	1,042	145
Operating profit margin	4.7%	4.2%
Efficiency Measures		
Asset turnover	1.61	1.45
Fixed-asset turnover	2.42	2.06
Receivables turnover	68.1	219.6
Average collection period (days)	5.36	1.66
Inventory turnover	4.10	3.75
Days in inventory	89.0	97.4
Leverage Measures		
Long-term debt ratio	30.9%	19.2%
Long-term debt-equity ratio	44.7%	23.7%
Total debt ratio	52.6%	42.2%
Times interest earned	6.95	10.84
Cash coverage ratio	9.62	16.47
Liquidity Measures		
Net working capital to assets	0.09	0.07
Current ratio	1.34	1.32
Quick ratio	0.23	0.17
Cash ratio	0.14	0.14
Growth Measures		
Payout ratio	0.57	0.22
Sustainable growth	6.5%	7.7%

*Authors' calculation.

before finally stabilizing. We know that ROA = asset turnover × operating profit margin. So what accounted for the fall in ROA? Figure 4.3 shows that the culprit was the decline in profit margin from 8.6% in 2005 to 5.7% in 2008. Perhaps Home Depot was forced to deal with greater price pressure from its competitors in those years. Here is where it may be useful to look at the experience of its different divisions.

This concludes our canter through Home Depot's financial statements.

4.10 The Role of Financial Ratios—and a Final Note on Transparency

Whenever two managers get together to talk business and finance, it's a good bet that they will refer to financial ratios. Let's drop in on two conversations.

Conversation 1   The CEO was musing out loud: "How are we going to finance this expansion? Would the banks be happy to lend us the $30 million that we need?"

"I've been looking into that," the financial manager replies. "Our current debt ratio is .3. If we borrow the full cost of the project, the ratio would be about .45. When we took out our last loan from the bank, we agreed that we would not allow our debt ratio to get above .5. So if we borrow to finance this project, we wouldn't have much leeway to respond to possible emergencies. Also, the rating agencies currently give our bonds

TABLE 4.9 Financial ratios and default risk by rating class, long-term debt

	Three-Year (2002–2004) Medians						
	AAA	**AA**	**A**	**BBB**	**BB**	**B**	**CCC**
EBIT interest coverage multiple	23.8	19.5	8.0	4.7	2.5	1.2	0.4
EBITDA interest coverage multiple	25.5	24.6	10.2	6.5	3.5	1.9	0.9
Funds from operations/total debt (%)	203.3	79.9	48.0	35.9	22.4	11.5	5.0
Free operating cash flow/total debt (%)	127.6	44.5	25.0	17.3	8.3	2.8	(2.1)
Total debt/EBITDA multiple	0.4	0.9	1.6	2.2	3.5	5.3	7.9
Return on capital (%)	27.6	27.0	17.5	13.4	11.3	8.7	3.2
Total debt/(total debt + equity) (%)	12.4	28.3	37.5	42.5	53.7	75.9	113.5

Note: EBITDA is earnings before interest, taxes, depreciation, and amortization. Standard & Poor's and Moody's, the two largest credit rating agencies, use slightly different labels for rating classes. For example, S&P's BBB rating is equivalent to Moody's Baa, BB is equivalent to Ba, and so on.
Source: Corporate Rating Criteria, Standard & Poor's, 2006.

an investment-grade rating. They too look at a company's leverage when they rate its bonds. I have a table here (Table 4.9), which shows that when firms are highly leveraged, their bonds receive a lower rating. I don't know whether the rating agencies would downgrade our bonds if our debt ratio increased to .45, but they might. That wouldn't please our existing bondholders, and it could raise the cost of any new borrowing."

"We also need to think about our interest cover, which is beginning to look a bit thin. Debt interest is currently covered three times, and if we borrowed the entire $30 million, interest cover would fall to about two times. Sure, we expect to earn additional profits on the new investment, but it could be several years before they come through. If we run into a recession in the meantime, we could find ourselves short of cash."

"Sounds to me as if we should be thinking about a possible equity issue," concluded the CEO.

Conversation 2 The CEO was not in the best of moods after his humiliating defeat at the company golf tournament by the manager of the packaging division: "I see our stock was down again yesterday," he growled. "It's now selling below book value, and the stock price is only six times earnings. I work my socks off for this company; you would think that our stockholders would show a little more gratitude."

"I think I can understand a little of our shareholders' worries," the financial manager replies. "Just look at our return on assets." It's only 6%, well below the cost of capital. Sure we are making a profit, but that profit does not cover the cost of the funds that investors provide. Our economic value added is actually negative. Of course, this doesn't necessarily mean that the assets could be used better elsewhere, but we should certainly be looking carefully at whether any of our divisions should be sold off or the assets redeployed.

"In some ways we're in good shape. We have very little short-term debt, and our current assets are three times our current liabilities. But that's not altogether good news because it also suggests that we may have more working capital than we need. I've been looking at our main competitors. They turn over their inventory 12 times a year compared with our figure of just 8 times. Also, their customers take an average of 45 days to pay their bills. Ours take 67. If we could just match their performance on these two measures, we would release $300 million that could be paid out to shareholders."

"Perhaps we could talk more about this tomorrow," said the CEO. "In the meantime I intend to have a word with the production manager about our inventory levels and with the credit manager about our collections policy. You've also got me thinking about whether we should sell off our packaging division. I've always worried about the divisional manager there. Spends too much time practicing his backswing and not enough worrying about his return on assets."

Transparency

Throughout this chapter we have assumed that financial statements are trustworthy. We assumed that accountants are following generally accepted accounting principles (GAAP) and not endorsing misleading numbers. We assumed that managers are not making up good "facts" for the financial statements or covering up bad ones. When these assumptions are correct, we say that the firm is *transparent,* because outsiders can assess its value and performance.

Unfortunately, dishonest managers with creamy compensation packages may seek to hide the truth from investors. When the truth comes out, there can be big trouble. Think back to the Enron scandal. Enron was in many ways an empty shell. Its stock price was supported more by investors' enthusiasm than by profitable operating businesses. The company inflated its apparent performance by borrowing aggressively through so-called *special-purpose entities (SPEs)* and hiding these debts. Much of the SPE borrowing was improperly excluded from Enron's financial statements.

The bad news started to leak out in the last months of 2001. In October, Enron announced a $1 billion write-off of its water and broadband business. In November, it recognized its SPE debt retroactively, which increased its acknowledged indebtedness by $658 million and reduced its claims of past earnings by $591 million. Its public debt was downgraded to junk status, and on December 2 it filed for bankruptcy.

Enron demonstrated the importance of transparency. If Enron had been more transparent to outsiders—that is, if they could have assessed its true profitability and prospects—its problems would have shown up right away in a falling stock price. That in turn would have generated extra scrutiny from security analysts, bond rating agencies, lenders, and investors.

With transparency, corporate troubles generally lead to corrective action. But the top management of a troubled and *opaque* company may be able to maintain its stock price and postpone the discipline of the market. Market discipline caught up with Enron only a month or two before bankruptcy.

Enron was only one in a series of accounting scandals that came to light in 2001 and 2002. A major goal of the Sarbanes-Oxley Act (SOX) is to increase transparency and ensure that companies and their accountants provide directors, lenders, and shareholders with the information they need to monitor progress. Among other things, the act set up the Public Company Accounting Oversight Board to oversee auditors; it bans accounting firms from offering their services to companies whose accounts they audit; it prohibits any individual from heading a firm's audit for more than 5 years; and it requires that the board's audit committee consist of directors who are independent of the company's management. Sarbanes-Oxley also requires that management (1) certify that the financial statements present a fair view of the firm's financial position and (2) demonstrate that the firm has adequate controls and procedures for financial reporting.

All this comes at a price. The costs of SOX and the burdens of meeting detailed regulations are pushing some corporations to return to private (versus public) ownership. Some observers also believe that these added regulatory demands have hurt the international competitiveness of U.S. financial markets.

Despite periodic accounting breakdowns, transparency in the United States and other developed economies is usually pretty good. Nevertheless, it pays to be careful and critical even in these countries. Take extra care in developing economies, where accounting standards are often lax.

SUMMARY

How do you measure whether a public corporation has delivered value for its shareholders? *(LO1)*

For a public corporation, this is relatively easy. Start with **market capitalization,** which equals price per share times the number of shares outstanding. The difference between market capitalization and the book value of equity measures the **market value added** by the firm's investments and operations. The book value of equity is the cumulative investment (including reinvested earnings) by shareholders in the company. The ratio of market value to book value is another way of expressing value added.

For private corporations, financial managers and analysts have to turn to other performance measures, because stock prices are not available.

What measures are used to assess financial performance? *(LO2)*

Financial managers and analysts track **return on equity (ROE),** which is the ratio of net income to shareholders' equity. But net income is calculated after interest expense, so ROE depends on the debt ratio. The **return on capital (ROC)** and the **return on assets (ROA)** are better measures of operating performance. These are the ratios of after-tax operating income to total capitalization (long-term debt plus shareholders' equity) and to total assets. ROC should be compared with the company's cost of capital. **EVA (economic value added** or residual income) deducts the cost of capital from operating income. If EVA is positive, then the firm's current operations are adding value for shareholders.

What are the standard measures of profitability, efficiency, leverage, and liquidity? *(LO3)*

Financial managers and analysts have to condense the enormous volume of information in a company's financial statements. They rely on a handful of ratios to summarize financial performance, operating efficiency, and financial strength. Look back at Table 4.6, which summarizes the most important ratios. Remember that the ratios sometimes appear under different names and may be calculated differently.

Profitability ratios measure return on investment. Leverage ratios measure how much the firm has borrowed and its obligations to pay interest. Efficiency ratios measure how intensively the firm uses its assets. Liquidity ratios measure how easily the firm can obtain cash.

Financial ratios crop up repeatedly in financial discussions and contracts. Banks and bondholders usually demand limits on debt ratios or interest coverage.

What determines the return on assets and equity? *(LO4)*

The **Du Pont system** links financial ratios together to explain the return on assets and equity. Return on assets is the product of asset turnover and operating profit margin. Return on equity is the product of the leverage ratio, asset turnover, operating profit margin, and debt burden.

What is sustainable growth? *(LO5)*

Sustainable growth is the rate at which the firm can grow without issuing shares or changing its debt ratio. Firms that reinvest more of their earnings can sustain faster growth. The sustainable growth rate is the product of the plowback ratio and return on equity (ROE). (The plowback ratio equals 1 minus the dividend payout ratio.) Of course, this growth rate is really sustainable only if ROE and plowback are maintained at current levels.

What are some potential pitfalls in financial statement analysis? *(LO6)*

Financial statement analysis will rarely be useful if done mechanically. Financial ratios do not provide final answers, although they should prompt the right questions. In addition, accounting entries do not always reflect current market values, and in rare cases accounting is not transparent, because unscrupulous managers make up good news and hide bad news in financial statements.

You will need a benchmark to assess a company's financial condition. Therefore, we usually compare financial ratios to the company's ratios in earlier years and to ratios of other firms in the same business.

LISTING OF EQUATIONS

4.1 $\text{Return on assets} = \dfrac{\text{after-tax operating income}}{\text{assets}}$

$$= \underbrace{\dfrac{\text{sales}}{\text{assets}}}_{\text{asset turnover}} \times \underbrace{\dfrac{\text{after-tax operating income}}{\text{sales}}}_{\text{operating profit margin}}$$

4.2

$$\text{ROE} = \frac{\text{net income}}{\text{equity}} = \underset{\substack{\uparrow \\ \text{leverage} \\ \text{ratio}}}{\frac{\text{assets}}{\text{equity}}} \times \underset{\substack{\uparrow \\ \text{asset} \\ \text{turnover}}}{\frac{\text{sales}}{\text{assets}}} \times \underset{\substack{\uparrow \\ \text{operating} \\ \text{profit margin}}}{\frac{\text{after-tax}}{\text{operating income}}} \times \underset{\substack{\uparrow \\ \text{"debt burden"}}}{\frac{\text{net income}}{\text{after-tax}}}$$

QUESTIONS

Mc Graw Hill **connect**
|FINANCE

QUIZ

1. **Calculating Ratios.** Here are simplified financial statements of Phone Corporation from a recent year: *(LO3)*

INCOME STATEMENT (Figures in millions of dollars)	
Net sales	13,193
Cost of goods sold	4,060
Other expenses	4,049
Depreciation	2,518
Earnings before interest and taxes (EBIT)	2,566
Interest expense	685
Income before tax	1,881
Taxes (at 35%)	658
Net income	1,223
Dividends	856

BALANCE SHEET (Figures in millions of dollars)	End of Year	Start of Year
Assets		
Cash and marketable securities	89	158
Receivables	2,382	2,490
Inventories	187	238
Other current assets	867	932
Total current assets	3,525	3,818
Net property, plant, and equipment	19,973	19,915
Other long-term assets	4,216	3,770
Total assets	27,714	27,503
Liabilities and shareholders' equity		
Payables	2,564	3,040
Short-term debt	1,419	1,573
Other current liabilities	811	787
Total current liabilities	4,794	5,400
Long-term debt and leases	7,018	6,833
Other long-term liabilities	6,178	6,149
Shareholders' equity	9,724	9,121
Total liabilities and shareholders' equity	27,714	27,503

Calculate the following financial ratios:

a. Long-term debt ratio
b. Total debt ratio
c. Times interest earned

       d. Cash coverage ratio

       e. Current ratio

       f. Quick ratio

       g. Operating profit margin

       h. Inventory turnover

       i. Days in inventory

       j. Average collection period

       k. Return on equity

       l. Return on assets

       m. Return on capital

       n. Payout ratio

2. **Market value.** Phone Corp.'s stock price was $84 at the end of the year. There were 205 million shares outstanding. What was the company's market capitalization and market value added? What was its market-to-book ratio? *(LO1)*

3. **EVA.** Phone Corp.'s cost of capital was 8.2%, the same as AT&T's cost of capital in Table 4.4. What was Phone Corp.'s economic value added? *(LO2)*

4. **Measuring Firm Performance.** *(LO2)*

    a. What would happen to Home Depot's economic value added if its cost of capital were 8% rather than the 7.5% value we assumed?

    b. Would this have any impact on its accounting profits?

    c. Which do you think is a better measure of the firm's performance?

5. **Measuring Firm Performance.** Suppose the broad stock market falls 5% in one day and Home Depot's stock price also falls by 5%. *(LO1)*

    a. What will happen to our assessment of market value added?

    b. Should this decline affect our assessment of the performance of Home Depot's managers?

    c. Would you feel differently about Home Depot's managers if the stock market were unchanged and Home Depot's stock fell by 5%?

6. **Sustainable Growth.** In Table 4.8, we report Home Depot's sustainable growth rate as 6.5%. *(LO5)*

    a. What would the sustainable growth rate be if Home Depot's plowback ratio rose to the same value as Lowe's?

    b. What would the sustainable growth rate be if Home Depot's return on equity were only 14%?

7. **Du Pont Analysis.** Use the data for Phone Corp. from Quiz Question 1 to confirm that ROA = asset turnover × operating profit margin. *(LO4)*

8. **Du Pont Analysis.** Use the data for Phone Corp. from Quiz Question 1 to demonstrate that ROE = leverage ratio × asset turnover ratio × operating profit margin × debt burden. *(LO4)*

PRACTICE PROBLEMS

9. **Asset Turnover.** In each case, choose the firm that you expect to have a higher asset turnover ratio. *(LO3)*

    a. Economics Consulting Group or Home Depot.

    b. Catalog Shopping Network or Neiman Marcus.

    c. Electric Utility Co. or Standard Supermarkets.

10. **Economic Value Added.** EVA will be positive whenever ROC is greater than the cost of capital. Explain why this is so. *(LO2)*

11. **Defining Ratios.** There are no universally accepted definitions of financial ratios, but some of the following ratios make no sense at all. Substitute correct definitions. *(LO3)*

    a. $\text{Debt-equity ratio} = \dfrac{\text{long-term debt}}{\text{long-term debt} + \text{equity}}$

    b. $\text{Return on equity} = \dfrac{\text{net incone}}{\text{average equity}}$

    c. $\text{Operating profit margin} = \dfrac{\text{after-tax operating income}}{\text{sales}}$

d. Inventory turnover $= \dfrac{\text{total sales}}{\text{average inventory}}$

e. Current ratio $= \dfrac{\text{current liabilities}}{\text{current assets}}$

f. Average collection period $= \dfrac{\text{sales}}{\text{average receivables}/365}$

g. Quick ratio $= \dfrac{\text{cash} + \text{marketable securities} + \text{receivables}}{\text{current liabilities}}$

12. **Current Liabilities.** Suppose that at year-end Home Depot had unused lines of credit which would have allowed it to borrow a further $300 million. Suppose also that it used this line of credit to borrow $300 million and invested the proceeds in marketable securities. Would the company have appeared to be (a) more or less liquid, (b) more or less highly leveraged? Calculate the appropriate ratios. *(LO3)*

13. **Current Ratio.** How would the following actions affect a firm's current ratio? *(LO3)*
    a. Inventory is sold at cost.
    b. The firm takes out a bank loan to pay its accounts due.
    c. A customer pays its accounts receivable.
    d. The firm uses cash to purchase additional inventories.

14. **Liquidity Ratios.** A firm uses $1 million in cash to purchase inventories. What will happen to its current ratio? Its quick ratio? *(LO3)*

15. **Receivables.** Chik's Chickens has average accounts receivable of $6,333. Sales for the year were $9,800. What is its average collection period? *(LO3)*

16. **Inventory.** Salad Daze maintains an inventory of produce worth $400. Its total bill for produce over the course of the year was $73,000. How old on average is the lettuce it serves its customers? *(LO3)*

17. **Inventory Turnover.** If a firm's inventory level of $10,000 represents 30 days' sales, what is the annual cost of goods sold? What is the inventory turnover ratio? *(LO3)*

18. **Leverage Ratios.** Lever Age pays an 8% rate of interest on $10 million of outstanding debt with face value $10 million. The firm's EBIT was $1 million. *(LO3)*
    a. What is times interest earned?
    b. If depreciation is $200,000, what is cash coverage?
    c. If the firm must retire $300,000 of debt for the sinking fund each year, what is its "fixed-payment cash-coverage ratio" (the ratio of cash flow to interest plus other fixed debt payments)?

19. **Du Pont Analysis.** Keller Cosmetics maintains an operating profit margin of 5% and asset turnover ratio of 3. *(LO4)*
    a. What is its ROA?
    b. If its debt-equity ratio is 1, its interest payments and taxes are each $8,000, and EBIT is $20,000, what is its ROE?

20. **Du Pont Analysis.** Torrid Romance Publishers has total receivables of $3,000, which represents 20 days' sales. Total assets are $75,000. The firm's operating profit margin is 5%. Find the firm's ROA and asset turnover ratio. *(LO4)*

21. **Leverage.** A firm has a long-term debt-equity ratio of .4. Shareholders' equity is $1 million. Current assets are $200,000, and the current ratio is 2. The only current liabilities are notes payable. What is the total debt ratio? *(LO3)*

22. **Leverage Ratios.** A firm has a debt-to-equity ratio of .5 and a market-to-book ratio of 2. What is the ratio of the book value of debt to the market value of equity? *(LO3)*

23. **Times Interest Earned.** In the past year, TVG had revenues of $3 million, cost of goods sold of $2.5 million, and depreciation expense of $200,000. The firm has a single issue of debt outstanding with book value of $1 million on which it pays an interest rate of 8%. What is the firm's times interest earned ratio? *(LO3)*

24. **Du Pont Analysis.** CFA Corp. has a debt-equity ratio that is lower than the industry average, but its cash coverage ratio is also lower than the industry average. What might explain this seeming contradiction? *(LO3)*

25. **Leverage.** Suppose that a firm has both floating-rate and fixed-rate debt outstanding. What effect will a decline in market interest rates have on the firm's times interest earned ratio? On

the market-value debt-to-equity ratio? On the basis of these answers, would you say that leverage has increased or decreased? *(LO3)*

26. **Interpreting Ratios.** In each of the following cases, explain briefly which of the two companies is likely to be characterized by the higher ratio: *(LO3)*

    a. Debt-equity ratio: a shipping company or a computer software company.
    b. Payout ratio: United Foods Inc. or Computer Graphics Inc.
    c. Ratio of sales to assets: an integrated pulp and paper manufacturer or a paper mill.
    d. Average collection period: Regional Electric Power Company or Z-Mart Discount Outlets.

27. **Using Financial Ratios.** For each category of financial ratios discussed in this chapter, give some examples of who would be likely to examine these ratios and why. *(LO6)*

CHALLENGE PROBLEMS

28. **Financial Statements.** As you can see, someone has spilled ink over some of the entries in the balance sheet and income statement of Transylvania Railroad. Can you use the following information to work out the missing entries? *(LO3)*

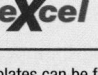

Templates can be found at
www.mhhe.com/bmm7e.

Long-term debt ratio	0.4
Times interest earned	8.0
Current ratio	1.4
Quick ratio	1.0
Cash ratio	0.2
Inventory turnover	5.0
Average collection period	73 days

INCOME STATEMENT
(Figures in millions of dollars)

Net sales	●●●
Cost of goods sold	●●●
Selling, general, and administrative expenses	10
Depreciation	20
Earnings before interest and taxes (EBIT)	●●●
Interest expense	●●●
Income before tax	●●●
Tax (35% of income before tax)	●●●
Net income	●●●

BALANCE SHEET
(Figures in millions of dollars)

	This Year	Last Year
Assets		
Cash and marketable securities	●●●	20
Receivables	●●●	34
Inventories	●●●	26
Total current assets	●●●	80
Net property, plant, and equipment	●●●	25
Total assets	●●●	105
Liabilities and shareholders' equity		
Accounts payable	25	20
Notes payable	30	35
Total current liabilities	●●●	55
Long-term debt	●●●	20
Shareholders' equity	●●●	30
Total liabilities and shareholders' equity	115	105

29. **Interpreting Financial Ratios.** *(LO3)*

    a. Turn back to Table 4.7. For the sample of industries in that table, plot operating profit margin again asset turnover in a scatter diagram. What is the apparent relationship between these two variables? Does this make sense to you?

    b. Now plot a scatter diagram of the current ratio versus quick ratio. Do these two measures of liquidity tend to move together? Would you conclude that once you know one of these ratios, there is little to be gained by calculating the other?

30. Company X does not raise any new finance during the year, but it generates a lot of earnings during the year, which are immediately reinvested. If you were calculating X's return on capital, would it make more sense to use capital at the start of the year or an average of the starting and ending capital? Would your answer change if X made a large issue of debt early in the year? Illustrate your answer with simple examples. *(LO2)*

WEB EXERCISE

1. Log on to finance.yahoo.com to find the latest simplified financial statements for Home Depot. Recalculate HD's financial ratios. What have been the main changes from those shown in these tables? If you owned some of HD's debt, would these changes make you feel more or less happy?

SOLUTIONS TO SELF-TEST QUESTIONS

4.1 Market capitalization is 75×14.5 million = $1,087.5 million. Market value added is $1,087.5 - $610 = $477.5 million. Market to book is 1,087.5/610 = 1.78. You can also calculate book value per share at $610/14.5 = $42.07, and use price per share to calculate market to book: $75/$42.07 = 1.78.

4.2 The cost of capital in dollars is $.115 \times $188 million = $21.62 million. EVA is $30 - $21.62 = $8.38 million.

4.3 After-tax operating income is calculated before interest expense. Net income is calculated after interest expense. Financial managers usually start with net income, so they add back after-tax interest to get after-tax operating income. After-tax operating income measures the profitability of the firm's investment and operations. If properly calculated, it is not affected by financing.

4.4 ROE measures return to equity as net income divided by the book value of equity. ROC and ROA measure the return to all investors, including interest paid as well as net income to shareholders. ROC measures return versus long-term debt and equity. ROA measures return versus total assets.

4.5 Average daily expenses are (43,764 + 15,907)/365 = $163.5 million. Accounts payable at the start of the year are $8,221 million. The average payment delay is therefore 8,221/163.5 = 50.3 days.

4.6 In industries with rapid asset turnover, competition forces prices down, reducing profit margins.

4.7 Nothing will happen to the long-term debt ratio computed using book values, since the face values of the old and new debt are equal. However, times interest earned and cash coverage will increase since the firm will reduce its interest expense.

4.8 a. The firm must compensate for its below-average profit margin with an above-average turnover ratio. Remember that ROA is the *product* of operating margin $\times$ turnover.

    b. If ROA equals the industry average but ROE exceeds the industry average, the firm must have above-average leverage. As long as ROA exceeds the borrowing rate, leverage will increase ROE.

4.9 a. The current ratio starts at 1.2/1.0 = 1.2. The transaction will reduce current assets to $.7 million and current liabilities to $.5 million. The current ratio increases to .7/.5 = 1.4. Net working capital is unaffected: Current assets and current liabilities fall by equal amounts.

    b. The current ratio is unaffected, since the firm merely exchanges one current asset (cash) for another (inventories). However, the quick ratio will fall since inventories are not included among the most liquid assets.

4.10

	Company A	Company B
1. Asset turnover	2.5	1.15
2. Operating profit margin, %	4.0	11.1
3. Return on assets, % (= 1 × 2)	10.0	12.7

Company A is Walmart; it generates a high volume of sales from its assets, but earns a relatively low profit margin on these sales. The reverse is true of Tiffany (company B). The two companies differ enormously in their asset turnover and profit margin, but much less in their return on assets.

MINICASE

Burchetts Green had enjoyed the bank training course, but it was good to be starting his first real job in the corporate lending group. Earlier that morning the boss had handed him a set of financial statements for The Hobby Horse Company, Inc. (HH). "Hobby Horse," she said, "has a $45 million loan from us due at the end of September, and it is likely to ask us to roll it over. The company seems to have run into some rough weather recently, and I have asked Furze Platt to go down there this afternoon and see what is happening. It might do you good to go along with her. Before you go, take a look at these financial statements and see what you think the problems are. Here's a chance for you to use some of that stuff they taught you in the training course."

Mr. Green was familiar with the HH story. Founded in 1990, it had rapidly built up a chain of discount stores selling materials for crafts and hobbies. However, last year a number of new store openings coinciding with a poor Christmas season had pushed the company into loss. Management had halted all new construction and put 15 of its existing stores up for sale.

Mr. Green decided to start with the 6-year summary of HH's balance sheet and income statement (Table 4.10). Then he turned to examine in more detail the latest position (Tables 4.11 and 4.12).

What appear to be the problem areas in HH? Do the financial ratios suggest questions that Ms. Platt and Mr. Green need to address?

TABLE 4.10 Financial highlights for The Hobby Horse Company, Inc., year ending March 31

	2011	2010	2009	2008	2007	2006
Net sales	3,351	3,314	2,845	2,796	2,493	2,160
EBIT	−9	312	256	243	212	156
Interest	37	63	65	58	48	46
Taxes	3	60	46	43	39	34
Net profit	−49	189	145	142	125	76
Earnings per share	−0.15	0.55	0.44	0.42	0.37	0.25
Current assets	669	469	491	435	392	423
Net fixed assets	923	780	753	680	610	536
Total assets	1,592	1,249	1,244	1,115	1,002	959
Current liabilities	680	365	348	302	276	320
Long-term debt	236	159	297	311	319	315
Stockholders' equity	676	725	599	502	407	324
Number of stores	240	221	211	184	170	157
Employees	13,057	11,835	9,810	9,790	9,075	7,825

TABLE 4.11

INCOME STATEMENT FOR THE HOBBY HORSE COMPANY, INC., FOR YEAR ENDING MARCH 31, 2011 (All items in millions of dollars)	
Net sales	3,351
Cost of goods sold	1,990
Selling, general, and administrative expenses	1,211
Depreciation expense	159
Earnings before interest and taxes (EBIT)	−9
Net interest expense	37
Taxable income	−46
Income taxes	3
Net income	−49
Allocation of net income	
Addition to retained earnings	−49
Dividends	0

Note: Column sums subject to rounding error.

TABLE 4.12

CONSOLIDATED BALANCE SHEET FOR THE HOBBY HORSE COMPANY, INC. (Figures in millions of dollars)		
Assets	**Mar. 31, 2011**	**Mar. 31, 2010**
Current assets		
Cash and marketable securities	14	72
Receivables	176	194
Inventories	479	203
Total current assets	669	469
Fixed assets		
Property, plant, and equipment (net of depreciation)	1,077	910
Less accumulated depreciation	154	130
Net fixed assets	923	780
Total assets	1,592	1,249
Liabilities and Shareholders' Equity	**Mar. 31, 2011**	**Mar. 31, 2010**
Current liabilities		
Debt due for repayment	484	222
Accounts payable	94	58
Other current liabilities	102	85
Total current liabilities	680	365
Long-term debt	236	159
Stockholders' equity		
Common stock and other paid-in capital	155	155
Retained earnings	521	570
Total stockholders' equity	676	725
Total liabilities and stockholders' equity	1,592	1,249

Note: Column sums subject to rounding error.

CHAPTER 5

The Time Value of Money

LEARNING OBJECTIVES

After studying this chapter, you should be able to:

(1) Calculate the future value to which money invested at a given interest rate will grow.

(2) Calculate the present value of a future payment.

(3) Calculate present and future values of a series of cash payments.

(4) Find the interest rate implied by present and future values.

(5) Compare interest rates quoted over different time intervals—for example, monthly versus annual rates.

(6) Understand the difference between real and nominal cash flows and between real and nominal interest rates.

RELATED WEB SITES FOR THIS CHAPTER CAN BE FOUND AT WWW.MHHE.COM/BMM7E.

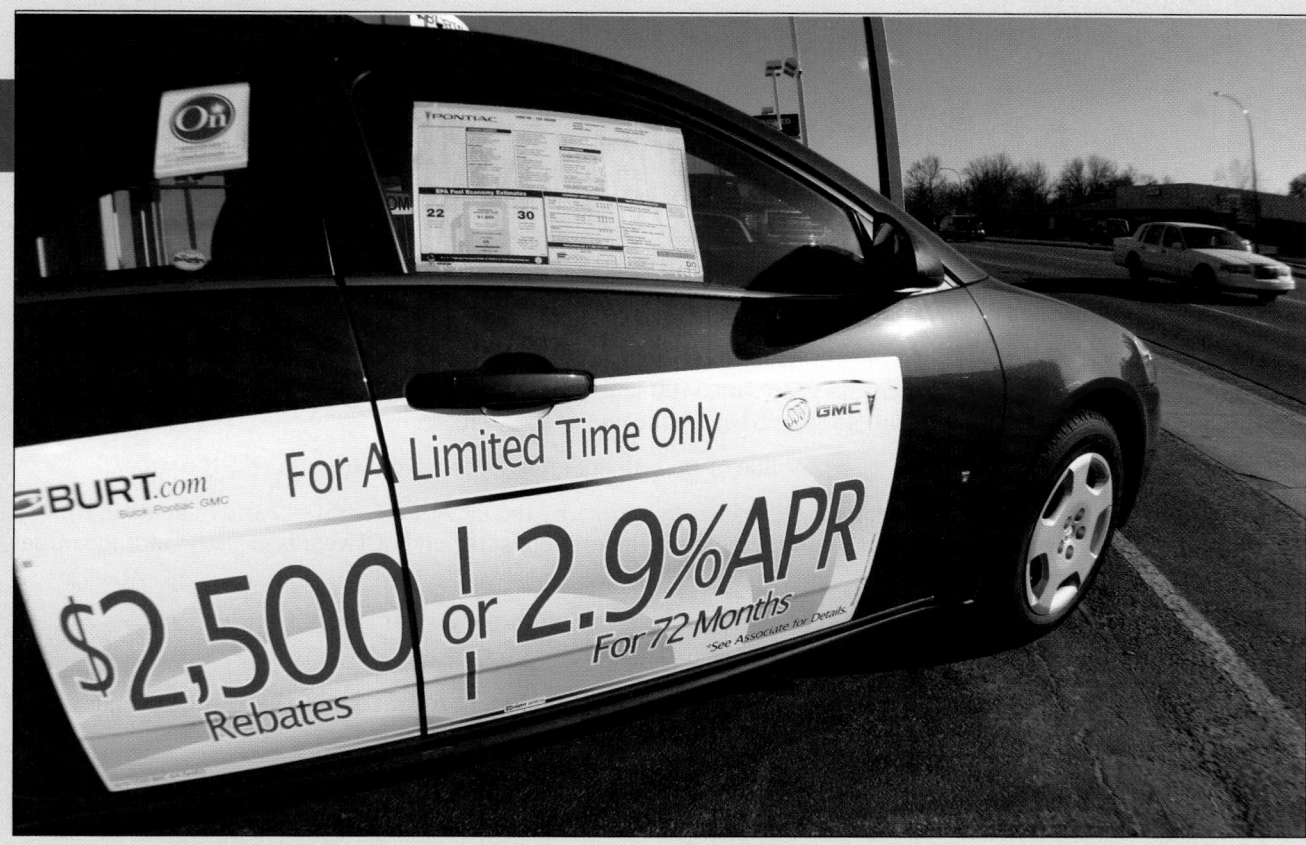

Do you truly understand what these figures mean? Would you be able to double check the dealer's calculations?

Companies invest in lots of things. Some are *tangible assets*—that is, assets you can kick, like factories, machinery, and offices. Others are *intangible assets,* such as patents or trademarks. In each case the company lays out some money now in the hope of receiving even more money later.

Individuals also make investments. For example, your college education may cost you $20,000 per year. That is an investment you hope will pay off in the form of a higher salary later in life. You are sowing now and expecting to reap later.

Companies pay for their investments by raising money and in the process assuming liabilities. For example, they may borrow money from a bank and promise to repay it with interest later. You also may have financed your investment in a college education by borrowing money that you plan to pay back out of that fat salary.

All these financial decisions require comparisons of cash payments at different dates. Will your future salary be sufficient to justify the current expenditure on college tuition? How much will you have to repay the bank if you borrow to finance your education?

In this chapter we take the first steps toward understanding the relationship between the values of dollars today and dollars in the future. We start by looking at how funds invested at a specific interest rate will grow over time. We next ask how much you would need to invest today to produce a specified future sum of money, and we describe some shortcuts for working out the value of a series of cash payments. Then we consider how inflation affects these financial calculations.

There is nothing complicated about these calculations, but if they are to become second nature, you should read the chapter thoroughly, work carefully through the examples (we have provided plenty), and make sure you tackle the self-test questions. We are asking you to make an investment now in return for a payoff later.

5.1   Future Values and Compound Interest

You have $100 invested in a bank account. Suppose banks are currently paying an interest rate of 6% per year on deposits. So after a year your account will earn interest of $6:

$$\text{Interest} = \text{interest rate} \times \text{initial investment}$$
$$= .06 \times \$100 = \$6$$

You start the year with $100 and you earn interest of $6, so the value of your investment will grow to $106 by the end of the year:

$$\text{Value of investment after 1 year} = \$100 + \$6 = \$106$$

Notice that the $100 invested grows by the factor $(1 + .06) = 1.06$. In general, for any interest rate r, the value of the investment at the end of 1 year is $(1 + r)$ times the initial investment:

$$\text{Value after 1 year} = \text{initial investment} \times (1 + r)$$
$$= \$100 \times (1.06) = \$106$$

What if you leave this money in the bank for a second year? Your balance, now $106, will continue to earn interest of 6%. So

$$\text{Interest in year 2} = .06 \times \$106 = \$6.36$$

You start the second year with $106, on which you earn interest of $6.36. So by the end of the year the value of your account will grow to $106 + $6.36 = $112.36.

In the first year your investment of $100 increases by a factor of 1.06 to $106; in the second year the $106 again increases by a factor of 1.06 to $112.36. Thus the initial $100 investment grows twice by a factor 1.06:

$$\text{Value of investment after 2 years} = \$100 \times 1.06 \times 1.06$$
$$= \$100 \times (1.06)^2 = \$112.36$$

If you keep your money invested for a third year, your investment multiplies by 1.06 each year for 3 years. By the end of the third year it will total $100 \times (1.06)^3 = \$119.10$, scarcely enough to put you in the millionaire class, but even millionaires have to start somewhere.

Clearly, if you invest your $100 for t years, it will grow to $\$100 \times (1.06)^t$. For an interest rate of r and a horizon of t years, the **future value (FV)** of your investment will be

$$\text{Future value (FV) of } \$100 = \$100 \times (1 + r)^t \qquad\qquad (5.1)$$

future value (FV)
Amount to which an investment will grow after earning interest.

Notice in our example that your interest income in the first year is $6 (6% of $100) and in the second year is $6.36 (6% of $106). Your income in the second year is higher because you now earn interest on *both* the original $100 investment *and* the $6 of interest earned in the previous year. Earning interest on interest is called *compounding* or **compound interest.** In contrast, if the bank calculated the interest only on your original investment, you would be paid **simple interest.** With simple interest the value of your investment would grow each year by .06 × $100 = $6.

compound interest
Interest earned on interest.

Table 5.1 and Figure 5.1 illustrate the mechanics of compound interest. Table 5.1 shows that in each year, you start with a greater balance in your account—your savings have been increased by the previous year's interest. As a result, your interest income also is higher.

simple interest
Interest earned only on the original investment; no interest is earned on interest.

Obviously, the higher the rate of interest, the faster your savings will grow. Figure 5.2 shows the balance in your savings account after a given number of years for several interest rates. Even a few percentage points added to the (compound) interest rate can dramatically affect the future balance. For example, after 10 years $100

TABLE 5.1 How your savings grow; the future value of $100 invested to earn 6% with compound interest

Year	Balance at Start of Year	Interest Earned during Year	Balance at End of Year
1	$100.00	.06 × $100.00 = $6.00	$106.00
2	$106.00	.06 × $106.00 = $6.36	$112.36
3	$112.36	.06 × $112.36 = $6.74	$119.10
4	$119.10	.06 × $119.10 = $7.15	$126.25
5	$126.25	.06 × $126.25 = $7.57	$133.82

FIGURE 5.1 A plot of the data in Table 5.1, showing the future values of an investment of $100 earning 6% with compound interest

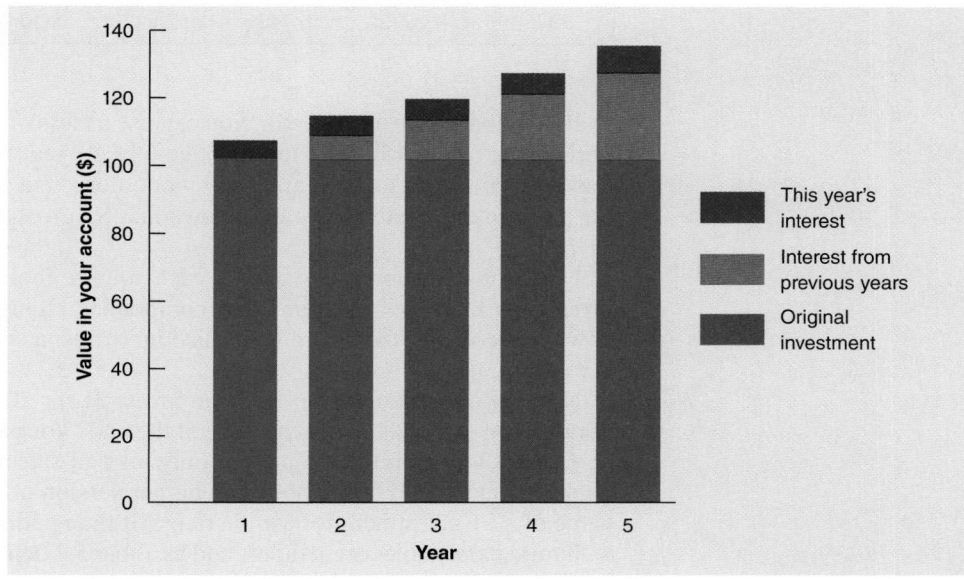

FIGURE 5.2 How an investment of $100 grows with compound interest at different interest rates

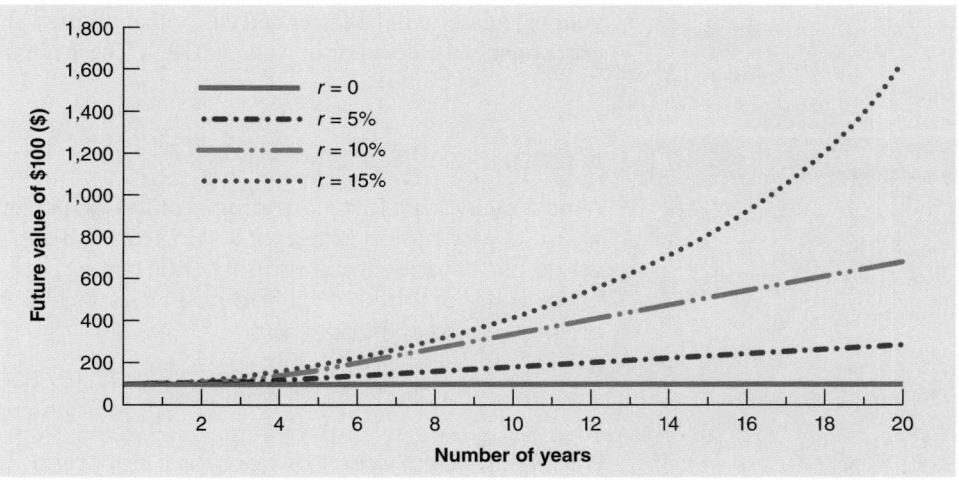

invested at 10% will grow to $100 \times (1.10)^{10} = \$259.37$. If invested at 5%, it will grow to only $100 \times (1.05)^{10} = \$162.89$.

Calculating future values is easy using almost any calculator. If you have the patience, you can multiply your initial investment by $1 + r$ (1.06 in our example) once for each year of your investment. A simpler procedure is to use the power key (the y^x key) on your calculator. For example, to compute $(1.06)^{10}$, enter 1.06, press the y^x key, enter 10, press =, and discover that the answer is 1.7908. (Try this!)

TABLE 5.2 An example of a future value table, showing how an investment of $1 grows with compound interest

Number of Years	Interest Rate per Year					
	5%	6%	7%	8%	9%	10%
1	1.0500	1.0600	1.0700	1.0800	1.0900	1.1000
2	1.1025	1.1236	1.1449	1.1664	1.1881	1.2100
3	1.1576	1.1910	1.2250	1.2597	1.2950	1.3310
4	1.2155	1.2625	1.3108	1.3605	1.4116	1.4641
5	1.2763	1.3382	1.4026	1.4693	1.5386	1.6105
10	1.6289	1.7908	1.9672	2.1589	2.3674	2.5937
20	2.6533	3.2071	3.8697	4.6610	5.6044	6.7275
30	4.3219	5.7435	7.6123	10.0627	13.2677	17.4494

If you don't have a calculator, you can use a table of future values such as Table 5.2. Let's use it to work out the future value of a 10-year investment at 6%. First find the row corresponding to 10 years. Now work along that row until you reach the column for a 6% interest rate. The entry shows that $1 invested for 10 years at 6% grows to $1.7908.

Notice that as you move across each *row* in Table 5.2, the future value of a $1 investment increases, as your funds compound at a higher interest rate. As you move down any *column*, the future value also increases, as your funds compound for a longer period.

Now try one more example. If you invest $1 for 20 years at 10% and do not withdraw any money, what will you have at the end? Your answer should be $6.7275.

Table 5.2 gives future values for only a small selection of years and interest rates. Table A.1 at the end of the book is a bigger version of Table 5.2. It presents the future value of a $1 investment for a wide range of time periods and interest rates.

Future value tables are tedious, and as Table 5.2 demonstrates, they show future values only for a limited set of interest rates and time periods. For example, suppose that you want to calculate future values using an interest rate of 7.835%. The power key on your calculator will be faster and easier than future value tables. A third alternative is to use a financial calculator or a spreadsheet. These are introduced in the next section.

EXAMPLE 5.1 ▶ Manhattan Island

Almost everyone's favorite example of the power of compound interest is the purchase of Manhattan Island for $24 in 1626 by Peter Minuit. Based on New York real estate prices today, it seems that Minuit got a great deal. But did he? Consider the future value of that $24 if it had been invested for 385 years (2011 minus 1626) at an interest rate of 8% per year:

$$\$24 \times (1.08)^{385} = \$177{,}157{,}000{,}000{,}000$$
$$= \$177.16 \text{ trillion}$$

Perhaps the deal wasn't as good as it appeared. The total value of land on Manhattan today is only a fraction of $177.16 trillion.

Though entertaining, this analysis is actually somewhat misleading. The 8% interest rate we've used to compute future values is high by historical standards. At a 3.5% interest rate, more consistent with historical experience, the future value of the $24 would be *dramatically* lower, only $24 × (1.035)^{385} = $13,560,000! On the other hand, we have understated the returns to Mr. Minuit and his successors: We have ignored all the rental income that the island's land has generated over the last three or four centuries.

All things considered, if we had been around in 1626, we would have gladly paid $24 for the island.

The power of compounding is not restricted to money. Foresters try to forecast the compound growth rate of trees, demographers the compound growth rate of population. A social commentator once observed that the number of lawyers in the United States is increasing at a higher compound rate than the population as a whole (3.6% versus .9% in the 1980s) and calculated that in about two centuries there will be more lawyers than people. In all these cases, the principle is the same: **Compound growth means that value increases each period by the factor (1 + growth rate). The value after *t* periods will equal the initial value times (1 + growth rate)^t. When money is invested at compound interest, the growth rate is the interest rate.**

Self-Test 5.1

Suppose that Peter Minuit did not become the first New York real estate tycoon but instead had invested his $24 at a 5% interest rate in New Amsterdam Savings Bank. What would have been the balance in his account after 5 years? 50 years?

Self-Test 5.2

In 1973 Gordon Moore, one of Intel's founders, predicted that the number of transistors that could be placed on a single silicon chip would double every 18 months, equivalent to an annual growth of 59% (i.e., $1.59^{1.5} = 2.0$). The first microprocessor was built in 1971 and had 2,250 transistors. By 2010 Intel chips contained 2.3 billion transistors, over 1 million times the number of transistors 39 years earlier. What has been the annual compound rate of growth in processing power? How does it compare with the prediction of Moore's law?

5.2 Present Values

Money can be invested to earn interest. If you are offered the choice between $100,000 now and $100,000 at the end of the year, you naturally take the money now to get a year's interest. Financial managers make the same point when they say that money in hand today has a *time value* or when they quote perhaps the most basic financial principle: **A dollar today is worth more than a dollar tomorrow.**

We have seen that $100 invested for 1 year at 6% will grow to a future value of $100 \times 1.06 = \$106$. Let's turn this around: How much do we need to invest *now* in order to produce $106 at the end of the year? In other words, what is the **present value (PV)** of the $106 payoff?

present value (PV)
Value today of a future cash flow.

To calculate future value, we multiply today's investment by 1 plus the interest rate, .06, or 1.06. To calculate present value, we simply reverse the process and divide the future value by 1.06:

$$\text{Present value} = \text{PV} = \frac{\text{future value}}{1.06} = \frac{\$106}{1.06} = \$100$$

What is the present value of, say, $112.36 to be received 2 years from now? Again we ask, How much would we need to invest now to produce $112.36 after 2 years? The answer is obviously $100; we've already calculated that at 6% $100 grows to $112.36:

$$\$100 \times (1.06)^2 = \$112.36$$

However, if we don't know, or forgot the answer, we just divide future value by $(1.06)^2$:

$$\text{Present value} = \text{PV} = \frac{\$112.36}{(1.06)^2} = \$100$$

In general, for a future value or payment t periods away, present value is

$$\text{Present value} = \frac{\text{future value after } t \text{ periods}}{(1 + r)^t} \qquad (5.2)$$

discounted cash flow (DCF)
Another term for the present value of a future cash flow.

To calculate present value, we *discounted* the future value at the interest rate r. The calculation is therefore termed a **discounted cash-flow (DCF)** calculation, and the interest rate r is known as the **discount rate.**

In this chapter we will be working through a number of more or less complicated DCF calculations. All of them involve a present value, a discount rate, and one or more future cash flows. If ever a DCF problem leaves you confused and flustered, just pause and write down which of these measures you know and which one you need to calculate.

discount rate
Interest rate used to compute present values of future cash flows.

EXAMPLE 5.2 ▶   Saving for a Future Purchase

Suppose you need $3,000 next year to buy a new computer. The interest rate is 8% per year. How much money should you set aside now in order to pay for the purchase? Just calculate the present value at an 8% interest rate of a $3,000 payment at the end of 1 year. To the nearest dollar, this value is

$$PV = \frac{\$3,000}{1.08} = \$2,778$$

Notice that $2,778 invested for 1 year at 8% will prove just enough to buy your computer:

$$\text{Future value} = \$2,778 \times 1.08 = \$3,000$$

The longer the time before you must make a payment, the less you need to invest today. For example, suppose that you can postpone buying that computer until the end of 2 years. In this case we calculate the present value of the future payment by dividing $3,000 by $(1.08)^2$:

$$PV = \frac{\$3,000}{(1.08)^2} = \$2,572$$

Thus you need to invest $2,778 today to provide $3,000 in 1 year but only $2,572 to provide the same $3,000 in 2 years.

You now know how to calculate future and present values: **To work out how much you will have in the future if you invest for t years at an interest rate r, multiply the initial investment by $(1 + r)^t$. To find the present value of a future payment, run the process in reverse and divide by $(1 + r)^t$.**

Present values are always calculated using compound interest. The ascending lines in Figure 5.2 showed the future value of $1 invested with compound interest. In contrast, present values decline, other things equal, when future cash payments are delayed. The longer you have to wait for money, the less it's worth today.

The descending line in Figure 5.3 shows the present value today of $100 to be received at some future date. Notice how even small variations in the interest rate can have a powerful effect on the value of distant cash flows. At an interest rate of 5%, a payment of $100 in year 20 is worth $37.69 today. If the interest rate increases to 10%, the value of the future payment falls by about 60% to $14.86.

The present value formula is sometimes written differently. Instead of dividing the future payment by $(1 + r)^t$, we could equally well multiply it by $1/(1 + r)^t$:

$$PV = \frac{\text{future payment}}{(1 + r)^t} = \text{future payment} \times \frac{1}{(1 + r)^t}$$

FIGURE 5.3 Present value of a future cash flow of $100. Notice that the longer you have to wait for your money, the less it is worth today.

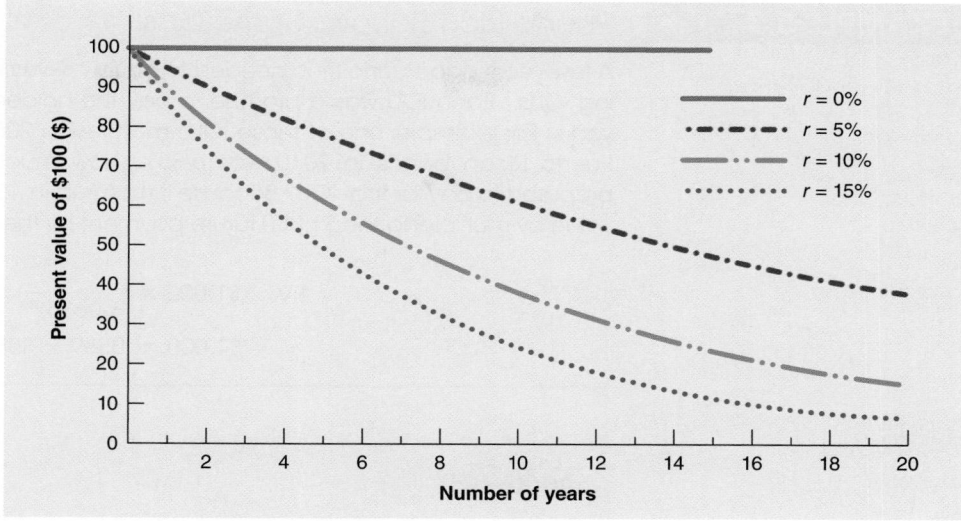

discount factor
Present value of a $1 future payment.

The expression $1/(1 + r)^t$ is called the **discount factor.** It measures the present value of $1 received in year t.

The simplest way to find the discount factor is to use a calculator, but financial managers sometimes find it convenient to use tables of discount factors. For example, Table 5.3 shows discount factors for a small range of years and interest rates. Table A.2 at the end of the book provides a set of discount factors for a wide range of years and interest rates.

Try using Table 5.3 to check our calculations of how much to put aside for that $3,000 computer purchase. If the interest rate is 8%, the present value of $1 paid at the end of 1 year is $.9259. So the present value of $3,000 is (to the nearest dollar)

$$PV = \$3,000 \times \frac{1}{1.08} = \$3,000 \times .9259 = \$2,778$$

which matches the value we obtained in Example 5.2.

What if the computer purchase is postponed until the end of 2 years? Table 5.3 shows that the present value of $1 paid at the end of 2 years is .8573. So the present value of $3,000 is

$$PV = \$3,000 \times \frac{1}{(1.08)^2} = \$3,000 \times .8573 = \$2,572$$

as we found in Example 5.2.

Notice that as you move along the rows in Table 5.3, moving to higher interest rates, present values decline. As you move down the columns, moving to longer discounting periods, present values again decline. (Why does this make sense?)

TABLE 5.3 An example of a present value table, showing the value today of $1 received in the future

Number of Years	Interest Rate per Year					
	5%	6%	7%	8%	9%	10%
1	0.9524	0.9434	0.9346	0.9259	0.9174	0.9091
2	0.9070	0.8900	0.8734	0.8573	0.8417	0.8264
3	0.8638	0.8396	0.8163	0.7938	0.7722	0.7513
4	0.8227	0.7921	0.7629	0.7350	0.7084	0.6830
5	0.7835	0.7473	0.7130	0.6806	0.6499	0.6209
10	0.6139	0.5584	0.5083	0.4632	0.4224	0.3855
20	0.3769	0.3118	0.2584	0.2145	0.1784	0.1486
30	0.2314	0.1741	0.1314	0.0994	0.0754	0.0573

EXAMPLE 5.3 ▶ Puerto Rico Borrows Some Cash

A few years ago, Puerto Rico needed to borrow several billion dollars. It did so by selling IOUs.[1] Each IOU was a promise to pay the holder $1,000 after some number of years. For example, one of those IOUs matured in 2056. The market interest rate on Puerto Rican bonds in 2010 was 6.35%. How much would investors have been prepared to pay for that IOU? Because it matured in 46 years, we calculate its present value by multiplying the $1,000 future payment by the 46-year discount factor:

$$PV = \$1,000 \times \frac{1}{(1.0635)^{46}}$$
$$= \$1,000 \times .0589 = \$58.90$$

Self-Test 5.3

Suppose that Puerto Rico had promised to pay $1,000 at the end of 30 years. If the market interest rate were 6.35%, how much would you have been prepared to pay for a 30-year IOU of $1,000?

EXAMPLE 5.4 ▶ Finding the Value of Free Credit

Kangaroo Autos is offering free credit on a $20,000 car. You pay $8,000 down and then the balance at the end of 2 years. Turtle Motors next door does not offer free credit but will give you $1,000 off the list price. If the interest rate is 10%, which company is offering the better deal?

Notice that you pay more in total by buying through Kangaroo, but since part of the payment is postponed, you can keep this money in the bank where it will continue to earn interest. To compare the two offers, you need to calculate the present value of your payments to Kangaroo. The *time line* in Figure 5.4 shows the cash payments. The first payment, $8,000, takes place today. The second payment, $12,000, takes place at the end of 2 years. To find its present value, we need to multiply by the 2-year discount factor. The total present value of the payments to Kangaroo is therefore

FIGURE 5.4 Drawing a time line can help us to calculate the present value of the payments to Kangaroo Autos.

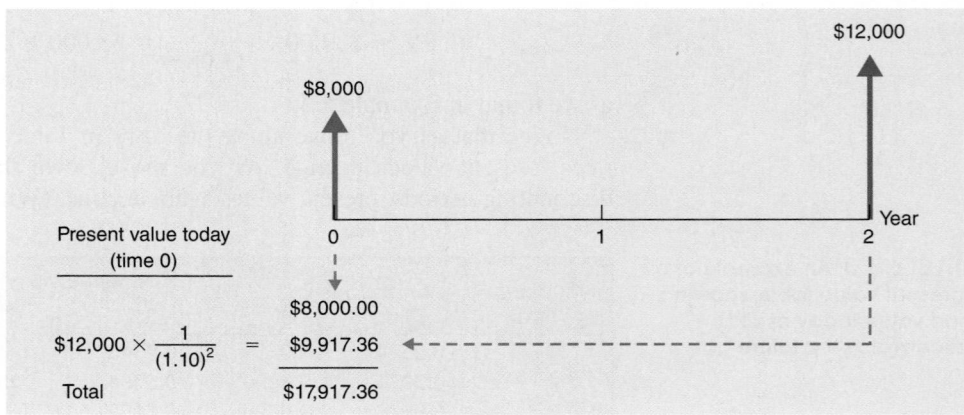

---

[1] "IOU" means "I owe you." Puerto Rico's IOUs are called *bonds*. Usually, bond investors receive a regular *interest* or *coupon* payment. This Puerto Rico bond will make only a single payment when it matures. It was therefore known as a *zero-coupon bond*. More on this in the next chapter.

An Introduction to Financial Calculators

The basic financial calculator uses five keys that correspond to the inputs for common problems involving the time value of money:

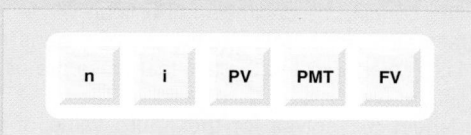

Each key represents the following input:

- *n* is the number of periods. (We have been using *t* to denote the length of time or the number of periods.)
- *i* is the interest rate, expressed as a percentage (not a decimal). For example, if the interest rate is 8%, you would enter 8, not .08. On some calculators, this key appears as *I/YR, I/Y,* or just *I.* (We have been using *r* to denote the interest rate.)
- *PV* is the present value
- *FV* is the future value
- *PMT* is the amount of any *recurring* payment (called an annuity). In single cash-flow problems such as those in Examples 5.1 and 5.2, *PMT* is zero.

Given any four of these inputs, the calculator will solve for the fifth. We can illustrate using Examples 5.1 and 5.2.

In Example 5.1, we calculated the future value of Peter Minuit's $24 investment if invested at 8% for 385 years. Our inputs would be as follows:

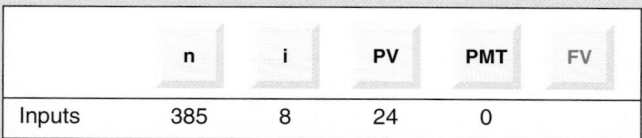

	n	i	PV	PMT	FV
Inputs	385	8	24	0	

For example, to enter the number of periods, type *385* and then press the *n* key. Notice that you enter a value of 0 for *PMT,* as there is no recurring cash flow, only a one-time initial payment of $24. Finally, there is no input for *FV;* We wish to solve for the future value given the other four inputs.

Now ask the calculator to compute *FV.* On some calculators, you just push *FV.* On others, you need to first press the

"compute" key, which may be labeled *CPT* or *COMP,* and then press *FV.* Your calculator should show a value of −$177.16 trillion, which, except for the minus sign, is the future value of $24.

Why does the minus sign appear? Most calculators treat cash flows as either inflows (shown as positive numbers) or outflows (negative numbers). For example, if you borrow $100 today at an interest rate of 12%, you receive money now (a *positive* cash flow), but you will have to pay back $112 in a year, a *negative* cash flow at that time. Therefore, the calculator displays *FV* as a negative number. The following time line of cash flows shows the reasoning employed. The final negative cash flow of $112 has the same present value as the $100 borrowed today.

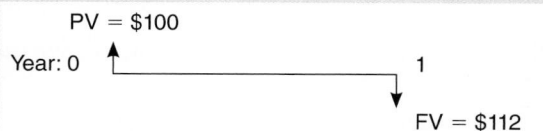

If, instead of borrowing, you were to *invest* $100 today to reap a future benefit, you would enter *PV* as a negative number (first press *100,* then press the +/− key to make the value negative, and finally press *PV* to enter the value into the *PV* register). In this case, *FV* would appear as a positive number, indicating that you will reap a cash inflow when your investment comes to fruition.

In Example 5.2, we consider a simple savings problem. We have a future goal in mind at a 2-year horizon, and we need to solve for the amount that you need to set aside today to meet that target. So our inputs look like this:

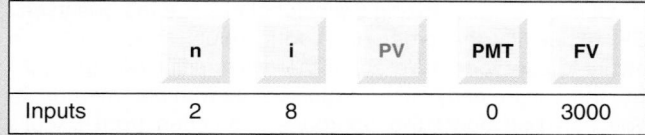

	n	i	PV	PMT	FV
Inputs	2	8		0	3000

Now compute *PV;* you should get an answer of −2572.02. Again, the answer is displayed as a negative number because you need to make a cash outflow today (an investment) of $2,572.02 in order to reap a cash flow of $3,000 in 2 years.

$$PV = \$8,000 + \$12,000 \times \frac{1}{(1.10)^2}$$
$$= \$8,000 + \$9,917.36 = \$17,917.36$$

Suppose you start with $17,917.36. You make a down payment of $8,000 to Kangaroo Autos and invest the balance of $9,917.36. At an interest rate of 10%, this will grow over 2 years to $9,917.36 × 1.10^2 = $12,000, just enough to make the final payment on your automobile. The total cost of $17,917.36 is a better deal than the $19,000 charged by Turtle Motors.

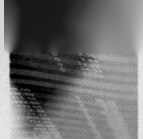

Excel's Interest Rate Functions

Just as financial calculators largely replaced interest rate tables in the 1980s, these calculators are today giving way to spreadsheets. Like financial calculators, spreadsheets provide built-in functions that solve the equations linking the five variables in a time-value-of-money problem: the number of periods, the interest rate per period, the present value, the future value, and any recurring payment (the annuity). For single cash-flow problems such as Examples 5.1 and 5.2, the recurring payment is zero. We will illustrate the use of these spreadsheets using Microsoft Excel.

The two Excel functions relevant for the single cash-flow problems in Examples 5.1 and 5.2 are:

Future value = FV(rate, nper, pmt, PV)
Present value = PV(rate, nper, pmt, FV)

As you can see, each spreadsheet formula requires four inputs—just as financial calculators require four inputs—and provides the solution for the fifth variable. Also, as with most calculators, the spreadsheet functions interpret cash inflows as positive values and cash outflows as negative values. Unlike financial calculators, however, most spreadsheets require that interest rates be input as decimals rather than whole numbers (e.g., .06 rather than 6%). Note also the use of = signs in front of the formulas to alert Excel to the fact that these are predefined formulas.

Spreadsheet 5.1 solves for the future value of the $24 spent to acquire Manhattan Island (Example 5.1). The interest rate is entered as a decimal in cell B3. The present value is entered as −24, representing the purchase price, and therefore the future value is a positive cash flow.

You can find this spreadsheet at www.mhhe.com/bmm7e.

SPREADSHEET 5.1 Finding the future value of $24 using a spreadsheet.

	A	B	C	D	F
1	Finding the future value of $24 using a spreadsheet				
2	INPUTS				
3	Interest rate	0.08			
4	Periods	385			
5	Payment	0			
6	Present value (PV)	-24			
7			Formula in cell B8		
8	Future value	$177,156,505,159,083	=FV(B3,B4,B5,B6)		
9					
10	Notice that we enter the present value in cell B6 as a negative number,				
11	since the "purchase price" is a cash outflow. The interest rate in cell B3				
12	is entered as a decimal, not a percentage.				
13					
14					

Of course, memorizing Excel functions like the one in cell B8, especially the order of its four inputs, may not come easily to everyone. (We admit that we're still working on it.) But there is an easy cure for those of us with bad memories. You can pull down the appropriate function from Excel's built-in functions, and you will be prompted for the necessary inputs. Spreadsheet 5.2 illustrates. Go to the Formula tab, click Financial formulas, and then select FV. The "Function Arguments" screen shown in Spreadsheet 5.2 should now appear.

SPREADSHEET 5.2
Using the financial function pull-down menu

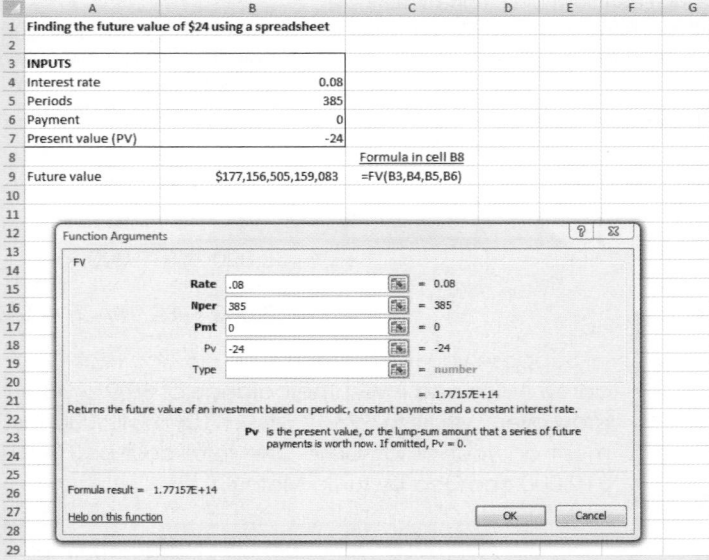

Now let's solve Example 5.2 in a spreadsheet. We can type the Excel function = PV(rate, nper, pmt, FV) = PV(.08, 2, 0, 3000), or we can select the PV function from the pull-down menu of financial functions and fill in our inputs as shown in the dialog box below.

Either way, you should get an answer of −$2,572. (Notice that you don't type the comma in 3,000 when entering the number in the spreadsheet. If you did, Excel would interpret the entry as two different numbers, 3 followed by zero.)

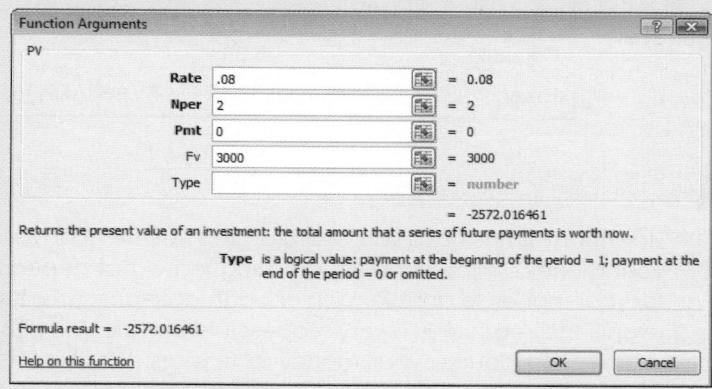

These calculations illustrate how important it is to use present values when comparing alternative patterns of cash payment. **You should *never* compare cash flows occurring at different times without first discounting them to a common date. By calculating present values, we see how much cash must be set aside today to pay future bills.**

Calculating present and future values can entail a considerable amount of tedious arithmetic. Fortunately, financial calculators and spreadsheets are designed with present value and future value formulas already programmed. They can make your work much easier. The two nearby boxes provide a short introduction to each of these tools.

Finding the Interest Rate

When we looked at Puerto Rico's IOUs in Example 5.3, we used the interest rate to compute a fair market price for each IOU. Sometimes, however, you are given the price and have to calculate the interest rate that is being offered.

For example, when Puerto Rico borrowed money, it did not announce an interest rate. It simply offered to sell each IOU for $58.90. Thus we know that

$$PV = \$1,000 \times \frac{1}{(1 + r)^{46}} = \$58.90$$

What is the interest rate?

There are several ways to approach this. You might use a table of discount factors. You need to find the interest rate for which the 46-year discount factor = .0589.

A better approach is to rearrange the equation and use your calculator:

$$\$58.90 \times (1 + r)^{46} = \$1,000$$

$$(1 + r)^{46} = \frac{\$1,000}{\$58.90} = 16.978$$

$$(1 + r) = (16.978)^{1/46} = 1.0635$$

$$r = .0635, \text{ or } 6.35\%$$

You can also use a financial calculator or a spreadsheet to find the interest rate. The inputs would be:

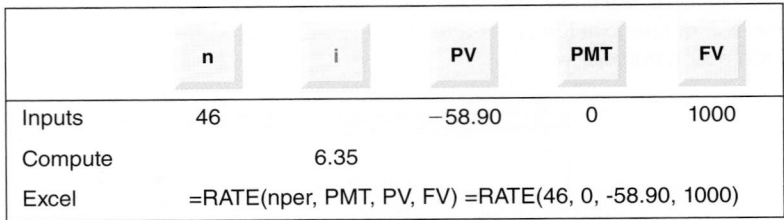

	n	i	PV	PMT	FV
Inputs	46		−58.90	0	1000
Compute		6.35			
Excel	=RATE(nper, PMT, PV, FV) =RATE(46, 0, -58.90, 1000)				

EXAMPLE 5.5   ▶   Double Your Money

How many times have you heard of an investment adviser who promises to double your money? Is this really an amazing feat? That depends on how long it will take for your money to double. With enough patience, your funds eventually will double even if they earn only a very modest interest rate. Suppose your investment adviser promises to double your money in 8 years. What interest rate is implicitly being promised?

The adviser is promising a future value of $2 for every $1 invested today. Therefore, we find the interest rate by solving for r as follows:

$$\text{Future value (FV)} = \text{PV} \times (1 + r)^t$$
$$\$2 = \$1 \times (1 + r)^8$$
$$1 + r = 2^{1/8} = 1.0905$$
$$r = .0905, \text{ or } 9.05\%$$

Self-Test 5.4

Use both a financial calculator and a spreadsheet to show that the interest rate in Example 5.5 is 9.05%.

5.3 Multiple Cash Flows

So far, we have considered problems involving only a single cash flow. This is obviously limiting. Most real-world investments, after all, will involve many cash flows over time. When there are many payments, you'll hear managers refer to a *stream of cash flows.*

Future Value of Multiple Cash Flows

Recall the computer you hope to purchase in 2 years (see Example 5.2). Now suppose that instead of putting aside one sum in the bank to finance the purchase, you plan to save some amount of money each year. You might be able to put $1,200 in the bank now, and another $1,400 in 1 year. If you earn an 8% rate of interest, how much will you be able to spend on a computer in 2 years?

The time line in Figure 5.5 shows how your savings grow. There are two cash inflows into the savings plan. The first cash flow will have 2 years to earn interest and therefore will grow to $1,200 \times (1.08)^2 = \$1,399.68$, while the second deposit, which comes a year later, will be invested for only 1 year and will grow to $1,400 \times (1.08) = \$1,512$. After 2 years, then, your total savings will be the sum of these two amounts, or $2,911.68.

FIGURE 5.5 Drawing a time line can help to calculate the future value of your savings.

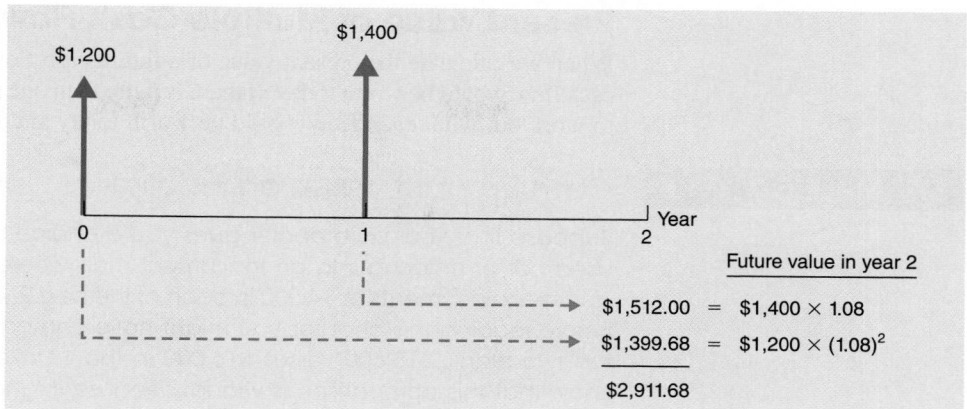

EXAMPLE 5.6 ▶ Even More Savings

Suppose that the computer purchase can be put off for an additional year and that you can make a third deposit of $1,000 at the end of the second year. How much will be available to spend 3 years from now?

Again we organize our inputs using a time line as in Figure 5.6. The total cash available will be the sum of the future values of all three deposits. Notice that when we save for 3 years, the first two deposits each have an extra year for interest to compound:

$$\$1,200 \times (1.08)^3 = \$1,511.65$$
$$\$1,400 \times (1.08)^2 = 1,632.96$$
$$\$1,000 \times (1.08) = \underline{1,080.00}$$
$$\text{Total future value} = \$4,224.61$$

Our examples show that problems involving multiple cash flows are simple extensions of single cash-flow analysis. **To find the value at some future date of a stream of cash flows, calculate what each cash flow will be worth at that future date and then add up these future values.**

As we will now see, a similar adding-up principle works for present value calculations.

FIGURE 5.6 To find the future value of a stream of cash flows, you just calculate the future value of each flow and then add them.

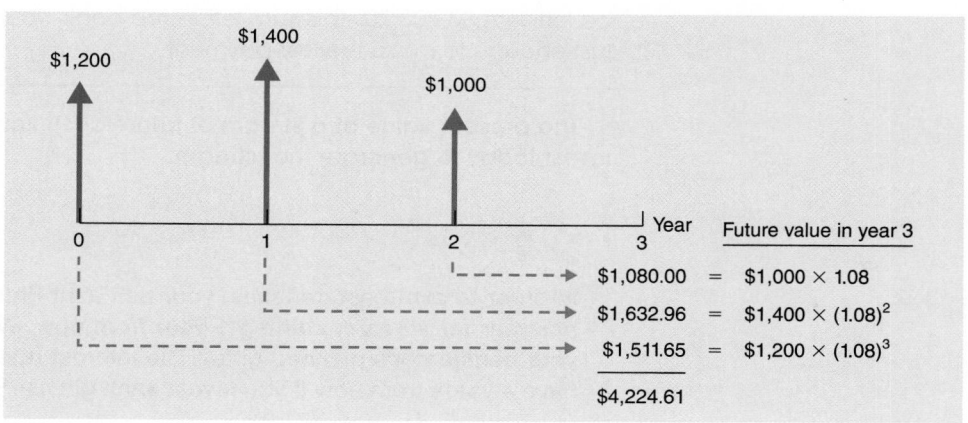

Present Value of Multiple Cash Flows

When we calculate the present value of a future cash flow, we are asking how much that cash flow would be worth today. If there is more than one future cash flow, we simply need to work out what each flow would be worth today and then add these present values.

EXAMPLE 5.7 ▶ Cash Up Front versus an Installment Plan

Suppose that your auto dealer gives you a choice between paying $15,500 for a used car or entering into an installment plan where you pay $8,000 down today and make payments of $4,000 in each of the next 2 years. Which is the better deal? Before reading this chapter, you might have compared the total payments under the two plans: $15,500 versus $16,000 in the installment plan. Now, however, you know that this comparison is wrong, because it ignores the time value of money. For example, the last installment of $4,000 is less costly to you than paying out $4,000 now. The true cost of that last payment is the present value of $4,000.

Assume that the interest rate you can earn on safe investments is 8%. Suppose you choose the installment plan. As the time line in Figure 5.7 illustrates, the present value of the plan's three cash flows is:

Present Value			
Immediate payment	$8,000	=	$ 8,000.00
Second payment	$4,000/1.08	=	3,703.70
Third payment	$4,000/(1.08)² =		3,429.36
Total present value		=	$15,133.06

Because the present value of the three payments is less than $15,500, the installment plan is in fact the cheaper alternative.

The installment plan's present value is the amount that you would need to invest now to cover the three payments. Let's check.

Here is how your bank balance would change as you make each payment:

Year	Initial Balance	− Payment	=	Remaining Balance	+	Interest Earned	=	Balance at Year-End
0	$ 15,133.06	$ 8,000		$ 7,133.06		$ 570.64		$ 7,703.70
1	7,703.70	4,000		3,703.70		296.30		4,000.00
2	4,000.00	4,000		0		0		0

If you start with the present value of $15,133.06 in the bank, you could make the first $8,000 payment and be left with $7,133.06. After 1 year, your savings account would receive an interest payment of $7,133.06 × .08 = $570.64, bringing your account to $7,703.70. Similarly, you would make the second $4,000 payment and be left with $3,703.70. This sum left in the bank would grow with interest to $4,000, just enough to make the last payment.

The present value of a stream of future cash flows is the amount you need to invest today to generate that stream.

Self-Test 5.5

In order to avoid estate taxes, your rich aunt Frederica will pay you $10,000 per year for 4 years, starting 1 year from now. What is the present value of your benefactor's planned gifts? The interest rate is 7%. How much will you have 4 years from now if you invest each gift at 7%?

FIGURE 5.7 To find the present value of a stream of cash flows, you just calculate the present value of each flow and then add them.

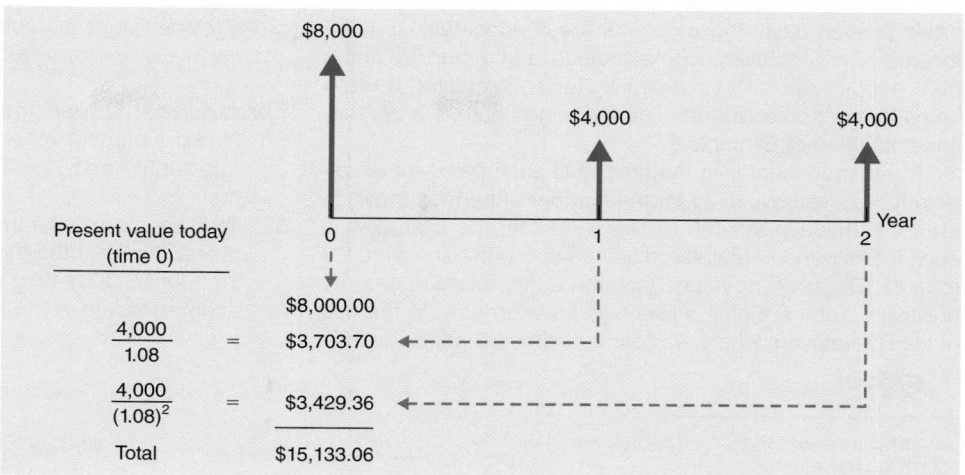

5.4 Level Cash Flows: Perpetuities and Annuities

Frequently, you may need to value a stream of equal cash flows. For example, a home mortgage might require the homeowner to make equal monthly payments for the life of the loan. For a 30-year loan, this would result in 360 equal payments. A 4-year car loan might require 48 equal monthly payments. Any such sequence of equally spaced, level cash flows is called an **annuity.** If the payment stream lasts forever, it is called a **perpetuity.**

annuity
Equally spaced level stream of cash flows, with a finite maturity.

perpetuity
Stream of level cash payments that never ends.

How to Value Perpetuities

Some time ago the British government borrowed by issuing loans known as consols. Consols are perpetuities. In other words, instead of repaying these loans, the British government pays the investors a fixed annual payment in perpetuity (forever).

How might we value such a security? Suppose that you could invest $100 at an interest rate of 10%. You would earn annual interest of $.10 \times \$100 = \$10$ per year and could withdraw this amount from your investment account each year without ever running down your balance. In other words, a $100 investment could provide a perpetuity of $10 per year. In general,

$$\text{Cash payment from perpetuity} = \text{interest rate} \times \text{present value}$$
$$C = r \times \text{PV}$$

We can rearrange this relationship to derive the present value of a perpetuity, given the interest rate r and the cash payment C:

$$\text{PV of perpetuity} = \frac{C}{r} = \frac{\text{cash payment}}{\text{interest rate}} \qquad (5.3)$$

Suppose some worthy person wishes to endow a chair in finance at your university. If the rate of interest is 10% and the aim is to provide $100,000 a year forever, the amount that must be set aside today is

$$\text{Present value of perpetuity} = \frac{C}{r} = \frac{\$100,000}{.10} = \$1,000,000$$

Two warnings about the perpetuity formula. First, at a quick glance you can easily confuse the formula with the present value of a single cash payment. A payment of $1 at the end of 1 year has a present value $1/(1 + r)$. The perpetuity has a value of $1/r$. These are quite different.

Multiple Cash Flows

While uneven cash-flow problems are conceptually straight-forward, they rapidly become tedious and prone to errors from "typos," even if you use a financial calculator. It really helps to use spreadsheets. The following figure is a spreadsheet solution of Example 5.7.

The spreadsheet lists the time until each payment in column A. This value is used for the number of periods (nper) in the PV formula in column C. The values for the cash flow in each future period are entered as negative numbers in the PV formula. The present values (column C) therefore appear as positive numbers. Column E shows an alternative to the use of the PV function, where we calculate present values directly.

You can find this spreadsheet at
www.mhhe.com/bmm7e.

An interactive version of this spreadsheet can be found at www.mhhe.com/bmm7e.

Spreadsheet Questions

5.1 Find the present value of the three payments at interest rates of 5% and 11%. Explain why the values change as they do.

5.2 Total payments over the 3 years are $16,000. What is the present value if the three payments are instead $6,000, $5,000, $5,000? Why does the present value fall? (Use an interest rate of 8%.)

	A	B	C	D	E
1	Finding the present value of multiple cash flows using a spreadsheet				
2					
3	Time until CF	Cash flow	Present value	Formula in Col C	Alternative formula for Col C
4	0	8000	$8,000.00	=PV($B$10, A4,0, -B4)	=B4/(1 + $B$10)^A4
5	1	4000	$3,703.70	=PV($B$10, A5,0, -B5)	=B5/(1 + $B$10)^A5
6	2	4000	$3,429.36	=PV($B$10, A6,0, -B6)	=B6/(1 + $B$10)^A6
7					
8	SUM		$15,133.06	=SUM(C4:C6)	=SUM(C4:C6)
9					
10	Discount rate:	0.08			
11					
12	Notice that the time until each payment is found in column A.				
13	Once we enter the formula for present value in cell C4, we can copy it to cells C5 and C6.				
14	The present value for other interest rates can be found by changing the entry in cell B10.				

Second, the perpetuity formula tells us the value of a regular stream of payments starting one period from now. Thus our endowment of $1 million would provide the university with its first payment of $100,000 one year hence. If the worthy donor wants to provide the university with an additional payment of $100,000 up front, he or she would need to put aside $1,100,000.

Sometimes you may need to calculate the value of a perpetuity that does not start to make payments for several years. For example, suppose that our philanthropist decides to provide $100,000 a year with the first payment 4 years from now. We know that in year 3, this endowment will be an ordinary perpetuity with payments starting at the end of 1 year. So our perpetuity formula tells us that in year 3 the endowment will be worth $100,000/r$. But it is not worth that much now. To find today's value we need to multiply by the 3-year discount factor. Thus, the "delayed" perpetuity is worth

$$\$100,000 \times \frac{1}{r} \times \frac{1}{(1 + r)^3} = \$1,000,000 \times \frac{1}{(1.10)^3} = \$751,315$$

Self-Test 5.6

A British government perpetuity pays £4 a year forever and is selling for £48. What is the interest rate?

How to Value Annuities

Let us return to Kangaroo Autos for (almost) the last time. Most installment plans call for level streams of payments. So let us suppose that Kangaroo now offers an "easy payment" scheme of $8,000 a year at the end of each of the next 3 years.

A level stream of cash flows that continues for a specified number of years is known as an *annuity*. The payments on the Kangaroo plan constitute a 3-year annuity. Figure 5.8 shows a time line of these cash flows and calculates the present value of each year's flow assuming an interest rate of 10%. You can see that the total present value of the payments is $19,894.82.

You can always value an annuity by calculating the present value of each cash flow and finding the total. However, it is usually quicker to use a simple formula which states that if the interest rate is r, then the present value of an annuity that pays C dollars a year for each of t periods is

$$\text{Present value of } t\text{-year annuity} = C\left[\frac{1}{r} - \frac{1}{r(1 + r)^t}\right] \qquad (5.4)$$

annuity factor
Present value of a $1 annuity.

The expression in brackets shows the present value of a t-year annuity of $1 starting in period 1. It is generally known as the t-year **annuity factor.** Therefore, another way to write the value of an annuity is

$$\text{Present value of } t\text{-year annuity} = \text{payment} \times \text{annuity factor}$$

You can use this formula to calculate the present value of the payments to Kangaroo. The annual payment (C) is $8,000, the interest rate (r) is 10%, and the number of years (t) is 3. Therefore,

$$\text{Present value} = C\left[\frac{1}{r} - \frac{1}{r(1 + r)^t}\right] = 8{,}000\left[\frac{1}{.10} - \frac{1}{.10(1.10)^3}\right] = \$19{,}894.82$$

This is exactly the same answer that we got by separately valuing each cash flow. If the number of periods is small, there is little to choose between the two methods, but when you are valuing long-term annuities, it is far easier to use the formula.

If you are wondering where the annuity formula comes from, look at Figure 5.9. It shows the payments and values of three investments.

Row 1   The investment in the first row provides a perpetual stream of $1 starting at the end of the first year. We have already seen that this perpetuity has a present value of $1/r$.

FIGURE 5.8 To find the value of an annuity, you can calculate the value of each cash flow. It is usually quicker to use the annuity formula.

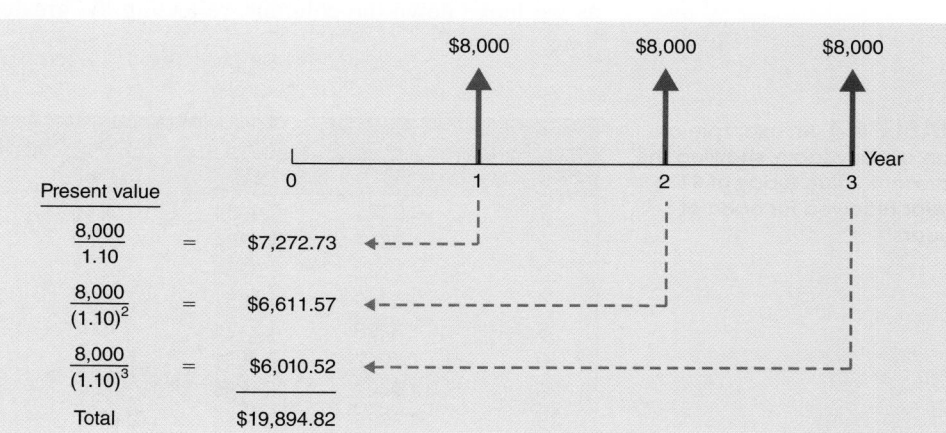

FIGURE 5.9 The value of an annuity is equal to the difference between the value of two perpetuities.

	Cash Flow						Present Value
Year:	**1**	**2**	**3**	**4**	**5**	**6 . . .**	
1. Perpetuity A	$1	$1	$1	$1	$1	$1 . . .	$\dfrac{1}{r}$
2. Perpetuity B				$1	$1	$1 . . .	$\dfrac{1}{r(1+r)^3}$
3. Three-year annuity	$1	$1	$1				$\dfrac{1}{r} - \dfrac{1}{r(1+r)^3}$

Row 2   Now look at the investment shown in the second row of Figure 5.9. It also provides a perpetual stream of $1 payments, but these payments don't start until year 4. This stream of payments is identical to the payments in row 1, except that they are delayed for an additional three years. In year 3, the investment will be an ordinary perpetuity with payments starting in 1 year and will therefore be worth $1/r$ in year 3. To find the value *today*, we simply multiply this figure by the 3-year discount factor. Thus

$$PV = \frac{1}{r} \times \frac{1}{(1+r)^3} = \frac{1}{r(1+r)^3}$$

Row 3   Finally, look at the investment shown in the third row of Figure 5.9. This provides a level payment of $1 a year for each of 3 years. In other words, it is a 3-year annuity. You can also see that, taken together, the investments in rows 2 and 3 provide exactly the same cash payments as the investment in row 1. Thus the value of our annuity (row 3) must be equal to the value of the row 1 perpetuity less the value of the delayed row 2 perpetuity:

$$\text{Present value of a 3-year \$1 annuity} = \frac{1}{r} - \frac{1}{r(1+r)^3}$$

Remembering formulas is about as difficult as remembering other people's birthdays. But as long as you bear in mind that an annuity is equivalent to the difference between an immediate and a delayed perpetuity, you shouldn't have any difficulty.

You can use a calculator or spreadsheet to work out annuity factors (we show you how momentarily), or you can use a set of annuity tables. Table 5.4 is an abridged annuity table (an extended version is shown in Table A.3 at the end of the book). Check that you can find the 3-year annuity factor for an interest rate of 10%.

Compare Table 5.4 with Table 5.3, which presented the present value of a *single* cash flow. In both tables, present values fall as we move across the rows to higher discount rates. But in contrast to those in Table 5.3, present values in Table 5.4 increase as we move down the columns, reflecting the greater number of payments made by longer annuities.

TABLE 5.4 An example of an annuity table, showing the present value today of $1 a year received for each of *t* years

Number	Interest Rate per Year					
of Years	**5%**	**6%**	**7%**	**8%**	**9%**	**10%**
1	0.9524	0.9434	0.9346	0.9259	0.9174	0.9091
2	1.8594	1.8334	1.8080	1.7833	1.7591	1.7355
3	2.7232	2.6730	2.6243	2.5771	2.5313	2.4869
4	3.5460	3.4651	3.3872	3.3121	3.2397	3.1699
5	4.3295	4.2124	4.1002	3.9927	3.8897	3.7908
10	7.7217	7.3601	7.0236	6.7101	6.4177	6.1446
20	12.4622	11.4699	10.5940	9.8181	9.1285	8.5136
30	15.3725	13.7648	12.4090	11.2578	10.2737	9.4269

Self-Test 5.7

If the interest rate is 8%, what is the 4-year discount factor? What is the 4-year annuity factor? What is the relationship between these two numbers? Explain.

EXAMPLE 5.8 ▶	Winning Big at the Lottery

In August 2006 eight lucky meatpackers from Nebraska pooled their money to buy Powerball lottery tickets and won a record $365 million. We suspect that the winners received unsolicited congratulations, good wishes, and requests for money from dozens of more or less worthy charities, relations, and newly devoted friends. In response, they could fairly point out that the prize wasn't really worth $365 million. That sum was to be paid in 30 equal annual installments of $12.167 million each. Assuming that the first payment occurred at the end of 1 year, what was the present value of the prize? The interest rate at the time was about 6%.

The present value of these payments is simply the sum of the present values of each annual payment. But rather than valuing the payments separately, it is much easier to treat them as a 30-year annuity. To value this annuity, we simply multiply $12.167 million by the 30-year annuity factor:

$$PV = 12.167 \times \text{30-year annuity factor}$$

$$= 12.167 \times \left[\frac{1}{r} - \frac{1}{r(1+r)^{30}} \right]$$

At an interest rate of 6%, the annuity factor is

$$\left[\frac{1}{.06} - \frac{1}{.06(1.06)^{30}} \right] = 13.7648$$

(We could also look up the annuity factor in Table A.3.) The present value of the cash payments is $12.167 × 13.7648 = $167.5 million, much less than the much-advertised prize, but still not a bad day's haul.

Lottery operators generally make arrangements for winners with big spending plans to take an equivalent lump sum. In our example the winners could either take the $365 million spread over 30 years or receive $167.5 million up front. Both arrangements have the same present value.

EXAMPLE 5.9 ▶	How Much Luxury and Excitement Can $53 Billion Buy?

Bill Gates is one of the world's richest persons, with wealth in 2010 reputed to be about $53 billion. Mr. Gates has devoted a large part of his fortune to the Bill and Melinda Gates Foundation; but suppose that he decides to allocate his entire remaining wealth to a life of luxury and entertainment (L&E). What annual expenditures on L&E could $53 billion support over a 30-year period? Assume that Mr. Gates can invest his funds at 6%.

The 30-year, 6% annuity factor is 13.7648. We set the present value of Mr. Gates's spending stream equal to his total wealth:

$$\text{Present value} = \text{annual spending} \times \text{annuity factor}$$
$$53,000,000,000 = \text{annual spending} \times 13.7648$$
$$\text{Annual spending} = 3,850,400,000, \text{ or about } 3.85 \text{ billion}$$

Using a financial calculator or spreadsheet, the inputs would be:

	n	i	PV	PMT	FV
Inputs	30	6	−53000000000		0
Compute				3,850,392,309	
Excel			=PMT(rate, nper, PV, FV) =PMT(.06, 30, -53000000000, 0)		

The answer is identical except for a little rounding error.

Warning to Mr. Gates: We haven't considered inflation. The cost of buying L&E will increase, so $3.85 billion won't buy as much L&E in 30 years as it will today. More on that later.

Self-Test 5.8

Suppose you retire at age 70. You expect to live 20 more years and to spend $55,000 a year during your retirement. How much money do you need to save by age 70 to support this consumption plan? Assume an interest rate of 7%.

EXAMPLE 5.10   ▶   Home Mortgages

Sometimes you may need to find the series of cash payments that would provide a given value today. For example, home purchasers typically borrow the bulk of the house price from a lender. The most common loan arrangement is a 30-year loan that is repaid in equal monthly installments. Suppose that a house costs $125,000 and that the buyer puts down 20% of the purchase price, or $25,000, in cash, borrowing the remaining $100,000 from a mortgage lender such as the local savings bank. What is the appropriate monthly mortgage payment?

The borrower repays the loan by making monthly payments over the next 30 years (360 months). The savings bank needs to set these monthly payments so that they have a present value of $100,000. Thus

$$\text{Present value} = \text{mortgage payment} \times \text{360-month annuity factor}$$
$$= \$100,000$$
$$\text{Mortgage payment} = \frac{\$100,000}{\text{360-month annuity factor}}$$

Suppose that the interest rate is 1% a month. Then

$$\text{Mortgage payment} = \frac{\$100,000}{\left[\dfrac{1}{.01} - \dfrac{1}{.01(1.01)^{360}}\right]} = \frac{\$100,000}{97.218} = \$1,028.61$$

The mortgage loan in Example 5.10 is an example of an *amortizing loan.* "Amortizing" means that part of the monthly payment is used to pay interest on the loan and part is used to reduce the amount of the loan. Table 5.5 illustrates a 4-year amortizing loan of $1,000 with an interest rate of 10% and annual payments starting in 1 year. The annual payment (annuity) that would repay the loan is $315.47. (Confirm this for yourself.) At the end of the first year, the interest payment is 10% of $1,000, or $100. So $100 of your first payment is used to pay interest, and the remaining $215.47 is used to reduce (or "amortize") the loan balance to $784.53.

TABLE 5.5 An example of an amortizing loan. If you borrow $1,000 at an interest rate of 10%, you would need to make an annual payment of $315.47 over 4 years to repay the loan with interest.

Year	Beginning-of-Year Balance	Year-End Interest Due on Balance	Year-End Payment	Amortization of Loan	End-of-Year Balance
1	$1,000.00	$100.00	$315.47	$215.47	$784.53
2	$784.53	$78.45	$315.47	$237.02	$547.51
3	$547.51	$54.75	$315.47	$260.72	$286.79
4	$286.79	$28.68	$315.47	$286.79	$0

Next year, the outstanding balance is lower, so the interest charge is only $78.45. Therefore, $315.47 − $78.45 = $237.02 can be applied to amortization. Amortization in the second year is higher than in the first, because the amount of the loan has declined and therefore less of the payment is taken up in interest. This procedure continues until the last year, when the amortization is just enough to reduce the outstanding balance on the loan to zero.

Because the loan is progressively paid off, the fraction of each payment devoted to interest steadily falls over time, while the fraction used to reduce the loan (the amortization) steadily increases. Figure 5.10 illustrates the amortization of the mortgage loan in Example 5.10. In the early years, almost all of the mortgage payment is for interest. Even after 15 years, the bulk of the monthly payment is interest.

Self-Test 5.9

What will be the monthly payment if you take out a $100,000 fifteen-year mortgage at an interest rate of 1% per month? How much of the first payment is interest, and how much is amortization?

Future Value of an Annuity

You are back in savings mode again. This time you are setting aside $3,000 at the end of every year. If your savings earn interest of 8% a year, how much will they be worth at the end of 4 years? We can answer this question with the help of the time line in Figure 5.11. Your first year's savings will earn interest for 3 years, the second will earn

FIGURE 5.10 Mortgage amortization. This figure shows the breakdown of mortgage payments between interest and amortization. Monthly payments within each year are summed, so the figure shows the annual payment on the mortgage.

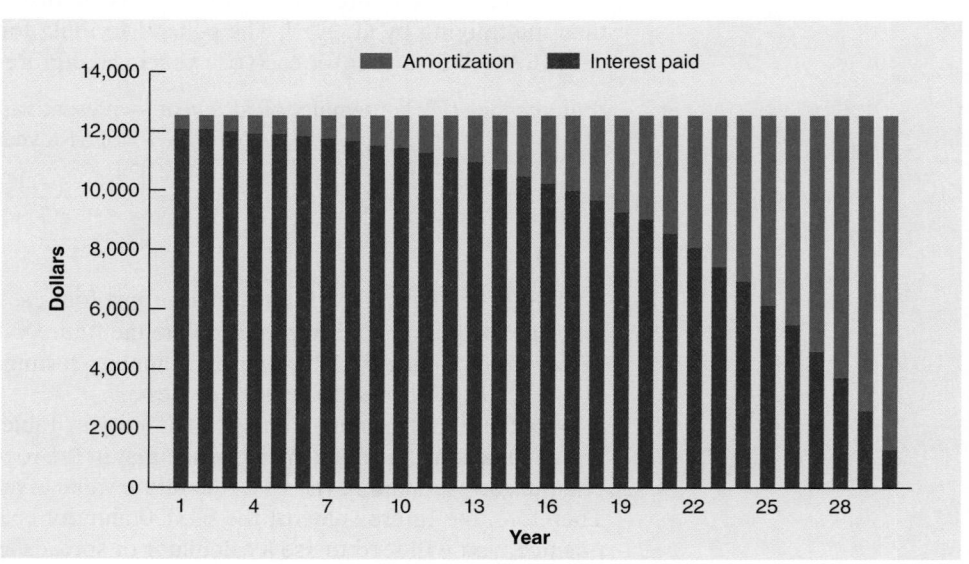

FIGURE 5.11 Calculating the future value of an ordinary annuity of $3,000 a year for 4 years (interest rate = 8%)

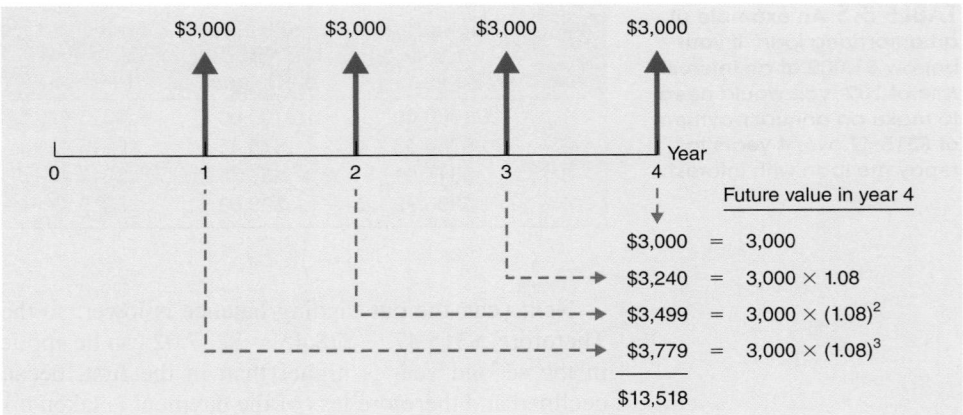

interest for 2 years, the third will earn interest for 1 year, and the final savings in year 4 will earn no interest. The sum of the future values of the four payments is

$$(\$3{,}000 \times 1.08^3) + (\$3{,}000 \times 1.08^2) + (\$3{,}000 \times 1.08) + \$3{,}000 = \$13{,}518$$

But wait a minute! We are looking here at a level stream of cash flows—an annuity. We have seen that there is a shortcut formula to calculate the *present* value of an annuity. So there ought to be a similar formula for calculating the *future* value of a level stream of cash flows.

Think first how much your stream of savings is worth today. You are setting aside $3,000 in each of the next 4 years. The *present* value of this 4-year annuity is therefore equal to

$$\text{PV} = \$3{,}000 \times \text{4-year annuity factor}$$
$$= \$3{,}000 \times \left[\frac{1}{.08} - \frac{1}{.08(1.08)^4} \right] = \$9{,}936$$

Now think how much you would have after 4 years if you invested $9,936 today. Simple! Just multiply by $(1.08)^4$:

$$\text{Value at end of year 4} = \$9{,}936 \times 1.08^4 = \$13{,}518$$

We calculated the future value of the annuity by first calculating the present value and then multiplying by $(1 + r)^t$. The general formula for the future value of a stream of cash flows of $1 a year for each of t years is therefore

Future value (FV) of annuity of $1 a year = present value of annuity of $1 a year $\times (1 + r)^t$

$$= \left[\frac{1}{r} - \frac{1}{r(1 + r)^t} \right] \times (1 + r)^t = \frac{(1 + r)^t - 1}{r}$$

$$(5.5)$$

If you need to find the future value of just four cash flows as in our example, it is a toss-up whether it is quicker to calculate the future value of each cash flow separately (as we did in Figure 5.11) or to use the annuity formula. If you are faced with a stream of 10 or 20 cash flows, there is no contest.

You can find the future value of an annuity in Table 5.6 or the more extensive Table A.4 at the end of the book. You can see that in the row corresponding to $t = 4$ and the column corresponding to $r = 8\%$, the future value of an annuity of $1 a year is $4.5061. Therefore, the future value of the $3,000 annuity is $3,000 × 4.5061 = $13,518. In practice, you will tend to use a calculator or spreadsheet to find these values.

TABLE 5.6 An example of a table showing the future value of an investment of $1 a year for each of *t* years

Number of Years	Interest Rate per Year					
	5%	**6%**	**7%**	**8%**	**9%**	**10%**
1	1.0000	1.0000	1.0000	1.0000	1.0000	1.0000
2	2.0500	2.0600	2.0700	2.0800	2.0900	2.1000
3	3.1525	3.1836	3.2149	3.2464	3.2781	3.3100
4	4.3101	4.3746	4.4399	4.5061	4.5731	4.6410
5	5.5256	5.6371	5.7507	5.8666	5.9847	6.1051
10	12.5779	13.1808	13.8164	14.4866	15.1929	15.9374
20	33.0660	36.7856	40.9955	45.7620	51.1601	57.2750
30	66.4388	79.0582	94.4608	113.2832	136.3075	164.4940

EXAMPLE 5.11 ▶ Saving for Retirement

In only 50 more years, you will retire. (That's right—by the time you retire, the retirement age will be around 70 years. Longevity is not an unmixed blessing.) Have you started saving yet? Suppose you believe you will need to accumulate $500,000 by your retirement date in order to support your desired standard of living. How much savings each year would be necessary to produce $500,000 at the end of 50 years? Let's say that the interest rate is 10% per year. You need to find how large the annuity in the following figure must be to provide a future value of $500,000:

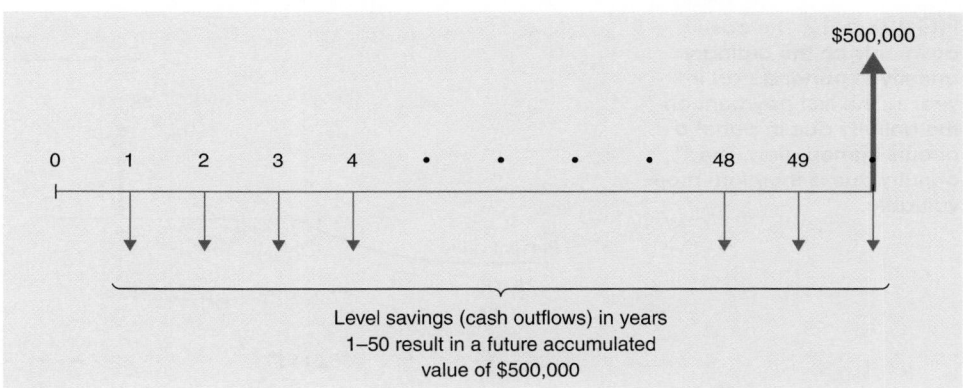

Level savings (cash outflows) in years
1–50 result in a future accumulated
value of $500,000

We know that if you were to save $1 each year your funds would accumulate to

$$\text{Future value (FV) of annuity of \$1 a year} = \frac{(1 + r)^t - 1}{r} = \frac{(1.10)^{50} - 1}{.10}$$

$$= \$1,163.91$$

We need to choose C to ensure that $C \times 1,163.91 = \$500,000$. Thus $C = \$500,000/1,163.91 = \$429.59$. This appears to be surprisingly good news. Saving $429.59 a year does not seem to be an extremely demanding savings program. Don't celebrate yet, however. The news will get worse when we consider the impact of inflation.

Self-Test 5.10

Find the required savings level in Example 5.11 using both a financial calculator and a spreadsheet. What would required savings be if the interest rate were only 5%? Why has the amount increased?

5.5 Annuities Due

Remember that our annuity formulas assume that the first cash flow does not occur until the end of the first period. The present value of an annuity is the value today of a stream of payments that starts in one period. Similarly, the future value of an annuity assumes that the first cash flow comes at the end of one period.

annuity due
Level stream of cash flows starting immediately.

But in many cases cash payments start immediately. For example, when Kangaroo Autos (see Figure 5.8) sells you a car on credit, it may insist that the first payment be made at the time of the sale. A level stream of payments starting immediately is known as an **annuity due.**

Figure 5.12 depicts the cash-flow streams of an ordinary annuity and an annuity due. Comparing panels *a* and *b*, you can see that each of the three cash flows in the annuity due comes one period earlier than the corresponding cash flow of the ordinary annuity. Therefore, each is discounted for one less period, and its present value increases by a factor of $(1 + r)$. Therefore,

$$\text{Present value of annuity due} = \text{present value of ordinary annuity} \times (1 + r) \quad \textbf{(5.6)}$$

Figure 5.12 shows that bringing the Kangaroo loan payments forward by 1 year increases their present value from $19,894.82 (as an ordinary annuity) to $21,884.30 (as an annuity due). Notice that $21,884.30 = $19,894.82 × 1.10.

FIGURE 5.12 The cash payments on the ordinary annuity in panel *a* start in year 1. The first payment on the annuity due in panel *b* occurs immediately. The annuity due is therefore more valuable.

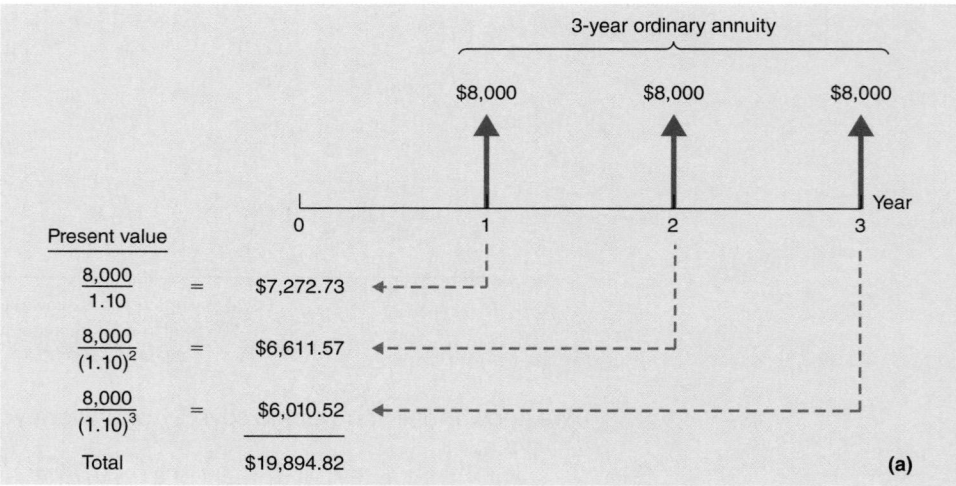

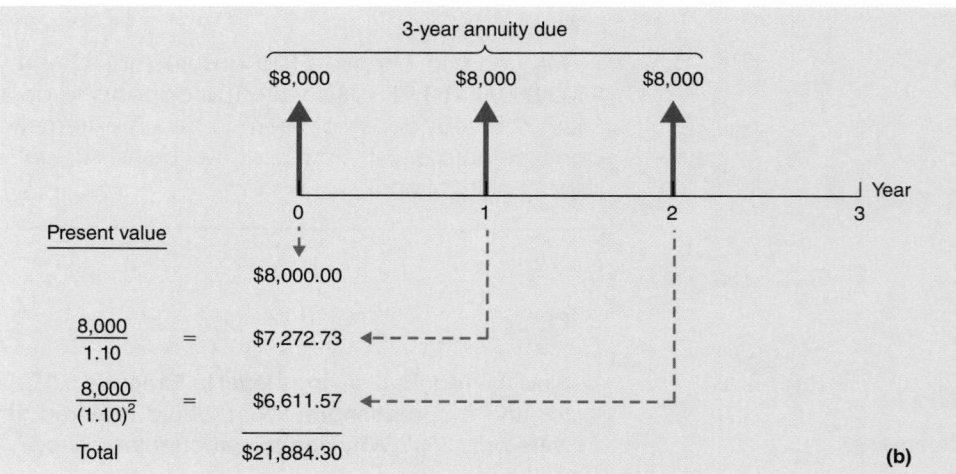

By the way, it is easy to deal with annuities due in your calculator or spreadsheets. Your calculator will have a "begin" key, possibly labeled BEG or BGN. If you push that key, the calculator will interpret all cash flows as coming at the beginning of each period. (Push the key again to return to ordinary annuity mode.) In Excel, if you enter a 1 at the end of a present value (or future value) function, the spreadsheet will interpret the annuity as an annuity due. For example, the present value of Kangaroo Auto's 3-year ordinary annuity was =PV(rate, nper, PMT, FV) =PV(.10, 3, 8000, 0) = $19,894.82. For an annuity due, we would add an extra 1 at the end of the function: =PV(.10, 3, 8000, 0, 1) = $21,884.30. The adjustment is the same for the other financial functions.

Self-Test 5.11

When calculating the value of the Powerball lottery prize in Example 5.8, we assumed that the first of the payments occurred at the end of 1 year. However, the winners of the lottery would not in fact have needed to wait a year before receiving their first payment. They would have gotten their first installment of $12.167 million up front, and the remaining payments would have been spread over the following 29 years. Recalculate the value of the prize.

You may also want to calculate the *future* value of an annuity due. If the first cash flow comes immediately, the future value of the cash-flow stream is greater, since each flow has an extra year to earn interest. For example, at an interest rate of 10%, the future value of an annuity due would be exactly 10% greater than the future value of an ordinary annuity. More generally,

Future value of annuity due = future value of ordinary annuity $\times\ (1\ +\ r)$ **(5.7)**

EXAMPLE 5.12 ▶ Future Value of Annuities versus Annuities Due

In Example 5.11, we showed that an annual savings stream of $429.59 invested for 50 years at 10% would satisfy a savings goal of $500,000. Suppose that you put aside the same annual amounts but you invested the money at the beginning rather than the end of each year. Your savings plan now looks as follows:

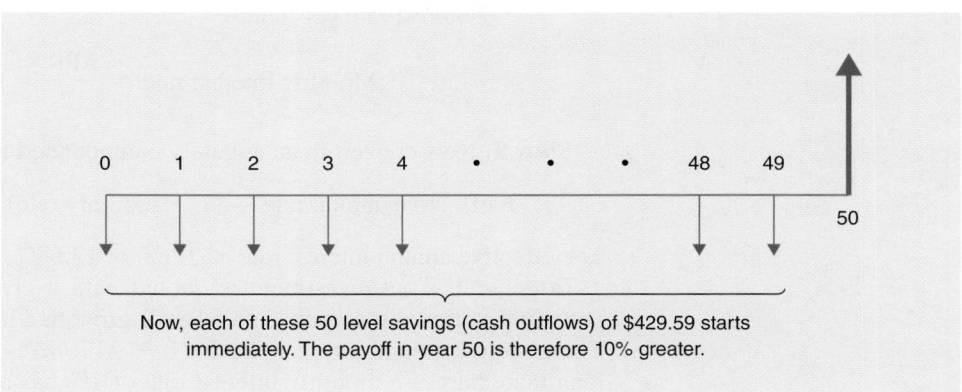

Now, each of these 50 level savings (cash outflows) of $429.59 starts immediately. The payoff in year 50 is therefore 10% greater.

How much would these annual savings provide by the end of year 50?

Easy. We know that the future value of an annuity due is equal to the future value of an ordinary annuity $\times\ (1\ +\ r)$. Therefore, if you make the first of your 50 annual investments immediately, then by the end of the 50 years your retirement savings will be 10% higher, $550,000.

5.6 Effective Annual Interest Rates

Thus far in this chapter we have mainly used *annual* interest rates to value a series of *annual* cash flows. But interest rates may be quoted for days, months, years, or any convenient interval. How should we compare rates when they are quoted for different periods, such as monthly versus annually?

Consider your credit card. Suppose you have to pay interest on any unpaid balances at the rate of 1% *per month*. What is it going to cost you if you neglect to pay off your unpaid balance for a year?

Don't be put off because the interest rate is quoted per month rather than per year. The important thing is to maintain consistency between the interest rate and the number of periods. If the interest rate is quoted as a percent per month, then we must define the number of periods in our future value calculation as the number of months. So if you borrow $100 from the credit card company at 1% per month for 12 months, you will need to repay $100 \times (1.01)^{12} = \$112.68$. Thus your debt grows after 1 year to $112.68. Therefore, we can say that the interest rate of 1% a month is equivalent to an **effective annual interest rate,** or *annually compounded rate,* of 12.68%.

effective annual interest rate
Interest rate that is annualized using compound interest.

In general, the effective annual interest rate is defined as the rate at which your money grows, allowing for the effect of compounding. Therefore, for the credit card,

$$1 + \text{effective annual rate} = (1 + \text{monthly rate})^{12}$$

When comparing interest rates, it is best to use effective annual rates. This compares interest paid or received over a common period (1 year) and allows for possible compounding during the period. Unfortunately, short-term rates are sometimes annualized by multiplying the rate per period by the number of periods in a year. In fact, truth-in-lending laws in the United States *require* that rates be annualized in this manner. Such rates are called **annual percentage rates (APRs).**[2] The interest rate on your credit card loan was 1% per month. Since there are 12 months in a year, the APR on the loan is $12 \times 1\% = 12\%$.

annual percentage rate (APR)
Interest rate that is annualized using simple interest.

If the credit card company quotes an APR of 12%, how can you find the effective annual interest rate? The solution is simple:

Step 1. Take the quoted APR and divide by the number of compounding periods in a year to recover the rate per period actually charged. In our example, the interest was calculated monthly. So we divide the APR by 12 to obtain the interest rate per month:

$$\text{Monthly interest rate} = \frac{\text{APR}}{12} = \frac{12\%}{12} = 1\%$$

Step 2. Now convert to an annually compounded interest rate:

$$1 + \text{effective annual rate} = (1 + \text{monthly rate})^{12} = (1 + .01)^{12} = 1.1268$$

The effective annual interest rate is .1268, or 12.68%.

In general, if an investment is quoted with a given APR and there are m compounding periods in a year, then $1 will grow to $\$1 \times (1 + \text{APR}/m)^m$ after 1 year. The effective annual interest rate is $(1 + \text{APR}/m)^m - 1$. For example, a credit card loan that charges a monthly interest rate of 1% has an APR of 12% but an effective annual interest rate of $(1.01)^{12} - 1 = .1268$, or 12.68%. To summarize: **The effective annual rate is the rate at which invested funds will grow over the course of a year. It equals the rate of interest per period compounded for the number of periods in a year.**

---

[2] The truth-in-lending laws apply to credit card loans, auto loans, home improvement loans, and some loans to small businesses. The term, APR, is not commonly used or quoted in the big leagues of finance.

TABLE 5.7 These investments all have an APR of 6%, but the more frequently interest is compounded, the higher is the effective annual rate of interest.

Compounding Period	Periods per Year (m)	Per-Period Interest Rate	Growth Factor of Invested Funds	Effective Annual Rate
1 year	1	6%	1.06	6.0000%
Semiannually	2	3	$1.03^2 = 1.0609$	6.0900
Quarterly	4	1.5	$1.015^4 = 1.061364$	6.1364
Monthly	12	.5	$1.005^{12} = 1.061678$	6.1678
Weekly	52	.11538	$1.0011538^{52} = 1.061800$	6.1800
Daily	365	.01644	$1.0001644^{365} = 1.061831$	6.1831
Continuous			$e^{.06} = 1.061837$	6.1837

EXAMPLE 5.13 ▶ The Effective Interest Rates on Bank Accounts

Back in the 1960s and 1970s federal regulation limited the (APR) interest rates banks could pay on savings accounts. Banks were hungry for depositors, and they searched for ways to increase the *effective* rate of interest that could be paid within the rules. Their solution was to keep the same APR but to calculate the interest on deposits more frequently. As interest is compounded at shorter and shorter intervals, less time passes before interest can be earned on interest. Therefore, the effective annually compounded rate of interest increases. Table 5.7 shows the calculations assuming that the maximum APR that banks could pay was 6%. (Actually, it was a bit less than this, but 6% is a nice round number to use for illustration.)

You can see from Table 5.7 how banks were able to increase the effective interest rate simply by calculating interest at more frequent intervals.

The ultimate step was to assume that interest was paid in a continuous stream rather than at fixed intervals. With 1 year's *continuous compounding,* $1 grows to e^{APR}, where $e = 2.718$ (a figure that may be familiar to you as the base for natural logarithms). Thus if you deposited $1 with a bank that offered a continuously compounded rate of 6%, your investment would grow by the end of the year to $(2.718)^{.06} = 1.061837, just a hair's breadth more than if interest were compounded daily.

Self-Test 5.12

A car loan requiring quarterly payments carries an APR of 8%. What is the effective annual rate of interest?

5.7 Inflation and the Time Value of Money

When a bank offers to pay 6% on a savings account, it promises to pay interest of $60 for every $1,000 you deposit. The bank fixes the number of dollars that it pays, but it doesn't provide any assurance of how much those dollars will buy. If the value of your investment increases by 6% while the prices of goods and services increase by 10%, you actually lose ground in terms of the goods you can buy.

Real versus Nominal Cash Flows

inflation
Rate at which prices as a whole are increasing.

Prices of goods and services continually change. Textbooks may become more expensive (sorry) while computers become cheaper. An overall general rise in prices is known as **inflation.** If the inflation rate is 5% per year, then goods that cost $1.00 a

TABLE 5.8 The consumer price index (CPI) shows how inflation has increased the cost of a typical family's purchases.

	CPI	Percent Change since 1950
1950	25.0	
1960	29.8	+ 19.2%
1970	39.8	+ 59.2
1980	86.3	+ 245.2
1990	133.8	+ 435.2
2000	174.0	+ 596.0
2010	219.2	+ 776.8

year ago typically cost $1.05 this year. The increase in the general level of prices means that the purchasing power of money has eroded. If a dollar bill bought one loaf of bread last year, the same dollar this year buys only part of a loaf.

Economists track the general level of prices using several different price indexes. The best known of these is the *consumer price index,* or *CPI.* This measures the number of dollars that it takes to buy a specified basket of goods and services that is supposed to represent the typical family's purchases.[3] Thus the percentage increase in the CPI from one year to the next measures the rate of inflation.

Table 5.8 shows the CPI for selected years. The base period for the index is 1982–1984, so the index shows the price level in each year as a percentage of the average price level during these 3 years. For example, the index in 1950 was 25.0. This means that on average $25 in 1950 would have bought the same quantity of goods and services as $100 in 1982–1984. By the end of 2010 the index had risen to 219.2. In other words, prices in 2010 were 8.77 times their level in 1950 (219.2/25.0 = 8.77).[4]

It is interesting to look at annual inflation rates over a somewhat longer period. These are shown in Figure 5.13. The peak year for inflation was 1918, when prices rose by 20%, but you can see that there have also been a few years when prices have fallen quite sharply.

As we write this in early 2011, all appears quiet on the inflation front. In the United States inflation is running at about 1% a year and a few countries are even experiencing falling prices, or *deflation.* This has led some economists to argue that inflation is dead; others are less sure.

FIGURE 5.13 Annual rates of inflation in the United States from 1900 to 2010

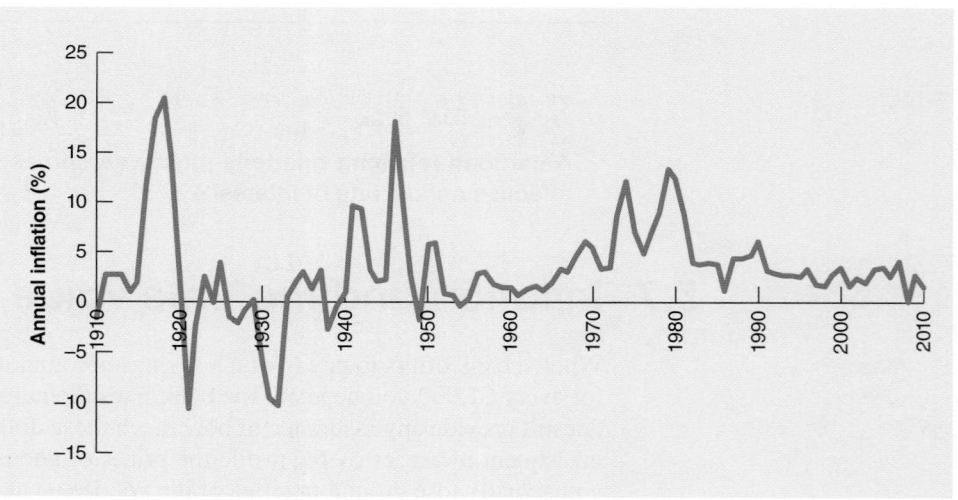

Source: Bureau of Labor Statistics.

---

[3] Don't ask how you buy a "basket" of services.

[4] The choice by the Bureau of Labor Statistics of 1982–1984 as a base period is arbitrary. For example, it could have set December 1950 as the base period. In this case the index would have been 100 in 1950 and 876.8 in 2010.

EXAMPLE 5.14 ▶ The Outrageous Price of Gasoline

Motorists in 2010, who were paying about $2.80 for a gallon of gasoline, may have looked back longingly to 1981, when they were paying just $1.40 a gallon. But how much had the real price of gasoline changed over this period? Let's check.

In 2010 the consumer price index was about 2.5 times its level in 1981. If the price of gasoline had risen in line with inflation, it would have cost 2.5 × $1.40 = $3.50 a gallon in 2010. That was the cost of gasoline in 1981 but measured in terms of 2010 dollars rather than 1981 dollars. Thus over this time period the real price of gasoline actually *declined* 20%, from $3.50 a gallon to $2.80.

Self-Test 5.13

Consider a telephone call to London that currently would cost $5. If the real price of telephone calls does not change in the future, how much will it cost you to make a call to London in 50 years if the inflation rate is 5% (roughly its average over the past 30 years)? What if inflation is 10%?

Economists sometimes talk about *current* **or** *nominal dollars* **versus** *constant* **or** *real dollars.* **Current or nominal dollars refer to the actual number of dollars of the day; constant or real dollars refer to the amount of purchasing power.**

Some expenditures are fixed in nominal terms and therefore *decline* in real terms when the CPI increases. Suppose you took out a 30-year house mortgage in 1990. The monthly payment was $800. It was still $800 in 2010, even though the CPI increased by a factor of 1.64 over those years (219.2/133.8 = 1.64).

What's the monthly payment for 2010 expressed in real 1990 dollars? The answer is $800/1.64, or $488 per month. The real burden of paying the mortgage was much less in 2010 than in 1990.

Self-Test 5.14

If a family spent $250 a week on their typical purchases in 1950, how much would those purchases have cost in 1980? If your salary in 1980 was $30,000 a year, what would be the real value of that salary in terms of 1950 dollars? Use the data in Table 5.8.

Inflation and Interest Rates

Whenever anyone quotes an interest rate, you can be fairly sure that it is a *nominal*, not a *real*, rate. It sets the actual number of dollars you will be paid with no offset for future inflation.

nominal interest rate
Rate at which money invested grows.

If you deposit $1,000 in the bank at a **nominal interest rate** of 6%, you will have $1,060 at the end of the year. But this does not mean you are 6% better off. Suppose that the inflation rate during the year is also 6%. Then the goods that cost $1,000 last year will now cost $1,000 × 1.06 = $1,060, so you've gained nothing:

$$\text{Real future value of investment} = \frac{\$1,000 \times (1 + \text{nominal interest rate})}{(1 + \text{inflation rate})}$$

$$= \frac{\$1,000 \times 1.06}{1.06} = \$1,000$$

real interest rate
Rate at which the purchasing power of an investment increases.

In this example, the nominal rate of interest is 6%, but the **real interest rate** is zero.
The real rate of interest is calculated by

$$1 + \text{real interest rate} = \frac{1 + \text{nominal interest rate}}{1 + \text{inflation rate}} \quad (5.8)$$

In our example both the nominal interest rate and the inflation rate were 6%. So

$$1 + \text{real interest rate} = \frac{1.06}{1.06} = 1$$

$$\text{Real interest rate} = 0$$

What if the nominal interest rate is 6% but the inflation rate is only 2%? In that case the real interest rate is $1.06/1.02 - 1 = .039$, or 3.9%. Imagine that the price of a loaf of bread is $1, so that $1,000 would buy 1,000 loaves today. If you invest that $1,000 at a nominal interest rate of 6%, you will have $1,060 at the end of the year. However, if the price of loaves has risen in the meantime to $1.02, then your money will buy you $1,060/1.02 = 1,039$ loaves. The real rate of interest is 3.9%.

Self-Test 5.15

a. Suppose that you invest your funds at an interest rate of 8%. What will be your real rate of interest if the inflation rate is zero? What if it is 5%?
b. Suppose that you demand a real rate of interest of 3% on your investments. What nominal interest rate do you need to earn if the inflation rate is zero? If it is 5%?

Here is a useful approximation. The real rate approximately equals the difference between the nominal rate and the inflation rate:[5]

$$\text{Real interest rate} \approx \text{nominal interest rate} - \text{inflation rate} \quad (5.9)$$

Our example used a nominal interest rate of 6%, an inflation rate of 2%, and a real rate of 3.9%. If we round to 4%, the approximation gives the same answer:

$$\text{Real interest rate} \approx \text{nominal interest rate} - \text{inflation rate}$$
$$\approx 6 - 2 = 4\%$$

The approximation works best when both the inflation rate and the real rate are small. When they are not small, throw the approximation away and do it right.

EXAMPLE 5.15 ▶   Real and Nominal Rates

In the United States in mid-2010, long-term high-grade corporate bonds offered a yield of about 5.1%. If inflation is expected to be about 1%, the *real* yield is

$$1 + \text{real interest rate} = \frac{1 + \text{nominal interest rate}}{1 + \text{inflation rate}} = \frac{1.051}{1.01} = 1.0406$$

$$\text{Real interest rate} = .0406, \text{ or } 4.06\%$$

The approximation rule gives a similar value of $5.1 - 1.0 = 4.1\%$. But the approximation would not have worked in the German hyperinflation of 1922–1923, when the inflation rate was well over 100% per *month* (at one point you needed 1 million marks to mail a letter), or in Zimbabwe in November 2008, when prices rose an average of 98% *per day*.

[5] The squiggle ($\approx$) means "approximately equal to."

Valuing Real Cash Payments

Think again about how to value future cash payments. Earlier in the chapter you learned how to value payments in current dollars by discounting at the nominal interest rate. For example, suppose that the nominal interest rate is 10%. How much do you need to invest now to produce $100 in a year's time? Easy! Calculate the present value of $100 by discounting by 10%:

$$PV = \frac{\$100}{1.10} = \$90.91$$

You get exactly the same result if you discount the *real* payment by the *real interest rate*. For example, assume that you expect inflation of 7% over the next year. The real value of that $100 is therefore only $100/1.07 = $93.46. In one year's time your $100 will buy only as much as $93.46 today. Also, with a 7% inflation rate the real rate of interest is only about 3%. We can calculate it exactly from the formula

$$1 + \text{real interest rate} = \frac{1 + \text{nominal interest rate}}{1 + \text{inflation rate}} = \frac{1.10}{1.07} = 1.028$$

$$\text{Real interest rate} = .028, \text{ or } 2.8\%$$

If we now discount the $93.46 real payment by the 2.8% real interest rate, we have a present value of $90.91, just as before:

$$PV = \frac{\$93.46}{1.028} = \$90.91$$

The two methods should always give the same answer.

Remember: **Current dollar cash flows must be discounted by the nominal interest rate; real cash flows must be discounted by the real interest rate.**

Mixing up nominal cash flows and real discount rates (or real rates and nominal flows) is an unforgivable sin. It is surprising how many sinners one finds.

Self-Test 5.16

You are owed $5,000 by a relative who will pay it back in 1 year. The nominal interest rate is 8%, and the inflation rate is 5%. What is the present value of your relative's IOU? Show that you get the same answer (a) discounting the nominal payment at the nominal rate and (b) discounting the real payment at the real rate.

EXAMPLE 5.16 ▶ How Inflation Might Affect Bill Gates

We showed earlier (Example 5.9) that at an interest rate of 6% Bill Gates could, if he wished, turn his $53 billion wealth into a 30-year annuity of $3.85 billion per year of luxury and excitement (L&E). Unfortunately, L&E expenses inflate just like gasoline and groceries. Thus Mr. Gates would find the purchasing power of that $3.85 billion steadily declining. If he wants the same luxuries in 2040 as in 2010, he'll have to spend less in 2010 and then increase expenditures in line with inflation. How much should he spend in 2010? Assume the long-run inflation rate is 3%.

Mr. Gates needs to calculate a 30-year *real* annuity. The real interest rate is a little less than 3%:

$$1 + \text{real interest rate} = \frac{1 + \text{nominal interest rate}}{1 + \text{inflation rate}}$$

$$= \frac{1.06}{1.03} = 1.029$$

so the real rate is 2.9%. The 30-year annuity factor at 2.9% is 19.8562. Therefore, annual spending (in 2010 dollars) should be chosen so that

$$\$53,000,000,000 = \text{annual spending} \times 19.8562$$
$$\text{Annual spending} = \$2,669,000,000$$

Mr. Gates could spend that amount on L&E in 1 year's time and 3% more (in line with inflation) in each subsequent year. This is only about 70% of the value we calculated when we ignored inflation. Life has many disappointments, even for tycoons.

Self-Test 5.17

You have reached age 60 with a modest fortune of $3 million and are considering early retirement. How much can you spend each year for the next 30 years? Assume that spending is stable in real terms. The nominal interest rate is 10%, and the inflation rate is 5%.

Real or Nominal?

Any present value calculation done in nominal terms can also be done in real terms, and vice versa. Most financial analysts forecast in nominal terms and discount at nominal rates. However, in some cases real cash flows are easier to deal with. In our example of Bill Gates, the *real* expenditures were fixed. In this case, it was easiest to use real quantities. On the other hand, if the cash-flow stream is fixed in nominal terms (for example, the payments on a loan), it is easiest to use all nominal quantities.

SUMMARY

If you invest money at a given interest rate, what will be the future value of your investment? (*LO1*)

An investment of $1 earning an interest rate of r will increase in value each period by the factor $(1 + r)$. After t periods its value will grow to $\$(1 + r)^t$. This is the **future value** of the $1 investment with compound interest.

What is the present value of a cash flow to be received in the future? (*LO2*)

The **present value** of a future cash payment is the amount that you would need to invest today to match that future payment. To calculate present value, we divide the cash payment by $(1 + r)^t$ or, equivalently, multiply by the **discount factor** $1/(1 + r)^t$. The discount factor measures the value today of $1 received in period t.

How can we calculate present and future values of streams of cash payments? (*LO3*)

A level stream of cash payments that continues indefinitely is known as a **perpetuity;** one that continues for a limited number of years is called an **annuity.** The present value of a stream of cash flows is simply the sum of the present value of each individual cash flow. Similarly, the future value of an annuity is the sum of the future value of each individual cash flow. Shortcut formulas make the calculations for perpetuities and annuities easy.

How can we find the interest rate implied by present and future values? (*LO4*)

The present value equals the discounted value of one or more future cash flows using the appropriate interest rate. Therefore, we solve for the interest rate that makes the discounted value of the future cash flows equal to the given present value. In some cases, this may require trial and error.

How should we compare interest rates quoted over different time intervals— for example, monthly versus annual rates? (*LO5*)	Interest rates for short time periods are often quoted as annual rates by multiplying the per-period rate by the number of periods in a year. These **annual percentage rates (APRs)** do not recognize the effect of compound interest, that is, they annualize assuming simple interest. The **effective annual rate** annualizes using compound interest. It equals the rate of interest per period compounded for the number of periods in a year.
What is the difference between real and nominal cash flows and between real and nominal interest rates? (*LO6*)	A dollar is a dollar, but the amount of goods that a dollar can buy is eroded by **inflation.** If prices double, the **real value of a dollar** halves. Financial managers and economists often find it helpful to reexpress future cash flows in terms of real dollars—that is, dollars of constant purchasing power. Be careful to distinguish the **nominal interest rate** and the **real interest rate**—that is, the rate at which the real value of the investment grows. Discount nominal cash flows (that is, cash flows measured in current dollars) at nominal interest rates. Discount real cash flows (cash flows measured in constant dollars) at real interest rates. *Never* mix and match nominal and real.

LISTING OF EQUATIONS

5.1   Future value = present value $\times (1 + r)^t$

5.2   Present value = $\dfrac{\text{future value after } t \text{ periods}}{(1 + r)^t}$

5.3   PV of perpetuity = $\dfrac{C}{r} = \dfrac{\text{cash payment}}{\text{interest rate}}$

5.4   Present value of *t*-year annuity = $C\left[\dfrac{1}{r} - \dfrac{1}{r(1 + r)^t}\right]$

5.5   Future value (FV) of annuity of \$1 a year = present value of annuity of \$1 a year $\times (1 + r)^t$

$$= \left[\dfrac{1}{r} - \dfrac{1}{r(1+r)^t}\right] \times (1+r)^t = \dfrac{(1+r)^t - 1}{r}$$

5.6   Present value of annuity due = $(1 + r) \times$ present value of annuity

5.7   Future value of annuity due = future value of ordinary annuity $\times (1 + r)$

5.8   1 + real interest rate = $\dfrac{1 + \text{nominal interest rate}}{1 + \text{inflation rate}}$

5.9   Real interest rate $\approx$ nominal interest rate $-$ inflation rate

QUESTIONS

QUIZ

1.   **Present Values.** Compute the present value of a \$100 cash flow for the following combinations of discount rates and times: (*LO2*)

   a. $r = 8\%, t = 10$ years.
   b. $r = 8\%, t = 20$ years.
   c. $r = 4\%, t = 10$ years.
   d. $r = 4\%, t = 20$ years.

2.   **Future Values.** Compute the future value of a \$100 cash flow for the same combinations of rates and times as in Quiz Question 1. (*LO1*)

3.   **Future Values.** In 1880 five aboriginal trackers were each promised the equivalent of 100 Australian dollars for helping to capture the notorious outlaw Ned Kelley. In 1993 the granddaughters of two of the trackers claimed that this reward had not been paid. The Victorian prime

minister stated that if this was true, the government would be happy to pay the $100. However, the granddaughters also claimed that they were entitled to compound interest. How much was each entitled to if the interest rate was 4%? What if it was 8%? (*LO1*)

4. **Future Values.** You deposit $1,000 in your bank account. If the bank pays 4% simple interest, how much will you accumulate in your account after 10 years? What if the bank pays compound interest? How much of your earnings will be interest on interest? (*LO1*)

5. **Present Values.** You will require $700 in 5 years. If you earn 5% interest on your funds, how much will you need to invest today in order to reach your savings goal? (*LO2*)

6. **Calculating Interest Rate.** Find the interest rate implied by the following combinations of present and future values: (*LO4*)

Present Value	Years	Future Value
$400	11	$684
183	4	249
300	7	300

7. **Present Values.** Would you rather receive $1,000 a year for 10 years or $800 a year for 15 years if (*LO3*)
    a. the interest rate is 5%?
    b. the interest rate is 20%?
    c. Why do your answers to (a) and (b) differ?

8. **Calculating Interest Rate.** Find the annual interest rate. (*LO4*)

Present Value	Future Value	Time Period
$100	$115.76	3 years
200	262.16	4
100	110.41	5

9. **Present Values.** What is the present value of the following cash-flow stream if the interest rate is 6%? (*LO3*)

Year	Cash Flow
1	$200
2	400
3	300

10. **Number of Periods.** How long will it take for $400 to grow to $1,000 at the interest rate specified? (*LO1*)
    a. 4%
    b. 8%
    c. 16%

11. **Calculating Interest Rate.** Find the effective annual interest rate for each case. (*LO5*)

APR	Compounding Period
12%	1 month
8	3
10	6

12. **Calculating Interest Rate.** Find the APR (the stated interest rate) for each case. (*LO5*)

Effective Annual Interest Rate	Compounding Period
10.00%	1 month
6.09	6
8.24	3

13. **Growth of Funds.** If you earn 6% per year on your bank account, how long will it take an account with $100 to double to $200? (*LO1*)

14. **Comparing Interest Rates.** Suppose you can borrow money at 8.6% per year (APR) compounded semiannually or 8.4% per year (APR) compounded monthly. Which is the better deal? (*LO5*)

15. **Calculating Interest Rate.** Lenny Loanshark charges "1 point" per week (that is, 1% per week) on his loans. What APR must he report to consumers? Assume exactly 52 weeks in a year. What is the effective annual rate? (*LO5*)

16. **Compound Interest.** Investments in the stock market have increased at an average compound rate of about 5% since 1900. It is now 2012.
    a. If you invested $1,000 in the stock market in 1900, how much would that investment be worth today? (*LO1*)
    b. If your investment in 1900 has grown to $1 million, how much did you invest in 1900? (*LO2*)

17. **Compound Interest.** Old Time Savings Bank pays 4% interest on its savings accounts. If you deposit $1,000 in the bank and leave it there, how much interest will you earn in the first year? The second year? The tenth year? (*LO1*)

18. **Compound Interest.** New Savings Bank pays 4% interest on its deposits. If you deposit $1,000 in the bank and leave it there, will it take more or less than 25 years for your money to double? You should be able to answer this without a calculator or interest rate tables. (*LO1*)

19. **Calculating Interest Rate.** A zero-coupon bond that will pay $1,000 in 10 years is selling today for $422.41. What interest rate does the bond offer? (*LO4*)

20. **Present Values.** A famous quarterback just signed a $15 million contract providing $3 million a year for 5 years. A less famous receiver signed a $14 million 5-year contract providing $4 million now and $2 million a year for 5 years. Who is better paid? The interest rate is 10%. (*LO3*)

PRACTICE PROBLEMS

21. **Compound Growth.** In mid-2010 a pound of apples cost $1.26, while oranges cost $1.10. Ten years earlier the price of apples was only $.92 a pound and that of oranges was $.70 a pound. What was the annual compound rate of growth in the price of the two fruits? If the same rates of growth persist in the future, what will be the price of apples in 2030? What about the price of oranges? (*LO6*)

22. **Loan Payments.** If you take out an $8,000 car loan that calls for 48 monthly payments starting after 1 month at an APR of 10%, what is your monthly payment? What is the effective annual interest rate on the loan? (*LO5*)

23. **Annuity Values.** (*LO3*)
    a. What is the present value of a 3-year annuity of $100 if the discount rate is 6%?
    b. What is the present value of the annuity in (a) if you have to wait 2 years instead of 1 year for the first payment?

24. **Annuities and Interest Rates.** Professor's Annuity Corp. offers a lifetime annuity to retiring professors. For a payment of $80,000 at age 65, the firm will pay the retiring professor $600 a month until death.
    a. If the professor's remaining life expectancy is 20 years, what is the monthly rate on this annuity? What is the effective annual rate? (*LO4*)
    b. If the monthly interest rate is .5%, what monthly annuity payment can the firm offer to the retiring professor? (*LO3*)

25. **Annuity Values.** You want to buy a new car, but you can make an initial payment of only $2,000 and can afford monthly payments of at most $400. (*LO3*)
    a. If the APR on auto loans is 12% and you finance the purchase over 48 months, what is the maximum price you can pay for the car?
    b. How much can you afford if you finance the purchase over 60 months?

26. **Calculating Interest Rate.** In a *discount interest loan,* you pay the interest payment up front. For example, if a 1-year loan is stated as $10,000 and the interest rate is 10%, the borrower "pays" $.10 \times \$10,000 = \$1,000$ immediately, thereby receiving net funds of $9,000 and repaying $10,000 in a year. (*LO5*)

    a. What is the effective interest rate on this loan?
    b. If you call the discount *d* (for example, *d* = 10% using our numbers), express the effective annual rate on the loan as a function of *d*.
    c. Why is the effective annual rate always greater than the stated rate *d?*

27. **Annuity Due.** Recall that an annuity due is like an ordinary annuity except that the first payment is made immediately instead of at the end of the first period. (*LO3*)

    a. Why is the present value of an annuity due equal to $(1 + r)$ times the present value of an ordinary annuity?
    b. Why is the future value of an annuity due equal to $(1 + r)$ times the future value of an ordinary annuity?

28. **Rate on a Loan.** If you take out an $8,000 car loan that calls for 48 monthly payments of $240 each, what is the APR of the loan? What is the effective annual interest rate on the loan? (*LO5*)

29. **Loan Payments.** Reconsider the car loan in the previous question. What if the payments are made in four annual year-end installments? What annual payment would have the same present value as the monthly payment you calculated? Use the same effective annual interest rate as in the previous question. Why is your answer not simply 12 times the monthly payment? (*LO5*)

30. **Annuity Value.** Your landscaping company can lease a truck for $8,000 a year (paid at year-end) for 6 years. It can instead buy the truck for $40,000. The truck will be valueless after 6 years. If the interest rate your company can earn on its funds is 7%, is it cheaper to buy or lease? (*LO3*)

31. **Annuity-Due Value.** Reconsider the previous problem. What if the lease payments are an annuity due, so that the first payment comes immediately? Is it cheaper to buy or lease? (*LO3*)

32. **Annuity Due.** A store offers two payment plans. Under the installment plan, you pay 25% down and 25% of the purchase price in each of the next 3 years. If you pay the entire bill immediately, you can take a 10% discount from the purchase price. Which is a better deal if you can borrow or lend funds at a 5% interest rate? (*LO3*)

33. **Annuity Value.** Reconsider the previous question. How will your answer change if the payments on the 4-year installment plan do not start for a full year? (*LO3*)

34. **Annuity and Annuity-Due Payments.** (*LO3*)

    a. If you borrow $1,000 and agree to repay the loan in five equal annual payments at an interest rate of 12%, what will your payment be?
    b. What if you make the first payment on the loan immediately instead of at the end of the first year?

35. **Valuing Delayed Annuities.** Suppose that you will receive annual payments of $10,000 for a period of 10 years. The first payment will be made 4 years from now. If the interest rate is 5%, what is the present value of this stream of payments? (*LO3*)

36. **Mortgage with Points.** Home loans typically involve "points," which are fees charged by the lender. Each point charged means that the borrower must pay 1% of the loan amount as a fee. For example, if the loan is for $100,000 and 2 points are charged, the loan repayment schedule is calculated on a $100,000 loan but the net amount the borrower receives is only $98,000. What is the effective annual interest rate charged on such a loan assuming loan repayment occurs over 360 months? Assume the interest rate is 1% per month. (*LO3*)

37. **Amortizing Loan.** You take out a 30-year $100,000 mortgage loan with an APR of 6% and monthly payments. In 12 years you decide to sell your house and pay off the mortgage. What is the principal balance on the loan? (*LO3*)

38. **Amortizing Loan.** Consider a 4-year amortizing loan. You borrow $1,000 initially, and repay it in four equal annual year-end payments. (*LO3*)

    a. If the interest rate is 8%, show that the annual payment is $301.92.
    b. Fill in the following table, which shows how much of each payment is interest versus principal repayment (that is, amortization), and the outstanding balance on the loan at each date.

Time	Loan Balance	Year-End Interest Due on Balance	Year-End Payment	Amortization of Loan
0	$1,000	$80	$301.92	$221.92
1	——	——	301.92	——
2	——	——	301.92	——
3	——	——	301.92	——
4	0	0	——	——

    c. Show that the loan balance after 1 year is equal to the year-end payment of $301.92 times the 3-year annuity factor.

39. **Annuity Value.** You've borrowed $4,248.68 and agreed to pay back the loan with monthly payments of $200. If the interest rate is 12% stated as an APR, how long will it take you to pay back the loan? What is the effective annual rate on the loan? (*LO3*)

40. **Annuity Value.** The $40 million lottery payment that you just won actually pays $2 million per year for 20 years. If the discount rate is 8% and the first payment comes in 1 year, what is the present value of the winnings? What if the first payment comes immediately? (*LO3*)

41. **Real Annuities.** A retiree wants level consumption in real terms over a 30-year retirement. If the inflation rate equals the interest rate she earns on her $450,000 of savings, how much can she spend in real terms each year over the rest of her life? (*LO6*)

42. **EAR versus APR.** You invest $1,000 at a 6% annual interest rate, stated as an APR. Interest is compounded monthly. How much will you have in 1 year? In 1.5 years? (*LO5*)

43. **Annuity Value.** You just borrowed $100,000 to buy a condo. You will repay the loan in equal monthly payments of $804.62 over the next 30 years. What monthly interest rate are you paying on the loan? What is the effective annual rate on that loan? What rate is the lender more likely to quote on the loan? (*LO3*)

44. **EAR.** If a bank pays 6% interest with continuous compounding, what is the effective annual rate? (*LO5*)

45. **Annuity Values.** You can buy a car that is advertised for $24,000 on the following terms: (a) pay $24,000 and receive a $2,000 rebate from the manufacturer; (b) pay $500 a month for 4 years for total payments of $24,000, implying zero percent financing. Which is the better deal if the interest rate is 1% per month? (*LO3*)

46. **Continuous Compounding.** How much will $100 grow to if invested at a continuously compounded interest rate of 10% for 8 years? What if it is invested for 10 years at 8%? (*LO5*)

47. **Future Values.** I now have $20,000 in the bank earning interest of .5% per month. I need $30,000 to make a down payment on a house. I can save an additional $100 per month. How long will it take me to accumulate the $30,000? (*LO3*)

48. **Perpetuities.** A local bank advertises the following deal: "Pay us $100 a year for 10 years and then we will pay you (or your beneficiaries) $100 a year *forever*." Is this a good deal if the interest rate available on other deposits is 6%? (*LO3*)

49. **Perpetuities.** A local bank will pay you $100 a year for your lifetime if you deposit $2,500 in the bank today. If you plan to live forever, what interest rate is the bank paying? (*LO4*)

50. **Perpetuities.** A property will provide $10,000 a year forever. If its value is $125,000, what must be the discount rate? (*LO4*)

51. **Applying Time Value.** You can buy property today for $3 million and sell it in 5 years for $4 million. (You earn no rental income on the property.) (*LO3*)

    a. If the interest rate is 8%, what is the present value of the sales price?

    b. Is the property investment attractive to you? Why or why not?

    c. Would your answer to (b) change if you also could earn $200,000 per year rent on the property?

52. **Applying Time Value.** A factory costs $400,000. You forecast that it will produce cash inflows of $120,000 in year 1, $180,000 in year 2, and $300,000 in year 3. The discount rate is 12%. Is the factory a good investment? Explain. (*LO3*)

53. **Applying Time Value.** You invest $1,000 today and expect to sell your investment for $2,000 in 10 years. (*LO1*)

    a. Is this a good deal if the discount rate is 6%?
    b. What if the discount rate is 10%?

54. **Calculating Interest Rate.** A store will give you a 3% discount on the cost of your purchase if you pay cash today. Otherwise, you will be billed the full price with payment due in 1 month. What is the implicit borrowing rate being paid by customers who choose to defer payment for the month? (*LO4*)

55. **Quoting Rates.** Banks sometimes quote interest rates in the form of "add-on interest." In this case, if a 1-year loan is quoted with a 20% interest rate and you borrow $1,000, then you pay back $1,200. But you make these payments in monthly installments of $100 each. What are the true APR and effective annual rate on this loan? Why should you have known that the true rates must be greater than 20% even before doing any calculations? (*LO5*)

56. **Compound Interest.** Suppose you take out a $1,000, 3-year loan using add-on interest (see previous problem) with a quoted interest rate of 20% per year. What will your monthly payments be? (Total payments are $1,000 + $1,000 × .20 × 3 = $1,600.) What are the true APR and effective annual rate on this loan? Are they the same as in the previous problem? (*LO5*)

57. **Calculating Interest Rate.** What is the effective annual rate on a 1-year loan with an interest rate quoted on a discount basis (see Practice Problem 26) of 20%? (*LO4*)

58. **Effective Rates.** First National Bank pays 6.2% interest compounded semiannually. Second National Bank pays 6% interest, compounded monthly. Which bank offers the higher effective annual rate? (*LO5*)

59. **Calculating Interest Rate.** You borrow $1,000 from the bank and agree to repay the loan over the next year in 12 equal monthly payments of $90. However, the bank also charges you a loan-initiation fee of $20, which is taken out of the initial proceeds of the loan. What is the effective annual interest rate on the loan taking account of the impact of the initiation fee? (*LO4*)

60. **Retirement Savings.** You believe you will need to have saved $500,000 by the time you retire in 40 years in order to live comfortably. If the interest rate is 6% per year, how much must you save each year to meet your retirement goal? (*LO3*)

61. **Retirement Savings.** How much would you need in the previous problem if you believe that you will inherit $100,000 in 10 years? (*LO3*)

62. **Retirement Savings.** You believe you will spend $40,000 a year for 20 years once you retire in 40 years. If the interest rate is 6% per year, how much must you save each year until retirement to meet your retirement goal? (*LO3*)

63. **Retirement Planning.** A couple thinking about retirement decide to put aside $3,000 each year in a savings plan that earns 8% interest. In 5 years they will receive a gift of $10,000 that also can be invested. (*LO3*)

    a. How much money will they have accumulated 30 years from now?
    b. If their goal is to retire with $800,000 of savings, how much extra do they need to save every year?

64. **Retirement Planning.** A couple will retire in 50 years; they plan to spend about $30,000 a year in retirement, which should last about 25 years. They believe that they can earn 8% interest on retirement savings. (*LO3*)

    a. If they make annual payments into a savings plan, how much will they need to save each year? Assume the first payment comes in 1 year.
    b. How would the answer to part (a) change if the couple also realize that in 20 years they will need to spend $60,000 on their child's college education?

65. **Real versus Nominal Dollars.** An engineer in 1950 was earning $6,000 a year. Today she earns $60,000 a year. However, on average, goods today cost 8.8 times what they did in 1950. What is her real income today in terms of constant 1950 dollars? (*LO6*)

66. **Real versus Nominal Rates.** If investors are to earn a 3% real interest rate, what nominal interest rate must they earn if the inflation rate is

    a. zero? (*LO6*)
    b. 4%? (*LO6*)
    c. 6%? (*LO6*)

67. **Real Rates.** If investors receive a 6% interest rate on their bank deposits, what real interest rate will they earn if the inflation rate over the year is
    a. zero? (*LO6*)
    b. 3%? (*LO6*)
    c. 6%? (*LO6*)

68. **Real versus Nominal Rates.** You will receive $100 from a savings bond in 3 years. The nominal interest rate is 8%.
    a. What is the present value of the proceeds from the bond? (*LO2*)
    b. If the inflation rate over the next few years is expected to be 3%, what will the real value of the $100 payoff be in terms of today's dollars? (*LO6*)
    c. What is the real interest rate? (*LO6*)
    d. Show that the real payoff from the bond [from part (b)] discounted at the real interest rate [from part (c)] gives the same present value for the bond as you found in part (a). (*LO6*)

69. **Real versus Nominal Dollars.** Your consulting firm will produce cash flows of $100,000 this year, and you expect cash flow to keep pace with any increase in the general level of prices. The interest rate currently is 6%, and you anticipate inflation of about 2%.
    a. What is the present value of your firm's cash flows for years 1 through 5? (*LO6*)
    b. How would your answer to (a) change if you anticipated no growth in cash flow? (*LO2*)

CHALLENGE PROBLEMS

70. **Real versus Nominal Annuities.** Good news: You will almost certainly be a millionaire by the time you retire in 50 years. Bad news: The inflation rate over your lifetime will average about 3%. (*LO6*)
    a. What will be the real value of $1 million by the time you retire in terms of today's dollars?
    b. What real annuity (in today's dollars) will $1 million support if the real interest rate at retirement is 2% and the annuity must last for 20 years?

71. **Real versus Nominal.** If the interest rate is 6% per year, how long will it take for your money to *quadruple* in value? If the inflation rate is 4% per year, what will be the change in the purchasing power of your money over this period? (*LO1, 6*)

72. **Inflation.** In the summer of 2007, Zimbabwe's official inflation rate was about 110% per month. What was the annual inflation rate? (*LO6*)

73. **Perpetuities.** British government 4% perpetuities pay £4 interest each year forever. Another bond, 2½% perpetuities, pays £2.50 a year forever. What is the value of 4% perpetuities if the long-term interest rate is 6%? What is the value of 2½% perpetuities? (*LO3*)

74. **Real versus Nominal Annuities.** (*LO6*)
    a. You plan to retire in 30 years and want to accumulate enough by then to provide yourself with $30,000 a year for 15 years. If the interest rate is 10%, how much must you accumulate by the time you retire?
    b. How much must you save each year until retirement in order to finance your retirement consumption?
    c. Now you remember that the annual inflation rate is 4%. If a loaf of bread costs $1 today, what will it cost by the time you retire?
    d. You really want to consume $30,000 a year in *real* dollars during retirement and wish to save an equal *real* amount each year until then. What is the real amount of savings that you need to accumulate by the time you retire?
    e. Calculate the required preretirement real annual savings necessary to meet your consumption goals. Compare with your answer to (b). Why is there a difference?
    f. What is the nominal value of the amount you need to save during the first year? (Assume the savings are put aside at the end of each year.) The thirtieth year?

75. **Retirement and Inflation.** Redo part (a) of Practice Problem 64, but now assume that the inflation rate over the next 50 years will average 5%. (*LO6*)
    a. What is the real annual savings the couple must set aside?
    b. How much do they need to save in nominal terms in the first year?
    c. How much do they need to save in nominal terms in the last year?
    d. What will be their nominal expenditures in the first year of retirement? The last?

76. **Perpetuities.** What is the value of a perpetuity that pays $100 every 3 months forever? The discount rate quoted on an APR basis is 6%. (*LO5*)

77. **Changing Interest Rates.** If the interest rate this year is 8% and the interest rate next year will be 10%, what is the future value of $1 after 2 years? What is the present value of a payment of $1 to be received in 2 years? (*LO1, 2*)

78. **Changing Interest Rates.** Your wealthy uncle established a $1,000 bank account for you when you were born. For the first 8 years of your life, the interest rate earned on the account was 6%. Since then, rates have been only 4%. Now you are 21 years old and ready to cash in. How much is in your account? (*LO1*)

Templates can be found at
www.mhhe.com/bmm7e.

79. **Real versus Nominal Cash Flows.**

    a. It is 2012, you've just graduated college, and you are contemplating your lifetime budget. You think your general living expenses will average around $50,000 a year. For the next 8 years, you will rent an apartment for $16,000 a year. After that, you will want to buy a house that should cost around $250,000. In addition, you will need to buy a new car roughly once every 10 years, costing around $30,000 each. In 25 years, you will have to put aside around $150,000 to put a child through college, and in 30 years you'll need to do the same for another child. In 50 years, you will retire, and will need to have accumulated enough savings to support roughly 20 years of retirement spending of around $35,000 a year on top of your social security benefits. The interest rate is 5% per year. What average salary will you need to earn to support this lifetime consumption plan? (*LO3*)

    b. Whoops! You just realized that the inflation rate over your lifetime is likely to average about 3% per year, and you need to redo your calculations. As a rough cut, it seems reasonable to assume that all relevant prices and wages will increase at around the rate of inflation. What is your new estimate of the required salary (in today's dollars)? (*LO6*)

Templates can be found at
www.mhhe.com/bmm7e.

80. **Amortizing Loans and Inflation.** Suppose you take out a $100,000, 20-year mortgage loan to buy a condo. The interest rate on the loan is 6%, and to keep things simple, we will assume you make payments on the loan annually at the end of each year. (*LO3*)

    a. What is your annual payment on the loan?

    b. Construct a mortgage amortization table in Excel similar to Table 5.5 in which you compute the interest payment each year, the amortization of the loan, and the loan balance each year. (Allow the interest rate to be an input that the user of the spreadsheet can enter and change.)

    c. What fraction of your initial loan payment is interest? What fraction is amortization? What about the last loan payment? What fraction of the loan has been paid off after 10 years (halfway through the life of the loan)?

    d. If the inflation rate is 2%, what is the real value of the first (year-end) payment? The last?

    e. Now assume the inflation rate is 8% and the real interest rate on the loan is unchanged. What must be the new nominal interest rate? Recompute the amortization table. What is the real value of the first (year-end) payment in this high-inflation scenario? The real value of the last payment?

    f. Comparing your answers to (d) and (e), can you see why high inflation rates might hurt the real estate market?

WEB EXERCISES

1. You can buy a car for $20,000, or you can lease it for 36 monthly payments of $350 each, with the first payment due immediately. At the end of the 36 months the car will be worth $10,000. Which alternative should you prefer if the interest rate (APR) is 12%? You can check your answer by logging on to the personal finance page of www.smartmoney.com and using the buy or lease calculator.

2. In Example 5.10 we showed you how to work out mortgage payments. Log on to the personal finance page of www.smartmoney.com and find the mortgage payment calculator. Assume a 20-year mortgage loan of $100,000 and an interest rate (APR) of 12%. What is the amount of

the monthly payment? Check that you get the same answer when using the annuity formula. Now look at how much of the first month's payment goes to reduce the size of the mortgage. How much of the payment by the tenth year? Can you explain why the figure changes? If the interest rate doubles, would you expect the mortgage payment to double? Check whether you are right.

3. You can find data on the consumer price index (CPI) on the Bureau of Labor Statistics Web site, www.bls.gov/cpi/home.htm. Tables of historical data can be formatted to provide either levels of the index or changes in the index (i.e., the rate of inflation). Construct a table of annual inflation rates since 1913. When did the USA last experience a year of deflation (i.e., falling prices)? Find the inflation rate in the latest year. Now log on to www.bloomberg.com, and on the first page find a measure of the short-term interest rate (e.g., the 2-year rate). Use the recent level of inflation to calculate the *real* interest rate. Consider the case of Herbert Protheroe, who in 1920 was an eligible bachelor with an income of $2,000 a year. What is that equivalent to today?

SOLUTIONS TO SELF-TEST QUESTIONS

5.1 Value after 5 years would have been $24 \times (1.05)^5 = \$30.63$; after 50 years, $24 \times (1.05)^{50} = \$275.22$.

5.2 Call g the annual growth rate of transistors over the 39-year period between 1971 and 2010. Then

$$2,250 \times (1 + g)^{39} = 2,300,000,000$$
$$(1 + g)^{39} = 1,022,222$$
$$1 + g = 1,022,222^{1/39} = 1.43$$

So the actual growth rate was $g = .43$, or 43%, not quite as high as Moore's prediction, but not so shabby either.

5.3 Multiply the $1,000 payment by the 30-year discount factor:

$$PV = \$1,000 \times \frac{1}{(1.0635)^{30}} = \$157.72$$

5.4 You invest $1 today, so this is the PV. The FV of the investment is $2, and the investment duration is 8 years. On your calculator, or in Excel, your inputs should be as follows:

	n	i	PV	PMT	FV
Inputs	8		−1	0	2
Compute		9.05			
Excel		=RATE(nper, PMT, PV, FV) =RATE(8, 0, -1, 2)			

5.5

Gift at Year	Present Value
1	10,000/(1.07) = $9,345.79
2	10,000/(1.07)² = 8,734.39
3	10,000/(1.07)³ = 8,162.98
4	10,000/(1.07)⁴ = 7,628.95
	$33,872.11

www.mhhe.com/bmm7e

Gift at Year	Future Value	
1	$10,000/(1.07)^3$ =	$12,250.43
2	$10,000/(1.07)^2$ =	11,449
3	$10,000/(1.07)$ =	10,700
4	$10,000$ =	10,000
		$44,399.43

5.6   The rate is $4/48 = .0833$, about 8.3%.

5.7   The 4-year discount factor is $1/(1.08)^4 = .7350$. The 4-year annuity factor is $[1/.08 - 1/(.08 \times 1.08^4)] = 3.3121$. This is the difference between the present value of a \$1 perpetuity starting next year and the present value of a \$1 perpetuity starting in year 5:

$$\text{PV (perpetuity starting next year)} = \frac{1}{.08} = 12.50$$

$$-\text{PV (perpetuity starting in year 5)} = \frac{1}{.08} \times \frac{1}{(1.08)^4} = 9.1879$$

$$=\text{PV (4-year annuity)} \quad\quad = 12.50 - 9.1879 = 3.3121$$

which matches the annuity factor.

5.8   You will need the present value at 7% of a 20-year annuity of \$55,000:

$$\text{Present value} = \text{annual spending} \times \text{annuity factor}$$

The annuity factor is $[1/.07 - 1/(.07 \times 1.07^{20})] = 10.5940$. Thus you need $\$55,000 \times 10.594 = \$582,670$.

5.9   Fifteen years means 180 months. Then

$$\text{Mortgage payment} = \frac{100,000}{\text{180-month annuity factor}}$$
$$= \frac{100,000}{83.32}$$
$$= \$1,200.17 \text{ per month}$$

\$1,000 of the payment is interest. The remainder, \$200.17, is amortization.

On a financial calculator or spreadsheet, your inputs should be as follows. Notice that our time period in this problem is 1 month; our payments are monthly, and our interest rate is for a 1-month period.

	n	i	PV	PMT	FV
Inputs	180	1	100000		0
Compute				−1200.17	
Excel	=PMT(rate, nper, PV, FV) =PMT(.01, 180, 100000, 0)				

5.10   On your calculator, or in Excel, your inputs should be as follows:

	n	i	PV	PMT	FV
Inputs	50	10	0		500000
Compute				−429.59	
Excel	=PMT(rate, nper, PV, FV) =PMT(.10, 50, 500000, 0)				

If the interest rate is instead only 5%, the future value of a 50-year, \$1 annuity will be

$$\frac{(1.05)^{50} - 1}{.05} = 209.348$$

Therefore, we need to choose the cash flow, C, so that $C \times 209.348 = \$500,000$. This requires that $C = \$500,000/209.348 = \$2,388.37$. (Try confirming this value on your calculator or in Excel.) This required savings level is much higher than we found in Example 5.11. At a 5% interest rate, current savings do not grow as rapidly as when the interest rate was 10%; with less of a boost from compound interest, we need to set aside greater amounts in order to reach the target of \$500,000.

5.11 We saw in Example 5.8 that the 30-year annuity factor for an ordinary annuity is 13.7648. Therefore, the 30-year annuity-due factor would be $13.7648 \times 1.06 = 14.5907$. The present value of the winnings would increase to $\$12.167 \times 14.5907 = \$177.5$ million. You can also put your calculator in *begin* mode; enter $n = 30$, $i = 6$, FV = 0, PMT = 12.167; and compute PV. Alternatively, in Excel use the formula =PV(.06, 30, 12.167, 0, 1). Starting the 30-year cash-flow stream immediately, rather than waiting 1 year, increases value by about \$10 million.

5.12 The quarterly rate is 8/4 = 2%. The effective annual rate is $(1.02)^4 - 1 = .0824$, or 8.24%.

5.13 The cost in dollars will increase by 5% each year, to a value of $\$5 \times (1.05)^{50} = \$57.34$. If the inflation rate is 10%, the cost will be $\$5 \times (1.10)^{50} = \$586.95$.

5.14 The CPI in 1980 was 3.452 times its value in 1950 (see Table 5.8). Therefore, purchases that cost \$250 in 1950 would have cost $\$250 \times 3.452 = \$863$ in 1980. The value of a 1980 salary of \$30,000, expressed in real 1950 dollars, is $\$30,000 \times (1/3.452) = \$8,691$.

5.15 a. If there's no inflation, real and nominal rates are equal at 8%. With 5% inflation, the real rate is $(1.08/1.05) - 1 = .02857$, a bit less than 3%.
b. If you want a 3% *real* interest rate, you need a 3% nominal rate if inflation is zero and an 8.15% rate if inflation is 5%. Note that $1.03 \times 1.05 = 1.0815$.

5.16 The present value is

$$PV = \frac{\$5,000}{1.08} = \$4,629.63$$

The real interest rate is 2.857% (see Self-Test 5.15a). The real cash payment is $\$5,000/(1.05) = \$4,761.90$. Thus,

$$PV = \frac{\$4,761.90}{1.02857} = \$4,629.63$$

5.17 Calculate the real annuity. The real interest rate is $1.10/1.05 - 1 = .0476$. We'll round to 4.8%. The real annuity is

$$\text{Annual payment} = \frac{\$3,000,000}{\text{30-year annuity factor}} = \frac{\$3,000,000}{\dfrac{1}{.048} - \dfrac{1}{.048(1.048)^{30}}} = \frac{\$3,000,000}{15.7292} = \$190,728$$

You can spend this much each year in dollars of constant purchasing power. The purchasing power of each dollar will decline at 5% per year, so you'll need to spend more in nominal dollars: $\$190,728 \times 1.05 = \$200,264$ in the second year, $\$190,728 \times 1.05^2 = \$210,278$ in the third year, and so on.

SOLUTIONS TO SPREADSHEET QUESTIONS

5.1

Interest rate	Present value
5%	\$15,438
8%	15,133
11%	14,850

5.2 \$14,916. While the total (undiscounted) payments remain \$16,000, part of the first payment in this example has been pushed to the next two years. This reduces present value.

MINICASE

Old Alfred Road, who is well-known to drivers on the Maine Turn-pike, has reached his seventieth birthday and is ready to retire. Mr. Road has no formal training in finance but has saved his money and invested carefully.

Mr. Road owns his home—the mortgage is paid off—and does not want to move. He is a widower, and he wants to bequeath the house and any remaining assets to his daughter.

He has accumulated savings of $180,000, conservatively invested. The investments are yielding 9% interest. Mr. Road also has $12,000 in a savings account at 5% interest. He wants to keep the savings account intact for unexpected expenses or emergencies.

Mr. Road's basic living expenses now average about $1,500 per month, and he plans to spend $500 per month on travel and hob-bies. To maintain this planned standard of living, he will have to rely on his investment portfolio. The interest from the portfolio is $16,200 per year (9% of $180,000), or $1,350 per month.

Mr. Road will also receive $750 per month in Social Security payments for the rest of his life. These payments are indexed for inflation. That is, they will be automatically increased in propor-tion to changes in the consumer price index.

Mr. Road's main concern is with inflation. The inflation rate has been below 3% recently, but a 3% rate is unusually low by histori-cal standards. His Social Security payments will increase with inflation, but the interest on his investment portfolio will not.

What advice do you have for Mr. Road? Can he safely spend all the interest from his investment portfolio? How much could he withdraw at year-end from that portfolio if he wants to keep its real value intact?

Suppose Mr. Road will live for 20 more years and is willing to use up all of his investment portfolio over that period. He also wants his monthly spending to increase along with inflation over that period. In other words, he wants his monthly spending to stay the same in real terms. How much can he afford to spend per month?

Assume that the investment portfolio continues to yield a 9% rate of return and that the inflation rate will be 4%.

Valuing Bonds

LEARNING OBJECTIVES

After studying this chapter, you should be able to:

1 Distinguish among a bond's coupon rate, current yield, and yield to maturity.

2 Find the market price of a bond given its yield to maturity, find a bond's yield given its price, and demonstrate why prices and yields move in opposite directions.

3 Show why bonds exhibit interest rate risk.

4 Understand why investors pay attention to bond ratings and demand a higher interest rate for bonds with low ratings.

RELATED WEB SITES FOR THIS CHAPTER CAN BE FOUND AT WWW.MHHE.COM/BMM7E.

Investment in new plant and equipment requires money—often a lot of money. Sometimes firms may be able to save enough out of previous earnings to cover the cost of investments, but often they need to raise cash from investors. In broad terms, we can think of two ways to raise new money from investors: borrow the cash or sell additional shares of common stock.

If companies need the money for just a short while, they may borrow it from a bank; if they need it to make long-term investments, they generally issue bonds, which are simply long-term loans. When companies issue bonds, they promise to make a series of fixed interest payments and then to repay the debt. As long as the company generates sufficient cash, the payments on a bond are certain. In this case bond valuation involves straightforward time-value-of-money computations. But there is some chance that even the most blue-chip company will fall on hard times and will not be able to repay its debts. Investors take this default risk into account when they price the bonds and demand a higher interest rate to compensate.

Companies are not the only bond issuers. State and local governments also raise money by selling bonds. So does the U.S. Treasury. Most investors would regard the risk of default on Treasury bonds as negligible, and therefore these issues offer a lower rate of interest than corporate bonds. Nevertheless, the interest rates on government bonds provide a benchmark for all interest rates. When government interest rates go up or down, corporate rates follow more or less proportionally. Therefore, in the first part of this chapter we focus on Treasury bonds and sidestep the issue of default.

We begin by showing you how to understand the bond pages in the financial press, and we

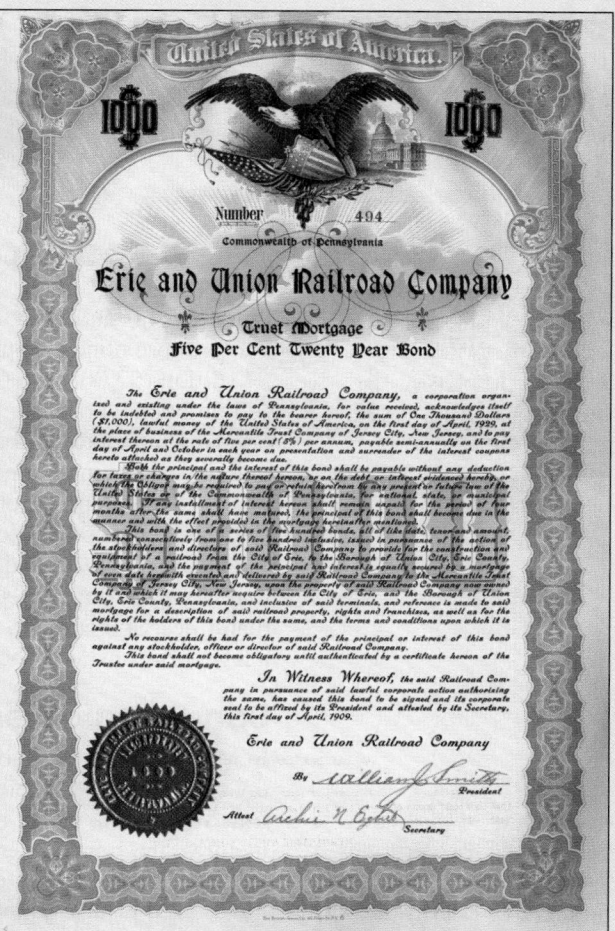

Bondholders once received a beautifully engraved certificate like this one issued by a railroad. Nowadays their ownership is simply recorded on an electronic database.

explain what bond dealers mean when they quote yields to maturity. We look at why short-term rates are usually lower (but sometimes higher) than long-term rates and why the longest-term bond prices are most sensitive to fluctuations in interest rates. We distinguish real (inflation-adjusted) interest rates and nominal (money) rates and explain how future inflation can affect interest rates.

Toward the end of the chapter we look at corporate bonds, which carry a possibility of default. We look at how bond ratings provide a guide to that default risk and how low-grade bonds offer higher promised yields. We will see that corporate bonds are more complex securities than government bonds. Some corporate bonds give the borrower an option to repay early; others can be exchanged for the company's common stock. Such complications affect the "spread" of corporate bond rates over interest rates on government bonds of similar maturities. In Chapter 14 we will look

in more detail at the securities that companies issue, and we will look further at some of these variations in bond design.

6.1 The Bond Market

bond
Security that obligates the issuer to make specified payments to the bondholder.

Governments and corporations borrow money by selling **bonds** to investors. The market for these bonds is huge. In 2011 public holdings of U.S. government bonds totaled $7 trillion ($7,000,000,000,000).[1] Companies also raise very large sums of money by selling bonds. For example, General Motors once borrowed $17 billion by an issue of bonds. The market for bonds is sophisticated and active. Bond traders frequently make massive trades motivated by tiny price discrepancies.

When governments or companies issue bonds, they promise to make a series of interest payments and then to repay the debt. But don't get the idea that all bonds are alike. For example, most bonds make a fixed interest payment, but in other cases the payment may go up or down as short-term interest rates change. Bonds may also have different maturities. Sometimes a company may borrow for only a few years, but there have been a few occasions when bonds have been issued with maturities of 100 years or more.

Bond Characteristics

face value
Payment at the maturity of the bond. Also called *principal* or *par value*.

coupon
The interest payments paid to the bondholder.

In May 2003 the U.S. government made a typical issue of a Treasury bond. It auctioned off to investors $18 billion of 3.625% bonds maturing in 2013. The bonds have a **face value** (also called the *principal* or *par value*) of $1,000. Each year until the bond matures, the bondholder receives an interest payment of 3.625% of the face value, or $36.25. This 3.625% interest payment is called the bond's **coupon.** In the old days, most bonds used to have coupons that the investor clipped off and mailed to the bond issuer to claim their payment. When the 3.625% coupon bond matures in 2013, the government must pay the $1,000 face value of the bond in addition to the final coupon payment.

At last count there were 204 different Treasury bonds. The prices at which you can buy and sell each of these bonds are shown each day in the financial press and on the Web. Table 6.1, which is compiled from *The Wall Street Journal*'s Web page, shows the prices for just a small sample of issues. The entry for the 3.625% bond maturing in May 2013 is highlighted.

Prices are generally quoted in 32nds rather than decimals. Thus for the 3.625% bond, the *asked price*—that is, the price that investors need to pay to buy the bond—is shown as 107:01. This means that the price is 107 and 1/32, or 107.03125% of face value. Therefore, each bond costs $1,070.3125. An investor who *already* owns the bond and wishes to *sell* it would receive the *bid price,* which is shown as 106:31. Just as the used-car dealer earns a living by reselling cars at higher prices than he paid for them, so the bond dealer needs to charge a *spread* between the bid and the asked price. Notice that the spread for these 3.625% bonds is only 2/32, or about .06% of the bond's value. Don't you wish that used-car dealers charged similar spreads?

The final column in the table shows the *asked yield to maturity*. This measures the return to investors if they buy the bond at the asked price and hold it to maturity in 2013. You can see that the 3.625% coupon Treasury bond offers a yield to maturity of 1.23%. We will explain shortly how this figure was calculated.

Self-Test 6.1

How much would an investor pay to buy one 4.75% Treasury bond of 2014 (see Table 6.1)? If a Treasury bond costs $1,106.25, how would this price be quoted?

---

[1] This figure includes Treasury notes (bonds maturing in 2 to 10 years) as well as long-term bonds maturing in more than 10 years.

TABLE 6.1 Sample Treasury bond quotes for May 14, 2010

Maturity	Coupon	Bid Price	Asked Price	Asked Yield, %
2012 May 15	1.375	101:05	101:06	0.78
2013 May 15	**3.625**	**106:31**	**107:01**	**1.23**
2014 May 15	4.75	111:22	111:23	1.70
2020 May 15	8.75	144:17	144:19	3.44
2025 Aug 15	6.875	133:07	133:11	3.94
2030 May 15	6.25	128:25	128:27	4.12
2040 May 15	4.375	100:28	100:29	4.32

Source: The Wall Street Journal Web site, **www.wsj.com**.

FIGURE 6.1 Cash flows to an investor in the 3.625% coupon bond maturing in the year 2013

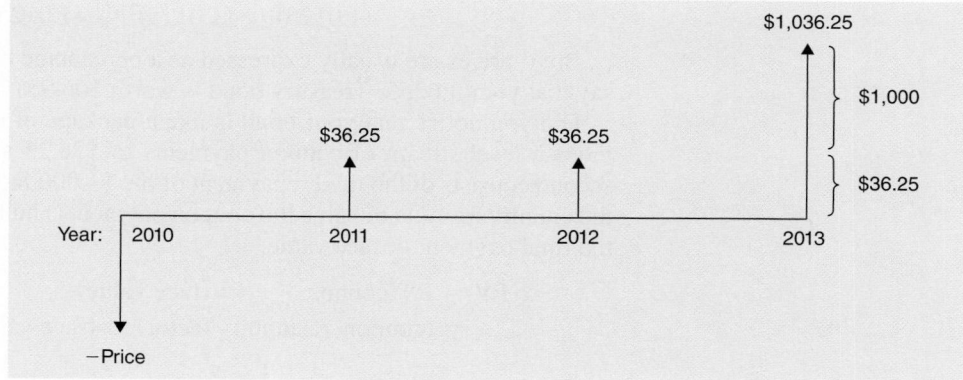

You can't buy Treasury bonds on the stock exchange. Instead, they are traded by a network of bond dealers, who quote bid and ask prices at which they are prepared to buy and sell. For example, suppose that in 2010 you decide to buy the "3.625s of 2013," that is, the 3.625% coupon bonds maturing in 2013. You approach a broker who checks the current price on her screen. If you are happy to go ahead with the purchase, your broker will contact a bond dealer and the trade is done.

If you plan to hold your bond until maturity, you can look forward to the cash flows shown in Figure 6.1. For the first 2 years, the cash flows equal the 3.625% coupon payment. Then, when the bond matures in 2013, you receive the $1,000 face value of the bond plus the final coupon payment.

Self-Test 6.2

Find the 8.75% coupon 2020 Treasury bond in Table 6.1.

a. How much does it cost to buy the bond?
b. If you already owned the bond, how much would a bond dealer pay you for it?
c. What annual interest payment does the bond make?
d. What is the bond's yield to maturity?

6.2 Interest Rates and Bond Prices

In Figure 6.1 we set out the cash flows from your 3.625% Treasury bond. The value of the bond is the present value of these cash flows. To find this value, you need to discount each future payment by the current interest rate.

The 3.625s were not the only Treasury bonds that matured in 2013. Almost identical bonds maturing at the same time offered an interest rate of about 1.25%. So, if the 3.625s had offered a lower return than 1.25%, no one would have been willing to hold them. Equally, if they had offered a *higher* return, everyone would have rushed to sell their other bonds and buy the 3.625s. In other words, if investors were on their toes, the 3.625s had to offer the same 1.25% rate of interest as similar Treasury bonds. You might recognize 1.25% as the opportunity cost of the funds invested in the bond, as we discussed in Chapter 1. This is the rate that investors could earn by placing their funds in similar securities rather than in this bond.

We can now calculate the present value of the 3.625s of 2013 by discounting the cash flows at 1.25%:

$$PV = \frac{\$36.25}{(1 + r)} + \frac{\$36.25}{(1 + r)^2} + \frac{\$1,036.25}{(1 + r)^3}$$

$$= \frac{\$36.25}{(1.0125)} + \frac{\$36.25}{(1.0125)^2} + \frac{\$1,036.25}{(1.0125)^3} = \$1,069.51$$

Bond prices are usually expressed as a percentage of their face value. Thus we can say that your 3.625% Treasury bond is worth 106.951% of face value.[2]

Did you notice that your bond is like a package of two investments? The first provides a level stream of coupon payments of $36.25 a year for each of 3 years. The second consists of the final repayment of the $1,000 face value. Therefore, you can use the annuity formula to value the coupon payments and then add on the present value of the final payment of face value:

$$PV = PV(\text{coupons}) + PV(\text{face value}) \tag{6.1}$$
$$= (\text{coupon} \times \text{annuity factor}) + (\text{face value} \times \text{discount factor})$$
$$= \$36.25 \times \left[\frac{1}{.0125} - \frac{1}{.0125(1.0125)^3} \right] + 1,000 \times \frac{1}{1.0125^3}$$
$$= \$106.09 + \$963.42 = \$1,069.51$$

If you need to value a bond with many years to run before maturity, it is usually easiest to value the coupon payments as an annuity and then add on the present value of the final payment.

Self-Test 6.3

Calculate the present value of a 6-year bond with a 9% coupon. The interest rate is 12%.

You can calculate bond prices easily using a financial calculator or spreadsheet. The trick is to recognize that the bond provides its owner *both* a recurring payment (the coupons) *and* an additional one-time cash flow (the face value). For this bond, the time to maturity is 3 years, annual coupon payment is $36.25, and face value is $1,000. The interest rate is 1.25%. Therefore, the inputs would be

	n	i	PV	PMT	FV
Inputs	3	1.25		36.25	1000
Compute			−1069.51		

Now compute PV, and you should get an answer of −1069.51, which is the initial cash outflow required to purchase the bond.

For an introduction to bond pricing using Excel, turn to the box on page 170.

---

[2] Our calculated value of $1,069.51 (106.951%) is a little lower than the asked price of 107 1/32% quoted in Table 6.1. We discounted at 1.25%, which is rounded up slightly from the asked yield to maturity of 1.2315%. Also, the bond's actual coupon is not $36.25 per year, but $18.125 every 6 months. In the next example, we'll show how to handle semiannual coupons.

EXAMPLE 6.1 ▶ Bond Prices and Semiannual Coupon Payments

When we valued our Treasury bond, we assumed that interest payments occur annually. This is the case for bonds in many European countries, but in the United States most bonds make coupon payments *semiannually*. So when you hear that a bond in the United States has a coupon rate of 3.625%, you can generally assume that the bond makes a payment of $36.25/2 = $18.125 every 6 months. Similarly, when investors in the United States refer to the bond's interest rate, they usually mean the semiannually compounded interest rate. Thus an interest rate quoted at 1.25% really means that the 6-month rate is 1.25/2 = .625%.[3] The actual cash flows on the Treasury bond are illustrated in Figure 6.2. To value the bond a bit more precisely, we should have discounted the series of semiannual payments by the semiannual rate of interest as follows:

$$PV = \frac{\$18.125}{(1.00625)} + \frac{\$18.125}{(1.00625)^2} + \frac{\$18.125}{(1.00625)^3} + \frac{\$18.125}{(1.00625)^4}$$
$$+ \frac{\$18.125}{(1.00625)^5} + \frac{\$1,018.125}{(1.00625)^6}$$
$$= \$1,069.72$$

Thus, once we allow for the fact that coupon payments are semiannual, the value of the 3.625s is 106.972% of face value, which is slightly higher than the value that we obtained when we assumed annual coupon payments.[4] Since semiannual coupon payments just add to the arithmetic, we will stick for the most part to our simplification and assume annual interest payments.

How Bond Prices Vary with Interest Rates

Figure 6.3 plots the interest rate on 10-year Treasury bonds from 1900 to 2010. Notice how much the interest rate fluctuates. For example, interest rates climbed steeply after 1979 when the Federal Reserve instituted a policy of tight money to rein in inflation. Within 2 years the rate on 10-year government bonds rose from 10% to 14%. Contrast this with 2008, when nervous investors fled to the safety of U.S. government bonds. By the end of that year, long-term Treasuries offered a measly 2.4% rate of interest.

As interest rates change, so do bond prices. For example, suppose that investors demanded an interest rate of 3.625% on 3-year Treasury bonds. What would be the price of the Treasury 3.625s of 2013? Just repeat our PV calculation with a discount rate of $r = .03625$:

$$PV \text{ at } 3.625\% = \frac{\$36.25}{(1.03625)} + \frac{\$36.25}{(1.03625)^2} + \frac{\$1,036.25}{(1.03625)^3} = \$1,000.00$$

Thus when the interest rate is the same as the coupon rate (3.625% in our example), the bond sells for its face value.

---

[3] You may have noticed that the semiannually compounded interest rate on the bond is also the bond's APR, although this term is not generally used by bond investors. To find the effective rate, we can use a formula that we presented in Section 5.6:

$$\text{Effective annual rate} = \left(1 + \frac{APR}{m}\right)^m - 1$$

where m is the number of payments each year. In the case of our Treasury bond,

$$\text{Effective annual rate} = \left(1 + \frac{.0125}{2}\right)^2 - 1 = 1.00625^2 - 1 = .01254, \text{ or } 1.254\%$$

[4] Why is the present value a bit higher in this case? Because now we recognize that half the annual coupon payment is received only 6 months into the year, rather than at year-end. Since part of the coupon income is received earlier, its present value is higher.

FIGURE 6.2 Cash flows to an investor in the 3.625% coupon bond maturing in 2013. The bond pays semiannual coupons, so there are two payments of $18.125 each year.

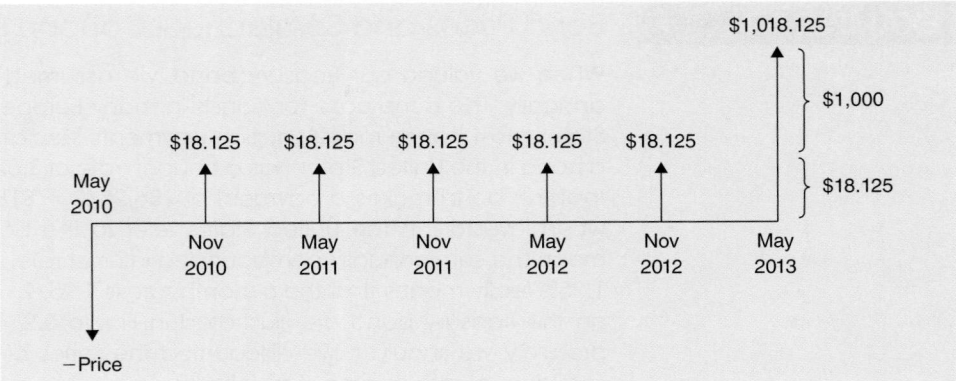

FIGURE 6.3 The interest rate on 10-year U.S. Treasury bonds, 1900-2010

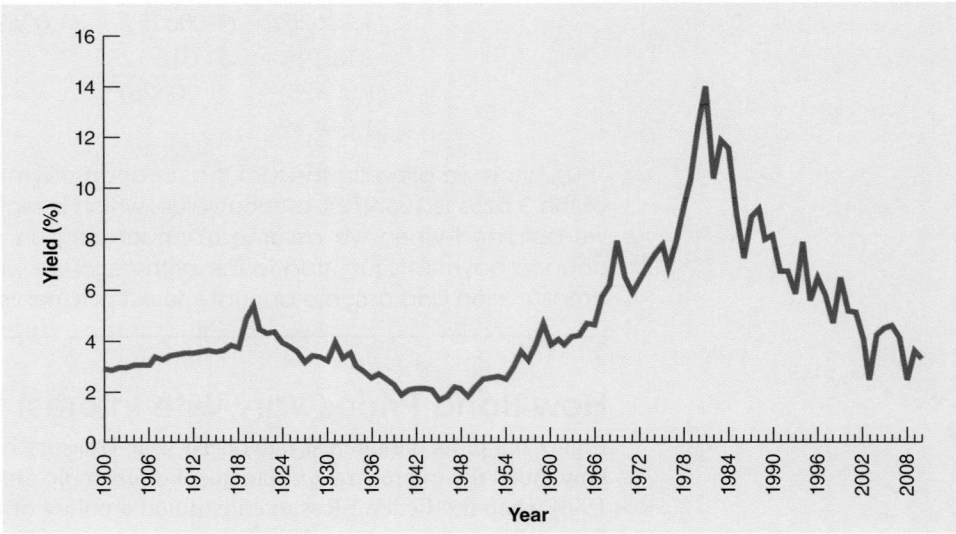

We first valued the Treasury bond using an interest rate of 1.25%, which is lower than the coupon rate. In that case the price of the bond was *higher* than its face value. We then valued it using an interest rate that is equal to the coupon and found that bond price equaled face value. You have probably already guessed that when the cash flows are discounted at a rate that is *higher* than the bond's coupon rate, the bond is worth *less* than its face value. The following example confirms that this is the case.

EXAMPLE 6.2 ▶ Interest Rates and Bond Prices

Investors will pay $1,000 for a 3.625%, 3-year Treasury bond when the interest rate is 3.625%. Suppose that the interest rate is higher than the coupon rate at (say) 8%. Now what is the value of the bond? Simple! We just repeat our calculation but with $r = .08$:

$$\text{PV at 8\%} = \frac{\$36.25}{(1.08)} + \frac{\$36.25}{(1.08)^2} + \frac{\$1,036.25}{(1.08)^3} = \$887.25$$

The bond sells for 88.725% of face value.

This is a general result. **When the market interest rate exceeds the coupon rate, bonds sell for less than face value. When the market interest rate is below the coupon rate, bonds sell for more than face value.**

**FIGURE 6.4 The value of
the 3.625% bond falls as
interest rates rise.**

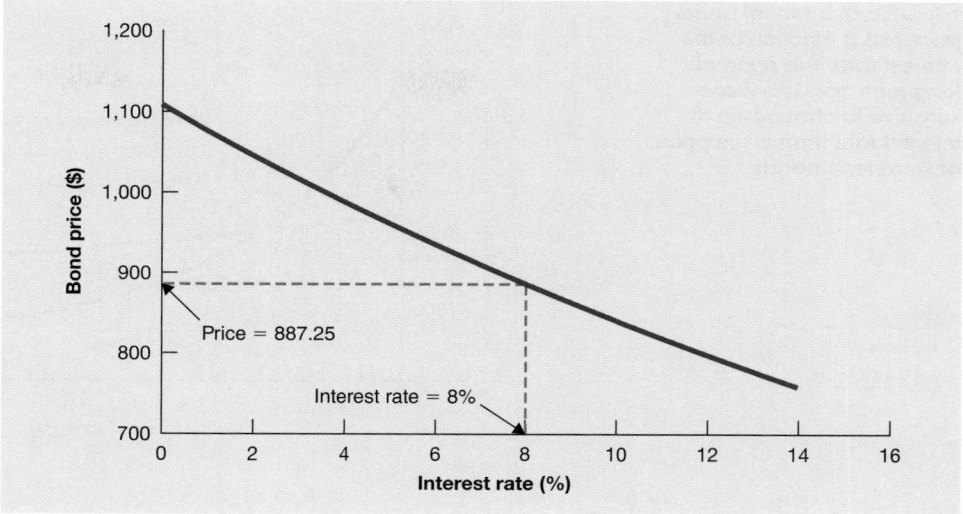

Suppose that interest rates rise. On hearing the news, bond investors appear disconsolate. Why? Don't they like higher interest rates? If you are not sure of the answer, look at Figure 6.4, which shows the present value of the 3.625% Treasury bond for different interest rates. For example, imagine yields soar from 1.25% to 8%. Our bond would then be worth only $887.25, creating a loss to bondholders of some 17%. Conversely, bondholders have reason to celebrate when market interest rates fall. You can see this also from Figure 6.4. For instance, if interest rates fall to .5%, the value of our 3.625% bond would increase to $1,092.82.

Figure 6.4 illustrates a fundamental relationship between interest rates and bond prices: **When the interest rate rises, the present value of the payments to be received by the bondholder falls and bond prices fall. Conversely, a decline in the interest rate increases the present value of those payments and results in a higher price.**

A warning! People sometimes confuse the interest, or coupon, *payment* on the bond with the *interest rate*—that is, the return that investors require. The $36.25 coupon payments on our Treasury bond are *fixed* when the bond is issued. The **coupon rate,** 3.625%, measures the coupon payment ($36.25) as a percentage of the bond's face value ($1,000) and is therefore also fixed. **However, the interest rate changes from day to day. These changes affect the *present value* of the coupon payments but not the payments themselves.**

coupon rate
Annual interest payment as a percentage of face value.

Interest Rate Risk

We have just seen that bond prices fluctuate as interest rates change. In other words, bonds exhibit **interest rate risk.** Bond investors cross their fingers that market interest rates will fall, so that the price of their bond will rise. If they are unlucky and the market interest rate rises, the value of their investment falls.

interest rate risk
The risk in bond prices due to fluctuations in interest rates.

A change in interest rates has only a modest impact on the value of near-term cash flows but a much greater impact on the value of distant cash flows. Therefore any change has a greater impact on the price of long-term bonds than the price of short-term bonds. For example, compare the two curves in Figure 6.5. The green line shows how the value of the 3-year, 3.625% coupon bond varies with the interest rate. The blue line shows how the price of a 30-year, 3.625% bond varies. You can see that the 30-year bond is more sensitive to interest rate fluctuations than the 3-year bond. This should not surprise you. If you buy a 3-year bond and rates then rise, you will be stuck with a bad deal—you could have got a better interest rate if you had waited. However, think how much worse it would be if the loan had been for 30 years rather than 3 years. The

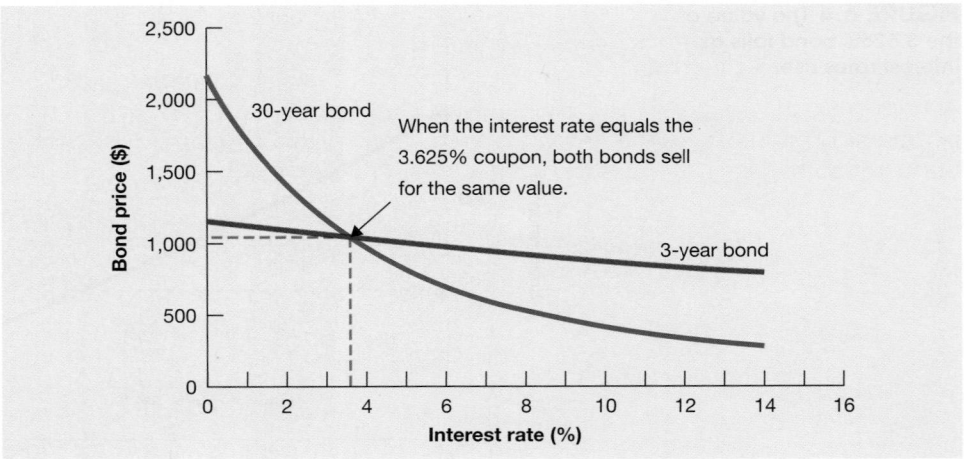

FIGURE 6.5 Plot of bond prices as a function of the interest rate. The price of long-term bonds is more sensitive to changes in the interest rate than is the price of short-term bonds.

longer the loan, the more income you have lost by accepting what turns out to be a low interest rate. This shows up in a bigger decline in the price of the longer-term bond. Of course, there is a flip side to this effect, which you can also see from Figure 6.5. When interest rates fall, the longer- term bond responds with a greater increase in price.

Self-Test 6.4

Suppose that the market interest rate rises overnight from 1.25% to 10%. Calculate the present values of the 3.625%, 3-year bond and of the 3.625%, 30-year bond both before and after this change in interest rates. Confirm that your answers correspond with Figure 6.5. Use your financial calculator or a spreadsheet. You can find a box on bond pricing using Excel on page 170.

6.3 Yield to Maturity

Suppose you are considering the purchase of a 3-year bond with a coupon rate of 10%. Your investment adviser quotes a price for the bond. How do you calculate the rate of return the bond offers?

For bonds priced at face value the answer is easy. The rate of return is the coupon rate. We can check this by setting out the cash flows on your investment:

	Cash Paid to You in Year:			
You Pay	**1**	**2**	**3**	**Rate of Return**
$1,000	$100	$100	$1,100	10%

Notice that in each year you earn 10% on your money ($100/$1,000). In the final year you also get back your original investment of $1,000. Therefore, your total return is 10%, the same as the coupon rate.

Now suppose that the market price of the 3-year bond is $1,136.16. Your cash flows are as follows:

	Cash Paid to You in Year:			
You Pay	**1**	**2**	**3**	**Rate of Return**
$1,136.16	$100	$100	$1,100	?

current yield
Annual coupon payments divided by bond price.

Notice that you are paying out $1,136.16 and receiving an annual income of $100. So your income as a proportion of the initial outlay is $100/$1,136.16 = .088, or 8.8%. This is sometimes called the bond's **current yield.**

However, your *total* return depends on both interest income and any capital gains or losses. A current yield of 8.8% may sound attractive only until you realize that the bond's price must fall. The price today is $1,136.16, but when the bond matures 3 years from now, the bond will sell for its face value, or $1,000. A price decline (i.e., a *capital loss*) of $136.16 is guaranteed, so the overall return over the next 3 years must be less than the 8.8% current yield.

Let us generalize. A bond that is priced above its face value is said to sell at a *premium.* Investors who buy a bond at a premium face a capital loss over the life of the bond, so the return on these bonds is always less than the bond's current yield. A bond priced below face value sells at a *discount.* Investors in discount bonds face a capital *gain* over the life of the bond; the return on these bonds is *greater* than the current yield: **Because it focuses only on current income and ignores prospective price increases or decreases, the *current* yield does not measure the bond's total rate of return. It overstates the return of premium bonds and understates that of discount bonds.**

yield to maturity
Interest rate for which the present value of the bond's payments equals the price.

We need a measure of return that takes account of both coupon payments and the change in a bond's value over its life. The standard measure is called **yield to maturity.** The yield to maturity is the answer to the following question: At what interest rate would the bond be correctly priced? **The yield to maturity is defined as the discount rate that makes the present value of the bond's payments equal to its price.**

If you can buy the 3-year bond at face value, the yield to maturity is the coupon rate, 10%. We can check this by noting that when we discount the cash flows at 10%, the present value of the bond is equal to its $1,000 face value:

$$\text{PV at } 10\% = \frac{\$100}{(1.10)} + \frac{\$100}{(1.10)^2} + \frac{\$1,100}{(1.10)^3} = \$1,000.00$$

But suppose the price of the 3-year bond is $1,136.16. In this case the yield to maturity is only 5%. At that discount rate, the bond's present value equals its actual market price, $1,136.16:

$$\text{PV at } 5\% = \frac{\$100}{(1.05)} + \frac{\$100}{(1.05)^2} + \frac{\$1,100}{(1.05)^3} = \$1,136.16$$

EXAMPLE 6.3 ▶ Calculating Yield to Maturity for the Treasury Bond

We found the value of the 3.625% coupon Treasury bond by discounting at a 1.25% interest rate. We could have phrased the question the other way around: If the price of the bond is $1,069.51, what is the bond's yield to maturity? To calculate the yield, we need to find the discount rate *r* that solves the following equation:

$$\text{Price} = \frac{\$36.25}{(1 + r)} + \frac{\$36.25}{(1 + r)^2} + \frac{\$1,036.25}{(1 + r)^3} = \$1,069.51$$

To compute the yield to maturity, most people use either a financial calculator or a spreadsheet. For this bond, the inputs would be:

	n	i	PV	PMT	FV
Inputs	3		−1069.51	36.25	1000
Compute		1.25			

Now compute *i*, and you should get an answer of 1.25%.

The yield to maturity is a measure of a bond's total return, including both coupon income and capital gain. If you buy the bond today and hold it to maturity, your return will be the yield to maturity. Bond investors often refer loosely to a bond's "yield." It's a safe bet that they are talking about its yield to maturity rather than its current yield.

The only *general* procedure for calculating yield to maturity is trial and error. You guess at an interest rate and calculate the present value of the bond's payments. If the present value is greater than the actual price, your discount rate must have been too low, so you try a higher interest rate (since a higher rate results in a lower PV). Conversely, if PV is less than price, you must reduce the interest rate. When a financial calculator or spreadsheet program finds a bond's yield to maturity, it uses a similar trial-and-error process.

EXAMPLE 6.4 ▶ Yield to Maturity with Semiannual Coupon Payments

Let's redo Example 6.3, but this time we recognize that the coupons are paid semiannually. Instead of three annual coupon payments of $36.25, the bond makes six semiannual payments of $18.125. Therefore, we can find the semiannual yield to maturity as follows:

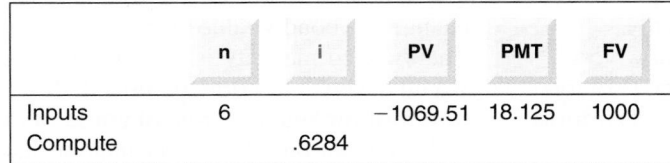

	n	i	PV	PMT	FV
Inputs	6		−1069.51	18.125	1000
Compute		.6284			

This yield to maturity, of course, is a 6-month, not an annual, rate. Bond dealers would typically annualize the semiannual rate by doubling it, so the yield to maturity would be quoted as .628 × 2 = 1.256%. The nearby box shows how to use spreadsheets to find bond prices and yields.

Self-Test 6.5

A 4-year maturity bond with a 14% coupon rate can be bought for $1,200. What is the yield to maturity if the coupon is paid annually? What if it is paid semiannually? You will need a spreadsheet or a financial calculator to answer this question.

6.4 Bond Rates of Return

The yield to maturity is defined as the discount rate that equates the bond's price to the present value of all its promised future cash flows. It measures the rate of return that you will earn if you buy the bond today and hold it to maturity. However, as interest rates fluctuate, the return that you earn in the interim may be very different from the yield to maturity. If interest rates rise in a particular week, month, or year, the price of your bond will fall and your return for that period will be lower than the yield to maturity. Conversely, if rates fall, the price of your bond will rise and your return will be higher. This is emphasized in the following example.

EXAMPLE 6.5 ▶ Rate of Return versus Yield to Maturity

On May 15, 2008, the U.S. Treasury sold $9 billion of 4.375% bonds maturing in February 2038. The bonds were issued at a price of 96.38% and offered a yield to maturity of 4.60%. This was the return to anyone buying at the issue price and holding the bonds to maturity. In the months following the issue the financial crisis reached its peak. Lehman Brothers filed for bankruptcy with assets of $691 billion, and the government poured money into rescuing Fannie Mae, Freddie Mac, AIG, and a host of banks. As investors rushed to the safety of Treasury bonds, their prices soared. By mid-December the price of the 4.375s of 2038 had reached 138.05% of face value and the yield had fallen to 2.5%. Anyone fortunate enough to have bought the bond at the issue price would have made a capital gain of $1,380.50 − $963.80 = $416.70. In addition, on August 15 the bond made its first coupon payment of $21.875 (this is the semiannual payment on the 4.375% coupon bond with a face value of $1,000). Our lucky investor would therefore have earned a 7-month **rate of return** of 45.5%:

rate of return
Total income per period per dollar invested.

$$\text{Rate of return} = \frac{\text{coupon income} + \text{price change}}{\text{investment}}$$

$$= \frac{\$21.875 + \$416.70}{\$963.80} = .455 = 45.5\%$$

Suddenly, government bonds did not seem quite so boring as before.

Self-Test 6.6

Suppose that you purchased 8% coupon, 10-year bonds for $1,324.4 when they were yielding 4% (we assume annual coupon payments). One year later you receive the annual coupon payment of $80, but the yield to maturity has risen to 6%. Confirm that the rate of return on your bond over the year is less than the original 4% yield to maturity.

Is there *any* connection between the yield to maturity and the rate of return during a particular period? Yes: If the bond's yield to maturity remains unchanged during the period, the bond price changes with time so that the total return on the bond is equal to the yield to maturity. The rate of return will be less than the yield to maturity if interest rates rise, and it will be greater than the yield to maturity if interest rates fall.

Self-Test 6.7

Suppose that you buy 8%, 2-year bonds for $1,036.67 when they yield 6%. At the end of the year they still yield 6%. Show that if you continue to hold the bond until maturity, your return in *each* of the two years will also be 6%.

The solid curve in Figure 6.6 plots the price of a 30-year maturity, 6% coupon bond over time assuming that its yield to maturity is currently 4% and does not change. The price declines gradually until the maturity date, when it finally reaches face value. In each period, the price decline offsets the coupon income by just enough to reduce total return to 4%. The dashed curve in Figure 6.6 shows the corresponding price path for a bond with a 2% coupon that sells at a discount to face value. In this case, the coupon income would provide less than a competitive rate of return, so the bond sells below face value. Its price gradually approaches face value, however, and the price gain each year brings its total return up to the market interest rate.

Bond Valuation

Excel and most other spreadsheet programs provide built-in functions to compute bond values and yields. They typically ask you to input both the date you buy the bond (called the *settlement date*) and the maturity date of the bond.

The Excel function for bond value is:

=PRICE(settlement date, maturity date, annual coupon rate, yield to maturity, redemption value as percent of face value, number of coupon payments per year)

(If you can't remember the formula, just remember that you can go to the Formulas tab in Excel, and from the Financial tab pull down the PRICE function, which will prompt you for the necessary inputs.) For our 3.625% coupon bond, we would enter the values shown in the spreadsheet below. Alternatively, we could simply enter the following function in Excel:

=PRICE(DATE(2010,5,15),DATE(2013,5,15),.03625, .0125, 100,1)

The DATE function in Excel, which we use for both the settlement and maturity dates, uses the format DATE(year, month,day).

Notice that the coupon rate and yield to maturity are expressed as decimals, not percentages. In most cases, redemption value will be 100 (i.e., 100% of face value), and the resulting price will be expressed as a percent of face value. Occasionally, however, you may encounter bonds that pay off at a premium or discount to face value. One example would be callable bonds, discussed at the end of the chapter.

The value of the bond assuming annual coupon payments is 106.951 of face value, or $1,069.51. If we wanted to assume semiannual coupon payments, as in Example 6.1, we would simply change the entry in cell B10 to 2 (see column D), and the bond value would change to 106.972% of face value, as we found in that example.

We have also assumed that the first coupon payment comes in exactly one period (either a year or a half-year). In

	A	B	C	D	E	F
1		3.625% annual		3.625% semi-annual		6% annual
2		coupon bond,		coupon bond,		coupon bond,
3		maturing May 2013	Formula in column B	maturing May 2013		30-year maturity
4						
5	Settlement date	5/15/2010	=DATE(2010,5,15)	5/15/2010		1/1/2000
6	Maturity date	5/15/2013	=DATE(2013,5,15)	5/15/2013		1/1/2030
7	Annual coupon rate	0.03625		0.03625		0.06
8	Yield to maturity	0.0125		0.0125		0.07
9	Redemption value (% of face value)	100		100		100
10	Coupon payments per year	1		2		1
11						
12						
13	Bond price (% of par)	106.951	=PRICE(B5,B6,B7,B8,B9,B10)	106.972		87.591

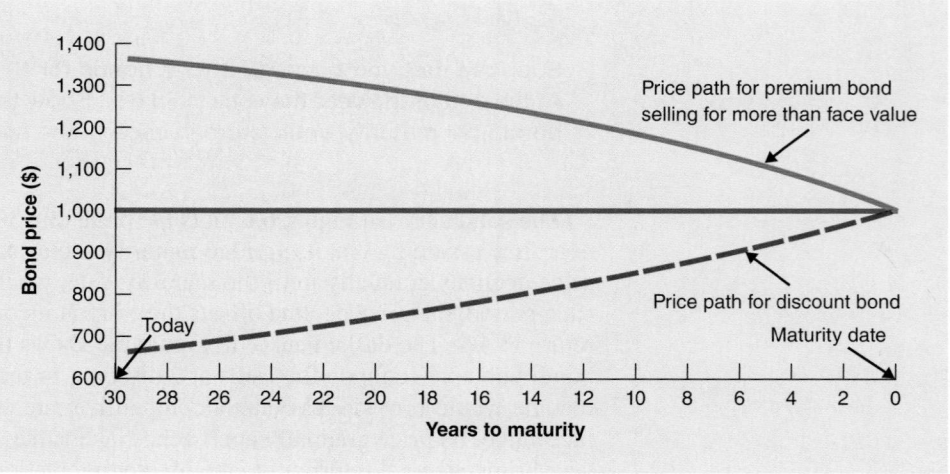

FIGURE 6.6 How bond prices change as they approach maturity, assuming an unchanged yield. Prices of both premium and discount bonds approach face value as their maturity date approaches.

other words, the settlement date is precisely at the beginning of the period. However, the PRICE function will make the necessary adjustments for intraperiod purchase dates.

Suppose now that you wish to find the price of a 30-year maturity bond with a coupon rate of 6% (paid annually) selling at a yield to maturity of 7%. You are not given a specific settlement or maturity date. You can still use the PRICE function to value the bond. Simply choose an arbitrary settlement date (January 1, 2000, is convenient) and let the maturity date be 30 years hence. The appropriate inputs appear in column F of the spreadsheet above, with the resulting price, 87.591% of face value, appearing in cell F13.

Excel also provides a function for yield to maturity. It is:

=YIELD(settlement date, maturity date, annual coupon rate, bond price, redemption value as percent of face value, number of coupon payments per year)

For example, to find the yield to maturity in Example 6.3, we would use column B of the following spreadsheet. If the coupons were paid semiannually, as in Example 6.4, we would change the entry for payments per year to 2 (see cell D8), and the yield would increase to 1.26%.

	A	B	C	D	E
1		**Annual coupons**		**Semiannual coupons**	
2					
3	Settlement date	5/15/2010		5/15/2010	
4	Maturity date	5/15/2013		5/15/2013	
5	Annual coupon rate	0.03625		0.03625	
6	Bond price	106.951		106.951	
7	Redemption value (% of face value)	100		100	
8	Coupon payments per year	1		2	
9					
10	**Yield to maturity (decimal)**	**0.0125**		**0.0126**	
11					
12					
13			The formula entered here is =YIELD(B3,B4,B5,B6,B7,B8)		
14					

You can find this spreadsheet at www.mhhe.com/bmm7e.

6.5 The Yield Curve

When you buy a bond, you buy a package of coupon payments plus the final repayment of face value. But sometimes it is inconvenient to buy things in packages. For example, perhaps you do not need a regular income and would prefer to buy just the final repayment. That's not a problem. The Treasury is prepared to split its bonds into a series of mini-bonds, each of which makes a single payment. These single-payment bonds are called *strips*.

The prices of strips are shown regularly in the financial press or on the Web. For example, in May 2010 it would have cost you $962.67 to buy a strip that just paid out $1,000 in May 2013. The yield on this 3-year mini-bond was 1.28%. In other words, $962.67 \times 1.0128^3 = \$1,000$.

yield curve

Plot of relationship between bond yields to maturity and time to maturity.

Bond investors often draw a plot of the relationship between bond yields and maturity. This is known as the **yield curve.** Treasury strips provide a convenient way to measure this yield curve. For example, if you look at Figure 6.7, you will see that in May 2010 one-year strips offered a yield to maturity of just .13%; those with 20 or more years to run provided a yield of about 4.6%. In this case, the yield curve sloped

FIGURE 6.7 Treasury strips are bonds that make a single payment. The yields on Treasury strips in May 2010 show that investors received a higher yield on longer-term bonds.

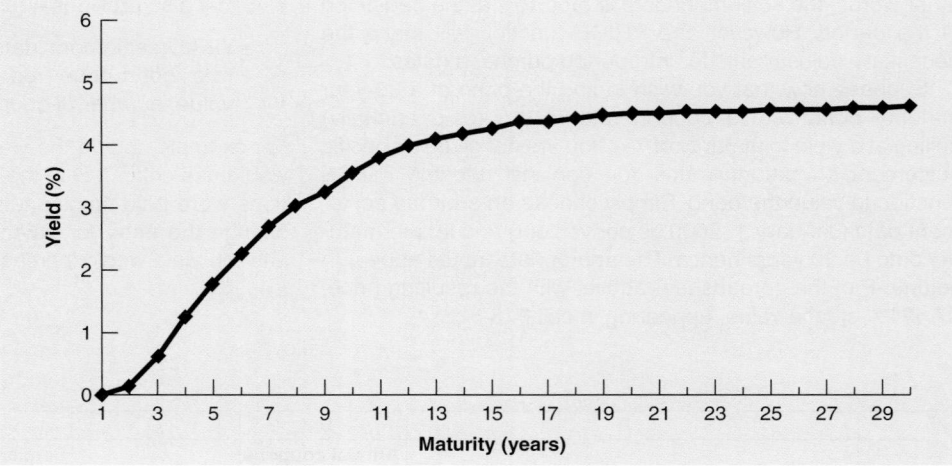

upward.[5] This is usually the case, though sometimes long-term bonds offer *lower* yields, so the curve slopes downward.

But that raises a question. If long-term bonds offered much higher yields, why didn't everyone buy them? Who were the (foolish?) investors who put their money into short-term Treasuries at such low yields?

Even when the yield curve is upward-sloping, investors might rationally stay away from long-term bonds for two reasons. First, the prices of long-term bonds fluctuate much more than prices of short-term bonds. We saw in Figure 6.5 that long-term bond prices are more sensitive to shifting interest rates. A sharp increase in interest rates could easily knock 20% or 30% off long-term bond prices. If investors don't like price fluctuations, they will invest their funds in short-term bonds unless they receive a higher yield to maturity on long-term bonds.

Second, short-term investors can profit if interest rates rise. Suppose you hold a 1-year bond. A year from now, when the bond matures, you can reinvest the proceeds and enjoy whatever rates the bond market offers then. These rates may be high enough to offset the first year's relatively low yield on the 1-year bond. Thus you often see an upward-sloping yield curve when future interest rates are expected to rise.

Self-Test 6.8

One-year Treasury bonds yield 5%, while 2-year bonds yield 6%. You are quite confident that in 1 year's time 1-year bonds will yield 8%. Would you buy the 2-year bond today? Show that there is a better strategy.

Nominal and Real Rates of Interest

In Chapter 5 we drew a distinction between nominal and real rates of interest. The cash flows on the Treasury bonds that we have been discussing are fixed in nominal terms. Investors are sure to receive a fixed interest payment each year, but they do not know what that money will buy them. The *real* interest rate on the Treasury bonds depends on the rate of inflation. For example, if the nominal rate of interest is 8% and the inflation rate is 4%, then the real interest rate is calculated as follows:

$$1 + \text{real interest rate} = \frac{1 + \text{nominal interest rate}}{1 + \text{inflation rate}} = \frac{1.08}{1.04} = 1.0385$$

$$\text{Real interest rate} = .0385 = 3.85\%$$

---

[5] Coupon bonds are like packages of strips. So investors often plot the yield curve using the yields on these packages. For example, you could plot the yields on the small sample of bonds in Table 6.1 against their maturity.

Since the inflation rate is uncertain, so is the real rate of interest on the Treasury bonds.

You *can* nail down a real rate of interest by buying an indexed bond, whose payments are linked to inflation. Indexed bonds have been available in some countries for many years, but they were almost unknown in the United States until 1997 when the U.S. Treasury began to issue inflation-indexed bonds known as *Treasury Inflation-Protected Securities,* or *TIPS.*[6] The real cash flows on TIPS are fixed, but the nominal cash flows (interest and principal) are increased as the consumer price index increases. For example, suppose the U.S. Treasury issues 3% coupon, 2-year TIPS. The *real* cash flows on the 2-year TIPS are therefore:

	Year 1	Year 2
Real cash flows	$30	$1,030

The *nominal* cash flows on TIPS depend on the inflation rate. For example, suppose inflation turns out to be 5% in year 1 and a further 4% in year 2. Then the *nominal* cash flows would be:

	Year 1	Year 2
Nominal cash flows	$30 × 1.05 = $31.50	$1,030 × 1.05 × 1.04 = $1,124.76

These cash payments are just sufficient to provide the holder with a 3% real rate of interest.

As we write this in May 2010, 10-year TIPS offer a yield of 1.2%. This yield is a *real* interest rate. It measures the amount of extra goods your investment will allow you to buy. The 1.2% real yield on TIPS is 2.2% less than the 3.4% yield on nominal 10-year Treasury bonds. If the annual inflation rate proves to be higher than 2.2%, you will earn a higher real return by holding TIPS; if the inflation rate is lower than 2.2%, the reverse will be true.

Real interest rates depend on the supply of savings and the demand for new investment. As this supply-demand balance changes, real interest rates change. But they do so gradually. We can see this by looking at the United Kingdom, where the government has issued indexed bonds since 1982. The red line in Figure 6.8 shows that the (real) interest rate on these bonds has fluctuated within a relatively narrow range.

FIGURE 6.8 The bottom line shows the real yield on long-term indexed bonds issued by the U.K. government. The top line shows the yield on U.K. government long-term nominal bonds. Notice that the real yield has been much more stable than the nominal yield.

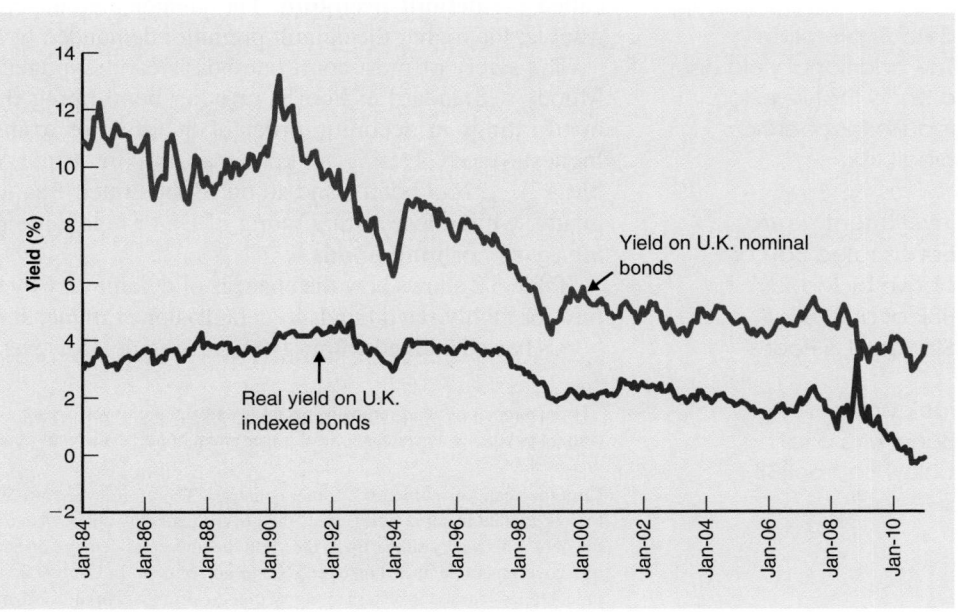

---

[6] Indexed bonds were not completely unknown in the United States before 1997. For example, in 1780 American Revolution soldiers were compensated with indexed bonds that paid the value of "five bushels of corn, 68 pounds and four-sevenths part of a pound of beef, ten pounds of sheep's wool, and sixteen pounds of sole leather."

Suppose that investors revise upward their forecast of inflation by 1%. How will this affect interest rates? If investors are concerned about the purchasing power of their money, the changed forecast should not affect the real rate of interest. The *nominal* interest rate must therefore rise by 1% to compensate investors for the higher inflation prospects.

The blue line in Figure 6.8 shows the nominal rate of interest in the United Kingdom since 1985. You can see that the nominal rate is much more variable than the real rate. For example, when investors were worried about inflation in the late 1980s, the nominal interest rate was about 7 percentage points above the real rate. Notice how low the real interest rate has been recently. By the fall of 2010 the yield on index bonds had fallen below zero.

6.6 Corporate Bonds and the Risk of Default

Our focus so far has been on U.S. Treasury bonds. But the federal government is not the only issuer of bonds. State and local governments borrow by selling bonds.[7] So do corporations. Many foreign governments and corporations also borrow in the United States. At the same time U.S. corporations may borrow dollars or other currencies by issuing their bonds in other countries. For example, they may issue dollar bonds in London that are then sold to investors throughout the world.

There is an important distinction between bonds issued by corporations and those issued by the U.S. Treasury. National governments don't go bankrupt—they just print more money.[8] So investors rarely worry that the U.S. Treasury will default on its bonds. However, there is some chance that corporations may get into financial difficulties and may default on their bonds. Thus the payments promised to corporate bondholders represent a best-case scenario: The firm will never pay more than the promised cash flows, but in hard times it may pay less.

default (or credit) risk
The risk that a bond issuer may default on its bonds.

The risk that a bond issuer may default on its obligations is called **default risk** (or **credit risk**). Companies need to compensate for this default risk by promising a higher rate of interest on their bonds. The difference between the promised yield on a corporate bond and the yield on a U.S. Treasury bond with the same coupon and maturity is called the **default premium.** The greater the chance that the company will get into trouble, the higher the default premium demanded by investors.

default premium
The additional yield on a bond that investors require for bearing credit risk.

The safety of most corporate bonds can be judged from bond ratings provided by Moody's, Standard & Poor's, or other bond-rating firms. Table 6.2 lists the possible bond ratings in declining order of quality. For example, the bonds that receive the highest Moody's rating are known as *Aaa* (or "triple A") bonds. Then come *Aa* ("double A"), *A, Baa* bonds, and so on. Bonds rated Baa and above are called **investment grade,** while those with a rating of Ba or below are referred to as *speculative grade, high-yield,* or **junk bonds.**[9]

investment grade
Bonds rated Baa or above by Moody's or BBB or above by Standard & Poor's.

Table 6.2 shows how the chances of default vary by bond rating. You can see that it is rare for highly rated bonds to default. For example, since 1981 only 6 in 1,000 triple-A bonds have defaulted within 10 years of issue. However, when an investment-grade bond

junk bond
Bond with a rating below Baa or BBB.

---

[7] These *municipal bonds* enjoy a special tax advantage; investors are exempt from federal income tax on the coupon payments on state and local government bonds. As a result, investors are prepared to accept lower yields on this debt.

[8] But they can't print money of other countries. Therefore, when a foreign government borrows dollars, investors worry that in some future crisis the government may not be able to come up with enough dollars to repay the debt. This worry shows up in the yield that investors demand on such debt. For example, in 2002, the Argentine government defaulted on over $100 billion of debt. In Chapter 2 we saw also how the Greek government's indebtedness caused investors to worry that governments in the eurozone might be forced to default on their euro borrowings.

[9] Rating agencies also distinguish between bonds in the same class. For example, the most secure A-rated bonds would be rated A1 by Moody's and A+ by Standard & Poor's. The least secure bonds in this risk class would be rated A3 by Moody's and A− by Standard & Poor's.

TABLE 6.2 Key to Moody's and Standard & Poor's bond ratings. The highest-quality bonds are rated triple A, then come double-A bonds, and so on.

Moody's	Standard & Poor's	Percent of Bonds Defaulting within 10 Years of Issue	Safety
Investment Grade Bonds			
Aaa	AAA	0.6%	The strongest rating; ability to repay interest and principal is very strong.
Aa	AA	0.8	Very strong likelihood that interest and principal will be repaid.
A	A	1.9	Strong ability to repay, but some vulnerability to changes in circumstances.
Baa	BBB	5.2	Adequate capacity to repay; more vulnerability to changes in economic circumstances.
High-Yield Bonds			
Ba	BB	16.0	Considerable uncertainty about ability to repay.
B	B	28.4	Likelihood of interest and principal payments over sustained periods is questionable.
Caa	CCC	} 50.3	Bonds that may already be in default or in danger of imminent default.
Ca	CC		
C	C	—	Little prospect for interest or principal on the debt ever to be repaid.

is downgraded or defaults, the shock waves can be considerable. For example, in May 2001 WorldCom sold $11.8 billion of bonds with an investment-grade rating. Within little more than a year WorldCom filed for bankruptcy, and its bondholders lost more than 80% of their investment. For low-grade issues, defaults are more common. For example, over half of the bonds that were rated CCC by Standard & Poor's at issue have defaulted within 10 years.[10]

Table 6.3 shows prices and yields to maturity on June 1, 2010, for a sample of the most heavily traded corporate bonds. Notice that, whereas prices of Treasury bonds are quoted in thirty-seconds, the prices of corporate bonds are quoted as decimals. As you would expect, corporate bonds offer higher yields than U.S. Treasuries. You can see that the yield differential rises as safety falls off.

Investors also prefer liquid bonds that they can easily buy and sell. So additionally we find that the heavily traded bonds are more highly prized and offer lower yields than their less liquid brethren. During the banking crisis of 2007–2009 the market for many corporate bonds effectively dried up and investors found it almost impossible to sell their holdings.

Figure 6.9 shows the yield spread between corporate bonds and Treasuries since 1953. During periods of uncertainty the spread shoots up. For example, as worries about the economy intensified in 2008, the promised yield on Baa bonds climbed to

TABLE 6.3 Prices and yields of a sample of heavily traded corporate bonds, June 1, 2010

Issuer Name	Coupon, %	Maturity	Moody's Rating	Last Price	Yield, %
JPMorgan Chase	3.700	Jan 2015	Aa	101.512	3.344
Cisco Systems	5.900	Feb 2039	A	109.106	5.280
Goldman Sachs	5.375	Mar 2020	A	96.287	5.878
Time Warner	4.875	Mar 2020	Baa	100.650	4.790
NewPage Corp.	11.375	Dec 2014	B	93.000	13.460
First Data Corp.	9.875	Sep 2015	Caa	80.125	15.494

Source: **www.wsj.com**.

---

[10] Standard & Poor's, "Default, Transition, and Recovery: 2008 Global Annual Corporate Default Study and Rating Transitions, February 2009," **www.standardandpoors.com**.

Insuring against Default

Wouldn't it be nice if you could insure yourself against a possible default on your bonds? Well, you can; you do so by buying a *credit default swap (CDS).* You pay an annual insurance premium or *spread,* and in return the insurer will make good any loss that you incur if there is a default. For a few cents you can even insure your Treasury bonds against default.

As you would expect, when investors become concerned about default, the cost of insurance soars. Look, for example, at the figure below, which shows the annual fee for insuring the senior bonds of Bank of America, Citigroup, and JPMorgan Chase. Notice that for the early years the spreads hover around .2%, but as the banking crisis reached its peak, the annual cost of insuring Citigroup debt reached nearly 7%.

Annual cost (CDS spread) of insuring 5-year senior bank bonds.

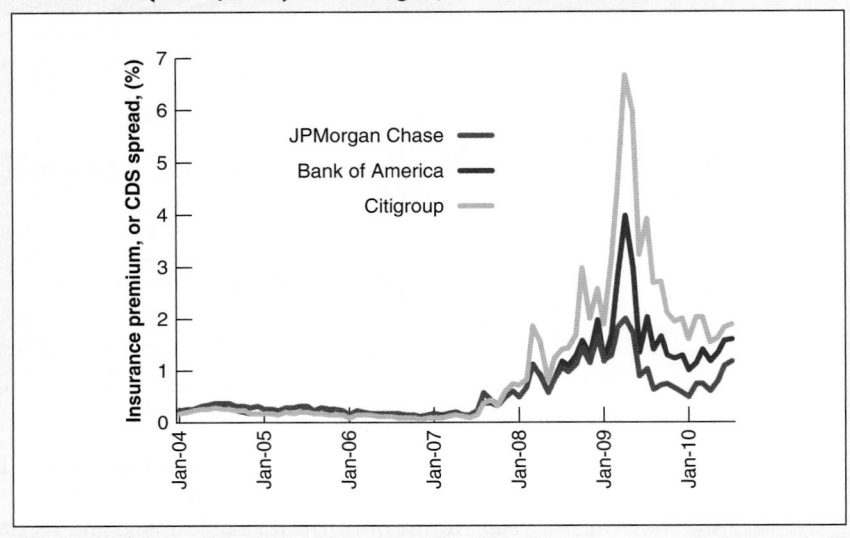

Source: online.thomsonreuters.com/datastream

6% above the yield on Treasuries. You might have been tempted by the higher promised yields on the lower-grade bonds. But remember, these bonds do not always keep their promises. By the way, you can, if you wish, insure your bonds against default. The nearby box explains how.

FIGURE 6.9 Yield spreads between corporate and 10-year Treasury bonds

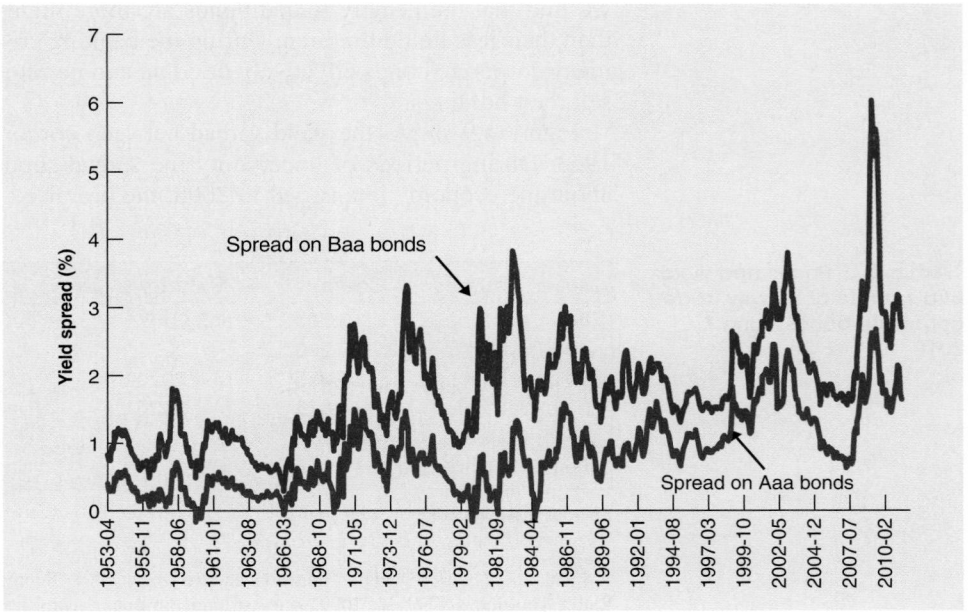

| EXAMPLE 6.6 ▶ | Promised versus Expected Yield to Maturity |

Bad Bet Inc. issued bonds several years ago with a coupon rate (paid annually) of 10% and face value of $1,000. The bonds are due to mature in 6 years. However, the firm is currently in bankruptcy proceedings, the firm has ceased to pay interest, and the bonds sell for only $200. Based on *promised* cash flow, the yield to maturity on the bond is 63.9%. (On your calculator, set PV = −200, FV = 1,000, PMT = 100, $n = 6$, and compute i.) But this calculation is based on the very unlikely possibility that the firm will resume paying interest and come out of bankruptcy. Suppose that the most likely outcome is that after 3 years of litigation, during which no interest will be paid, debtholders will receive 27 cents on the dollar—that is, they will receive $270 for each bond with $1,000 face value. In this case the expected return on the bond is 10.5%. (On your calculator, set PV = −200, FV = 270, PMT = 0, $n = 3$, and compute i.) When default is a real possibility, the promised yield can depart considerably from the expected return.

Variations in Corporate Bonds

Most corporate bonds are similar to the Treasury bonds that we examined earlier in the chapter. In other words, they promise to make a fixed nominal coupon payment for each year until maturity, at which point they also promise to repay the face value. However, you will find that there is greater variety in the design of corporate bonds. We will return to this issue in Chapter 14, but here are a few types of corporate bonds that you may encounter.

Zero-Coupon Bonds Corporations sometimes issue zero-coupon bonds. In this case, investors receive $1,000 face value at the maturity date but do not receive a regular coupon payment. In other words, the bond has a coupon rate of zero. The bonds are like Treasury strips. They are issued at prices well below face value, and the investor's return comes from the difference between the purchase price and the payment of face value at maturity.

Floating-Rate Bonds Sometimes the coupon rate can change over time. For example, floating-rate bonds make coupon payments that are tied to some measure of current market rates. The rate might be reset once a year to the current short-term Treasury rate plus 2%. So if the Treasury rate at the start of the year is 6%, the bond's coupon rate over the next year is set at 8%. This arrangement means that the bond's coupon rate always approximates current market interest rates.

Convertible Bonds If you buy a convertible bond, you can choose later to exchange it for a specified number of shares of common stock. For example, a convertible bond that is issued at face value of $1,000 may be convertible into 50 shares of the firm's stock. Because convertible bonds offer the opportunity to participate in any price appreciation of the company's stock, investors will accept lower interest rates on convertible bonds.

Bond issuers are always trying to devise new types of bonds that they hope will appeal to a particular clientele of investors. Just to give you a flavor of the inventiveness of financial managers, here is an example of one innovative bond.

Managers of life insurance companies agonize about the possibility of a pandemic or other disaster that results in a sharp increase in the death rate. In 2006 the French insurance company Axa sought to protect itself against this danger by issuing nearly €350 million of *mortality bonds*. Axa's bonds offered a tempting yield, but the bondholders will lose their entire investment if death rates for 2 consecutive years are 10% or more above expectations.

SUMMARY

What are the differences between the bond's coupon rate, current yield, and yield to maturity? (*LO1*)

A bond is a long-term debt of a government or corporation. When you own a bond, you receive a fixed interest payment each year until the bond matures. This payment is known as the coupon. The **coupon rate** is the annual coupon payment expressed as a fraction of the bond's **face value.** At maturity the bond's face value is repaid. In the United States most bonds have a face value of $1,000. The **current yield** is the annual coupon payment expressed as a percentage of the bond price. The **yield to maturity** measures the average rate of return to an investor who purchases the bond and holds it until maturity, accounting for coupon income as well as the difference between purchase price and face value.

How can one find the market price of a bond given its yield to maturity or find a bond's yield given its price? Why do prices and yields vary inversely? (*LO2*)

Bonds are valued by discounting the coupon payments and the final repayment by the yield to maturity on comparable bonds. The bond payments discounted at the bond's yield to maturity equal the bond price. You may also start with the bond price and ask what interest rate the bond offers. The interest rate that equates the present value of bond payments to the bond price is the yield to maturity. Because present values are lower when discount rates are higher, price and yield to maturity vary inversely.

Why do bonds exhibit interest rate risk? (*LO3*)

Bond prices are subject to **interest rate risk,** rising when market interest rates fall and falling when market rates rise. Long-term bonds exhibit greater interest rate risk than short-term bonds.

Why do investors pay attention to bond ratings and demand a higher interest rate for bonds with low ratings? (*LO4*)

Investors demand higher promised yields if there is a high probability that the borrower will run into trouble and default. **Credit risk** implies that the promised yield to maturity on the bond is higher than the expected yield. The additional yield investors require for bearing credit risk is called the **default premium.** Bond ratings measure the bond's credit risk.

LISTING OF EQUATIONS

6.1   Bond price = PV(coupons) + PV(face value)
   = (coupon × annuity factor) + (face value × discount factor)

6.2   Bond rate of return = $\dfrac{\text{coupon income} + \text{price change}}{\text{investment}}$

QUESTIONS

QUIZ

1. **Bond Yields.** A 30-year Treasury bond is issued with face value of $1,000, paying interest of $60 per year. If market yields increase shortly after the T-bond is issued, what happens to the bond's
    a. coupon rate? (*LO1*)
    b. price? (*LO1*)
    c. yield to maturity? (*LO1*)
    d. current yield? (*LO1*)

2. **Bond Yields.** If a bond with face value of $1,000 and a coupon rate of 8% is selling at a price of $970, is the bond's yield to maturity more or less than 8%? (*LO1*)

3. **Bond Yields.** A bond with face value $1,000 has a current yield of 6% and a coupon rate of 8%. What is the bond's price? (*LO1*)

4. **Bond Pricing.** A 6-year Circular File bond pays interest of $80 annually and sells for $950. What are its coupon rate and yield to maturity? (*LO2*)

5. **Bond Pricing.** If Circular File (see Quiz Question 4) wants to issue a new 6-year bond at face value, what coupon rate must the bond offer? (*LO2*)

6. **Bond Yields.** A bond has 8 years until maturity, a coupon rate of 8%, and sells for $1,100.
   a. What is the current yield on the bond? (*LO1*)
   b. What is the yield to maturity? (*LO2*)

7. **Coupon Rate.** General Matter's outstanding bond issue has a coupon rate of 10%, and it sells at a yield to maturity of 9.25%. The firm wishes to issue additional bonds to the public at face value. What coupon rate must the new bonds offer in order to sell at face value? (*LO2*)

8. **Financial Pages.** Turn back to Table 6.1. What is the current yield of the 8.75% 2020 maturity bond? Why is this more than its yield to maturity? (*LO1*)

PRACTICE PROBLEMS

9. **Bond Prices and Returns.** One bond has a coupon rate of 8%, another a coupon rate of 12%. Both bonds have 10-year maturities and sell at a yield to maturity of 10%. If their yields to maturity next year are still 10%, what is the rate of return on each bond? Does the higher coupon bond give a higher rate of return? (*LO2*)

10. **Bond Returns.** (*LO2*)
    a. If the bond in Quiz Question 6 has a yield to maturity of 8% 1 year from now, what will its price be?
    b. What will be the rate of return on the bond?
    c. If the inflation rate during the year is 3%, what is the real rate of return on the bond?

11. **Bond Pricing.** A General Electric bond carries a coupon rate of 8%, has 9 years until maturity, and sells at a yield to maturity of 7%.
    a. What interest payments do bondholders receive each year? (*LO1*)
    b. At what price does the bond sell? (Assume annual interest payments.) (*LO2*)
    c. What will happen to the bond price if the yield to maturity falls to 6%? (*LO2*)

12. **Bond Pricing.** A 30-year maturity bond with face value of $1,000 makes annual coupon payments and has a coupon rate of 8%. What is the bond's yield to maturity if the bond is selling for
    a. $900? (*LO2*)
    b. $1,000? (*LO2*)
    c. $1,100? (*LO2*)

13. **Bond Pricing.** Repeat the previous problem assuming semiannual coupon payments. (*LO2*)

14. **Bond Pricing.** Fill in the table below for the following zero-coupon bonds. The face value of each bond is $1,000. (*LO2*)

Price	Maturity (years)	Yield to Maturity
$300	30	—
300	—	8%
—	10	10

15. **Consol Bonds.** Perpetual Life Corp. has issued consol bonds with coupon payments of $60. (Consols pay interest forever and never mature. They are perpetuities.) If the required rate of return on these bonds at the time they were issued was 6%, at what price were they sold to the public? If the required return today is 10%, at what price do the consols sell? (*LO2*)

16. **Bond Pricing.** Sure Tea Co. has issued 9% annual coupon bonds that are now selling at a yield to maturity of 10% and current yield of 9.8375%. What is the remaining maturity of these bonds? (*LO2*)

17. **Bond Pricing.** Large Industries bonds sell for $1,065.15. The bond life is 9 years, and the yield to maturity is 7%. What must be the coupon rate on the bonds? (*LO2*)

18. **Bond Prices and Yields.**
    a. Several years ago, Castles in the Sand, Inc., issued bonds at face value at a yield to maturity of 7%. Now, with 8 years left until the maturity of the bonds, the company has run into hard

times and the yield to maturity on the bonds has increased to 15%. What has happened to the price of the bond? (*LO2*)

b. Suppose that investors believe that Castles can make good on the promised coupon payments, but that the company will go bankrupt when the bond matures and the principal comes due. The expectation is that investors will receive only 80% of face value at maturity. If they buy the bond today, what yield to maturity do they expect to receive? (*LO4*)

19. **Bond Returns.** You buy an 8% coupon, 10-year maturity bond for $980. A year later, the bond price is $1,200. (*LO2*)

a. What is the new yield to maturity on the bond?
b. What is your rate of return over the year?

20. **Bond Returns.** You buy an 8% coupon, 20-year maturity bond when its yield to maturity is 9%. A year later, the yield to maturity is 10%. What is your rate of return over the year? (*LO3*)

21. **Interest Rate Risk.** Consider three bonds with 8% coupon rates, all selling at face value. The short-term bond has a maturity of 4 years, the intermediate-term bond has maturity 8 years, and the long-term bond has maturity 30 years. (*LO3*)

a. What will happen to the price of each bond if their yields increase to 9%?
b. What will happen to the price of each bond if their yields decrease to 7%?
c. What do you conclude about the relationship between time to maturity and the sensitivity of bond prices to interest rates?

22. **Rate of Return.** A 2-year maturity bond with face value of $1,000 makes annual coupon payments of $80 and is selling at face value. What will be the rate of return on the bond if its yield to maturity at the end of the year is

a. 6%? (*LO3*)
b. 8%? (*LO3*)
c. 10%? (*LO3*)

23. **Rate of Return.** A bond that pays coupons annually is issued with a coupon rate of 4%, maturity of 30 years, and a yield to maturity of 7%. What rate of return will be earned by an investor who purchases the bond and holds it for 1 year if the bond's yield to maturity at the end of the year is 8%? (*LO3*)

24. **Credit Risk.** A bond's credit rating provides a guide to its risk. Long-term bonds rated Aa currently offer yields to maturity of 7.5%. A-rated bonds sell at yields of 7.8%. If a 10-year bond with a coupon rate of 7% is downgraded by Moody's from Aa to A rating, what is the likely effect on the bond price? (*LO4*)

25. **Real Returns.** Suppose that you buy a 1-year maturity bond for $1,000 that will pay you back $1,000 plus a coupon payment of $70 at the end of the year. What real rate of return will you earn if the inflation rate is

a. 2%? (*LO3*)
b. 4%? (*LO3*)
c. 6%? (*LO3*)
d. 8%? (*LO3*)

26. **Real Returns.** Now suppose that the bond in the previous problem is a TIPS (inflation-indexed) bond with a coupon rate of 4%. What will the cash flow provided by the bond be for each of the four inflation rates? What will be the real and nominal rates of return on the bond in each scenario? (*LO1*)

27. **Real Returns.** Now suppose the TIPS bond in the previous problem is a 2-year maturity bond. What will be the bondholder's cash flows in each year in each of the inflation scenarios? (*LO1*)

CHALLENGE PROBLEMS

28. **Interest Rate Risk.** Suppose interest rates increase from 8% to 9%. Which bond will suffer the greater percentage decline in price: a 30-year bond paying annual coupons of 8% or a 30-year zero-coupon bond? Can you explain intuitively why the zero exhibits greater interest rate risk even though it has the same maturity as the coupon bond? (*LO3*)

Templates can be found at
www.mhhe.com/bmm7e.

29. **Interest Rate Risk.** Consider two 30-year maturity bonds. Bond A has a coupon rate of 4%, while bond B has a coupon rate of 12%. Both bonds pay their coupons semiannually. (*LO3*)

   a. Construct an Excel spreadsheet showing the prices of each of these bonds for yields to maturity ranging from 2% to 15% at intervals of 1%. Column A should show the yield to maturity (ranging from 2% to 15%), and columns B and C should compute the prices of the two bonds (using Excel's bond price function) at each interest rate.

   b. In columns D and E, compute the percentage difference between the bond price and its value when yield to maturity is 8%.

   c. Plot the values in columns D and E as a function of the interest rate. Which bond's price is proportionally more sensitive to interest rate changes?

   d. Can you explain the result you found in part (c)? *Hint:* Is there any sense in which a bond that pays a high coupon rate has lower "average" or "effective" maturity than a bond that pays a low coupon rate?

Templates can be found at
www.mhhe.com/bmm7e.

30. **Yield Curve.** In Figure 6.7, we saw a plot of the yield curve on stripped Treasury bonds and pointed out that bonds of different maturities may sell at different yields to maturity. In principle, when we are valuing a stream of cash flows, each cash flow should be discounted by the yield appropriate to its particular maturity. Suppose the yield curve on (zero-coupon) Treasury strips is as follows:

Time to Maturity	YTM
1 year	4.0%
2	5.0
3–5	5.5
6–10	6.0

You wish to value a 10-year bond with a coupon rate of 10%, paid annually. (*LO2*)

   a. Set up an Excel spreadsheet to value each of the bond's annual cash flows using this table of yields. Add up the present values of the bond's 10 cash flows to obtain the bond price.

   b. What is the bond's yield to maturity?

   c. Compare the yield to maturity of the 10-year, 10% coupon bond to that of a 10-year zero-coupon bond or Treasury strip. Which is higher? Why does this result make sense given this yield curve?

WEB EXERCISES

1. Log on to www.investopedia.com to find a simple calculator for working out bond prices. Check whether a change in yield has a greater effect on the price of a long-term or a short-term bond.

2. When we plotted the yield curve in Figure 6.7, we used the prices of Treasury strips. You can find current prices of strips by logging on to the *Wall Street Journal* Web site (www.wsj.com) and clicking on Markets Data Center and then Bonds, Rates and Credit Markets. Try plotting the yields on stripped coupons against maturity. Do they currently increase or decline with maturity? Can you explain why? You can also use the *Wall Street Journal* site to compare the yields on nominal Treasury bonds with those on TIPS. Suppose that you are confident that inflation will be 3% per year. Which bonds are the better buy?

3. You can find the most recent bond rating for many companies by logging on to finance.yahoo.com and going to the Bond Center. Find the bond rating for some major companies. Were they investment-grade or below?

4. In Figure 6.9 we showed how bonds with greater credit risk have promised higher yields to maturity. This yield spread goes up when the economic outlook is particularly uncertain. You can check how much extra yield lower-grade bonds offer today by logging on to www.federalreserve.gov and comparing the yields on Aaa and Baa bonds. How does the spread in yields compare with the spread in November 2008 at the height of the financial crisis?

SOLUTIONS TO SELF-TEST QUESTIONS

6.1   The asked price is 111 $^{23}/_{32}$. So one bond would cost $1,117.19. If the bond cost $1,106.25, its price would be quoted as 110:20 (i.e., 110 $^{20}/_{32}$).

6.2   a. The asked price is 144 $^{19}/_{32}$% of face value, or $1445.94.
     b. The bid price is 144 $^{17}/_{32}$% of face value, or $1445.31.
     c. The annual coupon is 8.75% of face value, or $87.50, a year.
     d. The yield to maturity, based on the asked price, is given as 3.44%.

6.3   The coupon is 9% of $1,000, or $90 a year. First value the 6-year annuity of coupons:

$$PV = \$90 \times \text{(6-year annuity factor)}$$

$$= \$90 \times \left[\frac{1}{.12} - \frac{1}{.12(1.12)^6} \right]$$

$$= \$90 \times 4.1114 = \$370.03$$

Then value the final payment and add:

$$PV = \frac{\$1,000}{(1.12)^6} = \$506.63$$

$$PV \text{ of bond} = \$370.03 + \$506.63 = \$876.66$$

Using a financial calculator, your inputs would be: $n = 6$; $i = 12$; PMT = 90; FV = 1000. Now compute PV.

6.4   At an interest rate of 1.25%, the 3-year bond sells for $1,069.51. If the interest rate jumps to 10%, the bond price falls to $841.46, a decline of 21.3%. The 30-year bond sells for $1,591.11 when the interest rate is 1.25%, but its price falls to $399.03 at an interest rate of 10%, a much larger percentage decline of 74.9%. Thank goodness, interest rates rarely change by this amount overnight.

6.5   The yield to maturity assuming annual coupons is about 8%, because the present value of the bond's cash returns is $1,199, almost exactly $1,200, when discounted at 8%:

$$PV = PV(\text{coupons}) + PV(\text{final payment})$$

$$= (\text{coupon} \times \text{annuity factor}) + (\text{face value} \times \text{discount factor})$$

$$= \$140 \times \left[\frac{1}{.08} - \frac{1}{.08(1.08)^4} \right] + \$1,000 \times \frac{1}{1.08^4}$$

$$= \$463.70 + \$735.03 = \$1,199$$

To obtain a more precise solution on your calculator, these would be your inputs:

	Annual Payments	Semiannual Payments
n	4	8
PV	−1,200	−1,200
FV	1000	1000
PMT	140	70

Compute i to find yield to maturity (annual payments) = 7.97%. Yield to maturity (semiannual payments) = 4.026% per 6 months, which would be reported in the financial press as 8.05% annual yield.

6.6   With a yield of 4%, the 8% coupon, 10-year bond sells for $1,324.44. At the end of the year, the bond has only 9 years to maturity and investors demand an interest rate of 6%. Therefore, the value of the bond becomes $1,136.03. (On your calculator, input $n = 9$; $i = 6$; PMT = 80; FV = 1000; compute PV.)

    You therefore have received a coupon payment of $80 but have a capital *loss* of 1,324.44 − 1,136.03 = $188.41. Your total return is therefore (80 − 188.41)/1,324.44 = −.082, or −8.2%. Because interest rates rose over the year, your return was *less* than the yield to maturity.

6.7　　By the end of the year, the bond will have only 1 year left until maturity. So its price will be $1,080/1.06 = $1,018.87. You will therefore receive a coupon payment of $80 and make a capital loss of $1,036.67 − $1,018.87 = $17.80. Your total return over the year is (80 − 17.80)/1,036.67 = .060, or 6.0%. When the bond matures, you receive the face value of $1,000. So in the final year you receive a coupon payment of $80 and make a capital loss of $18.87. Your total return over this year is (80 − 18.87)/1,018.87 = .060, or 6.0%. When the yield to maturity does not change, your return is equal to the yield to maturity.

6.8　　If you invest in a 2-year bond, you will have $1,000 \times 1.06^2 = $1,123.60$. If you are right in your forecast about 1-year rates, then an investment in 1-year bonds will produce $1,000 \times 1.05 \times 1.08 = $1,134.00$ by the end of 2 years. You would do better to invest in the 1-year bond.

Valuing Stocks

LEARNING OBJECTIVES

After studying this chapter, you should be able to:

(1) Understand the stock trading reports on the Internet or in the financial pages of the newspaper.

(2) Calculate the present value of a stock given forecasts of future dividends and future stock price.

(3) Use stock valuation formulas to infer the expected rate of return on a common stock.

(4) Interpret price-earnings ratios.

(5) Understand what professionals mean when they say that there are no free lunches on Wall Street.

RELATED WEB SITES FOR THIS CHAPTER CAN BE FOUND AT WWW.MHHE.COM/BMM7E.

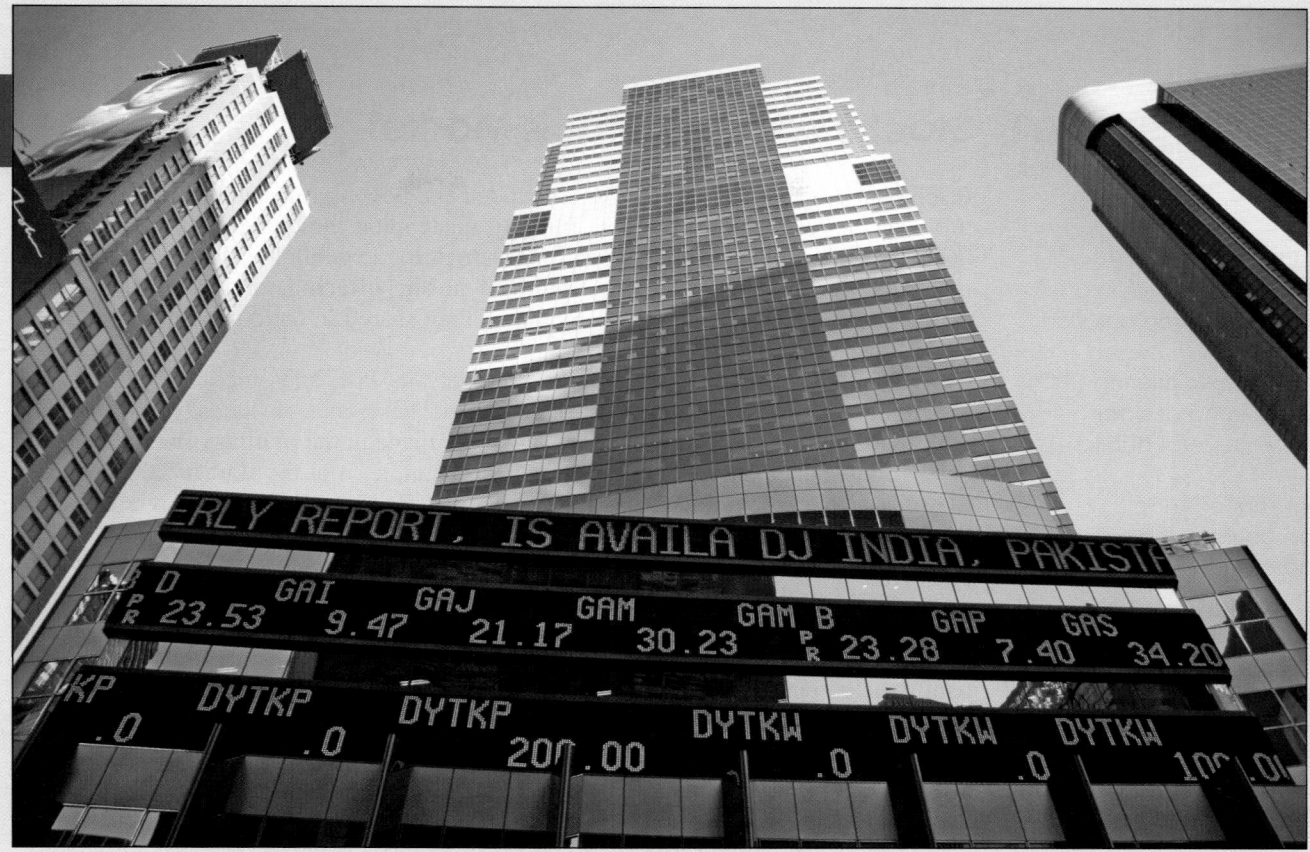

Share prices on the New York Stock Exchange. But what determines how much investors are prepared to pay for these shares?

A corporation can raise cash for investment by borrowing or by selling new shares of common stock to investors. If it borrows, it has a fixed obligation to repay the lender. If it issues shares, there is no fixed obligation, but the new stockholders become partial owners of the firm. All old and new stockholders share in its fortunes, in proportion to the number of shares that they hold. In this chapter, we take a first look at common stocks, the stock market, and the principles of stock valuation.

We start by looking at how stocks are bought and sold. Then we look at what determines stock prices and how stock valuation formulas can be used to infer the rate of return that investors are expecting. We will see how the firm's investment opportunities are reflected in its stock price and why stock market analysts focus so much attention on the price-earnings, or P/E, ratio of the company.

Why should you care how stocks are valued? After all, if you want to know the value of a firm's stock, you can look up the stock price on the Internet or in *The Wall Street Journal.* But you need to know what determines prices for at least two reasons. First, you may need to value the common stock of a business that is not traded on a stock exchange. For example, you may be the founder of a successful business that wishes to sell stock to the public for the first time. You and your advisers need to estimate the price at which those shares can be sold.

Second, in order to make good capital budgeting decisions, corporations need to have some understanding of how the market values firms. A project is attractive if it increases shareholder wealth. But you can't judge that unless you know how shares are valued.

There may be a third reason why you would like to know how stocks are valued. You may be hoping that the knowledge will allow you to make a killing on Wall Street. It's a pleasant thought, but we will see that even professional investors find it difficult to outsmart the competition and earn consistently superior returns.

7.1   Stocks and the Stock Market

common stock
Ownership shares in a publicly held corporation.

initial public offering (IPO)
First offering of stock to the general public.

primary offering
The corporation sells shares in the firm.

primary market
Market for the sale of new securities by corporations.

secondary market
Market in which previously issued securities are traded among investors.

In Chapter 1 we saw how FedEx was founded and how it grew and prospered. To fund this growth, FedEx needed capital. Initially, that capital came largely from borrowing, but in 1978 FedEx sold shares of **common stock** to the public for the first time. Those investors who bought shares in the **initial public offering,** or **IPO,** became part-owners of the business, and as shareholders they shared in the company's future successes and setbacks.[1]

A company's initial public offering is rarely its last, and since 1978 FedEx has raised more capital by selling additional shares. These sales of shares by the company are called **primary offerings** and are said to be made in the **primary market.**

Owning shares is a risky occupation. For example, if at the start of 2009 you had the misfortune to buy shares in Pacific Capital Bancorp or in the movie company RHI Entertainment, you would have lost 95% of your money by the year-end. You can understand, therefore, why investors would be reluctant to buy shares if they were forced to tie the knot with a particular company forever. So large companies usually arrange for their common stock to be listed on a stock exchange so that investors can trade shares among themselves. Exchanges are really markets for second-hand stocks, but they prefer to describe themselves as **secondary markets,** which sounds more important.

The two principal stock markets in the United States are the New York Stock Exchange (NYSE) and NASDAQ.[2] In addition, there are many computer networks called *electronic communication networks (ECNs),* that connect traders with each other. All of these markets compete vigorously for the business of traders and just as vigorously tout the advantages of their own trading venue. The volume of trades in these markets is immense. For example, every day the NYSE alone trades more than 3 billion shares with market value exceeding $70 billion.

Of course, there are stock exchanges in many other countries. Some are tiny, such as the Dar es Salaam exchange in Tanzania, which trades shares in just 10 companies. Others, such as the London, Tokyo, Frankfurt, and pan-European Euronext exchanges, trade the shares of thousands of firms.

Suppose that Ms. Jones, a longtime FedEx shareholder, no longer wishes to hold her shares in the company. She can sell them via a stock exchange to Mr. Brown, who wishes to increase his stake in the firm. The transaction merely transfers (partial) ownership of the firm from one investor to another. No new shares are created, and FedEx usually will neither care nor even be aware that such a trade has taken place.[3]

Ms. Jones and Mr. Brown do not buy or sell FedEx shares themselves. Instead, each must hire a brokerage firm with trading privileges on an exchange to arrange the transaction for them. Not so long ago, such trades would have involved hands-on negotiation. The broker would have had to agree on an acceptable price with a dealer in the stock or would have brought the trade to the floor of an exchange where a *specialist* in FedEx would have coordinated the transaction. But today the vast majority of trades are executed automatically and electronically, even on the more traditional exchanges.

When Ms. Jones and Mr. Brown decide to buy or sell FedEx stock, they need to give their brokers instructions about the price at which they are prepared to transact. Ms. Jones, who is anxious to sell quickly, might give her broker a *market order* to sell

---

[1] We use the terms "shares," "stock," and "common stock" interchangeably, as we do "shareholders" and "stockholders."

[2] This originally was an acronym for National Association of Security Dealers Automated Quotation system, but now is simply known as the NASDAQ market.

[3] Eventually, FedEx must know to whom it should send dividend checks, but this information is needed only when such payments are being prepared. In some cases, FedEx might care about a stock transaction, for example, if a large investor is building a big stake in the firm. But this is the exception.

FIGURE 7.1 A portion of the limit order book for Federal Express from the NYSE/ Archipelago exchange

stock at the best available price. On the other hand, Mr. Brown might give his broker a price limit at which he is willing to buy FedEx stock. If his order cannot be executed immediately, it is recorded in the exchange's *limit order book* until it can be executed.

Figure 7.1 shows a portion of the limit order book for FedEx from the Archipelago Exchange, an electronic market run by the NYSE. The bid prices on the left are the prices (and numbers of shares) at which investors are willing to buy. The Ask column presents offers to sell. The prices are arranged from best to worst, so the highest bids and lowest asks are at the top of the list. The broker might electronically enter Ms. Jones's market order to sell 100 shares on the Archipelago Exchange, where it would be automatically matched or *crossed* with the best offer to buy, which at that moment was $83.23 a share. Similarly, a market order to *buy* would be crossed with the best ask price, $83.27. The *bid-ask spread* at that moment was therefore 4 cents per share.

Reading Stock Market Listings

If you are thinking about buying shares in FedEx, you will wish to see its current price. Until recently, you probably would have looked for that information in *The Wall Street Journal* or the financial pages of your local newspaper. But those pages contain less and less information about individual stocks, and most investors today turn to the Internet for their information. For example, if you go to finance.yahoo.com, enter FedEx's ticker symbol, FDX, and ask to "Get Quotes," you will find recent trading data such as that presented in Figure 7.2.[4]

The most recent price at which the stock traded on August 3 was $83.75 per share, which was $.85 lower than its closing price the previous day, $84.60. The range of prices at which the stock traded that day, as well as over the previous 52 weeks, is provided. In the set of columns on the right, Yahoo tells us that the average daily trading volume over the last 3 months was 3,821,760 shares. Trading as of 9:47 A.M. on this

[4] Other good sources of trading data are **moneycentral.msn.com/investor/home.asp** or the online edition of *The Wall Street Journal* at **www.wsj.com** (look for the Market and then Market Data tabs).

**FedEx Corporation Common
Stock** (NYSE: FDX)

Last Trade:	**83.75**	Day's Range:	**83.61 − 84.46**
Trade Time:	**9:47AM EDT**	52wk Range:	**63.54 − 97.75**
Change:	**↓0.85 (1.00%)**	Volume:	**177,228**
Prev Close:	**84.60**	Avg Vol (3m)	**3,821,760**
Open:	**84.46**	Market Cap:	**26.34B**
Bid:	**83.73** × 200	P/E (ttm):	**22.24**
Ask:	**83.77** × 100	EPS (ttm):	**3.76**
1y Target Est:	**98.82**	Div & Yield:	**0.48 (0.60%)**

Source: Yahoo! Finance Web site, finance.yahoo.com

day totaled 177,228 shares. FedEx's *market cap* (shorthand for market capitalization) is the total value of its outstanding shares of stock, $26.34 billion. You will frequently hear traders referring to large-cap or small-cap firms, which is a convenient way to summarize the size of the company.

FedEx earned $3.76 per share in the past year. (The abbreviation "ttm" in the parentheses stands for *trailing 12 months*.) Therefore, the ratio of price per share to earnings per share, known as the *price-earnings multiple* or, equivalently, **P/E ratio,** is 83.75/3.76 = 22.24. The P/E ratio is a key tool of stock market analysts, and we will have much to say about it later in the chapter.

P/E ratio
Ratio of stock price to earnings per share.

The *dividend yield* tells you how much dividend income you would receive for every $100 invested in the stock. FedEx paid annual dividends of $.48 per share, so its yield was .48/83.75 = .6%. For every $100 invested in the stock, you would have received $.60 in dividends. Of course, this would not be the total rate of return on your investment, as you would also hope for some increase in the stock price. The dividend yield is thus much like the current yield of a bond. Both measures ignore prospective capital gains or losses.

The price at which you can buy shares in FedEx changes day to day and minute to minute. Remember, each share represents partial ownership in the firm, and share values will wax or wane with investors' perceptions of the prospects for the company. Figure 7.3 shows the share price of FedEx over a 6-month period in 2010. The price

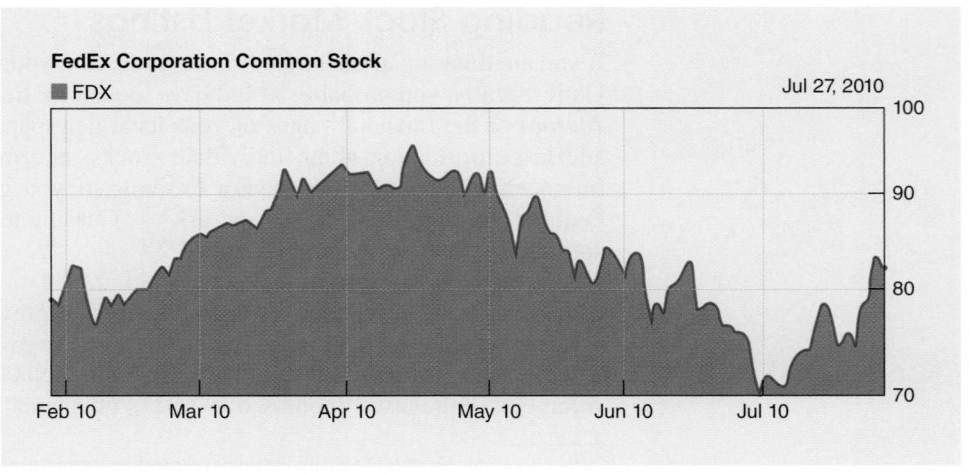

Source: Yahoo! Finance Web site, finance.yahoo.com

fell by over 25% in just 10 weeks, from $95 at the end of April to $70 in early July. Why would the price that investors were willing to pay for each share change so suddenly? And for that matter, why were they willing on August 2 to pay $84.60 a share for FedEx but only $26.25 a share for Microsoft? To answer these questions, we need to look at what determines value.

7.2 Market Values, Book Values, and Liquidation Values

Finding the value of FedEx stock may sound like a simple problem. Each quarter, the company publishes a balance sheet, which lists the value of the firm's assets and liabilities. The simplified balance sheet in Table 7.1 shows that in May 2010 the book value of all FedEx's assets—plant and machinery, inventories of materials, cash in the bank, and so on—was $24,902 million. FedEx's debt and other liabilities—money that it owes the banks, taxes that are due to be paid, and the like—amounted to $11,091 million. The difference between the value of the assets and the liabilities was $13,811 million. This was the **book value** of the firm's equity.[5] Book value records all the money that FedEx has raised from its shareholders plus all the earnings that have been plowed back on their behalf.

book value
Net worth of the firm according to the balance sheet.

Book value is a reassuringly definite number. But does the stock price equal book value? FedEx shares in May 2010 were selling at around $83, but as Table 7.2 shows, its book value per share was only $43.98. So the shares were worth about 1.9 times book value. This and the other cases shown in Table 7.2 tell us that investors in the stock market do *not* just buy and sell at book value per share.

TABLE 7.1

SIMPLIFIED BALANCE SHEET FOR FEDEX, MAY 31, 2010			
(Millions of dollars)			
Current assets	$ 7,284	Current liabilities	$ 4,645
Plant, equipment and other long-term assets	17,618	Debt and other long-term liabilities	6,446
		Shareholders' equity	13,811
Total assets	$24,902	Total liabilities and equity	$24,902

Note: Shares of stock outstanding: 314 million. Book value of equity (per share): 13,811/314 = $43.98

TABLE 7.2 Market values versus book values, August 2010

	Stock Price	Book Value per Share	Market-to-Book-Value Ratio
FedEx	$83.75	$43.98	1.9
Johnson & Johnson	58.29	19.19	3.0
Campbell Soup	36.97	3.23	11.4
PepsiCo	64.89	12.39	5.2
Walmart	51.20	17.49	2.9
Dow Chemical	25.59	14.22	1.8
Amazon	132.49	13.07	10.1
McDonald's	74.54	12.34	6.0
American Electric Power	36.11	27.70	1.3
GE	15.01	10.66	1.4

Source: Yahoo! Finance Web site, **finance.yahoo.com**.

---

[5] "Equity" is still another word for stock. Thus, stockholders are often referred to as *equity investors*.

liquidation value
Net proceeds that could
be realized by selling
the firm's assets and
paying off its creditors.

Investors know that accountants don't even try to estimate market values. The value of the assets reported on the firm's balance sheet is equal to their original (or "historical") cost less an allowance for depreciation. But that may not be a good guide to what the firm could sell its assets for today.

Well, maybe stock price equals **liquidation value** per share, that is, the amount of cash per share a company could raise if it sold off all its assets in secondhand markets and paid off all its debts. Wrong again. A successful company ought to be worth more than liquidation value. After all, that's the goal of bringing all those assets together in the first place.

The difference between a company's actual value and its book or liquidation value is often attributed to *going-concern value,* which refers to three factors:

1. *Extra earning power.* A company may have the ability to earn more than an adequate rate of return on assets. In this case the value of those assets will be higher than their book value or secondhand value.
2. *Intangible assets.* There are many assets that accountants don't put on the balance sheet. Some of these assets are extremely valuable. Take Johnson & Johnson, a health care product and pharmaceutical company. As you can see from Table 7.2, it sells at 3 times book value per share. Where did all that extra value come from? Largely from the cash flow generated by the drugs it has developed, patented, and marketed. These drugs are the fruits of a research and development (R&D) program that has grown to $7 billion per year. But U.S. accountants don't recognize R&D as an investment and don't put it on the company's balance sheet. Nevertheless, expertise, experience, and knowledge are crucial assets, and their values do show up in stock prices.
3. *Value of future investments.* If investors believe a company will have the opportunity to make very profitable investments in the future, they will pay more for the company's stock today. When eBay, the Internet auction house, first sold its stock to investors in 1998, the book value of shareholders' equity was about $100 million. Yet 1 day after the issue investors valued the equity at over $6 *billion.* In part, this difference reflected an intangible asset, eBay's unique platform for trading a wide range of goods over the Internet. But investors also judged that eBay was a *growth company.* In other words, they were betting that the company's know-how and brand name would allow it to expand internationally and make it easier for customers to trade and pay online. By 2010, eBay earned annual profits of $1.8 billion and had a market capitalization of $36 billion.

Market price is not the same as book value or liquidation value. Market value, unlike book value and liquidation value, treats the firm as a going concern.

It is not surprising that stocks virtually never sell at book or liquidation values. Investors buy shares on the basis of present and *future* earning power. Two key features determine the profits the firm will be able to produce: first, the earnings that can be generated by the firm's current tangible and intangible assets, and second, the opportunities the firm has to invest in lucrative projects that will increase future earnings.

> **EXAMPLE 7.1** ►   Amazon.com and Consolidated Edison
>
> Amazon.com, is a growth company. In 2010, its profit was $1,152 million. Yet investors in December 2010 were prepared to pay about 70 times that amount, or $81 billion, for Amazon's common stock. The value of the stock came from the company's market position, its highly regarded distribution system, and the promise of new related products that will generate increased future earnings. Amazon was a growth firm, because its market value depended so heavily on intangible assets and the anticipated profitability of new investments.
>
> Contrast this with Consolidated Edison (Con Ed), the electric utility servicing the New York City area. Con Ed is not a growth company. Its market is limited, and it is expanding capacity at a very deliberate pace. More important, it is a regulated

utility, so its returns on present and future investments are constrained. Con Ed's value derives mostly from the stream of income generated by its *existing* assets. Therefore, while Amazon shares in 2010 sold for 10.1 times book value, Con Ed shares sold at only about 1.3 times book value.

Investors refer to Amazon as a *growth stock* and Con Ed as an *income stock*. A few stocks, like Microsoft, offer both income and growth. Microsoft earns plenty from its current products. These earnings are part of what makes the stock attractive to investors. In addition, investors are willing to pay for the company's ability to invest profitably in new ventures that will increase future earnings.

Let's summarize. Just remember:

- *Book value* records what a company has paid for its assets, less a deduction for depreciation. It does not capture the true value of a business.
- *Liquidation value* is what the company could net by selling its assets and repaying its debts. It does not capture the value of a successful going concern.
- *Market value* is the amount that investors are willing to pay for the shares of the firm. This depends on the earning power of *today's* assets and the expected profitability of *future* investments.

The next question is, What determines market value?

Self-Test 7.1

In the 1970s, the computer industry was growing rapidly. In the 1980s, many new competitors entered the market, and computer prices fell. Computer makers in the last decade such as Dell, struggled with thinning profit margins and intense competition. How has the industry's market-value balance sheet changed over time? Have assets in place become proportionately more or less important? Do you think this progression is unique to the computer industry?

7.3 Valuing Common Stocks

Valuation by Comparables

When financial analysts need to value a business, they often start by identifying a sample of similar firms. They then examine how much investors in these companies are prepared to pay for each dollar of assets or earnings. This is often called *valuation by comparables*. Look, for example, at Table 7.3. The first column of numbers shows, for some well-known companies, the ratio of the market value of the equity to the book value. Notice that in each case market value is higher than book value.

The second column of numbers shows the market-to-book ratio for competing firms. For example, you can see from the second row of the table that the stock of the typical large pharmaceutical firm sells for three times its book value. If you did not have a market price for the stock of Johnson & Johnson (J&J), you might estimate that it would also sell at three times book value. In this case your estimate of J&J's market price would have been almost spot on.

An alternative would be to look at how much investors in other pharmaceutical stocks are prepared to pay for each dollar of earnings. The second row of Table 7.3 shows that the typical price-earnings (P/E) ratio for pharmaceutical stocks is 10.5. If you assumed that Johnson & Johnson should sell at a similar multiple of earnings, you would have gotten a value for the stock of $51, somewhat lower than its actual price of $58.29 in August 2010.

TABLE 7.3 Market-to-book-value ratios and price-earnings ratios for selected companies and their principal competitors, August 2010.

	Market-to-Book-Value Ratio		Price-Earnings Ratio	
	Company	Competitors*	Company	Competitors*
FedEx	1.9	5.2	22.2	29.8
Johnson & Johnson	3.0	3.0	11.8	10.5
Campbell Soup	11.4	4.7	16.1	14.0
Pepsico	5.2	4.1	16.6	17.5
Walmart	2.9	2.4	12.9	16.9
Dow Chemical	1.8	3.9	15.1	13.9
Amazon	10.1	2.8	54.9	20.5
McDonald's	6.0	2.5	16.7	18.8
American Electric Power	1.3	1.3	14.6	14.5
GE	1.4	2.5	15.1	17.6

*Figures are median ratios for competing companies.

Market-to-book and price-earnings ratios are the most popular rules of thumb for valuing common stocks, but financial analysts sometimes look at other multiples. For example, infant firms often do not have any earnings. So, rather than calculate a price-earnings ratio, analysts may look at the price-to-sales ratio for these firms. In the late 1990s, when dot-com companies were growing rapidly and losing lots of money, multiples were often based on the number of subscribers or Web-site visits.

There is nothing wrong with such rules of thumb if intelligently applied. Valuation by comparables worked well for Johnson & Johnson (and just about perfectly for American Electric Power). However, that is not the case for all the companies shown in Table 7.3. For example, if you had naïvely assumed that Amazon stock would sell at similar ratios to comparable dot-com stocks, you would have been out by a wide margin. Both the market-to-book ratio and the price-earnings ratio can vary considerably from stock to stock even for firms that are in the same line of business. To understand why this is so, we need to dig deeper and look at what determines a stock's market value.

Price and Intrinsic Value

In the previous chapter, we saw that the value of a bond is the present value of its coupon payments plus the present value of its final payment of face value. You can think of stocks in a similar way. Instead of receiving coupon payments, investors may receive dividends; and instead of receiving face value, they will receive the stock price at the time they sell their shares.

Consider, for example, an investor who buys a share of Blue Skies Inc. today and plans to sell it in 1 year. Call the predicted stock price in 1 year P_1, the expected dividend per share over the year DIV_1, and the discount rate for the stock's expected cash flows r. Remember, the discount rate reflects the risk of the stock. Riskier firms will have higher discount rates. Then the present value of the cash flows the investor will receive from Blue Skies is

$$V_0 = \frac{DIV_1 + P_1}{1 + r} \qquad (7.1)$$

intrinsic value
Present value of future cash payoffs from a stock or other security.

We call V_0 the **intrinsic value** of the share. Intrinsic value is just the present value of the cash payoffs anticipated by the investor in the stock.

To illustrate, suppose investors expect a cash dividend of $3 over the next year ($DIV_1$ = $3) and expect the stock to sell for $81 a year hence ($P_1$ = $81). If the discount rate is 12%, then intrinsic value is $75:

$$V_0 = \frac{3 + 81}{1.12} = \$75$$

You can think of intrinsic value as the "fair" price for the stock. If investors buy the stock for \$75, their expected rate of return will precisely equal the discount rate—in other words, their investment will just compensate them for the opportunity cost of their money.

To confirm this, note that the expected rate of return over the next year is the expected dividend plus the expected increase in price, $P_1 - P_0$, all divided by price at the start of the year, P_0. If the investor buys the shares for intrinsic value, then $P_0 = \$75$ and

$$\text{Expected return} = \frac{\text{DIV}_1 + P_1 - P_0}{P_0} = \frac{3 + 81 - 75}{75} = .12, \text{ or } 12\%$$

Notice that this expected return comes in two parts, the dividend and the capital gain:

Expected rate of return = expected dividend yield + expected capital gain

$$= \frac{\text{DIV}_1}{P_0} + \frac{P_1 - P_0}{P_0}$$

$$= \frac{3}{75} + \frac{81 - 75}{75}$$

$$= .04 + .08 = .12, \text{ or } 12\%$$

Of course, the actual return for Blue Skies may turn out to be more or less than investors expect. For example, in 2009, as the economy seemed to be emerging from a deep recession, one of the best-performing industries was automobiles, with a return exceeding 100%. This was almost certainly better than investors expected at the start of the year. At the other extreme, as oil prices fell, the share price of alternative energy firms declined on average by more than 10%. No investor at the start of the year would have purchased these shares anticipating such a loss. Never confuse the actual outcome with the expected outcome.

The dream of every investor is to buy shares at a bargain price, that is, a price less than intrinsic value. But in competitive markets, no price other than intrinsic value could survive for long. To see why, imagine that Blue Skies' current price were above \$75. Then the expected rate of return on Blue Skies stock would be *lower* than that on other securities of equivalent risk. (*Check this!*) Investors would bail out of Blue Skies stock and move into other securities. In the process they would force down the price of Blue Skies stock. If P_0 were less than \$75, Blue Skies stock would offer a *higher* expected rate of return than equivalent-risk securities. (*Check this, too.*) Everyone would rush to buy, forcing the price up to \$75. When the stock is priced correctly (that is, price equals present value), the *expected* rate of return on Blue Skies stock is also the rate of return that investors *require* to hold the stock. **At each point in time all securities of the same risk are priced to offer the same expected rate of return. This is a fundamental characteristic of prices in well-functioning markets. It is also common sense.**

Equation 7.1 is just a *definition* of intrinsic value, which works for any discount rate r. Now we can go beyond the definition and identify r as the expected rate of return on all securities at a given level of risk. If a stock is priced correctly, it will offer an expected rate of return equal to that of other equally risky stocks and price will equal intrinsic value:

$$P_0 = \frac{\text{DIV}_1 + P_1}{1 + r}$$

Thus today's price will equal the present value of dividend payments plus the present value of future price. But now we need to take a further step: How do we estimate the future price P_1?

Of course, many corporations do not pay cash dividends. Investors in a young, growing company may have to wait a decade or more before the firm matures and starts paying out cash to shareholders. Our formula for P_0 still applies to such firms if we set the immediate dividend DIV_1 equal to zero. In this case value depends on the subsequent dividends. But let's begin with a mature firm that is paying dividends now. We will say more about growth firms later.

The Dividend Discount Model

Our equation for stock price depends on $DIV_1 + P_1$, that is, next period's dividend and next period's price. Suppose you have forecast the dividend. How do you forecast the price P_1? We can answer this question by moving our stock-price equation forward one period and applying it in period 1. The equation then says that P_1 depends on the second period's dividend DIV_2 and the second-period price P_2. The second-period price P_2 in turn depends on the third period's dividend DIV_3 and the third-period price P_3, which depends on DIV_4 . . . you can see where this logic is going.

As it turns out, we can express a stock's intrinsic value (and, therefore, price) as the present value of *all* the forecasted future dividends paid by the company to its shareholders without referring to the future stock price. This is the **dividend discount model:**

dividend discount model
Discounted cash-flow model which states that today's stock price equals the present value of all expected future dividends.

$$P_0 = \text{present value of } (DIV_1, DIV_2, DIV_3, \ldots, DIV_t, \ldots)$$
$$= \frac{DIV_1}{1 + r} + \frac{DIV_2}{(1 + r)^2} + \frac{DIV_3}{(1 + r)^3} + \cdots + \frac{DIV_t}{(1 + r)^t} + \cdots$$

How far out in the future could we look? In principle, 40, 60, or 100 years or more—corporations are potentially immortal. However, far-distant dividends will not have significant present values. For example, the present value of $1 received in 30 years using a 10% discount rate is only $.057. Most of the value of established companies comes from dividends to be paid within a person's working lifetime.

How do we get from the one-period formula $P_0 = (DIV_1 + P_1)/(1 + r)$ to the dividend discount model? We look at increasingly long investment horizons.

Let's consider investors with different investment horizons. Each investor will value the share of stock as the present value of the dividends that she or he expects to receive plus the present value of the price at which the stock is eventually sold. Unlike bonds, however, the final horizon date for stocks is not specified—stocks do not "mature." Moreover, both dividends and final sales price can only be estimated. But the general valuation approach is the same. For a one-period investor, the valuation formula looks like this:

$$P_0 = \frac{DIV_1 + P_1}{1 + r}$$

A 2-year investor would value the stock as

$$P_0 = \frac{DIV_1}{1 + r} + \frac{DIV_2 + P_2}{(1 + r)^2}$$

and a 3-year investor would use the formula

$$P_0 = \frac{DIV_1}{1 + r} + \frac{DIV_2}{(1 + r)^2} + \frac{DIV_3 + P_3}{(1 + r)^3}$$

In fact we can look as far out into the future as we like. Suppose we call our horizon date H. Then the stock valuation formula would be

$$P_0 = \frac{DIV_1}{1 + r} + \frac{DIV_2}{(1 + r)^2} + \cdots + \frac{DIV_H + P_H}{(1 + r)^H} \qquad (7.2)$$

In words, the value of a stock is the present value of the dividends it will pay over the investor's horizon plus the present value of the expected stock price at the end of that horizon.

Does this mean that investors with different horizons will come to different conclusions about the value of the stock? No! Regardless of the investment horizon, the stock value will be the same. This is because the stock price at the horizon date is determined by expectations of dividends from that date forward. Therefore, as long as investors agree about a firm's prospects, they will also agree on its present value. Let's confirm this with an example.

EXAMPLE 7.2 ▶ Valuing Blue Skies Stock

Take Blue Skies. The firm is growing steadily, and investors expect both the stock price and the dividend to increase at 8% per year. Now consider three investors, Erste, Zweiter, and Dritter. Erste plans to hold Blue Skies for 1 year, Zweiter for 2, and Dritter for 3. Compare their payoffs:

	Year 1	Year 2	Year 3
Erste	$DIV_1 = 3$		
	$P_1 = 81$		
Zweiter	$DIV_1 = 3$	$DIV_2 = 3.24$	
		$P_2 = 87.48$	
Dritter	$DIV_1 = 3$	$DIV_2 = 3.24$	$DIV_3 = 3.50$
			$P_3 = 94.48$

Remember, we assumed that dividends and stock prices for Blue Skies are expected to grow at a steady 8%. Thus $DIV_2 = \$3 \times 1.08 = \$3.24$, $DIV_3 = \$3.24 \times 1.08 = \$3.50$, and so on.

Each investor requires the same 12% expected return. So we can calculate present value over Erste's 1-year horizon:

$$PV = \frac{DIV_1 + P_1}{1 + r} = \frac{\$3 + \$81}{1.12} = \$75$$

or Zweiter's 2-year horizon:

$$PV = \frac{DIV_1}{1 + r} + \frac{DIV_2 + P_2}{(1 + r)^2}$$
$$= \frac{\$3}{1.12} + \frac{\$3.24 + \$87.48}{(1.12)^2}$$
$$= \$2.68 + \$72.32 = \$75$$

or Dritter's 3-year horizon:

$$PV = \frac{DIV_1}{1 + r} + \frac{DIV_2}{(1 + r)^2} + \frac{DIV_3 + P_3}{(1 + r)^3}$$
$$= \frac{\$3}{1.12} + \frac{\$3.24}{(1.12)^2} + \frac{\$3.50 + \$94.48}{(1.12)^3}$$
$$= \$2.68 + \$2.58 + \$69.74 = \$75$$

All agree the stock is worth $75 per share. This illustrates our basic principle: The value of a common stock equals the present value of dividends received out to the investment horizon plus the present value of the forecast stock price at the horizon. Moreover, when you move the horizon date, the stock's present value should not change. The principle holds for horizons of 1, 3, 10, 20, and 50 years or more.

Self-Test 7.3

Refer to Self-Test 7.2. Assume that Androscoggin Copper's dividend and share price are expected to grow at a constant 5% per year. Calculate the current value of Androscoggin stock with the dividend discount model using a 3-year horizon. You should get the same answer as in Self-Test 7.2.

Look at Table 7.4, which continues the Blue Skies example for various time horizons, still assuming that the dividends are expected to increase at a steady 8% compound rate. The expected price increases at the same 8% rate. Each row in the table represents a present value calculation for a different horizon year. Note that total present value does not depend on the investment horizon. Figure 7.4 presents the same data in a graph. Each column shows the present value of the dividends up to the horizon and the present value of the price at the horizon. As the horizon recedes, the dividend stream accounts for an increasing proportion of present value but the *total* present value of dividends plus terminal price always equals $75.

TABLE 7.4 Value of Blue Skies

Horizon, Years	PV (Dividends)	+	PV (Terminal Price)	=	Value per Share
1	$ 2.68		$72.32		$75
2	5.26		69.74		75
3	7.75		67.25		75
10	22.87		52.13		75
20	38.76		36.24		75
30	49.81		25.19		75
50	62.83		12.17		75
100	73.02		1.98		75

FIGURE 7.4 Value of Blue Skies for different horizons

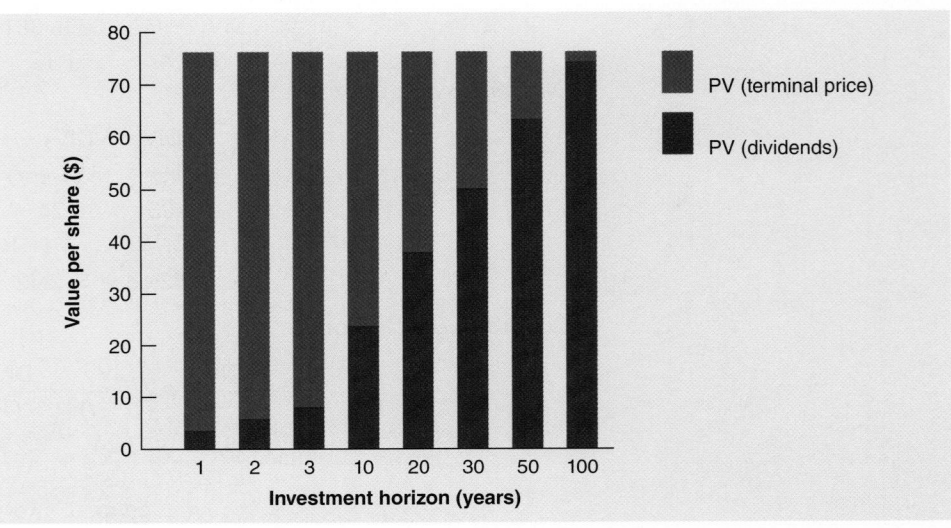

If the horizon is infinitely far away, then we can forget about the final horizon price—it has almost no present value—and simply say,

$$\text{Stock price} = \text{PV(all future dividends per share)}$$

This is the dividend discount model.

7.4 Simplifying the Dividend Discount Model

The Dividend Discount Model with No Growth

Consider a company that pays out all its earnings to its common shareholders. Such a company could not grow because it could not reinvest.[6] Stockholders might enjoy a generous immediate dividend, but they could not look forward to higher future dividends. The company's stock would offer a perpetual stream of equal cash payments, $\text{DIV}_1 = \text{DIV}_2 = \cdots = \text{DIV}_t = \cdots$.

The dividend discount model says that these no-growth shares should sell for the present value of a constant, perpetual stream of dividends. We learned how to do that calculation when we valued perpetuities in Chapter 5. Just divide the annual cash payment by the discount rate. The discount rate is the rate of return demanded by investors in other stocks with the same risk:

$$P_0 = \frac{\text{DIV}_1}{r}$$

Since our company pays out all its earnings as dividends, dividends and earnings are the same, and we could just as well calculate stock value by

$$\text{Value of a no-growth stock} = P_0 = \frac{\text{EPS}_1}{r}$$

where EPS_1 represents next year's earnings per share of stock. Thus some people loosely say, "Stock price is the present value of future earnings," and calculate value by this formula. Be careful—this is a special case.

Self-Test 7.4

Moonshine Industries has produced a barrel per week for the past 20 years but cannot grow because of certain legal hazards. It earns $25 per share per year and pays it all out to stockholders. The stockholders have alternative, equivalent-risk ventures yielding 20% per year on average. How much is one share of Moonshine worth? Assume the company can keep going indefinitely.

The Constant-Growth Dividend Discount Model

The dividend discount model requires a forecast of dividends for every year into the future, which poses a bit of a problem for stocks with potentially infinite lives. Unless we want to spend a lifetime forecasting dividends, we must use simplifying assumptions to reduce the number of estimates. As we have just seen, the simplest simplification assumes a no-growth perpetuity, which works only for no-growth shares.

Here's another simplification that finds a good deal of practical use. Suppose forecasted dividends grow at a constant rate into the indefinite future. If dividends grow at a steady rate, then instead of forecasting an infinite number of dividends, we need to forecast only the next dividend and the dividend growth rate.

---

[6] We assume it does not raise money by issuing new shares.

Recall Blue Skies Inc. It will pay a $3 dividend in 1 year. If the dividend grows at a constant rate of $g = .08$ (8%) thereafter, then dividends in future years will be

$$DIV_1 = \$3 \qquad\qquad\qquad = \$3.00$$
$$DIV_2 = \$3 \times (1 + g) = \$3 \times 1.08 = \$3.24$$
$$DIV_3 = \$3 \times (1 + g)^2 = \$3 \times 1.08^2 = \$3.50$$

Plug these forecasts of future dividends into the dividend discount model:

$$P_0 = \frac{DIV_1}{1 + r} + \frac{DIV_1(1 + g)}{(1 + r)^2} + \frac{DIV_1(1 + g)^2}{(1 + r)^3} + \frac{DIV_1(1 + g)^3}{(1 + r)^4} + \cdots$$
$$= \frac{\$3}{1.12} + \frac{\$3.24}{(1.12)^2} + \frac{\$3.50}{(1.12)^3} + \frac{\$3.78}{(1.12)^4} + \cdots$$
$$= \$2.68 + \$2.58 + \$2.49 + \$2.40 + \cdots$$

Although there is an infinite number of terms, each term is proportionately smaller than the preceding one as long as the dividend growth rate g is less than the discount rate r. Because the present value of far-distant dividends will be ever closer to zero, the sum of all of these terms is finite despite the fact that an infinite number of dividends will be paid. The sum can be shown to equal

$$P_0 = \frac{DIV_1}{r - g} \qquad\qquad (7.3)$$

constant-growth dividend discount model
Version of the dividend discount model in which dividends grow at a constant rate.

This equation is called the **constant-growth dividend discount model,** or the *Gordon growth model* after Myron Gordon, who did much to popularize it.[7]

EXAMPLE 7.3 ▶ Using the Constant-Growth Model to Value Aqua America

Aqua America (ticker symbol WTR) is a water utility serving parts of 14 states from Maine to Texas. In August 2010 its stock was selling for $19 a share. Since there were 137 million shares outstanding, investors were placing a total value on the stock of 137 million × $19 = $2.6 billion. Can we explain this valuation?

In 2010 Aqua America could point to a remarkably consistent growth record. For each of the past 15 years it had steadily increased its dividend payment (see Figure 7.5), and, with one minor hiccup, earnings had also grown steadily. The constant-growth model therefore seems tailor-made for valuing Aqua America's stock.

In 2010 investors were forecasting that in the following year Aqua America would pay a dividend of $.63 ($DIV_1 = \$.63$). The forecast growth in dividend was about 3.5% a year over the foreseeable future (we explain later where this figure comes from). If investors required a return of 6.8% from Aqua America's stock, then the constant-growth model gives a share value in 2010 (P_0) of just over $19:

$$P_0 = \frac{DIV_1}{r - g} = \frac{\$.63}{.068 - .035} = \$19.09$$

The constant-growth formula is similar to the formula for the present value of a perpetuity. Suppose you forecast no growth in dividends ($g = 0$). Then the dividend stream is a simple perpetuity, and the valuation formula is $P_0 = DIV_1/r$. This is precisely the formula you used in Self-Test 7.4 to value Moonshine, a no-growth common stock.

---

[7] Notice that the first dividend is assumed to come at the *end* of the first period and is discounted for a full period. If the stock has just paid a dividend DIV_0, then next year's dividend will be $(1 + g)$ times the dividend just paid. So another way to write the valuation formula is

$$P_0 = \frac{DIV_1}{r - g} = \frac{DIV_0 \times (1 + g)}{r - g}$$

FIGURE 7.5 Aqua America's dividends have grown steadily

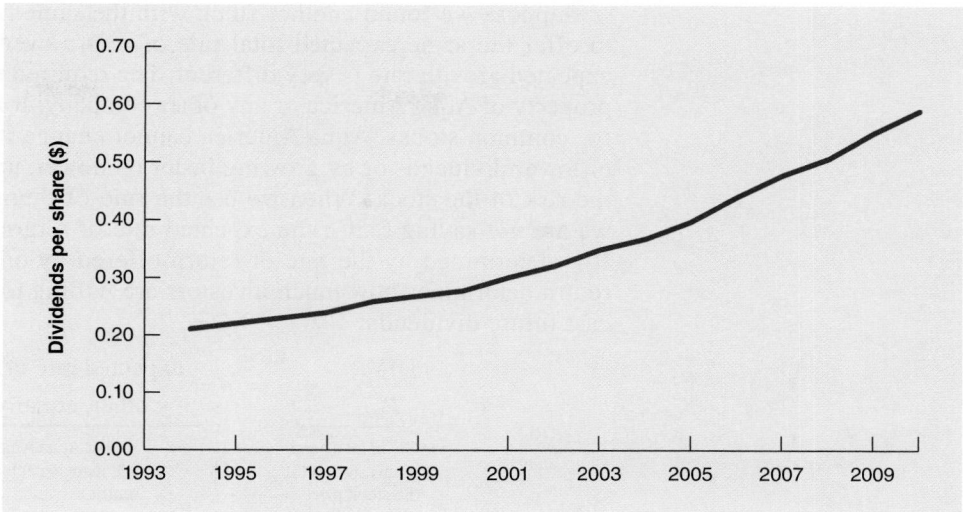

The constant-growth model generalizes the perpetuity formula to allow for constant growth in dividends. Notice that as g increases, the stock price also rises. However, the constant-growth formula is valid only when g is less than r. If someone forecasts perpetual dividend growth at a rate greater than investors' required return r, then two things happen:

1. The formula explodes. It gives crazy answers. (Try a numerical example.)
2. You know the forecast is wrong, because far-distant dividends would have incredibly high present values. (Again, try a numerical example. Calculate the present value of a dividend paid after 100 years, assuming $DIV_1 = \$.63$, $r = .068$, but $g = .20$.)

Estimating Expected Rates of Return

We argued earlier, in Section 7.3, that in competitive markets, common stocks with the same risk are priced to offer the same expected rate of return. But how do you figure out what that expected rate of return is?

It's not easy. Consensus estimates of future dividends, stock prices, or overall rates of return are not published in *The Wall Street Journal* or reported by TV newscasters. Economists argue about which statistical models give the best estimates. There are nevertheless some useful rules of thumb that can give sensible numbers.

One rule of thumb is based on the constant-growth dividend discount model, which forecasts a constant growth rate g in both future dividends and stock prices. That means expected capital gains equal g per year.

We can calculate the expected rate of return by rearranging the constant-growth formula as

$$r = \frac{DIV_1}{P_0} + g \qquad (7.4)$$

$$= \text{dividend yield} + \text{growth rate}$$

For Aqua America from Example 7.3, the expected first-year dividend is $.63 and the growth rate is 3.5%. With an initial stock price of $19.09, the expected rate of return is

$$r = \frac{DIV_1}{P_0} + g$$

$$= \frac{\$.63}{\$19.09} + .035 = .033 + .035 = .068, \text{ or } 6.8\%$$

Suppose we found another stock with the same risk as Aqua America. It ought to offer the same expected total rate of return even if its immediate dividend or expected growth rate is very different. The required rate of return is not the unique property of Aqua America or any other company; it is set in the worldwide market for common stocks. Aqua America cannot change its value of r by paying higher or lower dividends or by growing faster or slower, unless these changes also affect the risk of the stock. When we use the rule-of-thumb formula, $r = DIV_1/P_0 + g$, we are *not* saying that r, the expected rate of return, is *determined by* DIV_1 or g. It is determined by the rate of return offered by other equally risky stocks. That return determines how much investors are willing to pay for Aqua America's forecast future dividends:

$$\underbrace{\frac{DIV_1}{P_0} + g}_{\substack{\text{Given } DIV_1 \text{ and} \\ g, \text{ investors set} \\ \text{the stock price}}} = r = \underbrace{\substack{\text{expected rate of return offered} \\ \text{by other, equally risky stocks}}}_{\substack{\text{so that Aqua America offers an} \\ \text{adequate expected rate of} \\ \text{return } r}}$$

EXAMPLE 7.4 ▶ Aqua America Gets a Windfall

Suppose that a shift in water usage allows Aqua America to generate 5% per year future growth without sacrificing immediate dividends. Will that increase r, the expected rate of return?

This is good news for the firm's stockholders. The stock price will jump to

$$P_0 = \frac{DIV_1}{r - g} = \frac{\$.63}{.068 - .05} = \$35$$

But at the new price the stock will offer the same 6.8% expected return:

$$r = \frac{DIV_1}{P_0} + g$$

$$= \frac{\$.63}{\$35} + .05 = .068, \text{ or } 6.8\%$$

Aqua America's good news is reflected in a higher stock price today, not in a higher expected rate of return in the future. The unchanged expected rate of return corresponds to the firm's unchanged risk.

Self-Test 7.5

Androscoggin Copper can grow at 5% per year for the indefinite future. It's selling at $100, and next year's dividend is $5. What is the expected rate of return from investing in Carrabasset Mining common stock? Carrabasset and Androscoggin shares are equally risky.

Nonconstant Growth

Water companies and other utilities tend to have steady rates of growth and are therefore natural candidates for application of the constant-growth model. But many companies grow at rapid or irregular rates for several years before finally settling down. Obviously in such cases we can't use the constant-growth model to estimate value. However, there is an alternative approach. Set the *investment horizon* (year H) at the future year by which you expect the company's growth to settle down. Calculate the present value of dividends from now to the horizon year. Forecast the stock price in that year, and discount it also to present value. Then add up to get the total present value of dividends plus the ending stock price. The formula is

$$P_0 = \underbrace{\frac{DIV_1}{1 + r} + \frac{DIV_2}{(1 + r)^2} + \cdots + \frac{DIV_H}{(1 + r)^H}}_{\substack{\text{PV of dividends from} \\ \text{year 1 to horizon}}} + \underbrace{\frac{P_H}{(1 + r)^H}}_{\substack{\text{PV of stock price} \\ \text{at horizon}}}$$

The stock price in the horizon year is often called *terminal value*.

EXAMPLE 7.5 ▶ Estimating the Value of McDonald's Stock

In mid-2010 the price of McDonald's stock was nearly $70. The company earned about $4.50 a share and paid out about 40% of earnings as dividends. Let's see how we might use the dividend discount model to estimate McDonald's intrinsic value.

Investors in 2010 were optimistic about the prospects for McDonald's and were forecasting that earnings would grow over the next 5 years by 10% a year.[8] This growth rate is almost certainly higher than the return, *r*, that investors required from McDonald's stock, and it is implausible to suppose that such rapid growth could continue indefinitely. Therefore, we cannot use the simple constant-growth formula to value the shares. Instead, we will break the problem down into three steps:

Step 1: Value McDonald's dividends over the period of rapid growth.
Step 2: Estimate McDonald's stock price at the horizon year, when growth should have settled down.
Step 3: Calculate the present value of McDonald's stock by summing the present value of dividends up to the horizon year and the present value of the stock price at the horizon.

Step 1: Our first task is to value McDonald's dividends over the next 5 years. If dividends keep pace with the growth in earnings, then forecast earnings and dividends are as follows:

Year	1	2	3	4	5
Earnings	4.50	4.95	5.45	5.99	6.59
Dividends (40% of earnings)	1.80	1.98	2.18	2.40	2.64

In 2010 investors required a return of about 9% from McDonald's stock.[9] Therefore, the present value of the forecast dividends for years 1 to 5 was:

$$\text{PV of dividends years 1–5} = \frac{\$1.80}{1.09} + \frac{\$1.98}{(1.09)^2} + \frac{\$2.18}{(1.09)^3} + \frac{\$2.40}{(1.09)^4} + \frac{2.64}{(1.09)^5}$$

$$= \$8.41$$

Step 2: The trickier task is to estimate the price of McDonald's stock in the horizon year 5. The most likely scenario is that after year 5 growth will gradually settle down to a sustainable rate, but to keep life simple, we will assume that in year 6 the growth rate falls *immediately* to 6% a year.[10] Thus the forecast dividend in year 6 is

$$DIV_6 = 1.06 \times DIV_5 = 1.06 \times 2.64 = \$2.80$$

---

[8] Consensus analysts' forecasts are collected by Zack's, First Call, and IBES. They are available on the Web at **moneycentral.com** and **finance.yahoo.com**.

[9] For now, you can take this value purely as an assumption. In Chapter 12, we will show you how to estimate required returns. This value is about 4 percentage points higher than the 2010 yield to maturity on McDonald's long-term bonds. The stock requires a higher discount rate because it is riskier than the bonds.

[10] We will show shortly that if a company plows back a constant proportion of earnings and earns a constant return on these new investments, then earnings and dividends will grow by *g* = plowback ratio × return on new investment. Thus, if from year 5 onward McDonald's continues to reinvest 60% of its earnings and earns an ROE of 10% on this investment, earnings and dividends will grow by .6 × .10 = .06, or 6%.

and the expected price at the end of year 5 is

$$P_5 = \frac{DIV_6}{r - g} = \frac{\$2.80}{.09 - .06} = \$93.33$$

Step 3: Remember, the value of McDonald's today is equal to the present value of forecast dividends up to the horizon date plus the present value of the price at the horizon. Thus,

$$P_0 = PV(\text{dividends years 1–5}) + PV(\text{price in year 5})$$

$$= \$8.41 + \frac{\$93.33}{1.09^5} = \$69.07$$

A Reality Check   Our estimate of McDonald's value looks reasonable and almost matches McDonald's actual market price. But does it make you nervous to note that your estimate of the terminal price accounts for such a large proportion of the stock's value? It should. Only very minor changes in your assumptions about growth beyond year 5 could change your estimate of this terminal price by 10%, 20%, or 30%.

In the case of McDonald's we *know* what the market price really was in the middle of 2010, but suppose that you are using the dividend discount model to value a company going public for the first time or that you are wondering whether to buy Blue Skies' concatenator division. In such cases you do not have the luxury of looking up the market price in *The Wall Street Journal.* A valuation error of 30% could amount to serious money. Wise managers, therefore, check that their estimate of value is in the right ballpark by looking at what the market is prepared to pay for similar businesses. For example, suppose you can find mature, public companies whose scale, risk, and growth prospects today roughly match those projected for McDonald's at the investment horizon. You look back at Table 7.3 and discover that their stocks typically sell at 18.8 times recent earnings. Then you can reasonably guess that McDonald's value in year 5 will be about 18.8 times the earnings forecast for that year, that is, $18.8 \times \$6.59 = \$123.89$, somewhat higher than the $93.33 horizon value that we obtained from the dividend discount model.

Of course, these checks using price-earnings or price-to-book ratios are just an application of the *valuation by comparables* method introduced earlier in the chapter.

Self-Test 7.6

Suppose that on further analysis you decide that after year 5 McDonald's earnings and dividends will grow by a constant 5% a year. How does this affect your estimate of the value of McDonald's stock at year 0?

7.5 Growth Stocks and Income Stocks

We often hear investors speak of *growth stocks* and *income stocks.* They buy growth stocks primarily in the expectation of capital gains, and they are interested in the future growth of earnings rather than in next year's dividends. On the other hand, they buy income stocks principally for the cash dividends. Let us see whether these distinctions make sense.

Think back once more to Aqua America. It is expected to pay a dividend in 2011 of $.63 (DIV$_1$ = .63), and this dividend is expected to grow at a steady rate of 3.5% a year (g = .035). If investors require a return of 6.8% (r = .068), then the price of Aqua America should be

$$P_0 = DIV_1/(r - g) = .63/(.068 - .035) = \$19.09$$

But what determines the rate of dividend growth? Let's check. Aqua America starts 2011 with book equity of $8.35 a share. Suppose it earns a return on this equity (ROE) of 11% a year, matching its average return on equity during the past 15 years. Then earnings per share in 2011 will be

Earnings per share in 2011 = book equity per share at start of year
$\times$ return on equity
= $8.35 $\times$ .11 = $.919

The forecast dividend in 2011 is DIV_1 = $.63 a share, which leaves $.919 − $.63 = $.289 a share to be plowed back in new plant and equipment and other investments. The company's **payout ratio** (the fraction of earnings paid out as dividends) is, therefore, .63/.919 = .686, and its **plowback ratio** (the fraction of earnings reinvested in the firm) is .289/.919 = .314.

After reinvesting 31.4% of its earnings, the company will start year 2012 with additional equity per share equal to its plowback ratio times its earnings per share in 2011. We know that earnings per share equal the initial equity times the return on equity. Therefore:

Increase in book equity per share in 2012 = plowback ratio $\times$ earnings per share in 2011
= plowback ratio $\times$ [book equity per share at start of year $\times$ return on equity]
= .314 $\times$ [$8.35 $\times$ .11] = $.288

To find the growth rate in book equity we simply divide this increase in equity by the equity at the start of the year:

Growth rate = increase in book equity in 2012/book equity per share at start of year
= plowback ratio $\times$ [book equity per share at start of year $\times$ return on equity]/book equity per share at start of year
= plowback ratio $\times$ return on equity
= .314 $\times$ .11 = .035, or 3.5%

If Aqua America can continue to earn a return of 11% on its equity and plows back 31.4% of its earnings in new plant and equipment, then earnings and dividends will also continue to grow by 3.5%. This is the company's **sustainable growth rate,** because it is the rate of growth that the company can sustain from reinvested earnings per share without changing its leverage. (The sustainable growth rate is an old friend from Chapter 4.)

If a company earns a constant return on its equity and plows back a constant proportion of earnings, then the growth rate g is

$$g = \text{sustainable growth rate} = \text{return on equity} \times \text{plowback ratio} \quad (7.5)$$

What if Aqua America did not plow back *any* of its earnings into new plant and equipment? In that case it would pay out all of its earnings, $.919 a share, but would forgo any further growth in earnings and dividends:

g = sustainable growth rate = return on equity $\times$ plowback ratio = .11 $\times$ 0 = 0

We could recalculate the value of Aqua America assuming it paid out all its forecast earnings and forwent any growth:

$$P_0 = \frac{DIV_1}{r - g} = \frac{EPS_1}{r} = \frac{\$.919}{.068} = \$13.51$$

Thus, if Aqua America did not reinvest any of its earnings, its stock price would be not $19.09 but $13.51. The $13.51 represents the value of earnings from assets that are already in place. The rest of the stock price ($19.09 − $13.51 = $5.58) is the net present value of the *future* investments that Aqua America is expected to make.

Valuing Growth Opportunities

In April 2004 Google, the Internet search-engine provider, announced its plans to go public. Rather than selling shares at a fixed price, Google proposed to auction them to investors. Stock would be allotted to investors who were prepared to pay the most, but all those receiving stock would pay the same price.

The popularity of Google's sophisticated search technology created enormous interest in the issue, and investment managers and their advisers began to debate how much the stock was worth. Google's preliminary prospectus suggested a value of between $108 and $135 a share, which would have valued the equity at $29 billion to $36 billion.

If Google stock was sold at these prices, its share price would be more than 100 times its earnings. Clearly a stock price of $108 or more could not be justified by the stream of earnings generated by existing assets; it would make sense only if investors believed that Google had very valuable growth opportunities that would allow it to earn high returns on future investments. As *The Wall Street Journal* commented, "Sure, the company is making money hand over fist, and it has juicy margins and profits that are expanding rapidly. But . . . in the long run, Google likely will have to prove that it can continue to come up with new ways to profit from its dominant position in the Web-search business for its shares to be big winners."

It is notoriously difficult to guess what future opportunities may become available to a high-tech company. Rather than attempting to make detailed growth forecasts, many investors simply compared Google with rival companies such as Yahoo, whose stock was also trading at a price of around 100 times recent earnings.

As the date of the issue approached, a number of financial analysts expressed reservations about Google's suggested price range, and the company announced that it was reducing the number of shares on offer and cutting its estimate of the issue price to $85 from $95 a share. The auction took place in August, and after investors had submitted their bids, Google announced a sale price of $85, somewhat below the point at which the supply of shares equaled demand. It seemed that the pessimists had been right in their criticisms of the price range that Google had originally suggested. However, once trading started, investors rushed to buy. Google stock opened for trading at $100, within 5 months the price had doubled to just over $200, and in 2010 it was $500 a share. At that price, its total market capitalization was nearly identical to that of giants such as Procter & Gamble, whose earnings were more than double those of Google. Pessimists argued that such valuations were crazy, but optimists responded that Google was growing far faster than P&G and would continue to do so. It seems that valuing growth stocks is far from an exact science.

What if the company kept to its policy of reinvesting 31.4% of its profits but the forecast return on new investments was only 6.8%? In that case the sustainable growth rate would also be lower:

$$g = \text{sustainable growth rate} = \text{return on equity} \times \text{plowback ratio}$$
$$= .068 \times .314 = .0214, \text{ or } 2.14\%$$

If we plug this new figure into our valuation formula, we come up again with a value of $13.51 for Aqua America stock, no different from the value it would have if it chose not to grow at all:

$$P_0 = \frac{\text{DIV}_1}{r - g} = \frac{\$.63}{.068 - .0214} = \$13.51$$

Plowing earnings back into new investments may result in growth in earnings and dividends, but it does not add to the current stock price if that money is expected to earn only the return that investors require. Plowing earnings back *does* add value if investors believe that the reinvested earnings will earn a higher rate of return.

To repeat, if Aqua America did not reinvest any of its earnings, the value of its stock would simply derive from the stream of earnings from the existing assets. The price of its stock would be $13.51. If the company *did* reinvest each year but earned only the return that investors require, then those new investments would not add any value. The price of the stock would still be $13.51. Fortunately, investors believe that Aqua America has the opportunity to earn 11% on its new investments, somewhat above the 6.8% return that investors require. This is reflected in the $19.09 that investors are prepared to pay for the stock. The total value of Aqua America stock is equal to the value of its assets in place *plus* the **present value of its growth opportunities,** or **PVGO:**

present value of growth opportunities (PVGO)
Net present value of a firm's future investments.

Value of assets in place	$13.51
+ Present value of growth opportunities (PVGO)	5.58
= Total value of Aqua America's stock	$19.09

The superior prospects of Aqua America are reflected in its price-earnings ratio. With a stock price of $19.09 and forecast earnings of $.919, the P/E ratio is $19.09/$.919 = 20.8. If the company had no growth opportunities, its stock price would be only $13.51 and its P/E would be $13.51/$.919 = 14.7. The P/E ratio is, therefore, an indicator of Aqua's prospects and the profitability of its growth opportunities.

Does this mean that the financial manager should celebrate if the firm's stock sells at a high P/E? The answer is usually yes. The high P/E suggests that investors think that the firm has good growth opportunities. However, firms can have high P/E ratios not because the price is high but because earnings are temporarily depressed. A firm that earns *nothing* in a particular period will have an *infinite* P/E.

Of course, valuing stocks is always harder in practice than in principle. Forecasting cash flows and settling on an appropriate discount rate require skill and judgment. The difficulties are often greatest in the case of companies like Google or Amazon, whose value comes largely from growth opportunities rather than assets that are already in place. As the nearby box shows, in these cases there is plenty of room for disagreement about value.

Self-Test 7.7

Suppose that instead of plowing money back into lucrative ventures, Aqua America's management is investing at an expected return on equity of 5%, which is *below* the return of 6.8% that investors could expect to get from comparable securities.

a. Find the sustainable growth rate of dividends and earnings in these circumstances. Assume a 68.6% payout ratio.
b. Find the new value of its investment opportunities. Explain why this value is negative despite the positive growth rate of earnings and dividends.
c. If you were a corporate raider, would Aqua America be a good candidate for an attempted takeover?

Valuing Growth Stocks

We used the dividend discount model to value Aqua America and to distinguish the value of its growth opportunities from its assets in place. Aqua America was an easy target, because its profitability was stable and its growth moderate. What about young, risky, and rapidly growing companies? These companies usually pay no cash dividends, and their current growth rates cannot be sustained for the longer run. Here the dividend discount model still works logically—we could project dividends as zero out to some distant date when the firm matures and payout commences. But forecasting far-off dividends is more easily said than done. In these cases, it's more helpful to think about the value of a stock as the sum of the value of assets in place plus PVGO, the present value of growth opportunities.

The value per share of assets in place equals the firm's average future earnings if it does *not* grow, that is, EPS/r. So we can express the value of a growth stock as

$$P_0 = EPS/r + PVGO$$

If you can observe P_0 and calculate EPS/r, you can subtract and see how much value investors are assigning to growth.

Market-value balance sheet
Balance sheet showing market rather than book values of assets, liabilities, and stockholders' equity.

Market-Value Balance Sheets

Financial managers are not bound by generally accepted accounting principles. Sometimes they construct a **market-value balance sheet** to help identify sources of value. Table 7.5 shows the entries on such a balance sheet. Look at the assets in our

TABLE 7.5 A Market-Value Balance Sheet (All entries at current market, not book values.)

Current Assets	Current Liabilities
Assets in place	Debt and other long-term liabilities
Plant, equipment, and other tangible assets	
Intangible assets	Shareholders' equity
Growth opportunities = PV of future investment opportunities (PVGO)	
Total value	Total value

market-value balance sheet. Some of the entries will be familiar, for example, current assets. The market and book values of current assets are usually similar. In contrast, recall that book values of plant, equipment, and other long-term assets are recorded at historical cost, which for older assets can be much less than current value, particularly in periods of high inflation. Other assets may be obsolete and worth much less than historical cost. Also there will be intangible assets, such as going-concern value, that do not appear at all on the company's books.

The present value of growth opportunities (PVGO) never appears on a book balance sheet but belongs on a market-value balance sheet. For successful growth companies like Google, PVGO is far more valuable than assets in place. For mature companies like Con Ed, PVGO is relatively small and market value depends on assets in place. That is why Con Ed is an income stock.

The difference between the market and book values on the asset side of the balance sheet shows up in the market capitalization of the firm's stock and in the market-to-book ratio. A market-to-book ratio greater than 1 means that (1) the assets shown on the firm's books, are undervalued, (2) there are intangible assets not shown on the books, and/or (3) there are valuable future investment opportunities.

7.6 There Are No Free Lunches on Wall Street

We have explained how common stocks are valued. Does that mean that we have just given the game away and told you how to make an instant fortune on the stock market? We are sorry to disappoint you. It is not so easy to beat the market, and even highly paid pros find it very difficult to do so with any consistency.

Why is it so difficult to beat the market consistently? Let's look at two possible ways that you might attempt to do so.

Method 1: Technical Analysis

technical analysts
Investors who attempt to identify undervalued stocks by searching for patterns in past stock prices.

Some investors try to achieve superior returns by spotting and exploiting patterns in stock prices. These investors are known as **technical analysts.**

Technical analysis sounds plausible. For example, you might hope to beat the market by buying stocks when they are on their way up and by selling them on their way down. Unfortunately, it turns out that such simple rules don't work. A large price rise in one period may be followed by a further rise in the next period, but it is just as likely to be followed by a fall.

Look, for example, at Figure 7.6a. The horizontal axis shows the return on the New York Composite Index in one week (5 business days), while the vertical axis shows the return in the following week. Each point in the chart represents a different week over a recent 40-year period. If a market rise one week tended to be followed by a rise the next week, the points in the chart would plot along an upward-sloping line. But you can see that there was no such tendency; the points are scattered randomly across the chart. Statisticians sometimes measure the relationship between these changes by the coefficient of correlation. In our example, the correlation between the market movements in successive weeks is $-.022$—in other words, effectively zero. Figure 7.6b shows a similar plot for monthly (20-business-day) moves.

FIGURE 7.6a Each dot shows the returns on the New York Composite Index on two successive weeks between September 1970 and September 2010. The circled dot shows a weekly return of +3.1%, followed by +5.2% in the next week. The scatter diagram shows no significant relationship between returns on successive weeks.

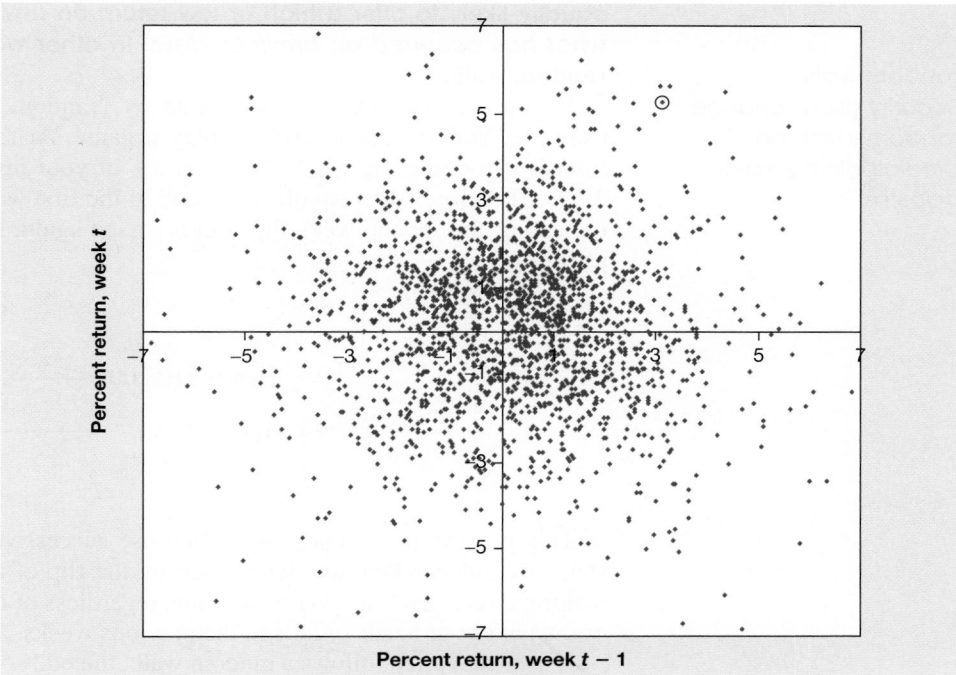

FIGURE 7.6b This scatter diagram shows that there is also no relationship between market returns in successive months.

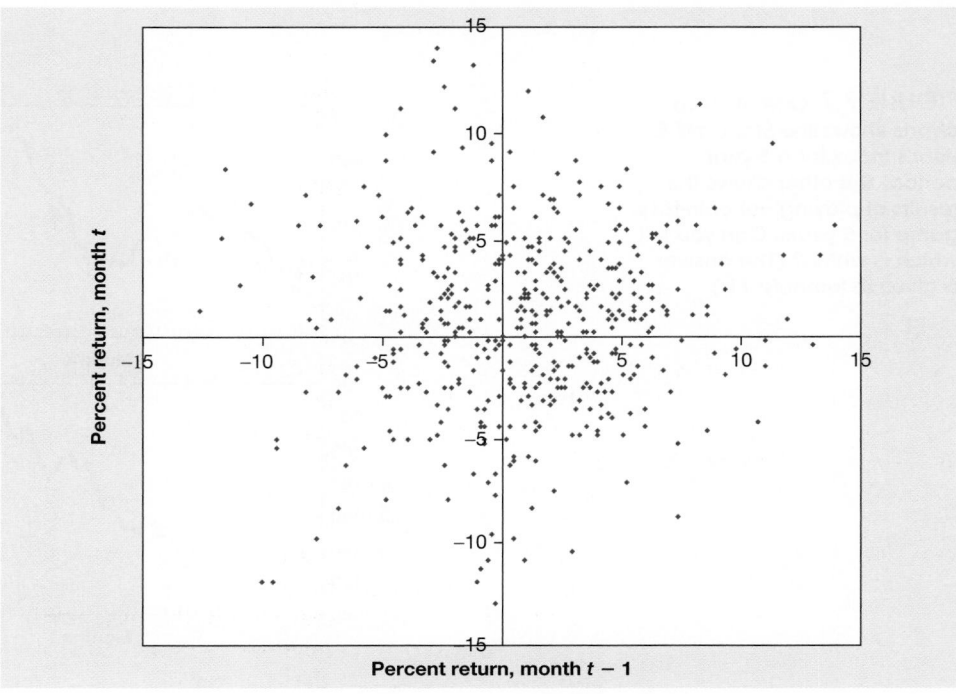

Again you can see that this month's change in the index gives you almost no clue as to the likely change next month. The correlation between successive monthly changes is −.004.

Financial economists and statisticians who have studied stock price movements have concluded that you won't get rich looking for consistent patterns in price changes. This seems to be so regardless of whether you look at the market as a whole (as we did in Figure 7.6) or at individual stocks. **Prices appear to wander randomly. They are equally likely to offer a high or low return on any particular day,** *regardless of what has occurred on previous days.* **In other words, prices seem to follow a random walk.**

random walk
Security prices change randomly, with no predictable trends or patterns.

If you are not sure what we mean by "random walk," consider the following example: You are given $100 to play a game. At the end of each week a coin is tossed. If it comes up heads, you win 3% of your investment; if it is tails, you lose 2.5%. Therefore, your payoff at the end of the first week is either $103 or $97.50. At the end of the second week the coin is tossed again. Now the possible outcomes are as follows:

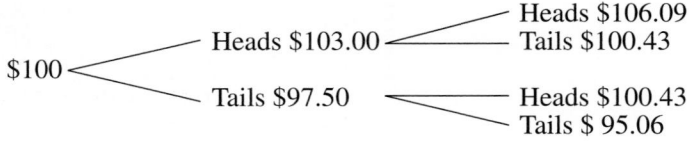

This process is a random walk because successive changes in the value of your stake are independent and determined by the flip of a fair coin. That is, the odds of making money each week are the same, regardless of the value at the start of the week or the pattern of heads or tails in the previous weeks.

If a stock's price follows a random walk, the odds of an increase or decrease during any day, month, or year do not depend *at all* on the stock's previous price moves. The historical path of prices gives no useful information about the future—just as a long series of recorded heads and tails gives no information about the next toss.

FIGURE 7.7 One of these charts shows the Standard & Poor's Index for a 5-year period. The other shows the results of playing our coin-toss game for 5 years. Can you tell which is which? (The answer is given in footnote 11.)

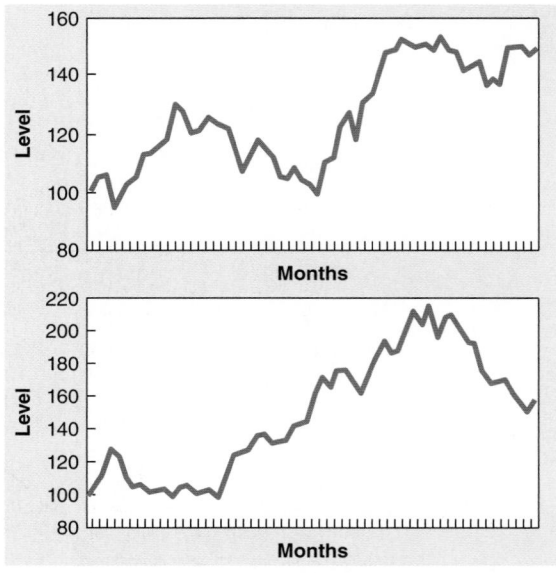

FIGURE 7.8 Cycles self-destruct as soon as they are recognized by investors. The stock price instantaneously jumps to the present value of the expected future price.

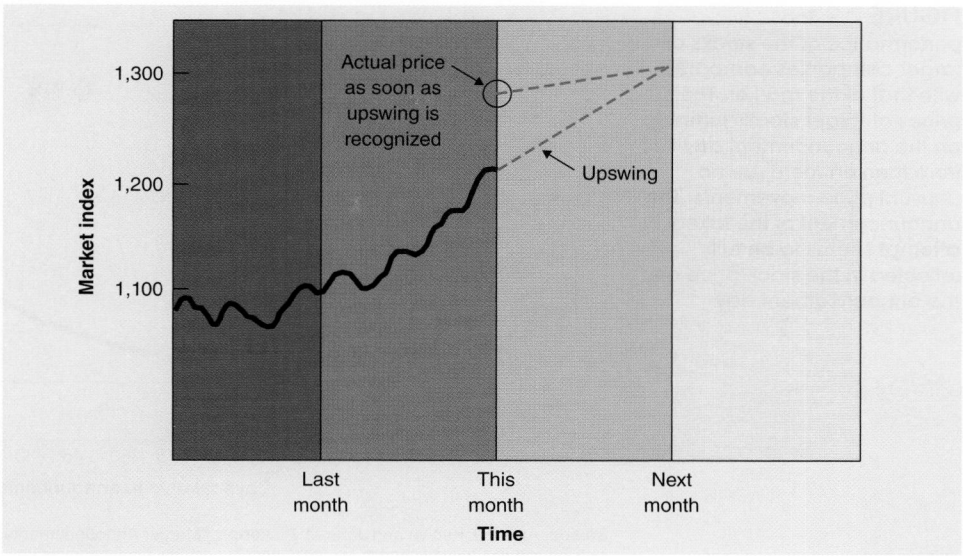

If you find it difficult to believe that stock prices could behave like our coin-tossing game, then look at the two charts in Figure 7.7. One of these charts shows the outcome from playing our game for 5 years; the other shows the actual performance of the S&P 500 Index for a 5-year period. Can you tell which one is which?[11]

Does it surprise you that stocks seem to follow a random walk? If so, imagine that it were not the case and that changes in stock prices were expected to persist for several months. Figure 7.8 provides a hypothetical example of such a predictable cycle. You can see that an upswing in the market started when the index was 1,100 and is expected to carry the price to 1,300 next month. What will happen when investors perceive this bonanza? Since stocks are a bargain at their current level, investors will rush to buy and, in so doing, will push up prices. They will stop buying only when stocks are fairly priced. **Thus, as soon as a cycle becomes apparent to investors, they immediately eliminate it by their trading.**

Don't confuse randomness in price *changes* with irrationality in the *level* of prices. If a stock is fairly priced, it will move only if new information changes the market perception of its fair price. But new information, by definition, is unrelated to earlier information.

Self-Test 7.8

True or false: If stock prices follow a random walk,

a. Successive stock prices are not related.
b. Successive stock price changes are not related.
c. Stock prices fluctuate above and below a normal long-run price.
d. The history of stock prices cannot be used to predict future returns to investors.

---

[11] The top chart in Figure 7.7 shows the real Standard & Poor's Index for the years 1980 through 1984. The bottom chart was generated by a series of random numbers. You may be among the 50% of our readers who guess right, but we bet it was just a guess.

FIGURE 7.9 The performance of the stocks of target companies compared with that of the market. The prices of target stocks jump up on the announcement day, but from then on there are no unusual price movements. The announcement of the takeover attempt seems to be fully reflected in the stock price on the announcement day.

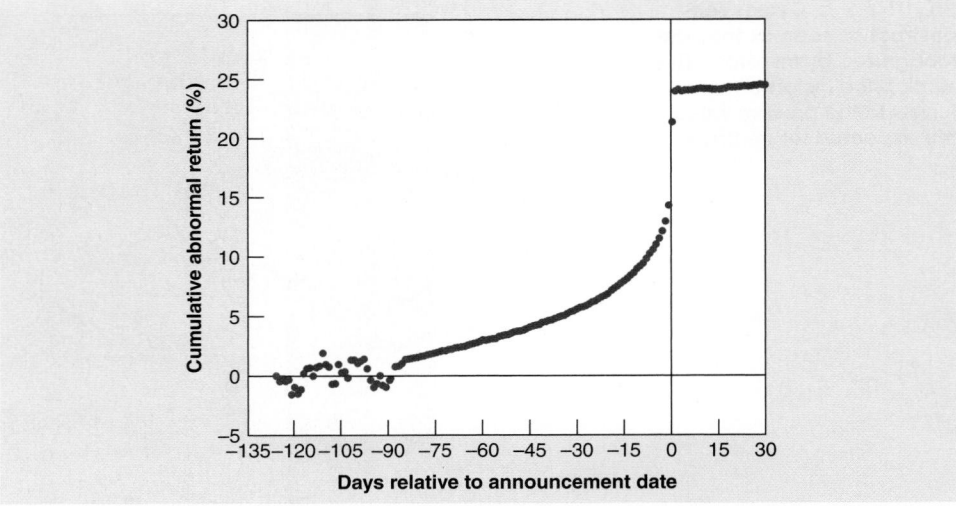

Source: Arthur J. Keown and John M. Pinkerton, "Merger Announcements and Insider Trading Activity," *Journal of Finance* 36 (September 1981); pp. 855–869. Used with permission of Wiley-Blackwell.

Method 2: Fundamental Analysis

fundamental analysts
Investors who attempt to find mispriced securities by analyzing fundamental information, such as accounting performance and earnings prospects.

You may not be able to earn superior returns just by studying past stock prices, but what about other types of information? After all, most investors don't just look at past stock prices. Instead, they try to gauge a firm's business prospects by studying the financial and trade press, the company's financial accounts, the president's annual statements, and other items of news. These investors are called **fundamental analysts,** in contrast to technical analysts who focus on past stock price movements.

Fundamental analysts are paid to uncover stocks for which price does not equal intrinsic value. If intrinsic value exceeds price, for example, the stock is a bargain and will offer a superior expected return. But what happens if there are many talented and competitive fundamental analysts? If one of them uncovers a stock that appears to be a bargain, it stands to reason that others will as well, and there will be a wave of buying that pushes up the price. In the end, their actions will eliminate the original bargain opportunity. To profit, your insights must be different from those of your competitors, and you must act faster than they can. This is a tall order.

To illustrate the challenge facing stock market analysts, look at Figure 7.9, which shows how stock prices react to one particular item of news—the announcement of a takeover. In most takeovers the acquiring company is willing to pay a hefty premium to induce the shareholders of the target company to give up their shares. You can see from Figure 7.9 that the stock price of the target company typically jumps up on the day that the public becomes aware of a takeover attempt (day 0 in the graph). However, this adjustment in the stock price is immediate; thereafter there is no further drift in the stock price, either upward or downward. By the time the acquisition has been made public, it is too late to buy.

Researchers have looked at the stock price reaction to many other types of news, such as earnings and dividend announcements, and plans to issue additional stock or repurchase existing stock. All this information seems to be rapidly and accurately reflected in the price of the stock, so it is impossible to make superior returns by buying or selling after the announcement.

A Theory to Fit the Facts

efficient market
Market in which prices reflect all available information.

Economists often refer to the stock market as an efficient market. By this they mean that the competition to find misvalued stocks is intense. So when new information comes out, investors rush to take advantage of it and thereby eliminate any profit opportunities. Professional investors express the same idea when they say that there are no free lunches on Wall Street.

It is useful to distinguish three types of information and three degrees of efficiency. The term *weak-form efficiency* describes a market in which prices already reflect all the information contained in past prices. In such a market, share price changes are random, and technical analysis that searches for patterns in past returns is valueless. Figure 7.6, which looked at successive weekly and monthly changes in the market index, is evidence in favor of weak-form efficiency.

Semistrong-form efficiency describes a market in which prices reflect not just the information contained in past prices but all publicly available information. In such a market it is impossible (or exceptionally difficult) to earn consistently superior returns simply by reading the financial press, studying the company's financial statements, and so on. Figure 7.9, which looked at the market reaction to merger announcements, was just one piece of evidence in favor of semistrong efficiency. As soon as information about the mergers became public, the stock prices jumped.

Finally, *strong-form efficiency* refers to a market where prices impound all available information. In such a market no investor, however hardworking, could expect to earn superior profits.

In fact, it appears that even professional investors, such as managers of mutual funds, do find it difficult to outperform the broad market consistently. Look, for example, at Figure 7.10, which shows the average performance of equity mutual funds over three decades. You can see that in some years these mutual funds did beat the market, but as often as not (in fact, in 24 of the 40 years since 1970) it was the other way around. Of course, it would be surprising if some of the managers were not smarter than others and were able to earn superior returns. But it seems hard to spot the smart ones, and the top-performing managers one year have about an average chance of falling on their face the next year.

FIGURE 7.10 Annual returns on the Wilshire 5000 Market Index and equity mutual funds, 1971–2010. The market index provided a higher return than the average mutual fund in 24 of the 40 years.

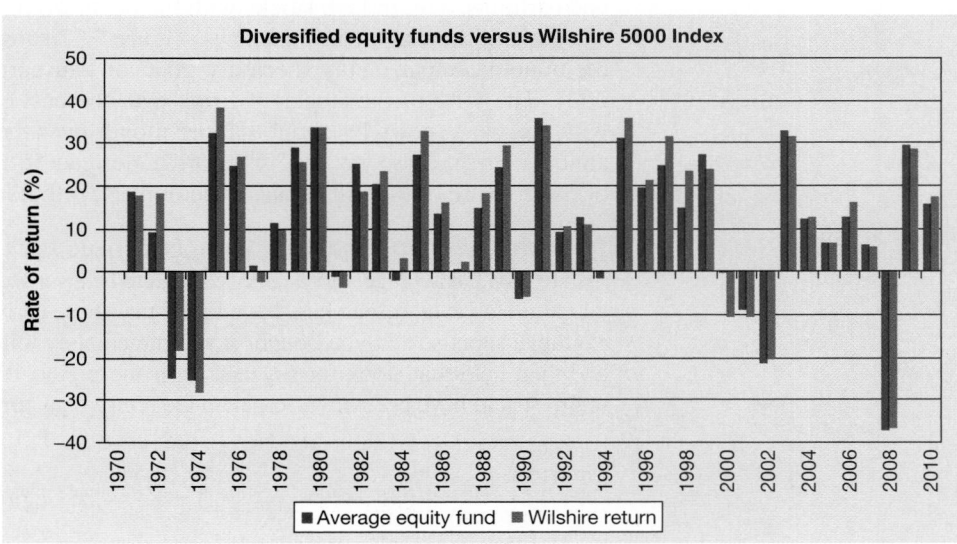

EXAMPLE 7.6 ▶ Performance of Money Managers

Forbes, a widely read investment magazine, publishes annually an "honor roll" of the most consistently successful mutual funds. Suppose that every year starting in 1975, you invested an equal sum in each of these successful funds when *Forbes* announced its honor roll. You would have outperformed the market in only 5 of the following 16 years, and your average annual return would have been more than 1% below the return on the market.[12]

As this kind of discouraging evidence has accumulated, many investors have given up the search for superior investment returns. Instead, they simply buy and hold index funds or exchange-traded portfolios (ETFs) that track the entire stock market. We discussed index funds and ETFs in Chapter 2. Recall that they provide maximum diversification, with very low management fees. Why pay higher fees to managers who attempt to "beat the market" but can't do so consistently? Corporate pension funds now invest over one-quarter of their U.S. equity holdings in index funds.

Self-Test 7.9

Technical analysts and fundamental analysts all try to earn superior returns in the stock market. Explain how their efforts help keep the market efficient.

7.7 Market Anomalies and Behavioral Finance

Market Anomalies

Almost without exception, early researchers concluded that the efficient-market hypothesis was a remarkably good description of reality. But eventually, cracks in its armor began to appear, and soon the finance journals were packed with evidence of anomalies, or seeming profit opportunities, that investors have apparently failed to exploit. We will look at just a few examples.

The Earnings Announcement Puzzle In an efficient stock market, a company's stock price should react instantly at the announcement of unexpectedly good or bad earnings. But, in fact, stocks with the best earnings news typically outperform the stocks with the worst earnings news. Figure 7.11 shows stock performance following the announcement of unexpectedly good or bad earnings during the years 1972 to 2001. The 10% of the stocks of firms with the best earnings news outperform those with the worst news by about 1% per month over the 6-month period following the announcement. It seems that investors underreact to the earnings announcement and become aware of the full significance only as further information arrives.

The New-Issue Puzzle When firms issue stock to the public, investors typically rush to buy. On average, those lucky enough to be awarded stock receive an immediate capital gain. However, researchers have found that these early gains often turn into losses. For example, suppose that you bought stock immediately following each initial public offering and then held that stock for 5 years. Over the period 1970 to 2008 your average annual return would have been 3.5% less than the return on a portfolio of similar-sized stocks.[13]

---

[12] See B. G. Malkiel, "Returns from Investing in Equity Mutual Funds 1971 to 1991," *Journal of Finance* 50 (June 1995), pp. 549–572.

[13] An excellent resource for data and analysis of initial public offerings is Professor Jay Ritter's Web page, **bear.cba.ufl.edu/ritter**.

FIGURE 7.11 Average stock returns over the 6 months following announcements of quarterly earnings. The 10% of stocks with the best earnings news (portfolio 10) outperformed those with the worst news (portfolio 1) by about 1% per month.

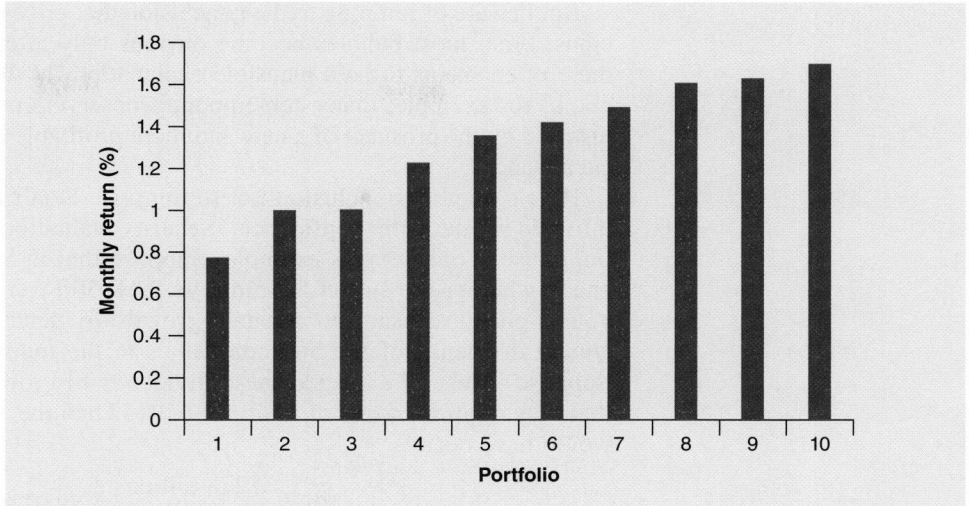

Source: Tarun Chordia and Lakshmanan Shivakumar, "Inflation Illusion and Post-Earnings-Announcement Drift," *Journal of Accounting Research* 43 (2005), pp. 521–556. Used with permission of John Wiley and Sons via Copyright Clearance Center, Inc.

The jury is still out on these studies of longer-term anomalies. We can't be sure whether they are important exceptions to the efficient-market theory or a coincidence that stems from the efforts of many researchers to find interesting patterns in the data. There may also be other explanations. Take, for example, the new-issue puzzle. Most new issues during the past 30 years have involved growth stocks with high market values and limited book assets. Perhaps the stocks performed badly not because they had just been issued but because all growth stocks happened to perform badly during this period. Of course, if that is true, we need to address another question: Why have growth stocks performed poorly over such a long period of time? We will come back to this question in Chapter 12.

Bubbles and Market Efficiency

Market anomalies, such as the earnings announcement puzzle, suggest that prices of individual stocks may occasionally get out of line. But are there also cases in which prices as a whole can no longer be justified? In the last few decades, we have witnessed several examples of apparent stock market *bubbles* when prices rose to levels hard to reconcile with reasonable outlooks for dividends and earnings.

Between 1985 and 1989, for example, the Japanese Nikkei index roughly quadrupled. But in 1990, interest rates rose and stock prices started to fall. By October the Nikkei had sunk to about half its peak, and by March 2009 it was down 80% from its peak value 19 years earlier.

The boom in Japanese stock prices was matched by an even greater explosion in land prices. For example, Ziemba and Schwartz document that the few hundred acres of land under the Emperor's Palace in Tokyo, evaluated at neighborhood land prices, was worth as much as all the land in Canada or California.[14] But then the real estate bubble also burst. By 2005 land prices in the six major Japanese cities had slumped to just 13% of their peak.

The dot-com bubble in the United States was almost as dramatic. The technology-heavy NASDAQ stock index rose 580% from the start of 1995 to its eventual high in March 2000. But then, as rapidly as it began, the boom ended, and by October 2002 the index had fallen 78% from its peak.

Looking back at these episodes, it seems difficult to believe that expected future cash flows could ever have been sufficient to justify the initial price run-ups. If that is the case, we have two important exceptions to the theory of efficient markets.

---

[14] See W. T. Ziemba and S. L. Schwartz, *Invest Japan* (Chicago: Probus Publishing Co., 1992), p. 109.

But beware of jumping to the conclusion that prices are always arbitrary and capricious. First, most bubbles become obvious only after they have burst. At the time, there often seems to be a plausible explanation for the price run-up. In the dot-com boom, for example, many contemporary observers rationalized stock-price gains as justified by the prospect of a new and more profitable economy, driven by technological advances.

Here's another conclusion not to jump to: Don't assume that anyone can know intrinsic value with confidence. Security valuation is intrinsically difficult and imprecise. Consider this example: Suppose that in September 2010 you wanted to check whether the stocks forming the S&P 500 were fairly priced. As a first stab, you might have used the constant-growth dividend discount model. In 2010, the annual dividends of the 500 companies in the index came to about $228 billion. Suppose investors expected these dividends to grow at a steady rate of 4.0% and that they required a rate of return of 6.3%. Then the value of the stocks in the index would have been

$$PV = \frac{\$228 \text{ billion}}{.063 - .04} = \$9,913 \text{ billion}$$

which was roughly their value in September 2010. But what if the dividend growth rate was only 3.5%? Then the value of the stocks would decline to

$$PV = \frac{\$228 \text{ billion}}{.063 - .035} = \$8,143 \text{ billion}$$

In other words, a reduction of just half a percentage point in the expected rate of dividend growth would reduce the value of common stocks by about 18%. Given this sensitivity of value to assumed growth rates, it is easy for investors to justify price run-ups when they are feeling optimistic about the future, and it is hard to identify bubbles—except of course in retrospect, at which point all bubbles seem to have been obvious.

Behavioral Finance

Why might prices depart from fundamental values? Some scholars believe that the answer to this question lies in behavioral psychology. People are not 100% rational 100% of the time. This shows up in two broad areas—their attitudes to risk and the way that they assess probabilities:

1. *Attitudes toward risk.* Psychologists have observed that, when making risky decisions, people are particularly loath to incur losses, even if those losses are small. Losers are liable to regret their actions and kick themselves for having been so foolish. To avoid this unpleasant possibility, individuals will tend to shun those actions that may result in loss.

   The pain of a loss seems to depend on whether it comes on the heels of earlier losses. Once investors have suffered a loss, they may be even more cautious not to risk a further loss. Conversely, just as gamblers are known to be more willing to take large bets when they are ahead, so investors may be more prepared to run the risk of a stock market dip after they have experienced a period of substantial gains. If they do then suffer a small loss, they at least have the consolation of being up on the year.

   You can see how this sort of behavior could lead to a stock-price bubble. For example, early investors in the technology firms that boomed during the dot-com bubble were big winners. They may have stopped worrying about the risk of loss. They may have thrown caution to the winds and piled even more investment into these companies, driving stock prices far above fundamental values. The day of reckoning came when investors woke up and realized how far above fundamental value prices had soared.

2. *Beliefs about probabilities.* Most investors do not have a Ph.D. in probability theory and may make common errors in assessing the probability of uncertain outcomes. Psychologists have found that, when judging the possible future outcomes, individuals commonly look back to what has happened in recent periods and then assume that this is representative of what may occur in the future. The temptation is to project recent experience into the future and to forget the lessons learned from the more distant past. For example, an investor who places too much weight on recent events may judge that glamorous growth companies are very likely to continue to grow rapidly, even though very high rates of growth cannot persist indefinitely.

A second common bias is overconfidence. Most of us believe that we are better-than-average drivers, and most investors think that they are better-than-average stockpickers. We know that two speculators who trade with one another cannot both make money from the deal; for every winner there must be a loser. But presumably investors are prepared to continue trading because each is confident that it is the other one who is the patsy.

You can see how such behavior may have reinforced the dot-com boom. As the bull market developed, it generated increased optimism about the future and stimulated demand for shares. The more that investors racked up profits on their stocks, the more confident they became in their views and the more willing they became to bear the risk that the next month might not be so good.

Now it is not difficult to believe that your uncle Harry or aunt Hetty may have become caught up in a scatty whirl of irrational exuberance,[15] but why didn't hard-headed professional investors bail out of the overpriced stocks and force their prices down to fair value? Perhaps they felt that it was too difficult to predict when the boom would end and that their jobs would be at risk if they moved aggressively into cash when others were raking up profits. In this case, sales of stock by the pros were simply not large enough to stem the tide of optimism that was sweeping the market.

It is too early to say how far behavioral finance scholars can help to sort out some of the puzzles and explain events like the dot-com boom. One thing, however, seems clear: It is relatively easy for statisticians to spot anomalies with the benefit of hindsight and for psychologists to provide an explanation for them. It is much more difficult for investment managers who are at the sharp end to spot and invest in mispriced securities. And that is the basic message of the efficient-market theory.

---

[15] The term "irrational exuberance" was coined by Alan Greenspan, former chairman of the Federal Reserve Board, to describe the dot-com boom. It was also the title of a book by Robert Shiller that examined the boom. See R. Shiller, *Irrational Exuberance* (New York City: Broadway Books, 2001).

SUMMARY

What information is included in stock trading reports? (*LO1*)

Large companies usually arrange for their stocks to be traded on a stock exchange. The stock listings report the stock's price, price change, volume, **dividend yield,** and **price-earnings (P/E)** ratio.

How can one calculate the present value of a stock given forecasts of future dividends and future stock price? (*LO2*)

Stockholders generally expect to receive (1) cash dividends and (2) capital gains or losses. The rate of return that they expect over the next year is defined as the expected dividend per share DIV_1 plus the expected increase in price $P_1 - P_0$, all divided by the price at the start of the year P_0.

Unlike the fixed interest payments that the firm promises to bondholders, the dividends that are paid to stockholders depend on the fortunes of the firm. That's why a company's common stock is riskier than its debt. The return that investors expect on any one stock is also the return that they demand on all stocks subject to the same degree of risk.

The present value of a share is equal to the stream of expected dividends per share up to some horizon date plus the expected price at this date, all discounted at the return that investors require. If the horizon date is far away, we simply say that stock price equals the present value of all future dividends per share. This is the **dividend discount model.**

How can stock valuation formulas be used to infer the expected rate of return on a common stock? (*LO3*)

If dividends are expected to grow forever at a constant rate g, then the expected return on the stock is equal to the dividend yield (DIV_1/P_0) plus the expected rate of dividend growth. The value of the stock according to this **constant-growth dividend discount model** is $P_0 = DIV_1/(r - g)$.

How should investors interpret price-earnings ratios? (*LO4*)

You can think of a share's value as the sum of two parts—the value of the assets in place and the **present value of growth opportunities,** that is, of future opportunities for the firm to invest in high-return projects. The price-earnings (P/E) ratio reflects the market's assessment of the firm's growth opportunities.

How does competition among investors lead to efficient markets? (*LO5*)

Competition between investors will tend to produce an **efficient market**—that is, a market in which prices rapidly reflect new information and investors have difficulty making consistently superior returns. Of course, we all *hope* to beat the market, but if the market is efficient, all we can rationally *expect* is a return that is sufficient on average to compensate for the time value of money and for the risks we bear.

The efficient-market theory comes in three flavors. The *weak form* states that prices reflect all the information contained in the past series of stock prices. In this case it is impossible to earn superior profits simply by looking for past patterns in stock prices. The *semistrong form* of the theory states that prices reflect all published information, so it is impossible to make consistently superior returns just by reading the newspaper, looking at the company's annual accounts, and so on. The *strong form* states that stock prices effectively impound all available information. This form tells us that private information is hard to come by, because in pursuing it you are in competition with thousands—perhaps millions—of active and intelligent investors. The best you can do in this case is to assume that securities are fairly priced.

The evidence for market efficiency is voluminous, and there is little doubt that skilled professional investors find it difficult to win consistently. Nevertheless, there remain some puzzling instances where markets do not seem to be efficient. Some financial economists attribute these apparent anomalies to behavioral foibles.

LISTING OF EQUATIONS

7.1 $V_0 = \dfrac{DIV_1 + P_1}{1 + r}$

7.2 $P_0 = \dfrac{DIV_1}{1 + r} + \dfrac{DIV_2}{(1 + r)^2} + \cdots + \dfrac{DIV_H + P_H}{(1 + r)^H}$

7.3 $P_0 = \dfrac{DIV_1}{r - g}$

7.4 $r = \dfrac{DIV_1}{P_0} + g =$ dividend yield + growth rate

7.5 $g =$ sustainable growth rate = return on equity $\times$ plowback ratio

QUESTIONS

QUIZ

1. **Dividend Discount Model.** Amazon.com has never paid a dividend, but in August 2010 the market value of its stock was $57 billion. Does this invalidate the dividend discount model? *(LO2)*

2. **Dividend Yield.** Favored stock will pay a dividend this year of $2.40 per share. Its dividend yield is 8%. At what price is the stock selling? *(LO1)*

3. **Preferred Stock.** Preferred Products has issued preferred stock with an $8 annual dividend that will be paid in perpetuity. *(LO2)*
   a. If the discount rate is 12%, at what price should the preferred sell?
   b. At what price should the stock sell 1 year from now?
   c. What is the dividend yield, the capital gains yield, and the expected rate of return of the stock?

4. **Constant-Growth Model.** Waterworks has a dividend yield of 8%. If its dividend is expected to grow at a constant rate of 5%, what must be the expected rate of return on the company's stock? *(LO3)*

5. **Dividend Discount Model.** How can we say that price equals the present value of all future dividends when many actual investors may be seeking capital gains and planning to hold their shares for only a year or two? Explain. *(LO2)*

6. **Rate of Return.** Steady As She Goes, Inc., will pay a year-end dividend of $3 per share. Investors expect the dividend to grow at a rate of 4% indefinitely.
   a. If the stock currently sells for $30 per share, what is the expected rate of return on the stock? *(LO3)*
   b. If the expected rate of return on the stock is 16.5%, what is the stock price? *(LO2)*

7. **Dividend Yield.** BMM Industries pays a dividend of $2 per quarter. The dividend yield on its stock is reported at 4.8%. What price is the stock selling at? *(LO1)*

8. **Forms of Efficient Markets.** Supply the missing words from the following list: *fundamental, semistrong, strong, technical, weak. (LO5)*

   There are three forms of the efficient market theory. Tests that have found there are no patterns in share price changes provide evidence for the _____ form of the theory. Evidence for the _____ form of the theory is provided by tests that look at how rapidly markets respond to new public information, and evidence for the _____ form of the theory is provided by tests that look at the performance of professionally managed portfolios. Market efficiency results from competition between investors. Many investors search for information about the company's business that would help them to value the stock more accurately. This is known as _____ analysis. Such research helps to ensure that prices reflect all available information. Other investors study past stock prices for recurrent patterns that would allow them to make superior profits. This is known as _____ analysis. Such research helps to eliminate any patterns.

9. **Information and Efficient Markets.** "It's competition for information that makes securities markets efficient." Is this statement correct? Explain. *(LO5)*

10. **Behavioral Finance.** Some finance scholars cite well-documented behavioral biases to explain apparent cases of market inefficiency. Describe two of these biases. *(LO5)*

PRACTICE PROBLEMS

11. **Stock Values.** Integrated Potato Chips paid a $1 per share dividend *yesterday*. You expect the dividend to grow steadily at a rate of 4% per year. *(LO2)*
    a. What is the expected dividend in each of the next 3 years?
    b. If the discount rate for the stock is 12%, at what price will the stock sell?
    c. What is the expected stock price 3 years from now?
    d. If you buy the stock and plan to hold it for 3 years, what payments will you receive? What is the present value of those payments? Compare your answer to (b).

12. **Constant-Growth Model.** A stock sells for $40. The next dividend will be $4 per share. If the rate of return earned on reinvested funds is a constant 15% and the company reinvests 40% of earnings in the firm, what must be the discount rate? *(LO3)*

13. **Constant-Growth Model.** Gentleman Gym just paid its annual dividend of $3 per share, and it is widely expected that the dividend will increase by 5% per year indefinitely. *(LO2)*

     a. What price should the stock sell at? The discount rate is 15%.

     b. How would your answer change if the discount rate were only 12%? Why does the answer change?

14. **Constant-Growth Model.** Arts and Crafts, Inc., will pay a dividend of $5 per share in 1 year. It sells at $50 a share, and firms in the same industry provide an expected rate of return of 14%. What must be the expected growth rate of the company's dividends? *(LO2)*

15. **Constant-Growth Model.** Eastern Electric currently pays a dividend of about $1.64 per share and sells for $27 a share. *(LO3)*

     a. If investors believe the growth rate of dividends is 3% per year, what rate of return do they expect to earn on the stock?

     b. If investors' required rate of return is 10%, what must be the growth rate they expect of the firm?

     c. If the sustainable growth rate is 5% and the plowback ratio is .4, what must be the rate of return earned by the firm on its new investments?

16. **Constant-Growth Model.** You believe that the Non-stick Gum Factory will pay a dividend of $2 on its common stock next year. Thereafter, you expect dividends to grow at a rate of 6% a year in perpetuity. If you require a return of 12% on your investment, how much should you be prepared to pay for the stock? *(LO2)*

17. **Negative Growth.** Horse and Buggy Inc. is in a declining industry. Sales, earnings, and dividends are all shrinking at a rate of 10% per year. *(LO2)*

     a. If $r = 15\%$ and $DIV_1 = \$3$, what is the value of a share?

     b. What price do you forecast for the stock next year?

     c. What is the expected rate of return on the stock?

     d. Can you distinguish between "bad stocks" and "bad companies"? Does the fact that the industry is declining mean that the stock is a bad buy?

18. **Constant-Growth Model.** Metatrend's stock will generate earnings of $6 per share this year. The discount rate for the stock is 15%, and the rate of return on reinvested earnings also is 15%. *(LO2)*

     a. Find both the growth rate of dividends and the price of the stock if the company reinvests the following fraction of its earnings in the firm: (i) 0%; (ii) 40%; (iii) 60%.

     b. Redo part (a) now assuming that the rate of return on reinvested earnings is 20%. What is the present value of growth opportunities for each reinvestment rate?

     c. Considering your answers to parts (a) and (b), can you briefly state the difference between companies experiencing growth versus companies with growth opportunities?

19. **Nonconstant Growth.** You expect a share of stock to pay dividends of $1.00, $1.25, and $1.50 in each of the next 3 years. You believe the stock will sell for $20 at the end of the third year. *(LO2)*

     a. What is the stock price if the discount rate for the stock is 10%?

     b. What is the dividend yield?

20. **Constant-Growth Model.** Here are data on two stocks, both of which have discount rates of 15%: *(LO2)*

	Stock A	Stock B
Return on equity	15%	10%
Earnings per share	$2.00	$1.50
Dividends per share	$1.00	$1.00

     a. What are the dividend payout ratios for each firm?

     b. What are the expected dividend growth rates for each firm?

     c. What is the proper stock price for each firm?

21. **P/E Ratios.** Web Cites Research projects a rate of return of 20% on new projects. Management plans to plow back 30% of all earnings into the firm. Earnings this year will be $3 per share, and investors expect a 12% rate of return on stocks facing the same risks as Web Cites. *(LO4)*

    a. What is the sustainable growth rate?
    b. What is the stock price?
    c. What is the present value of growth opportunities?
    d. What is the P/E ratio?
    e. What would the price and P/E ratio be if the firm paid out all earnings as dividends?
    f. What do you conclude about the relationship between growth opportunities and P/E ratios?

22. **Constant-Growth Model.** Fincorp will pay a year-end dividend of $2.40 per share, which is expected to grow at a 4% rate for the indefinite future. The discount rate is 12%. *(LO2)*

    a. What is the stock selling for?
    b. If earnings are $3.10 a share, what is the implied value of the firm's growth opportunities?

23. **P/E Ratios.** No-Growth Industries pays out all of its earnings as dividends. It will pay its next $4 per share dividend in a year. The discount rate is 12%. *(LO4)*

    a. What is the price-earnings ratio of the company?
    b. What would the P/E ratio be if the discount rate were 10%?

24. **Growth Opportunities.** Stormy Weather has no attractive investment opportunities. Its return on equity equals the discount rate, which is 10%. Its expected earnings this year are $4 per share. Find the stock price, P/E ratio, and growth rate of dividends for plowback ratios of

    a. zero. *(LO2)*
    b. .40. *(LO2)*
    c. .80. *(LO2)*

25. **Growth Opportunities.** Trend-Line Inc. has been growing at a rate of 6% per year and is expected to continue to do so indefinitely. The next dividend is expected to be $5 per share. *(LO2)*

    a. If the market expects a 10% rate of return on Trend-Line, at what price must it be selling?
    b. If Trend-Line's earnings per share will be $8, what part of Trend-Line's value is due to assets in place, and what part to growth opportunities?

26. **Market value balance sheets.** Construct a market-value balance sheet for FedEx, using the information in Table 7.1 and stock prices reported in Sections 7.1 and 7.2. Assume that market and book values are equal for current assets, current liabilities, and debt and other long-term liabilities. How much extra value shows up on the asset side of the balance sheet? *(LO1)*

27. **P/E Ratios.** Castles in the Sand generates a rate of return of 20% on its investments and maintains a plowback ratio of .30. Its earnings this year will be $4 per share. Investors expect a 12% rate of return on the stock.

    a. Find the price and P/E ratio of the firm. *(LO2)*
    b. What happens to the P/E ratio if the plowback ratio is reduced to .20? Why? *(LO4)*
    c. Show that if plowback equals zero, the earnings-price ratio, E/P, falls to the expected rate of return on the stock. *(LO4)*

28. **Dividend Growth.** Grandiose Growth has a dividend growth rate of 20%. The discount rate is 10%. The end-of-year dividend will be $2 per share. *(LO2)*

    a. What is the present value of the dividend to be paid in year 1? Year 2? Year 3?
    b. Could anyone rationally expect this growth rate to continue indefinitely?

29. **Stock Valuation.** Start-Up Industries is a new firm that has raised $200 million by selling shares of stock. Management plans to earn a 24% rate of return on equity, which is more than the 15% rate of return available on comparable-risk investments. Half of all earnings will be reinvested in the firm. *(LO2)*

    a. What will be Start-Up's ratio of market value to book value?
    b. How would that ratio change if the firm can earn only a 10% rate of return on its investments?

30. **Nonconstant Growth.** Planned Obsolescence has a product that will be in vogue for 3 years, at which point the firm will close up shop and liquidate the assets. As a result, forecast dividends are $DIV_1 = \$2$, $DIV_2 = \$2.50$, and $DIV_3 = \$18$. What is the stock price if the discount rate is 12%? *(LO2)*

31. **Nonconstant Growth.** Tattletale News Corp. has been growing at a rate of 20% per year, and you expect this growth rate in earnings and dividends to continue for another 3 years. *(LO2)*

   a. If the last dividend paid was $2, what will the next dividend be?

   b. If the discount rate is 15% and the steady growth rate after 3 years is 4%, what should the stock price be today?

32. **Nonconstant Growth.** Reconsider Tattletale News from the previous problem.

   a. What is your prediction for the stock price in 1 year? *(LO2)*

   b. Show that the expected rate of return equals the discount rate. *(LO3)*

33. **Interpreting the Efficient-Market Theory.** How would you respond to the following comments? *(LO5)*

   a. "Efficient market, my eye! I know lots of investors who do crazy things."

   b. "Efficient market? Balderdash! I know at least a dozen people who have made a bundle in the stock market."

   c. "The trouble with the efficient-market theory is that it ignores investors' psychology."

34. **Real versus Financial Investments.** Why do investments in financial markets almost always have zero NPVs, whereas firms can find many investments in their product markets with positive NPVs? *(LO5)*

35. **Investment Performance.** It seems that every month we read an article in *The Wall Street Journal* about a stockpicker with a marvelous track record. Do these examples mean that financial markets are not efficient? *(LO5)*

36. **Implications of Efficient Markets.** The president of Good Fortunes, Inc., states at a press conference that the company has a 30-year history of ever-increasing dividend payments. Good Fortunes is widely regarded as one of the best-run firms in its industry. Does this make the firm's stock a good buy? Explain. *(LO5)*

37. **Implications of Efficient Markets.** "Long-term interest rates are at record highs. Most companies, therefore, find it cheaper to finance with common stock or relatively inexpensive short-term bank loans." Discuss. *(LO5)*

38. **Expectations and Efficient Markets.** Geothermal Corp. just announced good news: Its earnings have increased by 20%. Most investors had anticipated an increase of 25%. Will Geothermal's stock price increase or decrease when the announcement is made? *(LO5)*

39. **Behavioral Finance.** In Section 7.6 we gave two examples of market anomalies (the earnings-announcement puzzle and the new-issue puzzle). Do you think that behavioral finance can help to explain these anomalies? *(LO5)*

CHALLENGE PROBLEMS

40. **Sustainable Growth.** Computer Corp. reinvests 60% of its earnings in the firm. The stock sells for $50, and the next dividend will be $2.50 per share. The discount rate is 15%. What is the rate of return on the company's reinvested funds? *(LO2)*

41. **Nonconstant Growth.** A company will pay a $2 per share dividend in 1 year. The dividend in 2 years will be $4 per share, and it is expected that dividends will grow at 5% per year thereafter. The expected rate of return on the stock is 12%. *(LO2)*

   a. What is the current price of the stock?

   b. What is the expected price of the stock in a year?

   c. Show that the expected return, 12%, equals dividend yield plus capital appreciation.

42. **Nonconstant Growth.** Phoenix Industries has pulled off a miraculous recovery. Four years ago it was near bankruptcy. Today, it announced a $1 per share dividend to be paid a year from now, the first dividend since the crisis. Analysts expect dividends to increase by $1 a year for another 2 years. After the third year (in which dividends are $3 per share) dividend growth is expected to settle down to a more moderate long-term growth rate of 6%. If the firm's investors expect to earn a return of 14% on this stock, what must be its price? *(LO2)*

43. **Nonconstant Growth.** Compost Science, Inc. (CSI), is in the business of converting Boston's sewage sludge into fertilizer. The business is not in itself very profitable. However, to induce CSI to

remain in business, the Metropolitan District Commission (MDC) has agreed to pay whatever amount is necessary to yield CSI a 10% return on investment. At the end of the year, CSI is expected to pay a $4 dividend. It has been reinvesting 40% of earnings and growing at 4% a year. *(LO2)*

   a. Suppose CSI continues on this growth trend. What is the expected rate of return for an investor who purchases the stock at the market price of $100?

   b. What part of the $100 price is attributable to the present value of growth opportunities?

   c. Now the MDC announces a plan for CSI to also treat Cambridge sewage. CSI's plant will therefore be expanded gradually over 5 years. This means that CSI will have to reinvest 80% of its earnings for 5 years. Starting in year 6, however, it will again be able to pay out 60% of earnings. What will be CSI's stock price once this announcement is made and its consequences for CSI are known?

Templates can be found at
www.mhhe.com/bmm7e.

44. **Nonconstant Growth.** Better Mousetraps has come out with an improved product, and the world is beating a path to its door. As a result, the firm projects growth of 20% per year for 4 years. By then, other firms will have copycat technology, competition will drive down profit margins, and the sustainable growth rate will fall to 5%. The most recent annual dividend was $DIV_0 = 1$ per share. *(LO2)*

   a. What are the expected values of DIV_1, DIV_2, DIV_3, and DIV_4?

   b. What is the expected stock price 4 years from now? The discount rate is 10%.

   c. What is the stock price today?

   d. Find the dividend yield, DIV_1/P_0.

   e. What will next year's stock price, P_1, be?

   f. What is the expected rate of return to an investor who buys the stock now and sells it in 1 year?

Templates can be found at
www.mhhe.com/bmm7e.

45. **Nonconstant Growth.** *(LO2)*

   a. Return to the previous problem, and compute the value of Better Mousetraps for assumed sustainable growth rates of 6% through 9%, in increments of .5%.

   b. Compute the percentage change in the value of the firm for each 1-percentage-point increase in the assumed final growth rate, g.

   c. What happens to the sensitivity of intrinsic value to changes in g? What do you conclude about the reliability of the dividend growth model when the assumed sustainable growth rate begins to approach the discount rate?

46. **Yield Curve and Efficient Markets.** If the yield curve is downward-sloping, meaning that long-term interest rates are lower than short-term interest rates, what might investors believe about future short-term interest rates? *(LO5)*

WEB EXERCISES

1. Review Table 7.2, which lists the market values of several firms. Update the table. Which company's value has changed by the greatest percentage since 2010, when the table was created? (*Hint:* Look for the price per share and the number of shares outstanding. The product of the two is total market capitalization.) Now calculate book value per share. Have the book values for any firm changed? Which seems to be more stable, book or market value? Why?

2. From finance.yahoo.com, obtain the price-earnings ratios of Adobe Systems (ADBE) and American Electric Power (AEP). Which of these two firms seems to be more of a "growth stock"? Now obtain a forecast of each firm's expected earnings per share in the coming year. You can find earnings forecasts on yahoo.com under "Analysts Estimates." What is the present value of growth opportunities for each firm as a fraction of the stock price? (Assume, for simplicity, that the required rate of return on the stocks is $r = 8\%$.) Are the relative values you obtain for PVGO consistent with the P/E ratios?

SOLUTIONS TO SELF-TEST QUESTIONS

7.1 Expected industry profitability has fallen. Thus the value of future investment opportunities has fallen relative to the value of assets in place. This happens in all growth industries sooner or later, as competition increases and profitable new investment opportunities shrink.

7.2 $P_0 = \dfrac{DIV_1 + P_1}{1 + r} = \dfrac{\$5 + \$105}{1.10} = \$100$

7.3   Since dividends and share price grow at 5%,

$$DIV_2 = \$5 \times 1.05 = \$5.25, DIV_3 = \$5 \times 1.05^2 = \$5.51$$

$$P_3 = \$100 \times 1.05^3 = \$115.76$$

$$P_0 = \dfrac{DIV_1}{1 + r} + \dfrac{DIV_2}{(1 + r)^2} + \dfrac{DIV_3 + P_3}{(1 + r)^3}$$

$$= \dfrac{\$5.00}{1.10} + \dfrac{\$5.25}{(1.10)^2} + \dfrac{\$5.51 + \$115.76}{(1.10)^3} = \$100$$

7.4 $P_0 = \dfrac{DIV}{r} = \dfrac{\$25}{.20} = \$125$

7.5   The two firms have equal risk, so we can use the data for Androscoggin to find the expected return on either stock:

$$r = \dfrac{DIV_1}{P_0} + g = \dfrac{\$5}{\$100} + .05 = .10, \text{ or } 10\%$$

7.6   The present value of dividends in years 1 to 5 is still \$8.41. However, with a lower terminal growth rate after year 5, the stock price in year 5 will be lower. If we assume a 5% growth rate, then the forecast dividend in year 6 is

$$DIV_6 = 1.05 \times DIV_5 = 1.05 \times 2.64 = \$2.772$$

and the expected price at the end of year 5 is

$$P_5 = \dfrac{DIV_6}{r - g} = \dfrac{\$2.772}{.09 - .05} = \$69.30$$

Therefore, present value is

$$P_0 = PV(\text{dividends years 1–5}) + PV(\text{price in year 5})$$

$$= \$8.41 + \dfrac{\$69.30}{1.09^5} = \$53.45$$

7.7   a. The sustainable growth rate is

$$g = \text{return on equity} \times \text{plowback ratio}$$
$$= .05 \times .314 = .0157, \text{ or } 1.57\%$$

     b. First value the company. At a 68.6% payout ratio, $DIV_1 = \$.63$ as before. Using the constant-growth model,

$$P_0 = \dfrac{\$.63}{.068 - .0157} = \$12.05$$

       which is \$1.46 per share less than the company's no-growth value of \$13.51. In this example Aqua America would be throwing away \$1.46 of potential value by investing in projects with unattractive rates of return.

     c. Sure. A raider could take over the company and generate a profit of \$1.46 per share just by halting all investments offering less than the 6.8% rate of return demanded by investors. This assumes the raider could buy the shares for \$13.51.

7.8   a. False. The *levels* of successive stock prices are related. If a stock is selling for \$100 per share today, the best guess of its price tomorrow is \$100.

     b. True. *Changes* in stock prices are unrelated. Whether a stock price increases or decreases today has no bearing on whether it will do so tomorrow.

     c. False. There is no such thing as a "normal" price. If there were, you could make easy profits by buying shares selling below their normal prices (which would tend to be rising back toward those normal levels) and selling shares currently selling above their normal prices. Under a random walk, prices are equally likely to rise or fall.

     d. True. Under a random walk, prices are equally likely to over- or underperform regardless of their past history.

7.9 Fundamental analysts ensure that stock prices reflect all publicly available information about the underlying value of the firm. If share prices deviate from their fundamental values, such analysts will generate buying or selling pressure that will return prices to their proper levels. Similarly, technical analysts ensure that if there is useful information in stock price history, it will be reflected in current share prices.

MINICASE

Terence Breezeway, the CEO of Prairie Home Stores, wondered what retirement would be like. It was almost 20 years to the day since his uncle Jacob Breezeway, Prairie Home's founder, had asked him to take responsibility for managing the company. Now it was time to spend more time riding and fishing on the old Lazy Beta Ranch.

Under Mr. Breezeway's leadership Prairie Home had grown slowly but steadily and was solidly profitable. (Table 7.6 shows earnings, dividends, and book asset values for the last 5 years.) Most of the company's supermarkets had been modernized and its brand name was well known.

Mr. Breezeway was proud of this record, although he wished that Prairie Home could have grown more rapidly. He had passed up several opportunities to build new stores in adjacent counties. Prairie Home was still just a family company. Its common stock was distributed among 15 grandchildren and nephews of Jacob Breezeway, most of whom had come to depend on generous regular dividends. The commitment to high dividend payout[16] had reduced the earnings available for reinvestment and thereby constrained growth.

Mr. Breezeway believed the time had come to take Prairie Home public. Once its shares were traded in the public market, the Breezeway descendants who needed (or just wanted) more cash to spend could sell off part of their holdings. Others with more interest in the business could hold on to their shares and be rewarded by higher future earnings and stock prices.

But if Prairie Home did go public, what should its shares sell for? Mr. Breezeway worried that shares would be sold, either by Breezeway family members or by the company itself, at too low a price. One relative was about to accept a private offer for $200, the current book value per share, but Mr. Breezeway had intervened and convinced the would-be seller to wait.

Prairie Home's value depended not just on its current book value or earnings but on its future prospects, which were good. One financial projection (shown in the top panel of Table 7.7) called for growth in earnings of over 100% by 2022. Unfortunately, this plan would require reinvestment of all of Prairie Home's earnings from 2016 to 2019. After that the company could resume its normal dividend payout and growth rate. Mr. Breezeway believed this plan was feasible.

He was determined to step aside for the next generation of top management. But before retiring, he had to decide whether to recommend that Prairie Home Stores "go public"—and before that decision he had to know what the company was worth.

The next morning he rode thoughtfully to work. He left his horse at the south corral and ambled down the dusty street to Mike Gordon's Saloon, where Francine Firewater, the company's CFO, was having her usual steak-and-beans breakfast. He asked Ms. Firewater to prepare a formal report to Prairie Home stockholders, valuing the company on the assumption that its shares were publicly traded.

Ms. Firewater asked two questions immediately. First, what should she assume about investment and growth? Mr. Breezeway suggested two valuations, one assuming more rapid expansion (as in the top panel of Table 7.7) and another just projecting past growth (as in the bottom panel of Table 7.7).

Second, what rate of return should she use? Mr. Breezeway said that 15%, Prairie Home's usual return on book equity, sounded right to him, but he referred her to an article in the *Journal of Finance* indicating that investors in rural supermarket chains, with risks similar to Prairie Home Stores, expected to earn about 11% on average.

---

[16] The company traditionally paid out cash dividends equal to 10% of start-of-period book value. See Table 7.6.

TABLE 7.6 Financial data for Prairie Home Stores, 2011–2015 (figures in millions)

	2011	2012	2013	2014	2015
Book value, start of year	$62.7	$66.1	$69.0	$73.9	$76.5
Earnings	9.7	9.5	11.8	11.0	11.2
Dividends	6.3	6.6	6.9	7.4	7.7
Retained earnings	3.4	2.9	4.9	2.6	3.5
Book value, end of year	66.1	69.0	73.9	76.5	80.0

Notes:
1. Prairie Home Stores has 400,000 common shares.
2. The company's policy is to pay cash dividends equal to 10% of start-of-year book value.

TABLE 7.7 Financial projections for Prairie Home Stores, 2016–2021 (figures in millions)

	2016	2017	2018	2019	2020	2021
			Rapid-Growth Scenario			
Book value, start of year	$80	$ 92	$105.8	$121.7	$139.9	$146.9
Earnings	12	13.8	15.9	18.3	21.0	22.0
Dividends	0	0	0	0	14	14.7
Retained earnings	12	13.8	15.9	18.3	7.0	7.4
Book value, end of year	92	105.8	121.7	139.9	146.9	154.3
			Constant-Growth Scenario			
Book value, start of year	$80	$84	$88.2	$92.6	$ 97.2	$102.1
Earnings	12	12.6	13.2	13.9	14.6	15.3
Dividends	8	8.4	8.8	9.3	9.7	10.2
Retained earnings	4	4.2	4.4	4.6	4.9	5.1
Book value, end of year	84	88.2	92.6	97.2	102.1	107.2

Notes:

1. Both panels assume earnings equal to 15% of start-of-year book value. This profitability rate is constant.

2. The top panel assumes all earnings are reinvested from 2016 to 2019. In 2020 and later years, two-thirds of earnings are paid out as dividends and one-third reinvested.

3. The bottom panel assumes two-thirds of earnings are paid out as dividends in all years.

4. Columns may not add up because of rounding.

CHAPTER 8

Net Present Value and Other Investment Criteria

LEARNING OBJECTIVES

After studying this chapter, you should be able to:

(1) Calculate the net present value of an investment.

(2) Use the net present value rule to analyze three common problems that involve competing projects: (a) when to postpone an investment expenditure, (b) how to choose between projects with unequal lives, and (c) when to replace equipment.

(3) Understand the payback rule and explain why it *doesn't* always make shareholders better off.

(4) Calculate the internal rate of return of a project and know what to look out for when using the internal rate of return rule.

(5) Calculate the profitability index and use it to choose between projects when funds are limited.

RELATED WEB SITES FOR THIS CHAPTER CAN BE FOUND AT WWW.MHHE.COM/BMM7E.

High tech businesses often require huge investments. How do companies decide which investments are worth undertaking?

The investment decision, also known as *capital budgeting,* is central to the success of the company. We have already seen that capital investments can sometimes absorb substantial amounts of cash; they also have very long-term consequences. The assets you buy today may determine the business you are in many years hence.

For some investment projects "substantial" is an understatement. Consider the following examples:

- By 2010, Verizon had already spent an estimated $23 billion rolling out its fiber-optic network, FiOS.

- The cost of bringing one new prescription drug to market is estimated to be $800 million.

- Rio Tinto is investing $3.6 billion to expand production at its Pilbara iron ore mine in Western Australia.

- Toyota's research and development costs for its hybrid gas-electric engine have been about $6 billion.

- Estimated production and marketing costs for the movie *Avatar* were about $400 million.

- The development costs of the Airbus A380 jumbo jet are estimated at around $15 billion.

Notice that many of these big capital projects require heavy investment in intangible assets. For example, almost all the cost of drug development is for research and testing. So is much of the cost of developing the hybrid auto. Any expenditure made in the hope of generating more cash later can be called a *capital investment project,* regardless of whether the cash outlay goes to tangible or intangible assets.

A company's shareholders prefer to be rich rather than poor. Therefore, they want the firm to invest in every project that is worth more than it costs. The difference between a project's value and its cost is termed the *net present value.* Companies can best help their shareholders by investing in projects with a *positive* net present value.

We start this chapter by showing how to calculate the net present value of some simple investment projects. Next we look at how to deal with cases in which a company must choose between two or more competing proposals; if it accepts one proposal, it cannot also take the other. For example, a company may need to choose between buying an expensive, durable machine or buying a cheap and short-lived one. We will show how the net present value criterion can be used to make such choices.

We also examine three other criteria that companies sometimes consider when evaluating investments. One of these, the *payback rule* is little better than a rule of thumb that companies may use to separate the no-brainers from the more marginal cases. We will spend relatively little time on the payback rule.

Instead of calculating a project's net present value, companies sometimes compare the expected rate of return from investing in a project with the return that shareholders could earn on equivalent-risk investments in the capital market.

Companies accept only those projects that provide a higher return than shareholders could earn for themselves. This rate of return rule generally gives the same answers as the net present value rule, but, as we shall see, it has some pitfalls. We explain three of these pitfalls in the body of the chapter, and in the appendix we describe a couple of tricks that can be used to circumvent them.

The other gauge of a project's worth is the *profitability index*. This measures the net present value of a project per dollar invested. The profitability index is less commonly used, but you will discover that it can be a handy tool when the company does not have enough money to take on every project that it would like to.

8.1 Net Present Value

In Chapter 5 you learned how to discount future cash payments to find their present value. We now apply these ideas to evaluate a simple investment proposal.

Suppose that you are in the real estate business. You are considering construction of an office block. The land would cost $50,000, and construction would cost a further $300,000. You foresee a shortage of office space and predict that a year from now you will be able to sell the building for $400,000. Thus you would be investing $350,000 now in the expectation of realizing $400,000 at the end of the year. Therefore, projected cash flows may be summarized in a simple time line as follows:

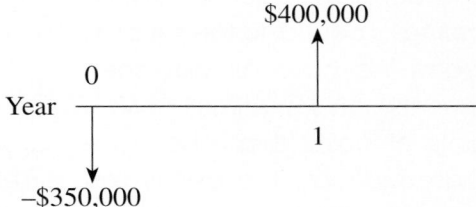

You should go ahead if the present value of the $400,000 payoff is greater than the investment of $350,000.

Assume for the moment that the $400,000 payoff is a sure thing. The office building is not the only way to obtain $400,000 a year from now. You could invest in 1-year U.S. Treasury notes. Suppose Treasury notes offer interest of 7%. How much would you have to invest in them in order to receive $400,000 at the end of the year? That's easy: You would have to invest

$$\$400{,}000 \times \frac{1}{1.07} = \$400{,}000 \times .9346 = \$373{,}832$$

Let's assume that as soon as you have purchased the land and laid out the money for construction, you decide to cash in on your project. How much could you sell it for? Since the property will be worth $400,000 in a year, investors would be willing to pay at most $373,832 for it now. That's all it would cost them to get the same $400,000 payoff by investing in government securities. Of course, you could always sell your property for less, but why sell for less than the market will bear?

Therefore, at an interest rate of 7%, the present value of the $400,000 payoff from the office building is $373,832.

The $373,832 present value is the only price that satisfies both buyer and seller. In general, the present value is the only feasible price, and the present value of the property is also its *market price* or *market value.*

To calculate present value, we discounted the expected future payoff by the rate of return offered by comparable investment alternatives. The discount rate—7% in our example—is often known as the **opportunity cost of capital.** It is called the *opportunity cost* because it is the return that is being given up by investing in the project.

opportunity cost of capital
Expected rate of return given up by investing in a project.

The building is worth $373,832, but this does not mean that you are $373,832 better off. You committed $350,000, and therefore your **net present value (NPV)** is $23,832. Net present value is found by subtracting the required initial investment from the present value of the project cash flows:

net present value (NPV)
Present value of cash flows minus investment.

$$\text{NPV} = \text{PV} - \text{required investment} \qquad (8.1)$$
$$= \$373,832 - \$350,000 = \$23,832$$

In other words, your office development is worth more than it costs—it makes a *net* contribution to value. **The net present value *rule* states that managers increase shareholders' wealth by accepting all projects that are worth more than they cost. Therefore, they should accept all projects with a positive net present value.**

A Comment on Risk and Present Value

In our discussion of the office development we assumed we knew the value of the completed project. Of course, you will never be *certain* about the future values of office buildings. The $400,000 represents the best *forecast,* but it is not a sure thing.

Therefore, our initial conclusion about how much investors would pay for the building is premature. Since they could achieve $400,000 risklessly by investing in $373,832 worth of U.S. Treasury notes, they would not buy your building for that amount. You would have to cut your asking price to attract investors' interest.

Here we can invoke a basic financial principle: **A risky dollar is worth less than a safe one.**

Most investors avoid risk when they can do so without sacrificing return. However, the concepts of present value and the opportunity cost of capital still apply to risky investments. It is still proper to discount the payoff by the rate of return offered by a comparable investment. But we have to think of *expected* payoffs and the *expected* rates of return on other investments.

Not all investments are equally risky. The office development is riskier than a Treasury note but is probably less risky than investing in a start-up biotech company. Suppose you believe the office development is as risky as an investment in the stock market and that you forecast a 12% rate of return for stock market investments. Then 12% would be the appropriate opportunity cost of capital. That is what you are giving up by not investing in comparable securities. You can now recompute NPV:

$$\text{PV} = \$400,000 \times \frac{1}{1.12} = \$400,000 \times .8929 = \$357,143$$
$$\text{NPV} = \text{PV} - \$350,000 = \$7,143$$

If other investors agree with your forecast of a $400,000 payoff and with your assessment of a 12% opportunity cost of capital, then the property ought to be worth $357,143 once construction is under way. If you tried to sell for more than that, there would be no takers, because the property would then offer a lower expected rate of return than the 12% available in the stock market. The office building still makes a net contribution to value, but it is much smaller than our earlier calculations indicated.

Self-Test 8.1

What is the office development's NPV if construction costs increase to $355,000? Assume the opportunity cost of capital is 12%. Is the development still a worthwhile investment? How high can development costs be before the project is no longer attractive? Now suppose that the opportunity cost of capital is 20% with construction costs of $355,000. Why is the office development no longer an attractive investment?

Valuing Long-Lived Projects

The net present value rule works for projects of any length. For example, suppose that you are approached by a possible tenant who is prepared to rent your office block for 3 years at a fixed annual rent of $25,000. You would need to expand the reception area and add some other tailor-made features. This would increase the initial investment to $375,000, but you forecast that after you have collected the third year's rent the building could be sold for $450,000. The projected cash flow (denoted C) in each year is shown below (the final cash flow is the sum of rental income plus the proceeds from selling the building).

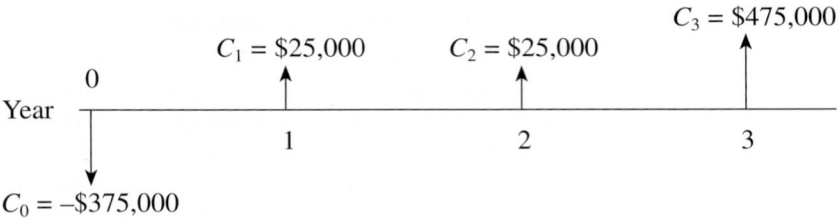

Notice that the initial investment shows up as a negative cash flow. That first cash flow, C_0, is $-\$375,000$. For simplicity, we will again assume that these cash flows are certain and that the opportunity cost of capital is $r = 7\%$.

Figure 8.1 shows a time line of the cash inflows and their present values. To find the present value of the project, we discount these cash inflows at the 7% opportunity cost of capital:

$$PV = \frac{C_1}{1 + r} + \frac{C_2}{(1 + r)^2} + \frac{C_3}{(1 + r)^3}$$

$$= \frac{\$25,000}{1.07} + \frac{\$25,000}{1.07^2} + \frac{\$475,000}{1.07^3} = \$432,942$$

The *net* present value of the revised project is NPV $= \$432,942 - \$375,000 = \$57,942$. Constructing the office block and renting it for 3 years makes a greater addition to your wealth than selling the office block at the end of the first year.

Of course, rather than subtracting the initial investment from the project's present value, you could calculate NPV directly, as in the following equation, where C_0 denotes the initial cash outflow required to build the office block.

$$NPV = C_0 + \frac{C_1}{1 + r} + \frac{C_2}{(1 + r)^2} + \frac{C_3}{(1 + r)^3}$$

$$= -\$375,000 + \frac{\$25,000}{1.07} + \frac{\$25,000}{1.07^2} + \frac{\$475,000}{1.07^3} = \$57,942$$

Let's check that the owners of this project really are better off. Suppose you put up $375,000 of your own money, commit to build the office building, and sign a lease that

FIGURE 8.1   **Cash flows and their present values for the office block project. Final cash flow of $475,000 is the sum of the rental income in year 3 plus the forecast sales price for the building.**

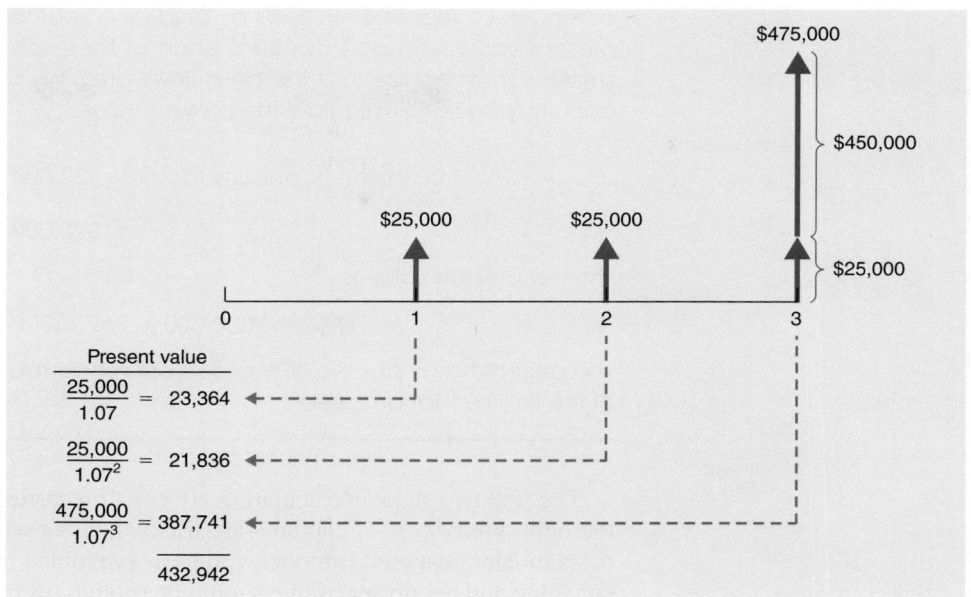

will bring in $25,000 a year for 3 years. Now you can cash in by selling the project to other investors.

Suppose you sell 1,000 shares in the project. Each share represents a claim to 1/1,000 of the future cash flows. Since the cash flows are certain, and the interest rate offered by other certain investments is 7%, investors will value each share at

$$\text{Price per share} = \frac{\$25}{1.07} + \frac{\$25}{1.07^2} + \frac{\$475}{1.07^3} = \$432.94$$

Thus you can sell the project to outside investors for $1,000 \times \$432.94 = \$432,940$, which, save for rounding, is exactly the present value we calculated earlier. Your net gain is

$$\text{Net gain} = \$432,942 - \$375,000 = \$57,942$$

which is the project's NPV. This equivalence should be no surprise, since the present value calculation is *designed* to calculate the value of future cash flows to investors in the capital markets.

Notice that in principle there could be a different opportunity cost of capital for each period's cash flow. In that case we would discount C_1 by r_1, the discount rate for 1-year cash flows; C_2 would be discounted by r_2; and so on. Here we assume that the cost of capital is the same regardless of the date of the cash flow. We do this for one reason only—simplicity. But we are in good company: With only rare exceptions firms decide on an appropriate discount rate and then use it to discount all cash flows from the project.

EXAMPLE 8.1   ▶   Valuing a New Computer System

Obsolete Technologies is considering the purchase of a new computer system to help handle its warehouse inventories. The system costs $50,000, is expected to last 4 years, and should reduce the cost of managing inventories by $22,000 a year. The opportunity cost of capital is 10%. Should Obsolete go ahead?

Don't be put off by the fact that the computer system does not generate any sales. If the expected cost savings are realized, the company's cash flows will be $22,000 a year higher as a result of buying the computer. Thus we can say that the computer increases cash flows by $22,000 a year for each of 4 years. To calculate present value, you can discount each of these cash flows by 10%. However, it is smarter to recognize that the cash flows are level, and therefore you can use the annuity formula to calculate the present value:

$$PV = \text{cash flow} \times \text{annuity factor} = \$22,000 \times \left[\frac{1}{.10} - \frac{1}{.10(1.10)^4} \right]$$

$$= \$22,000 \times 3.1699 = \$69,738$$

The net present value is

$$NPV = -\$50,000 + \$69,738 = \$19,738$$

The project has a positive NPV of $19,738. Undertaking it would increase the value of the firm by that amount.

The first two steps in calculating NPVs—forecasting the cash flows and estimating the opportunity cost of capital—are tricky, and we will have a lot more to say about them in later chapters. But once you have assembled the data, the calculation of present value and net present value should be routine. Here is another example.

EXAMPLE 8.2 ▶ Calculating Eurotunnel's NPV

One of the world's largest commercial investment projects was construction of the Channel Tunnel by the Anglo-French company Eurotunnel. Here is a chance to put yourself in the shoes of Eurotunnel's financial manager and find out whether the project looked like it would be a good deal for shareholders. The figures in column C of Table 8.1 are based on the forecasts of construction costs and revenues that the company provided to investors in 1986.

The Channel Tunnel project was not a safe investment. Indeed, the prospectus to the Channel Tunnel share issue cautioned investors that the project "involves significant risk and should be regarded at this stage as speculative. If for any reason the Project is abandoned or Eurotunnel is unable to raise the necessary finance, it is likely that equity investors will lose some or all of their money."

To be induced to invest in the project, investors needed a higher prospective rate of return than they could get on safe government bonds. Suppose investors expected a return of 13% from investments in the capital market that had a degree of risk similar to that of the Channel Tunnel. That was what investors were giving up when they provided the capital for the tunnel. To find the project's NPV we therefore discount the cash flows in Table 8.1 at 13%.

Since the tunnel was expected to take about 7 years to build, there are 7 years of negative cash flows in Table 8.1. To calculate NPV, you just discount all the cash flows, positive and negative, at 13% and sum the results. Call 1986 "year 0," call 1987 "year 1," and so on. Then

$$NPV = C_0 + \frac{C_1}{1 + r} + \frac{C_2}{(1 + r)^2} + \cdots$$

$$= -\pounds457 + \frac{-\pounds476}{1.13} + \frac{-\pounds497}{(1.13)^2} + \cdots + \frac{\pounds17,781}{(1.13)^{24}} = \pounds249.8 \text{ million}$$

We present the calculations in column D. (The nearby box provides additional discussion of how to calculate present values by using spreadsheets.) The net present value of the forecast cash flows is £249.8 million, making the tunnel a worthwhile project, though not by a wide margin, considering the planned investment of nearly £4 billion.

Present Values

Computer spreadsheets are tailor-made to calculate the present value of a series of cash flows. For example, the spreadsheet in Table 8.1, available at www.mhhe.com/bmm7e, sets up the Eurotunnel problem as an Excel spreadsheet. Cells D3 to D27 calculate the present value of each year's cash flows by discounting at 13% for the length of time given in column B. Cell D29 shows the sum of these separate present values.

Excel also provides a built-in function to calculate net present values. The formula is =NPV (discount rate, list of cash flows). So, instead of computing the present value of each cash flow separately and then summing, we could have used the NPV function in cell D31. The first entry in the function is the discount rate expressed as a decimal, in this case .13. That is followed by a list of the cash flows that appear in column C.

Why is the first entry in the cash-flow list cell C4 rather than C3, which contains the immediate cash flow, −457? It turns out that Excel always assumes the first cash flow comes after one period, the next after two periods, and so on. If the first cash flow actually comes immediately, as in our example, we do not want it discounted, nor do we want the other cash flows discounted for an extra period. Therefore, we don't include the immediate cash flow in the NPV function, instead adding it undiscounted to the present value of the other cash flows (see cells D31 and E31).

Be careful if you use the NPV function. If in doubt, discount each cash flow and then sum them, as we did in Cell D29.

Spreadsheet Questions

8.1 Try calculating Eurotunnel's NPV using the function =NPV(0.13,C3:C27). What do you find?

8.2 The value for NPV in Table 8.1 is exactly 1.13 times as large as the answer you should find for the previous question. Why does this make sense?

You can find this spreadsheet at www.mhhe.com/bmm7e.

TABLE 8.1 Forecast cash flows and present values in 1986 for the Channel Tunnel project. The investment at the time appeared to have a positive NPV of £249.8 million.

	A	B	C	D	E
1			Cash Flow		
2	Year	Time	(£ million)	PV at 13%	Formula in Column D
3	1986	0	−457	−457.0	=C3/1.13^B3
4	1987	1	−476	−421.2	=C4/1.13^B4
5	1988	2	−497	−389.2	=C5/1.13^B5
6	1989	3	−522	−361.8	=C6/1.13^B6
7	1990	4	−551	−337.9	=C7/1.13^B7
8	1991	5	−584	−317.0	=C8/1.13^B8
9	1992	6	−619	−297.3	=C9/1.13^B9
10	1993	7	211	89.7	=C10/1.13^B10
11	1994	8	489	183.9	=C11/1.13^B11
12	1995	9	455	151.5	=C12/1.13^B12
13	1996	10	502	147.9	=C13/1.13^B13
14	1997	11	530	138.2	=C14/1.13^B14
15	1998	12	544	125.5	=C15/1.13^B15
16	1999	13	636	129.8	=C16/1.13^B16
17	2000	14	594	107.3	=C17/1.13^B17
18	2001	15	689	110.2	=C18/1.13^B18
19	2002	16	729	103.2	=C19/1.13^B19
20	2003	17	796	99.7	=C20/1.13^B20
21	2004	18	859	95.2	=C21/1.13^B21
22	2005	19	923	90.5	=C22/1.13^B22
23	2006	20	983	85.3	=C23/1.13^B23
24	2007	21	1,050	80.6	=C24/1.13^B24
25	2008	22	1,113	75.6	=C25/1.13^B25
26	2009	23	1,177	70.8	=C26/1.13^B26
27	2010	24	17,781	946.4	=C27/1.13^B27
28					
29	Sum:			249.8	=SUM(D3:D27)
30					
31	Instead, use Excel's NPV function			249.8	=NPV(0.13,C4:C27) + C3

You can find this spreadsheet at www.mhhe.com/bmm7e.

Note: Cash flow for 2010 includes the value in 2010 of forecast cash flows in all subsequent years. Some of these figures involve guesswork because the prospectus reported accumulated construction costs including interest expenses.
Source: Eurotunnel Equity II Prospectus, October 1986. Reprinted with permission.

Of course, NPV calculations are only as good as the underlying cash-flow forecasts. The well-known Pentagon Law of Large Projects states that anything big takes longer and costs more than you're originally led to believe. As the law predicted, the tunnel proved much more expensive to build than anticipated in 1986, and the opening was delayed by more than a year. Revenues also were below forecast, and Eurotunnel did not even generate enough profits to pay the interest on its debt. Thus, with hindsight, the tunnel was a costly negative-NPV venture. By 2007, Eurotunnel was operating under French bankruptcy law and had to be restructured. Eventually, the firm was reorganized into a new company called Groupe Eurotunnel.

8.2 Using the NPV Rule to Choose among Projects

So far, the simple projects that we have considered involve take-it-or-leave-it decisions. But almost all real-world decisions entail either-or choices. You could use that vacant lot to build an apartment block, rather than the office block. You could build a 7-story office building or a 10-story one. You could heat it with oil or with natural gas. You could build it today or wait a year to start construction. Such choices are said to be *mutually exclusive.*

When choosing among mutually exclusive projects, calculate the NPV of each alternative and choose the highest positive-NPV project.

EXAMPLE 8.3 ▶	Choosing between Two Projects

It has been several years since your office last upgraded its office networking software. Two competing systems have been proposed. Both have an expected useful life of 3 years, at which point it will be time for another upgrade. One proposal is for an expensive, cutting-edge system, which will cost $800,000 and increase firm cash flows by $350,000 a year through increased productivity. The other proposal is for a cheaper, somewhat slower system. This system would cost only $700,000 but would increase cash flows by only $300,000 a year. If the cost of capital is 7%, which is the better option?

The following table summarizes the cash flows and the NPVs of the two proposals:

System	Cash Flows (Thousands of dollars)				NPV at 7%
	C_0	C_1	C_2	C_3	
Faster	−800	+350	+350	+350	118.5
Slower	−700	+300	+300	+300	87.3

In both cases, the software systems are worth more than they cost, but the faster system would make the greater contribution to value and therefore should be your preferred choice.

In Example 8.3 we assumed that the choice between the two networking systems did not affect any future decisions that you might wish to make. But sometimes the choices that you make today will have an impact on future opportunities. When that is the case, choosing between competing projects is trickier. Here are three important, but often challenging, problems:

• *The investment timing problem.* Should you buy a computer now or wait and think about it again next year? (Here, today's investment is competing with possible future investments.)

- *The choice between long- and short-lived equipment.* Should the company save money today by installing cheaper machinery that will not last as long? (Here, today's decision would accelerate a later investment in machine replacement.)
- *The replacement problem.* When should existing machinery be replaced? (Using it another year could delay investment in more modern equipment.)

We will look at each of these problems in turn.

Problem 1: The Investment Timing Decision

In Example 8.1 Obsolete Technologies is contemplating the purchase of a new computer system. The proposed investment has a net present value of almost $20,000, so it appears that the cost savings would easily justify the expense of the system. However, the financial manager is not persuaded. She reasons that the price of computers is continually falling and therefore suggests postponing the purchase, arguing that the NPV of the system will be even higher if the firm waits until the following year. Unfortunately, she has been making the same argument for 10 years, and the company is steadily losing business to competitors with more efficient systems. Is there a flaw in her reasoning?

This is a problem in investment timing. When is it best to commit to a positive-NPV investment? Investment timing problems all involve choices among mutually exclusive investments. You can either proceed with the project now or do so later. You can't do both.

Table 8.2 lays out the basic data for Obsolete. You can see that the cost of the computer is expected to decline from $50,000 today to $45,000 next year, and so on. The new computer system is expected to last for 4 years from the time it is installed. The present value of the savings *at the time of installation* is expected to be $70,000. Thus, if Obsolete invests today, it achieves an NPV of $70,000 − $50,000 = $20,000; if it invests next year, it will have an NPV of $70,000 − $45,000 = $25,000.

Isn't a gain of $25,000 better than one of $20,000? Well, not necessarily—you may prefer to be $20,000 richer *today* than $25,000 richer *next year*. Your decision should depend on the cost of capital. The fourth column of Table 8.2 shows the value today (year 0) of those net present values at a 10% cost of capital. For example, you can see that the discounted value of that $25,000 gain is $25,000/1.10 = $22,700. The financial manager has a point. It is worth postponing investment in the computer: Today's NPV is higher if she waits a year. But the investment should not be postponed indefinitely. You maximize net present value today by buying the computer in year 3.

Notice that you are involved in a trade-off. The sooner you can capture the $70,000 savings the better, but if it costs you less to realize those savings by postponing the investment, it may pay for you to wait. If you postpone purchase by 1 year, the gain from buying a computer rises from $20,000 to $25,000, an increase of 25%. Since the cost of capital is only 10%, it pays to postpone at least until year 1. If you postpone from year 3 to year 4, the gain rises from $34,000 to $37,000, a rise of just under 9%. Since this is less than the cost of capital, this postponement would not make sense. **The decision rule for investment timing is to choose the investment date that produces the highest net present value *today*.**

Self-Test 8.2

Unfortunately, Obsolete Technologies' business is shrinking as the company dithers and dawdles. Its chief financial officer realizes that the savings from installing the new computer will likewise shrink by $4,000 per year, from a present value of $70,000 now, to $66,000 next year, then to $62,000, and so on. Redo Table 8.2 with this new information. When should Obsolete buy the new computer?

TABLE 8.2 Obsolete Technologies: The gain from purchase of a computer is rising, but the NPV today is highest if the computer is purchased in year 3 (figures in thousands of dollars).

Year of Purchase	Cost of Computer	PV Savings	NPV at Year of Purchase ($r = 10\%$)	NPV Today	
0	$50	$70	$20	$20.0	
1	45	70	25	22.7	
2	40	70	30	24.8	
3	36	70	34	25.5	← optimal purchase date
4	33	70	37	25.3	
5	31	70	39	24.2	

Problem 2: The Choice between Long- and Short-Lived Equipment

Suppose the firm is forced to choose between two machines, A and B. The two machines are designed differently but have identical capacity and do exactly the same job. Machine A costs $15,000 and will last 3 years. It costs $4,000 per year to run. Machine B is an "economy" model, costing only $10,000, but it will last only 2 years and costs $6,000 per year to run.

Because the two machines produce exactly the same product, the only way to choose between them is on the basis of cost. Suppose we compute the present value of the costs:

	Costs (thousands of dollars)				
Year:	0	1	2	3	PV at 6%
Machine A	15	4	4	4	$25.69
Machine B	10	6	6	—	21.00

Should we take machine B, the one with the lower present value of costs? Not necessarily. All we have shown is that machine B offers 2 years of service for a lower total cost than 3 years of service from machine A. But is the *annual* cost of using B lower than that of A?

Suppose the financial manager agrees to buy machine A and pay for its operating costs out of her budget. She then charges the plant manager an annual amount for use of the machine. There will be three equal payments starting in year 1. Obviously, the financial manager has to make sure that the present value of these payments equals the present value of the costs of machine A, $25,690. When the discount rate is 6%, the payment stream with such a present value turns out to be $9,610 a year. In other words, the cost of buying and operating machine A over its 3-year life is equivalent to an annual charge of $9,610 a year for 3 years. This figure is therefore termed the **equivalent annual annuity** of operating machine A.

equivalent annual annuity The cash flow per period with the same present value as the cost of buying and operating a machine.

	Costs (thousands of dollars)				
Year:	0	1	2	3	PV at 6%
Machine A	15	4	4	4	$25.69
Equivalent annual annuity		9.61	9.61	9.61	25.69

How did we know that an annual charge of $9,610 has a present value of $25,690? The annual charge is a 3-year annuity. So we calculate the value of this annuity and set it equal to $25,690:

Equivalent annual annuity × 3-year annuity factor = PV of costs = $25,690

If the cost of capital is 6%, the 3-year annuity factor is 2.6730. So

$$\text{Equivalent annual annuity} = \frac{\text{present value of costs}}{\text{3-year annuity factor}} \qquad (8.2)$$

$$= \frac{\$25,690}{\text{3-year annuity factor}} = \frac{\$25,690}{2.6730} = \$9,610$$

If we make a similar calculation of costs for machine B, we get:

	Costs (thousands of dollars)			
Year:	0	1	2	PV at 6%
Machine B	10	6	6	$21.00
Equivalent annual annuity		11.45	11.45	21.00

We see now that machine A is better, because its equivalent annual annuity is less ($9,610 for A versus $11,450 for B). In other words, the financial manager could afford to set a lower *annual* charge for the use of A. **We thus have a rule for comparing assets with different lives: *Select the machine that has the lowest equivalent annual annuity.***

Think of the equivalent annual annuity as the level annual charge that is necessary to recover the present value of investment outlays and operating costs.[1] The annual charge continues for the life of the equipment. Calculate the equivalent annual annuity by dividing the present value by the annuity factor.

EXAMPLE 8.4 ▶ Equivalent Annual Annuity

You need a new car. You can either purchase one outright for $15,000 or lease one for 7 years for $3,000 a year. If you buy the car, it will be worth $500 to you in 7 years. The discount rate is 10%. Should you buy or lease? What is the maximum lease payment you would be willing to pay?

The present value of the cost of purchasing is

$$PV = \$15,000 - \frac{\$500}{(1.10)^7} = \$14,743$$

The equivalent annual cost of purchasing the car is therefore the annuity with this present value:

$$\text{Equivalent annual annuity} \times \text{7-year annuity factor at 10\%} = \text{PV costs of buying}$$
$$= \$14,743$$

$$\text{Equivalent annual annuity} = \frac{\$14,743}{\text{7-year annuity factor}} = \frac{\$14,743}{4.8684} = \$3,028$$

Therefore, the annual lease payment of $3,000 is less than the equivalent annual annuity of buying the car. You should be willing to pay up to $3,028 annually to lease.

EXAMPLE 8.5 ▶ Another Equivalent Annual Annuity

Low-energy lightbulbs typically cost $3.50, have a life of 9 years, and use about $1.60 of electricity a year. Conventional lightbulbs are cheaper to buy, for they cost only $.50. On the other hand, they last only about a year and use about $6.60 of energy. If the real discount rate is 5%, which product is cheaper to use?

---

[1] We have implicitly assumed that inflation is zero. If that is not the case, it would be better to calculate the equivalent annuities for machines A and B in real terms, using the real rate of interest to calculate the annuity factor.

To answer this question, you need first to convert the initial cost of each bulb to an annual figure and then to add in the annual energy cost.[2] The following table sets out the calculations:

	Low-Energy Bulb	Conventional Bulb
1. Initial cost, $	3.50	0.50
2. Estimated life, years	9	1
3. Annuity factor at 5%	7.1078	.9524
4. Equivalent annual annuity, $, =(1)/(3)	.49	.52
5. Annual energy cost, $	1.60	6.60
6. Total annual cost, $, = (4) + (5)	2.09	7.12
Assumption: Energy costs are incurred at the end of each year.		

It seems that a low-energy bulb provides an annual saving of about $7.12 − $2.09 = $5.03.

Problem 3: When to Replace an Old Machine

Our earlier comparison of machines A and B took the life of each machine as fixed. In practice, the point at which equipment is replaced reflects economics, not physical collapse. We usually decide when to replace. For example, we usually replace a car not when it finally breaks down but when it becomes more expensive and troublesome to keep up than a replacement.

Here is an example of a replacement problem: You are operating an old machine that will last 2 more years before it gives up the ghost. It costs $12,000 per year to operate. You can replace it now with a new machine that costs $25,000 but is much more efficient ($8,000 per year in operating costs) and will last for 5 years. Should you replace the machine now or stick with it for a while longer? The opportunity cost of capital is 6%.

We calculate the NPV of the new machine and its equivalent annual annuity in the following table:

			Costs (thousands of dollars)					
Year:	0	1	2	3	4	5	PV at 6%
New machine	25	8	8	8	8	8	$58.70
Equivalent annual annuity		13.93	13.93	13.93	13.93	13.93	58.70

The cash flows of the new machine are equivalent to an annuity of $13,930 per year. So we can equally well ask whether you would want to replace your old machine, which costs $12,000 a year to run, with a new one costing $13,930 a year. When the question is posed this way, the answer is obvious. As long as your old machine costs only $12,000 a year, why replace it with a new machine that costs $1,930 a year more?

Self-Test 8.3

Machines C and D are mutually exclusive and have the following investment and operating costs. Note that machine C lasts for only 2 years.

	Year:	0	1	2	3
C		$10,000	$1,100	$1,200	—
D		12,000	1,100	1,200	$1,300

---

[2] Our calculations ignore any environmental costs.

a. Calculate the equivalent annual annuity of each investment by using a discount rate of 10%. Which machine is the better buy?
b. Now suppose you have an existing machine. You can keep it going for 1 more year only, but it will cost $2,500 in repairs and $1,800 in operating costs. Is it worth replacing now with either C or D?

8.3 The Payback Rule

A project with a positive net present value is worth more than it costs. So whenever a firm invests in such a project, it is making its shareholders better off.

These days almost every large corporation calculates the NPV of proposed investments, but management may also consider other criteria when making investment decisions. We will look at three of these measures: the project's payback, its internal rate of return, and its profitability index. As we describe these measures, you will see that payback is no better than a very rough guide to an investment's worth. On the other hand, when properly used, the internal rate of return and profitability index lead to the same decisions as net present value.

We suspect that you have often heard conversations that go something like this: "A washing machine costs about $800. But we are currently spending $6 a week, or around $300 a year, at the laundromat. So the washing machine should pay for itself in less than 3 years." You have just encountered the payback rule.

payback period
Time until cash flows recover the initial investment in the project.

A project's **payback period** is the length of time before you recover your initial investment. For the washing machine the payback period was just under 3 years. **The payback rule states that a project should be accepted if its payback period is less than a specified cutoff period.** For example, if the cutoff period is 4 years, the washing machine makes the grade; if the cutoff is 2 years, it doesn't.

As a rough rule of thumb the payback rule may be adequate, but it is easy to see that it can lead to nonsensical decisions. For example, compare projects E and F. Project E has a 2-year payback and a large positive NPV. Project F also has a 2-year payback but a negative NPV. Project E is clearly superior, but the payback rule ranks both equally. This is because payback does not consider any cash flows that arrive after the payback period. A firm that uses the payback criterion with a cutoff of 2 or more years would accept both E and F despite the fact that only E would increase shareholder wealth.

	Cash Flows (dollars)				Payback Period,	NPV
Project	C_0	C_1	C_2	C_3	Years	at 10%
E	−2,000	+1,000	+1,000	+10,000	2	$7,249
F	−2,000	+1,000	+1,000	0	2	−264
G	−2,000	0	+2,000	0	2	−347

A second problem with payback is that it gives equal weight to all cash flows arriving *before* the cutoff period, despite the fact that the more distant flows are less valuable. For example, look at project G. It also has a payback period of 2 years, but it has an even lower NPV than project F. Why? Because its cash flows arrive later within the payback period.

To use the payback rule, a firm has to decide on an appropriate cutoff period. If it uses the same cutoff regardless of project life, it will tend to accept too many short-lived projects and reject too many long-lived ones. The payback rule will bias the firm against accepting long-term projects because cash flows that arrive after the payback period are ignored.

Earlier in the chapter we evaluated the Channel Tunnel project. Large construction projects of this kind inevitably have long payback periods. The cash flows that we presented in Table 8.1 implied a payback period of just over 14 years. But most firms that employ the payback rule use a much shorter cutoff period than this. If they used the payback rule mechanically, long-lived projects like the Channel Tunnel wouldn't have a chance.

The primary attraction of the payback criterion is its simplicity. But remember that the hard part of project evaluation is forecasting the cash flows, not doing the arithmetic. Today's spreadsheets make discounting a trivial exercise. Therefore, the payback rule saves you only the easy part of the analysis.

We have had little good to say about payback. So why do many companies continue to use it? Senior managers don't truly believe that all cash flows after the payback period are irrelevant. It seems more likely (and more charitable to those managers) that payback survives because the deficiencies are relatively unimportant or because there are some offsetting benefits. Thus managers may point out that payback is the simplest way to *communicate* an idea of project desirability. Investment decisions require discussion and negotiation between people from all parts of the firm, and it is important to have a measure that everyone can understand. Perhaps, also, managers favor quick payback projects even when the projects have lower NPVs because they believe that quicker profits mean quicker promotion. That takes us back to Chapter 1, where we discussed the need to align the objectives of managers with those of the shareholders.

In practice payback is most commonly used when the capital investment is small or when the merits of the project are so obvious that more formal analysis is unnecessary. For example, if a project is expected to produce constant cash flows for 10 years and the payback period is only 2 years, the project in all likelihood has a positive NPV.

Discounted Payback

Sometimes managers calculate the *discounted-payback period*. This is the number of periods before the present value of prospective cash flows equals or exceeds the initial investment. The discounted-payback measure asks, How long must the project last in order to offer a positive net present value? If the discounted payback meets the company's cutoff period, the project is accepted; if not, it is rejected. The discounted-payback rule has the advantage that it will never accept a negative-NPV project. On the other hand, it still takes no account of cash flows after the cutoff date, so a company that uses the discounted-payback rule risks rejecting good long-term projects.

Rather than automatically rejecting any project with a long discounted-payback period, many managers simply use the measure as a warning signal. These managers don't unthinkingly reject a project with a long discounted-payback period. Instead, they check that the proposer is not unduly optimistic about the project's ability to generate cash flows into the distant future. They satisfy themselves that the equipment truly has a long life or that competitors will not enter the market and eat into the project's cash flows.

Self-Test 8.4

A project costs $5,000 and will generate annual cash flows of $660 for 20 years. What is the payback period? If the interest rate is 6%, what is the discounted payback period? What is the project NPV? Should the project be accepted?

8.4 The Internal Rate of Return Rule

Instead of calculating a project's net present value, companies often prefer to ask whether the project's return is higher or lower than the opportunity cost of capital. For example, think back to the original proposal to build the office block. You planned to invest \$350,000 to get back a cash flow of $C_1 = \$400,000$ in 1 year. Therefore, you forecast a profit on the venture of $\$400,000 - \$350,000 = \$50,000$. In a one-period project like this one, it is easy to calculate the rate of return. Simply compute end-of-year profit per dollar invested in the project:

$$\text{Rate of return} = \frac{\text{profit}}{\text{investment}} = \frac{C_1 - \text{investment}}{\text{investment}} = \frac{\$400,000 - \$350,000}{\$350,000}$$

$$= .1429, \text{ or about } 14.3\%$$

The alternative of investing in a U.S. Treasury note would provide a return of only 7%. Thus the return on your office building is higher than the opportunity cost of capital.[3]

This suggests two rules for deciding whether to go ahead with an investment project:

1. *The NPV rule.* Invest in any project that has a positive NPV when its cash flows are discounted at the opportunity cost of capital.
2. *The rate of return rule.* Invest in any project offering a rate of return that is higher than the opportunity cost of capital.

Both rules set the same cutoff point. An investment that is on the knife edge with an NPV of zero will also have a rate of return that is just equal to the cost of capital.

Suppose that the rate of interest on Treasury notes is not 7% but 14.3%. Since your office project also offers a return of 14.3%, the rate of return rule suggests that there is now nothing to choose between taking the project and leaving your money in Treasury notes.

The NPV rule also tells you that if the interest rate is 14.3%, the project is evenly balanced with an NPV of zero:

$$\text{NPV} = C_0 + \frac{C_1}{1 + r} = -\$350,000 + \frac{\$400,000}{1.143} = 0$$

The project would make you neither richer nor poorer; it is worth what it costs. Thus the NPV rule and the rate of return rule both give the same decision on accepting the project.

A Closer Look at the Rate of Return Rule

We know that if the office project's cash flows are discounted at a rate of 7%, the project has a net present value of \$23,832. If they are discounted at a rate of 14.3%, it has an NPV of zero. In Figure 8.2 the project's NPV for a variety of discount rates is plotted. This is often called the *NPV profile* of the project. Notice two important things about Figure 8.2:

1. The project rate of return (in our example, 14.3%) is also the discount rate that would give the project a zero NPV. This gives us a useful definition: **The rate of return is the discount rate at which NPV equals zero.**
2. If the opportunity cost of capital is less than the project rate of return, then the NPV of your project is positive. If the cost of capital is greater than the project rate of return, then NPV is negative. Thus the rate of return rule and the NPV rule are equivalent.

Calculating the Rate of Return for Long-Lived Projects

There is no ambiguity in calculating the rate of return for an investment that generates a single payoff after one period. But how do we calculate return when the project produces cash flows in several periods? Just think back to the definition that we

---

[3] Recall that we are assuming the profit on the office building is risk-free. Therefore, the opportunity cost of capital is the rate of return on other risk-free investments.

FIGURE 8.2 The value of the office project is lower when the discount rate is higher. The project has a positive NPV if the discount rate is less than 14.3%.

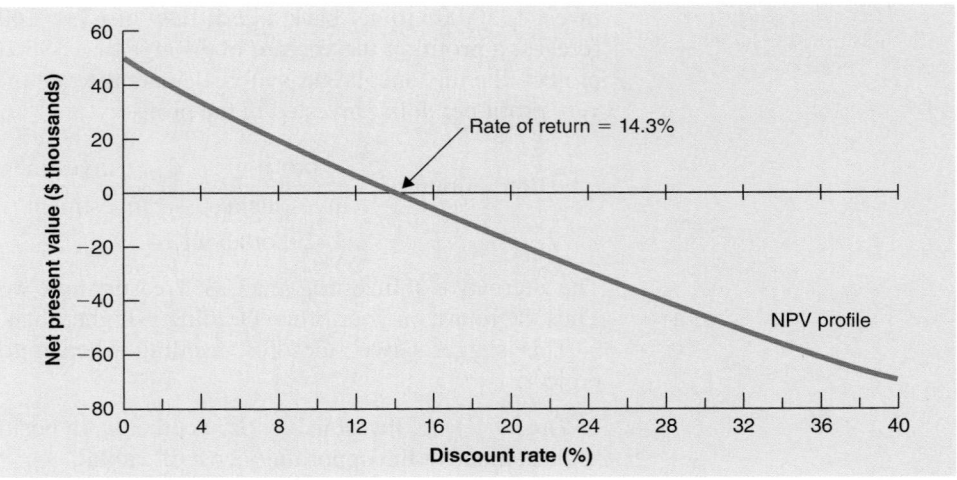

internal rate of return (IRR)
Discount rate at which project NPV = 0.

introduced above—*the project rate of return is also the discount rate that gives the project a zero NPV.* We can use this idea to find the return on a project that has many cash flows. **The discount rate that gives the project a zero NPV is known as the project's internal rate of return, or IRR. It is also termed the *discounted cash-flow (DCF) rate of return.***

Let's calculate the IRR for the revised office project. If you rent out the office block for 3 years, the cash flows are as follows:

Year:	0	1	2	3
Cash flows	−$375,000	+$25,000	+$25,000	+$475,000

The IRR is the discount rate at which these cash flows would have zero NPV. Thus,

$$\text{NPV} = -\$375,000 + \frac{\$25,000}{1 + \text{IRR}} + \frac{\$25,000}{(1 + \text{IRR})^2} + \frac{\$475,000}{(1 + \text{IRR})^3} = 0$$

There is no simple general method for solving this equation. You have to rely on a little trial and error. Let us arbitrarily try a zero discount rate. This gives an NPV of $150,000:

$$\text{NPV} = -\$375,000 + \frac{\$25,000}{1.0} + \frac{\$25,000}{(1.0)^2} + \frac{\$475,000}{(1.0)^3} = \$150,000$$

With a zero discount rate the NPV is positive. So the IRR must be greater than zero.

The next step might be to try a discount rate of 50%. In this case NPV is −$206,481:

$$\text{NPV} = -\$375,000 + \frac{\$25,000}{1.50} + \frac{\$25,000}{(1.50)^2} + \frac{\$475,000}{(1.50)^3} = -\$206,481$$

NPV is now negative. So the IRR must lie somewhere between zero and 50%. In Figure 8.3 we have plotted the net present values for a range of discount rates. You can see that a discount rate of 12.56% gives an NPV of zero. Therefore, the IRR is 12.56%. You can always find the IRR by plotting an NPV profile, as in Figure 8.3, but it is quicker and more accurate to let a spreadsheet or specially programmed financial calculator do the trial and error for you. The nearby boxes illustrate how to do so.

The rate of return rule tells you to accept a project if the rate of return exceeds the opportunity cost of capital. You can see from Figure 8.3 why this makes sense. Because the NPV profile is downward-sloping, the project has a positive NPV as long as the

FIGURE 8.3 The internal rate of return is the discount rate for which NPV equals zero.

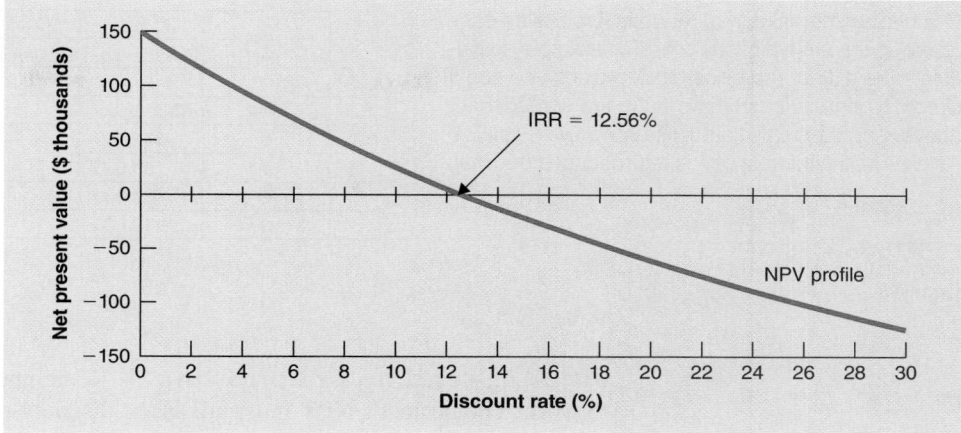

opportunity cost of capital is less than the project's 12.56% IRR. If the opportunity cost of capital is higher than the 12.56% IRR, NPV is negative. Therefore, when we compare the project IRR with the opportunity cost of capital, we are effectively asking whether the project has a positive NPV. This was true for our one-period office project. It is also true for our three-period office project. We conclude that **the rate of return rule will give the same answer as the NPV rule** *as long as the NPV of a project declines smoothly as the discount rate increases.*[4]

The usual agreement between the net present value and internal rate of return rules should not be a surprise. Both are *discounted cash-flow* methods of choosing between projects. Both are concerned with identifying those projects that make shareholders better off, and both recognize that companies always have a choice: They can invest in a project, or if the project is not sufficiently attractive, they can give the money back to shareholders and let them invest it for themselves in the capital market.

Self-Test 8.5

Suppose the cash flow in year 3 is only $420,000. Redraw Figure 8.3. How would the IRR change?

A Word of Caution

Some people confuse the internal rate of return on a project with the opportunity cost of capital. Remember that the project IRR measures the profitability of the project. It is an *internal* rate of return in the sense that it depends only on the project's own cash flows. The opportunity cost of capital is the standard for deciding whether to accept the project. It is equal to the return offered by equivalent-risk investments in the capital market.

Some Pitfalls with the Internal Rate of Return Rule

Many firms use the internal rate of return rule instead of net present value. We think that this is a pity. When used properly, the two rules lead to the same decision, but the rate of return rule has several pitfalls that can trap the unwary. Here are three examples.

---

[4] In Chapter 6 we showed how to calculate the yield to maturity on a bond. A bond's yield to maturity is simply its IRR by another name.

Internal Rate of Return

Calculating internal rate of return in Excel is as easy as listing the project cash flows. For example, to calculate the IRR of the office-block project, you could simply type in its cash flows as in the spreadsheet above, and then calculate IRR as we do in cell E4. As always, the interest rate is returned as a decimal.

You can find this spreadsheet at www.mhhe.com/bmm7e.

	A	B	C	D	E	F
1		Calculating IRR by using a spreadsheet				
2						
3	Year	Cash Flow				Formula
4	0	-375,000		IRR=	0.1256	=IRR(B4:B7)
5	1	25,000				
6	2	25,000				
7	3	475,000				

Pitfall 1: Lending or Borrowing?   Remember our condition for the IRR rule to work: The project's NPV must fall as the discount rate increases. Now consider the following projects:

	Cash Flows (dollars)			
Project	C_0	C_1	IRR, %	NPV at 10%
H	−100	+150	+50	+$36.4
I	+100	−150	+50	− 36.4

Each project has an IRR of 50%. In other words, if you discount the cash flows at 50%, both projects would have zero NPV.

Does this mean that the two projects are equally attractive? Clearly not. In the case of H we are paying out $100 now and getting $150 back at the end of the year. That is better than any bank account. But what about I? Here we are getting paid $100 now but we have to pay out $150 at the end of the year. That is equivalent to borrowing money at 50%.

If someone asked you whether 50% was a good rate of interest, you could not answer unless you also knew whether that person was proposing to lend or borrow at that rate. Lending money at 50% is great (as long as the borrower does not flee the country), but borrowing at 50% is not usually a good deal (unless, of course, you plan to flee the country). When you lend money, you want a *high* rate of return; when you borrow, you want a *low* rate of return.

If you plot a graph like Figure 8.2 for project I, you will find the NPV increases as the discount rate increases. *(Try it!)* Obviously, the rate of return rule will not work in this case.

Project I is a fairly obvious trap, but if you want to make sure you don't fall into it, calculate the project's NPV. For example, suppose that the cost of capital is 10%. Then the NPV of project H is +$36.4 and the NPV of project I is −$36.4. The NPV rule correctly warns us away from a project that is equivalent to borrowing money at 50%.

When NPV rises as the interest rate rises, the rate of return rule is reversed: A project is acceptable only if its internal rate of return is *less* than the opportunity cost of capital.

Pitfall 2: Mutually Exclusive Projects   We have seen that firms are seldom faced with take-it-or-leave-it projects. Usually they need to choose from a number of mutually exclusive alternatives. Given a choice between competing projects, you should accept the one that adds most to shareholder wealth. This is the one with the higher NPV.

But what about the rate of return rule? Would it make sense to just choose the project with the highest internal rate of return? Unfortunately, no. Mutually exclusive projects involve an additional pitfall for users of the IRR rule.[5]

---

[5] The other rule we've considered, payback, gives poor guidance even in the much simpler case of the accept-reject decision of a project considered in isolation. It is of no help in choosing among mutually exclusive projects.

Using Financial Calculators to Find NPV and IRR

We saw in Chapter 5 that the formulas for the present and future values of level annuities and one-time cash flows are built into financial calculators. However, as the example of the office block illustrates, most investment projects entail multiple cash flows that cannot be expected to remain level over time. Fortunately, many calculators are equipped to handle problems involving a sequence of uneven cash flows. In general, the procedure is quite simple. You enter the cash flows one by one into the calculator, and then you press the IRR key to find the project's internal rate of return. The first cash flow you enter is interpreted as coming immediately, the next cash flow is interpreted as coming at the end of one period, and so on. We can illustrate using the office block as an example. To find the project IRR, you would use the following sequence of keystrokes:

Hewlett-Packard HP-10B		Sharp EL-733A		Texas Instruments BA II Plus	
−375,000	CFj	−375,000	CFi		CF
25,000	CFj	25,000	CFi	2nd	[CLR Work]
25,000	CFj	25,000	CFi	−375,000	ENTER ↓
475,000	CFj	475,000	CFi	25,000	ENTER ↓
				25,000	ENTER ↓
				475,000	ENTER ↓
	[IRR/YR]		IRR		IRR
					CPT

The calculator should display the value 12.56%, the project's internal rate of return.

To calculate project NPV, the procedure is similar. You need to enter the discount rate in addition to the project cash flows, and then simply press the NPV key. Here is the specific sequence of keystrokes, assuming that the opportunity cost of capital is 7%:

Hewlett-Packard HP-10B		Sharp EL-733A		Texas Instruments BA II Plus	
−375,000	CFj	−375,000	CFi		CF
25,000	CFj	25,000	CFi	2nd	[CLR Work]
25,000	CFj	25,000	CFi	−375,000	ENTER ↓
475,000	CFj	475,000	CFi	25,000	ENTER ↓
7	I/YR	7	i	25,000	ENTER ↓
				475,000	ENTER ↓
	[NPV]		NPV		NPV
				7	ENTER
				↓	CPT

The calculator should display the value 57,942, the project's NPV when the discount rate is 7%.

By the way, you can check the accuracy of our earlier calculations using your calculator. Enter 50% for the discount rate (press 50, then press *i*) and then press the NPV key to find that NPV = −206,481. Enter 12.56 (the project's IRR) as the discount rate, and you will find that NPV is just about zero (it is not exactly zero, because we are rounding off the IRR to only two decimal places).

Think once more about the two office-block proposals from Section 8.1. You initially intended to invest $350,000 in the building and then sell it at the end of the year for $400,000. Under the revised proposal, you planned to invest $375,000, rent out the offices for 3 years at a fixed annual rent of $25,000, and then sell the building for $450,000. The following table shows the project cash flows, their IRRs, and their NPVs:

Year:	0	1	2	3	IRR	NPV at 7%
Initial proposal	−350,000	+400,000			14.29%	+$23,832
Revised proposal	−375,000	+25,000	+25,000	+475,000	12.56%	+$57,942

Both projects are good investments; both offer a positive NPV. But the revised proposal has the higher net present value and therefore is the better choice. Unfortunately, the superiority of the revised proposal doesn't show up as a higher rate of return. The IRR rule seems to say you should go for the initial proposal because it has the higher IRR. If you follow the IRR rule, you have the satisfaction of earning a 14.29% rate of return; if you use NPV, you are nearly $58,000 richer.

Figure 8.4 shows why the IRR rule gives the wrong signal. The figure plots the NPV of each project for different discount rates. These two NPV profiles cross at an interest rate of 11.72%. So if the opportunity cost of capital is higher than 11.72%, the initial proposal, with its rapid cash inflow, is the superior investment. If the cost of capital is lower than 11.72%, then the revised proposal dominates. Depending on the

FIGURE 8.4 The initial proposal offers a higher IRR than the revised proposal, but its NPV is lower if the discount rate is less than 11.72%.

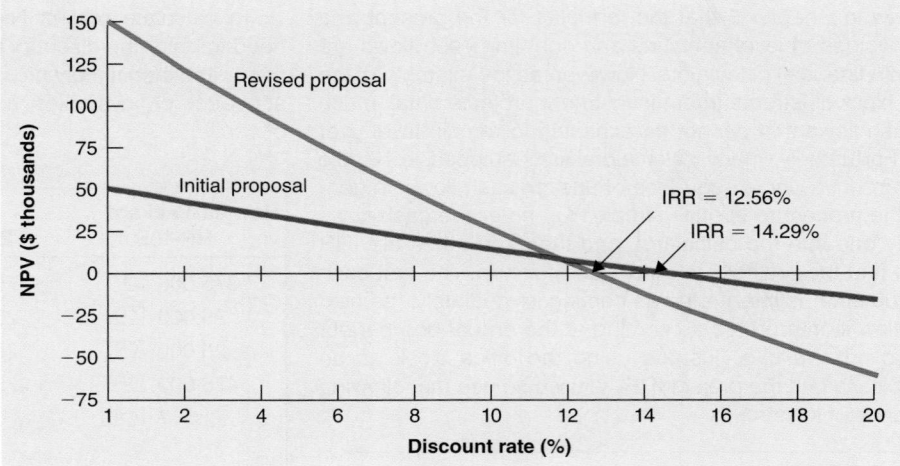

discount rate, either proposal may be superior. For the 7% cost of capital that we have assumed, the revised proposal is the better choice.

Now consider the IRR of each proposal. The IRR is simply the discount rate at which NPV equals zero, that is, the discount rate at which the NPV profile crosses the horizontal axis in Figure 8.4. As noted, these rates are 14.29% for the initial proposal and 12.56% for the revised proposal. However, as you can see from Figure 8.4, the higher IRR for the initial proposal does not mean that it has a higher NPV.

In our example both projects involved the same outlay, but the revised proposal had the longer life. The IRR rule mistakenly favored the quick payback project with the high percentage return but the lower NPV. **Remember, a high IRR is not an end in itself. You want projects that increase the value of the firm. Projects that earn a good rate of return for a long time often have higher NPVs than those that offer high percentage rates of return but die young.**

Self-Test 8.6

A rich, friendly, and probably slightly unbalanced benefactor offers you the opportunity to invest $1 million in two mutually exclusive ways. The payoffs are:

a. $2 million after 1 year, a 100% return.
b. $300,000 a year forever.

Neither investment is risky, and safe securities are yielding 7.5%. Which investment will you take? You can't take both, so the choices are mutually exclusive. Do you want to earn a high percentage return, or do you want to be rich? By the way, if you really had this investment opportunity, you'd have no trouble borrowing the money to undertake it.

Pitfall 2a: Mutually Exclusive Projects Involving Different Outlays

A similar misranking also may occur when comparing projects with the same lives but different outlays. In this case the IRR may mistakenly favor small projects with high rates of return but low NPVs. When you are faced with a straightforward either-or choice, the simple solution is to compare their NPVs. However, if you are determined to use the IRR rule, there is a way to do so. We explain how in the appendix.

Self-Test 8.7

Your wacky benefactor (see Self-Test 8.6) now offers you the choice of two opportunities:

a. Invest $1,000 today and quadruple your money—a 300% return—in 1 year with no risk.
b. Invest $1 million for 1 year at a guaranteed 50% return.

Which will you take? Do you want to earn a wonderful rate of return (300%), or do you want to be rich? Safe securities still yield 7.5%.

Pitfall 3: Multiple Rates of Return Here is a tricky problem. King Coal Corporation is considering a project to strip-mine coal. The project requires an investment of $210 million and is expected to produce a cash inflow of $125 million in the first 2 years, building up to $175 million in years 3 and 4. However, the company is obliged in year 5 to reclaim the land at a cost of $400 million. At a 20% opportunity cost of capital the project has an NPV of $5.9 million.

To find the IRR of King Coal's project, we have calculated the NPV for various discount rates and plotted the results in Figure 8.5. You can see that there are *two* discount rates at which NPV = 0. That is, *each* of the following statements holds:

$$\text{NPV} = -210 + \frac{\$125}{1.03} + \frac{125}{1.03^2} + \frac{175}{1.03^3} + \frac{175}{1.03^4} - \frac{400}{1.03^5} = 0$$

and

$$\text{NPV} = -210 + \frac{\$125}{1.25} + \frac{125}{1.25^2} + \frac{175}{1.25^3} + \frac{175}{1.25^4} - \frac{400}{1.25^5} = 0$$

In other words, the investment has an IRR of both 3% *and* 25%. The reason for this is the double change in the sign of the cash flows. There can be as many different internal rates of return as there are changes in the sign of the cash-flow stream.[6]

FIGURE 8.5 King Coal's project has two internal rates of return. NPV = 0 when the discount rate is either 3% or 25%.

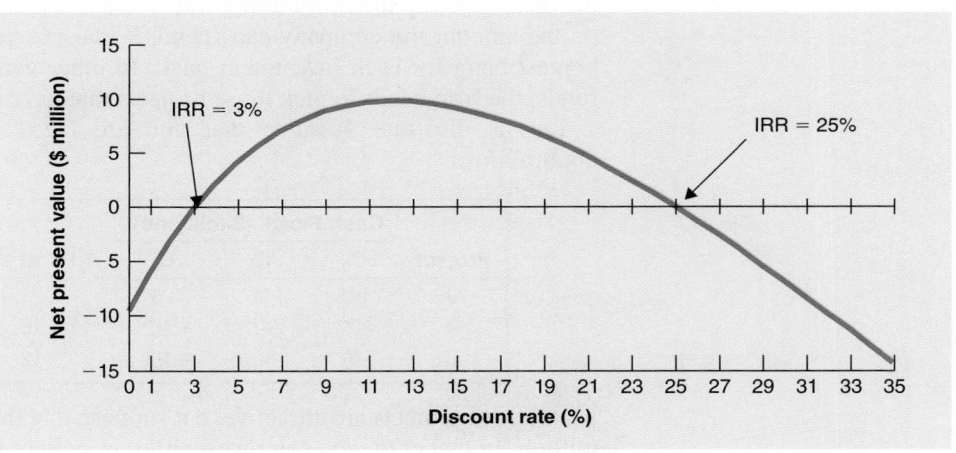

---

[6] There may be *fewer* IRRs than the number of sign changes. You may even encounter projects for which there is *no* IRR. For example, there is no IRR for a project that has cash flows of +$1,000 in year 0, −$3,000 in year 1, and +$2,500 in year 2. If you don't believe us, try plotting NPV for different discount rates. Can such a project ever have a negative NPV?

Is the coal mine worth developing? The simple IRR rule—accept if the IRR is greater than the cost of capital—won't help. For example, you can see from Figure 8.5 that with a low cost of capital (less than 3%) the project has a negative NPV. It has a positive NPV only if the cost of capital is between 3% and 25%.

Decommissioning and clean-up costs, which make King Coal's final cash flow negative, can sometimes be huge. Phillips Petroleum has estimated that it will need to spend $1 billion to remove its Norwegian offshore oil platforms. It can cost over $300 million to decommission a nuclear power plant. These are obvious examples where cash flows go from positive to negative, but you can probably think of a number of other cases where the company needs to plan for later expenditures. Ships periodically need to go into dry dock for a refit, hotels may receive a major facelift, machine parts may need replacement, and so on.

Whenever the cash-flow stream is expected to change sign more than once, the project typically has more than one IRR and there is no simple IRR rule. It is possible to get around the problem of multiple rates of return by calculating a *modified internal rate of return (MIRR)*. We explain how to do so in the appendix to this chapter. However, it would be much easier in such cases to abandon the IRR rule and just calculate project NPV.

8.5 The Profitability Index

profitability index
Ratio of net present value to initial investment.

The **profitability index measures** the net present value of a project *per dollar of investment:*

$$\text{Profitability index} = \frac{\text{net present value}}{\text{initial investment}} \qquad (8.3)$$

For example, our initial proposal to construct an office building involved an investment of $350,000 and had an NPV of $23,832. Its profitability index[7] was

$$\frac{23,832}{350,000} = .068$$

Any project with a positive profitability index must also have a positive NPV, so it would seem that either criterion must result in identical decisions. Why go to the trouble of calculating the profitability index? The answer is that whenever there is a limit on the amount the company can spend, it makes sense to concentrate on getting the biggest bang for each investment buck. In other words, when there is a shortage of funds, the firm needs to pick those projects that have the highest profitability index.

Let us illustrate. Assume that you are faced with the following investment opportunities:

	Cash Flows ($ millions)				
Project	C_0	C_1	C_2	NPV at 10%	Profitability Index
J	−10	+30	+5	21	21/10 = 2.1
K	−5	+5	+20	16	16/5 = 3.2
L	−5	+5	+15	12	12/5 = 2.4

All three projects are attractive, but suppose that the firm is limited to spending $10 million. In that case, you can invest either in project J *or* in projects K and L, but you can't invest in all three. The solution is to start with the project that has the highest

[7] Sometimes the profitability index is defined as the ratio of total present value (rather than *net* present value) to required investment. By this definition, all the profitability indexes calculated below are increased by 1. For example, the office building's profitability index would be PV/investment =373,832/350,000 = 1.068. Note that project rankings under either definition are identical.

profitability index and continue until you run out of money. In our example, K provides the highest NPV per dollar invested, followed by L. These two projects exactly use up the $10 million budget. Between them they add $28 million to shareholder wealth. The alternative of investing in J would have added only $21 million.

Capital Rationing

Economists use the term **capital rationing** to refer to a shortage of funds available for investment. In simple cases of capital rationing the profitability index can provide a measure of which projects to accept.[8] But that raises a question. Most large corporations can obtain very large sums of money on fair terms and at short notice. So why does top management sometimes tell subordinates that capital is limited and that they may not exceed a specified amount of capital spending? There are two reasons.

Soft Rationing

For many firms the limits on capital funds are "soft." By this we mean that the capital rationing is not imposed by investors. Instead, the limits are imposed by top management. For example, suppose that you are an ambitious, upwardly mobile junior manager. You are keen to expand your part of the business, and as a result you tend to overstate the investment opportunities. Rather than trying to determine which of your many bright ideas are truly worthwhile, senior management may find it simpler to impose a limit on the amount that you and other junior managers can spend. This limit forces you to set your own priorities.

Even if capital is not rationed, other resources may be. For example, very rapid growth can place considerable strains on management and the organization. A somewhat rough-and-ready response to this problem is to ration the amount of capital that the firm spends.

Hard Rationing

Soft rationing should never cost the firm anything. If the limits on investment become so tight that truly good projects are being passed up, then management should raise more money and relax the limits it has imposed on capital spending. But what if there is "hard rationing," meaning that the firm actually *cannot* raise the money it needs? In that case, it may be forced to pass up positive-NPV projects. With hard rationing you may still be interested in net present value, but you now need to select the package of projects that is within the company's resources and yet gives the highest net present value. This is when the profitability index can be useful.

Pitfalls of the Profitability Index

The profitability index is sometimes used to rank projects even when there is no soft or hard capital rationing. In this case the unwary user may be led to favor small projects over larger projects that have higher NPVs. The profitability index was designed to select projects with the most bang per buck—the greatest NPV per dollar spent. That's the right objective when bucks are limited. When they are not, a bigger bang is always better than a smaller one, even when more bucks are spent. Self-Test 8.8 is a numerical example.

---

[8] Unfortunately, when capital is rationed in more than one period, or when personnel, production capacity, or other resources are rationed in addition to capital, it isn't always possible to get the NPV-maximizing package just by ranking projects on their profitability index. Tedious trial and error may be called for, or linear programming methods may be used.

Self-Test 8.8

Calculate the profitability indexes of the two pairs of mutually exclusive investments in Self-Tests 8.6 and 8.7. Use a 7.5% discount rate. Does the profitability index give the right ranking in each case?

8.6 A Last Look

We've covered several investment criteria, each with its own nuances. If your head is spinning, you might want to take a look at Table 8.3, which gives an overview and summary of these decision rules.

Clearly, NPV is the gold standard. It is designed to tell you whether an investment will increase the value of the firm and by how much it will do so. It is the only rule that consistently can be used to rank and choose among mutually exclusive investments. The only instance in which NPV fails as a decision rule occurs when the firm faces capital rationing. In this case, there may not be enough cash to take every project with positive NPV, and the firm must then rank projects by the profitability index, that is, net present value per dollar invested.

For managers in the field, discounted cash-flow analysis is in fact the dominant tool for project evaluation. Table 8.4 provides a sample of the results of a large survey of CFOs. Notice that 75% of firms either always or almost always use NPV or IRR to evaluate projects. The dominance of these criteria is even stronger among larger, presumably more sophisticated, firms. Despite the clear advantages of discounted cash-flow methods, however, firms do use other investment criteria to evaluate projects. For example, just over half of corporations always or almost always compute a project's payback period. Profitability index is routinely computed by about 12% of firms.

What explains such wide use of presumably inferior decision rules? To some extent, these rules present rough reality checks on the project. As we noted in the introduction to the chapter, managers might want to consider some simple ways to describe project

TABLE 8.3 A comparison of investment decision rules

Criterion	Definition	Investment Rule	Comments
Net present value (NPV)	Present value of cash inflows minus present value of cash outflows	Accept project if NPV is positive. For mutually exclusive projects, choose the one with the highest (positive) NPV.	The "gold standard" of investment criteria. Only criterion necessarily consistent with maximizing the value of the firm. Provides proper rule for choosing among mutually exclusive investments. Only pitfall involves capital rationing, when one cannot accept all positive-NPV projects.
Internal rate of return (IRR)	The discount rate at which project NPV equals zero	Accept project if IRR is greater than opportunity cost of capital	If used properly, results in same accept-reject decision as NPV in the absence of project interactions. However, beware of the following pitfalls: IRR cannot rank mutually exclusive projects—the project with higher IRR may have lower NPV. The simple IRR rule cannot be used in cases of multiple IRRs or an upward-sloping NPV profile.
Payback period	Time until the sum of project cash flows equals the initial investment	Accept project if payback period is less than some specified number of years	A quick and dirty rule of thumb, with several critical pitfalls. Ignores cash flows beyond the acceptable payback period. Ignores discounting. Tends to improperly reject long-lived projects.
Profitability index	Ratio of net present value to initial investment	Accept project if profitability index is greater than 0. In case of capital rationing, accept projects with highest profitability index.	Results in same accept-reject decision as NPV in the absence of project interactions. Useful for ranking projects in case of capital rationing, but misleading in the presence of interactions. Cannot rank mutually exclusive projects.

TABLE 8.4 Capital budgeting techniques used in practice

Investment Criterion	Percentage of Firms That Always or Almost Always Use Criterion	Average Score on 0–4 Scale (0 = never use; 4 = always use)		
		All Firms	Small Firms	Large Firms
Internal rate of return	76	3.1	2.9	3.4
Net present value	75	3.1	2.8	3.4
Payback period	57	2.5	2.7	2.3
Profitability index	12	0.8	0.9	0.8

Source: Reprinted from the *Journal of Financial Economics,* Vol. 60, Issue 2–3, J. R. Graham and C. R. Harvey, "The Theory and Practice of Corporate Finance: Evidence from the Field," May 2001, pp. 187–243. © 2001 with permission from Elsevier Science.

profitability, even if they present obvious pitfalls. For example, managers talk casually about quick-payback projects in the same way that investors talk about high-P/E stocks. The fact that they talk about payback does not mean that the payback rule governs their decisions.

SUMMARY

What is the net present value of an investment, and how do you calculate it? (*LO1*)

The **net present value** of a project measures the difference between its value and cost. NPV is therefore the amount that the project will add to shareholder wealth. A company maximizes shareholder wealth by accepting all projects that have a positive NPV.

How can the net present value rule be used to analyze three common problems that involve competing projects: when to postpone an investment expenditure; how to choose between projects with unequal lives; and when to replace equipment? (*LO2*)

Sometimes a project may have a positive NPV if undertaken today but an even higher NPV if the investment is delayed. Choose between these alternatives by comparing their NPVs *today.*

When you have to choose between projects with different lives, you should put them on an equal footing by comparing the **equivalent annual annuity** of the two projects. When you are considering whether to replace an aging machine with a new one, you should compare the annual cost of operating the old one with the equivalent annual annuity of the new one.

Why doesn't the payback rule always make shareholders better off? (*LO3*)

The net present value rule and the rate of return rule both properly reflect the time value of money. But companies sometimes use rules of thumb to judge projects. One is the **payback rule,** which states that a project is acceptable if you get your money back within a specified period. The payback rule takes no account of any cash flows that arrive after the payback period and fails to discount cash flows within the payback period.

How is the internal rate of return of a project calculated, and what must one look out for when using the internal rate of return rule? (*LO4*)

Instead of asking whether a project has a positive NPV, many businesses prefer to ask whether it offers a higher return than shareholders could expect to get by investing in the capital market. Return is usually defined as the discount rate that would result in a zero NPV. This is known as the **internal rate of return,** or **IRR.** The project is attractive if the IRR exceeds the **opportunity cost of capital.**

There are some pitfalls in using the internal rate of return rule. Be careful about using the IRR when (1) the early cash flows are positive, (2) there is more than one change in the sign of the cash flows, or (3) you need to choose between two **mutually exclusive projects.**

How is the profitability index calculated, and how can it be used to choose between projects when funds are limited? (*LO5*)

If there is a shortage of capital, companies need to choose projects that offer the highest net present value per dollar of investment. This measure is known as the **profitability index.**

LISTING OF EQUATIONS

8.1   NPV = PV − required investment

8.2   Equivalent annual annuity = $\dfrac{\text{present value of costs}}{\text{annuity factor}}$

8.3   Profitability index = $\dfrac{\text{net present value}}{\text{initial investment}}$

QUESTIONS

connect
|FINANCE

QUIZ

Problems 1–8 refer to two projects with the following cash flows:

Year	Project A	Project B
0	−$200	−$200
1	80	100
2	80	100
3	80	100
4	80	

1. **IRR/NPV.** If the opportunity cost of capital is 11%, which of these projects is worth pursuing? (*LO1*)

2. **Mutually Exclusive Investments.** Suppose that you can choose only one of these projects. Which would you choose? The discount rate is still 11%. (*LO2*)

3. **IRR/NPV.** Which project would you choose if the opportunity cost of capital were 16%? (*LO1*)

4. **IRR.** What are the internal rates of return on projects A and B? (*LO4*)

5. **Investment Criteria.** In light of your answers to Quiz Questions 2–4, is there any reason to believe that the project with the higher IRR is the better project? (*LO4*)

6. **Profitability Index.** If the opportunity cost of capital is 11%, what is the profitability index for each project? Does the profitability index rank the projects correctly? (*LO5*)

7. **Payback.** What is the payback period of each project? (*LO3*)

8. **Investment Criteria.** Considering your answers to Quiz Questions 2, 3, and 7, is there any reason to believe that the project with the lower payback period is the better project? (*LO3*)

9. **NPV and IRR.** A project that costs $3,000 to install will provide annual cash flows of $800 for each of the next 6 years. Is this project worth pursuing if the discount rate is 10%? How high can the discount rate be before you would reject the project? (*LO1*)

10. **Payback.** A project that costs $2,500 to install will provide annual cash flows of $600 for the next 6 years. The firm accepts projects with payback periods of less than 5 years. Will the project be accepted? *Should* this project be pursued if the discount rate is 2%? What if the discount rate is 12%? Will the firm's decision change as the discount rate changes? (*LO3*)

11. **Profitability Index.** What is the profitability index of a project that costs $10,000 and provides cash flows of $3,000 in years 1 and 2 and $5,000 in years 3 and 4? The discount rate is 9%. (*LO5*)

12. **NPV.** A proposed nuclear power plant will cost $2.2 billion to build and then will produce cash flows of $300 million a year for 15 years. After that period (in year 15), it must be decommissioned at a cost of $900 million. What is project NPV if the discount rate is 5%? What if it is 18%? (*LO1*)

PRACTICE PROBLEMS

13. **NPV/IRR.** Consider projects A and B:

Project	Cash Flows (dollars)			NPV at 10%
	C_0	C_1	C_2	
A	−30,000	21,000	21,000	+$6,446
B	−50,000	33,000	33,000	+ 7,273

   Calculate IRRs for A and B. Which project does the IRR rule suggest is best? Which project is really best? (*LO4*)

14. **IRR.** You have the chance to participate in a project that produces the following cash flows:

C_0	C_1	C_2
+$5,000	+$4,000	−$11,000

   The internal rate of return is 13.6%. If the opportunity cost of capital is 12%, would you accept the offer? (*LO4*)

15. **NPV/IRR.**

   a. Calculate the net present value of the following project for discount rates of 0, 50, and 100%: (*LO1*)

C_0	C_1	C_2
−$6,750	+$4,500	+$18,000

   b. What is the IRR of the project? (*LO4*)

16. **IRR.** Marielle Machinery Works forecasts the following cash flows on a project under consideration. It uses the internal rate of return rule to accept or reject projects. Should this project be accepted if the required return is 12%? (*LO4*)

C_0	C_1	C_2	C_3
−$10,000	0	+$7,500	+$8,500

17. **NPV/IRR.** A new computer system will require an initial outlay of $20,000, but it will increase the firm's cash flows by $4,000 a year for each of the next 8 years. Is the system worth installing if the required rate of return is 9%? What if it is 14%? How high can the discount rate be before you would reject the project? (*LO1*)

18. **Investment Criteria.** If you insulate your office for $10,000, you will save $1,000 a year in heating expenses. These savings will last forever.

   a. What is the NPV of the investment when the cost of capital is 8%? 10%? (*LO1*)
   b. What is the IRR of the investment? (*LO4*)
   c. What is the payback period on this investment? (*LO3*)

19. **NPV versus IRR.** Here are the cash flows for two mutually exclusive projects:

Project	C_0	C_1	C_2	C_3
A	−$20,000	+$8,000	+$8,000	+$ 8,000
B	− 20,000	0	0	+ 25,000

   a. At what interest rates would you prefer project A to B? (*Hint:* Try drawing the NPV profile of each project.) (*LO1*)
   b. What is the IRR of each project? (*LO4*)

20. **Payback and NPV.** A project has a life of 10 years and a payback period of 10 years. What must be true of project NPV? (*LO3*)

21. **IRR/NPV.** Consider this project with an internal rate of return of 13.1%. Should you accept or reject the project if the discount rate is 12%? (*LO4*)

Year	Cash Flow
0	+$100
1	−60
2	−60

22. **Payback and NPV.**

    a. What is the payback period on each of the following projects? (*LO3*)

Project	Year:	0	1	2	3	4
			Cash Flows (dollars)			
A		−5,000	+1,000	+1,000	+3,000	0
B		−1,000	0	+1,000	+2,000	+3,000
C		−5,000	+1,000	+1,000	+3,000	+5,000

    b. Given that you wish to use the payback rule with a cutoff period of 2 years, which projects would you accept? (*LO3*)
    c. If you use a cutoff period of 3 years, which projects would you accept? (*LO3*)
    d. If the opportunity cost of capital is 10%, which projects have positive NPVs? (*LO1*)
    e. "Payback gives too much weight to cash flows that occur after the cutoff date." True or false? (*LO3*)

23. **Profitability Index.** Consider the following projects: (*LO5*)

Project	C_0	C_1	C_2
A	−$2,100	+$2,000	+$1,200
B	− 2,100	+ 1,440	+ 1,728

    a. Calculate the profitability index for A and B assuming a 22% opportunity cost of capital.
    b. Use the profitability index rule to determine which project(s) you should accept.

24. **Capital Rationing.** You are a manager with an investment budget of $8 million. You may invest in the following projects. Investment and cash-flow figures are in millions of dollars. (*LO5*)

Project	Discount Rate, %	Investment	Annual Cash Flow	Project Life, Years
A	10	3	1	5
B	12	4	1	8
C	8	5	2	4
D	8	3	1.5	3
E	12	3	1	6

    a. Why might these projects have different discount rates?
    b. Which projects should the manager choose?
    c. Which projects will be chosen if there is no capital rationing?

25. **Profitability Index versus NPV.** Consider these two projects: (*LO5*)

	C_0	C_1	C_2	C_3
A	−$36	+$20	+$20	+$20
B	− 50	+ 25	+ 25	+ 25

    a. Which project has the higher NPV if the discount rate is 10%?
    b. Which has the higher profitability index?

c. Which project is most attractive to a firm that can raise an unlimited amount of funds to pay for its investment projects? Which project is most attractive to a firm that is limited in the funds it can raise?

26. **Mutually Exclusive Investments.** Here are the cash flow forecasts for two *mutually exclusive* projects: (*LO2*)

	Cash Flows (dollars)	
Year	Project A	Project B
0	−100	−100
1	30	49
2	50	49
3	70	49

a. Which project would you choose if the opportunity cost of capital is 2%?
b. Which would you choose if the opportunity cost of capital is 12%?
c. Why does your answer change?

27. **Equivalent Annual Annuity.** A precision lathe costs $10,000 and will cost $20,000 a year to operate and maintain. If the discount rate is 10% and the lathe will last for 5 years, what is the equivalent annual cost of the tool? (*LO2*)

28. **Equivalent Annual Annuity.** A firm can lease a truck for 4 years at a cost of $30,000 annually. It can instead buy a truck at a cost of $80,000, with annual maintenance expenses of $10,000. The truck will be sold at the end of 4 years for $20,000. Which is the better option if the discount rate is 10%? (*LO2*)

29. **Multiple IRR.** Consider the following cash flows: (*LO4*)

C_0	C_1	C_2	C_3	C_4
−$22	+$20	+$20	+$20	−$40

a. Confirm that one internal rate of return on this project is (a shade above) 7%, and that the other is (a shade below) 34%.
b. Is the project attractive if the discount rate is 5%?
c. What if it is 20%? 40%?
d. Why is the project attractive at midrange discount rates but not at very high or very low rates?

30. **Equivalent Annual Cost.** Econo-Cool air conditioners cost $300 to purchase, result in electricity bills of $150 per year, and last for 5 years. Luxury Air models cost $500, result in electricity bills of $100 per year, and last for 8 years. The discount rate is 21%. (*LO2*)

a. What are the equivalent annual costs of the Econo-Cool and Luxury Air models?
b. Which model is more cost-effective?
c. Now you remember that the inflation rate is expected to be 10% per year for the foreseeable future. Redo parts (a) and (b).

31. **Investment Timing.** You can purchase an optical scanner today for $400. The scanner provides benefits worth $60 a year. The expected life of the scanner is 10 years. Scanners are expected to decrease in price by 20% per year. Suppose the discount rate is 10%. Should you purchase the scanner today or wait to purchase? When is the best purchase time? (*LO2*)

32. **Replacement Decision.** You are operating an old machine that is expected to produce a cash inflow of $5,000 in each of the next 3 years before it fails. You can replace it now with a new machine that costs $20,000 but is much more efficient and will provide a cash flow of $10,000 a year for 4 years. Should you replace your equipment now? The discount rate is 15%. (*LO2*)

33. **Replacement Decision.** A forklift will last for only 2 more years. It costs $5,000 a year to maintain. For $20,000 you can buy a new lift that can last for 10 years and should require maintenance costs of only $2,000 a year. (*LO2*)

a. If the discount rate is 4% per year, should you replace the forklift?
b. What if the discount rate is 12% per year? Why does your answer change?

CHALLENGE PROBLEMS

34. **NPV/IRR.** Growth Enterprises believes its latest project, which will cost $80,000 to install, will generate a perpetual growing stream of cash flows. Cash flow at the end of the first year will be $5,000, and cash flows in future years are expected to grow indefinitely at an annual rate of 5%.

    a. If the discount rate for this project is 10%, what is the project NPV? (*LO1*)

    b What is the project IRR? (*LO4*)

35. **Investment Timing.** A classic problem in management of forests is determining when it is most economically advantageous to cut a tree for lumber. When the tree is young, it grows very rapidly. As it ages, its growth slows down. Why is the NPV-maximizing rule to cut the tree when its growth rate equals the discount rate? (*LO2*)

36. **Multiple IRRs.** Strip Mining Inc. can develop a new mine at an initial cost of $5 million. The mine will provide a cash flow of $30 million in 1 year. The land then must be reclaimed at a cost of $28 million in the second year. (*LO4*)

    a. What are the IRRs of this project?

    b. Should the firm develop the mine if the discount rate is 10%? 20%? 350%? 400%?

Templates can be found at
www.mhhe.com/bmm7e.

37. **Investment Criteria.** A new furnace for your small factory will cost $27,000 a year to install and will require ongoing maintenance expenditures of $1,500 a year. But it is far more fuel-efficient than your old furnace and will reduce your consumption of heating oil by 2,400 gallons per year. Heating oil this year will cost $3 a gallon; the price per gallon is expected to increase by $.50 a year for the next 3 years and then to stabilize for the foreseeable future. The furnace will last for 20 years, at which point it will need to be replaced and will have no salvage value. The discount rate is 8%.

    a. What is the net present value of the investment in the furnace? (*LO1*)

    b. What is the IRR? (*LO4*)

    c. What is the payback period? (*LO3*)

    d. What is the equivalent annual cost of the furnace? (*LO2*)

    e. What is the equivalent annual savings derived from the furnace? (*LO2*)

    f. Compare the PV of the difference between the equivalent annual cost and savings to your answer to part (a). (*LO1*)

SOLUTIONS TO SELF-TEST QUESTIONS

8.1   Even if construction costs are $355,000, NPV is still positive:

$$\text{NPV} = \text{PV} - \$355,000 = \$357,143 - \$355,000 = \$2,143$$

Therefore, the project is still worth pursuing. The project is viable as long as construction costs are less than the PV of the future cash flow, that is, as long as construction costs are less than $357,143. However, if the opportunity cost of capital is 20%, the PV of the $400,000 sales price is lower and NPV is negative:

$$\text{PV} = \$400,000 \times \frac{1}{1.20} = \$333,333$$
$$\text{NPV} = \text{PV} - \$355,000 = -\$21,667$$

The present value of the future cash flow is not as high when the opportunity cost of capital is higher. The project would need to provide a higher payoff in order to be viable in the face of the higher opportunity cost of capital.

8.2

Year of Purchase	Cost of Computer	PV Savings	NPV at Year of Purchase	NPV Today
0	$50	$70	$20	$20
1	45	66	21	19.1
2	40	62	22	18.2
3	36	58	22	16.5
4	33	54	21	14.3
5	31	50	19	11.8

Purchase the new computer now.

8.3

	Year:	0	1	2	3	PV of Costs
C	Cash flows	$ 10,000	$1,100	$1,200		$11,992
	Equivalent annual annuity		6,910	6,910		11,992
D	Cash flows	12,000	1,100	1,200	$ 1,300	14,968
	Equivalent annual annuity		6,019	6,019	6,019	14,968

Machine D is the better buy. However, it's even better to keep the old machine going for 1 more year. That costs $4,300, which is less than D's equivalent annual cost, $6,019.

8.4   The payback period is $5,000/$660 = 7.6 years. Discounted payback is just over 11 years. Calculate NPV as follows. The present value of a $660 annuity for 20 years at 6% is

$$\text{PV annuity} = \$7{,}570$$
$$\text{NPV} = -\$5{,}000 + \$7{,}570 = +\$2{,}570$$

The project should be accepted.

8.5   The IRR is now about 8.3% because

$$\text{NPV} = -\$375{,}000 + \frac{\$25{,}000}{1.083} + \frac{\$25{,}000}{(1.083)^2} + \frac{\$420{,}000}{(1.083)^3} = 0$$

Note in Figure 8.6 that NPV falls to zero as the discount rate reaches 8.3%.

8.6   You want to be rich. The NPV of the long-lived investment is much larger.

$$\text{Short: NPV} = -\$1 + \frac{\$2}{1.075} = +\$.8605 \text{ million}$$
$$\text{Long: NPV} = -\$1 + \frac{\$.3}{.075} = +\$3 \text{ million}$$

FIGURE 8.6 NPV falls to zero at an interest rate of 8.3%.

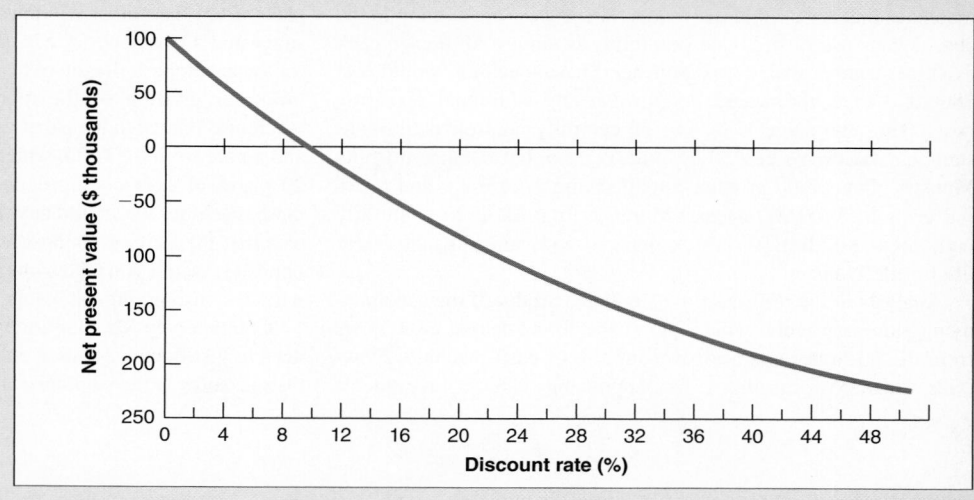

8.7   You want to be richer. The second alternative generates greater value at any reasonable discount rate. Other risk-free investments offer 7.5%. Therefore

$$NPV = -\$1,000 + \frac{\$4,000}{1.075} = +\$2,721$$

$$NPV = -\$1,000,000 + \frac{\$1,500,000}{1.075} = +\$395,349$$

8.8   The profitability index gives the correct ranking for the first pair, but the incorrect ranking for the second:

Project	PV	Investment	NPV	Profitability Index (NPV/Investment)
Short	$1,860,500	$1,000,000	$ 860,500	0.86
Long	4,000,000	1,000,000	3,000,000	3.0
Small	3,721	1,000	2,721	2.7
Large	1,395,349	1,000,000	395,349	0.395

SOLUTIONS TO SPREADSHEET QUESTIONS

8.1   NPV would be calculated as £221.08 million.

8.2   This value, £221.08 million, is 1.13 times as great as the value in Table 8.1 because each cash flow is discounted for one fewer period. The Excel NPV function assumes the first cash flow comes after one period. In this example, the first cash flow actually comes immediately.

MINICASE

Flowton Products enjoys a steady demand for stainless steel infiltrators used in a number of chemical processes. Revenues from the infiltrator division are $50 million a year and production costs are $47.5 million. However, the 10 high-precision Munster stamping machines that are used in the production process are coming to the end of their useful life. One possibility is simply to replace each existing machine with a new Munster. These machines would cost $800,000 each and would not involve any additional operating costs. The alternative is to buy 10 centrally controlled Skilboro stampers. Skilboros cost $1.25 million each, but compared to the Munster, they would produce a total saving in operator and material costs of $500,000 a year. Moreover, the Skilboro is sturdily built and would last 10 years, compared with an estimated 7-year life for the Munster.

Analysts in the infiltrator division have produced the accompanying summary table, which shows the forecast total cash flows from the infiltrator business over the life of each machine. Flowton's standard procedures for appraising capital investments involve calculating net present value, internal rate of return, and payback, and these measures are also shown in the table.

As usual, Emily Balsam arrived early at Flowton's head office. She had never regretted joining Flowton. Everything about the place, from the mirror windows to the bell fountain in the atrium, suggested a classy outfit. Ms. Balsam sighed happily and reached for the envelope at the top of her in-tray. It was an analysis from the infiltrator division of the replacement options for the stamper machines. Pinned to the paper was the summary table of cash flows and a note from the CFO, which read, "Emily, I have read through 20 pages of excruciating detail and I still don't know which of these machines we should buy. The NPV calculation seems to indicate that the Skilboro is best, while IRR and payback suggest the opposite. Would you take a look and tell me what we should do and why. You also might check that the calculations are OK."

Can you help Ms. Balsam by writing a memo to the CFO? You need to justify your solution and also to explain why some or all of the measures in the summary tables are inappropriate.

	Cash Flows (millions of dollars)				
Year:	0	1–7	8	9	10
Munster					
Investment	−8.0				
Revenues		50.0	0	0	0
Costs		47.5	0	0	0
Net cash flow	−8.0	2.5	0	0	0
NPV at 15%	$2.40 million				
IRR	24.5%				
Payback period	3.2 years				
Skilboro					
Investment	−12.5				
Revenues		50.0	50.0	50.0	50.0
Costs		47.0	47.0	47.0	47.0
Net cash flow	−12.5	3.0	3.0	3.0	3.0
NPV at 15%	$2.56 million				
IRR	20.2%				
Payback period	4.2 years				

APPENDIX More on the IRR Rule

In Section 8.4 we described several pitfalls that lie in wait for users of the IRR rule. However, there are some tricks that users of the rule may use to circumvent these hazards. In this appendix we show how you can adapt the IRR rule when you need to choose between competing projects or when there are multiple IRRs.

Using the IRR to Choose between Mutually Exclusive Projects

When you need to choose between mutually exclusive projects, a simple comparison of internal rates of return is liable to lead to poor decisions. We illustrated this by looking at two office building projects. Your initial proposal involved constructing the office building and then selling it. Under the revised proposal you would construct a more expensive building and rent it out before selling it at the end of 3 years. The cash flows from the two projects were as follows:

	Cash Flows					
	C_0	C_1	C_2	C_3	IRR	NPV at 7%
Initial proposal	−350,000	+400,000			14.29%	+$23,832
Revised proposal	−375,000	+25,000	+25,000	+475,000	12.56%	+$57,942

Although the initial proposal has the higher IRR, it has the lower net present value. If you were misled into choosing the initial rather than the revised proposal, you would have been more than $30,000 poorer.

You can salvage the IRR rule in these cases; you do so by calculating the IRR on the *incremental* cash flows, that is, the difference in cash flows between the two projects. Start with the smaller project, where you plan to invest $350,000 and sell the office building after 1 year. It has an IRR of 14.29%, which is well in excess of the 7% cost of capital. So you know that it is worthwhile. You now ask yourself whether it is worth investing the additional $25,000 and renting out the building for 3 years. Here are the incremental cash flows from doing so, together with their IRR and NPV:

Cash Flows:	C_0	C_1	C_2	C_3	IRR	NPV at 7%
Incremental cash flows	−25,000	−375,000	+25,000	+475,000	11.72%	+$34,110

The IRR on the incremental cash flows is 11.72%. Since this is greater than the opportunity cost of capital, you should prefer the revised proposal.

Using the Modified Internal Rate of Return when there are Multiple IRRs

Whenever there is more than one change in the sign of the cash flows, there is generally more than one internal rate of return and therefore no simple IRR rule. Companies sometimes get around this problem by calculating a *modified IRR (MIRR)*, which can then be compared with the cost of capital.

Think back to King Coal's strip-mining project. Its cash flows are as follows:

Cash Flows:	C_0	C_1	C_2	C_3	C_4	C_5
Cash flows, $ millions	−210	+125	+125	+175	+175	−400

The problem with the IRR rule arises because the cash flow in year 5 is negative. So let us try replacing the last two cash flows with a *single* year-4 cash flow that has the same present value. If the cost of capital is 20%, then we can replace the cash flows in years 4 and 5 with a single cash flow in year 4 of

$$+175 - \frac{400}{1.20} = -158$$

This figure is also negative. So we still have a problem. Therefore, we need to step back a further year and combine the last *three* cash flows into a single year-3 cash flow with the same present value:

$$+175 + \frac{175}{1.20} - \frac{400}{1.20^2} = +43$$

This value is positive, so if we use it in place of the last three cash flows, we will have only one change of sign. Now we can compute IRR using the *modified* cash-flow sequence:

Year:	0	1	2	3	4	5
Cash flows, $ millions	−210	+125	+125	+43	—	—

The modified IRR (MIRR) is the discount rate at which the net present value of these cash flows is zero:

$$-210 + \frac{125}{1 + \text{MIRR}} + \frac{125}{(1 + \text{MIRR})^2} + \frac{43}{(1 + \text{MIRR})^3} = 0$$

We solve to find that MIRR = .22, or 22%, which is greater than the cost of capital of 20%. If the modified IRR is greater than the cost of capital, then the project must have a positive NPV.

CHAPTER 9

Using Discounted Cash-Flow Analysis to Make Investment Decisions

LEARNING OBJECTIVES

After studying this chapter, you should be able to:

1. Identify the cash flows properly attributable to a proposed new project.

2. Calculate the cash flows of a project from standard financial statements.

3. Understand how the company's tax bill is affected by depreciation and how this affects project value.

4. Understand how changes in working capital affect project cash flows.

RELATED WEB SITES FOR THIS CHAPTER CAN BE FOUND AT WWW.MHHE.COM/BMM7E.

A working magnoosium mine. But how do you find its net present value?

Think of the problems that Toyota's managers face when considering whether to introduce a new model. What investment must be made in new plant and equipment? What will it cost to market and promote the new car? How soon can the car be put into production? What is the projected production cost? How much must be invested in inventories of raw materials and finished cars? How many cars can be sold each year and at what price? What credit arrangements should be given to dealers? How long will the model stay in production? When production comes to an end, can the plant and equipment be used elsewhere in the company? All of these issues affect the level and timing of project cash flows. In this chapter we continue our analysis of the capital budgeting decision by turning our focus to how the financial manager should prepare cash-flow estimates for use in net present value analysis.

In Chapter 8 you used the net present value rule to make a simple capital budgeting decision. You tackled the problem in four steps:

Step 1. Forecast the project cash flows.

Step 2. Estimate the opportunity cost of capital—that is, the rate of return that

your shareholders could expect to earn if they invested their money in the capital market.

Step 3. Use the opportunity cost of capital to discount the future cash flows. The project's present value (PV) is equal to the sum of the discounted future cash flows.

Step 4. Net present value (NPV) measures whether the project is worth more than it costs. To calculate NPV, you need to subtract the required investment from the present value of the future payoffs:

NPV = PV − required investment

You should go ahead with the project if it has a positive NPV.

We now need to consider how to apply the net present value rule to practical investment problems. The first step is to decide what to discount. We know the answer in principle: Discount cash flows. This is why capital budgeting is often referred to as *discounted cash-flow,* or *DCF,* analysis. But useful forecasts of cash flows do not arrive on a silver platter. Often the financial manager has to make do with raw data supplied by specialists in product design, production, marketing, and so on. In addition, most financial forecasts are prepared in accordance with accounting principles that do not necessarily recognize cash flows when they occur. These forecasts must also be adjusted.

We look first at what cash flows should be discounted. We then present an example designed to show how standard accounting information

can be used to compute cash flows and why cash flows and accounting income usually differ. The example will lead us to various further points, including the links between depreciation and taxes and the importance of tracking investments in working capital.

9.1 Identifying Cash Flows

Discount Cash Flows, Not Profits

Up to this point we have been concerned mainly with the mechanics of discounting and with the various methods of project appraisal. We have had almost nothing to say about the problem of *what* you should discount. The first and most important point is this: To calculate net present value, you need to discount cash flows, *not* accounting profits.

We stressed the difference between cash flows and profits in Chapter 3. Here we stress it again. Income statements are intended to show how well the firm has performed. They do not track cash flows.

If the firm lays out a large amount of money on a big capital project, you do not conclude that the firm performed poorly that year, even though a lot of cash is going out the door. Therefore, the accountant does not deduct capital expenditure when calculating the year's income but, instead, depreciates it over several years.

That is fine for computing year-by-year profits, but it could get you into trouble when working out net present value. For example, suppose that you are analyzing an investment proposal. It costs $2,000 and is expected to bring in a cash flow of $1,500 in the first year and $500 in the second. You think that the opportunity cost of capital is 10% and so calculate the present value of the cash flows as follows:

$$PV = \frac{\$1,500}{1.10} + \frac{\$500}{(1.10)^2} = \$1,776.86$$

The project is worth less than it costs; it has a negative NPV:

$$NPV = \$1,776.86 - \$2,000 = -\$223.14$$

The project costs $2,000 today, but accountants would not treat that outlay as an immediate expense. They would depreciate that $2,000 over 2 years and deduct the depreciation from the cash flow to obtain accounting income:

	Year 1	Year 2
Cash inflow	+$1,500	+$ 500
Less depreciation	− 1,000	− 1,000
Accounting income	+ 500	− 500

Thus an accountant would forecast income of $500 in year 1 and an accounting loss of $500 in year 2.

Suppose you were given this forecast income and loss and naively discounted them. Now NPV *looks* positive:

$$\text{Apparent NPV} = \frac{\$500}{1.10} + \frac{-\$500}{(1.10)^2} = \$41.32$$

Of course we know that this is nonsense. The project is obviously a loser; we are spending money today ($2,000 cash outflow), and we are simply getting our money back later ($1,500 in year 1 and $500 in year 2). We are earning a zero return when we could get a 10% return by investing our money in the capital market.

The message of the example is this: **When calculating NPV, recognize investment expenditures when they occur, not later when they show up as depreciation. Projects are financially attractive because of the cash they generate, either for distribution to shareholders or for reinvestment in the firm. Therefore, the focus of capital budgeting must be on cash flow, not profits.**

We saw another example of the distinction between cash flow and accounting profits in Chapter 3. Accountants try to show profit as it is earned, rather than when the company and the customer get around to paying their bills. For example, an income statement will recognize revenue when the sale is made, even if the bill is not paid for months. This practice also results in a difference between accounting profits and cash flow. The sale generates immediate profits, but the cash flow comes later.

EXAMPLE 9.1 ▶	Sales before Cash

Your firm's ace computer salesman closed a $500,000 sale on December 15, just in time to count it toward his annual bonus. How did he do it? Well, for one thing he gave the customer 180 days to pay. The income statement will recognize the sale in December, even though cash will not arrive until June.

The accountant takes care of this timing difference by adding $500,000 to accounts receivable in December and then reducing accounts receivable when the money arrives in June. (The total of accounts receivable is just the sum of all cash due from customers.)

You can think of the increase in accounts receivable as an investment—it's effectively a 180-day loan to the customer—and therefore a cash outflow. That investment is recovered when the customer pays. Thus financial analysts often find it convenient to calculate cash flow as follows:

December		June	
Sales	$500,000	Sales	0
Less investment in accounts receivable	−500,000	Plus recovery of accounts receivable	+$500,000
Cash flow	0	Cash flow	$500,000

Note that this procedure gives the correct cash flow of $500,000 in June.

It is not always easy to translate accounting data back into actual dollars. If you are in doubt about what is a cash flow, simply count the dollars coming in and take away the dollars going out.

Self-Test 9.1

A regional supermarket chain is deciding whether to install a tewgit machine in each of its stores. Each machine costs $250,000. Projected income per machine is as follows:

Year:	1	2	3	4	5
Sales	$250,000	$300,000	$300,000	$250,000	$250,000
Operating expenses	200,000	200,000	200,000	200,000	200,000
Depreciation	50,000	50,000	50,000	50,000	50,000
Accounting income	0	50,000	50,000	0	0

Why would a store continue to operate a machine in years 4 and 5 if it produces no profits? What are the cash flows from investing in a machine? Assume each tewgit machine has no salvage value at the end of its 5-year life.

Discount *Incremental* Cash Flows

A project's present value depends on the *extra* cash flows that it produces. So you need to forecast first the firm's cash flows if you go ahead with the project. Then forecast the cash flows if you *don't* accept the project. Take the difference and you have the extra (or *incremental*) cash flows produced by the project:

$$\text{Incremental cash flow} = \text{cash flow with project} - \text{cash flow without project}$$

EXAMPLE 9.2   ▶   Launching a New Product

Consider the decision by Sony to develop Playstation 4. If successful, the PS4 could lead to several billion dollars in profits.

But are these profits all incremental cash flows? Certainly not. Our with-versus-without principle reminds us that we need also to think about what the cash flows would be *without* the new system. By launching the new console, Sony will reduce demand for Playstation 3. The incremental cash flows therefore are

Cash flow with PS4 (including lower cash flow) from PS3)	−	cash flow without PS4 (with higher cash flow from PS3)

The trick in capital budgeting is to trace all the incremental flows from a proposed project. Here are some things to look out for.

Include All Indirect Effects   The decision to launch a new games console illustrates a common indirect effect. New products often damage sales of an existing product. Of course, companies frequently introduce new products anyway, usually because they believe that their existing product line is under threat from competition. Even if you don't go ahead with a new product, there is no guarantee that sales of the existing product line will continue at their present level. Sooner or later they will decline.

Sometimes a new project will *help* the firm's existing business. Suppose that you are the financial manager of an airline that is considering opening a new short-haul route from Peoria, Illinois, to Chicago's O'Hare Airport. When considered in isolation, the new route may have a negative NPV. But once you allow for the additional business that the new route brings to your other traffic out of O'Hare, it may be a very worthwhile investment. **To forecast incremental cash flow, you must trace out all indirect effects of accepting the project.**

Some capital investments have very long lives once all indirect effects are recognized. Consider the introduction of a new jet engine. Engine manufacturers often offer attractive pricing to achieve early sales, because once an engine is installed, 15 years' sales of replacement parts are almost ensured. Also, since airlines prefer to limit the number of different engines in their fleet, selling jet engines today improves sales tomorrow as well. Later sales will generate further demands for replacement parts. Thus the string of incremental effects from the first sales of a new model engine can run for 20 years or more.

Forget Sunk Costs   Sunk costs are like spilled milk: They are past and irreversible outflows. **Sunk costs remain the same whether or not you accept the project. Therefore, they do not affect project NPV.**

Unfortunately, managers often are influenced by sunk costs. A classic case occurred in 1971, when Lockheed sought a federal guarantee for a bank loan to continue development of the Tristar airplane. Lockheed and its supporters argued that it would be foolish to abandon a project on which nearly $1 billion had already been spent. This was a poor argument, however, because the $1 billion was sunk. The relevant questions were how much more needed to be invested and whether the finished product warranted the *incremental* investment.

Lockheed's supporters were not the only ones to appeal to sunk costs. Some of its critics claimed that it would be foolish to continue with a project that offered no prospect of a satisfactory return on that $1 billion. This argument too was faulty. The $1 billion was gone, and the decision to continue with the project should have depended only on the return on the incremental investment.

Include Opportunity Costs   Resources are almost never free, even when no cash changes hands. For example, suppose a new manufacturing operation uses land that could otherwise be sold for $100,000. This resource is costly; by using the land, you pass up the opportunity to sell it. There is no out-of-pocket cost, but there is an **opportunity cost,** that is, the value of the forgone alternative use of the land.

opportunity cost
Benefit or cash flow forgone as a result of an action.

This example prompts us to warn you against judging projects "before versus after" rather than "with versus without." A manager comparing before versus after might not assign any value to the land because the firm owns it both before and after:

Before	Take Project	After	Cash Flow, Before versus After
Firm owns land	⟶	Firm still owns land	0

The proper comparison, with versus without, is as follows:

Before	Take Project	After	Cash Flow, with Project
Firm owns land	⟶	Firm still owns land	0

Before	Do Not Take Project	After	Cash Flow, without Project
Firm owns land	⟶	Firm sells land for $100,000	$100,000

If you compare the cash flows with and without the project, you see that $100,000 is given up by undertaking the project. The original cost of purchasing the land is irrelevant—that cost is sunk. **The opportunity cost equals the cash that could be realized from selling the land now and therefore is a relevant cash flow for project evaluation.**

When the resource can be freely traded, its opportunity cost is simply the market price.[1] However, sometimes opportunity costs are difficult to estimate. Suppose that you go ahead with a project to develop Computer Nouveau, pulling your software team off their work on a new operating system that some existing customers are not-so-patiently awaiting. The exact cost of infuriating those customers may be impossible to calculate, but you'll think twice about the opportunity cost of moving the software team to Computer Nouveau.

net working capital
Current assets minus current liabilities.

Recognize the Investment in Working Capital   **Net working capital** (often referred to simply as *working capital*) is the difference between a company's short-term assets and its liabilities. The principal short-term assets are cash, accounts receivable (customers' unpaid bills), and inventories of raw materials and finished goods, and the principal short-term liabilities are accounts payable (bills that *you* have not paid), notes payable, and accruals (liabilities for items such as wages or taxes that have recently been incurred but have not yet been paid).

---

[1] If the value of the land to the firm were less than the market price, the firm would sell it. On the other hand, the opportunity cost of using land in a particular project cannot exceed the cost of buying an equivalent parcel to replace it.

Most projects entail an additional investment in working capital. For example, before you can start production, you need to invest in inventories of raw materials. Then, when you deliver the finished product, customers may be slow to pay and accounts receivable will increase. (Remember the computer sale described in Example 9.1. It required a $500,000, 6-month investment in accounts receivable.) Next year, as business builds up, you may need a larger stock of raw materials and you may have even more unpaid bills. **Investments in working capital, just like investments in plant and equipment, result in cash outflows.**

We find that working capital is one of the most common sources of confusion in forecasting project cash flows.[2] Here are the most common mistakes:

1. *Forgetting about working capital entirely.* We hope that you never fall into that trap.
2. *Forgetting that working capital may change during the life of the project.* Imagine that you sell $100,000 of goods per year and customers pay on average 6 months late. You will therefore have $50,000 of unpaid bills. Now you increase prices by 10%, so revenues increase to $110,000. If customers continue to pay 6 months late, unpaid bills increase to $55,000, and therefore you need to make an *additional* investment in working capital of $5,000.
3. *Forgetting that working capital is recovered at the end of the project.* When the project comes to an end, inventories are run down, any unpaid bills are (you hope) paid off, and you can recover your investment in working capital. This generates a cash *inflow.*

Remember Terminal Cash Flows   The end of a project almost always brings additional cash flows. For example, you might be able to sell some of the plant, equipment, or real estate that was dedicated to it. Also, as we just mentioned, you may recover some of your investment in working capital as you sell off inventories of finished goods and collect on outstanding accounts receivable.

Often, there are expenses to shutting down a project. For example, the decommissioning costs of nuclear power plants can soak up several hundred million dollars. Similarly, when a mine is exhausted, the surrounding environment may need rehabilitation. The mining company FCX has earmarked over $350 million to cover the future closure and reclamation costs of its New Mexico mines. Don't forget to include these terminal cash flows.

Beware of Allocated Overhead Costs   We have already mentioned that the accountant's objective in gathering data is not always the same as the project analyst's. A case in point is the allocation of overhead costs such as rent, heat, or electricity. These overhead costs may not be related to a particular project, but they must be paid for nevertheless. Therefore, when the accountant assigns costs to the firm's projects, a charge for overhead is usually made. But our principle of incremental cash flows says that in investment appraisal we should include only the *extra* expenses of the project.

A project may generate extra overhead costs, but then again it may not. We should be cautious about assuming that the accountant's allocation of overhead costs represents the *incremental* cash flow that would be incurred by accepting the project.

Self-Test 9.2

A firm is considering an investment in a new manufacturing plant. The site already is owned by the company, but existing buildings would need to be demolished. Which of the following should be treated as incremental cash flows?

---

[2] If you are not clear *why* working capital affects cash flow, look back to Chapter 3, where we gave a primer on working capital and a couple of simple examples.

> a. The market value of the site.
> b. The market value of the existing buildings.
> c. Demolition costs and site clearance.
> d. The cost of a new access road put in last year.
> e. Lost cash flows on other projects due to executive time spent on the new facility.
> f. Future depreciation of the new plant.

Discount Nominal Cash Flows by the Nominal Cost of Capital

Interest rates are usually quoted in *nominal* terms. If you invest $100 in a bank deposit offering 6% interest, then the bank promises to pay you $106 at the end of the year. It makes no promises about what that $106 will buy. The real rate of interest on the bank deposit depends on inflation. If inflation is 2%, that $106 will buy you only 4% more goods at the end of the year than your $100 could buy today. The nominal rate of interest is 6%, but the *real* rate is about 4%.[3]

If the discount rate is nominal, consistency requires that cash flows be estimated in nominal terms as well, taking account of trends in selling price, labor and materials costs, and so on. This calls for more than simply applying a single assumed inflation rate to all components of cash flow. Some costs or prices increase faster than inflation, some slower. For example, perhaps you have entered into a 5-year fixed-price contract with a supplier. No matter what happens to inflation over this period, this part of your costs is fixed in nominal terms.

Of course, there is nothing wrong with discounting real cash flows at the real interest rate, although this is not commonly done. We saw in Chapter 5 that real cash flows discounted at the real discount rate give exactly the same present values as nominal cash flows discounted at the nominal rate.

It should go without saying that you cannot mix and match real and nominal quantities. Real cash flows must be discounted at a real discount rate, nominal cash flows at a nominal rate. Discounting real cash flows at a nominal rate is a big mistake.

While the need to maintain consistency may seem like an obvious point, analysts sometimes forget to account for the effects of inflation when forecasting future cash flows. As a result, they end up discounting real cash flows at a nominal discount rate. This can grossly understate project values.

EXAMPLE 9.3 ▶ Cash Flows and Inflation

City Consulting Services is considering moving into a new office building. The cost of a 1-year lease is $8,000, paid immediately. This cost will increase in future years at the annual inflation rate of 3%. The firm believes that it will remain in the building for 4 years. What is the present value of its rental costs if the discount rate is 10%?

The present value can be obtained by discounting the nominal cash flows at the 10% discount rate as follows:

---

[3] Remember from Chapter 5,

$$\text{Real rate of interest} \approx \text{nominal rate of interest} - \text{inflation rate}$$

The exact formula is

$$1 + \text{real rate interest} = \frac{1 + \text{nominal rate of interest}}{1 + \text{inflation rate}} = \frac{1.06}{1.02} = 1.0392$$

Therefore, the real interest rate is .0392, or 3.92%.

Year	Cash Flow	Present Value at 10% Discount Rate
0	8,000	8,000
1	$8,000 \times 1.03 = 8,240$	$8,240/1.10 = 7,491$
2	$8,000 \times 1.03^2 = 8,487$	$8,487/(1.10)^2 = 7,014$
3	$8,000 \times 1.03^3 = 8,742$	$8,742/(1.10)^3 = \underline{6,568}$
		$29,073

Alternatively, the real discount rate can be calculated as $1.10/1.03 - 1 = .06796 = 6.796\%$.[4] The present value can then be computed by discounting the real cash flows at the real discount rate as follows:

Year	Real Cash Flow	Present Value at 6.796% Discount Rate
0	8,000	8,000
1	8,000	$8,000/1.06796 = 7,491$
2	8,000	$8,000/(1.06796)^2 = 7,014$
3	8,000	$8,000/(1.06796)^3 = \underline{6,568}$
		$29,073

Notice the real cash flow is a constant, since the lease payment increases at the rate of inflation. The present value of *each* cash flow is the same regardless of the method used to discount it. The sum of the present values is, of course, also identical.

Self-Test 9.3

Nasty Industries is closing down an outmoded factory and throwing all of its workers out on the street. Nasty's CEO is enraged to learn that the firm must continue to pay for workers' health insurance for 4 years. The cost per worker next year will be $2,400 per year, but the inflation rate is 4%, and health costs have been increasing at 3 percentage points faster than inflation. What is the present value of this obligation? The (nominal) discount rate is 10%.

Separate Investment and Financing Decisions

Suppose you finance a project partly with debt. How should you treat the proceeds from the debt issue and the interest and principal payments on the debt? Answer: You should *neither* subtract the debt proceeds from the required investment *nor* recognize the interest and principal payments on the debt as cash outflows. Regardless of the actual financing, you should view the project as if it were all equity-financed, treating all cash outflows required for the project as coming from stockholders and all cash inflows as going to them.

This procedure focuses exclusively on the *project* cash flows, not the cash flows associated with alternative financing schemes. It, therefore, allows you to separate the analysis of the investment decision from that of the financing decision. First, you ask whether the project has a positive net present value, assuming all-equity financing. Then you can undertake a separate analysis of the best financing strategy. Financing decisions are considered later in the text.

---

[4] We calculate the real discount rate to three decimal places to avoid confusion from rounding. Such precision is rarely necessary in practice.

9.2 Calculating Cash Flow

It is helpful to think of a project's cash flow as composed of three elements:

$$\text{Total cash flow} = \begin{aligned}&\text{cash flows from capital investments} \\ &+ \text{ operating cash flows} \\ &+ \text{ cash flows from changes in working capital}\end{aligned} \qquad \text{(9.1)}$$

We will look at each of these components in turn.

Capital Investment

To get a project off the ground, a company typically needs to make considerable up-front investments in plant, equipment, research, marketing, and so on. For example, development of a new car model typically involves expenditure of $500 million or more. This expenditure is a negative cash flow—negative because cash goes out the door.

When the model finally goes out of production, the company can either sell the plant and equipment or redeploy the assets elsewhere in the business. This salvage value (net of any taxes if the equipment is sold) represents a positive cash flow to the firm. However, remember our earlier comment that final cash flows can be negative if there are significant shutdown costs.

EXAMPLE 9.4 ▶ Cash Flow from Capital Investment

Slick Corporation plans to invest $800 million to develop the Mock4 razor blade. The specialized blade factory will run for 7 years until it is replaced by more advanced technology. At that point the machinery will be sold for $50 million. Taxes of $10 million will be assessed on the sale.

The initial cash flow from Slick's investment is −$800 million. In year 7, when the firm sells the land and equipment, there will be a net inflow of $50 million − $10 million = $40 million. Thus, the initial investment involves a negative cash flow, and the salvage value results in a positive flow.

Operating Cash Flow

Think back to the decision to launch a new car model. In such cases, operating cash flow consists of revenues from the sale of the new product less the costs of production and any taxes:

$$\text{Operating cash flow} = \text{revenues} - \text{costs} - \text{taxes}$$

Undoubtedly, the revenues are expected to outweigh the costs, and therefore operating cash flows are positive.

Many investments do not result in additional revenues; they are simply designed to reduce the costs of the company's existing operations. For example, a new computer system may provide labor savings, or a new heating system may be more energy-efficient than the one it replaces. Such projects also contribute to the operating cash flow of the firm—not by increasing revenues but by reducing costs. These cost savings therefore represent a positive cash flow.

EXAMPLE 9.5 ▶ Operating Cash Flow of Cost-Cutting Projects

Suppose a new heating system costs $100,000 but reduces heating costs by $30,000 a year. The firm's tax rate is 35%. The new system does not change revenues, but, thanks to the cost savings, income increases by $30,000. Therefore, incremental operating cash flow is:

Increase in (revenues less expenses)	$30,000
− Incremental tax at 35%	− 10,500
= Operating cash flow	+$19,500

Notice that because the cost savings increase profits, the company must pay more tax. The *net* increase in cash flow equals the after-tax cost savings:

$$(1 - .35) \times \$30,000 = \$19,500$$

Here is another matter that you need to look out for when calculating cash flow. When the firm calculates its taxable income, it makes a deduction for depreciation. This depreciation charge is an accounting entry. It affects the tax that the company pays, but it is not a cash expense and should not be deducted when calculating operating cash flow. (Remember from our earlier discussion that you want to discount cash flows, not profits.)

When you work out a project's cash flows, there are three possible ways to deal with depreciation.

Method 1: Dollars In Minus Dollars Out   Take only the items from the income statement that represent actual cash flows. This means that you start with cash revenues and subtract cash expenses and taxes paid. You do not, however, subtract a charge for depreciation because this does not involve cash going out the door. Thus,

$$\text{Operating cash flow} = \text{revenues} - \text{cash expenses} - \text{taxes} \qquad \textbf{(9.2)}$$

Method 2: Adjusted Accounting Profits   Alternatively, you can start with after-tax accounting profits and add back any depreciation deduction. This gives

$$\text{Operating cash flow} = \text{after-tax profit} + \text{depreciation} \qquad \textbf{(9.3)}$$

Method 3: Add Back Depreciation Tax Shield   Although the depreciation deduction is *not* a cash expense, it does affect the firm's tax payment, which certainly is a cash item. Each additional dollar of depreciation reduces taxable income by $1. So, if the firm's tax bracket is 35%, tax payments fall by $.35, and cash flow increases by the same amount. Financial managers often refer to this tax saving as the **depreciation tax shield.** It equals the product of the tax rate and the depreciation charge:

depreciation tax shield
Reduction in taxes attributable to depreciation.

$$\text{Depreciation tax shield} = \text{tax rate} \times \text{depreciation}$$

This suggests a third way to calculate operating cash flow. First, calculate net profit, assuming zero depreciation. This is equal to (revenues − cash expenses) × (1 − tax rate). Now add back the depreciation tax shield to find operating cash flow:

$$\text{Operating cash flow} = (\text{revenues} - \text{cash expenses}) \times (1 - \text{tax rate}) \qquad \textbf{(9.4)}$$
$$+ (\text{tax rate} \times \text{depreciation})$$

The following example confirms that the three methods all give the same figure for operating cash flow.

| EXAMPLE 9.6 ▶ | Operating Cash Flow |

A project generates revenues of $1,000, cash expenses of $600, and depreciation charges of $200 in a particular year. The firm's tax bracket is 35%. Net income is calculated as follows:

Revenues	1,000
− Cash expenses	600
− Depreciation expense	200
= Profit before tax	200
− Tax at 35%	70
= Net profit	130

Methods 1, 2, and 3 all show that operating cash flow is $330:

Method 1: Operating cash flow = revenues − cash expenses − taxes
$$= 1,000 + 600 - 70 = 330$$
Method 2: Operating cash flow = net profit + depreciation
$$= 130 + 200 = 330$$
Method 3: Operating cash flow = (revenues − cash expenses)
$$\times (1 - \text{tax rate}) + (\text{depreciation} \times \text{tax rate})$$
$$= (1,000 - 600) \times (1 - .35) + (200 \times .35) = 330$$

Self-Test 9.4

A project generates revenues of $600, expenses of $300, and depreciation charges of $200 in a particular year. The firm's tax bracket is 35%. Find the operating cash flow of the project by using all three approaches.

Changes in Working Capital

We pointed out earlier in the chapter that when a company builds up inventories of raw materials or finished product, the company's cash is reduced; the reduction in cash reflects the firm's investment in inventories. Similarly, cash is reduced when customers are slow to pay their bills—in this case, the firm makes an investment in accounts receivable. Investment in working capital, just like investment in plant and equipment, represents a negative cash flow. On the other hand, later in the life of a project, when inventories are sold off and accounts receivable are collected, the firm's investment in working capital is reduced as it converts these assets into cash.

| EXAMPLE 9.7 ▶ | Cash Flow from Changes in Working Capital |

Slick makes an initial (year 0) investment of $10 million in inventories of plastic and steel for its blade plant. Then in year 1 it accumulates an additional $20 million of raw materials. The total level of inventories is now $10 million + $20 million = $30 million, but the cash expenditure in year 1 is simply the $20 million addition to inventory. The $20 million investment in additional inventory results in a cash flow of − $20 million. Notice that the increase in working capital is an *investment* in the project. Like other investments, a buildup of working capital requires cash. Increases in the *level* of working capital therefore show up as *negative* cash flows.

Later on, say, in year 5, the company begins planning for the next-generation blade. At this point, it decides to reduce its inventory of raw material from $30 million to $25 million. This reduction in inventory investment frees up $5 million of cash, which is a positive cash flow. Therefore, the cash flows from inventory investment are −$10 million in year 0, −$20 million in year 1, and +$5 million in year 5.

These calculations can be summarized in a simple table, as follows:

Year:	0	1	2	3	4	5
1. Total working capital, year-end ($ million)	10	30	30	30	30	25
2. Change in working capital ($ million)	10	20	0	0	0	−5
3. Cash flow from changes in working capital	−10	−20	0	0	0	+5

In years 0 and 1, there is a net investment in working capital (line 2), corresponding to a negative cash flow (line 3), and an increase in the *level* of total working capital (line 1). In years 2 to 4, there is no investment in working capital, so its level remains unchanged at $30 million. But in year 5, the firm begins to disinvest in working capital, which provides a positive cash flow.

In general: **An *increase* in working capital is an investment and therefore implies a *negative* cash flow; a decrease in working capital implies a positive cash flow. The cash flow is measured by the *change* in working capital, not the *level* of working capital.**

9.3 An Example: Blooper Industries

Now that we have examined the basic pieces of a cash-flow analysis, let's try to put them together into a coherent whole. As the newly appointed financial manager of Blooper Industries, you are about to analyze a proposal for mining and selling a small deposit of high-grade magnoosium ore.[5] You are given the forecasts shown in the spreadsheet in Table 9.1. We will walk through the lines in the table.

Cash-Flow Analysis

Investment in Fixed Assets   Panel A of the spreadsheet summarizes our assumptions. Panel B details investments and disinvestments in fixed assets. The project requires an initial investment of $10 million, as shown in cell B14. After 5 years, the ore deposit is exhausted, so the mining equipment may be sold for $2 million (cell B3), a forecast that already reflects the likely impact of inflation.

When you sell the equipment, the IRS will check to see whether any taxes are due on the sale. Any difference between the sale price ($2 million) and the book value of the equipment will be treated as a taxable gain.

We assume that Blooper depreciates the equipment to a final value of zero. Therefore, the book value of the equipment when it is sold in year 6 will be zero, and you will be subject to taxes on the full $2 million proceeds. Your sale of the equipment will land you with an additional tax bill in year 6 of .35 × $2 million = $.70 million. The net cash flow from the sale in year 6 is therefore

Salvage value − tax on gain = $2 million − $.70 million = $1.30 million

This amount is recorded in cell H15.

---

[5] Readers have inquired whether magnoosium is a real substance. Here, now, are the facts: Magnoosium was created in the early days of television, when a splendid-sounding announcer closed a variety show by saying, "This program has been brought to you by Blooper Industries, proud producer of aleemiums, magnoosium, and stool." We forget the company, but the blooper really happened.

TABLE 9.1 Financial projections for Blooper's magnoosium mine (figures in thousands of dollars)

You can find this spreadsheet at www.mhhe.com/bmm7e.

	A	B	C	D	E	F	G	H
1	**A. Inputs**		Spreadsheet Name					
2	Initial investment	10,000	Investment					
3	Salvage value	2,000	Salvage					
4	Initial revenue	15,000	Initial_rev					
5	Initial expenses	10,000	Initial_exp					
6	Inflation rate	0.05	Inflation					
7	Discount rate	0.12	Disc_rate					
8	Acct receiv. as % of sales	1/6	A_R					
9	Inven. as % of expenses	0.15	Inv_pct					
10	Tax rate	0.35	Tax_rate					
11								
12	Year:	0	1	2	3	4	5	6
13	**B. Fixed assets**							
14	Investment in fixed assets	10,000						
15	Sales of fixed assets							1,300
16	CF, invest. in fixed assets	-10,000	0	0	0	0	0	1,300
17								
18	**C. Operating cash flow**							
19	Revenues		15,000	15,750	16,538	17,364	18,233	
20	Expenses		10,000	10,500	11,025	11,576	12,155	
21	Depreciation		2,000	2,000	2,000	2,000	2,000	
22	Pretax profit		3,000	3,250	3,513	3,788	4,078	
23	Tax		1,050	1,138	1,229	1,326	1,427	
24	Profit after tax		1,950	2,113	2,283	2,462	2,650	
25	Operating cash flow		3,950	4,113	4,283	4,462	4,650	
26								
27	**D. Working capital**							
28	Working capital	1,500	4,075	4,279	4,493	4,717	3,039	0
29	*Change* in working cap	1,500	2,575	204	214	225	-1,679	-3,039
30	CF, invest. in wk capital	-1,500	-2,575	-204	-214	-225	1,679	3,039
31								
32	**E. Project valuation**							
33	Total project cash flow	-11,500	1,375	3,909	4,069	4,238	6,329	4,339
34	Discount factor	1.0	0.8929	0.7972	0.7118	0.6355	0.5674	0.5066
35	PV of cash flow	-11,500	1,228	3,116	2,896	2,693	3,591	2,198
36	Net present value	4,223						

Row 16 summarizes the cash flows from investments in and sales of fixed assets. The entry in each cell equals the after-tax proceeds from asset sales (row 15) minus the investments in fixed assets (row 14).

Operating Cash Flow The company expects to be able to sell 750,000 pounds of magnoosium a year at a price of $20 a pound in year 1. That points to initial revenues of 750,000 × $20 = $15,000,000. But be careful; inflation is running at about 5% a year. If magnoosium prices keep pace with inflation, you should increase your forecast of the second-year revenues by 5%. Third-year revenues should increase by a further 5%, and so on. Row 19 in Table 9.1 shows revenues rising in line with inflation.

The sales forecasts in Table 9.1 are cut off after 5 years. That makes sense if the ore deposit will run out at that time. But if Blooper could make sales for year 6, you should include them in your forecasts. We have sometimes encountered financial managers who assume a project life of (say) 5 years, even when they confidently expect revenues for 10 years or more. When asked the reason, they explain that forecasting beyond 5 years is too hazardous. We sympathize, but you just have to do your best. Do not arbitrarily truncate a project's life.

Expenses in year 1 are $10,000 (cell C20). We assume that the expenses of mining and refining (row 20) also increase in line with inflation at 5% a year.

straight-line depreciation Constant depreciation for each year of the asset's accounting life.

We also assume for now that the company applies **straight-line depreciation** to the mining equipment over 5 years. This means that it deducts one-fifth of the initial $10 million investment from profits. Thus row 21 shows that the annual depreciation deduction is $2 million.

Pretax profit, shown in row 22, equals (revenues − expenses − depreciation). Taxes (row 23) are 35% of pretax profit. For example, in year 1,

$$\text{Tax} = .35 \times 3,000 = 1,050, \text{ or } \$1,050,000$$

Profit after tax (row 24) equals pretax profit less taxes.

The last row of panel C presents operating cash flow. We calculate cash flow as the sum of after-tax profits plus depreciation (method 2, above). Therefore, row 25 is the sum of rows 24 and 21.

Changes in Working Capital   Row 28 shows the *level* of working capital. As the project gears up in the early years, working capital increases, but later in the project's life, the investment in working capital is recovered and the level declines.

Row 29 shows the *change* in working capital from year to year. Notice that in years 1 to 4 the change is positive; in these years the project requires a continuing investment in working capital. Starting in year 5 the change is negative; there is a disinvestment as working capital is recovered. Cash flow associated with investments in working capital (row 30) is the negative of the change in working capital. Just like investment in plant and equipment, investment in working capital produces a negative cash flow, and disinvestment produces a positive cash flow.

Total Project Cash Flow   Total cash flow is the sum of cash flows from each of the three sources: Cash flow from investments in fixed assets and working capital, and operating cash flow. Therefore, total cash flow in row 33 is just the sum of rows 16, 25, and 30.

Calculating the NPV of Blooper's Project

You have now derived (in row 33) the forecast cash flows from Blooper's magnoosium mine. Suppose that investors expect a return of 12% from investments in the capital market with the same risk as the magnoosium project. This is the opportunity cost of the shareholders' money that Blooper is proposing to invest in the project. Therefore, to calculate NPV, you need to discount the cash flows at 12%.

Rows 34 and 35 set out the calculations. Remember that to calculate the present value of a cash flow in year t you can divide the cash flow by $(1 + r)^t$ or you can multiply by a discount factor that is equal to $1/(1 + r)^t$. Row 34 presents the discount factors for each year, and row 35 calculates the present value of each cash flow by multiplying the cash flow (row 33) times the discount factor. When all cash flows are discounted and added up, the magnoosium project is seen to offer a positive net present value of $4,223 thousand (cell B36), or about $4.2 million.

Now here is a small point that often causes confusion: To calculate the present value of the first year's cash flow, we divide by $(1 + r) = 1.12$. Strictly speaking, this makes sense only if all the sales and all the costs occur exactly 365 days, zero hours, and zero minutes from now. Of course the year's sales don't all take place on the stroke of midnight on December 31. However, when making capital budgeting decisions, companies are usually happy to pretend that all cash flows occur at 1-year intervals. They pretend this for one reason only—simplicity. When sales forecasts are sometimes little more than intelligent guesses, it may be pointless to inquire how the sales are likely to be spread out during the year.[6]

---

[6] Financial managers sometimes assume cash flows arrive in the middle of the calendar year, that is, at the end of June. This midyear convention is roughly equivalent to assuming cash flows are distributed evenly throughout the year. This is a bad assumption for some industries. In retailing, for example, most of the cash flow comes late in the year, as the holiday season approaches.

Further Notes and Wrinkles Arising from Blooper's Project

Before we leave Blooper and its magnoosium project, we should cover a few extra wrinkles.

Forecasting Working Capital   Table 9.1 shows that Blooper expects its magnoosium mine to produce revenues of $15,000 in year 1 and $15,750 in year 2. But Blooper will not actually receive these amounts in years 1 and 2, because some of its customers will not pay up immediately. We have assumed that, on average, customers pay with a 2-month lag, so that 2/12 of each year's sales are not paid for until the following year. These unpaid bills show up as accounts receivable. For example, in year 1 Blooper will have accounts receivable of $(2/12) \times 15,000 = \$2,500$.[7]

Consider now the mine's expenses. These are forecast at $10,000 in year 1 and $10,500 in year 2. But not all of this cash will go out of the door in these 2 years, for Blooper must produce the magnoosium before selling it. Each year, Blooper mines magnoosium ore, but some of this ore is not sold until the following year. The ore is put into inventory, and the accountant does not deduct the cost of its production until it is taken out of inventory and sold. We assume that 15% of each year's expenses represent an investment in inventory that took place in the previous year. Thus the investment in inventory is forecast at $.15 \times 10,000 = \$1,500$ in year 0 and at $.15 \times \$10,500 = \$1,575$ in year 1.

We can now see how Blooper arrives at its forecast of working capital:

	0	1	2	3	4	5	6
1. Receivables (2/12 × revenues)	$ 0	$2,500	$2,625	$2,756	$2,894	$3,039	0
2. Inventories (.15 × following year's expenses)	1,500	1,575	1,654	1,736	1,823	0	0
3. Working capital (1 + 2)	1,500	4,075	4,279	4,493	4,717	3,039	0

Note: Columns may not sum due to rounding.

Notice that working capital builds up in years 1 to 4, as sales of magnoosium increase. Year 5 is the last year of sales, so Blooper can reduce its inventories to zero in that year. In year 6 the company expects to collect any unpaid bills from year 5 and so in that year receivables also fall to zero. This decline in working capital increases cash flow. For example, in year 6 cash flow is increased as the $3,039 of outstanding bills are paid.

The construction of the Blooper spreadsheet is discussed further in the nearby box. Once the spreadsheet is set up, it is easy to try out different assumptions for working capital. For example, you can adjust the level of receivables and inventories by changing the values in cells B8 and B9.

A Further Note on Depreciation   We warned you earlier not to assume that all cash flows are likely to increase with inflation. The depreciation tax shield is a case in point, because the Internal Revenue Service lets companies depreciate only the amount of the original investment. For example, if you go back to the IRS to explain that inflation mushroomed since you made the investment and you should be allowed to depreciate more, the IRS won't listen. The *nominal* amount of depreciation is fixed, and therefore the higher the rate of inflation, the lower the *real* value of the depreciation that you can claim.

We assumed in our calculations that Blooper could depreciate its investment in mining equipment by $2 million a year. That produced an annual tax shield of

---

[7] For convenience, we assume that, although Blooper's customers pay with a lag, Blooper pays all its bills on the nail. If it didn't, these unpaid bills would be recorded as accounts payable. Working capital would be reduced by the amount of the accounts payable.

Year(s)	Recovery Period Class					
	3 Year	**5 Year**	**7 Year**	**10 Year**	**15 Year**	**20 Year**
1	33.33	20.00	14.29	10.00	5.00	3.75
2	44.45	32.00	24.49	18.00	9.50	7.22
3	14.81	19.20	17.49	14.40	8.55	6.68
4	7.41	11.52	12.49	11.52	7.70	6.18
5		11.52	8.93	9.22	6.93	5.71
6		5.76	8.92	7.37	6.23	5.28
7			8.93	6.55	5.90	4.89
8			4.46	6.55	5.90	4.52
9				6.56	5.91	4.46
10				6.55	5.90	4.46
11				3.28	5.91	4.46
12					5.90	4.46
13					5.91	4.46
14					5.90	4.46
15					5.91	4.46
16					2.95	4.46
17–20						4.46
21						2.23

Notes: ⁻
1. Tax depreciation is lower in the first year because assets are assumed to be in service for 6 months.
2. Real property is depreciated straight-line over 27.5 years for residential property and 39 years for nonresidential property.

$2 million × .35 = $.70 million per year for 5 years. These tax shields increase cash flows from operations and therefore increase present value. So if Blooper could get those tax shields sooner, they would be worth more, right? Fortunately for corporations, tax law allows them to do just that. It allows *accelerated depreciation.*

The rate at which firms are permitted to depreciate equipment is known as the **modified accelerated cost recovery system,** or **MACRS.** MACRS places assets into one of six classes, each of which has an assumed life. Table 9.2 shows the rate of depreciation that the company can use for each of these classes. Most industrial equipment falls into the 5- and 7-year classes. To keep life simple, we will assume that all of Blooper's mining equipment goes into 5-year assets. Thus Blooper can depreciate 20% of its $10 million investment in year 1. In the second year it can deduct depreciation of .32 × 10 = $3.2 million, and so on.[8]

How does MACRS depreciation affect the value of the depreciation tax shield for the magnoosium project? Table 9.3 gives the answer. Notice that MACRS does not affect the total amount of depreciation that is claimed. This remains at $10 million just as before. But MACRS allows companies to get the depreciation deduction earlier, which increases the present value of the depreciation tax shield from $2,523,000 to $2,583,000, an increase of $60,000. Before we recognized MACRS depreciation, we calculated project NPV as $4,223,000. When we recognize MACRS, we should increase that figure by $60,000.

All large corporations in the United States keep two sets of books, one for stockholders and one for the Internal Revenue Service. It is common to use straight-line depreciation on the stockholder books and MACRS depreciation on the tax books. Only the tax books are relevant in capital budgeting.

modified accelerated cost recovery system (MACRS) Depreciation method that allows higher tax deductions in early years and lower deductions later.

---

[8] You might wonder why the 5-year asset class provides a depreciation deduction in years 1 through 6. This is because the tax authorities assume that the assets are in service for only 6 months of the first year and 6 months of the last year. The total project life is 5 years, but that 5-year life spans parts of 6 calendar years. This assumption also explains why the depreciation allowance is lower in the first year than it is in the second.

MidAmerican's Wind Power Project

In 2005, MidAmerican Energy brought into operation in Iowa one of the largest wind farms in the world. The wind farm cost $386 million, contains 257 wind turbines, and has a capacity of 360.5 megawatts (MW). Wind speeds fluctuate, and most wind farms are expected to operate at an average of only 35% of their rated capacity. In this case, at an electricity price of $55 per megawatt-hour (MWh), the project will initially produce annual revenues of $60.8 million (i.e., .35 × 8,760 hours × 360.5 MW × $55 per MWh). A reasonable estimate of maintenance and other costs is about $18.9 million in the first year of operation. Thereafter, revenues and costs should increase with inflation by around 3% a year. Conventional power stations can be depreciated using 20-year MACRS, and their profits are taxed at 35%. A project such as this one might last 25 years and entail a cost of capital of 12%.

Wind power is more costly than conventional fossil-fuel power, but to encourage the development of renewable energy sources, the government provides several tax breaks to companies constructing wind farms. How large do these tax breaks need to be to make the wind farm viable for MidAmerican? We estimate that in the absence of any tax breaks the project would have a net present value of −$68 million. So any tax subsidy must have a value of at least $68 million to entice a private firm such as MidAmerican to undertake the project.

You can find our calculations at the Online Learning Center at www.mhhe.com/bmm7e. Once you're there, you might consider the following questions. Suppose the government believes that the national security and environmental benefits of being able to generate clean energy domestically are worth 25% of the value of the electricity produced. Does the subsidy make economic sense for the government? Some wind farm operators assume a capacity factor of 30% rather than 35%. If MidAmerican's plant achieves only this level of operation, how much larger would the tax subsidy need to be? If no tax breaks were available for wind farms, how high would electricity prices need to be before this plant would be viable (i.e., have a positive NPV)?

TABLE 9.3 The switch from straight-line to 5-year MACRS depreciation increases the value of Blooper's depreciation tax shield from $2,523,000 to $2,583,000 (figures in thousands of dollars).

Year	Straight-Line Depreciation			MACRS Depreciation		
	Depreciation	Tax Shield	PV Tax Shield at 12%	Depreciation	Tax Shield	PV Tax Shield at 12%
1	2,000	700	625	2,000	700	625
2	2,000	700	558	3,200	1,120	893
3	2,000	700	498	1,920	672	478
4	2,000	700	445	1,152	403	256
5	2,000	700	397	1,152	403	229
6	0	0	0	576	202	102
Totals	10,000	3,500	2,523	10,000	3,500	2,583

Note: Column sums subject to rounding error.

Self-Test 9.5

Suppose that Blooper's mining equipment could be put in the 3-year recovery period class. What is the present value of the depreciation tax shield? Confirm that the change in the value of the depreciation tax shield equals the increase in project NPV from question 9.1 of the Spreadsheet Solutions box.

More on Salvage Value When you sell equipment, you must pay taxes on the difference between the sales price and the book value of the asset. The book value in turn equals the initial cost minus cumulative charges for depreciation. It is common when figuring tax depreciation to assume a salvage value of zero at the end of the asset's depreciable life.

For reports to shareholders, however, positive expected salvage values are often recognized. For example, Blooper's financial statements might assume that its $10 million investment in mining equipment would be worth $2 million in year 6. In this case, the depreciation reported to shareholders would be based on the difference between the investment and the salvage value, that is, $8 million. Straight-line depreciation then would be $1.6 million annually.

The Blooper Spreadsheet Model

Discounted cash-flow analysis of proposed capital investments is clearly tailor-made for spreadsheet analysis. The formula view of the Excel spreadsheet used in the Blooper example appears below.

Notice that most of the entries in the spreadsheet are formulas rather than specific numbers. Once the relatively few input values are entered, the spreadsheet does most of the work. In panel A we enter only the initial investment (cell B2), the salvage value (cell B3), the initial levels of revenues and expenses (cells B4 and B5), and the other parameters.

Revenues and expenses in each year equal the value in the previous year times (1 + inflation rate), which is given in cell B6 as .05. For example, cell D19 equals C19 × 1.05. To make the spreadsheet easier to read, we have defined names for a few cells, such as B6 (*Inflation rate*) and B7 (*Discount rate*). These names can be assigned using the

Insert command and thereafter can be used to refer to specific cells.

Row 28 sets out the level of working capital, which is the sum of accounts receivable and inventories. Because inventories tend to rise with production, we set them equal to .15 times expenses recognized in the following year when the product is sold. Similarly, accounts receivable rise with sales, so we assume that they will be 2/12 times current year's revenues (in other words, that Blooper's customers pay, on average, 2 months after purchasing the product). Each entry in row 28 is the sum of these two quantities.

We calculate the discount factor in row 34 using the discount rate of 12%, compute present values of each cash flow in row 35, and add the present value of each cash flow to find project NPV in cell B36.

Once the spreadsheet is up and running, "what-if" analyses are easy. Here are a few questions to try your hand.

Formula view

	A	B	C	D	E	F	G	H
1	A. Inputs		Spreadsheet Name					
2	Initial investment	10,000	Investment					
3	Salvage value	2,000	Salvage					
4	Initial revenue	15,000	Initial_rev					
5	Initial expenses	10,000	Initial_exp					
6	Inflation rate	0.05	Inflation					
7	Discount rate	0.12	Disc_rate					
8	Acct receiv. as % of sales	=2/12	A_R					
9	Inven. as % of expenses	0.15	Inv_pct					
10	Tax rate	0.35	Tax_rate					
11								
12	Year:	0	1	2	3	4	5	6
13	B. Fixed assets							
14	Investment in fixed assets	=Investment						
15	Sales of fixed assets							=Salvage*(1-Tax_rate)
16	CF, invest. in fixed assets	=-B14+B15	=-C14+C15	=-D14+D15	=-E14+E15	=-F14+F15	=-G14+G15	=-H14+H15
17								
18	C. Operations							
19	Revenues		=Initial_rev	=C19*(1+Inflation)	=D19*(1+Inflation)	=E19*(1+Inflation)	=F19*(1+Inflation)	
20	Expenses		=Initial_exp	=C20*(1+Inflation)	=D20*(1+Inflation)	=E20*(1+Inflation)	=F20*(1+Inflation)	
21	Depreciation		=Investment/5	=Investment/5	=Investment/5	=Investment/5	=Investment/5	
22	Pretax profit		=C19-C20-C21	=D19-D20-D21	=E19-E20-E21	=F19-F20-F21	=G19-G20-G21	
23	Tax		=C22*Tax rate	=D22*Tax rate	=E22*Tax rate	=F22*Tax rate	=G22*Tax rate	
24	Profit after tax		=C22-C23	=D22-D23	=E22-E23	=F22-F23	=G22-G23	
25	Operating cash flow		=C21 + C24	=D21 + D24	=E21 + E24	=F21 + F24	=G21 + G24	
26								
27	D. Working capital							
28	Working capital	=Inv_pct*C20+A_R*B19	=Inv_pct*D20+A_R*C19	=Inv_pct*E20+A_R*D19	=Inv_pct*F20+A_R*E19	=Inv_pct*G20+A_R*F19	=Inv_pct*H20+A_R*G19	=Inv_pct*I20+A_R*H19
29	*Change* in working cap	=B28	=C28-B28	=D28-C28	=E28-D28	=F28-E28	=G28-F28	=H28-G28
30	CF, invest. in wk capital	=-B29	=-C29	=-D29	=-E29	=-F29	=-G29	=-H29
31								
32	E. Project valuation							
33	Total project cash flow	=B16+B30+B25	=C16+C30+C25	=D16+D30+D25	=E16+E30+E25	=F16+F30+F25	=G16+G30+G25	=H16+H30+H25
34	Discount factor	=1/(1+Disc_rate)^B12	=1/(1+Disc_rate)^C12	=1/(1+Disc_rate)^D12	=1/(1+Disc_rate)^E12	=1/(1+Disc_rate)^F12	=1/(1+Disc_rate)^G12	=1/(1+Disc_rate)^H12
35	PV of cash flow	=B33*B34	=C33*C34	=D33*D34	=E33*E34	=F33*F34	=G33*G34	=H33*H34
36	Net present value	=SUM(B35:H35)						

You can find this spreadsheet at www.mhhe.com/bmm7e.

Spreadsheet Questions

9.1 What happens to cash flow in each year and the NPV of the project if the firm uses MACRS depreciation assuming a 3-year recovery period? Assume year 1 is the first year that depreciation is taken.

9.2 Suppose the firm can economize on working capital by managing inventories more efficiently. If the firm can reduce inventories from 15% to 10% of next year's cost of goods sold, what will be the effect on project NPV?

9.3 What happens to NPV if the inflation rate falls from 5% to zero and the discount rate falls from 12% to 7% Given that the real discount rate is almost unchanged, why does project NPV increase? [To be consistent, you should assume that nominal salvage value will be lower in a zero-inflation environment. If you set (before-tax) salvage value to $1.492 million, you will maintain its real value unchanged.]

Brief solutions appear at the end of the chapter.

SUMMARY

How should the cash flows of a proposed new project be calculated? *(LO1)*

Here is a checklist to bear in mind when forecasting a project's cash flows:

- Discount cash flows, not profits.
- Estimate the project's *incremental* cash flows—that is, the difference between the cash flows with the project and those without the project.
- Include all indirect effects of the project, such as its impact on the sales of the firm's other products.
- Forget sunk costs.
- Include **opportunity costs,** such as the value of land that you could otherwise sell.
- Beware of allocated overhead charges for heat, light, and so on. These may not reflect the incremental effects of the project on these costs.
- Remember the investment in working capital. As sales increase, the firm may need to make additional investments in working capital, and as the project finally comes to an end, it will recover these investments.
- Treat inflation consistently. If cash flows are forecast in nominal terms (including the effects of future inflation), use a nominal discount rate. Discount real cash flows at a real rate.
- Do not include debt interest or the cost of repaying a loan. When calculating NPV, assume that the project is financed entirely by the shareholders and that they receive all the cash flows. This separates the investment decision from the financing decision.

How can the cash flows of a project be computed from standard financial statements? *(LO2)*

Project cash flow does not equal profit. You must allow for noncash expenses such as depreciation as well as changes in working capital.

How is the company's tax bill affected by depreciation, and how does this affect project value? *(LO3)*

Depreciation is not a cash flow. However, because depreciation reduces taxable income, it reduces taxes. This tax reduction is called the **depreciation tax shield. Modified accelerated cost recovery system (MACRS)** depreciation schedules allow more of the depreciation allowance to be taken in early years than is possible under **straight-line depreciation.** This increases the present value of the tax shield.

How do changes in working capital affect project cash flows? *(LO4)*

Increases in **net working capital** such as accounts receivable or inventory are investments and therefore use cash—that is, they reduce the net cash flow provided by the project in that period. When working capital is run down, cash is freed up, so cash flow increases.

LISTING OF EQUATIONS

9.1 Total cash flow = cash flows from capital investments
+ cash flows from changes in working capital
+ operating cash flows

9.2 Operating cash flow = revenues − cash expenses − taxes

9.3 Operating cash flow = after-tax profit + depreciation

9.4 Operating cash flow = (revenues − cash expenses) × (1 − tax rate) +
(tax rate × depreciation)

QUESTIONS

QUIZ

1. **Cash Flows.** A new project will generate sales of $74 million, costs of $42 million, and depreciation expense of $10 million in the coming year. The firm's tax rate is 35%. Calculate cash flow for the year by using all three methods discussed in the chapter, and confirm that they are equal. *(LO2)*

2. **Cash Flows.** Canyon Tours showed the following components of working capital last year: *(LO4)*

	Beginning	End of Year
Accounts receivable	$24,000	$23,000
Inventory	12,000	12,500
Accounts payable	14,500	16,500

   a. What was the change in net working capital during the year?
   b. If sales were $36,000 and costs were $24,000, what was cash flow for the year? Ignore taxes.

3. **Cash Flows.** Tubby Toys estimates that its new line of rubber ducks will generate sales of $7 million, operating costs of $4 million, and a depreciation expense of $1 million. If the tax rate is 35%, what is the firm's operating cash flow? Show that you get the same answer using all three methods to calculate operating cash flow. *(LO2)*

4. **Cash Flows.** We've emphasized that the firm should pay attention only to cash flows when assessing the net present value of proposed projects. Depreciation is a noncash expense. Why then does it matter whether we assume straight-line or MACRS depreciation when we assess project NPV? *(LO3)*

5. **Proper Cash Flows.** Quick Computing currently sells 10 million computer chips each year at a price of $20 per chip. It is about to introduce a new chip, and it forecasts annual sales of 12 million of these improved chips at a price of $25 each. However, demand for the old chip will decrease, and sales of the old chip are expected to fall to 3 million per year. The old chip costs $6 each to manufacture, and the new ones will cost $8 each. What is the proper cash flow to use to evaluate the present value of the introduction of the new chip? *(LO1)*

6. **Calculating Net Income.** The owner of a bicycle repair shop forecasts revenues of $160,000 a year. Variable costs will be $50,000, and rental costs for the shop are $30,000 a year. Depreciation on the repair tools will be $10,000. Prepare an income statement for the shop based on these estimates. The tax rate is 35%. *(LO2)*

7. **Cash Flows.** Calculate the operating cash flow for the repair shop in the previous problem using all three methods suggested in the chapter: (a) adjusted accounting profits; (b) cash inflow/cash outflow analysis; and (c) the depreciation tax shield approach. Confirm that all three approaches result in the same value for cash flow. *(LO2)*

8. **Cash Flows and Working Capital.** A house painting business had revenues of $16,000 and expenses of $9,000. There were no depreciation expenses. However, the business reported the following changes in working capital:

	Beginning	End
Accounts receivable	$1,200	$4,500
Accounts payable	700	300

   Calculate net cash flow for the business for this period. *(LO4)*

9. **Incremental Cash Flows.** A corporation donates a valuable painting from its private collection to an art museum. Which of the following are incremental cash flows associated with the donation? *(LO1)*

   a. The price the firm paid for the painting.
   b. The current market value of the painting.
   c. The deduction from income that it declares for its charitable gift.
   d. The reduction in taxes due to its declared tax deduction.

10. **Operating Cash Flows.** Laurel's Lawn Care, Ltd., has a new mower line that can generate revenues of $120,000 per year. Direct production costs are $40,000, and the fixed costs of maintaining the lawn mower factory are $15,000 a year. The factory originally cost $1 million and is being depreciated for tax purposes over 25 years using straight-line depreciation. Calculate the operating cash flows of the project if the firm's tax bracket is 35%. *(LO2)*

PRACTICE PROBLEMS

11. **Operating Cash Flows.** Talia's Tutus bought a new sewing machine for $40,000 that will be depreciated using the MACRS depreciation schedule for a 5-year recovery period. *(LO3)*
    a. Find the depreciation charge each year.
    b. If the sewing machine is sold after 3 years for $22,000, what will be the after-tax proceeds on the sale if the firm's tax bracket is 35%?

12. **Proper Cash Flows.** Conference Services Inc. has leased a large office building for $4 million per year. The building is larger than the company needs; two of the building's eight stories are almost empty. A manager wants to expand one of her projects, but this will require using one of the empty floors. In calculating the net present value of the proposed expansion, senior management allocates one-eighth of $4 million of building rental costs (i.e., $.5 million) to the project expansion, reasoning that the project will use one-eighth of the building's capacity. *(LO1)*
    a. Is this a reasonable procedure for purposes of calculating NPV?
    b. Can you suggest a better way to assess a cost of the office space used by the project?

13. **Cash Flows and Working Capital.** A firm had after-tax income last year of $1.2 million. Its depreciation expenses were $.4 million, and its total cash flow was $1.2 million. What happened to net working capital during the year? *(LO4)*

14. **Cash Flows and Working Capital.** The only capital investment required for a small project is investment in inventory. Profits this year were $10,000, and inventory increased from $4,000 to $5,000. What was the cash flow from the project? *(LO4)*

15. **Cash Flows and Working Capital.** A firm's balance sheets for year-end 2011 and 2012 contain the following data. What happened to investment in net working capital during 2012? All items are in millions of dollars. *(LO4)*

	Dec. 31, 2011	Dec. 31, 2012
Accounts receivable	32	36
Inventories	25	30
Accounts payable	12	26

16. **Salvage Value.** Quick Computing (from Quiz Question 5) installed its previous generation of computer chip manufacturing equipment 3 years ago. Some of that older equipment will become unnecessary when the company goes into production of its new product. The obsolete equipment, which originally cost $40 million, has been depreciated straight-line over an assumed tax life of 5 years, but it can be sold now for $18 million. The firm's tax rate is 35%. What is the after-tax cash flow from the sale of the equipment? *(LO3)*

17. **Salvage Value.** Your firm purchased machinery with a 7-year MACRS life for $10 million. The project, however, will end after 5 years. If the equipment can be sold for $4.5 million at the completion of the project, and your firm's tax rate is 35%, what is the after-tax cash flow from the sale of the machinery? *(LO3)*

18. **Depreciation and Project Value.** Bottoms Up Diaper Service is considering the purchase of a new industrial washer. It can purchase the washer for $6,000 and sell its old washer for $2,000. The new washer will last for 6 years and save $1,500 a year in expenses. The opportunity cost of capital is 16%, and the firm's tax rate is 40%. *(LO3)*
    a. If the firm uses straight-line depreciation to an assumed salvage value of zero over a 6-year life, what are the cash flows of the project in years 0 to 6? The new washer will in fact have zero salvage value after 6 years, and the old washer is fully depreciated.

b. What is project NPV?

c. What is NPV if the firm uses MACRS depreciation with a 5-year tax life?

19. **Equivalent Annual Cost.** What is the equivalent annual cost of the washer in the previous problem if the firm uses straight-line depreciation? *(LO2)*

20. **Cash Flows and NPV.** Johnny's Lunches is considering purchasing a new, energy-efficient grill. The grill will cost $40,000 and will be depreciated according to the 3-year MACRS schedule. It will be sold for scrap metal after 3 years for $10,000. The grill will have no effect on revenues but will save Johnny's $20,000 in energy expenses. The tax rate is 35%. *(LO2)*

a. What are the operating cash flows in years 1 to 3?

b. What are total cash flows in years 1 to 3?

c. If the discount rate is 12%, should the grill be purchased?

21. **Project Evaluation.** Revenues generated by a new fad product are forecast as follows:

Year	Revenues
1	$40,000
2	30,000
3	20,000
4	10,000
Thereafter	0

Expenses are expected to be 40% of revenues, and working capital required in each year is expected to be 20% of revenues in the following year. The product requires an immediate investment of $45,000 in plant and equipment. *(LO2)*

a. What is the initial investment in the product? Remember working capital.

b. If the plant and equipment are depreciated over 4 years to a salvage value of zero using straight-line depreciation, and the firm's tax rate is 40%, what are the project cash flows in each year?

c. If the opportunity cost of capital is 12%, what is project NPV?

d. What is project IRR?

Templates can be found at www.mhhe.com/bmm7e.

22. **Project Evaluation.** Suppose that Blooper's customers paid their bills with an average 3-month delay (instead of 2 months) and that Blooper's inventories were 20% rather than 15% of next year's expenses. *(LO4)*

a. Would project NPV be higher or lower than that in the worked example in the chapter?

b. Calculate Blooper's working capital in each year of its project.

c. What is the change in project NPV (use the Blooper spreadsheet)?

23. **Project Evaluation.** Kinky Copies may buy a high-volume copier. The machine costs $100,000 and will be depreciated straight-line over 5 years to a salvage value of $20,000. Kinky anticipates that the machine actually can be sold in 5 years for $30,000. The machine will save $20,000 a year in labor costs but will require an increase in working capital, mainly paper supplies, of $10,000. The firm's marginal tax rate is 35%, and the discount rate is 8%. Should Kinky buy the machine? *(LO2)*

24. **Project Evaluation.** Blooper Industries must replace its magnoosium purification system. Quick & Dirty Systems sells a relatively cheap purification system for $10 million. The system will last 5 years. Do-It-Right sells a sturdier but more expensive system for $12 million; it will last for 8 years. Both systems entail $1 million in operating costs; both will be depreciated straight-line to a final value of zero over their useful lives; neither will have any salvage value at the end of its life. The firm's tax rate is 35%, and the discount rate is 12%. Which system should Blooper install? (*Hint:* Check the discussion of equivalent annual annuities in the previous chapter.) *(LO2)*

25. **Project Evaluation.** The following table presents sales forecasts for Golden Gelt Giftware. The unit price is $40. The unit cost of the giftware is $25.

Year	Unit Sales
1	22,000
2	30,000
3	14,000
4	5,000
Thereafter	0

It is expected that net working capital will amount to 20% of sales in the following year. For example, the store will need an initial (year-0) investment in working capital of $.20 \times 22{,}000 \times \$40 = \$176{,}000$. Plant and equipment necessary to establish the giftware business will require an additional investment of $200,000. This investment will be depreciated using MACRS and a 3-year life. After 4 years, the equipment will have an economic and book value of zero. The firm's tax rate is 35%. What is the net present value of the project? The discount rate is 20%. *(LO4)*

26. **Project Evaluation.** Ilana Industries, Inc., needs a new lathe. It can buy a new high-speed lathe for $1 million. The lathe will cost $35,000 per year to run, but will save the firm $125,000 in labor costs, and will be useful for 10 years. Suppose that for tax purposes, the lathe will be depreciated on a straight-line basis over its 10-year life to a salvage value of $100,000. The actual market value of the lathe at that time also will be $100,000. The discount rate is 8%, and the corporate tax rate is 35%. What is the NPV of buying the new lathe? *(LO2)*

CHALLENGE PROBLEMS

27. **Project Evaluation.** The efficiency gains resulting from a just-in-time inventory management system will allow a firm to reduce its level of inventories permanently by $250,000. What is the most the firm should be willing to pay for installing the system? *(LO4)*

28. **Project Evaluation.** Better Mousetraps has developed a new trap. It can go into production for an initial investment in equipment of $6 million. The equipment will be depreciated straight-line over 6 years to a value of zero, but in fact it can be sold after 6 years for $500,000. The firm believes that working capital at each date must be maintained at a level of 10% of next year's forecast sales. The firm estimates production costs equal to $1.50 per trap and believes that the traps can be sold for $4 each. Sales forecasts are given in the following table. The project will come to an end in 5 years, when the trap becomes technologically obsolete. The firm's tax bracket is 35%, and the required rate of return on the project is 12%.

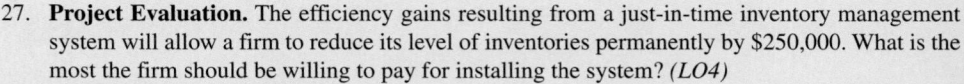
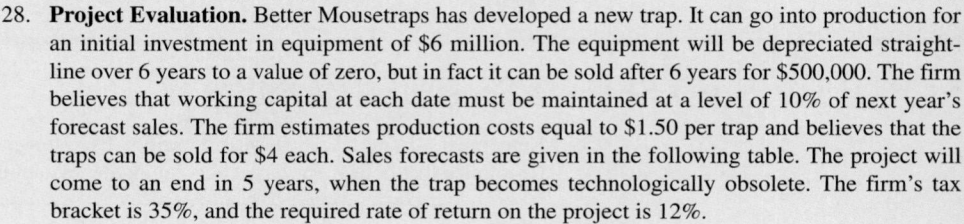

Year:	0	1	2	3	4	5	6	Thereafter
Sales (millions of traps)	0	.5	.6	1.0	1.0	.6	.2	0

a. What is project NPV? *(LO2)*
b. By how much would NPV increase if the firm depreciated its investment using the 5-year MACRS schedule? *(LO3)*

29. **Working Capital Management.** Return to the previous problem. Suppose the firm can cut its requirements for working capital in half by using better inventory control systems. By how much will this increase project NPV? *(LO4)*

30. **Project Evaluation.** PC Shopping Network may upgrade its modem pool. It last upgraded 2 years ago, when it spent $115 million on equipment with an assumed life of 5 years and an assumed salvage value of $15 million for tax purposes. The firm uses straight-line depreciation. The old equipment can be sold today for $80 million. A new modem pool can be installed today for $150 million. This will have a 3-year life and will be depreciated to zero using straight-line depreciation. The new equipment will enable the firm to increase sales by $25 million per year and decrease operating costs by $10 million per year. At the end of 3 years, the new equipment will be worthless. Assume the firm's tax rate is 35% and the discount rate for projects of this sort is 10%. *(LO2)*

a. What is the net cash flow at time 0 if the old equipment is replaced?
b. What are the incremental cash flows in years 1, 2, and 3?
c. What are the NPV and IRR of the replacement project?

31. **Project Evaluation.** In the Finance in Practice box on page 279 we described a major investment in windpower by MidAmerican Energy. Suppose that the company is now contemplating construction of a gas-fired power plant. The plant is likely to last 25 years and to have no salvage value. Depreciation allowances for tax purposes on the investment of $386 million will be calculated using the 20-year MACRS schedule.

If the plant could be operated 24 hours a day every day, it would produce each year 6.04 million megawatt-hours (MWh) of electricity. However, a more realistic estimate is that the plant will operate at an average of 60% of this notional capacity. In the first year of operation, the price of electricity is expected to average $66 per MWh, fuel costs are expected to be $38 per MWh, and labor and other costs are forecast to total $45 million. All prices and costs are expected to rise with inflation at 3% a year. The corporate tax rate is 35%. If the cost of capital is 12%, would you recommend that the company go ahead with the project? *(LO2)*

WEB EXERCISES

1. Go to finance.yahoo.com and obtain the financial statements for Ford (F) and Microsoft (MSFT). What were capital expenditures and sales for each firm? What were the ratios of capital expenditure to sales for the last 3 years for both companies? What were the sales and net capital expenditures relative to total assets? What might explain the variation in these ratios for these two large corporations? Did the company make an investment or disinvestment in working capital in each of the 3 years?

SOLUTIONS TO SELF-TEST QUESTIONS

9.1 Remember, discount cash flows, not profits. Each tewgit machine costs $250,000 right away. Recognize that outlay, but forget accounting depreciation. Cash flows per machine are:

Year:	0	1	2	3	4	5
Investment (outflow)	−250,000					
Sales		250,000	300,000	300,000	250,000	250,000
Operating expenses		−200,000	−200,000	−200,000	−200,000	−200,000
Cash flow	−250,000	+ 50,000	+100,000	+100,000	+ 50,000	+ 50,000

Each machine is forecast to generate $50,000 of cash flow in years 4 and 5. Thus it makes sense to keep operating for 5 years.

9.2 a,b. The site and buildings could have been sold or put to another use. Their values are opportunity costs, which should be treated as incremental cash outflows.
   c. Demolition costs are incremental cash outflows.
   d. The cost of the access road is sunk and not incremental.
   e. Lost cash flows from other projects are incremental cash outflows.
   f. Depreciation is not a cash expense and should not be included, except as it affects taxes. (Taxes are discussed later in this chapter.)

9.3 Actual health costs will be increasing at about 7% a year.

Year:	1	2	3	4
Cost per worker	$2,400	$2,568	$2,748	$2,940

The present value at 10% of these four cash flows is $8,377.

9.4 The tax rate is $T = 35\%$. Taxes paid will be

$$T \times (\text{revenue} - \text{expenses} - \text{depreciation}) = .35 \times (600 - 300 - 200) = \$35$$

Operating cash flow can be calculated as follows.

a. Revenue − expenses − taxes = 600 − 300 − 35 = $265

b. Net profit + depreciation = (600 − 300 − 200 − 35) + 200 = 65 + 200 = 265

c. (Revenues − cash expenses) × (1 − tax rate) + (depreciation × tax rate) = (600 − 300) × (1 − .35) +(200 × .35) = 265

9.5

Year	MACRS 3-Year Depreciation	Tax Shield	PV Tax Shield at 12%
1	3,333	1,167	1,042
2	4,445	1,556	1,240
3	1,481	518	369
4	741	259	165
Totals	10,000	3,500	2,816

The present value increases to 2,816, or $2,816,000.

SOLUTIONS TO SPREADSHEET QUESTIONS

9.1   NPV = $4,515

9.2   NPV = $4,459

9.3   NPV = $5,741. NPV rises because the real value of depreciation allowances and the depreciation tax shield is higher when the inflation rate is lower.

MINICASE

Jack Tar, CFO of Sheetbend & Halyard, Inc., opened the company confidential envelope. It contained a draft of a competitive bid for a contract to supply duffel canvas to the U.S. Navy. The cover memo from Sheetbend's CEO asked Mr. Tar to review the bid before it was submitted.

The bid and its supporting documents had been prepared by Sheetbend's sales staff. It called for Sheetbend to supply 100,000 yards of duffel canvas per year for 5 years. The proposed selling price was fixed at $30 per yard.

Mr. Tar was not usually involved in sales, but this bid was unusual in at least two respects. First, if accepted by the navy, it would commit Sheetbend to a fixed-price, long-term contract. Second, producing the duffel canvas would require an investment of $1.5 million to purchase machinery and to refurbish Sheetbend's plant in Pleasantboro, Maine.

Mr. Tar set to work and by the end of the week had collected the following facts and assumptions:

- The plant in Pleasantboro had been built in the early 1900s and is now idle. The plant was fully depreciated on Sheetbend's books, except for the purchase cost of the land (in 1947) of $10,000.
- Now that the land was valuable shorefront property, Mr. Tar thought the land and the idle plant could be sold, immediately or in the near future, for $600,000.
- Refurbishing the plant would cost $500,000. This investment would be depreciated for tax purposes on the 10-year MACRS schedule.

- The new machinery would cost $1 million. This investment could be depreciated on the 5-year MACRS schedule.
- The refurbished plant and new machinery would last for many years. However, the remaining market for duffel canvas was small, and it was not clear that additional orders could be obtained once the navy contract was finished. The machinery was custom-built and could be used only for duffel canvas. Its secondhand value at the end of 5 years was probably zero.
- Table 9.4 shows the sales staff's forecasts of income from the navy contract. Mr. Tar reviewed this forecast and decided that its assumptions were reasonable, except that the forecast used book, not tax, depreciation.
- But the forecast income statement contained no mention of working capital. Mr. Tar thought that working capital would average about 10% of sales.

Armed with this information, Mr. Tar constructed a spreadsheet to calculate the NPV of the duffel canvas project, assuming that Sheetbend's bid would be accepted by the navy.

He had just finished debugging the spreadsheet when another confidential envelope arrived from Sheetbend's CEO. It contained a firm offer from a Maine real estate developer to purchase Sheetbend's Pleasantboro land and plant for $1.5 million in cash.

Should Mr. Tar recommend submitting the bid to the navy at the proposed price of $30 per yard? The discount rate for this project is 12%.

TABLE 9.4 Forecast income statement for the U.S. Navy duffel canvas project (dollar figures in thousands, except price per yard)

Year:	1	2	3	4	5
1. Yards sold	100.00	100.00	100.00	100.00	100.00
2. Price per yard	30.00	30.00	30.00	30.00	30.00
3. Revenue (1 × 2)	3,000.00	3,000.00	3,000.00	3,000.00	3,000.00
4. Cost of goods sold	2,100.00	2,184.00	2,271.36	2,362.21	2,456.70
5. Operating cash flow (3 − 4)	900.00	816.00	728.64	637.79	543.30
6. Depreciation	250.00	250.00	250.00	250.00	250.00
7. Income (5 − 6)	650.00	566.00	478.64	387.79	293.30
8. Tax at 35%	227.50	198.10	167.52	135.72	102.65
9. Net income (7 − 8)	$422.50	$367.90	$311.12	$252.07	$190.65

Notes:

1. Yards sold and price per yard would be fixed by contract.
2. Cost of goods includes fixed cost of $300,000 per year plus variable costs of $18 per yard. Costs are expected to increase at the inflation rate of 4% per year.
3. Depreciation: A $1 million investment in machinery is depreciated straight-line over 5 years ($200,000 per year). The $500,000 cost of refurbishing the Pleasantboro plant is depreciated straight-line over 10 years ($50,000 per year).

Project Analysis

LEARNING OBJECTIVES

After studying this chapter, you should be able to:

(1) Appreciate the practical problems of capital budgeting in large corporations.

(2) Use sensitivity, scenario, and break-even analyses to see how project profitability would be affected by an error in your forecasts.

(3) Understand why an overestimate of sales is more serious for projects with high operating leverage.

(4) Recognize the importance of managerial flexibility in capital budgeting.

RELATED WEB SITES FOR THIS CHAPTER CAN BE FOUND AT WWW.MHHE.COM/BMM7E.

When undertaking capital investments, good managers maintain maximum flexibility.

It helps to use discounted cash-flow techniques to value new projects, but good investment decisions also require good data. Therefore, we start this chapter by thinking about how firms organize the capital budgeting operation to get the kind of information they need. In addition, we look at how they try to ensure that everyone involved works together toward a common goal.

Project evaluation should never be a mechanical exercise in which the financial manager takes a set of cash-flow forecasts and cranks out a net present value. Cash-flow estimates are just that—estimates. Financial managers need to look behind the forecasts to try to understand what makes the project tick and what could go wrong with it. A number of techniques have been developed to help managers identify the key assumptions in their analysis. These techniques involve asking a number of "what-if" questions. What if your market share turns out to be

higher or lower than you forecast? What if energy prices rise faster than you expect? In the second part of this chapter we show how managers use the techniques of sensitivity analysis, scenario analysis, and break-even analysis to help answer these what-if questions.

Books about capital budgeting sometimes create the impression that once the manager has made an investment decision, there is nothing to do but sit back and watch the cash flows develop. But since cash flows rarely proceed as anticipated, companies constantly need to modify their operations. If cash flows are better than anticipated, the project may be expanded; if they are worse, it may be scaled back or abandoned altogether. In the third section of this chapter we describe how good managers take account of these options when they analyze a project and why they are willing to pay money today to build in future flexibility.

10.1 How Firms Organize the Investment Process

In the previous chapter you learned how to evaluate a proposed investment such as the Blooper project. But potential projects and accurate cash-flow forecasts don't fall from the sky. Promising investment opportunities have to be identified, and they must fit in with the firm's strategic goals. To evaluate these opportunities properly, financial managers need unbiased cash-flow forecasts that have not been skewed to "sell" a project to upper management. Large firms in particular need to establish systems that facilitate effective communication across different parts of the organization.

For most sizable firms, investments are evaluated in two separate stages.

Stage 1: The Capital Budget

capital budget
List of planned investment projects.

Once a year, the head office generally asks each of its divisions and plants to provide a list of the investments that they would like to make.[1] These are gathered together into a proposed **capital budget.**

This budget is then reviewed and pruned by senior management and staff specializing in planning and financial analysis. Usually there are negotiations between the firm's senior management and its divisional management, and there may also be special analyses of major outlays or ventures into new areas. Once the budget has been approved, it generally remains the basis for planning over the ensuing year.

Many investment proposals bubble up from the bottom of the organization. But sometimes the ideas are likely to come from higher up. For example, the managers of plants A and B cannot be expected to see the potential benefits of closing their plants and consolidating production at a new plant C. We expect divisional management to propose plant C. Similarly, divisions 1 and 2 may not be eager to give up their own data processing operations to a large central computer. That proposal would come from senior management.

Senior management's concern is to see that the capital budget matches the firm's strategic plans. It needs to ensure that the firm is concentrating its efforts in areas where it has a real competitive advantage. As part of this effort, management must also identify declining businesses that should be sold or allowed to run down.

The firm's capital investment choices should reflect both "bottom-up" and "top-down" processes—capital budgeting and strategic planning, respectively. The two processes should complement each other. Plant and division managers, who do most of the work in bottom-up capital budgeting, may not see the forest for the trees. Strategic planners may have a mistaken view of the forest because they do not look at the trees.

Stage 2: Project Authorizations

The annual budget is important because it allows everybody to exchange ideas before attitudes have hardened and personal commitments have been made. However, the fact that your pet project has been included in the annual budget doesn't mean you have permission to go ahead with it. At a later stage you will need to draw up a detailed proposal setting out particulars of the project, engineering analyses, cash-flow forecasts, and present value calculations. If your project is large, this proposal may have to pass a number of hurdles before it is finally approved.

The type of backup information that you need to provide depends on the project category. For example, some firms use a fourfold breakdown:

1. *Outlays required by law or company policy,* for example, for pollution control equipment. These outlays do not need to be justified on financial grounds. The main

---

[1] Large firms may be divided into several divisions. For example, International Paper has divisions that specialize in printing paper, packaging, and forest products. Each of these divisions may be responsible for a number of plants.

issue is whether requirements are satisfied at the lowest possible cost. The decision is therefore likely to hinge on engineering analyses of alternative technologies.

2. *Maintenance or cost reduction,* such as machine replacement. Engineering analysis is also important in machine replacement, but new machines have to pay their own way. Here the firm faces the classical capital budgeting problems described in Chapters 8 and 9.

3. *Capacity expansion in existing businesses.* Projects in this category are less straightforward; these decisions may hinge on forecasts of demand, possible shifts in technology, and the reactions of competitors.

4. *Investment for new products.* Projects in this category are most likely to depend on strategic decisions. The first projects in a new area may not have positive NPVs if considered in isolation, but they may give the firm a valuable option to undertake follow-up projects. More about this later in the chapter.

Problems and Some Solutions

Valuing capital investment opportunities is hard enough when you can do the entire job yourself. In most firms, however, capital budgeting is a cooperative effort, and this brings with it some challenges.

Ensuring That Forecasts Are Consistent

Inconsistent assumptions often creep into investment proposals. For example, suppose that the manager of the furniture division is bullish (optimistic) on housing starts but the manager of the appliance division is bearish (pessimistic). This inconsistency makes the projects proposed by the furniture division look more attractive than those of the appliance division.

To ensure consistency, many firms begin the capital budgeting process by establishing forecasts of economic indicators, such as inflation and the growth in national income, as well as forecasts of particular items that are important to the firm's business, such as housing starts or the price of raw materials. These forecasts can then be used as the basis for all project analyses.

Eliminating Conflicts of Interest

In Chapter 1 we pointed out that while managers want to do a good job, they are also concerned about their own futures. If the interests of managers conflict with those of stockholders, the result is likely to be poor investment decisions. For example, new plant managers naturally want to demonstrate good performance right away. So they might propose quick-payback projects even if NPV is sacrificed. Unfortunately, many firms measure performance and reward managers in ways that encourage such behavior. If the firm always demands quick results, it is unlikely that plant managers will concentrate only on NPV.

Reducing Forecast Bias

Someone who is keen to get a project proposal accepted is also likely to look on the bright side when forecasting the project's cash flows. Such overoptimism is a common feature in financial forecasts. For example, think of large public expenditure proposals. How often have you heard of a new missile, dam, or highway that actually cost less than was originally forecast? Think back to the Eurotunnel project introduced in Chapter 8. The final cost of the project was far higher than initial forecasts. Overoptimism is not altogether bad. Psychologists stress that optimism and confidence are likely to increase effort, commitment, and persistence. The problem is that it is difficult for senior managers to judge the true prospects for each project.

Sometimes a head office seems actually to encourage project sponsors to overstate their case. For example, if middle managers believe that success depends on having the largest division rather than the most profitable one, they will propose large expansion projects that they do not believe have the largest possible net present value. Or if divisions must compete for limited resources, they will try to outbid each other for those resources. The fault in such cases is top management's—if lower-level managers are not rewarded on the basis of net present value and contribution to firm value, it should not be surprising that they focus their efforts elsewhere.

Other problems stem from sponsors' eagerness to obtain approval for their favorite projects. As the proposal travels up the organization, alliances are formed. Thus once a division has screened its own plants' proposals, the plants in that division unite in competing against outsiders. The result is that the head office may receive several thousand investment proposals each year, all essentially sales documents presented by united fronts and designed to persuade. The forecasts have been doctored to ensure that NPV appears positive.

Since it is difficult for senior management to evaluate each specific assumption in an investment proposal, capital investment decisions are effectively decentralized whatever the rules say. Some firms accept this; others rely on head office staff to check capital investment proposals.

Sorting the Wheat from the Chaff   Senior managers are continually bombarded with requests for funds for capital expenditures. All these requests are supported with detailed analyses showing that the projects have positive NPVs. How then can managers ensure that only worthwhile projects make the grade? One response of senior managers to this problem of poor information is to impose rigid expenditure limits on individual plants or divisions. These limits force the subunits to choose among projects. The firm ends up using capital rationing not because capital is unobtainable but as a way of decentralizing decisions.[2]

Senior managers might also ask some searching questions about why the project has a positive NPV. After all, if the project is so attractive, why hasn't someone already undertaken it? Will others copy your idea if it is so profitable? Positive NPVs are plausible only if your company has some competitive advantage.

Such an advantage can arise in several ways. You may be smart or lucky enough to be the first to the market with a new or improved product for which customers will pay premium prices. Your competitors eventually will enter the market and squeeze out excess profits, but it may take them several years to do so. Or you may have a proprietary technology or production cost advantage that competitors cannot easily match. You may have a contractual advantage such as the distributorship for a particular region. Or your advantage may be as simple as a good reputation and an established customer list.

Analyzing competitive advantage can also help ferret out projects that incorrectly appear to have a negative NPV. If you are the lowest-cost producer of a profitable product in a growing market, then you should invest to expand along with the market. If your calculations show a negative NPV for such an expansion, then you probably have made a mistake.

10.2 Some "What-If" Questions

"What-if" questions ask what will happen to a project in various circumstances. For example, what will happen if the economy enters a recession? What if a competitor enters the market? What if costs turn out to be higher than anticipated?

You might wonder why one would bother with these sorts of questions. For instance, suppose your project seems to have a positive NPV based on the best available forecasts, in which you have already factored in the chances of both positive and negative surprises. Won't you commit to this project regardless of possible future surprises? If things later don't work out as you had hoped, that is too bad, but you don't have a crystal ball.

---

[2] We discussed capital rationing in Chapter 8.

In fact, what-if analysis is crucial to capital budgeting. First recall that cash-flow estimates are just that—estimates. You often have the opportunity to improve on those estimates if you are willing to commit additional resources to the effort. For example, if you wish to improve the precision of an estimate of the demand for a product, you might conduct additional market research. Or if cost uncertainty is a concern, you might commission additional engineering studies to evaluate the feasibility of a novel production process. But how do you know when to keep sharpening your forecasts or where it is best to devote your efforts? What-if analysis can help identify the inputs that are most worth refining before you commit to a project. These will be the ones that have the greatest potential to alter project NPV.

Moreover, managers don't simply turn a key to start a project and then walk away and let the cash flows roll in. There are always surprises, adjustments, and refinements. What-if analysis indicates where the most likely need for adjustments will arise and where to undertake contingency planning. In this section, therefore, we examine some of the standard tools managers use when considering important types of what-if questions.

Sensitivity Analysis

sensitivity analysis
Analysis of the effects on project profitability of changes in sales, costs, and so on.

Uncertainty means that more things *can* happen than *will* happen. Therefore, whenever managers are given a cash-flow forecast, they try to determine what else might happen and the implications of those possible events. This is called **sensitivity analysis.**

Put yourself in the well-heeled shoes of the financial manager of the Finefodder supermarket chain. Finefodder is considering opening a new superstore in Gravenstein, and your staff members have prepared the figures shown in Table 10.1. To keep the example simple we have assumed no inflation. We have also assumed that the entire investment can be depreciated straight-line for tax purposes, we have neglected the working capital requirement, and we have ignored the fact that at the end of the 12 years you could sell off the land and buildings.

fixed costs
Costs that do not depend on the level of output.

Some of the costs of running a supermarket are fixed. For example, regardless of the level of output, you still have to heat and light the store and pay the store manager. These **fixed costs** are forecast to be $2 million per year.

Other costs vary with the level of sales. In particular, the lower the sales, the less food you need to buy. Also, if sales are lower than forecast, you can operate a smaller number of checkouts and reduce the staff needed to restock the shelves. The new superstore's variable costs are estimated at 81.25% of sales. Thus **variable costs** = .8125 × $16 million = $13 million (see cells C4 and D4).

variable costs
Costs that change as the level of output changes.

The initial investment of $5.4 million will be depreciated on a straight-line basis over the 12-year period, resulting in annual depreciation of $450,000 (cell C6). Profits are taxed at a rate of 40%.

TABLE 10.1 Cash-flow forecasts for Finefodder's superstore

You can find this spreadsheet at www.mhhe.com/bmm7e.

	A	B	C	D
1		**Year 0**	**Years 1-12**	**Formula in column C**
2	Initial investment	-5,400,000		
3	1. Sales		16,000,000	16000000
4	2. Variable costs		13,000,000	=$C$12*C3
5	3. Fixed costs		2,000,000	2000000
6	4. Depreciation		450,000	=-B2/12
7	5. Pretax profit		550,000	=C3-C4-C5-C6
8	6. Taxes (at 40%)		220,000	=0.4*C7
9	7. Profit after tax		330,000	=C7-C8
10	8. Cash flow from operations		780,000	=C6+C9
11				
12	Variable costs as proportion of sales		0.8125	0.8125
13	Discount rate		.08	0.08
14	12-year annuity factor		7.5361	=(1/$C$13)*(1 -1 /(1+$C$13)^12)
15	Net present value		478,141	=B2+C10*C14

TABLE 10.2 Sensitivity analysis for superstore project

Variable	Range			NPV		
	Pessimistic	Expected	Optimistic	Pessimistic	Expected	Optimistic
Investment	6,200,000	5,400,000	5,000,000	−120,897	+478,141	+777,660
Sales	14,000,000	16,000,000	18,000,000	−1,217,477	+478,141	+2,173,758
Variable cost as percent of sales	83	81.25	80	−787,920	+478,141	+1,382,470
Fixed cost	2,100,000	2,000,000	1,900,000	+25,976	+478,141	+930,306

Given these inputs, we add after-tax profit plus depreciation to obtain cash flow in periods 1 to 12 of $780,000 (cell C10). As an experienced financial manager, you recognize immediately that these cash flows constitute an annuity, and therefore you calculate the 12-year annuity factor at a discount rate of 8% (cell C14). The net present value of the project is calculated in cell C15 as

$$\text{NPV} = -\$5,400,000 + \$780,000 \times \text{12-year annuity factor} = \$478,141$$

It appears that the project is in fact viable, with a positive net present value. Before you agree to go ahead, however, you want to delve behind these forecasts and identify the key variables that will determine whether the project succeeds or fails.

You seem to have taken account of the important factors that will determine success or failure, but look out for things you may have forgotten. Perhaps there will be delays in obtaining planning permission, or perhaps you will need to undertake costly landscaping. The greatest dangers often lie in these *unknown* unknowns, or "unk-unks," as scientists call them.

Having found no unk-unks (no doubt you'll find them later), you look at how NPV may be affected if you have made a wrong forecast of sales, costs, and so on. To do this, you first obtain optimistic and pessimistic estimates for the underlying variables. These are set out in the left-hand columns of Table 10.2.

Next you see what happens to NPV under the optimistic or pessimistic forecasts for each of these variables. You recalculate project NPV under these various forecasts to determine which variables are most critical to NPV.

EXAMPLE 10.1 ▶ Sensitivity Analysis

The right-hand side of Table 10.2 shows the project's net present value if the variables are set *one at a time* to their optimistic and pessimistic values. For example, suppose fixed costs are $1.9 million rather than the forecast $2 million. To find NPV in this case, we simply substitute $1,900,000 in cell C5 of the spreadsheet, and discover that NPV rises to $930,306, a gain of approximately $452,000. The other entries in the three columns on the right in Table 10.2 similarly show how the NPV of the project changes when an input is changed.

Your project is by no means a sure thing. The principal uncertainties appear to be sales and variable costs. For example, if sales are only $14 million rather than the forecast $16 million (and all other forecasts are unchanged), then the project has an NPV of −$1.217 million. If variable costs are 83% of sales (and all other forecasts are unchanged), then the project has an NPV of −$787,920.

Self-Test 10.1

Recalculate cash flow as in Table 10.1, now assuming that variable costs are 83% of sales. Confirm that NPV will be −$787,920.

Value of Information Now that you know the project could be thrown badly off course by a poor estimate of sales, you might like to see whether it is possible to resolve some of this uncertainty. Perhaps your worry is that the store will fail to attract sufficient shoppers from neighboring towns. In that case, additional survey data and more careful analysis of travel times may be worthwhile.

On the other hand, there is less value to gathering additional information about fixed costs. Because the project is marginally profitable even under pessimistic assumptions about fixed costs, you are unlikely to be in trouble if you have misestimated that variable.

Limits to Sensitivity Analysis Your analysis of the forecasts for Finefodder's new superstore is an example of sensitivity analysis. Sensitivity analysis expresses cash flows in terms of unknown variables and then calculates the consequences of misestimating those variables. It forces the manager to identify the underlying factors, indicates where additional information would be most useful, and helps to expose confused or inappropriate forecasts.

Of course, there is no law stating which variables you should consider in your sensitivity analysis. For example, you may wish to look separately at labor costs and the costs of the goods sold. Or if you are concerned about a possible change in the corporate tax rate, you may wish to look at the effect of such a change on the project's NPV.

One drawback to sensitivity analysis is that it gives somewhat ambiguous results. For example, what exactly does *optimistic* or *pessimistic* mean? One department may be interpreting the terms in a different way from another. Ten years from now, after hundreds of projects, hindsight may show that one department's pessimistic limit was exceeded twice as often as the other's; but hindsight won't help you now while you're making the investment decision.

Another problem with sensitivity analysis is that the underlying variables are likely to be interrelated. For example, if sales exceed expectations, demand will likely be stronger than you anticipated and your profit margins will be wider. Or, if wages are higher than your forecast, both variable costs and fixed costs are likely to be at the upper end of your range.

Because of these connections, you cannot push *one-at-a-time* sensitivity analysis too far. It is impossible to obtain optimistic and pessimistic values for total *project* cash flows from the information in Table 10.2. Still, it does give a sense of which variables should be most closely monitored.

Scenario Analysis

scenario analysis
Project analysis given a particular combination of assumptions.

When variables are interrelated, managers often find it helpful to look at how their project would fare under different scenarios. **Scenario analysis** allows them to look at different but *consistent* combinations of variables. Forecasters generally prefer to give an estimate of revenues or costs under a particular scenario rather than to give some absolute optimistic or pessimistic value.

Suppose that you are worried that Stop and Scoff (S&S) may decide to build a new store in nearby Salome. That would reduce sales in your Gravenstein store by 15%, and you might be forced into a price war to keep the remaining business. Prices might be reduced to the point that variable costs equal 82% of revenue. Table 10.3 shows that under this scenario of *both* lower sales and smaller margins your new venture would no longer be worthwhile. A bit more research into S&S's intentions appears to be called for.

simulation analysis
Estimation of the probabilities of different possible outcomes, e.g., from an investment project.

An extension of scenario analysis is called **simulation analysis.** Here, instead of specifying a relatively small number of scenarios, a computer generates several hundred or thousand possible combinations of variables according to probability distributions specified by the analyst. Each combination of variables corresponds to one scenario. Project NPV and other outcomes of interest can be calculated for each

TABLE 10.3 Scenario analysis comparing NPV of superstore with and without competing store

You can find this spreadsheet at www.mhhe.com/bmm7e.

	A	B	C	D
1			\multicolumn{2}{c}{**Cash flows in years 1-12**}	
2		**Year 0**	**Base Case**	**Competing Store Scenario**
3	Initial investment	-5,400,000		
4	1. Sales		16,000,000	13,600,000
5	2. Variable costs		13,000,000	11,152,000
6	3. Fixed costs		2,000,000	2,000,000
7	4. Depreciation		450,000	450,000
8	5. Pretax profit		550,000	-2,000
9	6. Taxes (at 40%)		220,000	-800
10	7. Profit after tax		330,000	-1,200
11	8. Cash flow from operations		780,000	448,800
12				
13	Variable costs as proportion of sales		0.8125	0.8200
14	Discount rate		8%	8%
15	12-year annuity factor		7.5361	7.5361
16	Net present value		478,141	-2,017,808
17				
18	*Assumptions:* Competing store causes (1) a 15% decline in sales and (2) variable costs			
19	to increase to 82% of sales.			

combination of variables, and the entire probability distribution of outcomes can be constructed from the simulation results.

Self-Test 10.2

What is the basic difference between sensitivity analysis and scenario analysis?

10.3 Break-Even Analysis

When you undertake a sensitivity analysis of a project or when you look at alternative scenarios, you are asking how serious it would be if you have misestimated sales or costs. Managers sometimes prefer to rephrase this question and ask how far off the estimates could be before the project begins to lose money. This exercise is known as **break-even analysis.**

break-even analysis
Analysis of the level of sales at which the project breaks even.

For many projects, the make-or-break variable is sales volume. Therefore, managers most often focus on the break-even level of sales. However, you might also look at other variables, for example, at how high costs could be before the project goes into the red.

As it turns out, "losing money" can be defined in more than one way. Most often, the break-even condition is defined in terms of accounting profits. More properly, however, it should be defined in terms of net present value. We will start with accounting break-even, show that it can lead you astray, and then show how NPV break-even can be used as an alternative.

Accounting Break-Even Analysis

The *accounting break-even* point is the level of sales at which profits are zero or, equivalently, at which total revenues equal total costs. As we have seen, some costs are fixed regardless of the level of output. Other costs vary with the level of output.

When you first analyzed the superstore project, you came up with the following estimates:

Sales	$16	million
Variable costs	13	million
Fixed costs	2	million
Depreciation	0.45	million

TABLE 10.4 Income statement, break-even sales volume

Item	$ Thousands	
Revenues	13,067	
Variable costs	10,617	(81.25% of sales)
Fixed costs	2,000	
Depreciation	450	
Pretax profit	0	
Taxes	0	
Profit after tax	0	

Notice that variable costs are 81.25% of sales. So for each additional dollar of sales, costs increase by only $.8125. We can easily determine how much business the superstore needs to attract to avoid losses. If the store sells nothing, the income statement will show fixed costs of $2 million and depreciation of $450,000. Thus there will be an accounting *loss* before tax of $2.45 million. Each dollar of sales reduces this loss by $1.00 − $.8125 = $.1875. Therefore, to cover fixed costs plus depreciation, you need sales of 2.45 million/.1875 = $13.067 million. At this sales level, the firm will break even. More generally,

$$\text{Break-even level of revenues} = \frac{\text{fixed costs including depreciation}}{\text{additional profit from each additional dollar of sales}} \quad (10.1)$$

Table 10.4 shows the income statement with only $13.067 million of sales.

Figure 10.1 shows how the break-even point is determined. The blue 45-degree line shows the store's accounting revenues. The dashed cost line shows how costs vary with sales. If the store doesn't sell a cent, it still incurs fixed costs and depreciation amounting to $2.45 million. Each extra dollar of sales adds $.8125 to these costs. When sales are $13.067 million, the two lines cross, indicating that costs equal revenues. For lower sales, revenues are less than costs and the project is in the red; for higher sales, revenues exceed costs and the project moves into the black.

Is a project that breaks even in accounting terms an acceptable investment? If you are not sure about the answer, here's a possibly easier question: Would you be happy about an investment in a stock that after 5 years gave you a total rate of return of zero? We hope not. You might break even on such a stock, but a zero return does not compensate you for the time value of money or the risk that you have taken.

FIGURE 10.1 Accounting break-even analysis

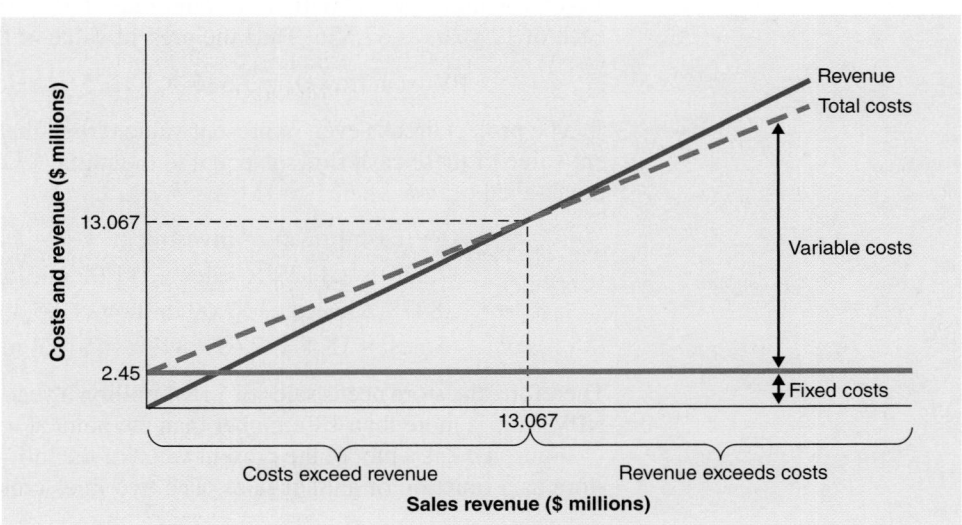

A project that simply breaks even on an accounting basis gives you your money back but does not cover the opportunity cost of the capital tied up in the project. A project that breaks even in accounting terms will surely have a negative NPV.

Let's check this with the superstore project. Suppose that in each year the store has sales of $13.067 million—just enough to break even on an accounting basis. What would be its operating cash flow?

$$\text{Operating cash flow} = \text{profit after tax} + \text{depreciation}$$
$$= 0 + \$450,000 = \$450,000$$

The initial investment is $5.4 million. In each of the next 12 years, the firm receives a cash flow of $450,000. So the firm gets its money back:

$$\text{Total operating cash flow} = \text{initial investment}$$
$$12 \times \$450,000 = \$5.4 \text{ million}$$

But revenues are *not* sufficient to repay the *opportunity cost* of that $5.4 million investment. NPV is negative.

NPV Break-Even Analysis

A manager who calculates an accounting-based measure of break-even may be tempted to think that any project that earns more than this figure will help shareholders. But projects that break even on an accounting basis are really making a loss—they are failing to cover the costs of capital employed. Managers who accept such projects are not helping their shareholders. Therefore, instead of asking what sales must be to produce an accounting profit, it is more useful to focus on the point at which NPV switches from negative to positive. This is called the **NPV break-even point.**

The cash flows of the superstore project in each year will depend on sales as follows:

1. Variable costs	81.25% of sales
2. Fixed costs	$2 million
3. Depreciation	$450,000
4. Pretax profit	$(.1875 \times \text{sales}) - \$2.45 \text{ million}$
5. Tax (at 40%)	$.40 \times (.1875 \times \text{sales} - \$2.45 \text{ million})$
6. Profit after tax	$.60 \times (.1875 \times \text{sales} - \$2.45 \text{ million})$
7. Cash flow (3 + 6)	$\$450,000 + .6 \times (.1875 \times \text{sales} - \$2.45 \text{ million})$
	$= .1125 \times \text{sales} - \$1.02 \text{ million}$

This cash flow will last for 12 years. So to find its present value we multiply by the 12-year annuity factor. With a discount rate of 8%, the present value of $1 a year for each of 12 years is $7.536. Thus the present value of the cash flows is

$$\text{PV(cash flows)} = 7.536 \times (.1125 \times \text{sales} - \$1.02 \text{ million})$$

The project breaks even in present value terms (that is, has a zero NPV) if the present value of these cash flows is equal to the initial $5.4 million investment. Therefore, break-even occurs when

$$\text{PV(cash flows)} = \text{investment}$$
$$7.536 \times (.1125 \times \text{sales} - \$1.02 \text{ million}) = \$5.4 \text{ million}$$
$$.8478 \times \text{sales} - \$7.69 \text{ million} = \$5.4 \text{ million}$$
$$\text{Sales} = (5.4 + 7.69)/.8478 = \$15.4 \text{ million}$$

Therefore, the store needs sales of $15.4 million a year for the investment to have a zero NPV. This is more than 18% higher than the point at which the project has zero profit.

Figure 10.2 is a plot of the present value of the inflows and outflows from the superstore as a function of annual sales. The two lines cross when sales are $15.4 million.

NPV break-even point
Level of sales at which project net present value becomes positive.

FIGURE 10.2 NPV break-even analysis

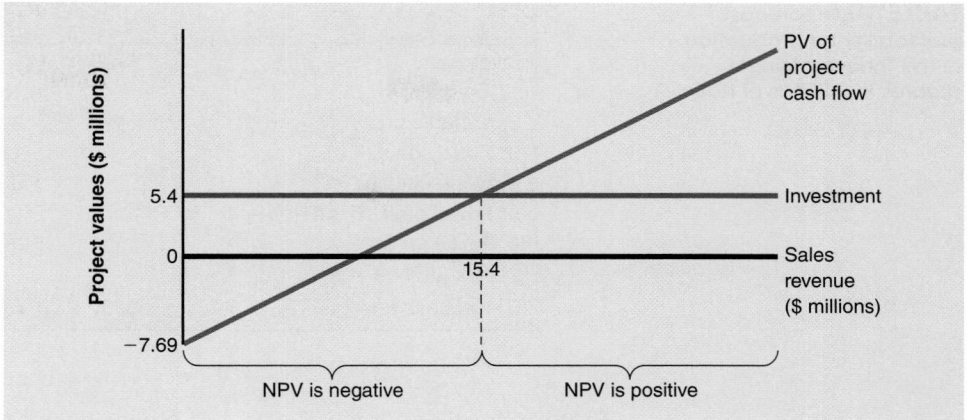

This is the point at which the project has zero NPV. As long as sales are greater than this, the present value of the inflows exceeds the present value of the outflows and the project has a positive NPV.[3]

Self-Test 10.3

What would be the NPV break-even level of sales if the capital investment was only $5 million?

EXAMPLE 10.2 ▶ Break-Even Analysis

We have said that projects that break even on an accounting basis are really making a loss—they are losing the opportunity cost of their investment. Here is a dramatic example. Lophead Aviation is contemplating investment in a new passenger aircraft, code-named the Trinova. Lophead's financial staff has gathered together the following estimates:

1. The cost of developing the Trinova is forecast at $900 million, and this investment can be depreciated in six equal annual amounts.
2. Production of the plane is expected to take place at a steady annual rate over the following 6 years.
3. The average price of the Trinova is expected to be $15.5 million.
4. Fixed costs are forecast at $175 million a year.
5. Variable costs are forecast at $8.5 million a plane.
6. The tax rate is 50%.
7. The cost of capital is 10%.

Lophead's financial manager has used this information to construct a forecast of the profitability of the Trinova program. This is shown in rows 1 to 7 of Table 10.5 (ignore row 8 for a moment).

How many aircraft does Lophead need to sell to break even? The answer depends on what is meant by "break even." In accounting terms the venture will break even when net profit (row 7 in the table) is zero. In this case,

$$(3.5 \times \text{planes sold}) - 162.5 = 0$$
$$\text{Planes sold} = 162.5/3.5 = 46.4$$

---

[3] Think back to our discussion of economic value added (EVA) in Chapter 4. A project that breaks even on a present value basis will have a positive accounting profit but zero economic value added. In other words, it will just cover *all* its costs, including the cost of capital.

TABLE 10.5 Forecast profitability for production of the Trinova airliner (figures in millions of dollars)

	Year 0	Years 1–6
Investment	$900	
1. Sales		15.5 × planes sold
2. Variable costs		8.5 × planes sold
3. Fixed costs		175
4. Depreciation		900/6 = 150
5. Pretax profit (1 − 2 − 3 − 4)		(7 × planes sold) − 325
6. Taxes (at 50%)		(3.5 × planes sold) − 162.5
7. Net profit (5 − 6)		(3.5 × planes sold) − 162.5
8. Net cash flow (4 + 7)	−$900	(3.5 × planes sold) − 12.5

Thus Lophead needs to sell about 46 planes a year, or a total of 280 planes over the 6 years to show a profit. With a price of $15.5 million a plane, Lophead will break even in accounting terms with annual revenues of 46.4 × $15.5 million = $719 million.

We would have arrived at the same answer if we had used our formula to calculate the break-even level of revenues. Notice that the variable cost of each plane is $8.5 million, which is 54.8% of the $15.5 million sale price. Therefore, each dollar of sales increases pretax profits by $1 − $.548 = $.452. Now we use the formula for the accounting break-even point:

$$\text{Break-even revenues} = \frac{\text{fixed costs including depreciation}}{\text{additional profit from each additional dollar of sales}}$$

$$= \frac{\$325 \text{ million}}{.452} = \$719 \text{ million}$$

If Lophead sells about 46 planes a year, it will recover its original investment, but it will not earn any return on the capital tied up in the project. Companies that earn a zero return on their capital can expect some unhappy shareholders. Shareholders will be content only if the company's investments earn at least the cost of the capital invested. True break-even occurs when the projects have zero NPV.

How many planes must Lophead sell to break even in terms of net present value? Development of the Trinova costs $900 million. If the cost of capital is 10%, the 6-year annuity factor is 4.3553. The last row of Table 10.5 shows that net cash flow (in millions of dollars) in years 1–6 equals (3.5 × planes sold − 12.5). We can now find the annual plane sales necessary to break even in terms of NPV:

$$4.3553(3.5 \times \text{planes sold} - 12.5) = 900$$
$$15.2436 \times \text{planes sold} - 54.44 = 900$$
$$\text{Planes sold} = 954.44/15.2436 = 62.6$$

Thus, while Lophead will break even in terms of accounting profits with sales of 46.4 planes a year (about 280 in total), it needs to sell 62.6 a year (or about 375 in total) to recover the opportunity cost of the capital invested in the project and break even in terms of NPV.

Our example may seem fanciful, but it is based loosely on reality. In 1971 Lockheed was in the middle of a major program to bring out the L-1011 TriStar airliner. This program was to bring Lockheed to the brink of failure, and it tipped Rolls-Royce (supplier of the TriStar engine) over the brink. In giving evidence to Congress, Lockheed argued that the TriStar program was commercially attractive and that sales would eventually exceed the break-even point of about 200 aircraft. But in calculating this break-even point, Lockheed appears to have ignored the opportunity cost of the huge capital investment in the project. Lockheed probably needed to sell about 500 aircraft to reach a zero net present value.[4]

Operating Leverage

A project's break-even point depends on both its *fixed* costs, which do not vary with sales, and the profit on each extra sale. Managers often face a trade-off between these variables. For example, we typically think of rental expenses as fixed costs. But supermarket companies sometimes rent stores with contingent rent agreements. This means that the amount of rent the company pays is tied to the level of sales from the store. Rent rises and falls along with sales. The store thus replaces a fixed cost with a *variable cost* that is linked to sales. Because a greater proportion of the company's expenses will fall when its sales fall, its break-even point is reduced.

Of course, a high proportion of fixed costs is not all bad. The firm whose costs are largely fixed fares poorly when demand is low, but it may make a killing during a boom. Let us illustrate.

Finefodder has a policy of hiring long-term employees who will not be laid off except in the most dire circumstances. For all intents and purposes, their salaries are fixed costs. Its rival, Stop and Scoff, has a much smaller permanent labor force and uses expensive temporary help whenever demand requires extra staff. A greater proportion of its labor expenses are therefore variable costs.

Suppose that if Finefodder adopted its rival's policy, fixed costs in its new super-store would fall from $2 million to $1.56 million but variable costs would rise from 81.25% to 84% of sales. Table 10.6 shows that with the normal level of sales, the two policies fare equally. In a slump a store that relies on temporary labor does better since its costs fall along with revenue. In a boom the reverse is true, and the store with the higher proportion of fixed costs has the advantage.

If Finefodder follows its normal policy of hiring long-term employees, each extra dollar of sales increases pretax profits by $1.00 - $.8125 = $.1875. If it uses temporary labor, an extra dollar of sales increases profits by only $1.00 - $.84 = $.16. As a result, a store with high fixed costs is said to have high **operating leverage.** High operating leverage magnifies the effect on profits of a fluctuation in sales.

We can measure a business's operating leverage by asking how much profits change for each 1% change in sales. The **degree of operating leverage,** often abbreviated as **DOL,** is this measure:

operating leverage
Degree to which costs are fixed.

degree of operating leverage (DOL)
Percentage change in profits given a 1% change in sales.

$$\text{DOL} = \frac{\text{percentage change in profits}}{\text{percentage change in sales}} \qquad (10.2)$$

TABLE 10.6 A store with high operating leverage performs relatively badly in a slump but flourishes in a boom (figures in thousands of dollars).

	High Fixed Costs			High Variable Costs		
	Slump	**Normal**	**Boom**	**Slump**	**Normal**	**Boom**
Sales	13,000	16,000	19,000	13,000	16,000	19,000
− Variable costs	10,563	13,000	15,438	10,920	13,440	15,960
− Fixed costs	2,000	2,000	2,000	1,560	1,560	1,560
− Depreciation	450	450	450	450	450	450
= Pretax profit	−13	550	1,112	70	550	1,030

---

[4] The true break-even point for the TriStar program is estimated in U. E. Reinhardt, "Break-Even Analysis for Lockheed's TriStar: An Application of Financial Theory," *Journal of Finance* 28 (September 1973), pp. 821–838.

For example, Table 10.6 shows that as the store moves from normal conditions to boom, sales increase from $16 million to $19 million, a rise of 18.75%. For the policy with high fixed costs, profits increase from $550,000 to $1,112,000, a rise of 102.2%. Therefore,

$$DOL = \frac{102.2}{18.75} = 5.45$$

The percentage change in sales is magnified more than fivefold in terms of the percentage impact on profits.

Now look at the operating leverage of the store if it uses the policy with low fixed costs but high variable costs. As the store moves from normal times to boom, profits increase from $550,000 to $1,030,000, a rise of 87.3%. Therefore,

$$DOL = \frac{87.3}{18.75} = 4.65$$

Because some costs remain fixed, a change in sales still generates a large percentage change in profits, but the degree of operating leverage is lower.

In fact, one can show that degree of operating leverage depends on fixed charges (including depreciation) in the following manner:[5]

$$DOL = 1 + \frac{\text{fixed costs}}{\text{profits}} \tag{10.3}$$

EXAMPLE 10.3 ▶   Operating Leverage

Suppose the firm adopts the high-fixed-cost policy. Then fixed costs including depreciation will be 2.00 + .45 = $2.45 million. Since the store produces profits of $.55 million at a normal level of sales, DOL should be

$$DOL = 1 + \frac{\text{fixed costs}}{\text{profits}} = 1 + \frac{2.45}{.55} = 5.45$$

This value matches the one we obtained by comparing the actual percentage changes in sales and profits.

Some companies have much higher fixed costs than others. Look, for example, at Table 10.7, which shows the average impact of a change in sales on profits for a sample of large U.S. companies. Steel producers appear to have relatively high fixed costs. A 1% change in sales has on average resulted in a 2.20% change in profits. By contrast, electric utilities appear to have low fixed costs. A 1% change in their sales has led to only a .56% change in profits.[6]

---

[5] This formula for DOL can be derived as follows. If sales increase by 1%, then variable costs also should increase by 1%, and profits will increase by .01 × (sales − variable costs) = .01 × (profits + fixed costs). Now recall the definition of DOL:

$$DOL = \frac{\text{percentage change in profits}}{\text{percentage change in sales}} = \frac{\text{change in profits/level of profits}}{.01}$$

$$= 100 \times \frac{\text{change in profits}}{\text{level of profits}} = 100 \times \frac{.01 \times (\text{profits} + \text{fixed costs})}{\text{level of profits}}$$

$$= 1 + \frac{\text{fixed costs}}{\text{profits}}$$

[6] You may be surprised to see electric utilities classified as exhibiting low operating leverage. But there is a good reason for this conclusion. While many electric utilities use nuclear or hydroelectric power, which have very high fixed costs and very low variable costs, they also require standby sources of power to be brought online only during peak demand periods. These standby technologies are less expensive to build (and so entail lower fixed costs) but use far more expensive energy sources (with high variable costs). A 1% change in total sales is far more likely to affect the use of that marginal standby technology than the core generating facilities.

TABLE 10.7 Estimated degree of operating leverage (DOL) for large U.S. companies by industry

High-Leverage Industries		Low-Leverage Industries	
	DOL		DOL
Steel	2.20	Electric utilities	.56
Railroad	1.99	Food	.79
Auto	1.57	Clothing	.88

Note: DOL is measured as the median ratio of the change in profits to the change in sales for firms in Standard & Poor's Composite Index, 1998–2008.

Notice that operating leverage will affect the risk of a project. The greater the degree of operating leverage, the greater the sensitivity of profits to variation in sales. **Risk depends on operating leverage. If a large proportion of costs is fixed, a shortfall in sales has a magnified effect on profits.**

We will have more to say about risk in the next three chapters.

Self-Test 10.5

Suppose that sales increase by 10% from the values in the normal scenario. Compute the percentage change in pretax profits from the normal level for both policies in Table 10.6. Compare your answers to the values predicted by the DOL formula.

10.4 Real Options and the Value of Flexibility

When you use discounted cash flow (DCF) to value a project, you implicitly assume that the firm will hold the assets passively. But managers are not paid to be dummies. After they have invested in a new project, they do not simply sit back and watch the future unfold. If things go well, the project may be expanded; if they go badly, the project may be cut back or abandoned altogether. Most tools for project analysis ignore these opportunities. For example, suppose the superstore's sales are at the low end of your forecasts. It would pay the company to close down the store rather than amass continuing losses.

Projects that can easily be modified in these ways are more valuable than those that don't provide such flexibility. The more uncertain the outlook, the more valuable this flexibility becomes.

The Option to Expand

The scientists at MacCaugh have developed a diet whiskey, and the firm is ready to go ahead with pilot production and test-marketing. The preliminary phase will take a year and cost $200,000. Management feels that there is only a 50–50 chance that the pilot production and market tests will be successful. If they are, then MacCaugh will build a $2 million production plant that will generate an expected annual cash flow in perpetuity of $480,000 after taxes. Given an opportunity cost of capital of 12%, project NPV in this case will be −$2 million + $480,000/.12 = $2 million. If the tests are not successful, MacCaugh will discontinue the project and the cost of the pilot production will be wasted.

Notice that MacCaugh's expenditure on the pilot program buys a valuable managerial option. The firm is not obliged to enter full production, but it has the option to do so depending on the outcome of the tests. If there is some doubt as to whether the project will take off, expenditure on the pilot operation could help the firm to avoid a costly mistake. Therefore, when it proposed the expenditure, MacCaugh's management was simply following the fundamental rule of swimmers: If you know the water temperature (and depth) dive in; if you don't, try putting a toe in first.

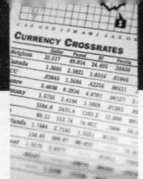
FedEx Buys an Option

In 2006, FedEx placed an order for 15 Boeing 777 Freighter transport planes for delivery in 2009–2011. Each freighter can carry 171,000 pounds of goods and can travel 2,200 miles farther than the MD-11F, FedEx's current primary long-haul plane. The freighter will allow FedEx to fly directly from its U.S. centers to its hubs in Asia and Europe with improved fuel economy and lower operating costs. The plane could have a big impact on FedEx's worldwide business.

If FedEx's long-haul air freight business continues to expand and the freighters are efficient and reliable, the company will want more of them. But it could not be sure they would be needed. Therefore, rather than placing additional firm orders in 2006, FedEx secured a place in the Boeing production line by acquiring *options* to buy an additional 15 aircraft at a predetermined price. These options did not commit the company to expand but gave it the flexibility to do so. By 2009 FedEx was sufficiently confident of its requirements that it decided to exercise its option. The additional planes will be delivered between 2013 and 2018.

---

decision tree
Diagram of sequential decisions and possible outcomes.

When faced with projects like this that involve future decisions, it is often helpful to draw a **decision tree** as in Figure 10.3. You can think of the problem as a game between MacCaugh and fate. Each square represents an action or decision by the company. Each circle represents an outcome revealed by fate. MacCaugh starts the play at the left-hand square. If it decides to test, then fate will cast the enchanted dice and decide the results of the test. Once the results are known, MacCaugh faces a second decision: Should it wind up the project, or should it invest $2 million and start full-scale production?

The second-stage decision is obvious: *Invest if the tests indicate that NPV is positive, and stop if they indicate that NPV is negative.* So now MacCaugh can move back to consider whether it should invest in the test program. This first-stage decision boils down to a simple problem: Should MacCaugh invest $200,000 now to obtain a 50% chance of a project with an NPV of $2 million a year later? At any reasonable discount rate the test program has a positive NPV.

You can probably now think of many other investments that take on added value because of the options they provide to expand in the future. For example:

- When designing a factory, it can make sense to provide extra land or floor space to reduce the future cost of a second production line.
- When building a four-lane highway, it may pay to build six-lane bridges so that the road can be converted later to six lanes if traffic proves higher than expected.
- An airline may acquire an option to buy a new aircraft (the nearby box explains how Federal Express bought options on the Boeing 777 freighter).

In each of these cases you are paying out money today to give you the option to invest in real assets at some time in the future. Managers therefore often refer to such

FIGURE 10.3 Decision tree for the diet-whiskey project

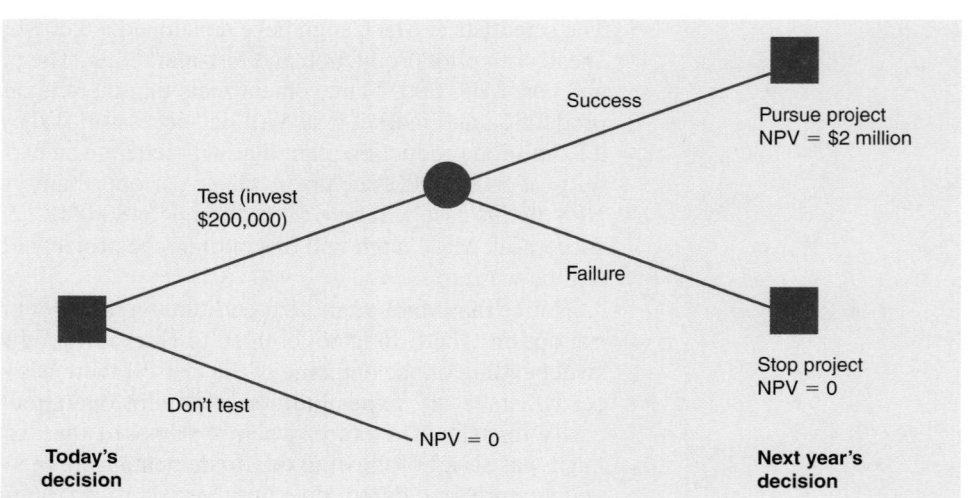

real options
Options to invest in, modify, or dispose of a capital investment project.

options as **real options.** These options do not show up in the assets that the company lists in its balance sheet, but investors are very aware of their existence. If a company has valuable real options that allow it to invest in profitable future projects, its market value will be higher than the value of its physical assets now in place. We consider the valuation of options in Chapter 23.

A Second Real Option: The Option to Abandon

If the option to expand has value, what about the decision to bail out? Projects don't just go on until assets expire of old age. The decision to terminate a project is usually taken by management, not by nature. Once the project is no longer profitable, the company will cut its losses and exercise its option to abandon the project.

Some assets are simpler to bail out of than others. Tangible assets are usually easier to sell than intangible ones. It helps to have active secondhand markets, which really exist only for standardized items. Real estate, airplanes, trucks, and certain machine tools are likely to be relatively easy to sell. On the other hand, the knowledge accumulated by a software company's research and development program is a specialized intangible asset and probably would not have significant abandonment value. (Some assets, such as old mattresses, even have *negative* abandonment value; you have to pay to get rid of them. It is costly to decommission nuclear power plants or to reclaim land that has been strip-mined.)

EXAMPLE 10.4 ▶ Abandonment Option

Suppose that the Widgeon Company must choose between two technologies for the manufacture of a new product, a Wankel-engined outboard motor:

1. Technology A uses custom-designed machinery to produce the complex shapes required for Wankel engines at low cost. But if the Wankel engine doesn't sell, this equipment will be worthless.
2. Technology B uses standard machine tools. Labor costs are much higher, but the tools can easily be sold if the motor doesn't sell.

Technology A looks better in an NPV analysis of the new product, because it is designed to have the lowest possible cost at the planned production volume. Yet you can sense the advantage of technology B's flexibility if you are unsure whether the new outboard will sink or swim in the marketplace.

Self-Test 10.6

Draw a decision tree showing how the choices open to the Widgeon Company depend on demand for the new product. Pick some plausible numbers to illustrate why it might make sense to adopt the more expensive technology B.

A Third Real Option: The Timing Option

Suppose that you have a project that could be a big winner or a big loser. The project's upside potential outweighs its downside potential, and it has a positive NPV if undertaken today. However, the project is not "now or never." So should you invest right away or wait? It's hard to say. If the project turns out to be a winner, waiting means the loss or deferral of its early cash flows. But if it turns out to be a loser, it would have been better to wait and get a better fix on the likely demand.

You can think of any project proposal as giving you the *option* to invest today. You don't have to exercise that option immediately. Instead, you need to weigh the value of the cash flows lost by delaying against the possibility that you will pick up some valuable information. Suppose, for example, you are considering development of a new oil field. At current oil prices the investment has a small positive NPV. But oil prices are highly volatile, occasionally halving or doubling in the space of a couple years. If a small decline in crude prices could push your project into the red, it might be better to wait a little before investing.

Our example illustrates why companies sometimes turn down apparently profitable projects. For example, suppose you approach your boss with a proposed project. It involves spending $1 million and has an NPV of $1,000. You explain to him how carefully you have analyzed the project, but nothing seems to convince him that the company should invest. Is he being irrational to turn down a positive-NPV project?

Faced by such marginal projects, it often makes sense to wait. One year later you may have much better information about the prospects for the project, and it may become clear whether it is really a winner or a loser. In the former case you can go ahead with confidence, but if it looks like a loser, the delay will have helped you to avoid a bad mistake.[7]

A Fourth Real Option: Flexible Production Facilities

A sheep is not a flexible production facility. It produces mutton and wool in roughly fixed proportions. If the price of mutton suddenly rises and that of wool falls, there is little that the farmer with a flock of sheep can do about it. Many manufacturing operations are different, for they have built-in flexibility to vary their output mix as demand changes. Since we have mentioned sheep, we might point to the knitwear industry as a case in which manufacturing flexibility has become particularly important in recent years. Fashion changes have made the pattern of demand in the knitwear industry notoriously difficult to predict, and firms have increasingly invested in computer-controlled knitting machines, which provide an option to vary the product mix as demand changes.

Companies also try to avoid becoming dependent on a single source of raw materials. For example, at current prices gas-fired industrial boilers may be cheaper to operate than oil-fired ones. Yet many companies prefer to buy boilers that can use either oil or natural gas, even though these dual-fired boilers cost more than a gas-fired boiler. The reason is obvious. If gas prices rise relative to oil prices, the dual-fired boiler gives the company a valuable option to exchange one asset (an oil-fired boiler) for another (a gas-fired boiler).

Self-Test 10.7

Investments in new products or production capacity often include an option to expand. What are other major types of options encountered in capital investment decisions?

---

[7] Does this conclusion contradict our earlier dictum (see Chapter 8) that the firm should accept all positive-NPV projects? No. Notice that the investment timing problem involves a choice among mutually exclusive alternatives. You can build the project today or next year, but not both. In such cases, we have seen that the right choice is the one with the *highest* NPV. The NPV of the project today, even if positive, may well be less than the NPV of deferring investment and keeping alive the option to invest later.

SUMMARY

How do large corporations go about selecting positive-NPV projects? *(LO1)*

For most large corporations there are two stages in the investment process: the preparation of the **capital budget,** which is a list of planned investments, and the authorization process for individual projects. This process is usually a cooperative effort.

Investment projects should never be selected through a purely mechanical process. Managers need to ask why a project should have a positive NPV. A positive NPV is plausible only if the company has some competitive advantage that prevents its rivals from stealing most of the gains.

How are sensitivity, scenario, and break-even analyses used to see the effect of an error in forecasts on project profitability? *(LO2)*

Good managers realize that the forecasts behind NPV calculations are imperfect. Therefore, they explore the consequences of a poor forecast and check whether it is worth doing some more homework. They use the following principal tools to answer these what-if questions:

- **Sensitivity analysis,** where one variable at a time is changed.
- **Scenario analysis,** where the manager looks at the project under alternative scenarios.
- **Simulation analysis,** an extension of scenario analysis in which a computer generates hundreds or thousands of possible combinations of variables.
- **Break-even analysis,** where the focus is on how far sales could fall before the project begins to lose money. Often the phrase "lose money" is defined in terms of accounting losses, but it makes more sense to define it as "failing to cover the opportunity cost of capital"—in other words, as a negative NPV.

Why is an overestimate of sales more serious for projects with high operating leverage? *(LO3)*

Operating leverage is the degree to which costs are fixed. A project's break-even point will be affected by the extent to which costs can be reduced as sales decline. If the project has mostly **fixed costs,** it is said to have *high operating leverage.* High operating leverage implies that profits are more sensitive to changes in sales.

Why is managerial flexibility important in capital budgeting? *(LO4)*

Some projects may take on added value because they give the firm the option to bail out if things go wrong or to capitalize on success by expanding. These options are known as **real options.** Other real options include the possibility to delay a project or to choose flexible production facilities. We showed how **decision trees** may be used to set out the possible choices.

LISTING OF EQUATIONS

10.1 Break-even level of revenues $= \dfrac{\text{fixed costs including depreciation}}{\text{additional profit from each additional dollar of sales}}$

10.2 $\text{DOL} = \dfrac{\text{percentage change in profits}}{\text{percentage change in sales}}$

10.3 $\text{DOL} = 1 + \dfrac{\text{fixed costs}}{\text{profits}}$

QUESTIONS

QUIZ

1. **Role of the Capital Budget.** How does the capital budget help mitigate the following potential problems? *(LO1)*
   a. Overoptimism by project sponsors.
   b. Inconsistent forecasts of macroeconomic variables.
   c. Capital budgeting organized solely as a bottom-up process.

2. **Fixed and Variable Costs.** In a slow year, Deutsche Burgers will produce 2 million hamburgers at a total cost of $3.5 million. In a good year, it can produce 4 million hamburgers at a total cost of $4.5 million. What are the fixed and variable costs of hamburger production? *(LO2)*

3. **Average Cost.** Reconsider Deutsche Burgers from Quiz Question 2. *(LO2)*
   a. What is the average cost per burger when the firm produces 1 million hamburgers?
   b. What is average cost when the firm produces 2 million hamburgers?
   c. Why is average cost lower when more burgers are produced?

4. **Sensitivity Analysis.** A project currently generates sales of $10 million, variable costs equal to 50% of sales, and fixed costs of $2 million. The firm's tax rate is 35%. What are the effects of the following changes on after-tax profits and cash flow? *(LO2)*
   a. Sales increase from $10 million to $11 million.
   b. Variable costs increase to 65% of sales.

PRACTICE PROBLEMS

5. **Sensitivity Analysis.** The project in the preceding problem will last for 10 years. The discount rate is 12%. *(LO2)*
   a. What is the effect on project NPV of each of the changes considered in the problem?
   b. If project NPV under the base-case scenario is $2 million, how much can fixed costs increase before NPV turns negative?
   c. How much can fixed costs increase before accounting profits turn negative?

6. **Sensitivity Analysis.** Emperor's Clothes Fashions can invest $5 million in a new plant for producing invisible makeup. The plant has an expected life of 5 years, and expected sales are 6 million jars of makeup a year. Fixed costs are $2 million a year, and variable costs are $1 per jar. The product will be priced at $2 per jar. The plant will be depreciated straight-line over 5 years to a salvage value of zero. The opportunity cost of capital is 10%, and the tax rate is 40%. *(LO2)*
   a. What is project NPV under these base-case assumptions?
   b. What is NPV if variable costs turn out to be $1.20 per jar?
   c. What is NPV if fixed costs turn out to be $1.5 million per year?
   d. At what price per jar would project NPV equal zero?

7. **Scenario Analysis.** The most likely outcomes for a particular project are estimated as follows:

Unit price:	$50
Variable cost:	$30
Fixed cost:	$300,000
Expected sales:	30,000 units per year

   However, you recognize that some of these estimates are subject to error. Suppose that each variable may turn out to be either 10% higher or 10% lower than the initial estimate. The project will last for 10 years and requires an initial investment of $1 million, which will be depreciated straight-line over the project life to a final value of zero. The firm's tax rate is 35% and the required rate of return is 12%. What is project NPV in the "best-case scenario," that is, assuming all variables take on the best possible value? What about the worst-case scenario? *(LO2)*

8. **Scenario Analysis.** Reconsider the best- and worst-case scenarios in the previous problem. Do the best- and worst-case outcomes when each variable is treated independently seem to be reasonable scenarios in terms of the combinations of variables? For example, if price is higher than predicted, is it more or less likely that cost is higher than predicted? What other relationships may exist among the variables? *(LO2)*

9. **Break-Even.** The following estimates have been prepared for a project under consideration:

Fixed costs:	$20,000
Depreciation:	$10,000
Price:	$2
Accounting break-even:	60,000 units

   What must be the variable cost per unit? *(LO2)*

10. **Break-Even.** Dime a Dozen Diamonds makes synthetic diamonds by treating carbon. Each diamond can be sold for $100. The materials cost for a standard diamond is $40. The fixed costs incurred each year for factory upkeep and administrative expenses are $200,000. The machinery costs $1 million and is depreciated straight-line over 10 years to a salvage value of zero. *(LO2)*

    a. What is the accounting break-even level of sales in terms of number of diamonds sold?

    b. What is the NPV break-even level of sales assuming a tax rate of 35%, a 10-year project life, and a discount rate of 12%?

11. **Break-Even.** Turn back to the previous problem. *(LO2)*

    a. Would the accounting break-even point in the first year of operation increase or decrease if the machinery were depreciated over a 5-year period?

    b. Would the NPV break-even point increase or decrease if the machinery were depreciated over a 5-year period?

12. **Break-Even.** You are evaluating a project that will require an investment of $10 million that will be depreciated over a period of 7 years. You are concerned that the corporate tax rate will increase during the life of the project. Would such an increase affect the accounting break-even point? Would it affect the NPV break-even point? *(LO2)*

13. **Break-Even.** Define the *cash-flow break-even point* as the sales volume (in dollars) at which cash flow equals zero. Is the cash-flow break-even level of sales higher or lower than the zero-profit (accounting) break-even point? *(LO2)*

14. **Break-Even and NPV.** If a project operates at cash-flow break-even (see the previous problem) for its entire life, is its NPV positive or negative? *(LO2)*

15. **NPV Break-Even.** Modern Artifacts can produce keepsakes that will be sold for $80 each. Nondepreciation fixed costs are $1,000 per year and variable costs are $60 per unit. *(LO2)*

    a. If the project requires an initial investment of $3,000 and is expected to last for 5 years and the firm pays no taxes, what are the accounting and NPV break-even levels of sales? The initial investment will be depreciated straight-line over 5 years to a final value of zero, and the discount rate is 10%.

    b. How do your answers change if the firm's tax rate is 35%?

16. **NPV Break-Even.** A financial analyst has computed both accounting and NPV break-even sales levels for a project using straight-line depreciation over a 6-year period. The project manager wants to know what will happen to these estimates if the firm uses MACRS depreciation instead. The capital investment will be in a 5-year recovery period class under MACRS rules (see Table 9.2). The firm is in a 35% tax bracket. *(LO2)*

    a. What (qualitatively) will happen to the accounting break-even level of sales in the first years of the project?

    b. What (qualitatively) will happen to NPV break-even level of sales?

    c. If you were advising the analyst, would the answer to (a) or (b) be important to you? Specifically, would you say that the switch to MACRS makes the project more or less attractive?

17. **NPV Break-Even.** Reconsider Finefodder's new superstore. Suppose that by investing an additional $600,000 initially in more efficient checkout equipment, Finefodder could reduce variable costs to 80% of sales. *(LO2)*

    a. Using the base-case assumptions (Table 10.1), find the NPV of this alternative scheme. *(Hint:* Remember to focus on the incremental cash flows from the project.)

    b. At what level of sales will accounting profits be unchanged if the firm invests in the new equipment? Assume the equipment receives the same 12-year straight-line depreciation treatment as in the original example. *(Hint:* Focus on the project's incremental effects on fixed and variable costs.)

    c. What is the NPV break-even point?

18. **Break-Even and NPV.** If the superstore project (see the previous problem) operates at accounting break-even, will net present value be positive or negative? *(LO2)*

19. **Operating Leverage.** You estimate that your cattle farm will generate $1 million of profits on sales of $4 million under normal economic conditions and that the degree of operating leverage is 8. What will profits be if sales turn out to be $3.5 million? What if they are $4.5 million? *(LO3)*

20. **Operating Leverage.** *(LO3)*
    a. What is the degree of operating leverage of Modern Artifacts (in problem 15) when sales are $7,000?
    b. What is the degree of operating leverage when sales are $12,000?
    c. Why is operating leverage different at these two levels of sales?

21. **Operating Leverage.** What is the lowest possible value for the degree of operating leverage for a profitable firm? Show with a numerical example that if Modern Artifacts (see Practice Problem 15a) has zero fixed costs, then DOL = 1 and in fact sales and profits are directly proportional, so that a 1% change in sales results in a 1% change in profits. *(LO3)*

22. **Operating Leverage.** A project has fixed costs of $1,000 per year, depreciation charges of $500 a year, revenue of $6,000 a year, and variable costs equal to two-thirds of revenues. *(LO3)*
    a. If sales increase by 10%, what will be the increase in pretax profits?
    b. What is the degree of operating leverage of this project?
    c. Confirm that the percentage change in profits equals DOL times the percentage change in sales.

23. **Project Options.** Your midrange guess as to the amount of oil in a prospective field is 10 million barrels, but in fact there is a 50% chance that the amount of oil is 15 million barrels and a 50% chance of 5 million barrels. If the actual amount of oil is 15 million barrels, the present value of the cash flows from drilling will be $8 million. If the amount is only 5 million barrels, the present value will be only $2 million. It costs $3 million to drill the well. Suppose that a seismic test that costs $100,000 can verify the amount of oil under the ground. Is it worth paying for the test? Use a decision tree to justify your answer. *(LO4)*

24. **Project Options.** A silver mine can yield 10,000 ounces of silver at a variable cost of $32 per ounce. The fixed costs of operating the mine are $40,000 per year. In half the years, silver can be sold for $48 per ounce; in the other years, silver can be sold for only $24 per ounce. Ignore taxes. *(LO4)*
    a. What is the average cash flow you will receive from the mine if it is always kept in operation and the silver always is sold in the year it is mined?
    b. Now suppose you can shut down the mine in years of low silver prices. What happens to the average cash flow from the mine?

25. **Project Options.** An auto plant that costs $100 million to build can produce a line of flex-fuel cars that will produce cash flows with a present value of $140 million if the line is successful but only $50 million if it is unsuccessful. You believe that the probability of success is only about 50%. You learn whether the line is successful immediately after building the plant. *(LO4)*
    a. Would you build the plant?
    b. Suppose that the plant can be sold for $95 million to another automaker if the auto line is not successful. Now would you build the plant?
    c. Illustrate the option to abandon in (b) using a decision tree.

26. **Production Options.** Explain why options to expand or contract production are most valuable when forecasts about future business conditions are most uncertain. *(LO4)*

CHALLENGE PROBLEMS

27. **Abandonment Option.** Hit or Miss Sports is introducing a new product this year. If its see-at-night soccer balls are a hit, the firm expects to be able to sell 50,000 units a year at a price of $60 each. If the new product is a bust, only 30,000 units can be sold at a price of $55. The variable cost of each ball is $30, and fixed costs are zero. The cost of the manufacturing equipment is $6 million, and the project life is estimated at 10 years. The firm will use straight-line depreciation over the 10-year life of the project. The firm's tax rate is 35%, and the discount rate is 12%. *(LO4)*

a. If each outcome is equally likely, what is expected NPV? Will the firm accept the project?

b. Suppose now that the firm can abandon the project and sell off the manufacturing equipment for $5.4 million if demand for the balls turns out to be weak. The firm will make the decision to continue or abandon after the first year of sales. Does the option to abandon change the firm's decision to accept the project?

28. **Expansion Option.** Now suppose that Hit or Miss Sports from the previous problem can expand production if the project is successful. By paying its workers overtime, it can increase production by 25,000 units; the variable cost of each ball will be higher, however, equal to $35 per unit. By how much does this option to expand production increase the NPV of the project? *(LO4)*

Templates can be found at
www.mhhe.com/bmm7e.

29. **Project Analysis.** New Energy is evaluating a new biofuel facility. The plant would cost $4,000 million to build and has the potential to produce up to 40 million barrels of synthetic oil a year. The product is a close substitute for conventional oil and would sell for the same price. The market price of oil currently is fluctuating around $100 per barrel, but there is considerable uncertainty about future prices. Variable costs for the organic inputs to the production process are estimated at $78 per barrel and are expected to be stable. In addition, annual upkeep and maintenance expenses on the facility will be $100 million regardless of the production level. The plant has an expected life of 15 years, and it will be depreciated using MACRS and a 10-year recovery period. Salvage value net of cleanup costs is expected to be negligible. Demand for the product is difficult to forecast. Depending on consumer acceptance, sales might range from 25 million to 35 million barrels annually. The discount rate is 12%, and New Energy's tax bracket is 35%.

a. Find the project NPV for the following combinations of oil price and sales volume. Which source of uncertainty seems most important to the success of the project? *(LO2)*

	Oil Price		
Annual sales	**$80/barrel**	**$100/barrel**	**$120/barrel**
25 million barrels			
30 million barrels			
35 million barrels			

b. At an oil price of $100, what level of annual sales, maintained over the life of the plant, is necessary for NPV break-even? (This will require trial and error unless you are familiar with more advanced features of Excel such as the Goal Seek command.) *(LO2)*

c. At an oil price of $100, what is the accounting break-even level of sales in each year? Why does it change each year? Does this notion of break-even seem reasonable to you? *(LO2)*

d. If each of the scenarios in the grid in part (a) is equally likely, what is the expected NPV of the facility? *(LO2)*

e. Why might the facility be worth building despite your answer to part (d)? *(LO4)*

WEB EXERCISE

1. Can you guess Dell's incremental cost for producing one computer? You probably have that amount in your wallet or purse! Let's estimate the sales break-even point and degree of operating leverage for Dell Computer (DELL). Go to the annual income statement, which you can find at finance.yahoo.com. Assume that selling, general, and administrative and depreciation expenses are fixed, and costs of goods sold are variable. Estimate the break-even level of sales for Dell for the last year (annual).

SOLUTIONS TO SELF-TEST QUESTIONS

10.1 Cash-flow forecasts for Finefodder's new superstore:

	Year 0	Years 1–12
Investment	−5,400,000	
1. Sales		16,000,000
2. Variable costs		13,280,000
3. Fixed costs		2,000,000
4. Depreciation		450,000
5. Pretax profit (1 − 2 − 3 − 4)		270,000
6. Taxes (at 40%)		108,000
7. Profit after tax		162,000
8. Cash flow from operations (4 + 7)		612,000
Net cash flow	−5,400,000	612,000

$$\text{NPV} = -\$5.4 \text{ million} + (7.5361 \times \$612,000) = -\$787,907$$

which matches the value in Table 10.2 except for minor rounding error in the annuity factor.

10.2 Both calculate how NPV depends on input assumptions. Sensitivity analysis changes inputs one at a time, whereas scenario analysis changes several variables at once. The changes should add up to a consistent scenario for the project as a whole.

10.3 With the lower initial investment, depreciation is also lower; it now equals $417,000 per year. Cash flow is now as follows:

1. Variable costs	81.25% of sales
2. Fixed costs	$2 million
3. Depreciation	$417,000
4. Pretax profit	(.1875 × sales) − $2.417 million
5. Tax (at 40%)	.4 × (.1875 × sales − $2.417 million)
6. Profit after tax	.6 × (.1875 × sales − $2.417 million)
7. Cash flow (3 + 6)	.6 × (.1875 × sales − $2.417 million) + $417,000
	= .1125 × sales − $1.033 million

Break-even occurs when

$$\text{PV (cash inflows)} = \text{investment}$$
$$7.536 \times (.1125 \times \text{sales} - \$1.033 \text{ million}) = \$5 \text{ million}$$
$$\text{Sales} = \$15.08 \text{ million}$$

10.4 Break-even analysis finds the level of sales or revenue at which NPV = 0. Sensitivity analysis changes these and other input variables to optimistic and pessimistic values and recalculates NPV.

10.5 Reworking Table 10.6 for the normal level of sales and 10% higher sales gives the following:

	High Fixed Costs		High Variable Costs	
	Normal	10% Higher Sales	Normal	10% Higher Sales
Sales	16,000	17,600	16,000	17,600
− Variable costs	13,000	14,300	13,440	14,784
− Fixed costs	2,000	2,000	1,560	1,560
− Depreciation	450	450	450	450
= Pretax profit	550	850	550	806

For the high-fixed-cost policy, profits increase by 54.5%, from $550,000 to $850,000. For the low-fixed-cost policy, profits increase by 46.5%. In both cases the percentage increase in profits equals DOL times the percentage increase in sales. This illustrates that DOL measures the sensitivity of profits to changes in sales.

FIGURE 10.4 Example of a decision tree for Widgeon Company

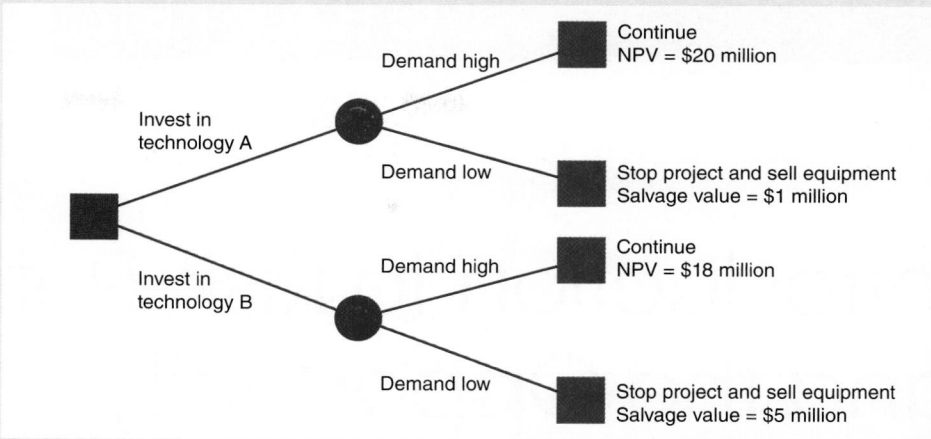

10.6 See Figure 10.4. Note that while technology A delivers the higher NPV if demand is high, technology B has the advantage of a higher salvage value if demand is unexpectedly low.

10.7 Abandonment options, options due to flexible production facilities, investment timing options.

MINICASE

Maxine Peru, the CEO of Peru Resources, hardly noticed the plate of savory quenelles de brochet and the glass of Corton Charlemagne '94 on the table before her. She was absorbed by the engineering report handed to her just as she entered the executive dining room.

The report described a proposed new mine on the North Ridge of Mt. Zircon. A vein of transcendental zirconium ore had been discovered there on land owned by Ms. Peru's company. Test borings indicated sufficient reserves to produce 340 tons per year of transcendental zirconium over a 7-year period.

The vein probably also contained hydrated zircon gemstones. The amount and quality of these zircons were hard to predict, since they tended to occur in "pockets." The new mine might come across one, two, or dozens of pockets. The mining engineer guessed that 150 pounds per year might be found. The current price for high-quality hydrated zircon gemstones was $3,300 per pound.

Peru Resources was a family-owned business with total assets of $45 million, including cash reserves of $4 million. The outlay required for the new mine would be a major commitment. Fortunately, Peru Resources was conservatively financed, and Ms. Peru believed that the company could borrow up to $9 million at an interest rate of about 8%.

The mine's operating costs were projected at $900,000 per year, including $400,000 of fixed costs and $500,000 of variable costs. Ms. Peru thought these forecasts were accurate. The big question marks seemed to be the initial cost of the mine and the selling price of transcendental zirconium.

Opening the mine, and providing the necessary machinery and ore-crunching facilities, was supposed to cost $10 million, but cost overruns of 10% or 15% were common in the mining business. In addition, new environmental regulations, if enacted, could increase the cost of the mine by $1.5 million.

There was a cheaper design for the mine, which would reduce its cost by $1.7 million and eliminate much of the uncertainty about cost overruns. Unfortunately, this design would require much higher fixed operating costs. Fixed costs would increase to $850,000 per year at planned production levels.

The current price of transcendental zirconium was $10,000 per ton, but there was no consensus about future prices.[8] Some experts were projecting rapid price increases to as much as $14,000 per ton. On the other hand, there were pessimists saying that prices could be as low as $7,500 per ton. Ms. Peru did not have strong views either way: Her best guess was that price would just increase with inflation at about 3.5% per year. (Mine operating costs would also increase with inflation.)

Ms. Peru had wide experience in the mining business, and she knew that investors in similar projects usually wanted a forecasted nominal rate of return of at least 14%.

You have been asked to assist Ms. Peru in evaluating this project. Lay out the base-case NPV analysis, and undertake sensitivity, scenario, or break-even analyses as appropriate. Assume that Peru Resources pays tax at a 35% rate. For simplicity, also assume that the investment in the mine could be depreciated for tax purposes straight-line over 7 years.

What forecasts or scenarios should worry Ms. Peru the most? Where would additional information be most helpful? Is there a case for delaying construction of the new mine?

---

[8] There were no traded forward or futures contracts on transcendental zirconium. See Chapter 24.

Introduction to Risk, Return, and the Opportunity Cost of Capital

LEARNING OBJECTIVES

After studying this chapter, you should be able to:

(1) Estimate the opportunity cost of capital for an "average-risk" project.

(2) Calculate returns and standard deviation of returns for individual common stocks or for a stock portfolio.

(3) Understand why diversification reduces risk.

(4) Distinguish between specific risk, which can be diversified away, and market risk, which cannot.

RELATED WEB SITES FOR THIS CHAPTER CAN BE FOUND AT WWW.MHHE.COM/BMM7E.

Investing in risky assets is not the same as gambling. After reading this chapter, you should be able to explain the difference.

In earlier chapters we skirted the issue of project risk; now it is time to confront it head-on. We can no longer be satisfied with vague statements like "The opportunity cost of capital depends on the risk of the project." We need to know how to measure risk, and we need to understand the relationship between risk and the cost of capital. These are the topics of the next two chapters.

Think for a moment what the cost of capital for a project means. It is the rate of return that shareholders could expect to earn if they invested in equally risky securities. So one way to estimate the cost of capital is to find securities that have the same risk as the project and then estimate the expected rate of return on these securities.

We start our analysis by looking at the rates of return earned in the past from different investments, concentrating on the *extra* return that investors have received for investing in risky rather than safe securities. We then show how to measure the risk of a portfolio, and we look again at past history to find out how risky it is to invest in the stock market.

Finally, we explore the concept of diversification. Most investors do not put all their eggs into one basket—they diversify. Thus investors are not concerned with the risk of each security in isolation; instead, they are concerned with how much it contributes to the risk of a diversified portfolio. We therefore need to distinguish between the risk that can be eliminated by diversification and the risk that cannot be eliminated.

11.1 Rates of Return: A Review

When investors buy a stock or a bond, their return comes in two forms: (1) a dividend or interest payment and (2) a capital gain or a capital loss. For example, suppose you bought the stock of IBM at the beginning of 2010 when its price was $130.90 a share. By the end of the year the value of that investment had appreciated to $146.76, giving a capital gain of $146.76 − $130.90 = $15.86. In addition, in 2010 IBM paid a dividend of $2.50 a share.

The *percentage* return on your investment was therefore

$$\text{Percentage return} = \frac{\text{capital gain} + \text{dividend}}{\text{initial share price}} \qquad (11.1)$$

$$= \frac{\$15.86 + \$2.50}{\$130.90} = .140, \text{ or } 14.0\%$$

The percentage return can also be expressed as the sum of the *dividend yield* and *percentage capital gain*. The dividend yield is the dividend expressed as a percentage of the stock price at the beginning of the year:

$$\text{Dividend yield} = \frac{\text{dividend}}{\text{initial share price}}$$

$$= \frac{\$2.50}{\$130.90} = .019, \text{ or } 1.9\%$$

Similarly, the percentage capital gain is

$$\text{Percentage capital gain} = \frac{\text{capital gain}}{\text{initial share price}}$$

$$= \frac{\$15.86}{\$130.90} = .121, \text{ or } 12.1\%$$

Thus the total return is the sum of 1.9% + 12.1% = 14.0%.

Remember that in Chapter 5 we made a distinction between the *nominal* rate of return and the *real* rate of return. The nominal return measures how much more money you will have at the end of the year if you invest today. The return that we just calculated for IBM stock is therefore a nominal return. The real rate of return tells you how much more you will be able to *buy* with your money at the end of the year. To convert from a nominal to a real rate of return, we use the following relationship:

$$1 + \text{real rate of return} = \frac{1 + \text{nominal rate of return}}{1 + \text{inflation rate}}$$

In 2010 inflation was 1.5%. So we calculate the real rate of return on IBM stock as follows:

$$1 + \text{real rate of return} = \frac{1.140}{1.015} = 1.123$$

Therefore, the real rate of return equals .123, or 12.3%.

Self-Test 11.1

Suppose you buy a bond for $1,020 with a 15-year maturity paying an annual coupon of $80. A year later interest rates have dropped and the bond's price has increased to $1,050. What are your nominal and real rates of return? Assume the inflation rate is 4%.

11.2 A Century of Capital Market History

When you invest in a stock, you don't know what return you will earn. But by looking at the history of security returns, you can get some idea of the return that investors might reasonably expect from investments in different types of securities and of the risks that they face. Let us look, therefore, at the risks and returns that investors have experienced in the past.

Market Indexes

market index
Measure of the investment performance of the overall market.

Investors can choose from an enormous number of different securities. For example, currently, about 2,300 common stocks trade on the New York Stock Exchange, and a further 2,900 are traded on the NASDAQ Stock Market.

Financial analysts can't track every stock, so they rely on **market indexes** to summarize the return on different classes of securities. The best-known stock market index in the United States is the **Dow Jones Industrial Average,** generally known as the *Dow.* The Dow tracks the performance of a portfolio that holds one share in each of 30 large firms. For example, suppose that the Dow starts the day at a value of 12,000 and then rises by 120 points to a new value of 12,120. Investors who own one share in each of the 30 companies make a capital gain of 120/12,000 = .01, or 1%.[1]

Dow Jones Industrial Average
Index of the investment performance of a portfolio of 30 "blue-chip" stocks.

The Dow Jones Industrial Average was first computed in 1896. Most people are used to it and expect to hear it on the 6 o'clock news. However, it is far from the best measure of the performance of the stock market. First, with only 30 large industrial stocks, it is not representative of the performance of stocks generally. Second, investors don't usually hold an equal number of shares in each company. For example, in 2010 there were 10.1 billion shares in General Electric and just under a billion in Du Pont. So on average investors did *not* hold the same number of shares in the two firms. Instead, they held over 10 times as many shares in General Electric as in Du Pont. It doesn't make sense, therefore, to look at an index that measures the performance of a portfolio with an equal number of shares in the two firms.

Standard & Poor's Composite Index
Index of the investment performance of a portfolio of 500 large stocks. Also called the *S&P 500.*

The **Standard & Poor's Composite Index,** better known as the *S&P 500,* includes the stocks of 500 major companies and is therefore a more comprehensive index than the Dow. Also, it measures the performance of a portfolio that holds shares in each firm in proportion to the number of shares that have been issued to investors. For example, the S&P portfolio would hold 10 times as many shares in General Electric as Du Pont. Thus the S&P 500 shows the *average* performance of investors in the 500 firms.

Only a small proportion of the publicly traded companies are represented in the S&P 500. However, these firms are among the largest in the country, and they account for about 75% of the market value of traded stocks. Therefore, success for professional investors usually means "beating the S&P."

Some stock market indexes, such as the Dow Jones Wilshire 5000, include an even larger number of stocks, while others focus on special groups of stocks such as the stocks of small companies. There are also stock market indexes for other countries, such as the Nikkei Index for Tokyo and the Financial Times (FT) Index for London. Morgan Stanley Capital International (MSCI) even computes a world stock market index. The Financial Times Company and Standard & Poor's have combined to produce their own world index.

The Historical Record

The historical returns of stock or bond market indexes can give us an idea of the typical performance of different investments. For example, Elroy Dimson, Paul Marsh,

---

[1] Stock market indexes record the market value of the portfolio. To calculate the total return on the portfolio, we need to add in any dividends that are paid.

and Mike Staunton have compiled measures of the investment performance of three portfolios of securities since 1900:

1. A portfolio of 3-month loans issued each week by the U.S. government. These loans are known as *Treasury bills.*
2. A portfolio of long-term *Treasury bonds* issued by the U.S. government and maturing in about 10 years.
3. A diversified portfolio of common stocks.

These portfolios are not equally risky. Treasury bills are about as safe an investment as you can make. Because they are issued by the U.S. government, you can be sure that you will get your money back. Their short-term maturity means that their prices are relatively stable. In fact, investors who wish to lend money for 3 months can achieve a certain payoff by buying 3-month bills. Of course, they can't be sure what that money will buy; there is still some uncertainty about inflation.

Long-term Treasury bonds are also certain to be repaid when they mature, but the prices of these bonds fluctuate more as interest rates vary. When interest rates fall, the value of long-term bonds rises; when rates rise, the value of the bonds falls.

Common stocks are the riskiest of the three groups of securities. When you invest in common stocks, there is no promise that you will get your money back. As a part-owner of the corporation, you receive what is left over after the bonds and any other debts have been repaid.

Figure 11.1 shows the performance of the three groups of securities assuming that all dividends or interest income had been reinvested in the portfolios. You can see that the performance of the portfolios fits our intuitive risk ranking. Common stocks were the riskiest investment, but they also offered the greatest gains. One dollar invested at the start of 1900 in a portfolio of common stocks would have grown to $21,765 by the end of 2010. At the other end of the spectrum, an investment in Treasury bills would have accumulated to only $74.

Table 11.1 shows the average of the annual returns from each of these portfolios. These returns are comparable to the return that we calculated for IBM. In other words, they include (1) dividends or interest and (2) any capital gains or losses.

maturity premium
Extra average return from investing in long- versus short-term Treasury securities.

The safest investment, Treasury bills, had the lowest rates of return—they averaged 4% a year. Long-term government bonds gave slightly higher returns than Treasury bills. This difference is called the **maturity premium.** Common stocks were in a class by themselves. Investors who accepted the risk of common stocks received on average an extra return of 7.4% a year over the return on Treasury bills. This

FIGURE 11.1 How an investment of $1 at the start of 1900 would have grown by the end of 2010 (index values plotted on log scale)

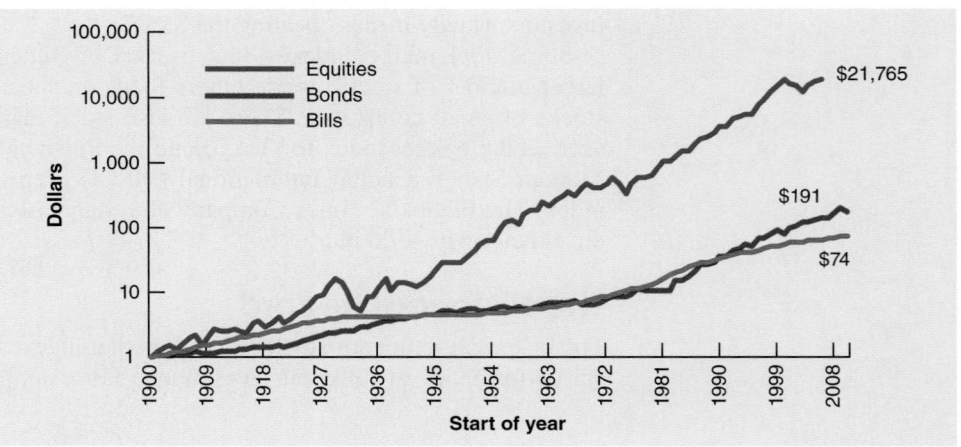

Source: Elroy Dimson, Paul Marsh, and Mike Staunton, *Triumph of the Optimists: 101 Years of Global Investment Returns* (Princeton, NJ: Princeton University Press, 2002). Updates courtesy of *Triumph*'s authors.

TABLE 11.1 Average rates of return on Treasury bills, government bonds, and common stocks, 1900–2010 (figures in percent per year)

Portfolio	Average Annual Rate of Return	Average Premium (Extra Return versus Treasury Bills)
Treasury bills	4.0	
Treasury bonds	5.2	1.2
Common stocks	11.4	7.4

Source: Elroy Dimson, Paul Marsh, and Mike Staunton, *Triumph of the Optimists: 101 Years of Global Equity Returns* (Princeton, NJ: Princeton University Press, 2002). Updates courtesy of *Triumph*'s authors.

risk premium
Expected return in excess of risk-free return as compensation for risk.

compensation for taking on the risk of common stock ownership is known as the market **risk premium:**

$$\frac{\text{Rate of return}}{\text{on common stocks}} = \frac{\text{interest rate on}}{\text{Treasury bills}} + \frac{\text{market risk}}{\text{premium}}$$

The historical record shows that investors have received a risk premium for holding risky assets. Average returns on high-risk assets are higher than those on low-risk assets.

You may ask why we look back over such a long period to measure average rates of return. The reason is that annual rates of return for common stocks fluctuate so much that averages taken over short periods are extremely unreliable. In some years investors in common stocks had a disagreeable shock and received a substantially lower return than they expected. In other years they had a pleasant surprise and received a higher-than-expected return. By averaging the returns across both the rough years and the smooth, we should get a fair idea of the typical return that investors might justifiably expect.

While common stocks have offered the highest average returns, they have also been riskier investments. Figure 11.2 shows the 111 annual rates of return on common stocks. The fluctuations in year-to-year returns on common stocks are remarkably wide. There were 2 years (1933 and 1954) when investors earned a return of more than 50%. However, Figure 11.2 shows that you can also lose money by investing in the stock market. The most dramatic case was the stock market crash of 1929–1932. Shortly after President Coolidge joyfully observed that stocks were "cheap at current prices," stocks rapidly became even cheaper. By July 1932 the Dow Jones Industrial Average had fallen in a series of slides by 89%.

FIGURE 11.2 Rates of return on common stocks, 1900–2010

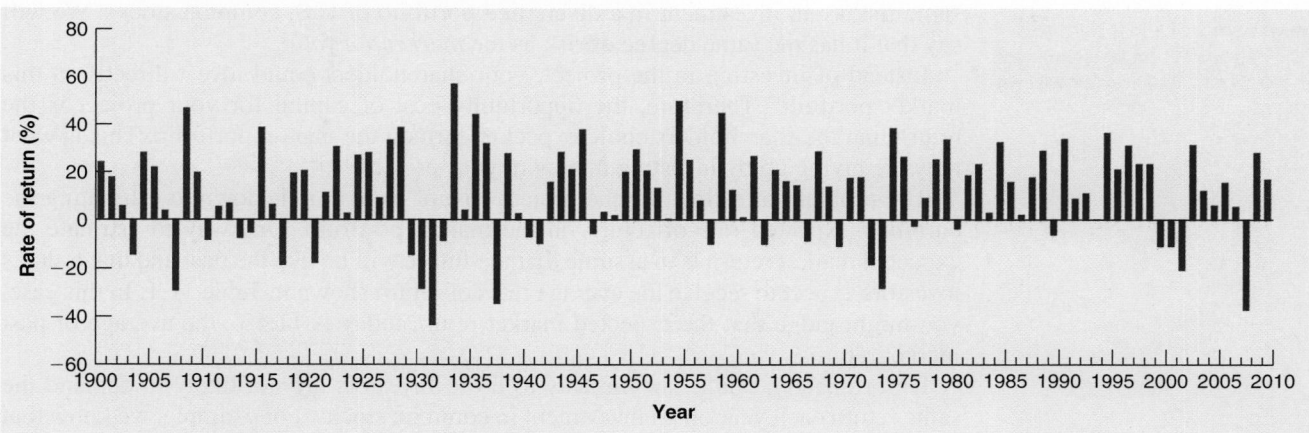

Source: Elroy Dimson, Paul Marsh, and Mike Staunton, *Triumph of the Optimists: 101 Years of Global Investment Returns* (Princeton, NJ: Princeton University Press, 2002). Updates courtesy of *Triumph*'s authors.

You don't have to look that far back to see that the stock market is a risky place. Investors who bought at the stock market peak in March 2000 saw little but falling stock prices over the next 2½ years. By October 2002 the S&P 500 had declined by 49%, while the tech-heavy NASDAQ market fell by 78%. But this was not the end of the roller-coaster ride. After recovering sharply, share prices plunged 57% between October 2007 and March 2009 as the banking crisis unfolded.

Bond prices also fluctuate, but far less than stock prices. The worst year for investors in our portfolio of Treasury bonds was 1967; their return that year was −9.2%.

Self-Test 11.2

Here are the average rates of return for common stocks and Treasury bills for four different periods:

	1900–1924	1925–1949	1950–1974	1975–2010
Stocks	9.5%	10.2%	11.1%	13.7%
Treasury bills	5.1	1.1	3.5	5.6

What was the risk premium on stocks for each of these periods?

Using Historical Evidence to Estimate Today's Cost of Capital

Think back now to Chapter 8, where we showed how firms calculate the present value of a new project by discounting the expected cash flows by the opportunity cost of capital. The opportunity cost of capital is the return that the firm's shareholders are giving up by investing in the project rather than in comparable risk alternatives.

Measuring the cost of capital is easy if the project is a sure thing. Since shareholders can obtain a surefire payoff by investing in a U.S. Treasury bill, the firm should invest in a risk-free project only if it can at least match the rate of interest on such a loan. If the project is risky—and most projects are—then the firm needs to at least match the return that shareholders could expect to earn if they invested in securities of similar risk. It is not easy to put a precise figure on this, but our skim through history provides an idea of the average return an investor might expect from an investment in risky common stocks.

Suppose there is an investment project that you *know*—don't ask how—has the same risk as an investment in a diversified portfolio of U.S. common stocks. We will say that it has the same degree of risk as the *market portfolio.*

Instead of investing in the project, your shareholders could invest directly in this market portfolio. Therefore, the opportunity cost of capital for your project is the return that the shareholders could expect to earn on the market portfolio. This is what they are giving up by investing money in your project.

The problem of estimating the project cost of capital boils down to estimating the currently expected rate of return on the market portfolio. One way to estimate the expected market return is to assume that the future will be like the past and that today's investors expect to receive the average rates of return shown in Table 11.1. In this case, you might judge that the expected market return today is 11.4%, the average of past market returns.

Unfortunately, this is *not* the way to do it. Investors are not likely to demand the same return each year on an investment in common stocks. For example, we know that the interest rate on safe Treasury bills varies over time. At their peak in 1981, Treasury bills offered a return of 14%, nearly 10 percentage points above the 4% average return on bills shown in Table 11.1.

What if you were called upon to estimate the expected return on common stocks in 1981? Would you have said 11.4%? That doesn't make sense. Who would invest in the risky stock market for an expected return of 11.4% when you could get a safe 14% from Treasury bills?

A better procedure is to take the *current* interest rate on Treasury bills plus 7.4%, the average *risk premium* shown in Table 11.1. In 1981, when the rate on Treasury bills was 14%, that would have given

$$\text{Expected market return (1981)} = \text{interest rate on Treasury bills (1981)} + \text{normal risk premium}$$

$$= 14 + 7.4 = 21.4\%$$

The first term on the right-hand side tells us the time value of money in 1981; the second term measures the compensation for risk. **The expected return on an investment provides compensation to investors both for waiting (the time value of money) and for worrying (the risk of the particular asset).**

What about today? As we write this in early 2011, Treasury bills offer a return of only 0.1%. This suggests that investors in common stocks are looking for a return of 7.5%:[2]

$$\text{Expected market return (2011)} = \text{interest rate on Treasury bills (2011)} + \text{normal risk premium}$$

$$= 0.1 + 7.4 = 7.5\%$$

These calculations assume that there is a normal, stable risk premium on the market portfolio, so the expected *future* risk premium can be measured by the average past risk premium. But even with more than 100 years of data, we can't estimate the market risk premium exactly; nor can we be sure that investors today are demanding the same reward for risk that they were in the early 1900s. All this leaves plenty of room for argument about what the risk premium *really* is.

Many financial managers and economists believe that long-run historical returns are the best measure available. Others have a gut instinct that investors don't need such a large risk premium to persuade them to hold common stocks. For example, surveys of financial economists and chief financial officers commonly suggest a risk premium that is 1% to 2% lower than the historical average.[3]

We may be able to gain some further insights into the question by looking at the experience of other countries. Figure 11.3 shows that the United States is roughly average in terms of the risk premium. Danish common stocks come bottom of the league; the average risk premium in Denmark is only 4.8%. Top of the form is Italy with a premium of 10.2%. Some of these variations between countries may reflect differences in risk. For example, Italian stocks have been particularly variable and investors may have required a higher return to compensate. But remember how difficult it is to make precise estimates of what investors expected. You probably would not be too far out if you concluded that the *expected* risk premium was the same in each country.

---

[2] In practice, things might be a bit more complicated. In 2010 short-term interest rates were unusually low and probably not appropriate for judging the required return on a long-term project. We will return to this problem in the next chapter.

[3] Unfortunately, it is difficult to interpret these surveys precisely, because respondents define the risk premium in different ways. For example, see P. Fernandez and J. del Campo, "Market Risk Premium Used in 2010 by Analysts and Companies," **ssrn.com/abstract=1609563**, and J. R. Graham and C. R. Harvey, "The Equity Risk Premium Amid a Global Financial Crisis," **ssrn.com/abstract=1405459**.

FIGURE 11.3 The risk premium in 18 countries, 1900–2010. The return on common stocks has averaged 7.0% more than the interest rate on bills.

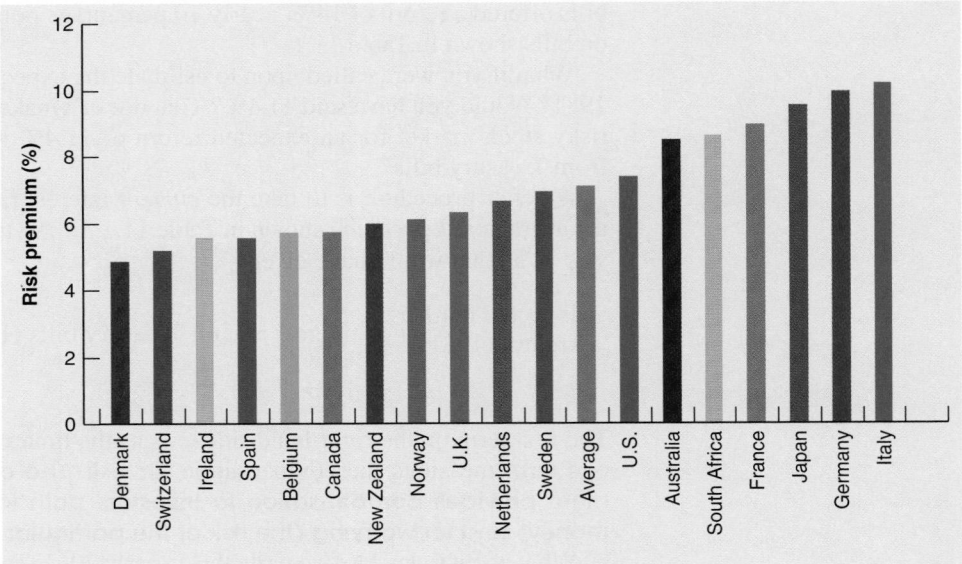

Source: Elroy Dimson, Paul Marsh, and Mike Staunton, *Triumph of the Optimists: 101 Years of Global Investment Returns* (Princeton, NJ: Princeton University Press, 2002). Updates courtesy of *Triumph*'s authors.

11.3 Measuring Risk

You now have some benchmarks. You know that the opportunity cost of capital for safe projects must be the rate of return offered by safe Treasury bills, and you know that the opportunity cost of capital for "average-risk" projects must be the expected return on the market portfolio. But you *don't* know how to estimate the cost of capital for projects that do not fit these two simple cases. Before you can do this, you need to understand more about investment risk.

The average fuse time for army hand grenades is 5 seconds, but that average hides a lot of potentially relevant information. If you are in the business of throwing grenades, you need some measure of the variation around the average fuse time.[4] Similarly, if you are in the business of investing in securities, you need some measure of how far the returns may differ from the average.

One way to present the spread of possible investment returns is by using histograms, such as the ones in Figure 11.4. The bars in each histogram show the number of years between 1900 and 2010 that the investment's return fell within a specific range. Look first at the performance of common stocks. Their risk shows up in the wide spread of outcomes. For example, you can see that in one year the return was between +55% and +60%, but there was also one year that investors lost between 40% and 45%.

The corresponding histograms for Treasury bonds and bills show that unusually high or low returns are much less common. Investors in these securities could have been much more confident of the outcome than common stockholders.

Variance and Standard Deviation

Investment risk depends on the dispersion or spread of possible outcomes. For example, Figure 11.4 showed that on past evidence there is greater uncertainty about the possible returns from common stocks than about the returns from bills or bonds. Sometimes a picture like Figure 11.4 tells you all you need to know about (past) dispersion. But in general, pictures do not suffice. The financial manager needs a

---

[4] We can reassure you; the variation around the standard fuse time is very small.

FIGURE 11.4 Historical returns on major asset classes, 1900–2010

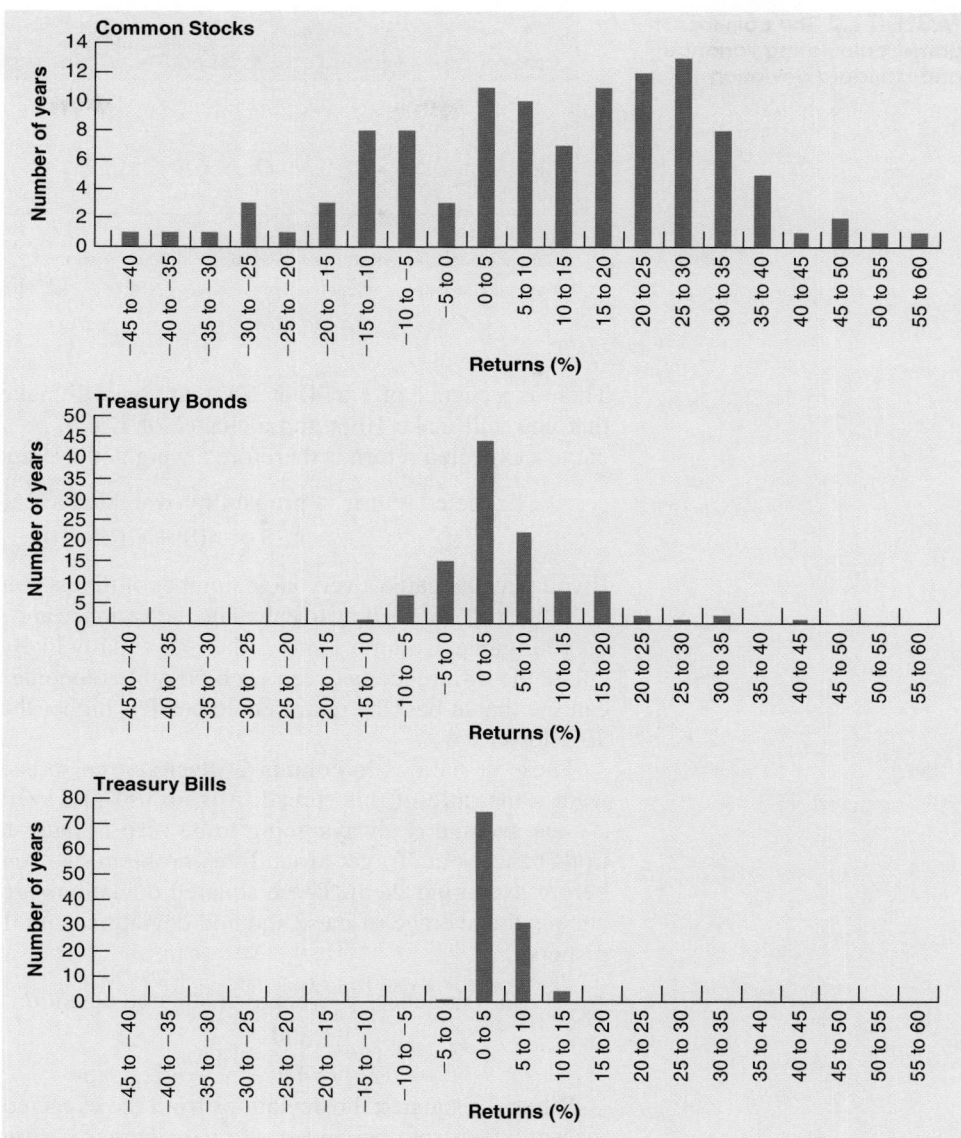

Source: Elroy Dimson, Paul Marsh, and Mike Staunton, *Triumph of the Optimists: 101 Years of Global Investment Returns* (Princeton, NJ: Princeton University Press, 2002). Updates courtesy of *Triumph*'s authors.

variance
Average value of squared deviations from mean. A measure of volatility.

standard deviation
Square root of variance. Another measure of volatility.

numerical measure of dispersion. The standard measures are **variance** and **standard deviation.** More variable returns imply greater investment risk. This suggests that some measure of dispersion will provide a reasonable measure of risk, and dispersion is precisely what is measured by variance and standard deviation.

Here is a very simple example showing how variance and standard deviation are calculated: Suppose that you are offered the opportunity to play the following game. You start by investing $100. Then two coins are flipped. For each head that comes up your starting balance will be *increased* by 20%, and for each tail that comes up your starting balance will be *reduced* by 10%. Clearly there are four equally likely outcomes:

- Head + Head: You make 20 + 20 = 40%
- Head + Tail: You make 20 − 10 = 10%
- Tail + Head: You make −10 + 20 = 10%
- Tail + Tail: You make −10 − 10 = −20%

TABLE 11.2 The coin-toss game; calculating variance and standard deviation

(1) Percent Rate of Return	(2) Deviation from Expected Return	(3) Squared Deviation
+40	+30	900
+10	0	0
+10	0	0
−20	−30	900

Notes:
1. Variance = average of squared deviations = 1,800/4 = 450.
2. Standard deviation = square root of variance = $\sqrt{450}$ = 21.2, about 21%.

There is a chance of 1 in 4, or .25, that you will make 40%; a chance of 2 in 4, or .5, that you will make 10%; and a chance of 1 in 4, or .25, that you will lose 20%. The game's expected return is therefore a weighted average of the possible outcomes:

$$\text{Expected return} = \text{probability-weighted average of possible outcomes}$$
$$= (.25 \times 40) + (.5 \times 10) + (.25 \times -20) = +10\%$$

If you play the game a very large number of times, your average return should be 10%.

Table 11.2 shows how to calculate the variance and standard deviation of the returns on your game. Column 1 shows the four equally likely outcomes. In column 2 we calculate the difference between each possible outcome and the expected outcome. You can see that at best the return could be 30% higher than expected; at worst it could be 30% lower.

These deviations in column 2 illustrate the spread of possible returns. But if we want a measure of this spread, it is no use just averaging the deviations in column 2—the average is always going to be zero because the positive and negative deviations cancel out. To get around this problem, we *square* the deviations in column 2 before averaging them. These squared deviations are shown in column 3. The variance is the average of these squared deviations and therefore is a natural measure of dispersion:

$$\text{Variance} = \text{average of squared deviations around the average} \qquad \textbf{(11.2)}$$
$$= \frac{1,800}{4} = 450$$

When we squared the deviations from the expected return, we changed the units of measurement from *percentages* to *percentages squared.* Our last step is to get back to percentages by taking the square root of the variance. This is the standard deviation:

$$\text{Standard deviation} = \text{square root of variance} \qquad \textbf{(11.3)}$$
$$= \sqrt{450} = 21\%$$

Because standard deviation is simply the square root of variance, it too is a natural measure of risk. If the outcome of the game had been certain, the standard deviation would have been zero because there would then be no deviations from the expected outcome. The actual standard deviation is positive because we *don't* know what will happen.

Now think of a second game. It is the same as the first except that each head means a 35% gain and each tail means a 25% loss. Again there are four equally likely outcomes:

- Head + Head: You gain 70%
- Head + Tail: You gain 10%
- Tail + Head: You gain 10%
- Tail + Tail: You lose 50%

For this game, the expected return is 10%, the same as that of the first game, but it is more risky. For example, in the first game, the worst possible outcome is a loss of 20%, which is 30% worse than the expected outcome. In the second game the downside is a loss of 50%, or 60% below the expected return. This increased spread of outcomes shows up in the standard deviation, which is double that of the first game, 42% versus 21%. By this measure the second game is twice as risky as the first.

A Note on Calculating Variance

When we calculated variance in Table 11.2, we recorded separately each of the four possible outcomes. An alternative would have been to recognize that in two of the four possible cases the outcomes are the same. In other words, if you were to play the game a large number of times, you would find that on 50% of the occasions the deviation from the expected return is 0%, 25% of the time it is +30%, and the remaining 25% of the time it is −30%. This suggests a simple way to calculate variance: Just weight each squared deviation by its probability:

Self-Test 11.3

Calculate the variance and standard deviation of the second (higher-risk) coin-tossing game.

$$\text{Variance} = \text{sum of squared deviations weighted by probabilities}$$
$$= .25 \times 30^2 + .5 \times 0 + .25 \times (-30)^2 = 450$$

Measuring the Variation in Stock Returns

When estimating the spread of possible outcomes from investing in the stock market, most financial analysts start by assuming that the spread of returns in the past is a reasonable indication of what could happen in the future. Therefore, they calculate the standard deviation of past returns. To illustrate, suppose that you were presented with the data for stock market returns shown in Table 11.3. The average return over the 6 years from 2005 to 2010 was 6.00%. This is just the sum of the returns over the 6 years divided by 6 (36.00/6 = 6.00%).

Column 2 in Table 11.3 shows the difference between each year's return and the average return. For example, in 2010 the return of 17.16% on common stocks was

TABLE 11.3 The average return and standard deviation of stock market returns, 2005–2010

Year	Rate of Return, %	Deviation from Average Return, %	Squared Deviation
2005	6.38	0.38	0.14
2006	15.77	9.77	95.52
2007	5.62	−0.38	0.15
2008	−37.23	−43.23	1,869.23
2009	28.30	22.30	497.48
2010	17.16	11.16	124.65
Total	36.00		2,587.17
Average return = 36.00/6 = 6.00%			
Variance = average of squared deviations = 2,587.17/6 = 431.19			
Standard deviation = square root of variance = 20.77%			

Source: Elroy Dimson, Paul Marsh, and Mike Staunton, *Triumph of the Optimists: 101 Years of Global Investment Returns* (Princeton, NJ: Princeton University Press, 2002). Updates courtesy of *Triumph's* authors.

TABLE 11.4 Standard deviation of returns, 1900–2010

Portfolio	Standard Deviation, %
Treasury bills	2.8
Long-term government bonds	8.6
Common stocks	20.0

Source: Elroy Dimson, Paul Marsh, and Mike Staunton, *Triumph of the Optimists: 101 Years of Global Investment Returns* (Princeton, NJ: Princeton University Press, 2002). Updates courtesy of *Triumph*'s authors.

above the 6-year average by 11.16%. In column 3 we square these deviations from the average. The variance is then the average of these squared deviations:[5]

$$\text{Variance} = \text{average of squared deviations}$$
$$= \frac{2{,}587.17}{6} = 431.19$$

Since standard deviation is the square root of the variance,

$$\text{Standard deviation} = \text{square root of variance}$$
$$= \sqrt{431.19} = 20.77\%$$

It is difficult to measure the risk of securities on the basis of just six past outcomes. Therefore, Table 11.4 lists the annual standard deviations for our three portfolios of securities over the period 1900–2010. As expected, Treasury bills were the least variable security, and common stocks were the most variable. Treasury bonds hold the middle ground.

Of course, there is no reason to believe that the market's variability should stay the same over many years. Indeed many people believe that in recent years the stock market has become more volatile due to irresponsible speculation by . . . (fill in here the name of your preferred guilty party). Figure 11.5 provides a chart of the volatility of the U.S. stock market for each year from 1900 to 2010.[6] Notice how volatility spiked

FIGURE 11.5 Annualized standard deviation of weekly percent changes in the Dow Jones Industrial Average, 1900–2010

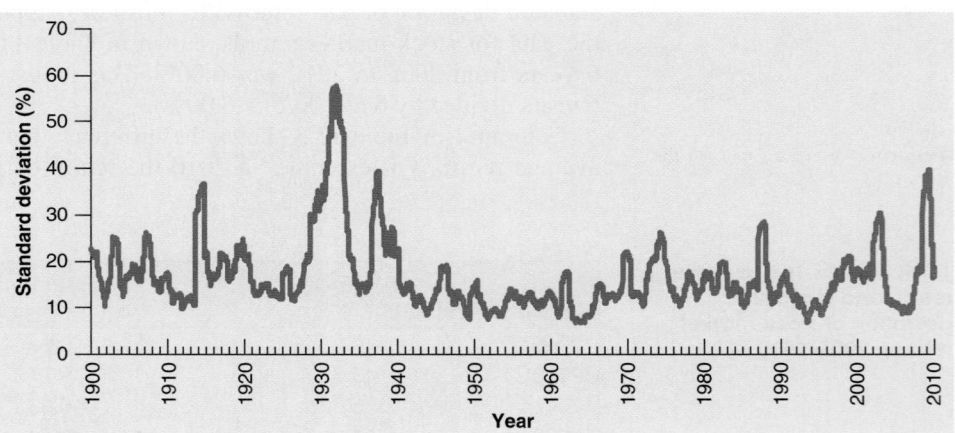

Source: Ibbotson Associates, www.ibbotson.com

---

[5] *Technical note:* When variance is estimated from a sample of observed returns, it is common to add the squared deviations and divide by $N - 1$, rather than N, where N is the number of observations. This procedure adjusts the estimate for what is called *the loss of a degree of freedom*. We will ignore this fine point, emphasizing the interpretation of variance as an average squared deviation. In any event, the correction for the lost degree of freedom is negligible when there are plentiful observations. For example, with 100 years of data, the difference between dividing by 99 or 100 will affect the estimated variance by only 1% (i.e., a factor of 1.01).

[6] We converted the weekly variance to an annual variance by multiplying by 52. In other words, the variance of annual returns is 52 times that of weekly returns. The longer you hold a security, the more risk you have to bear.

upward during the Great Crash of 1929. The past decade has also experienced unusually high volatility as the dot-com boom unwound in 2002 and as the banking crisis reached its climax in 2009. But recent years have also seen some of the most tranquil stock prices. Market volatility, it seems, may rise and fall, but there is little sign of an upward trend.

11.4 Risk and Diversification

Diversification

We can calculate our measures of variability equally well for individual securities and portfolios of securities. Of course, the level of variability over 100 years is less interesting for specific companies than for the market portfolio because it is a rare company that faces the same business risks today as it did a century ago.

Table 11.5 presents estimated standard deviations for some well-known common stocks for a recent 5-year period.[7] The standard deviation of the market portfolio in these years was 16.3%, a little below the long-term average. However, the standard deviation of the returns on most of our stocks was much higher than 16.3%. Most stocks are substantially more variable than the market portfolio; only a handful are less variable.

This raises an important question: The market portfolio is made up of individual stocks, so why isn't its variability equal to the average variability of its components? The answer is that **diversification** *reduces variability*.

Selling umbrellas is a risky business; you may make a killing when it rains, but you are likely to lose your shirt in a heat wave. Selling ice cream is no safer; you do well in the heat wave, but business is poor in the rain. Suppose, however, that you invest in both an umbrella shop and an ice cream shop. By diversifying your investment across the two businesses, you make an average level of profit come rain or shine.

Portfolio diversification works because prices of different stocks do not move exactly together. Statisticians make the same point when they say that stock price changes are less than perfectly correlated. Diversification works best when the returns are negatively correlated, as is the case of our umbrella and

diversification
Strategy designed to reduce risk by spreading the portfolio across many investments.

TABLE 11.5 Standard deviations for selected common stocks, May 2005–April 2010

Ford Motor	77.4%
Dow Chemical	55.5
Amazon.com	49.0
Newmont	38.5
Starbucks	35.8
Dell	35.7
Boeing	30.0
Microsoft	25.5
Disney	23.7
Pfizer	22.0
IBM	20.5
McDonald's	17.7
ExxonMobil	17.6
Campbell Soup	16.9
Walmart	16.6
S&P	16.3
Consolidated Edison	15.9

---

[7] We pointed out earlier that five annual observations are insufficient to give a reliable estimate of variability. Therefore, these estimates are derived from 60 monthly rates of return, and then the monthly variance is multiplied by 12.

ice cream businesses. When one business does well, the other does badly. Unfortunately, in practice, stocks that are negatively correlated are as rare as pecan pie in Budapest.

Asset versus Portfolio Risk

The history of returns on different asset classes provides compelling evidence of a risk–return trade-off and suggests that the variability of the rates of return on each asset class is a useful measure of risk. However, volatility of returns can be a misleading measure of risk for an *individual* asset held as part of a portfolio. To see why, consider the following example.

Suppose there are three equally likely outcomes, or *scenarios,* for the economy: a recession, normal growth, and a boom. An investment in an auto stock will have a rate of return of −8% in a recession, 5% in a normal period, and 18% in a boom. Auto firms are *cyclical:* They do well when the economy does well. In contrast, gold firms are often said to be *countercyclical,* meaning that they do well when other firms do poorly. Suppose that stock in a gold mining firm will provide a rate of return of 20% in a recession, 3% in a normal period, and −20% in a boom. These assumptions are summarized in Table 11.6.

It appears that gold is the more volatile investment. The difference in return across the boom and bust scenarios is 40% (−20% in a boom versus +20% in a recession), compared to a spread of only 26% for the auto stock. In fact, we can confirm the higher volatility by measuring the variance or standard deviation of returns of the two assets. The calculations are set out in Table 11.7.

Since all three scenarios are equally likely, the expected return on each stock is simply the average of the three possible outcomes.[8] For the auto stock the expected

TABLE 11.6 Rate of return assumptions for two stocks

Scenario	Probability	Rate of Return, %	
		Auto Stock	Gold Stock
Recession	1/3	−8	+20
Normal	1/3	+5	+3
Boom	1/3	+18	−20

TABLE 11.7 Expected return and volatility for two stocks

Scenario	Auto Stock			Gold Stock		
	Rate of Return, %	Deviation from Expected Return, %	Squared Deviation	Rate of Return, %	Deviation from Expected Return, %	Squared Deviation
Recession	−8	−13	169	+20	+19	361
Normal	+5	0	0	+3	+2	4
Boom	+18	+13	169	−20	−21	441
Expected return	$\frac{1}{3}(-8 + 5 + 18) = 5\%$			$\frac{1}{3}(+20 + 3 - 20) = 1\%$		
Variance*	$\frac{1}{3}(169 + 0 + 169) = 112.7$			$\frac{1}{3}(361 + 4 + 441) = 268.7$		
Standard deviation (=√variance)	$\sqrt{112.7} = 10.6\%$			$\sqrt{268.7} = 16.4\%$		

*Variance = average of squared deviations from the expected value.

---

[8] If the probabilities were not equal, we would need to weight each outcome by its probability in calculating the expected outcome and the variance.

return is 5%; for the gold stock it is 1%. The variance is the average of the squared deviations from the expected return, and the standard deviation is the square root of the variance.

Self-Test 11.4

Suppose the probability of the recession or boom is .30, while the probability of a normal period is .40. Would you expect the variance of returns on these two investments to be higher or lower? Why? Confirm by calculating the standard deviation of the auto stock. (Refer back to Section 11.3 if you are unsure of how to do this.)

The gold mining stock offers a lower expected rate of return than the auto stock and *more* volatility—a loser on both counts, right? Would anyone be willing to hold gold mining stocks in an investment portfolio? The answer is a resounding yes.

To see why, suppose you do believe that gold is a lousy asset, and therefore you hold your entire portfolio in the auto stock. Your expected return is 5% and your standard deviation is 10.6%. We'll compare that portfolio to a partially diversified one, invested 75% in autos and 25% in gold. For example, if you have a $10,000 portfolio, you could put $7,500 in autos and $2,500 in gold.

First, we need to calculate the return on this portfolio in each scenario. The portfolio return is the weighted average of returns on the individual assets with weights equal to the proportion of the portfolio invested in each asset. For a portfolio formed from only two assets,

$$\text{Portfolio rate of return} = \left(\begin{array}{c} \text{fraction of portfolio} \\ \text{in first asset} \end{array} \times \begin{array}{c} \text{rate of return} \\ \text{on first asset} \end{array} \right) \quad (11.4)$$
$$+ \left(\begin{array}{c} \text{fraction of portfolio} \\ \text{in second asset} \end{array} \times \begin{array}{c} \text{rate of return} \\ \text{on second asset} \end{array} \right)$$

For example, autos have a weight of .75 and a rate of return of −8% in the recession, and gold has a weight of .25 and a return of 20% in a recession. Therefore, the portfolio return in the recession is the following weighted average:[9]

$$\text{Portfolio return in recession} = [.75 \times (-8\%)] + (.25 \times 20\%)$$
$$= -1\%$$

Table 11.8 expands Table 11.6 to include the portfolio of the auto stock and the gold mining stock. The expected returns and volatility measures are summarized at the bottom of the table. The surprising finding is this: When you shift part of your funds from the auto stock to the more volatile gold mining stock, your portfolio variability actually *decreases*. In fact, the volatility of the auto-plus-gold stock portfolio is considerably less than the volatility of *either* stock separately. This is the payoff to diversification.

We can understand this more clearly by focusing on asset returns in the two extreme scenarios, boom and recession. In the boom, when auto stocks do best, the poor return on gold reduces the performance of the overall portfolio. However, when auto stocks are stalling in a recession, gold shines, providing a substantial positive return that boosts portfolio performance. The gold stock offsets the swings in the

[9] Let's confirm this. Suppose you invest $7,500 in autos and $2,500 in gold. If the recession hits, the rate of return on autos will be −8%, and the value of the auto investment will fall by 8% to $6,900. The rate of return on gold will be 20%, and the value of the gold investment will rise 20% to $3,000. The value of the total portfolio falls from its original value of $10,000 to $6,900 + $3,000 = $9,900, which is a rate of return of −1%. This matches the rate of return given by the formula for the weighted average.

TABLE 11.8 Rates of return for two stocks and a portfolio

Scenario	Probability	Rate of Return, %		Portfolio Return, %*
		Auto Stock	**Gold Stock**	
Recession	1/3	−8	+20	−1.0
Normal	1/3	+5	+3	+4.5
Boom	1/3	+18	−20	+8.5
Expected return		5	1	4
Variance		112.7	268.7	15.2
Standard deviation		10.6	16.4	3.9

* Portfolio return = (.75 × auto stock return) + (.25 × gold stock return)

performance of the auto stock, reducing the best-case return but improving the worst-case return. The inverse relationship between the returns on the two stocks means that returns are more stable when the gold mining stock is added to an all-auto portfolio.

A gold stock is really a *negative-risk* asset to an investor starting with an all-auto portfolio. Adding it to the portfolio reduces the volatility of returns. The *incremental* risk of the gold stock (that is, the *change* in overall risk when gold is added to the portfolio) is *negative* despite the fact that gold returns are highly volatile.

In general, the incremental risk of a stock depends on whether its returns tend to vary with or against the returns of the other assets in the portfolio. Incremental risk does not just depend on a stock's volatility. If returns do not move closely with those of the rest of the portfolio, the stock will reduce the volatility of portfolio returns.

We can summarize as follows:

1. Investors care about the expected return and risk of their *portfolio* of assets. The risk of the overall portfolio can be measured by the volatility of returns, that is, the variance or standard deviation.
2. The standard deviation of the returns of an individual security measures how risky that security would be if held in isolation. But an investor who holds a portfolio of securities is interested only in how each security affects the risk of the entire portfolio. The contribution of a security to the risk of the portfolio depends on how the security's returns vary with the investor's other holdings. Thus a security that is risky if held in isolation may nevertheless serve to reduce the variability of the portfolio if its returns do not move in lockstep with the rest of the portfolio.

EXAMPLE 11.1 ▶ Ford and Newmont Mining

Our example of the auto and gold mining stocks was entirely fanciful. But we can make the same point by looking at two real auto and gold mining companies, Ford Motor and Newmont Mining. We will focus on a period in which the two stocks had roughly similar standard deviations. Suppose that in April 2005 you invested your savings in the stock of Ford. The orange line in Figure 11.6 shows how the value of your portfolio would have fluctuated over the following 40 months. The risk shows up in the wide spread of monthly returns. For example, there were 7 months when you would have lost more than 10% of your capital. The standard deviation of Ford's returns during this period amounted to 30.4% a year.

The blue line in Figure 11.6 shows a similar picture of the performance of Newmont Mining stock over the same period. The fluctuations in this stock were only slightly less than those of Ford. The standard deviation of the returns on Newmont stock was 29.6% a year.

FIGURE 11.6 The values of investments in the stock of Newmont Mining or Ford have been very variable. But the two stocks have not moved in lockstep. Investors could have reduced variability by dividing their money equally between the two stocks.

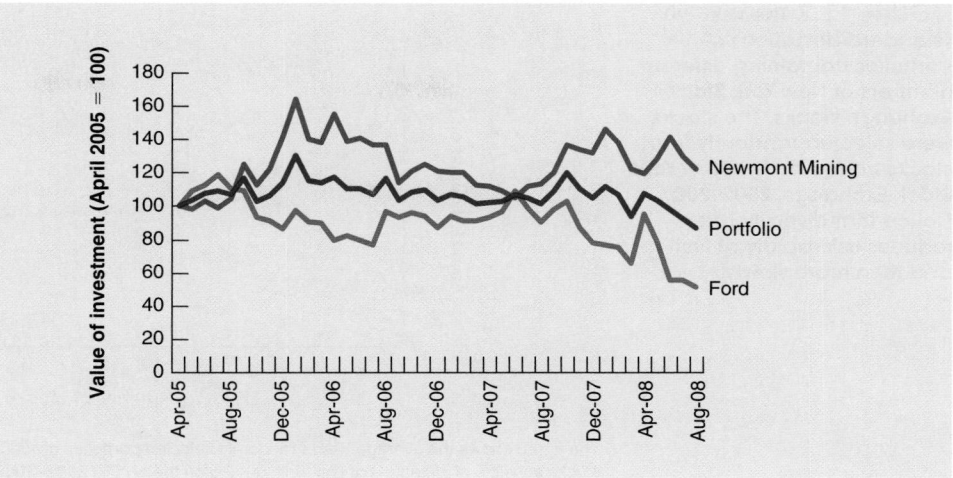

Although both stocks had their ups and downs, the two stocks have not moved in exact lockstep.[10] As often as not, a decline in the value of one stock was offset by a rise in the price of the other. So if you had split your portfolio between the two stocks, you could have reduced the monthly fluctuations in the value of your savings. You can see from the green line in Figure 11.6 that if your portfolio had been evenly divided between Ford and Newmont Mining, there would have been many more months when the return was just middling and far fewer cases of extreme returns. Take April 2006, for example. This was a fairly poor month for investors in Ford; its stock price fell that month by 11.4%. Fortunately, the price of Newmont rose by 12.5%, leaving the value of your combined holding little changed. By diversifying between the two stocks, you would have reduced the standard deviation of the returns on your investment to 23.3% a year.

Self-Test 11.5

An investor is currently fully invested in gold mining stocks. Which action would do more to reduce portfolio risk: diversification into silver mining stocks or into automotive stocks? Why?

Market Risk versus Specific Risk

Our examples illustrate that even a little diversification can provide a substantial reduction in variability. Suppose you calculate and compare the standard deviations of randomly chosen one-stock portfolios, two-stock portfolios, five-stock portfolios, and so on. You can see from Figure 11.7 that diversification can cut the variability of returns by about half. But you can get most of this benefit with relatively few stocks: The improvement is slight when the number of stocks is increased beyond, say, 20 or 30.

---

[10] Statisticians calculate a *correlation coefficient* as a measure of how closely two series move together. If Ford's and Newmont's stock moved in perfect lockstep, the correlation coefficient between the returns would be 1.0. If their returns were completely unrelated, the correlation would be zero. If the returns on two stocks tend to move inversely, that is, if one stock usually is up when the other is down, the correlation coefficient will be negative. If returns move in perfect but inverse lockstep, the correlation coefficient will be −1.0. But negative correlations are unusual. Because most firms have a common dependence on the overall economy, correlations between stock returns are typically positive. The correlation between the returns on Ford and Newmont Mining was .21.

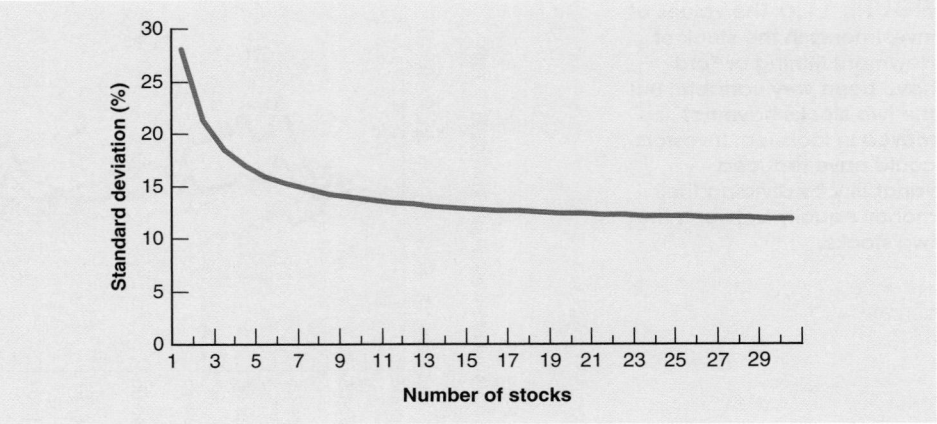

The figure shows the average risk of randomly selected portfolios divided equally among *N* stocks. The group of stocks consists of all those continuously quoted on the NYSE, 2002–2007.

Figure 11.7 also illustrates that no matter how many securities you hold, you cannot eliminate all risk. There remains the danger that the market—including your portfolio—will plummet.

The risk that can be eliminated by diversification is called **specific risk.** The risk that you can't avoid regardless of how much you diversify is generally known as **market risk** or *systematic risk.* *Specific risk* **arises because many of the perils that surround an individual company are peculiar to that company and perhaps its direct competitors.** *Market risk* **stems from economywide perils that threaten all businesses. Market risk explains why stocks have a tendency to move together, so even well-diversified portfolios are exposed to market movements.**

Figure 11.8 divides risk into its two parts—specific risk and market risk. If you have only a single stock, specific risk is very important; but once you have a portfolio of 30 or more stocks, diversification has done most of what it can to eliminate risk. **For a reasonably well-diversified portfolio, only market risk matters.**

specific risk
Risk factors affecting
only that firm. Also
called *diversifiable risk.*

market risk
Economywide
(macroeconomic)
sources of risk that affect
the overall stock market.
Also called *systematic risk.*

11.5 Thinking about Risk

How can you tell which risks are specific and diversifiable? Where do market risks come from? Here are three messages to help you think clearly about risk.

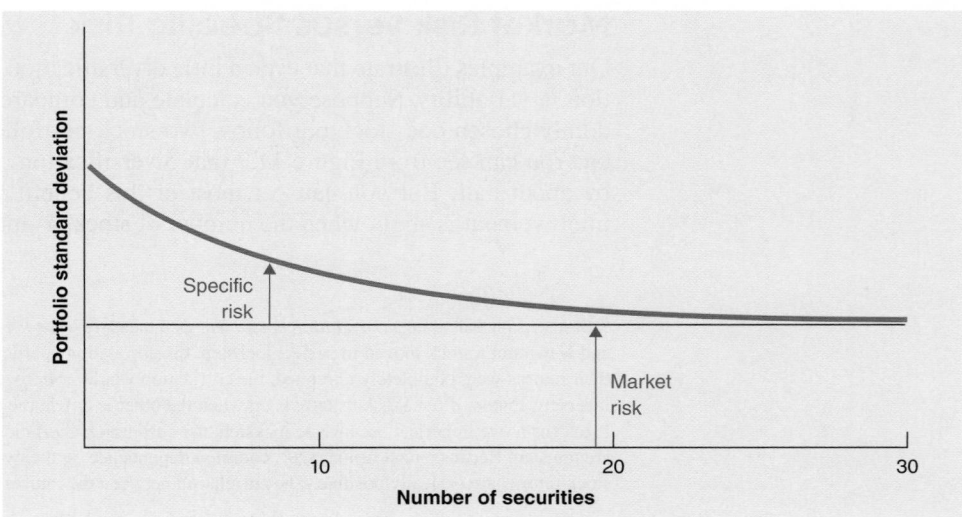

Message 1: Some Risks Look Big and Dangerous but Really Are Diversifiable

Managers confront risks "up close and personal." They must make decisions about particular investments. The failure of such an investment could cost a promotion, bonus, or otherwise steady job. Yet that same investment may not seem risky to an investor who can stand back and combine it in a diversified portfolio with many other assets or securities.

EXAMPLE 11.2 ▶ Wildcat Oil Wells

You have just been promoted to director of exploration, Western Hemisphere, of MPS Oil. The manager of your exploration team in far-off Costaguana has appealed for $20 million extra to drill in an even steamier part of the Costaguanan jungle. The manager thinks there may be an "elephant" field worth $500 million or more hidden there. But the chance of finding it is at best 1 in 10, and yesterday MPS's CEO sourly commented on the $100 million already "wasted" on Costaguanan exploration.

Is this a risky investment? For you it probably is; you may be a hero if oil is found and a goat otherwise. But MPS drills hundreds of wells worldwide; for the company as a whole, it's the *average* success rate that matters. Geologic risks (is there oil or not?) should average out. The risk of a worldwide drilling program is much less than the apparent risk of any single wildcat well.

Back up one step, and think of the investors who buy MPS stock. The investors may hold other oil companies too, as well as companies producing steel, computers, clothing, cement, and breakfast cereal. They naturally—and realistically—assume that your successes and failures in drilling oil wells will average out with the thousands of independent bets made by the companies in their portfolio.

Therefore, the risks you face in Costaguana do not affect the rate of return they demand for investing in MPS Oil. Diversified investors in MPS stock will be happy if you find that elephant field, but they probably will not notice if you fail and lose your job. In any case, they will not demand a higher *average* rate of return for worrying about geologic risks in Costaguana.

EXAMPLE 11.3 ▶ Fire Insurance

Would you be willing to write a $100,000 fire insurance policy on your neighbor's house? The neighbor is willing to pay you $100 for a year's protection, and experience shows that the chance of fire damage in a given year is substantially less than 1 in 1,000. But if your neighbor's house is damaged by fire, you would have to pay up.

Few of us have deep enough pockets to insure our neighbors, even if the odds of fire damage are very low. Insurance seems a risky business if you think policy by policy. But a large insurance company, which may issue a million policies, is concerned only with average losses, which can be predicted with excellent accuracy.

Self-Test 11.6

Imagine a laboratory at IBM, late at night. One scientist speaks to another.

"You're right, Watson, I admit this experiment will consume all the rest of this year's budget. I don't know what we'll do if it fails. But if this yttrium–magnoosium alloy superconducts, the patents will be worth millions."

Would this be a good or bad investment for IBM? Can't say. But from the ultimate investors' viewpoint this is *not* a risky investment. Explain why.

Message 2: Market Risks Are Macro Risks

We have seen that diversified portfolios are not exposed to the specific risks of individual stocks but are exposed to the uncertain events that affect the entire securities market and the entire economy. These are macroeconomic, or "macro," factors such as changes in interest rates, industrial production, inflation, foreign exchange rates, and energy costs. These factors affect most firms' earnings and stock prices. When the relevant macro risks turn generally favorable, stock prices rise and investors do well; when the same variables go the other way, investors suffer.

You can often assess relative market risks just by thinking through exposures to the business cycle and other macro variables. The following businesses have substantial macro and market risks:

- *Airlines.* Because business travel falls during a recession, and individuals postpone vacations and other discretionary travel, the airline industry is subject to the swings of the business cycle. On the positive side, airline profits really take off when business is booming and personal incomes are rising.
- *Machine tool manufacturers.* These businesses are especially exposed to the business cycle. Manufacturing companies that have excess capacity rarely buy new machine tools to expand. During recessions, excess capacity can be quite high.

Here, on the other hand, are two industries with less than average macro exposures:

- *Food companies.* Companies selling staples, such as breakfast cereal, flour, and dog food, find that demand for their products is relatively stable in good times and bad.
- *Electric utilities.* Business demand for electric power varies somewhat across the business cycle, but by much less than demand for air travel or machine tools. Also, many electric utilities' profits are regulated. Regulation cuts off upside profit potential but also gives the utilities the opportunity to increase prices when demand is slack.

Remember, investors holding diversified portfolios are mostly concerned with macroeconomic risks. They do not worry about microeconomic risks peculiar to a particular company or investment project. Micro risks wash out in diversified portfolios. Company managers may worry about both macro and micro risks, but only the former affect the cost of capital.

Self-Test 11.7

Which company of each of the following pairs would you expect to be more exposed to macro risks?

a. A luxury Manhattan restaurant or an established Burger Queen franchise?
b. A paint company that sells through small paint and hardware stores to do-it-yourselfers or a paint company that sells in large volumes to Ford, GM, and Chrysler?

Message 3: Risk Can Be Measured

Delta Airlines clearly has more exposure to macro risks than food companies such as Kellogg or General Mills. These are easy cases. But is IBM stock a riskier investment than ExxonMobil? That's not an easy question to reason through. We can, however, *measure* the risk of IBM and ExxonMobil by looking at how their stock prices fluctuate.

We've already hinted at how to do this. Remember that diversified investors are concerned with market risks. The movements of the stock market sum up the net effects of all relevant macroeconomic uncertainties. If the market portfolio of all traded stocks is up in a particular month, we conclude that the net effect of macroeconomic news is positive. Remember, the performance of the market is barely affected by a firm-specific event. These cancel out across thousands of stocks in the market.

How do we measure the risk of a single stock, like IBM or ExxonMobil? We do not look at the stocks in isolation, because the risks that loom when you're up close to a single company are often diversifiable. Instead we measure the individual stock's sensitivity to the fluctuations of the overall stock market. We will show you how this works in the next chapter.

SUMMARY

How can one estimate the opportunity cost of capital for an "average-risk" project? *(LO1)*

Over the past century the return on the **Standard & Poor's Composite Index** of common stocks has averaged 7.4% a year higher than the return on safe Treasury bills. This is the **risk premium** that investors have received for taking on the risk of investing in stocks. Long-term bonds have offered a higher return than Treasury bills but less than stocks.

If the risk premium in the past is a guide to the future, we can estimate the expected return on the market today by adding that 7.4% expected risk premium to today's interest rate on Treasury bills. This would be the opportunity cost of capital for an average-risk project, that is, one with the same risk as a typical share of common stock.

How is the standard deviation of returns for individual common stocks or for a stock portfolio calculated? *(LO2)*

The spread of outcomes on different investments is commonly measured by the **variance** or **standard deviation** of the possible outcomes. The variance is the average of the squared deviations around the average outcome, and the standard deviation is the square root of the variance. The standard deviation of the returns on a market portfolio of common stocks has averaged around 20% a year.

Why does diversification reduce risk? *(LO3)*

The standard deviation of returns is generally higher on individual stocks than it is on the market. Because individual stocks do not move in exact lockstep, much of their risk can be diversified away. By spreading your portfolio across many investments, you smooth out the risk of your overall position. The risk that can be eliminated through diversification is known as **specific risk.**

What is the difference between specific risk, which can be diversified away, and market risk, which cannot? *(LO4)*

Even if you hold a well-diversified portfolio, you will not eliminate all risk. You will still be exposed to macroeconomic changes that affect most stocks and the overall stock market. These macro risks combine to create **market risk**—that is, the risk that the market as a whole will slump.

Stocks are not all equally risky. But what do we mean by a "high-risk stock"? We don't mean a stock that is risky if held in isolation; we mean a stock that makes an above-average contribution to the risk of a diversified portfolio. In other words, investors don't need to worry much about the risk that they can diversify away; they *do* need to worry about risk that can't be diversified. This depends on the stock's sensitivity to macroeconomic conditions.

LISTING OF EQUATIONS

11.1 $\text{Percentage return} = \dfrac{\text{capital gain} + \text{dividend}}{\text{initial share price}}$

11.2 Variance = average of squared deviations around the average

11.3 Standard deviation = square root of variance

11.4 Portfolio rate of return $=$ $\left(\begin{array}{c}\text{fraction of portfolio} \\ \text{in first asset}\end{array} \times \begin{array}{c}\text{rate of return} \\ \text{on first asset}\end{array}\right)$

$+ \left(\begin{array}{c}\text{fraction of portfolio} \\ \text{in second asset}\end{array} \times \begin{array}{c}\text{rate of return} \\ \text{on second asset}\end{array}\right)$

QUESTIONS

|FINANCE

QUIZ

1. **Rate of Return.** A stock is selling today for $40 per share. At the end of the year, it pays a dividend of $2 per share and sells for $44. What is the total rate of return on the stock? What are the dividend yield and percentage capital gain? (*LO2*)

2. **Rate of Return.** Return to Quiz Question 1. Suppose the year-end stock price after the dividend is paid is $36. What are the dividend yield and percentage capital gain in this case? Why is the dividend yield unaffected? (*LO2*)

3. **Real versus Nominal Returns.** You purchase 100 shares of stock for $40 a share. The stock pays a $2 per share dividend at year-end. What is the rate of return on your investment for the end-of-year stock prices listed below? What is your real (inflation-adjusted) rate of return? Assume an inflation rate of 4%. (*LO2*)

    a. $38
    b. $40
    c. $42

4. **Real versus Nominal Returns.** The Costaguanan stock market provided a rate of return of 95%. The inflation rate in Costaguana during the year was 80%. In the United States, in contrast, the stock market return was only 12%, but the inflation rate was only 2%. Which country's stock market provided the higher real rate of return? (*LO2*)

5. **Real versus Nominal Returns.** The inflation rate in the United States has averaged 3.1% a year since 1900. What was the average real rate of return on Treasury bills, Treasury bonds, and common stocks in that period? Use the data in Table 11.1. (*LO2*)

6. **Real versus Nominal Returns.** Do you think it is possible for risk-free Treasury bills to offer a negative nominal interest rate? Might they offer a negative real expected rate of return? (*LO2*)

7. **Market Indexes.** The accompanying table shows annual stock prices on the Costaguanan Stock Exchange for 2005–2010. Construct two stock market indexes, one using weights as in the Dow Jones Industrial Average, the other using weights as in the Standard & Poor's Composite Index. (*LO2*)

Annual prices in Costaguanan pegos for trading on the Sulaco Stock Exchange (Only five stocks were traded at the start of 2005.)					
	San Tomé Mining, 184 million*	**Sulaco Markets, 42 million***	**National Central Railway, 64 million***	**Minerva Shipping, 38 million***	**Azuera, Inc., 16 million***
2005	55.10	80.00	21.45	82.50	135.00
2006	58.15	144.62	24.04	115.52	151.22
2007	58.45	135.93	26.53	138.90	166.99
2008	52.43	74.61	23.53	121.02	149.42
2009	52.50	75.01	32.46	174.62	177.27
2010	54.82	67.22	34.48	164.48	165.52

* Number of shares outstanding.

8. **Stock Market History.** (*LO1*)

    a. What was the average rate of return on large U.S. common stocks from 1900 to 2010?
    b. What was the average risk premium on large stocks?
    c. What was the standard deviation of returns on the market portfolio?

PRACTICE PROBLEMS

9. **Risk Premiums.** Here are stock market and Treasury bill percentage returns between 2006 and 2010: (*LO1*)

Year	Stock Market Return	T-Bill Return
2006	15.77	4.80
2007	5.61	4.66
2008	−37.23	1.60
2009	28.30	0.10
2010	17.16	0.12

   a. What was the risk premium on common stock in each year?
   b. What was the average risk premium?
   c. What was the standard deviation of the risk premium?

10. **Market Indexes.** In 1990, the Dow Jones Industrial Average was at a level of about 2,600. In 2010, it was about 10,000. Would you expect the Dow in 2010 to be more or less likely to move up or down by more than 40 points in a day than in 1990? Does this mean the market was riskier in 2010 than it was in 1990? (*LO2*)

11. **Maturity Premiums.** Investments in long-term government bonds produced a negative average return during the period 1977–1981. How should we interpret this? Did bond investors in 1977 expect to earn a negative maturity premium? What do these 5 years' bond returns tell us about the normal future maturity premium? (*LO1*)

12. **Risk Premiums.** What will happen to the opportunity cost of capital if investors suddenly become especially conservative and less willing to bear investment risk? (*LO1*)

13. **Risk Premiums and Discount Rates.** Top hedge fund manager Diana Sauros believes that a stock with the same market risk as the S&P 500 will sell at year-end at a price of $50. The stock will pay a dividend at year-end of $2. What price should she be willing to pay for the stock today? (*Hint:* Start by checking today's 1-year Treasury rates.) (*LO1*)

14. **Scenario Analysis.** The common stock of Leaning Tower of Pita, Inc., a restaurant chain, will generate the following payoffs to investors next year: (*LO2*)

	Dividend	Stock Price
Boom	$8	$240
Normal economy	4	90
Recession	0	0

   The company goes out of business if a recession hits. Calculate the expected rate of return and standard deviation of return to Leaning Tower of Pita shareholders. Assume for simplicity that the three possible states of the economy are equally likely. The stock is selling today for $80.

15. **Portfolio Risk.** Who would view the stock of Leaning Tower of Pita (see Practice Problem 14) as a risk-reducing investment—the owner of a gambling casino or a successful bankruptcy lawyer? Explain. (*LO3*)

16. **Scenario Analysis.** The common stock of Escapist Films sells for $25 a share and offers the following payoffs next year: (*LO3*)

	Dividend	Stock Price
Boom	0	$18
Normal economy	$1	26
Recession	3	34

   Calculate the expected return and standard deviation of Escapist. All three scenarios are equally likely. Then calculate the expected return and standard deviation of a portfolio half invested in Escapist and half in Leaning Tower of Pita (from Practice Problem 14). Show that the portfolio standard deviation is lower than either stock's. Explain why this happens.

17. **Scenario Analysis.** Consider the following scenario analysis: (*LO2*)

		Rate of Return	
Scenario	Probability	Stocks	Bonds
Recession	.20	−5%	+14%
Normal economy	.60	+15	+8
Boom	.20	+25	+4

   a. Is it reasonable to assume that Treasury bonds will provide higher returns in recessions than in booms?
   b. Calculate the expected rate of return and standard deviation for each investment.
   c. Which investment would *you* prefer?

18. **Portfolio Analysis.** Use the data in the previous problem and consider a portfolio with weights of .60 in stocks and .40 in bonds. (*LO3*)

   a. What is the rate of return on the portfolio in each scenario?
   b. What are the expected rate of return and standard deviation of the portfolio?
   c. Would you prefer to invest in the portfolio, in stocks only, or in bonds only?

19. **Risk Premium.** If the stock market return next year turns out to be −20%, what will happen to our estimate of the "normal" risk premium? Does this make sense? (*LO1*)

20. **Diversification.** In which of the following situations would you get the largest reduction in risk by spreading your portfolio across two stocks? (*LO3*)

   a. The stock returns vary with each other.
   b. The stock returns are independent.
   c. The stock returns vary against each other.

21. **Market Risk.** Which firms of each pair below would you expect to have greater market risk? (*LO4*)

   a. General Steel or General Food Supplies.
   b. Club Med or General Cinemas.

22. **Risk and Return.** A stock will provide a rate of return of either −18% or +26%.

   a. If both possibilities are equally likely, calculate the expected return and standard deviation. (*LO2*)
   b. If Treasury bills yield 4% and investors believe that the stock offers a satisfactory expected return, what must the market risk of the stock be? (*LO4*)

23. **Specific versus Market Risk.** Sassafras Oil is staking all its remaining capital on wildcat exploration off the Côte d'Huile. There is a 10% chance of discovering a field with reserves of 50 million barrels. If it finds oil, it will immediately sell the reserves to Big Oil, at a price depending on the state of the economy. Thus the possible payoffs are as follows: (*LO4*)

	Value of Reserves, per Barrel	Value of Reserves, 50 Million Barrels	Value of Dryholes
Boom	$4	$200,000,000	0
Normal economy	5	250,000,000	0
Recession	6	300,000,000	0

   Is Sassafras Oil a risky investment for a diversified investor in the stock market—compared, say, to the stock of Leaning Tower of Pita, described in Practice Problem 14? Explain.

24. **Diversification.** Go to our Online Learning Center at www.mhhe.com/bmm7e, and link to the material for Chapter 11, where you will find a spreadsheet containing 5 years of monthly rates of return on ExxonMobil (XOM), BP, and Walmart (WMT). (*LO3*)

   a. What was the average return and standard deviation of returns for each firm?
   b. What was the correlation of returns between each pair of firms? Try using Excel's CORREL function, which calculates the correlation between two series of numbers. Which pair of firms exhibits the highest correlation of returns? Is this surprising?
   c. Now imagine that you held an equally weighted portfolio of ExxonMobil and Walmart (that is, a portfolio with equal dollar investments in each stock). Compute the portfolio's rate of

return for each month, and calculate the standard deviation of the portfolio's monthly rate of return. How does the portfolio standard deviation compare to the average of the standard deviations of each component stock?

d. Repeat part (c), but this time calculate the results for a portfolio of BP and ExxonMobil. Comparing your answers to (c) and (d), which pair of firms provides greater benefits from diversification? Relate your answer to the correlation coefficients you found in part (a).

WEB EXERCISES

1. Go to finance.yahoo.com, and find the monthly rates of return over a 2-year period for five companies of your choice. Now assume you form each month an equally weighted portfolio of the five firms (i.e., a portfolio with equal investments in each firm). What is the rate of return each month on your portfolio? Compare the standard deviation of the monthly portfolio return to that of each firm and to the average standard deviation across the five firms. What do you conclude about portfolio diversification?

2. Return to the monthly returns of the five companies you chose in the previous question.

   a. Using the Excel functions for average (AVERAGE) and sample standard deviation (STDEV), calculate the average and the standard deviation of the returns for each of the firms.

   b. Using Excel's correlation function (CORREL), find the correlations between each pair of five stocks. What are the highest and lowest correlations?

   c. Try finding correlations between pairs of stocks in the same industry. Are the correlations higher than those you found in part (b)? Is this surprising?

3. A large mutual-fund group such as Fidelity offers a variety of funds. Some, called *sector funds,* specialize in particular industries; others, known as *index funds,* simply invest in the market index. Log on to www.fidelity.com and look up the standard deviation of returns on the Fidelity Spartan 500 Index Fund, which replicates the S&P 500. Now find the standard deviation of fund returns for different industry (sector) funds. Are they larger or smaller than the index fund? How do you interpret your findings?

SOLUTIONS TO SELF-TEST QUESTIONS

11.1 The bond price at the end of the year is $1,050. Therefore, the capital gain on each bond is $1,050 − $1,020 = $30. Your dollar return is the sum of the income from the bond, $80, plus the capital gain, $30, or $110. The rate of return is

$$\frac{\text{Income plus capital gain}}{\text{Original price}} = \frac{80 + 30}{1,020} = .108, \text{ or } 10.8\%$$

Real rate of return is

$$\frac{1 + \text{nominal return}}{1 + \text{inflation rate}} - 1 = \frac{1.108}{1.04} - 1 = .065, \text{ or } 6.5\%$$

11.2 The risk premium on stocks is the average return in excess of Treasury bills. It was 4.4% in period 1, 9.1% in period 2, 7.6% in period 3, and 8.1% in period 4.

11.3

Rate of Return	Deviation	Squared Deviation
+70%	+60%	3,600
+10	0	0
+10	0	0
−50	−60	3,600
Variance = average of squared deviations = 7,200/4 = 1,800		
Standard deviation = square root of variance = $\sqrt{1,800}$ = 42.4, about 42%		

11.4   The standard deviation should decrease because there is now a lower probability of the more extreme outcomes. The expected rate of return on the auto stock is now

$$[.3 \times (-8\%)] + (.4 \times 5\%) + (.3 \times 18\%) = 5\%$$

The variance is

$$[.3 \times (-8 - 5)^2] + [.4 \times (5 - 5)^2] + [.3 \times (18 - 5)^2] = 101.4$$

The standard deviation is $\sqrt{101.4} = 10.07\%$, which is lower than the value assuming equal probabilities of each scenario.

11.5   The gold mining stock's returns are more highly correlated with the silver mining company than with a car company. As a result, the automotive firm will offer a greater diversification benefit. The power of diversification is lowest when rates of return are highly correlated, performing well or poorly in tandem. Shifting part of the portfolio from one such firm to another has little impact on overall risk.

11.6   The success of this project depends on the experiment. Success does *not* depend on the performance of the overall economy. The experiment creates a diversifiable risk. A portfolio of many stocks will embody "bets" on many such specific risks. Some bets will work out and some will fail. Because the outcomes of these risks do not depend on common factors, such as the overall state of the economy, the risks will tend to cancel out in a well-diversified portfolio.

11.7   a.   The luxury restaurant will be more sensitive to the state of the economy because expense account meals will be curtailed in a recession. Burger Queen meals should be relatively recession-proof.

b.   The paint company that sells to the auto producers will be more sensitive to the state of the economy. In a downturn, auto sales fall dramatically as consumers stretch the lives of their cars. In contrast, in a recession, more people "do it themselves," which makes paint sales through small stores more stable and less sensitive to the economy.

CHAPTER 12

Risk, Return, and Capital Budgeting

LEARNING OBJECTIVES

After studying this chapter, you should be able to:

(1) Measure and interpret the market risk, or beta, of a security.

(2) Relate the market risk of a security to the rate of return that investors demand.

(3) Calculate the opportunity cost of capital for a project.

RELATED WEB SITES FOR THIS CHAPTER CAN BE FOUND AT WWW.MHHE.COM/BMM7E.

In Chapter 11 we began to come to grips with the topic of risk. We made the distinction between *specific* risk and macro, or *market,* risk. Specific risk arises from events that affect only the individual firm or its immediate competitors; it can be eliminated by diversification. But regardless of how much you diversify, you cannot avoid the macroeconomic events that create market risk. This is why investors do not require a higher rate of return to compensate for specific risk but do need a higher return to persuade them to take on market risk.

How can you measure the market risk of a security or a project? We will see that market risk is usually measured by the sensitivity of the investment's returns to fluctuations in the market. We will also see that the risk premium investors demand should be proportional to this sensitivity. This relationship between risk and return is a useful way to estimate the return that investors expect from investing in common stocks.

Finally, we will distinguish between the risk of the company's securities and the risk of an individual project. We will also consider what

Professor William F. Sharpe receiving the Nobel Prize in Economics.   The prize was for Sharpe's development of the capital asset pricing model. This model shows how risk should be measured and provides a formula relating risk to the opportunity cost of capital.

managers should do when the risk of the project is different from that of the company's existing business.

12.1   Measuring Market Risk

market portfolio
Portfolio of all assets in the economy. In practice a broad stock market index is used to represent the market.

beta
Sensitivity of a stock's return to the return on the market portfolio.

Changes in interest rates, government spending, oil prices, foreign exchange rates, and other macroeconomic events affect almost all companies and the returns on almost all stocks. We can therefore assess the impact of "macro" news by tracking the rate of return on a **market portfolio** of all securities. If the market is up on a particular day, then the net impact of macroeconomic changes must be positive. We know the performance of the market reflects only macro events, because firm-specific events—that is, specific risks—average out when we look at the combined performance of thousands of companies and securities.

In principle the market portfolio should contain all assets in the world economy—not just stocks but bonds, foreign securities, real estate, and so on. In practice, however, financial analysts make do with indexes of the stock market, such as the Standard & Poor's Composite Index (the S&P 500).[1]

Our task here is to define and measure the risk of *individual* common stocks. You can probably see where we are headed. Risk depends on exposure to macroeconomic events and can be measured as the sensitivity of a stock's returns to fluctuations in returns on the market portfolio. This sensitivity is called the stock's **beta.** Beta is often written as the Greek letter β.

Measuring Beta

In the last chapter we looked at the variability of several individual securities. Dow Chemical had one of the highest standard deviations, and Consolidated Edison had the lowest. If you had held Dow Chemical on its own, your returns would have varied nearly four times as much as they would have if you had held Con Ed. But wise investors don't put all their eggs in just one basket: They reduce their risk by diversification. An investor with a diversified portfolio will be interested in the effect each stock has on the risk of the entire portfolio.

Diversification can eliminate the risk that is unique to individual stocks but not the risk that the market as a whole may decline, carrying your stocks with it.

Some stocks are less affected than others by market fluctuations. Investment managers talk about "defensive" and "aggressive" stocks. Defensive stocks are not very sensitive to market fluctuations and therefore have low betas. In contrast, aggressive stocks amplify any market movements and have higher betas. If the market goes up, it is good to be in aggressive stocks; if it goes down, it is better to be in defensive stocks (and better still to have your money in the bank).

Aggressive stocks have high betas, betas greater than 1.0, meaning that their returns tend to respond more than one for one to changes in the return of the overall market. The betas of defensive stocks are less than 1.0. The returns of these stocks vary less than one for one with market returns. The average beta of all stocks is—no surprises here—1.0 exactly.

Now we'll show you how betas are measured.

EXAMPLE 12.1 ▶	Measuring Beta for Turbot-Charged Seafoods

Suppose we look back at the trading history of Turbot-Charged Seafoods and pick out 6 months when the return on the market portfolio was plus or minus 1%.

Month	Market Return, %	Turbot-Charged Seafood's Return, %	
1	+1	+ .8	
2	+1	+1.8	Average = .8%
3	+1	− .2	
4	−1	−1.8	
5	−1	+ .2	Average = −.8
6	−1	− .8	

---

[1] We discussed the most popular stock market indexes in Section 11.2.

FIGURE 12.1 This figure is a plot of the data presented in the table in Example 12.1. Each point shows the performance of Turbot-Charged Seafoods stock when the overall market is either up or down by 1%. On average, Turbot-Charged moves in the same direction as the market, but not as far. Therefore, Turbot-Charged's beta is less than 1.0. We can measure beta by the slope of a line fitted to the points in the figure. In this case it is .8.

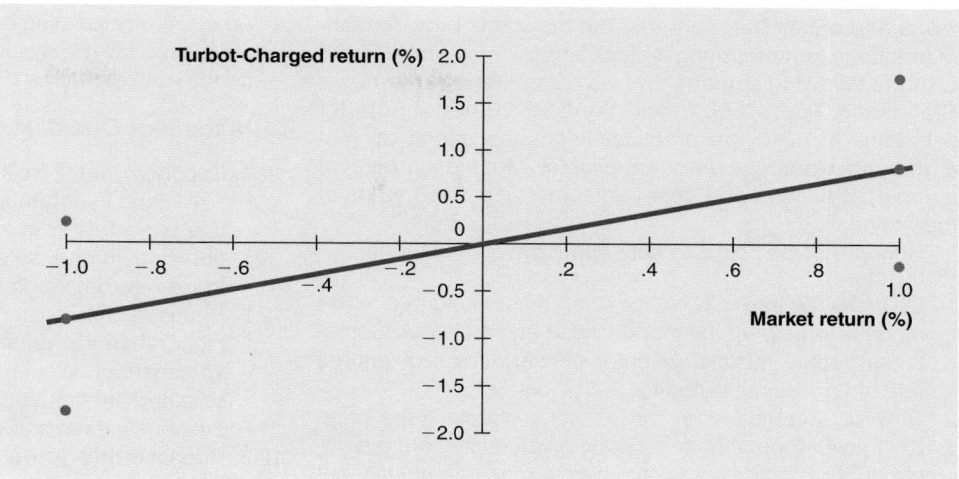

Look at Figure 12.1, where these observations are plotted. We've drawn a line through the average performance of Turbot when the market is up or down by 1%. *The slope of this line is Turbot's beta.* You can see right away that the beta is .8, because on average Turbot stock gains or loses .8% when the market is up or down by 1%. Notice that a 2-percentage-point difference in the market return (-1 to $+1$) generates on average a 1.6-percentage-point difference for Turbot shareholders ($-.8$ to $+.8$). The ratio, $1.6/2 = .8$, is beta.

In 4 months, Turbot's returns lie above or below the line in Figure 12.1. The distance from the line shows the response of Turbot's stock returns to news or events that affected Turbot but did *not* affect the overall market. For example, in month 2, investors in Turbot stock benefited from good macroeconomic news (the market was up 1%) and also from some favorable news specific to Turbot. The market rise gave a boost of .8% to Turbot stock (beta of .8 times the 1% market return). Then firm-specific news gave Turbot stockholders an extra 1% return, for a total return that month of 1.8%.

As this example illustrates, we can break down common stock returns into two parts: the part explained by market returns and the firm's beta, and the part due to news that is specific to the firm. Fluctuations in the first part reflect market risk; fluctuations in the second part reflect specific risk.

Of course, diversification can get rid of the specific risks. That's why wise investors, who don't put all their eggs in one basket, will look to Turbot's less-than-average beta and call its stock "defensive."

Self-Test 12.1

Here are 6 months' returns to stockholders in the Anchovy Queen restaurant chain:

Month	Market Return, %	Anchovy Queen Return, %
1	+1	+2.0
2	+1	+0
3	+1	+1.0
4	−1	−1.0
5	−1	+0
6	−1	−2.0

Draw a figure like Figure 12.1 and check the slope of the fitted line. What is Anchovy Queen's beta?

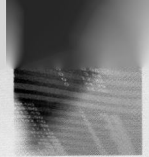

Calculating Risk

Excel and most other spreadsheet programs provide built-in functions for computing a stock's beta. In columns B and C of the following spreadsheet we have entered returns for Standard & Poor's 500 Index (the S&P 500) and Ford for 6 months in 2010. (In practice, estimates based on just 6 months would be *very* unreliable. Most estimates of standard deviation and beta use something like 5 years of monthly data.)

Here are some points to note about the spreadsheet:

1. *Columns B and C.* Notice that these columns show monthly *returns* for the market index and the stock. Sometimes people mistakenly enter prices instead of returns and get nonsensical results.
2. *Row 10.* Footnote 5 in the previous chapter (see page 327) pointed out that in estimating variability from a sample of observations, it is common to make an adjustment for what is called *the loss of a degree of freedom.* In this case the appropriate formula for standard deviation would be STDEV(C3:C8).
3. *Row 11.* We have converted monthly standard deviations to annual figures by multiplying by the square root of 12 (the number of months in a year).

4. *Row 12.* In calculating beta, it is important to enter first the addresses for the stock returns (C3:C8) and then those for the market returns (B3:B8).

Spreadsheet Questions

12.1. Suppose that Ford's return in June 2010 had been −4%, and its return in July 2010 had been 15%. Would you expect its beta to be more or less than the value obtained in the spreadsheet? Reestimate beta with these new data, and confirm your intuition.

12.2. Suppose that Ford's return in each month had been 1% higher than the values presented in the accompanying spreadsheet. Would Ford's beta differ from the value obtained in the spreadsheet? Reestimate beta with these new data, and confirm your intuition.

12.3. Suppose that you add 1 more month of data to your spreadsheet and find that in October 2010, Ford was down 5% while the market was up 5%. Would you expect Ford's beta to be more or less than the value obtained in the spreadsheet? Reestimate beta with this new data point, and confirm your intuition.

You can find this spreadsheet at
www.mhhe.com/bmm7e.

	A	B	C	D
1		Returns, percent		Formula used in
2	Month	S&P 500	Ford	Column C
3	Sep-10	5.74	4.43	
4	Aug-10	−4.74	−11.59	
5	Jul-10	6.88	26.69	
6	Jun-10	−5.39	−14.07	
7	May-10	−8.20	−9.91	
8	Apr-10	1.48	3.58	
9				
10	Standard deviation (monthly)	5.75	13.99	=STDEVP(C3:C8)
11	Standard deviation, annualized	19.91	48.47	=C10*SQRT(12)
12	Beta		2.15	=SLOPE(C3:C8,B3:B8)
13	Correlation		0.88	=CORREL(C3:C8,B3:B8)

Real life doesn't serve up numbers quite as convenient as those in our examples so far. However, the procedure for measuring real companies' betas is exactly the same:

1. Observe rates of return, usually monthly, for the stock and the market.
2. Plot the observations as in Figure 12.1.
3. Fit a line showing the average return to the stock at different market returns.

Beta is the slope of the fitted line.

This may sound like a lot of work, but in practice computers do it for you. The nearby box shows how to use the SLOPE function in Excel to calculate a beta. Here are two real examples.

Betas for Dow Chemical and Consolidated Edison

Each point in Figure 12.2*a* shows the return on Dow Chemical stock and the return on the market index in a different month. For example, the circled point shows that in March 2009, Dow Chemical's stock price rose by 19.7%, whereas the market index rose by 8.5%. Notice that more often than not Dow outperformed the market when the

FIGURE 12.2 (a) Each point in this figure shows the returns on Dow Chemical common stock and the overall market in a particular month between June 2005 and May 2010. Dow's beta is the slope of the line fitted to these points. Dow has a very high beta of 2.28. (b) In this plot of 60 months' returns for Con Ed and the overall market, the slope of the fitted line is much less than Dow's beta in (a). Con Ed has a relatively low beta of .32.

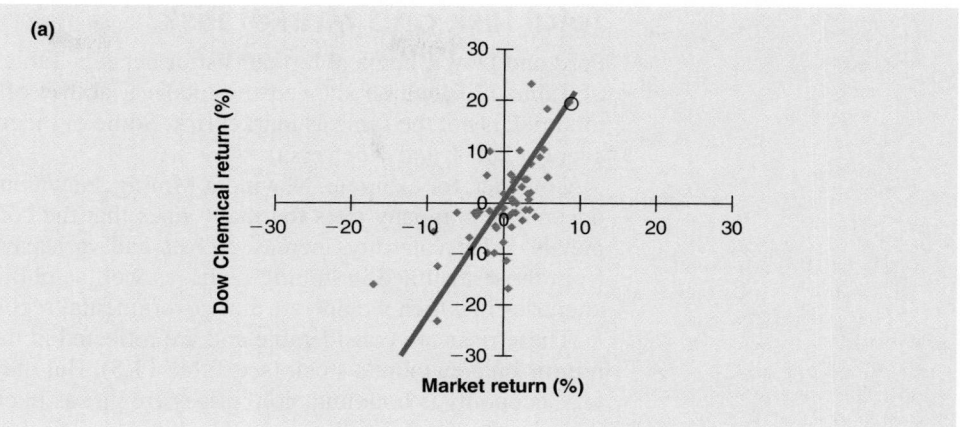

(a)

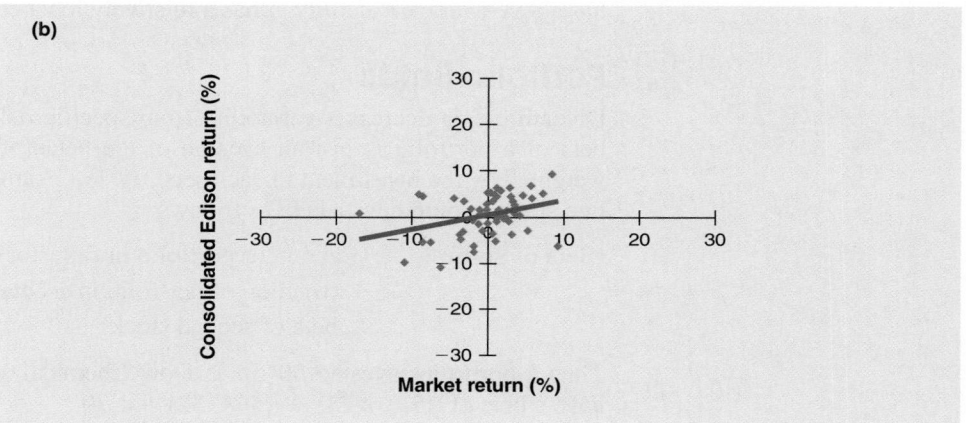

(b)

index rose and underperformed the market when the index fell. Thus Dow was a relatively aggressive, high-beta stock.

We have drawn a line of best fit through the points in the figure.[2] The slope of this line is 2.28. For each extra 1% rise in the market, Dow's stock price moved on average an extra 2.28%. For each extra 1% fall in the market, Dow's stock price fell an extra 2.28%. Thus Dow's beta was 2.28.

Of course, Dow's stock returns are not perfectly related to market returns. The company was also subject to specific risk, which shows up in the scatter of points around the line. Sometimes Dow flew south while the market went north, or vice versa.

Figure 12.2*b* shows a similar plot of the monthly returns for Consolidated Edison. In contrast to Dow Chemical, Con Ed was a defensive, low-beta stock. It was not highly sensitive to market movements, usually lagging when the market rose and yet doing better (or less badly) when the market fell. The slope of the line of best fit shows that on average an extra 1% change in the index resulted in an extra .32% change in the price of Con Ed stock. Thus ConEd's beta was .32.

Estimates of beta can be accessed easily, for example, at finance.yahoo.com, but you may find it interesting to look at Table 12.1, which shows how past market movements have affected several well-known stocks. Consolidated Edison had almost the lowest beta: Its stock return was .32 times as sensitive as the average stock to market movements. Dow Chemical was near the other extreme: Its return was 2.28 times as sensitive as the average stock to market movements.

---

[2] The line of best fit is usually known as a *regression* line. The slope of the line can be calculated using *ordinary least squares* regression. The dependent variable is the return on the stock (Dow Chemical). The independent variable is the return on the market index, in this case the S&P 500.

Total Risk and Market Risk

Ford and Dow Chemical top our list of betas in Table 12.1. They were also at the top of Table 11.6, which showed the total variability of the same group of stocks. But total risk is not the same as market risk. Some of the most variable stocks have below-average betas, and vice versa.

Consider, for example, Newmont Mining. Newmont is the world's largest gold producer. The company cites the many risks that the company faces as "gold and other metals' price volatility, increased costs and variances in ore grade or recovery rates from those assumed in mining plans, as well as political and operational risks in the countries in which we operate and governmental regulation and judicial outcomes."

These risks are considerable and are reflected in the high standard deviation of the returns on Newmont's stock (see Table 11.5). But they are not macro risks. When the U.S. economy is booming, gold prices are just as likely to slump, and a mine in some distant part of the world may well be hit by political unrest. So, while Newmont stock has above-average volatility, it has a relatively low beta.

Portfolio Betas

Diversification decreases variability from specific risk but not from market risk. The beta of a portfolio is just an average of the betas of the securities in the portfolio, weighted by the investment in each security. For example, a portfolio comprising only two stocks would have a beta as follows:

Beta of portfolio = (fraction of portfolio in first stock × beta of first stock)   **(12.1)**
                        + (fraction of portfolio in second stock
                        × beta of second stock)

Thus a portfolio invested 50–50 in Dow Chemical and Consolidated Edison would have a beta of (.5 × 2.28) + (.5 × .32) = 1.30.

A well-diversified portfolio of stocks all with betas of 2.28, like Dow Chemical, would still have a portfolio beta of 2.28. However, most of the individual stocks' specific risk would be diversified away. The market risk would remain, and such a portfolio would end up 2.28 times as variable as the market. For example, if the market

TABLE 12.1 Betas for selected common stocks, May 2005–April 2010

	Beta
Ford	2.53
Dow Chemical	2.28
Starbucks	1.36
Dell	1.33
Boeing	1.28
Disney	1.16
Microsoft	.97
IBM	.76
Pfizer	.68
McDonald's	.62
Heinz	.61
Newmont Mining	.59
Johnson & Johnson	.57
ExxonMobil	.42
Campbell Soup	.37
Consolidated Edison	.32
Walmart	.24

Note: Betas are calculated from 5 years of monthly data.

has an annual standard deviation of 20%, a fully diversified portfolio with beta of 2.28 has a standard deviation of 2.28 × 20 = 45.6%.

Portfolios with betas between 0 and 1.0 tend to move in the same direction as the market but not as far. A well-diversified portfolio of low-beta stocks like Consolidated Edison, all with betas of .32, has almost no specific risk and is relatively unaffected by market movements. Such a portfolio is .32 times as variable as the market.

Of course, on average stocks have a beta of 1.0. A well-diversified portfolio including all kinds of stocks, with an average beta of 1.0, has the same variability as the market index.

Self-Test 12.2

Suppose you invested an equal amount in each of the stocks shown in Table 12.1. Calculate the beta of your portfolio.

EXAMPLE 12.2 ▶ How Risky Are Mutual Funds?

You don't have to be wealthy to own a diversified portfolio. You can buy shares in one of the more than 8,000 mutual funds in the United States.

Investors buy shares of the funds, and the funds use the money to buy portfolios of securities. The returns on the portfolios are passed back to the funds' owners in proportion to their shareholdings. Therefore, the funds act like investment cooperatives, offering even the smallest investors diversification and professional management at low cost.

Let's look at the betas of two mutual funds that invest in stocks. Figure 12.3a plots the monthly returns of Vanguard's Explorer mutual fund and of the S&P index for 5 years ending in April 2010. You can see that the stocks in the Explorer fund had above-average sensitivity to market changes: They had on average a beta of 1.15.

If the Explorer fund had no specific risk, its portfolio would have been 1.15 times as variable as the market portfolio. But the fund manager wanted to beat the market, not to hold it. So the fund had not diversified away all the specific risk; there is still some scatter about the line in Figure 12.3a. As a result, the variability of the fund was somewhat more than 1.15 times that of the market.

FIGURE 12.3a The slope of the fitted line shows that investors in the Vanguard Explorer mutual fund bore market risk greater than that of the S&P 500 portfolio. Explorer's beta was 1.15. This was the average beta of the individual common stocks held by the fund. Investors also bore some specific risk, however; note the scatter of Explorer's returns above and below the fitted line.

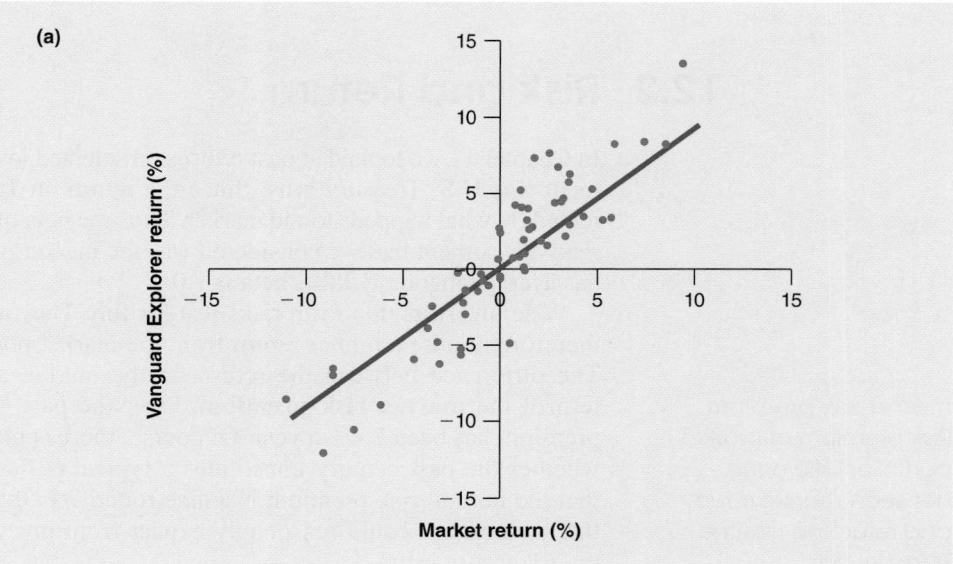

FIGURE 12.3*b* The Vanguard 500 Portfolio is a fully diversified index fund designed to track the performance of the market. Note the fund's beta (1.0) and the absence of specific risk. The fund's returns lie almost precisely on the fitted line relating its returns to those of the S&P 500 portfolio.

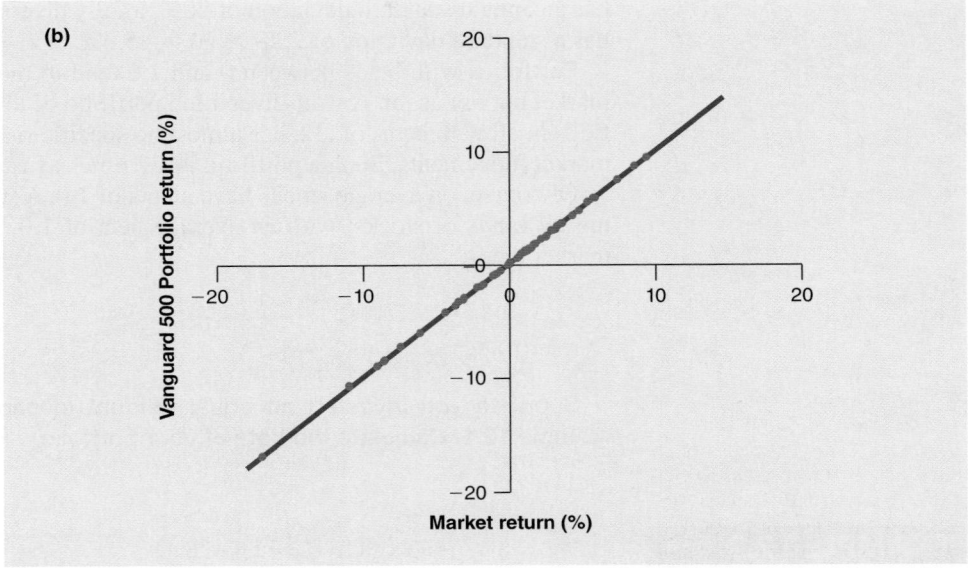

Figure 12.3*b* shows the same sort of plot for Vanguard's Index Trust 500 Portfolio mutual fund. Notice that this fund has a beta of 1.0 and only a tiny residual of specific risk—the fitted line fits almost exactly because an *index fund* is designed to track the market as closely as possible. The managers of the fund do not attempt to pick good stocks but just work to achieve full diversification at very low cost. The index fund is *fully diversified.* Investors in this fund buy the market as a whole and don't have to worry at all about specific risk.

Self-Test 12.3

Suppose you could achieve full diversification in a portfolio constructed from stocks with an average beta of .5. If the standard deviation of the market is 20% per year, what is the standard deviation of the portfolio return?

12.2 Risk and Return

In Chapter 11 we looked at past returns on selected investments. The least risky investment was U.S. Treasury bills. Since the return on Treasury bills is fixed, it is unaffected by what happens to the market. Thus the beta of Treasury bills is zero. The *most* risky investment that we considered was the market portfolio of common stocks. This has average market risk: Its beta is 1.0.

Wise investors don't run risks just for fun. They are playing with real money and therefore require a higher return from the market portfolio than from Treasury bills. The difference between the return on the market and the interest rate on bills is termed the **market risk premium.** Over the past century the average market risk premium has been 7.4% a year. Of course, there is plenty of scope for argument as to whether the past century constitutes a typical period, but we will just assume here that the normal risk premium is a nice round 7%, that is, 7% is the additional return that an investor could reasonably expect from investing in the stock market rather than Treasury bills.

market risk premium
Risk premium of market portfolio. Difference between market return and return on risk-free Treasury bills.

FIGURE 12.4 **(a)** Here we begin the plot of expected rate of return against beta. The first benchmarks are Treasury bills (beta = 0) and the market portfolio (beta = 1.0). We assume a Treasury bill rate of 3% and a market return of 10%. The market risk premium is 10 − 3 = 7%. **(b)** A portfolio split evenly between Treasury bills and the market will have beta = .5 and an expected return of 6.5% (point *X*). A portfolio invested 20% in the market and 80% in Treasury bills has beta = .2 and an expected rate of return of 4.4% (point *Y*). Note that the expected rate of return on any portfolio mixing Treasury bills and the market lies on a straight line. The risk premium is proportional to the portfolio beta.

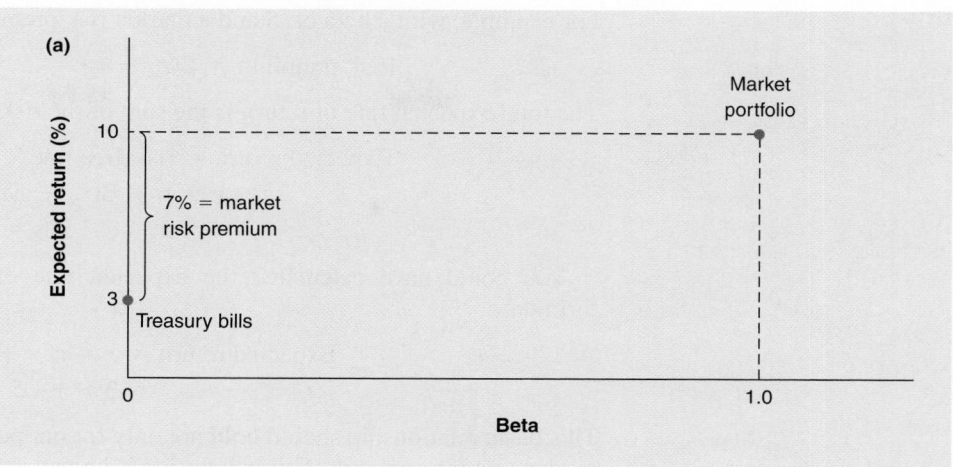

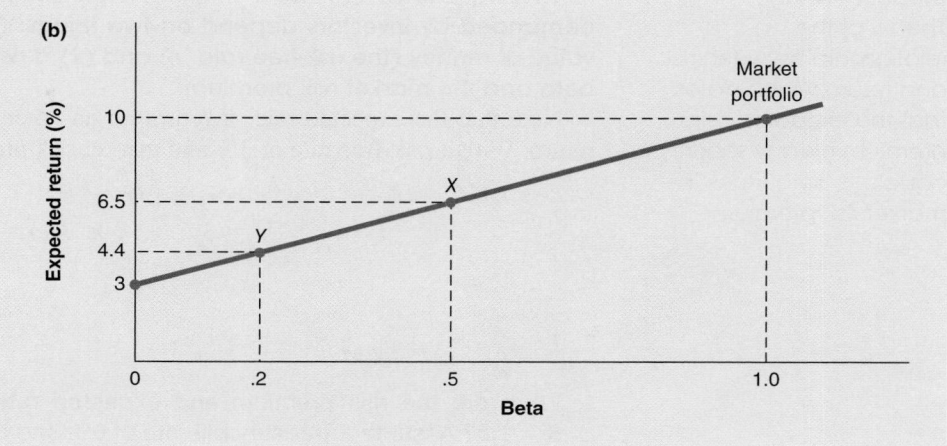

In Figure 12.4*a* we have plotted the risk and expected return from Treasury bills and the market portfolio. You can see that Treasury bills have a beta of zero and a risk-free return; we'll assume that return is 3%. The market portfolio has a beta of 1.0 and an assumed expected return of 10%.[3]

Now, given these two benchmarks, what expected rate of return should an investor require from a portfolio that is equally divided between Treasury bills and the market? Halfway between, of course. Thus in Figure 12.4*b* we have drawn a straight line through the Treasury bill return and the expected market return. The portfolio (marked with an *X*) would have a beta of .5 and an expected return of 6.5%. This includes a risk premium of 3.5% above the Treasury bill return of 3%.

You can calculate this return as follows: Start with the difference between the expected market return r_m and the Treasury bill rate r_f. This is the expected market risk premium:

$$\text{Market risk premium} = r_m - r_f = 10\% - 3\% = 7\%$$

Beta measures risk relative to the market. Therefore, the expected risk premium equals beta times the market risk premium:

$$\text{Risk premium} = r - r_f = \beta(r_m - r_f)$$

---

[3] We assumed that the risk premium on the market is about 7%. With a 3% Treasury bill rate, the expected market return would be 3 + 7 = 10%.

For example, with a beta of .5 and a market risk premium of 7%,

$$\text{Risk premium} = \beta(r_m - r_f) = .5 \times 7\% = 3.5\%$$

The total expected rate of return is the sum of the risk-free rate and the risk premium:

$$\text{Expected return} = \text{risk-free rate} + \text{risk premium} \qquad \textbf{(12.2)}$$
$$r = r_f + \beta(r_m - r_f)$$
$$= 3\% + 3.5\% = 6.5\%$$

You could have calculated the expected rate of return in one step from this formula:

$$\text{Expected return} = r = r_f + \beta(r_m - r_f)$$
$$= 3\% + (.5 \times 7\%) = 6.5\%$$

capital asset pricing model (CAPM)
Theory of the relationship between risk and return which states that the expected risk premium on any security equals its beta times the market risk premium.

This basic relationship should hold not only for our portfolios of Treasury bills and the market, but for *any* asset. This conclusion is known as the **capital asset pricing model,** or **CAPM.** The CAPM has a simple interpretation: **The expected rates of return demanded by investors depend on two things: (1) compensation for the time value of money (the risk-free rate r_f) and (2) a risk premium, which depends on beta and the market risk premium.**

Note that the expected rate of return on an asset with $\beta = 1.0$ is just the market return. With a risk-free rate of 3% and market risk premium of 7%,

$$r = r_f + \beta(r_m - r_f)$$
$$= 3\% + (1 \times 7\%) = 10\%$$

Self-Test 12.4

What are the risk premium and expected rate of return on a stock with $\beta = 1.5$? Assume a Treasury bill rate of 6% and a market risk premium of 7%.

Why the CAPM Makes Sense

The CAPM assumes that the stock market is dominated by well-diversified investors who are concerned only with market risk. That is reasonable in a stock market where trading is dominated by large institutions and even small fry can diversify at very low cost. The following example shows why in this case the CAPM makes sense.

EXAMPLE 12.3 ▶   How Would You Invest $1 Million?

Have you ever daydreamed about receiving a $1 million check, no strings attached, from an unknown benefactor? Let's daydream about how you would invest it.

We have two good candidates: Treasury bills, which offer an absolutely safe return, and the market portfolio (possibly via the Vanguard index fund discussed earlier in this chapter). The market has generated superior returns on average, but those returns have fluctuated a lot. (Look back to Figure 11.4.) So your investment policy is going to depend on your tolerance for risk.

If you're a wimp, you may invest only part of your money in the market portfolio and lend the remainder to the government by buying Treasury bills. Suppose that you invest 20% of your money in the market portfolio and put the other 80% in U.S. Treasury bills. Then the beta of your portfolio will be a mixture of the beta of the market ($\beta_{market} = 1.0$) and the beta of the T-bills ($\beta_{T\text{-bills}} = 0$):

$$\text{Beta of portfolio} = \left(\begin{array}{c}\text{proportion} \\ \text{in market}\end{array} \times \begin{array}{c}\text{beta of} \\ \text{market}\end{array}\right) + \left(\begin{array}{c}\text{proportion} \\ \text{in T-bills}\end{array} \times \begin{array}{c}\text{beta of} \\ \text{T-bills}\end{array}\right)$$

$$\beta = (.2 \times \beta_{market}) \qquad\qquad + (.8 \times \beta_{T\text{-bills}})$$
$$= (.2 \times 1.0) \qquad\qquad + (.8 \times 0) = .20$$

The fraction of funds that you invest in the market also affects your expected return. If you invest your entire million in the market portfolio, you earn the full market risk premium. But if you invest only 20% of your money in the market, you earn only 20% of the risk premium.

$$\begin{array}{c}\text{Expected} \\ \text{risk premium} \\ \text{on portfolio}\end{array} = \left(\begin{array}{c}\text{proportion} \\ \text{in market}\end{array} \times \begin{array}{c}\text{market risk} \\ \text{premium}\end{array}\right) + \left(\begin{array}{c}\text{proportion} \\ \text{in T-bills}\end{array} \times \begin{array}{c}\text{risk premium} \\ \text{on T-bills}\end{array}\right)$$

$$= (.2 \times \text{expected market risk premium}) + (.8 \times 0)$$
$$= .2 \times \text{expected market risk premium}$$
$$= .2 \times 7 = 1.4\%$$

The expected return on your portfolio is equal to the risk-free interest rate plus the expected risk premium:

$$\text{Expected portfolio return} = r_{portfolio} = 3 + 1.4 = 4.4\%$$

In Figure 12.4*b* we show the beta and expected return on this portfolio by the letter *Y*.

The Security Market Line

security market line
Relationship between
expected return and
beta.

Example 12.3 illustrates a general point: By investing some proportion of your money in the market portfolio and lending (or borrowing)[4] the balance, you can obtain any combination of risk and expected return along the sloping line in Figure 12.5. This line is generally known as the **security market line.**

Self-Test 12.5

How would you construct a portfolio with a beta of .25? What is the expected return to this strategy? Assume Treasury bills yield 6% and the market risk premium is 7%.

The security market line describes the expected returns and risks from investing different fractions of your funds in the market. It also sets a standard for other investments. Investors will be willing to hold other investments only if they offer

---

[4] Notice that the security market line extends above the market return at $\beta = 1.0$. How would you generate a portfolio with, say, $\beta = 2.0$? It's easy, but it's risky. Suppose you borrow $1 million and invest the loan plus $1 million in the market portfolio. That gives you $2 million invested and a $1 million liability. Your portfolio now has a beta of 2.0:

$$\text{Beta of portfolio} = (\text{proportion in market} \times \text{beta of market}) + (\text{proportion in loan} \times \text{beta of loan})$$
$$\beta = (2 \times \beta_{market}) + (-1 \times \beta_{loan})$$
$$= (2 \times 1.0) + (-1 \times 0) = 2$$

Notice that the proportion in the loan is negative because you are borrowing, not lending money.

By the way, borrowing from a bank or stockbroker would not be difficult or unduly expensive as long as you put up your $2 million stock portfolio as security for the loan.

Can you calculate the risk premium and the expected rate of return on this borrow-and-invest strategy?

FIGURE 12.5 The security market line shows how expected rate of return depends on beta. According to the capital asset pricing model, expected rates of return for all securities and all portfolios lie on this line.

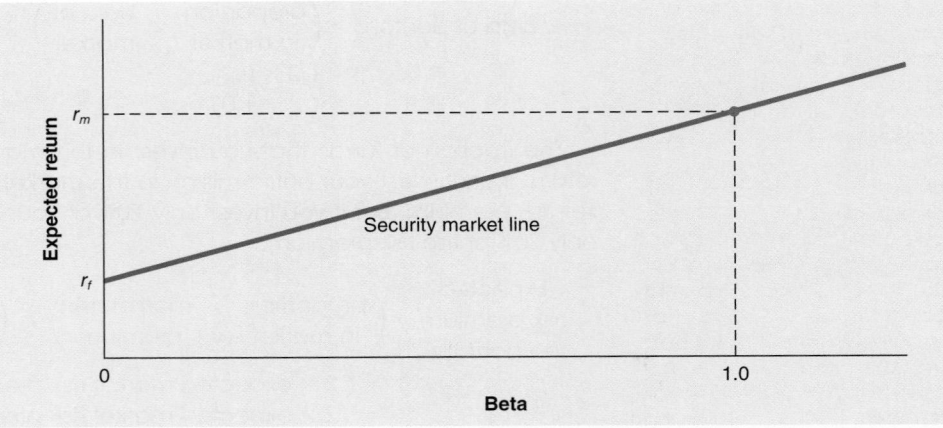

equally good prospects. Thus the required risk premium for *any* investment is given by the security market line:

Risk premium on investment = beta × expected market risk premium

Look back to Figure 12.4*b*, which suggests that an individual common stock with $\beta = .5$ must offer a 6.5% expected rate of return when Treasury bills yield 3% and the market risk premium is 7%. You can now see why this has to be so. If that stock offered a lower rate of return, nobody would buy even a little of it—they could get 6.5% just by investing 50–50 in Treasury bills and the market. And if nobody wants to hold the stock, its price has to drop. A lower price means a better buy for investors, that is, a higher rate of return. The price will fall until the stock's expected rate of return is pushed up to 6.5%. At that price and expected return the CAPM holds.

If, on the other hand, our stock offered more than 6.5%, diversified investors would want to buy more of it. That would push the price up and the expected return down to the levels predicted by the CAPM.

This reasoning holds for stocks with any beta. That's why the CAPM makes sense, and why the expected risk premium on an investment should be proportional to its beta.

Self-Test 12.6

Suppose you invest $400,000 in Treasury bills and $600,000 in the market portfolio. What is the return on your portfolio if bills yield 6% and the expected return on the market is 13%? What does the return on this portfolio imply for the expected return on individual stocks with betas of .6?

How Well Does the CAPM Work?

The basic idea behind the capital asset pricing model is that investors expect a reward for both waiting and worrying. The greater the worry, the greater the expected return. If you invest in a risk-free Treasury bill, you just receive the rate of interest. That's the reward for waiting. When you invest in risky stocks, you can expect an extra return or risk premium for worrying. The capital asset pricing model states that this risk premium is equal to the stock's beta times the market risk premium. Therefore,

Expected return on stock = risk-free interest rate + (beta × market risk premium)
$$r = r_f + \beta(r_m - r_f)$$

How well does the CAPM work in practice? Do the returns on stocks with betas of .5 on average lie halfway between the return on the market portfolio and the interest

FIGURE 12.6 The capital asset pricing model states that the expected risk premium from any investment should lie on the security market line. The dots show the actual average risk premium from portfolios with different betas. The high-beta portfolios generated higher returns, just as predicted by the CAPM. But the high-beta portfolios plotted below the market line and the low-beta portfolios plotted above. A line fitted to the 10 portfolio returns would be "flatter" than the security market line.

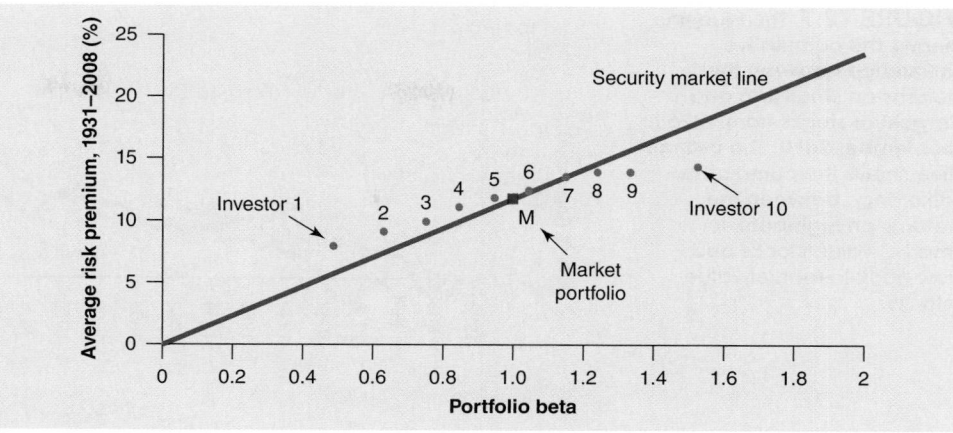

Source: This material is reprinted with permission from Institutional Investor, Inc. It originally appeared in the Fall 1993 issue of the *Journal of Portfolio Management* 20. It is illegal to make unauthorized copies of this article. For more information please visit www.iijournals.com. All Rights Reserved.

rate on Treasury bills? Unfortunately, the evidence is conflicting. Let's look back to the actual returns earned by investors in low-beta stocks and in high-beta stocks.

Imagine that in 1931 ten investors gathered together in a Wall Street bar and agreed to establish investment trust funds for their children. Each investor decided to follow a different strategy. Investor 1 opted to buy the 10% of the New York Stock Exchange stocks with the lowest estimated betas; investor 2 chose the 10% with the next-lowest betas; and so on, up to investor 10, who proposed to buy the stocks with the highest betas. They also planned that at the end of each year they would reestimate the betas of all NYSE stocks and reconstitute their portfolios. And so they parted with much cordiality and good wishes.

In time the 10 investors all passed away, but their children agreed to meet in early 2009 in the same bar to compare the performance of their portfolios. Figure 12.6 shows how they fared. Investor 1's portfolio turned out to be much less risky than the market; its beta was only .49. However, investor 1 also realized the lowest return, 8.0% above the risk-free rate of interest. At the other extreme, the beta of investor 10's portfolio was 1.53, about three times that of investor 1's portfolio. But investor 10 was rewarded with the highest return, averaging 14.3% a year above the interest rate. So over this 77-year period returns did indeed increase with beta.

As you can see from Figure 12.6, the market portfolio over the same 77-year period provided an average return of 11.8% above the interest rate[5] and (of course) had a beta of 1.0. The CAPM predicts that the risk premium should increase in proportion to beta, so the returns of each portfolio should lie on the upward-sloping security market line in Figure 12.6. Since the market provided a risk premium of 11.8%, investor 1's portfolio, with a beta of .49, should have provided a risk premium of 5.8% and investor 10's portfolio, with a beta of 1.53, should have given a premium of 18.1%. You can see that, while high-beta stocks performed better than low-beta stocks, the difference was not as great as the CAPM predicts.

Figure 12.6 provides broad support for the CAPM, though it suggests that the line relating return to beta has been too flat. But recent years have been less kind to the CAPM. For example, if the 10 friends had invested their cash in 1966 rather than 1931, there would have been very little relation between their portfolio returns and beta.[6] Does this imply that there has been a fundamental change in the relation between

---

[5] In Figure 12.6 the stocks in the "market portfolio" are weighted equally. Since the stocks of small firms have provided higher average returns than those of large firms, the risk premium on an equally weighted index is higher than that on a value-weighted index. This is one reason for the difference between the 11.8% market risk premium in Figure 12.6 and the 7.4% premium reported in Table 11.1.

[6] During this later period, the returns to the first seven investors increased in line with beta. However, the highest beta portfolios performed poorly.

FIGURE 12.7 The blue line shows the cumulative difference between the returns on small-firm and large-firm stocks from 1926 to September 2010. The orange line shows the cumulative difference between the returns on high-book-to-market-value stocks and low-book-to-market-value stocks.

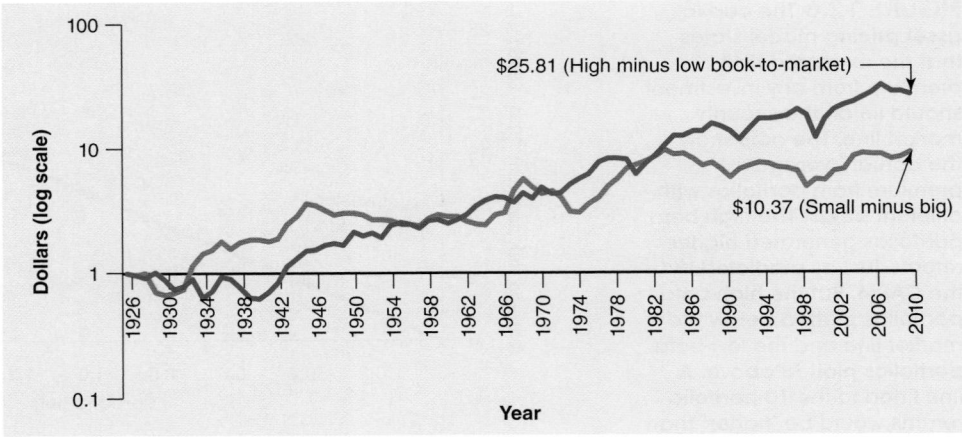

Source: **mba.tuck.dartmouth.edu/pages/faculty/ken.french/data_library.html.** Used by permission of Kenneth R. French.

risk and return in the last 40 years, or did high-beta stocks just happen to perform worse during these years than investors expected? It is hard to be sure.

There is little doubt that the CAPM is too simple to capture everything that is going on in the market. For example, look at Figure 12.7. The orange line shows the cumulative difference between the returns on small-firm stocks and large-firm stocks. If you had bought the shares with the smallest market capitalizations and sold those with the largest capitalizations, this is how your wealth would have changed. You can see that small-cap stocks did not always do well, but over the long haul their owners have made substantially higher returns. Since the end of 1926 the average annual difference between the returns on the two groups of stocks has been 3.8%. Now look at the blue line in Figure 12.7, which shows the cumulative difference between the returns on value stocks and growth stocks. *Value stocks* here are defined as those with high ratios of book value to market value. *Growth stocks* are those with low ratios of book to market. Notice that value stocks have provided a higher long-run return than growth stocks. Since 1926 the average annual difference between returns on value and growth stocks has been 4.9%.

The superior performance of small-firm stocks and value stocks does not fit well with the CAPM, which predicts that beta is the *only* reason that expected returns differ. If investors *expected* the returns to depend on firm size or book-to-market ratios, then the simple version of the capital asset pricing model cannot be the whole truth.

What's going on here? It is hard to say. Defenders of the capital asset pricing model emphasize that it is concerned with *expected* returns, whereas we can observe only *actual* returns. Actual returns reflect expectations, but they also embody lots of "noise"—the steady flow of surprises that conceal whether on average investors have received the returns that they expected. Thus, when we observe that in the past small-firm stocks and value stocks have provided superior performance, we can't be sure whether this was simply a coincidence or whether investors have required a higher return to hold these stocks.

Such debates have prompted headlines like "Is Beta Dead?" in the business press. It is not the first time that beta has been declared dead, but the CAPM remains the leading model for estimating required returns. Only strong theories can have more than one funeral.

The CAPM is not the only model of risk and return. It has several brothers and sisters as well as second cousins. However, the CAPM captures in a simple way two fundamental ideas. First, almost everyone agrees that investors require some extra return for taking on risk. Second, investors appear to be concerned principally with the market risk that they cannot eliminate by diversification. That is why financial managers rely on the capital asset pricing model as a good rule of thumb.

TABLE 12.2 Expected rates of return

	Beta	Expected Return
Ford	2.53	20.7%
Dow Chemical	2.28	19.0
Starbucks	1.36	12.5
Dell	1.33	12.3
Boeing	1.28	12.0
Disney	1.16	11.1
Microsoft	.97	9.8
IBM	.76	8.3
Pfizer	.68	7.8
McDonald's	.62	7.3
Heinz	.61	7.3
Newmont Mining	.59	7.1
Johnson & Johnson	.57	7.0
ExxonMobil	.42	5.9
Campbell Soup	.37	5.6
Consolidated Edison	.32	5.2
Walmart	.24	4.7

Note: Expected return $= r = r_f + \beta(r_m - r_f) = 3\% + \beta \times 7\%$.

Using the CAPM to Estimate Expected Returns

To calculate the returns that investors are expecting from particular stocks, we need three numbers—the risk-free interest rate, the expected market risk premium, and beta. Suppose that the interest rate on Treasury bills is about 3% and the market risk premium is about 7%. Now look back to Table 12.1, where we gave you betas of several stocks. Table 12.2 puts these numbers together to give an estimate of the expected return from each stock. Let's take Dell Computer as an example:

$$\text{Expected return on Dell} = \text{risk-free interest rate} + \left(\text{beta} \times \frac{\text{expected market}}{\text{risk premium}} \right)$$

$$r = 3\% + (1.33 \times 7\%) = 12.3\%$$

Of our sample of companies, Ford had the highest beta. Investors in Ford required compensation for taking on the extra market risk. Table 12.2 suggests that Ford's expected rate of return was around 20%, considerably higher than Dell's.

12.3 Capital Budgeting and Project Risk

We have seen that the firm faces a trade-off. It can either buy new plant and equipment or return cash to its shareholders, who can then invest the money for themselves in the capital market. When the company invests the cash, shareholders can't invest these funds in the capital market. The return that shareholders give up by keeping their money in the company is therefore called the *opportunity cost of capital.* Shareholders need the company to earn at least the opportunity cost of capital on its investments.

We have referred loosely to the return that investors could expect to earn by buying securities. But there are thousands of different securities that investors can buy. The expected return on each of these securities depends on its risk. So we need to redefine the opportunity cost of capital for a project, *r,* as the expected return on a security that has a similar level of risk to that of the project. The capital asset pricing model tells us how to calculate this.

company cost of capital
Expected rate of return demanded by investors in a company, determined by the average risk of the company's securities.

Company versus Project Risk

Many companies estimate the rate of return required by investors in their securities and use this **company cost of capital** to discount the cash flows on all new projects. Because investors require a higher rate of return from a risky company, risky firms will have a higher company cost of capital and will set a higher discount rate for their new investment opportunities. For example, on past evidence Dell has a beta of 1.33; the corresponding expected rate of return is about 12.3% (see Table 12.2). According to the company cost of capital rule, Dell should use a 12.3% cost of capital to calculate project NPVs.

This is a step in the right direction, but we must take care when the firm has issued securities other than equity.[7] Moreover, this approach can get a firm in trouble if its new projects do not have the same risk as its existing business. Dell's beta reflects investors' estimate of the risk of the computer hardware business, and its company cost of capital is the return that investors require for taking on this risk. If Dell is considering an expansion of its regular business, it makes sense to discount expected cash flows by the company cost of capital. But suppose Dell is wondering whether to branch out into production of pharmaceuticals. Its beta tells us nothing about the **project cost of capital.** That depends on the risk of the pharmaceutical business and the return that shareholders require from investing in such a business.

project cost of capital
Minimum acceptable expected rate of return on a project given its risk.

Self-Test 12.7

Dell is contemplating an expansion of its existing business. The investment is forecast to produce cash flows of $50 million a year for each of 10 years. What is its present value? Use data from Table 12.2.

The project cost of capital depends on the use to which that capital is put. Therefore, it depends on the risk of the project—not on the risk of the company. If a company invests in a low-risk project, it should discount the cash flows at a correspondingly low cost of capital. If it invests in a high-risk project, those cash flows should be discounted at a high cost of capital. Many companies use the company cost of capital as a measure of the return that they require on a "typical" capital investment. They then adjust the required return up or down depending on the risk of the particular project.

Self-Test 12.8

The company cost of capital for Dell Computer is about 12.3% (see Table 12.2); for Pfizer it is about 7.8%. What would be the more reasonable discount rate for Dell to use for a proposed move into pharmaceutical production? Why?

EXAMPLE 12.4 ▶ Estimating the Opportunity Cost of Capital for a Project

Suppose that Dell is contemplating investment in a new project. You have forecast the cash flows on the project and calculated that the internal rate of return is 11%. We assume that Treasury bills offer a return of 3% and that the expected market risk premium is 7%. Should Dell go ahead with the project?

To answer this question, you need the opportunity cost of capital, *r*. You start with the *project's* beta. For example, if the project is a sure thing, its beta is zero and the cost of capital equals the interest rate on Treasury bills:

$$r = r_f + \beta(r_m - r_f) = 3 + (0 \times 7) = 3\%$$

---

[7] This is not too serious a problem with Dell, because it is financed primarily by common stock. Therefore, the risk of its assets is similar to the risk of its stock. But most companies issue a mix of debt and common stock.

If the project offers an expected return of 11% when the cost of capital is 3%, Dell should obviously go ahead.[8] But if you had compared this project's return with Dell's 12.3% *company* cost of capital, you would have wrongly concluded that it was not worthwhile.

Surefire projects rarely occur outside finance texts. So let's think about the cost of capital if the project has the same risk as the market portfolio. In this case beta is 1.0, and the cost of capital is the expected return on the market:

$$r = 3 + (1.0 \times 7) = 10\%$$

The project appears less attractive than before but still worth doing.

The project is attractive because, as Figure 12.8 shows, its expected rate of return lies above the security market line. The project offers a higher return than investors can reasonably expect elsewhere on equally risky investments. Therefore, it is a positive-NPV investment.

The security market line provides a standard for project acceptance. If the project's expected return lies above the security market line, then it is higher than investors could expect to earn by investing their funds in the capital market, and the project is an attractive investment opportunity.

Determinants of Project Risk

We have seen that the company cost of capital is the correct discount rate for projects that have the same risk as the company's existing business but *not* for those projects that are safer or riskier than the company's average. How do we know whether a project is unusually risky? Estimating project risk is never going to be an exact science, but here are two things to bear in mind.

First, we saw in Chapter 10 that operating leverage increases the risk of a project. When a large fraction of your costs is fixed, any change in revenues can have a dramatic effect on earnings. Therefore, projects that involve high fixed costs tend to have higher betas.

Second, many people intuitively associate risk with the variability of earnings. But much of this variability reflects diversifiable risk. Lone prospectors in search of gold look forward to extremely uncertain future earnings, but whether they strike it rich is not likely to depend on the performance of the rest of the economy. These investments (like Newmont Mining) have a high standard deviation but a low beta.

FIGURE 12.8 The expected return of this project is more than the expected return one could earn on stock market investments with the same market risk (beta). Therefore, the project's expected return lies above the security market line, and the project should be accepted.

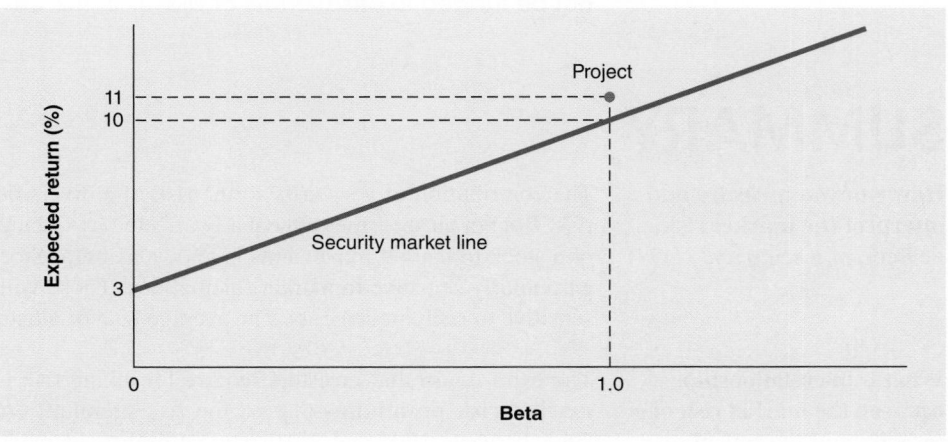

---

[8] In Chapter 8 we described some special cases where you should prefer projects that offer a *lower* internal rate of return than the cost of capital. We assume here that your project is a "normal" one and that you prefer high IRRs to low ones.

What matters is the strength of the relationship between the firm's earnings and the aggregate earnings of all firms. Cyclical businesses, whose revenues and earnings are strongly dependent on the state of the economy, tend to have high betas and a high cost of capital. By contrast, businesses that produce essentials, such as food, beer, and cosmetics, are less affected by the state of the economy. They tend to have low betas and a low cost of capital.

Don't Add Fudge Factors to Discount Rates

Risk to an investor arises because an investment adds to the spread of possible portfolio returns. To a diversified investor, risk is predominantly market risk. But in everyday usage *risk* simply means "bad outcome." People think of the "risks" of a project as the things that can go wrong. For example,

- A geologist looking for oil worries about the risk of a dry hole.
- A pharmaceutical manufacturer worries about the risk that a new drug which reverses balding may not be approved by the Food and Drug Administration.
- The owner of a hotel in a politically unstable part of the world worries about the political risk of expropriation.

Managers sometimes add fudge factors to discount rates to account for worries such as these.

This sort of adjustment makes us nervous. First, the bad outcomes we cited appear to reflect diversifiable risks that would not affect the expected rate of return demanded by investors. Second, the need for an adjustment in the discount rate usually arises because managers fail to give bad outcomes their due weight in cash-flow forecasts. They then try to offset that mistake by adding a fudge factor to the discount rate. For example, if a manager is worried about the possibility of a bad outcome such as a dry hole in oil exploration, he or she may reduce the value of the project by using a higher discount rate. That's not the way to do it. Instead, the possibility of the dry hole should be included in the calculation of the expected cash flows to be derived from the well. Suppose that there is a 50% chance of a dry hole and a 50% chance that the well will produce oil worth $20 million. Then the *expected* cash flow is not $20 million but $(.5 \times 0) + (.5 \times 20) = \$10$ million. You should discount the $10 million expected cash flow at the opportunity cost of capital; it does not make sense to discount the $20 million using a fudged discount rate.

Expected cash-flow forecasts should already reflect the probabilities of *all* possible outcomes, good and bad. If the cash-flow forecasts are prepared properly, the discount rate should reflect only the market risk of the project. It should not be fudged to offset errors or biases in the cash-flow forecast.

SUMMARY

How can you measure and interpret the market risk, or beta, of a security? *(LO1)*

The contribution of a security to the risk of a diversified portfolio depends on its market risk. But not all securities are equally affected by fluctuations in the market. The sensitivity of a stock to market movements is known as **beta.** Stocks with a beta greater than 1.0 are particularly sensitive to market fluctuations. Those with a beta of less than 1.0 are not so sensitive to such movements. The average beta of all stocks is 1.0.

What is the relationship between the market risk of a security and the rate of return that investors demand of that security? *(LO2)*

The extra return that investors require for taking risk is known as the risk premium. The **market risk premium**—that is, the risk premium on the **market portfolio**—averaged 7.4% between 1900 and 2010. The **capital asset pricing model** states that the expected risk premium of an investment should be proportional to both its beta and the market risk premium. The expected rate of return from any investment is equal to the risk-free interest rate plus the risk premium, so the **CAPM** boils down to

$$r = r_f + \beta(r_m - r_f)$$

The **security market line** is the graphical representation of the CAPM equation. The security market line relates the expected return investors demand of a security to its beta.

How can a manager calculate the opportunity cost of capital for a project? (*LO3*)

The opportunity cost of capital is the return that investors give up by investing in the project rather than in securities of equivalent risk. Financial managers use the capital asset pricing model to estimate the opportunity cost of capital. The **company cost of capital** is the expected rate of return demanded by investors in a company. It depends on the *average* risk of the company's assets and operations.

The opportunity cost of capital is determined by the use to which the capital is put. Therefore, required rates of return depend on the risk of the project, not on the risk of the firm's existing business. The **project cost of capital** is the minimum acceptable expected rate of return on a project given its risk.

Your cash-flow forecasts should already factor in the chances of pleasant and unpleasant surprises. Potential bad outcomes should be reflected in the discount rate only to the extent that they affect beta.

LISTING OF EQUATIONS

12.1   Beta of portfolio = (fraction of portfolio in first stock × beta of first stock)
+ (fraction of portfolio in second stock × beta of second stock)

12.2   Expected return = risk-free rate + risk premium
$$r = r_f + \beta(r_m - r_f)$$

QUESTIONS

QUIZ

1.   **Risk and Return.** True or false? Explain or qualify as necessary. (*LO2*)
   a.   Investors demand higher expected rates of return on stocks with more variable rates of return.
   b.   The capital asset pricing model predicts that a security with a beta of zero will provide an expected return of zero.
   c.   An investor who puts $10,000 in Treasury bills and $20,000 in the market portfolio will have a portfolio beta of 2.0.
   d.   Investors demand higher expected rates of return from stocks with returns that are highly exposed to macroeconomic changes.
   e.   Investors demand higher expected rates of return from stocks with returns that are very sensitive to fluctuations in the stock market.

2.   **Diversifiable Risk.** In light of what you've learned about market versus diversifiable (specific) risks, explain why an insurance company has no problem in selling life insurance to individuals but is reluctant to issue policies insuring against flood damage to residents of coastal areas. Why don't the insurance companies simply charge coastal residents a premium that reflects the actuarial probability of damage from hurricanes and other storms? (*LO1*)

3.   **Specific versus Market Risk.** Figure 12.9 plots monthly rates of return from 2006 to 2010 for the Snake Oil mutual fund. Was this fund well-diversified? Explain. (*LO1*)

4.   **Risk and Return.** Suppose that the risk premium on stocks and other securities did in fact rise with total risk (that is, the variability of returns) rather than just market risk. Explain how investors could exploit the situation to create portfolios with high expected rates of return but low levels of risk. (*LO2*)

5.   **CAPM and Hurdle Rates.** A project under consideration has an internal rate of return of 14% and a beta of .6. The risk-free rate is 4%, and the expected rate of return on the market portfolio is 14%. (*LO3*)
   a.   Should the project be accepted?
   b.   Should the project be accepted if its beta is 1.6?
   c.   Why does your answer change?

FIGURE 12.9 Monthly rates of return for the Snake Oil mutual fund and the Standard & Poor's Composite Index. See Quiz Question 3.

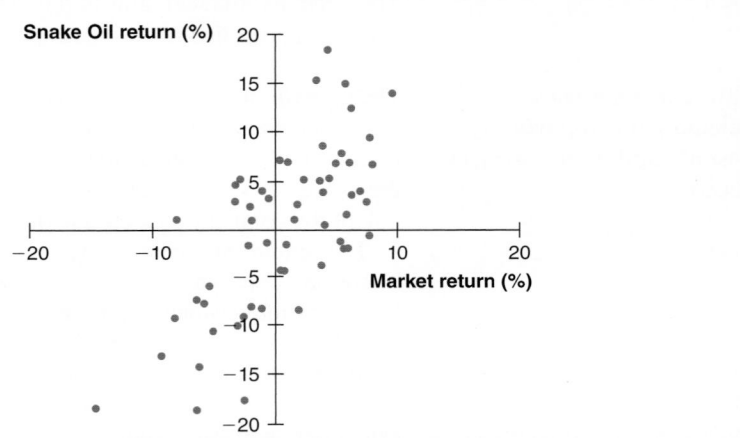

PRACTICE PROBLEMS

6. **CAPM and Valuation.** You are considering acquiring a firm that you believe can generate expected cash flows of $10,000 a year forever. However, you recognize that those cash flows are uncertain. (*LO2*)

   a. Suppose you believe that the beta of the firm is .4. How much is the firm worth if the risk-free rate is 4% and the expected rate of return on the market portfolio is 11%?

   b. By how much will you overvalue the firm if its beta is actually .6?

7. **CAPM and Expected Return.** If the risk-free rate is 6% and the expected rate of return on the market portfolio is 13%, is a security with a beta of 1.25 and an expected rate of return of 16% overpriced or underpriced? (*LO2*)

8. **Using Beta.** Investors expect the market rate of return this year to be 14%. A stock with a beta of .8 has an expected rate of return of 12%. If the market return this year turns out to be 10%, what is your best guess as to the rate of return on the stock? (*LO1*)

9. **Specific versus Market Risk.** Figure 12.10 shows plots of monthly rates of return on three stocks versus the stock market index. The beta and standard deviation of each stock is given beside its plot. (*LO1*)

   a. Which stock is safest for a diversified investor?

   b. Which stock is safest for an undiversified investor who puts all her funds in one of these stocks?

   c. Consider a portfolio with equal investments in each stock. What would this portfolio's beta have been?

   d. Consider a well-diversified portfolio made up of stocks with the same beta as Ford. What are the beta and standard deviation of this portfolio's return? The standard deviation of the market portfolio's return is 20%.

   e. What is the expected rate of return on each stock? Use the capital asset pricing model with a market risk premium of 8%. The risk-free rate of interest is 4%.

10. **Calculating Beta.** Following are several months' rates of return for Tumblehome Canoe Company. Prepare a plot like Figure 12.1. What is Tumblehome's beta? (*LO1*)

Month	Market Return, %	Tumblehome Return, %
1	0	+1
2	0	−1
3	−1	−2.5
4	−1	−0.5
5	+1	+2
6	+1	+1
7	+2	+4
8	+2	+2
9	−2	−2
10	−2	−4

FIGURE 12.10 These plots show monthly rates of return for (a) Ford, (b) Disney, and (c) Newmont Mining, plus the market portfolio. See Practice Problem 9.

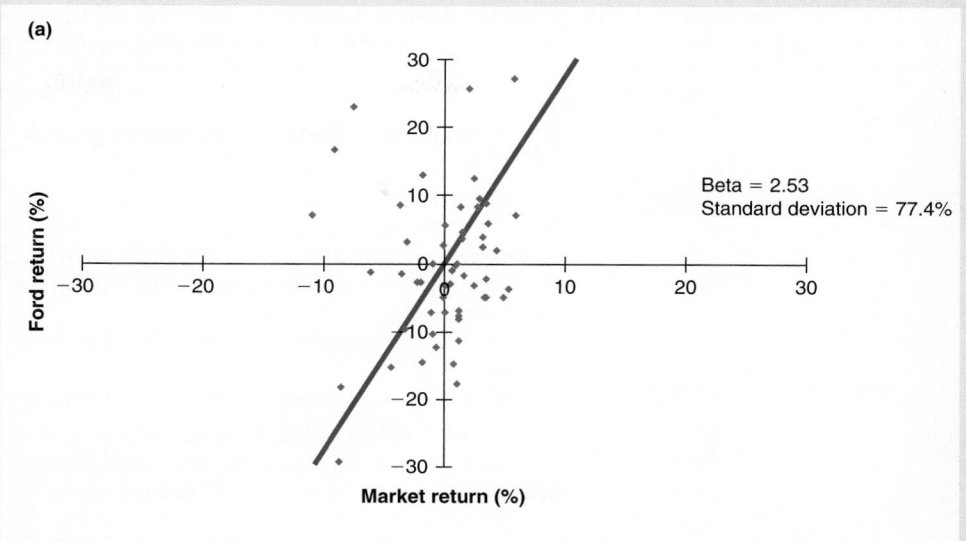

(a)

Beta = 2.53
Standard deviation = 77.4%

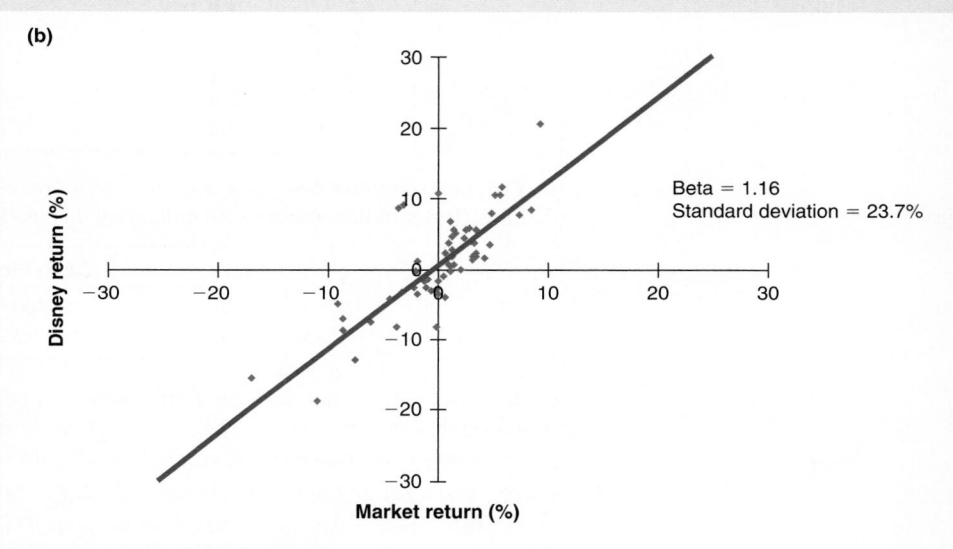

(b)

Beta = 1.16
Standard deviation = 23.7%

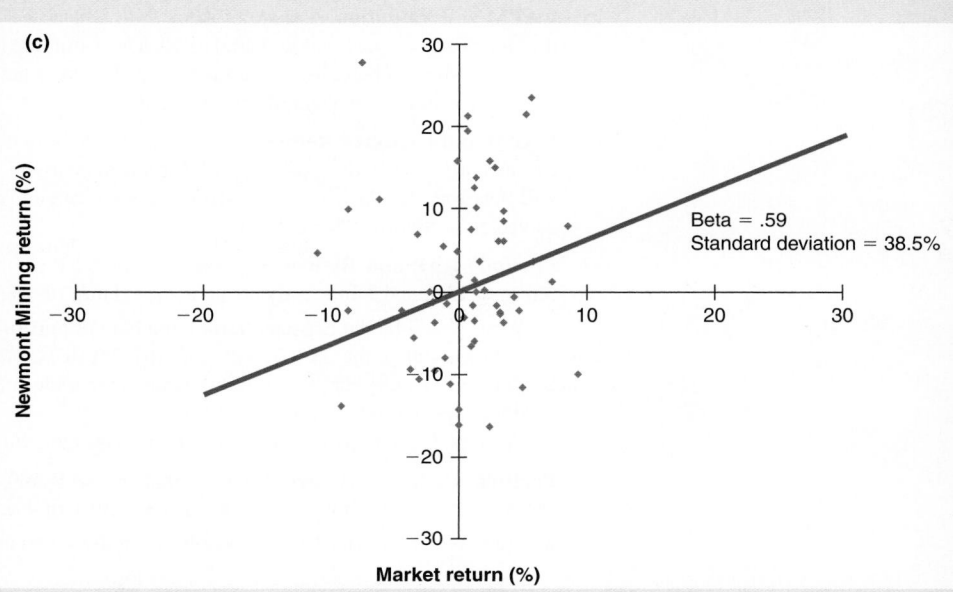

(c)

Beta = .59
Standard deviation = 38.5%

11. **Expected Returns.** Consider the following two scenarios for the economy and the returns in each scenario for the market portfolio, an aggressive stock A, and a defensive stock D. (*LO2*)

		Rate of Return	
Scenario	Market	Aggressive Stock A	Defensive Stock D
Bust	−8%	−10%	−6%
Boom	32	38	24

a. Find the beta of each stock. In what way is stock D defensive?
b. If each scenario is equally likely, find the expected rate of return on the market portfolio and on each stock.
c. If the T-bill rate is 4%, what does the CAPM say about the fair expected rate of return on the two stocks?
d. Which stock seems to be a better buy on the basis of your answers to (a) through (c)?

12. **CAPM and Cost of Capital.** Draw the security market line when the Treasury bill rate is 4% and the market risk premium is 7%. What are the project costs of capital for new ventures with betas of .75 and 1.75? Which of the following capital investments have positive NPVs? (*LO3*)

Project	Beta	Internal Rate of Return, %
P	1.0	14
Q	0	6
R	2.0	18
S	0.4	7
T	1.6	20

13. **CAPM and Valuation.** You are a consultant to a firm evaluating an expansion of its current business. The cash-flow forecasts (in millions of dollars) for the project are as follows: (*LO3*)

Years	Cash Flow
0	−100
1–10	+ 15

On the basis of the behavior of the firm's stock, you believe that the beta of the firm is 1.4. Assuming that the rate of return available on risk-free investments is 4% and that the expected rate of return on the market portfolio is 12%, what is the net present value of the project?

14. **CAPM and Cost of Capital.** Reconsider the project in the preceding problem. What is the project IRR? What is the cost of capital for the project? Does the accept–reject decision using IRR agree with the decision using NPV? (*LO3*)

15. **CAPM and Valuation.** A share of stock with a beta of .75 now sells for $50. Investors expect the stock to pay a year-end dividend of $2. The T-bill rate is 4%, and the market risk premium is 7%. If the stock is perceived to be fairly priced today, what must be investors' expectation of the price of the stock at the end of the year? (*LO2*)

16. **CAPM and Expected Return.** Reconsider the stock in the preceding problem. Suppose investors actually believe the stock will sell for $52 at year-end. Is the stock a good or bad buy? What will investors do? At what point will the stock reach an "equilibrium" at which it again is perceived as fairly priced? (*LO2*)

17. **Portfolio Risk and Return.** Suppose that the S&P 500, with a beta of 1.0, has an expected return of 13% and T-bills provide a risk-free return of 5%. (*LO2*)
a. What would be the expected return and beta of portfolios constructed from these two assets with weights in the S&P 500 of (i) 0; (ii) .25; (iii) .5; (iv) .75; (v) 1.0?
b. On the basis of your answer to (a), what is the trade-off between risk and return, that is, how does expected return vary with beta?
c. What does your answer to (b) have to do with the security market line relationship?

18. **Portfolio Risk and Return.** Suppose that the S&P 500, with a beta of 1.0, has an expected return of 10% and T-bills provide a risk-free return of 4%. (*LO1*)
a. How would you construct a portfolio from these two assets with an expected return of 8%?

b. How would you construct a portfolio from these two assets with a beta of .4?

c. Show that the risk premiums of the portfolios in (a) and (b) are proportional to their betas.

19. **CAPM and Valuation.** You are considering the purchase of real estate that will provide perpetual income that should average $50,000 per year. How much will you pay for the property if you believe its market risk is the same as the market portfolio's? The T-bill rate is 5%, and the expected market return is 12.5%. (*LO3*)

20. **Risk and Return.** According to the CAPM, would the expected rate of return on a security with a beta less than zero be more or less than the risk-free interest rate? Why would investors be willing to invest in such a security? (*Hint:* Look back to the auto and gold example in Chapter 11). (*LO2*)

21. **CAPM and Expected Return.** The following table shows betas for several companies. Calculate each stock's expected rate of return using the CAPM. Assume the risk-free rate of interest is 5%. Use a 7% risk premium for the market portfolio. (*LO2*)

Company	Beta
Cisco	1.22
Apple	1.44
Hershey	.39
Coca-Cola	.59

22. **CAPM and Expected Return.** Stock A has a beta of .5, and investors expect it to return 5%. Stock B has a beta of 1.5, and investors expect it to return 13%. Use the CAPM to find the market risk premium and the expected rate of return on the market. (*LO2*)

23. **CAPM and Expected Return.** If the expected rate of return on the market portfolio is 13% and T-bills yield 6%, what must be the beta of a stock that investors expect to return 10%? (*LO2*)

24. **Project Cost of Capital.** Suppose Cisco is considering a new investment in the common stock of a chocolate company. Which of the betas shown in the table in Problem 21 is most relevant in determining the required rate of return for this venture? Explain why the expected return to Cisco stock is *not* the appropriate required return. (*LO3*)

25. **Risk and Return.** True or false? Explain or qualify as necessary. (*LO2*)

a. The expected rate of return on an investment with a beta of 2.0 is twice as high as the expected rate of return of the market portfolio.

b. The contribution of a stock to the risk of a diversified portfolio depends on the market risk of the stock.

c. If a stock's expected rate of return plots below the security market line, it is underpriced.

d. A diversified portfolio with a beta of 2.0 is twice as volatile as the market portfolio.

e. An undiversified portfolio with a beta of 2.0 is twice as volatile as the market portfolio.

26. **CAPM and Expected Return.** A mutual fund manager expects her portfolio to earn a rate of return of 11% this year. The beta of her portfolio is .8. If the rate of return available on risk-free assets is 4% and you expect the rate of return on the market portfolio to be 14%, should you invest in this mutual fund? (*LO2*)

27. **Required Rate of Return.** Reconsider the mutual fund manager in the previous problem. Explain how you would use a stock index mutual fund and a risk-free position in Treasury bills (or a money market mutual fund) to create a portfolio with the same risk as the manager's but with a higher expected rate of return. What is the rate of return on that portfolio? (*LO2*)

28. **Required Rate of Return.** In view of your answer to the preceding problem, explain why a mutual fund must be able to provide an expected rate of return in excess of that predicted by the security market line for investors to consider the fund an attractive investment opportunity. (*LO2*)

29. **CAPM.** We Do Bankruptcies is a law firm that specializes in providing advice to firms in financial distress. It prospers in recessions when other firms are struggling. Consequently, its beta is negative, −.2. (*LO2*)

a. If the interest rate on Treasury bills is 5% and the expected return on the market portfolio is 15%, what is the expected return on the shares of the law firm according to the CAPM?

b. Suppose you invested 90% of your wealth in the market portfolio and the remainder of your wealth in the shares in the law firm. What would be the beta of your portfolio?

CHALLENGE PROBLEMS

30. **Leverage and Portfolio Risk.** Footnote 4 in the chapter asks you to consider a borrow-and-invest strategy in which you use $1 million of your own money and borrow another $1 million to invest $2 million in a market index fund. If the risk-free interest rate is 4% and the expected rate of return on the market index fund is 12%, what is the risk premium and expected rate of return on the borrow-and-invest strategy? Why is the risk of this strategy twice that of simply investing your $1 million in the market index fund? (*LO2*)

Templates can be found at www.mhhe.com/bmm7e.

31. **Beta.** Go to our Online Learning Center at www.mhhe.com/bmm7e, and link to the material for Chapter 12, where you will find a spreadsheet containing 5 years of monthly rates of return on Dell Computer (DELL), Consolidated Edison (ED), and the S&P 500. (*LO1*)

   a. Calculate the beta of each firm. Use Excel's SLOPE function, which fits a regression line through a scatter diagram of two series of numbers.
   b. Does the relative magnitude of each beta make sense in terms of the business risk of the two firms? Explain.

WEB EXERCISE

1. **Betas and Expected Stock Returns**   You can find estimates of stock betas by logging on to finance.yahoo.com and looking at a company's profile. Try comparing the stock betas of Google (GOOG), The Home Depot (HD), Du Pont (DD), Altria Group (MO), and Caterpillar (CAT). Once you have read Section 12.2, use the capital asset pricing model to estimate the expected return for each of these stocks. You will need a figure for the current Treasury bill rate. You can find this also on finance.yahoo.com by clicking on *Bonds—Rates*. Assume for your estimates a market risk premium of 7%.

2. **Fund Betas**   Log on to www.fidelity.com and look at the list of mutual funds that are managed by Fidelity. Some of these funds, such as the Aggressive Growth Fund, appear from their names to be high-risk. Others, such as the Balanced Fund, appear to be low-risk. Pick several apparent high- and low-risk funds and then check whether their betas really do match the fund's name.

SOLUTIONS TO SELF-TEST QUESTIONS

12.1   See Figure 12.11. Anchovy Queen's beta is 1.0.

12.2   A portfolio's beta is just a weighted average of the betas of the securities in the portfolio. In this case the weights are equal, since an equal amount is assumed invested in each of the stocks in Table 12.1. The average beta of these stocks is 0.95.

12.3   The standard deviation of a fully diversified portfolio's return is proportional to its beta. The standard deviation in this case is $.5 \times 20 = 10\%$.

12.4 $r = r_f + \beta(r_m - r_f) = 6 + (1.5 \times 7) = 16.5\%$

12.5   Put 25% of your money in the market portfolio and the rest in Treasury bills. The portfolio's beta is .25 and its expected return is

$$r_{\text{portfolio}} = (.75 \times 6) + (.25 \times 13) = 7.75\%$$

The expected return also may be computed as

$$r_f + \beta(r_m - r_f) = 6 + .25 \times 7 = 7.75\%$$

12.6 $r_{\text{portfolio}} = (.4 \times 6) + (.6 \times 13) = 10.2\%$. This portfolio's beta is .6, since $600,000, which is 60% of the investment, is in the market portfolio. Investors in a stock with a beta of .6 would not buy it unless it also offered a rate of return of 10.2% and would rush to buy if it offered more. The stock price would adjust until the stock's expected rate of return was 10.2%.

FIGURE 12.11 Each point shows the performance of Anchovy Queen stock when the market is up or down by 1%. On average, Anchovy Queen stock follows the market; it has a beta of 1.0.

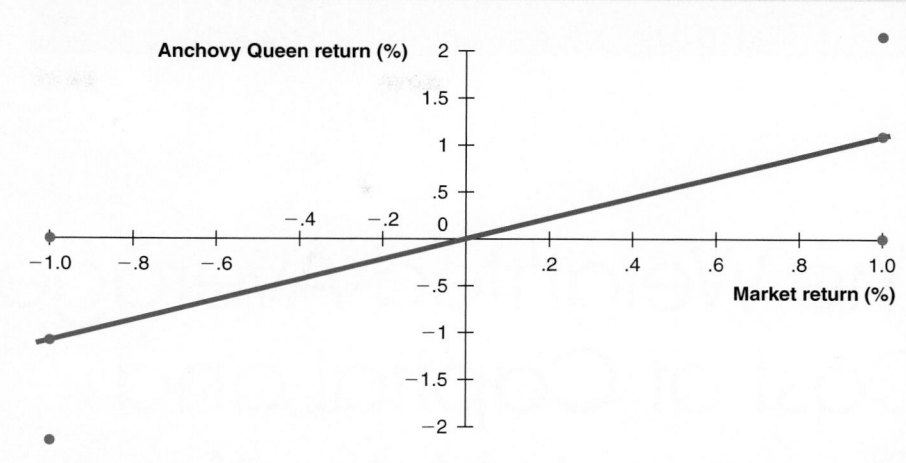

12.7 Present value = $50 million × 10-year annuity factor at 12.3% = $279.1 million.

12.8 Dell should use Pfizer's cost of capital, 7.8%. Dell's company cost of capital tells us what expected rate of return investors demand from the computer hardware business. This is not the appropriate project cost of capital for its proposed venture into pharmaceuticals.

SOLUTIONS TO SPREADSHEET QUESTIONS

12.1 We would expect beta to fall from the value obtained in the spreadsheet. Ford's return in June (when the market fell) is not as bad as originally assumed, and its return in July (when the market rose) is not as good as originally assumed. In both cases, Ford's returns are less responsive to the market. In fact, beta falls from 2.15 to 1.46.

12.2 Ford's beta is precisely the same as the original value. Increasing the assumed return in each month by a constant does not change the typical *responsiveness* of Ford to variation in the return of the market index.

12.3 If in the additional month of data Ford is down 5% while the market is up 5%, we would expect beta to fall. In this month, Ford's stock moved in opposition to the market index. Adding this observation therefore reduces our estimate of Ford's typical response to market movements. In fact, beta falls to 1.78.

The Weighted-Average Cost of Capital and Company Valuation

LEARNING OBJECTIVES

After studying this chapter, you should be able to:

1. Calculate a firm's capital structure.

2. Estimate the required rates of return on the securities issued by the firm.

3. Calculate the weighted-average cost of capital.

4. Understand when the weighted-average cost of capital is—or isn't—the appropriate discount rate for a new project.

5. Use the weighted-average cost of capital to value a business given forecasts of its future cash flows.

RELATED WEB SITES FOR THIS CHAPTER CAN BE FOUND AT WWW.MHHE.COM/BMM7E.

Geothermal Corporation was founded to produce electricity from geothermal energy trapped under the earth. How should Geothermal determine its cost of capital?

I n the last chapter you learned how to use the capital asset pricing model to estimate the expected return on a company's common stock. If the firm is financed wholly by common stock, then the stockholders own all the firm's assets and are entitled to all the cash flows. In this case, the return required by investors in the common stock equals the company cost of capital.[1]

Most companies, however, are financed by a mixture of securities, including common stock, bonds, preferred stock, or other securities. Each of these securities has different risks and therefore investors in them look for different rates of return. In these circumstances, the company cost of capital is no longer the same as the expected return on the common stock. It depends on the expected return from *all* the securities that the company has issued.

The cost of capital also depends on taxes, because interest payments made by a corporation are tax-deductible expenses. Therefore, the company cost of capital is usually calculated as a weighted average of the *after-tax* cost of debt interest and the "cost of equity," that is, the expected rate of return on the firm's common stock. The weights are the fractions of debt and equity in the firm's capital structure. Managers refer to the firm's *weighted-average* cost of capital, or *WACC* (rhymes with "quack").

Managers use the weighted-average cost of capital to evaluate average-risk investment projects. "Average risk" means that the project's risk matches the risk of the firm's existing assets and operations. This chapter explains how the weighted-average cost of capital is calculated in practice.

Managers calculating WACC can get bogged down in formulas. We want you to understand *why* WACC works, not just how to calculate it. Let's start with "Why?" We'll listen in as a young financial manager struggles to recall the rationale for project discount rates.

[1] Investors will invest in the firm's securities only if they offer the same expected return as other equally risky securities. When securities are properly priced, the return that investors can expect from their investments is therefore also the return that they *require*.

13.1   Geothermal's Cost of Capital

Jo Ann Cox, a recent graduate of a prestigious eastern business school, poured a third cup of black coffee and tried again to remember what she once knew about project hurdle rates. Why hadn't she paid more attention in Finance 101? Why had she sold her finance text the day after passing the finance final?

Costas Thermopolis, her boss and CEO of Geothermal Corporation, had told her to prepare a financial evaluation of a proposed expansion of Geothermal's production. She was to report at 9:00 Monday morning. Thermopolis, whose background was geophysics, not finance, not only expected a numerical analysis but also expected her to explain it to him.

Thermopolis had founded Geothermal in 1996 to produce electricity from geothermal energy trapped deep under Nevada. The company had pioneered this business and had obtained perpetual production rights for a large tract on favorable terms from the U.S. government. When the oil shock in 2007–2008 drove up energy prices worldwide, Geothermal became an exceptionally profitable company. It was currently reporting a rate of return on book assets of 25% per year.

Now, in 2012, production rights were no longer cheap. The proposed expansion would cost $30 million and should generate a perpetual after-tax cash flow of $4.5 million annually. The projected rate of return was 4.5/30 = .15, or 15%, much less than the profitability of Geothermal's existing assets. However, once the new project was up and running, it would be no riskier than Geothermal's present business.

Jo Ann realized that 15% was not necessarily a bad return—though of course 25% would have been better. Fifteen percent might still exceed Geothermal's cost of capital, that is, exceed the expected rate of return that outside investors would demand to invest money in the project. If the cost of capital was less than the 15% expected return, expansion would be a good deal and would generate net value for Geothermal and its stockholders.

Jo Ann remembered how to calculate the cost of capital for companies that used only common stock financing. Briefly she sketched the argument.

"I need the expected rate of return investors would require from Geothermal's real assets—the wells, pumps, generators, etc. That rate of return depends on the assets' risk. However, the assets aren't traded in the stock market, so I can't observe how risky they have been. I can only observe the risk of Geothermal's common stock.

"But if Geothermal issues only stock—no debt—then owning the stock means owning the assets, and the expected return demanded by investors in the stock must also be the cost of capital for the assets." She jotted down the following identities:

Value of business = value of stock

Risk of business = risk of stock

Rate of return on business = rate of return on stock

Investors' required return from business = investors' required return from stock

If there were no company debt, this would be the right discount rate for Geothermal's expansion plan.

Unfortunately, Geothermal had borrowed a substantial amount of money; its stockholders did *not* have unencumbered ownership of Geothermal's assets. The expansion project would also justify some extra debt finance. Jo Ann realized that she would have to look at Geothermal's **capital structure**—its mix of debt and equity financing—and consider the expected rates of return required by debt as well as equity investors.

Geothermal had issued 22.65 million shares, now trading at $20 each. Thus shareholders valued Geothermal's equity at $20 × 22.65 million = $453 million. In addition, the company had issued bonds with a market value of $194 million. The market value of the company's debt and equity was therefore $194 + $453 = $647 million. Debt was 194/647 = .3, or 30% of the total.

capital structure
The mix of long-term debt and equity financing.

"Geothermal's worth more to investors than either its debt or its equity," Jo Ann mused. "But I ought to be able to find the overall value of Geothermal's business by adding up the debt and equity." She sketched a rough balance sheet:

Assets		Liabilities and Shareholders' Equity		
Market value of assets = value of Geothermal's existing business	$647	Market value of debt	$194	(30%)
		Market value of equity	453	(70%)
Total value	$647	Total value	$647	(100%)

"Holy Toledo, I've got it!" Jo Ann exclaimed. "If I bought *all* the securities issued by Geothermal, debt as well as equity, I'd own the entire business. That means . . ." She jotted again:

$$\text{Value of business} = \frac{\text{value of portfolio of all the firm's}}{\text{debt and equity securities}}$$

$$\text{Risk of business} = \text{risk of portfolio}$$

$$\text{Rate of return on business} = \text{rate of return on portfolio}$$

$$\frac{\text{Investors' required return on business}}{\text{(company cost of capital)}} = \frac{\text{investors' required return on}}{\text{portfolio}}$$

"All I have to do is calculate the expected rate of return on a portfolio of all the firm's securities. That's easy. The debt's yielding 8%, and Fred, that nerdy banker, says that equity investors want 14%. Suppose he's right. The portfolio would contain 30% debt and 70% equity, so . . ."

$$\text{Portfolio return} = (.3 \times 8\%) + (.7 \times 14\%) = 12.2\%$$

It was all coming back to her now. The company cost of capital is just a weighted average of returns on debt and equity, with weights depending on relative market values of the two securities.

"But there's one more thing. Interest is tax-deductible. If Geothermal pays $1 of interest, taxable income is reduced by $1, and the firm's tax bill drops by 35 cents (assuming a 35% tax rate). The net cost is only 65 cents. So the after-tax cost of debt is not 8%, but $.65 \times 8 = 5.2\%$.

"Now I can finally calculate the weighted-average cost of capital:

$$\text{WACC} = (.3 \times 5.2\%) + (.7 \times 14\%) = 11.4\%$$

"Looks like the expansion's a good deal. Fifteen's better than 11.4. But I sure need a break."

13.2 The Weighted-Average Cost of Capital

Jo Ann's conclusions were important. It should be obvious by now that the choice of the discount rate can be crucial, especially when the project involves large capital expenditures or is long-lived. The nearby box describes how a major investment in a power station—an investment with both a large capital expenditure and very long life—turned on the choice of the discount rate.

Think again what the company cost of capital is, and what it is used for. We *define* it as the opportunity cost of capital for the firm's existing assets; we *use* it to value new assets that have the same risk as the old ones. The company cost of capital is the minimum acceptable rate of return when the firm expands by investing in average-risk projects.

We first introduced the opportunity cost of capital in Chapter 1. "Opportunity cost" is a shorthand reminder that when the firm invests rather than returning cash to shareholders, the shareholders lose the opportunity to invest in financial markets. If the corporation acts in the shareholders' interests, it will invest their money only if it

Choosing the Discount Rate

Shortly before the British government began to sell off the electricity industry to private investors, controversy erupted over the industry's proposal to build a 1,200-megawatt nuclear power station known as Hinkley Point C. The government argued that a nuclear station would both diversify the sources of electricity generation and reduce sulfur dioxide and carbon dioxide emissions. Protesters emphasized the dangers of nuclear accidents and attacked the proposal as "bizarre, dated and irrelevant."

At the public inquiry held to consider the proposal, opponents produced some powerful evidence that the nuclear station was also a very high cost option. Their principal witness, Professor Elroy Dimson, argued that the government-owned power company had employed an unrealistically low figure for the opportunity cost of capital. Had the company used a more plausible figure, the cost of building and operating the nuclear station would have been higher than that of a comparable station based on fossil fuels.

The reason why the choice of discount rate was so important was that nuclear stations are expensive to build but cheap to operate. If capital is cheap (i.e., the discount rate is low), then the high up-front cost is less serious. But if the cost of capital is high, then the high initial cost of nuclear stations made them uneconomic.

Evidence produced at the inquiry suggested that the construction cost of a nuclear station was £1,527 million (or about $2.3 billion), while the cost of a comparable nonnuclear station was only £895 million. However, power stations last about 40 years, and, once built, nuclear stations cost much less to operate than nonnuclear stations. If operated at 75% of theoretical capacity, the running costs of the nuclear station would be about £63 million a year, compared with running costs of £168 million a year for the nonnuclear station.

The following table shows the cost advantage of the nuclear power station at different (real) discount rates. At a 5% discount rate, which was the figure used by the government, the present value of the costs of the nuclear option was nearly £1 billion lower than that of a station based on fossil fuels. But with a discount rate of 16%, which was the figure favored by Professor Dimson, the position was almost exactly reversed, so the government could save nearly £1 billion by refusing the power company permission to build Hinkley Point C and relying instead on new fossil-fuel power stations.

Eight years after the inquiry, the proposal to construct Hinkley Point C continued to gather dust, and British Energy, the privatized electric utility, declared that it had no plans to build a new nuclear power station in the near future.

Present value of the cost advantage to a nuclear rather than a fossil-fuel station (figures in billions of pounds)

Real Discount Rate	Present Value of the Cost Advantage of the Nuclear Station
5%	0.9
8	0.2
10	−0.1
12	−0.4
14	−0.7
16	−0.9
18	−1.2

Technical Notes:
1. Present values are measured at the date that the power station comes into operation.
2. The above table assumes for simplicity that construction costs for nuclear stations are spread evenly over the 8 years before the station comes into operation, while the costs for fossil-fuel stations are assumed to be spread evenly over the 4 years before operation. As a result the present value of the costs of the two stations may differ slightly from the more precise estimates produced by Professor Dimson.

Source: Adapted from Elroy Dimson, "The Discount Rate for a Power Station," *Energy Economics*, Volume 11, Issue 3, pp. 175–180. © 1989 with permission from Elsevier Science.

can find projects that offer higher rates of return than investors could achieve on their own. Therefore, the expected rates of return on investments in financial markets determine the cost of capital for corporate investments.

The company cost of capital is the opportunity cost of capital for the company as a whole. We discussed the company cost of capital in Chapter 12, but did not explain how to measure it when the firm has raised different types of debt and equity financing or how to adjust it for the tax-deductibility of interest payments. The weighted-average cost of capital formula handles these complications.

Calculating Company Cost of Capital as a Weighted Average

When only common stock is outstanding, calculating the company cost of capital is straightforward, though not always easy. For example, a financial manager could estimate beta and calculate shareholders' required rate of return using the capital asset pricing model (CAPM). This would be the expected rate of return investors require on the company's existing assets and operations and also the expected return they will require on new investments that do not change the company's market risk.

But most companies issue debt as well as equity. **The company cost of capital is a *weighted average* of the returns demanded by debt and equity investors. The weighted average is the expected rate of return investors would demand on a portfolio of all the firm's outstanding securities.**

Let's review Jo Ann Cox's calculations for Geothermal. To avoid complications, we'll ignore taxes for the next two or three pages. The total market value of Geothermal, which we denote as V, is the sum of the values of the outstanding debt D and the equity E. Thus firm value is $V = D + E = \$194$ million $+ \$453$ million $= \$647$ million. Debt accounts for 30% of the value and equity accounts for the remaining 70%. If you held all the shares and all the debt, your investment in Geothermal would be $V = \$647$ million. Between them, the debt- and equityholders own *all* the firm's assets. So V is also the value of these assets—the value of Geothermal's existing business.

Suppose that Geothermal's equity investors require a 14% rate of return on their investment in the stock. What rate of return must a new project provide in order that all investors—both debtholders and stockholders—earn a fair rate of return? The debtholders require a rate of return of $r_{debt} = 8\%$. So each year the firm will need to pay interest of $r_{debt} \times D = .08 \times \$194$ million $= \$15.52$ million. The shareholders, who have invested in a riskier security, require an expected return of $r_{equity} = 14\%$ on their investment of $\$453$ million. Thus in order to keep shareholders happy, the company needs additional income of $r_{equity} \times E = .14 \times \$453$ million $= \$63.42$ million. To satisfy both the debtholders and the shareholders, Geothermal needs to earn $\$15.52$ million $+ \$63.42$ million $= \$78.94$ million. This is equivalent to earning a return of $r_{assets} = 78.94/647 = .122$, or 12.2%.

Figure 13.1 illustrates the reasoning behind our calculations. The figure shows the amount of income needed to satisfy the debt and equity investors. Notice that debtholders account for 30% of Geothermal's capital structure but receive less than 30% of its expected income. On the other hand, they bear less than a 30% share of risk, since they have first cut at the company's income and also first claim on its assets if the company gets in trouble. Shareholders expect a return of more than 70% of Geothermal's income because they bear correspondingly more risk.

However, if you buy *all* Geothermal's debt and equity, you own its assets lock, stock, and barrel. You receive all the income and bear all the risks. The expected rate of return you'd require on this portfolio of securities is the same return you'd require from unencumbered ownership of the business. This rate of return—12.2%, ignoring taxes—is therefore the company cost of capital and the required rate of return from an equal-risk expansion of the business.

FIGURE 13.1 Geothermal's debtholders account for 30% of the company's capital structure, but they get a smaller share of income because their return is guaranteed by the company. Geothermal's stockholders bear more risk and receive, on average, greater return. Of course, if you buy all the debt and all the equity, you get all the income.

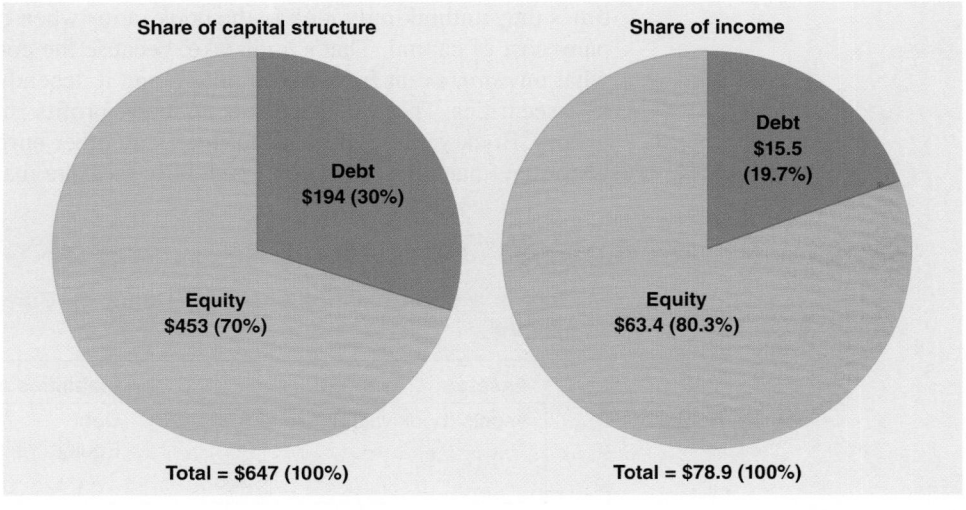

Share of capital structure

Debt
$194 (30%)

Equity
$453 (70%)

Total = $647 (100%)

Share of income

Debt
$15.5
(19.7%)

Equity
$63.4 (80.3%)

Total = $78.9 (100%)

The bottom line (still ignoring taxes) is

Company cost of capital = weighted average of debt and equity returns

The underlying algebra is simple. Debtholders need income of ($r_{\text{debt}} \times D$), and the equity investors need expected income of ($r_{\text{equity}} \times E$). The *total* income that is needed is ($r_{\text{debt}} \times D$) + ($r_{\text{equity}} \times E$). The amount of their combined existing investment in the company is V. So to calculate the return that is needed on the assets, we simply divide the income by the investment:

$$r_{\text{assets}} = \frac{\text{total income}}{\text{value of investment}}$$

$$= \frac{(D \times r_{\text{debt}}) + (E \times r_{\text{equity}})}{V} = \left(\frac{D}{V} \times r_{\text{debt}}\right) + \left(\frac{E}{V} \times r_{\text{equity}}\right)$$

For Geothermal,

$$r_{\text{assets}} = (.30 \times 8\%) + (.70 \times 14\%) = 12.2\%$$

This figure is the expected return demanded by investors in the firm's assets.

Self-Test 13.1

Hot Rocks Corp., one of Geothermal's competitors, has issued long-term bonds with a market value of $50 million and an expected return of 9%. It has 4 million shares outstanding trading for $10 each. At this price the shares offer an expected return of 17%. What is the weighted-average cost of capital for Hot Rocks's assets and operations? Assume Hot Rocks pays no taxes.

Use Market Weights, Not Book Weights

The company cost of capital is the expected rate of return that investors demand from the company's assets and operations. **The cost of capital must be based on what investors are actually willing to pay for the company's outstanding securities—that is, based on the securities' *market* values.**

Market values usually differ from the values recorded by accountants in the company's books. The book value of Geothermal's equity reflects money raised in the past from shareholders or reinvested by the firm on their behalf. If investors recognize Geothermal's excellent prospects, the market value of equity may be much higher than book, and the debt ratio will be lower when measured in terms of market values rather than book values.

Financial managers use book debt-to-value ratios for various purposes, and sometimes they unthinkingly look to the book ratios when calculating weights for the company cost of capital. That's a mistake, because the company cost of capital measures what *investors* want from the company, and it depends on how they value the company's securities. That value depends on future profits and cash flows, not on accounting history. Book values, while useful for many other purposes, measure only cumulative historical financings; they don't generally measure market values accurately.

Self-Test 13.2

Here is a book balance sheet for Duane S. Burg Associates. Figures are in millions.

Assets		Liabilities and Shareholders' Equity	
Assets (book value)	$75	Debt	$25
		Equity	50
	$75		$75

Unfortunately, the company has fallen on hard times. The 6 million shares are trading for only $4 apiece, and the market value of its debt securities is 20% below the face (book) value. Because of the company's large cumulative losses, it will pay no taxes on future income.

Suppose shareholders now demand a 20% expected rate of return. The bonds are now yielding 14%. What is the weighted-average cost of capital?

Taxes and the Weighted-Average Cost of Capital

So far our examples have ignored taxes. When you calculate a project's NPV, you need to discount the cash flows *after* tax assuming that the project is wholly equity-financed. That is exactly the approach that we used in Chapter 9, when we valued Blooper's investment in the magnoosium mine. Sometimes you may encounter companies that forecast cash flows *before* tax and then try to compensate for this by using a higher discount rate. It doesn't work; there is no simple adjustment to the discount rate that will allow you to discount pretax cash flows.

Taxes are also important because most companies are financed by both equity and debt. The interest payments on this debt are deducted from income before tax is calculated. Therefore, the cost to the company is reduced by the amount of this tax saving.

The interest rate on Geothermal's debt is $r_{debt} = 8\%$. However, with a corporate tax rate of $T_c = .35$, the government bears 35% of the cost of the interest payments. The government doesn't send the firm a check for this amount, but the income tax that the firm pays is reduced by 35% of its interest expense. Therefore, Geothermal's after-tax cost of debt is only $100 - 35 = 65\%$ of the 8% pretax cost:

$$\text{After-tax cost of debt} = (1 - \text{tax rate}) \times \text{pretax cost}$$
$$= (1 - T_c) \times r_{debt}$$
$$= (1 - .35) \times 8\% = 5.2\%$$

We can now adjust our calculation of Geothermal's cost of capital to recognize the tax savings associated with interest payments:

$$\text{Company cost of capital, after-tax} = (.3 \times 5.2\%) + (.7 \times 14\%) = 11.4\%$$

weighted-average cost of capital (WACC)
Expected rate of return on a portfolio of all the firm's securities, adjusted for tax savings due to interest payments.

Now we're back to the **weighted-average cost of capital,** or **WACC.** The general formula is

$$\text{WACC} = \left[\frac{D}{V} \times (1 - T_c)r_{debt}\right] + \left(\frac{E}{V} \times r_{equity}\right) \tag{13.1}$$

Self-Test 13.3

Criss-Cross Industries has earnings before interest and taxes (EBIT) of $10 million. Interest payments are $2 million, and the corporate tax rate is 35%. Construct a simple income statement to show that the debt interest reduces the taxes the firm owes to the government. How much more tax would Criss-Cross pay if it were financed solely by equity?

EXAMPLE 13.1 ▶ Weighted-Average Cost of Capital for Dow Chemical

In Chapter 12 we showed how the capital asset pricing model can be used to estimate the expected return on Dow Chemical common stock. We will now use this estimate to figure out the company's weighted-average cost of capital.

Step 1. *Calculate the value of each security as a proportion of firm value.* The company has outstanding 1,150 million shares, which in mid-2010 had a market value of about $26.50 each. The total market value of Dow's equity was $E = 1{,}150 \times \$26.50 = \$30{,}475$ million. The company's latest balance sheet showed that it had borrowed $D = \$19{,}152$ million. So the total value of Dow's securities is $V = D + E = \$19{,}152 + \$30{,}475 = \$49{,}627$ million. Debt as a proportion of the total value is $D/V = \$19{,}152/\$49{,}627 = .39$, and equity as a proportion of the total is $\$30{,}475/\$49{,}627 = .61$.

Step 2. *Determine the required rate of return on each security.* In Chapter 12 we estimated that Dow's shareholders required a return of 19.0%. The average yield on Dow's debt was about 6.3%.

Step 3. *Calculate a weighted average of the after-tax return on the debt and the return on the equity.*[2] The weighted-average cost of capital is

$$\text{WACC} = \left[\frac{D}{V} \times (1 - T_c)r_{\text{debt}}\right] + \left(\frac{E}{V} \times r_{\text{equity}}\right)$$
$$= [.39 \times (1 - .35)6.3\%] + (.61 \times 19.0\%) = 13.2\%$$

Self-Test 13.4

Calculate WACC for Hot Rocks (Self-Test 13.1) and Burg Associates (Self-Test 13.2) assuming the companies face a 35% corporate income tax rate.

What If There Are Three (or More) Sources of Financing?

We have simplified our discussion of the cost of capital by assuming the firm has only two classes of securities: debt and equity. Even if the firm has issued other classes of securities, our general approach to calculating WACC remains unchanged. We simply calculate the weighted-average after-tax return of each security type.

For example, suppose the firm also has outstanding preferred stock. Preferred stock has some of the characteristics of both common stock and fixed-income securities. Like bonds, preferred stock promises to pay a given, usually level, stream of dividends. Unlike bonds, however, there is no maturity date for the preferred stock. The promised dividends constitute a perpetuity as long as the firm stays in business. Moreover, a failure to come up with the cash to pay the dividends does not push the firm into bankruptcy. Instead, any unpaid dividends simply cumulate; the common stockholders do not receive dividends until the accumulated preferred dividends have been paid. Finally, unlike interest payments, preferred stock dividends are not considered tax-deductible expenses.

How would we calculate WACC for a firm with preferred stock as well as common stock and bonds outstanding? Using P to denote the value of preferred stock, we simply generalize Equation 13.1 for WACC as follows:

$$\text{WACC} = \left[\frac{D}{V} \times (1 - T_c)r_{\text{debt}}\right] + \left(\frac{P}{V} \times r_{\text{preferred}}\right) + \left(\frac{E}{V} \times r_{\text{equity}}\right) \quad \textbf{(13.1a)}$$

---

[2] Financial managers often use "equity" to refer to common stock, even though a firm's equity strictly includes both common and preferred stock. We continue to use r_{equity} to refer specifically to the expected return on the common stock.

Wrapping Up Geothermal

We now turn one last time to Jo Ann Cox and Geothermal's proposed expansion. We want to make sure that she—and you—know how to *use* the weighted-average cost of capital.

Remember that the proposed expansion costs $30 million and should generate a perpetual cash flow of $4.5 million per year. A simple cash-flow worksheet might look like this:[3]

Revenue	$10.00 million
− Operating expenses	− 3.08
= Pretax operating cash flow	6.92
− Tax at 35%	− 2.42
After-tax cash flow	$ 4.50 million

Note that these cash flows do not include the tax benefits of using debt. Geothermal's managers and engineers forecast revenues, costs, and taxes as if the project were to be all-equity financed. The interest tax shields generated by the project's actual debt financing are not forgotten, however. They are accounted for by using the *after-tax* cost of debt in the weighted-average cost of capital.

Project net present value is calculated by discounting the cash flow (which is a perpetuity) at Geothermal's 11.4% weighted-average cost of capital:

$$NPV = -30 + \frac{4.5}{.114} = +\$9.5 \text{ million}$$

Expansion will thus add $9.5 million to the net wealth of Geothermal's owners.

Checking Our Logic

Any project offering a rate of return more than 11.4% will have a positive NPV, assuming that the project has the same risk and financing as Geothermal's business. A project offering exactly 11.4% would just break even; it would generate just enough cash to satisfy both debtholders and stockholders.

Let's check that out. Suppose the proposed expansion had revenues of only $8.34 million and after-tax cash flows of $3.42 million:

Revenue	$8.34 million
− Operating expenses	− 3.08
= Pretax operating cash flow	5.26
− Tax at 35%	− 1.84
After-tax cash flow	$3.42 million

With an investment of $30 million, the internal rate of return on this perpetuity is exactly 11.4%:

$$\text{Rate of return} = \frac{3.42}{30} = .114, \text{ or } 11.4\%$$

and NPV is exactly zero:

$$NPV = -30 + \frac{3.42}{.114} = 0$$

When we calculated Geothermal's weighted-average cost of capital, we recognized that the company's debt ratio was 30%. When Geothermal's analysts use the

---

[3] For this example we ignore depreciation, a noncash but tax-deductible expense. (If the project were really perpetual, why depreciate?)

weighted-average cost of capital to evaluate the new project, they are *assuming* that the $30 million additional investment would support the issue of additional debt equal to 30% of the investment, or $9 million. The remaining $21 million is provided by the shareholders either in the form of reinvested earnings or through the issue of additional shares.

The following table shows how the cash flows would be shared between the debtholders and shareholders assuming still that the project has zero NPV. We start with the pretax operating cash flow of $5.26 million:

Cash flow before tax and interest	$5.26 million
− Interest payment (.08 × $9 million)	− .72
= Pretax cash flow	4.54
− Tax at 35%	− 1.59
After-tax cash flow	$2.95 million

Project cash flows before tax and interest are forecast to be $5.26 million. Out of this figure, Geothermal needs to pay interest of 8% of $9 million, which comes to $.72 million. This leaves a pretax cash flow of $4.54 million, on which the company must pay tax. Taxes equal .35 × 4.54 = $1.59 million. Shareholders are left with $2.95 million, just enough to give them the 14% return that they need on their $21 million investment. (Note that 2.95/21 = .14, or 14%.) Therefore, everything checks out.

If a project has zero NPV when the expected cash flows are discounted at the weighted-average cost of capital, then the project's cash flows are just sufficient to give debtholders and shareholders the returns they require.

13.3 Measuring Capital Structure

We have explained the formula for calculating the weighted-average cost of capital. We will now look at some of the practical problems in applying that formula. Suppose that the financial manager of Big Oil has asked you to estimate the firm's weighted-average cost of capital. Your first step is to work out Big Oil's capital structure. But where do you get the data?

Financial managers usually start with the company's accounts, which show the book value of debt and equity, whereas the weighted-average cost of capital formula calls for their *market* values. A little work and a dash of judgment are needed to go from one to the other.

Table 13.1 shows the debt and equity issued by Big Oil. The firm has borrowed $200 million from banks and has issued a further $200 million of long-term bonds. These bonds have a coupon rate of 8% and mature at the end of 12 years. Finally, there are 100 million shares of common stock outstanding, each with a par value of $1. But the accounts also recognize that Big Oil has in past years plowed back into the firm $300 million of retained earnings. The total book value of the equity shown in the accounts is $100 million + $300 million = $400 million.

The figures shown in Table 13.1 are taken from Big Oil's annual accounts and are therefore book values. Sometimes the differences between book values and market values are negligible. For example, consider the $200 million that Big Oil owes the bank. The interest rate on bank loans is usually linked to the general level of interest rates. Thus if interest rates rise, the rate charged on Big Oil's loan also rises to

TABLE 13.1 The *book* values of Big Oil's debt and equity (dollar figures in millions)

Bank debt	$200	25.0%
Long-term bonds (12-year maturity, 8% coupon)	200	25.0
Common stock (100 million shares, par value $1)	100	12.5
Retained earnings	300	37.5
Total	$800	100.0%

TABLE 13.2 The market values of Big Oil's debt and equity (dollar figures in millions)

Bank debt	$ 200.0	12.6%
Long-term bonds	185.7	11.7
Total debt	385.7	24.3
Common stock (100 million shares at $12)	1,200.0	75.7
Total	$1,585.7	100.0%

maintain the loan's value. As long as Big Oil is reasonably sure to repay the loan, it is worth close to $200 million. Most financial managers most of the time are willing to accept the book value of bank debt as a fair approximation of its market value.

What about Big Oil's long-term bonds? Since the bonds were originally issued, long-term interest rates have risen to 9%.[4] We can calculate the value today of each bond as follows.[5] There are 12 coupon payments of $.08 \times 200 = \$16$ million and then repayment of face value 12 years out. Thus the final cash payment to the bondholders is $216 million. All the bond's cash flows are discounted back at the *current* interest rate of 9%:

$$PV = \frac{16}{1.09} + \frac{16}{(1.09)^2} + \frac{16}{(1.09)^3} + \cdots + \frac{216}{(1.09)^{12}} = \$185.7$$

Therefore, the bonds are worth only $185.7 million, 93% of their face value.

If you used the book value of Big Oil's long-term debt rather than its market value, you would be a little bit off in your calculation of the weighted-average cost of capital, but probably not seriously so.

The really big errors are likely to arise if you use the book value of equity rather than its market value. The $400 million book value of Big Oil's equity measures the total amount of cash that the firm has raised from shareholders in the past or has retained and invested on their behalf. But perhaps Big Oil has been able to find projects that were worth more than they originally cost, or perhaps the value of the assets has increased with inflation. Perhaps investors see great future investment opportunities for the company. All these considerations determine what investors are willing to pay for Big Oil's common stock.

Big Oil's stock price is $12 a share. Thus the total *market value* of the stock is

Number of shares $\times$ share price $= 100$ million $\times$ $12 = \$1,200$ million

In Table 13.2 we show the market values of Big Oil's debt and equity. You can see that debt accounts for 24.3% of company value ($D/V = .243$) and equity accounts for 75.7% ($E/V = .757$). These are the proportions to use when calculating the weighted-average cost of capital. Notice that if you looked only at the book values shown in the company accounts, you would mistakenly conclude that debt and equity each accounted for 50% of value.

> ## Self-Test 13.5
>
> Here is the capital structure shown in Executive Fruit's *book* balance sheet:
>
> | | | |
> |---|---:|---:|
> | Debt | $4.1 million | 45.0% |
> | Preferred stock | 2.2 | 24.2 |
> | Common stock | 2.8 | 30.8 |
> | Total | $9.1 million | 100.0% |
>
> Explain why the percentage weights given above should *not* be used in calculating Executive Fruit's WACC.

---

[4] If Big Oil's bonds are traded, you can simply look up their price. But many bonds are not regularly traded, and in such cases you need to infer their price by calculating the bond's value using the rate of interest offered by similar bonds.

[5] We assume that coupon payments are annual. Most bonds in the United States actually pay interest twice a year.

13.4 Calculating the Weighted-Average Cost of Capital

To calculate Big Oil's weighted-average cost of capital, you first need the rate of return that investors require from each security.

The Expected Return on Bonds

We know that Big Oil's bonds offer a yield to maturity of 9%. As long as the company does not go belly-up, that is the rate of return investors can expect to earn from holding Big Oil's bonds. If there is any chance that the firm may be unable to repay the debt, however, the yield to maturity of 9% represents the most favorable outcome and the *expected* return is lower than 9%.

For most large and healthy firms, the probability of bankruptcy is sufficiently low that financial managers are content to take the promised yield to maturity on the bonds as a measure of the expected return. But beware of assuming that the yield offered on the bonds of Fly-by-Night Corporation is the return that investors could *expect* to receive.

The Expected Return on Common Stock

Estimates Based on the Capital Asset Pricing Model   In the last chapter we showed you how to use the capital asset pricing model to estimate the expected rate of return on common stock. The capital asset pricing model tells us that investors demand a higher rate of return from stocks with high betas. The formula is

$$\text{Expected return on stock} = \text{risk-free interest rate} + \left(\text{stock's beta} \times \text{expected market risk premium}\right)$$

Financial managers and economists measure the risk-free rate of interest by the yield on Treasury bills. To measure the expected market risk premium, they usually look back at capital market history, which suggests that investors have received about an extra 7% a year from investing in common stocks rather than Treasury bills. Yet wise financial managers use this evidence with considerable humility, for who is to say whether investors in the past received more or less than they expected or whether investors today require a higher or lower reward for risk than their parents did?

Let's suppose Big Oil's common stock beta is estimated at .85, the risk-free interest rate (r_f) is 6%, and the expected market risk premium ($r_m - r_f$) is 7%. Then the CAPM would put Big Oil's cost of equity at

$$\text{Cost of equity} = r_{\text{equity}} = r_f + \beta(r_m - r_f)$$
$$= 6\% + .85(7\%) = 12\%$$

Self-Test 13.6

Jo Ann Cox decides to check whether Fred, the nerdy banker, was correct in claiming that Geothermal's cost of equity is 14%. She estimates Geothermal's beta at 1.20. The risk-free interest rate is 6%, and the long-run average market risk premium is 7.6%. What is the expected rate of return on Geothermal's common stock, assuming of course that the CAPM is true? Recalculate Geothermal's weighted-average cost of capital.

Estimates Based on the Dividend Discount Model   Whenever you are given an estimate of the expected return on a common stock, always look for ways to check whether it is reasonable. One check on the estimates provided by the CAPM can be obtained from the dividend discount model (DDM). In Chapter 7 we showed you how to use the constant-growth DDM formula to estimate the return that investors expect from different common stocks. Remember the formula: If dividends are expected to grow indefinitely at a constant rate g, then the price of the stock is equal to

$$P_0 = \frac{\text{DIV}_1}{r_{\text{equity}} - g}$$

where P_0 is the current stock price, DIV_1 is the forecast dividend at the end of the year, and r_{equity} is the expected return from the stock. We can rearrange this formula to provide an estimate of r_{equity}:

$$r_{\text{equity}} = \frac{\text{DIV}_1}{P_0} + g \qquad\qquad (13.2)$$

In other words, the expected return on equity is equal to the dividend yield (DIV_1/P_0) plus the expected perpetual growth rate in dividends (g).

This constant-growth dividend discount model is widely used in estimating expected rates of return on common stocks of public utilities. Utility stocks have a fairly stable growth pattern and are therefore tailor-made for the constant-growth formula.

Remember that the constant-growth formula will get you into trouble if you apply it to firms with very high current rates of growth. Such growth cannot be sustained indefinitely. Using the formula in these circumstances will lead to an over-estimate of the expected return.

Beware of False Precision   Do not expect estimates of the cost of equity to be precise. In practice you can't know whether the capital asset pricing model fully explains expected returns or whether the assumptions of the dividend discount model hold exactly. Even if your formulas were right, the required inputs would be noisy and subject to error. Thus a financial analyst who can confidently locate the cost of equity in a band of 2 or 3 percentage points is doing pretty well. In this endeavor it is perfectly okay to conclude that the cost of equity is, say, "about 15%" or "somewhere between 14% and 16%."[6]

Sometimes accuracy can be improved by estimating the cost of equity or WACC for an industry or a group of comparable companies. This cuts down the "noise" that plagues single-company estimates. Suppose, for example, that Jo Ann Cox is able to identify three companies with investments and operations similar to Geothermal's. The average WACC for these three companies would be a valuable check on her estimate of WACC for Geothermal alone.

Or suppose that Geothermal is contemplating investment in oil refining. For this venture Geothermal's existing WACC is probably not right; it needs a discount rate reflecting the risks of the refining business. It could therefore try to estimate WACC for a sample of oil refining companies. If too few "pure-play" refining companies were available—most oil companies invest in production and marketing as well as refining—an industry WACC for a sample of large oil companies could be a useful check or benchmark.

The Expected Return on Preferred Stock

Preferred stock that pays a fixed annual dividend can be valued from the perpetuity formula:

$$\text{Price of preferred} = \frac{\text{dividend}}{r_{\text{preferred}}}$$

---

[6] The calculations in this chapter have been done to one or two decimal places just to avoid confusion from rounding.

where $r_{preferred}$ is the appropriate discount rate for the preferred stock. Therefore, we can infer the required rate of return on preferred stock by rearranging the valuation formula to

$$r_{preferred} = \frac{dividend}{price\ of\ preferred} \qquad (13.3)$$

For example, if a share of preferred stock sells for $20 and pays a dividend of $2 per share, the expected return on preferred stock is $r_{preferred} = \$2/\$20 = 10\%$, which is simply the dividend yield.

Adding It All Up

Once you have worked out Big Oil's capital structure and estimated the expected return on its securities, you require only simple arithmetic to calculate the weighted-average cost of capital. Table 13.3 summarizes the necessary data. Now all you need to do is plug the data in Table 13.3 into the weighted-average cost of capital formula:

$$WACC = \left[\frac{D}{V} \times (1 - T_c)r_{debt}\right] + \left(\frac{E}{V} \times r_{equity}\right)$$
$$= [.243 \times (1 - .35)\ 9\%] + (.757 \times 12\%) = 10.5\%$$

Suppose that Big Oil needs to evaluate a project with the same risk as its existing business. If the project would also support a 24.3% debt ratio, the 10.5% weighted-average cost of capital is the appropriate discount rate for the cash flows.

Real-Company WACCs

Big Oil is entirely hypothetical. Therefore you might be interested in looking at Table 13.4, which gives some estimates of the weighted-average cost of capital for a sample of real companies. As you do so, remember that any estimate of the cost of capital for a single company can be way off the true cost. You should always check your estimate by looking at the cost of capital for a group of similar companies.[7]

13.5 Interpreting the Weighted-Average Cost of Capital

When You Can and Can't Use WACC

The weighted-average cost of capital is the rate of return that the firm must expect to earn on its average-risk investments in order to provide a fair expected return to all its security holders. Strictly speaking, the weighted-average cost of capital is an appropriate discount rate only for a project that is a carbon copy

TABLE 13.3 Data needed to calculate Big Oil's weighted-average cost of capital (dollar figures in millions)

Security Type	Capital Structure		Required Rate of Return
Debt	$D = \$\ 385.7$	$D/V = .243$	$r_{debt} = .09$, or 9%
Common stock	$E = \$1,200.0$	$E/V = .757$	$r_{equity} = .12$, or 12%
Total	$V = \$1,585.7$		

Note: Corporate tax rate $= T_c = .35$.

---

[7] Notice that Ford's WACC is about average despite its very high cost of equity. This results from the company's very high debt ratio. Should Ford use a WACC of 8% when valuing a proposal to expand its operations? The answer is yes if a 79% debt ratio really is a sensible target capital structure. But if you believe that this debt ratio does not constitute a desirable long-term capital structure for Ford, then you would need to recalculate WACC with a different ratio.

of the firm's existing business. But often it is used as a companywide benchmark discount rate; the benchmark is adjusted upward for unusually risky projects and downward for unusually safe ones.

There is a good musical analogy here. Most of us, lacking perfect pitch, need a well-defined reference point, like middle C, before we can sing on key. But anyone who can carry a tune gets *relative* pitches right. Businesspeople have good intuition about *relative* risks, at least in industries they are used to, but not about absolute risk or required rates of return. Therefore, they set a company- or industrywide cost of capital as a benchmark. This is not the right hurdle rate for everything the company does, but judgmental adjustments can be made for more risky or less risky ventures.

Some Common Mistakes

One danger with the weighted-average formula is that it tempts people to make logical errors. Think back to your estimate of the cost of capital for Big Oil:

$$\text{WACC} = \left[\frac{D}{V} \times (1 - T_c)r_{\text{debt}}\right] + \left(\frac{E}{V} \times r_{\text{equity}}\right)$$
$$= [.243 \times (1 - .35)\,9\%] + (.757 \times 12\%) = 10.5\%$$

Now you might be tempted to say to yourself: "Aha! Big Oil has a good credit rating. It could easily push up its debt ratio to 50%. If the interest rate is 9% and the required return on equity is 12%, the weighted-average cost of capital would be

$$\text{WACC} = [.50 \times (1 - .35)\,9\%] + (.50 \times 12\%) = 8.9\%$$

At a discount rate of 8.9%, we can justify a lot more investment."

That reasoning will get you into trouble. First, if Big Oil increased its borrowing, the lenders would almost certainly demand a higher rate of interest on the debt. Second, as the borrowing increased, the risk of the common stock would also increase and therefore the stockholders would demand a higher return.

There are actually two costs of debt finance. The explicit cost of debt is the rate of interest that bondholders demand. But there is also an implicit cost,

TABLE 13.4 Calculating the weighted-average cost of capital for selected companies

	Expected Return on Equity, %	Interest Rate on Debt, %	Proportion of Equity (E/V)	Proportion of Debt (D/V)	WACC, %
Dow Chemical	19.0	6.30	.61	.39	13.2
Starbucks	12.5	6.30	.97	.03	12.3
Dell	12.3	4.60	.88	.12	11.2
Boeing	12.0	4.60	.79	.21	10.1
Disney	11.1	4.60	.86	.14	9.9
Microsoft	9.8	3.50	.98	.02	9.7
Ford	20.7	7.25	.21	.79	8.0
IBM	8.3	4.55	.88	.12	7.7
McDonald's	7.3	4.65	.87	.13	6.8
Newmont Mining	7.1	6.25	.85	.15	6.7
Johnson & Johnson	7.0	3.50	.92	.08	6.6
Heinz	7.3	6.25	.74	.26	6.4
Pfizer	7.8	4.55	.70	.30	6.4
ExxonMobil	5.9	3.50	.98	.02	5.8
Campbell Soup	5.6	4.60	.85	.15	5.2
Consolidated Edison	5.2	6.20	.55	.45	4.7
Walmart	4.7	4.20	.84	.16	4.4

Notes:
1. Expected return on equity is taken from Table 12.2.
2. Interest rate on debt is calculated from yields on similarly rated bonds.
3. D is the book value of the firm's debt, and E is the market value of equity.
4. WACC = (D/V) × (1 − .35) × r_{debt} + (E/V) × r_{equity}.

because borrowing increases the required return to equity. When you jumped to the conclusion that Big Oil could lower its weighted-average cost of capital to 8.9% by borrowing more, you were recognizing only the explicit cost of debt and not the implicit cost.

Self-Test 13.7

Jo Ann Cox's boss has pointed out that Geothermal proposes to finance its expansion entirely by borrowing at an interest rate of 8%. He argues that this is therefore the appropriate discount rate for the project's cash flows. Is he right?

How Changing Capital Structure Affects Expected Returns

We will illustrate how changes in capital structure affect expected returns by focusing on the simplest possible case, where the corporate tax rate T_c is zero.

Think back to our earlier example of Geothermal. Geothermal, you may remember, has the following market-value balance sheet:

Assets		Liabilities and Shareholders' Equity		
Assets = value of Geothermal's existing business	$647	Debt	$194	(30%)
		Equity	453	(70%)
Total value	$647	Value	$647	(100%)

Geothermal's debtholders require a return of 8%, and the shareholders require a return of 14%. Since we assume here that Geothermal pays no corporate tax, its weighted-average cost of capital is simply the expected return on the firm's assets:

$$\text{WACC} = r_{\text{assets}} = (.3 \times 8\%) + (.7 \times 14\%) = 12.2\%$$

This is the return you would expect if you held all Geothermal's securities and therefore owned all its assets.

Now think what will happen if Geothermal borrows an additional $97 million and uses the cash to buy back and retire $97 million of its common stock. The revised market-value balance sheet is

Assets		Liabilities and Shareholders' Equity		
Assets = value of Geothermal's existing business	$647	Debt	$291	(45%)
		Equity	356	(55%)
Total value	$647	Value	$647	(100%)

If there are no corporate taxes, the change in capital structure does not affect the total cash that Geothermal pays out to its security holders and it does not affect the risk of those cash flows. Therefore, if investors require a return of 12.2% on the total package of debt and equity before the financing, they must require the same 12.2% return on the package afterward. The weighted-average cost of capital is therefore unaffected by the change in the capital structure.

Is that surprising? After all, the required return on debt is lower than the required return on equity, so you might expect the additional borrowing to *reduce* the weighted-average cost of capital. The reason that it does not do so is that the return on the individual securities changes. Since the company has more debt than before, the debt is riskier and debtholders are likely to demand a higher return. Increasing the amount of debt also makes the equity riskier and increases the return that shareholders require. We will return to this point in Chapter 16.

What Happens When the Corporate Tax Rate Is Not Zero

We have shown that when there are no corporate taxes, the weighted-average cost of capital is unaffected by a change in capital structure. Unfortunately, taxes can complicate the picture.[8] For the moment, just remember:

- **The weighted-average cost of capital is the right discount rate for average-risk capital investments.**
- **The weighted-average cost of capital is the return the company needs to earn after tax in order to satisfy all its security holders.**
- **If the firm increases its debt ratio, both the debt and the equity will become more risky. The debtholders and equityholders require a higher return to compensate for the increased risk.**

13.6 Valuing Entire Businesses

Investors routinely buy and sell shares of common stock. Companies frequently buy and sell entire businesses. Do the discounted cash-flow formulas that we used in Chapter 7 to value Blue Skies' stock also work for entire businesses?

Sure! As long as the company's debt ratio is expected to remain fairly constant, you can treat the company as one big project and discount its cash flows by the weighted-average cost of capital. The result is the combined value of the company's debt and equity. If you want to know just the value of the equity, you must remember to subtract the value of the debt from the company's total value.

Suppose that you are interested in buying Establishment Industry's concatenator manufacturing operation. The problem is to figure out what it is worth. Table 13.5 sets out your forecasts for the next 6 years. Row 8 shows the expected cash flow from operations. This is equal to the expected profit after tax plus depreciation. Remember, depreciation is not a cash outflow, and therefore you need to add it back when calculating the operating cash flow. Row 9 in the table shows the forecast investments in plant and working capital.

free cash flow
Cash flow that is not required for investment in fixed assets or working capital and is therefore available to investors.

The operating cash flow *less* investment expenditures is the amount of cash that the business can pay out to investors after paying for all investments necessary for growth. This is the concatenator division's **free cash flow** (row 10 in the table). Notice that the free cash flow is negative in the early years. Is that a bad sign? Not really. The business is running a cash deficit not because it is unprofitable but because it is growing so fast. Rapid growth is good news, not bad, as long as the business is earning more than the cost of capital on its investments.

The forecast cash flows in Table 13.5 did not include a deduction for debt interest. But we will not forget that acquisition of the concatenator business will support additional debt. We will recognize that fact by discounting the free cash flows by the weighted-average cost of capital, which reflects both the firm's capital structure and the tax deductibility of its interest payments.

---

[8] There's nothing wrong with our formulas and examples, *provided* that the tax deductibility of interest payments doesn't change the aggregate risk of the debt and equity investors. However, if the tax savings from deducting interest are treated as safe cash flows, the formulas get more complicated. If you really want to dive into the tax-adjusted formulas showing how WACC changes with capital structure, we suggest Chapter 19 in R. A. Brealey, S. C. Myers, and F. Allen, *Principles of Corporate Finance,* 10th ed. (New York: Irwin/McGraw-Hill, 2011).

TABLE 13.5 Forecasts of operating cash flow and investment for the concatenator manufacturing division (thousands of dollars). Rapid expansion means that free cash flow is negative in the early years, because investment outstrips the cash flow from operations. Free cash flow turns positive when growth slows down.

	Year					
	1	2	3	4	5	6
1. Sales	1,189	1,421	1,700	2,020	2,391	2,510
2. Costs	1,070	1,279	1,530	1,818	2,152	2,260
3. Earnings before interest, taxes, depreciation, and amortization (EBITDA) = 1 − 2	119	142	170	202	239	250
4. Depreciation	45	59	76	99	128	136
5. Profit before tax = 3 − 4	74	83	94	103	111	114
6. Tax at 35%	25.9	29.1	32.9	36.1	38.9	39.9
7. Profit after tax = 5 − 6	48.1	54.0	61.1	67.0	72.2	74.1
8. Operating cash flow = 4 + 7	93.1	113.0	137.1	166.0	200.2	210.1
9. Investment in plant and working capital	166.7	200.0	240.0	200.0	160.0	130.6
10. Free cash flow = 8 − 9	−73.6	−87.1	−102.9	−34.1	40.2	79.5

Suppose that a sensible capital structure for the concatenator operation is 60% equity and 40% debt.[9] You estimate that the required rate of return on the equity is 12% and that the business could borrow at an interest rate of 5%. The weighted-average cost of capital is therefore

$$\text{WACC} = \left[\frac{D}{V} \times (1 - T_c) r_{\text{debt}} \right] + \left(\frac{E}{V} \times r_{\text{equity}} \right)$$
$$= [.4 \times (1 - .35)5\%] + (.6 \times 12\%) = 8.5\%$$

Calculating the Value of the Concatenator Business

The value of the concatenator operation is equal to the discounted value of the free cash flows (FCFs) out to a horizon year plus the forecasted value of the business at the horizon, also discounted back to the present. That is,

$$\text{PV} = \underbrace{\frac{\text{FCF}_1}{1 + \text{WACC}} + \frac{\text{FCF}_2}{(1 + \text{WACC})^2} + \cdots + \frac{\text{FCF}_H}{(1 + \text{WACC})^H}}_{\text{PV (free cash flows)}} + \underbrace{\frac{\text{PV}_H}{(1 + \text{WACC})^H}}_{+ \text{PV (horizon value)}}$$

Of course, the concatenator business will continue to grow after the horizon, but it's not practical to forecast free cash flow year by year to infinity. PV_H stands in for the value of free cash flows in periods $H + 1$, $H + 2$, and so on.

Horizon years are often chosen arbitrarily. Sometimes the boss tells everybody to use 10 years because that's a nice round number. We have picked year 5 as the horizon year because the business is expected to settle down to steady growth of 5% a year from then on.

There are several common formulas or rules of thumb for estimating horizon value. Let's try the constant-growth formula that we introduced in Chapter 7:

$$\text{Horizon value} = \frac{\text{free cash flow in year 6}}{r - g} = \frac{79.5}{.085 - .05} = \$2,271.4 \text{ thousand}$$

---

[9] By this we mean that it makes sense to finance 40% of the *present value* of the business by debt. Remember that we use market-value weights to compute WACC. Debt as a proportion of *book value* may be more or less than 40%.

We now have all we need to calculate the value of the concatenator business today. We add up the present values of the free cash flows in the first 5 years and that of the horizon value:

PV (business) = PV (free cash flows years 1–5) + PV (horizon value)

$$= -\frac{73.6}{1.085} - \frac{87.1}{(1.085)^2} - \frac{102.9}{(1.085)^3} - \frac{34.1}{(1.085)^4} + \frac{40.2}{(1.085)^5} + \frac{2,271.4}{(1.085)^5}$$

= \$1,290.4 thousand

Notice that when we use the weighted-average cost of capital to value a company, we are asking, "What is the combined value of the company's debt and equity?" If you need to value the equity, you must subtract the value of any outstanding debt. Suppose that the concatenator business has been partly financed with \$516,000 of debt, 40% of the overall value of about \$1,290,000. Then the equity in the business is worth only \$1,290,000 − \$516,000 = \$774,000.

Self-Test 13.8

Managers often use rules of thumb to check their estimates of horizon value. Suppose you observe that the value of the debt plus equity of a typical mature concatenator producer is nine times its EBITDA. (EBITDA is defined at line 3 of Table 13.5.) If your operation sold in year 5 at a similar multiple of EBITDA, how would your estimate of the *present* value of the operation change?

SUMMARY

Why do firms compute weighted-average costs of capital? (*LO4*)

They need a standard discount rate for average-risk projects. An "average-risk" project is one that has the same risk as the firm's existing assets and operations.

What about projects that are not average? (*LO4*)

The **weighted-average cost of capital** can still be used as a benchmark. The benchmark is adjusted up for unusually risky projects and down for unusually safe ones.

How do firms compute weighted-average costs of capital? (*LO3*)

Here's the WACC formula one more time:

$$\text{WACC} = \left[\frac{D}{V} \times (1 - T_c)r_{\text{debt}} \right] + \left(\frac{E}{V} \times r_{\text{equity}} \right)$$

The WACC is the expected rate of return on the portfolio of debt and equity securities issued by the firm. The required rate of return on each security is weighted by its proportion of the firm's total market value (not book value). Since interest payments reduce the firm's income tax bill, the required rate of return on debt is measured after tax, as $r_{\text{debt}} \times (1 - T_c)$.

How do firms measure capital structure? (*LO1*)

Capital structure is the proportion of each source of financing in total market value. The WACC formula is usually written assuming the firm's capital structure includes just two classes of securities, debt and equity. If there is another class, say preferred stock, the formula expands to include it. In other words, we would estimate $r_{\text{preferred}}$, the rate of return demanded by preferred stockholders, determine P/V, the fraction of market value accounted for by preferred, and add $r_{\text{preferred}} \times P/V$ to the equation. Of course the weights in the WACC formula always add up to 1. In this case $D/V + P/V + E/V = 1$.

How are the costs of debt and equity calculated? (*LO3*)

The cost of debt (r_{debt}) is the market interest rate demanded by bondholders. In other words, it is the rate that the company would pay on *new* debt issued to finance its investment projects. The cost of preferred ($r_{\text{preferred}}$) is just the preferred dividend divided by the market price of a preferred share.

The tricky part is estimating the cost of equity (r_{equity}), the expected rate of return on the firm's shares. Financial managers use the capital asset pricing model to estimate expected return. But for mature, steady-growth companies, it can also make sense to use the constant-growth dividend discount model. Remember, estimates of expected return are less reliable for a single firm's stock than for a sample of comparable-risk firms. Therefore, managers also consider WACCs calculated for industries.

What happens when capital structure changes? (*LO4*)

The rates of return on debt and equity will change. For example, increasing the debt ratio will increase the risk borne by both debt and equity investors and cause them to demand higher returns. However, this does *not* necessarily mean that the overall WACC will increase, because more weight is put on the cost of debt, which is less than the cost of equity. In fact, if we ignore taxes, the overall **cost of capital** will stay constant as the fractions of debt and equity change. This is discussed further in Chapter 16.

Can WACC be used to value an entire business? (*LO5*)

Just think of the business as a very large project. Forecast the business's operating cash flows (after-tax profits plus depreciation), and subtract the future investments in plant and equipment and in net working capital. The resulting **free cash flows** can then be discounted back to the present at the weighted-average cost of capital. Of course, the cash flows from a company may stretch far into the future. Financial managers therefore typically produce detailed cash flows only up to some horizon date and then estimate the remaining value of the business at the horizon.

LISTING OF EQUATIONS

13.1 $\text{WACC} = \left[\dfrac{D}{V} \times (1 - T_c)r_{debt} \right] + \left(\dfrac{E}{V} \times r_{equity} \right)$

13.1a $\text{WACC} = \left[\dfrac{D}{V} \times (1 - T_c)r_{debt} \right] + \left(\dfrac{P}{V} \times r_{preferred} \right) + \left(\dfrac{E}{V} \times r_{equity} \right)$

13.2 $r_{equity} = \dfrac{DIV_1}{P_0} + g$

13.3 $r_{preferred} = \dfrac{dividend}{price\ of\ preferred}$

QUESTIONS

QUIZ

1. **Cost of Debt.** Micro Spinoffs, Inc., issued 20-year debt a year ago at par value with a coupon rate of 8%, paid annually. Today, the debt is selling at $1,050. If the firm's tax bracket is 35%, what is its after-tax cost of debt? (*LO2*)

2. **Cost of Preferred Stock.** Micro Spinoffs also has preferred stock outstanding. The stock pays a dividend of $4 per share, and the stock sells for $40. What is the cost of preferred stock? (*LO2*)

3. **Calculating WACC.** Suppose Micro Spinoffs's cost of equity is 12%. What is its WACC if equity is 50%, preferred stock is 20%, and debt is 30% of total capital? (*LO3*)

4. **Cost of Equity.** Reliable Electric is a regulated public utility, and it is expected to provide steady growth of dividends of 5% per year for the indefinite future. Its last dividend was $5 per share; the stock sold for $60 per share just after the dividend was paid. What is the company's cost of equity? (*LO2*)

5. **Calculating WACC.** Reactive Industries has the following capital structure. Its corporate tax rate is 35%. What is its WACC? (*LO3*)

Security	Market Value	Required Rate of Return
Debt	$20 million	6%
Preferred stock	10 million	8
Common stock	50 million	12

6. **Company versus Project Discount Rates.** Geothermal's WACC is 11.4%. Executive Fruit's WACC is 12.3%. Now Executive Fruit is considering an investment in geothermal power production. Should it discount project cash flows at 12.3%? Why or why not? (*LO4*)

7. **Company Valuation.** Icarus Airlines is proposing to go public, and you have been given the task of estimating the value of its equity. Management plans to maintain debt at 30% of the company's present value, and you believe that at this capital structure the company's debtholders will demand a return of 6% and stockholders will require 11%. The company is forecasting that next year's operating cash flow (depreciation plus profit after tax at 40%) will be $68 million and that investment expenditures will be $30 million. Thereafter, operating cash flows and investment expenditures are forecast to grow by 4% a year. (*LO5*)
   a. What is the total value of Icarus?
   b. What is the value of the company's equity?

PRACTICE PROBLEMS

8. **WACC.** The common stock of Buildwell Conservation & Construction, Inc., has a beta of .90. The Treasury bill rate is 4%, and the market risk premium is estimated at 8%. BCCI's capital structure is 30% debt, paying a 5% interest rate, and 70% equity. What is BCCI's cost of equity capital? Its WACC? Buildwell pays tax at 40%. (*LO3*)

9. **WACC and NPV.** BCCI (see the previous problem) is evaluating a project with an internal rate of return of 12%. Should it accept the project? If the project will generate a cash flow of $100,000 a year for 8 years, what is the most BCCI should be willing to pay to initiate the project? (*LO5*)

10. **Company Valuation.** You need to estimate the value of Buildwell Conservation (see Practice Problem 8). You have the following forecasts (in millions of dollars) of Buildwell's profits and of its future investments in new plant and working capital: (*LO5*)

	Year			
	1	2	3	4 ...
Earnings before interest, taxes, depreciation, and amortization (EBITDA)	80	100	115	120
Depreciation	20	30	35	40
Pretax profit	60	70	80	80
Investment	12	15	18	20

From year 5 onward, EBITDA, depreciation, and investment are expected to remain unchanged at year-4 levels. Estimate the company's total value and the separate values of its debt and equity.

11. **Calculating WACC.** Find the WACC of William Tell Computers. The total book value of the firm's equity is $10 million; book value per share is $20. The stock sells for a price of $30 per share, and the cost of equity is 15%. The firm's bonds have a face value of $5 million and sell at a price of 110% of face value. The yield to maturity on the bonds is 9%, and the firm's tax rate is 40%. (*LO3*)

12. **WACC.** Nodebt, Inc., is a firm with all-equity financing. Its equity beta is .80. The Treasury bill rate is 4%, and the market risk premium is expected to be 10%. What is Nodebt's asset beta? What is Nodebt's weighted-average cost of capital? The firm is exempt from paying taxes. (*LO3*)

13. **Cost of Debt.** A financial analyst at Dawn Chemical notes that the firm's total interest payments this year were $10 million while total debt outstanding was $80 million, and he concludes that the cost of debt was 12.5%. What is wrong with this conclusion? (*LO2*)

14. **Cost of Equity.** Bunkhouse Electronics is a recently incorporated firm that makes electronic entertainment systems. Its earnings and dividends have been growing at a rate of 30%, and the current dividend yield is 2%. Its beta is 1.2, the market risk premium is 8%, and the risk-free rate is 4%. (*LO2*)
    a. Calculate two estimates of the firm's cost of equity.
    b. Which estimate seems more reasonable to you? Why?

15. **Cost of Debt.** Olympic Sports has two issues of debt outstanding. One is a 9% coupon bond with a face value of $20 million, a maturity of 10 years, and a yield to maturity of 10%. The coupons are paid annually. The other bond issue has a maturity of 15 years, with coupons also paid annually, and a coupon rate of 10%. The face value of the issue is $25 million, and the issue sells for 94% of par value. The firm's tax rate is 35%. (*LO2*)
    a. What is the before-tax cost of debt for Olympic?
    b. What is Olympic's after-tax cost of debt?

16. **Capital Structure.** Examine the following book-value balance sheet for University Products, Inc. What is the capital structure of the firm on the basis of market values? The preferred stock currently sells for $15 per share and the common stock for $20 per share. There are 1 million common shares outstanding. (*LO1*)

BOOK VALUE BALANCE SHEET (all values in millions)			
Assets		**Liabilities and Net Worth**	
Cash and short-term securities	$ 1	Bonds, coupon = 8%, paid annually (maturity = 10 years, current yield to maturity = 9%)	$10.0
Accounts receivable	3	Preferred stock (par value $20 per share)	2.0
Inventories	7	Common stock (par value $.10)	.1
Plant and equipment	21	Additional paid-in stockholders' equity	9.9
		Retained earnings	10.0
Total	$32	Total	$32.0

17. **Calculating WACC.** Turn back to University Products's balance sheet from the previous problem. If the preferred stock pays a dividend of $2 per share, the beta of the common stock is .8, the market risk premium is 10%, the risk-free rate is 6%, and the firm's tax rate is 40%, what is University's weighted-average cost of capital? (*LO3*)

18. **Project Discount Rate.** University Products is evaluating a new venture into home computer systems (see Practice Problems 16 and 17). The internal rate of return on the new venture is estimated at 13.4%. WACCs of firms in the personal computer industry tend to average around 14%. Should the new project be pursued? Will University Products make the correct decision if it discounts cash flows on the proposed venture at the firm's WACC? (*LO4*)

19. **Cost of Capital.** The total market value of Okefenokee Real Estate Company is $6 million, and the total value of its debt is $4 million. The treasurer estimates that the beta of the stock currently is 1.2 and that the expected risk premium on the market is 10%. The Treasury bill rate is 4%. (*LO3*)
    a. What is the required rate of return on Okefenokee stock?
    b. What is the beta of the company's existing portfolio of assets? The debt is perceived to be virtually risk-free.
    c. Estimate the weighted-average cost of capital assuming a tax rate of 40%.
    d. Estimate the discount rate for an expansion of the company's present business.
    e. Suppose the company wants to diversify into the manufacture of rose-colored glasses. The beta of optical manufacturers with no debt outstanding is 1.4. What is the required rate of return on Okefenokee's new venture? (You should assume that the risky project will not enable the firm to issue any additional debt.)

CHALLENGE PROBLEMS

Templates can be found at
www.mhhhe.com/bmm7e.

20. **Changes in Capital Structure.** Look again at our calculation of Big Oil's WACC. Suppose Big Oil is excused from paying taxes. How would its WACC change? Now suppose Big Oil makes a large stock issue and uses the proceeds to pay off all its debt. How would the cost of equity change? *(LO2)*

21. **Changes in Capital Structure.** Refer again to Challenge Problem 20. Suppose Big Oil starts from the financing mix in Table 13.3, and then borrows an additional $200 million from the bank. It then pays out a special $200 million dividend, leaving its assets and operations unchanged. What happens to Big Oil's WACC, still assuming it pays no taxes? What happens to the cost of equity? *(LO1)*

22. **WACC and Taxes.** "The after-tax cost of debt is lower when the firm's tax rate is higher; therefore, the WACC falls when the tax rate rises. Thus, with a lower discount rate, the firm must be worth more if its tax rate is higher." Explain why this argument is wrong. *(LO5)*

23. **Cost of Capital.** An analyst at Dawn Chemical notes that its cost of debt is far below that of equity. He concludes that it is important for the firm to maintain the ability to increase its borrowing because if it cannot borrow, it will be forced to use more expensive equity to finance some projects. This might lead it to reject some projects that would have seemed attractive if evaluated at the lower cost of debt. Comment on this reasoning. *(LO4)*

WEB EXERCISE

1. Estimate the weighted-average cost of capital for Eastman Kodak, Home Depot, Altria, Caterpillar, Intel, and Du Pont. You can estimate the expected stock returns for these companies by using the betas shown on finance.yahoo.com. You can also use Yahoo! Finance to find the relative proportions of equity and debt for each company. Remember, though, to use the market value of the equity, not its book value. Finding the yield on the debt is a little trickier. One possibility it to log on to www.bondsonline.com to find the current level of Treasury yields and the yield spreads (i.e., the extra yield for bonds with different ratings). An alternative is to look at the yields shown in the bonds section of Yahoo! Finance. Note: As we write this, Moody's ratings for the six companies vary from B for Eastman Kodak, to Baa for Home Depot and Altria, to A for Caterpillar, Intel, and Du Pont.

SOLUTIONS TO SELF-TEST QUESTIONS

13.1   Hot Rocks's 4 million common shares are worth $40 million. Its market value balance sheet is:

Assets		Liabilities and Shareholders' Equity		
Assets	$90	Debt	$50	(56%)
		Equity	40	(44%)
Value	$90	Value	$90	

$$WACC = (.56 \times 9\%) + (.44 \times 17\%) = 12.5\%$$

We use Hot Rocks's pretax return on debt because the company pays no taxes.

13.2   Burg's 6 million shares are now worth only 6 million $\times$ $4 = $24 million. The debt is selling for 80% of book, or $20 million. The market value balance sheet is:

Assets		Liabilities and Shareholders' Equity		
Assets	$44	Debt	$20	(45%)
		Equity	24	(55%)
Value	$44	Value	$44	

$$WACC = (.45 \times 14\%) + (.55 \times 20\%) = 17.3\%$$

Note that this question ignores taxes.

13.3   Compare the two income statements, one for Criss-Cross Industries and the other for a firm with identical EBIT but no debt in its capital structure. (All figures in millions.)

	Criss-Cross	**Firm with No Debt**
EBIT	$10.0	$10.0
Interest expense	2.0	0.0
Taxable income	8.0	10.0
Taxes owed	2.8	3.5
Net income	5.2	6.5
Total income accruing to debt- & equityholders	7.2	6.5

Notice that Criss-Cross pays $.7 million less in taxes than its debt-free counterpart. Accordingly, the total income available to debt- plus equityholders is $.7 million higher.

13.4   For Hot Rocks,

$$WACC = [.56 \times 9 \times (1 - .35)] + (.44 \times 17) = 10.8\%$$

For Burg Associates,

$$WACC = [.45 \times 14 \times (1 - .35)] + (.55 \times 20) = 15.1\%$$

13.5   WACC measures the expected rate of return demanded by debt and equity investors in the firm (plus a tax adjustment capturing the tax-deductibility of interest payments). Thus the calculation must be based on what investors are actually paying for the firm's debt and equity securities. In other words, it must be based on market values.

13.6   From the CAPM:

$$\begin{aligned} r_{equity} &= r_f + \beta_{equity}(r_m - r_f) \\ &= 6\% + 1.20(7.6\%) = 15.1\% \\ WACC &= .3(1 - .35)\, 8\% + .7(15.1\%) = 12.13\% \end{aligned}$$

13.7   Jo Ann's boss is wrong. The ability to borrow at 8% does not mean that the cost of capital is 8%. The firm could not finance a stand-alone project with 8% debt. This analysis ignores the side effects of the borrowing, for example, that at the higher indebtedness of the firm the equity will be riskier and, therefore, the equityholders will demand a higher rate of return on their investment.

13.8   Estimated horizon value for the concatenator business is 9 × year-5 EBITDA = 9 × 239 = $2,151 thousand. PV (horizon value) is $2,151/(1.085)^5 = $1,430.5 thousand. Adding in the PV of free cash flows for years 1 to 5 gives a present value for the business of $1,210.3 thousand.

MINICASE

Bernice Mountaindog was glad to be back at Sea Shore Salt. Employees were treated well. When she had asked a year ago for a leave of absence to complete her degree in finance, top management promptly agreed. When she returned with an honors degree, she was promoted from administrative assistant (she had been secretary to Joe-Bob Brinepool, the president) to treasury analyst.

Bernice thought the company's prospects were good. Sure, table salt was a mature business, but Sea Shore Salt had grown steadily at the expense of its less well known competitors. The company's brand name was an important advantage, despite the difficulty most customers had in pronouncing it rapidly.

Bernice started work on January 2, 2011. The first 2 weeks went smoothly. Then Mr. Brinepool's cost of capital memo (see Figure 13.2) assigned her to explain Sea Shore Salt's weighted-average cost of capital to other managers. The memo came as a surprise to Bernice, so she stayed late to prepare for the questions that would surely come the next day.

FIGURE 13.2 Mr. Brinepool's cost of capital memo

Sea Shore Salt Company
Spring Vacation Beach, Florida

CONFIDENTIAL MEMORANDUM

DATE: January 15, 2011
TO: S.S.S. Management
FROM: Joe-Bob Brinepool, President
SUBJECT: Cost of Capital

This memo states and clarifies our company's long-standing policy regarding hurdle rates for capital investment decisions. There have been many recent questions, and some evident confusion, on this matter.

Sea Shore Salt evaluates replacement and expansion investments by discounted cash flow. The discount or hurdle rate is the company's after-tax weighted-average cost of capital.

The weighted-average cost of capital is simply a blend of the rates of return expected by investors in our company. These investors include banks, bondholders, and preferred stock investors in addition to common stockholders. Of course many of you are, or soon will be, stockholders of our company.

The following table summarizes the composition of Sea Shore Salt's financing.

	Amount (in millions)	Percent of Total	Rate of Return
Bank loan	$120	20%	8%
Bond issue	80	13.3	7.75
Preferred stock	100	16.7	6
Common stock	300	50	16
	$600	100%	

The rates of return on the bank loan and bond issue are of course just the interest rates we pay. However, interest is tax-deductible, so the after-tax interest rates are lower than shown above. For example, the after-tax cost of our bank financing, given our 35% tax rate, is 8(1 − .35) = 5.2%.

The rate of return on preferred stock is 6%. Sea Shore Salt pays a $6 dividend on each $100 preferred share.

Our target rate of return on equity has been 16% for many years. I know that some newcomers think this target is too high for the safe and mature salt business. But we must all aspire to superior profitability.

Once this background is absorbed, the calculation of Sea Shore Salt's weighted-average cost of capital (WACC) is elementary:

$$\text{WACC} = 8(1 - .35)(.20) + 7.75(1 - .35)(.133) + 6(.167) + 16(.50) = 10.7\%$$

The official corporate hurdle rate is therefore 10.7%.

If you have further questions about these calculations, please direct them to our new Treasury Analyst, Ms. Bernice Mountaindog. It is a pleasure to have Bernice back at Sea Shore Salt after a year's leave of absence to complete her degree in finance.

Bernice first examined Sea Shore Salt's most recent balance sheet, summarized in Table 13.6. Then she jotted down the following additional points:

- The company's bank charged interest at current market rates, and the long-term debt had just been issued. Book and market values could not differ by much.
- But the preferred stock had been issued 35 years ago, when interest rates were much lower. The preferred stock, originally issued at a book value of $100 per share, was now trading for only $70 per share.
- The common stock traded for $40 per share. Next year's earnings per share would be about $4 and dividends per share probably $2. (10 million shares of common stock are outstanding.) Sea Shore Salt had traditionally paid out 50% of earnings as dividends and plowed back the rest.
- Earnings and dividends had grown steadily at 6% to 7% per year, in line with the company's sustainable growth rate:

$$\text{Sustainable growth rate} = \frac{\text{return on equity}}{} \times \frac{\text{plowback ratio}}{}$$
$$= 4/30 \times .5$$
$$= .067, \text{ or } 6.7\%$$

- Sea Shore Salt's beta had averaged about .5, which made sense, Bernice thought, for a stable, steady-growth business. She made a quick cost of equity calculation by using the capital asset pricing model (CAPM). With current interest rates of about 7%, and a market risk premium of 7%,

$$\text{CAPM cost of equity} = r_E = r_f + \beta(r_m - r_f)$$
$$= 7\% + .5(7\%) = 10.5\%$$

This cost of equity was significantly less than the 16% decreed in Mr. Brinepool's memo. Bernice scanned her notes apprehensively. What if Mr. Brinepool's cost of equity was wrong? Was there some other way to estimate the cost of equity as a check on the CAPM calculation? Could there be other errors in his calculations?

Bernice resolved to complete her analysis that night. If necessary, she would try to speak with Mr. Brinepool when he arrived at his office the next morning. Her job was not just finding the right number. She also had to figure out how to explain it all to Mr. Brinepool.

TABLE 13.6 Sea Shore Salt's balance sheet, taken from the company' 2010 balance sheet (figures in millions)

Assets		Liabilities and Net Worth	
Working capital	$200	Bank loan	$120
Plant and equipment	360	Long-term debt	80
Other assets	40	Preferred stock	100
		Common stock, including retained earnings	300
Total	$600	Total	$600

Notes:
1. At year-end 2010, Sea Shore Salt had 10 million common shares outstanding.
2. The company had also issued 1 million preferred shares with book value of $100 per share. Each share receives an annual dividend of $6.

CHAPTER 14

Introduction to Corporate Financing

RELATED WEB SITES FOR THIS CHAPTER CAN BE FOUND AT WWW.MHHE.COM/BMM7E.

LEARNING OBJECTIVES

After studying this chapter, you should be able to:

(1) Explain why managers should assume that the securities they issue are fairly priced.

(2) Summarize the changing ways that U.S. firms have financed their growth.

(3) Interpret shareholder equity accounts in the firm's financial statements.

(4) Describe voting procedures for the election of a firm's board of directors and other matters.

(5) Describe the major classes of securities sold by the firm.

GM and Chrysler went bankrupt, but Ford managed to raise and keep enough financing to survive the recent financial crisis and recession. It's time to start learning about financing.

Up to this point we have concentrated almost exclusively on the firm's capital expenditure decisions. Now we move to the other side of the balance sheet to look at how the firm can finance those capital expenditures. To put it crudely, you have learned how to spend money; now you must learn how to raise it. In the next few chapters, therefore, we assume that the firm has already decided on which investment projects to accept, and we focus on the best way to finance these projects.

You will find that in some ways financing decisions are more complicated than investment decisions. You'll need to learn about the wide variety of securities that companies can issue. But there are also ways in which financing decisions are easier than investment decisions. For example, financing decisions do not have the same degree of finality as investment decisions. When Ford Motor Company decides to issue a bond, it knows that it can buy it back later if second thoughts arise. It would be far more difficult

for Ford to dismantle or sell an auto factory that is no longer needed.

In later chapters we will look at some of the classic finance problems, such as how much firms should borrow and what dividends they should pay their shareholders. In this chapter we set the scene with a brief overview of the types of long-term finance.

We begin our discussion of financing with a basic conceptual point. It is easier to make shareholders wealthier through your investment decisions than by your financing decisions. As we explain, competition between investors makes it difficult to find misvalued securities.

We then introduce you to the principal sources of finance, and we show how they are used by corporations. It is customary to classify these sources of finance as debt or equity. However, we will see that a simple division of sources of finance into debt and equity would miss the enormous variety of financing instruments that companies use today.

14.1 Creating Value with Financing Decisions

Smart investment decisions make shareholders wealthier. So do smart financing decisions. For example, if your company can borrow at 3% when the going rate is 4%, you have done your shareholders a good turn.

Unfortunately, this is more easily said than done. The problem is that competition in financial markets is more intense than in most product markets. In product markets, companies regularly find competitive advantages that allow positive-NPV investments. For example, a company may have only a few competitors that specialize in the same line of business in the same geographical area. Or it may be able to capitalize on patents or technology or on customer recognition and loyalty. All this opens up the opportunity to make superior profits and find projects with positive NPVs.

But there are few protected niches in *financial* markets. You can't patent the design of a new security. Moreover, in these markets you always face fast-moving competition, including all the other corporations seeking funds, to say nothing of the state, local, and federal governments, financial institutions, individuals, and foreign firms and governments that also come to New York, London, or Tokyo for financing. The investors who supply financing are numerous, and they are smart. Most likely, these investors can assess values of securities at least as well as you can.

Of course, when you borrow, you would like to pay less than the going rate of interest. But if the loan is a good deal for your shareholders, it must be a bad deal for the lenders. So what are the chances that your firm could consistently trick investors into overpaying for its securities? Pretty slim. In general, firms should assume that the securities they issue sell for their true values.

But what do we mean by *true value?* It is a potentially slippery phrase. True value does not mean ultimate future value—we do not expect investors to be fortune-tellers. It means a price that incorporates all the information *currently* available to investors. We came across this idea in Chapter 7, when we introduced the concept of *efficient capital markets* and showed how difficult it is for investors to obtain consistently superior performance. In an efficient capital market all securities are fairly priced given the information available to investors. In that case the sale of securities at their market price can never be a positive-NPV transaction.

All this means that it's harder to make or lose money by smart or stupid financing strategies. It is difficult to make money—that is, to find cheap financing—because the investors who supply the financing demand fair terms. At the same time, it's harder to lose money because competition among investors prevents any one of them from demanding more than fair terms.

Just remember as you read the following chapters: There are few free lunches on Wall Street. . . . and few easy answers for the financial manager who must decide which securities to issue.

14.2 Patterns of Corporate Financing

internally generated funds
Cash reinvested in the firm: depreciation plus earnings not paid out as dividends

Firms have three broad sources of cash: They can plow back part of their profits, or they can raise money from external sources by an issue of either shares or debt. Look, for example, at Figure 14.1, which shows how FedEx and Dow Chemical have generated cash. In each panel the green line shows the percentage yearly addition to the firm's capital that was provided by the sale of shares. The orange line shows the addition that came from new issues of long- or short-term debt, and the blue line shows the contribution from **internally generated funds** (defined as depreciation plus earnings that are not paid out as dividends[1]).

---

[1] Remember that depreciation is a *noncash* expense. This means that it is treated as an expense even though it does not represent a use of cash. Therefore, we add it back to earnings to find the cash flow generated by the firm.

FIGURE 14.1 Sources of funds for FedEx and Dow Chemical

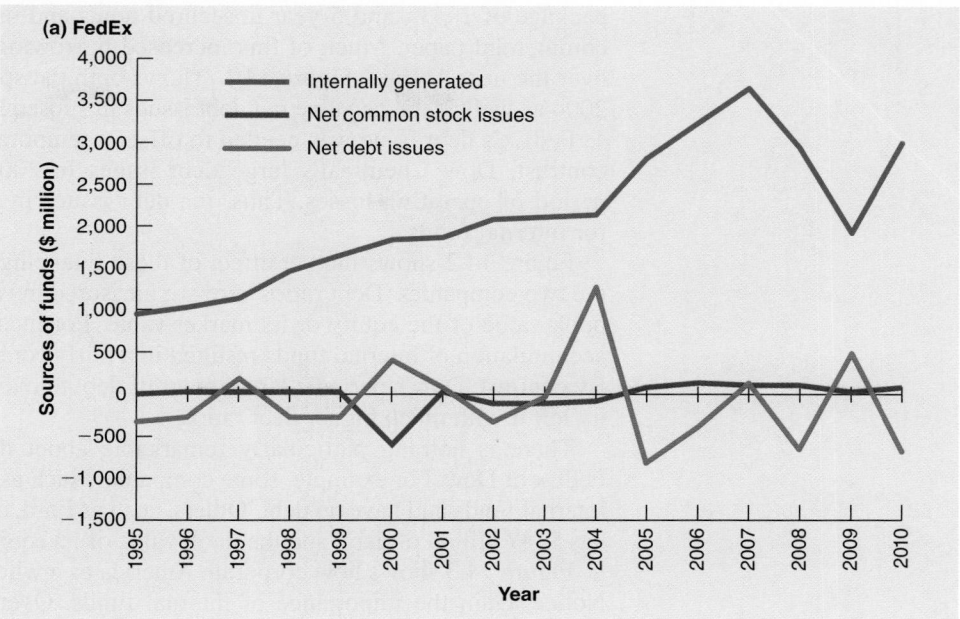

(a) FedEx

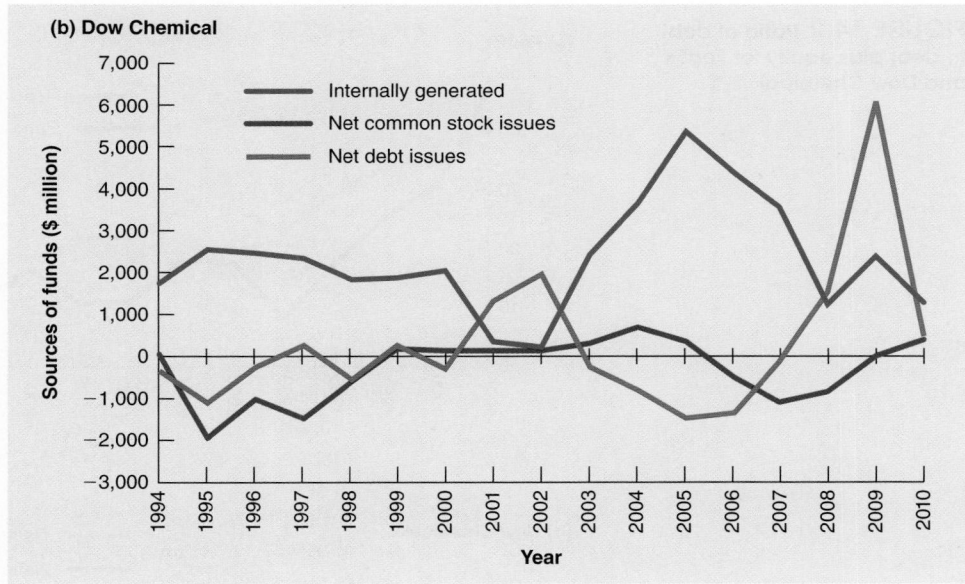

(b) Dow Chemical

There are both some similarities and some differences in our two examples. Let's start with the similarities. By far the largest source of cash for both companies came from plowing back profits. The gap between this internally generated cash and the cash that the company needs is called the **financial deficit.** To make up the deficit, the company must either sell new equity or borrow. Neither FedEx nor Dow raised significant amounts of cash by selling new shares. In fact, as often as not they *used* cash to buy back shares that had been issued in earlier years. In Figure 14.1 these repurchases show up as negative issues of common stock. (Dow did make an issue of preferred stock in 2009. This is not shown in Figure 14.1.).

Instead of issuing equity, both companies have made occasional large new issues of debt, but they have done so for somewhat different reasons. For example, in 2004 FedEx bought Kinko's for $2.4 billion in cash. To help pay for this purchase, FedEx sold $1.9 billion of short-term debt, called *commercial paper*. It then issued a

financial deficit
Difference between the cash companies need and the amount generated internally.

package of 1-, 3-, and 5-year unsecured notes and used the proceeds to pay off the commercial paper. Much of this increased borrowing was also subsequently repaid over the next 4 years. Figure 14.1*a* shows both the spike in FedEx's debt issuance in 2004 as well as the negative net debt issues in subsequent years.

FedEx's debt issue was needed to offset a temporary increase in expenditures. In contrast, Dow Chemical's large debt issues in 2001 and 2002 coincided with a period of operating losses. Thus, the debt issues in those years largely substituted for internal funds.

Figure 14.2 shows the net effect of these financing decisions on the debt ratios of the two companies. Debt ratios here are measured in two ways: alternatively using the book value of the equity or its market value. For most of this period FedEx's steady accumulation of internal funds resulted in a fairly continuous decline in the debt ratio. By contrast, Dow's periodic large issues of debt to make up for shortfalls in profitability left it with much higher debt ratios.

There is nothing particularly remarkable about the financial structure of either FedEx or Dow. For example, some companies, such as Google, rely almost entirely on internal funds and have no debt. Others, such as Ford, are at the opposite extreme. Ford has $147 billion of debt, and the book value of its equity is negative at −$8 billion.[2]

Figure 14.3 shows how corporate America as a whole has financed its investments. Notice again the importance of internal funds. Over the 15-year period, internally

FIGURE 14.2 Ratio of debt to debt plus equity for FedEx and Dow Chemical

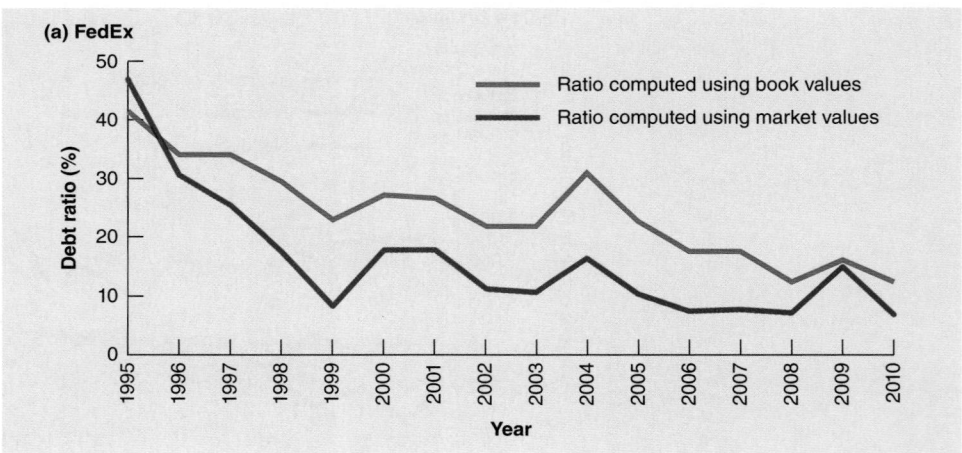

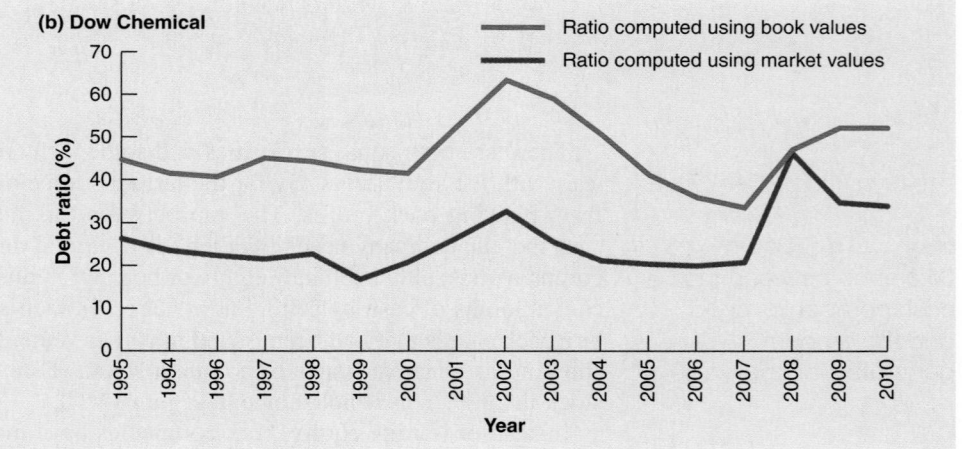

---

[2] In other words, Ford's accumulated losses exceed the total cumulative amount that it has raised from shareholders.

FIGURE 14.3 **Sources of funds for U.S. nonfinancial corporations, 1995–2010**

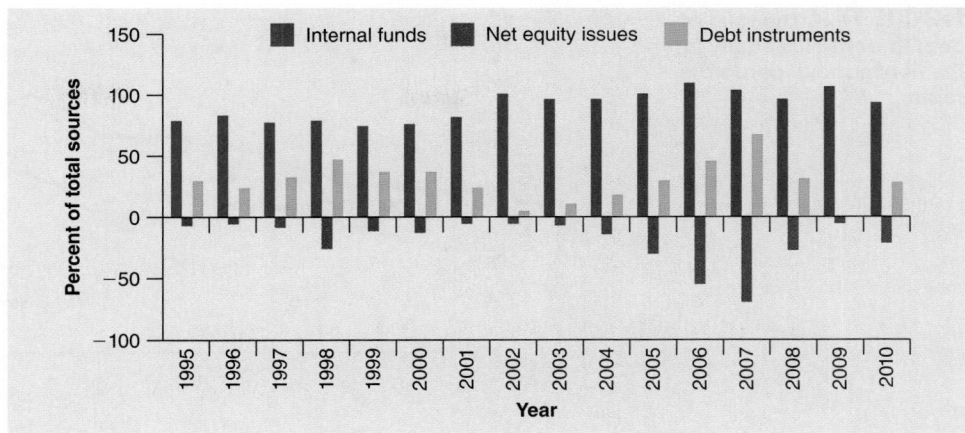

Source: Board of Governors of the Federal Reserve System, Division of Research and. Statistics, "Flow of Funds Accounts," Table F.102 at **www.federalreserve.gov/releases/z1/current/data.htm**.

generated cash covered 87% of corporate capital requirements. The gap was more than made up by borrowing.[3] Equity issues in each year were negative; firms used some of their new cash to buy back stock.

Do Firms Rely Too Heavily on Internal Funds?

Some observers worry that firms rely too heavily on internal funds. They believe that managers might think more carefully about spending money if they had to ask investors for it. Think back to Chapter 1, where we pointed out that a firm is a team, consisting of managers, shareholders, debtholders, and so on. The shareholders and debtholders would like to monitor management to make sure that it is pulling its weight and truly maximizing market value. It is costly for individual investors to keep check on management, but large financial institutions are specialists in monitoring. So when the firm goes to the bank for a large loan or makes a public issue of stock or bonds, managers know that they had better have all the answers. If they want a quiet life, they will avoid going to the capital market to raise money and they will retain sufficient earnings to be able to meet unanticipated demands for cash.

We do not mean to paint managers as loafers. There are also rational reasons for relying on internally generated funds. For example, the costs of issuing new securities are avoided. Moreover, the announcement of a new equity issue is usually bad news for investors, who worry that management may be trying to sell overpriced stock.[4] Raising equity capital from internal sources avoids the costs and the bad omens associated with equity issues.

Are Firms Issuing Too Much Debt?

We have seen that rather than sell additional common stock, firms have on average issued debt and used part of the proceeds to buy back some of their stock. Has this policy resulted in an increase in the proportion of debt that companies use?

Figure 14.4 provides some long-term perspective on the question. If all U.S. manufacturing corporations were merged into a single gigantic firm, this would be its ratio

---

[3] The *type* of debt that firms use varies from year to year. For example, in 2009 the financial crisis led firms to repay bank debt and to issue instead huge amounts of corporate bonds. These variations do not show up in Figure 14.3.

[4] Managers have insiders' insights and naturally are tempted to issue stock when the stock price looks good to them, that is, when they are less optimistic than outside investors. The outside investors realize all this and will buy a new issue only at a discount from the preannouncement price. Stock issues are discussed further in the next chapter.

FIGURE 14.4 The ratio of debt to debt plus equity for the nonfinancial corporate sector

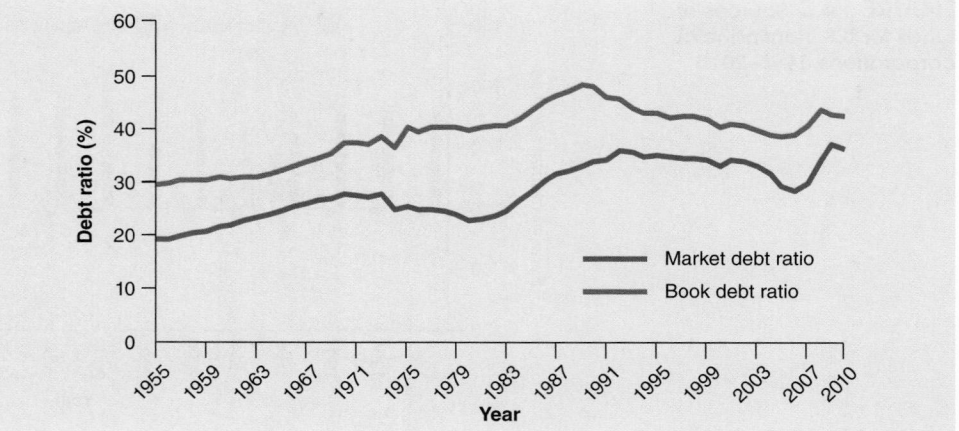

Source: Board of Governors of the Federal Reserve System, Division of Research and Statistics, "Flow of Funds Accounts," Table B.102 at **www.federalreserve.gov/releases/z1/current/data.htm**.

of debt to total capital. Debt ratios are lower when computed from market rather than book values. This is because the market value of equity is substantially greater than book value for most firms. Debt ratios using either measure, however, generally have increased since 1955.[5] Notice the especially sharp rise in the market debt ratio in 2008–2009 as equity values plunged during the financial crisis.

Should we be worried that book debt ratios are higher today than they were 50 years ago? It is true that high debt ratios mean that more companies are likely to fall into financial distress when a serious recession hits the economy. Undoubtedly GM, Chrysler, Washington Mutual, and the many other companies that faced insolvency in the recent recession would all have been in a stronger position if they had carried less debt. But it does not always follow that less risk is better. Finding the optimal debt ratio is like finding the optimal speed limit; we can agree that accidents at 30 miles per hour are less dangerous, other things being equal, than accidents at 60 miles per hour, but we do not therefore set the national speed limit at 30. Speed has benefits as well as risks. So does debt, as we will see in Chapter 16.

Self-Test 14.1

"Since internal funds provide the bulk of industry's needs for capital, the securities markets serve little function." Does the speaker have a point?

14.3 Common Stock

We will now look more closely at the different sources of finance, starting with common stock. We will stick with our example of Dow Chemical.

Most major corporations are far too large to be owned by one investor. For example, you would need to lay your hands on about $42 billion if you wanted to own the whole of Dow. Dow is owned by about 650,000 different investors, each of whom holds a number of shares of common stock. These investors are therefore known as *shareholders,* or *stockholders.* At the end of 2010 Dow had outstanding 1.167 billion shares of common stock. Thus, if you were to buy one Dow share, you would own 1/167,000,000,

---

[5] The rise in debt ratios in the first part of the period was not due to stock repurchases, since these were relatively uncommon until the mid-1980s.

or about .00000009%, of the company. Of course, a large pension fund might hold many thousands of Dow shares.

The 1.167 billion shares held by investors are not the only shares that have been issued by Dow. The company has also issued a further 5 million shares, which it later bought back from investors. These repurchased shares are held in the company's treasury and are known as **treasury stock.** The shares held by investors are said to be **issued and outstanding shares.** By contrast, the 5 million treasury shares are said to be *issued but not outstanding.*

If Dow wishes to raise more money, it can sell more shares. However, there is a limit to the number that it can issue without the approval of the current shareholders. The maximum number of shares that can be issued is known as the **authorized share capital**—for Dow, this is 1.5 billion shares. Since Dow has already issued 1.172 billion shares, it can issue about 330 million more without shareholders' approval.

Table 14.1 shows how the investment by Dow's common stockholders is recorded in the company's books. The price at which each share is recorded is known as its **par value.** In Dow's case each share has a par value of $2.50. Thus the total par value of the issued shares is 1.172 billion shares × $2.50 per share = $2.931 billion. Par value has little economic significance.[6]

The price at which new shares are sold to investors almost always exceeds par value. The difference is entered into the company's accounts as **additional paid-in capital,** or *capital surplus.* For example, if Dow sold an additional 1 million shares at $20 a share, the par value of the common stock would increase by 1 million × $2.50 = $2.5 million and additional paid-in capital would increase by 1 million × ($20 − $2.50) = $17.5 million. You can see from this example that the funds raised from the stock issue are divided between par value and additional paid-in capital. Since the choice of par value in the first place was immaterial, so is the allocation between par value and additional paid-in capital.

Besides buying new stock, shareholders also indirectly contribute new capital to the firm whenever profits that could be paid out as dividends are instead plowed back into the company. Table 14.1 shows that the cumulative amount of such **retained earnings** is $17.736 billion.

Dow's books also show the amount that the company has spent to repurchase its own stock. The repurchase of the 5 million shares cost Dow $.239 billion. This is money that has in effect been returned to shareholders. Companies sometimes spend huge sums repurchasing shares.

The sum of the par value, additional paid-in capital, and retained earnings, less repurchased stock and some miscellaneous other adjustments, is known as the *net common equity* of the firm. It equals the total amount contributed directly by shareholders

treasury stock
Stock that has been repurchased by the company and held in its treasury.

issued shares
Shares that have been issued by the company.

outstanding shares
Shares that have been issued by the company and are held by investors.

authorized share capital
Maximum number of shares that the company is permitted to issue.

par value
Value of security shown in the company's accounts.

additional paid-in capital
Difference between issue price and par value of stock. Also called *capital surplus.*

retained earnings
Earnings not paid out as dividends.

TABLE 14.1 Book value of common stockholders' equity of Dow Chemical, December 31, 2010 (figures in billions)

Common shares ($2.50 par value per share)	$ 2.931
Additional paid-in capital	2.286
Retained earnings	17.736
Treasury shares at cost	(.239)
Other	(4.875)
Net common equity	17.839
Note:	
Authorized shares	1.5
Issued shares, of which	1.172
Outstanding shares	1.167
Treasury shares	.005

[6] Some companies issue shares with no par value, in which case the stock is listed in the accounts at an arbitrarily determined figure.

when the firm issued new stock and indirectly when it plowed back part of its earnings. The book value of Dow's net common equity is $17.839 billion. With 1.167 billion shares outstanding this is equivalent to 17.839/1.167 = $15.29 a share. But, the market value of Dow's stock is about $34, much higher than its book value. Evidently investors believe that Dow's assets are worth much more than they originally cost.

Self-Test 14.2

Generic Products has had one stock issue in which it sold 100,000 shares to the public at $15 per share. Can you fill in the following table?

Common shares ($1 par value per share)	_____
Additional paid-in capital	_____
Retained earnings	_____
Net common equity	$4,500,000

Ownership of the Corporation

A corporation is owned by its common stockholders. As we saw in Chapter 2, over one-third of the stock is held by individual U.S. investors and nonprofit organizations. The remainder belongs to financial institutions such as mutual funds, pension funds, and insurance companies. Their holdings are summarized again in Figure 14.5.

What do we mean when we say that the stockholders *own* the corporation? First, the stockholders are entitled to whatever profits are left over after the lenders have received their entitlement. Usually the company pays out part of these profits as dividends and plows back the remainder into new investments. Shareholders hope that these investments will enable the company to earn higher profits and pay higher dividends in the future.

Second, shareholders have the ultimate control over how the company is run. This does not mean that shareholders can do whatever they like. For example, the bank that lends to the company may place restrictions on how much extra borrowing the company can undertake. However, the contract with the bank can never restrict *all* the actions that the company might wish to undertake. The shareholders retain the residual rights of control over these decisions.

Occasionally, the company must get shareholder approval before it can take certain actions. For example, it needs shareholder agreement to increase the authorized capital or to merge with another company. On most other matters, shareholder control boils down to the right to vote on appointments to the board of directors.

FIGURE 14.5 Holdings of corporate equities, third quarter, 2010

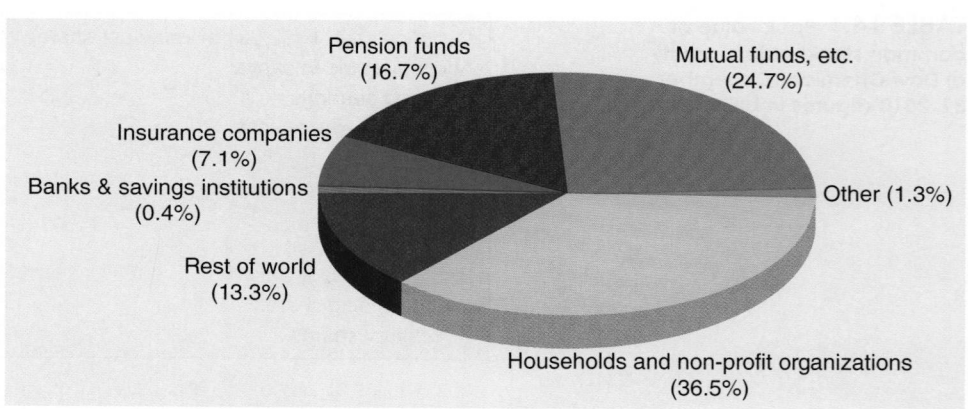

Source: Board of Governors of the Federal Reserve System, Division of Research and Statistics, "Flow of Funds Accounts," table L.213 at **www.federalreserve.gov/releases/z1/current/data.htm**.

The board of directors usually consists of the company's top management as well as *outside directors,* who are not employed by the firm. The board is there to look after shareholders' interests. It appoints and oversees the management of the firm and meets to vote on such matters as a new share issue or the payment of a dividend. Most of the time the board will go along with the management, but in crisis situations it can be very independent. For example, boards will not usually hesitate to replace a failing chief executive.

Voting Procedures

majority voting
Voting system in which each director is voted on separately.

cumulative voting
Voting system in which all votes that one shareholder is allowed to cast can be cast for one candidate for the board of directors.

In most companies stockholders elect directors by a system of **majority voting.** In this case each director is voted on separately, and stockholders can cast one vote for each share they own. In some companies directors are elected by **cumulative voting.** The directors are then voted on jointly, and the stockholders can, if they choose, cast all their votes for just one candidate. For example, suppose that there are five directors to be elected and you own 100 shares. You therefore have a total of $5 \times 100 = 500$ votes. Under majority voting you can cast a maximum of 100 votes for any one candidate. With a cumulative voting system you can cast all 500 votes for your favorite candidate. Cumulative voting makes it easier for a minority group of the stockholders to elect a director to represent their interests. That is why minority groups devote so much effort to campaigning for cumulative voting.

On many issues a simple majority of the votes cast is enough to carry the day, but there are some decisions that require a "supermajority" of, say, 75% of those eligible to vote. For example, a supermajority vote is sometimes needed to approve a merger. This makes it difficult for the firm to be taken over and therefore helps to protect the incumbent management.

proxy contest
Takeover attempt in which outsiders compete with management for shareholders' votes.

Shareholders can either vote in person or appoint a proxy to vote. The issues on which they are asked to vote are rarely contested, particularly in the case of large publicly traded firms. Occasionally, however, there are **proxy contests** in which outsiders compete with the firm's existing management and directors for control of the corporation. But the odds are stacked against the outsiders, for the insiders can get the firm to pay all the costs of presenting their case and obtaining votes.

Classes of Stock

Most companies in the United States issue just one class of common stock. But a few, such as Ford Motor and Google, have issued two classes of shares with different voting rights. For example, suppose that a firm needs fresh capital, but its management does not want to give up its controlling interest. The existing shares could be labeled "class A," and then "class B" shares with limited voting rights could be issued to outside investors.

preferred stock
Stock that takes priority over common stock in regard to dividends.

In some countries it is fairly common for firms to issue two classes of stock with different voting rights. That may be a good thing if the controlling shareholders then use their influence to improve profitability. However, you can see the dangers here. If an idle or incompetent management has a large block of votes, it may use these votes to stay in control. Or if another corporation has a controlling stake, it may exercise its influence to gain a business advantage.

14.4 Preferred Stock

net worth
Book value of common stockholders' equity plus preferred stock.

Usually when investors talk about equity or stock, they are referring to common stock. But Dow Chemical has also issued 4 million shares of **preferred stock,** and this too is part of the company's equity. The sum of Dow's common equity and preferred stock is known as its **net worth.**

For most companies preferred stock is much less important than common stock. However, it can be a useful method of financing in mergers and certain other special situations.

Like debt, preferred stock promises a series of fixed payments to the investor, and with relatively few exceptions preferred dividends are paid in full and on time. Nevertheless, preferred stock is legally an equity security. This is because payment of a preferred dividend is within the discretion of the directors. The only obligation is that no dividends can be paid on the common stock until the preferred dividend has been paid.[7] If the company goes out of business, the preferred stockholders get in the queue after the debtholders but before the common stockholders.

Preferred stock rarely confers full voting privileges. This is an advantage to firms that want to raise new money without sharing control of the firm with the new shareholders. However, if there is any matter that affects their place in the queue, preferred stockholders usually get to vote on it. Most issues also provide the holder with some voting power if the preferred dividend is skipped.

Companies cannot deduct preferred dividends when they calculate taxable income. Like common stock dividends, preferred dividends are paid from after-tax income. For most industrial firms this is a serious deterrent to issuing preferred. However, regulated public utilities can take tax payments into account when they negotiate with regulators the rates they charge customers. So they can effectively pass the tax disadvantage of preferred on to the consumer. Preferred stock also has a particular attraction for banks, for regulators allow banks to lump preferred in with common stock when calculating whether they have sufficient equity capital.

Preferred stock does have one tax advantage. If one corporation buys another's stock, only 30% of the dividends it receives is taxed. This rule applies to dividends on both common and preferred stock, but it is most important for preferred, for which returns are dominated by dividends rather than capital gains.

Suppose that your firm has surplus cash to invest. If it buys a bond, the interest will be taxed at the company's tax rate of 35%. If it buys a preferred share, it owns an asset like a bond (the preferred dividends can be viewed as "interest"), but the effective tax rate is only 30% of 35%, $.30 \times .35 = .105$, or 10.5%. It is no surprise that most preferred shares are held by corporations.

If you invest your firm's spare cash in a preferred stock, you will want to make sure that when it is time to sell the stock, it won't have plummeted in value. One problem with garden-variety preferred stock that pays a fixed dividend is that the preferred's market prices go up and down as interest rates change (because present values fall when rates rise). So one ingenious banker thought up a wrinkle: Why not link the dividend on the preferred stock to interest rates so that it goes up when interest rates rise and vice versa? The result is known as **floating-rate preferred.** If you own floating-rate preferred, you know that any change in interest rates will be counterbalanced by a change in the dividend payment, so the value of your investment is protected.

floating-rate preferred
Preferred stock paying dividends that vary with short-term interest rates.

Self-Test 14.3

A company in a 35% tax bracket can buy a bond yielding 10% or a preferred stock of the same firm that is priced to yield 8%. Which will provide the higher after-tax yield?

---

[7] These days this obligation is usually cumulative. In other words, before the common stockholders get a cent, the firm must pay any preferred dividends that have been missed in the past.

14.5 Corporate Debt

When they borrow money, companies promise to make regular interest payments and to repay the principal (that is, the original amount borrowed). **However, corporations have limited liability. By this we mean that the promise to repay the debt is not always kept. If the company gets into deep water, the company has the right to default on the debt and to hand over the company's assets to the lenders.**

Clearly it will choose bankruptcy only if the value of the assets is less than the amount of the debt. In practice, when companies go bankrupt, this handover of assets is far from straightforward. For example, when Pacific Gas and Electric filed for bankruptcy in 2004, the bankruptcy court was faced with several thousand creditors all jostling for a better place in the queue. By the time the company had emerged from bankruptcy 3 years later, it had agreed to make 2,100 separate payments resolving $8.4 billion of agreed claims and had set aside a further $1.8 billion for claims that were still under dispute.

Because lenders are not regarded as owners of the firm, they don't normally have any voting power. Also, the company's payments of interest are regarded as a cost and are therefore deducted from taxable income. Thus interest is paid out of *before-tax* income, whereas dividends on common and preferred stock are paid out of *after-tax* income. This means that the government provides a tax subsidy on the use of debt, which it does not provide on stock.

Debt Comes in Many Forms

Some orderly scheme of classification is essential to cope with the almost endless variety of debt issues. We will walk you through the major distinguishing characteristics.

Interest Rate   The interest payment, or *coupon,* on most long-term loans is fixed at the time of issue. If a $1,000 bond is issued with a coupon of 10%, the firm continues to pay $100 a year regardless of how interest rates change. You may also encounter zero-coupon bonds. In this case the firm does not make a regular interest payment. It just makes a single payment at maturity. Obviously, investors pay less for zero-coupon bonds.

> **prime rate**
> Benchmark interest rate charged by banks.

Most loans from a bank and some long-term loans carry a *floating interest rate.* For example, your firm may be offered a loan at "1 percent over prime." The **prime rate** is the benchmark interest rate charged by banks to large customers with good to excellent credit. (But the largest and most creditworthy corporations can, and do, borrow at *less* than prime.) The prime rate is adjusted up and down with the general level of interest rates. When the prime rate changes, the interest on your floating-rate loan also changes.

Floating-rate loans are not always tied to the prime rate. Often they are tied to the rate at which international banks lend to one another. This is known as the *London Interbank Offered Rate,* or *LIBOR.*

> *Self-Test 14.4*
>
> Would you expect the price of a 10-year floating-rate bond to be more or less sensitive to changes in interest rates than the price of a 10-year maturity fixed-rate bond?

> **funded debt**
> Debt with more than 1 year remaining to maturity.

Maturity   **Funded debt** is any debt repayable more than 1 year from the date of issue. Debt due in less than a year is termed *unfunded* and is carried on the balance sheet as a current liability. Unfunded debt is often described as short-term debt, and funded debt is described as long-term, although it is clearly artificial to call a 364-day debt short-term and a 366-day debt long-term (except in leap years).

There are corporate bonds of nearly every conceivable maturity. For example, Bristol Myers Squibb has issued bonds that do not mature until 2097. Some British banks have issued perpetuities—that is, bonds which may survive forever. At the other extreme we find firms borrowing literally overnight.

Repayment Provisions   Long-term loans are commonly repaid in a steady regular way, perhaps after an initial grace period. For bonds that are publicly traded, this is done by means of a **sinking fund.** Each year the firm puts aside a sum of cash into a sinking fund that is then used to buy back the bonds. When there is a sinking fund, investors are prepared to lend at a lower rate of interest. They know that they are more likely to be repaid if the company sets aside some cash each year than if the entire loan has to be repaid on one specified day.

Suppose that a company issues a 6%, 30-year bond at a price of $1,000. Five years later interest rates have fallen to 4%, and the price of the bond has risen dramatically. If you were the company's treasurer, wouldn't you like to be able to retire the bonds and issue some new bonds at the lower interest rate? Well, with some bonds, known as **callable bonds,** the company does have the option to buy them back for the *call price.*[8] Of course, holders of these callable bonds know that the company will wish to buy the issue back if interest rates fall, and therefore the price of the bond will not rise above the call price.

Figure 14.6 shows the risk of a call to the bondholder. The blue line is the value of a 30-year, 6% "straight," that is, noncallable, bond; the orange line is the value of a bond with the same coupon rate and maturity but callable at $1,060 (i.e., 106% of face value). At very high interest rates the risk that the company will call the bonds is negligible, and the values of the two bonds are nearly identical. As rates fall, the straight bond continues to increase steadily in value, but since the capital appreciation of the callable bond is limited by the call price, its capital appreciation will lag behind that of the straight bond.

A callable bond gives the *company* the option to retire the bonds early. But some bonds give the *investor* the right to demand early repayment. During the 1990s many loans to Asian companies gave the lenders a repayment option. Consequently, when the Asian crisis struck in 1997, these companies were faced by a flood of lenders

sinking fund
Fund established to retire debt before maturity.

callable bond
Bond that may be repurchased by firm before maturity at specified call price.

FIGURE 14.6 Prices of callable versus straight debt. When interest rates fall, bond prices rise. But the price of the callable bond (orange line) is limited by the call price.

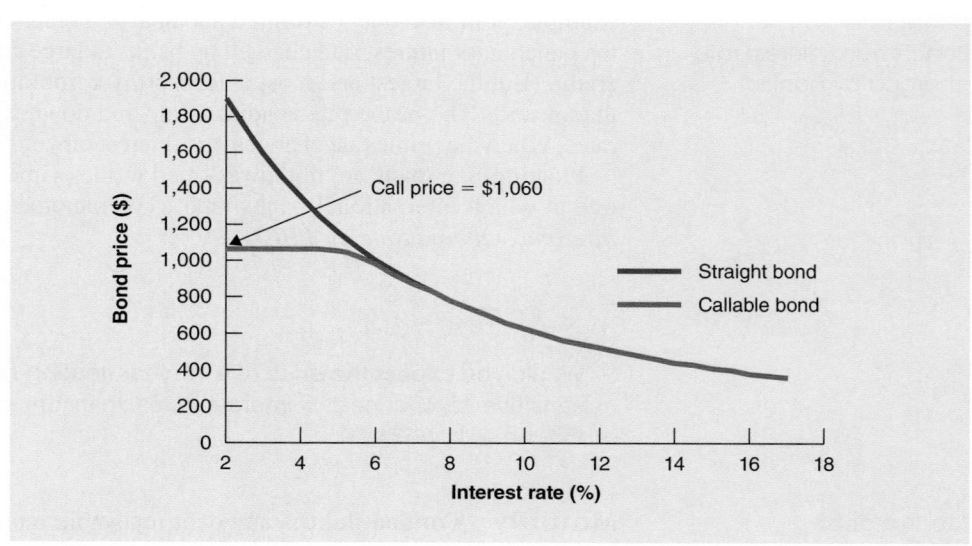

_____

[8] Sometimes callable bonds specify a period during which the firm is not allowed to call the bond if the purpose is simply to issue another bond at a lower interest rate.

demanding their money back. Needless to say, companies that were already struggling to survive did not appreciate this additional burden.

> ## Self-Test 14.5
>
> **Suppose Dow Chemical is considering two issues of 20-year maturity coupon bonds; one issue will be callable, the other not. For a given coupon rate, will the callable or noncallable bond sell at the higher price? If the bonds are both to be sold to the public at face value, which bond must have the higher coupon rate?**

subordinated debt
Debt that may be repaid in bankruptcy only after senior debt is paid.

Seniority   Some debts are **subordinated.** In the event of default the subordinated lender gets in line behind the firm's general creditors. The subordinated lender holds a junior claim and is paid only after all senior creditors are satisfied.

When you lend money to a firm, you can assume that you hold a senior claim unless the debt agreement says otherwise. However, this does not always put you at the front of the line, for the firm may have set aside some of its assets specifically for the protection of other lenders. That brings us to our next classification.

Security   When you borrow to buy your home, the savings and loan company will take out a mortgage on the house. The mortgage acts as security for the loan. If you default on the loan payments, the S&L can seize your home.

secured debt
Debt that has first claim on specified collateral in the event of default.

When companies borrow, they also may set aside certain assets as security for the loan. These assets are termed *collateral,* and the debt is said to be **secured.** In the event of default, the secured lender has first claim on the collateral; unsecured lenders have a general claim on the rest of the firm's assets but only a junior claim on the collateral.

Default Risk   Seniority and security do not guarantee payment. A debt can be senior and secured but still as risky as a dizzy tightrope walker—it depends on the value and the risk of the firm's assets. In Chapter 6 we showed how the safety of most corporate bonds can be judged from bond ratings provided by rating agencies such as Moody's and Standard & Poor's. Bonds that are rated "triple-A" seldom default. At the other extreme, many speculative-grade (or "junk") bonds may be teetering on the brink.

As you would expect, investors demand a high return from low-rated bonds. We saw evidence of this in Chapter 6, where Figure 6.9 compares the yields on default-free U.S. Treasury bonds with those on corporate bonds in various rating classes. The lower-rated bonds do in fact offer higher promised yields to maturity.

Country and Currency   These days capital markets know few national boundaries and many large firms in the United States borrow abroad. For example, an American company may choose to finance a new plant in Switzerland by borrowing Swiss francs from a Swiss bank, or it may expand its Dutch operation by issuing a bond in Holland. Also many foreign companies come to the United States to borrow dollars, which are then used to finance their operations throughout the world.

In addition to these national capital markets, there is an international capital market centered mainly in London. Banks from all over the world have branches in London. They include such giants as Citicorp, UBS, Deutsche Bank, Mitsubishi UFJ, HSBC, and BNP Paribas. One reason they are there is to collect deposits in the major currencies. For example, suppose an Arab sheikh has just received payment in dollars for a large sale of oil to the United States. Rather than depositing the check in the United States, he may choose to open a dollar account with a bank in London. Dollars held in a bank outside the United States came to be known as **eurodollars.** Similarly, yen held outside Japan were termed euroyen, and so on.

eurodollars
Dollars held on deposit in a bank outside the United States.

The London bank branch that is holding the sheikh's dollar deposit may temporarily lend those dollars to a company, in the same way that a bank in the United States may relend dollars that have been deposited with it. Thus a company can either borrow dollars from a bank in the United States or borrow dollars from a bank in London.[9]

eurobond
Bond that is marketed internationally.

If a firm wants to make an issue of long-term bonds, it can choose to do so in the United States. Alternatively, it can sell the bonds to investors in several countries. Because these international issues have usually been marketed by the London branches of international banks, they have traditionally been known as **eurobonds.** A eurobond may be denominated in dollars, yen, or any other currency. Unfortunately, when the single European currency was established it was called the *euro.* It is easy, therefore, to confuse a *eurobond* (a bond that is sold internationally) with a bond that is denominated in *euros.*

private placement
Sale of securities to a limited number of investors without a public offering.

Public versus Private Placements   Publicly issued bonds are sold to anyone who wishes to buy, and once they have been issued, they can be freely traded in the securities markets. In a **private placement,** the issue is sold directly to a small number of banks, insurance companies, or other investment institutions. Privately placed bonds cannot be resold to individuals in the United States and can be resold only to other qualified institutional investors. However, there is increasingly active trading *among* these investors.

We will have more to say about the difference between public issues and private placements in the next chapter.

protective covenant
Restriction on a firm to protect bondholders.

Protective Covenants   When investors lend to a company, they know that they might not get their money back. But they expect that the company will use their money well and not take unreasonable risks. To help ensure this, lenders usually impose a number of conditions, or **protective covenants,** on companies that borrow from them. An honest firm is willing to accept these conditions because it knows that they enable the firm to borrow at a reasonable rate of interest.

Companies that borrow in moderation are less likely to get into difficulties than those that are up to the gunwales in debt. So lenders usually restrict the amount of extra debt that the firm can issue. Lenders are also eager to prevent others from pushing ahead of them in the queue if trouble occurs. So they will not allow the company to create new debt that is senior to them or to put aside assets for other lenders.

The story of Marriott in the nearby box illustrates what can happen when bondholders are not sufficiently careful about the conditions they impose.

Self-Test 14.6

In 1987 RJR Nabisco, the food and tobacco giant, had $5 billion of A-rated debt outstanding. In that year the company was taken over, and $19 billion of debt was issued and used to buy back equity. The debt ratio skyrocketed, and the debt was downgraded to a BB rating. The holders of the previously issued debt were furious, and one filed a lawsuit claiming that RJR had violated an *implicit* obligation not to undertake major financing changes at the expense of existing bondholders. Why did these bondholders believe they had been harmed by the massive issue of new debt? What type of *explicit* restriction would you have wanted if you had been one of the original bondholders?

---

[9] Because the Federal Reserve requires banks in the United States to keep interest-free reserves, there is in effect a tax on dollar deposits in the United States. Overseas dollar deposits are free of this tax, and therefore banks can afford to charge the borrower slightly lower interest rates.

Marriott Plan Enrages Holders of Its Bonds

Marriott Corp. has infuriated bond investors with a restructuring plan that may be a new way for companies to pull the rug out from under bondholders.

Prices of Marriott's existing bonds have plunged as much as 30% in the past two days in the wake of the hotel and food-services company's announcement that it plans to separate into two companies, one burdened with virtually all of Marriott's debt.

On Monday, Marriott said that it will divide its operations into two separate businesses. One, Marriott International Inc., is a healthy company that will manage Marriott's vast hotel chain; it will get most of the old company's revenue, a larger share of the cash flow and will be nearly debt-free.

The second business, called Host Marriott Corp., is a debt-laden company that will own Marriott hotels along with other real estate and retain essentially all of the old Marriott's $3 billion of debt.

The announcement stunned and infuriated bondholders, who watched nervously as the value of their Marriott bonds tumbled and as Moody's Investors Service Inc. downgraded the bond to the junk-bond category from investment-grade.

Price Plunge

In trading, Marriott's 10% bonds that mature in 2012, which Marriott sold to investors just six months ago, were quoted yesterday at about 80 cents on the dollar, down from 110 Friday. The price decline translates into a stunning loss of $300 for a bond with a $1,000 face amount.

Marriott officials concede that the company's spinoff plan penalizes bondholders. However, the company notes that, like all public corporations, its fiduciary duty is to stockholders, not bondholders. Indeed, Marriott's stock jumped 12% Monday. (It fell a bit yesterday.)

Bond investors and analysts worry that if the Marriott spinoff goes through, other companies will soon follow suit by separating debt-laden units from the rest of the company. "Any company that fears it has underperforming divisions that are dragging down its stock price is a possible candidate" for such a restructuring, says Dorothy K. Lee, an assistant vice president at Moody's.

If the trend heats up, investors said, the Marriott restructuring could be the worst news for corporate bondholders since RJR Nabisco Inc.'s managers shocked investors in 1987 by announcing they were taking the company private in a record $25 billion leveraged buy-out. The move, which loaded RJR with debt and tanked the value of RJR bonds, triggered a deep slump in prices of many investment-grade corporate bonds as investors backed away from the market.

Strong Covenants May Re-Emerge

Some analysts say the move by Marriott may trigger the re-emergence of strong covenants, or written protections, in future corporate bond issues to protect bondholders against such restructurings as the one being engineered by Marriott. In the wake of the RJR buy-out, many investors demanded stronger covenants in new corporate bond issues.

Some investors blame themselves for not demanding stronger covenants. "It's our own fault," said Robert Hickey, a bond fund manager at Van Kampen Merritt. In their rush to buy bonds in an effort to lock in yields, many investors have allowed companies to sell bonds with covenants that have been "slim to none," Mr. Hickey said.

lease
Long-term rental agreement.

A Debt by Any Other Name The word *debt* sounds straightforward, but companies enter into a number of financial arrangements that look suspiciously like debt yet are treated differently in the accounts. Some of these obligations are easily identifiable. For example, accounts payable are simply obligations to pay for goods that have already been delivered and are therefore like a short-term debt.

Other arrangements are not so easy to spot. For example, instead of borrowing money to buy equipment, many companies **lease** or rent it on a long-term basis. In this case the firm promises to make a series of payments to the lessor (the owner of the equipment). This is just like the obligation to make payments on an outstanding loan. What if the firm can't make the payments? The lessor can then take back the equipment, which is precisely what would happen if the firm had *borrowed* money from the lessor, using the equipment as collateral for the loan.

Postretirement health benefits and pension promises can also be huge liabilities. For example, at the start of 2010 Ford faced an estimated $12 billion deficit on its pension plan. That is a debt which the company will eventually need to pay.

There is nothing underhanded about these obligations. They are clearly shown on the company's balance sheet as a liability. Sometimes, however, companies go to considerable lengths to ensure that investors do not know how much they have borrowed. For example, Enron was able to borrow $658 million by setting up *special-purpose entities (SPEs),* which raised cash by a mixture of equity and debt and then used that debt to help fund the parent company. None of this debt showed up on Enron's balance sheet.

EXAMPLE 14.1 ▶   The Terms of Procter & Gamble's Bond Issue

Now that you are familiar with some of the jargon, you might like to look at an example of a bond issue. Table 14.2 is a summary of the terms of a bond issue in 2009 by Procter & Gamble. We have added some explanatory notes.

TABLE 14.2 Procter & Gamble's Debt Issue

Comment	Description of Bond
1. Interest of 3.15% will be payable on March 1 and September 1 of each year. Thus every 6 months each note will pay interest of $(.0315/2) \times \$1,000 = \$15.75$.	ISSUE Procter & Gamble 3.150% Notes.
2. Investors will be repaid the $1,000 face value in 2015.	DUE September 1, 2015.
3. Moody's bond rating is Aa, the second-highest-quality rating.	RATING—Aa.
4. A trustee is appointed to look after investors' interest.	TRUSTEE Issued under an indenture between P&G and The Bank of New York Mellon Trust Company.
5. The bonds are registered. The registrar keeps a record of who owns the bonds.	REGISTERED Issued in registered, book-entry form only.
6. The company is not obliged to repay any of the bonds on a regular basis before maturity.	SINKING FUND None.
7. The company has the option to buy back the notes. The redemption price is the greater of $1,000 or the value of an equivalent Treasury bond.	CALLABLE in whole or in part at any time.
8. The notes are senior debt, ranking equally with all P&G's other unsecured senior debt.	SENIORITY
9. The notes are not secured; that is, no assets have been set aside to protect the noteholders in the event of default. However, if P&G sets aside assets to protect any other bondholders, the notes will also be secured by these assets. This is termed a *negative pledge clause.*	SECURITY The notes are unsecured. However, "if P&G shall incur, assume or guarantee any Debt . . . it will secure . . . , the debt securities then outstanding equally and ratably with . . . such Debt."
10. The principal amount of the issue was $500,000. The notes were sold at 99.77% of their principal value. After deducting the payment to the underwriters, the company received $994.20 per bond.	OFFERED $500,000 at 99.77% (proceeds to Company 99.42%).
11. The book runners are the managing underwriters to the issue and maintain the book of securities sold.	JOINT BOOK-RUNNING MANAGERS Goldman, Sachs, J.P. Morgan, and Morgan Stanley.

Innovation in the Debt Market

We have discussed domestic bonds and eurobonds, fixed-rate and floating-rate loans, secured and unsecured loans, senior and junior loans, and much more. You might think that this gives you all the choice you need. Yet almost every day companies and their advisers dream up new types of debt. Here is one example of a bond that proved popular until the financial crisis of 2007–2009.

The Rise and Fall of Asset-Backed Bonds   Instead of borrowing money directly, companies sometimes bundle a group of loans and then sell the cash flows from these loans. This issue is known as an *asset-backed bond.* For example, automobile loans, student loans, and credit card receivables have all been bundled together and remarketed as asset-backed bonds. However, by far the most common application has been in the field of mortgage lending.

Suppose your company has made a large number of mortgage loans to buyers of homes or commercial real estate. However, you don't want to wait until the loans are paid off; to get your hands on the money now, you can sell *mortgage pass-through certificates* backed by the mortgage loans. The holders of these certificates are buying a share of the payments made by the underlying pool of mortgages. For example, if interest rates fall and the mortgages are repaid early, holders of the pass-through certificates are also repaid early. That is not generally popular with these holders, for they get their money back just when they don't want it—when interest rates are low.

Sometimes, instead of issuing one class of pass-through certificates, companies issue several different classes of security, known as *collateralized debt obligations* (or *CDOs*). For example, any mortgage payments might be used first to pay off the class of security holders called *senior* investors and only then will other, *junior* classes start to be repaid.

By 2007 over half of the new issues of CDOs involved exposure to subprime mortgages. Because the mortgages were packaged together, senior investors in these CDOs were protected against the risk of default on any particular mortgage. However, even the senior tranches were exposed to the risk of an economy-wide slump in the housing market that would lead to widespread defaults

Economic catastrophe struck in the summer of 2007, when the investment bank Bear Stearns revealed that two of its hedge funds had invested heavily in CDOs that became nearly worthless when mortgage default rates rose. Bear Stearns was rescued with help from the Federal Reserve, but the incident signaled the start of the credit crunch and the collapse of the CDO market. In 2008 issues of CDOs fell by nearly 90%.

There is a great variety of potential security designs. As long as you can convince investors of its attractions, you can issue a callable, subordinated, floating-rate bond denominated in euros. Rather than combining features of existing securities, you may be able to create an entirely new one. We can imagine a copper mining company issuing preferred shares on which the dividend fluctuates with the world copper price. We know of no such security, but it is perfectly legal to issue it and—who knows?—it might generate considerable interest among investors.

Variety is intrinsically good. People have different tastes, levels of wealth, rates of tax, and so on. Why not offer them a choice? Of course, the problem is the expense of designing and marketing new securities. But if you can think of a new security that will appeal to investors, you may be able to issue it on especially favorable terms and thus increase the value of your company.

14.6 Convertible Securities

warrant
Right to buy shares from a company at a stipulated price before a set date.

We have seen that companies sometimes have the option to repay an issue of bonds before maturity. There are also cases in which *investors* have an option. The most dramatic case is provided by a **warrant,** which is *nothing but* an option. Companies often issue warrants and bonds in a package.

EXAMPLE 14.2 ▶ Warrants

Macaw Bill wishes to make a bond issue, which could include some warrants as a "sweetener." Each warrant might allow you to purchase one share of Macaw stock at a price of $50 any time during the next 5 years. If Macaw's stock performs well, that option could turn out to be very valuable. For instance, if the stock price at the end of the 5 years is $80, then you pay the company $50 and receive in exchange a share worth $80. Of course, an investment in warrants also has its perils. If the price of Macaw stock fails to rise above $50, then the warrants expire worthless.

convertible bond
Bond that the holder may exchange for a specified amount of another security

A **convertible bond** gives its owner the option to exchange the bond for a predetermined number of common shares. The convertible bondholder hopes that the company's share price will zoom up so that the bond can be converted at a big profit. But if the shares zoom down, there is no obligation to convert; the bondholder remains just that. Not surprisingly, investors value this option to keep the bond or exchange it for shares, and therefore a convertible bond sells at a higher price than a comparable bond that is not convertible.

The convertible is rather like a package of a bond and a warrant. But there is an important difference: When the owners of a convertible wish to exercise their options to buy shares, they do not pay cash—they just exchange the bond for shares of the stock.

Companies may also issue convertible preferred stock. In this case the investor receives preferred stock with fixed dividend payments but has the option to exchange this preferred stock for the company's common stock. The preferred stock issued by Dow Chemical is convertible into common stock.

These examples do not exhaust the options encountered by the financial manager. In fact, once you read Chapter 23 and learn how to analyze options, you will find that they are all around you.

SUMMARY

Why should firms assume that the securities they issue are fairly priced? *(LO1)*

Managers want to raise money at the lowest possible cost, but their ability to find cheap financing is limited by the intense competition between investors. As a result of this competition, securities are likely to be fairly priced given the information available to investors. Such a market is said to be *efficient.*

What are recent trends in firms' use of different sources of finance? *(LO2)*

Internally generated cash is the principal source of company funds. Some people worry about that; they think that if management does not go to the trouble of raising money, it may be profligate in spending it.

In recent years, net equity issues have often been negative; that is, companies have repurchased more equity than they have issued. At the same time companies have issued large quantities of debt. However, large levels of **internally generated funds** in this period allowed book equity to increase despite the share repurchases, with the result that the ratio of long-term debt to book value of equity was fairly stable.

What information is contained in the shareholders' equity account in the firm's financial statements? *(LO3)*

The stockholders' equity account breaks down the book value of equity into **par value, additional paid-in capital, retained earnings,** and **treasury stock.** For most purposes, the allocation among the first three categories is not important. These accounts also show the total number of shares issued as well as shares repurchased by the company.

What procedures are used for elections to a firm's board of directors and other matters put to shareholders? *(LO4)*

Most companies use a **majority voting** system in which each director is voted on separately and stockholders cast one vote for each share they own. Less commonly, firms employ **cumulative voting,** which means that all directors are voted on jointly and stockholders may cast all their votes for just one candidate. On most issues put to the shareholders, a majority of votes is usually enough to prevail, but for some decisions a supermajority is required.

What are the major classes of securities issued by firms to raise capital? *(LO5)*

A company can issue a variety of securities such as common stock, preferred stock, and bonds. The **common stockholders** own the company. By this we mean that they are entitled to whatever profits are left over after other investors have been paid and that they have the ultimate control over how the company is run. Because shareholdings in the United States are usually widely dispersed, managers get to make most of the decisions. Managers may be given strong financial incentives to perform well, and their actions are monitored by the board of directors.

Preferred stock offers a fixed dividend but the company has the discretion not to pay it. It can't, however, then pay a dividend on the common stock. Despite its name, preferred stock is not a popular source of finance, but it is useful in special situations.

When companies issue **bonds,** they promise to make a series of interest payments and to repay the principal. However, this liability is limited. Stockholders have the right to default on their obligation and to hand over the assets to the debtholders. Unlike dividends on common stock and preferred stock, the interest payments on debt are regarded as a cost and therefore they are paid out of before-tax income. Here are some forms of debt:

- *Fixed-rate* and *floating-rate* debt.
- *Funded (long-term)* and *unfunded (short-term)* debt.
- *Callable* and *sinking-fund* debt.
- *Senior* and *subordinated* debt.
- *Secured* and *unsecured* debt.
- *Investment grade* and *junk* debt.
- *Domestic bonds* and *eurobonds.*
- *Publicly traded* debt and *private placements.*

The fourth source of finance consists of options and optionlike securities. The simplest option is a **warrant,** which gives its holder the right to buy a share from the firm at a set price by a set date. Warrants are often sold in combination with other securities. **Convertible bonds** give their holder the right to convert the bond to shares. They therefore resemble a package of straight debt and a warrant.

QUESTIONS

connect FINANCE

QUIZ

1. **Equity Accounts.** The authorized share capital of the Alfred Cake Company is 100,000 shares. The equity is currently shown in the company's books as follows: *(LO3)*

Common stock ($1 par value)	$ 60,000
Additional paid-in capital	10,000
Retained earnings	30,000
Common equity	100,000
Treasury stock (2,000 shares)	5,000
Net common equity	$ 95,000

   a. How many shares are issued?
   b. How many are outstanding?
   c. How many more shares can be issued without the approval of shareholders?

2. **Equity Accounts.** *(LO3)*
   a. Look back at Quiz Question 1. Suppose that the company issues 10,000 shares at $4 a share. Which of the above figures would change?
   b. What would happen to the company's books if instead it bought back 1,000 shares at $4 per share?

3. **Financing Terms.** Fill in the blanks by choosing the appropriate term from the following list: *lease, funded, floating-rate, eurobond, convertible, subordinated, call, sinking fund, prime rate, private placement, public issue, senior, unfunded, eurodollar rate, warrant, debentures, term loan. (LO5)*
   a. Debt maturing in more than 1 year is often called _____ debt.
   b. An issue of bonds that is sold simultaneously in several countries is traditionally called a(n) _____.
   c. If a lender ranks behind the firm's general creditors in the event of default, the loan is said to be _____.
   d. In many cases a firm is obliged to make regular contributions to a(n) _____, which is then used to repurchase bonds.
   e. Some bonds give the firm the right to repurchase or _____ the bonds at specified prices.
   f. The benchmark interest rate that banks charge to their customers with good credit is generally termed the _____.
   g. The interest rate on bank loans is often tied to short-term interest rates. These loans are usually called _____ loans.

h. Where there is a(n) _____, securities are sold directly to a small group of institutional investors. These securities cannot be resold to individual investors. In the case of a(n) _____, debt can be freely bought and sold by individual investors.

i. A long-term rental agreement is called a(n) _____.

j. A(n) _____ bond can be exchanged for shares of the issuing corporation.

k. A(n) _____ gives its owner the right to buy shares in the issuing company at a predetermined price.

4. **Financing Trends.** True or false? Explain. *(LO2)*

a. In several recent years, nonfinancial corporations in the United States have repurchased more stock than they have issued.

b. A corporation pays tax on only 30% of the common or preferred dividends it receives from other corporations.

c. Because of the tax advantage, a large fraction of preferred shares is held by corporations.

5. **Preferred Stock.** In what ways is preferred stock like long-term debt? In what ways is it like common stock? *(LO5)*

PRACTICE PROBLEMS

6. **Voting for Directors.** If there are 10 directors to be elected and a shareholder owns 100 shares, indicate the maximum number of votes that he or she can cast for a favorite candidate under

a. majority voting. *(LO4)*

b. cumulative voting. *(LO4)*

7. **Voting for Directors.** The shareholders of the Pickwick Paper Company need to elect five directors. There are 400,000 shares outstanding. How many shares do you need to own to *ensure* that you can elect at least one director if the company has

a. majority voting? *(LO4)*

b. cumulative voting? *(LO4)*

(*Hint:* How many votes in total will be cast? How many votes are required to ensure that at least one-fifth of votes are cast for your choice?)

8. **Equity Accounts.** Look back at Table 14.1. *(LO3)*

a. Suppose that Dow Chemical issues 100 million shares at $25 share. Rework Table 14.1 to show the company's equity after the issue.

b. Suppose that Dow *subsequently* repurchased 50 million shares at $40 a share. Rework part (a) to show the effect of the further change.

9. **Equity Accounts.** Common Products has just made its first issue of stock. It raised $2 million by selling 200,000 shares of stock to the public. These are the only shares outstanding. The par value of each share was $2. Fill in the following table: *(LO3)*

Common shares (par value)	_____
Additional paid-in capital	_____
Retained earnings	_____
Net common equity	$2,500,000

10. **Protective Covenants.** Why might a bond agreement limit the amount of assets that the firm can lease? *(LO5)*

11. **Bond Yields.** Other things equal, will the following provisions increase or decrease the yield to maturity at which a firm can issue a bond? *(LO5)*

a. A call provision.

b. A restriction on further borrowing.

c. A provision of specific collateral for the bond.

d. An option to convert the bonds into shares.

12. **Income Bonds.** *Income bonds* are unusual. Interest payments on such bonds may be skipped or deferred if the firm's income is insufficient to make the payment. In what way are these bonds like preferred stock? Why might a firm choose to issue an income bond instead of preferred stock? *(LO5)*

13. **Preferred Stock.** Preferred stock of financially strong firms sometimes sells at lower yields than the bonds of those firms. For weaker firms, the preferred stock has a higher yield. What might explain this pattern? *(LO5)*

WEB EXERCISES

1. Pick two companies [Caterpillar (CAT) and Union Pacific (UNP) could be good candidates], and compare their sources of funds and financial structures. You can find summary cash-flow statements and balance sheets on finance.yahoo.com, but you may also find it useful to go to the companies' Web sites. What factors might explain the difference in the companies' financing patterns?

2. In Figure 14.3 we summarized the sources and uses of funds for U.S. nonfinancial corporations. The data for this figure can be found on www.federalreserve.gov/releases/z1/current/data.htm. Look at Table F.102 for the latest year. Find "total internal funds" (which appeared in row 9 at the time we last looked) and "net funds raised in markets" (row 38). What proportion of the funds that companies needed in the latest year was generated internally, and how much had to be raised on the financial markets? Is this the usual pattern? Now look at "net new equity issues" (row 39). Were companies on average issuing new equity or buying their shares back?

3. Construct a table similar to Table 14.1 for a company of your choice by looking up its annual report on the Web. What is the difference between the company's outstanding and issued shares? Explain. Has the company in the past raised more money by issuing new shares or by plowing back earnings? Is that typical of U.S. public companies (see Section 14.2)?

SOLUTIONS TO SELF-TEST QUESTIONS

14.1 Capital markets provide liquidity for investors. Because individual stockholders can always lay their hands on cash by selling shares, they are prepared to invest in companies that retain earnings rather than pay them out as dividends. Well-functioning capital markets allow the firm to serve all its stockholders simply by maximizing value. Capital markets also provide managers with information. Without this information, it would be very difficult to determine opportunity costs of capital or to assess financial performance.

14.2 Par value of common shares must be $1 \times 100,000$ shares $= \$100,000$. Additional paid-in capital is $(\$15 - \$1) \times 100,000 = \$1,400,000$. Since book value is $4,500,000, retained earnings must be $3,000,000. Therefore, the accounts look like this:

Common shares ($1 par value per share)	$100,000
Additional paid-in capital	1,400,000
Retained earnings	3,000,000
Net common equity	$4,500,000

14.3 The corporation's after-tax yield on the bonds is $10\% - (.35 \times 10\%) = 6.5\%$. The after-tax yield on the preferred is $8\% - [.35 \times (.30 \times 8\%)] = 7.16\%$. The preferred stock provides the higher after-tax rate despite its lower before-tax rate.

14.4 Because the coupon on floating-rate debt adjusts periodically to current market conditions, the bondholder is less vulnerable to changes in market yields. The coupon rate paid by the bond is not locked in for as long a period of time. Therefore, prices of floaters should be less sensitive to changes in market interest rates.

14.5   The callable bond will sell at a lower price. Investors will not pay as much for the callable bond since they know that the firm may call it away from them if interest rates fall. Thus they know that their capital gains potential is limited, which makes the bond less valuable. If both bonds are to sell at face value, the callable bond must pay a higher coupon rate as compensation to the investor for the firm's right to call the bond.

14.6   The extra debt makes it more likely that the firm will not be able to make good on its promised payments to its creditors. If the new debt is not junior to the already-issued debt, then the original bondholders suffer a loss when their bonds become more susceptible to default risk. A protective covenant limiting the amount of new debt that the firm can issue would have prevented this problem. Investors, having witnessed the problems of the RJR bondholders, generally demanded the covenant on future debt issues.

How Corporations Raise Venture Capital and Issue Securities

LEARNING OBJECTIVES

After studying this chapter, you should be able to:

(1) Understand how venture capital firms design successful deals.

(2) Understand how firms make initial public offerings and the costs of such offerings.

(3) Know what is involved when established firms make a general cash offer or a private placement of securities.

(4) Explain the role of the underwriter in an issue of securities.

(5) Describe the terms of a rights issue.

RELATED WEB SITES FOR THIS CHAPTER CAN BE FOUND AT WWW.MHHE.COM/BMM7E.

Trading opens on NASDAQ for shares in Google.

Bill Gates and Paul Allen founded Microsoft in 1975, when both were around 20 years old. Eleven years later Microsoft shares were sold to the public for $21 a share and immediately zoomed to $35. The largest shareholder was Bill Gates, whose shares in Microsoft then were worth $350 million.

In 1976 two college dropouts, Steve Jobs and Steve Wozniak, sold their most valuable possessions, a van and a couple of calculators, and used the cash to start manufacturing computers in a garage. In 1980, when Apple Computer went public, the shares were offered to investors at $22 and jumped to $36. At that point, the shares owned by the company's two founders were worth $414 million.

In 1996 two Stanford computer science students, Larry Page and Sergey Brin, decided to collaborate to develop a Web search engine. To help turn their idea into a commercial product, the two friends succeeded in raising almost $1 million from several wealthy investors, and this was later supplemented by funding from two *venture capital* firms that specialized in

helping young start-up businesses. The company, now named Google, went public in 2004 at a price of $85 a share, putting a value on the enterprise of $23 billion.

Such stories illustrate that the most important asset of a new firm may be a good idea. But that is not all you need. To take an idea from the drawing board to a prototype and through to large-scale production requires ever greater amounts of capital.

To get a new company off the ground, entrepreneurs may rely on their own savings and personal bank loans. But this is unlikely to be sufficient to build a successful enterprise. *Venture capital* firms specialize in providing new equity capital to help firms over the awkward adolescent period before they are large enough to "go public." In the first part of this chapter we will explain how venture capital firms do this.

If the firm continues to be successful, there is likely to come a time when it needs to tap a wider source of capital. At this point it will make its first public issue of common stock. This is known as an *initial public offering,* or *IPO.* In the second section of the chapter we will describe what is involved in an IPO.

A company's initial public offering is seldom its last. In Chapter 14 we saw that internally generated cash is not usually sufficient to satisfy the firm's needs. Established companies make up the deficit by issuing more equity or debt. The remainder of this chapter looks at this process.

15.1 Venture Capital

You have taken a big step. With a couple of friends, you have formed a corporation to open a number of fast-food outlets, offering innovative combinations of national dishes such as sushi with sauerkraut, curry Bolognese, and chow mein with Yorkshire pudding. Breaking into the fast-food business costs money, but, after pooling your savings and borrowing to the hilt from the bank, you have raised $100,000 and purchased 1 million shares in the new company. At this *zero-stage* investment, your company's assets are $100,000 plus the *idea* for your new product.

That $100,000 is enough to get the business off the ground, but if the idea takes off, you will need more capital to pay for new restaurants. Many start-ups continue to grow with funds provided directly by managers or by their friends and families. Some thrive using bank loans and reinvested earnings. But, particularly if your start-up combines high-risk, sophisticated technology and substantial investment, you will probably need to find an investor who is prepared to back an untried company in return for part of the profits. Equity capital in young businesses is known as **venture capital,** and it is provided by specialist venture capital firms, wealthy individuals, and investment institutions such as pension funds.

Most entrepreneurs are able to spin a plausible yarn about their company. But it is as hard to convince a venture capitalist to invest in your business as it is to get a first novel published. Your first step is to prepare a *business plan*. This describes your product, the potential market, the production method, and the resources—time, money, employees, plant, and equipment—needed for success. It helps if you can point to the fact that you are prepared to put your money where your mouth is. By staking all your savings in the company, you *signal* your faith in the business.

The venture capital company knows that the success of a new business depends on the effort its managers put in. Therefore, it will try to structure any deal so that you have a strong incentive to work hard. For example, if you agree to accept a modest salary (and look forward instead to increasing the value of your investment in the company's stock), the venture capital company knows you will be committed to working hard. However, if you insist on a watertight employment contract and a fat salary, you won't find it easy to raise venture capital.

You are unlikely to persuade a venture capitalist to give you all at once as much money as you need. Rather, the firm will probably offer you enough to reach the next major checkpoint. Suppose you can convince the venture capital company to buy 1 million new shares for $.50 each. This will give it one-half ownership of the firm: It owns 1 million shares, and you and your friends also own 1 million shares. Because the venture capitalist is paying $500,000 for a claim to half your firm, it is placing a $1 million value on the business. After this *first-stage* financing, your company's balance sheet looks like this:

FIRST-STAGE MARKET-VALUE BALANCE SHEET (figures in millions)			
Assets		**Liabilities and Shareholders' Equity**	
Cash from new equity	$ .5	New equity from venture capital	$ .5
Other assets	.5	Your original equity	.5
Value	$1.0	Value	$1.0

Suppose that 2 years later your business has grown to the point at which it needs a further injection of equity. This *second-stage* financing might involve the issue of a further 1 million shares at $1 each. Some of these shares might be bought by the original backers and some by other venture capital firms. The balance sheet after the new financing would then be as follows:

SECOND-STAGE MARKET-VALUE BALANCE SHEET (figures in millions)			
Assets		**Liabilities and Shareholders' Equity**	
Cash from new equity	$1	New equity from second-stage financing	$1
Other assets	2	Equity from first stage	1
		Your original equity	1
Value	$3	Value	$3

Notice that the value of the initial 1 million shares owned by you and your friends has now been marked up to $1 million. Does this begin to sound like a money machine? It was so only because you have made a success of the business and new investors are prepared to pay $1 to buy a share in the business. When you started out, it wasn't clear that sushi and sauerkraut would catch on. If it hadn't caught on, the venture capital firm could have refused to put up more funds.

You are not yet in a position to cash in on your investment, but your gain is real. The second-stage investors have paid $1 million for a one-third share in the company. (There are now 3 million shares outstanding, and the second-stage investors hold 1 million shares.) Therefore, at least these impartial observers—who are willing to back up their opinions with a large investment—must have decided that the company was worth at least $3 million. Your one-third share is therefore also worth $1 million.

Venture Capital Companies

Some young companies grow with the aid of equity investment provided by wealthy individuals known as *angel investors*. Many others raise capital from specialist venture capital firms, which pool funds from a variety of investors, seek out fledgling companies to invest in, and then work with these companies as they try to grow. In addition, some large technology firms such as Intel and Johnson & Johnson act as *corporate venturers* by providing capital to new innovative companies.

Most venture capital funds are organized as limited private partnerships with a fixed life of about 10 years. Pension funds and other investors are the limited partners. The management company, which is the general partner, is responsible for making and overseeing the investments and, in return, receives a fixed fee as well as a share of the profits. You will find that these venture capital partnerships are often lumped together with similar partnerships that provide funds for companies in distress or that buy out whole companies and then take them private. The general term for these activities is *private equity investing.*

Venture capital firms are not passive investors. They are usually represented on each company's board of directors, they help to recruit senior managers for the company, and they provide ongoing advice. This advice can be very valuable to businesses in their early years and helps them to bring their products more quickly to market.

For every 10 first-stage venture capital investments, only 2 or 3 may survive as successful, self-sufficient businesses, and only 1 may pay off big. From these statistics come two rules of success in venture capital investment. First, don't shy away from uncertainty; accept a low probability of success. But don't buy into a business unless you can see the *chance* of a big, public company in a profitable market. There's no sense taking a big risk unless the reward is big if you win. Second, cut your losses; identify losers early, and if you can't fix the problem—by replacing management, for example—don't throw good money after bad.

Very few new businesses make it big, but those that do can be very profitable. So venture capitalists keep sane by reminding themselves of the success stories—those who got in on the ground floor of firms like Genentech, Intel and FedEx.[1]

15.2 The Initial Public Offering

For many successful start-ups there comes a time when they need more capital than can comfortably be provided by a small number of individuals or venture capitalists. At this point one solution is to sell the business to a larger firm. But many entrepreneurs do not fit easily into a corporate bureaucracy and would prefer instead to remain the boss. In this case, the company may choose to raise money by selling shares to the public. **A firm is said to** *go public* **when it sells its first issue of shares in a general offering to investors. This first sale of stock is called an initial public offering, or IPO.**

initial public offering (IPO)
First offering of stock to the general public.

An IPO is called a *primary* offering when new shares are sold to raise additional cash for the company. It is a *secondary* offering when the company's founders and the venture capitalist cash in on some of their gains by selling shares. A secondary offer therefore is no more than a sale of shares from the early investors in the firm to new investors, and the cash raised in a secondary offer does not flow to the company. Of course, IPOs can be and commonly are both primary and secondary: The firm raises new cash at the same time that some of the already existing shares in the firm are sold to the public.

Some of the biggest secondary offerings have involved governments selling off stock in nationalized enterprises. For example, the Japanese government raised $12.6 billion by selling its stock in Nippon Telegraph and Telephone, and the Italian government took in $19.3 billion from the sale of its shares in the electricity company Enel. Even these two issues were dwarfed by the 2006 IPO of the state-owned Industrial and Commercial Bank of China, which raised $22 billion.

We have seen that companies may make an IPO to raise new capital or to enable the existing shareholders to cash out, but there may be other benefits to going public. For example, the company's stock price provides a readily available yardstick of performance and allows the firm to reward the management team with stock options. And, because information about the company becomes more widely available, the firm can diversify its sources of finance and reduce its borrowing cost.

While there are advantages to having a market for your shares, we should not give the impression that firms everywhere aim to go public. In many countries it is common for businesses to remain privately owned. Even in the United States many firms choose to remain as private, unlisted companies. They include some very large operations, such as Bechtel, Cargill, and Levi Strauss. Also, you should not think of the issue process in the United States as a one-way street; public firms often go into reverse and return to being privately owned. For a somewhat extreme example, consider the food service company Aramark. It began life in 1936 as a private company and went public in 1960. In 1984 the management bought out the company and took it private, and it remained private until 2001, when it had its second public offering. But the experiment did not last long, for 6 years later Aramark was the object of yet another buyout that took the company private once again.

---

[1] Fortunately, the successes seem to have outweighed the failures. Cambridge Associates estimated that net returns on venture capital funds averaged 24% a year for the 20 years ending in March 2010.

Managers often chafe at the red tape involved in running a public company and at the unrelenting pressure from shareholders to report increasing earnings. These complaints have become more vocal since the passage of the Sarbanes-Oxley Act. This act has sought to prevent a repeat of the corporate scandals that brought about the collapse of Enron and WorldCom, but a consequence has been an increased reporting burden on small public companies and a rise in the number of companies reverting to private ownership.

Arranging a Public Issue

underwriter
Firm that buys an issue of securities from a company and resells it to the public.

Once a firm decides to go public, the first task is to select the underwriters. **Underwriters are investment banking firms that act as financial midwives to a new issue. Usually they play a triple role—first providing the company with procedural and financial advice, then buying the stock, and finally reselling it to the public.** A small IPO may have only one underwriter, but larger issues usually require a syndicate of underwriters who buy the issue and resell it.

In the typical underwriting arrangement, called a *firm commitment,* the underwriters buy the securities from the firm and then resell them to the public. The underwriters receive payment in the form of a **spread**—that is, they are allowed by the company to sell the shares at a slightly higher price than they paid for them. But the underwriters also accept the risk that they won't be able to sell the stock at the agreed offering price. If that happens, they will be stuck with unsold shares and must get the best price they can for them. In the more risky cases, the underwriter may not be willing to enter into a firm commitment and handles the issue on a *best efforts* basis. In this case the underwriter agrees to sell as much of the issue as possible but does not guarantee the sale of the entire issue.

spread
Difference between public offer price and price paid by underwriter.

Before any stock can be sold to the public, the company must register the issue with the Securities and Exchange Commission (SEC). This involves preparation of a detailed and sometimes cumbersome registration statement, which contains information about the proposed financing and the firm's history, existing business, and plans for the future. The SEC does not evaluate the wisdom of an investment in the firm, but it does check the registration statement for accuracy and completeness. The firm must also comply with the "blue-sky" laws of each state, so named because they seek to protect the public against firms that fraudulently promise the blue sky to investors.[2]

prospectus
Formal summary that provides information on an issue of securities.

The first part of the registration statement is distributed to the public in the form of a preliminary **prospectus.** One function of the prospectus is to warn investors about the risks involved in any investment in the firm. Some investors have joked that if they read prospectuses carefully, they would never dare buy any new issue. The appendix to this chapter provides a streamlined version of a possible prospectus for your restaurant business.

The company and its underwriters also need to set the issue price. To gauge how much the stock is worth, they may undertake discounted cash-flow calculations like those described in Chapter 7. They also look at the price-earnings ratios of the shares of the firm's principal competitors.

Before settling on the issue price, the underwriters generally arrange a "roadshow," which gives the underwriters and the company's management an opportunity to talk to potential investors. These investors may then offer their reaction to the issue, suggest what they think is a fair price, and indicate how much stock they would be prepared to buy. This allows the underwriters to build up a book of likely orders. Although investors are not bound by their indications, they know that if they want to maintain a good relationship with the underwriters, they must be careful not to renege on their expressions of interest.

underpricing
Issuing securities at an offering price set below the true value of the security.

The managers of the firm are eager to secure the highest possible price for their stock, but the underwriters are likely to be cautious because they will be left with any unsold stock if they overestimate investor demand. As a result, underwriters typically try to underprice the initial public offering. **Underpricing,** they argue, is needed to

---

[2] Sometimes states go beyond blue-sky laws in their efforts to protect their residents. When Apple Computer Inc. made its first public issue, the Massachusetts state government decided the offering was too risky for its residents and therefore banned the sale of the shares to investors in the state. The state relented later, after the issue was out and the price had risen. Massachusetts investors obviously did not appreciate this "protection."

tempt investors to buy stock and to reduce the cost of marketing the issue to customers. **Underpricing represents a cost to the existing owners since the new investors are allowed to buy shares in the firm at a favorable price.**

Sometimes new issues are dramatically underpriced. For example, when the prospectus for the IPO of eBay was first published, the underwriters indicated that the company would sell 3.5 million shares at a price between $14 and $16 each. However, the enthusiasm for eBay's Web-based auction system was such that the underwriters increased the issue price to $18. The next morning dealers were flooded with orders to buy eBay; over 4.5 million shares traded, and the stock closed the day at a price of $47.375.

The experience of eBay is not typical, but it is common to see the stock price increase significantly from the issue price in the days following the sale. For example, one study of more than 12,000 new issues between 1960 and 2009 found an average first-day price rise of 16.9%.[3] Such immediate price jumps suggest that investors would have been prepared to pay much more than they did for the shares.

EXAMPLE 15.1 ▶ Underpricing of IPOs

Suppose an IPO is a secondary issue and the firm's founders sell part of their holding to investors. Clearly, if the shares are sold for less than their true worth, the founders will suffer an opportunity loss.

But what if the IPO is a primary issue that raises new cash for the company? Do the founders care whether the shares are sold for less than their market value? The following example illustrates that they do care.

Suppose Cosmos.com has 2 million shares outstanding and now offers a further 1 million shares to investors at $50. On the first day of trading the share price jumps to $80, so the shares that the company sold for $50 million are now worth $80 million. The total market capitalization of the company is 3 million × $80 = $240 million.

The value of the founders' shares is equal to the total value of the company less the value of the shares that have been sold to the public—in other words, $240 million − $80 million = $160 million. The founders might justifiably rejoice at their good fortune. However, if the company had issued shares at a higher price, it would have needed to sell fewer shares to raise the $50 million that it needs and the founders would have retained a larger share of the company. For example, suppose that the outside investors, who put up $50 million, received shares that were *worth* only $50 million. In that case the value of the founders' shares would be $240 million − $50 million = $190 million.

The effect of selling shares below their true value is to transfer $30 million of value from the founders to the investors who buy the new shares.

Unfortunately, underpricing does not mean that anyone can become wealthy by buying stock in IPOs. If an issue is underpriced, everybody will want to buy it and the underwriters will not have enough stock to go around. You are therefore likely to get only a small share of these hot issues. If it is overpriced, other investors are unlikely to want it and the underwriter will be only too delighted to sell it to you. This phenomenon is known as the *winner's curse*.[4] It implies that, unless you can spot which issues are underpriced, you are likely to receive a small proportion of the cheap issues and a large proportion of the expensive ones. Since the dice are loaded against uninformed investors, they will play the game only if there is substantial underpricing on average.

---

[3] These figures are provided on Jay Ritter's home page, **bear.cba.ufl.edu/ritter**.

[4] The highest bidder in an auction is the participant who places the highest value on the auctioned object. Therefore, it is likely that the winning bidder has an overly optimistic assessment of true value. Winning the auction suggests that you have overpaid for the object—this is the winner's curse. In the case of IPOs, your ability to "win" an allotment of shares may signal that the stock is overpriced.

| **EXAMPLE 15.2** ▶ | Underpricing of IPOs and Investor Returns |

Suppose that an investor will earn an immediate 10% return on underpriced IPOs and lose 5% on overpriced IPOs. But because of high demand, you may get only half the shares you bid for when the issue is underpriced. Suppose you bid for $1,000 of shares in two issues, one overpriced and the other underpriced. You are awarded the full $1,000 of the overpriced issue but only $500 worth of shares in the underpriced issue. The net gain on your two investments is $(.10 \times \$500) - (.05 \times \$1,000) = 0$. Your net profit is zero, despite the fact that, on average, the IPOs are underpriced (10% underpricing versus 5% overpricing). You have suffered the winner's curse: You "win" a larger allotment of shares when they are overpriced.

Self-Test 15.2

What is the percentage profit earned by an investor who can identify the underpriced issues in Example 15.2? Who are such investors likely to be?

flotation costs
The costs incurred when a firm issues new securities to the public.

The costs of a new issue are termed **flotation costs.** Underpricing is not the only flotation cost. In fact, when people talk about the cost of a new issue, they often think only of the *direct costs* of the issue. For example, preparation of the registration statement and prospectus involves management, legal counsel, and accountants, as well as underwriters and their advisers. There is also the underwriting spread. (Remember, underwriters make their profit by selling the issue at a higher price than they paid for it.) For most issues between $20 million and $80 million, the spread is 7%.

Look at the blue bars (corresponding to IPOs) in Figure 15.1. These show the direct costs of going public. For all but the smallest IPOs the underwriting spread and administrative costs are likely to absorb 7% to 8% of the proceeds from the issue. For the very largest IPOs, these direct costs may amount to only 5% of the proceeds.

FIGURE 15.1 Total direct costs as a percentage of gross proceeds, 2004–2008. The total direct costs for initial public offerings (IPOs), seasoned equity offerings (SEOs), convertible bonds, and straight bonds are composed of underwriter spreads and other direct expenses.

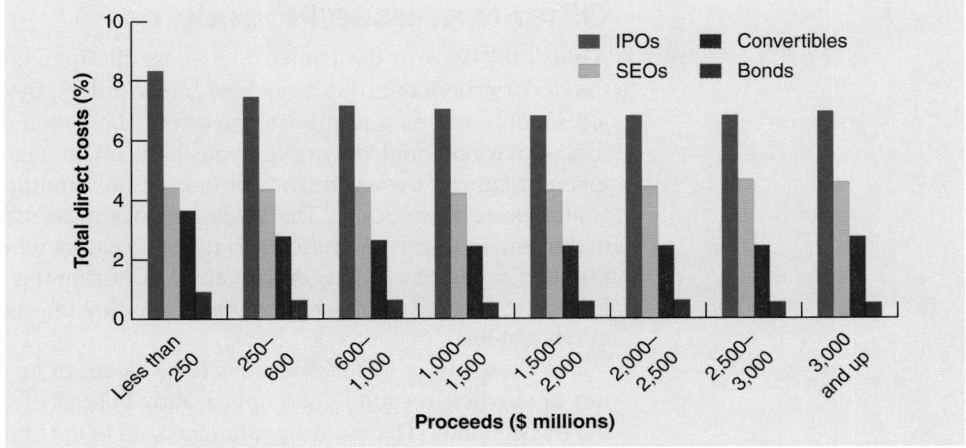

Source: We are grateful to Nickolay Gantchev for undertaking these calculations, which update tables in Immoo Lee, Scott Lochhead, Jay Ritter, and Quanshui Zhao, "The Costs of Raising Capital," *Journal of Financial Research* 19 (Spring 1996), pp. 59–74. Used with permission. Updates courtesy of Nickolay Gantchev.

EXAMPLE 15.3 ▶ Costs of an IPO

The largest U.S. IPO was the $19.7 billion sale of stock by the credit card company Visa in 2008. A syndicate of 45 underwriters acquired a total of 446.6 million Visa shares for $42.768 each and then resold them to the public at an offering price of $44. The underwriters' spread was therefore $44 − $42.768 = $1.232. The firm also paid a total of $45.5 million in legal fees and other costs.[5] Therefore, the direct costs of the Visa issue were as follows:

Direct Expenses	
Underwriting spread	(446.6 million × $1.232) = $550.2 million
Other expenses	45.5
Total direct expenses	$595.7 million

The total amount of money raised by the issue was 446.6 million × $44 = $19,650 million. Of this sum 3% was absorbed by direct expenses (that is, 595.7/19,650 = .030).

In addition to these direct costs, there was the cost of underpricing. By the end of the first day's trading Visa's stock price had risen to $56.50, so investors valued Visa shares at 446.6 × $56.50 = $25,233 million. In other words, Visa sold stock for $25,233 − $19,650 = $5,583 less than its market value. This was the cost of underpricing.

Managers commonly focus only on the direct costs of an issue. But, when we add in the cost of underpricing, the *total* cost of the Visa issue as a proportion of the market value of the shares was ($595.7 + $5,583)/$25,233 = .24, or 24%.

Self-Test 15.3

Suppose that the underwriters acquired Visa shares for $45 and sold them to the public at an offering price of $47. If all other features of the offer were unchanged (and investors still valued the stock at $56.50 a share), what would have been the direct costs of the issue and the costs of underpricing? What would have been the total costs (direct costs plus underpricing) as a proportion of the market value of the shares?

Other New-Issue Procedures

Almost all IPOs in the United States use the bookbuilding method. In other words, the underwriters build up a book of likely orders, buy the issue from the company at a discount, and then resell it to investors. This method is in some ways like an auction, since potential buyers indicate how many shares they are prepared to buy at given prices. However, the indications are not binding and are used only as a guide to fix the price of the issue. The advantage of the bookbuilding method is that it allows underwriters to give preference to those investors whose bids are most helpful in setting the issue price and to offer them a reward in the shape of underpricing. But critics of the method point to the dangers of allowing the underwriters to decide who is allotted stock.

An alternative way to issue stock is by means of an open auction. In this case, investors are invited to submit their bids, stating both an offering price and how many shares they wish to buy. The securities are then sold to the highest bidders. Most governments,

---

[5] These figures do not capture all administrative costs. For example, they do not include management time spent on the issue.

including the U.S. Treasury, sell their bonds by auction. In the United States, auctions of common stock are fairly rare. However, in 2004 Google simultaneously raised eyebrows and $1.7 billion in the world's largest IPO to be sold by auction.

The Underwriters

We have described underwriters as playing a triple role—providing advice, buying a new issue from the company, and reselling it to investors. Underwriters don't just help the company to make its initial public offering; they are called in whenever a company wishes to raise cash by selling securities to the public.

Successful underwriting requires considerable experience and financial muscle. If a large issue fails to sell, the underwriters may be left with a loss of several hundred million dollars and some very red faces. Underwriting in the United States is therefore dominated by the major investment banking firms, which specialize in underwriting new issues, dealing in securities, and arranging mergers.

They include such giants as Citigroup, JPMorgan, Bank of America, Merrill Lynch, and Goldman Sachs. Large foreign banks, such as Barclays, Deutsche Bank, and UBS, are also heavily involved in underwriting securities that are sold internationally.

Underwriting is not always fun. In April 2008 the British bank HBOS offered its shareholders two new shares at a price of £2.75 for each five shares that they currently held.[6] The underwriters to the issue guaranteed that at the end of 8 weeks they would buy any new shares that the stockholders did not want. At the time of the offer HBOS shares were priced at about £5, so the underwriters felt confident that they would not have to honor their pledge. Unfortunately, they reckoned without the turbulent market in bank shares that year. The bank's shareholders worried that the money they were asked to provide would largely go to bailing out the bondholders and depositors. By the end of the 8 weeks the price of HBOS stock had slumped below the issue price, and the underwriters were left with 932 million unwanted shares worth £3.6 billion.

Companies get to make only one IPO, but underwriters are in the business all the time. Wise underwriters, therefore, realize that their reputation is on the line and will not handle an issue unless they believe the facts have been presented fairly to investors. If a new issue goes wrong and the stock price crashes, the underwriters can find themselves very unpopular with their clients. For example, in 1999 the software company VA Linux went public at $30 a share. The next day trading opened at $299 a share, but then the price began to sag. Within 2 years it had fallen below $2. Disgruntled VA Linux investors sued the underwriters for overhyping the issue. VA Linux investors were not the only ones to feel aggrieved. Investment banks soon found themselves embroiled in a major scandal as evidence emerged that they had deliberately oversold many of the issues that they underwrote during the dot-com boom years. There was further embarrassment when it emerged that several well-known underwriters had engaged in "spinning"—that is, allocating stock in popular new issues to managers of their important corporate clients. The underwriter's seal of approval for a new issue no longer seemed as valuable as it once had.

15.3 General Cash Offers by Public Companies

seasoned offering
Sale of securities by a firm that is already publicly traded.

After the initial public offering a successful firm will continue to grow, and from time to time it will need to raise more money by issuing stock or bonds. An issue of additional stock by a company whose stock already is publicly traded is called a **seasoned offering.** Any issue of securities needs to be formally approved by the firm's board of directors.

---

[6] This arrangement is known as a *rights issue*. We describe rights issues later in the chapter.

rights issue
Issue of securities offered only to current stockholders.

If a stock issue requires an increase in the company's authorized capital, it also needs the consent of the stockholders.

Public companies can issue securities either by making a general cash offer to investors at large or by making a **rights issue,** which is limited to existing shareholders. In the latter case, the company offers the shareholders the opportunity, or *right,* to buy more shares at an "attractive" price. For example, if the current stock price is $100, the company might offer investors an additional share at $50 for each share they hold. Suppose that before the issue an investor has one share worth $100 and $50 in the bank. If the investor takes up the offer of a new share, that $50 of cash is transferred from the investor's bank account to the company's. The investor now has two shares that are a claim on the original assets worth $100 and on the $50 cash that the company has raised. So the two shares are worth a total of $150, or $75 each.

EXAMPLE 15.4   ▶   Rights Issues

We have already come across one example of a rights issue—the offer by the British bank HBOS, which ended up in the hands of its underwriters. Let us look more closely at another issue.

In May 2010, the British gas and electricity company National Grid needed to raise over £3 billion. It did so by offering its existing shareholders the right to buy two new shares for every five that they currently held. The new shares were priced at £3.35 each, some 44% below the preannouncement price of £5.95.

Before the issue, National Grid had about 2.5 billion shares outstanding, which were priced at £5.95 each. So investors valued the company at $2.5 \times £5.95 =$ £14.875 billion. The new issue increased the total number of shares by $(2/5) \times$ 2.5 billion = 1 billion and therefore raised 1 billion $\times$ £3.35 = £3.35 billion. In effect, the issue increased the total value of the company to 14.875 + 3.35 = £18.225 billion and reduced the value of each share to £18.225/3.5 = £5.207.

Suppose that just before the issue you hold five shares of National Grid valued at $5 \times £5.95 = £29.75$. If you decide to take up the rights offer, you would need to lay out $2 \times £3.35 = £6.70$ and the value of your shareholding would increase by exactly £6.70 to $7 \times £5.207 = £36.45$. You would get what you paid for.

In some countries the rights issue is the most common or only method for issuing stock, but in the United States rights issues are now very rare. We therefore will concentrate on the mechanics of the general cash offer.

General Cash Offers and Shelf Registration

general cash offer
Sale of securities open to all investors by an already-public company.

When a public company makes a **general cash offer** of debt or equity, it essentially follows the same procedure used when it first went public. This means that it must first register the issue with the SEC and draw up a prospectus.[7] Before settling on the issue price, the underwriters will usually contact potential investors and build up a book of likely orders. The company will then sell the issue to the underwriters, and they in turn will offer the securities to the public.

Companies do not need to prepare a separate registration statement every time they issue new securities. Instead, they are allowed to file a single registration statement covering financing plans for up to 2 years into the future. The actual issues can then be sold to the public with scant additional paperwork, whenever the firm needs cash or

---

[7] The procedure is similar when a company makes an international issue of bonds or equity, but as long as these issues are not sold publicly in the United States, they do not need to be registered with the SEC.

shelf registration
A procedure that allows firms to file one registration statement for several issues of the same security.

thinks it can issue securities at an attractive price. This is called **shelf registration**—the registration is put "on the shelf," to be taken down, dusted off, and used as needed.

Think of how you might use shelf registration when you are a financial manager. Suppose that your company is likely to need up to $200 million of new long-term debt over the next year or so. It can file a registration statement for that amount. It now has approval to issue up to $200 million of debt, but it isn't obliged to issue any. Nor is it required to work through any *particular* underwriters—the registration statement may name the underwriters the firm thinks it may work with, but others can be substituted later.

Now you can sit back and issue debt as needed, in bits and pieces if you like. Suppose JPMorgan comes across an insurance company with $10 million ready to invest in corporate bonds, priced to yield, say, 7.3%. If you think that's a good deal, you say OK and the deal is done, subject to only a little additional paperwork. JPMorgan then resells the bonds to the insurance company, hoping for a higher price than it paid for them.

Here is another possible deal. Suppose you think you see a window of opportunity in which interest rates are "temporarily low." You invite bids for $100 million of bonds. Some bids may come from large investment bankers acting alone, others from ad hoc syndicates. But that's not your problem; if the price is right, you just take the best deal offered.

Thus shelf registration offers several advantages:

1. Securities can be issued in dribs and drabs without incurring excessive costs.
2. Securities can be issued on short notice.
3. Security issues can be timed to take advantage of "market conditions" (although any financial manager who can reliably identify favorable market conditions could make a lot more money by quitting and becoming a bond or stock trader instead).
4. The issuing firm can make sure that underwriters compete for its business.

Not all companies eligible for shelf registration actually use it for all their public issues. Sometimes they believe they can get a better deal by making one large issue through traditional channels, especially when the security to be issued has some unusual feature or when the firm believes it needs the investment banker's counsel or stamp of approval on the issue. Thus shelf registration is less often used for issues of common stock than for garden-variety corporate bonds.

Costs of the General Cash Offer

Whenever a firm makes a cash offer, it incurs substantial administrative costs. Also, the firm needs to compensate the underwriters by selling them securities below the price that they expect to receive from investors. Look back at Figure 15.1, which shows the average underwriting spread and administrative costs for several types of security issues in the United States.

You can see that issue costs are higher for equity than for debt securities. Issue costs are higher for equity than for debt because administrative costs are somewhat greater and also because underwriting stock is riskier than underwriting bonds. The underwriters demand additional compensation for the greater risk they take in buying and reselling equity.

Market Reaction to Stock Issues

Because stock issues usually throw a sizable number of new shares onto the market, it is widely believed that they must temporarily depress the stock price. If the proposed issue is very large, this price pressure may, it is thought, be so severe as to make it almost impossible to raise money.

This belief in price pressure implies that a new issue depresses the stock price temporarily below its true value. However, that view doesn't appear to fit very well with the notion of market efficiency. If the stock price falls solely because of increased supply, then that stock would offer a higher return than comparable stocks and investors would be attracted to it as ants to a picnic.

Economists who have studied new issues of common stock have generally found that the announcement of the issue does result in a decline in the stock price. For industrial issues in the United States this decline amounts to about 3%.[8] While this may not sound overwhelming, such a price drop can be a large fraction of the money raised. Suppose that a company with a market value of equity of $5 billion announces its intention to issue $500 million of additional equity and thereby causes the stock price to drop by 3%. The loss in value is .03 × $5 billion, or $150 million. That's 30% of the amount of money raised (.30 × $500 million = $150 million).

What's going on here? Is the price of the stock simply depressed by the prospect of the additional supply? Possibly, but here is an alternative explanation.

Suppose managers (who have better information about the firm than outside investors) know that their stock is undervalued. If the company sells new stock at this low price, it will give the new shareholders a good deal at the expense of the old shareholders. In these circumstances managers might be prepared to forgo the new investment rather than sell shares at too low a price.

If managers know that the stock is *overvalued,* the position is reversed. If the company sells new shares at the high price, it will help its existing shareholders at the expense of the new ones. Managers might be prepared to issue stock even if the new cash were just put in the bank.

Of course investors are not stupid. They can predict that managers are more likely to issue stock when they think it is overvalued, and therefore they mark the price of the stock down accordingly. **The tendency for stock prices to decline at the time of an issue may have nothing to do with increased supply. Instead, the stock issue may simply be a *signal* that well-informed managers believe the market has overpriced the stock.**[9]

15.4 The Private Placement

private placement
Sale of securities to a limited number of investors without a public offering.

Whenever a company makes a public offering, it must register the issue with the SEC. It could avoid this costly process by selling the issue privately. There are no hard-and-fast definitions of a **private placement,** but the SEC has insisted that the security should be restricted largely to knowledgeable investors.

One disadvantage of a private placement is that the investor cannot easily resell the security. This is less important to institutions such as life insurance companies, which invest huge sums of money in corporate debt for the long haul. In 1990 the SEC relaxed its restrictions on who could buy unregistered issues. Under this rule, Rule 144a, large financial institutions can trade unregistered securities among themselves.

As you would expect, it costs less to arrange a private placement than to make a public issue. That might not be so important for the very large issues where costs are less significant, but it is a particular advantage for companies making smaller issues.

Another advantage of the private placement is that the debt contract can be custom-tailored for firms with special problems or opportunities. Also, if the firm wishes later to change the terms of the debt, it is much simpler to do this with a private placement where only a few investors are involved.

Therefore, it is not surprising that private placements occupy a particular niche in the corporate debt market, namely, loans to small and medium-sized firms. These are

---

[8] See, for example, P. Asquith and D. W. Mullins, "Equity Issues and Offering Dilution," *Journal of Financial Economics* 15 (January–February 1986), pp. 61–90; R. W. Masulis and A. N. Korwar, "Seasoned Equity Offerings: An Empirical Investigation," *Journal of Financial Economics* 15 (January–February 1986), pp. 91–118; and W. H. Mikkelson and M. M. Partch, "Valuation Effects of Security Offerings and the Issuance Process," *Journal of Financial Economics* 15 (January–February 1986), pp. 31–60.

[9] This explanation was developed in S. C. Myers and N. S. Majluf, "Corporate Financing and Investment Decisions When Firms Have Information That Investors Do Not Have," *Journal of Financial Economics* 13 (1984), pp. 187–222.

the firms that face the highest costs in public issues, that require the most detailed investigation, and that may require specialized, flexible loan arrangements.

We do not mean that large, safe, and conventional firms should rule out private placements. Enormous amounts of capital are sometimes raised by this method. For example, in 2005, Berkshire Hathaway, the investment company controlled by Warren Buffett, borrowed $3.75 billion in a private placement. Nevertheless, the advantages of private placement—avoiding registration costs and establishing a direct relationship with the lender—are generally more important to smaller firms.

Of course these advantages are not free. Lenders in private placements have to be compensated for the risks they face and for the costs of research and negotiation. They also have to be compensated for holding an asset that is not easily resold. All these factors are rolled into the interest rate paid by the firm. It is difficult to generalize about the differences in interest rates between private placements and public issues, but a typical yield differential is on the order of half a percentage point.

SUMMARY

How do venture capital firms design successful deals? *(LO1)*

Infant companies raise **venture capital** to carry them through to the point at which they can make their first public issue of stock. Venture capital firms try to structure the financing to avoid conflicts of interest. If both the entrepreneur and the venture capital investors have an important equity stake in the company, they are likely to pull in the same direction. The entrepreneur's willingness to take that stake also *signals* management's confidence in the company's future. In addition, most venture capital is provided in stages that keep the firm on a short leash and force it to prove at each stage that it deserves the additional funds.

How do firms make initial public offerings, and what are the costs of such offerings? *(LO2)*

The **initial public offering** is the first sale of shares in a general offering to investors. The sale of the securities is usually managed by an underwriting firm that buys the shares from the company and resells them to the public. The **underwriter** helps to prepare a **prospectus,** which describes the company and its prospects. The costs of an IPO include direct costs, such as legal and administrative fees, as well as the **underwriting spread**—the difference between the price the underwriter pays to acquire the shares from the firm and the price the public pays the underwriter for those shares. Another major implicit cost is the **underpricing** of the issue—that is, shares are typically sold to the public somewhat below the true value of the security. This discount is reflected in abnormally high average returns to new issues on the first day of trading.

What are some of the significant issues that arise when established firms make a general cash offer or a private placement of securities? *(LO3)*

There are always economies of scale in issuing securities. It is cheaper to go to the market once for $100 million than to make two trips for $50 million each. Consequently, firms "bunch" security issues. This may mean relying on short-term financing until a large issue is justified. Or it may mean issuing more than is needed at the moment to avoid another issue later.

A **seasoned offering** may depress the stock price. The extent of this price decline varies, but for issues of common stocks by industrial firms the fall in the value of the existing stock may amount to a significant proportion of the money raised. The likely explanation for this pressure is the information the market reads into the company's decision to issue stock.

Shelf registration often makes sense for debt issues by blue-chip firms. Shelf registration reduces the time taken to arrange a new issue, it increases flexibility, and it may cut underwriting costs. It seems best suited for debt issues by large firms that are happy to switch between investment banks. It seems least suited for issues of unusually risky securities or for issues by small companies that most need a close relationship with an investment bank.

Private placements are well-suited for small, risky, or unusual firms. The special advantages of private placement stem from avoiding registration expenses and a more direct relationship with the lender. These are not worth as much to blue-chip borrowers.

What is the role of the underwriter in an issue of securities? *(LO4)*

Underwriters manage the sale of the securities and advise on the price at which the issue is sold. They then buy the securities from the issuing company, and resell them to the public. The difference between the price at which the underwriter buys the securities and the price at which they are resold is the underwriter's spread. Underwriting firms have expertise in such sales because they are in the business all the time, whereas the company raises capital only occasionally.

What is a rights issue? *(LO5)*

Unlike a general cash offering, a rights issue is an offer to buy shares that is made only to existing shareholders. The shares are priced at a substantial discount to current market value, which ensures that the shareholders will either exercise the rights themselves or sell them to other investors. In either case, the firm raises funds when the right is exercised.

QUESTIONS

QUIZ

1. **Underwriting.** *(LO3)*
   a. Is a rights issue more likely to be used for an initial public offering or for subsequent issues of stock?
   b. Is a private placement more likely to be used for issues of seasoned stock or seasoned bonds by an industrial company?
   c. Is shelf registration more likely to be used for issues of unseasoned stocks or bonds by a large industrial company?

2. **Underwriting.** Each of the following terms is associated with one of the events beneath. Can you match them up? *(LO3)*
   a. Shelf registration
   b. Firm commitment
   c. Rights issue

   A. The underwriter agrees to buy the issue from the company at a fixed price.
   B. The company offers to sell stock to existing stockholders.
   C. Several issues of the same security may be sold under the same registration.

3. **Underwriting Costs.** For each of the following pairs of issues, state which issue you would expect would involve the lower proportionate underwriting and administrative costs, other things equal. *(LO3)*
   a. A large issue/a small issue.
   b. A bond issue/a common stock issue.
   c. A small private placement of bonds/a small general cash offer of bonds.

4. **IPO Costs.** Why are the issue costs for debt issues generally less than those for equity issues? *(LO2)*

5. **Venture Capital.** Why do venture capital companies prefer to advance money in stages? *(LO1)*

6. **IPOs.** Your broker calls and says that you can get 500 shares of an imminent IPO at the offering price. Should you buy? Are you worried about the fact that your broker called *you?* *(LO2)*

PRACTICE PROBLEMS

7. **IPO Underpricing.** Having heard about IPO underpricing, I put in an order to my broker for 1,000 shares of every IPO he can get for me. After 3 months, my investment record is as follows: *(LO2)*

IPO	Shares Allocated to Me	Price per Share	Initial Return
A	500	$10	7%
B	200	20	12
C	1,000	8	−2
D	0	12	23

a. What is the average underpricing of this sample of IPOs?
b. What is the average initial return on my "portfolio" of shares purchased from the four IPOs I bid on? Calculate the average initial return, weighting by the amount of money invested in each issue.
c. Why have I performed so poorly relative to the average initial return on the full sample of IPOs? What lessons do you draw from my experience?

8. **IPO Costs.** Moonscape has just completed an initial public offering. The firm sold 3 million shares at an offer price of $8 per share. The underwriting spread was $.50 a share. The price of the stock closed at $12 per share at the end of the first day of trading. The firm incurred $100,000 in legal, administrative, and other costs. What were flotation costs as a fraction of funds raised? Were flotation costs for Moonscape higher or lower than is typical for IPOs of this size (see Figure 15.1)? *(LO2)*

9. **IPO Costs.** Look at the illustrative new issue prospectus in the appendix. *(LO2)*
a. Is this issue a primary offering, a secondary offering, or both?
b. What are the direct costs of the issue as a percentage of the total proceeds? Are these more than the average for an issue of this size?
c. Suppose that on the first day of trading the price of Hotch Pot stock is $15 a share. What are the *total* costs of the issue as a percentage of the market price?
d. After paying her share of the expenses, how much will the firm's president, Emma Lucullus, receive from the sale? What will be the value of the shares that she retains in the company?

10. **Flotation Costs.** "For small issues of common stock, the costs of flotation amount to about 15% of the proceeds. This means that the opportunity cost of external equity capital is about 15 percentage points higher than that of retained earnings." Does this follow? *(LO2)*

11. **Flotation Costs.** When Microsoft went public, the company sold 2 million new shares (the primary issue). In addition, existing shareholders sold .8 million shares (the secondary issue) and kept 21.1 million shares. The new shares were offered to the public at $21, and the underwriters received a spread of $1.31 a share. At the end of the first day's trading the market price was $35 a share. *(LO2)*
a. How much money did the company receive before paying its portion of the direct costs?
b. How much did the existing shareholders receive from the sale before paying their portion of the direct costs?
c. If the issue had been sold to the underwriters for $30 a share, how many shares would the company have needed to sell to raise the same amount of cash?
d. How much better off would the existing shareholders have been?

12. **Flotation Costs.** The market value of the marketing research firm Fax Facts is $600 million. The firm issues an additional $100 million of stock, but as a result the stock price falls by 2%. What is the cost of the price drop to existing shareholders as a fraction of the funds raised? *(LO2)*

13. **Flotation Costs.** Young Corporation stock currently sells for $30 per share. There are 1 million shares currently outstanding. The company announces plans to raise $3 million by offering shares to the public at a price of $30 per share. *(LO2)*
a. If the underwriting spread is 6%, how many shares will the company need to issue in order to be left with net proceeds of $3 million?
b. If other administrative costs are $60,000, what is the dollar value of the total direct costs of the issue?
c. If the share price falls by 3% at the announcement of the plans to proceed with a seasoned offering, what is the dollar cost of the announcement effect?

14. **Private Placements.** You need to choose between the following types of issues: *(LO3)*
• *A public issue of $10 million face value of 10-year debt.* The interest rate on the debt would be 8.5%, and the debt would be issued at face value. The underwriting spread would be 1.5%, and other expenses would be $80,000.

- *A private placement of $10 million face value of 10-year debt.* The interest rate on the private placement would be 9%, but the total issuing expenses would be only $30,000.
  a. What is the difference in the proceeds to the company net of expenses?
  b. Other things equal, which is the better deal?
  c. What other factors beyond the interest rate and issue costs would you wish to consider before deciding between the two offers?

15. **Rights.** Pandora, Inc., makes a rights issue at a subscription price of $5 a share. One new share can be purchased for every four shares held. Before the issue there were 10 million shares outstanding and the share price was $6. *(LO5)*
    a. What is the total amount of new money raised?
    b. What is the expected stock price after the rights are issued?

16. **Rights.** Practice Problem 15 contains details of a rights offering by Pandora. Suppose that the company had decided to issue the new stock at $4 instead of $5 a share. How many new shares would it have needed to raise the same sum of money? Recalculate the answers to Practice Problem 15. Show that Pandora's shareholders are just as well off if it issues the shares at $4 a share rather than the $5 assumed in Practice Problem 15. *(LO5)*

17. **Rights.** Consolidated Jewels needs to raise $2 million to pay for its Diamonds in the Rough campaign. It will raise the funds by offering 200,000 rights, each of which entitles the owner to buy one new share. The company currently has outstanding 1 million shares priced at $20 each. *(LO5)*
    a. What must be the subscription price on the rights the company plans to offer?
    b. What will be the share price after the rights issue?
    c. What is the value of a right to buy one share?
    d. How many rights would be issued to an investor who currently owns 1,000 shares?
    e. Show that the investor who currently holds 1,000 shares is unaffected by the rights issue. Specifically, show that the value of the rights plus the value of the 1,000 shares after the rights issue equals the value of the 1,000 shares before the rights issue.

18. **Rights.** Associated Breweries is planning to market unleaded beer. To finance the venture, it proposes to make a rights issue with a subscription price of $10. One new share can be purchased for each two shares held. The company currently has outstanding 100,000 shares priced at $40 a share. Assuming that the new money is invested to earn a fair return, give values for the following: *(LO5)*
    a. Number of new shares.
    b. Amount of new investment.
    c. Total value of company after issue.
    d. Total number of shares after issue.
    e. Share price after the issue.

CHALLENGE PROBLEMS

19. **Venture Capital.** Here is a difficult question. Pickwick Electronics is a new high-tech company financed entirely by 1 million ordinary shares, all of which are owned by George Pickwick. The firm needs to raise $1 million now for stage 1 and, assuming all goes well, a further $1 million at the end of 5 years for stage 2.

    First Cookham Venture Partners is considering two possible financing schemes:
    - Buying 2 million shares now at their current valuation of $1.
    - Buying 1 million shares at the current valuation and investing a further $1 million at the end of 5 years at whatever the shares are worth.

    The outlook for Pickwick is uncertain, but as long as the company can secure the additional finance for stage 2, it will be worth either $2 million or $12 million after completing stage 2. (The company will be valueless if it cannot raise the funds for stage 2.) Show the possible payoffs for Mr. Pickwick and First Cookham, and explain why one scheme might be preferred. Assume an interest rate of zero. *(LO1)*

WEB EXERCISES

1. In the appendix to this chapter we provide a flavor of an IPO prospectus, but you can see what an actual prospectus or registration statement looks like. We suggest that you first log on to finance.yahoo.com and click on the *Investing* tab to find a recent IPO by a U.S. company. Now log on to the SEC's huge database at www.sec.gov/edgar/searchedgar/webusers.htm. Edgar can be a bit complicated, but the final IPO prospectus should be shown as Form 424B4. On the basis of this prospectus, do you think the stock looks like an attractive investment? Which parts of the statement appear most useful? Which seem the least useful? What were the direct expenses of the issue?

2. We describe underpricing as part of the costs of a new issue. Jay Ritter's home page (bear.cba .ufl.edu/ritter) is a mine of information on IPO underpricing. Look up his table of underpricing by year. Is underpricing less of a problem now than in the boom IPO years of 1998–2000? Now look at Jay Ritter's table of "money-left-on-the-table." Which company provided the greatest 1-day dollar gains to investors?

SOLUTIONS TO SELF-TEST QUESTIONS

15.1 Unless the firm can secure second-stage financing, it is unlikely to succeed. If the entrepreneur is going to reap any reward on his own investment, he needs to put in enough effort to get further financing. By accepting only part of the necessary venture capital, management increases its own risk and reduces that of the venture capitalist. This decision would be costly and foolish if management lacked confidence that the project would be successful enough to get past the first stage. A credible signal by management is one that only managers who are truly confident can afford to provide. However, words are cheap and there is little to be lost by saying that you are confident (although if you are proved wrong, you may find it difficult to raise money a second time).

15.2 If an investor can distinguish between overpriced and underpriced issues, she will bid only on the underpriced ones. In this case she will purchase only issues that provide a 10% gain. However, the ability to distinguish these issues requires considerable insight and research. The return to the informed IPO participant may be viewed as a return on the resources expended to become informed.

15.3

Underwriting spread = 446.6 million × $2	$ 893.2 million
Other expenses	45.5
Total direct expenses	$ 938.7 million
Underpricing = 446.6 million × ($56.50 − $47)	4,242.7
Total expenses	$ 5,181.4 million
Market value of issue = 446.6 × $56.50	$25,232.9 million

Expenses as a proportion of market value = $5,181.4/25,232.9 = .205, or 20.5%.

MINICASE

Mutt.Com was founded in 2009 by two graduates of the University of Wisconsin with help from Georgina Sloberg, who had built up an enviable reputation for backing new start-up businesses. Mutt.Com's user-friendly system was designed to find buyers for unwanted pets. Within 3 years the company was generating revenues of $3.4 million a year and, despite racking up sizable losses, was regarded by investors as one of the hottest new e-commerce businesses. The news that the company was preparing to go public therefore generated considerable excitement.

The company's entire equity capital of 1.5 million shares was owned by the two founders and Ms. Sloberg. The initial public offering involved the sale of 500,000 shares by the three existing shareholders, together with the sale of a further 750,000 shares by the company in order to provide funds for expansion.

The company estimated that the issue would involve legal fees, auditing, printing, and other expenses of $1.3 million, which would be shared proportionately between the selling shareholders and the company. In addition, the company agreed to pay the underwriters a spread of $1.25 per share (this cost also would be shared).

The roadshow had confirmed the high level of interest in the issue, and indications from investors suggested that the entire issue could be sold at a price of $24 a share. The underwriters, however, cautioned about being too greedy on price. They pointed out that indications from investors were not the same as firm orders. Also, they argued, it was much more important to have a successful issue than to have a group of disgruntled shareholders. They therefore suggested an issue price of $18 a share.

That evening Mutt.Com's financial manager decided to run through some calculations. First, she worked out the net receipts to the company and the existing shareholders assuming that the stock was sold for $18 a share. Next, she looked at the various costs of the IPO and tried to judge how they stacked up against the typical costs for similar IPOs. That brought her up against the question of underpricing. When she had raised the matter with the underwriters that morning, they had dismissed the notion that the initial day's return on an IPO should be considered part of the issue costs. One of the members of the underwriting team had asked: "The underwriters want to see a high return and a high stock price. Would Mutt.Com prefer a low stock price? Would that make the issue less costly?" Mutt.Com's financial manager was not convinced but felt that she should have a good answer. She wondered whether underpricing was only a problem because the existing shareholders were selling part of their holdings. Perhaps the issue price would not matter if they had not planned to sell.

APPENDIX   Hotch Pot's New-Issue PROSPECTUS[10]

Prospectus

> 800,000 Shares
> Hotch Pot, Inc.
> Common Stock ($.01 par value)

Of the 800,000 shares of Common Stock offered hereby, 500,000 shares are being sold by the Company and 300,000 shares are being sold by the Selling Stockholders. See "Principal and Selling Stockholders." The Company will not receive any of the proceeds from the sale of shares by the Selling Stockholders.

Before this offering there has been no public market for the Common Stock. **These securities involve a high degree of risk. See "Certain Factors."**

THESE SECURITIES HAVE NOT BEEN APPROVED OR DISAPPROVED BY THE SECURITIES AND EXCHANGE COMMISSION NOR HAS THE COMMISSION PASSED ON THE ACCURACY OR ADEQUACY OF THIS PROSPECTUS. ANY REPRESENTATION TO THE CONTRARY IS A CRIMINAL OFFENSE.

	Price to Public	Underwriting Discount	Proceeds to Company*	Proceeds to Selling Shareholders†
Per share	$12.00	$1.30	$10.70	$10.70
Total†	$9,600,000	$1,040,000	$5,350,000	$3,210,000

* Before deducting expenses payable by the Company estimated at $400,000, of which $250,000 will be paid by the Company and $150,000 by the Selling Stockholders.
† The Company and the Selling Shareholders have granted to the Underwriters options to purchase up to 120,000 additional shares at the initial public offering price less the underwriting discount, solely to cover overallotment.

The Common Stock is offered, subject to prior sale, when, as, and if delivered to and accepted by the Underwriters and subject to approval of certain legal matters by their counsel and by counsel for the Company and the Selling Shareholders. The Underwriters reserve the right to withdraw, cancel, or modify such offer and reject orders in whole or in part.

Silverman Pinch Inc.   **April 1, 2012**

No person has been authorized to give any information or to make any representations, other than as contained therein, in connection with the offer contained in this Prospectus, and, if given or made,

---

[10] Real prospectuses would be much longer than our simple example. You can get a better impression of the contents of a prospectus by looking at some real ones. These are available on the SEC's site **www.sec.gov/edgar/searchedgar/webusers.htm**. For example, take a look at the prospectus dated 6/29/2010 for the IPO of the electric car company, Tesla Motors. Notice the mixture of useful information and redundant qualification.

such information or representations must not be relied upon. This Prospectus does not constitute an offer of any securities other than the registered securities to which it relates or an offer to any person in any jurisdiction where such an offer would be unlawful. The delivery of this Prospectus at any time does not imply that information herein is correct as of any time subsequent to its date.

IN CONNECTION WITH THIS OFFERING, THE UNDERWRITER MAY OVERALLOT OR EFFECT TRANSACTIONS WHICH STABILIZE OR MAINTAIN THE MARKET PRICE OF THE COMMON STOCK OF THE COMPANY AT A LEVEL ABOVE THAT WHICH MIGHT OTHERWISE PREVAIL IN THE OPEN MARKET. SUCH STABILIZING, IF COMMENCED, MAY BE DISCONTINUED AT ANY TIME.

Prospectus Summary

The following summary information is qualified in its entirety by the detailed information and financial statements appearing elsewhere in this Prospectus.

The Company: Hotch Pot, Inc., operates a chain of 140 fast-food outlets in the United States offering unusual combinations of dishes.

The Offering: Common Stock offered by the Company 500,000 shares; Common Stock offered by the Selling Stockholders 300,000 shares; Common Stock to be outstanding after this offering 3,500,000 shares.

Use of Proceeds: For the construction of new restaurants and to provide working capital.

The Company

Hotch Pot, Inc., operates a chain of 140 fast-food outlets in Illinois, Pennsylvania, and Ohio. These restaurants specialize in offering an unusual combination of foreign dishes.

The Company was organized in Delaware in 2002.

Use of Proceeds

The Company intends to use the net proceeds from the sale of 500,000 shares of Common Stock offered hereby, estimated at approximately $5 million, to open new outlets in midwest states and to provide additional working capital. It has no immediate plans to use any of the net proceeds of the offering for any other specific investment.

Dividend Policy

The Company has not paid cash dividends on its Common Stock and does not anticipate that dividends will be paid on the Common Stock in the foreseeable future.

Certain Factors

Investment in the Common Stock involves a high degree of risk. The following factors should be carefully considered in evaluating the Company:

Substantial Capital Needs The Company will require additional financing to continue its expansion policy. The Company believes that its relations with its lenders are good, but there can be no assurance that additional financing will be available in the future.

Competition The Company is in competition with a number of restaurant chains supplying fast food. Many of these companies are substantially larger and better capitalized than the Company.

Capitalization

The following table sets forth the capitalization of the Company as of December 31, 2011, and as adjusted to reflect the sale of 500,000 shares of Common Stock by the Company.

	Actual	As Adjusted
	(in thousands)	
Long-term debt	$ –	$ –
Stockholders' equity	30	35
Common stock—$.01 par value, 3,000,000 shares outstanding, 3,500,000 shares outstanding, as adjusted		
Paid-in capital	1,970	7,315
Retained earnings	3,200	3,200
Total stockholders' equity	5,200	10,550
Total capitalization	$5,200	$10,550

Selected Financial Data

[*The Prospectus typically includes a summary income statement and balance sheet.*]

Management's Analysis of Results of Operations and Financial Condition

Revenue growth for the year ended December 31, 2011, resulted from the opening of ten new restaurants in the Company's existing geographic area and from sales of a new range of desserts, notably crepe suzette with custard. Sales per customer increased by 20% and this contributed to the improvement in margins.

During the year the Company borrowed $600,000 from its banks at an interest rate of 2% above the prime rate.

Business

Hotch Pot, Inc., operates a chain of 140 fast-food outlets in Illinois, Pennsylvania, and Ohio. These restaurants specialize in offering an unusual combination of foreign dishes. 50% of company's revenues derived from sales of two dishes, sushi and sauerkraut and curry bolognese. All dishes are prepared in three regional centers and then frozen and distributed to the individual restaurants.

Management

The following table sets forth information regarding the Company's directors, executive officers, and key employees:

Name	Age	Position
Emma Lucullus	28	President, Chief Executive Officer, & Director
Ed Lucullus	33	Treasurer & Director

Emma Lucullus Emma Lucullus established the Company in 2002 and has been its Chief Executive Officer since that date.

Ed Lucullus Ed Lucullus has been employed by the Company since 2002.

Executive Compensation

The following table sets forth the cash compensation paid for services rendered for the year 2011 by the executive officers:

Name	Capacity	Cash Compensation
Emma Lucullus	President and Chief Executive Officer	$130,000
Ed Lucullus	Treasurer	$ 95,000

Certain Transactions

At various times between 2002 and 2011 First Cookham Venture Partners invested a total of $1.5 million in the Company. In connection with this investment, First Cookham Venture Partners was granted certain rights to registration under the Securities Act of 1933, including the right to have their shares of Common Stock registered at the Company's expense with the Securities and Exchange Commission.

Principal and Selling Stockholders

The following table sets forth certain information regarding the beneficial ownership of the Company's voting Common Stock as of the date of this prospectus by (i) each person known by the Company to be the beneficial owner of more than 5% of its voting Common Stock, and (ii) each director of the Company who beneficially owns voting Common Stock. Unless otherwise indicated, each owner has sole voting and dispositive power over his shares.

Name of Beneficial Owner	Shares Beneficially Owned prior to Offering		Shares to Be Sold	Shares Beneficially Owned after Offering	
	Number	Percent		Number	Percent
Emma Lucullus	400,000	13.3	25,000	375,000	12.9
Ed Lucullus	400,000	13.3	25,000	375,000	12.9
First Cookham Venture Partners	1,700,000	66.7	250,000	1,450,000	50.0
Hermione Kraft	200,000	6.7	—	200,000	6.9

Lock-Up Agreements

The holders of the Common Stock have agreed with the Underwriter not to sell, pledge, or otherwise dispose of their shares, other than as specified in this Prospectus, for a period of 180 days after the date of the Prospectus without the prior consent of Silverman Pinch.

Description of Capital Stock

The Company's authorized capital stock consists of 10,000,000 shares of voting Common Stock.

As of the date of this Prospectus, there are 4 holders of record of the Common Stock.

Under the terms of one of the Company's loan agreements, the Company may not pay cash dividends on Common Stock except from net profits without the written consent of the lender.

Underwriting

Subject to the terms and conditions set forth in the Underwriting Agreement, the Underwriter, Silverman Pinch Inc., has agreed to purchase from the Company and the Selling Stockholders 800,000 shares of Common Stock.

There is no public market for the Common Stock. The price to the public for the Common Stock was determined by negotiation between the Company and the Underwriter and was based on, among other things, the Company's financial and operating history and condition, its prospects, and the prospects for its industry in general, the management of the Company, and the market prices of securities for companies in businesses similar to that of the Company.

Legal Matters

The validity of the shares of Common Stock offered by the Prospectus is being passed on for the Company by Cameron, Merkel, and Sarkozy and for the Underwriter by Harper Berlusconi.

Legal Proceedings

Hotch Pot was served in January 2012 with a summons and complaint in an action commenced by a customer who alleges that consumption of the Company's products caused severe nausea and loss of feeling in both feet. The Company believes that the complaint is without foundation.

Experts

The consolidated financial statements of the Company have been so included in reliance on the reports of Hooper Firebrand, independent accountants, given on the authority of that firm as experts in auditing and accounting.

Financial Statements

[*Text and tables omitted.*]

CHAPTER 16

Debt Policy

LEARNING OBJECTIVES

After studying this chapter, you should be able to:

(1) Show why capital structure does not affect firm value in perfect capital markets.

(2) Show why the tax system encourages debt finance and calculate the value of interest tax shields.

(3) Show how costs of financial distress can lead to an optimal capital structure.

(4) Explain why financial slack is valuable and might influence optimal capital structure.

RELATED WEB SITES FOR THIS CHAPTER CAN BE FOUND AT WWW.MHHE.COM/BMM7E.

River Cruises is reviewing its capital structure. More debt would increase the expected return on its shares, but would it add value?

A firm's basic financial resource is the stream of cash flows produced by its assets and operations. When the firm is financed entirely by common stock, all those cash flows belong to the stockholders. When it issues both debt and equity, the firm splits the cash flows into two streams, a relatively safe stream that goes to the debtholders and a more risky one that goes to the stockholders.

The firm's mix of securities is known as its *capital structure*. Look at Table 16.1. You can see that in some industries companies borrow much more heavily than in others. Most high-tech firms, such as Intel and Microsoft, rely almost wholly on equity finance. So do most biotech, software, and Internet companies. At the other extreme, hotels and airlines rely much more on debt than on equity.[1]

Capital structure is not immutable. Firms can change their capital structure, sometimes almost overnight. Later in the chapter you will see how Sealed Air Corporation did just that.

Shareholders want management to choose the mix of securities that maximizes firm value.

But is there an optimal capital structure? We must consider the possibility that no combination has any greater appeal than any other. Perhaps the really important decisions concern the company's assets, and decisions about capital structure are mere details—matters to be attended to but not worried about.

In the first part of the chapter we will look at examples in which capital structure *doesn't* matter. After that we will put back some of the things that do make a difference, such as taxes, bankruptcy, and the signals that your financing decisions may send to investors. We will then draw up a checklist for financial managers who need to decide on the firm's capital structure.

The appendix to the chapter contains a brief discussion of what happens when firms cannot pay their debts and enter bankruptcy proceedings.

---

[1] Airlines actually had negative equity on their books in 2009, as a result of massive losses incurred in the recession of 2008–2009. Thus the ratio of debt to debt plus equity for airlines was greater than 1. The *market* value of airline equity was positive, however. The airlines' market-value debt ratio was less than 1.

TABLE 16.1 Median ratios of debt to total capital for a sample of nonfinancial industries, 2009

Industry	Debt Ratio
Internet information providers	.01
Major integrated oil and gas	.10
Biotechnology	.12
Semiconductors	.13
Communication equipment	.18
Consumer appliances	.25
Railroads	.42
Gas utilities	.47
Hotels	.58
Airlines	1.10

Note: Debt to total capital ratio = $D/(D + E)$ where D and E are the book values of long-term debt and equity.
Source: Compustat.

16.1 How Borrowing Affects Value in a Tax-Free Economy

> It is after the ball game and the pizza man is delivering a pizza to Yogi Berra. "Should I cut it into four slices as usual, Yogi?" asks the pizza man. "No," replies Yogi, "Cut it into eight; I'm hungry tonight."

capital structure
The mix of long-term debt and equity financing.

If you understand why more slices won't sate Yogi's appetite, you will have no difficulty understanding when a company's choice of **capital structure** does not increase the underlying value of the firm.

Think of a simple balance sheet, with all entries expressed as current market values:

Assets	Liabilities and Stockholders' Equity
Value of cash flows from the firm's real assets and operations	Market value of debt
	Market value of equity
Value of firm	Value of firm

The right- and left-hand sides of a balance sheet are always equal. (Balance sheets have to balance!) Therefore, if you add up the market values of all the firm's debt and equity securities, you can calculate the value of all the future cash flows from the firm's real assets and operations.

In fact, the value of those cash flows *determines* the value of the firm and therefore determines the aggregate value of all the firm's outstanding debt and equity securities. If the firm changes its capital structure, say, by using more debt and less equity financing, overall value should not change.

Think of the left-hand side of the balance sheet as the size of the pizza; the right-hand side determines how it is sliced. A company can slice its cash flow into as many parts as it likes, but the value of those parts will always sum back to the value of the unsliced cash flow. (Of course, we have to make sure that none of the cash-flow stream is lost in the slicing. We cannot say "The value of a pizza is independent of how it is sliced" if the slicer is also a nibbler.)

The basic idea here (the value of a pizza does not depend on how it is sliced) has various applications. Yogi Berra got friendly chuckles for his misapplication. Franco Modigliani and Merton Miller received Nobel Prizes for applying it to corporate financing. Modigliani and Miller, always referred to as "MM," showed in 1958 that the value of a firm does not depend on how its cash flows are "sliced." More precisely, they demonstrated the following proposition: **When there are no taxes and capital markets function well, the market value of a company does not depend on its capital structure. In other words, financial managers cannot increase value by changing the mix of securities used to finance the company.**

Of course, this MM proposition rests on some important simplifying assumptions. For example, capital markets have to be "well functioning." This means that investors can trade securities without restrictions and can borrow or lend on the same terms as the firm. It also means that capital markets are efficient, so securities are fairly priced given the information available to investors. (We discussed market efficiency in Chapter 7.) MM's proposition also assumes that there are no distorting taxes, and it ignores the costs encountered if a firm borrows too much and lands in financial distress.

The firm's capital structure decision does matter if these assumptions are not true or if other practical complications are encountered. But the best way to *start* thinking about capital structure is to work through MM's argument. *To keep things as simple as possible, we will ignore taxes until further notice.*

MM's Argument

Cleo, the president of River Cruises, is reviewing that firm's capital structure with Antony, the financial manager. Table 16.2 shows the current position. The company has no debt and all its operating income is paid as dividends to the shareholders. The *expected* earnings and dividends per share are $1.25, but this figure is by no means certain—it could turn out to be more or less than $1.25. For example, earnings could fall to $.75 in a slump or they could jump to $1.75 in a boom.

The price of each share is $10. The firm expects to produce a level stream of earnings and dividends in perpetuity. No growth is forecast, so stockholders' expected return is equal to the dividend yield—that is, the expected dividend per share divided by the price, $1.25/$10.00 = .125, or 12.5%.

Cleo has come to the conclusion that shareholders would be better off if the company had equal proportions of debt and equity. She therefore proposes to issue $500,000 of debt at an interest rate of 10% and to use the proceeds to repurchase 50,000 shares. This is called a **restructuring.** Notice that the $500,000 raised by the new borrowing does not stay in the firm. It goes right out the door to shareholders in order to repurchase and retire 50,000 shares. Therefore, the assets and investment policy of the firm are not affected. Only the financing mix changes.

restructuring
Process of changing the firm's capital structure without changing its real assets.

What would MM say about this new capital structure? Suppose the change is made. Operating income is the same, so the value of the "pie" is fixed at $1 million. With $500,000 in new debt outstanding, the remaining common shares must be worth $500,000, that is, 50,000 shares at $10 per share. The total value of the debt and equity is still $1 million.

TABLE 16.2 River Cruises is entirely equity-financed. Although it expects to have an income of $125,000 in perpetuity, this income is not certain. This table shows the return to the stockholder under different assumptions about operating income. We assume no taxes.

Data			
Number of shares	100,000		
Price per share	$10		
Market value of shares	$1 million		

	State of the Economy		
	Slump	**Normal**	**Boom**
Operating income	$75,000	125,000	175,000
Earnings per share	$.75	1.25	1.75
Return on shares	7.5%	12.5%	17.5%
		Expected outcome	

Since the value of the firm is the same, common shareholders are no better or worse off than before. River Cruises shares still trade at $10 each. The overall value of River Cruises' equity falls from $1 million to $500,000, but shareholders have also received $500,000 in cash.

Antony points all this out: "The restructuring doesn't make our stockholders any richer or poorer, Cleo. Why bother? Capital structure doesn't matter."

Self-Test 16.1

Suppose River Cruises issues $350,000 of new debt (rather than $500,000) and uses the proceeds to repurchase and retire common stock. How does this affect price per share? How many shares will be left outstanding?

How Borrowing Affects Earnings per Share

Cleo is unconvinced. She prepares Table 16.3 and Figure 16.1 to show how borrowing $500,000 could increase earnings per share. Comparison of Tables 16.2 and 16.3 shows that "normal" earnings per share increase to $1.50 (versus $1.25) after the restructuring. Table 16.3 also shows more "upside" (earnings per share of $2.50 versus $1.75) and more "downside" ($.50 versus $.75).

The orange line in Figure 16.1 shows how earnings per share would vary with operating income under the firm's current all-equity financing. It is therefore simply a plot of the data in Table 16.2. The blue line shows how earnings per share would vary if the company moves to equal proportions of debt and equity. It is therefore a plot of the data in Table 16.3.

Cleo reasons as follows: "It is clear that debt could either increase or reduce the return to the equityholder. In a slump the return to the equityholder is reduced by the use of debt, but otherwise it is *increased.* We could be heading for a recession but it doesn't look likely. Maybe we could help our shareholders by going ahead with the debt issue."

As financial manager, Antony replies as follows: "I agree that borrowing will increase earnings per share as long as there's no slump." But we're not really doing anything for shareholders that they can't do on their own. Suppose River Cruises does *not* borrow. In that case an investor could go to the bank, borrow $10, and then invest $20 in two shares. Such an investor would put up only $10 of her own money. Table 16.4 shows how the payoffs on this $10 investment vary with River Cruises'

TABLE 16.3 River Cruises is wondering whether to issue $500,000 of debt at an interest rate of 10% and repurchase 50,000 shares. This table shows the return to the shareholder under different assumptions about operating income. Returns to shareholders are increased in normal and boom times but fall more in slumps.

Data			
Number of shares	50,000		
Price per share	$10		
Market value of shares	$500,000		
Market value of debt	$500,000		

Outcomes			
	State of the Economy		
	Slump	**Normal**	**Boom**
Operating income	$75,000	125,000	175,000
Interest	$50,000	50,000	50,000
Equity earnings	$25,000	75,000	125,000
Earnings per share	$.50	1.50	2.50
Return on shares	5%	15%	25%
		Expected outcome	

FIGUR 16.1 Borrowing increases River Cruises' earnings per share (EPS) when operating income is greater than $100,000 but reduces it when operating income is less than $100,000. Expected EPS rises from $1.25 to $1.50.

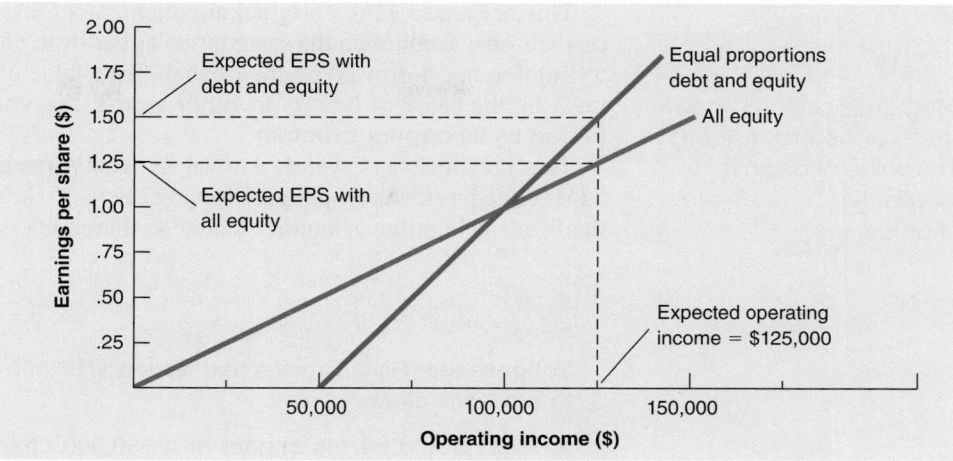

operating income. You can see that these payoffs are exactly the same as the investor would get by buying one share in the company after the restructuring. (Compare the last two lines of Tables 16.3 and 16.4.) It makes no difference whether shareholders borrow directly or whether River Cruises borrows on their behalf. Therefore, if River Cruises goes ahead and borrows, it will not allow investors to do anything that they could not do already, and so it cannot increase the value of the firm.

"We can run the same argument in reverse and show that investors also won't be any *worse* off after the restructuring. Imagine an investor who owns two shares in the company before the restructuring. If River Cruises borrows money, there is some chance that the return on the shares will be lower than before. If that possibility is not to our investor's taste, he can buy one share in the restructured company and also invest $10 in the firm's debt. Table 16.5 shows how the payoff on this investment varies with River Cruises' operating income. You can see that these payoffs are exactly the same as the investor got before the restructuring. (Compare the last lines of Tables 16.2 and 16.5.) By lending half of his capital (by investing in River Cruises' debt), the investor exactly offsets the company's borrowing. So if River Cruises goes ahead and borrows, it won't *stop* investors from doing anything that they could previously do."

TABLE 16.4 Individual investors can replicate River Cruises' borrowing by borrowing on their own. In this example we assume that River Cruises has not restructured. However, the investor can put up $10 of her own money, borrow $10 more, and buy two shares at $10 apiece. This generates the same rates of return as in Table 16.3.

	State of the Economy		
	Slump	**Normal**	**Boom**
Earnings on two shares	$1.50	2.50	3.50
Less interest at 10%	$1.00	1.00	1.00
Net earnings on investment	$ .50	1.50	2.50
Return on $10 investment	5%	15%	25%
		Expected outcome	

TABLE 16.5 Individual investors can also undo the effects of River Cruises' borrowing. Here the investor buys one share for $10 and lends out $10 more. Compare these rates of return to the original returns of River Cruises in Table 16.2.

	State of the Economy		
	Slump	**Normal**	**Boom**
Earnings on one share	$ .50	1.50	2.50
Plus interest at 10%	$1.00	1.00	1.00
Net earnings on investment	$1.50	2.50	3.50
Return on $20 investment	7.5%	12.5%	17.5%
		Expected outcome	

This re-creates MM's original argument.[2] As long as investors can borrow or lend on their own account on the same terms as the firm, they are not going to pay more for a firm that has borrowed on their behalf. The value of the firm after the restructuring must be the same as before. **In other words, the value of the firm must be unaffected by its capital structure.**

This conclusion is widely known as **MM's proposition I.** It is also called the **MM debt-irrelevance proposition,** because it shows that under ideal conditions the firm's debt policy shouldn't matter to shareholders.

Self-Test 16.2

Suppose that River Cruises had issued $750,000 of debt, using the proceeds to buy back stock.

a. What would be the impact of a $50,000 change in operating income on earnings per share?
b. Show how a conservative investor could "undo" the change in River Cruises' capital structure by varying the investment strategy shown in Table 16.5. *Hint:* The investor will have to lend $3 for every dollar invested in River Cruises' stock.

How Borrowing Affects Risk and Return

Figure 16.2 summarizes the implications of MM's debt irrelevance proposition for River Cruises. The upper circles represent firm value; the lower circles, expected, or "normal," operating income. Restructuring does not affect the size of the circles, because the amount and risk of operating income are unchanged. Thus if the firm raises $500,000 in debt and uses the proceeds to repurchase and retire shares, the remaining shares *must* be worth $500,000, and the total value of debt and equity *must* stay at $1 million.

The two bottom circles in Figure 16.2 are also the same size. But notice that the bottom right circle shows that shareholders can expect to earn more than half of River Cruises' normal operating income. They get more than half of the expected income "pie." Does that mean shareholders are better off? MM say no. Why? Because shareholders bear more risk.

Look again at Tables 16.2 and 16.3. Restructuring does not affect operating income, regardless of the state of the economy. Therefore, debt financing does not affect the **operating risk** or, equivalently, the **business risk** of the firm. But with less equity outstanding, a change in operating income has a greater impact on earnings per share. Suppose operating income drops from $125,000 to $75,000. Under all-equity financing, there are 100,000 shares; so earnings per share fall by $.50. With 50% debt, there are only 50,000 shares outstanding; so the same drop in operating income reduces earnings per share by $1.

You can see now why the use of debt finance is known as **financial leverage** and a firm that has issued debt is described as a *levered firm.* The debt increases the uncertainty about percentage stock returns. If the firm is financed entirely by equity, a decline of $50,000 in operating income reduces the return on the shares by 5 percentage points. If the firm issues debt, then the same decline of $50,000 in operating income reduces the return on the shares by 10 percentage points. (Compare Tables 16.2 and 16.3.) In other words, the effect of leverage is to double the magnitude of the upside and downside in the return on River Cruises' shares. Whatever the beta of the firm's shares before the restructuring, it would be twice as high afterward.

---

[2] There are many more general—and technical—proofs of the MM proposition. We will not pursue them here.

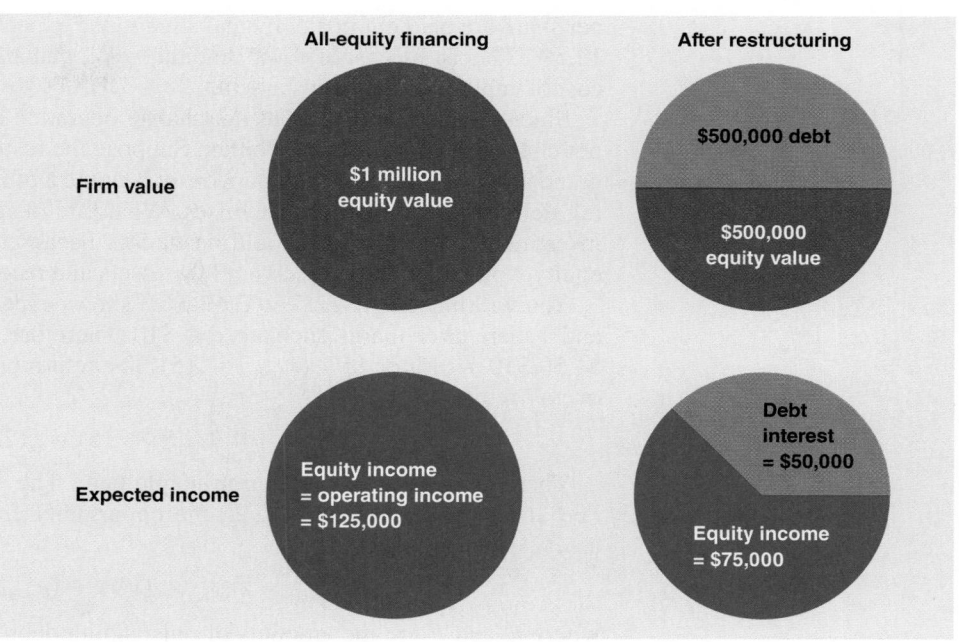

FIGURE 16.2 "Slicing the pie" for River Cruises. The circles on the left assume the company has no debt. The circles on the right reflect the proposed restructuring. The restructuring splits firm value (top circles) 50–50. Shareholders get more than 50% of expected, or "normal," operating income (bottom circles), but only because they bear financial risk. Note that restructuring does not affect total firm value or operating income.

financial risk
Risk to shareholders resulting from the use of debt.

Debt finance does not affect the operating risk but it does add financial risk. With only half the equity to absorb the same amount of operating risk, risk per share must double.[3]

Consider now the implications of MM's proposition I for the expected return on River Cruises' stock. Before the proposed debt issue, the expected stream of earnings and dividends per share is $1.25. Since investment in the shares is risky, the shareholders require a return of 12.5%, or 2.5% above the interest rate. So the share price (which for a perpetuity is equal to the expected dividend divided by the required return) is $1.25/.125 = $10. The good news is that after the debt issue, expected earnings and dividends rise to $1.50. The bad news is that the risk of the shares has now doubled. So instead of being content with a return of 2.5% above the interest rate, shareholders now demand a return of 5% more than the interest rate—that is, a required return of 10 + 5 = 15%. The benefit from the rise in dividends is exactly canceled out by the rise in the required return. The share price after the debt issue is $1.50/.15 = $10, exactly the same as before.

	Current Structure: All Equity	Proposed Structure: Equal Debt and Equity
Expected earnings per share	$1.25	$1.50
Share price	$10	$10
Expected return on share	12.5%	15.0%

Thus leverage increases the expected return to shareholders, but it also increases the risk. The two effects cancel, leaving shareholder value unchanged.

Debt and the Cost of Equity

What is River Cruises' cost of capital? With all-equity financing, the answer is easy. Stockholders pay $10 per share and expect earnings per share of $1.25. If the earnings

---

[3] Think back to Section 10.3, where we showed that fixed costs increase the variability in a firm's profits. These fixed costs are said to provide *operating leverage*. It is exactly the same with debt. Debt interest is a fixed cost, and therefore debt magnifies the variability of profits after interest. These fixed interest charges create financial leverage.

per share are paid out in a perpetual stream, the expected return is $1.25/10 = .125, or 12.5%. This is the cost of equity capital, r_{equity}, and also r_{assets}, the expected return and cost of capital for the firm's assets.

Since the restructuring does not change operating earnings or firm value, it should not change the cost of capital either. Suppose the restructuring takes place. Also, by a grand stroke of luck you simultaneously become a billionaire and buy *all* the outstanding debt and equity of River Cruises. What rate of return should you expect on this investment? Your answer should be 12.5%, because once you own all the debt and equity, you will effectively own all the assets and receive all the operating income.

You will indeed get 12.5%. Table 16.3 shows expected earnings per share of $1.50 and a share price that is unchanged at $10. Therefore, the expected return on equity is $1.50/$10 = .15, or 15% ($r_{equity} = .15$). The return on debt is 10% ($r_{debt} = .10$). Your overall return is

$$(.5 \times .10) + (.5 \times .15) = .125 = r_{assets}$$

There is obviously a general principle here: The appropriate weighted average of r_{debt} and r_{equity} takes you to r_{assets}, the opportunity cost of capital for the company's assets. The formula is

$$r_{assets} = (r_{debt} \times D/V) + (r_{equity} \times E/V)$$

where D and E are the amounts of outstanding debt and equity and V equals overall firm value, the sum of D and E. Remember that D, E, and V are market values, not book values.

This formula does not quite match the weighted-average cost of capital (WACC) formula presented in Chapter 13 because at this point we are still ignoring taxes.[4] Don't worry, we'll get to WACC in a moment. First let's look at the implications of MM's debt-irrelevance proposition for the cost of equity.

MM's proposition I states that the firm's choice of capital structure does not affect the firm's operating income or the value of its assets. So r_{assets}, the expected return on the package of debt and equity, is unaffected.

However, we have just seen that leverage does increase the risk of the equity and the return that shareholders demand. To see how the expected return on equity varies with leverage, we simply rearrange the formula for the company cost of capital as follows:

$$r_{equity} = r_{assets} + \frac{D}{E}(r_{assets} - r_{debt}) \tag{16.1}$$

which in words says that

$$\begin{array}{l}\text{Expected} \\ \text{return} \\ \text{on equity}\end{array} = \begin{array}{l}\text{expected} \\ \text{return} \\ \text{on assets}\end{array} + \left[\begin{array}{l}\text{debt-} \\ \text{equity} \\ \text{ratio}\end{array} \times \left(\begin{array}{l}\text{expected} \\ \text{return on} \\ \text{assets}\end{array} - \begin{array}{l}\text{expected} \\ \text{return on} \\ \text{debt}\end{array}\right)\right]$$

MM's proposition II
The required rate of return on equity increases as the firm's debt-equity ratio increases.

This is **MM's proposition II.** It states that the expected rate of return on the common stock of a levered firm increases in proportion to the debt-equity ratio (D/E), expressed in market values. Note that $r_{equity} = r_{assets}$ if the firm has no debt.

EXAMPLE 16.1 ▶   River Cruises' Cost of Equity

We can check out MM's proposition II for River Cruises. Before the decision to borrow,

$$r_{equity} = r_{assets} = \frac{\text{expected operating income}}{\text{market value of all securities}}$$

$$= \frac{125,000}{1,000,000} = .125, \text{ or } 12.5\%$$

---

[4] See Sections 13.1 and 13.2.

If the firm goes ahead with its plan to borrow, the expected return on assets, r_{assets}, is still 12.5%. So the expected return on equity is

$$
\begin{aligned}
r_{\text{equity}} &= r_{\text{assets}} + \frac{D}{E}(r_{\text{assets}} - r_{\text{debt}}) \\
&= .125 + \frac{500{,}000}{500{,}000}(.125 - .10) \\
&= .15, \text{ or } 15\%
\end{aligned}
$$

We pointed out in Chapter 13 that you can think of a debt issue as having an explicit cost and an implicit cost. The explicit cost is the rate of interest charged on the firm's debt. **But debt also increases financial risk and causes shareholders to demand a higher return on their investment. Once you recognize this implicit cost, debt is no cheaper than equity—the return that investors require on their assets is unaffected by the firm's borrowing decision.** Be sure to remember this point whenever you hear some layperson say "Debt is cheaper than equity."

Self-Test 16.3

When the firm issues debt, why does r_{assets}, the company cost of capital, remain fixed while the expected return on equity, r_{equity}, changes? Why is it not the other way around?

The implications of MM's proposition II are shown in Figure 16.3. No matter how much the firm borrows, the expected return on the package of debt and equity, r_{assets}, is unchanged, but the expected rate of return on the separate parts of the package does change. How is this possible? Because the proportions of debt and equity in the package are also changing. More debt means that the cost of equity increases, but at the same time the *amount* of equity is less.

In Figure 16.3 we have drawn the rate of interest on the debt as constant no matter how much the firm borrows. That is not wholly realistic. It is true that most large, conservative companies could borrow a little more or less without noticeably affecting the interest rate that they pay. But at higher debt levels lenders become concerned that they may not get their money back and they demand higher rates of interest. Figure 16.4 modifies Figure 16.3 to take account of this. You can see that as the firm borrows more, the risk of default increases and the firm has to pay higher rates of interest. Proposition II continues to predict that the expected return on the package of debt and

FIGURE 16.3 **MM's proposition II with a fixed interest rate on debt. The expected return on River Cruises' equity rises in line with the debt-equity ratio. The weighted average of the expected returns on debt and equity is constant, equal to the expected return on assets.**

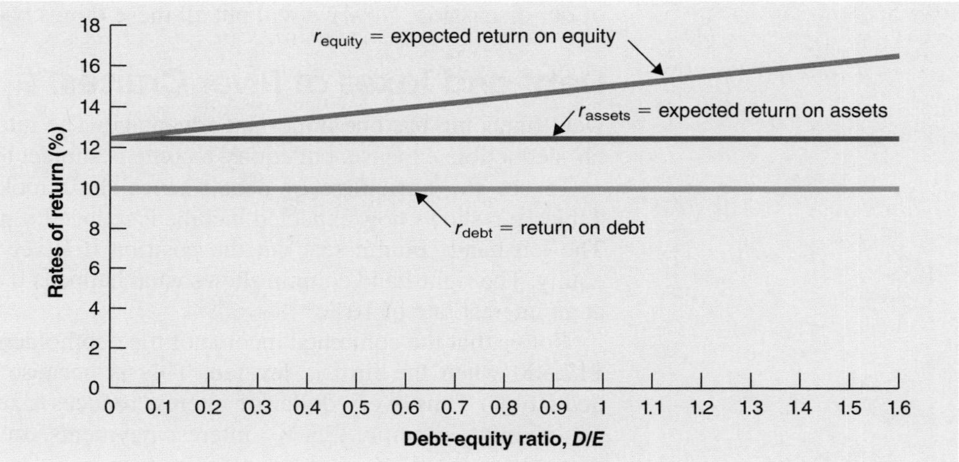

FIGURE 16.4 MM's proposition II when debt is not risk-free. As the debt-equity ratio increases, debtholders demand a higher expected rate of return to compensate for the risk of default. The expected return on equity increases more slowly when debt is risky because the debtholders take on part of the risk. The expected return on the package of debt and equity, r_{assets}, remains constant.

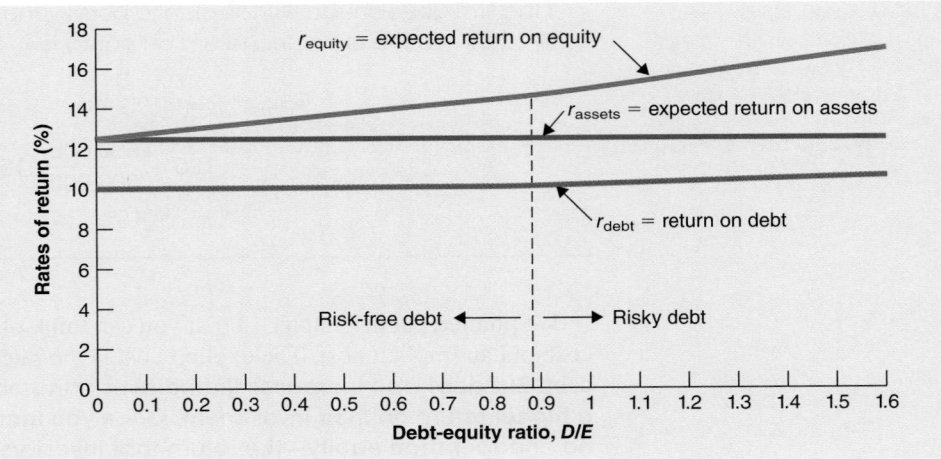

equity does not change. However, the slope of the r_{equity} line now tapers off as D/E increases. Why? Essentially because holders of risky debt begin to bear part of the firm's operating risk. As the firm borrows more, more of that risk is transferred from stockholders to bondholders.

Figures 16.3 and 16.4 wrap up our discussion of MM's leverage-irrelevance proposition. Because overall firm value is constant, the average return on the firm's debt and equity securities is also constant, regardless of the fraction of debt financing. This result follows from MM's assumptions that capital markets are well functioning and taxes are absent. Now it's time to put taxes back into the picture.

16.2 Capital Structure and Corporate Taxes

The MM propositions suggest that debt policy should not matter. Yet financial managers do worry about debt policy, and for good reasons. Now we are ready to see why.

If debt policy were *completely* irrelevant, actual debt ratios would vary randomly from firm to firm and from industry to industry. Yet almost all airlines, utilities, and real estate development companies rely heavily on debt. And so do many firms in capital-intensive industries like steel, aluminum, chemicals, and mining. On the other hand, it is rare to find a drug or software company that is not predominantly equity-financed. Glamorous growth companies seldom use much debt, despite rapid expansion and often heavy requirements for capital.

The explanation of these patterns lies partly in the things that we have so far left out of our discussion. Now we will put all these things back in, starting with taxes.

Debt and Taxes at River Cruises

Debt financing has one important advantage: The interest that the company pays is a tax-deductible expense, but equity income is subject to corporate tax.

To see the advantage of debt finance, let's look once again at River Cruises. Table 16.6 shows how expected income is reduced if profits are taxed at a rate of 35%. The left-hand column sets out the position if River Cruises is financed entirely by equity. The right-hand column shows what happens if the firm issues $500,000 of debt at an interest rate of 10%.

Notice that the combined income of the debtholders and equityholders is higher by $17,500 when the firm is levered. This is because the interest payments are tax-deductible. Thus every dollar of interest reduces taxes by $.35. The total amount of tax savings is simply .35 × interest payments. In the case of River Cruises, the

TABLE 16.6 Since debt interest is tax-deductible, River Cruises' debtholders and equityholders expect to receive a higher combined income when the firm is leveraged

	Zero Debt	$500,000 of Debt
Expected operating income	$125,000	$125,000
Debt interest at 10%	0	50,000
Before-tax income	125,000	75,000
Tax at 35%	43,750	26,250
After-tax income	81,250	48,750
Combined debt and equity income (debt interest + after-tax income)	81,250	98,750

interest tax shield

Tax savings resulting from deductibility of interest payments.

interest tax shield is $.35 \times \$50,000 = \$17,500$ each year. In other words, the "pie" of after-tax income that is shared by debt and equity investors increases by $17,500 relative to the zero-debt case. Since the debtholders receive no more than the going rate of interest, all the benefit of this interest tax shield is captured by the shareholders.

The interest tax shield is a valuable asset. Let's see how much it could be worth. Suppose that River Cruises plans to replace its bonds when they mature and to keep "rolling over" the debt indefinitely. It therefore looks forward to a permanent stream of tax savings of $17,500 per year. These savings depend only on the corporate tax rate and on the ability of River Cruises to earn enough to cover interest payments. So the risk of the tax shield is likely to be small. If we wish to compute the present value of all the future tax savings associated with permanent debt, we should discount the interest tax shields at a relatively low rate.

But what rate? The most common assumption is that the risk of the tax shields is the same as that of the interest payments generating them. Thus we discount at 10%, the expected rate of return demanded by investors who are holding the firm's debt. If the debt is permanent, then the firm can look forward to annual savings of $17,500 in perpetuity. Their present value is

$$\text{PV tax shield} = \frac{\$17,500}{.10} = \$175,000$$

This is what the tax savings are worth to River Cruises.

How does company value change? We continue to assume that if the firm is all-equity-financed, the shareholders will demand a 12.5% return and therefore the company will be valued at $81,250/.125 = \$650,000.[5] But if River Cruises issues $500,000 of permanent debt, the package of all the firm's securities increases by the value of the tax shield to $650,000 + \$175,000 = \$825,000$.

Let us generalize. The interest payment each year equals the rate of interest times the amount borrowed, or $r_{debt} \times D$. The annual tax saving is the corporate tax rate T_c times the interest payment. Therefore,

$$\text{Annual tax shield} = \text{corporate tax rate} \times \text{interest payment}$$
$$= T_c \times (r_{debt} \times D)$$

If the tax shield is perpetual, we use the perpetuity formula to calculate its present value:

$$\text{PV tax shields} = \frac{\text{annual tax shield}}{r_{debt}} = \frac{T_c \times (r_{debt} \times D)}{r_{debt}} = T_c D \qquad (16.2)$$

We will use this simple formula (PV tax shields $= T_c D$) in the rest of the River Cruises example. We do so for simplicity. In fact, the formula almost always *overstates* the value of interest tax shields. First, the firm may not borrow permanently. Second, it may run into future losses and not pay income taxes. If that happens, there

---

[5] The firm was worth $1 million when the corporate tax rate was zero (see Table 16.2). It is worth only $650,000 when all-equity-financed because 35% of income is lost to taxes.

are no taxes for interest to shield. Third, the formula assumes that the amount of debt is fixed regardless of how well the firm performs. It's more reasonable to assume that the firm will *rebalance* its capital structure over time to keep its debt *ratio* more or less constant. If the firm thrives and its value increases, it can borrow more. If the firm hits hard times and value decreases, it can gradually pay down debt to a more comfortable level. Rebalancing means future debt and interest tax shields are no longer fixed amounts; they vary with the firm's performance, and therefore should be discounted at a rate higher than the cost of debt.

The simple formula nevertheless summarizes an important point. It tells us that interest tax shields can add significant value to the firm and its shareholders.

Self-Test 16.4

In the year ending January 2010, Walmart paid out $2,065 million as debt interest. How much more tax would Walmart have paid if the firm had been entirely equity-financed? What would be the present value of Walmart's interest tax shield if the company planned to keep its borrowing permanently at the 2010 level? Assume an interest rate of 6% and a corporate tax rate of 35%.

How Interest Tax Shields Contribute to the Value of Stockholders' Equity

MM's proposition I amounts to saying that "the value of the pizza does not depend on how it is sliced." The pizza is the firm's assets, and the slices are the debt and equity claims. If we hold the pizza constant, then a dollar more of debt means a dollar less of equity value.

But there is really a third slice—the government's. MM would still say that the value of the pizza—in this case the company value *before* taxes—is not changed by slicing. But anything the firm can do to reduce the size of the government's slice obviously leaves more for the others. One way to do this is to borrow money. This reduces the firm's tax bill and increases the cash payments to the investors. The value of their investment goes up by the present value of the tax savings.

In a no-tax world, MM's proposition I states that the value of the firm is unaffected by capital structure. But MM also modified proposition I to recognize corporate taxes:

Value of levered firm = value if all-equity-financed + present value of tax shield

In the special case of permanent debt,

$$\text{Value of levered firm} = \text{value if all-equity-financed} + T_c D \qquad (16.3)$$

This "corrected" formula is illustrated in Figure 16.5. It implies that borrowing increases firm value and shareholders' wealth.

Corporate Taxes and the Weighted-Average Cost of Capital

We have shown that when there are corporate taxes, debt provides the company with a valuable tax shield. Few companies explicitly calculate the present value of interest tax shields associated with a particular borrowing policy. The tax shields are not forgotten, however, because they show up in the discount rate used to evaluate capital investments.

Since debt interest is tax-deductible, the government in effect pays 35% of the interest cost. So to keep its investors happy, the firm has to earn the *after-tax* rate of interest on its debt plus the return required by shareholders. Once we recognize the tax benefit of debt, the weighted-average cost of capital formula (see Chapter 13 for a review if you need one) becomes

$$\text{WACC} = (1 - T_c)r_{\text{debt}}\left(\frac{D}{D+E}\right) + r_{\text{equity}}\left(\frac{E}{D+E}\right)$$

FIGURE 16.5 The heavy blue line shows how the interest tax shields affect the market value of the firm. Additional borrowing decreases corporate income tax payments and increases the cash flows available to investors. Thus market value increases.

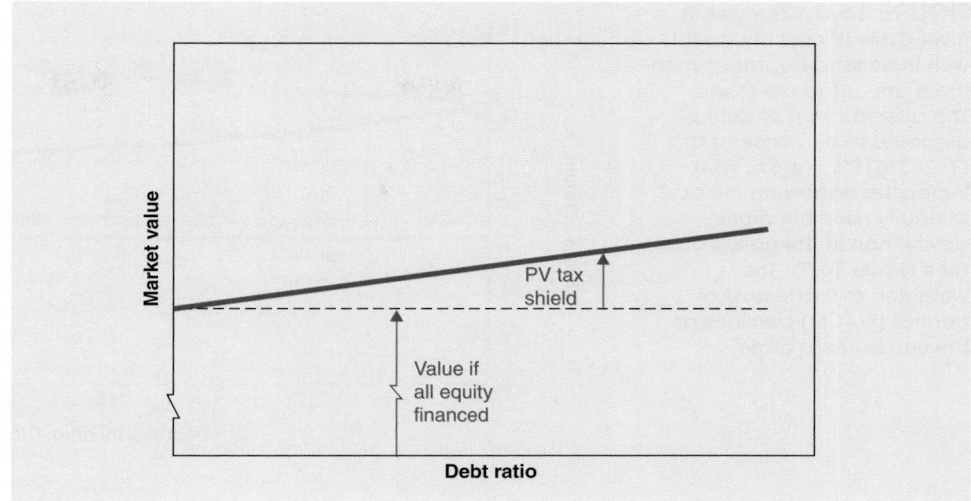

Notice that when we allow for the tax advantage of debt, the weighted-average cost of capital depends on the *after-tax* rate of interest $(1 - T_c) \times r_{debt}$.

EXAMPLE 16.2 ▶ WACC and Debt Policy

We can use the weighted-average cost of capital formula to see how leverage affects River Cruises' cost of capital if the company pays corporate tax. When a company has no debt, the weighted-average cost of capital and the return required by shareholders are identical. In the case of River Cruises the WACC with all-equity financing is 12.5%, and the value of the firm is $650,000.

Now let us calculate the weighted-average cost of capital if River Cruises issues $500,000 of permanent debt (D = $500,000). Company value increases by PV tax shield = $175,000, from $650,000 to $825,000 (meaning that $D + E$ = $825,000). Therefore the value of equity must be $825,000 − $500,000 = $325,000 ($E$ = $325,000).

Table 16.6 shows that when River Cruises borrows, the expected equity income is $48,750. So the expected return to shareholders is 48,750/325,000 = 15% (r_{equity} = .15). The interest rate is 10% (r_{debt} = .10), and the corporate tax rate is 35% (T_c = .35). This is all the information we need to see how leverage affects River Cruises' weighted-average cost of capital:

$$\text{WACC} = (1 - T_c)r_{debt}\left(\frac{D}{D + E}\right) + r_{equity}\left(\frac{E}{D + E}\right)$$

$$= (1 - .35).10\left(\frac{500,000}{825,000}\right) + .15\left(\frac{325,000}{825,000}\right) = .0985, \text{ or } 9.85\%$$

We saw earlier that if there are no corporate taxes, the weighted-average cost of capital is unaffected by borrowing. But when there are corporate taxes, debt provides the company with a new benefit—the interest tax shield. In this case leverage reduces the weighted-average cost of capital (in River Cruises' case from 12.5% to 9.85%).

Figure 16.6 repeats Figure 16.3 except that now we have allowed for the effect of taxes on River Cruises' cost of capital. You can see that as the company borrows more, the expected return on equity rises, but the rise is less rapid than in the absence of taxes. The after-tax cost of debt is only 6.5%. As a result, the weighted-average cost of capital declines. For example, if the company has debt of $500,000, the equity is worth $325,000 and the debt/equity ratio (D/E) is $500,000/$325,000 = 1.54. Figure 16.6 shows that with this amount of debt the weighted-average cost of capital is 9.85%, the same figure that we calculated above.

FIGURE 16.6 Changes in River Cruises' cost of capital with increased leverage when there are corporate taxes. The after-tax cost of debt is assumed to be constant at $(1 - .35)10\% = 6.5\%$. With increased borrowing the cost of equity rises, but more slowly than in the no-tax case (see Figure 16.3). The weighted-average cost of capital (WACC) declines as the firm borrows more.

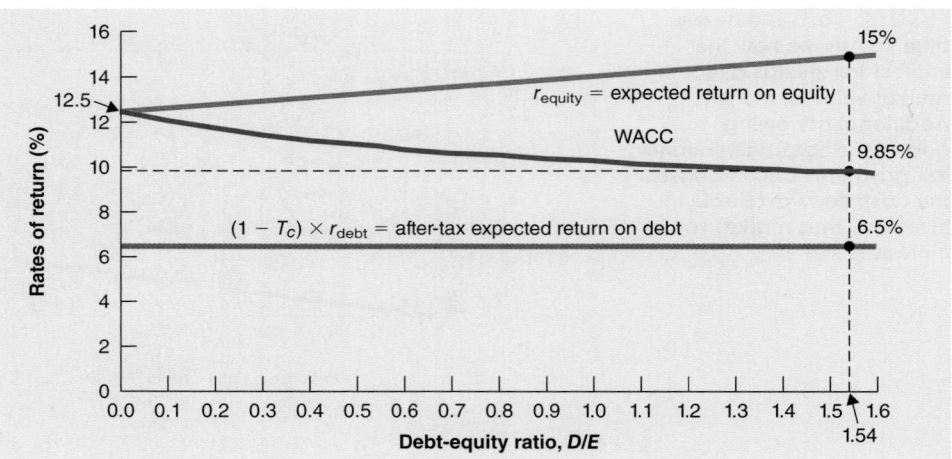

Again, we must nag and remind you that we have used the simple formula (PV tax shields = T_cD). The formula assumes that tax shields are fixed, safe, and permanent. But the message from Figure 16.6 still stands even if these assumptions are relaxed.[6] Interest tax shields increase firm value and reduce the after-tax WACC.

The Implications of Corporate Taxes for Capital Structure

If borrowing provides an interest tax shield, the implied optimal debt policy appears to be embarrassingly extreme: All firms should borrow to the hilt. This maximizes firm value and minimizes the weighted-average cost of capital.

MM were not that fanatical about it. No one would expect the gains to apply at extreme debt ratios. For example, if a firm borrows heavily, all its operating income may go to pay interest and therefore there are no corporate taxes to be paid. There is no point in such firms borrowing any more.

There may also be some tax *disadvantages* to borrowing, for bondholders have to pay personal income tax on any interest they receive. The top rate of tax on bond interest is 35%. On the other hand, stockholders currently are taxed at only 15% on both dividends and capital gains. Capital gains have the additional advantage that they are not taxed until the stock is sold. (The delay reduces the present value of the tax payment.)

All this suggests that there may come a point at which the tax savings from debt level off and may even decline. But it doesn't explain why highly profitable companies with large tax bills often thrive with little or no debt. There are clearly factors besides tax to consider. One such factor is the likelihood of financial distress.

16.3 Costs of Financial Distress

Financial distress occurs when promises to creditors are broken or honored with difficulty. Sometimes financial distress leads to bankruptcy. Sometimes it means only skating on thin ice.

---

[6] If the firm rebalances its capital structure to keep its market-value debt ratio constant, then the expected rate of return on equity increases more rapidly with D/E than in Figure 16.6. The after-tax WACC still declines, however. If you want a more detailed analysis of formulas for cost of equity and WACC, check out Chapter 19 in R. A. Brealey, S. C. Myers, and F. Allen, *Principles of Corporate Finance,* 10th ed. (New York: McGraw-Hill Irwin), 2011.

costs of financial distress
Costs arising from
bankruptcy or distorted
business decisions
before bankruptcy.

As we will see, financial distress is costly. Investors know that levered firms may run into financial difficulty, and they worry about the **costs of financial distress.** That worry is reflected in the current market value of the levered firm's securities. Even the most blue-chip firms are concerned about how their debt is perceived by investors. They know that they will be charged a lower rate of interest if the probability of default is minimal, and they are therefore anxious to maintain an investment-grade rating.

Even if the firm is not now in financial distress, investors factor the potential for future distress into their assessment of current value. This means that the overall value of the firm is

$$\text{Overall market value} = \text{value if all-equity-financed} + \text{PV tax shield} - \text{PV costs of financial distress}$$

The present value of the costs of financial distress depends both on the probability of distress and on the magnitude of the costs encountered if distress occurs.

Figure 16.7 shows how the trade-off between the tax benefits of debt and the costs of distress determines optimal capital structure. Think of a firm like River Cruises, which starts with no debt but considers moving to higher and higher debt levels, holding its assets and operations constant. **At moderate debt levels the probability of financial distress is trivial, and therefore the tax advantages of debt dominate. But at some point additional borrowing causes the probability of financial distress to increase rapidly and the potential costs of distress begin to take a substantial bite out of firm value. The theoretical optimum is reached when the present value of tax savings from further borrowing is just offset by increases in the present value of costs of distress.**

trade-off theory
Debt levels are chosen
to balance interest tax
shields against the costs
of financial distress.

This is called the **trade-off theory** of optimal capital structure. The theory says that managers will try to increase debt levels to the point where the value of additional interest tax shields is exactly offset by the additional costs of financial distress.

Now let's take a closer look at financial distress.

Bankruptcy Costs

In principle, bankruptcy is merely a legal mechanism for allowing creditors (that is, lenders) to take over the firm when the decline in the value of its assets triggers a default on outstanding debt. If the company cannot pay its debts, the company is turned over to the creditors, who become the new owners; the old stockholders are left with nothing. Bankruptcy is not the *cause* of the decline in the value of the firm. It is the result.

In practice, of course, anything involving courts and lawyers cannot be free. The fees involved in a bankruptcy proceeding are paid out of the remaining value of the

FIGURE 16.7 The trade-off theory of capital structure. The curved blue line shows how the market value of the firm at first increases as the firm borrows but finally decreases as the costs of financial distress become more and more important. The optimal capital structure balances the costs of financial distress against the value of the interest tax shields generated by borrowing.

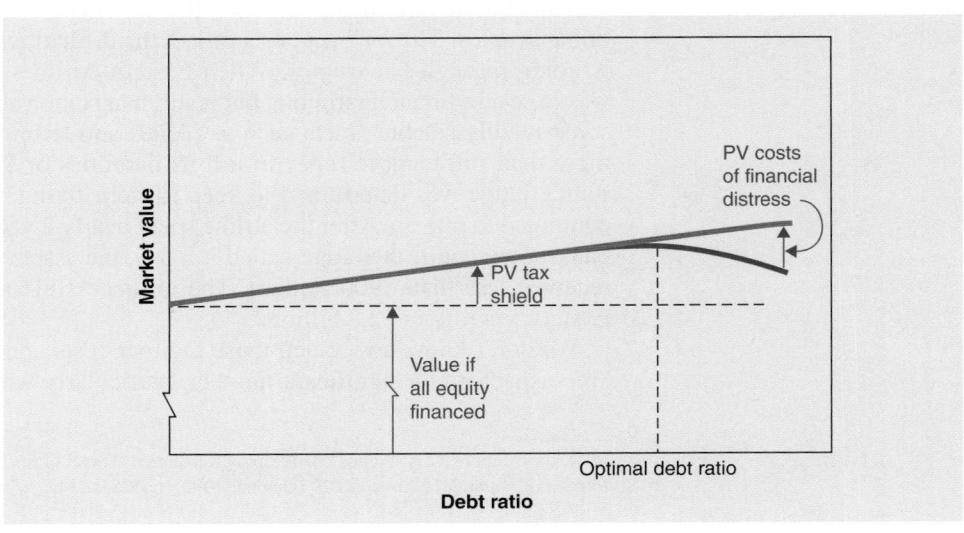

firm's assets. Creditors end up with what is left after paying the lawyers and other court expenses. If there is a possibility of bankruptcy, the current market value of the firm is reduced by the present value of these potential costs.

It is easy to see how increased leverage affects the costs of financial distress. The more the firm owes, the higher the chance of default and therefore the greater the expected value of the associated costs. This reduces the current market value of the firm.

Creditors foresee the costs and realize that if default occurs, the bankruptcy costs will come out of the value of the firm. For this they demand compensation in advance in the form of a higher promised interest rate. This reduces the possible payoffs to stockholders and reduces the current market value of their shares.

Self-Test 16.5

Suppose investors foresee $2 million of legal costs if the firm defaults on its bonds. How does this affect the value of the firm's bonds if bankruptcy occurs? How does the possibility of default affect the interest rate demanded by bondholders *today?* How does this possibility affect today's value of the firm's common stock?

When large firms file for bankruptcy, they usually do so under an arrangement called *Chapter 11.* The purpose of Chapter 11 is to nurse the firm back to health and enable it to face the world again. This requires approval of a reorganization plan for who gets what; under the plan each class of creditors needs to give up its claim in exchange for new securities or a mixture of new securities and cash. The challenge is to design a new capital structure that will satisfy the creditors and allow the firm to solve the business problems that got it into trouble in the first place. Sometimes it proves possible to satisfy both demands and the patient emerges fit and healthy. Often, however, the proceedings involve costly delays and legal tangles, and the business continues to deteriorate.

Bankruptcy costs can add up fast. The failed energy giant Enron paid nearly $1 billion in legal, accounting, and other professional fees during the time that it spent in bankruptcy. The costs of sorting out the 65,000 claims on the assets of Lehman Brothers are forecast to reach a record $1.5 billion.

Of course, these are exceptional cases, for only the largest firms can lay their hands on a billion dollars when bankrupt. But daunting as such numbers may seem, bankruptcy costs average only about 3% of the value of a firm in the year before bankruptcy.[7] The proportion is typically higher for small firms than for large ones; it seems that there are significant economies of scale in going bankrupt.

Thus far we have discussed only the *direct* (that is, legal and administrative) costs of bankruptcy. The *indirect* costs reflect the difficulties of running a company while it is going through bankruptcy. When Eastern Airlines entered bankruptcy in 1989, it was in severe financial trouble, but it still had some valuable, profit-making routes and some readily salable assets such as planes and terminal facilities. These assets were more than sufficient to repay in full its liabilities of $3.7 billion. However, the bankruptcy judge was determined to keep Eastern flying. Unfortunately, Eastern's losses continued to pile up. After the airline spent nearly 2 years under the "protection" of the bankruptcy court, the judge called it a day, the assets were sold off, and the creditors received less than $900 million. The unsuccessful attempt at resuscitation had cost Eastern's creditors $2.8 billion.

We don't know how much these indirect costs add to the expenses of bankruptcy. We suspect it is a significant number, particularly when bankruptcy proceedings are

---

[7] See, for example, L. A. Weiss, "Bankruptcy Resolution: Direct Costs and Violation of Priority of Claims," *Journal of Financial Economics* 27 (October 1990), pp. 285–314.

prolonged. Perhaps the best evidence is the reluctance of creditors to force a firm into bankruptcy. In principle, they would be better off to end the agony and seize the assets as soon as possible. But, instead, creditors often overlook defaults in the hope of nursing the firm over a difficult period. They do this in part to avoid the costs of bankruptcy. There is an old financial saying, "Borrow $1,000 and you've got a banker. Borrow $10,000,000 and you've got a partner."

Costs of Bankruptcy Vary with Type of Asset

Suppose your firm's only asset is a large downtown hotel, mortgaged to the hilt. A recession hits, occupancy rates fall, and the mortgage payments cannot be met. The lender takes over and sells the hotel to a new owner and operator. The stock is worthless and you use the firm's stock certificates for wallpaper.

What is the cost of bankruptcy? In this example, probably very little. The value of the hotel is, of course, much less than you hoped, but that is due to the lack of guests, not to bankruptcy. Bankruptcy does not damage the hotel itself. The direct bankruptcy costs are restricted to items such as legal and court fees, real estate commissions, and the time the lender spends sorting things out.

Suppose we repeat the story of Heartbreak Hotel for Fledgling Electronics. Everything is the same, except for the underlying assets. Fledgling is a high-tech going concern, and much of its value reflects investors' belief that its research team will come up with profitable ideas. Fledgling is a "people business"; its most important assets go down in the elevator and into the parking lot every night.

If Fledgling gets into trouble, the stockholders may be reluctant to put up money to cash in on those profitable ideas—why should they put up cash which will simply go to pay off the banks? Failure to invest is likely to be much more serious for Fledgling than for a company like Heartbreak Hotel.

If Fledgling finally defaults on its debt, the lender would find it much more difficult to cash in by selling the assets. In fact, if trouble comes, many of those assets may drive into the sunset and never come back.

Some assets, like good commercial real estate, can pass through bankruptcy and reorganization largely unscathed; the values of other assets are likely to be considerably diminished. The losses are greatest for intangible assets that are linked to the continuing prosperity of the firm. That may be why debt ratios are low in the biotech industry, where company values depend on continued success in research and development. It may also explain the low debt ratios in many service companies, whose main asset is their skilled labor. The moral of these examples is this: **Do not think only about whether borrowing is likely to bring trouble. Think also of the value that may be lost if trouble comes.**

Self-Test 16.6

For which of the following companies would the costs of financial distress be most serious? Why?

- A 3-year-old biotech company. So far the company has no products approved for sale, but its scientists are hard at work developing a breakthrough drug.
- An oil production company with 50 producing wells and 20 million barrels of proven oil reserves.

Financial Distress without Bankruptcy

Not every firm that gets into trouble goes bankrupt. As long as the firm can scrape up enough cash to pay the interest on its debt, it may be able to postpone bankruptcy for many years. Eventually the firm may recover, pay off its debt, and escape bankruptcy altogether.

A narrow escape from bankruptcy does *not* mean that costs of financial distress are avoided. When a firm is in trouble, suppliers worry that they may not be paid, potential customers fear that the firm will not be able to honor its warranties,[8] and employees start slipping out for job interviews. The firm's bondholders and stockholders both want it to recover, but in other respects their interests may be in conflict. In times of financial distress the security holders are like many political parties—united on generalities but threatened by squabbling on any specific issue. **Financial distress is costly when these conflicts get in the way of running the business. Stockholders are tempted to forsake the usual objective of maximizing the overall market value of the firm and to pursue narrower self-interest instead. They are tempted to play games at the expense of their creditors. These games add to the costs of financial distress.**

Think of a company—call it Double-R Nutting—which is teetering on the brink of bankruptcy. It has large debts and large losses. Double-R's assets have little value, and if its debts were due today, Double-R would default, leaving the firm bankrupt. The debtholders would perhaps receive a few cents on the dollar, and the shareholders would be left with nothing.

But suppose the debts are not due yet. That grace period explains why Double-R's shares still have value. There could be a stroke of luck that will rescue the firm and allow it to pay off its debts with something left over. That's a long shot—unless firm value increases sharply, the stock will be valueless. But the owners have a secret weapon: They control investment and operating strategy.

The First Game: Bet the Bank's Money   Suppose Double-R has the opportunity to take a wild gamble. If it does not come off, the shareholders will be no worse off; the company will probably go under anyway. But if the gamble does succeed, there will be more than enough assets to pay off the debt and the surplus will go into the shareholders' pockets. You can see why management might want to take the chance. In taking the gamble, they are essentially betting the debtholders' money, but if Double-R does hit the jackpot, the equityholders get most of the loot.

This was essentially the situation facing Federal Express while it was still struggling in 1974. It had only $5,000 left in its checking account but needed $24,000 for its weekly jet fuel payment. Fred Smith took the incentive to gamble literally. He took the firm's remaining $5,000 and boarded a plane for Las Vegas, where he won $27,000. When asked how he had mustered the nerve to do this, he replied, "What difference did it make? Without the funds for the fuel companies, we couldn't have flown anyway."[9] The effects of such distorted incentives to take on risk are usually not this blatant, but the results can be the same.

These kinds of warped capital investment strategies are costly for the bondholders and for the firm as a whole. Why are they associated with financial distress? Because the temptation to follow such strategies is strongest when the odds of default are high. A healthy firm would never invest in Double-R's lousy gamble, since it would be gambling with its own money, not the bondholders'. A healthy firm's creditors would not be vulnerable to this type of game.

The Second Game: Don't Bet Your Own Money   We have just seen how shareholders, acting in their narrow self-interest, may take on risky, unprofitable projects. These are errors of commission. We will now illustrate how conflicts of interest may also lead to errors of omission.

---

[8] In an attempt to stave off Chrysler's bankruptcy, the U.S. government sought to reassure the firm's customers by backing the warranties on its vehicles.

[9] Roger Frock, *Changing How the World Does Business, FedEx's Incredible Journey to Success: The Inside Story* (San Francisco: Berrett-Koehler Publishers, 2006).

Suppose Double-R uncovers a relatively safe project with a positive NPV. Unfortunately, the project requires a substantial investment. Double-R will need to raise this extra cash from its shareholders. Although the project has a positive NPV, the profits may not be sufficient to rescue the company from bankruptcy. If that is so, all the profits from the new project will be used to help pay off the company's debt, and the shareholders will get no return on the cash they put up. Although it is in the firm's interest to go ahead with the project, it is not in the *owners'* interest, and the project will be passed up. A recent example of this problem occurred during the financial crisis when many banks, threatened with failure, discovered that their shareholders were reluctant to come to the rescue. The shareholders reasoned that any cash that they contributed would simply be used to get existing debtholders and the government off the hook.

These examples illustrate a general point. The value of any investment opportunity to the firm's *stockholders* is reduced because project benefits must be shared with the bondholders. Thus it may not be in the stockholders' self-interest to contribute fresh equity capital even if that means forgoing positive-NPV opportunities.

These two games illustrate potential conflicts of interest between stockholders and debtholders. The conflicts, which theoretically affect all levered firms, become much more serious when firms are staring bankruptcy in the face. **If the probability of default is high, managers and stockholders will be tempted to take on excessively risky projects. At the same time, stockholders may refuse to contribute more equity capital even if the firm has safe, positive-NPV opportunities. Stockholders would rather take money out of the firm than put new money in.**

loan covenant
Agreement between firm and lender requiring the firm to fulfill certain conditions to safeguard the loan.

The company knows that lenders will demand a higher rate of interest if they are worried that games will be played at their expense. So to reassure lenders that its intentions are honorable, the firm will commonly agree to **loan covenants.** For example, it may promise to limit future borrowing and not to pay excessive dividends. Of course, no amount of fine print can cover every possible game that the company might play. For instance, no contract can ensure that companies will accept all positive-NPV investments and reject negative ones.

We do not mean to leave the impression that managers and stockholders always succumb to temptation unless restrained. Usually they refrain voluntarily, not only because of a sense of fair play but also on pragmatic grounds: A firm or individual that makes a killing today at the expense of a creditor will be coldly received when the time comes to borrow again. Aggressive game playing is done only by firms in extreme financial distress (and sometimes by out-and-out crooks). Firms limit borrowing precisely because they don't wish to land in distress and be exposed to the temptation to play.

Self-Test 16.7

We have described two games that might be played by firms in financial distress. Why are the games costly? How does the possibility that the game might be played at some point in the future affect today's capital structure decisions?

We have now completed our review of the building blocks of the trade-off theory of optimal capital structure. In the next section we will sum up that theory and briefly cover a competing "pecking order" theory.

16.4 Explaining Financing Choices

The Trade-Off Theory

Financial managers often think of the firm's debt-equity decision as a trade-off between interest tax shields and the costs of financial distress. Of course, there is controversy about how valuable interest tax shields are and what kinds of financial trouble are most threatening, but these disagreements are only variations on a theme. Thus Figure 16.7 illustrates the debt-equity trade-off.

This trade-off theory predicts that target debt ratios will vary from firm to firm. Companies with safe, tangible assets and plenty of taxable income to shield ought to have high target ratios. Unprofitable companies with risky, intangible assets ought to rely primarily on equity financing.

All in all, this trade-off theory of capital structure tells a comforting story. It avoids extreme predictions and rationalizes moderate debt ratios. But what are the facts? Can the trade-off theory of capital structure explain how companies actually behave?

The answer is yes and no. On the yes side, the trade-off theory successfully explains many of the industry differences in capital structure that we encountered in Table 16.1. For example, high-tech growth companies, whose assets are risky and mostly intangible, normally use relatively little debt. Utilities or hotels can and do borrow heavily because their assets are tangible and relatively safe.

On the no side, there are other things the trade-off theory cannot explain. It cannot explain why some of the most successful companies thrive with little debt. Consider, for example, Microsoft, which is basically all-equity-financed. Granted, Microsoft's most valuable assets are intangible: the fruits of its research and development. We know that intangible assets and conservative capital structures should go together. But Microsoft also has a very large corporate income tax bill ($6.3 billion in 2010) and the highest possible credit rating. It could borrow enough to save tens of millions of tax dollars without raising a whisker of concern about possible financial distress.

Our example illustrates an odd fact about real-life capital structures: The most profitable companies generally borrow the least. Here the trade-off theory fails, for it predicts exactly the reverse. Under the trade-off theory, high profits should mean more debt-servicing capacity and more taxable income to shield and therefore should result in a *higher* debt ratio.

Self-Test 16.8

Rank these industries in order of predicted debt ratios under the trade-off theory of capital structure: (a) Internet software; (b) auto manufacturing; (c) regulated electric utilities.

A Pecking Order Theory

There is an alternative theory which could explain why profitable companies borrow less. It is based on *asymmetric information*—managers know more than outside investors about the profitability and prospects of the firm. Thus investors may not be able to assess the true value of a new issue of securities by the firm. They may be especially reluctant to buy newly issued common stock, because they worry that the new shares will turn out to be overpriced.

Such worries can explain why the announcement of a stock issue can drive down the stock price.[10] If managers know more than outside investors, they will be tempted to time stock issues when their companies' stock is *overpriced*—in other words, when the managers are relatively pessimistic. On the other hand, optimistic managers will see their companies' shares as *underpriced* and decide *not* to issue. You can see why investors would learn to interpret the announcement of a stock issue as a "pessimistic manager" signal and mark down the stock price accordingly. You can also see why optimistic financial managers—and most managers *are* optimistic!—would view a common stock issue as a relatively expensive source of financing.

---

[10] We described this "announcement effect" in Chapter 15.

All these problems are avoided if the company can finance with internal funds, that is, with earnings retained and reinvested. But if external financing is required, the path of least resistance is debt, not equity. Issuing debt seems to have a trifling effect on stock prices. There is less scope for debt to be misvalued and therefore a debt issue is a less worrisome signal to investors.

pecking order theory
Firms prefer to issue debt rather than equity if internal finance is insufficient.

These observations suggest a **pecking order theory** of capital structure. It goes like this:

1. Firms prefer internal finance. Reinvesting internally generated cash does not send adverse signals that could lower the stock price.
2. If external finance is required, firms issue debt first and issue equity only as a last resort. This pecking order arises because an issue of debt is less likely than an equity issue to be interpreted by investors as a bad omen.

In this story, there is no clear target debt-equity mix, because there are two kinds of equity, internal and external. The first is at the top of the pecking order, and the second is at the bottom. The pecking order explains why the most profitable firms generally borrow less; it is not because they have low target debt ratios but because they don't need outside money. Less profitable firms issue debt because they do not have sufficient internal funds for their capital investment program and because debt is first in the pecking order for *external* finance.

The pecking order theory does not deny that taxes and financial distress can be important factors in the choice of capital structure. However, the theory says that these factors are less important than managers' preference for internal over external funds and for debt financing over new issues of common stock.

For most U.S. corporations, internal funds finance the majority of new investment, and most external financing comes from debt. These aggregate financing patterns are consistent with the pecking order theory. Yet the pecking order seems to work best for mature firms. Fast-growing high-tech firms often resort to a series of common stock issues to finance their investments. Of course you wouldn't expect the pecking order to apply to firms with extremely valuable growth opportunities. Such firms have good reasons to issue stock; they are credible issuers. Stock issues by growth firms do not send the same pessimistic signal as issues by mature firms.

The Two Faces of Financial Slack

Other things equal, it's better to be at the top of the pecking order than at the bottom. Firms that have worked down the pecking order and need external equity may end up living with excessive debt or bypassing good investments because shares can't be sold at what managers consider a fair price.

financial slack
Ready access to cash or debt financing.

When asked about what factors are uppermost in their minds when they think about debt policy, financial managers commonly mention the tax advantage of debt and the importance of maintaining the firm's credit rating. But they place even greater emphasis on the need to retain flexibility so that the company has access to funds for pursuing new projects when they come along.[11] In other words, they place a high value on **financial slack.** Having financial slack means having cash, marketable securities, and ready access to the debt markets or to bank financing. Ready access basically requires conservative financing so that potential lenders see the company's debt as a safe investment.

In the long run, a company's value rests more on its capital investment and operating decisions than on financing. Therefore, you want to make sure your firm has sufficient financial slack so that financing is quickly available for good investments. Financial slack is most valuable to firms with plenty of positive-NPV growth opportunities. That is another reason why growth companies usually aspire to conservative capital structures.

---

[11] J. R. Graham and C. R. Harvey, "The Theory and Practice of Corporate Finance: Evidence from the Field." *Journal of Financial Economics* 61 (2001), pp. 187–243.

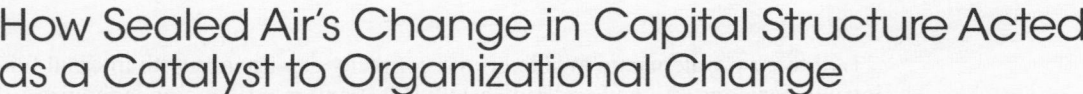

How Sealed Air's Change in Capital Structure Acted as a Catalyst to Organizational Change

Sealed Air Corporation manufactures a wide variety of packaging materials such as plastic packing bubbles and Jiffy padded envelopes.

As it entered 1989, Sealed Air was very conservatively financed with $33 million in total debt and over $54 million in cash. Thus the company was a net lender, not a borrower. However, in June of that year Sealed Air dramatically changed its capital structure by paying a special one-time dividend of $40 a share. With about 8.25 million shares trading, the total cash payout amounted to almost $330 million, or close to 90% of the total market value of the firm's common stock. To help finance this special dividend, the company borrowed a total of $307 million. Thus, the company went overnight from a net lender to a very heavy borrower. Debt now amounted to 125% of the book value of the assets and 65% of their market value.

Until the change in capital structure Sealed Air's performance was no better than that of the industry as a whole. But the change was a prelude to a sharp improvement in the company's operating performance. In the following 5 years, operating profit increased by 70% while the asset base grew by only 9%. This improvement in profitability was more than matched by the company's stock market performance. The initial effect of Sealed Air's announced change in capital structure was a jump of 10% in the stock price. Over the next 5½ years the stock outperformed the market by 400%.

What then motivated the change in capital structure and what role, if any, did this change play in the company's subsequent performance?

Some of the gains from the change in capital structure may have come from the fact that the company was able to offset the interest payments against tax. But this does not appear to have been a primary motive. Instead, the change appears to have been management's response to the realization that life at Sealed Air was in many respects too comfortable. For years patents had insulated the company from competition. Cash was plentiful. So the company never needed to think hard about requests to invest in new projects, and there was no sense of urgency in removing inefficiencies. In the management's view it would take nothing less than a "crisis" to shake employees out of their complacency. The change in capital structure was just such a crisis.

The sharp increase in debt levels meant that cash was no longer abundant for it was now needed to pay the debtholders and was literally essential to the company's survival. Thus managers now felt under pressure to make those efficiency gains that previously had not seemed worthwhile. As employees became aware of the need for more effective operations, it was possible to decentralize decision making within the company and to install a more effective system of performance measurement and compensation. The result was a sharp increase in profit margins and a reduction in the working capital and fixed assets employed to generate each dollar of sales. It seemed that the capital structure change had succeeded in kickstarting a remarkable improvement in Sealed Air's performance.

Source: Adapted from K. H. Wruck, "Financial Policy as a Catalyst for Organizational Change: Sealed Air Corporation's Leveraged Special Dividend," *Journal of Applied Corporate Finance* 7 (Winter 1995), pp. 20–37. Used with permission of John Wiley and Sons via Copyright Clearance Center, Inc.

However, there is also a dark side to financial slack. Too much of it may encourage managers to take it easy, expand their perks, or empire-build with cash that should be paid back to stockholders. Michael Jensen has stressed the tendency of managers with ample free cash flow (or unnecessary financial slack) to plow too much cash into mature businesses or ill-advised acquisitions. "The problem," Jensen says, "is how to motivate managers to disgorge the cash rather than investing it below the cost of capital or wasting it in organizational inefficiencies."[12]

If that's the problem, then maybe debt is an answer. Scheduled interest and principal payments are contractual obligations of the firm. Debt forces the firm to pay out cash. Perhaps the best debt level would leave just enough cash in the bank, after debt service, to finance all positive-NPV projects, with not a penny left over.

We do not recommend this degree of fine-tuning, but the idea is valid and important. For some firms, the threat of financial distress may have a good effect on managers' incentives. After all, skating on thin ice can be useful if it makes the skater concentrate. Likewise, managers of highly levered firms are more likely to work harder, run a leaner operation, and think more carefully before they spend money.

The nearby box tells the story of how Sealed Air Corporation borrowed more than $300 million, using the proceeds of the loan to pay a special cash dividend to shareholders. The net effect was an increase in debt from a trivial level to fully 65% of the

---

[12] M. C. Jensen, "Agency Costs of Free Cash Flow, Corporate Finance and Takeovers," *American Economic Review* 26 (May 1986), p. 323.

total value of the firm. The dramatic increase in debt committed the firm to pay out large sums of money as interest, leaving it with little opportunity to fritter its cash away in pursuit of a comfortable life. Sealed Air showed great improvements in efficiency after the change in capital structure.

SUMMARY

What is the goal of the capital structure decision? What is the financial manager trying to do? When would capital structure *not* matter? *(LO1)*

The goal is to maximize the overall market value of all the securities issued by the firm. Think of the financial manager as taking all the firm's real assets and selling them to investors as a package of securities. Some financial managers choose the simplest package possible: all-equity financing. Others end up issuing dozens of types of debt and equity securities. The financial manager must try to find the particular combination that maximizes the market value of the firm. If firm value increases, common stockholders will benefit.

But capital structure does not necessarily affect firm value. Modigliani and Miller's (MM's) famous **debt-irrelevance proposition** states that firm value can't be increased by changing **capital structure.** Therefore, the proportions of debt and equity financing don't matter. **Financial leverage** does increase the expected rate of return to shareholders, but the risk of their shares increases proportionally. MM show that the extra return and extra risk balance out, leaving shareholders no better or worse off.

Of course, MM's argument rests on simplifying assumptions. For example, it assumes efficient, well-functioning capital markets and ignores taxes and costs of financial distress. But even if these assumptions are incorrect in practice, MM's proposition is important. It exposes logical traps that financial managers sometimes fall into, particularly the idea that debt is "cheap financing" because the explicit cost of debt (the interest rate) is less than the cost of equity. Debt has an implicit cost too, because increased borrowing increases **financial risk** and the cost of equity. When both costs are considered, debt is not cheaper than equity. MM show that if there are no corporate income taxes, the firm's weighted-average cost of capital does not depend on the amount of debt financing.

How do corporate income taxes modify MM's leverage-irrelevance proposition? *(LO2)*

Debt interest is a tax-deductible expense. Thus borrowing creates an **interest tax shield,** which equals the marginal corporate tax rate T_c times the interest payment $r_{debt} \times D$. If debt is fixed and permanent,

$$\text{PV tax shield} = \frac{T_c(r_{debt} \times D)}{r_{debt}} = T_c D$$

Of course, interest tax shields are valuable only for companies that are making profits and paying taxes.

If interest tax shields are valuable, why don't all taxpaying firms borrow as much as possible? *(LO3)*

The more firms borrow, the higher the odds of financial distress. The **costs of financial distress** can be broken down as follows:

- Direct bankruptcy costs, primarily legal and administrative costs.
- Indirect bankruptcy costs, reflecting the difficulty of managing a company when it is in bankruptcy proceedings.
- Costs of the threat of bankruptcy, such as poor investment decisions resulting from conflicts of interest between debtholders and stockholders.

Combining interest tax shields and costs of financial distress leads to a **trade-off theory** of optimal capital structure. The trade-off theory says that financial managers should increase debt to the point where the value of additional interest tax shields is just offset by additional costs of possible financial distress.

The trade-off theory says that firms with safe, tangible assets and plenty of taxable income should operate at high debt levels. Less profitable firms, or firms with risky, intangible assets, ought to borrow less.

What's the pecking order theory? *(LO4)*

The **pecking order theory** says that firms prefer internal financing (that is, earnings retained and reinvested) over external financing. If external financing is needed, they prefer to issue debt rather than issue new shares. The pecking order theory starts with the observation that managers know more than outside investors about the firm's value and prospects. Investors realize that firms may seek to issue equity when their stock is overvalued and therefore mark down the stock price when an equity issue is announced. Internal financing avoids this problem. If external financing is necessary, debt is the first choice.

The pecking order theory says that the amount of debt a firm issues will depend on its need for external financing. The theory also suggests that financial managers should try to maintain at least some **financial slack,** that is, a reserve of ready cash or unused borrowing capacity.

On the other hand, too much financial slack may lead to slack managers. High debt levels (and the threat of financial distress) can create strong incentives for managers to work harder, conserve cash, and avoid negative-NPV investments.

Is there a rule for finding optimal capital structure? *(LO3, 4)*

Sorry, there are no simple answers for capital structure decisions. Debt may be better than equity in some cases, worse in others. But there are at least four dimensions for the financial manager to think about.

- *Taxes.* How valuable are interest tax shields? Is the firm likely to continue paying taxes over the full life of a debt issue? Safe, consistently profitable firms are most likely to stay in a taxpaying position.
- *Risk.* Financial distress is costly even if the firm survives it. Other things equal, financial distress is more likely for firms with high business risk. That is why risky firms typically issue less debt.
- *Asset type.* If distress does occur, the costs are generally greatest for firms whose value depends on intangible assets. Such firms generally borrow less than firms with safe, tangible assets.
- *Financial slack.* How much is enough? More slack makes it easy to finance future investments, but it may weaken incentives for managers. More debt, and therefore less slack, increases the odds that the firm may have to issue stock to finance future investments.

LISTING OF EQUATIONS

16.1 $r_{\text{equity}} = r_{\text{assets}} + \dfrac{D}{E}(r_{\text{assets}} - r_{\text{debt}})$

16.2 PV tax shields $= \dfrac{\text{annual tax shield}}{r_{\text{debt}}} = \dfrac{T_c \times (r_{\text{debt}} \times D)}{r_{\text{debt}}} = T_c D$

16.3 Value of levered firm = value if all-equity-financed $+ T_c D$

QUESTIONS

QUIZ

1. **MM's Leverage-Irrelevance Proposition.** True or false? MM's leverage-irrelevance proposition says: *(LO1)*
    a. The value of the firm does not depend on the fraction of debt versus equity financing.
    b. As financial leverage increases, the value of the firm increases by just enough to offset the additional financial risk absorbed by equity.
    c. The cost of equity increases with financial leverage only when the risk of financial distress is high.
    d. If the firm pays no taxes, the weighted-average cost of capital does not depend on the debt ratio.

2. **Effects of Leverage.** Increasing financial leverage can increase both the cost of debt (r_{debt}) and the cost of equity (r_{equity}). How can the overall cost of capital stay constant? (Assume the firm pays no taxes.) *(LO1)*

3. **Tax Shields.** What is an interest tax shield? How does it increase the size of the "pie" for after-tax income stockholders? Explain. (*Hint:* Construct a simple numerical example showing how financial leverage affects the total cash flow available to debt and equity investors. Be sure to hold pretax operating income constant.) *(LO2)*

4. **Value of Tax Shields.** Establishment Industries borrows $800 million at an interest rate of 7.6%. It expects to maintain this debt level into the far future. What is the present value of interest tax shields? Establishment will pay tax at an effective rate of 35%. *(LO2)*

5. **Trade-Off Theory.** What is the trade-off theory of optimal capital structure? How does it define the optimal debt ratio? *(LO3)*

6. **Financial Distress.** Give three examples of the types of costs incurred by firms in financial distress. *(LO3)*

7. **Pecking Order Theory.** What is the pecking order theory of optimal capital structure? If the theory is correct, what types of firms would you expect to operate at high debt levels? *(LO4)*

8. **Financial Slack.** Why is financial slack valuable? (*Hint:* What does the pecking order theory say about financial slack? Are there circumstances where too much financial slack might actually reduce the market value of the firm?) *(LO4)*

9. **Earnings and Leverage.** Suppose that River Cruises, which currently is all-equity-financed, issues $250,000 of debt and uses the proceeds to repurchase 25,000 shares. Assume that the firm pays no taxes and that debt finance has no impact on its market value. Rework Table 16.3 to show how earnings per share and share return now vary with operating income. *(LO1)*

10. **Debt Irrelevance.** Suppose an investor is unhappy with River Cruises' decision to borrow $250,000 (see the previous question). What modifications can she make to her own investment portfolio to offset the effects of the firm's additional borrowing? *(LO1)*

11. **Leverage and P/E Ratio.** Calculate the ratio of price to expected earnings for River Cruises both before and after it borrows the $250,000 (see Question 9). Why does the P/E ratio fall after the increase in leverage? *(LO1)*

12. **Tax Shields.** Now suppose that the corporate tax is $T_c = .35$. Demonstrate that when River Cruises borrows the $250,000, the combined after-tax income of its debtholders and equityholders increases (compared to all-equity financing) by 35% of the firm's interest expense regardless of the state of the economy. *(LO2)*

PRACTICE PROBLEMS

13. **Equity Return and Leverage.** The common stock and debt of Northern Sludge are valued at $70 million and $30 million, respectively. Investors currently require a 16% return on the common stock and an 8% return on the debt. If Northern Sludge issues an additional $10 million of common stock and uses this money to retire debt, what happens to the expected return on the stock? Assume that the change in capital structure does not affect the risk of the debt and that there are no taxes. *(LO1)*

14. **Earnings and Leverage.** Reliable Gearing currently is all-equity-financed. It has 10,000 shares of equity outstanding, selling at $100 a share. The firm is considering a capital restructuring. The low-debt plan calls for a debt issue of $200,000 with the proceeds used to buy back stock. The high-debt plan would exchange $400,000 of debt for equity. The debt will pay an interest rate of 10%. The firm pays no taxes. *(LO1)*

    a. What will be the debt-to-equity ratio after each contemplated restructuring?

    b. If earnings before interest and tax (EBIT) will be either $90,000 or $130,000, what will be earnings per share for each financing mix for both possible values of EBIT? If both scenarios are equally likely, what is expected (i.e., average) EPS under each financing mix? Is the high-debt mix preferable?

    c. Suppose that EBIT is $100,000. What is EPS under each financing mix? Why are they the same in this particular case?

15. **Leverage and Risk Premiums.** Astromet is financed entirely by common stock and has a beta of 1.0. The firm pays no taxes. The stock has a price-earnings multiple of 10 and is priced to offer a 10% expected return. The company decides to repurchase half the common stock and substitute an equal value of debt. *(LO1)*

    Assume that the debt yields a *risk-free* 5%. Calculate

    a. the beta of the common stock after the refinancing.
    b. the required return and risk premium on the common stock before the refinancing.
    c. the required return and risk premium on the common stock after the refinancing.
    d. the required return on the debt.
    e. the required return on the company (i.e., stock and debt combined) after the refinancing.

    Assume that the operating profit of the firm is expected to remain constant. Give

    f. the percentage increase in earnings per share after the refinancing.
    g. the new price-earnings multiple. (*Hint:* Has anything happened to the stock price?)

16. **Leverage and Capital Costs.** Hubbard's Pet Foods is financed 80% by common stock and 20% by bonds. The expected return on the common stock is 12%, and the rate of interest on the bonds is 6%. Assume that the bonds are default-free and that there are no taxes. Now assume that Hubbard's issues more debt and uses the proceeds to retire equity. The new financing mix is 60% equity and 40% debt. If the debt is still default-free, what happens to the expected rate of return on equity? What happens to the expected return on the package of common stock and bonds? *(LO1)*

17. **Leverage and Capital Costs.** "MM totally ignore the fact that as you borrow more, you have to pay higher rates of interest." Explain carefully whether this is a valid objection. *(LO1)*

18. **Debt Irrelevance.** What's wrong with the following arguments? *(LO1)*

    a. As the firm borrows more and debt becomes risky, both stock- and bondholders demand higher rates of return. Thus by *reducing* the debt ratio we can reduce *both* the cost of debt and the cost of equity, making everybody better off.
    b. Moderate borrowing doesn't significantly affect the probability of financial distress or bankruptcy. Consequently, moderate borrowing won't increase the expected rate of return demanded by stockholders.
    c. A capital investment opportunity offering a 10% internal rate of return is an attractive project if it can be 100% debt-financed at an 8% interest rate.
    d. The more debt the firm issues, the higher the interest rate it must pay. That is one important reason why firms should operate at conservative debt levels.

19. **Leverage and Capital Costs.** A firm currently has a debt-equity ratio of 1/2. The debt, which is virtually riskless, pays an interest rate of 6%. The expected rate of return on the equity is 12%. What would happen to the expected rate of return on equity if the firm reduced its debt-equity ratio to 1/3? Assume the firm pays no taxes. *(LO1)*

20. **Leverage and Capital Costs.** If an increase in the debt-equity ratio makes both debt and equity more risky, how can the cost of capital remain unchanged? *(LO1)*

21. **Tax Shields.** Look back to Table 3.3 where we provided a summary 2009 income statement for Home Depot. If the tax rate is 35%, what is Home Depot's annual interest tax shield? What is the present value of the annual tax shield if the company plans to maintain its current debt level indefinitely? Assume a discount rate of 8%. *(LO2)*

22. **WACC.** Here is Establishment Industries' market-value balance sheet (figures in millions):

Net working capital	$ 550	Debt	$ 800
Long-term assets	2,150	Equity	1,900
Value of firm	$2,700		$2,700

The debt is yielding 7%, and the cost of equity is 14%. The tax rate is 35%. Investors expect this level of debt to be permanent. *(LO2)*

a. What is Establishment's WACC?
b. How would the market-value balance sheet change if Establishment retired all its debt? (Hint: look back at Quiz Question 4.)

23. **Tax Shields and WACC.** Here are book- and market-value balance sheets of the United Frypan Company:

Book-Value Balance Sheet			
Net working capital	$ 20	Debt	$ 40
Long-term assets	80	Equity	60
	$ 100		$ 100

Market-Value Balance Sheet			
Net working capital	$ 20	Debt	$ 40
Long-term assets	140	Equity	120
	$ 160		$ 160

Assume that MM's theory holds except for taxes. There is no growth, and the $40 of debt is expected to be permanent. Assume a 35% corporate tax rate. *(LO2)*

a. How much of the firm's value is accounted for by the debt-generated tax shield?

b. What is United Frypan's after-tax WACC if $r_{debt} = 8\%$ and $r_{equity} = 15\%$?

c. Now suppose that Congress passes a law that eliminates the deductibility of interest for tax purposes after a grace period of 5 years. What will be the new value of the firm, other things equal? Assume an 8% borrowing rate.

24. **Bankruptcy.** What are the drawbacks of operating a firm that is close to bankruptcy? Give some examples. *(LO3)*

25. **Costs of Financial Distress.** The Salad Oil Storage Company (SOS) has financed a large part of its facilities with long-term debt. There is a significant risk of default, but the company is not on the ropes yet. Explain *(LO3)*

a. why SOS stockholders could lose by investing in a positive-NPV project financed by an equity issue.

b. why SOS stockholders could gain by investing in a highly risky, negative-NPV project.

26. **Financial Distress.** Explain how financial distress can lead to conflicts of interest between debt and equity investors. Then explain how these conflicts can lead to costs of financial distress. *(LO3)*

27. **Costs of Financial Distress.** For which of the following firms would you expect the costs of financial distress to be highest? Explain briefly. *(LO3)*

a. A computer software company that depends on skilled programmers to produce new products.

b. A shipping company that operates a fleet of modern oil tankers.

28. **Trade-Off Theory.** Smoke and Mirrors currently has EBIT of $25,000 and is all-equity-financed. EBIT is expected to stay at this level indefinitely. The firm pays corporate taxes equal to 35% of taxable income. The discount rate for the firm's projects is 10%. *(LO3)*

a. What is the market value of the firm?

b. Now assume the firm issues $50,000 of debt paying interest of 6% per year, using the proceeds to retire equity. The debt is expected to be permanent. What will happen to the total value of the firm (debt plus equity)?

c. Recompute your answer to (b) under the following assumptions: The debt issue raises the probability of bankruptcy. The firm has a 30% chance of going bankrupt after 3 years. If it does go bankrupt, it will incur bankruptcy costs of $200,000. The discount rate is 10%. Should the firm issue the debt?

29. **Pecking Order Theory.** Alpha Corp. and Beta Corp. both produce turbo encabulators. Both companies' assets and operations are growing at the same rate, and their annual capital expenditures are about the same. However, Alpha Corp. is the more efficient producer and is consistently more profitable. According to the pecking order theory, which company should have the higher debt ratio? Explain. *(LO4)*

30. **Financial Slack.** Look back to the Sealed Air example in the box in Section 16.4. What was the value of financial slack to Sealed Air before its restructuring? What does the success of the restructuring say about optimal capital structure? Would you recommend that all firms restructure as Sealed Air did? *(LO4)*

CHALLENGE PROBLEMS

31. **Costs of Financial Distress.** Let's go back to the Double-R Nutting Company. Suppose that Double-R's bonds have a face value of $50. Its current *market-value* balance sheet is

Assets		Liabilities and Equity	
Net working capital	$20	Bonds outstanding	$25
Fixed assets	10	Common stock	5
Total assets	$30	Total liabilities and shareholders' equity	$30

Who would gain or lose from the following maneuvers? *(LO3)*

a. Double-R pays a $10 cash dividend.

b. Double-R halts operations, sells its fixed assets for $6, and converts net working capital into $20 cash. It invests its $26 in Treasury bills.

c. Double-R encounters an investment opportunity requiring a $10 initial investment with NPV = $0. It borrows $10 to finance the project by issuing more bonds with the same security, seniority, and so on, as the existing bonds.

d. Double-R finances the investment opportunity in part (c) by issuing more common stock.

32. **Trade-Off Theory.** Ronald Masulis[13] has analyzed the stock price impact of *exchange offers* of debt for equity or vice versa. In an exchange offer, the firm offers to trade freshly issued securities for seasoned securities in the hands of investors. Thus a firm that wanted to move to a higher debt ratio could offer to trade new debt for outstanding shares. A firm that wanted to move to a more conservative capital structure could offer to trade new shares for outstanding debt securities. Masulis found that debt-for-equity exchanges were good news (stock price increased on announcement) and equity-for-debt exchanges were bad news. *(LO3)*

a. Are these results consistent with the trade-off theory of capital structure?

b. Are the results consistent with the evidence that investors regard announcements of (i) stock issues as bad news, (ii) stock repurchases as good news, and (iii) debt issues as no news or, at most, trifling disappointments?

33. **Pecking Order Theory.** Construct a simple example to show that a firm's existing stockholders gain if it can sell overpriced stock to new investors and invest the cash in a zero-NPV project. Who loses from these actions? If investors are aware that managers are likely to issue stock when it is overpriced, what will happen to the stock price when the issue is announced? *(LO4)*

34. **Pecking Order Theory.** When companies announce an issue of common stock, the share price typically falls. When they announce an issue of debt, there is typically only a negligible change in the stock price. Can you explain why? *(LO4)*

35. **Taxes.** MM's proposition I suggests that in the absence of taxes it makes no difference whether the firm borrows on behalf of its shareholders or whether they borrow directly. However, if there are corporate taxes, this is no longer the case. Construct a simple example to show that with taxes it is better for the firm to borrow than for the shareholders to do so. *(LO2)*

36. **Taxes.** MM's proposition I, when modified to recognize corporate taxes, suggests that there is a tax advantage to firm borrowing. If there is a tax advantage to firm borrowing, there is also a tax *disadvantage* to firm lending. Explain why. *(LO2)*

37. **Tax Shields and WACC.** River Cruises' management now understands that the trade-off theory of optimal capital structure implies managers will increase debt as long as the value of additional interest tax shields exceeds the additional costs of potential financial distress. This trade-off gives rise to the hump-shaped curve in Figure 16.7, where the value of the firm is maximized at the optimal debt level. What will the curve of WACC as a function of debt level look like? *(LO2)*

a. Start with a no-tax economy. Continue to assume that River Cruises' required return on assets is 12.5% and return on debt is 10%. In a spreadsheet, calculate r_{equity}, WACC, and r_{debt} for debt-equity ratios ranging from 0 to 2.5 in increments of .1. Does WACC vary with the *D/E* ratio? Compare your plot to Figure 16.3.

e**X**cel

Templates can be found at
www.mhhe.com/bmm7e.

---

[13] R. W. Masulis, "The Effects of Capital Structure Change on Security Prices: A Study of Exchange Offers," *Journal of Financial Economics* 8 (June 1980), pp. 139–77, and "The Impact of Capital Structure Change on Firm Value," *Journal of Finance* 38 (March 1983), pp. 107–26.

b. Now assume the corporate tax rate is 35%. Repeat part (a). What happens to WACC as *D/E* increases? What seems to be the optimal capital structure?

c. What considerations are missing that would affect the optimal capital structure seemingly implied by part (b)?

WEB EXERCISES

1. Log on to finance.yahoo.com and click the "Key Statistics" link for Pfizer (PFE) and Coca-Cola (KO). Construct the debt ratio, debt/(debt + equity), for both firms. Now calculate their debt ratios by using the market value of equity but assuming that book value of debt approximates its market value. How does debt as a proportion of firm value change as you switch from book to market values?

2. On finance.yahoo.com find the profiles for PepsiCo (PEP) and IBM (IBM), and then look at each firm's annual balance sheet and income statement under "Financials." Calculate the present value of the interest tax shield contributed by each company's long-term debt. Now suppose that each issues $3 billion more of long-term debt and uses the proceeds to repurchase equity. How would the interest tax shield change? In each case assume that the debt is fixed and permanent.

SOLUTIONS TO SELF-TEST QUESTIONS

16.1   Price per share will stay at $10, so with $350,000, River Cruises can repurchase 35,000 shares, leaving 65,000 outstanding. The remaining value of equity will be $650,000. Overall firm value stays at $1 million. Shareholders' wealth is unchanged: They start with shares worth $1 million, receive $350,000, and retain shares worth $650,000.

16.2   a.

Data			
Number of shares	25,000		
Price per share	$10		
Market value of shares	$250,000		
Market value of debt	$750,000		

	State of the Economy		
	Slump	**Normal**	**Boom**
Operating income, dollars	75,000	125,000	175,000
Interest, dollars	75,000	75,000	75,000
Equity earnings, dollars	0	50,000	100,000
Earnings per share, dollars	0	2.00	4.00
Return on shares	0%	20%	40%

Every change of $50,000 in operating income leads to a change in the return to equityholders of 20%. This is double the swing in equity returns when debt was only $500,000.

b. The stockholder should lend out $3 for every $1 invested in River Cruises' stock. For example, he could buy one share for $10 and then lend $30. The payoffs are:

	State of the Economy		
	Slump	**Normal**	**Boom**
Earnings on one share, dollars	0	2.00	4.00
Plus interest at 10%, dollars	3.00	3.00	3.00
Net earnings, dollars	3.00	5.00	7.00
Return on $40 investment	7.5%	12.5%	17.5%

16.3   Business risk is unaffected by capital structure. As the financing mix changes, whatever equity is outstanding must absorb the fixed business risk of the firm. The less equity, the more risk absorbed per share. Therefore, as capital structure changes, r_{assets} is held fixed while r_{equity} adjusts.

16.4   Walmart's borrowing reduced taxable profits by $2,065 million. With a tax rate of 35%, tax was reduced by .35 × $2,065 = $722.8 million. If the borrowing is permanent, Walmart will save this amount of tax each year. The present value of the tax savings would be $722.8/.06 = $12,045 million.

16.5   In bankruptcy bondholders will receive $2 million less. This lowers the expected cash flow from the bond and reduces its present value. Therefore, the bonds will be priced lower and must offer a higher interest rate. This higher rate is paid by the firm today. It comes out of stockholders' income. Thus common stock value falls.

16.6   The biotech company. Its assets are all intangible. If bankruptcy threatens and the best scientists accept job offers from other firms, there may not be much value remaining for the biotech company's debt and equity investors. On the other hand, bankruptcy would have little or no effect on the value of 50 producing oil wells and of the oil reserves still in the ground.

16.7   The conflicts are costly because they lead to poor investment decisions. The more debt the firm has today, the greater the chance of poor decisions in the future. Investors foresee this possibility and reduce today's market value of the firm.

16.8   The electric utility has the most stable cash flow. It also has the highest reliance on tangible assets that would not be impaired by a bankruptcy. It should have the highest debt ratio. The software firm has the least dependence on tangible assets and the most on assets that have value only if the firm continues as an ongoing concern. It probably also has the most unpredictable cash flows. It should have the lowest debt ratio.

MINICASE

In March 2013 the management team of Londonderry Air (LA) met to discuss a proposal to purchase five shorthaul aircraft at a total cost of $25 million. There was general enthusiasm for the investment, and the new aircraft were expected to generate an annual cash flow of $4 million for 20 years.

The focus of the meeting was on how to finance the purchase. LA had $20 million in cash and marketable securities (see table), but Ed Johnson, the chief financial officer, pointed out that the company needed at least $10 million in cash to meet normal outflow and as a contingency reserve. This meant that there would be a cash deficiency of $15 million, which the firm would need to cover either by the sale of common stock or by additional borrowing. While admitting that the arguments were finely balanced, Mr. Johnson recommended an issue of stock. He pointed out that the airline industry was subject to wide swings in profits and the firm should be careful to avoid the risk of excessive borrowing. He estimated that in market value terms the long-term debt ratio was about 59% and that a further debt issue would raise the ratio to 62%.

Mr. Johnson's only doubt about making a stock issue was that investors might jump to the conclusion that management believed

Summary financial statements for Londonderry Air, 2012 (Figures are book values, in millions of dollars.)

Balance Sheet			
Bank debt	$ 50	Cash	$ 20
Other current liabilities	20	Other current assets	20
10% bond, due 2032*	100	Fixed assets	250
Stockholders' equity†	120		
Total liabilities	$ 290	Total assets	$ 290
Income Statement			
Gross profit	$57.5		
Depreciation	20.0		
Interest	7.5		
Pretax profit	30.0		
Tax	10.5		
Net profit	19.5		
Dividend	6.5		

* The yield to maturity on LA debt currently is 6%.
† LA has 10 million shares outstanding, with a market price of $10 a share. LA's equity beta is estimated at 1.25, the market risk premium is 8%, and the Treasury bill rate is 3%.

the stock was overpriced, in which case the announcement might prompt an unjustified selloff by investors. He stressed therefore that the company needed to explain carefully the reasons for the issue. Also, he suggested that demand for the issue would be enhanced if at the same time LA increased its dividend payment. This would provide a tangible indication of management's confidence in the future.

These arguments cut little ice with LA's chief executive. "Ed," she said, "I know that you're the expert on all this, but everything you say flies in the face of common sense. Why should we want to sell more equity when our stock has fallen over the past year by nearly a fifth? Our stock is currently offering a dividend yield of 6.5%, which makes equity an expensive source of capital. Increasing the dividend would simply make it more expensive. What's more, I don't see the point of paying out more money to the stockholders at the same time that we are asking *them* for cash. If we hike the dividend, we will need to increase the amount of the stock issue; so we will just be paying the higher dividend out of the shareholders' own pockets. You're also ignoring the question of

dilution. Our equity currently has a book value of $12 a share; it's not playing fair by our existing shareholders if we now issue stock for around $10 a share.

"Look at the alternative. We can borrow today at 6%. We get a tax break on the interest, so the after-tax cost of borrowing is .65 × 6 = 3.9%. That's about half the cost of equity. We expect to earn a return of 15% on these new aircraft. If we can raise money at 3.9% and invest it at 15%, that's a good deal in my book.

"You finance guys are always talking about risk, but as long as we don't go bankrupt, borrowing doesn't add any risk at all.

"Ed, I don't want to push my views on this—after all, you're the expert. We don't need to make a firm recommendation to the board until next month. In the meantime, why don't you get one of your new business graduates to look at the whole issue of how we should finance the deal and what return we need to earn on these planes?"

Evaluate Mr. Johnson's arguments about the stock issue and dividend payment as well as the reply of LA's chief executive. Who is correct? What is the required rate of return on the new planes?

APPENDIX 　Bankruptcy Procedures

Firms that issue debt always bear a risk that when the debt comes due, they will not be able to pay their creditors. At that point, the firm may be forced into bankruptcy. We conclude this chapter with a brief overview of the bankruptcy process.

A corporation that cannot pay its debts will often try to come to an informal agreement with its creditors. This is known as a **workout.** A workout may take several forms. For example, the firm may negotiate an *extension,* that is, an agreement with its creditors to delay payments. Or the firm may negotiate a *composition,* in which the firm makes partial payments to its creditors in exchange for relief of its debts.

The advantage of a negotiated agreement is that the costs and delays of formal bankruptcy are avoided. However, the larger the firm and the more complicated its capital structure, the less likely it is that a negotiated settlement can be reached.

If the firm cannot get an agreement, then it may have no alternative but to file for **bankruptcy.**[14] Under the federal bankruptcy system the firm has a choice of procedures. In about two-thirds of the cases a firm will file for, or be forced into, bankruptcy under Chapter 7 of the 1978 Bankruptcy Reform Act. Then the firm's assets are **liquidated**—that is, sold—and the proceeds are used to pay creditors.

There is a ranking order of unsecured creditors.[15] First come claims for expenses that arise after bankruptcy is filed, such as attorneys' fees or employee compensation earned after the filing. If such postfiling claims did not receive priority, no firm in bankruptcy proceedings could continue to operate. Next come claims for wages and employee benefits earned in the period immediately prior to the filing. Taxes are next in line, together with debts to some government agencies such as the Small Business Administration or the Pension Benefit Guarantee Corporation. Finally come general unsecured claims such as bonds or unsecured trade debt.

The alternative to a liquidation is to seek a **reorganization,** which keeps the firm as a going concern and usually compensates creditors with new securities in the reorganized firm. Such reorganizations are generally in the shareholders' interests—they have little to lose if things deteriorate further and everything to gain if the firm recovers.

Firms attempting reorganization seek refuge under Chapter 11 of the Bankruptcy Reform Act. Chapter 11 is designed to keep the firm alive and operating and to protect the value of its assets while

workout
Agreement between a company and its creditors establishing the steps the company must take to avoid bankruptcy.

bankruptcy
The reorganization or liquidation of a firm that cannot pay its debts.

liquidation
Sale of bankrupt firm's assets.

reorganization
Restructuring of financial claims on failing firm to allow it to keep operating.

---

[14] Occasionally creditors will allow the firm to petition for bankruptcy after it has reached an agreement with the creditors. This is known as a *prepackaged bankruptcy.* The court simply approves the agreed workout plan.

[15] Secured creditors have the first priority to the collateral pledged for their loans.

a plan of reorganization is worked out. During this period, other proceedings against the firm are halted and the company is operated by existing management or by a court-appointed trustee.

The responsibility for developing a plan of reorganization may fall on the debtor firm. If no trustee is appointed, the firm has 120 days to present a plan to creditors. If this deadline is *not* met, or if a trustee is appointed, anyone can submit a plan—the trustee, for example, or a committee of creditors.

The reorganization plan is basically a statement of who gets what; each class of creditors gives up its claim in exchange for new securities. (Sometimes creditors receive cash as well.) The problem is to design a new capital structure for the firm that will (1) satisfy the creditors and (2) allow the firm to solve the *business* problems that got the firm into trouble in the first place. Sometimes only a plan of baroque complexity can satisfy these two requirements.

The reorganization plan goes into effect if it is accepted by creditors and confirmed by the court. Acceptance requires approval by a majority of each class of creditor. Once a plan is accepted, the court normally approves it, provided that *each* class of creditors has approved it and that the creditors will be better off under the plan than if the firm's assets were liquidated and distributed. The court may, under certain conditions, confirm a plan even if one or more classes of creditors vote against it. This is known as a *cram-down*.

The interests of the different classes of creditors do not always coincide. For example, junior creditors may threaten to slow the process as a way of extracting concessions from senior creditors. The senior creditors may take less than 100 cents on the dollar and give something to junior creditors in order to expedite the process and reach an agreement.

Chapter 11 proceedings are often successful, and the patient emerges fit and healthy. But in other cases cure proves impossible and the assets are liquidated. Sometimes the firm may emerge from Chapter 11 for a brief period before it is once again submerged by disaster and back in bankruptcy. For example, TWA came out of bankruptcy at the end of 1993 and was back again less than 2 years later, prompting jokes about "Chapter 22." TWA has plenty of company in this regard. In recent years, about 80% of large firms have emerged from bankruptcy proceedings with a second life, but nearly one-third of those reorganized firms met with failure within 5 years.[16] Among other notable "serial failures" are Planet Hollywood, Grand Union, Memorex, Continental Airlines, and Harvard Industries, which had the rare distinction of achieving a "Chapter 44."

The Choice between Liquidation and Reorganization

Here is an idealized view of the bankruptcy decision. Whenever a payment is due to creditors, management checks the value of the firm. If the firm is worth more than the promised payment, the firm pays up (if necessary, raising the cash by an issue of shares). If not, the equity is worthless, and the firm defaults on its debt and petitions for bankruptcy. If in the court's judgment the assets of the bankrupt firm can be put to better use elsewhere, the firm is liquidated and the proceeds are used to pay off the creditors. Otherwise, the creditors simply become the new owners and the firm continues to operate.

In practice, matters are rarely so simple. For example, we observe that firms often petition for bankruptcy even when the equity has a positive value. Moreover, the bankruptcy court may decide to keep the firm on life support even when the assets could be used more efficiently elsewhere. There are several reasons for this.

First, although the reorganized firm is legally a new entity, it is entitled to any tax-loss carry-forwards belonging to the old firm. If the firm is liquidated rather than reorganized, any tax-loss carry-forwards disappear. Thus there is an incentive to continue in operation even if assets are better used by another firm.

Second, if the firm's assets are sold off, it is easy to determine what is available to pay the creditors. However, when the company is reorganized, it needs to conserve cash as far as possible. Therefore, claimants are generally paid in a mixture of cash and securities. This makes it less easy to judge whether they have received their entitlement. For example, each bondholder may be offered $300 in cash and $700 in a new bond which pays no interest for the first 2 years and a low rate of interest thereafter. A bond of this kind in a company that is struggling to survive may not be worth much, but the bankruptcy court usually looks at the face value of the new bonds and may therefore regard the bondholders as paid in full.

---

[16] "The Firms That Can't Stop Failing," *The Economist,* September 7, 2002.

Senior creditors who know they are likely to get a raw deal in a reorganization are likely to press for a liquidation. Shareholders and junior creditors prefer a reorganization. They hope that the court will not interpret the pecking order too strictly and that they will receive some crumbs.

Third, although shareholders and junior creditors are at the bottom of the pecking order, they have a secret weapon: they can play for time. Bankruptcies of large companies often take several years before a plan is presented to the court and agreed to by each class of creditor. When they use delaying tactics, the junior claimants are betting on a turn of fortune that will rescue their investment. On the other hand, the senior creditors know that time is working against them, so they may be prepared to accept a smaller payoff as part of the price for getting a plan accepted. Also, prolonged bankruptcy cases are costly. (While their cases are extreme, we've seen that the Enron and Lehman bankruptcies each generated $1 billion or more in legal and administrative costs.) Senior claimants may see their money seeping into lawyers' pockets and therefore decide to settle quickly.

Fourth, while a reorganization plan is being drawn up, the company is allowed to buy goods on credit and borrow money. Postpetition creditors (those who extend credit to a firm already in bankruptcy proceedings) have priority over the old creditors, and their debt may even be secured by assets that are already mortgaged to existing debtholders. This also gives the prepetition creditors an incentive to settle quickly, before their claim on assets is diluted by the new debt.

Finally, profitable companies may file for Chapter 11 bankruptcy to protect themselves against "burdensome" suits. For example, in 1982 Manville Corporation was threatened by 16,000 damage suits alleging injury from asbestos. Manville filed for bankruptcy under Chapter 11, and the bankruptcy judge agreed to put the damage suits on hold until the company was reorganized. This took 6 years. Of course, legislators worry that these actions are contrary to the original intent of the bankruptcy acts.

The U.S. bankruptcy system is often described as debtor-friendly. In some other countries, the bankruptcy regime is designed to recover as much cash as possible for the lenders. While critics of Chapter 11 complain about the costs of saving businesses that are not worth saving, commentators elsewhere bemoan the fact that their bankruptcy laws are causing the breakup of potentially healthy businesses.

Appendix Questions

1. **Bankruptcy.** True or false?
   a. When a company becomes bankrupt, it is usually in the interests of the equityholders to seek a liquidation rather than a reorganization.
   b. A reorganization plan must be presented for approval by each class of creditor.
   c. The Internal Revenue Service has first claim on the company's assets in the event of bankruptcy.
   d. In a reorganization, creditors may be paid off with a mixture of cash and securities.
   e. When a company is liquidated, one of the most valuable assets to be sold is often the tax-loss carry-forward.

2. **Bankruptcy.** Explain why equity can sometimes have a positive value even when companies petition for bankruptcy.

CHAPTER 17

Payout Policy

LEARNING OBJECTIVES

After studying this chapter, you should be able to:

(1) Describe how dividends are paid and how corporations decide how much to pay.

(2) Explain how stock repurchases are used to distribute cash to investors.

(3) Explain why dividend increases and repurchases are good news for investors and why dividend cuts are bad news.

(4) Explain why payout policy would not affect shareholder value in perfect and efficient financial markets.

(5) Show how market imperfections, especially the different tax treatment of dividends and capital gains, can affect payout policy.

RELATED WEB SITES FOR THIS CHAPTER CAN BE FOUND AT WWW.MHHE.COM/BMM7E.

In 2010 Union Pacific paid out $600 million in dividends and used $1.2 billion to repurchase stock. How do companies decide on the payout to shareholders?

Shareholders invest in the corporation when they buy newly issued shares and when the corporation reinvests earnings on the shareholders' behalf. The shareholders do not usually demand a prompt cash return on this investment. Some long-established companies have never paid a cash dividend. Sooner or later, however, most corporations do pay out cash to their shareholders. They pay dividends, or they use cash to buy back previously issued shares.

How much should a corporation pay out in a given year? Should the payout come as dividends or share repurchases? The answers to these two questions are the corporation's *payout policy*.

We start the chapter with a discussion of how dividends are paid and how firms repurchase their stock. We explain why dividend increases usually convey good news to investors, and why dividend cuts convey bad news. Then we explain why payout policy should not affect shareholder wealth in an ideal world with perfect and efficient financial markets.

That leads us to the real-world complications that could favor one payout policy over another. Taxes are probably at the head of the list. Also, shareholders of mature, cash-cow firms often worry that managers will waste cash on empire-building and negative-NPV projects. In these cases a commitment to pay a generous cash dividend is reassuring.

17.1 How Corporations Pay Out Cash to Shareholders

Corporations pay out cash to their shareholders in two ways. They can pay a cash dividend or repurchase some outstanding shares. Figure 17.1 shows annual repurchases and dividends in the United States since 1980. You can see that stock repurchases were rare before the mid-1980s but have since become far more common. In 2009, some of the more active stock repurchasers included Walmart ($7.3 billion), IBM ($7.4 billion), and Microsoft ($8.2 billion). The repurchase champion, however, is ExxonMobil, which bought back more than $125 billion of its shares in the 5 years ending in 2009. In 2009, repurchases and dividends in the United States were just about equal, and together amounted to about 85% of total corporate earnings.

Most mature, profitable companies pay cash dividends. By contrast, growth companies typically pay small or no dividends. The no-dividend group includes household names such as Sun Microsystems, Oracle, Amazon, and Google. The no-dividend group also includes companies that used to pay dividends but have fallen on hard times and been forced to cut back dividends to conserve cash. An example is Ford Motor Company, which paid regular dividends for decades but cut its dividend to zero in 2006.

Paying Dividends

cash dividend
Payment of cash by the firm to its shareholders.

In May 2010, Union Pacific's board of directors met and decided to authorize a regular quarterly **cash dividend** of $.33 per share, an increase of $.06 from the previous year's quarterly dividend of $.27. The term *regular* indicated that the directors expected to maintain or increase the dividend in the future. Instead of increasing the regular dividend, they could have kept it at $.27 and authorized a *special* dividend. Investors realize that special dividends probably won't be repeated.

Some of Union Pacific's shareholders may have welcomed the cash, but others preferred to reinvest the dividend in the company. To help these investors, Union Pacific offered an automatic dividend reinvestment plan, or DRIP. If a shareholder belonged to this plan, his or her dividends were automatically used to buy additional shares.[1]

Who receives the Union Pacific dividend? That may seem an obvious question, but shares trade constantly, and the firm's records of who owns its shares are never fully

FIGURE 17.1 Dividends and stock repurchases in the United States, 1980–2008 (figures in $ billions).

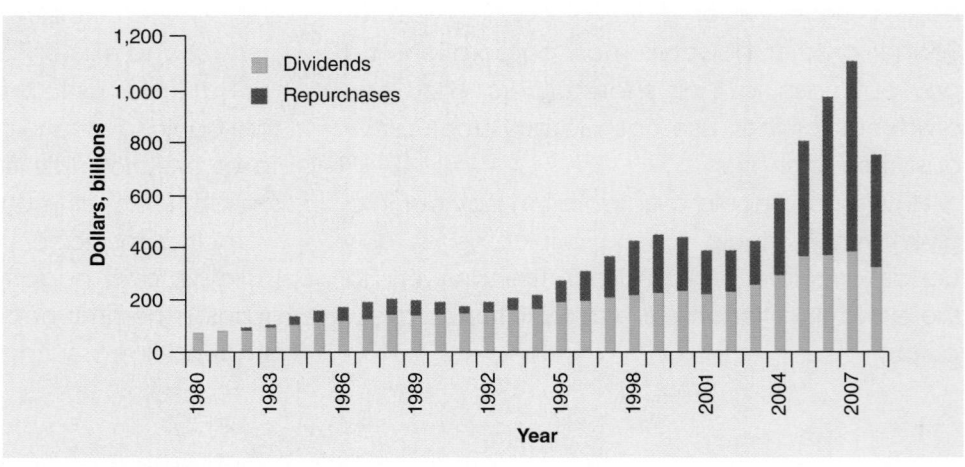

Source: Capital IQ Compustat, www.compustat.com.

---

[1] Often the new shares in an automatic dividend investment plan are issued at a small discount of around 5% from the market price; the firm offers this sweetener because it saves the underwriting costs of a regular share issue. Sometimes 10% or more of total dividends are reinvested under such plans.

FIGURE 17.2 The key dates for Union Pacific's quarterly dividend.

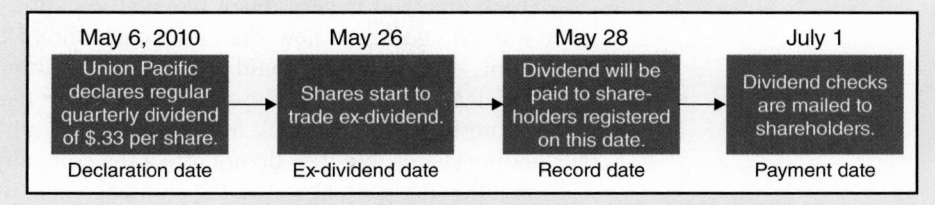

May 6, 2010	May 26	May 28	July 1
Union Pacific declares regular quarterly dividend of $.33 per share.	Shares start to trade ex-dividend.	Dividend will be paid to share-holders registered on this date.	Dividend checks are mailed to shareholders.
Declaration date	Ex-dividend date	Record date	Payment date

ex-dividend
Without dividend. Buyer of a stock after the ex-dividend date does not receive the most recently declared dividend.

up to date. So corporations have to specify a particular day's roster of shareholders who qualify to receive each dividend. Union Pacific announced that it would send a dividend check on July 1 (the *payment date*) to all shareholders recorded in its books on May 28 (the *record date*).

On May 26, two days before the record date, Union Pacific stock began to trade **ex-dividend.** Investors who bought shares on or after that date did not have their purchases registered by the record date and were not entitled to the dividend. Other things equal, a stock is worth less if you miss out on the dividend. So when a stock "goes ex-dividend," its price falls by about the amount of the dividend.

Figure 17.2 illustrates the sequence of the key dividend dates. This sequence is the same whenever companies pay a dividend (though of course the actual dates will differ).

Self-Test 17.1

Mick Milekin buys 100 shares of Junk Bombs, Inc., on Tuesday, June 2. The company has declared a dividend of $1 per share payable on June 30 to shareholders of record as of Wednesday, June 3. If the ex-dividend date is June 1, is Mick entitled to the dividend? When will the checks go out in the mail?

Limitations on Dividends

Suppose that an unscrupulous board decided to sell all the firm's assets and distribute the money as dividends. That would not leave anything in the kitty to pay the firm's debts.

State law helps to protect the firm's creditors against excessive dividend payments. For example, most states prohibit a company from paying dividends if doing so would make the company insolvent.[2] Also, companies are not allowed to pay a dividend if it cuts into legal capital. *Legal capital* is generally defined as the par value of the outstanding shares.[3]

Banks and other lenders may also demand dividend restrictions, particularly if they are worried about the borrower's creditworthiness. We mentioned that Ford eliminated its dividend in 2006. Ford had lost billions and had been forced to borrow heavily to finance its recovery plan. Its loan agreements prohibit dividends. Thus Ford's stockholders can forget about dividends until the company's health improves and its debt can be paid off or renegotiated.

stock dividends and splits
Distributions of additional shares to a firm's stockholders.

Stock Dividends and Stock Splits

Union Pacific's dividend was in cash, but companies sometimes declare **stock dividends.** For example, the firm could declare a stock dividend of 10%. In this case it would send each shareholder one additional share for each 10 that the shareholder owns.

---

[2] The statutes define insolvency in different ways. In some cases, it just means an inability to meet immediate obligations; in other cases, it means a deficiency of assets compared with all outstanding fixed liabilities.

[3] Where there is no par value, legal capital consists of part or all of the receipts from past share issues.

A stock dividend is very much like a **stock split.** In both cases the shareholder is given a fixed number of new shares for each one held. For example, in a two-for-one stock split, each investor would receive one additional share for each share already held. The investor ends up with two shares rather than one. A two-for-one stock split is therefore like a 100% stock dividend. Both result in a doubling of the number of outstanding shares, but they do not affect the company's assets, profits, or total value.[4]

More often than not, however, the announcement of a stock split does result in a rise in the market price of the stock, even though investors are aware that the company's business is not affected. Perhaps low-priced shares are particularly favored by investors, or maybe investors take the decision as a signal of management's confidence in the future.[5]

EXAMPLE 17.1   ▶   Stock Dividends and Splits

Amoeba Products has issued 2 million shares currently selling at $15 each. Thus investors place a total market value on Amoeba of $30 million. The company now declares a 50% stock dividend. This means that each shareholder will receive one new share for every two shares that are currently held. So the total number of Amoeba shares will increase from 2 million to 3 million. The company's assets are not changed by this paper transaction and are still worth $30 million. The value of each share after the stock dividend is therefore $30/3 = $10.

If Amoeba split its stock three for two, the effect would be the same.[6] In this case two shares would split into three. (Amoeba's motto is "Divide and conquer.") So each shareholder has 50% more shares with the same total value. Other things equal, share price must decline by a third.

17.2 Stock Repurchases

Another way for the firm to hand back cash to its stockholders is to repurchase some of its shares. For example, when Union Pacific announced its dividend increase in May 2010, it also announced plans to repurchase up to 32 million of its shares over the following 2 years. The company can keep these reacquired shares in its treasury and resell them if it needs money later. The shares can also be issued to managers who exercise stock options.

stock repurchase
Firm buys back stock from its shareholders.

There are four main ways to implement a **stock repurchase:**

1. *Open-market repurchase.* The firm announces that it plans to buy stock in the secondary market, just like any other investor. This is by far the most common

---

[4] Unusually high stock prices can make trading difficult for some individual investors who are accustomed to buying shares in round lots of 100 shares each. So a corporation with stock that is selling for, say, $240 per share could use a six-for-one split to pull the price down into a more convenient "trading range" of around $40. It seems that sometimes individual investors may favor stocks with low prices and that companies respond to this change in demand by splitting their stock. See M. Baker. R. Greenwood, and J. Wurgler, "Catering through Nominal Share Prices," *Journal of Finance* 64 (December 2009), pp. 2559–2590. Sometimes companies with very low stock prices use a *reverse split* to increase price per share. For example, a corporation with a share price of $4 could use a 1-for-10 reverse split (1 new share in exchange for every 10 old shares) to get stock price up to $40.

[5] See E. F. Fama, L. Fisher, M. Jensen, and R. Roll, "The Adjustment of Stock Prices to New Information," *International Economic Review* 10 (February 1969), pp. 1–21. For evidence that companies which split their stock have above-average earnings prospects, see P. Asquith, P. Healy, and K. Palepu, "Earnings and Stock Splits," *Accounting Review* 64 (July 1989), pp. 387–403.

[6] The distinction between stock dividends and stock splits is a technical one. A stock dividend is shown on the balance sheet as a transfer from retained earnings to par value and additional paid-in capital. A split is shown as a proportional reduction in the par value of each share. Neither affects the total book value of stockholders' equity.

method. There are limits on how many of its own shares a firm can purchase on a given day, so repurchases are spread out over several months or years.
2. *Tender offer.* The firm offers to buy back a stated number of shares at a fixed price. If enough shareholders accept the offer, the deal is done.
3. *Auction.* The firm states a range of prices at which it is prepared to repurchase. Shareholders submit offers declaring how many shares they are prepared to sell at each price, and the firm calculates the lowest price at which it can buy the desired number of shares.
4. *Direct negotiation.* The firm may negotiate repurchase of a block of shares from a major shareholder. The most notorious examples are *greenmail transactions,* in which the target of an attempted takeover buys out the hostile bidder. "Greenmail" means that the shares are repurchased at a generous price that makes the bidder happy to leave the target alone.

Why Repurchases Are Like Dividends

To see why share repurchase is similar to a dividend, look at panel A of Table 17.1, which shows the market value of Hewlard Pocket's assets and liabilities. Shareholders hold 100,000 shares worth in total $1 million, so the price per share equals $1 million/100,000 = $10. This is the price just before the current dividend is paid.

Pocket is proposing to pay a dividend of $1 a share. With 100,000 shares outstanding, that amounts to a total payout of $100,000. Panel B shows the effect of this dividend payment. The cash account is reduced by $100,000, and the market value of the firm's assets falls to $900,000. Since there are still 100,000 shares outstanding, share price falls to $9. Suppose that before the dividend payment you owned 1,000 shares of Pocket worth $10,000. After the payment you would have $1,000 in cash and 1,000 shares worth $9,000.

Rather than paying out $100,000 as a dividend, Pocket could use the cash to buy back 10,000 shares at $10 each. Panel C shows what happens. The firm's assets fall to $900,000, just as in panel B, but only 90,000 shares remain outstanding, so the price per share remains at $10. If you owned 1,000 shares before the repurchase, you would own 1% of the company. If you then sold 100 of your shares to Pocket, you would still own 1% of the company. Your sales would put $1,000 of cash in your wallet, and you

TABLE 17.1 Cash dividend versus share repurchase. Hewlard Pocket's market-value balance sheet.

Assets		Liabilities and Shareholders' Equity	
A. Original balance sheet			
Cash	$ 150,000	Debt	$ 0
Other assets	850,000	Equity	1,000,000
Value of firm	$1,000,000	Value of firm	$1,000,000
Shares outstanding = 100,000			
Price per share = $1,000,000/100,000 = $10			
B. After cash dividend of $1 per share			
Cash	$ 50,000	Debt	$ 0
Other assets	850,000	Equity	900,000
Value of firm	$ 900,000	Value of firm	$ 900,000
Shares outstanding = 100,000			
Price per share = $900,000/100,000 = $9			
C. After $100,000 stock repurchase program			
Cash	$ 50,000	Debt	$ 0
Other assets	850,000	Equity	900,000
Value of firm	$ 900,000	Value of firm	$ 900,000
Shares outstanding = 90,000			
Price per share = $900,000/90,000 = $10			

would keep 900 shares worth $9,000. Your position is exactly the same with the share repurchase (panel C of Table 17.1) as with the cash dividend (panel B): Shares worth $9,000 and cash of $1,000.

It's not surprising that a cash dividend and a share repurchase are equivalent transactions. In both cases the firm pays out cash, which goes into shareholders' wallets. The assets left in the company are the same in each case. The number of shares is reduced by repurchases, however, and the price per share is higher than it is when the cash is paid out as dividends.

Self-Test 17.2

What would Table 17.1 look like if the dividend changes to $1.50 per share and the share repurchase to $150,000?

Repurchases and Share Valuation

Now here is a question that often causes confusion. We stated in Chapter 7 that the value of a share of stock is equal to the discounted value of the stream of dividends paid on that stock. If companies also hand back cash to their shareholders in the form of repurchases, does our simple dividend discount model still hold? The answer is yes, but we need to explain why.

Think again about how you would value the stock of Hewlard Pocket. We'll suppose that it has just paid a dividend of $1 per share. The stock is ex-dividend. The next dividend is in year 1.[7] Pocket is expected to continue to pay annual dividends of $100,000 in perpetuity. Since there are 100,000 shares outstanding, this works out to a dividend of $1 a share. If the cost of equity is 11.1%, the discounted value of this dividend stream is $1/.111 = $9.

Pocket now announces that it will not pay a dividend in year 1 but will instead use the $100,000 it would have paid out to repurchase 10,000 shares at that time. From year 2 onward it will resume paying annual dividends of $100,000.[8] The new policy does not change the aggregate amount of cash going out to shareholders. Therefore, the one-time switch to share repurchase in year 1 should not affect share value. Let's check that the dividend discount model continues to give a present value of $9 a share.

After the company has repurchased the stock in year 1, the number of outstanding shares will fall to 90,000. Therefore, there is no dividend payment in year 1, but the dividend per share *from year 2 onward* will be $100,000/90,000 = $1.11. The present value of this perpetual stream *in year 1* is $1.11/.111 = $10, and its value *in year 0* is $10/1.11 = $9.[9]

So our dividend discount model still holds. The price of a share is the PV of future dividends *per share*. The only trick is to remember that share repurchases reduce the number of shares and increase future dividends per share. You can also calculate PV per share by first calculating the firm's overall market capitalization, which depends on the *total* cash paid out to both present and future shareholders, and then dividing by the number of shares currently outstanding.

---

[7] We assume annual dividends for simplicity. Most cash dividends are paid quarterly.

[8] Have we cheated by assuming a $100,000 dividend forever? No. The actual payout could be higher or lower, but it doesn't matter. You can check by asking what happens if Pocket performs unexpectedly well over the next year and is able to increase payout to $111,000. Construct a table like Table 17.1 to show that shareholders in year 1 are just as well off with $111,000 in repurchases as $111,000 of cash dividends. In fact, shareholders are indifferent between repurchases and cash dividends at any level of payout, at least in the simple examples that we're doing now. Some complications come later in the chapter.

[9] Since the price of the share in year 1 is $10, the cost of repurchasing 10,000 shares is $100,000. Everything checks.

17.3 How Do Corporations Decide How Much to Pay Out?

In 2004 a survey asked senior executives about their firms' dividend policies. Figure 17.3 summarizes the executives' responses. Three features stand out:

1. Managers are reluctant to make dividend changes that may have to be reversed, and they are willing to raise new financing if necessary to maintain payout.
2. Managers "smooth" dividends and hate to cut them back. Dividends tend to follow the growth in long-run, sustainable earnings. Transitory fluctuations in earnings rarely affect dividend payouts.
3. Managers focus more on dividend *changes* than on absolute levels. Thus paying a $2 dividend is an important financial decision if last year's dividend was $1, but it's no big deal if last year's dividend was $2.

Corporations that pay regular dividends sometimes act as though they have a *target payout ratio,* say 40% of earnings. A 40% target ratio does *not* imply that each year's dividends equal 40% of each year's earnings, however. Dividends in that case would be just as volatile as earnings. We know, on the contrary, that dividends are smoothed.

Think instead of the *target dividend* as a percentage of *expected* or *normal* earnings, not this year's actual earnings. For example, suppose that the financial manager forecasts average income of $5 per share over the next 2 or 3 years. If the target payout ratio is 40%, the target dividend is 40% of $5, or $2.

If the current dividend is less than the target, then the dividend is increased gradually toward the target. But what if the firm hits hard times and expected earnings fall, leaving the current dividend *higher* than the target dividend? In this case, the dividend would probably not be cut immediately, but just left alone. Financial managers don't cut regular dividends unless the cut is forced by heavy losses or dangerously high debt.

Financial managers do not have to choose between cash dividends and repurchases. They can do both. Large, mature corporations that pay cash dividends also repurchase regularly. Many smaller firms and growth firms pay no cash dividends but do repurchase, either regularly or sporadically. The number of firms that pay regular cash dividends but never repurchase is tiny.[10]

FIGURE 17.3 A survey of financial executives suggested that their firms were reluctant to cut the dividend and tried to maintain a smooth series of payments.

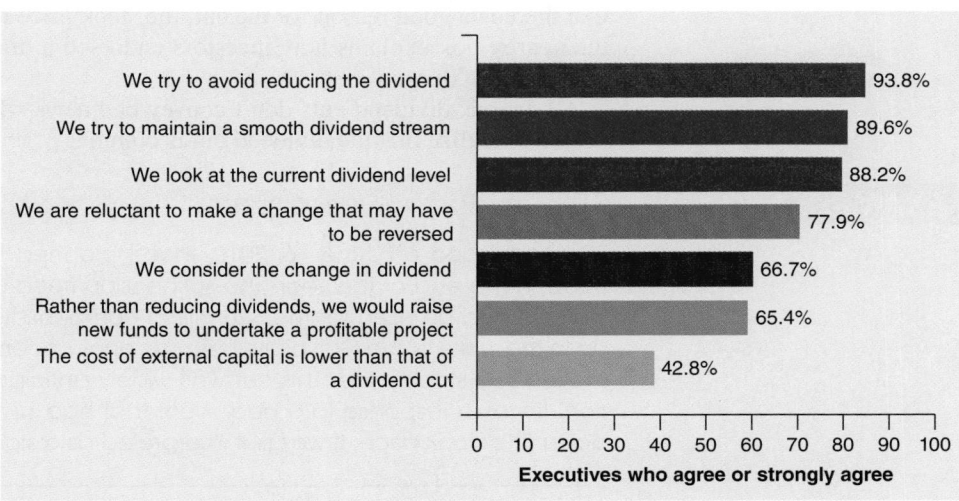

Source: A. Brav, J. R. Graham, C. R. Harvey, and R. Michaely, "Payout Policy in the 21st Century," *Journal of Financial Economics* 77 (September 2005), pp. 483–527. Used with permission of Elsevier Science via Copyright Clearance Center, Inc.

---

[10] Douglas Skinner examined over 7,000 firms and found only 141 that paid regular dividends but never repurchased. See his paper "The Evolving Relation between Earnings, Dividends and Stock Repurchases," *Journal of Financial Economics* 87 (March 2008), pp. 582–609.

Firms that do pay cash dividends stabilize the dividends. Cash dividends evolve smoothly, except in times of serious trouble. Repurchases are not smoothed in the same way. Therefore, it is not surprising to find that repurchases are far more volatile than dividends. They mushroom during boom times, as firms accumulate excess cash, but wither in recessions. Look back at Figure 17.1, and you will see that repurchases fell far more dramatically than dividends in the financial crisis of 2008.

The Information Content of Dividends and Repurchases

In some countries, you cannot rely on the information that companies provide. Secrecy and multilayered corporate organizations make financial statements next to meaningless. Some say that creative accounting makes the situation in the United States scarcely better.

If transparency is limited, dividends can provide clues about a company's true prospects. When a firm that reports good earnings also commits to a cash dividend, it is putting its money where its mouth is. Financial statements may be manipulated, but dividends require the firm to come up with cash; if the firm's cash flow cannot back up its dividend payout, it will ultimately have to reduce its investments or turn to investors for additional debt or equity financing. This can be costly. We can understand, therefore, why investors believe in the **information content of dividends.**

It is no surprise, therefore, to find that announcements of dividend increases are good news (stock price rises) and that dividend cuts are usually taken as bad news (stock price typically falls). For example, Healy and Palepu found that the announcement of a company's first dividend caused an immediate price increase of 4% on average.[11] Such announcements are obviously good news for investors. The news is good not because investors simply "like dividends." It is good because announcements of dividend increases send positive signals about future income. **Managers don't increase dividends unless they are confident that income will be high enough to cover the dividend with room to spare. A dividend increase conveys that confidence to investors. A dividend cut, on the other hand, conveys a *lack* of confidence.** Even investors who otherwise prefer low-payout policies might find that a cut in the dividend is unwelcome news about the firm's prospects.

There are exceptions. Not *all* dividend cuts are bad news; if investors are convinced that there is a good reason for the cut, the stock price may be unscathed. For example, the nearby box explains how investors endorsed a drastic dividend cut announced in 2009 by J.P. Morgan.

Of course, dividend cuts don't convey bad news when the news is already out and investors realize that the dividend cut is coming.

information content of dividends
Dividend increases send good news about future cash flow and earnings. Dividend cuts send bad news.

EXAMPLE 17.2 ▶   BP's Dividend Suspension

BP announced on June 16, 2010, that it planned to suspend dividends at least through the end of the year. The suspension freed up roughly $7.8 billion in cash, which could be used for the $20 billion compensation fund that BP agreed to set up in the wake of the Gulf oil spill. Yet the announcement of the dividend cut barely moved BP's stock price. This cut was widely anticipated, so it wasn't new information. It was a response to a bad event that had *already* happened and knocked down BP's stock price. It was not interpreted as a signal of *new* bad news about BP.

Announcements of share repurchase programs are also good news for investors. But repurchase programs may not be repeated, unlike dividend increases, which imply

[11] See P. Healy and K. Palepu, "Earnings Information Conveyed by Dividend Initiations and Omissions," *Journal of Financial Economics* 21 (1988), pp. 149–175.

Good News: J.P. Morgan Cuts Its Dividend to a Nickel

On February 23, 2009, J.P. Morgan cut its quarterly dividend from 38¢ to a nickel (5¢) per share. The cut was a surprise to investors, but the bank's share price *increased* by about 5%.

Usually dividend cuts or omissions are bad news, because investors infer trouble. Investors take the cut as a signal of a cash or earnings shortfall—and they are usually right. Managers know that cuts will be treated as bad news, so they usually put off cuts until enough bad news accumulates to force them to act. For example, General Motors, which lost $39 billion in 2007 and $31 billion in 2008, continued paying quarterly dividends of 25¢ per share until June 2008, when it cut its dividend to zero.

J.P. Morgan Chase, however, acted from a position of relative strength. It remained profitable when other large U.S. banks were announcing horrific losses. Its CEO James Dimon explained that the dividend cut would save $5 billion a year and prepare it for a worst-case recession. It would also "put the bank in a position to pay back more quickly the $25 billion that it took from the government under the Troubled Asset Relief Program." J.P. Morgan has said it was encouraged to take the money and didn't need it.

Thus investors interpreted the dividend cut as a signal of confidence, not of distress.

Source: R. Sidel and M. Rieker, "J.P. Morgan Makes 87% Cut in its Dividend to a Nickel," *The New York Times*, February 24, 2009, pp. C1, C3.

---

a longer-run commitment. Therefore, the information content of a repurchase program is usually less than the information content of dividends.[12]

Companies repurchase shares when they have accumulated more cash than they can invest profitably or when they undertake to substitute debt for equity. Shareholders are often relieved to see companies paying out the excess cash rather than frittering it away on unprofitable investments. Of course, investors would be less thrilled if their favorite growth company suddenly announced a repurchase program because its managers could not think of anything better to do with its cash.

17.4 The Payout Controversy

It seems clear that a change in payout may provide information about management's confidence in the firm, and so may affect the stock price. But this change in stock price would happen anyway as the information eventually seeps out through other channels. Can payout policy *itself* change the underlying value of the firm's common stock, or is it just a signal about underlying value?

This can be a difficult question to tackle, because payout decisions are often intertwined with other financing or investment decisions. Some firms pay low dividends because management is optimistic about the firm's future and wishes to retain earnings for expansion. In this case the payout decision is a by-product of the firm's capital budgeting decision. Another firm might finance capital expenditures largely by borrowing. This frees up cash that can be paid out to shareholders. In this case the payout decision is a by-product of the borrowing decision.

We wish to isolate payout policy from other problems of financial management. The precise question we should ask is, What is the effect of a change in dividend policy, *given the firm's capital budgeting and borrowing decisions?*

Suppose that the firm proposes to increase its dividend. The cash to finance that dividend increase has to come from somewhere. If we fix the firm's investment outlays and borrowing, there is only one possible source—an issue of stock or a reduction in stock repurchases. Suppose instead that the firm decides to reduce its dividend. In that case it would have extra cash. If investment outlays and borrowing are fixed, there is only one possible way that this cash can be used—to increase repurchases or reduce stock issues. **Thus dividend policy involves a trade-off between higher or lower cash dividends and the issue or repurchase of stock.**

---

[12] But repurchases do suggest that the firm's managers, who ought to know more than investors, believe that the company's stock is worth more than the market's current assessment. A study of open-market stock repurchase programs found that stock prices increased by 2% on average when the programs were announced. See R. Comment and G. Jarrell, "The Relative Signaling Power of Dutch-Auction and Fixed Price Self-Tender Offers and Open Market Share Repurchases," *Journal of Finance* 46 (September 1991), pp. 1243–1271.

One nice feature of economics is that it can accommodate not just two but three opposing points of view. And so it is with payout policy. On one side there is a group that believes high dividends increase value. On the other side there is a group that believes high dividends bring high taxes and therefore reduce firm value. And in the center there is a middle-of-the-road party that believes payout policy makes no difference. Let's start with the middle-of-the-roaders.

Why Dividends Are Irrelevant in Perfect and Efficient Capital Markets

Franco Modigliani and Merton Miller (MM), who proved that financing doesn't matter in perfect financial markets, founded the middle-of-the-road party when they also proved that dividend policy doesn't matter in perfect financial markets.[13] We have already seen the common sense of MM's argument in Table 17.1, which shows that investors should not care whether a firm distributes cash by dividends or share repurchases.

MM would admit that payout policy *may* matter, not just because of the information content of dividends and repurchases but also because of taxes and market imperfections. But first we take a more thorough look at **MM's dividend-irrelevance proposition.**

MM's dividend-irrelevance proposition
Under ideal conditions, the value of the firm is unaffected by dividend policy.

We can illustrate MM's views about payout policy by considering the Pickwick Paper Company, which had set aside $100 million in cash to construct a new paper mill. But Pickwick's directors now propose to use the $100 million to increase the dividend payment. If Pickwick is to continue to build its new mill, that cash needs to be replaced. If the borrowing is fixed, the money must come from the sale of new shares. The combination of the dividend payment and the new issue of shares leaves Pickwick and its shareholders in exactly the same position that they started from. All that has happened is that Pickwick has put an extra $100 million in investors' pockets (the dividend payment) and then taken it out again (the share issue). In other words, Pickwick is simply recycling cash. To suggest that this makes investors better off is like advising the cook to cool the kitchen by leaving the refrigerator door open.

After Pickwick pays the additional dividend and replaces the cash by selling new shares, the company value is unchanged. The old shareholders now have an extra $100 million of cash in their pockets, but they have given up a stake in the firm to those investors who buy the newly issued shares. The new stockholders are putting up $100 million and therefore will demand to receive shares *worth* $100 million. Since the total value of the company is the same, the value of the old stockholders' stake in the company falls by this $100 million. Thus the extra dividend that the old stockholders receive just offsets the loss in the value of the shares that they hold.

Does it make any difference to the old stockholders that they receive an extra dividend payment plus an offsetting capital loss? It might if that were the only way they could get their hands on the cash. But as long as there are efficient capital markets, they can raise cash by selling shares. Thus Pickwick's old shareholders can "cash in" either by persuading the management to pay a higher dividend or by selling some of their shares. In either case there will be the same transfer of value from the old to the new stockholders. Because **investors do not need dividends to convert their shares to cash, they will not pay higher prices for firms with higher dividend payouts. In other words, payout policy will have no impact on the value of the firm. This is MM's argument.**

The example of the Pickwick Paper Company showed that the firm cannot make shareholders better off simply by increasing the proportion of earnings paid out as dividends. But the same argument also works in reverse: If investment and borrowing are held constant, any *reduction* in dividends must be balanced by a *purchase* of stock. For

[13] M. H. Miller and F. Modigliani, "Dividend Policy, Growth and the Valuation of Shares," *Journal of Business* 34 (October 1961), pp. 411–433.

example, suppose that Old Curiosity Shops has $100 million surplus cash which it had been proposing to pay out to shareholders as a dividend. If Old Curiosity now decides not to pay this dividend, then the surplus cash can be used to buy back some of the company's shares. The shareholders miss out on $100 million of dividend payments but they receive $100 million from the sale to the company of part of their shareholdings.

Thus MM's irrelevance argument holds both for increases in dividends and for reductions. **As these examples illustrate, payout policy is a trade-off between cash dividends and the issue or repurchase of common stock. In a perfect capital market, the payout decision would have no impact on firm value.**

These examples may seem artificial at first, for we do not observe firms scheduling a stock issue with every dividend payment. But there are many firms that pay dividends and also issue stock from time to time. They could avoid the stock issues by paying lower dividends and retaining more funds in the firm. Many other firms use unwanted cash to repurchase shares. They could instead use the cash to increase the dividend.

Of course our examples of dividend irrelevance have ignored taxes, issue costs, and a variety of other real-world complications. We will turn to these intricacies shortly, but before we do, we note that the crucial assumption in our proof is that the sale or purchase of shares occurs at a fair price. The shares that Pickwick sells to raise $100,000 must actually be worth $100,000; those that Old Curiosity buys for $100,000 must also be worth that figure. In other words, dividend irrelevance assumes efficient capital markets.

If you'd like another example, look back at Table 17.1 and the comparison between the share prices of Hewlard Pocket after paying a cash dividend and after spending the same amount of money to repurchase shares. Pocket's shareholders were as well off with one payout policy as the other. Notice the trade-off, however: Lower cash dividends enable higher repurchases. (We were implicitly holding investment and borrowing policy constant.) We could run the trade-off the other way, too, with higher dividends offset by share issues. Again shareholders would not care.

EXAMPLE 17.3 ▶ Dividend Irrelevance

The columns labeled "Old Dividend Plan" in Table 17.2 show that Consolidated Pasta is currently expected to pay annual dividends of $10 a share in perpetuity. Shareholders expect a 10% rate of return from Consolidated stock, and therefore the value of each share is

$$PV = \frac{10}{1.10} + \frac{10}{(1.10)^2} + \frac{10}{(1.10)^3} + \cdots = \frac{10}{.10} = \$100$$

Consolidated has issued 1 million shares. So the total forecast dividend payment in each year is 1 million × $10 = $10 million, and the total value of Consolidated Pasta equity is 1 million × $100 = $100 million. The president, Al Dente, has read that the value of a share depends on the dividends it pays. That suggests an

---

TABLE 17.2 Consolidated Pasta is currently expected to pay a dividend of $10 million in perpetuity. However, the president is proposing to pay a one-time bumper dividend of $20 million in year 1. To replace the lost cash, the firm will need to issue more shares, and the dividends that will need to be diverted to the new shareholders will exactly offset the effect of the higher dividend in year 1.

	Old Dividend Plan		Revised Dividend Plan	
	Year 1	**Year 2 On**	**Year 1**	**Year 2 On**
Total dividend payments ($ million)	10	10	20	10
Total dividends paid to old shareholders ($ million)	10	10	20	9
Total dividends paid to new shareholders ($ million)	—	—	—	1

Note: New shareholders are putting up $10 million of cash at the end of year 1. Since they require a return of 10%, the total dividends paid to the new shares (starting in year 2) must be 10% of $10 million, or $1 million.

easy way to keep shareholders happy—increase next year's dividend to $20 per share. That way, he reasons, share price should rise by the present value of the increase in the first-year dividend to a new value of

$$PV = \frac{20}{1.10} + \frac{10}{(1.10)^2} + \frac{10}{(1.10)^3} + \cdots = \frac{10}{1.10} + \frac{10}{.10} = \$109.91$$

The president's heart is obviously in the right place. Unfortunately, his head isn't. Let's see why.

Consolidated is proposing to pay out an extra $10 million in dividends. It can't do that *and* earn the same profits in the future, unless it also replaces the lost cash by an issue of shares. The new shareholders who provide this cash will require a return of 10% on their investment. So Consolidated will need to pay $1 million a year of dividends to the new shareholders ($1 million/$10 million = .10, or 10%). This is shown in the last line of Table 17.2.

As long as the company replaces the extra cash it pays out, it will continue to earn the same profits and to pay out $10 million of dividends each year from year 2. However, $1 million of this total will be needed to satisfy the new shareholders, leaving only $9 million (or $9 a share) for the original shareholders. Now recalculate the value of the original shares under the revised dividend plan:

$$PV = \frac{20}{1.10} + \frac{9}{(1.10)^2} + \frac{9}{(1.10)^3} + \cdots = \frac{11}{1.10} + \frac{9}{.10} = \$100$$

The value of the shares is unchanged. The extra cash dividend in year 1 is exactly offset by the reduction of dividends per share in later years. This reduction is necessary because some of the money paid out as dividends in later years is diverted to the new shareholders.[14]

The Assumptions behind Dividend Irrelevance

Many stockholders and businesspeople find it difficult to accept the suggestion that dividend policy is irrelevant. When faced with MM's argument, they often reply that dividends are cash in hand while capital gains are at best in the bush. It may be true, they say, that the recipient of an extra cash dividend forgoes an equal capital gain, but if the dividend is safe and the capital gain is risky, isn't the stockholder ahead?

It's correct that dividends are more predictable than capital gains. Managers can stabilize dividends but they cannot control stock price. From this it seems a small step to conclude that increased dividends make the firm less risky.[15] But the important point is, once again, that as long as investment policy and borrowing are held constant, a firm's *overall* cash flows are the same regardless of payout policy. The risks borne by *all* the firm's stockholders are likewise fixed by its investment and borrowing policies and unaffected by dividend policy.

If we really believed that existing stockholders are better off by trading a risky asset for cash, then we would also have to argue that the new stockholders—those who trade cash for the newly issued shares—are worse off. But this doesn't make sense: The new

---

[14] Notice that at the end of year 1, when the new shareholders purchase their shares, the dividend per share they can look forward to receiving will be $9; since this dividend is expected to be a perpetuity, the share price at that time will be $9/.10 = $90. So the new shareholders will receive $10,000,000/$90 = 111,111 shares. Consistent with Table 17.2, the new shareholders therefore will receive total dividend payments of 111,111 × $9 = $1 million and the old shareholders will receive total dividend payments of 1 million × $9 = $9 million. Notice also that after the extra $10 million dividend is paid in year 1, the share price falls to $90, and the value of the shares held by the original shareholders falls by exactly $10 million to $90 million.

[15] In that case one might also argue that interest payments are even more predictable, so a company's risk would be reduced by increasing the proportion of profits paid out as interest. How would you respond to that suggestion?

stockholders are bearing risk, but they are getting paid for it. They are willing to buy because the new shares are priced to offer an expected return that compensates for the risk.

MM's argument for the irrelevance of dividend policy does not assume a world of certainty; it assumes an efficient capital market. Market efficiency means that the transfers of ownership created by shifts in dividend policy are carried out on fair terms. And since the *overall* value of (old and new) stockholders' equity is unaffected, nobody gains or loses.

17.5 Why Dividends May Increase Value

MM's conclusions follow from their assumptions of perfect and efficient capital markets. However, nobody claims their model is an exact description of the so-called real world. Thus the impact of payout policy finally boils down to arguments about imperfections and inefficiencies.

Those who believe that dividends are good argue that some investors have a natural preference for high-payout stocks. For example, some financial institutions are legally restricted from holding stocks lacking established dividend records. Trusts and endowment funds may prefer high-dividend stocks because dividends are regarded as spendable "income," whereas capital gains are "additions to principal," which may not be spent.

In addition, there is a natural clientele of investors, including the elderly, who look to their stock portfolios for a steady source of cash to live on. In principle this cash can be generated from stocks paying no dividends at all; the investors can just sell off a small fraction of their holdings from time to time. But that can be inconvenient and lead to heavy transaction costs.

Behavioral psychology may also help to explain why some investors prefer to receive regular dividends rather than sell small amounts of stock. We are all liable to succumb to temptation. Some of us may hanker after fattening foods, while others may be dying for a drink. We could seek to control these cravings by willpower, but that can be a painful struggle. Instead, it may be easier to set simple rules for ourselves ("cut out chocolate," or "wine only with meals"). In just the same way, we may welcome the self-discipline that comes from limiting our spending to dividend income.

All this may well be true, but it does not follow that you can increase the value of *your* firm by increasing dividend payout. Smart managers already have recognized that there is a clientele of investors who would be prepared to pay a premium for high-payout stocks. **There are natural clienteles for high-payout stocks, but it does not follow that any particular firm can benefit by increasing its dividends. The high-dividend clienteles already have plenty of high-dividend stocks to choose from.**

Suppose that the CEO of a software company announces at a press conference a plan to enter the market for mint toothpaste. When you ask why, the CEO points out that millions of people buy mint toothpaste. You would doubt the CEO's business sanity. So why should you believe that because there is a clientele of investors who like high payouts, your company can increase value by manufacturing a high payout? That clientele was probably satisfied long ago.

Perhaps the most persuasive argument in favor of a high-payout policy is that it prevents managers from wasting funds. Suppose a company has plenty of cash but few profitable investment opportunities. Shareholders may fear that the money will be plowed back into building a larger empire rather than a more profitable one. In such cases, generous dividends or share repurchases deprive the managers of excess cash and encourage a more careful, value-oriented investment policy.

The nearby box describes how Microsoft announced the largest cash distribution in corporate history. By 2004, the company's investment opportunities had diminished, and investors were, therefore, happy to see Microsoft distribute its cash mountain.

Microsoft's Payout Bonanza

By 2004 Microsoft had amassed a $61 billion pile of cash. The company's operations were throwing off a further $15 billion of cash each year, far in excess of the company's opportunities for new profitable investments. So, unless Microsoft took some strong action, it looked as if its cash mountain could only continue to grow.

Microsoft's solution was to announce the largest cash distribution in corporate history, involving a total payout of $75 billion over 4 years. The company doubled its regular dividend to about $3.5 billion a year. In addition, the company proposed a one-off special dividend of $32 billion. Finally, up to $30 billion of cash was to be used to buy back stock over a period of 4 years.

The timing of Microsoft's dividend payouts was apparently motivated by taxes. The top tax rate on qualifying dividends was cut from 39.6% to 15% in 2003.

Self-Test 17.3

The Altria Group pays a generous cash dividend. Suppose an investor in Altria does not need a regular income. What could she do? If there were no trading costs, would she have any reason to care about Altria's payout policy? What if there is a brokerage fee on the purchase of new shares? What if Altria has a dividend reinvestment plan that allows the investor to buy shares at a 5% discount?

17.6 Why Dividends May Reduce Value

The low-dividend creed is simple. Companies can convert dividends into capital gains by shifting their dividend policy. If dividends are taxed more heavily than capital gains, such financial alchemy should be welcomed by any taxpaying investor. Firms should pay the lowest cash dividend they can get away with. Surplus cash should be used to repurchase shares.

Table 17.3 illustrates this. It assumes that dividends are taxed at a rate of 40% but that capital gains are taxed at only 20%. The stocks of firms A and B are equally risky, and investors demand an expected *after-tax* rate of return of 10% on each. Investors expect A to be worth $112.50 per share next year. The share price of B is expected to be only $102.50, but a $10 dividend is also forecast, so the total pretax payoff is the same, $112.50.

Both stocks offer the same pretax dollar payoff. Yet B's stock sells for less than A's. The reason is obvious: Investors are willing to pay more for stock A because its return comes in the form of low-taxed capital gains. After tax, both stocks offer the same 10% expected return despite the fact that B's *pretax* return is higher.

Suppose the management of firm B eliminates the $10 dividend and uses the cash to repurchase stock instead. We saw earlier that a stock repurchase is equivalent to a cash dividend, but now we need to recognize that it is treated differently by the tax

TABLE 17.3 Effects of a shift in dividend policy when dividends are taxed more heavily than capital gains. The high-payout stock (firm B) must sell at a lower price in order to provide the same after-tax return.

	Firm A	Firm B
Next year's price	$112.50	$102.50
Dividend	$ 0	$ 10.00
Total *pretax* payoff	$112.50	$112.50
Today's stock price	$100	$ 97.78
Capital gain	$ 12.50	$ 4.72
Before-tax rate of return (%)	$\frac{12.5}{100} = .125 = 12.5\%$	$\frac{14.72}{97.78} = .1505 = 15.05\%$
Tax on dividend at 40%	$0	.40 × $10 = $4.00
Tax on capital gain at 20%	.20 × $12.50 = $2.50	.20 × $4.72 = $.94
Total after-tax income (dividends plus capital gains less taxes)	(0 + 12.50) − 2.50 = $10.00	(10 + 4.72) − (4.00 + .94) = $9.78
After-tax rate of return (%)	$\frac{10}{100} = .10 = 10\%$	$\frac{9.78}{97.78} = .10 = 10\%$

authorities. Stockholders who sell shares back to their firm pay tax only on any capital gains realized in the sale. By substituting a repurchase for a dividend, B's new policy would reduce the taxes paid by stockholders, and its stock price should rise.[16]

Self-Test 17.4

Look again at Table 17.3. What would happen to the price and pretax rate of return on stock B if the tax on capital gains were eliminated?

Taxation of Dividends and Capital Gains under Current Tax Law

If dividends are taxed more heavily than capital gains, why should any firm ever pay a cash dividend? If cash is to be distributed to stockholders, isn't share repurchase the best channel for doing so?

In the United States, the case for low dividends was strongest before 1986. The top rate of tax on dividends was then 50%, while realized capital gains were taxed at 20%. However, the top rates of tax on both dividends and capital gains were later reduced to 15%, minimizing the tax advantages of repurchases over dividends. Late in 2010, Congress agreed to extend these rates through 2012, so at least for the immediate future, the tax case for low dividends has been weakened.

There is, however, one way that tax law still favors capital gains. Taxes on dividends have to be paid immediately, but taxes on capital gains can be deferred until shares are sold and the capital gains are realized. Stockholders can choose when to sell their shares and thus when to pay the capital gains tax.[17] The longer they wait, the less the present value of the capital gains tax liability.[18] Thus the *effective* capital gains tax rate can be less than the statutory rate.

The distinction between dividends and capital gains is less important for pension funds, endowments, and some other financial institutions that operate free of all taxes and therefore have no reason to prefer capital gains to dividends or vice versa. Only corporations have a tax reason to *prefer* dividends. They pay corporate income tax on only 30% of any dividends received.[19] Thus the effective tax rate on dividends received by large corporations is 30% of 35% (the marginal rate of corporate income tax), or 10.5%. But they have to pay a 35% tax on the full amount of any capital gain.

The implications of these tax rules for payout policy are pretty simple. Capital gains have advantages to many investors, but they are far less advantageous than they were 30 or 40 years ago. Consequently, it is less easy today to make convincing arguments in favor of one kind of payout rather than another.

---

[16] The tax authorities have rules intended to prevent tax avoidance by substitution of repurchases for dividends. These rules are not applied to public corporations. But a private corporation that eliminates dividends and repurchases shares on a regular basis may find the repurchases reclassified as dividends for tax purposes.

[17] If the stock is willed to your heirs, capital gains escape taxation altogether.

[18] Suppose the discount rate is 6%, and an investor in a 15% capital gains tax bracket has a $100 capital gain. If the stock is sold today, the capital gains tax will be $15. If sale is deferred 1 year, the tax due on that $100 gain still will be $15, but by virtue of delaying the sale for a year, the present value of the tax falls to $15/1.06 = $14.15. The effective tax rate falls to 14.15%. The longer the sale is deferred, the lower the effective tax rate.

[19] The percentage of dividend income on which tax is paid depends on the firm's ownership share in the company paying the dividend. If the share is less than 20%, taxes are paid on 30% of dividends received.

SUMMARY

How are dividends paid, and how do companies decide how much to pay? *(LO1)*

Dividends come in many forms. The most common is the regular **cash dividend,** but sometimes companies pay a special cash dividend, and sometimes they pay a **stock dividend.** A firm is not free to pay dividends at will. For example, it may have accepted restrictions on dividends as a condition for borrowing money.

Dividends do not go up and down with every change in the firm's earnings. Instead, managers aim for smooth dividends and increase dividends gradually as earnings grow.

How are repurchases used to distribute cash to shareholders? *(LO2)*

Corporations also distribute cash by repurchasing shares. **Stock repurchases** have grown rapidly in recent years, but they do not replace dividends. Mature firms that pay dividends also repurchase shares. On the other hand, thousands of U.S. corporations pay no dividends at all. When they pay out cash, they do so exclusively through repurchases.

Why are dividend increases and repurchases usually good news for investors? Why are dividend cuts bad news? *(LO3)*

Managers do not increase dividends unless they are confident that the firm will generate enough earnings to cover the payout. Announcement of a dividend conveys the managers' confidence to investors. Dividend cuts convey lack of confidence. Managers generally avoid them unless their firms are in trouble. This **information content of dividends** is the main reason that stock prices respond to dividend changes.

Repurchases are usually also good news. For example, announcement of a repurchase program can reveal managers' view that their company's stock is a "good buy" at the current price.

Cash payouts by dividends and repurchases can also reassure investors who worry that managers might otherwise spend the money on empire-building and negative-NPV projects.

Why would payout policy not affect firm value in an ideal world? *(LO4)*

If we hold the company's investment policy and capital structure constant, then payout policy is a trade-off between cash dividends and the issue or repurchase of common stock. In an ideally simple and perfect world, the choice would have no effect on market value. An increased cash dividend would require more shares issued or fewer shares repurchased. The increased cash in shareholder's wallets would be exactly offset by a lower share price. This is the **MM dividend-irrelevance proposition.**

How might differences in the tax treatment of dividends and capital gains affect payout policy? *(LO5)*

In the United States, individual investors currently pay tax on dividend income at a top rate of 15%. The top capital gains rate is also 15%, but the investor pays no tax on capital gains until his or her shares are actually sold. The longer the wait before the sale, the lower the present value of the tax. Thus capital gains have a tax advantage for investors. The advantage was much greater in the 1970s and early 1980s, when the top tax rate on dividends was 50% and the top rate on capital gains only 20%.

If dividend income is taxed more heavily than capital gains, investors should demand a higher pretax rate of return on high-dividend stocks. Instead of paying high dividends, corporations should shift to repurchases.

QUESTIONS

QUIZ

1. **Dividend sequence.** Cash Cow International paid a regular quarterly dividend of $.075 a share. *(LO1)*

    a. Connect each of the following dates to the correct term:

May 7	Record date
June 6	Payment date
June 7	Ex-dividend date
June 11	Last with-dividend date
July 2	Declaration date

   b. On one of these dates the stock price is likely to fall by about the amount of the dividend. Why?

   c. The stock price in early January was $27. What was the prospective dividend yield?

   d. The annual earnings per share were forecast at around $1.90. What was the percentage payout ratio?

2. **Splits and Dividends.** Shares in Raven Products are selling for $80 per share. There are 1 million shares outstanding. What will be the share price in each of the following situations? Ignore taxes. *(LO1)*

   a. The stock splits five for four.

   b. The company pays a 25% stock dividend.

   c. The company repurchases 100,000 shares.

3. **Institutional Background.** True or false? If false, correct the statement. *(LO1)*

   a. A corporation cannot pay a dividend if its legal capital is impaired or if it is insolvent.

   b. There is no important difference between a regular and a special dividend.

   c. The effective tax rate on capital gains can be less than the stated rate.

   d. Corporations settle on a target payout ratio and in every year pay out that fraction of the year's earnings.

   e. Managers and investors are more concerned with dividend changes than dividend levels.

   f. Future stock price will be higher when a corporation distributes cash by repurchases rather than cash dividends.

4. **Dividend Irrelevance.** You own 2,000 shares of Patriot Corporation, which is about to double its dividend from $.75 to $1.50 per share. You do not need the extra dividend income, but you don't want to sell out. What would you do to offset the dividend increase? *(LO4)*

5. **Dividend Policy.** Big Bend Tubing's dividend was $2.20 last year. Big Bend's target payout ratio is 50%. This year's earnings per share are $5. But Pablo Donoso, the CFO, worries about higher raw-material costs and forecasts average future earnings of only $4 per share over the next 3 years. Should Mr. Donoso cut or increase this year's dividend? How does your answer change if forecast average earnings are $3, $5, or $7? *(LO1)*

6. **Information Content of Dividends.** Why are dividend increases typically good news for investors and dividend cuts bad news? Explain briefly. *(LO3)*

7. **Dividends versus Repurchases.** What is the tax reason for *not* paying generous cash dividends? *(LO5)*

PRACTICE PROBLEMS

8. **DRIPs.** A firm considers initiating an aggressive dividend reinvestment plan (DRIP) in which it allows its investors to use dividends to buy shares at a discount of 40% from current market value. The firm's financial manager argues that the policy will benefit shareholders by giving them the opportunity to buy additional shares at a deep discount and will benefit the firm by providing a source of cash. Is the manager correct? *(LO4)*

9. **Cash Dividends.** The stock of Payout Corp. will go ex-dividend tomorrow. The dividend will be $0.50 per share, and there are 20,000 shares of stock outstanding. The market-value balance sheet for Payout is shown on the following table. *(LO1)*

   a. What price is Payout stock selling for today?

   b. What price will it sell for tomorrow? Ignore taxes.

Assets		Liabilities and Equity	
Cash	$100,000	Equity	$1,000,000
Fixed assets	900,000		

10. **Repurchases.** Now suppose that Payout from Practice Problem 9 announces its intention to repurchase $10,000 worth of stock instead of paying out the dividend. *(LO2)*

   a. What effect will the repurchase have on an investor who currently holds 100 shares and sells 1 of those shares back to the company in the repurchase?

   b. Compare the effects of the repurchase to the effects of the cash dividend that you worked out in Problem 9.

11. **Stock Dividend.** Now suppose that Payout again changes its mind and decides to issue a 1% stock dividend instead of either issuing the cash dividend or repurchasing 1% of the outstanding stock. How would this action affect a shareholder who owns 100 shares of stock? Compare with your answers to Practice Problems 9 and 10. *(LO1)*

12. **Dividend Irrelevance.** Suppose Al Dente from Example 17.3 changes his mind and cuts out Consolidated's year-1 dividend entirely, instead spending $10 million to buy back stock. Are shareholders any better or worse off than if Consolidated had paid out $10 million as cash dividends? *(Hints:* How many shares will be repurchased? The purchase price at year 1 will be $110.) *(LO4)*

13. **Information.** Which of the following newspaper headlines would have the greatest positive impact on stock price? Explain. *(LO3)*

   a. "Growler Corporation announces a $1 increase in its regular dividend."

   b. "Growler Corporation announces a $1 special dividend."

   c. "Growler Corporation wins lawsuit and collects cash amounting to $1 per Growler share. Growler plans to use the cash in a stock buyback program."

14. **Stock Dividends and Splits.** Suppose that you own 1,000 shares of Nocash Corp. and the company is about to pay a 25% stock dividend. The stock currently sells at $100 per share. *(LO1)*

   a. What will be the number of shares that you hold and the total value of your equity position after the dividend is paid?

   b. What will happen to the number of shares that you hold and the value of your equity position if the firm splits five for four instead of paying the stock dividend?

15. **Dividend Policy.** In 2011, Arborio Farms earned $3.60 per share and paid a cash dividend of $1.20 per share, exactly in line with its target payout ratio of 33%. Arborio's earnings per share in the next 6 years were $3.30 in 2012, $3.60 in 2013, $4.00 in 2014, $4.68 in 2015, $4.00 in 2016, and $4.05 in 2017. Make a prediction of Arborio's dividends per share in these years. You can make additional assumptions if that is helpful, but make sure your prediction is reasonable. *(LO1)*

16. **Dividends and Taxes.** Good Values, Inc., is all-equity-financed. The total market value of the firm currently is $100,000, and there are 2,000 shares outstanding. Ignore taxes. *(LO1)*

   a. The firm has declared a $5 per share dividend. The stock will go ex-dividend tomorrow. At what price will the stock sell today? Tomorrow?

   b. Now assume that the tax rate on dividend income is 30%, and the tax rate on capital gains is zero. At what price will the stock sell, taking account of the taxation of dividends?

17. **Repurchases and Taxes.** Now suppose that instead of paying a dividend Good Values (from the previous problem) plans to repurchase $10,000 worth of stock. *(LO5)*

   a. What will be the stock price before and after the repurchase?

   b. Suppose an investor who holds 200 shares sells 20 of her shares back to the firm. If there are no taxes on dividends or capital gains, show that she should be indifferent between the repurchase and the dividend.

   c. Show that if dividends are taxed at 30% and capital gains are not taxed, the value of the firm is higher if it pursues the share repurchase instead of the dividend.

18. **Dividends and Taxes.** Investors require an after-tax rate of return of 10% on their stock investments. Assume that the tax rate on dividends is 30% while capital gains escape taxation. A firm

will pay a $2 per share dividend 1 year from now, after which it is expected to sell at a price of $20. *(LO5)*

a. Find the current price of the stock.

b. Find the expected before-tax rate of return for a 1-year holding period.

c. Now suppose that the dividend will be $3 per share. If the expected after-tax rate of return is still 10%, and investors still expect the stock to sell at $20 in 1 year, at what price must the stock now sell?

d. What is the before-tax rate of return? Why is it now higher than in part (b)?

19. **Dividends and Taxes.** The expected pretax return on three stocks is divided between dividends and capital gains in the following way: *(LO5)*

Stock	Expected Dividend	Expected Capital Gain
A	$ 0	$10
B	5	5
C	10	0

a. If each stock is priced at $100, what are the expected net returns on each stock to (i) a pension fund that does not pay taxes, (ii) a corporation paying tax at 35%, and (iii) an individual with an effective tax rate of 15% on dividends and 10% on capital gains?

b. Suppose that investors pay 50% tax on dividends and 20% tax on capital gains. If stocks are priced to yield an 8% return *after tax,* what would A, B, and C each sell for? Assume the expected dividend is a level perpetuity.

20. **Signaling.** It is well documented that stock prices tend to rise when firms announce an increase in their dividend payouts. How then can it be said that dividend policy is irrelevant? *(LO3)*

21. **Dividend Irrelevance.** Respond to the following two statements. *(LO4)*

a. "MM say that investors are equally happy with a dollar of dividends and a dollar of capital gains. That's crazy. Everyone knows that dividends are stable and capital gains risky. I'll take the dividend any day."

b. "Safer companies tend to pay more generous dividends. Therefore a company can reduce the risk of its shares by increasing dividend payout."

22. **Dividends versus Repurchases.** Prowler Corporation wants to increase its debt ratio without changing its operations or capital investment outlays. Obviously Prowler will have to increase borrowing, but how should it reduce equity? What would you recommend? *(LO5)*

CHALLENGE PROBLEMS

23. **Dividends versus Repurchases.** Big Industries has the following market-value balance sheet. The stock currently sells for $20 a share, and there are 1,000 shares outstanding. The firm will either pay a $1 per share dividend or repurchase $1,000 worth of stock. Ignore taxes. *(LO4)*

Assets		Liabilities and Equity	
Cash	$ 2,000	Debt	$10,000
Fixed assets	28,000	Equity	20,000

a. What will be the subsequent price per share under each alternative (dividend versus repurchase)?

b. If total earnings of the firm are $2,000 a year, find earnings per share under each alternative.

c. Find the price-earnings ratio under each alternative.

d. Adherents of the "dividends-are-good" school sometimes point to the fact that stocks with high-dividend-payout ratios tend to sell at above-average price-earnings multiples. Is this evidence convincing? Discuss this argument with regard to your answers to parts (a) to (c).

24. **Dividends and Taxes.** Shares in Growth Products Inc. are priced at $100. Investors expect the total *pretax* rate of return to be 10%. The tax rate on both capital gains and dividends is 15%. *(LO5)*

 a. If the entire return on the shares is in the form of dividends, what is the investor's annualized *after-tax* rate of return for a holding period of 1 year? 5 years? 10 years? 20 years?

 b. What is the investor's annualized *after-tax* rate of return for each holding period if all of the pretax return is in the form of capital gains?

 c. Explain why capital gains may be preferred to dividends even if the tax rate on the two are equal.

WEB EXERCISES

1. Go to finance.yahoo.com. Under the *Investing* tab, choose *Industries*. Find the dividend yield and payout ratio of the typical firm in the biotech industry and the electric utilities industry. Which is higher? Can you come up with a good explanation for the difference?

2. Log on to www.earnings.com and click on the *Dividends* tab to find a recent list of dividend declarations. What is the meaning of each event? What is the typical interval between each event?

SOLUTIONS TO SELF-TEST QUESTIONS

17.1 The ex-dividend date is June 1. Therefore, Mick buys the stock ex-dividend and will not receive the dividend. The checks will be mailed on June 30.

17.2

Assets		Liabilities and Equity	
After cash dividend			
Cash	$ 0	Debt	$ 0
Other assets	850,000	Equity	850,000
Value of firm	$850,000	Value of firm	$850,000
Shares outstanding = 100,000			
Price per share = $850,000/100,000 = $8.50			
After stock repurchase			
Cash	$ 0	Debt	$ 0
Other assets	850,000	Equity	850,000
Value of firm	$850,000	Value of firm	$850,000
Shares outstanding = 85,000			
Price per share = $850,000/85,000 = $10			

If a dividend is paid, the stock price falls by the amount of the dividend. If the company instead uses the cash for a share repurchase, the stock price remains unchanged but, with fewer shares left outstanding, the market value of the firm falls by the same amount as it would have if the dividend had been paid.

17.3 An investor who prefers a zero-dividend policy can reinvest any dividends received. This will cause the value of the shares held to be unaffected by payouts. The price drop on the ex-dividend date is offset by the reinvestment of the dividends. However, if the investor had to pay brokerage fees on the newly purchased shares, she would be harmed by a high-payout policy since part of the proceeds of the dividends would go toward paying the broker. On the other hand, if the firm offers a dividend reinvestment plan (DRIP) with a 5% discount, she is better off with a high-dividend policy. The DRIP is like a "negative trading cost." She can increase the value of her stock by 5% of the dividend just by participating in the DRIP. Of course, her gain is at the expense of shareholders that do not participate in the DRIP.

17.4   The price of the stock will equal the after-tax cash flows discounted by the required (after-tax) rate of return:

$$P = \frac{102.50 + 10 \times (1 - .4)}{1.10} = 98.64$$

Notice that the after-tax proceeds from the stock would increase by the amount that previously went to pay capital gains taxes, $.20 \times \$4.72 = \$.944$. The present value of this tax saving is $\$.944/1.10 = \$.86$. Therefore, the price increases to $\$97.78 + \$.86 = \$98.64$. The pretax rate of return falls to $(102.50 - 98.64 + 10)/98.64 = .1405$, or 14.05%, but the after-tax rate of return remains at 10%.

MINICASE

George Liu, the CEO of Penn Schumann, was a creature of habit. Every month he and Jennifer Rodriguez, the company's chief financial officer, met for lunch and an informal chat at Pierre's. Nothing was ever discussed until George had finished his favorite *escalope de foie gras chaude*. At their last meeting in March he had then toyed thoughtfully with his glass of Chateau Haut-Brion Blanc before suddenly asking, "What do you think we should be doing about our payout policy?"

Penn Schumann was a large and successful pharmaceutical company. It had an enviable list of highly profitable drugs, many of which had 5 or more further years of patent protection. Earnings in the latest 4 years had increased rapidly, but it was difficult to see that such rates of growth could continue. The company had traditionally paid out about 40% of earnings as dividends, though the figure in 2011 was only 35%. Penn was spending over $4 billion a year on R&D, but the strong operating cash flow and conservative dividend policy had resulted in a buildup of cash. Penn's recent income statements, balance sheets, and cash-flow statements are summarized in Tables 17.4 to 17.6.

The problem, as Mr. Liu explained, was that Penn's dividend policy was more conservative than that of its main competitors. "Share prices depend on dividends," he said. "If we raise our dividend, we'll raise our share price, and that's the name of the game." Ms. Rodriguez suggested that the real issue was how much cash the company wanted to hold. The current cash holding was more than adequate for the company's immediate needs. On the other hand, the research staff had been analyzing a number of new compounds with promising applications in the treatment of liver diseases. If this research were to lead to a marketable product, Penn would need to make a large investment. In addition, the company might require cash for possible acquisitions in the biotech field. "What worries me," Ms. Rodriguez said, "is that investors don't give us credit for this and think that we are going to fritter away the cash on negative-NPV investments or easy living. I don't think we should commit to paying out high dividends, but perhaps we could use some of our cash to repurchase stock."

"I don't know where anyone gets the idea that we fritter away cash on easy living," replied Mr. Liu, as he took another sip of wine,

"but I like the idea of buying back our stock. We can tell shareholders that we are so confident about the future that we believe buying our own stock is the best investment we can make." He scribbled briefly on his napkin. "Suppose we bought back 50 million shares at $105. That would reduce the shares outstanding to 488 million. Net income last year was nearly $4.8 billion, so earnings per share would increase to $9.84. If the price-earnings multiple stays at 11.8, the stock price should rise to $116. That's an increase of over 10%." A smile came over Mr. Liu's face. "Wonderful, he exclaimed, "here comes my *homard à la nage*. Let's come back to this idea over dessert."

Evaluate the arguments of Jennifer Rodriguez and George Liu. Do you think the company is holding too much cash? If you do, how do you think it could be best paid out?

TABLE 17.4 Penn Schumann, Inc., balance sheet (figures in millions of dollars)

	2011	2010
Cash and short-term investments	7,061	5,551
Receivables	2,590	2,214
Inventory	1,942	2,435
Total current assets	11,593	10,200
Property, plant, & equipment	21,088	19,025
Less accumulated depreciation	5,780	4,852
Net fixed assets	15,308	14,173
Total assets	26,901	24,373
Payables	6,827	6,215
Short-term debt	1,557	2,620
Total current liabilities	8,384	8,835
Long-term debt	3,349	3,484
Shareholders' equity	15,168	12,054
Total liabilities and equity	26,901	24,373
Note:		
Shares outstanding, millions	538	516
Market price per share ($)	105	88

TABLE 17.5 Penn Schumann, Inc., income statement (figures in millions of dollars)

	2011	2010
Revenue	16,378	13,378
Costs	8,402	7,800
Depreciation	928	850
EBIT	7,048	4,728
Interest	323	353
Tax	1,933	1,160
Net income	4,792	3,215
Dividends	1,678	1,350
Earnings per share ($)	8.91	6.23
Dividends per share ($)	3.12	2.62

TABLE 17.6 Penn Schumann, Inc., statement of cash flows (figures in millions of dollars)

	2011
Net income	4,792
Depreciation	928
Decrease (increase) in receivables	(376)
Decrease (increase) in inventories	493
Increase (decrease) in payables	612
Total cash from operations	6,449
Capital expenditures	(2,063)
Increase (decrease) in short-term debt	(1,063)
Increase (decrease) in long-term debt	(135)
Dividends paid	(1,678)
Cash provided by financing activities	(2,876)
Net increase in cash	1,510

CHAPTER 18

Long-Term Financial Planning

LEARNING OBJECTIVES

After studying this chapter, you should be able to:

1 Describe the contents and uses of a financial plan.

2 Construct a simple financial planning model.

3 Estimate the effect of growth on the need for external financing.

RELATED WEB SITES FOR THIS CHAPTER CAN BE FOUND AT WWW.MHHE.COM/BMM7E.

Financial planners don't guess the future; they prepare for it.

It's been said that a camel looks like a horse designed by a committee. If a firm made every decision piecemeal, it would end up with a financial camel. That is why smart financial managers consider the overall effect of future investment and financing decisions.

Think back to Chapter 1, where we discussed the job of the financial manager. The manager must consider what investments the firm should undertake and how the firm should raise the cash to pay for those investments. By now you know a fair amount about how to make investment decisions that increase shareholder value and about the different securities that the firm can issue. But because new investments need to be paid for, those decisions cannot be made independently. They must add up to a sensible whole. That's why financial planning is needed. The financial plan allows managers to think about the implications of alternative financial

strategies and to tease out any inconsistencies in the firm's goals.

Financial planning also helps managers avoid some surprises and consider how they should react to surprises that *cannot* be avoided. In Chapter 10 we stressed that good financial managers insist on understanding what makes projects work and what could go wrong with them. The same approach should be taken when investment and financing decisions are considered as a whole.

Finally, financial planning helps establish goals to motivate managers and provide standards for measuring performance.

We start the chapter by summarizing what financial planning involves, and we describe the contents of a typical financial plan. We then discuss the use of financial models in the planning process. Finally, we examine the relationship between a firm's growth and its need for new financing.

18.1 What Is Financial Planning?

planning horizon
Time horizon for a
financial plan.

Firms must plan for both the short term and the long term. Short-term planning rarely looks further ahead than the next 12 months. It seeks to ensure that the firm has enough cash to pay its bills and that short-term borrowing and lending are arranged to the best advantage. We discuss short-term planning in the next chapter.

Here we are concerned with long-term planning, where a typical **planning horizon** is 5 years, although some firms look out 10 years or more. For example, it can take at least 10 years for an electric utility to design, obtain approval for, build, and test a major generating plant.

Long-term financial planning focuses on the firm's long-term goals, the investment that will be needed to meet those goals, and the finance that must be raised. But you can't think about these things without also tackling other important issues. For example, you need to consider possible dividend policies, for the more that is paid out to shareholders, the more external financing that will be needed. You also need to think about what is an appropriate debt ratio for the firm. A conservative capital structure may mean greater reliance on new share issues. The financial plan is used to enforce consistency in the way that these questions are answered and to highlight the choices that the firm needs to make. Finally, by establishing a set of consistent goals, the plan enables subsequent evaluation of the firm's performance in meeting those goals.

Financial Planning Focuses on the Big Picture

Many of the firm's capital expenditures are proposed by plant managers. But the final budget must also reflect strategic plans made by senior management. Positive-NPV opportunities occur in those businesses where the firm has a real competitive advantage. Strategic plans need to identify such businesses and look to expand them. The plans also seek to identify businesses to sell or liquidate as well as businesses that should be allowed to run down. Of course, these decisions are not the sole province of the financial manager. The company's chief executive together with specialists in functional areas, such as marketing, production, and human resources, will be closely involved in the planning process. The final plan will also be subject to the approval of the board of directors.

Strategic planning involves capital budgeting on a grand scale. In this process, you need to look at the investment by each line of business and avoid getting bogged down in details. Of course, some individual projects are large enough to have significant individual impact. For example, the telecom giant Verizon is currently in the midst of a project to spend billions of dollars to deploy fiber-optic-based broadband technology to its residential customers; you can bet that this project was explicitly analyzed as part of its long-range financial plan. Normally, however, planners do not work on a project-by-project basis. Smaller projects are aggregated into a unit that is treated as a single project.

At the beginning of the planning process the corporate staff might ask each division to submit three alternative business plans covering the next 5 years:

1. A *best-case* or aggressive growth plan calling for heavy capital investment and rapid growth of existing markets.
2. A *normal growth* plan in which the division grows with its markets but not significantly at the expense of its competitors.
3. A plan of *retrenchment* if the firm's markets contract. This is planning for lean economic times.

The plan will contain a summary of capital expenditures, working capital requirements, as well as strategies to raise funds for these investments.

Why Build Financial Plans?

Firms spend considerable energy, time, and resources building elaborate financial plans. What do they get for this investment?

Contingency Planning   Planning is not just forecasting. Forecasting concentrates on the most likely outcomes, but planners need to worry about unlikely events as well as likely ones. If you think ahead about what could go wrong, then you are less likely to ignore the danger signals and you can respond faster to trouble.

Companies have developed a number of ways of asking "what-if" questions about both individual projects and the overall firm. For example, as we saw in Chapter 10, managers often work through the consequences of their decisions under different scenarios. One scenario might envisage high interest rates contributing to a slowdown in world economic growth and lower commodity prices. A second scenario might involve a buoyant domestic economy, high inflation, and a weak currency.

The idea is to formulate responses to inevitable surprises. What will you do, for example, if sales in the first year turn out to be 10% below forecast? A good financial plan should help you adapt as events unfold.

Considering Options   Planners need to think whether there are opportunities for the company to exploit its existing strengths by moving into a wholly new area. Often they may recommend entering a market for "strategic" reasons—that is, not because the immediate investment has a positive net present value but because it establishes the firm in a new market and creates options for possibly valuable follow-on investments.

For example, Verizon's costly fiber-optic initiative would never be profitable strictly in terms of its most common current uses for phone or conventional Internet applications. But the new technology gives Verizon *options* to offer services that may be highly valuable in the future, such as the rapid delivery of an array of home entertainment services. The justification for the huge investment lies in these potential growth options.

Forcing Consistency   Financial plans draw out the connections between the firm's plans for growth and the financing requirements. For example, a forecast of 25% growth might require the firm to issue securities to pay for necessary capital expenditures, while a 5% growth rate might enable the firm to finance capital expenditures by using only reinvested profits.

Financial plans should help to ensure that the firm's goals are mutually consistent. For example, the chief executive might say that she is shooting for a profit margin of 10% and sales growth of 20%, but financial planners need to think whether the higher sales growth may require price cuts that will reduce profit margin.

Moreover, a goal that is stated in terms of accounting ratios is not operational unless it is translated back into what that means for business decisions. For example, a higher profit margin can result from higher prices, lower costs, or a move into new, high-margin products. Why then do managers define objectives in this way? In part, such goals may be a code to communicate real concerns. For example, a target profit margin may be a way of saying that in pursuing sales growth, the firm has allowed costs to get out of control.

The danger is that everyone may forget the code and the accounting targets may be seen as goals in themselves. No one should be surprised when lower-level managers focus on the goals for which they are rewarded. For example, when Volkswagen set a goal of 6.5% profit margin, some VW groups responded by developing and promoting expensive, high-margin cars. Less attention was paid to marketing cheaper models, which had lower profit margins but higher sales volume. As soon as this became apparent, Volkswagen announced that it would de-emphasize its profit margin goal and would instead focus on return on investment. It hoped that this would encourage managers to get the most profit out of every dollar of invested capital.

18.2 Financial Planning Models

Financial planners often use a financial planning model to help them explore the consequences of alternative strategies. These models range from simple models, such as the one presented later in this chapter, to models that incorporate hundreds of equations.

Financial planning models support the financial planning process by making it easier and cheaper to construct forecast financial statements. The models automate an important part of planning that would otherwise be boring, time-consuming, and labor-intensive.

Programming these financial planning models used to consume large amounts of computer time and high-priced talent. These days standard spreadsheet programs such as Excel can be used to solve complex financial planning problems.

Components of a Financial Planning Model

A completed financial plan for a large company is a substantial document. A smaller corporation's plan would have the same elements but less detail. For the smallest businesses, financial plans may be entirely in the financial managers' heads. The basic elements of the plans will be similar, however, for firms of any size.

Financial plans include three components: inputs, the planning model, and outputs. The relationship among these components is represented in Figure 18.1. Let's look at them in turn.

Inputs The inputs to the financial plan consist of the firm's current financial statements and its forecasts about the future. Usually, the principal forecast is the likely growth in sales, since many of the other variables such as labor requirements and inventory levels are tied to sales. These forecasts are only in part the responsibility of the financial manager. Obviously, the marketing department will play a key role in forecasting sales. In addition, because sales will depend on the state of the overall economy, large firms will seek forecasting help from firms that specialize in preparing macroeconomic and industry forecasts.

The Planning Model The financial planning model calculates the implications of the manager's forecasts for profits, new investment, and financing. The model consists of equations relating output variables to forecasts. For example, the equations can show how a change in sales is likely to affect costs, working capital, fixed assets, and financing requirements. The financial model could specify that the total cost of goods produced may increase by 80 cents for every $1 increase in total sales, that accounts receivable will be a fixed proportion of sales, and that the firm will need to increase fixed assets by 8% for every 10% increase in sales.

pro formas
Projected or forecast financial statements.

Outputs The output of the financial model consists of financial statements such as income statements, balance sheets, and statements describing sources and uses of cash. These statements are called **pro formas,** which means that they are forecasts based on the inputs and the assumptions built into the plan. Usually the output of financial models also includes many of the financial ratios we discussed in Chapter 4. These ratios indicate whether the firm will be financially fit and healthy at the end of the planning period.

FIGURE 18.1 The components of a financial plan

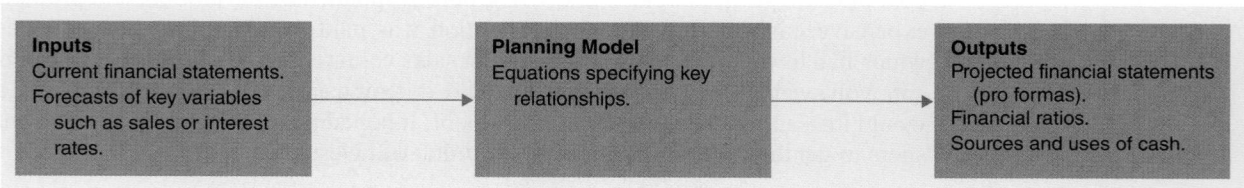

Inputs	Planning Model	Outputs
Current financial statements. Forecasts of key variables such as sales or interest rates.	Equations specifying key relationships.	Projected financial statements (pro formas). Financial ratios. Sources and uses of cash.

TABLE 18.1 Financial statements of Executive Cheese Company for past year

INCOME STATEMENT		
Sales		$ 1,200
Costs		1,000
Net income		$ 200
BALANCE SHEET (YEAR-END)		
Assets	$2,000	Debt	$ 800
		Equity	1,200
Total	$2,000	Total	$ 2,000

Percentage of Sales Models

We can illustrate the basic components of a planning model with a very simple example. In the next section we will start to add some complexity.

Suppose that Executive Cheese has prepared the simple balance sheet and income statement shown in Table 18.1. The firm's financial planners forecast that total sales next year will increase by 10% from this year's level. They expect that costs will be a fixed proportion of sales, so they too will increase by 10%. Almost all the forecasts for Executive Cheese are proportional to the forecast of sales. Such models are therefore called **percentage of sales models.** The result is the pro forma, or forecast, income statement in Table 18.2, which shows that next year's income will be $200 × 1.10 = $220.

percentage of sales model Planning model in which sales forecasts are the driving variables and most other variables are proportional to sales.

Executive Cheese has no spare capacity, and in order to sustain this higher level of output, it must increase plant and equipment by 10%, or $200. Therefore, the left-hand side of the balance sheet, which lists total assets, must increase to $2,200. What about the right-hand side? The firm must decide how it intends to finance its new assets. Suppose that it decides to maintain a fixed debt-equity ratio. Then both debt and equity would grow by 10%, as shown in the pro forma balance sheet in Table 18.2. Notice that this implies that the firm must issue $80 in additional debt. On the other hand, no equity needs to be issued. The 10% increase in equity can be accomplished by retaining $120 of earnings.

This raises a question, however. If income is forecast at $220, why does equity increase by only $120? The answer is that the firm must be planning to pay a dividend of $220 − $120 = $100. Notice that this dividend payment is not chosen independently but is a *consequence* of the other decisions. Given the company's need for funds and its decision to maintain the debt-equity ratio, dividend policy is completely determined. Any other dividend payment would be inconsistent with the two conditions that (1) the right-hand side of the balance sheet increase by $200 and (2) both debt and equity increase in the same proportion. For this reason we call dividends the **balancing item,** or *plug.* The balancing item is the variable that adjusts to make the sources of funds equal to the uses.

balancing item Variable that adjusts to maintain the consistency of a financial plan. Also called *plug.*

Of course, most firms would be reluctant to vary dividends simply because they have a temporary need for cash; instead, they like to maintain a steady progression of

TABLE 18.2 Pro forma financial statements of Executive Cheese

PRO FORMA INCOME STATEMENT		
Sales		$ 1,320
Costs		1,100
Net income		$ 220
PRO FORMA BALANCE SHEET (YEAR-END)		
Assets	$2,200	Debt	$ 880
		Equity	1,320
Total	$2,200	Total	$ 2,200

dividends. In this case Executive Cheese could commit to some other dividend payment and allow the debt-equity ratio to vary. The amount of debt would therefore become the balancing item.

EXAMPLE 18.1   ▶   Balancing Item

Suppose the firm commits to a dividend level of $180 and raises any extra money it needs by an issue of debt. In this case the amount of debt becomes the balancing item. With the dividend set at $180, reinvested earnings would be only $40, so the firm would have to issue $160 in new debt to help pay for the additional $200 of assets. Table 18.3, panel A, is the new balance sheet.

Now suppose instead that the firm commits to the $180 dividend but decides that it will issue at most $100 in new debt. In that case, new equity issues become the balancing item. With $40 of earnings reinvested and $100 of new debt, an additional $60 of equity needs to be raised to support the total addition of $200 to the firm's assets. Table 18.3, panel B, is the resulting balance sheet.

Is one of these plans better than the others? It's hard to give a simple answer. The choice of dividend payment depends partly on how investors will interpret the decision. If last year's dividend was only $50, investors might regard a dividend payment of $100 as a sign of a confident management; if last year's dividend was $150, investors might not be so content with a payment of $100. The alternative of paying $180 in dividends and making up the shortfall by issuing more debt leaves the company with a debt-equity ratio of 77%. That is unlikely to make your bankers edgy, but you may worry about how long you can continue to finance expansion predominantly by borrowing.

Our example shows how experiments with a financial model, including changes in the model's balancing item, can raise important financial questions. But the model does not answer these questions. **Financial models ensure *consistency* between growth assumptions and financing plans, but they do not identify the best financing plan.**

Self-Test 18.1

Suppose that the firm decides to maintain its debt-equity ratio at 800/1,200 = 2/3. It is committed to increasing assets by 10% to support the forecast increase in sales, and it strongly believes that a dividend payment of $180 is in the best interests of the firm. What must be the balancing items? What is the implication for the firm's financing activities in the next year?

An Improved Model

Now that you have grasped the idea behind financial planning models, we can move on to a more sophisticated example.

Table 18.4 shows the financial statements for Executive Fruit Company in 2011. Judging by these figures, the company is ordinary in almost all respects. Its earnings before interest and taxes were 10% of sales revenue. Net income was $96,000 after payment of taxes and 10% interest on $400,000 of long-term debt. The company paid out two-thirds of its net income as dividends.

TABLE 18.3 Pro forma balance sheets. *A:* Dividends are fixed, and debt is the balancing item. *B:* Dividends and debt are fixed, and equity issues are the balancing item.

	Panel A				Panel B		
Assets	$2,200	Debt	$ 960	Assets	$2,200	Debt	$ 900
		Equity	1,240			Equity	1,300
Total	$2,200	Total	$2,200	Total	$2,200	Total	$2,200

TABLE 18.4 Financial statements for Executive Fruit Co., 2011 (figures in thousands)

INCOME STATEMENT, 2011		
		Comment
Revenue	$ 2,000	
Cost of goods sold	1,800	90% of sales
EBIT	200	Difference = 10% of sales
Interest	40	10% of debt
Earnings before taxes	160	EBIT − interest
State and federal tax	64	40% of (EBIT − interest)
Net income	$ 96	EBIT − interest − taxes
Dividends	$ 64	Payout ratio = $^2/_3$
Additions to retained earnings	$ 32	Net income − dividends
BALANCE SHEET (YEAR-END, 2011)		
Assets		
Net working capital	$ 200	10% of sales
Fixed assets	800	40% of sales
Total assets	$ 1,000	50% of sales
Liabilities and shareholders' equity		
Long-term debt	$ 400	
Shareholders' equity	600	
Total liabilities and shareholders' equity	$ 1,000	Equals total assets

Next to each item on the financial statements in Table 18.4 we have entered a comment about the relationship between that variable and sales. In most cases, the comment gives the value of each item as a percentage of sales. This may be useful for forecasting purposes. For example, it would be reasonable to assume that cost of goods sold will remain at 90% of sales even if sales grow by 10% next year. Similarly, it is reasonable to assume that net working capital will remain at 10% of sales.

On the other hand, the fact that long-term debt was 20% of sales in 2011 does not mean that we should assume that this ratio will continue to hold next year. Many alternative financing plans with varying combinations of debt issues, equity issues, and dividend payouts may be considered without affecting the firm's operations.

Now suppose that you are asked to prepare pro forma financial statements for Executive Fruit for 2012. You are told to assume that (1) sales and operating costs are expected to be up 10% over 2011, (2) interest rates will remain at their current level, (3) the firm will stick to its traditional dividend policy of paying out two-thirds of earnings, and (4) Executive will need 10% more fixed assets and net working capital next year to support the higher sales volume.

In Table 18.5 we present the resulting first-stage pro forma calculations for Executive Fruit. These calculations show what would happen if the size of the firm increases along with projected sales, but at this preliminary stage the plan does not specify a particular mix of new security issues.

Without any security issues, the balance sheet will not balance: Assets increase to $1,100,000, while debt plus shareholders' equity amounts to only $1,036,000. Somehow the firm will need to raise an extra $64,000 to help pay for the increase in assets that is necessary to support the higher projected level of sales in 2012. In this first pass, external financing is the balancing item. Given the firm's growth forecasts and its dividend policy, the financial plan calculates *how much* money the firm needs to raise but does not yet specify how those funds will be raised.

In the second-stage pro forma, the firm must decide on the financing mix that best meets its needs for additional funds. It must choose some combination of new debt or new equity that supports the contemplated acquisition of additional assets. For example, it could issue $64,000 of equity or debt, or it could choose to maintain its long-term debt-equity ratio at two-thirds by issuing both debt and equity.

TABLE 18.5 First-stage pro forma statements for Executive Fruit Co., 2012 (figures in thousands)

PRO FORMA INCOME STATEMENT, 2012		
		Comment
Revenue	$ 2,200	10% higher
Cost of goods sold	1,980	10% higher
EBIT	220	10% higher
Interest	40	Unchanged
Earnings before taxes	180	EBIT − interest
State and federal tax	72	40% of (EBIT − interest)
Net income	$ 108	EBIT − interest − taxes
Dividends	$ 72	$2/3$ of net income
Additions to retained earnings	$ 36	Net income − dividends
PRO FORMA BALANCE SHEET (YEAR-END, 2012)		
Assets		
Net working capital	$ 220	10% higher
Fixed assets	880	10% higher
Total assets	$ 1,100	10% higher
Liabilities and shareholders' equity		
Long-term debt	$ 400	Temporarily held fixed
Shareholders' equity	636	Increased by earnings retained during year
Total liabilities and shareholders' equity	$ 1,036	Sum of debt plus equity
Required external financing	$ 64	Balancing item or plug (= $1,100 − $1,036)

Table 18.6 shows the second-stage pro forma balance sheet if the required funds are raised by issuing $64,000 of debt. Therefore, in Table 18.6, debt is treated as the balancing item. Notice that while the plan requires the firm to specify a financing plan *consistent* with its growth projections, it does not provide guidance as to the *best* financing mix.

Table 18.7 sets out the firm's sources and uses of funds. It shows that working capital must be increased by $20,000 and fixed assets by $80,000 compared to their level a year earlier. The firm reinvested $36,000 of this year's profits, so $64,000 must be raised in the capital markets. Under the financing plan presented in Table 18.6, the firm borrows the entire $64,000.

We have spared you the trouble of actually calculating the figures necessary for Tables 18.5 through 18.7. The calculations do not take more than a few minutes for this simple example, *provided* you set up the calculations correctly and make no arithmetic mistakes. If that time requirement seems trivial, remember that in reality you probably would be asked for five similar sets of statements covering each year from 2012 to 2016. Probably you would be asked for alternative projections under different

TABLE 18.6 Second-stage pro forma balance sheet for Executive Fruit Co., year-end 2012 (figures in thousands)

		Comment
Assets		
Net working capital	$ 220	10% higher
Fixed assets	880	10% higher
Total assets	$1,100	10% higher
Liabilities and shareholders' equity		
Long-term debt	$ 464	16% higher (new borrowing = $64; this is the balancing item)
Shareholders' equity	636	Increased by reinvested earnings
Total liabilities and shareholders' equity	$1,100	Again equals total assets

TABLE 18.7 Statement of sources and uses of funds for Executive Fruit, 2012 (figures in thousands)

Sources		Uses	
Retained earnings	$ 36	Investment in working capital	$ 20
New borrowing	64	Investment in fixed assets	80
Total sources	$100	Total uses	$100

assumptions (for example, 5% instead of 10% growth rate of revenue) or different financial strategies (for example, freezing dividends at their 2012 level of $64,000). This would be far more time-consuming. Moreover, actual plans will have many more line items than this simple one. Building a model and letting the computer toil in your place have obvious attractions.

Spreadsheet 18.1 is the spreadsheet we used for the Executive Fruit model. Column E contains the values that appear in Table 18.4. Columns F and G are pro forma statements using the growth rate given in cell B3. The spreadsheet recognizes that additional debt issued in one year will result in increased interest expenses in the following year. For example, interest expense in 2013 is 10% of the debt outstanding at the end of 2012.

Column H presents the formulas used to obtain each value in column G. Notice that we assume the firm will maintain its dividend payout ratio at 2/3 and that debt will be the balancing item, increasing in each year by required external financing (row 24). Required external financing in 2012 equals total assets required to support that year's sales (cell F17) minus the previous year's assets (cell E17) minus earnings reinvested

You can find this spreadsheet at www.mhhe.com/bmm7e.

SPREADSHEET 18.1 Executive Fruit spreadsheet

	A	B	C	D	E	F	G	H
1	**A. Model inputs**				**Base year**			**Formula**
2				*Income Statement*	**2011**	**2012**	**2013**	**for column G**
3	Growth rate	.10		Revenue	2,000	2,200.0	2,420.0	=F3*(1+$B3)
4	Tax rate	0.4		Cost of goods sold	1,800	1,980.0	2,178.0	=G3*$B$8
5	Interest rate	0.1		EBIT	200	220.0	242.0	=G3-G4
6	NWC/sales ratio	0.1		Interest expense	40	40.0	46.4	=$B$5*F20
7	Fixed assets/sales	0.4		Earnings before taxes	160	180.0	195.6	=G5-G6
8	COGS/sales	0.9		Taxes	64	72.0	78.2	=$B$4*G7
9	Payout ratio	2/3		Net income	96	108.0	117.4	=G7-G8
10				Dividends	64	72.0	78.2	=G9*$B$9
11				Addn. to retained earnings	32	36.0	39.1	=G9-G10
12								
13				*Balance Sheet (year end)*				
14				Assets				
15				Net working capital	200	220.0	242.0	=$B$6*G3
16				Fixed assets	800	880.0	968.0	=$B$7*G3
17				Total assets	1,000	1,100.0	1,210.0	=G15+G16
18								
19				Liabilities and equity				
20				Long-term debt (note a)	400	464.0	534.9	=F20+G24
21				Shareholders' equity (note b)	600	636.0	675.1	=F21+G11
22				Total liab. & share. equity	1,000	1,100.0	1,210.0	=G20+G21
23								
24				Required external financing		64.0	70.9	=G17-F17-G11
25								
26								
27	Notes:							
28	(a): Long-term debt, the balancing item, increases by required external financing.							
29	(b): Shareholders' equity equals its value in the previous year plus reinvested earnings.							

TABLE 18.8 Required external financing for Executive Fruit. Higher growth rates require greater amounts of external capital.

Growth Rate, %	Required External Financing, $ Thousands
0	−32
2	−12.8
3.33	0
5	16
10	64
15	112
20	160

during the year (cell F11). Shareholders' equity (cell F21) equals its previous value plus reinvested earnings.

Now that the spreadsheet is set up, it is easy to explore the consequences of various assumptions. For example, you can change the assumed growth rate (cell B3) or experiment with different policies, such as changing the dividend-payout ratio or forcing debt or equity finance (or both) to absorb the required external financing.

EXAMPLE 18.2 ▶   What Happens If the Growth Rate Changes?

Let's use the spreadsheet to explore the effect of sales growth on the need for external financing. We can alter the assumed growth rate in cell B3 and see the effect on required external financing in cell F24. For example, we saw in Spreadsheet 18.1 that when the growth rate was 10%, required external financing was $64,000. In our model, assets are proportional to sales, so when we assume a higher growth rate of sales, assets also increase at a faster rate. The additional funds necessary to pay for those additional assets imply greater external financing.

Table 18.8 shows how required external financing responds to a change in the growth rate. Notice that at a 3.33% growth rate, required external financing is zero. At higher growth rates, the firm requires external financing; at lower rates, reinvested earnings exceed the addition to assets and there is a surplus of funds from internal sources; this shows up as negative required external financing. Later in the chapter, we will explore the limits to internal growth more systematically.

Self-Test 18.2

a. Suppose that Executive Fruit is committed to a 10% growth rate and to paying out two-thirds of its profits as dividends. However, it now also wishes to maintain its debt-equity ratio at $2/3$. What are the implications for external financing in 2012?

b. If the company is prepared to reduce dividends paid in 2012 to $60,000, how much external financing would be needed?

18.3 Planners Beware

Pitfalls in Model Design

The Executive Fruit model is still too simple for practical application. You probably have already noticed several ways to improve it. For example, we ignored depreciation of fixed assets. Depreciation is important because it provides a tax shield. If Executive Fruit deducts depreciation before calculating its tax bill, it could plow back more money into new investments and would need to borrow less. We've also simplified the firm's borrowing plans, ignoring short-term debt and assuming that the firm will be able to issue small amounts of long-term debt as needed at a fixed interest rate regardless of changes in its leverage.

You would certainly want to make these obvious improvements. But beware: There is always the temptation to make a model bigger and more detailed. You may end up with an exhaustive model that is too cumbersome for routine use.

Excessive detail gets in the way of the intended use of corporate planning models, which is to project the financial consequences of a variety of strategies and assumptions. The fascination of detail, if you give in to it, distracts attention from crucial decisions like stock issues and dividend policy and allocation of capital by business area.

The Assumption in Percentage of Sales Models

When forecasting Executive Fruit's capital requirements, we assumed that both fixed assets and working capital increase proportionately with sales. For example, the orange line in Figure 18.2 shows that net working capital is a constant 10% of sales.

Percentage of sales models are useful first approximations for financial planning. However, in reality, assets may not be proportional to sales. For example, we will see in Chapter 19 that important components of working capital such as inventories and cash balances will generally rise *less* than proportionately with sales. Suppose that Executive Fruit looks back at past variations in sales and estimates that on average a $1 rise in sales requires only a $.075 increase in net working capital. The blue line in Figure 18.2 shows the level of working capital that would now be needed for different levels of sales. To allow for this in the Executive Fruit model, we would need to set net working capital equal to ($50,000 + .075 × sales).

A further complication is that fixed assets such as plant and equipment are typically not added in small increments as sales increase. Instead, the picture is more likely to resemble Figure 18.3. If Executive Fruit's factories are operating at less than full capacity (point *A,* for example), then the firm can expand sales without any additional investment in plant. Ultimately, however, if sales continue to increase, say beyond point *B,* Executive Fruit will need to add new capacity. This is shown by the occasional large changes to fixed assets in Figure 18.3. These "lumpy" changes to fixed assets need to be recognized when devising the financial plan. If there is considerable excess capacity, even rapid sales growth may not require big additions to fixed assets. On the other hand, if the firm is already operating at capacity, even small sales growth may call for large investment in plant and equipment.

FIGURE 18.2 Net working capital as a function of sales. The orange line shows net working capital equal to .10 × sales. The blue line depicts net working capital as $50,000 + .075 × sales, so that it increases less than proportionately with sales.

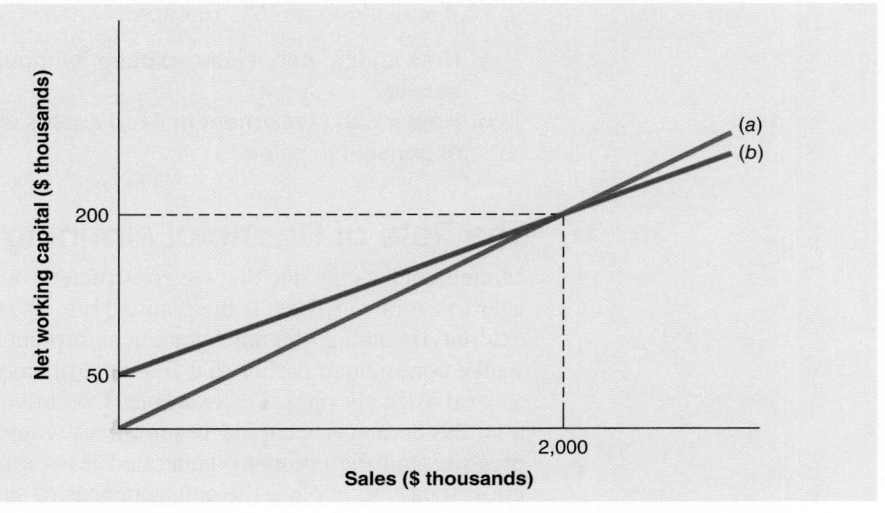

FIGURE 18.3 If factories are operating below full capacity, sales can increase without investment in fixed assets (point *A*). Beyond some sales level (point *B*), new capacity must be added.

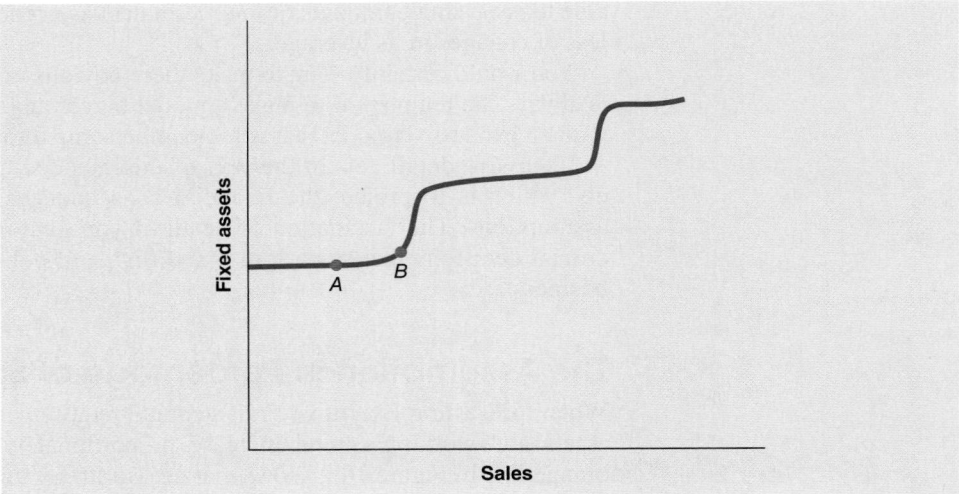

EXAMPLE 18.3 ▶   Required External Funds and Excess Capacity

Suppose that Carter Tools has $50 million invested in fixed assets and generates sales of $60 million. The company is currently working at 80% of capacity. Suppose that a 50% increase in sales is forecast. How much investment in fixed assets would be required?

Sales can increase *without* the need for new investments in fixed assets until the company is at 100% of capacity. Therefore, sales can increase to $60 million × 100/80 = $75 million before the firm reaches full capacity given its current level of fixed assets. At full capacity, therefore, the ratio of assets to sales would be $50 million/$75 million = ⅔.

The 50% increase in forecast sales would imply a sales level of $60 million × 1.5 = $90 million. To support this level of sales, the company needs at least $90 million × ⅔ = $60 million of fixed assets. This calls for a $10 million investment in additional fixed assets.

Self-Test 18.3

Suppose that at its current level of assets and sales, Carter Tools in Example 18.3 is working at 75% of capacity.

a. How much can sales expand without any further investment in fixed assets?
b. How much investment in fixed assets would be required to support a 50% expansion in sales?

The Role of Financial Planning Models

Models such as the one that we constructed for Executive Fruit help the financial manager to avoid surprises. If the planned rate of growth will require the company to raise external financing, the manager can start planning how best to do so.

We commented earlier that financial planners are concerned about unlikely events as well as likely ones. For example, Executive Fruit's manager may wish to consider how the company's capital requirement would change if profit margins come under pressure and the company generated less cash from its operations. Planning models make it easy to explore the consequences of such events.

However, there are limits to what you can learn from planning models. Although they help to trace through the consequences of alternative plans, they do not tell you which plan is best. For example, we saw that Executive Fruit is proposing to grow its sales and earnings per share. Is that good news for shareholders? Well, not necessarily; it depends on the opportunity cost of the additional capital that the company needs to achieve that growth. In 2012 the company proposes to invest $100,000 in fixed assets and working capital. Table 18.5 showed that this extra investment is expected to generate $12,000 of additional net income, equivalent to a return of 12% on the new investment.[1] If the cost of that capital is less than 12%, the new investment will have a positive NPV and will add to shareholder wealth. But suppose that the cost of capital is higher at, say, 15%. In this case Executive Fruit's investment makes shareholders *worse off,* even though the company is recording steady growth in earnings per share and dividends. Executive Fruit's planning model tells us how much money the firm must raise to fund the planned growth, but it cannot tell us whether that growth contributes to shareholder value. Nor can it tell us whether the company should raise the cash by issuing new debt or equity.

Self-Test 18.4

Which of the following questions will a financial plan help to answer?

a. Is the firm's assumption for asset growth consistent with its plans for debt and equity issues and dividend policy?
b. Will accounts receivable increase in direct proportion to sales?
c. Will the contemplated debt-equity mix maximize the value of the firm?

18.4 External Financing and Growth

Financial *plans* force managers to be consistent in their goals for growth, investments, and financing. The nearby box describes how one company was brought to its knees in part by fundamental inconsistences between its growth strategy and its financing plans.

Financial *models,* such as the one that we have developed for Executive Fruit, can help managers trace through the financial consequences of their growth plans and avoid such disasters. But there is a danger that the complexities of a full-blown financial model can obscure the basic issues. Therefore, managers also use some simple rules of thumb to draw out the relationship between a firm's growth objectives and its requirement for external financing.

Recall that in 2011 Executive Fruit ended the year with $1,000,000 of fixed assets and net working capital, and it had $2,000,000 of sales. In other words, each dollar of sales required $.50 of net assets. The company forecasts that sales in 2012 will increase by $200,000. Therefore, if the ratio of net assets to sales remains constant, assets in 2012 will need to rise by $.50 × $200,000 = $100,000.[2] Part of this increase can be financed by reinvested earnings, which in 2012 are $36,000. So the amount of external financing needed is

$$\text{Required external financing} = (\text{net assets/sales}) \times \text{increase in sales} - \text{reinvested earnings}$$
$$= (.50 \times 200,000) - 36,000 = \$64,000$$

Sometimes it is useful to write this calculation in terms of growth rates. Executive Fruit's forecast increase in sales is equivalent to a rise of 10%. So, if net assets are a

---

[1] We assume this additional income is a perpetuity.

[2] However, remember our earlier warning that the ratio of net assets to sales may change as the firm grows.

The Collapse of Vivendi: A Failure in Planning

In 1994 39-year-old Jean-Marie Messier became CEO of the French company Generale des Eaux. He immediately set out to transform it from a sleepy water and sewage business into a multinational media and telecommunications group. The company, now renamed Vivendi, entered into a series of major acquisitions, including a $42 billion purchase of Seagram, owner of Universal Studios. To finance its expansion, Vivendi increased its borrowing to $35 billion, and it increased its leverage further by repurchasing 104 million shares for $6.3 billion. Confident that its share price would rise, the company raised the stakes even more by selling a large number of put options on its own stock.

Vivendi's strategy made it very vulnerable to any decline in operating cash flow. As profits began to evaporate, the company faced a severe cash shortage. Its banks were reluctant to extend further credit, and its bonds were downgraded to junk status. By July 2002 the share price had fallen to less than 10% of its level 2 years earlier. With the company facing imminent bankruptcy, M. Messier was ousted and the new management set about slashing costs and selling assets to reduce the debt burden.*

Vivendi's problems were exacerbated by considerable waste and ostentatious extravagance, but its brush with bankruptcy was a result of a lack of financial planning. The company's goals for growth were unsustainable, and it had few options for surviving a decline in operating cash flow.

---

*The rise and fall of Vivendi is chronicled in J. Johnson and M. Orange, *The Man Who Tried to Buy the World: Jean-Marie Messier and Vivendi Universal* (Portfolio, 2003).

---

constant proportion of sales, the higher sales volume will also require a 10% addition to net assets. Thus

$$\text{New investment} = \text{growth rate} \times \text{initial assets}$$
$$\$100,000 = .10 \times \$1,000,000$$

Part of the funds to pay for the new assets is provided by reinvested earnings. The remainder must come from external financing. Therefore,

$$\text{Required external financing} = \text{new investment} - \text{reinvested earnings} \qquad \textbf{(18.1)}$$
$$= (\text{growth rate} \times \text{assets}) - \text{reinvested earnings}$$

This simple equation highlights that the amount of external financing depends on the firm's projected growth. The faster the firm grows, the more it needs to invest and therefore the more it needs to raise new capital.

In the case of Executive Fruit,

$$\text{Required external financing} = (.10 \times \$1,000,000) - \$36,000$$
$$= \$100,000 - \$36,000 = \$64,000$$

If Executive Fruit's assets remain a constant percentage of sales, then the company needs to raise $64,000 to produce a 10% addition to sales.

The sloping line in Figure 18.4 illustrates how required external financing increases with the growth rate. At low growth rates, the firm generates more funds than necessary for expansion. In this sense, its requirement for further external funds is negative. It may choose to use its surplus to pay off some of its debt or buy back its stock. In fact, the vertical intercept in Figure 18.4, at zero growth, is the negative of the addition

FIGURE 18.4 External financing and growth

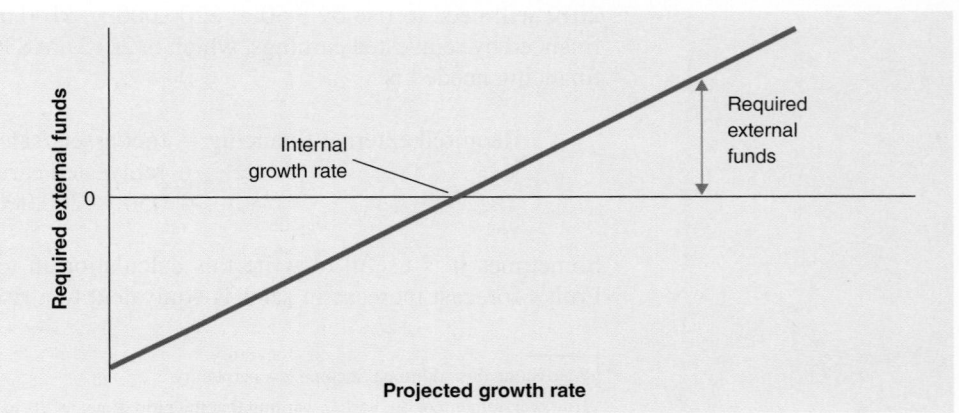

to retained earnings. When growth is zero, no funds are needed for expansion, so all that addition is surplus.

As the firm's projected growth rate increases, more funds are needed to pay for the necessary investments. Therefore, the plot in Figure 18.4 is upward-sloping. For high rates of growth the firm must issue new securities to pay for new investments.

Where the sloping line crosses the horizontal axis, external financing is zero: The firm is growing as fast as possible without resorting to new security issues. This is called the **internal growth rate.** The growth rate is "internal" because it can be maintained without resorting to additional external sources of capital.

Notice that if we set required external financing to zero, we can solve for the internal growth rate as

internal growth rate
Maximum rate of growth without external financing.

$$\text{Internal growth rate} = \frac{\text{reinvested earnings}}{\text{assets}}$$

Thus the firm's rate of growth without additional external sources of capital will equal the ratio of reinvested earnings to assets. This means that a firm with a high volume of reinvested earnings relative to its assets can generate a higher growth rate without needing to raise more capital.

We can gain more insight into what determines the internal growth rate by multiplying the top and bottom of the expression for internal growth by *net income* and *equity* as follows:

$$\text{Internal growth rate} = \frac{\text{reinvested earnings}}{\text{net income}} \times \frac{\text{net income}}{\text{equity}} \times \frac{\text{equity}}{\text{assets}}$$

$$= \text{plowback ratio} \times \text{return on equity} \times \frac{\text{equity}}{\text{assets}} \quad (18.2)$$

A firm can achieve a higher growth rate without raising external capital if (1) it plows back a high proportion of its earnings, (2) it has a high return on equity (ROE), and (3) it has a low debt-to-asset ratio.

EXAMPLE 18.4 ▶ Internal Growth for Executive Fruit

Executive Fruit has chosen a plowback ratio of ⅓. Equity outstanding at the start of 2012 is 600, and outstanding assets are 1,000. Executive Fruit's return on equity[3] is ROE = 16.67%, and its ratio of equity to assets is 600/1,000 = .60. If it is unwilling to raise new capital, its maximum growth rate is

$$\text{Internal growth rate} = \text{plowback ratio} \times \text{ROE} \times \frac{\text{equity}}{\text{assets}}$$

$$= \frac{1}{3} \times .1667 \times .60 = .033, \text{ or } 3.33\%$$

Look back at Table 18.8 and you will see that at this growth rate, external financing is in fact zero. This growth rate is much lower than the 10% growth Executive Fruit projects, which explains its need for external financing.

---

[3] Actually, calculating ROE to find the internal growth rate can be a bit tricky. Executive Fruit is forecasting a growth rate of 10% and an ROE of 108/600 = 18%, but if it grows more slowly, sales, net income and ROE will be lower. In other words, ROE may depend on the growth rate. We saw in Table 18.8 that a growth rate of 3.33% implies external financing of zero; we will choose the ROE corresponding to the internal growth rate of 3.33%. If you input .0333 as the growth rate in the Executive Fruit spreadsheet (Spreadsheet 18.1), you will find that net income in 2012 is $100,000 while equity outstanding at the beginning of 2012 (end of 2011) is $600,000, which implies an ROE of 100/600 = .1667. Notice that although it is common to calculate ROE by dividing income by either end-of-year or year-average shareholders' equity, neither of those conventions will work in this application. To find the internal growth rate, we need to view ROE as analogous to the rate of return on a stock, that is, as money earned *during* the year per dollar of shareholders' equity at the *start* of the year.

sustainable growth rate
Steady rate at which a
firm can grow without
changing leverage;
plowback ratio × return
on equity.

Instead of focusing on the maximum growth rate that can be supported without *any* external financing, firms also may be interested in the growth rate that can be sustained without additional *equity* issues. Of course, if the firm is able to issue enough debt, virtually any growth rate can be financed. It makes more sense to assume that the firm has settled on an optimal capital structure that it will maintain even as equity is augmented by reinvested earnings. The firm issues only enough debt to keep its debt-equity ratio constant. The **sustainable growth rate** is the highest growth rate the firm can maintain without increasing its financial leverage. It turns out that the sustainable growth rate depends only on the plowback ratio and return on equity:[4]

$$\text{Sustainable growth rate} = \text{plowback ratio} \times \text{return on equity} \qquad (18.3)$$

You may remember this formula from Chapter 7, where we first used it when we looked at the valuation of the firm and the dividend discount model.

EXAMPLE 18.5 ▶ Sustainable Growth Rate

Executive Suites, Inc., currently has an equity-to-asset ratio of .8. Its ROE is 18%. The firm currently reinvests one-third of its earnings back into the firm. Moreover, if it plans to keep leverage unchanged, it will issue an additional 20 cents of debt for every 80 cents of reinvested earnings. Given this policy, its maximum growth rate is

$$\text{Sustainable growth rate} = \text{plowback ratio} \times \text{ROE}$$
$$= 1/3 \times .18 = .06, \text{ or } 6\%$$

If the firm is willing to plow back a higher proportion of its earnings, it can issue more debt without increasing its leverage. Both the greater reinvested profits and the additional debt issues would allow it to grow more rapidly. You can confirm in the following Self-Test problem [see part (b)] that if the firm increases its plowback ratio, its sustainable growth rate will be higher.

Self-Test 18.5

Suppose Executive Suites reduces the dividend payout ratio to 25%. Calculate its growth rate assuming (a) that no new debt or equity will be issued and (b) that the firm maintains its debt-to-equity ratio at .25.

---

[4] Here is a proof:

$$\text{Required equity issues} = \text{growth rate} \times \text{assets} - \text{reinvested earnings} - \text{new debt issues}$$

We find the sustainable growth rate by setting required new equity issues to zero and solving for growth:

$$\text{Sustainable growth rate} = \frac{\text{reinvested earnings} + \text{new debt issues}}{\text{assets}}$$

$$= \frac{\text{reinvested earnings} + \text{new debt issues}}{\text{debt} + \text{equity}}$$

However, because both debt and equity are growing at the same rate, new debt issues must equal reinvested earnings multiplied by the ratio of debt to equity, *D/E*. Therefore, we can write the sustainable growth rate as

$$\text{Sustainable growth rate} = \frac{\text{reinvested earnings} \times (1 + D/E)}{\text{debt} + \text{equity}}$$

$$= \frac{\text{reinvested earnings} \times (1 + D/E)}{\text{equity} \times (1 + D/E)} = \frac{\text{reinvested earnings}}{\text{equity}}$$

$$= \frac{\text{reinvested earnings}}{\text{net income}} \times \frac{\text{net income}}{\text{equity}} = \text{plowback} \times \text{ROE}$$

SUMMARY

What are the contents and uses of a financial plan? *(LO1)*

Most firms take financial planning seriously and devote considerable resources to it. The tangible product of the planning process is a financial plan describing the firm's financial strategy and projecting its future consequences by means of **pro forma** balance sheets, income statements, and statements of sources and uses of funds. The plan establishes financial goals and is a benchmark for evaluating subsequent performance. Usually it also describes why that strategy was chosen and how the plan's financial goals are to be achieved.

Planning, if it is done right, forces the financial manager to think about events that could upset the firm's progress and to devise strategies to be held in reserve for counterattack when unfortunate surprises occur. Planning is more than forecasting, because forecasting deals with the most likely outcome. Planners also have to think about events that may occur even though they are unlikely.

In long-range, or strategic, planning, the **planning horizon** is usually 5 years or more. This kind of planning deals with aggregate decisions; for example, the planner would worry about whether the broadax division should commit to heavy capital investment and rapid growth, but not whether the division should choose machine tool A versus tool B. In fact, planners must be constantly on guard against the fascination of detail, because giving in to it means slighting crucial issues like investment strategy, debt policy, and the choice of a target dividend payout ratio.

The plan is the end result. The process that produces the plan is valuable in its own right. Planning forces the financial manager to consider the combined effects of all the firm's investment and financing decisions. This is important because these decisions interact and should not be made independently.

How are financial planning models constructed? *(LO2)*

There is no theory or model that leads straight to *the* optimal financial strategy. Consequently, financial planning proceeds by trial and error. Many different strategies may be projected under a range of assumptions about the future before one strategy is finally chosen. The dozens of separate projections that may be made during this trial-and-error process generate a heavy load of arithmetic and paperwork. Firms have responded by developing corporate planning models to forecast the financial consequences of specified strategies and assumptions about the future. One very simple starting point may be a **percentage of sales model,** in which many key variables are assumed to be directly proportional to sales. Planning models are efficient and widely used. But remember that there is not much finance in them. Their primary purpose is to produce accounting statements. The models do not search for the best financial strategy but only trace out the consequences of a strategy specified by the model user.

What is the effect of growth on the need for external financing? *(LO3)*

Higher growth rates will lead to greater need for investments in fixed assets and working capital. The **internal growth rate** is the maximum rate at which the firm can grow if it relies entirely on reinvested profits to finance its growth, that is, the maximum rate of growth without requiring external financing. The **sustainable growth rate** is the rate at which the firm can grow without changing its leverage ratio.

LISTING OF EQUATIONS

18.1 Required external financing = growth rate $\times$ assets $-$ reinvested earnings

18.2 Internal growth rate = plowback ratio $\times$ return on equity $\times \dfrac{\text{equity}}{\text{assets}}$

18.3 Sustainable growth rate = plowback ratio $\times$ return on equity

QUESTIONS

QUIZ

1. **Financial Planning.** True or false? Explain. *(LO1)*
   a. Financial planning should attempt to minimize risk.
   b. The primary aim of financial planning is to obtain better forecasts of future cash flows and earnings.
   c. Financial planning is necessary because financing and investment decisions interact and should not be made independently.
   d. Firms' planning horizons rarely exceed 3 years.
   e. Individual capital investment projects are not considered in a financial plan unless they are very large.
   f. Financial planning requires accurate and consistent forecasting.
   g. Financial planning models should include as much detail as possible.

2. **Financial Models.** What are the dangers and disadvantages of using a financial model? Discuss. *(LO1)*

3. **Using Financial Plans.** Corporate financial plans are often used as a basis for judging subsequent performance. What can be learned from such comparisons? What problems might arise and how might you cope with such problems? *(LO1)*

4. **Growth Rates.** Find the sustainable and internal growth rates for a firm with the following ratios: asset turnover = 1.40; profit margin = 5%; payout ratio = 25%; equity/assets = .60. *(LO3)*

5. **Percentage of Sales Models.** Percentage of sales models usually assume that costs, fixed assets, and working capital all increase at the same rate as sales. When do you think that these assumptions do not make sense? Would you feel happier using a percentage of sales model for short-term or long-term planning? *(LO2)*

6. **Relationships among Variables.** Comebaq Computers is aiming to increase its market share by slashing the price of its new range of personal computers. Are costs and assets likely to increase or decrease as a proportion of sales? Explain. *(LO2)*

7. **Balancing Items.** What are the possible choices of balancing items when using a financial planning model? Discuss whether some are generally preferable to others. *(LO2)*

8. **Financial Targets.** Managers sometimes state a target growth rate for sales or earnings per share. Do you think that either makes sense as a corporate goal? If not, why do you think that managers focus on them? *(LO1)*

PRACTICE PROBLEMS

9. **Percentage of Sales Models.** Here are the abbreviated financial statements for Planners Peanuts:

INCOME STATEMENT, 2012	
Sales	$2,000
Cost	1,500
Net income	$ 500

BALANCE SHEET, YEAR-END					
	2011	2012		2011	2012
Assets	$ 2,500	$ 3,000	Debt	$ 833	$ 1,000
			Equity	1,667	2,000
Total	$ 2,500	$ 3,000	Total	$ 2,500	$ 3,000

   If sales increase by 20% in 2013 and the company uses a strict percentage of sales planning model (meaning that all items on the income and balance sheet also increase by 20%), what must be the balancing item? What will be its value? *(LO2)*

10. **Required External Financing.** If the dividend payout ratio in Practice Problem 9 is fixed at 50%, calculate the required total external financing for growth rates in 2013 of 15%, 20%, and 25%. *(LO3)*

11. **Feasible Growth Rates.** What is the maximum possible growth rate for Planners Peanuts (see Practice Problem 9) if the payout ratio remains at 50% and

    a. no external debt or equity is to be issued. *(LO3)*
    b. the firm maintains a fixed debt ratio but issues no equity. *(LO3)*

12. **Using Percentage of Sales.** Eagle Sports Supply has the following financial statements. Assume that Eagle's assets are proportional to its sales. *(LO2)*

INCOME STATEMENT, 2012	
Sales	$950
Costs	250
Interest	50
Taxes	150
Net income	$500

BALANCE SHEET, YEAR-END					
	2011	2012		2011	2012
Assets	$ 2,700	$ 3,000	Debt	$ 900	$ 1,000
			Equity	1,800	2,000
Total	$ 2,700	$ 3,000	Total	$ 2,700	$ 3,000

    a. Find Eagle's required external funds if it maintains a dividend payout ratio of 70% and plans a growth rate of 15% in 2013.
    b. If Eagle chooses not to issue new shares of stock, what variable must be the balancing item? What will its value be?
    c. Now suppose that the firm plans instead to increase long-term debt only to $1,100 and does not wish to issue any new shares of stock. Why must the dividend payment now be the balancing item? What will its value be?

13. **Feasible Growth Rates.** *(LO3)*

    a. What is the internal growth rate of Eagle Sports (see Practice Problem 12) if the dividend payout ratio is fixed at 70% and the equity-to-asset ratio is fixed at $^2/_3$?
    b. What is the sustainable growth rate?

14. **Building Financial Models.** How would Executive Fruit's financial model change if the dividend payout ratio were cut to $^1/_3$? Use the revised model to generate a new financial plan for 2012 assuming that debt is the balancing item. Show how the financial statements given in Table 18.6 would change. What would be required external financing? *(LO2)*

Templates can be found at
www.mhhe.com/bmm7e.

15. **Required External Financing.** Executive Fruit's financial manager believes that sales in 2012 could rise by as much as 20% or by as little as 5%. *(LO3)*

    a. Recalculate the first-stage pro forma financial statements (Table 18.5) under these two assumptions. How does the rate of growth in revenues affect the firm's need for external funds?
    b. Assume any required external funds will be raised by issuing long-term debt and that any surplus funds will be used to retire such debt. Prepare the completed (second-stage) pro forma balance sheet.

Templates can be found at
www.mhhe.com/bmm7e.

16. **Building Financial Models.** The following tables contain financial statements for Dynastatics Corporation. Although the company has not been growing, it now plans to expand and will increase net fixed assets (that is, assets net of depreciation) by $200,000 per year for the next 5 years and forecasts that the ratio of revenues to total assets will remain at 1.50. Annual depreciation is 10% of net fixed assets at the end of the year. Fixed costs are expected to remain at $56,000 and variable costs at 80% of revenue. The company's policy is to pay out two-thirds of net income as dividends and to maintain a book debt ratio of 25% of total capital. *(LO2)*

    a. Produce a set of financial statements for 2013. Assume that net working capital will equal 50% of fixed assets.
    b. Now assume that the balancing item is debt and that no equity is to be issued. Prepare a completed pro forma balance sheet for 2013. What is the projected debt ratio for 2013?

INCOME STATEMENT, 2012
(figures in thousands of dollars)

Revenue	$1,800
Fixed costs	56
Variable costs (80% of revenue)	1,440
Depreciation	80
Interest (8% of beginning-of-year debt)	24
Taxable income	200
Taxes (at 40%)	80
Net income	$ 120
Dividends $80	
Addition to retained earnings $40	

BALANCE SHEET, YEAR-END
(figures in thousands of dollars)

	2012
Assets	
Net working capital	$ 400
Fixed assets	800
Total assets	$1,200
Liabilities and shareholders' equity	
Debt	$ 300
Equity	900
Total liabilities and shareholders' equity	$1,200

17. **Sustainable Growth.** Plank's Plants had net income of $2,000 on sales of $50,000 last year. The firm paid a dividend of $500. Total assets were $100,000, of which $40,000 was financed by debt. *(LO3)*

    a. What is the firm's sustainable growth rate?
    b. If the firm grows at its sustainable growth rate, how much debt will be issued next year?
    c. What would be the maximum possible growth rate if the firm did not issue any debt next year?

18. **Sustainable Growth.** A firm has decided that its optimal capital structure is 100% equity financed. It perceives its optimal dividend policy to be a 40% payout ratio. Asset turnover is sales/assets = .8, the profit margin is 10%, and the firm has a target growth rate of 5%. *(LO3)*

    a. Is the firm's target growth rate consistent with its other goals?
    b. If not, by how much does it need to increase asset turnover to achieve its goals?
    c. How much would it need to increase the profit margin instead?

19. **Internal Growth.** Go Go Industries is growing at 30% per year. It is all-equity-financed and has total assets of $1 million. Its return on equity is 25%. Its plowback ratio is 40%. *(LO3)*

    a. What is the internal growth rate?
    b. What is the firm's need for external financing this year?
    c. By how much would the firm increase its internal growth rate if it reduced its payout ratio to zero?
    d. By how much would such a move reduce the need for external financing? What do you conclude about the relationship between dividend policy and requirements for external financing?

20. **Sustainable Growth.** A firm's profit margin is 10%, and its asset turnover ratio is .6. It has no debt, has net income of $10 per share, and pays dividends of $4 per share. What is the sustainable growth rate? *(LO3)*

21. **Internal Growth.** An all-equity-financed firm plans to grow at an annual rate of at least 10%. Its return on equity is 18%. What is the maximum possible dividend payout rate the firm can maintain without resorting to additional equity issues? *(LO3)*

22. **Internal Growth.** Suppose the firm in the previous question has a debt-equity ratio of $^1/_3$. What is the maximum dividend payout ratio it can maintain without resorting to any external financing? *(LO3)*

23. **Internal Growth.** A firm has an asset turnover ratio of 2.0. Its plowback ratio is 50%, and it is all-equity-financed. What must its profit margin be if it wishes to finance 10% growth using only internally generated funds? *(LO3)*

24. **Internal Growth.** If the profit margin of the firm in the previous problem is 6%, what is the maximum payout ratio that will allow it to grow at 8% without resorting to external financing? *(LO3)*

25. **Internal Growth.** If the profit margin of the firm in Practice Problem 23 is 6%, what is the maximum possible growth rate that can be sustained without external financing? *(LO3)*

26. **Using Percentage of Sales.** The 2012 financial statements for Growth Industries are presented below. Sales and costs in 2013 are projected to be 20% higher than in 2012. Both current assets and accounts payable are projected to rise in proportion to sales. The firm is currently operating at full capacity, so it plans to increase fixed assets in proportion to sales. What external financing will be required by the firm? Interest expense in 2013 will equal 10% of long-term debt outstanding at the start of the year. The firm will maintain a dividend payout ratio of .40. *(LO2)*

INCOME STATEMENT, 2012	
Sales	$200,000
Costs	150,000
EBIT	50,000
Interest expense	10,000
Taxable income	40,000
Taxes (at 35%)	14,000
Net income	$ 26,000
Dividends	10,400
Addition to retained earnings	15,600

BALANCE SHEET, YEAR-END, 2012			
Assets		**Liabilities**	
Current assets		Current liabilities	
Cash	$ 3,000	Accounts payable	$ 10,000
Accounts receivable	8,000	Total current liabilities	$ 10,000
Inventories	29,000	Long-term debt	100,000
Total current assets	$ 40,000	Stockholders' equity	
Net plant and equipment	160,000	Common stock plus additional paid-in capital	15,000
		Retained earnings	75,000
		Total liabilities plus	
Total assets	$200,000	stockholders' equity	$200,000

CHALLENGE PROBLEMS

27. **Capacity Use and External Financing.** Now suppose that the fixed assets of Growth Industries (from the previous problem) are operating at only 75% of capacity. What is required external financing over the next year? *(LO3)*

Templates can be found at www.mhhe.com/bmm7e.

28. **Capacity Use and External Financing.** If Growth Industries from Practice Problem 26 is operating at only 75% of capacity, how much can sales grow before the firm will need to raise any external funds? Assume that once fixed assets are operating at capacity, they will need to grow thereafter in direct proportion to sales. *(LO3)*

29. **Internal Growth.** We will see in Chapter 19 that for many firms, cash and inventory needs may grow less than proportionally with sales. When we recognize this fact, will the firm's internal growth rate be higher or lower than the level predicted by the following formula: *(LO3)*

$$\text{Internal growth rate} = \frac{\text{reinvested earnings}}{\text{assets}}$$

Templates can be found at
www.mhhe.com/bmm7e.

30. **Spreadsheet Problem.** Use Spreadsheet 18.1 to answer the following questions about Executive Fruit: *(LO2)*

a. What would be required external financing if the growth rate is 15% and the dividend payout ratio is 60%?

b. Given the assumptions in part (a), what would be the amount of debt and equity issued if the firm wants to maintain its debt-equity ratio at a level of $2/3$?

c. What formulas would you put in cells H20 and H21 (as well as the corresponding cells in columns F and G) of Spreadsheet 18.1 to maintain the debt-equity ratio at $2/3$ while forcing the balance sheet to balance (that is, forcing debt + equity = total assets)?

WEB EXERCISES

1. Log on to finance.yahoo.com, and compare Wendy's International (WEN) and McDonald's (MCD) internal growth rates and sustainable growth rates by using recent annual data. (Note that the internal growth rate is calculated by using the earnings reinvested in the firm in the current year, not total retained earnings from the balance sheet.) Yahoo also shows the earnings growth that analysts are forecasting for each firm. Are the forecasts supported by the past performance of each firm?

2. Go to finance.yahoo.com. Find the (annual) balance sheet and income statement for American Electric Power (AEP). Suppose the company plans on 4% revenue growth over the next year. Under a percentage of sales approach, where assets and costs (except for depreciation) are proportional to sales, find AEP's required external funding over the next year. Assume that it will maintain the same dividend-payout ratio as in the current year and that its average tax rate will be the same next year as it was in the most recent year.

3. Log on to finance.yahoo.com, and click on *Investing* and then *Industries*. The industry browser provides some financial ratios for different sectors. What is the sustainable rate of growth for each sector if the firms maintain their plowback ratio and return on equity? (*Note:* Although Yahoo does not report the plowback ratio, you can work it out from the P/E and dividend yield.) Do you think that those industries with a high return on equity can continue to earn such a high return on new investment?

SOLUTIONS TO SELF-TEST QUESTIONS

18.1 Total assets will rise to $2,200. The debt-equity ratio is to be maintained at $2/3$. Therefore, debt rises by $80 to $880, and equity rises by $120 to $1,320. Net income will be $220. (See Table 18.2.) If the dividend is fixed at $180, reinvested earnings will be $40. Therefore, the firm needs to issue $120 − $40 = $80 of new equity and $80 of new debt.

18.2 a. The *total amount* of external financing is unchanged, since the dividend payout is unchanged. The $100,000 increase in total assets will now be financed by a mixture of debt and equity. If the debt-equity ratio is to remain at $2/3$, the firm will need to increase equity by $60,000 and debt by $40,000. Since reinvested earnings already increase shareholders' equity by $36,000, the firm would issue an additional $24,000 of new equity and $40,000 of debt.

b. If dividends are reduced from $72,000 to $60,000, then required external funds fall by $12,000, from $64,000 to $52,000.

18.3 a. The company currently runs at 75% of capacity given the current level of fixed assets. Sales can increase until the company is at 100% of capacity; therefore, sales can increase to $60 million × (100/75) = $80 million.

b. If sales were to increase by 50% to $90 million, new fixed assets would need to be added. The ratio of assets to sales when the company is operating at 100% of capacity [from part (a)] is $50 million/$80 million = $5/8$. Therefore, to support sales of $90 million, the company needs at least $90 million × $5/8$ = $56.25 million of fixed assets. This calls for a $6.25 million investment in additional fixed assets.

18.4   a. This question is answered by the planning model. Given assumptions for asset growth, the model will show the need for external financing, and this value can be compared to the firm's plans for such financing.

      b. Such a relationship may be assumed and built into the model. However, the model does not help to determine whether it is a reasonable assumption.

      c. Financial models do not shed light on the best capital structure. They can tell us only whether contemplated financing decisions are consistent with asset growth.

18.5   a. The equity-to-asset ratio is .8. If the payout ratio were reduced to 25%, the maximum growth rate assuming no external financing would be $.75 \times 18\% \times .8 = 10.8\%$.

      b. If the firm also can issue enough debt to maintain its equity-to-asset ratio unchanged, the sustainable growth rate will be $.75 \times 18\% = 13.5\%$.

MINICASE

Garnett Jackson, the founder and CEO of Tech Tune-Ups, stared out the window as he finished his customary peanut butter and jelly sandwich, contemplating the dilemma currently facing his firm. Tech Tune-Ups is a start-up firm, offering a wide range of computer services to its clients, including online technical assistance, remote maintenance and backup of client computers through the Internet, and virus prevention and recovery. The firm has been highly successful in the 2 years since it was founded; its reputation for fair pricing and good service is spreading, and Mr. Jackson believes the firm is in a good position to expand its customer base rapidly. But he is not sure that the firm has the financing in place to support that rapid growth.

Tech Tune-Ups' main capital investments are its own powerful computers, and its major operating expense is salary for its consultants. To a reasonably good approximation, both of these factors grow in proportion to the number of clients the firm serves.

Currently, the firm is a privately held corporation. Mr. Jackson and his partners, two classmates from his undergraduate days, have contributed $250,000 in equity capital, largely raised from their parents and other family members. The firm has a line of credit with a bank that allows it to borrow up to $400,000 at an interest rate of 8%. So far, the firm has used $200,000 of its credit line. If and when the firm reaches its borrowing limit, it will need to raise equity capital and will probably seek funding from a venture capital firm. The firm is growing rapidly, requiring continual investment in additional computers, and Mr. Jackson is concerned that it is approaching its borrowing limit faster than anticipated.

Mr. Jackson thumbs through past financial statements and estimates that each of the firm's computers, costing $10,000, can support revenues of $80,000 per year but that the salary and benefits paid to each consultant using one of the computers is $70,000. Sales revenue in 2011 was $1.2 million, and sales are expected to grow at a 20% annual rate in the next few years. The firm pays taxes at a rate of 35%. Its customers pay their bills with an average delay of 3 months, so accounts receivable at any time are usually around 25% of that year's sales.

Mr. Jackson and his co-owners receive minimal formal salary from the firm, instead taking 70% of profits as a "dividend," which accounts for a substantial portion of their personal incomes. The remainder of the profits are reinvested in the firm. If reinvested profits are not sufficient to support new purchases of computers, the firm borrows the required additional funds using its line of credit with the bank.

Mr. Jackson doesn't think Tech Tune-Ups can raise venture funding until after 2013. He decides to develop a financial plan to determine whether the firm can sustain its growth plans using its line of credit and reinvested earnings until then. If not, he and his partners will have to consider scaling back their hoped-for rate of growth, negotiate with their bankers to increase the line of credit, or consider taking a smaller share of profits out of the firm until further financing can be arranged.

Mr. Jackson wiped the last piece of jelly from the keyboard and settled down to work.

Can you help Mr. Jackson develop a financial plan? Do you think his growth plan is feasible?

CHAPTER 19

Short-Term Financial Planning

LEARNING OBJECTIVES

After studying this chapter, you should be able to:

(1) Understand why the firm needs to invest in net working capital.

(2) Show how long-term financing policy affects short-term financing requirements.

(3) Trace a firm's sources and uses of cash and evaluate its need for short-term borrowing.

(4) Develop a short-term financing plan that meets the firm's need for cash.

(5) Identify several major sources of short-term financing.

RELATED WEB SITES FOR THIS CHAPTER CAN BE FOUND AT WWW.MHHE.COM/BMM7E.

Short-term financial planning ensures that you have enough cash on hand to pay the bills.

Much of this book is devoted to long-term financial decisions such as capital budgeting and the choice of capital structure. These decisions are called *long-term* for two reasons. First, they usually involve long-lived assets or liabilities. Second, they are not easily reversed and thus may commit the firm to a particular course of action for several years.

Short-term financial decisions generally involve short-lived assets and liabilities, and usually they are easily reversed. Compare, for example, a 60-day bank loan for $50 million with a $50 million issue of 20-year bonds. The bank loan is clearly a short-term decision. The firm can repay it 2 months later and be right back where it started. A firm might conceivably issue a 20-year bond in January and retire it in March, but it would be extremely inconvenient and expensive to do so. In practice, such a bond issue is a long-term decision, not only because of the bond's 20-year maturity but also because the decision to issue it cannot be reversed on short notice.

A financial manager responsible for short-term financial decisions does not have to look far into the future. The decision to take the 60-day bank loan could properly be based on cash-flow forecasts for the next few months only. The bond issue decision will normally reflect forecast cash requirements 5, 10, or more years into the future.

Short-term financial decisions do not involve many of the difficult conceptual issues encountered elsewhere in this book. In a sense, short-term decisions are easier than long-term decisions—but they are not less important. A firm can identify extremely valuable capital investment opportunities, find the precise optimal debt ratio, follow the perfect dividend policy, and yet founder because no one bothers to raise the cash to pay this year's bills. Hence the need for short-term planning.

We start by showing how long-term financing decisions, introduced in the previous chapter, affect the firm's short-term financial planning problem. Next we review the components of working capital and describe the cash conversion cycle that dictates the types and amount of working capital a firm might maintain. We demonstrate how financial managers forecast month-by-month cash requirements or surpluses and how they develop short-term financing strategies. We conclude with an examination of various sources of short-term finance.

19.1 Links between Long-Term and Short-Term Financing

When you plan your personal finances, you have to choose which factors are central to your decision making and which are merely distractions. Often, this will depend on your time horizon. For example, at very long horizons such as for retirement planning, you don't think too carefully about when you will need to purchase your next car. At shorter horizons, covering perhaps the next 3 to 5 years, specific big-ticket items such as that potential car purchase need to be accounted for explicitly. At the shortest horizons, your planning might involve details down to the balances you maintain in your checking account.

It is the same with firms. When formulating long-term financial plans such as those considered in the previous chapter, firms may plan year by year. They often will be content with rules of thumb that relate average levels of fixed and short-term assets to annual sales, and not worry so much about seasonal variations in these relationships. In such cases, the likelihood that accounts receivable rise as sales peak in the Christmas season would be a needless detail that would distract from more important strategic decisions. But these considerations become crucial when firms focus on their near-term needs for cash and working capital. Short-term financing issues are conceptually easier than those involved in capital budgeting, but woe to the firm that takes them for granted.

Short-term financing needs are tied to the firm's long-term decisions. For example, businesses require capital—that is, money invested in plant, machinery, inventories, accounts receivable, and all the other assets it takes to run a company efficiently. Typically, these assets are not purchased all at once but are obtained gradually over time as the firm grows. The total cost of these assets is called the firm's *total capital requirement.*

Figure 19.1 illustrates the growth in the firm's total capital requirements. The upward-sloping line shows that as the business grows, it is likely to need additional fixed assets and current assets. You can think of this trendline as showing the base level of capital that is required. In addition to this base capital requirement, there may be seasonal fluctuations in the business that require an additional investment in current assets. Thus the wavy line in the illustration shows that the total capital requirement peaks late in each year. In practice, there would also be week-to-week and month-to-month fluctuations in the capital requirement, but these are not shown in Figure 19.1.

FIGURE 19.1 The firm's total capital requirement grows over time. It also exhibits seasonal variation around the trend.

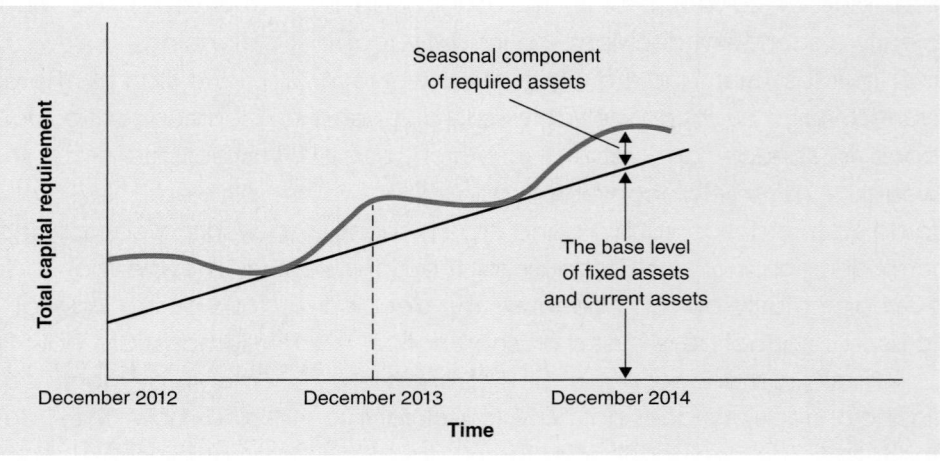

FIGURE 19.2 Alternative approaches to long- versus short-term financing: (a) relaxed strategy, where the firm is always a short-term lender; (b) middle-of-the-road policy; (c) restrictive policy, where the firm is always a short-term borrower

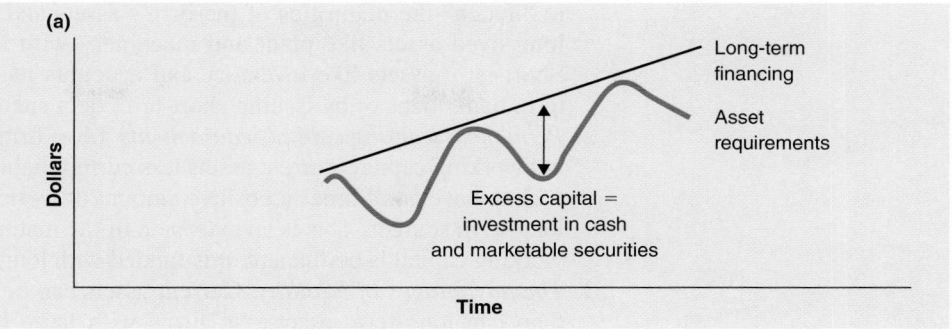

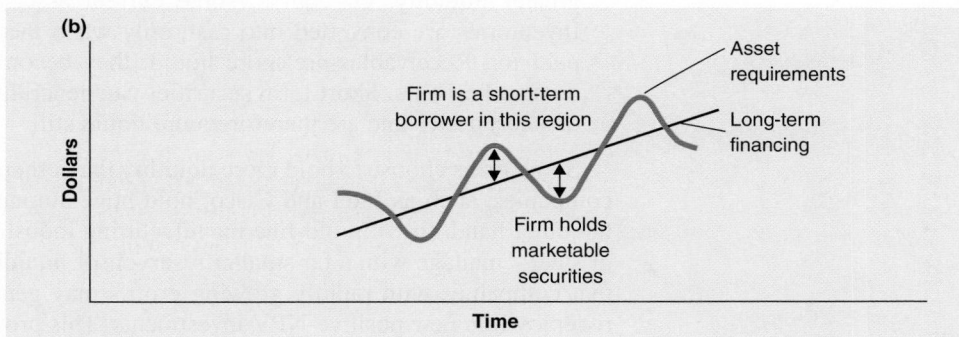

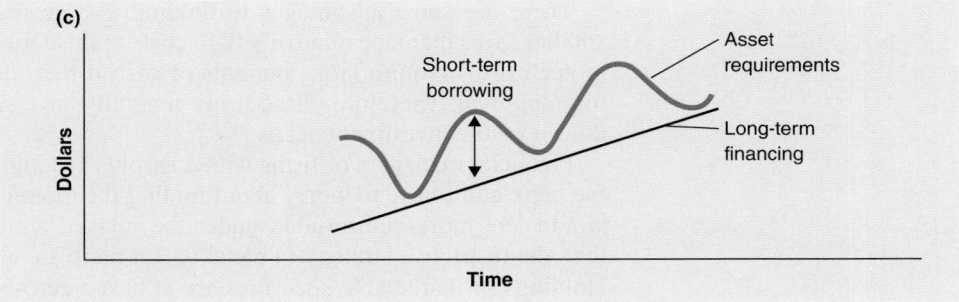

The total capital requirement can be met through either long- or short-term financing. When long-term financing does not cover the total capital requirement, the firm must raise short-term capital to make up the difference. When long-term financing *more* than covers the total capital requirement, the firm has surplus cash available for short-term investment. Thus the difference between the long-term financing raised and the total capital requirement determines whether the firm is a short-term borrower or lender.

The three panels in Figure 19.2 illustrate this. Each depicts a different long-term financing strategy. The "relaxed strategy" in panel *a* implies a permanent short-term cash surplus. This surplus will be invested in marketable securities. The "restrictive" policy illustrated in panel *c* implies a permanent need for short-term borrowing. Finally, panel *b* illustrates an intermediate strategy: The firm has spare cash that it can lend out during the part of the year when total capital requirements are relatively low, but it is a borrower during the rest of the year when capital requirements are relatively high.

What is the *best* level of long-term financing relative to the total capital requirement? It is hard to say. We can make several practical observations, however:

1. *Matching maturities.* When financial managers are asked the most important reason for choosing short-term rather than long-term debt, they generally say that they try

to "match" the maturities of the firm's assets and liabilities.[1] That is, they finance long-lived assets like plant and machinery with long-term borrowing and equity. Short-term assets like inventory and accounts receivable are financed with short-term bank loans or by issuing short-term debt such as commercial paper.

2. *Permanent working capital requirements.* Most firms have a permanent investment in net working capital (current assets less current liabilities). By this we mean that they *plan* to have at all times a positive amount of working capital. This is financed from long-term sources. This is an extension of the maturity-matching principle. Since the working capital is permanent, it is funded with long-term sources of financing.

3. *The advantages of liquidity.* Current assets can be converted into cash more easily than can long-term assets. So firms with large holdings of current assets enjoy greater liquidity. Of course, some current assets are more liquid than others. Inventories are converted into cash only when the goods are produced, sold, and paid for. Receivables are more liquid; they become cash as customers pay their outstanding bills. Short-term securities can generally be sold if the firm needs cash on short notice and are therefore more liquid still.

Some firms choose to hold more liquidity than others. For example, many high-tech companies, such as Intel and Cisco, hold huge amounts of short-term securities. On the other hand, firms in old-line manufacturing industries—such as chemicals, paper, or steel—manage with a far smaller reservoir of liquidity.[2] Why is this? One reason is that companies with rapidly growing profits may generate cash faster than they can redeploy it in new positive-NPV investments. This produces a surplus of cash that can be invested in short-term securities.

There are some advantages to holding a large reservoir of cash, particularly for smaller firms that face relatively high costs to raise funds on short notice. For example, biotech firms require large amounts of cash if their drugs succeed in gaining regulatory approval. Therefore, these firms generally have substantial cash holdings to fund their possible investment needs.

Financial managers of firms with a surplus of long-term financing and with cash in the bank don't have to worry about finding the money to pay next month's bills. They would feel more comfortable under the relaxed strategy illustrated in Figure 19.2*a* than the restrictive strategy in panel *c*. But there are also costs to having surplus cash. Holdings of marketable securities are at best a zero-NPV investment for a taxpaying firm.[3] Also, managers of firms with large cash surpluses may be tempted to run a less tight ship. The box nearby describes how the fashion company L. A. Gear was able to use its cash to survive 6 years of large losses and to employ a variety of radical, though ultimately unsuccessful, strategies to stave off bankruptcy. For shareholders, it may be best for firms with excess cash to go on a diet and use the money to retire some of their long-term securities. Indeed, we saw in Chapter 17 that Microsoft reduced its cash mountain by paying a special dividend and repurchasing its stock.

Pinkowitz and Williamson looked at the value that investors place on a firm's cash and found that on average shareholders valued a dollar of cash at $1.20.[4] Investors

---

[1] A survey by Graham and Harvey found that 63% of managers believed that maturity matching was the most important factor in their choice of debt maturity. See J. R. Graham and C. R. Harvey, "The Theory and Practice of Corporate Finance: Evidence from the Field," *Journal of Financial Economics* 61 (2001) pp. 187–243.

[2] Look back at Table 4.7. You can see that the firms in the computer and electronic industry have the highest quick ratio.

[3] Why do we say *at best* zero NPV? Not because we worry that the Treasury bills may be overpriced. Instead, we worry that when the firm holds Treasury bills, the interest income is subject to double taxation, first at the corporate level and then again at the personal level when the income is passed through to investors as dividends. The extra layer of taxation can make corporate holdings of Treasury bills a negative-NPV investment even if the bills would provide a fair rate of interest to an individual investor.

[4] L. Pinkowitz and R. Williamson, "The Market Value of Cash," *Journal of Applied Corporate Finance* 19 (2007), pp. 74–81.

placed a particularly high value on liquidity in the case of firms with plenty of growth opportunities. At the other extreme, Pinkowitz and Williamson found that when a firm was likely to face financial distress, a dollar of cash within the firm was often worth less than a dollar to the shareholders.

19.2 Working Capital

Much of short-term financial planning focuses on variation in working capital. Short-term or *current* assets and liabilities such as cash, accounts receivable, inventories, and accounts payable vary considerably as firms move through a cycle in which raw materials are purchased, goods are produced and sold, and customers pay their bills. In order to plan for this variation, it is best to begin by considering the various components of working capital and the factors that determine the level of each component.

The Components of Working Capital

Short-term, or *current,* assets and liabilities are collectively known as *working capital.* Table 19.1 gives a breakdown of current assets and liabilities for all manufacturing corporations in the United States in 2010. Total current assets were $2,137 billion, and total current liabilities were $1,485 billion.

Current Assets One important current asset is *accounts receivable.* Accounts receivable arise because companies do not usually expect customers to pay for their purchases immediately. These unpaid bills are a valuable asset that companies expect to be able to turn into cash in the near future. The bulk of accounts receivable consists of unpaid bills from sales to other companies and are known as *trade credit.* The remainder arises from the sale of goods to the final consumer. These are known as *consumer credit.*

Another important current asset is *inventory.* Inventories may consist of raw materials, work in process, or finished goods awaiting sale and shipment. Table 19.1 shows that firms in the United States have about the same amount invested in inventories as in accounts receivable.

The remaining current assets are cash and marketable securities. The cash consists partly of dollar bills, but most of the cash is in the form of bank deposits. These may be *demand deposits* (money in checking accounts that the firm can pay out immediately) and *time deposits* (money in savings accounts that can be paid out only with a delay). The principal marketable security is *commercial paper* (short-term unsecured debt sold by other firms). Other securities include *Treasury bills,* which are short-term debts sold by the U.S. government, and state and local government securities. Large firms usually invest directly in these securities; smaller firms may invest through a money market mutual fund that holds a package of short-term securities.

In managing their cash companies face much the same problem you do. There are always advantages to holding large amounts of ready cash—there is less risk of running out of cash and having to borrow more on short notice. On the other hand,

TABLE 19.1 Current assets and liabilities, U.S. manufacturing corporations, fourth quarter 2010 (figures in billions)

Current Assets		Current Liabilities	
Cash	$ 352	Short-term loans	$ 138
Marketable securities	174	Accounts payable	472
Accounts receivable	602	Accrued income taxes	26
Inventories	621	Current payments due on long-term debt	115
Other current assets	386	Other current liabilities	734
Total	$2,137	Total	$1,485

Notes: Net working capital (current assets − current liabilities) = $2,137 − $1,485 = $652 billion. Column sums subject to rounding error.
Source: U.S. Department of Commerce, *Quarterly Financial Report for Manufacturing, Mining and Trade Corporations,* March 2011, **www.census.gov/prod/www/abs/qfr-mm.html**.

The Rise and Fall of L. A. Gear

Fashion company L. A. Gear was one of the stars of the 1980s. Teenie boppers loved its pink sequined sneakers and its silver and gold lamé workout shoes. Investors preferred the 1300% growth in the company's stock price in the space of 4 years. But as the company failed to react to changes in fashion during the 1990s, sales and profits fell away rapidly. In January 1998 L. A. Gear filed for Chapter 11 bankruptcy. The decline of L. A. Gear illustrates how a company's liquid assets can provide the financial slack that allows it to evade market discipline and survive repeated losses.

The first table below summarizes the changes in L. A. Gear's profitability and its assets. The first two rows of the table show that after 1990 L. A. Gear's sales declined sharply and the firm produced losses for the rest of its life. The remaining rows show the company's assets. Since L. A. Gear farmed out shoe and clothing production, it had few fixed assets and owned largely cash, receivables, and inventory. As sales declined, two things happened. First, the company was able to reduce its inventory of finished goods. Second, customers paid off their outstanding bills. Thus, despite making steady losses, the company's holdings of cash and short-term securities initially increased.

The second table shows L. A. Gear's capital structure. Notice that after 1991 the company had almost no short-term bank debt, so that it was largely free from the discipline that is exerted whenever a company has to approach its bank for a loan to be renewed. As losses cumulated, common equity dwindled and the debt ratio climbed to 92%. Yet even in 1996 the company's cash holdings were over eight times that year's interest payments.

Because the company could liquidate its inventories and receivables and had no maturing debt, it was able to survive 6 years of large losses and to try a variety of radical new strategies, including a new emphasis on performance athletic shoes and then on children's shoes. All these strategies were ultimately unsuccessful. A company with large fixed assets that are not so easily liquidated would have found it less easy to survive so long.

Source: The decline of L. A. Gear is chronicled in H. DeAngelo, L. DeAngelo, and K. H. Wruck, "Asset Liquidity, Debt Covenants, and Managerial Discretion in Financial Distress: The Collapse of L. A. Gear," *Journal of Financial Economics* 64 (April 2002), pp. 3–34. Used with permission of Elsevier via Copyright Clearance Center, Inc.

Sales, Income, and Assets of L. A. Gear 1989–1996 (figures in $ millions)								
	1989	1990	1991	1992	1993	1994	1995	1996
Sales	617	820	619	430	398	416	297	196
Net income	55	31	−66	−72	−33	−22	−51	−62
Cash & securities	0	3	1	84	28	50	36	34
Receivables	101	156	112	56	73	77	47	24
Inventory	140	161	141	62	110	58	52	33
Current assets	257	338	297	230	220	194	138	93

	1989	1990	1991	1992	1993	1994	1995	1996
Bank debt	37	94	20	0	4	1	1	0
Long-term debt	0	0	0	0	50	50	50	50
Preferred stock	0	0	100	100	100	100	108	116
Common equity	168	206	132	88	47	18	−41	−111

there is a cost to holding idle cash balances rather than putting the money to work earning interest.

Now take a look at Figure 19.3, which shows the relative importance of current assets in different industries. For example, current assets constitute over half of the total assets of telecom companies, while they account for less than 10% of the assets of railroads. For some companies "current assets" means principally inventory; for others it means accounts receivable or cash and securities. For example, you can see that inventory accounts for the majority of the current assets of retail firms, receivables are more important for oil companies, and cash and short-term securities make up the bulk of the current assets of telecom and software companies.

Current Liabilities   We have seen that a typical company's principal current asset consists of unpaid bills. One firm's credit must be another's debit. Therefore, it is not surprising that a company's principal current liability generally consists of *accounts payable*—that is, outstanding payments due to other companies.

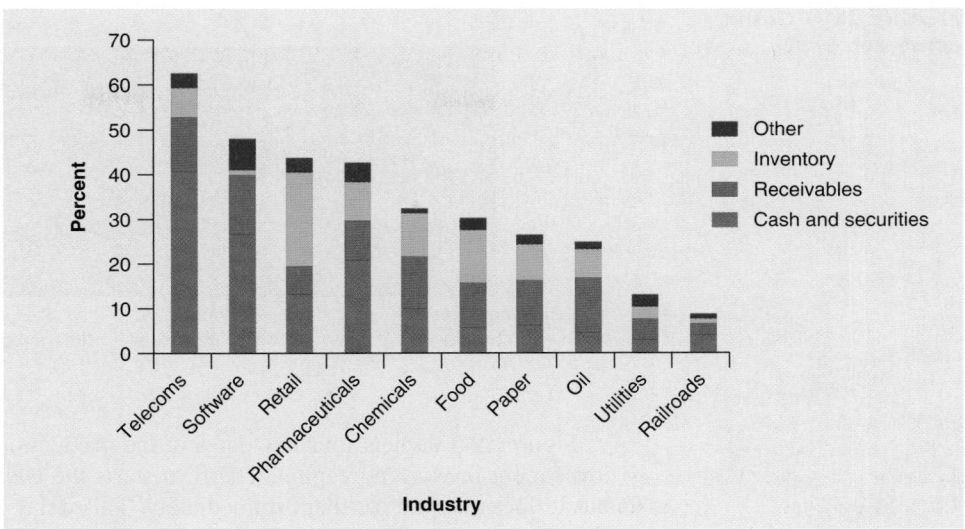

FIGURE 19.3 Current assets as a percentage of total assets in different industries. Figures are the mean percentages for firms in the S&P Composite Index in 2009.

The other major current liability consists of short-term borrowing. We will have more to say about this later in the chapter.

Working Capital and the Cash Conversion Cycle

net working capital
Current assets minus current liabilities. Often called *working capital*.

The difference between current assets and current liabilities is known as **net working capital,** but financial managers often refer to the difference simply (but imprecisely) as *working capital*. Usually current assets exceed current liabilities—that is, firms have positive net working capital. For U.S. manufacturing companies, current assets are on average about 40% higher than current liabilities.

To see why firms need net working capital, imagine a small company, Simple Souvenirs, that makes small novelty items for sale at gift shops. It buys raw materials such as leather, beads, and rhinestones for cash, processes them into finished goods like wallets or costume jewelry, and then sells these goods on credit. Figure 19.4 shows the whole cycle of operations.

If you prepare the firm's balance sheet at the beginning of the process, you see cash (a current asset). If you delay a little, you find the cash replaced first by inventories of raw materials and then by inventories of finished goods (also current assets). When the goods are sold, the inventories give way to accounts receivable (another current asset), and finally, when the customers pay their bills, the firm takes out its profit and replenishes the cash balance.

The components of working capital constantly change with the cycle of operations, but the amount of working capital is fixed. This is one reason why net working capital is a useful summary measure of current assets or liabilities.

FIGURE 19.4 Simple cycle of operations

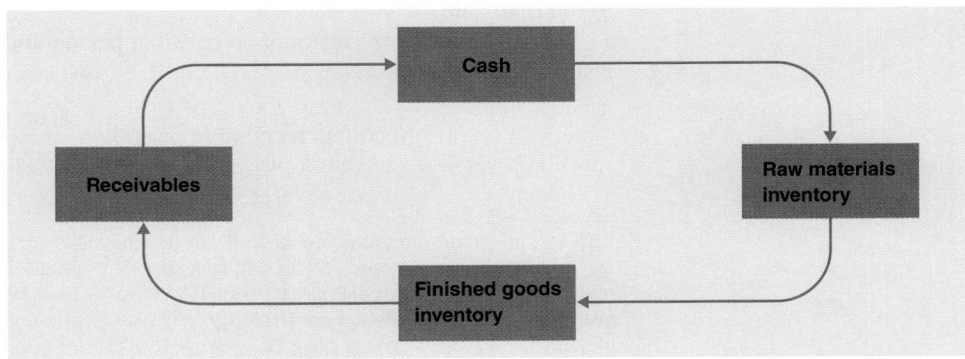

FIGURE 19.5 Cash
conversion cycle

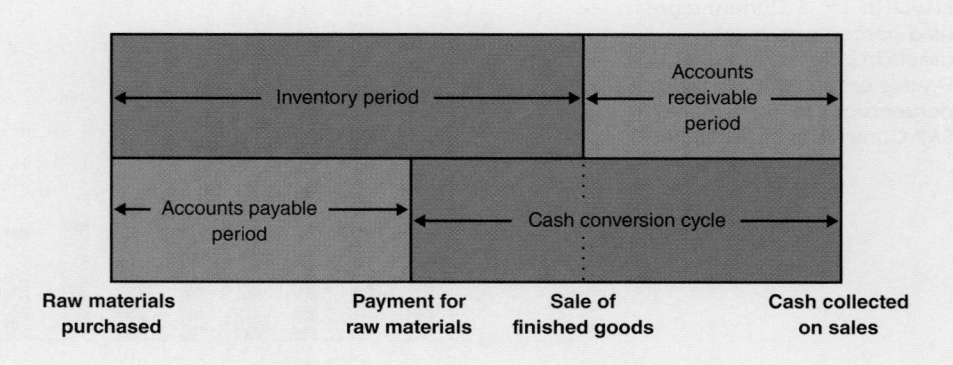

Figure 19.5 depicts four key dates in the production cycle that influence the firm's investment in working capital. The firm starts the cycle by purchasing raw materials, but it does not pay for them immediately. This delay is the *accounts payable period.* The firm processes the raw material and then sells the finished goods. The delay between the initial investment in inventories and the sale date is the *inventory period.* Some time after the firm has sold the goods, its customers pay their bills. The delay between the date of sale and the date at which the firm is paid is the *accounts receivable period.*

The top part of Figure 19.5 shows that the *total* delay between initial purchase of raw materials and ultimate payments from customers is the sum of the inventory and accounts receivable periods: First the raw materials must be purchased, processed, and sold, and then the bills must be collected. However, the *net* time that the company is out of cash is reduced by the time it takes to pay its own bills. The length of time between the firm's payment for its raw materials and the collection of payment from the customer is known as the firm's **cash conversion cycle.** To summarize,

cash conversion cycle
Period between firm's
payment for materials
and collection on its
sales.

$$\text{Cash conversion cycle} = (\text{inventory period} + \text{receivables period}) \\ - \text{accounts payable period}$$

The longer the production process, the more cash the firm must keep tied up in inventories. Similarly, the longer it takes customers to pay their bills, the higher the value of accounts receivable. On the other hand, if a firm can delay paying for its own materials, it may reduce the amount of cash it needs. In other words, accounts payable reduce net working capital.

In Chapter 4 we showed you how the firm's financial statements can be used to estimate the inventory period, also called *days' sales in inventory:*

$$\text{Inventory period} = \frac{\text{inventory}}{\text{annual cost of goods sold}/365}$$

The denominator in this equation is the firm's daily output. The ratio of inventory to daily output measures the average number of days from the purchase of the inventories to the final sale.

We can estimate the accounts receivable period and the accounts payable period in a similar way:[5]

$$\text{Accounts receivable period} = \frac{\text{accounts receivable}}{\text{annual sales}/365}$$

---

[5] Because inventories are valued at cost, we divide inventory levels by cost of goods sold rather than sales revenue to obtain the inventory period. This way, both numerator and denominator are measured by cost. The same reasoning applies to the accounts payable period. On the other hand, because accounts receivable are valued at product price, we divide average receivables by daily sales revenue to find the receivables period.

$$\text{Accounts payable period} = \frac{\text{accounts payable}}{\text{annual cost of goods sold}/365}$$

Of course, the cash conversion cycle is much shorter in some businesses than in others. For example, look at Table 19.2, which shows the average length of the cycle for the sample of industries that we looked at earlier.

EXAMPLE 19.1 ▶ Cash Conversion Cycle

The following table provides the information necessary to compute the cash conversion cycle for manufacturing firms in the United States in 2010. We can use the table to answer four questions: How long on average does it take U.S. manufacturing firms to produce and sell their product? How long does it take to collect bills? How long does it take to pay bills? And what is the cash conversion cycle?

These data can be used to calculate the cash conversion cycle for U.S. manufacturing firms in 2010 (figures in billions)

Income Statement Data		Balance Sheet Data	
Sales	$5,773	Inventory	$569
Cost of goods sold	5,184	Accounts receivable	559
		Accounts payable	415

Note: Cost of goods sold includes selling, general, and administrative expenses.
Source: U.S. Department of Commerce, *Quarterly Financial Report for Manufacturing, Mining and Trade Corporations,* March 2011, Tables 1.0 and 1.1.

The delays in collecting cash are given by the inventory and receivables periods. The delay in paying bills is given by the payables period. The net delay in collecting payments is the cash conversion cycle. We calculate these periods as follows:

$$\text{Inventory period} = \frac{\text{inventory}}{\text{annual cost of goods sold}/365}$$

$$= \frac{569}{5,184/365} = 40.1 \text{ days}$$

$$\text{Receivables period} = \frac{\text{accounts receivable}}{\text{annual sales}/365}$$

$$= \frac{559}{5,773/365} = 35.3 \text{ days}$$

$$\text{Payables period} = \frac{\text{accounts payable}}{\text{annual cost of goods sold}/365}$$

$$= \frac{415}{5,184/365} = 29.2 \text{ days}$$

The cash conversion cycle is

Inventory period + receivables period − payables period
= 40.1 + 35.3 − 29.2 = 46.2 days

It is therefore taking U.S. manufacturing companies an average of about 7 weeks from the time they lay out money on inventories to collect payment from their customers.

TABLE 19.2 Average cash conversion cycle (days) for selected industries, 2009

Industry	Inventory Period	+ Accounts Receivable Period	− Accounts Payable Period	= Cash Conversion Cycle
Telecoms	82.2	88.1	56.4	113.9
Software	8.2	76.4	68.3	16.3
Retail	79.6	13.1	37.9	54.8
Pharmaceuticals	208.7	56.8	89.9	175.7
Chemicals	68.4	58.8	67.5	59.7
Food	55.8	35.5	40.5	50.8
Paper	60.0	48.6	36.7	72.0
Oil	19.7	29.4	42.1	7.1
Utilities	40.0	53.6	46.6	47.0
Railroads	16.4	30.5	34.4	12.5

Self-Test 19.1

a. Would you expect Tiffany, which sells fine jewelry, or Target, which sells a wide range of household goods at attractive prices, to have the higher cash conversion cycle? Why?

b. Use the following data to calculate the cash conversion cycle of each firm (all values are in millions of dollars). What factor has the greatest impact on the difference in their conversion cycles?

	Tiffany	Target
Sales	2,709	65,357
Cost of goods sold	1,179	45,583
Inventories	1,428	7,179
Accounts receivable	165	6,966
Accounts payable	299	9,631

The Working Capital Trade-Off

Of course the cash conversion cycle is not cast in stone. To a large extent it is within management's control. Working capital can be *managed*. For example, accounts receivable are affected by the terms of credit the firm offers to its customers. You can cut the amount of money tied up in receivables by getting tough with customers who are slow in paying their bills. (You may find, however, that in the future they take their business elsewhere.) Similarly, the firm can reduce its investment in inventories of raw materials. (Here the risk is that it may one day run out of inventories and production will grind to a halt.)

These considerations show that investment in working capital has both costs and benefits. For example, the cost of the firm's investment in receivables is the interest that could have been earned if customers had paid their bills earlier. The firm also forgoes interest income when it holds idle cash balances rather than putting the money to work in marketable securities. The cost of holding inventory includes not only the opportunity cost of capital but also storage and insurance costs and the risk of spoilage or obsolescence. All of these **carrying costs** encourage firms to hold current assets to a minimum.

carrying costs
Costs of maintaining current assets, including opportunity cost of capital.

While carrying costs discourage large investments in current assets, a low level of current assets makes it more likely that the firm will face **shortage costs.** For example, if the firm runs out of inventory of raw materials, it may have to shut down production. Similarly, a producer holding a small finished goods inventory is more likely to be caught short, unable to fill orders promptly. There are also disadvantages to holding small "inventories" of cash. If the firm runs out of cash, it may have to sell securities and incur unnecessary trading costs. The firm may also maintain too low a level of accounts receivable. If the firm tries to minimize accounts receivable by restricting credit sales, it

shortage costs
Costs incurred from shortages in current assets.

may lose customers. **An important job of the financial manager is to strike a balance between the costs and benefits of current assets, that is, to find the level of current assets that minimizes the sum of carrying costs and shortage costs.**

In Chapter 4 we pointed out that when managers review the performance of each part of their business, they often deduct the cost of the capital employed from its profits. This measure is known as *residual income* or *economic value added (EVA),* which is the term coined by the consulting firm Stern Stewart. Firms that employ EVA to measure performance have often discovered that they can make large savings on working capital. Herman Miller Corporation, the furniture manufacturer, found that after it introduced EVA, employees became much more conscious of the cash tied up in inventories. One sewing machine operator commented:

> We used to have these stacks of fabric sitting here on the tables until we needed them. . . . We were going to use the fabric anyway, so who cares that we're buying it and stacking it up there? Now no one has excess fabric. They only have stuff we're working on today. And it's changed the way we connect with suppliers, and we're having [them] deliver fabric more often.[6]

The company also started to look at how rapidly customers paid their bills. It found that any time an item was missing from an order, the customer would delay payment until all the pieces had been delivered. When the company cleared up the problem of missing items, it made its customers happier and it collected the cash faster.[7]

We will look more carefully at the costs and benefits of working capital in the next two chapters.

Self-Test 19.2

How will the following affect the size of the firm's optimal investment in current assets?

a. The interest rate rises from 6% to 8%.
b. A just-in-time inventory system is introduced that reduces the risk of inventory shortages.
c. Customers pressure the firm for a more lenient credit sales policy.

19.3 Tracing Changes in Cash and Working Capital

Table 19.3 compares 2010 and 2011 year-end balance sheets for Dynamic Mattress Company. Table 19.4 shows the firm's income statement for 2011. Note that Dynamic's cash balance increased from $4 million to $5 million in 2011. What caused this increase? Did the extra cash come from Dynamic Mattress Company's additional long-term borrowing? From reinvested earnings? From cash released by reducing inventory? Or perhaps it came from extra credit extended by Dynamic's suppliers. (Note the increase in accounts payable.)

The correct answer? All of the above. There is rarely any point in linking a particular source of funds with a particular use. Instead, financial analysts list the various sources and uses of cash in a statement like the one shown in Table 19.5. The statement shows that Dynamic *generated* cash from the following sources:

1. It issued $7 million of long-term debt.
2. It reduced inventory, releasing $1 million.

---

[6] A. Ehrbar, *EVA: The Real Key to Creating Wealth* (New York: John Wiley & Sons, 1998), pp. 130–131.

[7] A. Ehrbar and G. Bennett Stewart III, "The EVA Revolution," *Journal of Applied Corporate Finance* 12 (Summer 1999), pp. 18–31.

TABLE 19.3 Year-end balance sheets for Dynamic Mattress Company (figures in millions)

Assets	2010	2011	Liabilities and Shareholders' Equity	2010	2011
Current assets			Current liabilities		
Cash	$ 4	$ 5	Bank loans	$ 5	$ 0
Marketable securities	0	5	Accounts payable	20	27
Inventory	26	25	Total current liabilities	$25	$ 27
Accounts receivable	25	30	Long-term debt	5	12
Total current assets	$55	$ 65	Net worth (equity and retained earnings)	65	76
Fixed assets			Total liabilities and owners' equity	$95	$115
Gross investment	$56	$ 70			
Less depreciation	16	20			
Net fixed assets	$40	$ 50			
Total assets	$95	$115			

3. It increased its accounts payable, in effect borrowing an additional $7 million from its suppliers.
4. By far the largest source of cash was Dynamic's operations, which generated $16 million. Note that the $12 million net income reported in Table 19.4 understates cash flow because depreciation is deducted in calculating income. Depreciation is *not* a cash outlay. Thus it must be added back in order to obtain operating cash flow.

Dynamic *used* cash for the following purposes:

1. It paid a $1 million dividend. (*Note:* The $11 million increase in Dynamic's equity is due to reinvested earnings: $12 million of equity income less the $1 million dividend.)
2. It repaid a $5 million short-term bank loan.
3. It invested $14 million. This shows up as the increase in gross fixed assets in Table 19.3.
4. It purchased $5 million of marketable securities.
5. It allowed accounts receivable to expand by $5 million. In effect, it lent this additional amount to its customers.

> ### Self-Test 19.3
>
> How will the following affect *cash* and *net working capital*?
>
> a. The firm takes out a short-term bank loan and uses the funds to pay off some of its accounts payable.
> b. The firm uses cash on hand to buy raw materials.
> c. The firm repurchases outstanding shares of stock.
> d. The firm sells long-term bonds and puts the proceeds in its bank account.

TABLE 19.4 2011 income statement for Dynamic Mattress Company (figures in millions)

Sales	$350
Operating costs	321
Depreciation	4
EBIT	25
Interest	1
Pretax income	24
Tax at 50%	12
Net income	$ 12

Note: Dividend = $1 million; reinvested earnings = $11 million.

TABLE 19.5 Sources and uses of cash for Dynamic Mattress Company (figures in millions)

Sources	
Issued long-term debt	$ 7
Reduced inventories	1
Increased accounts payable	7
Cash from operations	
Net income	12
Depreciation	4
Total sources	$31
Uses	
Repaid short-term bank loan	$ 5
Invested in fixed assets	14
Purchased marketable securities	5
Increased accounts receivable	5
Dividend	1
Total uses	$30
Increase in cash balance	$ 1

19.4 Cash Budgeting

The financial manager's task is to forecast *future* sources and uses of cash. These forecasts serve two purposes. First, they alert the financial manager to future cash needs. Second, the cash-flow forecasts provide a standard, or budget, against which subsequent performance can be judged.

There are several ways to produce a quarterly cash budget. Many large firms have developed elaborate "corporate models"; others use a spreadsheet program to plan their cash needs. The procedures of smaller firms may be less formal. But no matter what method is chosen, there are three common steps to preparing a cash budget:

Step 1. Forecast the sources of cash. The largest inflow of cash comes from payments by the firm's customers.

Step 2. Forecast uses of cash.

Step 3. Calculate whether the firm is facing a cash shortage or surplus.

The financial *plan* sets out a strategy for investing cash surpluses or financing any deficit.

We will illustrate these issues by continuing the example of Dynamic Mattress.

Forecast Sources of Cash

Most of Dynamic's cash inflow comes from the sale of mattresses. We therefore start with a sales forecast by quarter for 2012:[8]

Quarter:	First	Second	Third	Fourth
Sales ($ million)	87.5	78.5	116	131

But unless customers pay cash on delivery, sales become accounts receivable before they become cash. Cash flow comes from *collections* on accounts receivable.

Most firms keep track of the average time it takes customers to pay their bills. From this they can forecast what proportion of a quarter's sales is likely to be converted into cash in that quarter and what proportion is likely to be carried over to the next quarter as accounts receivable. This proportion depends on the lags with which customers pay their bills. For example, if customers wait 1 month to pay their bills, then on average one-third of each quarter's bills will not be paid until the following quarter. If the payment delay is 2 months, then two-thirds of quarterly sales will be collected in the following quarter.

---

[8] For simplicity, we present a quarterly forecast. However, most firms would forecast by month instead of by quarter. Sometimes weekly or even daily forecasts are made.

Suppose that 80% of sales are collected in the immediate quarter and the remaining 20% in the next. Panel A of Spreadsheet 19.1 shows forecast collections under this assumption.

In the first quarter, for example, collections from current sales are 80% of $87.5 million, or $70 million. But the firm also collects 20% of the previous quarter's sales, or .20 × $75 million = $15 million. Therefore, total collections are $70 million + $15 million = $85 million.

Dynamic started the first quarter with $30 million of accounts receivable. The quarter's sales of $87.5 million were *added* to accounts receivable, but $85 million of collections were *subtracted*. Therefore, as Spreadsheet 19.1 shows, Dynamic ended the quarter with accounts receivable of $30 million + $87.5 million − $85 million = $32.5 million. The general formula is

Ending accounts receivable = beginning accounts receivable + sales − collections

Panel B of Spreadsheet 19.1 shows forecast sources and uses of cash for Dynamic Mattress. Collection of receivables is the main source, but it is not the only one. Perhaps the firm plans to dispose of some land or expects a tax refund or payment of

SPREADSHEET 19.1 Dynamic Mattress's cash budget for 2010
(figures in millions of dollars)

You can find this spreadsheet at www.mhhe.com/bmm7e.

	A	B	C	D	E
1	Quarter:	First	Second	Third	Fourth
2					
3	**A. Accounts Receivable**				
4	Receivables (beginning of period)	30.0	32.5	30.7	38.2
5	Sales	87.5	78.5	116.0	131.0
6	Collections				
7	On sales in current period (80%)	70.0	62.8	92.8	104.8
8	On sales in previous period (20%)[a]	15.0	17.5	15.7	23.2
9	Total collections	85.0	80.3	108.5	128.0
10	Receivables (end of period) = Rows 4+5-9	32.5	30.7	38.2	41.2
11					
12	**B. Cash Budget**				
13	Sources of cash				
14	Collections of accounts receivable (row 9)	85.0	80.3	108.5	128.0
15	Other	1.5	0.0	12.5	0.0
16	Total collections	86.5	80.3	121.0	128.0
17	Uses of cash				
18	Payments of accounts payable	65.0	60.0	55.0	50.0
19	Labor & other expenses	30.0	30.0	30.0	30.0
20	Capital expenses	32.5	1.3	5.5	8.0
21	Taxes, interest, and dividends	4.0	4.0	4.5	5.0
22	Total uses	131.5	95.3	95.0	93.0
23					
24	**Net cash inflow = Sources - Uses**	-45.0	-15.0	26.0	35.0
25					
26	**C. Short-term financing requirements**				
27	Cash at start of period	5.0	-40.0	-55.0	-29.0
28	+ Net cash inflow (from row 24)	-45.0	-15.0	26.0	35.0
29	= Cash at end of period[b]	-40.0	-55.0	-29.0	6.0
30	Minimum operating balance	5.0	5.0	5.0	5.0
31	Cumulative financing required[c] (Row 30 - 29)	45.0	60.0	34.0	-1.0
32					
33					

[a] Sales in the fourth quarter of the previous year were $75 million.
[b] Firms cannot literally hold a negative amount of cash. This line shows the amount of cash the firm will have to raise to pay its bills.
[c] A negative sign indicates that no short-term financing is required. Instead the firm has a cash surplus.

an insurance claim. All such items are included as "other" sources. It is also possible that you may raise additional capital by borrowing or selling stock, but we don't want to prejudge that question. Therefore, for the moment we just assume that Dynamic will not raise further long-term finance.

Forecast Uses of Cash

There always seem to be many more uses for cash than there are sources. Panel B of Spreadsheet 19.1 shows how Dynamic expects to use cash. For simplicity, we condense the uses into four categories:

1. *Payments of accounts payable.* Dynamic has to pay its bills for raw materials, parts, electricity, and so on. The cash-flow forecast assumes all these bills are paid on time, although Dynamic could probably delay payment to some extent. Delayed payment is sometimes called *stretching your payables.* Stretching is one source of short-term financing, but for most firms it is an expensive source, because by stretching they lose discounts given to firms that pay promptly. (This is discussed in more detail in Chapter 20.)
2. *Labor, administrative, and other expenses.* This category includes all other regular business expenses.
3. *Capital expenditures.* Note that Dynamic Mattress plans a major outlay of cash in the first quarter to pay for a long-lived asset.
4. *Taxes, interest, and dividend payments.* This includes interest on currently outstanding long-term debt and dividend payments to stockholders.

The forecast net inflow of cash (sources minus uses) is shown in row 24. Note the large negative figure for the first quarter: a $45 million forecast *outflow.* There is a smaller forecast *outflow* in the second quarter and then substantial cash inflows in the second half of the year.

The Cash Balance

So far, Dynamic Mattress does not know how much it will have to borrow or, for that matter, if it will have to borrow at all. These calculations are presented in panel C, which shows how much financing Dynamic will have to raise if its cash-flow forecasts are right. It starts the year with $5 million in cash. There is a $45 million cash outflow in the first quarter, which in the absence of external financing would create a $40 million cash shortfall at the end of the period (row 29). This deficit is carried to the beginning of the next quarter (cell C27). At the very least, Dynamic must obtain $40 million of additional financing just to cover the forecast cash deficit. This would leave the firm with a forecast cash balance of exactly zero at the start of the second quarter.

However, most financial managers would regard a planned cash balance of zero as driving too close to the edge of the cliff. They establish a *minimum operating cash balance* to absorb unexpected cash inflows and outflows. We assume in Spreadsheet 19.1 that Dynamic's minimum operating cash balance is $5 million. That means it has to raise $45 million instead of $40 million in the first quarter and $15 million more in the second quarter. Thus its *cumulative* financing requirement is $60 million in the second quarter. Fortunately, this is the peak; the cumulative requirement declines in the third quarter when its $26 million net cash inflow reduces its cumulative financing requirement to $34 million. (Notice that cumulative short-term financing falls by the net cash inflow in that quarter from row 24.) In the final quarter Dynamic is out of the woods. Its $35 million net cash inflow is enough to eliminate short-term financing and actually increase cash balances above the $5 million minimum acceptable balance.

Before moving on, we offer two general observations about this example:

1. The large cash outflows in the first two quarters do not necessarily spell trouble for Dynamic Mattress. In part they reflect the capital investment made in the first quarter: Dynamic is spending $32.5 million, but it should be acquiring an asset

worth that much or more. The cash outflows also reflect low sales in the first half of the year; sales recover in the second half.[9] If this is a predictable seasonal pattern, the firm should have no trouble borrowing to help it get through the slow months.

2. Spreadsheet 19.1 is only a best guess about future cash flows. It is a good idea to think about the *uncertainty* in your estimates. For example, you could undertake a sensitivity analysis, in which you inspect how Dynamic's cash requirements would be affected by a shortfall in sales or by a delay in collections.

Self-Test 19.4

Calculate Dynamic Mattress's quarterly cash receipts, net cash inflow, and cumulative short-term financing required if customers pay for only 60% of purchases in the current quarter and pay the remaining 40% in the following quarter.

You can find this spreadsheet at www.mhhe.com/bmm7e.

Our next step will be to develop a short-term financing plan that addresses the forecast requirements in the most economical way possible. Before presenting such a plan, however, we should pause briefly to point out that short-term financial planning, like long-term planning, is best done on a computer. Spreadsheet 19.2 presents the formula

SPREADSHEET 19.2 Dynamic Mattress's cash budget (formula view)

	A	B	C	D	E
1	Quarter:	**First**	**Second**	**Third**	**Fourth**
2					
3	**A. Accounts Receivable**				
4	Receivables (beginning of period)	30	=B10	=C10	=D10
5	Sales	87.5	78.5	116	131
6	Collections				
7	On sales in current period (80%)	=0.8*B5	=0.8*C5	=0.8*D5	=0.8*E5
8	On sales in previous period (20%)	=0.2*75	=0.2*B5	=0.2*C5	=0.2*D5
9	Total collections	=B7+B8	=C7+C8	=D7+D8	=E7+E8
10	Receivables (end of period)	=B4+B5-B9	=C4+C5-C9	=D4+D5-D9	=E4+E5-E9
11					
12	**B. Cash Budget**				
13	**Sources of cash**				
14	Collections of accts receivable	=B9	=C9	=D9	=E9
15	Other	1.5	0	12.5	0
16	Total sources	=B14+B15	=C14+C15	=D14+D15	=E14+E15
17	**Uses**				
18	Payments of accounts payable	65	60	55	50
19	Labor & other expenses	30	30	30	30
20	Capital expenses	32.5	1.3	5.5	8
21	Taxes, interest, and dividends	4	4	4.5	5
22	Total uses	=SUM(B18:B21)	=SUM(C18:C21)	=SUM(D18:D21)	=SUM(E18:E21)
23					
24	**Net cash inflow = Sources - Uses**	=B16-B22	=C16-C22	=D16-D22	=E16-E22
25					
26	**C. Short-term Financing Requirements**				
27	Cash at start of period	5	=B29	=C29	=D29
28	+ Net cash inflow	=B24	=C24	=D24	=E24
29	= Cash at end of period	=B27+B28	=C27+C28	=D27+D28	=E27+E28
30	Minimum operating balance	5	=B30	=C30	=D30
31	Cumulative financing required	=B30-B29	=C30-C29	=D30-D29	=E30-E29
32					
33					

---

[9] Maybe people buy more mattresses late in the year when the nights are longer.

view of Spreadsheet 19.1. Examine the entries and note which items are inputs (for example, rows 18 to 21) and which are calculated from equations. The formulas also indicate the links from one panel to another. For example, collections of receivables are calculated in panel A, row 9, and passed through as inputs in panel B, row 14. Similarly, net cash inflow in panel B, row 24, is passed along to panel C, row 28.

Once the spreadsheet is set up, it becomes easy to explore the consequences of many "what-if" questions. For example, Self-Test 19.4 asked you to recalculate the quarterly cash receipts, net cash inflow, and cumulative short-term financing required if the firm's collections on accounts receivable slow down. You can obviously do this by hand, but it is quicker and easier to do it in a spreadsheet—especially when there might be dozens of scenarios that you need to work through!

19.5 A Short-Term Financing Plan

Dynamic's cash budget defines its problem. Its financial manager must find short-term financing to cover the firm's forecast cash requirements. There are dozens of sources of short-term financing, but for simplicity we will consider only two: obtaining bank loans or stretching payables.

We assume that Dynamic can borrow up to $40 million from its bank at an interest rate of 8% per year, or 2% per quarter. It can borrow and repay the loan whenever it wants to, but it may not exceed its credit limit.

Alternatively, Dynamic can raise capital by putting off paying its bills. The financial manager believes that Dynamic can defer the following amounts in each quarter:

Quarter:	First	Second	Third	Fourth
Amount deferrable ($ million)	52	48	44	40

That is, $52 million can be saved in the first quarter by *not* paying bills in that quarter. (*Note:* Spreadsheet 19.1 was prepared assuming these bills *are* paid in the first quarter.) If deferred, these payments *must* be made in the second quarter. Similarly, $48 million of the second quarter's bills can be deferred to the third quarter, and so on.

Stretching payables is often costly, however, even if no ill will is incurred.[10] This is because many suppliers offer discounts for prompt payment, so Dynamic loses the discount if it pays late. In this example we assume the lost discount is 5% of the amount deferred. In other words, if a $52 million payment is delayed in the first quarter, the firm must pay 5% more, or $54.6 million, in the next quarter. This is like borrowing at an annual interest rate of over 20% (because $1.05^4 - 1 = .216$, or 21.6%).

Dynamic Mattress's Financing Plan

With these two options, the short-term financing strategy is obvious: Use the lower-cost bank loan first. Stretch payables only if you can't borrow enough from the bank.

Spreadsheet 19.3 shows the resulting plan. Panel A (cash requirements) sets out the cash that needs to be raised in each quarter. Panel B (cash raised) describes the various sources of financing the firm plans to use. Panels C and D describe how the firm will use net cash inflows when they turn positive. Panel E keeps track of the bank loan.

In the first quarter the plan calls for borrowing the full amount available from the bank ($40 million). In addition, the firm sells the $5 million of marketable securities it held at the end of 2011. Thus under this plan it raises the necessary $45 million in the first quarter.

---

[10] In fact, ill will is likely to be incurred. Firms that stretch payments risk being labeled as credit risks. Since stretching is so expensive, suppliers reason that customers will resort to it only when they cannot obtain credit at reasonable rates elsewhere. Suppliers naturally are reluctant to act as the lender of last resort.

SPREADSHEET 19.3
Dynamic Mattress's financing plan (figures in millions of dollars)

You can find this spreadsheet at www.mhhe.com/bmm7e.

	A	B	C	D	E
1	Quarter:	First	Second	Third	Fourth
2	**A. Cash requirements**				
3	Cash required for operations[a]	45.00	15.00	-26.00	-35.00
4	Interest on bank loan[b]	0.00	0.80	0.80	0.63
5	Interest on stretched payables[c]	0.00	0.00	0.79	0.00
6	Total cash required	45.00	15.80	-24.41	-34.37
7					
8	**B. Cash raised in quarter**				
9	Bank loan	40.00	0.00	0.00	0.00
10	Stretched payables	0.00	15.80	0.00	0.00
11	Securities sold	5.00	0.00	0.00	0.00
12	Total cash raised	45.00	15.80	0.00	0.00
13					
14	**C. Repayments**				
15	Of stretched payables	0.00	0.00	15.80	0.00
16	Of bank loan	0.00	0.00	8.61	31.39
17					
18	**D. Addition to cash balances**	0.00	0.00	0.00	2.98
19					
20	**E. Bank loan**				
21	Beginning of quarter	0.00	40.00	40.00	31.39
22	End of quarter	40.00	40.00	31.39	0.00

[a] A negative cash requirement implies positive cash flow from operations. This row is derived from row 24 of Spreadsheet 19.1.
[b] The interest rate on the bank loan is 2% per quarter applied to the bank loan outstanding at the start of the quarter. Thus the interest due in the second quarter is .02 × $40 million = $.8 million.
[c] The "interest" cost of the stretched payables is 5% of the amount of payment deferred. For example, in the third quarter, 5% of the $15.8 million stretched in the second quarter is about $.8 million.

In the second quarter, an additional $15 million must be raised to cover the net cash outflow predicted in Spreadsheet 19.1. In addition, $.8 million must be raised to pay interest on the bank loan. Therefore, the plan calls for Dynamic to maintain its bank borrowing and to stretch $15.8 million in payables. Notice that in the first two quarters, when net cash flow from operations is negative, the firm maintains its cash balance at the minimum acceptable level. Additions to cash balances are zero. Similarly, repayments of outstanding debt are zero. In fact outstanding debt rises in each of these quarters.

In the third and fourth quarters, the firm generates a cash-flow surplus, so the plan calls for Dynamic to pay off its debt. First it pays off stretched payables, as it is required to do, and then it uses any remaining cash-flow surplus to pay down its bank loan. In the third quarter, all of the net cash inflow is used to reduce outstanding short-term borrowing. In the fourth quarter, the firm pays off its remaining short-term borrowing and uses the extra $2.98 million to increase its cash balances.

> *Self-Test 19.5*
>
> Revise Dynamic Mattress's short-term financial plan assuming it can borrow up to $45 million through its bank loan. Assume that the firm will still sell its $5 million of short-term securities in the first quarter.

Evaluating the Plan

Does the plan shown in Spreadsheet 19.3 solve Dynamic's short-term financing problem? No—the plan is feasible, but Dynamic can probably do better. The most glaring weakness of this plan is its reliance on stretching payables, an extremely expensive financing device. Remember that it costs Dynamic 5% *per quarter* to delay paying bills—more than a 20%

per year effective annual interest rate. This first plan should merely stimulate the financial manager to search for cheaper sources of short-term borrowing.

The financial manager would ask several other questions as well. For example:

1. Does Dynamic need a larger reserve of cash or marketable securities to guard against, say, its customers stretching *their* payables (thus slowing down collections on accounts receivable)?
2. Does the plan yield satisfactory current and quick ratios?[11] Its bankers may be worried if these ratios deteriorate.
3. Are there hidden costs to stretching payables? Will suppliers begin to doubt Dynamic's creditworthiness?
4. Does the plan for 2012 leave Dynamic in good financial shape for 2013? (Here the answer is yes, since Dynamic will have paid off all short-term borrowing by the end of the year.)
5. Should Dynamic try to arrange long-term financing for the major capital expenditure in the first quarter? This seems sensible, following the rule of thumb that long-term assets deserve long-term financing. It would also dramatically reduce the need for short-term borrowing. A counterargument is that Dynamic is financing the capital investment *only temporarily* by short-term borrowing. By year-end, the investment is paid for by cash from operations. Thus Dynamic's initial decision not to seek immediate long-term financing may reflect a preference for ultimately financing the investment with retained earnings.
6. Perhaps the firm's operating and investment plans can be adjusted to make the short-term financing problem easier. Is there any easy way of deferring the first quarter's large cash outflow? For example, suppose that the large capital investment in the first quarter is for new mattress-stuffing machines to be delivered and installed in the first half of the year. The new machines are not scheduled to be ready for full-scale use until August. Perhaps the machine manufacturer could be persuaded to accept 60% of the purchase price on delivery and 40% when the machines are installed and operating satisfactorily.

Short-term financing plans must be developed by trial and error. You lay out one plan, think about it, and then try again with different assumptions on financing and investment alternatives. You continue until you can think of no further improvements.

19.6 Sources of Short-Term Financing

Dynamic solved the greater part of its cash shortage by borrowing from a bank. Banks offer various types of loans and one type may make more sense for you than another. Also, banks are not the only source of short-term borrowing. For example, firms may obtain loans from finance companies, which specialize in lending to businesses and individuals. Unlike banks, finance companies obtain funds through selling securities rather than through deposits. Firms may also raise money by selling their own short-term debt directly to investors. Let's look at some of these alternative sources of short-term financing.

Bank Loans

line of credit
Agreement by a bank that a company may borrow at any time up to an established limit.

The simplest and most common source of short-term finance is a loan from a bank. Companies sometimes wait until they need the money before they apply for a bank loan, but in the majority of cases the firm will arrange a **line of credit** that permits it to borrow from the bank up to an agreed limit. For example, in 2009, Chipotle Mexican

---

[11] These ratios are discussed in Chapter 4.

Grill entered into a $25 million unsecured *credit facility* with Bank of America. This was in the form of a revolving credit agreement. The company can borrow and repay whenever it wants until 2014, as long as it does not exceed the agreed limit. In return, the company agreed to pay the bank a commitment fee of up to .5% on any unused amount.

Many bank loans have durations of only a few months. For example, a firm may need a loan to cover a seasonal increase in inventories, and the loan is then repaid as the goods are sold. Such a loan is described as *self-liquidating,* in other words, the sale of goods provides the cash to repay the loan. However, banks also make *term loans,* which last for several years.

Some bank loans are too large for a single lender. In these cases the borrower may pay an arrangement fee to a lead bank, which then parcels out the loan or credit line among a syndicate of banks. For example, when the mining company BHP Billiton needed to raise $45 billion to finance its (ultimately unsuccessful) takeover bid for Potash, six banks from around the world agreed to provide the money.

Most short-term bank loans are made at a fixed rate of interest, which is often quoted as a discount. For example, if the interest rate on a 1-year loan is stated as a discount of 5%, the borrower receives $100 − $5 = $95 and undertakes to pay $100 at the end of the year. The return on such a loan is not 5% but 5/95 = .0526, or 5.26%.

For longer-term bank loans the interest rate is usually linked to the general level of interest rates. A common benchmark is the London Interbank Offered Rate (LIBOR), which is the interest rate at which the major international banks borrow dollars from one another.[12] Thus, if the rate is set at "1% over LIBOR," the borrower may pay 5% in the first 3 months when LIBOR is 4%, 6% in the next 3 months when LIBOR is 5%, and so on.

Figure 19.6 shows the 3-month LIBOR rate and the equivalent Treasury bill rate. Their difference, usually called the TED spread, indicates the financial strength of the banking sector. When banks are in trouble, the rates at which they are prepared to lend to each other will naturally increase. While the TED spread was below .5% for the early part of the decade, at the height of the banking crisis it spiked to 4.65%.

FIGURE 19.6 Interest rates on 3-month Treasury bills and LIBOR. The orange line shows how the spread between the two rates (the TED spread) leapt up during the banking crisis.

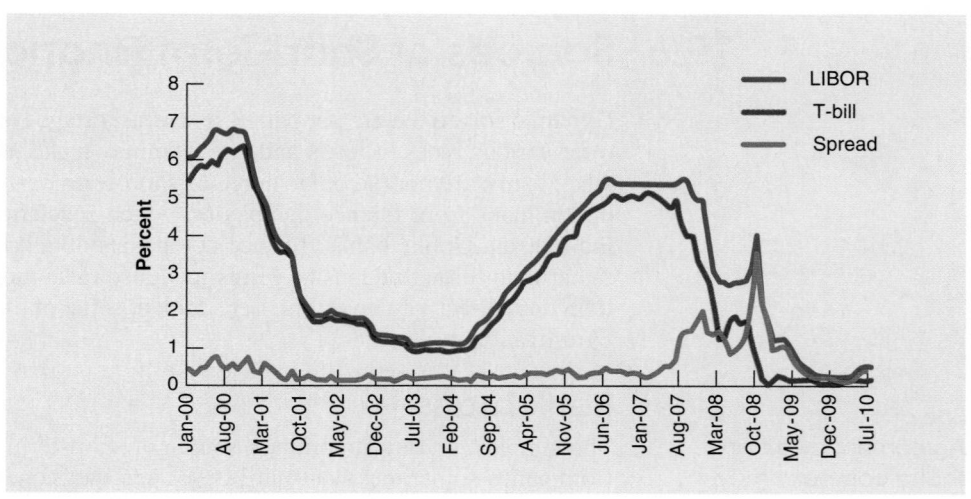

Secured Loans

If a bank is concerned about a firm's credit risk, the firm will need to provide security or collateral for the loan. Sometimes this security will include both current and fixed assets. However, if the bank is lending on a short-term basis, the collateral is generally restricted to liquid assets such as receivables, inventories, or securities. For example, a firm may decide to borrow short-term money secured by its accounts receivable. When its customers pay their bills, it can use the cash collected to repay the loan.

Banks will not usually lend the full value of the assets that are used as security. So a firm that puts up $100,000 of receivables as security may find that the bank is prepared to lend only $75,000. The safety margin (or *haircut,* as it is called) is likely to be even larger in the case of loans that are secured by inventory.

Accounts Receivable Financing When a loan is secured by receivables, the firm *assigns* the receivables to the bank. If the firm fails to repay the loan, the bank can collect the receivables from the firm's customers and use the cash to pay off the debt. However, the firm is still responsible for the loan even if the receivables ultimately cannot be collected. The risk of default on the receivables is therefore borne by the firm.

An alternative procedure is to *sell* the receivables at a discount to a financial institution known as a *factor* and let it collect the money. In other words, some companies solve their financing problem by borrowing on the strength of their current assets; others solve it by selling their current assets. Once the firm has sold its receivables, the factor bears all the responsibility for collecting on the accounts. Therefore, the factor plays three roles: It administers collection of receivables, takes responsibility for bad debts, and provides finance.

EXAMPLE 19.2 ▶ Factoring

To illustrate factoring, suppose that the firm sells its accounts receivable to a factor at a 2% discount. This means that the factor pays 98 cents for each dollar of accounts receivable. If the average collection period is 1 month, then in a month the factor should be able to collect $1 for every 98 cents it paid today. Therefore, the implicit interest rate is 2/98 = 2.04% per month, which corresponds to an effective annual interest rate of $(1.0204)^{12} - 1 = .274$, or 27.4%.

While factoring would appear from this example to be an expensive source of financing for the firm, part of the apparently steep interest rate represents payment for the assumption of default risk and for the cost of running the credit operation.

Inventory Financing Banks also lend on the security of inventory, but they are choosy about the inventory they will accept. They want to make sure that they can identify and sell it if you default. Automobiles and other standardized nonperishable commodities are good security for a loan; work in progress and ripe strawberries are poor collateral.

Banks need to monitor companies to be sure they don't sell their assets and run off with the money. Consider, for example, the story of the great salad oil swindle. Fifty-one banks and companies made loans of nearly $200 million to the Allied Crude Vegetable Oil Refining Corporation in the belief that these loans were secured by valuable salad oil. Unfortunately, they did not notice that Allied's tanks contained false compartments which were mainly filled with seawater. When the fraud was discovered, the president of Allied went to jail and the 51 lenders stayed out in the cold looking for their $200 million. The nearby box presents a similar story that illustrates the potential pitfalls of secured lending. Here, too, the loans were not as "secured" as they appeared: The supposed collateral did not exist.

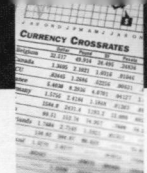

The Hazards of Secured Bank Lending

The National Safety Council of Australia's Victoria Division had been a sleepy outfit until John Friedrich took over. Under its new management, NSC members trained like commandos and were prepared to go anywhere and do anything. They saved people from drowning, fought fires, found lost bushwalkers, and went down mines. Their lavish equipment included 22 helicopters, 8 aircraft, and a mini-submarine. Soon the NSC began selling its services internationally.

Unfortunately the NSC's paramilitary outfit cost millions of dollars to run—far more than it earned in revenue. Friedrich bridged the gap by borrowing $A236 million of debt. The banks were happy to lend because the NSC's debt appeared well secured. At one point the company showed $A107 million of receivables (that is, money owed by its customers), which it pledged as security for bank loans. Later checks revealed that many of these customers did not owe the NSC a cent. In other cases banks took comfort in the fact that their loans were secured by containers of valuable rescue gear. There were more than 100 containers stacked around the NSC's main base. Only a handful contained any equipment, but these were the ones that the bankers saw when they came to check that their loans were safe. Sometimes a suspicious banker would ask to inspect a particular container. Friedrich would then explain that it was away on exercise, fly the banker across the country in a light plane, and point to a container well out in the bush. The container would of course be empty, but the banker had no way to know that.

Six years after Friedrich was appointed CEO, his massive fraud was uncovered. But a few days before a warrant could be issued, Friedrich disappeared. Although he was eventually caught and arrested, he shot himself before he could come to trial. Investigations revealed that Friedrich was operating under an assumed name, having fled from his native Germany, where he was wanted by the police. Many rumors continued to circulate about Friedrich. He was variously alleged to have been a plant of the CIA and the KGB, and the NSC was said to have been behind an attempted counter-coup in Fiji. For the banks there was only one hard truth: Their loans to the NSC, which had appeared so well secured, would never be repaid.

Source: Adapted from T. Sykes, *The Bold Riders* (St. Leonards, NSW, Australia: Allen & Unwin, 1994), chap. 7.

To protect themselves against this sort of risk, lenders often insist on *field warehousing.* An independent warehouse company hired by the bank supervises the inventory pledged as collateral for the loan. As the firm sells its product and uses the revenue to pay back the loan, the bank directs the warehouse company to release the inventory back to the firm. If the firm defaults on the loan, the bank keeps the inventory and sells it to recover the debt.

Commercial Paper

commercial paper
Short-term unsecured notes issued by firms.

When banks lend money, they provide two services. They match up would-be borrowers and lenders, and they check that the borrower is likely to repay the loan. Banks recover the costs of providing these services by charging borrowers on average a higher interest rate than they pay to lenders. These services are less necessary for large, well-known companies that regularly need to raise large amounts of cash. These companies have increasingly found it profitable to bypass the bank and to sell short-term debt, known as **commercial paper,** directly to large investors. Banks have been forced to respond by reducing the interest rates on their loans to blue-chip customers.

In the United States commercial paper has a maximum maturity of 270 days; longer maturities would require registration with the Securities and Exchange Commission. However, most paper matures in 60 days or less. Commercial paper is not secured, but companies generally back their issue of paper by arranging a special backup line of credit with a bank. This guarantees that they can find the money to repay the paper, and the risk of default is therefore small.

Since investors are reluctant to buy paper that does not have the highest credit rating, companies cannot rely on the commercial paper market to provide them with short-term capital if their credit standing deteriorates. For example, when the rating services downrated the commercial paper of Ford and General Motors, both companies were forced to reduce sharply the amount of paper that they had issued and to rely instead on the long-term debt market. Ford Credit had $42 billion of commercial paper outstanding at the end of 2000; by 2009 it had cut that amount to $6.4 billion.

Recent years have not been kind to the commercial paper market. When Lehman Brothers went bankrupt in 2008, it defaulted on its outstanding commercial paper. The commercial paper market seized up; many companies either found it impossible to issue commercial paper or were obliged to pay very high rates of interest. The resulting inter- ruption of credit to the corporate sector was a major cause of the recession that followed the financial crisis. Even before the crisis, however, all was not well. In 2001 two large California utilities, Pacific Gas & Electric and Southern California Edison, became the first companies for 10 years to default on their nonfinancial commercial paper. In the wake of these events, the market for commercial paper shrank.

SUMMARY

Why do firms need to invest in net working capital? *(LO1)*

Short-term financial planning is concerned with the management of the firm's short-term, or *current,* assets and liabilities. The most important current assets are cash, marketable securities, inventory, and accounts receivable. The most important current liabilities are bank loans and accounts payable. The difference between current assets and current liabili- ties is called **net working capital.**

Net working capital arises from lags between the time the firm obtains the raw materi- als for its product and the time it finally collects its bills from customers. The **cash conversion cycle** is the length of time between the firm's payment for materials and the date that it gets paid by its customers. The cash conversion cycle is partly within manage- ment's control. For example, it can choose to have a higher or lower level of inventories. Management needs to trade off the benefits and costs of investing in current assets. Higher investments in current assets entail higher **carrying costs** but lower expected **shortage costs.**

How does long-term financing policy affect short-term financing requirements? *(LO2)*

The nature of the firm's short-term financial planning problem is determined by the amount of long-term capital it raises. A firm that issues large amounts of long-term debt or com- mon stock, or that retains a large part of its earnings, may find that it has permanent excess cash. Other firms raise relatively little long-term capital and end up as permanent short- term debtors. Most firms attempt to find a golden mean by financing all fixed assets and part of current assets with equity and long-term debt. Such firms may invest cash surpluses during part of the year and borrow during the rest of the year.

How does the firm's sources and uses of cash relate to its need for short-term borrowing? *(LO3)*

The starting point for short-term financial planning is an understanding of sources and uses of cash. Firms forecast their net cash requirement by forecasting collections on accounts receivable, adding other cash inflows, and subtracting all forecast cash outlays. If the fore- cast cash balance is insufficient to cover day-to-day operations and to provide a buffer against contingencies, you will need to find additional finance.

How do firms develop a short-term financing plan that meets their need for cash? *(LO4)*

The search for the best short-term financial plan inevitably proceeds by trial and error. The financial manager must explore the consequences of different assumptions about cash requirements, interest rates, limits on financing from particular sources, and so on. Firms are increasingly using computerized financial models to help in this process.

What are some of the major sources of short-term financing? *(LO5)*

A major source of short-term financing is bank loans. Often, firms pay a regular fee for a **line of credit** that allows them to borrow from the bank up to an agreed amount. Other important sources of short-term finance are **commercial paper**, secured loans such as accounts receivable or inventory financing, and factoring.

QUESTIONS

connect |FINANCE

QUIZ

1. **Working Capital Management.** Indicate how each of the following six different transactions that Dynamic Mattress might make would affect (i) cash and (ii) net working capital. *(LO1)*

   a. Paying out a $2 million cash dividend.
   b. A customer paying a $2,500 bill resulting from a previous sale.
   c. Paying $5,000 previously owed to one of its suppliers.
   d. Borrowing $1 million long-term and investing the proceeds in inventory.
   e. Borrowing $1 million short-term and investing the proceeds in inventory.
   f. Selling $5 million of marketable securities for cash.

2. **Short-Term Financial Plans.** Fill in the blanks in the following statements. *(LO3)*

   a. A firm has a cash surplus when its _____ exceeds its _____. The surplus is normally invested in _____.
   b. In developing the short-term financial plan, the financial manager starts with a(n) _____ budget for the next year. This budget shows the _____ generated or absorbed by the firm's operations and also the minimum _____ needed to support these operations. The financial manager may also wish to invest in _____ as a reserve for unexpected cash requirements.

3. **Sources and Uses of Cash.** State how each of the following events would affect the firm's balance sheet. State whether each change is a source or use of cash. *(LO3)*

   a. An automobile manufacturer increases production in response to a forecast increase in demand. Unfortunately, the demand does not increase.
   b. Competition forces the firm to give customers more time to pay for their purchases.
   c. The firm sells a parcel of land for $100,000. The land was purchased 5 years earlier for $200,000.
   d. The firm repurchases its own common stock.
   e. The firm pays its quarterly dividend.
   f. The firm issues $1 million of long-term debt and uses the proceeds to repay a short-term bank loan.

4. **Cash Conversion Cycle.** What effect will the following events have on the cash conversion cycle? *(LO1)*

   a. Higher financing rates induce the firm to reduce its level of inventory.
   b. The firm obtains a new line of credit that enables it to avoid stretching payables to its suppliers.
   c. The firm factors its accounts receivable.
   d. A recession occurs, and the firm's customers increasingly stretch their payables.

5. **Managing Working Capital.** A new computer system allows your firm to more accurately monitor inventory and anticipate future inventory shortfalls. As a result, the firm feels more able to pare down its inventory levels. What effect will the new system have on working capital and on the cash conversion cycle? *(LO1)*

6. **Cash Conversion Cycle.** Calculate the accounts receivable period, accounts payable period, inventory period, and cash conversion cycle for the following firm: *(LO1)*

   Income statement data:

Sales	5,000
Cost of goods sold	4,200

   Balance sheet data:

Inventory	550
Accounts receivable	110
Accounts payable	270

7. **Cash Conversion Cycle.** What effect will the following have on the cash conversion cycle? *(LO1)*

   a. Customers are given a larger discount for cash transactions.
   b. The inventory turnover ratio falls from 8 to 6.
   c. New technology streamlines the production process.

d. The firm adopts a policy of reducing outstanding accounts payable.
e. The firm starts producing more goods in response to customers' advance orders instead of producing for inventory.
f. A temporary glut in the commodity market induces the firm to stock up on raw materials while prices are low.

PRACTICE PROBLEMS

8. **Factoring.** A firm sells its $1,000,000 receivables to a factor for $960,000. The average collection period is 1 month. What is the effective annual rate on this arrangement? *(LO5)*

9. **Factoring.** A firm sells its accounts receivables to a factor at a 1.5% discount. The average collection period is 1 month. What is the implicit effective annual interest rate on the factoring arrangement? Suppose the average collection period is 1.5 months. How does this affect the implicit effective annual interest rate? *(LO5)*

10. **Cash conversion cycle.** A firm is considering several policy changes to increase sales. It will increase the variety of goods it keeps in inventory, but this will increase inventory by $10,000. It will offer more liberal sales terms, but this will result in average receivables increasing by $65,000. These actions are expected to increase sales by $800,000 per year, and cost of goods will remain at 80% of sales. Because of the firm's increased purchases for its own production needs, average payables will increase by $35,000. What effect will these changes have on the firm's cash conversion cycle? *(LO1)*

11. **Sources and uses of cash.** Create the statement of sources and uses of cash from the following entries: *(LO3)*

Net income	$1,500
Dividends	900
Additions to inventory	120
Additions to receivables	150
Depreciation	90
Reduction in payables	550
Net issuance of long-term debt	300
Sale of fixed assets	60

12. **Short-term financial policy.** What will be the effect of each of the following transactions on cash, net working capital, and the current ratio? Assume that the current ratio is above 1.0. *(LO4)*

a. The firm borrows $1,000 in a short-term loan from its bank and pays $500 in accounts payable.
b. The firm factors $1,000 in receivables at a 4% discount.
c. The firm issues $1,000 in long-term bonds and uses the proceeds to pay $800 in payables and purchase $200 in marketable securities.

13. **Lines of credit.** The chapter notes that firms commonly pay commitment fees to banks when obtaining a line of credit. Yet when the line is first taken out, it commonly is not drawn down (i.e., the firm does not initiate any borrowing from its line). Why do these firms pay for something that seems to be not currently needed? *(LO5)*

14. **Forecasting Collections.** Here is a forecast of sales by National Bromide for the first 4 months of 2012 (figures in thousands of dollars):

Month:	1	2	3	4
Cash sales	15	24	18	14
Sales on credit	100	120	90	70

On average, 50% of credit sales are paid for in the current month, 30% in the next month, and the remainder in the month after that. What are expected cash collections in months 3 and 4? *(LO4)*

15. **Forecasting Payments.** If a firm pays its bills with a 30-day delay, what fraction of its purchases will be paid for in the current quarter? In the following quarter? What if its payment delay is 60 days? *(LO4)*

16. **Short-Term Planning.** Paymore Products places orders for goods equal to 75% of its sales forecast in the next quarter. What will be orders in each quarter of the year if the sales forecasts for the next five quarters are as follows: *(LO4)*

	Quarter in Coming Year				Following Year
	First	**Second**	**Third**	**Fourth**	**First Quarter**
Sales forecast	$372	$360	$336	$384	$384

17. **Forecasting Payments.** Calculate Paymore's cash payments to its suppliers under the assumption that the firm pays for its goods with a 1-month delay. Therefore, on average, two-thirds of purchases are paid for in the quarter that they are purchased, and one-third are paid in the following quarter. *(LO4)*

18. **Forecasting Collections.** Now suppose that Paymore's customers pay *their* bills with a 2-month delay. What is the forecast for Paymore's cash receipts in each quarter of the coming year? Assume that sales in the last quarter of the previous year were $336. *(LO4)*

19. **Forecasting Net Cash Flow.** Assuming that Paymore's labor and administrative expenses are $65 per quarter and that interest on long-term debt is $40 per quarter, work out the net cash inflow for Paymore for the coming year using a table like Spreadsheet 19.1, panel B. *(LO4)*

20. **Short-Term Financing Requirements.** Suppose that Paymore's cash balance at the start of the first quarter is $40 and its minimum acceptable cash balance is $30. Work out the short-term financing requirements for the firm in the coming year using a table like Spreadsheet 19.1, panel C. The firm pays no dividends. *(LO4)*

21. **Short-Term Financing Plan.** Now assume that Paymore can borrow up to $100 from a line of credit at an interest rate of 2% per quarter. Prepare a short-term financing plan. Use Spreadsheet 19.3 to guide your answer. *(LO4)*

22. **Short-Term Plan.** Recalculate Dynamic Mattress's financing plan (Spreadsheet 19.3) assuming that the firm wishes to maintain a minimum cash balance of $10 million instead of $5 million. Assume the firm can convince the bank to extend its line of credit to $45 million. *(LO4)*

Templates can be found at
www.mhhe.com/bmm7e.

23. **Sources and Uses of Cash.** The accompanying tables show Dynamic Mattress's year-end 2009 balance sheet and its income statement for 2010. Use these tables (and Table 19.3) to work out a statement of sources and uses of cash for 2010. *(LO4)*

YEAR-END BALANCE SHEET FOR 2009			
(figures in millions of dollars)			
Assets		**Liabilities**	
Current assets		Current liabilities	
Cash	4	Bank loans	4
Marketable securities	2	Accounts payable	15
Inventory	20	Total current liabilities	19
Accounts receivable	22	Long-term debt	5
Total current assets	48	Net worth (equity and retained earnings)	60
Fixed assets			
Gross investment	50		
Less depreciation	14	Total liabilities and net worth	84
Net fixed assets	36		
Total assets	84		

INCOME STATEMENT FOR 2010 (figures in millions of dollars)	
Sales	300
Operating costs	−285
	15
Depreciation	−2
EBIT	13
Interest	−1
Pretax income	12
Tax at 50%	−6
Net income	6

Note: Dividend = $1 million, and reinvested earnings = $5 million.

CHALLENGE PROBLEM

Templates can be found at www.mhhe.com/bmm7e.

24. **Cash Budget.** The following data are from the budget of Ritewell Publishers. Half the company's sales are transacted on a cash basis. The other half are paid for with a 1-month delay. The company pays all of its credit purchases with a 1-month delay. Credit purchases in January were $30, and total sales in January were $180. *(LO4)*

	February	March	April
Total sales	200	220	180
Cash purchases	70	80	60
Credit purchases	40	30	40
Labor and administrative expenses	30	30	30
Taxes, interest, and dividends	10	10	10
Capital expenditures	100	0	0

Complete the following cash budget:

	February	March	April
Sources of cash			
Collections on current sales			
Collections on accounts receivable			
Total sources of cash			
Uses of cash			
Payments of accounts payable			
Cash purchases			
Labor and administrative expenses			
Capital expenditures			
Taxes, interest, and dividends			
Total uses of cash			
Net cash inflow			
Cash at start of period	100		
+ Net cash inflow			
= Cash at end of period			
+ Minimum operating cash balance	100	100	100
= Cumulative short-term financing required			

WEB EXERCISES

1. Log on to finance.yahoo.com and find the condensed balance sheets and income statements for Merck (MRK) and Consolidated Edison (ED). Calculate the net working capital and the cash conversion cycle, discussed in Section 19.2, for each firm. By how much would the investment in working capital fall if each firm could reduce its cash conversion cycle by 1 day?

2. We mentioned that the interest rate on longer-term bank loans is not usually fixed for the term of the loan but is adjusted up or down as the general level of interest rates changes. Often the interest rate is linked to the London Interbank Offered Rate (LIBOR), which is the interest rate at which major international banks lend to one another. Two alternatives are to link it to the federal funds rate or the bank's prime rate. Suppose you are offered the choice of a 3-year loan at 1.5% above 3-month LIBOR, at the bank's prime rate, or at 1.25% above federal funds. Which would you prefer? Log on to www.bloomberg.com to find current rates.

SOLUTIONS TO SELF-TEST QUESTIONS

19.1 One would expect Tiffany's to have the longer conversion cycle. It holds an inventory of expensive jewelry that can take a long time to sell. Target's wares are "priced to sell." In fact, the calculations below show that the difference in the two firms' cash conversion cycles is driven primarily by their extremely different inventory periods.

	Tiffany	Target
Sales	2,709	65,357
COGS	1,179	45,583
Inventories	1,428	7,179
Accounts receivable	165	6,966
Accounts payable	299	9,631
Inventory period	442.1	57.5
Receivables period	22.2	38.9
Payables period	92.6	77.1
Cash conversion cycle	371.8	19.3

19.2 a. An increase in the interest rate will increase the cost of carrying current assets. The effect is to reduce the optimal level of such assets.
      b. The just-in-time system lowers the expected level of shortage costs and reduces the amount of goods the firm ought to be willing to keep in inventory.
      c. If the firm decides that more lenient credit terms are necessary to avoid lost sales, it must then expect customers to pay their bills more slowly. Accounts receivable will increase.

19.3 a. This transaction merely substitutes one current liability (short-term debt) for another (accounts payable). Neither cash nor net working capital is affected.
      b. This transaction will increase inventory at the expense of cash. Cash falls but net working capital is unaffected.
      c. The firm will use cash to buy back the stock. Both cash and net working capital will fall.
      d. The proceeds from the sale will increase both cash and net working capital.

19.4

Quarter:	First	Second	Third	Fourth
Accounts receivable				
Receivables (beginning of period)	30.0	35.0	31.4	46.4
Sales	87.5	78.5	116.0	131.0
Collections*	82.5	82.1	101.0	125.0
Receivables (end of period)	35.0	31.4	46.4	52.4
Cash budget				
Sources of cash				
Collections of accounts receivable	82.5	82.1	101.0	125.0
Other	1.5	0.0	12.5	0.0
Total sources	84.0	82.1	113.5	125.0
Uses				
Payments of accounts payable	65.0	60.0	55.0	50.0
Labor and administrative expenses	30.0	30.0	30.0	30.0
Capital expenses	32.5	1.3	5.5	8.0
Taxes, interest, and dividends	4.0	4.0	4.5	5.0
Total uses	131.5	95.3	95.0	93.0
Net cash inflow	−47.5	−13.2	18.5	32.0
Short-term financing requirements				
Cash at start of period	5.0	−42.5	−55.7	−37.2
+ Net cash inflow	−47.5	−13.2	18.5	32.0
= Cash at end of period	−42.5	−55.7	−37.2	−5.2
Minimum operating balance	5.0	5.0	5.0	5.0
Cumulative short-term financing required	47.5	60.7	42.2	10.2

*Sales in fourth quarter of the previous year totaled $75 million.

19.5 The major change in the plan is the substitution of the extra $5 million of borrowing from the bank in the second quarter and the corresponding reduction in the stretched payables. This substitution is advantageous because the bank loan is a cheaper source of funds. Notice that the cash balance at the end of the year is higher under this plan than in the original plan.

Quarter:	First	Second	Third	Fourth
Cash requirements				
1. Cash required for operations	45	15	−26.0	−35
2. Interest on line of credit	0	0.8	0.9	0.6
3. Interest on stretched payables	0	0	0.5	0
4. Total cash required	45	15.8	−24.6	−34.4
Cash raised				
5. Bank loan	40	5	0	0
6. Stretched payables	0	10.8	0	0
7. Securities sold	5	0	0	0
8. Total cash raised	45	15.8	0	0
Repayments				
9. Of stretched payables	0	0	10.8	0
10. Of bank loan	0	0	13.8	31.2
Increase in cash balances				
11. Addition to cash balances	0	0	0	3.2
Bank loan				
12. Beginning of quarter	0	40	45	31.2
13. End of quarter	40	45	31.2	0

MINICASE

Capstan Autos operated an East Coast dealership for a major Japanese car manufacturer. Capstan's owner, Sidney Capstan, attributed much of the business's success to its no-frills policy of competitive pricing and immediate cash payment. The business was basically a simple one—the firm imported cars at the beginning of each quarter and paid the manufacturer at the end of the quarter. The revenues from the sale of these cars covered the payment to the manufacturer and the expenses of running the business, as well as providing Sidney Capstan with a good return on his equity investment.

By the fourth quarter of 2015 sales were running at 250 cars a quarter. Since the average sale price of each car was about $20,000, this translated into quarterly revenues of 250 × $20,000 = $5 million. The average cost to Capstan of each imported car was $18,000. After paying wages, rent, and other recurring costs of $200,000 per quarter and deducting depreciation of $80,000, the company was left with earnings before interest and taxes (EBIT) of $220,000 a quarter and net profits of $140,000.

The year 2016 was not a happy year for car importers in the United States. Recession led to a general decline in auto sales, while the fall in the value of the dollar shaved profit margins for many dealers in imported cars. Capstan more than most firms foresaw the difficulties ahead and reacted at once by offering 6 months' free credit while holding the sale price of its cars constant. Wages and other costs were pared by 25% to $150,000 a quarter, and the company effectively eliminated all capital expenditures. The policy appeared successful. Unit sales fell by 20% to 200 units a quarter, but the company continued to operate at a satisfactory profit (see table).

The slump in sales lasted for 6 months, but as consumer confidence began to return, auto sales began to recover. The company's new policy of 6 months' free credit was proving sufficiently popular that Sidney Capstan decided to maintain the policy. In the third quarter of 2016 sales had recovered to 225 units; by the fourth quarter they were 250 units; and by the first quarter of the next year they had reached 275 units. It looked as if by the second quarter of 2017 the company could expect to sell 300 cars. Earnings before interest and tax were already in excess of their previous high, and Sidney Capstan was able to congratulate himself on weathering what looked to be a tricky period. Over the 18-month period the firm had earned net profits of over half a million dollars, and the equity had grown from just over $1.5 million to about $2 million.

Sidney Capstan was first and foremost a superb salesman and always left the financial aspects of the business to his financial manager. However, there was one feature of the financial statements that disturbed Sidney Capstan—the mounting level of debt, which by the end of the first quarter of 2017 had reached $9.7 million. This unease turned to alarm when the financial manager phoned to say that the bank was reluctant to extend further credit and was even questioning its current level of exposure to the company.

Mr. Capstan found it impossible to understand how such a successful year could have landed the company in financial difficulties. The company had always had good relationships with its bank, and the interest rate on its bank loans was a reasonable 8% a year (or about 2% a quarter). Surely, Mr. Capstan reasoned, when the bank saw the projected sales growth for the rest of 2017, it would realize that there were plenty of profits to enable the company to start repaying its loans.

Mr. Capstan kept coming back to three questions: Was his company really in trouble? Could the bank be right in its decision to withhold further credit? And why was the company's indebtedness increasing when its profits were higher than ever?

SUMMARY INCOME STATEMENT
(all figures except unit sales in thousands of dollars)

	Year: 2015	2016				2017
Quarter:	4	1	2	3	4	1
1. Number of cars sold	250	200	200	225	250	275
2. Unit price	20	20	20	20	20	20
3. Unit cost	18	18	18	18	18	18
4. Revenues (1 × 2)	5,000	4,000	4,000	4,500	5,000	5,500
5. Cost of goods sold (1 × 3)	4,500	3,600	3,600	4,050	4,500	4,950
6. Wages and other costs	200	150	150	150	150	150
7. Depreciation	80	80	80	80	80	80
8. EBIT (4 − 5 − 6 − 7)	220	170	170	220	270	320
9. Net interest	4	0	76	153	161	178
10. Pretax profit (8 − 9)	216	170	94	67	109	142
11. Tax (.35 × 10)	76	60	33	23	38	50
12. Net profit (10 − 11)	140	110	61	44	71	92

SUMMARY BALANCE SHEETS (figures in thousands of dollars)		
	End of 3rd Quarter 2015	End of 1st Quarter 2017
Cash	10	10
Receivables	0	10,500
Inventory	4,500	5,400
Total current assets	4,510	15,910
Fixed assets, net	1,760	1,280
Total assets	6,270	17,190
Bank loan	230	9,731
Payables	4,500	5,400
Total current liabilities	4,730	15,131
Shareholders' equity	1,540	2,059
Total liabilities plus equity	6,270	17,190

CHAPTER 20

Working Capital Management

LEARNING OBJECTIVES

After reading this chapter, you should be able to:

(1) Describe the usual steps in a firm's credit management policy.

(2) Measure the implicit interest rate on credit sales.

(3) Describe how firms assess the probability that a customer will pay its bills.

(4) Decide whether it makes sense to grant credit to customers.

(5) Cite the costs and benefits of holding inventories and cash balances.

(6) Compare the different techniques that firms use to make and receive payments.

(7) Compare alternatives for investing excess funds over short horizons.

RELATED WEB SITES FOR THIS CHAPTER CAN BE FOUND AT WWW.MHHE.COM/BMM7E.

Amazon's warehouses are stacked with over $3 billion of inventory. What are the benefits and costs of this inventory?

Most of this book is devoted to long-term financial decisions such as capital budgeting and the choice of capital structure. In the previous chapter, we started our analysis of short-term planning decisions by looking at how firms ensure that they have enough cash to pay their bills. It is now time to look more closely at the management of short-term assets and liabilities, known collectively as *working capital.*

There are four principal types of current assets. All need to be managed. We begin with accounts receivable. Companies frequently sell goods on credit, so it may be weeks or even months before they receive payment. The unpaid bills show up in the balance sheet as accounts receivable. We will explain how the company's credit manager sets the terms of payment, decides which customers should be offered credit, and ensures that they pay promptly.

The second major short-term asset is inventory. To do business, firms need reserves of raw materials, work in progress, and finished goods.

But these inventories can be expensive to store, and they tie up capital. Inventory management involves a trade-off between these costs and benefits. In manufacturing companies, the production manager is most likely to make this judgment without direct input from the financial manager. Therefore, we spend less time on this topic than on the management of the other components of working capital.

Our next task is to discuss the firm's cash balances. The first problem is to decide how much cash the firm should retain and, therefore, how much can be invested in interest-bearing securities. The second is to ensure that cash payments are handled efficiently. You want to collect payments as quickly as possible and put them to work earning interest. We will describe some of the techniques that firms use to move money around efficiently.

Finally, we describe some of the firm's choices for how to invest excess funds in a variety of short-term securities, which are the fourth major component of working capital.

20.1 Accounts Receivable and Credit Policy

trade credit
Bills awaiting payment from one company to another.

consumer credit
Bills awaiting payment from final customer to a company.

We start our tour of current assets with the firm's accounts receivable. When one company sells goods to another, it does not usually expect to be paid immediately. The unpaid bills, or **trade credit,** compose the bulk of accounts receivable. The remainder is made up of **consumer credit,** bills awaiting payment by the final customer.

Credit management involves the following five steps:

1. You must establish the terms of sale on which you propose to sell your goods. For example, how long will you give customers to pay their bills? Will you offer a discount for immediate payment?
2. You must decide what evidence you require that the customer owes you money. For example, is a signed receipt enough, or do you insist on a formal IOU?
3. You must determine which customers are likely to pay their bills. This is called *credit analysis.*
4. You must decide on credit policy. How much credit will you extend to each customer? How much risk are you prepared to take on marginally creditworthy prospects?
5. Finally, you have to collect the money when it becomes due. What do you do about reluctant payers or deadbeats?

We discuss these topics in turn.

Terms of Sale

terms of sale
Credit, discount, and payment terms offered on a sale.

Whenever you sell goods, you need to set the **terms of sale.** For example, if you are supplying goods to a wide variety of irregular customers, you may require cash on delivery (COD). And if you are producing goods to the customer's specification or incurring heavy delivery costs, then it may be sensible to ask for cash before delivery (CBD).

In many other cases, payment is not made until after delivery, so the buyer receives *credit.* Each industry seems to have its own typical credit arrangements. These arrangements have a rough logic. For example, the seller will naturally demand earlier payment if its customers are financially less secure, if their accounts are small, or if the goods are perishable or quickly resold.

When you buy goods on credit, the supplier will state a final payment date. To encourage you to pay *before* the final date, it is common to offer a cash discount for prompt settlement. For example, a manufacturer may require payment within 30 days but offer a 5% discount to customers who pay within 10 days. These terms would be referred to as 5/10, net 30:

5	/	10,		net 30
↑		↑		↑
percent discount for early payment		number of days that discount is available		number of days before payment is due

Similarly, if a firm sells goods on terms of 2/30, net 60, customers receive a 2% discount for payment within 30 days or else must pay in full within 60 days. If the terms are simply net 30, then customers must pay within 30 days of the invoice date and no discounts are offered for early payment.

Self-Test 20.1

Suppose that a firm sells goods on terms of 2/10, net 20. On May 1 you buy goods from the company with an invoice value of $20,000. How much would you need to pay if you took the cash discount? What is the latest date on which the cash discount is available? By what date should you pay for your purchase if you decide not to take the cash discount?

For many items that are bought regularly, it is inconvenient to require separate payment for each delivery. A common solution is to pretend that all sales during the month in fact occur at the end of the month (EOM). Thus goods may be sold on terms of 8/10, *EOM,* net 60. This allows the customer a cash discount of 8% if the bill is paid within 10 days of the end of the month; otherwise, the full payment is due within 60 days of the invoice date.

A firm that buys on credit is in effect borrowing from its supplier. It saves cash today but will have to pay later. This is an implicit loan from the supplier. Of course, if it is free, a loan is always worth having. But if you pass up a cash discount, then the loan may prove to be very expensive. For example, a customer who buys on terms of 3/10, net 30, may decide to forgo the cash discount and pay on the thirtieth day. The customer obtains an extra 20 days' credit by deferring payment from 10 to 30 days after the sale but pays about 3% more for the goods. This is equivalent to borrowing money at a rate of 74.3% a year. To see why, consider an order of $100. If the firm pays within 10 days, it gets a 3% discount and pays only $97. If it waits the full 30 days, it pays $100. The extra 20 days of credit increase the payment by the fraction 3/97 = .0309, or 3.09%. Therefore, the implicit interest charged to extend the trade credit is 3.09% *per 20 days.* There are 365/20 = 18.25 twenty-day periods in a year, so the effective annual rate of interest on the loan is $(1.0309)^{18.25} - 1 = .743$, or 74.3%.

The general formula for calculating the implicit annual interest rate for customers who do not take the cash discount is

$$\text{Effective annual rate} = \left(1 + \frac{\text{discount}}{\text{discounted price}}\right)^{365/\text{extra days credit}} - 1 \quad \textbf{(20.1)}$$

The discount divided by the discounted price is the percentage increase in price paid by a customer who forgoes the discount. In our example, with terms of 3/10, net 30, the percentage increase in price is 3/97 = .0309, or 3.09%. This is the implicit rate of interest *per period.* The period of the loan is the number of extra days of credit that you can obtain by forgoing the discount. In our example, this is 20 days. To annualize this rate, we compound the per-period rate by the number of periods in a year.

Of course any firm that delays payment beyond day 30 gains a cheaper loan but damages its reputation for creditworthiness.

EXAMPLE 20.1 ▶   Trade Credit Rates

What is the implied interest rate on the trade credit if the discount for early payment is 5/10, net 60?

The cash discount in this case is 5% and customers who choose not to take the discount receive an extra 60 − 10 = 50 days credit. So the effective annual interest is

$$\text{Effective annual rate} = \left(1 + \frac{\text{discount}}{\text{discounted price}}\right)^{365/\text{extra days credit}} - 1$$

$$= \left(1 + \frac{5}{95}\right)^{365/50} - 1 = .454, \text{ or } 45.4\%$$

In this case the customer who does not take the discount is effectively borrowing money at an annual interest rate of 45.4%.

You might wonder why the effective interest rate on trade credit is typically so high. At such steep effective rates, most purchasers will choose to pay early and receive the discount. Those who don't are probably strapped for cash. It makes sense to charge these firms a high rate of interest.

Self-Test 20.2

What would be the effective annual interest rate in Example 20.1 if the terms of sale were 5/10, net 50? Why is the rate higher?

Credit Agreements

open account
Agreement whereby sales are made with no formal debt contract.

The terms of sale define the amount of any credit but not the nature of the contract. Repetitive sales are almost always made on **open account** and involve only an implicit contract. There is simply a record in the seller's books and a receipt signed by the buyer.

Sometimes you might want a clear commitment from the buyer before you deliver the goods. In this case the common procedure is to arrange a *commercial draft.* This is simply jargon for an order to pay.[1] It works as follows: The seller prepares a draft ordering payment by the customer and sends this draft to the customer's bank. If immediate payment is required, the draft is termed a *sight draft;* otherwise, it is known as a *time draft.* Depending on whether it is a sight or a time draft, the customer either tells the bank to pay up or acknowledges the debt by adding the word "accepted" and a signature. Once accepted, a time draft is like a postdated check and is called a *trade acceptance.* This trade acceptance is then forwarded to the seller, who holds it until the payment becomes due.

If your customer's credit is shaky, you may ask the customer to arrange for a bank to accept the time draft. In this case, the bank guarantees the customer's debt, and the draft is called a *banker's acceptance.* Banker's acceptances are often used in overseas trade. They are actively bought and sold in the money market, the market for short-term high-quality debt.

If you sell goods to a customer who proves unable to pay, you cannot get your goods back. You simply become a general creditor of the company, in common with other unfortunates. You can avoid this situation by making a *conditional sale,* so that ownership of the goods remains with the seller until full payment is made. The conditional sale is common in Europe. In the United States it is used only for goods that are bought on installment. In this case, if the customer fails to make the agreed number of payments, then the equipment can be immediately repossessed by the seller.

Credit Analysis

credit analysis
Procedure to determine the likelihood a customer will pay its bills.

There are a number of ways to find out whether customers are likely to pay their debts, that is, to carry out **credit analysis.** The most obvious indication is whether they have paid promptly in the past. Prompt payment is usually a good omen, but beware of the customer who establishes a high credit limit on the basis of small payments and then disappears, leaving you with a large unpaid bill.

If you are dealing with a new customer, you will probably check with a credit agency. Dun & Bradstreet, which is by far the largest of these agencies, provides credit ratings on a huge number of domestic and foreign firms. In addition to its rating service, Dun & Bradstreet provides on request a full credit report on a potential customer.

Credit agencies usually report the experience that other firms have had with your customer, but you can also get this information by contacting those firms directly or through a credit bureau.

Your bank can also make a credit check. It will contact the customer's bank and ask for information on the customer's average bank balance, access to bank credit, and general reputation.

---

[1] For example, a check is an example of a draft. Whenever you write a check, you are ordering the bank to make a payment.

In addition to checking with your customer's bank, it might make sense to discover what everybody else in the financial community thinks about your customer's credit standing. Does that sound expensive? Not if your customer is a public company. You just look at the Moody's or Standard & Poor's rating for the customer's bonds.[2] You can also compare prices of these bonds with the prices of other firms' bonds. (Of course the comparisons should be between bonds of similar maturity, coupon, and so on.)

If you don't wish to rely on the judgment of others, you can do your own homework. Ideally this would involve a detailed analysis of the company's business prospects and financing, but this is usually too expensive. Therefore, credit analysts concentrate on the company's financial statements, using rough rules of thumb to judge whether the firm is a good credit risk. The rules of thumb are based on *financial ratios*. Chapter 4 described how these ratios are calculated and interpreted.

Numerical Credit Scoring   Analyzing credit risk is like detective work. You have a lot of clues—some important, some fitting into a neat pattern, others contradictory. You must weigh these clues to come up with an overall judgment.

When the firm has a small, regular clientele, the credit manager can easily handle the process informally and make a judgment about what are often termed the *five Cs of credit:*

1. The customer's *character.*
2. The customer's *capacity* to pay.
3. The customer's *capital.*
4. The *collateral* provided by the customer.[3]
5. The *condition* of the customer's business.

When the company is dealing directly with consumers or with a large number of small trade accounts, some streamlining is essential. In these cases it may make sense to use a scoring system to prescreen credit applications.

If you apply for a credit card or a bank loan, you will probably be asked to complete a questionnaire that provides details about your job, home, and financial health. This information is then used to calculate an overall credit score.[4] If you do not make the grade on the score, you are likely to be refused credit or subjected to a more detailed analysis. In a similar way, banks and the credit departments of industrial firms also use mechanical credit-scoring systems to assess the financial health of potential customers.

Suppose that you are given the task of developing a credit-scoring system that will help to decide when it makes sense to extend credit to the firm's customers. You start by comparing the financial statements of companies that went bankrupt over a 40-year period with those of surviving firms. Figure 20.1 shows what you find. Panel *a* illustrates that, as early as 4 years before they went bankrupt, failing firms were earning a much lower return on assets (ROA) than firms that survived. Panel *b* shows that on average they also had a high ratio of liabilities to assets, and panel *c* shows that EBITDA (earnings before interest, taxes, and depreciation) was low relative to the firms' total liabilities. Thus bankrupt firms were less profitable (low ROA), were more highly leveraged (high ratio of liabilities to assets), and generated relatively little cash (low ratio of EBITDA to liabilities). In each case, these indicators of the firms' financial health steadily deteriorated as bankruptcy approached.

William Beaver, Maureen McNichols, and Jung-Wu Rhie studied these firms and concluded that these variables could be used together to estimate the likelihood of

---

[2] We described bond ratings in Chapter 6, Section 6.6.

[3] For example, the customer can offer bonds as collateral. These bonds can then be seized by the seller if the customer fails to pay.

[4] The most commonly used consumer credit score is the FICO score developed by Fair Isaac Corp., which uses data provided by any one of three credit bureaus—Experian, Trans Union, or Equifax.

FIGURE 20.1 Financial ratios of failing and nonfailing firms

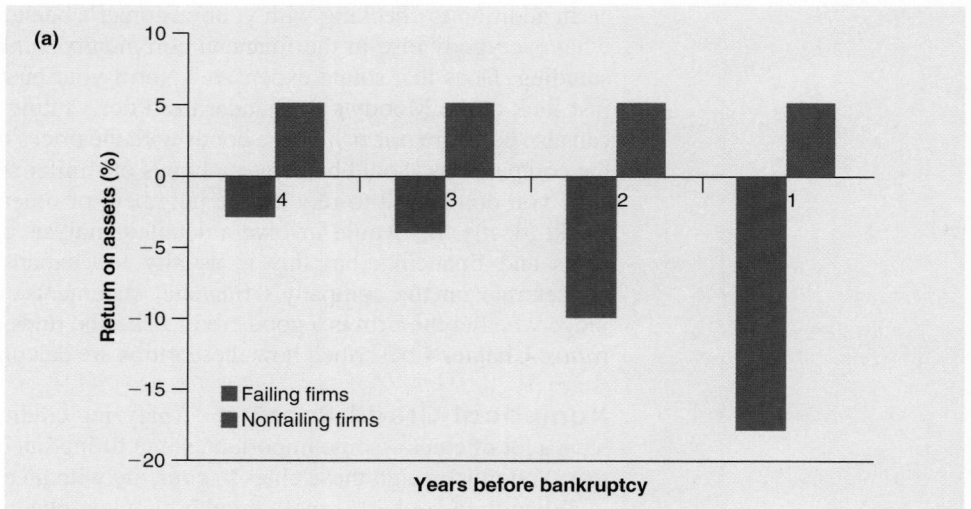

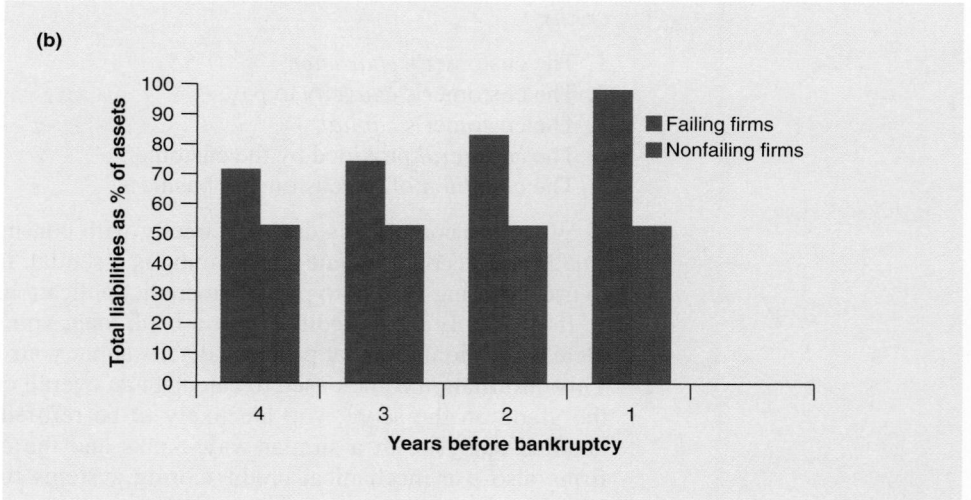

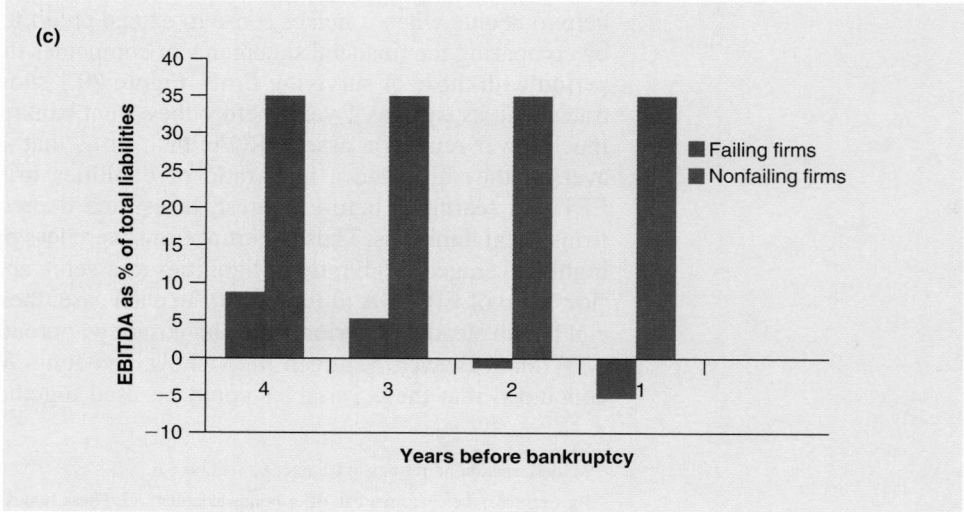

Source: W. H. Beaver, M. F. McNichols, and J.-W. Rhie, "Have Financial Statements Become Less Informative? Evidence from the Ability of Financial Ratios to Predict Bankruptcy," *Review of Accounting Studies* 10 (2005), pp. 93–122.

bankruptcy. The chance of failing during the next year relative to the odds of not failing was best estimated by the following equation:[5]

$$\text{Log(relative chance of failure)} = -6.445 - 1.192 \times \text{ROA} + 2.307 \times \frac{\text{liabilities}}{\text{assets}}$$

$$-.346 \times \frac{\text{EBITDA}}{\text{liabilities}}$$

A variety of similar techniques have been used to develop credit-scoring systems. The model that we have just described uses the technique of *hazard analysis*. An early, and still widely used approach, the famous Z-score model developed by Edward Altman uses *multiple discriminant analysis* to separate the creditworthy sheep from the impecunious goats.[6] His analysis suggested that a firm's financial ratios could be combined as follows into a summary measure of creditworthiness, now commonly known as a *Z score:*[7]

$$Z = 3.3 \times \frac{\text{EBIT}}{\text{total assets}} + 1.0 \times \frac{\text{sales}}{\text{total assets}} + .6 \times \frac{\text{market value of equity}}{\text{total book debt}} +$$

$$1.4 \times \frac{\text{retained earnings}}{\text{total assets}} + 1.2 \times \frac{\text{working capital}}{\text{total assets}}$$

Altman found that most bankrupt firms had Z scores below 2.7 before they went bankrupt, while most nonbankrupt firms had Z scores above this level.

EXAMPLE 20.2 ▶ The *Z*-Score Model

Consider a firm with the following financial ratios:

$$\frac{\text{EBIT}}{\text{Total assets}} = .12 \qquad \frac{\text{Sales}}{\text{Total assets}} = 1.4 \qquad \frac{\text{Market value of equity}}{\text{Total book debt}} = .9$$

$$\frac{\text{Retained earnings}}{\text{Total assets}} = .4 \qquad \frac{\text{Working capital}}{\text{Total assets}} = .12$$

The firm's *Z* score is

$$(3.3 \times .12) + (1.0 \times 1.4) + (.6 \times .9) + (1.4 \times .4) + (1.2 \times .12) = 3.04$$

This score is above the cutoff level for predicting bankruptcy, and it would therefore be considered favorably in an evaluation of the firm's creditworthiness.

The nearby box describes how statistical scoring systems can provide timely first-cut estimates of creditworthiness. These assessments can streamline the credit decision and free up labor for other, less mechanical tasks.

The Credit Decision

You have taken the first three steps toward an effective credit operation. In other words, you have fixed your terms of sale; you have decided whether to sell on open account

---

[5] See W. H. Beaver, M. F. McNichols, and J.-W. Rhie, "Have Financial Statements Become Less Informative? Evidence from the Ability of Financial Ratios to Predict Bankruptcy," *Review of Accounting Studies* 10 (2005), pp. 93–122.

[6] See E. I. Altman, "Financial Ratios and the Prediction of Corporate Bankruptcy," *Journal of Finance* 23 (September 1968), pp. 589–609.

[7] EBIT is earnings before interest and taxes. E. I. Altman, "Financial Ratios, Discriminant Analysis and the Prediction of Corporate Bankruptcy," *Journal of Finance* 23 (September 1968), pp. 589–609.

FINANCE IN PRACTICE

Credit Scoring: What Your Lender Won't Tell You

To hear bankers tell it, credit scoring is the best thing to happen to small-business borrowers since the invention of compound interest. Forget haggling over things like how well your business is doing or what your competitors are up to. Just hand in some predetermined data about yourself and your company, let the computer crunch the numbers, and voilà: Out comes a "credit score" that predicts the chances that you'll actually pay off the loan. Score high enough, and you get approved, sometimes within minutes.

Scoring is already ubiquitous in consumer lending, and 22 of the 25 biggest players in the small-business loan market use the system, according to Fair, Isaac & Co., a pioneer in the development of credit-scoring software. Almost any loan of $50,000 or less issued by a national financial services company will have gone through a credit-scoring system.

Credit-scoring models assign points for up to 20 factors. The more points you get, the better credit risk you represent. The best-known credit-scoring models are provided by Fair, Isaac. The score on its Small Business Scoring Service ranges from 50 to 350, with most small businesses falling into the 150 to 250 area. While lenders set their own cutoff points, if you score above 220, that's generally good, while scores below 170 are considered high risk.

The overriding factor in a small-business credit score is your personal credit history. Specifically, the system looks at whether you pay your personal bills on time. The later you pay, the fewer points you get, and the more bills you pay late, the more your score gets knocked down.

The next key input is how much credit you've already got access to and balances on your accounts. If lines of credit are maxed out, lenders worry that there is little room to maneuver if the business runs into trouble. Other major red flags include bankruptcies, debts turned over to a collection agency, liens, and even overdue child-support payments. You can even get penalized for shopping too hard for credit.

Finally, specific business characteristics are weighed. They include the size of the company, its age, the industry in which it does business, and whether it's a corporation, partnership, or sole proprietorship. A sole prop gets fewer points than a partnership, and a partnership gets fewer points than a corporation. After all, if you're a sole proprietor and you get hit by a bus, all bets are off on your business. By the same token, a manufacturer gets higher points than bars or restaurants because it's less likely to go under quickly.

Source: V. M. Kahn, "Credit Scoring: What Your Lender Won't Tell You," *BusinessWeek,* May 22, 2000, p. F30. Used with permission of Bloomberg L.P.

---

credit policy
Standards set to determine the amount and nature of credit to extend to customers.

or to ask your customers to sign an IOU; and you have established a procedure for estimating the probability that each customer will pay up. Your next step is to decide on **credit policy.**

If there is no possibility of repeat orders, the credit decision is relatively simple. Figure 20.2 summarizes your choice. On the one hand, you can refuse credit and pass up the sale. In this case you make neither profit nor loss. The alternative is to offer credit. If you offer credit and the customer pays, you benefit by the profit margin on the sale. If the customer defaults, you lose the cost of the goods delivered. **The decision to offer credit depends on the probability of payment. You should grant credit if the expected profit from doing so is greater than the profit from refusing.**

Suppose that the probability that the customer will pay up is p. If the customer does pay, you receive additional revenues (REV) and you deliver goods that you

FIGURE 20.2 If you refuse credit, you make neither profit nor loss. If you offer credit, there is a probability p that the customer will pay and you will make REV − COST and there is a probability $(1 − p)$ that the customer will default and you will lose COST.

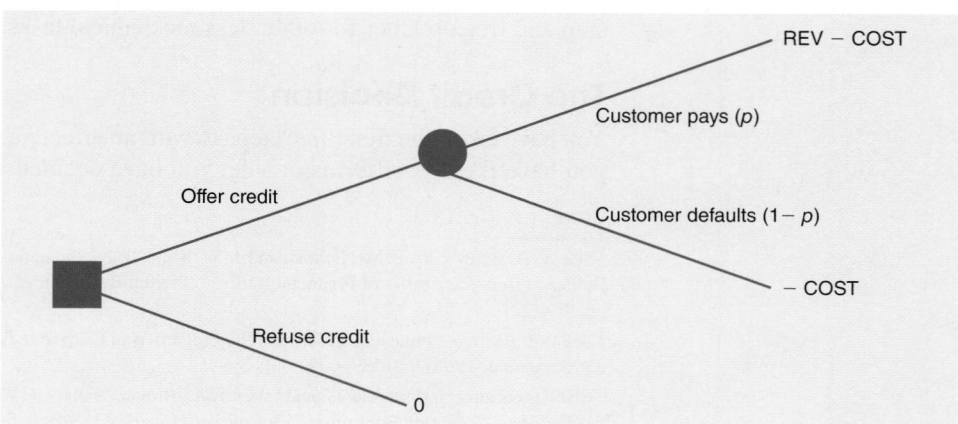

incurred costs to produce; your net gain is the present value of REV − COST. Unfortunately, you can't be certain that the customer will pay; there is a probability $(1 − p)$ of default. Default means you receive nothing but still incur the additional costs of the delivered goods. The *expected profit*[8] from the two sources of action is therefore as follows:

Action	Expected Profit
Refuse credit:	0
Grant credit:	$p \times PV(REV − COST) − (1 − p) \times PV(COST)$

You should grant credit if the expected profit from doing so is positive.

EXAMPLE 20.3 ▶ The Credit Decision

Consider the case of the Cast Iron Company. On each nondelinquent sale Cast Iron receives revenues with a present value of $1,200 and incurs costs with a present value of $1,000. Therefore, the company's expected profit if it offers credit is

$$p \times PV(REV − COST) − (1 − p) \times PV(COST) = p \times 200 − (1 − p) \times 1{,}000$$

If the probability of collection is 5/6, Cast Iron can expect to break even:

$$\text{Expected profit} = 5/6 \times 200 − (1 − 5/6) \times 1{,}000 = 0$$

Thus Cast Iron's policy should be to grant credit whenever the chances of collection are better than 5 out of 6.

In this last example, the net present value of granting credit is positive if the probability of collection exceeds 5/6. In general, this break-even probability can be found by setting the net present value of granting credit equal to zero and solving for p. It turns out that the formula for the break-even probability is simply the ratio of the present value of costs to revenues:

$$p \times PV(REV − COST) − (1 − p) \times PV(COST) = 0$$

Break-even probability of collection, then, is

$$p = \frac{PV(COST)}{PV(REV)}$$

and the break-even probability of *default* is

$$(1 − p) = 1 − PV(COST)/PV(REV) = PV(PROFIT)/PV(REV)$$

In other words, the break-even probability of default is simply the profit margin on each sale. If the default probability is larger than the profit margin, you should not extend credit.

Think what this implies. Companies that operate on low profit margins should be cautious about granting credit to high-risk customers. Firms with high margins can afford to deal with more doubtful ones.

---

[8] Notice that we use the present values of costs and revenues. This is because there sometimes are significant lags between costs incurred and revenues generated. Also, while we follow convention in referring to the "expected profit" of the decision, it should be clear that our equation for expected profit is in fact the net present value of the decision to grant credit. As we emphasized in Chapter 1, the manager's task is to add value, not to maximize accounting profits.

Self-Test 20.3

What is the break-even probability of collection if the present value of the revenues from the sale is $1,100 rather than $1,200? Why does the break-even probability increase? Use your answer to decide whether firms that sell high-profit-margin or low-margin goods should be more willing to issue credit.

So far we have ignored the possibility of repeat orders. But one of the reasons for offering credit today is that you may get yourself a good, regular customer.

Suppose Cast Iron has been asked to extend credit to a new customer. You can find little information on the firm, and you believe that the probability of payment is no better than .8. If you grant credit, the expected profit on this order is

$$\text{Expected profit on initial order} = p \times \text{PV(REV} - \text{COST)} - (1 - p) \times \text{PV(COST)}$$
$$= (.8 \times 200) - (.2 \times 1,000) = -\$40$$

You decide to refuse credit.

This is the correct decision *if* there is no chance of a repeat order. But now consider future periods. If the customer does pay up, there will be a reorder next year. Having paid once, the customer will seem less of a risk. For this reason, any repeat order is very profitable.

Think back to Chapter 10, and you will recognize that the credit decision bears many similarities to our earlier discussion of real options. By granting credit now, the firm retains the option to grant credit on an entire sequence of potentially profitable repeat sales. This option can be very valuable and can tilt the decision toward granting credit. Even a dubious prospect may warrant some initial credit if there is a chance that the company will develop into a profitable steady customer.

EXAMPLE 20.4 ▶ Credit Decisions with Repeat Orders

To illustrate, let's look at an extreme case. Suppose that if a customer pays up on the first sale, you can be *sure* you will have a regular and completely reliable customer. In this case, the value of such a customer is not the profit on one order but an entire stream of profits from repeat purchases. For example, suppose that the customer will make one purchase each year from Cast Iron. If the discount rate is 10% and the profit on each order is $200 a year, then the present value of an indefinite stream of business from a good customer is not $200 but $200/.10 = $2,000. There is a probability p that Cast Iron will secure a good customer with a value of $2,000. There is a probability of $(1 - p)$ that the customer will default, resulting in a loss of $1,000. So, once we recognize the benefits of securing a good and permanent customer, the expected profit from granting credit is

$$\text{Expected profit} = (p \times 2,000) - (1 - p) \times 1,000$$

This is positive for any probability of collection above .33. Thus the break-even probability falls from 5/6 to 1/3. **If one sale may lead to profitable repeat sales, the firm should be inclined to grant credit on the initial purchase.**

Self-Test 20.4

How will the break-even probability vary with the discount rate? Try a rate of 20% in Example 20.4. What is the intuition behind your answer?

Of course, real-life situations are generally far more complex than our simple examples. Customers are not all good or all bad. Many pay late consistently; you get your money, but it costs more to collect and you lose a few months' interest. And estimating the probability that a customer will pay up is far from an exact science. Then there is uncertainty about repeat sales. There may be a good chance that the customer will give you further business, but you can't be sure of that and you can't know for how long she or he will continue to buy from you.

Like almost all financial decisions, credit allocation involves a strong dose of judgment. Our examples are intended as reminders of the issues involved rather than as cookbook formulas. Here are the basic things to remember:

1. *Maximize profit.* As credit manager your job is not to minimize the number of bad accounts; it is to maximize profits. You are faced with a trade-off. The best that can happen is that the customer pays promptly; the worst is default. In the one case the firm receives the full additional revenues from the sale less the additional costs; in the other it receives nothing and loses the costs. You must weigh the chances of these alternative outcomes. If the margin of profit is high, you are justified in a liberal credit policy; if it is low, you cannot afford many bad debts.

2. *Concentrate on the dangerous accounts.* You should not expend the same effort on analyzing all credit decisions. If an application is small or clear-cut, your decision should be largely routine; if it is large or doubtful, you may do better to move straight to a detailed credit appraisal. Most credit managers don't make credit decisions on an order-by-order basis. Instead, they set a credit limit for each customer. The sales representative is required to refer the order for approval only if the customer exceeds this limit.

3. *Look beyond the immediate order.* Sometimes it may be worth accepting a relatively poor risk as long as there is a likelihood that the customer will grow into a regular and reliable buyer. (This is why credit card companies are eager to sign up college students even though few students can point to an established credit history.) New businesses must be prepared to incur more bad debts than established businesses because they have not yet formed relationships with low-risk customers. This is part of the cost of building up a good customer list.

Collection Policy

It would be nice if all customers paid their bills by the due date. But they don't, and since you may also "stretch" your payables, from time to time, you can't altogether blame them.

Slow payers impose two costs on the firm. First, they require the firm to spend more resources in collecting payments. They also force the firm to invest more in working capital. Recall from Chapter 4 that accounts receivable are proportional to the average collection period (also known as days' sales in receivables):

$$\text{Accounts receivable} = \text{daily sales} \times \text{average collection period}$$

collection policy
Procedures to collect and monitor receivables.

aging schedule
Classification of accounts receivable by time outstanding.

When your customers stretch payables, you end up with a longer collection period and a greater investment in accounts receivable. That's why you need a **collection policy.**

The credit manager keeps a record of payment experiences with each customer. In addition, the manager monitors overdue payments by drawing up a schedule of the aging of receivables. The **aging schedule** classifies accounts receivable by the length of time they are outstanding. This may look roughly like Table 20.1. The table shows that customer A, for example, is fully current: There are no bills outstanding for more than a month. Customer Z, however, might present problems, as there are $15,000 in bills that have been outstanding for more than 3 months.

TABLE 20.1 An aging
schedule of receivables

Customer's Name	Less than 1 Month	1–2 Months	2–3 Months	More than 3 Months	Total Owed
A	$ 10,000	$ 0	$ 0	$ 0	$ 10,000
B	8,000	3,000	0	0	11,000
.	.	.	.	.	.
.	.	.	.	.	.
.	.	.	.	.	.
Z	5,000	4,000	6,000	15,000	30,000
Total	$200,000	$40,000	$15,000	$43,000	$298,000

Self-Test 20.5

Suppose a customer who buys goods on terms 1/10, net 45, always forgoes the cash discount and pays on the 45th day after sale. If the firm typically buys $10,000 of goods a month, spread evenly over the month, what will the aging schedule look like?

When a customer is in arrears, the usual procedure is to send a *statement of account* and to follow this at intervals with increasingly insistent letters, telephone calls, or fax messages. If none of these has any effect, most companies turn the debt over to a collection agency or an attorney.

Large firms can reap economies of scale in record keeping, billing, and so on, but the small firm may not be able to support a fully fledged credit operation. However, it can obtain some scale economies by farming out part of the job to a *factor.* The factor and its client's firm agree on credit limits for each customer, and the client notifies each customer that the factor has purchased the debt (i.e., the trade credit). The factor then takes on the responsibility (and risk) of collecting the bills and pays the invoice value to the client minus a fee of 1% or 2%. Aside from gaining the economies that come from specializing in collection for a large number of manufacturers, factors see many more transactions than any single firm and so may be better placed to judge the creditworthiness of each customer.

There is always a potential conflict of interest between the collection department and the sales department. Sales representatives commonly complain that they no sooner win new customers than the collection department frightens them off with threatening letters. The collection manager, on the other hand, bemoans the fact that the sales force is concerned only with winning orders and does not care whether the goods are subsequently paid for. This conflict is another example of the agency problem introduced in Chapter 1. **Good collection policy balances conflicting goals. The company wants cordial relations with its customers. It also wants them to pay their bills on time.**

There are instances of cooperation between sales managers and the financial managers who worry about collections. For example, the specialty chemicals division of a major pharmaceutical company actually made a business loan to an important customer that had been suddenly cut off by its bank. The pharmaceutical company bet that it knew its customer better than the customer's bank did—and the pharmaceutical company was right. The customer arranged alternative bank financing, paid back the pharmaceutical company, and became an even more loyal customer. It was a nice example of financial management supporting sales.

It is not common for suppliers to make business loans in this way, but they lend money *indirectly* whenever they allow a delay in payment. Trade credit can be an important source of funds for indigent customers that cannot obtain a bank loan. But that raises an important question: If the bank is unwilling to lend, does it make sense for you, the supplier, to continue to extend trade credit? Here are two possible reasons that it may make sense: First, as in the case of our pharmaceutical company, you may have more information than the bank about the customer's business. Second, you need to look beyond the immediate transaction and recognize that your firm may stand to lose some profitable future sales if the customer goes out of business.[9]

20.2 Inventory Management

The second important current asset is *inventory*. Inventories may consist of raw materials, work in process, or finished goods awaiting sale and shipment. Firms are not obliged to carry these inventories. For example, they could buy materials day by day, as needed. But then they would pay higher prices for ordering in small lots, and they would risk production delays if the materials were not delivered on time. They can avoid that risk by ordering more than the firm's immediate needs. Similarly, firms could do away with inventories of finished goods by producing only what they expect to sell tomorrow. But this also could be a dangerous strategy. A producer with only a small inventory of finished goods is more likely to be caught short and unable to fill orders if demand is unexpectedly high. Moreover, a large inventory of finished goods may allow longer, more economical production runs.

But there are also costs to holding inventories that must be set against these benefits. These are called *carrying costs*. For example, money tied up in inventories does not earn interest; storage and insurance must be paid for; and there may be a risk of spillage or obsolescence. Therefore, production managers need to strike a sensible balance between the benefits of holding inventory and the costs.

EXAMPLE 20.5 ▶   Inventory Management

Here is a simple inventory problem. Akron Wire Products uses 255,000 tons a year of wire rod. Suppose that it orders Q tons at a time from the manufacturer. Just before delivery, its inventories of wire have run down to zero. Just *after* delivery, it has an inventory of Q tons. Thus, Akron's inventory of wire rod roughly follows the sawtooth pattern in Figure 20.3.

There are two costs to holding this inventory. First, there are carrying costs, such as the cost of storage, and the cost of the capital that is tied up in inventory. Suppose these costs work out to an annual figure of about $55 per ton. The second type of cost is the order cost. Each order that Akron places with the manufacturer involves a fixed handling and delivery charge of $450.

FIGURE 20.3 A simple inventory rule. The company waits until inventories of materials are exhausted and then reorders a constant quantity.

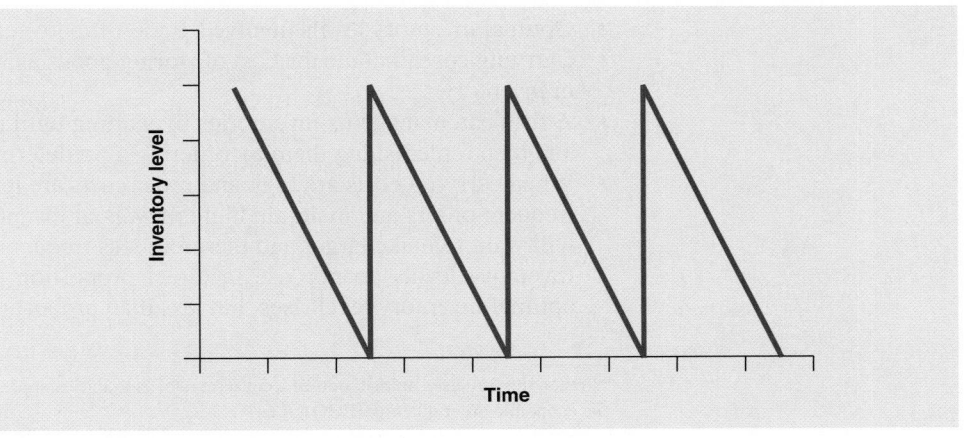

---

[9] Of course, banks also need to recognize the possibility of continuing business from the firm. The question therefore is whether suppliers have a *greater* stake in the firm's continuing prosperity. For some evidence on the determinants of the supply and demand for trade credit, see M. A. Petersen and R. G. Rajan, "Trade Credit: Theories and Evidence," *Review of Financial Studies* 10 (Fall 1997), pp. 661–692.

FIGURE 20.4 As the inventory order size increases, order costs fall and inventory carrying costs rise. Total costs are minimized when the saving in order costs equals the increase in carrying costs.

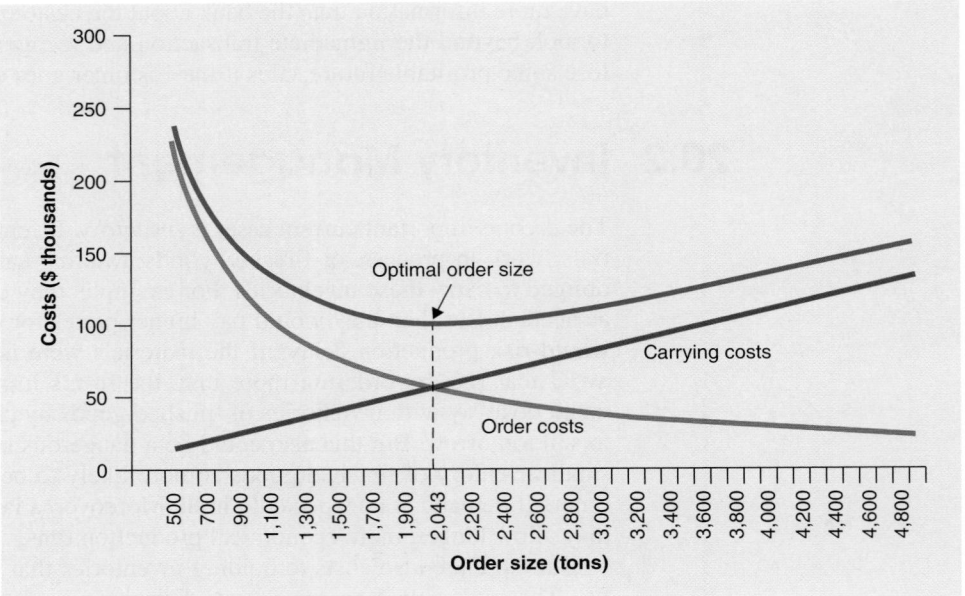

Here, then, is the kernel of the inventory problem: As Akron increases its order size, the number of orders falls but average inventory rises. Figure 20.4 shows that cost related to the number of orders declines, though at a decreasing rate, while carrying cost related to inventory size rises. It is worth increasing order size as long as the decline in order cost outweighs the rise in carrying cost. The optimal inventory policy is one in which these two effects exactly offset each other. In our example, this occurs when the firm places about 250 orders a year (roughly one order every working day) and the size of each order is Q = 2,043 tons. The optimal order size (2,043 tons in our example) is known as the *economic order quantity*, or *EOQ*.[10]

In calculating the economic order quantity for Akron Wire, we made several unrealistic assumptions. For instance, most firms do not use up their inventory of raw material at a constant rate, and they would not wait until stocks had completely run out before replenishing them. But this simple model does capture some essential features of inventory management:

• Optimal inventory levels involve a trade-off between carrying costs and order costs.
• Carrying costs include the cost of storing goods as well as the cost of capital tied up in inventory.
• A firm can manage its inventories by waiting until they reach some minimum level and then replenishing them by ordering a predetermined quantity.
• When carrying costs are high and order costs are low, it makes sense to place more frequent orders and maintain higher levels of inventory. If order costs are high, you will want to make larger and therefore less frequent orders.
• Inventory levels do not rise in direct proportion to sales. As sales increase, the optimal inventory level rises, but less than proportionately.

---

[10] When the firm uses up materials at a constant rate, as in our example, there is a simple formula for calculating the economic order quantity (EOQ). It is:

$$\text{Optimal order size} = Q = \sqrt{\frac{2 \times \text{sales} \times \text{cost per order}}{\text{carrying cost}}}$$

In our example, $Q = \sqrt{\dfrac{2 \times 255{,}000 \times 450}{55}} = 2{,}043$ tons.

just-in-time approach
System of inventory management that requires minimal inventories of materials and very frequent deliveries by suppliers.

Corporations today get by with lower levels of inventory than they used to. Thirty years ago, inventories held by U.S. companies accounted for 12% of firm assets. Today the figure is about 8%. One way that companies have reduced inventory levels is by moving to a **just-in-time approach.** Just-in-time was pioneered by Toyota in Japan. Toyota keeps inventories of auto parts to a minimum by ordering supplies only as they are needed. Thus deliveries of components to its plants are made throughout the day at intervals as short as 1 hour. Toyota is able to operate successfully with such low inventories only because it has a set of plans to ensure that strikes, traffic snarl-ups, or other hazards don't halt the flow of components and bring production to a standstill. Many companies in the United States have learned from Toyota's example and have pared their investment in inventories.

Firms are also finding that they can reduce their inventories of finished goods by producing their goods to order. For example, Dell Computer discovered that it did not need to keep a large stock of finished machines. Its customers are able to use the Internet to specify what features they want on their PC. The computer is then assembled to order and shipped to the customer.[11]

20.3 Cash Management

Short-term securities pay interest; cash doesn't. So why do corporations and individuals hold billions of dollars in cash and demand deposits? Why, for example, don't you take all *your* cash and invest it in interest-bearing securities? The answer of course is that cash gives you more *liquidity* than do securities. You can use it to buy things. It is hard enough to get New York cab drivers to give you change for a $20 bill, but try asking them to split a Treasury bill.

When you have only a small proportion of your wealth in cash, a little extra can be extremely useful; when you have a substantial holding, any additional liquidity is not worth much. Therefore, as financial manager you want to hold cash balances up to the point where the marginal value of the liquidity is equal to the value of the interest forgone.

In choosing between cash and short-term securities, the financial manager faces a task like that of the production manager. After all, cash is just another raw material that you need to do business, and there are costs and benefits to holding large "inventories" of cash. If the cash were invested in securities, it would earn interest. On the other hand, you can't use those securities to pay the firm's bills. If you had to sell them every time you needed to pay a bill, you could incur heavy transaction costs. The financial manager must trade off the cost of keeping an inventory of cash (the lost interest) against the benefits (the saving on transaction costs).

For very large firms, the transaction costs of buying and selling securities are trivial compared with the opportunity cost of holding idle cash balances. Suppose that the interest rate is 4% per year, or roughly 4/365 = .011% per day. Then the daily interest earned on $1 million is .00011 × $1,000,000 = $110. Even at a cost of $50 per transaction, which is generous, it pays to buy Treasury bills today and sell them tomorrow rather than to leave $1 million idle overnight.

A corporation such as Walmart with about $400 billion of annual sales, has an average daily cash flow of $400,000,000,000/365 = $1,096 million. Firms of this size end up buying or selling securities once a day, every day, unless by chance they have only a small positive cash balance at the end of the day.

Banks have developed a variety of ways to help such firms invest idle cash. For example, they may provide *sweep programs,* in which the bank automatically "sweeps"

---

[11] These examples of just-in-time and build-to-order production are taken from T. Murphy, "JIT When ASAP Isn't Good Enough," *Ward's Auto World,* May 1999, pp. 67–73; R. Schreffler, "Alive and Well," *Ward's Auto World,* May 1999, pp. 73–77; "A Long March: Mass Customization," *The Economist,* July 14, 2001, pp. 63–65.

surplus funds into a higher-interest account. Why then do these large firms hold any significant amounts of cash in non-interest-bearing accounts? For two reasons: First, cash may be left in accounts to compensate banks for the services they provide. Second, large corporations may have literally hundreds of accounts with dozens of different banks. It is often less expensive to leave idle cash in some of these accounts than to monitor each account daily and make daily transfers between them.

One major reason for the proliferation of bank accounts is decentralized management. If you give a subsidiary operating freedom to manage its own affairs, you must also give it the right to spend and receive cash. Good cash management nevertheless implies some degree of centralization. You cannot maintain your desired inventory of cash if all the subsidiaries in the group are responsible for their own private pools of cash. And you certainly want to avoid situations in which one subsidiary is investing its spare cash at 8% while another is borrowing at 10%. It is not surprising, therefore, that even in highly decentralized companies there is generally central control over cash balances and bank relations.

Check Handling and Float

Traditionally, most large bills in the United States have been paid with checks. But check handling is a cumbersome and labor-intensive task, and it can take several days for a check to clear. Suppose, for example, that you renew your auto insurance by writing a check for $600, which you mail to your insurance company. A day or so later the insurance company receives your check and deposits it in its bank account. But this money isn't available to the company immediately. The company's bank won't actually have the money in hand until it sends the check to your bank and receives payment. Since the bank has to wait, it makes the insurance company wait too—usually 1 or 2 business days. Until the check has been presented and cleared, that $600 will continue to sit in your bank account.

Checks that have been mailed but not yet cleared are known as *float*. In our example, float provided you with an extra $600 in your bank account while the check went first to the insurance company, then to the company's bank, and finally to your own bank. This may make float seem like a marvelous invention, but unfortunately it can also work in reverse. Every time someone writes *you* a check, you have to wait several days after depositing it before you may spend the money.

However, changes in federal law in the last several years have helped to speed up collections. The Check Clearing for the 21st Century Act, usually known as "Check 21," allows banks to send digital images of checks to one another rather than sending the checks themselves. So fewer cargo planes and trucks need to crisscross the country to take bundles of checks from one bank to another.

Firms that receive a large volume of checks have devised a number of ways to ensure that the cash becomes available as quickly as possible. For example, a retail chain may arrange for each branch to deposit receipts in a collection account at a local bank. Surplus funds are then periodically transferred electronically to a **concentration account** at one of the company's principal banks. There are two reasons that concentration banking allows the company to gain quicker use of its funds. First, because the store is nearer to the bank, transfer times are reduced. Second, since the customer's check is likely to be drawn on a local bank, the time taken to clear the check is also reduced.

Concentration banking is often combined with a **lock-box system.** In this case the firm's customers are instructed to send their payments to a regional post-office box. The local bank then takes on the administrative chore of emptying the box and depositing the checks in the company's local deposit account.

---

concentration account
Customers make payments to a regional collection center, which then transfers funds to an account at a principal bank.

lock-box system
System whereby customers send payments to a post-office box, and a local bank collects and processes checks.

EXAMPLE 20.6 ▶ Lock-Box Systems

Suppose that you are thinking of opening a lock box. The local bank shows you a map of mail delivery times. From that and knowledge of your customers' locations, you come up with the following data:

> Average number of daily payments to lock box = 150
> Average size of payment   = $1,200
> Rate of interest *per day*   = .02%
> Saving in mailing time   = 1.2 days
> Saving in processing time   = .8 day

On this basis, the lock box would reduce collection float by

$$150 \text{ items per day} \times \$1,200 \text{ per item} \times (1.2 + .8) \text{ days saved} = \$360,000$$

Invested at .02% per day, that gives a daily return of

$$.0002 \times \$360,000 = \$72$$

The bank's charge for operating the lock-box system depends on the number of checks processed. Suppose that the bank charges $.26 per check. That works out to $150 \times \$.26 = \$39$ per day. You are ahead by $72 − $39 = $33 per day, plus whatever your firm saves from not having to process the checks itself.

Self-Test 20.6

How will the following conditions affect the price that a firm should be willing to pay for a lock-box service?

a. **The average size of its payments increases.**
b. **The number of payments per day increases (with no change in average size of payments).**
c. **The interest rate increases.**
d. **The average mail time saved by the lock-box system increases.**
e. **The processing time saved by the lock-box system increases.**

Other Payment Systems

There are a variety of ways besides checks that you can pay for larger purchases or send payments to another location. Some of the more important payment methods are set out in Table 20.2.

Figure 20.5 compares use of these payment systems around the world. Payment patterns vary widely across countries. For example, look at the bottom (blue) portion of the bars in the figure. Checks are virtually unheard of in the Netherlands, Sweden, or Germany. Most payments in these countries are made by debit cards or credit transfer. By contrast, Americans love to write checks. Each year, U.S. individuals and firms make about 27 billion payments by check. But even in the United States, check writing is steadily giving way to electronic payments. Over 50% of U.S. households now use direct payment for recurring expenditures, and nearly three-quarters of employees are paid by direct deposit.

In fact, the use of checks continues to decline around the world as the market share of credit and debit cards continues to grow. In addition, mobile phone technology and

TABLE 20.2 Small face-to-face purchases are commonly paid for in cash, but here are some of the other ways that you can pay your bills.

Check When you write a check, you are instructing your bank to pay a specified sum on demand to the particular firm or person named on the check.

Credit card A credit card, such as a Visa card or MasterCard, gives you a line of credit that allows you to make purchases up to a stated limit. At the end of each month, either you pay the credit card company for these purchases or you will be charged interest on any outstanding balance.

Charge card (or travel and entertainment card) A charge card may look like a credit card and you can spend money with it like a credit card. But with a charge card the day of reckoning comes at the end of each month, when you must pay for all purchases that you have made. In other words, you must pay off your entire balance every month.

Debit card A debit card allows you to have your purchases from a store charged directly to your bank account. The deduction is usually made electronically and is immediate. Often, debit cards may also be used to make withdrawals from a cash machine (ATM).

Credit transfer With a credit transfer you ask your bank to set up a standing order to make a regular set payment to a supplier. For example, standing orders are often used to make regular fixed mortgage payments.

Direct payment A direct payment (also called direct debit) is an instruction to your bank to allow a company to collect varying amounts from your account, as long as you have been given advance notice of the collection amounts and dates. For example, an electric utility company may ask you to set up a direct debit that allows it to receive automatic payment of your electricity bills from your bank account.

FIGURE 20.5 How purchases are paid for: Percentage of total *volume* of cashless transactions. (Data exclude small usage of card-based e-money.)

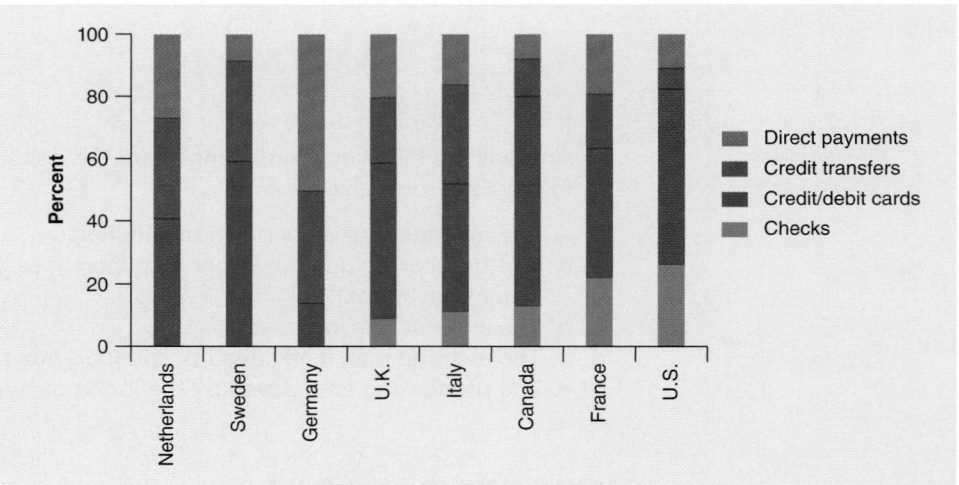

Source: Bank for International Settlements, "Statistics on Payment and Settlement Systems in Selected Countries," **www.bis.org/publ,** December 2009.

the Internet are encouraging the development of new infant payment systems. Here are just two examples:

- Electronic bill presentment and payment (or EBPP) allows companies to bill customers and receive payments through the Internet. Already in Finland, two out of three people regard the Internet as the most typical medium for paying bills.
- Stored value cards (or e-money) let you transfer funds to a card that can be used pretty much as electronic cash.

Electronic Funds Transfer

As we've just noted, throughout the world payments are increasingly being made electronically. The most familiar forms of electronic payment are the credit card and debit card, but there are three other important ways that money can travel electronically. It can do so by direct payment, direct deposit, or wire transfer. Figure 20.6 shows the proportion of firms using each of these methods.

FIGURE 20.6 Methods used by companies to make and receive electronic payments

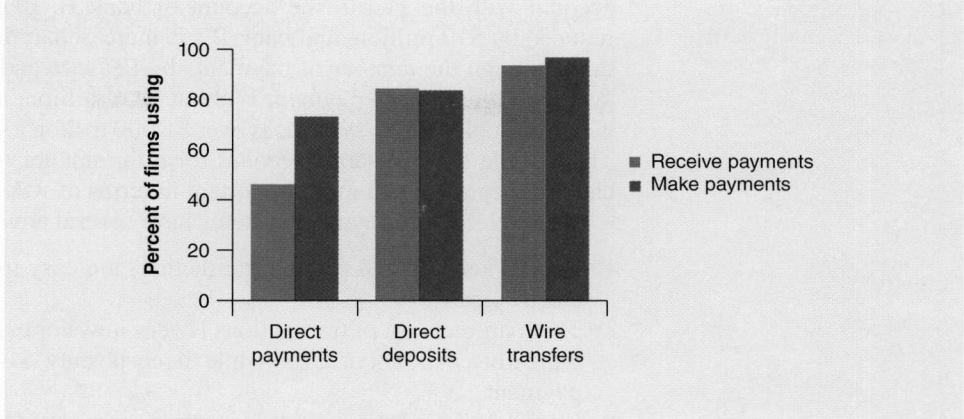

Source: *A Treasurer's Guide to U.S. Cash Management,* Association for Financial Professionals, Report of Survey Results, August 2000.

Automated Clearing House (ACH)
An electronic network for cash transfers in the United States.

Direct payment systems are used for recurring expenditures, such as utility bills, insurance premiums, and mortgage or loan payments. For example, if you have taken out a student loan, you may have authorized the lender to take the payment directly from your bank account each month. The student loan company simply needs to provide its bank with a file showing details of each student, the amount to be debited, and the date. The payment then travels electronically through the **Automated Clearing House (ACH)** system. You are saved from the chore of writing regular checks, and the firm knows exactly when the cash is coming in and avoids the labor-intensive process of handling thousands of checks.

The Automated Clearing House system also allows money to flow in the reverse direction. Thus, while a *direct payment* transaction provides an automatic debit, a *direct deposit* constitutes an automatic credit. Direct deposits are used to make bulk payments such as wages or dividends. Again the company provides its bank with a file of instructions. The bank then debits the company's account and transfers the cash via the Automated Clearing House to the bank accounts of the firm's employees or shareholders. ACH transactions have grown dramatically in recent years. You can see from Table 20.3 that the total value of these transactions in the United States has overtaken that of checks.

The third method of electronic payment is wire transfer. Most large-value payments between companies are made electronically through Fedwire or CHIPS (Clearing House Interbank Payments System). Fedwire is operated by the Federal Reserve and connects nearly 10,000 financial institutions to the Fed and so to each other.[12] CHIPS, the other electronic payment system, is owned by the banks and used mainly for cross-border payments. Wire transfers allow fast and secure movement of very large sums of money. For example, suppose bank A wires the Fed to transfer $10 million from its

TABLE 20.3 Use of payment systems in the United States, 2009

	Number of Payments, millions	Value of Payments, $ trillions
Checks	24,000	32
ACH	19,000	37
Fedwire	125	608
CHIPS	85	364

Source: **www.federalreserve.gov, www.nacha.com,** and **www.chips.org.**

---

[12] Fedwire is a *real-time, gross settlement system,* which means that each transaction over Fedwire is settled individually and immediately. With a net settlement system, transactions are put into a pot and periodically netted off before being settled. CHIPS is an example of a net system that settles at frequent intervals.

account with the Fed to the account of bank B. Bank A's account is immediately reduced by $10 million, and bank B's is increased at the same time. Table 20.3 shows that although the *number* of payments by Fedwire and CHIPS is relatively small, the average value of each payment is about $4.6 million, and the total value of payments going through the two systems is over $1,000 trillion a year ($1,000,000,000,000,000). Thus, while these systems account for a far smaller *number* of transactions than do checks, they are much more important in terms of *value.*

These electronic payment systems have several advantages:

- Record keeping and routine transactions are easy to automate when money moves electronically.
- The marginal cost of transactions is very low. For example, a transfer using Fedwire typically costs about $20, while it costs only a few cents to make each ACH payment.
- Float is reduced. For example, cash managers at Occidental Petroleum found that one plant was paying out about $8 million a month several days early to avoid any risk of late fees if checks were delayed in the mail. The solution was obvious: The plant's managers switched to paying large bills electronically; that way they could ensure payments arrived exactly on time.

International Cash Management

Cash management in domestic firms is child's play compared with that in large multinational corporations operating in dozens of different countries, each with its own currency, banking system, and legal structure.

A single centralized cash management system is an unattainable ideal for these companies, although they are edging toward it. For example, suppose that you are treasurer of a large multinational company with operations throughout Europe. You could allow the separate businesses to manage their own cash, but that would be costly and would almost certainly result in each one accumulating little hoards of cash. The solution is to set up a regional system. In this case the company establishes a local concentration account with a bank in each country. Any surplus cash is swept daily into central multicurrency accounts in London or another European banking center. This cash is then invested in marketable securities or used to finance any subsidiaries that have a cash shortage.

Payments can also be made out of the regional center. For example, to pay wages in each European country, the company just needs to send its principal bank a computer file with details of the payments to be made. The bank then finds the least costly way to transfer the cash from the company's central accounts and arranges for the funds to be credited on the correct day to the employees in each country.

Most large multinationals have several banks in each country, but the more banks they use, the less control they have over their cash balances. So development of regional cash management systems favors banks that can offer a worldwide branch network. These banks can also afford the high costs of setting up computer systems for handling cash payments and receipts in different countries.

20.4 Investing Idle Cash: The Money Market

money market
Market for short-term financial assets.

When firms have excess funds, they can invest the surplus in a variety of securities in the **money market,** the market for short-term financial assets. Larger firms usually invest directly in these securities. However, smaller firms often park their spare cash in a money market mutual fund, which holds a portfolio of money market investments.

Only fixed-income securities with maturities less than 1 year are considered to be part of the money market. In fact, however, most instruments in the money market have considerably shorter maturity. Limiting maturity has two advantages for the cash manager. Recall from Chapter 6 that risk due to interest rate fluctuations increases with maturity. Very short-term securities, therefore, have almost no interest rate risk. Second, it is far easier to gauge the risk of default over short horizons. One need not worry as much about deterioration in financial strength over a 90-day horizon as over the 30-year life of a bond. These considerations imply that high-quality money market securities are a safe "parking spot" to keep idle balances until they are converted back to cash.

Most money market securities are also highly marketable or *liquid,* meaning that it is easy and cheap to sell the asset for cash. This property, too, is an attractive feature of securities used as temporary investments until cash is needed.

Some of the important instruments of the money market are:

Treasury bills. Treasury bills are issued weekly by the U.S. government and mature in 4 weeks, 3 months, 6 months, and (since June 2008) 12 months. They are the safest and most liquid money market instrument.

Commercial paper. This is short-term, usually unsecured, debt of large and well-known companies. While maturities can range up to 270 days before registration with the SEC is required, most commercial paper is issued with maturities of less than 2 months. Because there is no active trading in commercial paper, it has low marketability. Therefore, it would not be an appropriate investment for a firm that could not hold it until maturity. Both Moody's and Standard & Poor's rate commercial paper in terms of the default risk of the issuer.

Certificates of deposit. CDs are time deposits at banks, usually in denominations greater than $100,000. Unlike demand deposits (checking accounts), time deposits cannot be withdrawn from the bank on demand: The bank pays interest and principal only at the maturity of the deposit. However, short-term CDs (with maturities less than 3 months) are actively traded, so a firm can easily sell the security if it needs cash.

Repurchase agreements. Also known as *repos,* repurchase agreements are, in effect, collateralized loans. A government bond dealer sells Treasury securities to an investor, with an agreement to repurchase them at a later date at a higher price. The increase in price serves as implicit interest, so the investor in effect is lending money to the dealer, first giving money to the dealer and later getting it back with interest. The bills serve as collateral for the loan: If the dealer fails, and cannot buy back the bill, the investor can keep it. Repurchase agreements are usually very short-term, with maturities of only a few days.

Interest rates on short-term loans (loans of less than 1 year) are often quoted on a so-called *discount basis.* For example, a $95,000 loan might require repayment of $100,000 in 1 year. On a discount basis, the rate would be *quoted* as the discount from face value, in this case 5%. The actual interest rate is a bit higher than this. You pay interest of $5,000 on a $95,000 loan, so the interest rate is $5,000/$95,000 = .0526, or 5.26%. You should be aware that rates in the money market also are typically quoted on a discount basis.

EXAMPLE 20.7 ▶ Money Market Rates

A Treasury bill with face value $100,000 and maturity 6 months is sold for $98,000. The rate on this bill on a discount basis would be quoted as 4%. The actual discount from face value is 2% semiannually, or 4% on an annualized basis. Notice also that money market rates are annualized using simple, not compound, interest. The *effective* annual rate on this half-year investment can be found by solving

$$98,000 \times (1 + r)^{1/2} = 100,000$$

which implies that $r = .0412$, or 4.12%.

Yields on Money Market Investments

When we value long-term debt, it is important to take account of default risk. Almost anything may happen in 30 years, and even today's most respectable company may get into trouble eventually. Therefore, corporate bonds offer higher yields than Treasury bonds.

Short-term debt is not risk-free either. During the financial crisis seven companies stopped payments on their commercial paper. They included Lehman Brothers, which defaulted on a record $3 billion of paper. Fortunately, such examples are exceptions; in general, the danger of default is less for money market securities issued by corporations than for corporate bonds. There are two reasons for this. First, as we pointed out above, the range of possible outcomes is smaller for short-term investments. Even though the distant future may be clouded, you can usually be confident that a particular company will survive for at least the next month. Second, for the most part only well-established companies can borrow in the money market. If you are going to lend money for just a few days, you can't afford to spend too much time in evaluating the loan. Thus, you will consider only blue-chip borrowers.

Despite the high quality of money market investments, there are often significant differences in yield between corporate and U.S. government securities. Why is this? One answer is the risk of default. Another is that the investments have different degrees of liquidity, or "moneyness." Investors like Treasury bills because they are easily turned into cash on short notice. Securities that cannot be converted so quickly and cheaply into cash need to offer relatively high yields.

During times of market turmoil investors may place a higher value on having ready access to cash. On these occasions the yield on illiquid securities can increase dramatically. This happened in 2007, when banks across the world revealed huge losses in the U.S. subprime mortgage market. Fearful that some banks would be forced into sales of their positions, investors shrank from illiquid securities, and there was a "flight to quality." The spread between the yields on commercial paper and Treasury bills increased to over 100 basis points (1.00%), four times its level at the beginning of the year.

The International Money Market

In addition to the domestic money market, there is also an international market for short-term dollar investments, which is known as the *eurodollar* market. Eurodollars have nothing to do with the euro, the currency of the European Monetary Union (EMU). They are simply dollars deposited in a bank in Europe. For example, suppose that an American auto producer buys 1,000 ounces of palladium from Xstrata, the European mining giant. It pays for the purchase with a check for $1.5 million drawn on JPMorgan Chase. Xstrata then deposits the check with its account at Barclays Bank in London. As a result, Barclays has an asset in the form of a $1.5 million credit in its account with JPMorgan Chase. It also has an offsetting liability in the form of a dollar deposit. Since that dollar deposit is placed in Europe, it is called a eurodollar deposit.[13]

Just as there is both a domestic U.S. money market and a eurodollar market, so there is both a domestic Japanese money market and a market in London for euroyen. So if a U.S. corporation wishes to make a short-term investment in yen, it can deposit the yen with a bank in Tokyo or it can make a euroyen deposit in London. Similarly, there is both a domestic money market in the euro area as well as a money market for euros in London. And so on.

Major international banks in London lend dollars to one another at the *London Interbank Offered Rate* (LIBOR). Similarly, they lend yen to each other at the yen LIBOR interest rate, and they lend euros at the euro interbank offered rate, or Euribor. These interest rates are used as a benchmark for pricing many types of short-term loans in the United States and in other countries. For example, a corporation in the United States may issue a floating-rate note with interest payments tied to dollar LIBOR.

---

[13] Xstrata could equally well deposit the check with the London branch of a U.S. bank or a Japanese bank. It would still have made a eurodollar deposit.

SUMMARY

What are the usual steps in credit management? *(LO1)*

The first step in credit management is to set normal **terms of sale.** This means that you must decide the length of the payment period and the size of any cash discounts. In most industries these conditions are fairly standardized.

Your second step is to decide the form of the contract with your customer. Most domestic sales are made on **open account.** In this case the only evidence that the customer owes you money is the entry in your ledger and a receipt signed by the customer. Sometimes, you may require a more formal commitment before you deliver the goods. For example, the supplier may arrange for the customer to provide a trade acceptance.

The third task is to assess each customer's creditworthiness. When you have made an assessment of the customer's credit standing, the fourth step is to establish sensible credit policy. Finally, once the credit policy is set, you need to establish a collection policy to identify and pursue slow payers.

How do we measure the implicit interest rate on credit? *(LO2)*

The effective interest rate for customers who buy goods on credit rather than taking the discount for quicker payment is

$$\left(1 + \frac{\text{discount}}{\text{discounted price}}\right)^{365/\text{extra days credit}} - 1$$

How do firms assess the probability that a customer will pay? *(LO3)*

Credit analysis is the process of deciding which customers are likely to pay their bills. There are various sources of information: your own experience with the customer, the experience of other creditors, the assessment of a credit agency, a check with the customer's bank, the market value of the customer's securities, and an analysis of the customer's financial statements. Firms that handle a large volume of credit information often use a formal system for combining the various sources into an overall credit score.

How do firms decide whether it makes sense to grant credit to a customer? *(LO4)*

Credit policy refers to the decision to extend credit to a customer. The job of the credit manager is not to minimize the number of bad debts; it is to maximize profits. This means that you need to weigh the odds that the customer will pay, providing you with a profit, against the odds that the customer will default, resulting in a loss. Remember not to be too shortsighted when reckoning the expected profit. It is often worth accepting the marginal applicant if there is a chance that the applicant may become a regular and reliable customer.

If credit is granted, the next problem is to set a **collection policy.** This requires tact and judgment. You want to be firm with the truly delinquent customer, but you don't want to offend the good one by writing demanding letters just because a check has been delayed in the mail. You will find it easier to spot troublesome accounts if you keep a careful **aging schedule** of outstanding accounts.

What are the costs and benefits of holding inventories and cash? *(LO5)*

The benefit of higher inventory levels is the reduction in order costs associated with restocking and the reduced chances of running out of material. The costs are the carrying costs, which include the cost of space, insurance, spoilage, and the opportunity cost of the capital tied up in inventory. Cash provides liquidity, but it doesn't pay interest. Securities pay interest, but you can't use them to buy things. As financial manager you want to hold cash up to the point where the incremental or marginal benefit of liquidity is equal to the cost of holding cash, that is, the interest that you could earn on securities.

What are some of the ways that companies receive and make payments? *(LO6)*

When you mail a check, it may take several days before it is presented and cleared. During this time the money will continue to sit in your bank account. Checks that have been mailed but not yet cleared are known as *float.* Unfortunately, float also works in reverse. Every time someone writes *you* a check, there is a delay before the money ends up in your bank account. Companies that receive a large volume of checks employ techniques such as **lock-box banking** and **concentration accounts** to speed up the process of depositing and clearing checks.

Check usage is on the decline. Instead, money increasingly travels electronically. For example, your mortgage payment will probably be taken directly *from* your bank account each month, and your salary will probably be paid directly *into* your account. Large-value payments between companies are made electronically by means of the Fedwire and CHIPS systems. The number of payments going through these two systems is quite small, but their value is huge.

Where do firms invest excess funds until they are needed to pay bills? *(LO7)*

Firms can invest idle cash in the **money market,** the market for short-term financial assets. These assets tend to be short-term, low risk, and highly liquid, making them ideal instruments in which to invest funds for short periods of time before cash is needed. The most important money market instruments are Treasury bills, commercial paper, certificates of deposit and repurchase agreements.

LISTING OF EQUATIONS

20.1   Effective annual rate $= \left(1 + \dfrac{\text{discount}}{\text{discounted price}}\right)^{365/\text{extra days credit}} - 1$

QUESTIONS

|FINANCE

QUIZ

1. **Trade Credit Rates.** Company X sells on a 1/20, net 60, basis. Customer Y buys goods with an invoice of $1,000. *(LO2)*
    a. How much can company Y deduct from the bill if it pays on day 20?
    b. How many extra days of credit can company Y receive if it passes up the cash discount?
    c. What is the effective annual rate of interest if Y pays on the due date rather than day 20?

2. **Terms of Sale.** Complete the following passage by selecting the appropriate terms from the following list (some terms may be used more than once): *acceptance, open, commercial, trade, the United States, his or her own, draft, account, bank, banker's, the customer's. (LO1)*

    Most goods are sold on _____ _____. In this case the only evidence of the debt is a record in the seller's books and a signed receipt. An alternative is for the seller to arrange a(n) _____ _____ ordering payment by the customer. In order to obtain the goods, the customer must acknowledge this order and sign the document. This signed acknowledgment is known as a(n) _____ _____. Sometimes the seller may also ask _____ _____ bank to sign the document. In this case it is known as a(n) _____ _____.

3. **Terms of Sale.** For each pair below, indicate which firm you would expect to grant shorter or longer credit periods. *(LO4)*
    a. One firm sells hardware; the other sells bread.
    b. One firm's customers have an inventory turnover ratio of 10; the other's customers have turnover of 15.
    c. One firm sells mainly to electric utilities; the other to fashion boutiques.

4. **Payment Lag.** The lag between purchase date and the date at which payment is due is known as the *terms lag.* The lag between the due date and the date on which the buyer actually pays is termed the *due lag,* and the lag between the purchase and actual payment dates is the *pay lag.* Thus

    Pay lag = terms lag + due lag

    State how you would expect the following events to affect each type of lag: *(LO1)*
    a. The company imposes a service charge on late payers.
    b. A recession causes customers to be short of cash.
    c. The company changes its terms from net 10 to net 20.

5. **Trade Credit Rates.** A firm currently offers terms of sale of 3/20, net 40. What effect will the following actions have on the implicit interest rate charged to customers that pass up the cash discount? State whether the implicit interest rate will increase or decrease. *(LO2)*
   a. The terms are changed to 4/20, net 40.
   b. The terms are changed to 3/30, net 40.
   c. The terms are changed to 3/20, net 30.

6. **Float.** On January 25, Coot Company has $250,000 deposited with a local bank. On January 27, the company writes and mails checks of $20,000 and $60,000 to suppliers. At the end of the month, Coot's financial manager deposits a $45,000 check received from a customer in the morning mail and picks up the end-of-month account summary from the bank. The manager notes that only the $20,000 payment of the 27th has cleared the bank. What is the company's available balance with its bank? *(LO6)*

7. **Float.** Most banks now allow you to pay your bills over the Internet. You log on to your account to tell the bank which payments it should send out on your behalf. Whereas most banks charge you for writing paper checks, they do not charge for this Internet bill-paying service and, in fact, do not even charge you for their cost of postage. Why are the banks willing to provide this service to you for no fee? *(LO6)*

8. **Float.** General Products writes checks that average $20,000 daily. These checks take an average of 6 days to clear. It receives payments that average $22,000 daily. It takes 3 days before these checks are available to the firm. What would be General Products's annual savings if it could obtain access to the payments it receives within 2 days? The interest rate is 6% per year. *(LO6)*

9. **Lock Boxes.** Anne Teak, the financial manager of a furniture manufacturer, is considering operating a lock-box system. She forecasts that 400 payments a day will be made to lock boxes with an average payment size of $2,000. The bank's charge for operating the lock boxes is $.40 a check. The interest rate is .015% per day. *(LO6)*
   a. If the lock box makes the cash available 2 days earlier, is it worthwhile to adopt the system?
   b. What minimum reduction in the time to collect and process each check is needed to justify use of the lock-box system?

10. **Cash Management.** Complete the passage that follows by choosing the appropriate terms from the following list: *lock-box banking. Fedwire, concentration banking. (LO6)*

    Firms can increase their cash resources by speeding up collections. One way to do this is to arrange for payments to be made to regional offices which pay the checks into local banks. This is known as _____. Surplus funds are then transferred from the local bank to one of the company's main banks. Transfers can be made electronically through the _____ system. Another technique is to arrange for a local bank to collect the checks directly from a post office. This is known as _____.

PRACTICE PROBLEMS

11. **Trade Credit and Receivables.** A firm offers terms of 3/15, net 30. Currently, two-thirds of all customers take advantage of the trade discount; the remainder pay bills at the due date. *(LO2)*
    a. What will be the firm's typical value for its accounts receivable period? (See Chapter 19, Section 19.2, for a review of the accounts receivable period.)
    b. What is the average investment in accounts receivable if annual sales are $20 million?
    c. What would likely happen to the firm's accounts receivable period if it changed its terms to 4/15, net 30?

12. **Terms of Sale.** Microbiotics currently sells all of its frozen dinners cash on delivery but believes it can increase sales by offering supermarkets 1 month of free credit. The price per carton is $50, and the cost per carton is $40. *(LO4)*
    a. If unit sales will increase from 1,000 cartons to 1,060 per month, should the firm offer the credit? The interest rate is 1% per month, and all customers will pay their bills.
    b. What if the interest rate is 1.5% per month?
    c. What if the interest rate is 1.5% per month but the firm can offer the credit only as a special deal to new customers, while old customers will continue to pay cash on delivery?

13. **Credit Decision/Repeat Sales.** Locust Software sells computer training packages to its business customers at a price of $101. The cost of production (in present value terms) is $96. Locust sells its packages on terms of net 30 and estimates that about 7% of all orders will be uncollectible. An order comes in for 20 units. The interest rate is 1% per month. *(LO4)*
   a. Should the firm extend credit if this is a one-time order? The sale will not be made unless credit is extended.
   b. What is the break-even probability of collection?
   c. Now suppose that if a customer pays this month's bill, it will place an identical order in each month indefinitely and can be safely assumed to pose no risk of default. Should credit be extended?
   d. What is the break-even probability of collection in the repeat-sales case?

14. **Credit Decision.** Look back at Example 20.3. Cast Iron's costs have increased from $1,000 to $1,050. Assuming that there is no possibility of repeat orders, and that the probability of successful collection from the customer is $p = .95$, answer the following: *(LO4)*
   a. Should Cast Iron grant or refuse credit?
   b. What is the break-even probability of collection?

15. **Credit Analysis.** Financial ratios were described in Chapter 4. If you were the credit manager, to which financial ratios would you pay most attention? *(LO3)*

16. **Credit Decision.** The Branding Iron Company sells its irons for $60 apiece wholesale. Production cost is $50 per iron. There is a 25% chance that a prospective customer will go bankrupt within the next half-year. The customer orders 1,000 irons and asks for 6 months' credit. Should you accept the order? Assume an 8% per year discount rate, no chance of a repeat order, and that the customer will pay either in full or not at all. *(LO4)*

17. **Credit Policy.** As treasurer of the Universal Bed Corporation, Aristotle Procrustes is worried about his bad debt ratio, which is currently running at 6%. He believes that imposing a more stringent credit policy might reduce sales by 5% and reduce the bad debt ratio to 4%. If the cost of goods sold is 80% of the selling price, should Mr. Procrustes adopt the more stringent policy? *(LO4)*

18. **Credit Decision/Repeat Sales.** Surf City sells its network browsing software for $15 per copy to computer software distributors and allows its customers 1 month to pay their bills. The cost of the software is $10 per copy. The industry is very new and unsettled, however, and the probability that a new customer granted credit will go bankrupt within the next month is 25%. The firm is considering switching to a cash-on-delivery credit policy to reduce its exposure to defaults on trade credit. The discount rate is 1% per month. *(LO4)*
   a. Should the firm switch to a cash-on-delivery policy? If it does so, its sales will fall by 40%.
   b. How would your answer change if a customer that is granted credit and pays its bills can be expected to generate repeat orders with negligible likelihood of default for each of the next 6 months? Similarly, customers that pay cash also will generate on average 6 months of repeat sales.

Templates can be found at
www.mhhe.com/bmm7e.

19. **Credit Policy.** A firm currently makes only cash sales. It estimates that allowing trade credit on terms of net 30 would increase monthly sales from 100 to 110 units per month. The price per unit is $101, and the cost (in present value terms) is $80. The interest rate is 1% per month. *(LO4)*
   a. Should the firm change its credit policy?
   b. Would your answer to (a) change if 5% of all customers will fail to pay their bills under the new credit policy?
   c. What if 5% of only the *new* customers fail to pay their bills? The current customers take advantage of the 30 days of free credit but remain safe credit risks.

20. **Lock Boxes.** Sherman's Sherbet currently takes about 6 days to collect and deposit checks from customers. A lock-box system could reduce this time to 4 days. Collections average $15,000 daily. The interest rate is .02% per day. *(LO6)*
   a. By how much will the lock-box system reduce float?
   b. What is the daily interest savings of the system?
   c. Suppose the lock-box service is offered for a fixed monthly fee instead of payment per check. What is the maximum monthly fee that Sherman's should be willing to pay for this service? (Assume a 30-day month.)

21. **Lock Boxes.** The financial manager of JAC Cosmetics is considering opening a lock box in Pittsburgh. Checks cleared through the lock box will amount to $300,000 per month. The lock box will make cash available to the company 3 days earlier. *(LO6)*

    a. Suppose that the bank offers to run the lock box for a $25,000 compensating balance. Is the lock box worthwhile?

    b. Suppose that the bank offers to run the lock box for a fee of $.10 per check cleared instead of a compensating balance. What must the average check size be for the fee alternative to be less costly? Assume an interest rate of 6% per year.

    c. Why did you need to know the interest rate to answer (b) but not to answer (a)?

22. **Collection Policy.** Major Manufacturing currently has one bank account located in New York to handle all of its collections. The firm keeps an additional cash balance with the bank of $300,000 to pay for these services. It is considering opening a bank account with West Coast National Bank to speed up collections from its many California-based customers. Major estimates that the West Coast account would reduce collection time by 1 day on the $1 million a day of business that it does with its California-based customers. If it opens the account, it can reduce the balance with its New York bank to $200,000 since it will do less business in New York. However, West Coast also will require additional cash balances of $200,000. Should Major open the new account? *(LO6)*

23. **Cash Management.** Suppose that the rate of interest increases from 4% to 8% per year. Would firms' cash balances go up or down relative to sales? Explain. *(LO5)*

CHALLENGE PROBLEMS

24. **Credit Analysis.** Use the data in Example 20.3. Now suppose, however, that 10% of Cast Iron's customers are slow payers and that slow payers have a probability of 30% of defaulting on their bills. If it costs $5 to determine whether a customer has been a prompt or slow payer in the past, should Cast Iron undertake such a check? (*Hint:* What is the expected savings from the credit check? It will depend on both the probability of uncovering a slow payer and the savings from denying these payers credit.) *(LO3)*

25. **Credit Analysis.** Look back at the previous problem, but now suppose that if a customer defaults on a payment, you can eventually collect about half the amount owed to you. Will you be more or less tempted to pay for a credit check once you account for the possibility of partial recovery of debts? *(LO3)*

Templates can be found at
www.mhhe.com/bmm7e.

26. **Credit Policy.** Jim Khana, the credit manager of Velcro Saddles, is reappraising the company's credit policy. Velcro sells on terms of net 30. Cost of goods sold is 85% of sales. Velcro classifies customers on a scale of 1 to 4. During the past 5 years, the collection experience was as follows:

Classification	Defaults as Percentage of Sales	Average Collection Period in Days for Nondefaulting Accounts
1	0	45
2	2	42
3	10	50
4	20	85

The average interest rate was 15%. What conclusions (if any) can you draw about Velcro's credit policy? Should the firm deny credit to any of its customers? What other factors should be taken into account before changing this policy? *(LO4)*

27. **Credit Analysis.** Galenic, Inc., is a wholesaler for a range of pharmaceutical products. Before deducting any losses from bad debts, Galenic operates on a profit margin of 5%. For a long time the firm has employed a numerical credit-scoring system based on a small number of key ratios. This has resulted in a bad debt ratio of 1%.

Galenic has recently commissioned a detailed statistical study of the payment record of its customers over the past 8 years and, after considerable experimentation, has identified five variables that could form the basis of a new credit-scoring system. On the evidence of the past 8 years, Galenic calculates that for every 10,000 accounts it would have experienced the following default rates:

Credit Score under Proposed System	Number of Accounts		
	Defaulting	Paying	Total
Better than 80	60	9,100	9,160
Worse than 80	40	800	840
Total	100	9,900	10,000

By refusing credit to firms with a poor credit score (worse than 80) Galenic calculates that it would reduce its bad debt ratio to 60/9,160, or just under .7%. While this may not seem like a big deal, Galenic's credit manager reasons that this is equivalent to a decrease of one-third in the bad debt ratio and would result in a significant improvement in the profit margin. *(LO3)*

a. What is Galenic's current profit margin, allowing for bad debts?

b. Assuming that the firm's estimates of default rates are right, how would the new credit-scoring system affect profits?

c. Why might you suspect that Galenic's estimates of default rates will not be realized in practice?

d. Suppose that one of the variables in the proposed new scoring system is whether the customer has an existing account with Galenic (new customers are more likely to default). How would this affect your assessment of the proposal? (*Hint:* Think about repeat sales.)

WEB EXERCISES

For Exercises 1 to 4, obtain financial statements for the firms either from the company Web sites or from a service such as finance.google.com *or* finance.yahoo.com.

1. Look at the financial statements of Ann Taylor Stores (ANN) and Buckle, Inc. (BKE), two fashion-clothing retailers. Compare the inventory level and turnover of each. What might explain the differences you uncover?

2. Check out the recent performance of two very nice coffee shops with attached free reading rooms: Barnes & Noble, Inc. (BKS), and Borders Group (BGP). These firms are sometimes characterized as "inventory businesses." Why? How does their inventory management compare?

3. Compare and contrast the accounts receivable turnover and days' sales outstanding for Peets Coffee & Tea, Inc. (PEET), and the casino and gaming firm Wynn Resorts (WYNN). Read the business description for information that may explain the level of each company's investment in accounts receivable.

4. Calculate the Z score for Ford (F) over the last 3 years. What do you think has happened to its bond rating over this period?

5. When credit managers need a credit check on a small business, they often look up the Dun & Bradstreet report on the company. You can see a sample Comprehensive Report by logging on to **www.dnb.com**. On the basis of this report, would you be prepared to extend credit to this company? Why or why not?

6. Credit scoring is widely used to rate applicants for personal loans. Several Web sites provide a free calculator that you can use to estimate your FICO score. Try varying some of the inputs and see how your credit rating changes. How much would the rating change if you missed a loan payment?

7. Log on to the Web page of a major bank such as Wells Fargo (www.wellsfargo.com) or Bank of America (www.bankofamerica.com). How do these banks help corporations to manage their cash? For example, check out each bank's Treasury management services. Among their offerings, you will find lock-box services as well as electronic check processing.

SOLUTIONS TO SELF-TEST QUESTIONS

20.1 To get the cash discount, you have to pay the bill within 10 days, that is, by May 11. With the 2% discount, the amount that needs to be paid by May 11 is $20,000 \times .98 = \$19,600$. If you forgo the cash discount, you do not have to pay your bill until May 21, but on that date the amount due is $20,000.

20.2 The cash discount in this case is 5%, and customers who choose not to take the discount receive an extra $50 - 10 = 40$ days credit. So the effective annual interest is

$$\text{Effective annual rate} = \left(1 + \frac{\text{discount}}{\text{discounted price}} \right)^{365/\text{extra days credit}} - 1$$

$$= \left(1 + \frac{5}{95} \right)^{365/40} - 1 = .597, \text{ or } 59.7\%$$

In this case the customer who does not take the discount is effectively borrowing money at an annual interest rate of 59.7%. This is higher than the rate in Example 20.1 because fewer days of credit are obtained by forfeiting the discount.

20.3 The present value of costs is still $1,000. Present value of revenues is now $1,100. The break-even probability is defined by

$$p \times 100 - (1 - p) \times 1,000 = 0$$

which implies that $p = .909$. The break-even probability is higher because the profit margin is now lower. The firm cannot afford as high a bad debt ratio as before since it is not making as much on its successful sales. We conclude that high-margin goods will be offered with more liberal credit terms.

20.4 The higher the discount rate the less important are future sales. Because the present value of repeat sales is lower, the break-even probability on the initial sale is higher. For instance, we saw that the break-even probability was 1/3 when the discount rate was 10%. When the discount rate is 20%, the present value of a perpetual flow of repeat sales falls to $200/.20 = \$1,000$, and the break-even probability increases to 1/2:

$$1/2 \times \$1,000 - 1/2 \times \$1,000 = 0$$

20.5 The customer pays bills 45 days after the invoice date. Because goods are purchased daily, at any time there will be bills outstanding with "ages" ranging from 1 to 45 days. At any time, the customer will have 30 days' worth of purchases, or $10,000, outstanding for a period of up to 1 month and have 15 days' worth of purchases, or $5,000, outstanding for between 1 month and 45 days. The aging schedule will appear as follows:

Age of Account	Amount
<1 month	$10,000
1–2 months	5,000

20.6 The benefit of the lock-box system, and the price the firm should be willing to pay for the system, is higher when:
   a. Payment size is higher (since interest is earned on more funds).
   b. Payments per day are higher (since interest is earned on more funds).
   c. The interest rate is higher (since the cost of float is higher).
   d. Mail time saved is higher (since more float is saved).
   e. Processing time saved is higher (since more float is saved).

MINICASE

George Stamper, a credit analyst with Micro-Encapsulators Corp. (MEC), needed to respond to an urgent e-mail request from the southeast sales office. The local sales manager reported that she had an opportunity to clinch an order from Miami Spice (MS) for 50 encapsulators at $10,000 each. She added that she was particularly keen to secure this order since MS was likely to have a continuing need for 50 encapsulators a year and could therefore prove a very valuable customer. However, orders of this size to a new customer generally required head office agreement, and it was therefore George's responsibility to make a rapid assessment of MS's creditworthiness and to approve or disapprove the sale.

Mr. Stamper knew that MS was a medium-sized company with a patchy earnings record. After growing rapidly in the 1980s, MS had encountered strong competition in its principal markets and earnings had fallen sharply. Mr. Stamper was not sure exactly to what extent this was a bad omen. New management had been brought in to cut costs, and there were some indications that the worst was over for the company. Investors appeared to agree with this assessment, for the stock price had risen to $5.80 from its low of $4.25 the previous year. Mr. Stamper had in front of him MS's latest financial statements, which are summarized in Table 20.4. He rapidly calculated a few key financial ratios and the company's Z score.

Mr. Stamper also made a number of other checks on MS. The company had a small issue of bonds outstanding, which were rated B by Moody's. Inquiries through MEC's bank indicated that MS had unused lines of credit totaling $5 million but had entered into discussions with its bank for a renewal of a $15 million bank loan that was due to be repaid at the end of the year. Telephone calls to MS's other suppliers suggested that the company had recently been 30 days late in paying its bills.

Mr. Stamper also needed to take into account the profit that the company could make on MS's order. Encapsulators were sold on standard terms of 2/30, net 60. So if MS paid promptly, MEC would receive additional revenues of $50 \times \$9,800 = \$490,000$. However, given MS's cash position, it was more than likely that it would forgo the cash discount and would not pay until sometime after the 60 days. Since interest rates were about 8%, any such delays in payment could reduce the present value to MEC of the revenues. Mr. Stamper also recognized that there were production and transportation costs in filling MS's order. These worked out at $475,000, or $9,500 a unit. Corporate profits were taxed at 35%.

QUESTIONS

1. What can you say about Miami Spice's creditworthiness?
2. What is the break-even probability of default? How is it affected by the delay before MS pays its bills?
3. How should George Stamper's decision be affected by the possibility of repeat orders?

TABLE 20.4 Miami Spice: Summary financial statements (figures in millions of dollars)

	2012	2011
Assets		
Current assets		
Cash and marketable securities	5.0	12.2
Accounts receivable	16.2	15.7
Inventories	27.5	32.5
Total current assets	48.7	60.4
Fixed assets		
Property, plant, and equipment	228.5	228.1
Less accumulated depreciation	129.5	127.6
Net fixed assets	99.0	100.5
Total assets	147.7	160.9
Liabilities and Shareholders' Equity		
Current liabilities		
Debt due for repayment	22.8	28.0
Accounts payable	19.0	16.2
Total current liabilities	41.8	44.2
Long-term debt	40.8	42.3
Shareholders' equity		
Common stock*	10.0	10.0
Retained earnings	55.1	64.4
Total shareholders' equity	65.1	74.4
Total liabilities and shareholders' equity	147.7	160.9
Income Statement		
Revenue	149.8	134.4
Cost of goods sold	131.0	124.2
Other expenses	1.7	8.7
Depreciation	8.1	8.6
Earnings before interest and taxes	9.0	−7.1
Interest expense	5.1	5.6
Income taxes	1.4	−4.4
Net income	2.5	−8.3
Allocation of net income		
Addition to retained earnings	1.5	−9.3
Dividends	1.0	1.0

* 10 million shares, $1 par value.

CHAPTER 21

Mergers, Acquisitions, and Corporate Control

LEARNING OBJECTIVES

After studying this chapter, you should be able to:

(1) Explain why it may make sense for companies to merge.

(2) Estimate the gains and costs of mergers to the acquiring firm.

(3) Describe ways that companies change their ownership or management.

(4) Describe takeover defenses.

(5) Explain some of the motivations for leveraged and management buyouts of the firm.

(6) Summarize the evidence on whether mergers increase efficiency and on how the gains from mergers are distributed between shareholders of the acquired and acquiring firms.

RELATED WEB SITES FOR THIS CHAPTER CAN BE FOUND AT WWW.MHHE.COM/BMM7E.

Panasonic, a consumer electronics giant, acquired rival Sanyo for around $9 billion. What are the gains and costs of company mergers?

The scale and pace of merger activity have often been remarkable. For example, Table 21.1 lists just a few recent mergers. Notice that many of the largest mergers have involved firms in different countries. Look also at Figure 21.1, which shows the number of mergers involving U.S. companies for each year from 1962 to 2009. In 2006, a record year for mergers, there were nearly 12,000 deals, with a total value of $1.5 trillion. During periods of intense merger activity financial managers spend considerable time either searching for firms to acquire or worrying whether some other firm is about to take over their company.

When one company buys another, it is making an investment, and the basic principles of capital investment decisions apply. You should go ahead with the purchase if it makes a net contribution to shareholders' wealth. But mergers are often awkward transactions to evaluate, and you have to be careful to define benefits and costs properly.

Many marriages between companies are amicable, but sometimes one party is dragged kicking and screaming to the altar. We review these hostile takeovers and the principal methods of attack and defense.

When a firm is taken over, its management is usually replaced. That is why we describe takeovers as part of a broader market for corporate control. Activity in this market goes far beyond ordinary acquisitions. Ownership or management also changes if there is a proxy contest, a leveraged buyout, or a divestiture. We therefore look at these ways to change control of the firm.

We close the chapter with a discussion of who gains and loses from mergers, and we discuss whether mergers are beneficial on balance.

FIGURE 21.1 The number of mergers in the United States, 1962–2009

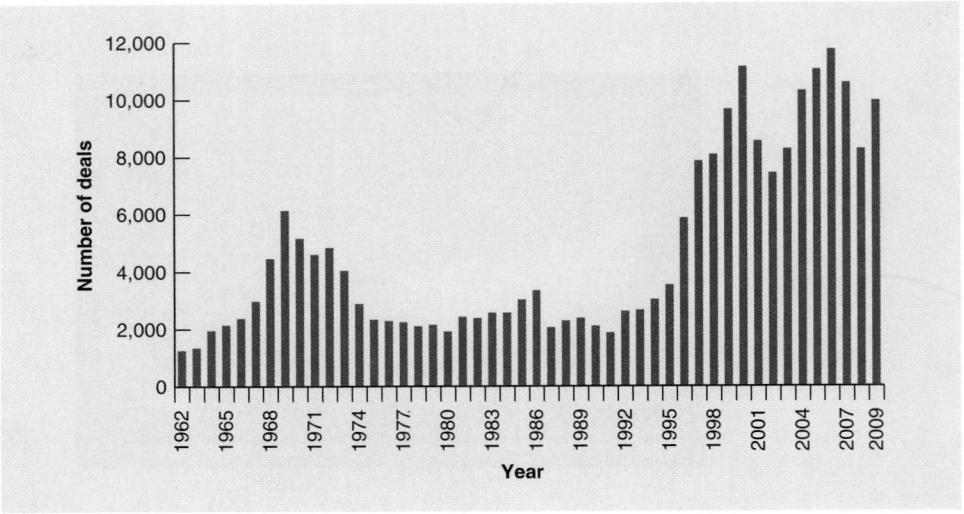

Source: **www.mergerstat.com**.

21.1 Sensible Motives for Mergers

Mergers are often categorized as *horizontal, vertical,* or *conglomerate.* A horizontal merger is one that takes place between two firms in the same line of business; the merged firms are former competitors. Most recent mergers have been of this type. For example, the financial crisis led to a number of mammoth bank mergers, such as those between Bank of America and Merrill Lynch and between Wells Fargo and Wachovia. Other headline-grabbing horizontal mergers have brought together pharmaceutical companies, such as the combinations of Pfizer and Wyeth and of Merck and Schering-Plough.

A *vertical merger* involves companies at different stages of production. The buyer expands back toward the source of raw materials or forward in the direction of the ultimate consumer. Thus, a soft-drink manufacturer might buy a sugar producer (expanding backward) or a fast-food chain as an outlet for its product (expanding forward). A recent example of a vertical merger is the acquisition of Tele Atlas by its fellow Dutch firm Tom Tom. Tom Tom, the world's largest maker of car navigation devices, plans to use Tele Atlas's digital map data to provide real-time updates to its sat-nav systems.

TABLE 21.1 Some important recent mergers

Industry	Acquiring Company	Selling Company	Payment, $ billions
Insurance	Berkshire Hathaway	Sun Life Financial	109
Pharmaceuticals	Pfizer	Wyeth	67
Pharmaceuticals	Roche (Switzerland)	Genentech	44
Pharmaceuticals	Merck	Schering-Plough	38
Oil	ExxonMobil	XTO Energy	32
Railroads	Berkshire Hathaway	Burlington Northern Santa Fe	30
Pharmaceuticals	Sanofi-Aventis (France)	Genzyme	20
Food	Kraft	Cadbury (United Kingdom)	19
Telecommunications	Comcast	NBC Universal	14
Electronics	Panasonic (Japan)	Sanyo (Japan)	9

A *conglomerate merger* involves companies in unrelated lines of business. For example, the Indian company Tata Group is a huge, widely diversified company. In recent years its acquisitions have been as diverse as Eight O'Clock Coffee, Corus Steel, Jaguar Land Rover, and the Ritz Carlton, Boston. No U.S. company is as diversified as Tata, but in the 1960s and 1970s it was common in the United States for unrelated businesses to merge. The number of U.S. conglomerate mergers declined in the 1980s. In fact much of the action in the 1980s came from breaking up the conglomerates that had been formed 10 to 20 years earlier.

Self-Test 21.1

Are the following hypothetical mergers horizontal, vertical, or conglomerate?

a. IBM acquires Dell Computer.
b. Dell Computer acquires Safeway (a supermarket chain).
c. Safeway acquires Campbell Soup.
d. Campbell Soup acquires IBM.

Many mergers and acquisitions are motivated by possible gains in efficiency from combining operations. These mergers create *synergies*. By this we mean that the two firms are worth more together than apart.

It would be convenient if we could say that certain types of mergers are more likely to result in synergies and create wealth for the shareholders. Unfortunately, there are no such simple generalizations. Many mergers that appear to make sense nevertheless fail because managers cannot handle the complex task of integrating two firms with different production processes, pay structures, and accounting methods. Moreover, the value of most businesses depends on *human* assets—managers, skilled workers, scientists, and engineers. If these people are not happy in their new roles in the merged firm, the best of them will leave. Beware of paying too much for assets that go down in the elevator and out to the parking lot at the close of each business day.

Consider the $38 billion merger between Daimler-Benz and Chrysler. Although it was hailed as a model for consolidation in the auto industry, the early years were bedevilled by conflicts between two very different cultures:

> German management-board members had executive assistants who prepared detailed position papers on any number of issues. The Americans didn't have assigned aides and formulated their decisions by talking directly to engineers or other specialists. A German decision worked its way through the bureaucracy for final approval at the top. Then it was set in stone. The Americans allowed midlevel employees to proceed on their own initiative, sometimes without waiting for executive-level approval.
>
> . . . Cultural integration also was proving to be a slippery commodity. The yawning gap in pay scales fueled an undercurrent of tension. The Americans earned two, three, and, in some cases, four times as much as their German counterparts. But the expenses of U.S. workers were tightly controlled compared with the German system. Daimler-side employees thought nothing of flying to Paris or New York for a half-day meeting, then capping the visit with a fancy dinner and a night in an expensive hotel. The Americans blanched at the extravagance.[1]

Nine years after acquiring Chrysler, Daimler threw in the towel and announced that it was offloading an 80% stake in Chrysler to a leveraged-buyout firm, Cerberus Capital Management. Daimler actually paid Cerberus $677 million to take Chrysler off its hands. Cerberus in return assumed about $18 billion in pension and employee health care liabilities and agreed to invest $6 billion in Chrysler and its finance subsidiary.

These observations illustrate the difficulties in realizing the benefits of merger. There are also occasions when the merger does achieve the intended synergies, but

---

[1] Bill Vlasic and Bradley A. Stertz, "Taken for a Ride," *BusinessWeek,* June 5, 2000. Reprinted with special permission © 2000 The McGraw-Hill Companies, Inc.

Those Elusive Synergies

When three of Japan's largest banks combined to form Mizuho Bank, it brought together assets of $1.5 trillion, more than twice those of the world leader Deutsche Bank. The name "Mizuho" means "rich rice harvest," and the bank's management forecast that the merger would create a rich harvest of synergies. In a message to shareholders, the bank president claimed that the merger would create "a comprehensive financial services group that will surge forward in the 21st century." He predicted that the bank would "lead the new era through cutting-edge comprehensive financial services . . . by exploiting to the fullest extent the Group's enormous strengths, which are backed by a powerful customer base and state-of-the-art financial and information technologies." The cost of putting the banks together was forecast at ¥130 billion, but management predicted future benefits of ¥466 billion a year.

Within a few months of the announcement reports began to emerge of squabbles between the three partners. One problem area was IT. Each of the three merging banks had a different supplier for its computer system. At first it was proposed to use just one of these three systems, but then the banks decided to connect the three different systems together by using "relay" computers.

Three years after the initial announcement the new company opened for business on April 1, 2002. Five days later, computer glitches resulted in a spectacular foul-up. Some 7,000 of the bank's cash machines did not work; 60,000 accounts were debited twice for the same transaction; and millions of bills went unpaid. *The Economist* reported that 2 weeks later Tokyo Gas, the biggest gas company, was still missing ¥2.2 billion in payments and the top telephone company, NTT, which was looking for ¥12.7 billion, was forced to send its customers receipts marked with asterisks in place of figures, since it did not know which of about 760,000 bills had been paid.

One of the objects behind the formation of Mizuho was to exploit economies in its IT systems. The launch fiasco illustrated dramatically that it is easier to predict such merger synergies than to realize them.

Source: The creation of Mizuho Bank and its launch problems are described in "Undispensable: A Fine Merger Yields One Fine Mess," *The Economist,* April 25, 2002 © The Economist Newspaper Limited, London (April 25, 2002).

the buyer nevertheless loses because it pays too much. For example, the buyer may overestimate the value of stale inventory or underestimate the costs of renovating old plant and equipment, or it may overlook the warranties on a defective product.

With these caveats in mind, we will now consider some possible sources of synergy.

Economies of Scale

Just as most of us believe that we would be happier if only we were a little richer, so managers always seem to believe their firm would be more competitive if only it were just a little bigger. They hope for *economies of scale,* that is, the opportunity to spread fixed costs across a larger volume of output. The banking industry provides many examples. As a result of bank regulation, the United States had too many small, local banks. When these regulations were relaxed, some banks grew by systematically buying up other banks and streamlining their operations. When Bank of New York and Mellon Financial Corporation merged in 2007, management forecast annual cost savings of $700 million, or over 8% of the current combined costs. Management anticipated that the merger would allow the two companies to share services and technology and would permit a reduction in staff from 40,000 to about 36,000. (Some of these savings involved senior management. For example, there were two chief financial officers before the merger and only one afterward.) Beware of overly optimistic predictions of cost savings, however. The nearby box tells the story of one bank merger that resulted in a spectacular debacle rather than the predicted synergies.

These economies of scale are the natural goal of horizontal mergers. But they have been claimed in conglomerate mergers, too. The architects of these mergers have pointed to the economies that come from sharing central services such as accounting, financial control, and top-level management.

Economies of Vertical Integration

Large companies commonly like to gain as much control and coordination as possible over the production process by expanding back toward the output of the raw material and forward to the ultimate consumer. One way to achieve this is to merge with a supplier or a customer.

Vertical integration has fallen out of fashion recently. Many companies are finding it more efficient to *outsource* many of their activities. For example, back in the 1950s and 1960s, General Motors was thought to have a cost advantage over its competitors because it produced a greater fraction of its components in-house. By the 1990s Ford and Chrysler had the advantage. They could buy the parts more cheaply from outside suppliers. This was partly because the outside suppliers tended to use nonunion labor. But it also appears that manufacturers have more bargaining power when they are dealing with independent suppliers rather than with another part of the corporate family. In 1998 GM decided to spin off Delphi, its automotive parts division, as a separate company. After the spin-off, GM continued to buy parts from Delphi in large volumes, but it negotiated the purchases at arm's length.

Combining Complementary Resources

Many small firms are acquired by large firms that can provide the missing ingredients necessary for the firm's success. The small firm may have a unique product but lack the engineering and sales organization necessary to produce and market it on a large scale. The firm could develop engineering and sales talent from scratch, but it may be quicker and cheaper to merge with a firm that already has ample talent. The two firms have *complementary resources*—each has what the other needs—so it may make sense for them to merge. Also the merger may open up opportunities that neither firm would pursue otherwise.

In recent years many of the major pharmaceutical firms have faced the loss of patent protection on their more profitable products and have not had an offsetting pipeline of promising new compounds. This has prompted an increasing number of acquisitions of biotech firms. For example, in 2008 Eli Lilly acquired ImClone Systems. Lilly paid $6.5 billion for ImClone, a premium of some 50% over the company's earlier market value. But Lilly's CEO claimed that the acquisition would "broaden Lilly's portfolio of marketed cancer therapies and boost Lilly's oncology pipeline with up to three promising targeted therapies in Phase III in 2009." At the same time ImClone obtained the resources necessary to bring its products to market.

Mergers as a Use for Surplus Funds

Suppose that your firm is in a mature industry. It is generating a substantial amount of cash, but it has few profitable investment opportunities. Ideally such a firm should distribute the surplus cash to shareholders by increasing its dividend payment or by repurchasing its shares. Unfortunately, energetic managers are often reluctant to shrink their firm in this way.

If the firm is not willing to purchase its own shares, it can instead purchase someone else's. Thus firms with a surplus of cash and a shortage of good investment opportunities often turn to mergers *financed by cash* as a way of deploying their capital.

Firms that have excess cash and do not pay it out or redeploy it by acquisition often find themselves targets for takeover by other firms that propose to redeploy the cash for them. During the oil price slump of the early 1980s, many cash-rich oil companies found themselves threatened by takeover. This was not because their cash was a unique asset. The acquirers wanted to capture the companies' cash flow to make sure it was not frittered away on negative-NPV oil exploration projects. We return to this *free-cash-flow* motive for takeovers later in the chapter.

Eliminating Inefficiencies

Cash is not the only asset that can be wasted by poor management. There are always firms with unexploited opportunities to cut costs and increase sales and earnings. Such firms are natural candidates for acquisition by other firms with better management. In some instances "better management" may simply mean the determination to force painful cuts or realign the company's operations. Notice that the motive for such acquisitions has nothing to do with benefits from combining two firms. Acquisition is simply the mechanism by which a new management team replaces the old one.

A merger may not be the only way to improve management, but sometimes there is no simple and practical alternative. Managers are naturally reluctant to fire or demote themselves, and stockholders of large public firms do not usually have much *direct* influence on how the firm is run or who runs it.

If this motive for merger is important, one would expect to observe that acquisitions often precede a change in the management of the target firm. This seems to be the case. For example, Martin and McConnell found that the chief executive is four times more likely to be replaced in the year after a takeover than during earlier years.[2] The firms that they studied had generally been poor performers. Apparently many of these firms fell on bad times and were rescued by merger.

21.2 Dubious Reasons for Mergers

The benefits that we have described so far all make economic sense. Other arguments sometimes given for mergers are more dubious. Here are two.

Diversification

We have suggested that the managers of a cash-rich company may prefer to see that cash used for acquisitions. That is why we often see cash-rich firms in stagnant industries merging their way into fresh woods and pastures new. But what about diversification as an end in itself? It is obvious that diversification reduces risk. Isn't that a gain from merging?

The trouble with this argument is that diversification is easier and cheaper for the stockholder than for the corporation. Why should firm A buy firm B to diversify when the shareholders of firm A can buy shares in firm B to diversify their own portfolios? It is far easier and cheaper for individual investors to diversify than it is for firms to combine operations.

The Bootstrap Game

During the 1960s some conglomerate companies made acquisitions that offered no evident economic gains. Nevertheless, the conglomerates' aggressive strategy produced several years of rising earnings per share. To see how this can happen, let us look at the acquisition of Muck and Slurry by the well-known conglomerate World Enterprises.

EXAMPLE 21.1 ▶ The Bootstrap Game

The position before the merger is set out in the first two columns of Table 21.2. Notice that because Muck and Slurry has relatively poor growth prospects, its stock sells at a lower price-earnings ratio than World Enterprises (line 3). The merger, we assume, produces no economic benefits, so the firms should be worth exactly the same together as apart. The value of World Enterprises after the merger is therefore equal to the sum of the separate values of the two firms (line 6).

Since World Enterprises stock is selling for double the price of Muck and Slurry stock (line 2), World Enterprises can acquire the 100,000 Muck and Slurry shares for 50,000 of its own shares. Thus World will have 150,000 shares outstanding after the merger.

World's total earnings double as a result of the acquisition (line 5), but the number of shares increases by only 50%. Its earnings *per share* rise from $2.00 to $2.67. We call this a *bootstrap effect* because there is no real gain created by the merger and no increase in the two firms' combined value. Since World's stock price is unchanged by the acquisition of Muck and Slurry, the price-earnings ratio falls (line 3).

---

[2] K. J. Martin and J. J. McConnell, "Corporate Performance, Corporate Takeovers, and Management Turnover," *Journal of Finance* 46 (June 1991), pp. 671–687.

TABLE 21.2 Impact of merger on market value and earnings per share of World Enterprises

	World Enterprises (before merger)	Muck and Slurry	World Enterprises (after acquiring Muck and Slurry)
1. Earnings per share	$2	$2	$2.67
2. Price per share	$40	$20	$40
3. Price-earnings ratio	20	10	15
4. Number of shares	100,000	100,000	150,000
5. Total earnings	$200,000	$200,000	$400,000
6. Total market value	$4,000,000	$2,000,000	$6,000,000
7. Current earnings per dollar invested in stock (line 1 divided by line 2)	$.05	$.10	$.067

Note: When World Enterprises purchases Muck and Slurry, there are no gains. Therefore, total earnings and total market value should be unaffected by the merger. But earnings *per share* increase. World Enterprises issues only 50,000 of its shares (priced at $40) to acquire the 100,000 Muck and Slurry shares (priced at $20).

Before the merger, $1 invested in World Enterprises bought 5 cents of current earnings and rapid growth prospects. On the other hand, $1 invested in Muck and Slurry bought 10 cents of current earnings but slower growth prospects. If the *total* market value is not altered by the merger, then $1 invested in the merged firm gives World shareholders 6.7 cents of immediate earnings but slower growth than before the merger. Muck and Slurry shareholders get lower immediate earnings but faster growth. Neither side gains or loses *provided* that everybody understands the deal.

Financial manipulators sometimes try to ensure that the market does *not* understand the deal. Suppose that investors are fooled by the exuberance of the president of World Enterprises and mistake the 33% postmerger increase in earnings per share for *sustainable* growth. If they do, the price of World Enterprises stock rises and the shareholders of both companies receive something for nothing.

You should now see how to play the bootstrap game. Suppose that you manage a company enjoying a high price-earnings ratio. The reason it is high is that investors anticipate rapid growth in future earnings. You achieve this growth not by capital investment, product improvement, or increased operating efficiency but by purchasing slow-growing firms with low price-earnings ratios. The long-run result will be slower growth and a depressed price-earnings ratio, but in the short run earnings per share can increase dramatically. If this fools investors, you may be able to achieve the higher earnings per share without suffering a decline in your price-earnings ratio. But in order to *keep* fooling investors, you must continue to expand by merger *at the same compound rate.* Obviously you cannot do this forever; one day expansion must slow down or stop. Then earnings growth will cease, and your house of cards will fall. **Buying a firm with a lower P/E ratio can increase earnings per share. But the increase should not result in a higher share price. The short-term increase in earnings should be offset by lower future earnings growth.**

Self-Test 21.2

Suppose that Muck and Slurry has even worse growth prospects than in our example and its share price is only $10. Recalculate the effects of the merger in this case. You should find that earnings per share increase by a greater amount, since World Enterprises can now buy the same *current* earnings for fewer shares.

21.3 The Mechanics of a Merger

Buying a company is a much more complicated affair than buying a piece of machinery. We are not going to get into the tax or accounting complexities here, but we will describe the different forms that an acquisition can take and the way that an acquisition can be stymied by an antitrust ruling.

The Form of Acquisition

There are three ways for one firm to acquire another. One possibility is to *merge* the two companies into one, in which case the acquiring company assumes *all* the assets and *all* the liabilities of the other. The acquired firm ceases to exist, and its former shareholders receive cash and/or securities in the acquiring firm. In many mergers there is a clear acquiring company, whose management then runs the enlarged firm. Sometimes a merger is presented as a "merger of equals," but even in these cases one firm's management usually comes out on top.

merger
Combination of two firms into one, with the acquirer assuming assets and liabilities of the target firm.

A **merger** must have the approval of at least 50% of the shareholders of each firm.[3] Approval is not always guaranteed. For example, when Charles River Laboratories in 2010 proposed a $1.6 billion tie-up with Shanghai-based WuXi PharmaTech, its share price slumped and some major institutional shareholders voiced their opposition to the deal. With a week to go before its shareholders' meeting, success for CRL was looking doubtful and the company decided to break off the marriage.

An alternative procedure is for the acquiring firm to buy the target firm's stock in exchange for cash, shares, or other securities. The acquired firm may continue to exist as a separate entity, but it is now owned by the acquirer. The approval and cooperation of the target firm's managers are generally sought, but even if they resist, the acquirer can attempt to purchase a majority of the outstanding shares. By offering to buy shares directly from shareholders, the acquiring firm can bypass the target firm's management altogether. The offer to purchase stock is called a **tender offer.** If the tender offer is successful, the buyer obtains control and can, if it chooses, toss out incumbent management.

tender offer
Takeover attempt in which outsiders directly offer to buy the stock of the firm's shareholders.

The third approach is to buy the target firm's assets. In this case ownership of the assets needs to be transferred, and payment is made to the selling firm rather than directly to its stockholders. Usually, the target firm sells only some of its assets, but occasionally it sells *all* of them. In this case, the selling firm continues to exist as an independent entity, but it becomes an empty shell—a corporation engaged in no business activity.

acquisition
Takeover of a firm by purchase of that firm's common stock or assets.

The terminology of mergers and acquisitions (M&A) can be confusing. These phrases are used loosely to refer to any kind of corporate combination or takeover. But strictly speaking, *merger* means the combination of all the assets and liabilities of two firms. The purchase of the stock or assets of another firm is an **acquisition.**

Mergers, Antitrust Law, and Popular Opposition

Mergers may be blocked by the federal government if they are thought to be anticompetitive or to create too much market power. Thus, when the video-rental giant Blockbuster proposed to merge with its smaller rival Hollywood Video, the Federal Trade Commission (FTC) made it clear that it would likely block the deal. In the face of this opposition, the two companies broke off their engagement.

Companies that do business outside the United States also have to worry about foreign antitrust laws. For example, GE's $46 billion takeover bid for Honeywell was blocked by the European Commission, which argued that the combined company would have too much power in the aircraft industry.

---

[3] Corporate charters and state laws sometimes specify a higher percentage.

Often, trustbusters will object to a merger but then relent if the companies agree to divest certain assets and operations. For instance, when the organic grocer Whole Foods Market acquired its closest rival, Wild Oats Markets, the FTC required the company to sell the Wild Oats brand and 13 stores.

Mergers may also be stymied by political pressures and popular resentment even when no formal antitrust issues arise. For example, the news in 2005 that Pepsi Cola might bid for Danone aroused considerable hostility in France. The prime minister added his support to opponents of the merger and announced that the French government was drawing up a list of strategic industries that should be protected from foreign ownership. It was unclear whether yogurt production would be one of these strategic industries.

Economic nationalism is not confined to Europe. In 2005 the China National Offshore Oil Corporation (CNOOC) felt obliged to withdraw its bid for Unocal, after what it described as "unprecedented political opposition" in Congress. The following year Congress voiced its opposition to the takeover of Britain's P&O by the Dubai company, DP World. The acquisition went ahead only after P&O's ports in the United States were excluded from the deal.

21.4 Evaluating Mergers

If you are given the responsibility for evaluating a proposed merger, you must think hard about the following two questions:

1. Is there an overall economic gain to the merger? In other words, is the merger value-enhancing? Are the two firms worth more together than apart?
2. Do the terms of the merger make my company and its shareholders better off? There is no point in merging if the cost is too high and all the economic gain goes to the other company.

Answering these deceptively simple questions is rarely easy. Some economic gains can be nearly impossible to quantify, and complex merger financing can obscure the true terms of the deal. But the basic principles for evaluating mergers are not too difficult.

Mergers Financed by Cash

We will concentrate on a simple numerical example. Your company, Cislunar Foods, is considering acquisition of a smaller food company, Targetco. Cislunar is proposing to finance the deal by purchasing all of Targetco's outstanding stock for $19 per share. Some financial information on the two companies is given in the left and center columns of Table 21.3.

TABLE 21.3 Cislunar Foods is considering an acquisition of Targetco. The merger would increase the companies' combined earnings by $4 million.

	Cislunar Foods	Targetco	Combined Companies	
Revenues	$150	$20	$172	(+2)
Operating costs	118	16	132	(−2)
Earnings	$ 32	$ 4	$ 40	(+4)
Cash	$ 55	$ 2.5		
Other assets' book value	185	17.0		
Total assets	$240	$19.5		
Price per share	$ 48	$16		
Number of shares	10.0	2.5		
Market value	$480	$40		

Note: Figures in millions except price per share.

Question 1   Why would Cislunar and Targetco be worth more together than apart? Suppose that operating costs can be reduced by combining the companies' marketing, distribution, and administration. Revenues can also be increased in Targetco's region. The rightmost column of Table 21.3 contains projected revenues, costs, and earnings for the two firms operating together: annual operating costs postmerger will be $2 million less than the sum of the separate companies' costs, and revenues will be $2 million more. Therefore, projected earnings increase by $4 million.[4] We will assume that the increased earnings are the only synergy to be generated by the merger.

The economic gain to the merger is the present value of the extra earnings. If the earnings increase is permanent (a level perpetuity) and the cost of capital is 20%,

$$\text{Economic gain} = \text{PV(increased earnings)} = \frac{4}{.20} = \$20 \text{ million}$$

This additional value is the basic motivation for the merger.

Question 2   What are the terms of the merger? What is the cost to Cislunar and its shareholders?

Targetco's management and shareholders will not consent to the merger unless they receive at least the stand-alone value of their shares. They can be paid in cash or by new shares issued by Cislunar. In this case we are considering a cash offer of $19 per Targetco share, $3 per share over the prior share price. Targetco has 2.5 million shares outstanding, so Cislunar will have to pay out $47.5 million, a premium of $7.5 million over Targetco's prior market value. On these terms, Targetco stockholders will capture $7.5 million out of the $20 million gain from the merger. That ought to leave $12.5 million for Cislunar.

This is confirmed in the Cash Purchase column of Table 21.4. Start at the *bottom* of the column, where the total market value of the merged firms is $492.5 million. This is derived as follows:

Cislunar market value prior to merger	$480 million
Targetco market value	40
Present value of gain to merger	20
Less Cash paid out to Targetco shareholders	−47.5
Postmerger market value	$492.5 million

The postmerger share price for Cislunar will be $49.25, an increase of $1.25 per share. There are 10 million shares now outstanding, so the total increase in the value of Cislunar shares is $12.5 million.

Now let's summarize. The merger makes sense for Cislunar for two reasons. First, the merger adds $20 million of overall value. Second, the terms of the merger give only $7.5 million of that $20 million overall gain to Targetco's stockholders, leaving $12.5 million for Cislunar. You could say that the *cost* of acquiring Targetco is $7.5 million, the difference between the cash payment and the value of Targetco as a separate company:

$$\text{Cost} = \text{cash paid out} - \text{Targetco value} = \$47.5 - 40 = \$7.5 \text{ million}$$

Of course, the Targetco stockholders are ahead by $7.5 million. *Their gain is your cost.* As we've already seen, Cislunar stockholders come out $12.5 million ahead. This is the merger's NPV for Cislunar:

$$\text{NPV} = \text{economic gain} - \text{cost} = \$20 - 7.5 = \$12.5 \text{ million}$$

Writing down the economic gain and cost of a merger in this way separates the motive for the merger (the economic gain, or value added) from the terms of the merger (the *division* of the gain between the two merging companies).

---

[4] To keep things simple, the example ignores taxes and assumes that both companies are all-equity-financed. We also ignore the interest income that could have been earned by investing the cash used to finance the merger.

TABLE 21.4 Financial forecasts after the Cislunar-Targetco merger. The left column assumes a cash purchase at $19 per Targetco share. The right column assumes Targetco stockholders receive one new Cislunar share for every three Targetco shares.

	Cash Purchase	Exchange of Shares
Earnings	$ 40	$ 40
Cash	$ 10	$ 57.5
Other assets' book value	202	202
Total assets	$212	$259.5
Price per share	$ 49.25	$ 49.85
Number of shares	10.0	10.833
Market value	$492.5	$540

Note: Figures in millions except price per share.

Self-Test 21.3

Killer Shark Inc. makes a surprise cash offer of $22 a share for Goldfish Industries. Before the offer, Goldfish was selling for $18 a share. Goldfish has 1 million shares outstanding. What must Killer Shark believe about the present value of the improvement it can bring to Goldfish's operations?

Mergers Financed by Stock

What if Cislunar wants to conserve its cash for other investments and therefore decides to pay for the Targetco acquisition with new Cislunar shares? The deal calls for Targetco shareholders to receive one Cislunar share in exchange for every three Targetco shares.

It's the same merger, but the financing is different. The right column of Table 21.4 works out the consequences. Again, start at the *bottom* of the column. Note that the market value of Cislunar's shares after the merger is $540 million, $47.5 million higher than in the cash deal, because that cash is kept rather than paid out to Targetco shareholders. On the other hand, there are more shares outstanding, since 833,333 new shares have to be issued in exchange for the 2.5 million Targetco shares (a 1-to-3 ratio). Therefore, the price per share is 540/10.833 = $49.85, which is 60 cents higher than in the cash offer.

Why do Cislunar stockholders do better from the share exchange? The economic gain from the merger is the same, but the Targetco stockholders capture less of it. They get 833,333 shares at $49.85, or $41.5 million, a premium of only $1.5 million over Targetco's prior market value:

$$\text{Cost} = \text{value of shares issued} - \text{Targetco value}$$
$$= \$41.5 - 40 = \$1.5 \text{ million}$$

The merger's NPV to Cislunar's original shareholders is

$$\text{NPV} = \text{economic gain} - \text{cost} = 20 - 1.5 = \$18.5 \text{ million}$$

Note that Cislunar stock rises by $1.85 from its prior value. The total increase in value for Cislunar's original shareholders, who retain 10 million shares, is $18.5 million.

Evaluating the terms of a merger can be tricky when there is an exchange of shares. The target company's shareholders will retain a stake in the merged firms, so you have to figure out what the firm's shares will be worth *after* the merger is announced and its benefits appreciated by investors. Notice that we started with the total market value of Cislunar and Targetco postmerger, took account of the merger terms (833,333 new shares issued), and worked back to the postmerger share price. Only then could we work out the division of the merger gains between the two companies.

There is a key distinction between cash and stock for financing mergers. If cash is offered, the cost of the merger is not affected by the size of the merger gains. If stock is offered, the cost depends on the gains because the gains show up in the postmerger share price, and these shares are used to pay for the acquired firm.

Stock financing also mitigates the effects of over- or undervaluation of either firm. Suppose, for example, that A overestimates B's value as a separate entity, perhaps because it has overlooked some hidden liability. Thus A makes too generous an offer. Other things equal, A's stockholders are better off if it is a stock rather than a cash offer. With a stock offer, the inevitable bad news about B's value will fall partly on B's former stockholders.

Self-Test 21.4

Suppose Targetco shareholders demand 1 Cislunar share for every 2.5 Targetco shares. Otherwise, they will not accept the merger. Under these revised terms, is the merger still a good deal for Cislunar?

A Warning

The cost of a merger is the premium the acquirer pays for the target firm over its value as a separate company. If the target is a public company, you can measure its separate value by multiplying its stock price by the number of outstanding shares. Watch out, though: If investors expect the target to be acquired, its stock price may overstate the company's separate value. The target company's stock price may already have risen in anticipation of a premium to be paid by an acquiring firm.

Another Warning

Some companies begin their merger analyses with a forecast of the target firm's future cash flows. Any revenue increases or cost reductions attributable to the merger are included in the forecasts, which are then discounted back to the present and compared with the purchase price:

$$\text{Estimated net gain} = \text{DCF valuation of target including merger benefits} - \text{cash required for acquisition}$$

This is a dangerous procedure. Even the brightest and best-trained analyst can make large errors in valuing a business. The estimated net gain may come up positive not because the merger makes sense, but simply because the analyst's cash-flow forecasts are too optimistic. On the other hand, a good merger may not be pursued if the analyst fails to recognize the target's potential as a stand-alone business.

A better procedure *starts* with the target's current and stand-alone market value and concentrates instead on the *changes* in cash flow that would result from the merger. **Always ask why the two firms should be worth more together than apart. Remember, *you add value only if you can generate additional economic benefits— some competitive edge that other firms can't match and that the target firm's managers can't achieve on their own.***

It makes sense to keep an eye on the value that investors place on the gains from merging. If A's stock price falls when the deal is announced, investors are sending a message that the merger benefits are doubtful *or* that A is paying too much for these benefits.

21.5 The Market for Corporate Control

The shareholders are the owners of the firm. But most shareholders do not feel like the boss, and with good reason. Try buying a share of IBM stock and marching into the boardroom for a chat with your employee, the chief executive officer.

The *ownership* and *management* of large corporations are almost always separated. Shareholders do not directly appoint or supervise the firm's managers. They elect the board of directors, who act as their agents in choosing and monitoring the managers of the firm. Shareholders have a direct say in very few matters. Control of the firm is in the hands of the managers, subject to the general oversight of the board of directors.

This system of governance creates potential *agency costs.* Agency costs occur when managers or directors take actions adverse to shareholders' interests.

The temptation to take such actions may be ever-present, but there are many forces and constraints working to keep managers' and shareholders' interests in line. As we pointed out in Chapter 1, managers' paychecks in large corporations are almost always tied to the profitability of the firm and the performance of its shares. Boards of directors take their responsibilities seriously—they may face lawsuits if they don't—and therefore are reluctant to rubber-stamp obviously bad financial decisions.

But what ensures that the board has engaged the most talented managers? What happens if managers are inadequate? What if the board of directors is derelict in monitoring the performance of managers? Or what if the firm's managers are fine but resources of the firm could be used more efficiently by merging with another firm? Can we count on managers to pursue arrangements that would put them out of jobs?

These are all questions about *the market for corporate control,* the mechanisms by which firms are matched up with management teams and owners who can make the most of the firm's resources. You should not take a firm's current ownership and management for granted. If it is possible for the value of the firm to be enhanced by changing management or by reorganizing under new owners, there will be incentives for someone to make a change.

There are four ways to change the management of a firm. These are (1) a successful proxy contest in which a group of stockholders votes in a new group of directors, who then pick a new management team; (2) the purchase of one firm by another in a merger or acquisition; (3) a leveraged buyout of the firm by a private group of investors; and (4) a divestiture, in which a firm either sells part of its operations to another company or spins it off as an independent firm.

We will review briefly each of these methods.

21.6 Method 1: Proxy Contests

Shareholders elect the board of directors to keep watch on management and replace unsatisfactory managers. If the board is lax, shareholders are free to elect a different board. In theory this ensures that the corporation is run in the best interests of shareholders.

In practice things are not so clear-cut. Ownership in large corporations is widely dispersed. Usually even the largest single shareholder holds only a small fraction of the shares. Most shareholders have little notion who is on the board or what the members stand for. Management, on the other hand, deals directly with the board and has a personal relationship with its members. In many corporations, management sits on the committee that nominates candidates for the board. It is not surprising that some boards seem less than aggressive in forcing managers to run a lean, efficient operation and to act primarily in the interests of shareholders.

proxy contest
Takeover attempt in which outsiders compete with management for shareholders' votes. Also called *proxy fight.*

When a group of investors believe that the board and its management team should be replaced, they can launch a **proxy contest.** A *proxy* is the right to vote another shareholder's shares. In a proxy contest, the dissident shareholders attempt to obtain enough proxies to elect their own slate to the board of directors. Once the new board is in control, management can be replaced and company policy changed. A proxy fight is therefore a direct contest for control of the corporation.

The problem with proxy fights is that they can cost millions of dollars. Dissidents who engage in them must use their own money, but management can draw on the corporation's funds and lines of communication with shareholders to defend itself. Given the costs of mounting a proxy fight, shareholders often register their discontent simply by voting against the reelection of existing directors. This can send a powerful signal. When Disney shareholders voted 43% of the shares against the reelection of Michael Eisner, the company's autocratic chairman, he heard the message and resigned the next day.

In 2010 the SEC adopted a *proxy access* rule to make it easier for dissident shareholders to put their own nominations for the board of directors to shareholder vote. This rule would have greatly reduced the cost of a proxy contest. However, proxy access was successfully challenged in court in 2011. This initiative promises to be an ongoing controversy.

Institutional shareholders, such as large hedge funds, have become more aggressive in pressing for managerial accountability and have been able to gain concessions by threatening proxy fights. For example, in 2008 shareholder activist Carl Icahn indicated his intention to put himself forward for nomination to the board of Motorola. Icahn controlled less than 7% of the votes and failed to prevent the reelection of the existing board. Nevertheless, the pressure from Icahn had an effect: Motorola agreed to nominate two new board members and to consult with Icahn about a possible spin off of the company's handset division.[5]

21.7 Method 2: Takeovers

If the management of one firm believes that another company's management is not acting in the best interests of investors, it can go over the heads of that firm's management and make a *tender offer* directly to its stockholders. The management of the target firm may advise its shareholders to accept the offer and sell their shares, or it may fight the bid in the hope that the acquirer will either raise its offer or walk away from the deal. If the tender offer is successful, the new owner can then install its own management team. Thus, corporate takeovers are the arenas where contests for corporate control are often fought.

Of course, these battles for corporate control don't always result in the intended improvements to management. Hubris, excessive belief in one's own ability, has led many managers into unsuccessful acquisitions. Take the case of Jean-Marie Messier, the CEO of Vivendi, whom we first encountered in Chapter 18. Messier attempted to turn Vivendi into "the world's preferred creator and provider of entertainment, education and personalized services to customers, at any time, and across all distribution platforms and devices." Vivendi entered into a series of major acquisitions, including the purchase of Seagram, which in turn owned Universal Studios. Messier's ambitions earned him the nickname "J6M," which, spelled out, stood for "Jean-Marie Messier, *moi-même, maitre du monde*"—"myself master of the world." Unfortunately, however, profits collapsed, the firm faced imminent bankruptcy, and Messier was ousted.[6]

Anglo-Saxon countries used to have a near-monopoly on hostile takeovers. That is no longer the case. Takeover activity in Europe now exceeds that in the United States, and in recent years some of the most bitterly contested takeovers have involved European companies. For example, Mittal's $27 billion takeover of fellow steel-producer Arcelor resulted from a fierce and highly politicized 5-month battle. Arcelor used every defense in the book—including inviting a Russian company to become a leading shareholder.

---

[5] In Chapter 1 we saw that, in the same year, Carl Icahn used the threat of a proxy fight to gain seats on the board of Yahoo.

[6] The rise and fall of Vivendi is chronicled in J. Johnson and M. Orange, *The Man Who Tried to Buy the World: Jean-Marie Messier and Vivendi Universal* (Portfolio, 2003).

Mittal is now based in Europe, but it began operations in Indonesia. This illustrates another change in the merger market: Acquirers are no longer confined to the major industrialized countries. They now include Brazilian, Russian, Indian, and Chinese companies. We have already encountered some of the recent acquisitions of U.S. and British companies by the Indian conglomerate Tata Group. Other examples include IBM's personal computer business, which was bought by the Chinese company Lenovo, and Inco, the Canadian nickel producer, which is now owned by Brazil's Vale.

In the United States the rules of merger warfare are largely set by federal and state laws,[7] and the courts act as referee to see that contests are conducted fairly. We will look at one recent contest that illustrates the tactics and weapons employed.

EXAMPLE 21.2 ▶ Oracle Bids for PeopleSoft

Hostile takeover bids are relatively uncommon in high-tech industries where an acrimonious takeover battle may cause many of the target's most valued staff to leave. Investors were therefore startled in June 2003 when the software giant Oracle Corp. announced a $5.1 billion cash tender offer for its rival PeopleSoft. The offer price of $16 a share was only a very modest 6% above the recent price of PeopleSoft stock. PeopleSoft's CEO angrily rejected the bid as dramatically undervaluing the business and accused Oracle of trying to disrupt PeopleSoft's business and to thwart its recently announced plan to merge with its smaller rival J.D. Edwards & Co. PeopleSoft immediately filed a suit claiming that Oracle's management had engaged in "acts of unfair trade practices" and had "disrupted PeopleSoft's customer relationships." In another suit J.D. Edwards claimed that Oracle had wrongly "interfered with its proposed merger with PeopleSoft" and demanded $1.7 billion in compensatory damages.

Oracle's bid was the opening salvo in a battle that was to last 18 months. Some of the key dates in this battle are set out in Table 21.5. PeopleSoft had several defenses at its disposal. First, it had in place a **poison pill,** which would allow it to flood the market with additional shares if a predator acquired 20% of the stock. Second, the company instituted a customer-assurance program that offered customers money-back guarantees if an acquirer were to reduce customer support. At one point in the takeover battle the potential liability under this program reached nearly $1.6 billion. Third, elections to the PeopleSoft board were staggered, so different directors came up for reelection in different years. This meant that it would take two annual meetings to replace a majority of PeopleSoft's board.

Oracle not only had to overcome PeopleSoft's defenses but also had to clear possible antitrust roadblocks. Connecticut's attorney general instituted an antitrust action to block Oracle's bid, in part to protect his state's considerable investment in PeopleSoft software, and announced that he was seeking to assemble a coalition of other states and customers as well. Then an investigation of the deal by the U.S. Department of Justice ruled that the deal was anticompetitive. Normally such an objection is enough to kill a deal, but Oracle was persistent and successfully appealed the ruling in a federal court.

While these battles were being fought out, Oracle revised its offer four times. It upped its offer first to $19.50 and then to $26 a share. Then, in an effort to put pressure on PeopleSoft shareholders, Oracle *reduced* its offer to $21 a share, citing a drop of 28% in the price of PeopleSoft's shares. Six months later it raised the offer again to $24 a share, warning investors that it would walk away if the offer was not accepted by PeopleSoft's board or a majority of the PeopleSoft shareholders.

Sixty-one percent of PeopleSoft's shareholders indicated that they wished to accept this last offer, but before Oracle could gain control of PeopleSoft, it still

poison pill
Measure taken by a target firm to avoid acquisition; for example, the right of existing shareholders to buy additional shares at an attractive price if a bidder acquires a large holding.

---

[7] The principal federal act regulating takeovers is the Williams Act of 1968.

TABLE 21.5 Some key dates in the Oracle/PeopleSoft takeover battle

Date	Event
June 6, 2003	Oracle offers cash of $16 a share for PeopleSoft stock, a premium of 6%.
June 18, 2003	Oracle increases offer to $19.50 a share.
February 4, 2004	Oracle raises offer to $26 a share.
February 26, 2004	Justice Department files suit to block deal. Oracle announces plans to appeal.
May 16, 2004	Oracle *reduces* offer to $21 a share.
September 9, 2004	Oracle wins appeal in a federal court against Department of Justice antitrust ruling.
September 27, 2004	Hearing begins in Delaware court on Oracle's request to overturn PeopleSoft's poison pill.
November 1, 2004	Oracle raises offer to $24 a share. Accepted by 61% of PeopleSoft shares.
November 23, 2004	Oracle announces plans to mount a proxy fight by naming four nominees for PeopleSoft's board.
December 13, 2004	Oracle raises offer to $26.50 a share. Accepted by PeopleSoft's board.

needed the company to get rid of the poison pill and customer-assurance scheme. That meant putting pressure on PeopleSoft's management, which had continued to reject every approach. Oracle tried two tactics. First, it initiated a proxy fight to change the composition of PeopleSoft's board. Second, it filed a suit in a Delaware court alleging that PeopleSoft's management had breached its fiduciary duty by trying to thwart Oracle's offer and not giving it "due consideration." The lawsuit asked the court to require that PeopleSoft dismantle its takeover defenses, including the poison-pill plan and the customer-assurance program.

PeopleSoft's CEO had at one point said that he "could imagine no price nor combination of price and other conditions to recommend accepting the offer." But with 61% of PeopleSoft's shareholders wishing to take up Oracle's latest offer, it was becoming less easy for the company to keep saying no, and many observers were starting to question whether PeopleSoft's management was acting in the shareholders' interest. If management showed itself deaf to shareholders' interests, the court could well rule in favor of Oracle or disgruntled shareholders might vote to change the composition of the PeopleSoft board. PeopleSoft's directors therefore decided to be less intransigent and testified at the Delaware trial that they would consider negotiating with Oracle if it were to offer $26.50 or $27 a share. This was the breakthrough that Oracle was looking for. It upped its offer immediately to $26.50 a share, PeopleSoft lifted its defenses, and within a month 97% of PeopleSoft's shareholders had agreed to the bid. After 18 months of punch and counterpunch the battle for PeopleSoft was over.

---

shark repellent
Amendment to a company charter made to forestall takeover attempts.

What are the lessons? First, the example illustrates some of the stratagems of merger warfare. Firms like PeopleSoft that are worried about being taken over usually prepare their defenses in advance. Often they will persuade shareholders to agree to **shark-repellent** changes to the corporate charter. For example, the charter may be amended to require that any merger must be approved by a *supermajority* of 80% of the shares rather than the normal 50%.

Firms frequently deter potential bidders by devising poison pills, which make the company unappetizing. For example, the poison pill may give existing shareholders the right to buy the company's shares at half-price as soon as a bidder acquires more than 15% of the shares. The bidder is not entitled to the discount. Thus the bidder resembles Tantalus—as soon as it has acquired 15% of the shares, control is lifted away from its reach.

The battle for PeopleSoft illustrates the strength of poison pills and other takeover defenses. Oracle's offensive still gained ground, but with great expense and at a very slow pace. But eventually the pressure on PeopleSoft's management became overwhelming. Unless it could demonstrate that it was acting in the shareholders' interests, it risked having the poison pill removed by the court. The second reason that the company caved in was the increasing pressure from its shareholders, including some large institutions, who wished to accept Oracle's offer.

21.8 Method 3: Leveraged Buyouts

leveraged buyout (LBO)
Acquisition of the firm by a private group using substantial borrowed funds.

management buyout (MBO)
Acquisition of the firm by its own management in a leveraged buyout.

Leveraged buyouts, or **LBOs,** differ from ordinary acquisitions in two ways. First, a large fraction of the purchase price is debt-financed. Some, perhaps all, of this debt is junk, that is, below investment grade. Second, the shares of the LBO no longer trade on the open market. The remaining equity in the LBO is privately held by a small group of (usually institutional) investors and is known as *private equity.* When this group is led by the company's management, the acquisition is called a **management buyout (MBO).** Many LBOs are in fact MBOs.

In the 1970s and 1980s many management buyouts were arranged for unwanted divisions of large, diversified companies. Smaller divisions outside the companies' main lines of business often lacked top management's interest and commitment, and divisional management chafed under corporate bureaucracy. Many such divisions flowered when spun off as MBOs. Their managers, pushed by the need to generate cash for debt service and encouraged by a substantial personal stake in the business, found ways to cut costs and compete more effectively.

During the 1980s private-equity activity shifted to buyouts of entire businesses, including large, mature public corporations. The largest, most dramatic, and best-documented LBO of them all was the $25 billion takeover of RJR Nabisco in 1988 by Kohlberg Kravis Roberts (KKR). The players, tactics, and controversies of LBOs are writ large in this case.

EXAMPLE 21.3 ▶ RJR Nabisco[8]

On October 28, 1988, the board of directors of RJR Nabisco revealed that Ross Johnson, the company's chief executive officer, had formed a group of investors prepared to buy all the firm's stock for $75 per share in cash and take the company private. Johnson's group was backed up and advised by Shearson Lehman Hutton, the investment bank subsidiary of American Express.

RJR's share price immediately moved to about $75, handing shareholders a 36% gain over the previous day's price of $56. At the same time RJR's bonds fell, since it was clear that existing bondholders would soon have a lot more company.

Johnson's offer lifted RJR onto the auction block. Once the company was in play, its board of directors was obliged to consider other offers, which were not long coming. Four days later, a group of investors led by LBO specialists Kohlberg Kravis Roberts bid $90 per share, $79 in cash plus preferred stock valued at $11.

The bidding finally closed on November 30, some 32 days after the initial offer was revealed. In the end it was Johnson's group against KKR. KKR offered $109 per share, after adding $1 per share (roughly $230 million) at the last hour. The KKR bid

---

[8] The story of the RJR Nabisco buyout is reconstructed by B. Burrough and J. Helyar in *Barbarians at the Gate: The Fall of RJR Nabisco* (New York: Harper & Row, 1990) and is the subject of a movie with the same title.

was $81 in cash, convertible subordinated debentures valued at about $10, and preferred shares valued at about $18. Johnson's group bid $112 in cash and securities.

But the RJR board chose KKR. True, Johnson's group had offered $3 per share more, but its security valuations were viewed as "softer" and perhaps overstated. Also, KKR's planned asset sales were less drastic; perhaps their plans for managing the business inspired more confidence. Finally, the Johnson group's proposal contained a management compensation package that seemed extremely generous and had generated an avalanche of bad press.

But where did the merger benefits come from? What could justify offering $109 per share, about $25 billion in all, for a company that only 33 days previously had been selling for $56 per share?

KKR and other bidders were betting on two things. First, they expected to generate billions of additional dollars from interest tax shields, reduced capital expenditures, and sales of assets not strictly necessary to RJR's core businesses. Asset sales alone were projected to generate $5 billion. Second, they expected to make those core businesses significantly more profitable, mainly by cutting back on expenses and bureaucracy. Apparently there was plenty to cut, including the RJR "Air Force," which at one point operated 10 corporate jets.

In the year after KKR took over, new management was installed. This group sold assets and cut back operating expenses and capital spending. There were also layoffs. As expected, high interest charges meant a net loss of $976 million for 1989, but pretax operating income actually increased, despite extensive asset sales, including the sale of RJR's European food operations.

While management was cutting costs and selling assets, prices in the junk bond market were rapidly declining, implying much higher future interest charges for RJR and stricter terms on any refinancing. In mid-1990 KKR made an additional equity investment, and later that year the company announced an offer of cash and new shares in exchange for $753 million of junk bonds. By 1993 the burden of debt had been reduced from $26 billion to $14 billion. For RJR, the world's largest LBO, it seemed that high debt was a temporary, not permanent, virtue.

Barbarians at the Gate?

The buyout of RJR crystallized views on LBOs, the junk bond market, and the takeover business. For many it exemplified all that was wrong with finance in the 1980s, especially the willingness of "raiders" to carve up established companies, leaving them with enormous debt burdens, basically in order to get rich quick.

There was plenty of confusion, stupidity, and greed in the LBO business. Not all the people involved were nice. On the other hand, LBOs generated enormous increases in market value, and most of the gains went to selling stockholders, not raiders. For example, the biggest winners in the RJR Nabisco LBO were the company's stockholders.

We should therefore consider briefly where these gains may have come from before we try to pass judgment on LBOs. There are several possibilities.

The Junk Bond Markets   LBOs and debt-financed takeovers may have been driven by artificially cheap funding from the junk bond markets. With hindsight it seems that investors in junk bonds underestimated the risks of default. Default rates climbed painfully between 1989 and 1991, yields rose dramatically, and new issues dried up. For a while junk-financed LBOs disappeared from the scene.

Leverage and Taxes   As we explained in Chapter 16, borrowing money saves taxes. But taxes were not the main driving force behind LBOs. The value of interest tax shields was just not big enough to explain the observed gains in market value.

Of course, if interest tax shields were the main motive for LBOs' high debt, then LBO managers would not be so concerned to pay off debt. We saw that this was one of the first tasks facing RJR Nabisco's new management.

Other Stakeholders   It is possible that the gain to the selling stockholders is just someone else's loss and that no value is generated overall. Therefore, we should look at the total gain to *all* investors in an LBO, not just the selling stockholders.

Bondholders are the obvious losers. The debt they thought was well-secured may turn into junk when the borrower goes through an LBO. We noted how market prices of RJR Nabisco debt fell sharply when Ross Johnson's first LBO offer was announced. But again, the value losses suffered by bondholders in LBOs are not nearly large enough to explain stockholder gains.

Leverage and Incentives   Managers and employees of LBOs work harder and often smarter. They have to generate cash to service the extra debt. Moreover, managers' personal fortunes are riding on the LBO's success. They become owners rather than organization men or women.

It is hard to measure the payoff from better incentives, but there is some evidence of improved operating efficiency in LBOs. Kaplan, who studied 48 management buyouts between 1980 and 1986, found average increases in operating income of 24% over the following 3 years. Ratios of operating income and net cash flow to assets and sales increased dramatically. He observed cutbacks in capital expenditures but not in employment. Kaplan suggests that these operating changes "are due to improved incentives rather than layoffs or managerial exploitation of shareholders through inside information."[9]

Free Cash Flow   The free-cash-flow theory of takeovers is basically that mature firms with a surplus of cash will tend to waste it. This contrasts with standard finance theory, which says that firms with more cash than positive-NPV investment opportunities should give the cash back to investors through higher dividends or share repurchases. But we see firms like RJR Nabisco spending on corporate luxuries and questionable capital investments. One benefit of LBOs is to put such companies on a diet and force them to pay out cash to service debt.

The free-cash-flow theory predicts that mature, "cash cow" companies will be the most likely targets of LBOs. We can find many examples that fit the theory, including RJR Nabisco. The theory says that the gains in market value generated by LBOs are just the present values of the future cash flows that would otherwise have been frittered away.[10]

We do not endorse the free-cash-flow theory as the sole explanation for LBOs. We have mentioned several other plausible rationales, and we suspect that most LBOs are driven by a mixture of motives. Nor do we say that all LBOs are beneficial. On the contrary, there are many mistakes and a good many LBOs have ended in bankruptcy, including in recent years such well-known names as Chrysler, Tropicana, Chicago Tribune, Wickes Furniture, and Masonite. However, we do take issue with those who portray LBOs *simply* as Wall Street barbarians breaking up the traditional strengths of corporate America. In many cases LBOs have generated true gains.

The buyout of RJR Nabisco illustrates how during the merger boom of the 1980s even very large companies were not immune from attack by a rival management team. What made such attacks possible was the ability of the bidder to finance the takeover

---

[9] S. Kaplan, "The Effects of Management Buyouts on Operating Performance and Value," *Journal of Financial Economics* 24 (October 1989), pp. 217–254.

[10] The free-cash-flow theory's chief proponent is Michael Jensen. See M. C. Jensen, "The Eclipse of the Public Corporation," *Harvard Business Review* 67 (September–October 1989), pp. 61–74, and "The Agency Costs of Free Cash Flow, Corporate Finance and Takeovers," *American Economic Review* 76 (May 1986), pp. 323–329.

with large amounts of junk bonds. But by the end of the decade the merger environment had changed. Many of the obvious targets had disappeared and the battle for RJR Nabisco highlighted the increasing cost of victory. Institutions were reluctant to increase their holdings of junk bonds. Moreover, the market for these bonds had depended to a remarkable extent on one individual, Michael Milken, of the investment bank Drexel Burnham Lambert. By the late 1980s Milken and his employer were in trouble. Milken was indicted by a grand jury on 98 counts and was subsequently sentenced to jail. Drexel filed for bankruptcy, but by that time the junk bond market was moribund and the finance for highly leveraged buyouts had largely dried up.[11] Finally, in reaction to the perceived excesses of the merger boom, the state legislatures and the courts began to lean against hostile takeovers.

Eventually, LBO activity began to recover, encouraged by low interest rates and (until August 2007) easy access to debt financing. CEOs and CFOs, pressured to meet short-term earnings targets, have been attracted by the prospect of escaping from the goldfish bowl and into private ownership. In addition, for public companies the costs of meeting the requirements of the Sarbanes-Oxley Act and other detailed regulations have helped to push corporations to return to private (rather than public) ownership.

21.9   Method 4: Divestitures, Spin-Offs, and Carve-Outs

In the market for corporate control, fusion—mergers and acquisitions—gets the most publicity. But fission—the divestiture of assets or entire businesses—can be just as important. Often one firm may sell part of its business to another firm. For example, in 2007, Ford announced the sale of Aston Martin, its luxury-car producer, for $924 million.

Instead of selling part of their operations, companies sometimes *spin off* a business by separating it from the parent firm and distributing to their shareholders the stock in the newly independent company. For example, in 2009 Time Warner spun off its investment in AOL. Time Warner's shareholders received shares in the new company and could trade their AOL shares as well as those of the slimmed-down Time Warner.

Carve-outs are similar to spin-offs except that shares in the new company are not given to existing stockholders but, instead, are sold in a public offering. Sometimes companies carve out a small proportion of the company to establish a market in the subsidiary and subsequently spin off the remainder of the shares. The nearby box describes how the computer company, Palm, was first carved and then spun.

The most frequent motive for spin-offs is improved efficiency. Companies sometimes refer to a business as being a "poor fit." By spinning off a poor fit, the management of the parent company can concentrate on its main activity. If each business must stand on its own feet, there is no risk that funds will be siphoned off from one in order to support unprofitable investments in the other. Moreover, if the two parts of the business are independent, it is easy to see the value of each and to reward managers accordingly.

21.10   The Benefits and Costs of Mergers

Merger activity comes in waves and is concentrated in a relatively small number of industries. This urge to merge frequently seems to be prompted by deregulation and by changes in technology or the pattern of demand. Take the merger wave of the 1990s,

---

[11] For a history of the role of Milken in the development of the junk bond market, see C. Bruck, *The Predator's Ball: The Junk Bond Raiders and the Man Who Staked Them* (New York: Simon and Schuster, 1988).

How Palm Was Carved and Spun

When 3Com acquired U.S. Robotics in 1997, it also became the owner of Palm, a small start-up business developing handheld computers. It was a lucky purchase, for over the next 3 years the Palm Pilot came to dominate the market for handheld computers. But as Palm began to take up an increasing amount of management time, 3Com concluded that it needed to return to its knitting and focus on its basic business of selling computer network systems. It therefore announced that it would carve out 5% of its holding of Palm through an initial public offering. At the same time it published plans to spin off the remaining 95% of Palm shares later in 2000 by giving 3Com shareholders about 1.5 Palm shares for each 3Com share that they owed.

The Palm carve-out occurred at close to the peak of the high-tech boom and got off to a dazzling start. The shares were issued in the IPO at $38 each. On the first day of trading the stock price touched $165 before closing at $95. Therefore, anyone owning a share of 3Com stock could look forward later in the year to receiving about 1.5 shares of Palm worth $1.5 \times 95 = \$142.50$. But apparently 3Com's shareholders were not fully convinced that their newfound wealth was for real, for on the same day 3Com's stock price closed at $82, or more than $60 a share *less* than the market value of the shares in Palm that they were due to receive.*

Three years after 3Com spun off its holding in Palm, Palm itself entered the spin-off business by giving shareholders stock in PalmSource, a subsidiary that was responsible for developing and licensing the Palm operating system. The remaining business, renamed palmOne, would focus on making mobile gadgets. The company gave three reasons for its decision to split into two. First, like 3Com's management, Palm's management believed that the company would benefit from clarity of focus and mission. Second, it argued that shareholder value could "be enhanced if investors could evaluate and choose between both businesses separately, thereby attracting new and different investors." Finally, it seemed that Palm's rivals were reluctant to buy software from a company that competed with them in making handheld hardware.

---

*This difference would seem to present an arbitrage opportunity. An investor who bought 1 share of 3Com and sold short 1.5 shares of Palm would receive an immediate cash flow of $60 *and* own 3Com's other assets for free. The difficulty in executing this arbitrage is explored in O. A. Lamont and R. H. Thaler, "Can the Market Add and Subtract? Mispricing in Tech Stock Carve-Outs," *Journal of Political Economy* 111 (April 2003), pp. 227–268.

---

for example. Deregulation of telecoms and banking earlier in the decade led to a spate of mergers in both industries that has continued to the present. Elsewhere, the decline in military spending brought about a number of mergers between defense companies until the Department of Justice decided to call a halt. And in the entertainment industry the prospective advantages from controlling both content and distribution led to mergers between such giants as AOL and Time Warner.

There are undoubtedly good acquisitions and bad acquisitions, but economists find it hard to agree on whether acquisitions are beneficial *on balance*. In general, shareholders of the target firm make a healthy gain. For example, one study found that following the announcement of the bid, the stock price of the target company jumped by 16% on average.[12] On the other hand, it appears that investors expected the acquiring companies to just about break even, for the price of their shares fell by .7%. The value of the total package—buyer plus seller—increased by 1.8%. Of course, these are averages; selling shareholders, for example, have sometimes obtained much higher returns. When Hewlett-Packard won its takeover battle to buy data-storage company 3Par, it paid a premium of 230%, or about $1.5 billion, for 3Par's stock.

Since buyers roughly break even and sellers make substantial gains, it seems that there are positive overall benefits from mergers. But not everybody is convinced. Some believe that investors analyzing mergers pay too much attention to short-term earnings gains and don't notice that these gains are at the expense of long-term prospects.

Since we can't observe how companies would have fared in the absence of a merger, it is difficult to measure the effects on profitability. However, several studies of merger activity suggest that mergers *do* seem to improve real productivity. For example, Healy, Palepu, and Ruback examined 50 large mergers and found an average increase in the companies' pretax returns of 2.4 percentage points.[13] They argue that this gain

---

[12] See G. Andrade, M. Mitchell, and E. Stafford, "New Evidence and Perspectives on Mergers," *Journal of Economic Perspectives* 15 (Spring 2001), pp. 103–120.

[13] See P. Healy, K. Palepu, and R. Ruback, "Does Corporate Performance Improve after Mergers?" *Journal of Financial Economics* 31 (April 1992), pp. 135–175. The study examined the pretax returns of the merged companies relative to industry averages.

came from generating a higher level of sales from the same assets. There was no evidence that the companies were mortgaging their long-term futures by cutting back on long-term investments; expenditures on capital equipment and research and development tracked the industry average.

If you are concerned with public policy toward mergers, you do not want to look only at their impact on the shareholders of the companies concerned. For instance, we have already seen that in the case of RJR Nabisco some part of the shareholders' gain was at the expense of the bondholders and the Internal Revenue Service (through the enlarged interest tax shield). The acquirer's shareholders may also gain at the expense of the target firm's employees, who in some cases are laid off or are forced to take pay cuts after takeovers.

Perhaps the most important effect of acquisition is felt by the managers of companies that are not taken over. For example, one effect of LBOs was that the managers of even the largest corporations could not feel safe from challenge. Perhaps the threat of takeover spurs the whole of corporate America to try harder. Unfortunately, we don't know whether on balance the threat of merger makes for more active days or more sleepless nights.

The threat of takeover may be a spur to inefficient management, but it is also costly. The companies need to pay for the services provided by the investment bankers, lawyers, and accountants. In addition, mergers can soak up large amounts of management time and effort. When a company is planning a takeover, it can be difficult to give as much attention as one should to the firm's existing business.

Even if the gains to the community exceed these costs, one wonders whether the same benefits could not be achieved more cheaply another way. For example, are leveraged buyouts necessary to make managers work harder? Perhaps the problem lies in the way that many corporations reward and penalize their managers. Perhaps many of the gains from takeover could be captured by linking management compensation more closely to performance.

SUMMARY

Why may it make sense for companies to merge? *(LO1)*

A merger may be undertaken in order to replace an inefficient management. But sometimes two businesses may be more valuable together than apart. Gains may stem from economies of scale, economies of vertical integration, the combination of complementary resources, or redeployment of surplus funds. We don't know how frequently these benefits occur, but they do make economic sense. Sometimes mergers are undertaken to diversify risks or artificially increase growth of earnings per share. These motives are dubious.

How should the gains and costs of mergers to the acquiring firm be measured? *(LO2)*

A merger generates an economic gain if the two firms are worth more together than apart. The *gain* is the difference between the value of the merged firm and the value of the two firms run independently. The *cost* is the premium that the buyer pays for the selling firm over its value as a separate entity. When payment is in the form of shares, the value of this payment naturally depends on what those shares are worth after the merger is complete. You should go ahead with the merger if the gain exceeds the cost.

In what ways do companies change the composition of their ownership or management? *(LO3)*

If the board of directors fails to replace an inefficient management, there are four ways to effect a change: (1) Shareholders may engage in a **proxy contest** to replace the board; (2) the firm may be taken over by another; (3) the firm may be purchased by a private group of investors in a leveraged buyout; or (4) it may sell off part of its operations to another company.

What are some takeover defenses? *(LO4)*

Mergers are often amicably negotiated between the management and directors of the two companies; but if the seller is reluctant, the would-be buyer can decide to make a tender offer for the stock. We sketched some of the offensive and defensive tactics used in take-over battles. These defenses include **shark repellents** (changes in the company charter meant to make a takeover more difficult to achieve) and **poison pills** (measures that make takeover of the firm more costly).

What are some of the motivations for leveraged and management buyouts of the firm? *(LO5)*

In a **leveraged buyout (LBO)** or **management buyout (MBO),** all public shares are repurchased and the company "goes private." LBOs tend to involve mature businesses with ample cash flow and modest growth opportunities. LBOs and other debt-financed take-overs are driven by a mixture of motives, including (1) the value of interest tax shields; (2) transfers of value from bondholders, who may see the value of their bonds fall as the firm piles up more debt; and (3) the opportunity to create better incentives for managers and employees, who have a personal stake in the company. In addition, many LBOs have been designed to force firms with surplus cash to distribute it to shareholders rather than plowing it back. Investors feared such companies would otherwise channel free cash flow into negative-NPV investments.

Do mergers increase efficiency, and how are the gains from mergers distributed between shareholders of the acquired and acquiring firms? *(LO6)*

We observed that when the target firm is acquired, its shareholders typically win: Target firms' shareholders earn abnormally large returns. The bidding firm's shareholders roughly break even. This suggests that the typical merger generates positive net benefits, but competition among bidders and active defense by management of the target firm pushes most of the gains toward selling shareholders.

QUESTIONS

QUIZ

1. **Merger Motives.** Which of the following motives for mergers make economic sense? *(LO1)*
   a. Merging to achieve economies of scale.
   b. Merging to reduce risk by diversification.
   c. Merging to redeploy cash generated by a firm with ample profits but limited growth opportunities.
   d. Merging to increase earnings per share.

2. **Merger Motives.** Explain why it might or might not make good sense for Northeast Heating and Northeast Air Conditioning to merge into one company. *(LO1)*

3. **Empirical Facts.** True or false? *(LO6)*
   a. Sellers almost always gain in mergers.
   b. Buyers almost always gain in mergers.
   c. Firms that do unusually well tend to be acquisition targets.
   d. Merger activity in the United States varies dramatically from year to year.
   e. On average, mergers produce substantial economic gains.
   f. Tender offers require the approval of the selling firm's management.
   g. The cost of a merger is always independent of the economic gain produced by the merger.

4. **Merger Tactics.** Connect each term to its correct definition or description. *(LO4)*

   A. LBO
   B. Poison pill
   C. Tender offer
   D. Shark repellent
   E. Proxy contest

   1. Attempt to gain control of a firm by winning the votes of its stockholders.
   2. Changes in corporate charter designed to deter unwelcome takeover.
   3. Shareholders are issued rights to buy shares if bidder acquires large stake in the firm.
   4. Offer to buy shares directly from stockholders.
   5. Company or business bought out by private investors, largely debt-financed.

5. **LBO Facts.** True or false? *(LO5)*

   a. One of the first tasks of an LBO's financial manager is to pay down debt.

   b. Leveraged buyouts reduce the free cash flow available to the firm.

   c. Targets for LBOs in the 1980s tended to be profitable companies in mature industries with limited investment opportunities.

PRACTICE PROBLEMS

6. **Merger Gains.** Acquiring Corp. is considering a takeover of Takeover Target Inc. Acquiring has 10 million shares outstanding, which sell for $40 each. Takeover Target has 5 million shares outstanding, which sell for $20 each. If the merger gains are estimated at $25 million, what is the highest price per share that Acquiring should be willing to pay to Takeover Target shareholders? *(LO2)*

7. **Mergers and P/E Ratios.** If Acquiring Corp. from Practice Problem 6 has a price-earnings ratio of 12 and Takeover Target has a P/E ratio of 8, what should be the P/E ratio of the merged firm? Assume in this case that the merger is financed by an issue of new Acquiring Corp. shares. Takeover Target will get one Acquiring share for every two Takeover Target shares held. *(LO1)*

8. **Merger Gains and Costs.** Velcro Saddles is contemplating the acquisition of Pogo Ski Sticks, Inc. The values of the two companies as separate entities are $20 million and $10 million, respectively. Velcro Saddles estimates that by combining the two companies, it will reduce marketing and administrative costs by $500,000 per year in perpetuity. Velcro Saddles is willing to pay $14 million cash for Pogo. The opportunity cost of capital is 8%. *(LO2)*

   a. What is the gain from merger?

   b. What is the cost of the cash offer?

   c. What is the NPV of the acquisition under the cash offer?

9. **Stock versus Cash Offers.** Suppose that instead of making a cash offer as in Practice Problem 8, Velcro Saddles considers offering Pogo shareholders a 50% holding in Velcro Saddles. *(LO2)*

   a. What is the value of the stock in the merged company held by the original Pogo shareholders?

   b. What is the cost of the stock alternative?

   c. What is its NPV under the stock offer?

10. **Merger Gains.** Immense Appetite, Inc., believes that it can acquire Sleepy Industries and improve efficiency to the extent that the market value of Sleepy will increase by $5 million. Sleepy currently sells for $20 a share, and there are 1 million shares outstanding. *(LO2)*

    a. Sleepy's management is willing to accept a cash offer of $25 a share. Can the merger be accomplished on a friendly basis?

    b. What will happen if Sleepy's management holds out for an offer of $28 a share?

11. **Mergers and P/E Ratios.** Castles in the Sand currently sells at a price-earnings multiple of 10. The firm has 2 million shares outstanding, and sells at a price per share of $40. Firm Foundation has a P/E multiple of 8, has 1 million shares outstanding, and sells at a price per share of $20. *(LO1)*

    a. If Castles acquires the other firm by exchanging one of its shares for every two of Firm Foundation, what will be the earnings per share of the merged firm?

    b. What should be the P/E of the new firm if the merger has no economic gains? What will happen to Castles's price per share? Show that shareholders of neither Castles nor Firm Foundation realize any change in wealth.

    c. What will happen to Castles's price per share if the market does not realize that the P/E ratio of the merged firm ought to differ from Castles's premerger ratio?

    d. How are the gains from the merger split between shareholders of the two firms if the market is fooled as in part (c)?

12. **Stock versus Cash Offers.** Sweet Cola Corp. (SCC) is bidding to take over Salty Dog Pretzels (SDP). SCC has 3,000 shares outstanding, selling at $50 per share. SDP has 2,000 shares outstanding, selling at $17.50 a share. SCC estimates the economic gain from the merger to be $15,000. *(LO2)*

    a. If SDP can be acquired for $20 a share, what is the NPV of the merger to SCC?

b. What will SCC sell for when the market learns that it plans to acquire SDP for $20 a share? What will SDP sell for? What are the percentage gains to the shareholders of each firm?

c. Now suppose that the merger takes place through an exchange of stock. On the basis of the premerger prices of the firms, SCC sells for $50, so instead of paying $20 cash, SCC issues .40 of its shares for every SDP share acquired. What will be the price of the merged firm?

d. What is the NPV of the merger to SCC when it uses an exchange of stock? Why does your answer differ from part (a)?

CHALLENGE PROBLEMS

13. **Bootstrap Game.** The Muck and Slurry merger has fallen through (see Section 21.2). But World Enterprises is determined to report earnings per share of $2.67. It therefore acquires the Wheelrim and Axle Company. You are given the following facts:

	World Enterprises	Wheelrim and Axle	Merged Firm
Earnings per share	$2	$2.50	$2.67
Price per share	$40	$25	_____
Price-earnings ratio	20	10	_____
Number of shares	100,000	200,000	_____
Total earnings	$200,000	$500,000	_____
Total market value	$4,000,000	$5,000,000	_____

Once again there are no gains from merging. In exchange for Wheelrim and Axle shares, World Enterprises issues just enough of its own shares to ensure its $2.67 earnings per share objective. *(LO1)*

a. Complete the above table for the merged firm.

b. How many shares of World Enterprises are exchanged for each share of Wheelrim and Axle?

c. What is the cost of the merger to World Enterprises?

d. What is the change in the total market value of those World Enterprises shares that were outstanding before the merger?

Templates can be found at
www.mhhe.com/bmm7e.

14. **Merger Gains and Costs.** As treasurer of Leisure Products, Inc., you are investigating the possible acquisition of Plastitoys. You have the following basic data:

	Leisure Products	Plastitoys
Forecast earnings per share	$5	$1.50
Forecast dividend per share	$3	$.80
Number of shares	1,000,000	600,000
Stock price	$90	$20

You estimate that investors currently expect a steady growth of about 6% in Plastitoys's earnings and dividends. You believe that Leisure Products could increase Plastitoys's growth rate to 8% per year, without any additional capital investment required. *(LO2)*

a. What is the gain from the acquisition?

b. What is the cost of the acquisition if Leisure Products pays $25 in cash for each share of Plastitoys?

c. What is the cost of the acquisition if Leisure Products offers one share of Leisure Products for every three shares of Plastitoys?

d. How would the cost of the cash offer and the share offer alter if the expected growth rate of Plastitoys were not increased by the merger?

WEB EXERCISE

1. Look at a recent example of a merger announcement, and log on to the Web site of the acquiring company. What reasons does the acquirer give for buying the target? How does it intend to pay for the target—with cash, shares, or a mixture of the two? Can you work out how much the target's shareholders will gain from the offer? Is it more or less than would be the case for an average merger? Now log on to finance.yahoo.com and find out what happened to the stock price of the acquiring company when the merger was announced. Were shareholders pleased with the announcement?

SOLUTIONS TO SELF-TEST QUESTIONS

21.1   a. Horizontal merger. IBM is in the same industry as Dell Computer.
       b. Conglomerate merger. Dell Computer and Safeway are in different industries.
       c. Vertical merger. Safeway is expanding backward to acquire one of its suppliers, Campbell Soup.
       d. Conglomerate merger. Campbell Soup and IBM are in different industries.

21.2   Given current earnings of $2 a share and a share price of $10, Muck and Slurry would have a market value of $1,000,000 and a price-earnings ratio of only 5. It can be acquired for only half as many shares of World Enterprises, 25,000 shares. Therefore, the merged firm will have 125,000 shares outstanding and earnings of $400,000, resulting in earnings per share of $3.20, higher than the $2.67 value in the third column of Table 21.2.

21.3   The cost of the merger is $4 million: the $4 per share premium offered to Goldfish shareholders times 1 million shares. If the merger has positive NPV to Killer Shark, the gain must be greater than $4 million.

21.4   Yes. Look again at Table 21.4. Total market value is still $540 million, but Cislunar will have to issue 1 million shares to complete the merger. Total shares in the merged firm will be 11 million. The postmerger share price is $49.09, so Cislunar and its shareholders still come out ahead.

MINICASE

McPhee Food Halls operated a chain of supermarkets in the west of Scotland. The company had had a lackluster record, and since the death of its founder in late 2004, it had been regarded as a prime target for a takeover bid. In anticipation of a bid, McPhee's share price moved up from £4.90 in March to a 12-month high of £5.80 on June 10, despite the fact that the London stock market index as a whole was largely unchanged.

Almost nobody anticipated a bid coming from Fenton, a diversified retail business with a chain of clothing and department stores. Though Fenton operated food halls in several of its department stores, it had relatively little experience in food retailing. Fenton's management had, however, been contemplating a merger with McPhee for some time. The managers not only felt that they could make use of McPhee's food retailing skills within their department stores, but they also believed that better management and inventory control in McPhee's business could result in cost savings worth £10 million.

Fenton's offer of 8 Fenton shares for every 10 McPhee shares was announced after the market close on June 10. Since McPhee had 5 million shares outstanding, the acquisition would add an additional 5 × (8/10) = 4 million shares to the 10 million Fenton shares that were already outstanding. While Fenton's management believed that it would be difficult for McPhee to mount a successful takeover defense, the company and its investment bankers privately agreed that the company could afford to raise the offer if it proved necessary.

Investors were not persuaded of the benefits of combining a supermarket with a department store company, and on June 11 Fenton's shares opened lower and drifted down £.10 to close the day at £7.90. McPhee's shares, however, jumped to £6.32 a share.

Fenton's financial manager was due to attend a meeting with the company's investment bankers that evening, but before doing so, he decided to run the numbers once again. First he reestimated the gain and cost of the merger. Then he analyzed that day's fall in Fenton's stock price to see whether investors believed there were any gains to be had from merging. Finally, he decided to revisit the issue of whether Fenton could afford to raise its bid at a later stage. If the effect was simply a further fall in the price of Fenton stock, the move could be self-defeating.

CHAPTER 22

International Financial Management

LEARNING OBJECTIVES

After studying this chapter, you should be able to:

(1) Understand the difference between spot and forward exchange rates.

(2) Understand the basic relationships between spot exchange rates, forward exchange rates, interest rates, and inflation rates.

(3) Formulate simple strategies to protect the firm against exchange rate risk.

(4) Perform an NPV analysis for projects with cash flows in foreign currencies.

RELATED WEB SITES FOR THIS CHAPTER CAN BE FOUND AT WWW.MHHE.COM/BMM7E.

Coca-Cola does business around the world. What new issues does international business raise for the financial manager?

Thus far we have talked mostly about doing business at home. But many companies have substantial overseas interests. Of course, the objectives of international financial management are still the same. You want to buy assets that are worth *more* than they cost, and you want to pay for them by issuing liabilities that are, if possible, worth *less* than the money raised. But when you try to apply these criteria to an international business, you come up against some new wrinkles.

You must, for example, know how to deal with more than one currency. Therefore we open this chapter with a look at foreign exchange markets.

The financial manager must also remember that interest rates differ from country to country.

For example, in September 2010, the 1-year interest rate was about .2% in the United States, 4.7% in Australia, and 11.0% in Brazil. We will discuss the reasons for these differences in interest rates, along with some of the implications for financing overseas operations.

Exchange rate fluctuations can knock companies off course and transform black ink into red. We will therefore discuss how firms can protect themselves against exchange risks.

We will also discuss how international companies decide on capital investments. How do they choose the discount rate? You'll find that the basic principles of capital budgeting are the same as those for domestic projects, but there are a few pitfalls to watch for.

22.1 Foreign Exchange Markets

An American company that imports goods from France will probably need to exchange its dollars for euros in order to pay for its purchases. Another company exporting to France will probably receive euros, which it then sells in exchange for dollars. Both firms must make use of the foreign exchange market, where currencies are traded.

The foreign exchange market has no central marketplace. All business is conducted via computer terminals and telephone. The principal dealers are the large commercial banks, and a corporation that wants to buy or sell currency usually does so through a commercial bank.

Turnover in the foreign exchange markets is huge. In London alone nearly $1.9 trillion of currency changes hands each day. That is equivalent to an annual turnover of around $500 trillion ($500,000,000,000,000). New York accounts for a further $800 billion of turnover per day. Compare this with the trading volume of the New York Stock Exchange, where about $70 billion of stock typically changes hands on any given day.

Spot Exchange Rates

exchange rate
Amount of one currency needed to purchase one unit of another.

Suppose you ask someone the price of bread. He may tell you that you can buy two loaves for a dollar, or he may say that one loaf costs 50 cents. If you ask a foreign exchange dealer to quote you a price for Ruritanian pesos, she may tell you that you can buy 100 pesos for a dollar or that 1 peso costs $.01. The first quote (the number of pesos that you can buy for a dollar) is known as an *indirect quote* of the **exchange rate.** The second quote (the number of dollars that it costs to buy 1 peso) is known as a *direct quote.* Of course, both quotes provide the same information. If you can buy 100 pesos for a dollar, then you can easily calculate that the cost of buying 1 peso is 1/100 = $.01.

(Ruritania is a fictional country, which for arithmetic convenience has a currency that trades for exactly 100 pesos per U.S. dollar. We will use Ruritania in several examples below.)

Table 22.1 shows the exchange rate for several actual countries on September 17, 2010. The second column of the table shows the name of the currency and its common abbreviation. For example, the Mexican peso is usually abbreviated as MXN and the U.S. dollar as USD. By custom, the prices of most currencies are expressed as indirect quotes. Thus the third column of Table 22.1 shows that

TABLE 22.1 Exchange rates in September 2010

Country	Currency	Exchange Rate
Europe		
Euro zone countries	Euro (EUR or €)	1.30440*
Sweden	Krona (SEK)	7.05820
Switzerland	Franc (CHF)	1.00940
United Kingdom	Pound (GBP or £)	1.56380*
Americas		
Brazil	Real (BRL)	1.71550
Canada	Dollar (CAD)	1.03260
Mexico	Peso (MXN)	12.8344
Asia/Africa		
Australia	Dollar (AUD)	1.06840
China	Yuan (CNY)	6.72300
China (Hong Kong)	Dollar (HKD)	7.76340
India	Rupee (INR)	45.8300
Japan	Yen (JPY or ¥)	85.6600
South Africa	Rand (ZAR)	7.15460
South Korea	Won (KRW)	1,160.00

* Direct quotes (number of U.S. dollars per unit of foreign currency). Other quotes are indirect (units of foreign currency per U.S. dollar).
Source: Financial Times, September 17, 2010, available at **www.ft.com.**

you could buy 12.8344 Mexican pesos for 1 dollar. This is sometimes written as MXN12.8344 = USD1.

To complicate matters, there are two currencies whose prices are generally expressed as direct quotes. These are the euro and the British pound. For example, you can see that it cost $1.3044 to buy 1 euro. We therefore write the euro exchange rate as USD1.3044 = EUR1.

Self-Test 22.1

Use the exchange rates in Table 22.1. How many euros can you buy for 1 dollar (an indirect quote)? How many dollars can you buy for 1 yen (a direct quote)?

EXAMPLE 22.1 ▶ A Yen for Trade

How many yen will it cost a Japanese importer to purchase $10,000 worth of oranges from a California farmer? How many dollars will that farmer need in order to buy and import a Japanese tractor priced in Japan at 4.5 million yen?

The exchange rate is JPY85.6600 = USD1. The $10,000 of oranges will require the Japanese importer to come up with 10,000 × 85.66 = 856,600 yen. The tractor will require the American importer to come up with 4,500,000/85.66 = $52,533.

spot rate of exchange Exchange rate for an immediate transaction.

The exchange rates in the last column of Table 22.1 are the prices of currency for immediate delivery. These are known as **spot rates of exchange.** For example, the spot rate of exchange for Brazilian reals is BRL1.71550 = USD1. In other words, it costs 1.71550 Brazilian reals to buy 1 dollar for immediate delivery.

Exchange rates are generally quoted against the dollar. For example, Table 22.1 shows that $1 can buy either 85.66 Japanese yen or 1,160 Korean won. This implies that 85.66 yen are equivalent to 1,160 won and, therefore, that 1 yen is equivalent to 1,160/85.66 = 13.54 won. An exchange rate between two currencies other than the U.S. dollar is known as a *cross-rate*. In our example, the cross-rate of exchange between the Japanese yen and the South Korean won is KRW13.54 = JPY1.

Cross-rates between any two currencies are locked down by the exchange rate for each currency versus the U.S. dollar. Otherwise, investors could make an easy, risk-free arbitrage profit. For example, suppose that a (really stupid) bank quotes a rate of KRW10 = JPY1. Here's what you do: You take $1 and exchange it for 1,160 Korean won, which you then use to buy 1,160/10 = 116 Japanese yen. These in turn can be exchanged back to U.S. dollars for 116/85.66 = $1.354. You have just taken advantage of a misalignment of prices to make a surefire 35% profit.[1] Of course, in real life you and other investors would transact with millions of dollars, not with one dollar at a time. The bank would be forced to revise its quote in short order.

Self-Test 22.2

Use the exchange rates in Table 22.1. What is the cross-rate between the Mexican peso and the Hong Kong dollar? How could you make money if a bank quoted you a rate of 1.75 pesos per Hong Kong dollar?

Most countries allow their currencies to *float,* so the exchange rate fluctuates from minute to minute and day to day. When the currency increases in value, which means that

---

[1] In practice foreign exchange dealers quote a spread between the prices at which they are prepared to buy and sell foreign currency, and this spread would reduce your profit. The spread is very small on large trades, but it is a major cost for small transactions by individuals.

you need less of the foreign currency to buy 1 dollar, the currency is said to *appreciate.* When you need more of the currency to buy 1 dollar, the currency is said to *depreciate.*

Self-Test 22.3

Table 22.1 shows that the exchange rate for the Swiss franc in September 2010 was CHF1.00940 = USD1. A year earlier, the spot rate of exchange for the Swiss franc was CHF1.036 = USD1. Thus, in 2010 you could buy fewer Swiss francs for your dollar than a year earlier. Did the Swiss franc appreciate or depreciate?

Some countries try to avoid fluctuations in the value of their currency and seek instead to maintain a fixed exchange rate. But fixed rates seldom last forever. If everybody tries to sell the currency, eventually the country will be forced to allow the currency to depreciate. When this happens, exchange rates can change dramatically. In December 2001, when Argentina gave up defending its fixed exchange rate versus the U.S. dollar, the value of the Argentinian peso fell by over 70% in a few months.

Forward Exchange Rates

Fluctuations in exchange rates can get companies into hot water. For example, suppose you have agreed to buy a consignment of machinery from Ruritania. The machinery will be delivered at the end of 12 months at a cost of 100 million Ruritanian pesos (RUPs). Currently, 1 dollar buys 100 pesos (RUP100 = USD1). So, if the exchange rate does not change, the machinery will cost you $1 million. But what if the peso appreciates? For example, suppose that when you come to buy the pesos at the end of the year, one dollar buys only 80 pesos (RUP80 = USD1). Then the *dollar* cost of your machinery has risen to $1.25 million (100 million/80 = $1.25 million).

You can avoid this exchange rate risk and fix your dollar cost by *buying forward,* that is, by arranging *now* to buy pesos at a prespecified price on a future date. This arrangement is called a foreign exchange *forward contract.* Suppose you enter into a forward contract with a bank to buy 100 million pesos 12 months from now at a price of RUP105 = USD1. You don't pay anything now; you simply fix today the price that you will pay in the future. After 12 months, the bank pays you 100 million pesos and you hand over in exchange $.952 million (100 /105 = $.952 million).[2]

The spot exchange rate is the rate that you pay to obtain foreign currency today. The exchange rates in Table 22.1 are all spot exchange rates. The price of currency for delivery at a future date is called the **forward exchange rate.** The forward exchange rate is not usually the same as the spot rate. In our example 1 dollar bought 100 Ruritanian pesos in the spot market but 105 pesos in the forward market. In this case, the peso is said to trade at a forward *discount* relative to the dollar. It's a discount because pesos are cheaper—more pesos per dollar—if purchased forward rather than spot. If each dollar bought *fewer* pesos in the forward market, the peso would trade at a forward *premium* relative to the dollar.

A forward purchase or sale is a made-to-order transaction between you and the bank. It can be for any currency, any amount, and any delivery day. You could buy, say, 99,999 Vietnamese dong or 101,000 Haitian gourdes for a year and a day forward as long as you can find a bank ready to deal. There is also an organized market for currency for future delivery known as the currency *futures* market. Futures contracts are highly standardized versions of forward contracts—they exist only for the main currencies, they are for specified amounts, and the choice of delivery dates is limited. But trading is

forward exchange rate
Exchange rate for a future transaction.

---

[2] If the forward exchange rate is RUP105 = USD1, then 1 peso will cost you 1/105 = $.00952, and 100 million pesos will cost 100 million × $.00952 = $.952 million.

easy on futures exchanges—you don't have to negotiate a one-off contract with a bank. Almost everything we will say about the pricing of forward contracts applies also to futures. We will describe futures markets in greater detail in Chapter 24.

Self-Test 22.4

A skiing vacation in Switzerland costs 1,500 Swiss francs.

a. How many dollars does that represent? Use the exchange rates in Table 22.1.
b. Suppose that the dollar depreciates by 10% relative to the Swiss franc, so each dollar buys 10% fewer Swiss francs than before. What is the new indirect exchange rate?
c. If the Swiss vacation continues to cost the same number of Swiss francs, what will happen to the cost in dollars?

22.2 Some Basic Relationships

The financial manager of an international business must cope with fluctuations in exchange rates and must be aware of the distinction between spot and forward exchange rates. She must also recognize that two countries may have different interest rates. To develop a consistent international financial policy, the financial manager needs to understand how exchange rates are determined and why one country may have a lower interest rate than another.

To keep life as simple as possible, we will stick with our fictitious company doing business in Ruritania. Here are four basic questions that its financial manager needs to consider:

1. Why is the interest rate in Ruritania not the same as the rate in the United States?
2. What is the relationship between the spot exchange rate for the peso today and the expected exchange rate at some future date?
3. How do different rates of inflation in Ruritania and the United States affect each country's interest rate and the exchange rate?
4. What explains the difference between the forward exchange rate for the peso and the spot rate?

These are complex issues, but as a first cut we suggest that you think of spot and forward exchange rates, interest rates, and inflation rates as being linked as shown in Figure 22.1.

FIGURE 22.1 Some simple theories linking spot and forward exchange rates, interest rates, and inflation rates

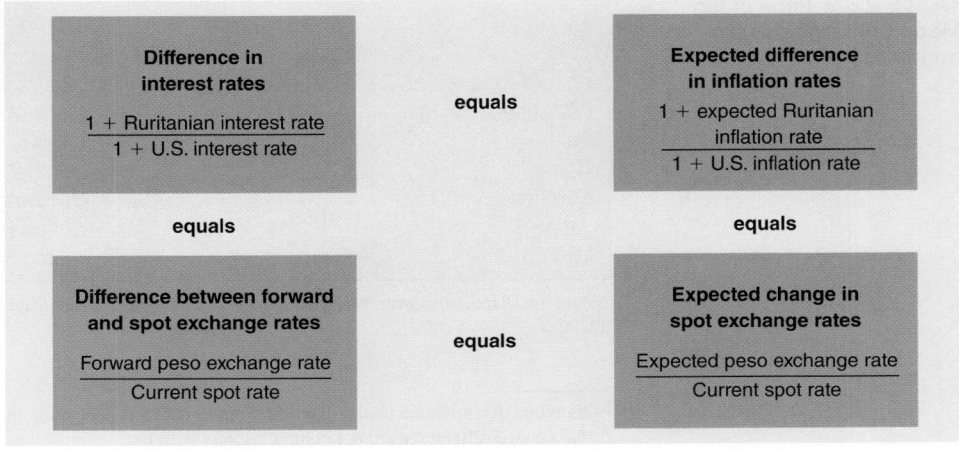

Exchange Rates and Inflation

Consider first the relationship between changes in the exchange rate and inflation rates (the two boxes on the right of Figure 22.1). The idea here is simple: If one country suffers a higher rate of inflation than another, then the value of that country's currency will decline.

But let's slow down and consider *why* changes in inflation and spot interest rates are linked. Suppose you notice that gold can be bought in New York for $1,200 an ounce and sold in Ruritania for 130,000 pesos an ounce. If there are no restrictions on the transport of gold, you could be onto a good thing. You buy gold for $1,200 and take it on the first plane to Ruritania, where you sell it for 130,000 pesos. The current exchange rate for the Ruritanian peso is RUP100 = USD1. So you can exchange your 130,000 pesos for 130,000/100 = $1,300. You have made a gross profit of $100 an ounce. Of course, you have to pay transportation and insurance costs, but there should still be something left over for you.

You returned from your trip with a surefire profit. But surefire profits rarely exist, and when they do exist, they don't last long. As others notice the disparity between the price of gold in Ruritania and the price in New York, the price will be forced down in Ruritania (or up in New York) until the profit opportunity disappears. This ensures that the dollar price of gold is the same in the two countries.

Our conclusion that gold is worth the same regardless of currency is an example of the **law of one price.** Just as the price of goods in Walmart must be roughly the same as the price of goods in Target, so the prices of goods in Ruritania when converted into dollars should be roughly the same as the prices in the United States:

$$\text{Dollar price of goods in U.S.} = \frac{\text{Peso price of goods in Ruritania}}{\text{Number of pesos per dollar}}$$

Gold is a standard and easily transportable commodity, but the same forces push the domestic and foreign prices of other goods toward equality. Those goods that can be bought more cheaply abroad will be imported, which will force down the price of the domestic product. Those goods that can be produced more cheaply at home will be exported, and that will force down the price of the foreign product.

No one who has compared prices in foreign stores with prices at home really believes that the law of one price holds exactly. Look at Table 22.2, which shows the local price of a Big Mac in different countries converted into dollars. You can see that the price varies considerably across countries. For example, in Norway Big Macs cost almost twice as much as in the United States, but in China they are around half the U.S. price.[3]

law of one price
Theory that prices of goods in all countries should be equal when translated to a common currency.

TABLE 22.2 Price of Big Mac hamburgers in different countries

Country	Local Price Converted to U.S. Dollars	Country	Local Price Converted to U.S. Dollars
Argentina	3.56	Norway	7.20
Australia	3.84	Russia	2.33
China	1.95	South Korea	2.82
Euro area	4.33	Switzerland	6.19
Japan	3.67	United Kingdom	3.48
Mexico	2.50	United States	3.73

"When the Chips Are Down: The Latest Big Mac Index Suggests the Euro Is Still Overvalued," *The Economist,* July 22, 2010.

---

[3] Of course, it could also be that Big Macs come with a bigger smile in Norway. If the quality of the hamburgers or the service differs, we are not comparing like with like.

purchasing power parity (PPP)
Theory that the cost of living in different countries is equal and that exchange rates adjust to offset inflation differentials across countries.

This suggests a possible way to make a quick buck. Why don't you buy a hamburger-to-go in China for $1.95 and take it for resale in Norway, where the price in dollars is $7.20? The answer, of course, is that the gain would not cover the costs. The law of one price works very well for commodities like gold, where transportation costs are small. It works far less well for Big Macs and also badly for haircuts and appendectomies, which cannot be transported at all.

We need a weaker version of the law of one price, a diluted law that captures the main idea but allows for exceptions. The weaker version is **purchasing power parity,** or **PPP.** PPP states that although some goods, such as Big Macs and haircuts, may cost different amounts in different countries, the overall cost of living should be similar. PPP implies that the relative costs of living in two countries will not be affected by differences in their inflation rates. Instead, different inflation rates in local currencies will be offset by changes in exchange rates.

If purchasing power parity holds, then your forecast of the difference in inflation rates is also your best forecast of the change in the spot rate of exchange. For example, suppose you need a forecast of the exchange rate for the Ruritanian peso. Purchasing power parity says that you should focus on the difference between the inflation rates in Ruritania and the United States.

The current exchange rate for the peso is RUP100 = USD1. If the cost of living is the same in Ruritania and the United States, then 100 pesos buys the same bundle of goods and services as $1. Suppose that economists are forecasting an inflation rate of 6% in Ruritania and 1% in the United States. Then at the end of 1 year 106 pesos will buy the same quantity of goods as $1.01, and $1 will have the same purchasing power as RUP100 × (1.06/1.01) = RUP105. Purchasing power parity implies that the expected exchange rate at the end of the year is RUP105 = USD1. Since inflation is expected to be higher in Ruritania, the peso is forecast to depreciate.

Look back at the two right-hand boxes in Figure 22.1. We can now fill in those boxes for the Ruritanian peso:[4]

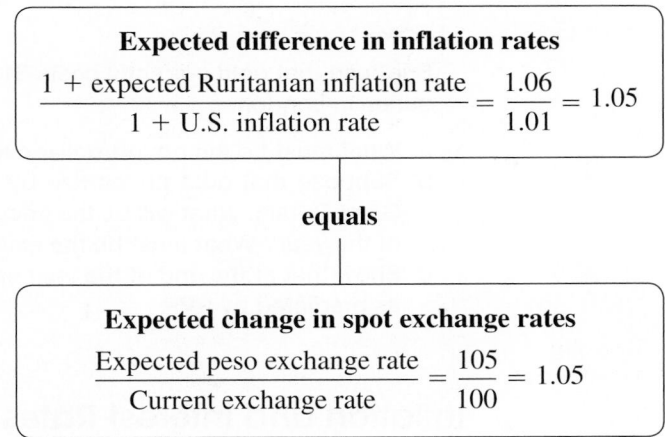

Now we have some helpful advice for the U.S. company doing business in Ruritania. If the financial manager needs to forecast the future spot exchange rate for Ruritanian pesos, he or she can use the difference in expected inflation rates in Ruritania versus in the United States.

---

[4] A warning: Notice that the relationships in Figure 22.1 all apply to *indirect* exchange rates, i.e., foreign currency per dollar. Remember that the pound/U.S. dollar and euro/U.S. dollar exchange rates are conventionally expressed as direct rates. To use our formulas for euros and pounds, you must first convert the quoted rates to indirect rates.

Real and Nominal Exchange Rates

Financial managers distinguish nominal exchange rates from real exchange rates. *Nominal exchange rates* tell you how many euros or yen or pounds you can buy for your dollar. *Real exchange rates* measure the quantity of goods you can buy for that dollar in Europe or Japan or the United Kingdom. For example, if the value of the Ruritanian peso declines, you will be able to purchase more pesos for your dollar, but if Ruritania experiences higher inflation, those pesos may buy you only the same amount of goods. In this case the *nominal* exchange rate has declined but the *real* exchange rate is unchanged. Purchasing power parity theory implies that any change in the nominal exchange rate will be offset by a change in the relative price of goods in the two countries, leaving the real exchange rate unaffected.

Figure 22.2 plots the nominal and real exchange rates since 1900 in three countries. For example, the first plot shows that in 2010 one pound (£1) bought only 33% of the dollars that it did a century earlier. But this decline in the nominal value of the pound was offset by the higher inflation rate in the United Kingdom. The plot shows that just over a century later the inflation-adjusted, or real, exchange rate was little changed. The plots for France and Italy tell a similar story.

Of course, purchasing power parity theory is not the whole truth, and in the short term real exchange rates do change, sometimes quite sharply. For example, the real value of the pound fell by more than one-quarter between the end of 2007 and the end of 2008. U.S. tourists to Britain found that their dollar bought more than it had in earlier years. Such changes in real exchange rates can be a major headache for anyone making short-term currency forecasts. But if you are a financial manager called on to make a long-term forecast of an exchange rate, you probably can't do much better than to assume that changes in the nominal value of the currency will offset the difference in inflation rates. That is the message of purchasing power parity theory.

Self-Test 22.5

Suppose that gold currently costs $1,000 an ounce in New York and £600 an ounce in London.

a. What must be the pound/dollar exchange rate?
b. Suppose that gold prices rise by 2% in the United States and by 5% in Great Britain. What will be the price of gold in the two currencies at the end of the year? What must be the exchange rate at the end of the year?
c. Show that at the end of the year each dollar buys about 3% more pounds, as predicted by PPP.

Inflation and Interest Rates

Suppose that a bank deposit earns interest of 3% in the United States and 8.1% in Ruritania. What might explain such a difference?

We can start by looking back to Chapter 5, where we distinguished nominal and real rates of interest. Bank deposits promise you a fixed nominal rate of interest, but they don't promise what that money will buy. If you invest $100 for a year at an interest rate of 3%, you will have 3% more dollars at the end of the year than you did at the start. But you may not be 3% better off. Some of the gain would be needed to compensate for inflation.

In our example, the nominal rate of interest is higher in Ruritania than in the United States, but if the inflation rate is also higher, then the real rates of interest may be much closer than the nominal rates. For example, suppose that the expected inflation rate is 1% in the United States and 6% in Ruritania. Then

FIGURE 22.2 Nominal versus real exchange rates in (a) the United Kingdom, (b) France, and (c) Italy. December 1899 = 1. (Values are shown on log scale.)

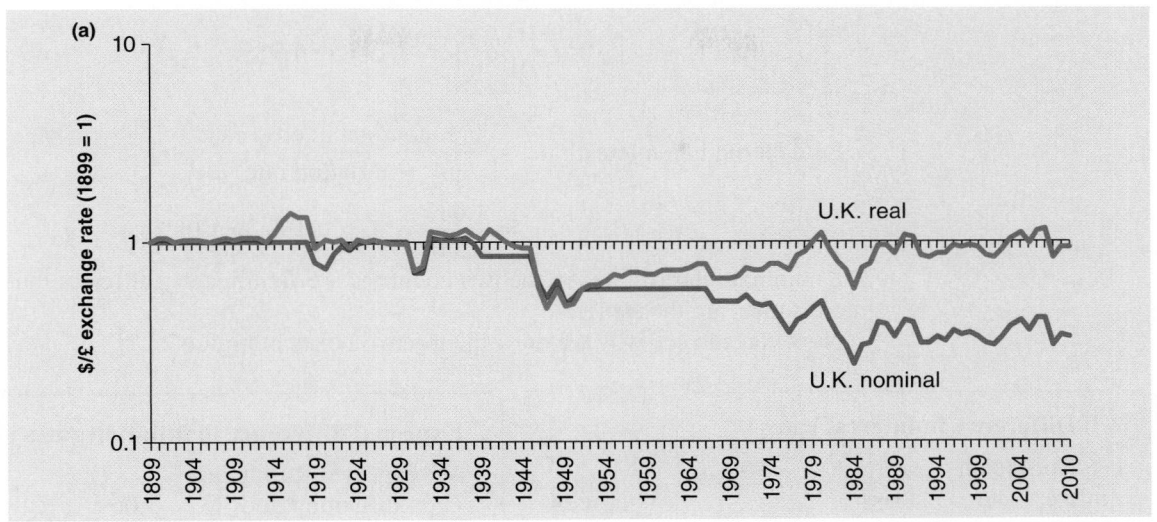

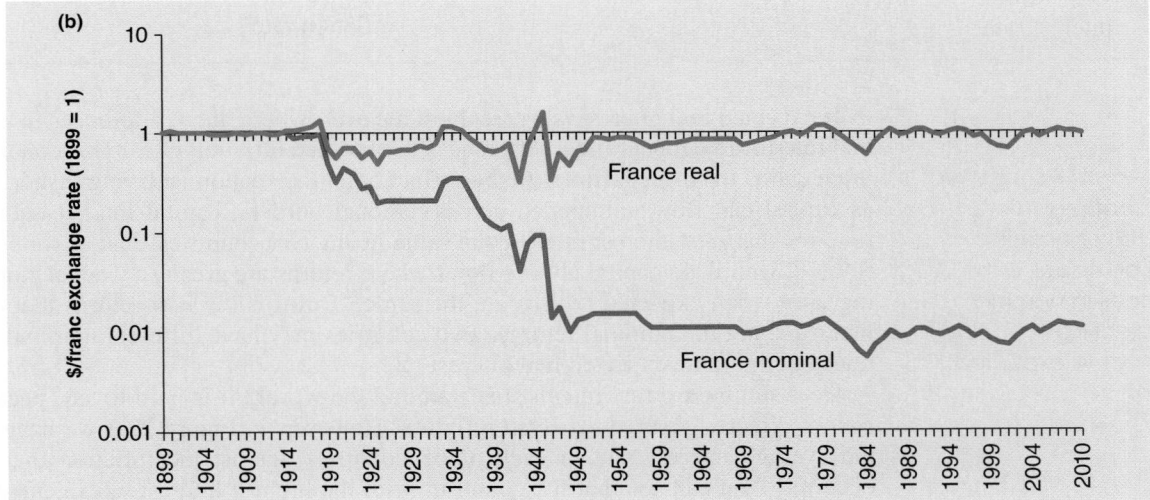

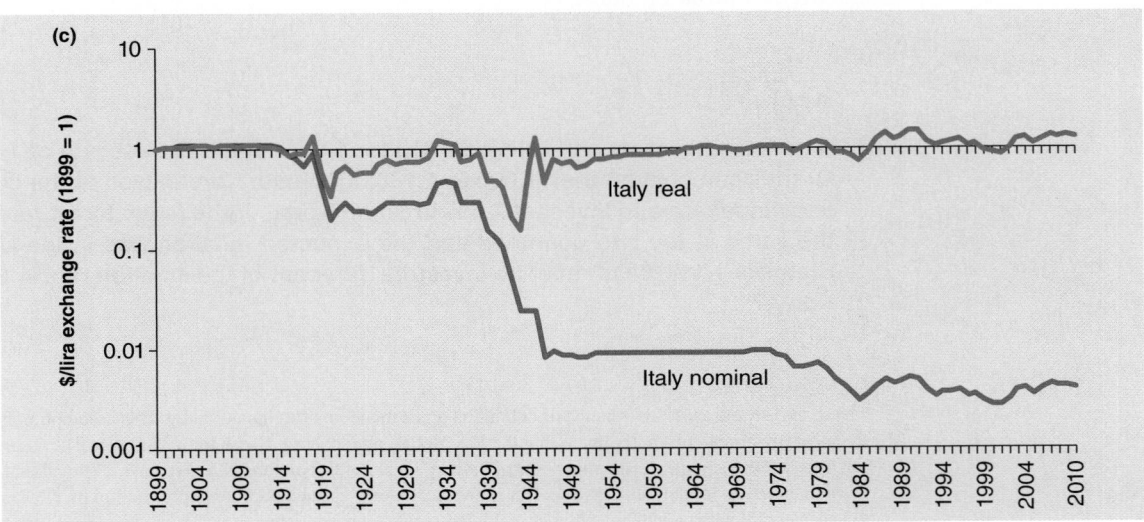

Source: E. Dimson, P. R. Marsh, and M. Staunton, *Triumph of the Optimists: 101 Years of Global Investment Returns* (Princeton, NJ: Princeton University Press, 2002) Updates courtesy of *Triumph's* authors.

$$\text{Real U.S. interest rate} = \frac{1 + \text{nominal interest rate}}{1 + \text{inflation rate}} - 1$$

$$= \frac{1.03}{1.01} - 1 = .0198, \text{ or } 1.98\%$$

and

$$\text{Real Ruritanian interest rate} = \frac{1 + \text{nominal interest rate}}{1 + \text{inflation rate}} - 1$$

$$= \frac{1.081}{1.06} - 1 = .0198, \text{ or } 1.98\%$$

The nominal interest rates in the two countries are significantly different, but the real interest rates are the same.

Now you can see why we drew the top two boxes in Figure 22.1:

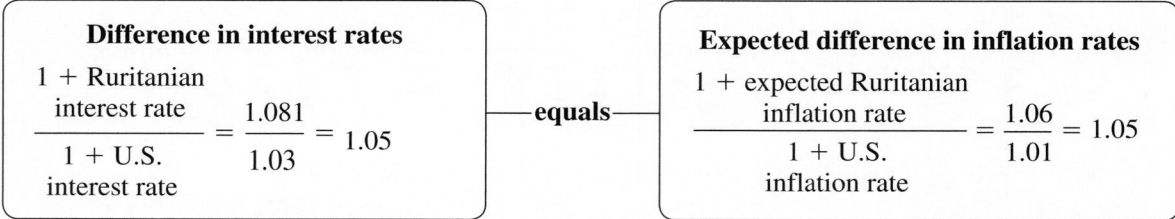

If expected real interest rates are the same everywhere, then differences in the nominal interest rate must reflect differences in expected inflation rates. This conclusion is often called the **international Fisher effect,** after the economist Irving Fisher. As long as capital can flow unimpeded across national borders, capital market equilibrium requires that *real* interest rates be the same in any two countries. Just as water always flows downhill, so capital always flows where returns are greatest. Capital stops flowing only when expected returns are the same.[5] But it is the *real* returns that concern investors, not the nominal returns. Two countries may have different nominal interest rates but the same expected real interest rate.

international Fisher effect Theory that real interest rates in all countries should be equal, with differences in nominal rates reflecting differences in expected inflation.

How similar are real interest rates around the world? It is hard to say, because we cannot directly observe *expected* inflation. However, in Figure 22.3 we have plotted the average interest rate in each of 65 countries against the inflation that in fact occurred. You can see that the countries with the highest interest rates generally had the highest inflation rates.

Self-Test 22.6

American investors can invest $1,000 for 1 year at an interest rate of 1.25%. Or they can convert the $1,000 to 1,160,000 South Korean won at the current exchange rate and invest at 2.6% in South Korea. If the real interest rates are the same in the two countries and the expected inflation rate in the United States is 1.1%, what must be investors' forecast of the inflation rate in South Korea?

---

[5] Here we assume away any chance of default on loans made in a foreign currency. This assumption is fine for the most important currencies, including the U.S. dollar, pound, euro, Swiss franc, and yen. The assumption is not acceptable for some developing countries where local politics are unstable. We have assumed that loans in Ruritanian pesos are default-risk-free. But if investors worry about default or expropriation by the Ruritanian government, they may demand a higher real interest rate on peso loans.

FIGURE 22.3 Countries with the highest interest rates generally have the highest inflation. In this diagram each of the 65 points represents the experience of a different country.

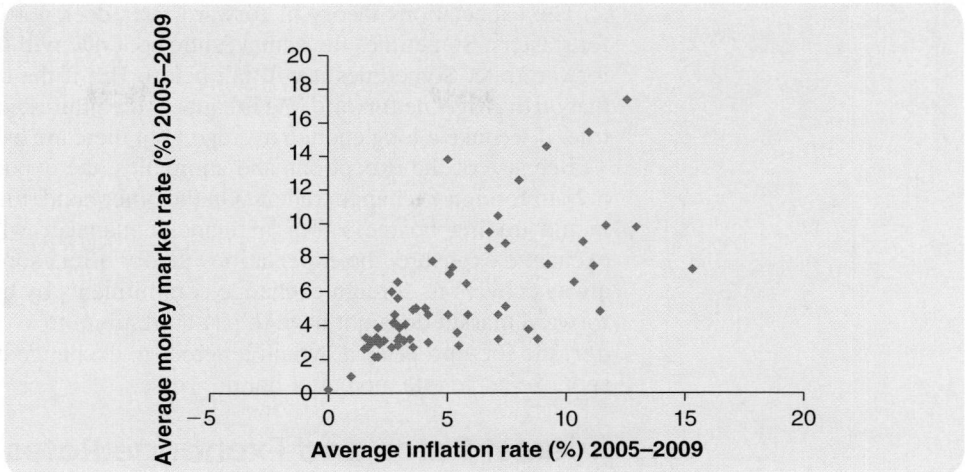

The Forward Exchange Rate and the Expected Spot Rate

If you buy Ruritanian pesos forward, you get more pesos for your U.S. dollar than if you buy them spot. So the peso is selling at a forward discount. Now let us think how this discount may be related to expected changes in spot rates of exchange.

The spot rate for the peso is RUP100 = USD1, and the 1-year forward rate is RUP105 = USD1. Would you sell pesos forward if you expected them to rise in value? Probably not. You would be tempted to wait until the end of the year and get a better price (more pesos) in the spot market. If other traders felt the same way, nobody would sell pesos forward. Everybody would want to buy, so the number of pesos that you could get for your dollar in the forward market would fall. On the other hand, if traders expected the peso to fall sharply in value, they might be reluctant to *buy* forward and, in order to attract buyers, the number of pesos that you could buy for a U.S. dollar in the forward market would need to rise.[6] Trading would stabilize when the forward rate adjusts to equal the expected future spot rate.

This is the reasoning behind the **expectations theory of exchange rates,** which predicts that the forward rate equals the expected future spot exchange rate. Put another way, we can say that the *percentage* difference between the forward rate and today's spot rate is equal to the expected *percentage* change in the spot rate:

This is the third leg of our quadrilateral in Figure 22.1.

expectations theory of exchange rates
Theory that expected spot exchange rate equals the forward rate.

Difference between forward and spot exchange rates	**Expected change in spot exchange rate**
$\dfrac{\text{Forward peso exchange rate}}{\text{Current spot rate}} = \dfrac{105}{100} = 1.05$	$\dfrac{\text{Expected peso exchange rate}}{\text{Current spot rate}} = \dfrac{105}{100} = 1.05$

—equals—

---

[6] This reasoning ignores risk. If a forward purchase reduces your risk sufficiently, you *might* be prepared to buy forward even if you expected to pay more as a result. Similarly, if a forward sale reduces risk, you *might* be prepared to sell forward even if you expected to receive less as a result.

The expectations theory of forward rates does not imply that managers are perfect forecasters. Sometimes the actual future spot rate will turn out to be above the previous forward rate. Sometimes it will fall below. But if the theory is correct, we should find that *on average* the forward rate is equal to the future spot rate. This prediction is roughly true, if we take a long enough average,[7] but there are exceptions and anomalies.[8]

Because of the exceptions and anomalies, the expectations hypothesis is not much help to foreign exchange traders. On the other hand, financial managers are not usually in the trading business. For a financial manager who consistently hedges foreign exchange exposure, the expectations theory offers some reassurance. A company that always covers its foreign exchange commitments by buying or selling currency in the forward market does not have to pay a premium to avoid exchange rate risk: *On average,* the forward price at which it agrees to exchange currency will equal the eventual spot exchange rate, no better but no worse.

Interest Rates and Exchange Rates

Now let's move on to a result that does not require qualification or appeals to long-run averages: the relationship between interest rates and exchange rates, known as *covered interest rate parity,* almost always works, even in the short run.

You are an investor with $1 million to invest for 1 year. The interest rate in Ruritania is 8.1%, and in the United States it is 3%. Is it better to invest your money in Ruritania or in the United States?

The answer seems obvious: Isn't it better to earn an interest rate of 8.1% than 3%? But appearances may be deceptive. If you lend in Ruritania, you first need to convert your $1 million into pesos. When the loan is repaid at the end of the year, you need to convert your pesos back into U.S. dollars. Of course, you don't know what the exchange rate will be at the end of the year, but you can fix the future value of your pesos by selling them forward. If the forward rate of exchange is sufficiently low, you may do just as well keeping your money in the United States.

Let's check which loan is the better deal:

- *U.S. dollar loan.* The rate of interest on a U.S. dollar loan is 3%. Therefore, at the end of the year, you get $1 million × 1.03 = $1.03 million.
- *Ruritanian peso loan.* The current (spot) rate of exchange is RUP100 = USD1. Therefore, you can convert your million dollars into RUP100 million. The interest rate on a peso loan is 8.1%, so at the end of the year you will have RUP100 million × 1.081 = RUP108.1 million. You don't know what the exchange rate will be at the end of the year, but that doesn't matter. You can nail down the rate at which you convert your pesos back into U.S. dollars. The 1-year forward exchange rate is RUP105 = USD1. Therefore, by selling the pesos forward, you make sure that you will get RUP108.1/105 = $1.03 million.

Thus the two investments offer exactly the same rate of return. They have to, because they are both risk-free. If the domestic interest rate were different from the "covered" foreign rate, you would have a money machine: You could borrow in the market with the lower rate and lend in the market with the higher rate.

---

[7] It seems that companies are sometimes prepared to give up return in order to *buy* forward currency and other times they are prepared to give up return in order to *sell* forward currency. The forward rate *overstates* the likely future spot rate about half the time, and about half the time it *understates* the likely spot rate. The over- and underpredictions average out in the long run.

[8] Scholars who have studied exchange rates have found that forward rates typically exaggerate the likely change in the spot rate. When the forward rate appears to predict a sharp rise in the spot rate, the forward rate tends to overestimate the rise in the spot rate. When the forward rate appears to predict a fall, it tends to overestimate this fall. There is even evidence that, when the forward rate predicts a rise, the spot rate is more likely to fall than rise. For a readable discussion of this puzzling finding, see K. A. Froot and R. H. Thaler, "Anomalies: Foreign Exchange," *Journal of Political Economy* 4 (1990), pp. 179–192.

We now have the final leg of our quadrilateral in Figure 22.1:

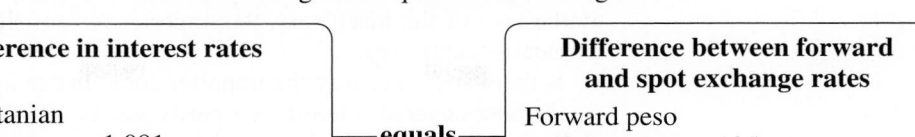

| **Difference in interest rates** | | **Difference between forward and spot exchange rates** |

$$\frac{1 + \text{Ruritanian interest rate}}{1 + \text{U.S. interest rate}} = \frac{1.081}{1.03} = 1.05 \qquad \text{—equals—} \qquad \frac{\text{Forward peso exchange rate}}{\text{Current spot rate}} = \frac{105}{100} = 1.05$$

interest rate parity
Theory that forward premium equals interest rate differential.

This link between the forward exchange rate and the difference in interest rates is called **interest rate parity.** Whereas the other relationships shown in Figure 22.1 tend to hold approximately, interest rate parity almost always holds with great precision. This should not be surprising, since there would be easy opportunities for riskless arbitrage whenever parity is violated. In fact, foreign currency dealers set the forward exchange rate by looking at the difference between the interest rates on deposits in different currencies.

Interest rate parity also holds an important lesson for managers. International capital markets and currency markets function well and offer no free lunches. You can't assume that it is cheaper to borrow in a currency with a low nominal rate of interest. If you hedge or "cover" your exchange rate exposure, interest rate parity implies that the all-in cost of borrowing will be the same in any currency.[9] If you don't cover, exchange rate movements can easily erase the apparent advantage of a low interest rate.

Interest rate parity means that covered interest rates are the same in all major currencies. A financial manager who attempts to borrow in currencies with low interest rates can profit only by taking a bet on future exchange rates.

Self-Test 22.7

By 2012 Ruritanian exchange rates had moved to RUP120 = USD1 (spot) and RUP126.92 = USD1 (1-year forward). One-year interest rates were 4% in the United States and 10% in Ruritania. Confirm covered interest rate parity.

22.3 Hedging Exchange Rate Risk

Transaction Risk

Firms with international operations are subject to exchange rate risk. As exchange rates fluctuate, the dollar value of their revenues or expenses also fluctuates. It is useful to distinguish two types of exchange rate risk: *transaction risk* and *economic risk.*

Transaction risk arises when the firm agrees to pay or receive a known amount of foreign currency. For example, our importer of machinery was committed to pay RUP100 million at the end of 12 months. If the value of the peso appreciates rapidly over this period, that machinery will cost more dollars than the importer expected.

Transaction risk is easily identified and hedged. For every peso our importer is committed to pay, she can buy 1 peso forward. If she buys RUP100 million forward, the importer fixes the entire dollar cost of the machinery and avoids the risk of an appreciation of the peso.

Of course, it is possible that the peso will *depreciate* sharply over the year,[10] in which case the importer would regret that she did not wait to buy the peso more cheaply

---

[9] A covered foreign interest rate means that you borrow or lend in a foreign currency and hedge the exchange rate risk by entering a forward currency contract. In our example, you could lend RUP100 million, which grows with 8.1% interest to RUP108.1 million. You therefore would sell RUP108.1 million forward to lock in the dollar value of your year-end proceeds.

[10] By this we mean that the peso falls by more than predicted by the forward rate.

in the spot market. Unfortunately, you cannot have your cake and eat it. By fixing the dollar cost of the machinery, the importer forfeits the chance of pleasant, as well as unpleasant, surprises.

Is there any other way the importer could hedge against exchange rate loss? Think again how covered interest rate parity works. The financial manager could borrow dollars, convert them into pesos today, put the proceeds in a Ruritanian bank deposit, and withdraw them at the end of the year to pay her bill. Interest rate parity tells us that the cost of borrowing dollars, buying pesos in the spot market, and leaving them on deposit is exactly the same as the cost of buying pesos forward.

What is the cost of protection against currency risk? You sometimes hear managers say that it is equal to the difference between the forward rate and *today's* spot rate. This is wrong. If our importer did not hedge, she would pay the spot price for pesos when the payment is due at the end of the year. Therefore, the cost of hedging is the difference between the forward rate and the expected spot rate when payment is due.

Should companies hedge, or should they just sit back and absorb currency fluctuations? We generally vote for hedging. First, it makes life simpler for the firm and allows it to concentrate on its own business. Second, it does not cost much. (In fact, the cost is zero if the forward rate equals the expected spot rate, as our simple theories imply.) Third, the foreign exchange market seems reasonably efficient, at least for the major currencies. Speculation should be a zero-sum game, barring the unlikely case where the financial manager knows more than the pros who make the foreign exchange market.

Economic Risk

Even if a firm neither owes nor is owed foreign currency, it still may be affected by currency fluctuations. Consider, for example, the competitive position of foreign auto producers such as Volkswagen and Toyota when the value of the U.S. dollar fell dramatically in 2006 and 2007. These firms faced a difficult choice between maintaining the dollar price of their product, thus accepting a reduced price in their home currency, or raising the dollar price and becoming less competitive against U.S. producers such as Ford and GM. *Economic exposure* to the exchange rate arises because exchange rate fluctuations affect competitive positions.

One solution is for the company to undertake *operational hedging* by balancing production closely with sales. For example, 38% of Ford's sales are outside North America, but so is 44% of its production. It gains protection from currency risks because its costs and revenues in different currencies are more or less balanced.

Japanese auto manufacturers have less operational hedging. For example, Toyota produces 63% of its output in Japan but only 37% is sold there. Exchange rate fluctuations are potentially a more serious risk for Toyota than for Ford. On the other hand, the Japanese auto companies operate in a wider range of markets than U.S. firms. They have therefore diversified away some of their currency risks.

Operational hedging rarely eliminates all currency risk. Think again of Toyota. It is a net exporter of autos to North America and is therefore exposed to a decline in the value of the dollar. So, in addition to its operational hedging, Toyota also mitigates exchange rate risk by using *financial hedges.* For example, it borrows large amounts in dollars rather than yen. So, if the dollar falls, the pressure on Toyota's profits is offset in part by a reduction in the number of yen needed to service the dollar debt.

Self-Test 22.8

A Ford dealer in the United States never needs to buy or sell foreign currency. Does that mean it has no currency risk? Explain.

22.4 International Capital Budgeting

Net Present Values for Foreign Investments

Exports by the soft-drink manufacturer Ecsy-Cola Corporation have risen to the point that it is considering establishing a small manufacturing and sales operation overseas in Ruritania. Ecsy-Cola's decision to invest overseas should be based on the same criteria as a decision to invest in the United States. The company needs to forecast the incremental cash flows from the project, discount the cash flows at the opportunity cost of capital, and accept those projects with a positive NPV.

Suppose Ecsy-Cola's Ruritanian facility is expected to generate the following cash flows *in Ruritanian pesos:*

	0	1	2	3	4	5
Cash flow (millions of pesos)	−380	100	125	150	175	200

The interest rate in the United States is 3%. Ecsy's financial manager estimates that the company requires an additional expected return of 10% to compensate for the risk of the project, so the opportunity cost of capital for the project is $3 + 10 = 13\%$.

Notice that Ecsy's opportunity cost of capital is stated in terms of the return on a dollar-denominated investment but the cash flows are given in pesos. A project that offers a 13% expected return in pesos could fall far short of offering the required return in dollars if the value of the peso is expected to decline. Conversely, a project that offers an expected return of less than 13% in pesos may be worthwhile if the peso is likely to appreciate.

You cannot compare the project's return measured in one currency with the return that you require from investing in another currency. If the opportunity cost of capital is measured as a dollar-denominated return, cash flows should also be forecast in dollars.

To translate the peso cash flows into dollars, Ecsy needs a forward exchange rate. Where does this come from? Forward exchange rates for longer than a year are not usually quoted in the financial press, but they can be estimated using interest rate parity. For example, suppose that the financial manager looks in the newspaper and finds that the current exchange rate is RUP100 = USD1 and that the interest rate is 3% in the United States and 8.1% in Ruritania. Thus, the manager sees right away that the peso is likely to sell at a forward discount of 5% a year. For example, the 1-year forward rate is

$$\text{Forward rate for year 1} = \text{Spot rate in year 0} \times \frac{1 + \text{peso interest rate}}{1 + \text{dollar interest rate}}$$

$$= \text{RUP100/USD1} \times \frac{1.081}{1.03} = \text{RUP104.95/USD1}$$

The implied forward exchange rates for each year of the project are calculated similarly, as follows:[11]

Year	Forward Exchange Rate (RUP per USD)
1	$100 \times (1.081/1.03) = \text{RUP104.95/USD1}$
2	$100 \times (1.081/1.03)^2 = \text{RUP110.15/USD1}$
3	$100 \times (1.081/1.03)^3 = \text{RUP115.60/USD1}$
4	$100 \times (1.081/1.03)^4 = \text{RUP121.33/USD1}$
5	$100 \times (1.081/1.03)^5 = \text{RUP127.33/USD1}$

---

[11] We assume that the 3% and 8.1% interest rates are the same for longer maturities.

The financial manager can use these forward exchange rates to convert the peso cash flows into dollars:

Year:	0	1	2	3	4	5
Cash flow (millions of pesos)	−380	100	125	150	175	200
Forward exchange rate (pesos to the dollar)	100	104.95	110.15	115.60	121.33	127.33
Cash flow (millions of dollars)	−3.8	.9528	1.1348	1.2976	1.4424	1.5707

Now the manager discounts these dollar cash flows at the 13% dollar cost of capital:

$$NPV = -3.8 + \frac{.9528}{1.13} + \frac{1.1348}{1.13^2} + \frac{1.2976}{1.13^3} + \frac{1.4424}{1.13^4} + \frac{1.5707}{1.13^5}$$

$$= \$.568 \text{ million, or } \$568{,}000$$

Notice that the manager discounted cash flows at 13%, not at the U.S. risk-free interest rate of 3%. The cash flows are risky, so a risk-adjusted interest rate is appropriate. The positive NPV tells the manager that the project is worth undertaking; it increases shareholder wealth by $568,000.

Notice also that the firm does *not* have to forecast the future peso/dollar exchange rate to translate its peso cash flows into dollar equivalents. It instead uses the forward exchange rates implied by the interest rate differential in the two countries. No currency forecast is needed, because the company can hedge its foreign exchange exposure.

If it does hedge, for example, by selling pesos forward, then its peso cash flows will be brought back into dollars at the forward exchange rates implied by the interest rate differential. In other words, the firm can, if it chooses, nail down the dollar cash flows that we have just calculated. The decision to accept or reject the project therefore is separate from the firm's particular view about the future exchange rate.

What if the management actually expects the peso to appreciate rather than depreciate? Should it use its own forecasts of the future exchange rate instead of the forward exchange rates implied by interest rate parity? No! For a project to be attractive, it must be able to stand on its own, based on *hedged* cash flows. It would be foolish for a firm to accept a poor project just because it forecasts exchange rate appreciation. If management is confident in its predictions of future exchange rates, it would be better to speculate on the currency directly rather than use a negative-NPV project to gain exposure to the currency. (Of course, before it speculates, management ought to think very carefully about why it believes its exchange rate forecast is superior to the market's. After all, Ecsy's comparative advantage is presumably in manufacturing fizzy drinks, not in exchange rate speculation.)

Self-Test 22.9

Suppose that the nominal interest rate in Ruritania is 6% rather than 8.1%. The spot exchange rate is still RUP100 = USD1, and the expected peso cash flows on Ecsy's project are also the same as before.

a. What do you deduce about the likely difference in the inflation rates in Ruritania and the United States?

b. Would you now be able to buy more or fewer pesos in the forward market than when the peso interest rate was 8.1%?

c. Do you think that the NPV of Ecsy's project will now be higher or lower than the figure we calculated above? Check your answer by calculating NPV under this new assumption.

Political Risk

So far we have focused on the management of exchange rate risk, but managers also worry about *political risk*. They worry that a government will change the rules of the game, breaking a promise or an understanding, after the investment is made. Of course, political risks are not confined to overseas investments. Businesses in every country are exposed to the risk of unanticipated actions by governments. But in some parts of the world foreign companies are particularly vulnerable.

Consultancy services offer analyses of political and economic risks and draw up country rankings.[12] For example, Table 22.3 is an extract from the January 2010 political risk rankings provided by the PRS Group. Each country is scored on 12 dimensions and a total score is calculated. Finland comes top of the class overall, while Somalia languishes at the bottom.

Some managers dismiss political risk as an act of God, like a hurricane or earthquake. But the most successful multinational companies structure their business to reduce political risk. Foreign governments are not likely to expropriate a local business if it cannot operate without the support of its parent. For example, the foreign subsidiaries of American computer software or pharmaceutical companies would have relatively little value if they were cut off from the know-how of their parents. Such operations are much less likely to be expropriated than, say, a mining operation that can be operated as a stand-alone venture.

We are not recommending that you turn your silver mine into a pharmaceutical company, but you may be able to plan your overseas manufacturing operations to improve your bargaining position with foreign governments. For example, Ford has integrated its overseas operations so that the manufacture of components, subassemblies, and complete automobiles is spread across plants in a number of countries. None of these plants would have much value on its own, and Ford can switch production between plants if the political climate in one country deteriorates.

TABLE 22.3 Political risk scores for a sample of countries - January 2010

	Total
Maximum score	100
COUNTRY	
Finland	92.0
Australia	88.5
Switzerland	86.0
Germany	85.5
United States	82.5
Japan	82.0
France	79.5
United Kingdom	76.5
Brazil	68.5
China, Peoples' Rep.	65.5
Russia	64.5
India	63.5
Pakistan	44.5
Somalia	24.5

Source: PRS Group, "International Country Risk Guide, July 2007," **www.prsgroup.com**.

---

[12] For a discussion of these services, see C. Erb, C. R. Harvey, and T. Viskanta, "Political Risk, Financial Risk, and Economic Risk," *Financial Analysts Journal* 52 (1996), pp. 28–46. Campbell Harvey's Web page (**www.duke.edu/~charvey**) is also a useful source of information on political risk.

Multinational corporations have also devised financing arrangements to help keep foreign governments honest. For example, suppose your firm is contemplating an investment of $500 million to reopen the San Tomé silver mine in Costaguana with modern machinery, smelting equipment, and shipping facilities.[13] The Costaguanan government agrees to invest in roads and other infrastructure and to take 20% of the silver produced by the mine in lieu of taxes. The agreement is to run for 25 years.

The project's NPV on these assumptions is quite attractive. But what happens if a new government comes into power 5 years from now and imposes a 50% tax on "any precious metals exported from the Republic of Costaguana"? Or changes the government's share of output from 20% to 50%? Or simply takes over the mine "with fair compensation to be determined in due course by the Minister of Natural Resources of the Republic of Costaguana"?

No contract can absolutely restrain sovereign power. But you can arrange project financing to make these acts as painful as possible for the foreign government. For example, you might set up the mine as a subsidiary corporation, which then borrows a large fraction of the required investment from a consortium of major international banks. If your firm guarantees the loan, make sure the guarantee stands only if the Costaguanan government honors its contract. The government will be reluctant to break the contract if doing so causes a default on the loans and undercuts the country's credit standing with the international banking system.

The Cost of Capital for Foreign Investment

We did not say how Ecsy-Cola arrived at a 13% dollar discount rate for its Ruritanian project. That depends on the risk of overseas investment and the reward that investors require for taking this risk. Unfortunately, there is no tidy theory of risk and return in an international context.[14]

Remember that the risk of an investment cannot be considered in isolation; it depends on the securities that the investor holds in his or her portfolio. For example, suppose Ecsy-Cola's shareholders invest mainly in companies that do business in the United States. They could view the Ruritanian market, though volatile, as driven by different forces and therefore a diversifiable risk. If the correlation between the Ruritanian and U.S. markets is relatively low, an investment in the Ruritanian soft-drink business would appear to be a relatively low-risk project to Ecsy-Cola's shareholders. That would not be true of a Ruritanian company, whose shareholders are already exposed to the fortunes of the Ruritanian market.[15]

Avoiding Fudge Factors

We don't pretend that we can put an absolutely precise figure on the cost of capital for foreign investment. But we disagree with the practice of *automatically* increasing the domestic cost of capital when foreign investment is considered.

Some financial managers automatically mark up the required return for foreign investment because it is more costly to manage an operation in a foreign country and

---

[13] The early history of the San Tomé mine is described in Joseph Conrad's *Nostromo*.

[14] Why is there no tidy theory? One fundamental reason is that economists have never been able to agree on what makes one country different from another. Is it just that they have different currencies? Or is it that their citizens have different tastes and consume different things? Or is it that they are subject to different regulations and taxes? The answers to these questions affect the relationship among security prices in different countries.

[15] One can imagine an integrated world in which all investors diversify worldwide, regardless of their domiciles. In this ideal case, U.S. and Ruritanian investors would view the risks of Ecsy-Cola's investment identically. But in reality investors' portfolios are strongly weighted toward their home countries. This weighting is called a "home bias." We do not yet have an integrated world capital market.

because they worry about the risks of expropriation, foreign exchange restrictions, or unfavorable tax changes. In other words, they add a fudge factor to the discount rate to offset these costs and risks.

Those managers should leave the discount rate alone and reduce expected cash flows instead. For example, let's go back to Ecsy-Cola's cash-flow forecast of 100 million Ruritanian pesos in year 1. Now the company gets word of a proposed 100 million peso "incorporation fee" to be imposed in "the first year of operations for all new foreign investments." The odds that the fee will be imposed are judged at 5%.

Now the *expected* cash flow for year 1 is not 100 million pesos but .95 × 100 million = 95 million pesos. Ecsy should recalculate NPV using this forecast. It should make similar cash-flow adjustments for possible political risks in later years.

Adjusting cash flows brings management's assumptions about political risks out in the open for scrutiny and sensitivity analysis. There may be some discount rate fudge factor that gives the correct NPV, but financial managers have no practical way of knowing what the fudge factor is until the cash flows are adjusted and NPV is recalculated. Once the adjusted NPV is in hand, the fudge factor is not needed.

SUMMARY

What is the difference between spot and forward exchange rates? *(LO1)*

The **exchange rate** is the amount of one currency needed to purchase one unit of another currency. The **spot rate of exchange** is the exchange rate for an immediate transaction. The **forward rate** is the exchange rate for a forward transaction, that is, a transaction at a specified future date.

What are the basic relationships between spot exchange rates, forward exchange rates, interest rates, and inflation rates? *(LO2)*

To produce order out of chaos, the international financial manager needs some model of the relationships between exchange rates, interest rates, and inflation rates. Four very simple theories prove useful:

- In its strict form, **purchasing power parity** states that $1 must have the same purchasing power in every country. You only need to take a vacation abroad to know that this doesn't square well with all the facts. Nevertheless, *on average*, changes in exchange rates tend to match differences in inflation rates and, if you need a long-term forecast of the exchange rate, it is difficult to do much better than to assume that the exchange rate will offset the effect of any differences in the inflation rates.
- In an open world capital market *real* rates of interest would have to be the same. Thus differences in *nominal* interest rates result from differences in expected inflation rates. This **international Fisher effect** suggests that firms should not simply borrow where interest rates are lowest. Those countries are also likely to have the lowest inflation rates and the strongest currencies.
- The **expectations theory of exchange rates** tells us that the forward rate equals the expected spot rate (though it is very far from being a perfect forecaster of the spot rate).
- **Interest rate parity theory** states that the interest differential between two countries must be equal to the difference between the forward and spot exchange rates. In the international markets, arbitrage ensures that parity almost always holds.

What are some simple strategies to protect the firm against exchange rate risk? *(LO3)*

Our simple theories about forward rates have two practical implications for the problem of hedging overseas operations. First, the expectations theory suggests that hedging exchange risk is on average costless. Second, there are two ways to hedge against exchange risk: One is to buy or sell currency forward; the other is to lend or borrow abroad. Interest rate parity tells us that the cost of the two methods should be the same.

How do we perform an NPV analysis for projects with cash flows in foreign currencies? *(LO4)*

Overseas investment decisions are no different in principle from domestic decisions. You need to forecast the project's cash flows and then discount them at the opportunity cost of capital. But it is important to remember that if the opportunity cost of capital is stated in dollars, the cash flows must also be converted to dollars. This requires a forecast of foreign exchange rates. We suggest that you rely on the simple parity relationships and use the interest rate differential to produce these forecasts.

QUESTIONS

QUIZ

1. **Exchange Rates.** Use Table 22.1 to answer the following questions. *(LO1)*
   a. How many euros can you buy for $100? How many dollars can you buy for 100 euros?
   b. How many Swiss francs can you buy for $100? How many dollars can you buy for 100 Swiss francs?
   c. If the British pound depreciates with respect to the dollar, will the exchange rate quoted in Table 22.1 increase or decrease?
   d. Is a United States or a Canadian dollar worth more?

2. **Exchange Rate Relationships.** Look at Table 22.1. *(LO2)*
   a. How many Brazilian reals do you get for your dollar?
   b. If the 1-year forward rate on the real is BRL1.834 = USD1, is the real at a forward discount or premium?
   c. If the 1-year interest rate on dollars is 1%, what do you think is the interest rate on the real?
   d. According to the expectations theory, what is the expected spot rate for the real in 1 year's time?
   e. According to purchasing power parity, what is the difference in the expected rate of price inflation in the United States and the rate in Brazil?

3. **Exchange Rate Relationships.** Define each of the following theories in a sentence or simple equation. *(LO2)*
   a. Interest rate parity theory.
   b. Expectations theory of forward rates.
   c. Law of one price.
   d. International Fisher effect (relationship between interest rates in different countries).

4. **Purchasing Power Parity.** The following table shows the local prices of a Grande Latte coffee in Starbucks in 2009: *(LO2)*

	Price of Coffee	Exchange Rate
U.K.	GBP2.35	USD1.60 = GBP1
Japan	JPY420	JPY91 = USD1
Canada	CAD3.75	CAD1.08 = USD1
China	CNY28	CNY6.83 = USD1
U.S.	USD3.75	

Source: **blogs.reuters.com**, September 25, 2009.

   a. Calculate the dollar price of a latte in each city. Does purchasing power parity hold?
   b. What would the local price of a latte need to be in each city to ensure that the cost was the same as in New York? In each case state whether the currency would need to appreciate or depreciate to equalize the prices.

5. **Foreign Currency Management.** Rosetta Stone, the treasurer of International Reprints, Inc., has noticed that the interest rate in Japan is below the rates in most other countries. She is therefore suggesting that the company should make an issue of Japanese yen bonds. What considerations ought she first take into account? *(LO3)*

6. **Hedging Exchange Rate Risk.** An importer in the United States is due to take delivery of silk scarves from Europe in 6 months. The price is fixed in euros. Which of the following transactions could eliminate the importer's exchange risk? *(LO3)*

   a. Buy euros forward.

   b. Sell euros forward.

   c. Borrow euros, buy dollars at the spot exchange rate.

   d. Sell euros at the spot exchange rate, lend dollars.

PRACTICE PROBLEMS

7. **Currency Risk.** Sanyo produces audio and video consumer goods and exports a large fraction of its output to the United States under its own name and the Fisher brand name. It prices its products in yen, meaning that it seeks to maintain a fixed price in terms of yen. Suppose the yen moves from JPY85.66 = USD1 to JPY82.00 = USD1. What currency risk does Sanyo face? How can it reduce its exposure? *(LO3)*

8. **Managing Exchange Rate Risk.** A firm in the United States is due to receive payment of 1 million Australian dollars in 8 years' time. It would like to protect itself against a decline in the value of the Australian dollar but finds it difficult to arrange a forward sale for such a long period. Is there any other way that it can protect itself? *(LO3)*

9. **Expectations Theory.** If the basic relationships in Section 22.1 hold, then what will be the relationship between the expected change in the Ruritanian/dollar exchange rate and the interest rates in the United States and Ruritania? Suppose that you were confident that the exchange rate would not change over the coming year. Does this open up a profit opportunity? *(LO2)*

10. **Exchange Rate Risk.** An American investor buys 100 shares of London Enterprises at a price of £50 when the exchange rate is USD2 = GBP1. A year later the shares are selling at £52. No dividends have been paid. *(LO3)*

   a. What is the rate of return to an American investor if the exchange rate is still USD2 = GBP1?

   b. What if the exchange rate is USD2.20 = GBP1?

   c. What if the exchange rate is USD1.80 = GBP1?

11. **Interest Rate Parity.** Look at Table 22.1. If the 3-month forward exchange rate is USD1.55 = GBP1 and the 3-month interest rate on dollars is 3.5% (effective annual rate), what do you think is the 3-month sterling (U.K.) interest rate? Explain what would happen if the rate were substantially above your figure. (*Hint:* In your calculations remember to convert the annually compounded interest rate into a rate for 3 months.) *(LO2)*

12. **Expectations Theory.** In 2010 many investors borrowed money in countries such as the United States and Japan, where interest rates were low, and invested the money in countries such as Australia and South Africa, where rates were high. This is called a "carry trade." What is the risk in these carry trades? Could you eliminate this risk by entering into a forward exchange contract and still make money? Explain. *(LO2)*

13. **Interest Rate Parity.** Suppose the interest rate on 1-year loans in the United States is 3% while in the United Kingdom the interest rate is 5%. The spot exchange rate is USD1.67 = GBP1 and the 1-year forward rate is USD1.64 = GBP1. In what country would you choose to borrow? To lend? Can you profit from this situation? *(LO2)*

14. **Purchasing Power Parity.** Suppose that the inflation rate in the United States is 4% and in Canada it is 5%. What would you expect is happening to the exchange rate between the United States and Canadian dollars? *(LO2)*

15. **Cross Rates.** Look at Table 22.1. How many Mexican pesos can you buy for $1? How many yen can you buy? What rate do you think a Japanese bank would quote for buying or selling Mexican pesos? Explain what would happen if it quoted a rate that was substantially less than your figure. *(LO1)*

16. **International Capital Budgeting.** Suppose that you do use your own views about exchange rates when valuing an overseas investment proposal. Specifically, suppose that you believe that the peso will depreciate by 2% per year. Recalculate the NPV of Ecsy's project. *(LO4)*

17. **Currency Risk.** You have bid for a possible export order that would provide a cash inflow of €1 million in 6 months. The spot exchange rate is USD1.30 = EUR1, and the 1-year forward rate is USD1.28 = EUR1. There are two sources of uncertainty: (1) The euro could appreciate or depreciate, and (2) you may or may not receive the export order. Illustrate in each case the profits or losses that you would make if you sell €1 million forward by filling in the following table. Assume that the exchange rate in 1 year will be either USD1.20 = EUR1 or USD1.40 = EUR1. *(LO3)*

	Total Profit/Loss	
Spot Rate	**Receive Order**	**Lose Order**
USD1.20 = EUR1	_____	_____
USD1.40 = EUR1	_____	_____

18. **Managing Currency Risk.** General Gadget Corp. (GGC) is a U.S.-based multinational firm that makes electrical coconut scrapers. These gadgets are made only in the United States using local inputs. The scrapers are sold mainly to Asian and West Indian countries where coconuts are grown. *(LO3)*

    a. If GGC sells scrapers in Trinidad, what is the currency risk faced by the firm?
    b. In what currency should GGC borrow funds to pay for its investment in order to mitigate its foreign exchange exposure?
    c. Suppose that GGC begins manufacturing its products in Trinidad using local (Trinidadian) inputs and labor. How does this affect its exchange rate risk?

19. **Currency Risk.** The following table shows a breakdown of sales and costs for four Swiss companies. Swatch produces watches; Lindt & Sprüngli, chocolate; Nestlé, food; and Roche, pharmaceuticals. Discuss the currency exposure that comes from each of their operations. Which company do you think would be most affected by an increase in the value of the dollar? What about an increase in the value of the euro? *(LO3)*

	Percentage of total sales or costs in the United States and the Euro area			
	U.S. sales	**U.S. costs**	**Euro-area sales**	**Euro-area costs**
Swatch Group	8%	2%	25%	10%
Lindt & Sprüngli	23	14	58	67
Nestlé	27	27	27	27
Roche	45	35	35	10

CHALLENGE PROBLEMS

20. **International Capital Budgeting.** An American firm is evaluating an investment in Mexico. The project costs 500 million pesos, and it is expected to produce an income of 250 million pesos a year in real terms for each of the next 3 years. The expected inflation rate in Mexico is 4% a year, and the firm estimates that an appropriate discount rate for the project would be about 8% above the risk-free rate of interest. Calculate the net present value of the project in U.S. dollars. Exchange rates are given in Table 22.1. The interest rate is about 4.5% in Mexico and 1.5% in the United States. *(LO4)*

21. **Currency Risk.** The current exchange rate is USD2 = GBP1. Cookham Industries is a large British firm that exports computer games to the United States. If the dollar depreciates relative to the pound, Cookham will increase the dollar price it charges its U.S. customers. But it cannot raise its U.S. price enough to fully offset any dollar depreciation because if it does so, it will lose customers to its U.S. competitors. Its rule of thumb is that for every 10-cent increase in the exchange rate (e.g., from USD2 = GBP1 to USD2.10 = GBP1) it will increase prices by $5 (e.g., from $200 to $205 per game). Given this rule, it will lose only some of its U.S. sales. Suppose its forecast of annual sales in the United States as a function of the dollar price is

$$\text{Quantity sold} = 1,000,000 - 100 \times \text{price in dollars}$$

Answer the questions below. *(LO3)*

a. Plot the British pound value of Cookham's revenue from its U.S. sales as a function of the exchange rate for exchange rates ranging from USD1.50 = GBP1 to USD3.00 = GBP1. What is its exchange rate exposure?

b. Suppose each exchange rate scenario in part (a) is equally likely. What would Cookham's expected dollar revenue be? What would be its pound revenue in each scenario if it sold forward that number of U.S. dollars at a forward exchange rate of USD2 = GBP1? Does this seem like an effective hedge?

WEB EXERCISES

1. There are plenty of good sites that show current and past spot rates of exchange. You can even add a currency converter to your Google home page. Forward rates are less easy to come by, but the Bank of England Web site gives spot and forward rates for the pound (we suggest that you download the forward rate itself rather than the forward premium). Can you deduce from these whether the interest rate is higher in the United States than in the United Kingdom? *Warning:* Look out for the difference between direct and indirect quotes.

2. Log on to www.prsgroup.com, and get a free sample of the *International Country Risk Guide.* For which characteristics does the United States score well? For which does it score badly? Is Finland still close to top of the class?

SOLUTIONS TO SELF-TEST QUESTIONS

22.1 Direct quote: USD1.30440 = EUR1
Indirect quote: 1/1.3044, or EUR.7666 = USD1
Indirect quote: JPY85.66 = USD1
Direct quote: 1/85.66, or USD.0117 = JPY1

22.2 One Hong Kong dollar is worth 12.8344/7.7634 = 1.6532 Mexican pesos (and one peso is worth 7.7634/12.8344 = .6049 Hong Kong dollars). If a bank quotes 1.75 pesos per Hong Kong dollar, you could take one U.S. dollar, buy 7.7634 Hong Kong dollars, and then exchange the Hong Kong dollars for 7.7634 × 1.75 = 13.586 pesos. Then you could change the pesos back into 13.586/12.8344 = 1.0586 U.S. dollars. The profit is $.0586.

22.3 The dollar buys fewer Swiss francs, so the franc has appreciated with respect to the dollar.

22.4 a. 1,500/1.0094 = $1,486.
b. Indirect exchange rate: $1 = .9 × 1.0094 = .9085 francs.
c. 1,500/.9085 = $1,651. The dollar price increases.

22.5 a. Since the gold price must be the same in the two countries, GBP600 = USD1,000. Therefore GBP.6 = USD1. The direct quote would be 1/.6 = USD1.667 = GBP1.0.
b. In the United States, price = $1,000 × 1.02 = $1,020. In Great Britain, price = £600 × 1.05 = £630. The new exchange rate is, therefore, USD1,020 = GBP630, or USD1.619 = GBP1.
c. Initially $1 buys 1/1.667 = £.6. At the end of the year, $1 buys 1/1.619 = £.6177, which is 3% higher than the original value of £.6.

22.6 The real interest rate in the United States is 1.0125/1.011 − 1 = .0015, or 0.15%. If the real rate is the same in South Korea, then expected inflation must be (1 + nominal rate)/(1 + real rate) − 1 = 1.026/1.0015 − 1 = .0245, or 2.45%.

22.7 Suppose you want Ruritanian pesos next year. You can put $1 aside, earn interest at 4%, and buy pesos at the forward price of 126.92. You end up with 1 × 1.04 × 126.92 = 132 pesos. As the alternative, you can buy 120 pesos at spot and earn 10% in Ruritania. You end up in exactly the same place, with 120 × 1.1 = 132 pesos.

22.8   If the euro or the yen depreciates against the dollar, then foreign cars are likely to become cheaper. The Ford dealer therefore has economic risk even though it never needs to buy or sell foreign currency.

22.9   a.   If real interest rates are the same in the two countries, the difference in the inflation rates is now $1.06/1.03 - 1 = .0291$, or 2.91%.

   b.   Less. For example, the 1-year forward rate should now be $(1.06/1.03) \times 100$, or RUP102.91 = USD1. A dollar now buys fewer pesos in the forward market than before (or, equivalently, each peso is now worth more dollars in the forward market).

   c.   The peso cash inflows from Ecsy's project can now be exchanged for more dollars. So net present value increases:

Year:	0	1	2	3	4	5
Cash flow (millions of pesos)	−380	100	125	150	175	200
Forward exchange rate (pesos to the dollar)	100	102.91	105.91	108.99	112.17	115.44
Cash flow (millions of dollars)	−3.8	.9717	1.1802	1.3762	1.5601	1.7326
PV at 13%	−3.8	.8599	.9243	.9538	.9569	.9404

NPV = $.835 million

MINICASE

"Jumping jackasses! Not another one!" groaned George Luger. It was a memo from the CEO of DVR Importers dated December 31, 2007. It was the third memo from the CEO that he had received that day. It read as follows:

> From: CEO's Office
>
> To: Company Treasurer
>
> George,
>
> I have been looking at some of our foreign exchange deals and they don't seem to make sense.
>
> First, we have been buying yen forward to cover the cost of our imports. You have explained that this insures us against the risk that the dollar may depreciate over the next year, but it is incredibly expensive insurance. Each dollar buys only 108.173 yen when we buy forward, compared with the current spot rate of 111.715 yen to the dollar. We could save a fortune by buying yen as and when we need them rather than buying them forward.
>
> Another possibility has occurred to me. If we are worried that the dollar may depreciate (or do I mean "appreciate"?), why don't we buy yen at the low spot rate of ¥111.715 to the dollar and then put them on deposit until we have to pay for the DVRs? That way we can make sure that we get a good rate for our yen.
>
> I am also worried that we are missing out on some cheap financing. We are paying about 6% to borrow dollars for one year, but Ben Hur was telling me at lunch that we could get a one-year yen loan for about 2%. I find that a bit surprising, but if that's the case, why don't we repay our dollar loans and borrow yen instead?
>
> Perhaps we could discuss these ideas at next Wednesday's meeting. I would be interested in your views on the matter.
>
> Jill Edison

How should George respond to Jill's memo? For example,

1. Is the forward purchase of the yen "incredibly expensive insurance?"

2. Would the company be better if it purchased yen and "then put them on deposit?"

3. Should the company "repay its dollar loans and borrow yen instead?"

CHAPTER 23

Options

LEARNING OBJECTIVES

After studying this chapter, you should be able to:

(1) Calculate the payoff to buyers and sellers of call and put options.

(2) Understand the determinants of option values.

(3) Recognize options in capital investment proposals.

(4) Identify options that are provided in financial securities.

RELATED WEB SITES FOR THIS CHAPTER CAN BE FOUND AT WWW.MHHE.COM/BMM7E.

Just another day on the options exchange. But why does the financial manager of an industrial company need to understand options?

When the Chicago Board Options Exchange (CBOE) was established in 1973, few observers guessed what a success it would be. Today the CBOE and its younger rival, the International Securities Exchange (ISE), each trade options to buy or sell over 60 billion shares of stock a year. In addition to trading options on individual stocks, you can now trade options on stock indexes, bonds, commodities, and foreign exchange.

You will see that options can be valuable tools for managing the risk characteristics of an investment portfolio. But why should the financial manager of an industrial company read further? There are several reasons. First, most capital budgeting projects have options embedded in them that allow the company to expand at a future date or to bail out. These options enable the company to profit if things go well but give downside protection when they don't.

Second, many of the securities that firms issue include an option. For example, companies often issue convertible bonds. The holder has the option to exchange the bond for common stock. Some corporate bonds also contain a call provision, meaning that the issuer has the option to buy back the bond from the investor.

Finally, managers routinely use currency, commodity, and interest rate options to protect the firm against a variety of risks. (We will have more to say about this in Chapter 24.)

In one chapter we can provide you with only a brief introduction to options. Our first goal is to explain how options work and how option value is determined. Then we will tell you how to recognize some of the options that crop up in capital investment proposals and in company financing.

23.1 Calls and Puts

call option
Right to buy an asset at a specified exercise price on or before the expiration date.

A **call option** gives its holder the right to buy stock for a fixed *exercise price* (also called the *strike price*) on or before a specified expiration date.[1] For example, if you buy a call option on Google stock with an expiration date in January and an exercise price of $460, you have the right to buy the stock at a price of $460 any time until January.

You need not exercise a call option; it will be profitable to do so only if the share price exceeds the exercise price. If it does not, the option will be left unexercised and will be valueless. But suppose that when the option expires, Google shares are selling above the exercise price, say, at $520. In this case you will choose to exercise your option to pay $460 for shares worth $520. Your payoff will equal the difference between the $520 for which you can sell the shares and the $460 that you pay when you exercise the option. More generally, when the stock price is greater than the exercise price, the payoff from your call option is equal to the difference between the stock price and the exercise price.

In summary, the value of the call option at expiration is as follows:

Stock Price at Expiration	Value of Call at Expiration
Greater than exercise price	Stock price − exercise price
Less than exercise price	Zero

Of course, that payoff is not all profit: You have to pay for the option. The price of the call is known as the option *premium*. Option buyers pay the premium for the right to exercise later. Your *profit* equals the ultimate payoff to the call option (which may be zero) minus the initial premium.

EXAMPLE 23.1 ▶ Call Options on Google

In July 2010 a call option on Google stock with a January 2011 expiration and an exercise price of $460 sold for $42.50. If you bought this call, you gained the right to purchase Google shares for $460 at any time until the option expired the following January. The price of Google stock in July was $460. If the stock price did not rise by January, the call would not be worth exercising and you would lose your investment of $42.50. On the other hand, even a relatively modest rise in the stock price could give you a rich profit on your option. For example, if Google sold for $520 in January, the proceeds from exercising the call would be

$$\text{Proceeds} = \text{stock price} - \text{exercise price} = \$520 - \$460 = \$60$$

and the net profit on the call would be

$$\text{Profit} = \text{Proceeds} - \text{original investment} = \$60 - \$42.50 = \$17.50$$

In 6 months, you would have earned a return of $17.50/$42.50 = .41, or 41%.

---

put option
Right to sell an asset at a specified exercise price on or before the expiration date.

Whereas a call option gives you the right to buy a share of stock, a **put option** gives you the right to *sell* it for the exercise price. If you own a put on a share of stock and the stock price turns out to be greater than the exercise price, you will not want to exercise your option to sell the shares for the exercise price. The put will be left unexercised and will expire valueless. But if the stock price turns out to be less than the exercise price, it will pay to buy the share in the market at the low price and then exercise your option to sell it for the exercise price. The put would then be worth the difference between the exercise price and the stock price.

---

[1] In some cases, the option can be exercised only on one particular day, and it is then conventionally known as a *European call;* in other cases, it can be exercised on or before that day, and it is known as an *American call.*

| EXAMPLE 23.2 | ▶ | Put Options on Google |

In July 2010 it cost $41 to buy a put option on Google stock with a January 2011 expiration and an exercise price of $460. Suppose that Google is selling for $400 when the put option expires. Then if you hold the put, you can buy a share of stock in the market for $400 and exercise your right to sell it for $460. The put will be worth $460 − $400 = $60. Because you paid $41 for the put originally, your net profit is $60 − $41 = $19. As a put buyer, your worry is that the stock price will rise above the $460 exercise price. If that happens, you will let the put option expire worthless and you will lose the $41 that you originally paid for it.

In general, the value of the put option at expiration is as follows:

Stock Price at Expiration	Value of Put at Expiration
Greater than exercise price	Zero
Less than exercise price	Exercise price − stock price

Table 23.1 shows how the values of Google calls and puts are affected by the level of the stock price on the expiration date. You can see that once the stock price is above the exercise price, the call value rises dollar for dollar with the stock price, and once the stock price is below the exercise price, the put value rises a dollar for each dollar *decrease* in the stock price. Figure 23.1 plots the values of each option on the expiration date.

Table 23.2 shows the prices of nine options on Google stock in July 2010. Notice that for any particular expiration date, call options are worth more when the exercise price is lower, while puts are worth more when the exercise price is higher. This makes sense: You would rather have the right to buy at a low price and the right to sell at a high price. Notice also that for any particular exercise price the longer-dated options are the most valuable. This also makes sense. An option that expires in January 2012 gives you everything that a shorter-dated option offers and more. Naturally, you would be prepared to pay for the chance to keep your options open for as long as possible.

Self-Test 23.1

a. What will be the proceeds and net profits (i.e., net of the option premium) to an investor who purchases the September-expiration Google call options with exercise price of $490 if the stock price at expiration is $400? What if the stock price at expiration is $550? Use the data in Table 23.2.

b. Now answer part (a) for an investor who purchases a September-expiration Google put option with exercise price $490.

Selling Calls and Puts

The traded options that you see quoted in the financial pages are not sold by the companies themselves but by other investors. If one investor buys an option on Google

TABLE 23.1 **How the value of a Google option on its expiration date varies with the price of the stock on that date (exercise price = $460)**

Stock Price:	$400	$430	$460	$490	$520
Call value	0	0	0	$30	$60
Put value	$60	$30	0	0	0

FIGURE 23.1 Values of call options and put options on Google stock on option expiration date (exercise price = $460)

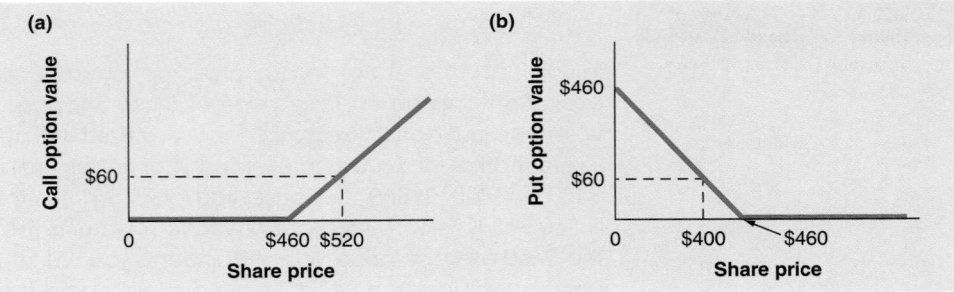

stock, some other investor must be on the other side of the bargain. We will look now at the position of the investor who sells an option.[2]

We have already seen that the Google calls that expire in January 2011 with an exercise price of $460 are trading at $42.50. Thus if you *sell* the January call option on Google stock, the buyer pays you $42.50. However, in return you promise to sell Google shares at a price of $460 to the call buyer if he decides to exercise his option. The option seller's obligation to *sell* Google is just the other side of the coin to the option holder's right to *buy* the stock. The buyer pays the option premium for the right to exercise; the seller *receives* the premium but may be required at a later date to deliver the stock for an exercise price that is less than the market price of the stock. If the share price is below the exercise price of $460 when the option expires in January, holders of the call will not exercise their option and you, the seller, will have no further liability. However, if the price of Google is greater than $460, it will pay the buyer to exercise and you must give up your shares for $460 each. You lose the difference between the share price and the $460 that you receive from the buyer.

Suppose that Google's stock price turns out to be $520. In this case the buyer will exercise the call option and will pay $460 for stock that can be resold for $520. The buyer therefore has a payoff of $60. Of course, that positive payoff for the buyer means a negative payoff for you the seller, for you are obliged to deliver Google stock worth $520 for only $460. This $60 loss more than wipes out the $42.50 that you were originally paid for selling the option.

In general, the seller's loss is the buyer's gain, and vice versa. Figure 23.2a shows the payoffs to the call option seller. Note that this figure is just Figure 23.1a drawn upside down.

The position of an investor who sells the Google put option can be shown in just the same way by standing Figure 23.1b on its head. The put *buyer* has the right to sell a share for $460; so the *seller* of the put has agreed to pay $460 for the share if the put buyer should demand it. Clearly the seller will be safe as long as the share price

TABLE 23.2 Examples of options on Google shares in July 2010 when Google stock was selling for $460

Expiration Date	Exercise Price	Call Price	Put Price
September 2010	$430	$41.20	$11.05
	460	22.50	22.20
	490	10.10	39.36
January 2011	430	65.98	27.20
	460	42.50	41.00
	490	28.80	51.60
January 2012	430	96.00	56.10
	460	80.00	69.80
	490	68.00	84.20

---

[2] The option seller is known as the *writer.*

FIGURE 23.2 Payoffs to sellers of call and put options on Google stock (exercise price = $460)

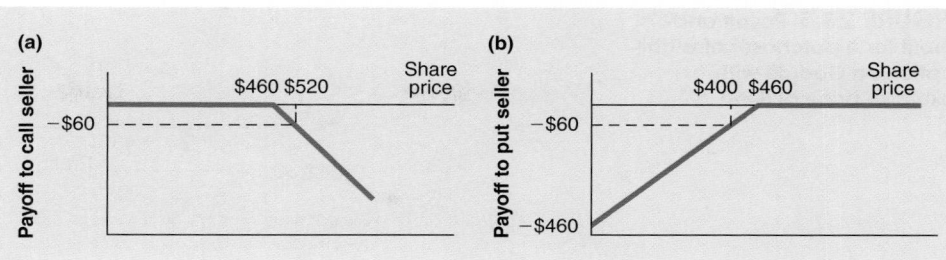

remains above $460 but his payoff will be negative if the share price falls below this figure. The worst thing that can happen to the put seller is for the stock to be worthless. The seller would then be obliged to pay $460 for a worthless stock. The payoff to the seller would be −$460. Note that the advantage always lies with the option buyer, and the obligation lies with the seller. Therefore, the buyer must pay the seller to acquire the option.

Table 23.3 summarizes the rights and obligation of buyers and sellers of calls and puts.

Self-Test 23.2

a. What will be the proceeds and net profits to an investor who sells the September-expiration Google call options with exercise price of $490 if the stock price at expiration is $460? What if the stock price at expiration is $520? Use the data in Table 23.2.

b. Now answer part (a) for an investor who sells a September-expiration Google put option with exercise price $490.

Payoff Diagrams Are Not Profit Diagrams

Figures 23.1 and 23.2 show only the possible *payoffs* when the option expires; they do not account for the initial cost of buying the option or the initial proceeds from selling it.

This is a common point of confusion. For example, the payoff diagram in Figure 23.1a makes purchase of a call look like a sure thing—the payoff is at worst zero, with plenty of upside if Google's stock price goes above $460 by January 2011. But compare this with the *profit diagram* in Figure 23.3, which subtracts the $42.50 cost of the call in July 2010 from the payoff at expiration. The call buyer loses money at all share prices less than $460 + $42.50 = $502.50.

Take another example: The payoff diagram in Figure 23.2b makes selling a put look like a sure loser—the *best* payoff is zero. But the profit diagram in Figure 23.4, which recognizes the $41 received by the seller, shows that the seller gains at all prices above $460 − $41 = $419.

Profit diagrams like those in Figures 23.3 and 23.4 may be helpful to the options beginner, but options experts rarely draw them. Now that you've graduated from the first options class, we won't draw them either. We will stick to payoff diagrams, because you have to focus on payoffs at expiration to understand options and to value them properly.

TABLE 23.3 Rights and obligations of various option positions

	Buyer	Seller
Call option	Right to buy asset	Obligation to sell asset
Put option	Right to sell asset	Obligation to buy asset

FIGURE 23.3 Payoff and profit for a purchaser of a call option on Google with exercise price of $460

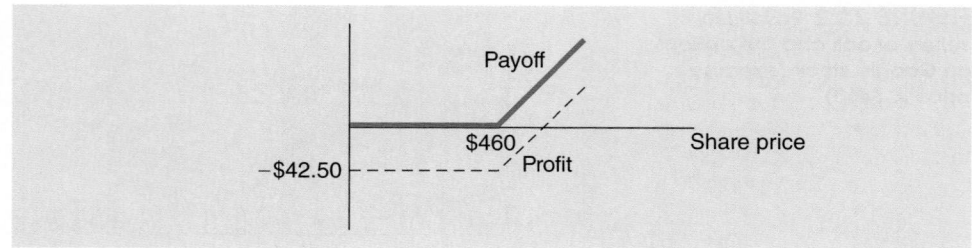

FIGURE 23.3 Payoff and profit for a purchaser of a call option on Google with exercise price of $460

Financial Alchemy with Options

Options can be used to modify the risk characteristics of a portfolio. Suppose, for example, that you are generally optimistic about Google's prospects but you perceive enough risk that a large investment in the stock would cause you sleepless nights. Here is a strategy that might appeal to you: Buy the stock, but also buy a put option on the stock with exercise price $460. If the stock price rises from its current level of $460, your put turns out to be worthless but you win on your investment in the stock. If the stock price falls, your losses are limited, since the put gives you the right to sell your stock for the $460 exercise price. Thus the value of your stock-plus-put position cannot be less than $460.

Here is another way to view your overall position. You hold the stock and the put option. The ultimate value of each component of the portfolio is as follows:

	Stock Price < $460	Stock Price ≥ $460
Value of stock	Stock price	Stock price
Value of put option	$460 − stock price	0
Total value	$460	Stock price

No matter how far the stock price falls, the total value of your portfolio cannot fall below the $460 exercise price.

The value of your position when the option expires is graphed in Figure 23.5. You have downside protection at $460, but still share in any increase in the stock price. This strategy is called a *protective put,* because the put option gives protection against losses. Of course, such protection is not free. Look again at Table 23.2 and you will find the cost of such protection. "Stock price insurance" at a level of $460 between July 2010 and January 2011 cost $41 per share; this was the price of a put option with exercise price $460 and January expiration.

Some More Option Magic

Look again at Figure 23.5, which shows the possible payoffs at expiration from holding both a share of Google stock and a put option to sell it for $460. Does this picture look somewhat familiar? It should. Turn back to panel *a* of Figure 23.2, which shows

FIGURE 23.4 Payoff and profit for a seller of a put option on Google with exercise price of $460

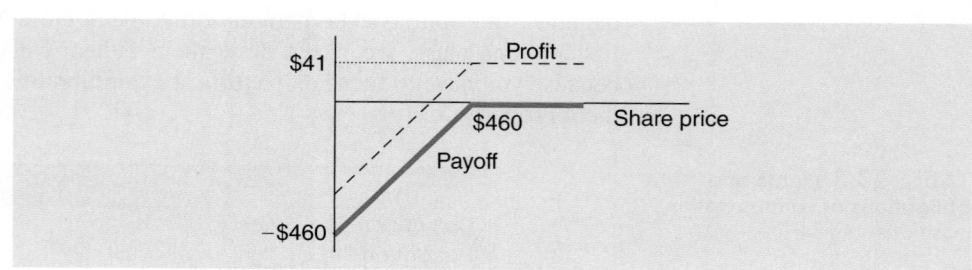

FIGURE 23.5 Payoff to protective put strategy. If the ultimate stock price exceeds $460, the put is valueless but you own the stock. If it is less than $460, you can sell the stock for the exercise price.

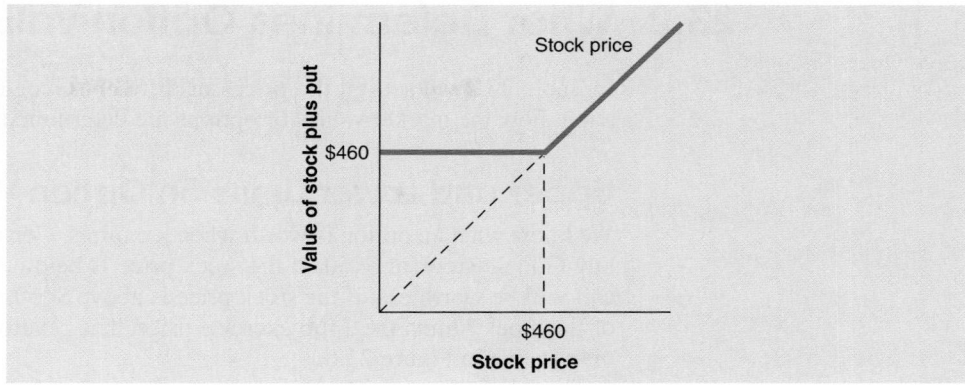

the payoffs from holding a call option on Google stock with an exercise price of $460. The only difference between the two sets of payoffs is that the combination of the stock and put option always provides exactly $460 more than the call option. In other words, regardless of the final stock price, holding the stock plus a put option gives the same payoff as an alternative strategy of buying a call option plus investing the present value of $460 in a bank deposit.

Think what happens if you follow this second strategy. If the stock price is below $460 when the option expires, your call option will be valueless but you will still have $460 in the bank. On the other hand, if the stock price rises above $460, you will take your money out of the bank, use it to exercise the call, and own the stock. The following table confirms that this second investment package gives you exactly the same payoffs as you get from holding the stock and a put option:

	Payoffs at Expiration	
	Stock price < $460	Stock price > $460
Call option	0	Stock price − $460
Bank deposit paying $460	$460	$460
Total value	$460	Stock price

If you plan to hold each of these packages until the options expire, the packages must sell for the same price today. This gives us a fundamental relationship between the value of a call and the value of a put:[3]

Value of stock + value of put = value of call + present value of exercise price

This basic relationship between share price, call and put values, and the present value of the exercise price is called *put-call parity.*

Self-Test 23.3

A 1-year *call* option on Witterman stock with an exercise price of $60 costs $8.05. The stock price is $55 and the interest rate on a bank deposit is 4%. What is the value of a 1-year *put* option on Witterman with an exercise price of $60?

---

[3] This relationship assumes that the two options have the same exercise price and expiration date. Note that the present value of the exercise price is simply the amount that you would need to set aside in a bank deposit in order to receive the exercise price at expiration.

23.2 What Determines Option Values?

In Table 23.2 we set out the prices of different Google options. But we said nothing about how the market values of options are determined. It is time that we did so.

Upper and Lower Limits on Option Values

We know what an option is worth when it expires. Consider, for example, the option to buy Google stock at $460. If the stock price is below $460 at the expiration date, the call will be worthless; if the stock price is above $460, the call will be worth the value of the stock minus the $460 exercise price. The relationship is depicted by the heavy orange line in Figure 23.6.

Even before expiration, the price of the option can never remain *below* the heavy orange line in Figure 23.6. For example, if our option were priced at $20 and the stock at $520, it would pay any investor to buy the option, exercise it for an additional $460, and then sell the stock for $520. That would give a "money machine" with a profit of $520 − ($20 + $460) = $40. Money machines can't last. The demand for options from investors using this strategy would quickly force the option price up at least to the heavy orange line in the figure. The heavy orange line is therefore a lower limit on the market price of the option. Thus

$$\text{Lower limit on value of call option} = \text{the greater of } zero \text{ or } (stock\ price - exercise\ price)$$

The diagonal blue line in Figure 23.6, which is the plot of the stock price, is the *upper* limit to the option price. Why? Because the stock itself gives a higher final payoff whatever happens. If when the option expires the stock price ends up above the exercise price, the option is worth the stock price *less* the exercise price. If the stock price ends up below the exercise price, the option is worthless but the stock's owner still has a valuable security. Thus the extra payoff to holding the stock rather than the option is as follows:

Stock Price at Expiration	Stock Payoff	Option Payoff	Extra Payoff from Holding Stock rather than Option
Greater than $460	Stock price	Stock price − $460	$460
Less than or equal to $460	Stock price	$0	Stock price

The Determinants of Option Value

The option price must lie between the upper and lower limits in Figure 23.6. In fact, the price will lie on a curved, upward-sloping line like the dashed curve shown in the figure. This line begins its travels where the upper and lower bounds meet (at zero). Then it rises, gradually becoming parallel to the lower bound. This line tells us an important fact about option values: Given the exercise price, *the value of a call option increases as the stock price increases.*

That should be no surprise. Owners of call options are clearly happy when the stock price is much higher than the exercise price and are willing to pay more for options that are "in the money." If you look back at the prices of the Google options, you will see that the price of the call is higher when the stock price is above the exercise price. But let us look more carefully at the shape and location of the dashed line. Three points, A, B, and C, are marked on the dashed line. As we explain

FIGURE 23.6 Value of a call before its expiration date (dashed line). The value depends on the stock price. The call is always worth more than its value if exercised now (heavy orange line). It is never worth more than the stock price itself (blue line).

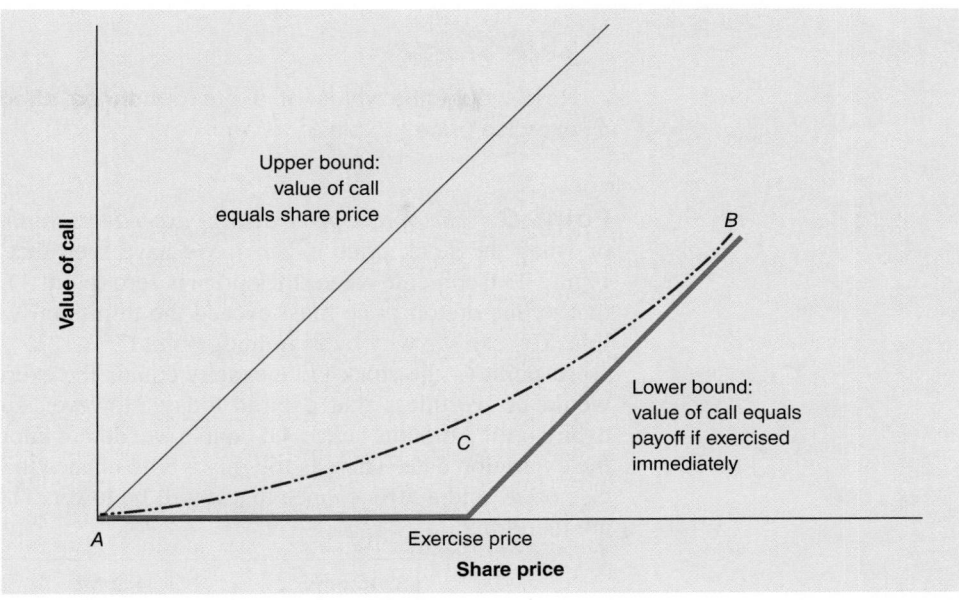

each point, you will see why the option price has to behave as the dashed line predicts.

Point A   *When the stock is worthless, the option is worthless.* A stock price of zero means that there is no possibility the stock will ever have any future value.[4] If so, the option is sure to expire unexercised and worthless, and it is worthless today.

Point B   *When the stock price becomes very high, the option price approaches the stock price less the present value of the exercise price.* Notice that the dashed line representing the option price in Figure 23.6 eventually becomes parallel to the ascending heavy orange line representing the lower bound on the option price. The reason is as follows: The higher the stock price, the greater the odds that the option will eventually be exercised. If the stock price is high enough, exercise becomes a virtual certainty; the probability that the stock price will fall below the exercise price before the option expires becomes trivial.

If you own an option that you know will be exchanged for a share of stock, you effectively own the stock now. The only difference is that you don't have to pay for the stock (by handing over the exercise price) until later, when formal exercise occurs. In these circumstances, buying the call is equivalent to buying the stock now with deferred payment and delivery. The value of the call is therefore equal to the stock price less the present value of the exercise price.[5]

This brings us to another important point about options. Investors who acquire stock by way of a call option are buying on "installment credit." They pay the purchase price of the option today, but they do not pay the exercise price until they actually exercise the option. The delay in payment is particularly valuable if interest rates are high and the option has a long maturity. Thus *the value of a call option increases with both the rate of interest and the time to expiration.*

---

[4] If a stock can be worth something in the future, then investors will pay *something* for it today, although possibly a very small amount.

[5] We assume here that the stock pays no dividends until after the option expires. If dividends were paid, you *would* care about when you get to own the stock because the option holder misses out on any dividends.

Self-Test 23.4

How would the value of a put option be affected by an increase in the exercise price? Explain.

Point C *The option price always exceeds its minimum value* (except at expiration or when the stock price is zero). We have seen that the dashed and heavy lines in Figure 23.6 coincide when stock price is zero (point *A*), but elsewhere the lines diverge; that is, the option price must exceed the minimum value given by the heavy orange line. You can see why by examining point *C*.

At point *C*, the stock price exactly equals the exercise price. The option therefore would be worthless if it expired today. However, suppose that the option will not expire until 3 months hence. Of course, we do not know what the stock price will be at the expiration date. There is roughly a 50% chance that it will be higher than the exercise price, and a 50% chance that it will be lower. The possible payoffs to the option are therefore:

Outcome	Payoff
Stock price rises (50% probability)	Stock price − exercise price (option is exercised)
Stock price falls (50% probability)	Zero (option expires worthless)

If there is some chance of a positive payoff, and if the worst payoff is zero, then the option must be valuable. That means the option price at point *C* exceeds its lower bound, which at point *C* is zero. In general, the option price will exceed the lower bound as long as there is time left before expiration.

One of the most important determinants of the *height* of the dashed curve (that is, of the difference between actual and lower-bound value) is the likelihood of substantial movements in the stock price. An option on a stock whose price is unlikely to change by more than 1% or 2% is not worth much; an option on a stock whose price may halve or double is very valuable.

For example, suppose that a call option has an exercise price of $460 and the stock price will be either $400 or $520 when the option expires. The possible payoffs to the option are as follows:

Stock price at expiration	$400	$520
Call value at expiration	0	$ 60

Now suppose that the value of the stock when the option expires can be $340 or $580. The *average* of the possible stock prices is the same as before, but the volatility is greater. In this case the payoffs to the call are:

Stock price at expiration	$340	$580
Call value at expiration	0	$120

A comparison of the two cases highlights the valuable asymmetry that options offer. If the stock price turns out to be below the exercise price when the option expires, the option is valueless regardless of whether the shortfall is a cent or a dollar. However, the option holder reaps all the benefits of stock price advances. Thus in our example the option is worth only $60 if the stock price reaches $520, but it is worth $120 if the stock price rises to $580. Therefore, volatility helps the option holder.

TABLE 23.4 What the price of a call option depends on

If the following variables increase, . . .	. . . the value of a call option will
Stock price	Increase
Exercise price	Decrease
Interest rate	Increase
Time to expiration	Increase
Volatility of stock price	Increase

The probability of large stock price changes during the remaining life of an option depends on two things: (1) the variability of the stock price *per unit of time* and (2) the length of time until the option expires. Other things equal, you would like to hold an option on a volatile stock. Given volatility, you would like to hold an option with a long life ahead of it, since that longer life means that there is more opportunity for the stock price to change. The value of an option increases with both the variability of the share price and the time to expiration.

It's a rare person who can keep all these properties straight at first reading. Therefore, we have summed them up in Table 23.4.

Self-Test 23.5

Rework our numerical example for a put option with an exercise price of $460. Show that put options also are more valuable when the stock price is more volatile.

Option-Valuation Models

If you want to value an option, you need to go beyond the qualitative statements of Table 23.4; you need an exact option-valuation model—a formula that you can plug numbers into and come up with a figure for option value.

Valuing complex options is a high-tech business and well beyond the scope of this book. Our aim here is not to make you into instant option whizzes, but we can illustrate the basics of option valuation by walking you through an example. The trick to option valuation is to find a combination of borrowing and an investment in the stock that exactly replicates the option. The nearby box illustrates a simple version of one of these option-valuation models.

This model achieves simplicity by assuming that the share price can take on only two values at the expiration date of the option. This assumption is clearly unrealistic, but it turns out that the same approach can be generalized to allow for a large number of possible future share prices rather than just the two values in our example.

In 1973 Fischer Black, Myron Scholes, and Robert Merton came up with a formula which showed that even when share prices are changing continuously, you can still replicate an option by a series of levered investments in the stock. The Black-Scholes formula is regularly used by option traders, investment bankers, and financial managers to value a wide variety of options. Scholes and Merton shared the 1997 Nobel Prize in economics for their work on the development of this formula.[6] The box on page 657 shows you how to set up a Black-Scholes calculator in Excel.

Today, there are many ever-more-sophisticated variants on the Black-Scholes formula that can better capture some aspect of real-life markets. As computer power continues to increase, these models can be made more complex and increasingly accurate.

---

[6] Fischer Black passed away in 1995.

A Simple Option-Valuation Model

It is July 2010, and you are contemplating the purchase of a call option on Google stock. The call has a January 2011 expiration date and an exercise price of $460. Google's stock price is also currently $460, so the option will be valueless unless the stock price appreciates over the next 6 months. The outlook for Google is uncertain, and all you know is that at the end of the 6 months the price will either fall by one-quarter to $345 or rise by one-third to $613.33. Finally, the rate of interest on a bank loan at this time is about 1.5% for 6 months.

The following table depicts the outlook for three alternative investments:

Google Stock		Call Option		Bank Loan	
July	January	July	January	July	January
$460<	$613.33	?<	$153.33	$100<	$101.50
	$345		$0		$101.50

The first investment is Google stock. Its current price is $460, but the price could rise to $613.33 or fall to $345. The second investment is the call option. When the call expires in January, the option will be valueless if the stock price falls to $345, and it will be worth $613.33 − $460 = $153.33 if the stock price rises to $613.33. We don't know (yet) what the call is worth today, so for the time being we put a question mark against the July value. Our third investment is a bank loan at an interest rate of 1.5% for 6 months. The payoff on the $100 bank loan is $101.50 no matter what happens to the price of Google stock.

Consider now two investment strategies. The first (strategy A) is to buy 7 call options. The second (strategy B) is to buy 4 Google shares and to borrow the present value of $1,380 from the bank. Table 23.5 shows the possible payoffs from the two strategies. Notice that when you borrow from the bank, you receive a *positive* cash flow now but have a *negative flow* when the loan is repaid in January.

You can see that *regardless of whether the stock price falls to $345 or rises to $613.33,* the payoffs from the two strategies are identical. To put it another way, you can exactly replicate an investment in call options by a combination of a bank loan and an investment in the stock.* If two investments give the same payoffs in all circumstances, then their value must be the same today. In other words, the cost of buying 7 call options must be exactly the same as borrowing PV($1,380) from the bank and buying 4 Google shares:

$$\text{Price of 7 calls} = \$1,840 - \$1,359.61 = \$480.39$$

$$\text{Price of 1 call} = \frac{\$480.39}{7} = \$68.63$$

Presto! You have just valued a call option.[†]

---

* The only tricky part in valuing the Google option was to work out the number of shares that were needed to replicate the call option. Fortunately, there is a simple formula which says that the number of shares needed is equal to

$$\frac{\text{Spread of possible option prices}}{\text{Spread of possible stock prices}} = \frac{\$153.33 - 0}{\$613.33 - \$345} = \frac{4}{7}$$

To replicate 1 call option, you need to buy 4/7 of a share. To replicate 7 calls, you need to buy 4 shares of stock.

† Notice that the actual price of the Google call in July 2010 was $42.50, quite a bit lower than our simple estimate of the option's value. It looks as if we have overestimated the spread of possible future stock prices.

TABLE 23.5 It is possible to replicate the payoffs from Google call options by borrowing to invest in Google stock.

	Cash Flow in July 2010	Payoff in January If Stock Price Equals:	
		$345	$613.33
Strategy A			
Buy 7 calls	?	$ 0	+$1,073.33
Strategy B			
Buy 4 shares	−$1,840.00	+$1,380	+$2,453.33
Borrow PV($1,380)	+$1,359.61	−$1,380	−$1,380.00
	−$ 480.39	$ 0	+$1,073.33

Note: PV($1,380) paid 6 months from now is $1,380/1.015 = $1,359.61

Self-Test 23.6

Use the nearby Finance in Practice box as a model to help you answer this question. Suppose that the price of Fly-by-Night stock is $30 and could either double to $60 or halve to $15 over the next 3 months. Show that the following two strategies have exactly the same payoffs regardless of whether the stock price rises or falls: *Strategy A*—Buy three call options with an exercise price of $30; *Strategy B*—Buy two shares and borrow the present value of $30. What is your cash outflow today if you follow strategy B? What does this tell you about the value of three call options? Assume that the interest rate is 1% per 3 months.

Using the Black-Scholes Formula

You may like to try your hand at using the Black-Scholes option-pricing formula to value the Google option. A number of Web sites include a Black-Scholes calculator (see, for example, www.numa.com, and look for the options calculator). But it takes only a few moments to construct your own Excel program to calculate Black-Scholes values. The following spreadsheet shows how you do it. First, type in the formulas shown on the right side of the spreadsheet in cells E2 to E8. Now enter the data for the Google January 2011 call in cells B2 to B6. Notice that the values for the standard deviation and interest rate are entered as decimals.* On past evidence, the standard deviation of Google's annual returns has been about 30%, so we enter the standard deviation in cell B2 as .30, not 30. The last two lines of the output column show that the Black-Scholes formula gives a value of $42.04 for the Google call option, almost exactly the same as its market price in July 2010. (Don't worry about the other lines of output.)

Spreadsheet Questions

1. Use the option pricing spreadsheet to calculate the value of the call option at stock prices ranging from $300 to $600 at intervals of $25.
2. Plot the values as a function of the stock price. How does your graph compare to the plot in Figure 23.4?

You can find this spreadsheet at www.mhhe.com/bmm7e.

	A	B	C	D	E	F	G	H	I	J
1	**INPUTS**			**OUTPUTS**			**FORMULA FOR OUTPUT IN COLUMN E**			
2	Standard deviation (annual)	0.300		PV(Ex. Price)	453.2515		B6/(1+B4)^B3			
3	Maturity (in years)	0.500		d1	.1757		(LN(B5/E2)+(0.5*B2^2)*B3)/(B2*SQRT(B3))			
4	Risk-free rate (effective annual rate)	0.03		d2	−.0364		E3-B2*SQRT(B3)			
5	Stock price	460		N(d1)	.5697		NORMSDIST(E3)			
6	Exercise price	460		N(d2)	.4855		NORMSDIST(E4)			
7				B/S call value	42.04		B5*E5 − E2*E6			
8				B/S put value	35.29		E7+E2 − B5			

* Chapter 11 described how to calculate standard deviations. Notice also that in cell E2, we compute the present value of the exercise price by treating the interest rate as an effective annual yield. You should be aware, however, that many Black-Scholes calculators require that the interest rate be expressed as a continuously compounded rate. See Chapter 5, Table 5.7, if you need a review of continuous compounding.

23.3 Spotting the Option

In our discussion so far we may have given you the impression that financial managers are concerned only with traded options to buy or sell shares. But once you have learned to recognize the different kinds of options, you will find that they are everywhere. Unfortunately, they rarely come with a large label attached. Often the trickiest part of the problem is to identify the option.

We will start by looking briefly at options on real assets and then turn to options on financial assets. You should find that you have already encountered many of these options in earlier chapters.

Options on Real Assets

In Chapter 10 we pointed out that the capital investment projects that you accept today may affect the opportunities you have tomorrow. Today's capital budgeting decisions need to recognize these future opportunities.

Other things equal, a capital investment project that generates new opportunities is more valuable than one that doesn't. A flexible project—one that doesn't commit management to a fixed operating strategy—is more valuable than an inflexible one. When a project is flexible or generates new opportunities for the firm, it is said to contain **real options.**

real options

Options to invest in, modify, or dispose of a capital investment project.

If you look out for real options, you'll find them almost everywhere. The nearby Finance in Practice box provides an illustration of a firm that took real options into account in an important capital budgeting decision. In Chapter 10 we looked at several ways that companies may build future flexibility into a project. Here is a brief reminder of two types of real options that we introduced in that chapter.

Allegheny Acquires a Real Option

Allegheny Corporation acquired open gas-fired power plants in Mississippi and Tennessee. These plants were expected to sit idle most of the year and, when operating, to produce electricity at a cost at least 50% higher than the most efficient state-of-the-art facilities. Allegheny's decision to build these power plants resulted from a sophisticated application of real options analysis.

The firm observed that electricity prices in an increasingly free energy market can be wildly volatile. For example, during some power shortages in the Midwest during the hot summer months the cost of 1 megawatt-hour of electricity has increased briefly from a typical level of $40 to several thousand dollars. The option to obtain additional energy in these situations obviously would be quite valuable.

Allegheny concluded that it would pay to acquire some cheap power plants, even if they were relatively high-cost electricity producers. Most of the time, the plants will sit idle, with market prices for electricity below the marginal cost of production. But every so often, when electricity prices spike, the plants can be fired up to produce electricity—at a great profit. Even if they operate only a few weeks a year, they can be positive-NPV investments.

These plants are in effect call options on electrical power. The options are currently out of the money, but the possibility that power prices will increase makes these calls worth more than their price. The decision to build them therefore makes the firm more valuable.

The Option to Expand   Many capital investment proposals include an option to expand in the future. For instance, some of the world's largest oil reserves are found in the tar sands of Athabasca, Canada. Unfortunately, in many cases the cost of extracting oil is higher than the current market price and higher than most people's estimate of the likely price in the future. Yet oil companies have been prepared to pay considerable sums for these tracts of barren land. The reason? Ownership of the tar sands gives the companies an option. If prices remain below the cost of extraction, the Athabasca sands will remain undeveloped. But if prices rise above the cost of extraction those land purchases could prove very valuable. Thus, ownership gives the companies a real option—a call option to extract the oil.

The Option to Abandon   Suppose that you need a new plant ready to produce turboencabulators in 3 years. You have a choice of designs. If design A is chosen construction must start immediately. Design B is more expensive but you can wait a year before breaking ground.

If you know with certainty that the plant will be needed, you should opt for design A. But suppose that there is some possibility that demand for turboencabulators will fall off and that in a year's time you will decide the plant is not required. Then design B may be preferable because it gives you the option to bail out at low cost any time during the next 12 months.

You can think of the option to abandon as a put option. The exercise price of the put is the amount that you could recover if you abandon the project. The abandonment option makes design B more attractive by limiting the downside exposure. The more uncertain is the need for the new plant, the more valuable is the downside protection offered by the option to abandon.

Self-Test 23.7

A real estate developer buys 70 acres of land in a rural area, planning to build a subdivision on the land if and when the population from the city begins to expand into the area. If population growth is less than anticipated, the developer believes that the land can be sold to a country club that would build a golf course on the property.

a. In what way does the possibility of sale to the country club provide a put option to the developer?
b. What is the exercise price of the option? The asset value?
c. How does the golf course option increase the NPV of the land project to the developer?

Options on Financial Assets

The Google options that we considered earlier were sold by one group of investors to another. They had no effect on the company's cash flows. However, firms may also issue options to their managers or investors, and these do have a potential impact on the companies' cash flows. Here are a few examples.

Executive Stock Options In 2010 Larry Ellison, the CEO of Oracle, was paid a salary of $250,000, but that figure was dwarfed by the award of stock options and shares worth $68.4 million. The amount of Larry Ellison's compensation is unusual, but these days the chief executives of most major U.S. corporations are compensated largely with stock options.

These stock options are valuable and therefore are an expense just like salaries and wages. The Financial Accounting Standards Board (FASB) now requires companies to use an option-valuation model, such as the Black-Scholes model, to estimate the fair value of option grants and to recognize this value when calculating expenses. For example, in fiscal 2010 Oracle granted options to its directors, management, and employees to buy 61 million shares of the company's stock. Oracle's accounts showed that according to the Black-Scholes model the total value of these options was $375 million.

Stock options, such as those provided by Oracle, are an important part of managers' compensation. There is nothing wrong with that if the options encourage managers to work hard to increase the value of their companies' stock. However, in recent years some companies illegally boosted the value of the stock options that they have given to managers by backdating the grant of their executive stock options. The nearby box discusses the backdating scandal.

warrant
Right to buy shares from a company at a stipulated price before a set date.

Warrants A **warrant** is a long-term call option on the company's stock. For example, in return for helping to bail out the Bank of America in 2008, the U.S. Treasury received 150 million Bank of America warrants. Each warrant entitled the Treasury to buy one share in the bank for $13.30 at any time before January 2019.

In March 2010 the Treasury sold the warrants to investors for $8.35 each. At that time the price of Bank of America stock was $16.40 a share. So investors who bought the warrants would realize a profit if the stock price rose above $13.30 + $8.35 = $21.65.

Warrants are sometimes issued when a firm becomes bankrupt; the bankruptcy court offers the firm's bondholders warrants in the reorganized company as part of the settlement. At other times warrants are given to underwriters as part of their compensation for managing an issue of securities. When a company issues a bond, it will occasionally add some warrants as a "sweetener." Since these warrants are valuable to investors, they are prepared to pay a higher price for a package of bonds and warrants than for the bond on its own. Managers sometimes look with delight at this higher price, forgetting that in return the company has incurred a liability to sell its shares to the warrant holders at what, with hindsight, may turn out to be a low price.

convertible bond
Bond that the holder may exchange for a specified amount of security.

Convertible Bonds The **convertible bond** is a close relative of the bond-warrant package. It allows the bondholder to exchange the bond for a given number of shares of common stock. Therefore, it is a package of a straight bond and a call option. The exercise price of the call option is the value of the "straight bond" (that is, a bond that is not convertible). It will be profitable to convert if the value of the stock to which the investor is entitled exceeds the value of the straight bond.

The owner of a convertible bond owns a bond and a call option on the firm's stock. So does the owner of a package of a bond and a warrant. However, there are differences, the most important being that a convertible bond's owner must give up the bond to exercise the option. The owner of a package of bonds and warrants exercises the warrants for cash and keeps the bond.

The Options Backdating Scandal

In 2007 the SEC investigated a number of instances in which companies had backdated the stock options that they granted to senior executives. Evidence of this practice had appeared 2 years earlier in an academic paper,* and it was subsequently highlighted in a Wall Street Journal *article entitled "The Perfect Payday." The following extract is taken from this article.*

On a summer day in 2002, shares of Affiliated Computer Services Inc. sank to their lowest level in a year. Oddly, that was good news for Chief Executive Jeffrey Rich.

His annual grant of stock options was dated that day, entitling him to buy stock at that price for years. Had they been dated a week later, when the stock was 27% higher, they'd have been far less rewarding. It was the same through much of Mr. Rich's tenure: In a striking pattern, all six of his stock-option grants from 1995 to 2002 were dated just before a rise in the stock price, often at the bottom of a steep drop.

Just lucky? A *Wall Street Journal* analysis suggests the odds of this happening by chance are extraordinarily remote— around one in 300 billion. The odds of winning the multistate Powerball lottery with a $1 ticket are one in 146 million.

Suspecting such patterns aren't due to chance, the Securities and Exchange Commission is examining whether some option grants carry favorable grant dates for a different reason: They were backdated.

Stock options give recipients a right to buy company stock at a set price, called the exercise price or strike price. The

right usually doesn't vest for a year or more, but then it continues for several years. The exercise price is usually the stock's 4 p.m. price on the date of the grant, an average of the day's high and low, or the 4 p.m. price the day before. Naturally, the lower it is, the more money the recipient can potentially make someday by exercising the options.

The *Journal's* analysis raises questions about one of the most lucrative stock-option grants ever. On Oct. 13, 1999, William W. McGuire, CEO of giant insurer UnitedHealth Group Inc., got an enormous grant in three parts that—after adjustment for later stock splits—came to 14.6 million options. So far, he has exercised about 5% of them, for a profit of about $39 million. As of late February he had 13.87 million unexercised options left from the October 1999 tranche. His profit on those, if he exercised them today, would be about $717 million more.

The 1999 grant was dated the very day UnitedHealth stock hit its low for the year. Grants to Dr. McGuire in 1997 and 2000 were also dated on the day with those years' single lowest closing price. A grant in 2001 came near the bottom of a sharp stock dip. In all, the odds of such a favorable pattern occurring by chance would be one in 200 million or greater.[†]

Source: C. Forelle and J. Bandler, "The Perfect Payday; Some CEOs Reap Millions by Landing Stock Options When They Are Most Valuable; Luck—or Something Else?" *The Wall Street Journal,* March 18, 2006, p. A1. Used with permission of Dow Jones & Company, Inc. via Copyright Clearance Center, Inc.

---

* E. Lie, "On the Timing of CEO Stock Option Awards," *Management Science* 51 (2005), pp. 802–812.

[†] Postcript: In December 2007 Dr. McGuire agreed to pay back $620 million in stock-option gains and retirement pay. He was also barred from serving as an officer or director of a public company for 10 years.

EXAMPLE 23.3 ▶ Convertible Bonds

In March 2009, the giant aluminum company Alcoa issued $575 million of 5.25% convertible bonds maturing in 2014. Each of these bonds can be converted before maturity into 155.49 shares of Alcoa stock. In other words, the owner of the convertible has the option to return the bond to Alcoa and receive 155.49 shares in exchange. The number of shares that are received for each bond is called the bond's *conversion ratio.* The conversion ratio of the Alcoa bond is 155.49.

In order to receive 155.49 shares of Alcoa stock, you must surrender bonds with a face value of $1,000. Therefore, to receive *one* share, you have to surrender a face amount of $1,000/155.49 = $6.43. This figure is called the *conversion price.* Anybody who originally bought the bond at $1,000 in order to convert it into 155.49 shares paid the equivalent of $6.43 a share.

As we write this in July 2010, Alcoa's stock price is $10.40. So, if investors were obliged to convert their bond today, their investment would be worth 155.49 × $10.40 = $1,617. This is the bond's *conversion value.* Of course, investors do not need to convert in 2010. They obviously hope that Alcoa's stock price will zoom up, making conversion even more profitable. But they have the comfort of knowing that if the stock price zooms down, they can choose not to convert and simply hold on to the bond. The value of the bond if it could not be converted is known as its *bond value.* If Alcoa's bond could not be converted, it would probably sell in July 2010 for about its face value of $1,000.

Since the owner of the convertible always has the option *not* to convert, bond value establishes a lower bound, or floor, to the price of a convertible. Of course, this floor is not completely flat. If the firm falls on hard times, the bond may not be worth much. In the extreme case where the firm becomes worthless, the bond is also worthless.

When the firm does well, conversion value exceeds bond value. In this case the investor would choose to convert if forced to make an immediate choice. Bond value exceeds conversion value when the firm does poorly. In these circumstances the investor would hold on to the bonds if forced to choose. Convertible holders do not have to make a now-or-never choice for or against conversion. They can wait and then, with the benefit of hindsight, take whatever course turns out to give them the highest payoff. Thus a convertible is always worth more than both its bond value and its conversion value (except when time runs out at the bond's maturity).

We stated earlier that it is useful to think of a convertible bond as a package of a straight bond and an option to buy the common stock in exchange for the straight bond. The value of this call option is equal to the difference between the convertible's market price and its bond value.

Self-Test 23.8

a. What would be the conversion value of the Alcoa convertible bond if the stock price rose to $12? What would happen to its conversion price?

b. Suppose that a straight (nonconvertible) bond issued by Alcoa had been priced to yield 7%. What would be the bond value of the 5.25% convertibles in 2010? (Assume annual coupon payments and remaining time to maturity is exactly four years.)

---

callable bond
Bond that may be repurchased by the issuer before maturity at specified call price.

Callable Bonds   Unlike warrants and convertibles, which give the *investor* an option, a **callable bond** gives an option to the *issuer.* A company that issues a callable bond has an option to buy the bond back at the stated exercise or "call" price. Therefore, you can think of a callable bond as a *package* of a straight bond (a bond that is not callable) and a call option held by the issuer.

The option to call the bond is obviously attractive to the issuer. If interest rates decline and bond prices rise, the company has the opportunity to repurchase the bond at a fixed call price. Therefore, the option to call the bond puts a ceiling on the bond price.

Of course, when the company issues a callable bond, investors are aware of this ceiling on the bond price and will pay less for a callable bond than for a straight bond. The difference between the value of a straight bond and a callable bond with the same coupon rate and maturity is the value of the call option that investors have given to the company:

Value of callable bond = value of straight bond − value of the issuer's call option

---

Self-Test 23.9

"Puttable bonds" allow the investor to redeem the bond at face value or let the bond remain outstanding until maturity. Suppose a 20-year puttable bond is issued with the investor allowed after 5 years to redeem the bond at face value.

a. On what asset is the option written? (What asset do the option holders have the right to sell?)

b. What is the exercise price of the option?

c. In what circumstances will the option be exercised?

d. Does the put option make the bond more or less valuable?

SUMMARY

What is the payoff to buyers and sellers of call and put options? *(LO1)*

There are two basic types of options. A **call option** is the right to buy an asset at a specific exercise price on or before the exercise date. A **put** is the right to sell an asset at a specific exercise price on or before the exercise date. The payoff to a call is the value of the asset minus the exercise price if the difference is positive, and zero otherwise. The payoff to a put is the exercise price minus the value of the asset if the difference is positive, and zero otherwise. The payoff to the seller of an option is the negative of the payoff to the option buyer.

What are the determinants of option values? *(LO2)*

The value of a call option depends on the following considerations:

- To exercise the call option you must pay the exercise price. Other things equal, the less you are obliged to pay, the better. Therefore, the value of the option is higher when the exercise price is low relative to the stock price.
- Investors who buy the stock by way of a call option are buying on installment credit. They pay the purchase price of the option today but they do not pay the exercise price until they exercise the option. The higher the rate of interest and the longer the time to expiration, the more this "free credit" is worth.
- No matter how far the stock price falls, the owner of the call cannot lose more than the price of the call. On the other hand, the more the stock price rises above the exercise price, the greater the profit on the call. Therefore, the option holder does not lose from increased variability if things go wrong, but gains if they go right. The value of the option increases with the variability of stock returns. Of course, the longer the time to the final exercise date, the more opportunity there is for the stock price to vary.

What options may be present in capital investment proposals? *(LO3)*

The importance of building flexibility into investment projects (discussed in Chapter 10) can be reformulated in the language of options. For example, many capital investments provide the flexibility to expand capacity in the future if demand turns out to be unusually buoyant. They are in effect providing the firm with a call option on the extra capacity. Firms also think about alternative uses for their assets if things go wrong. The option to abandon a project is a put option; the put's exercise price is the value of the project's assets if shifted to an alternative use. The ability to expand or to abandon are both examples of **real options.**

What options may be provided in financial securities? *(LO4)*

Many of the securities that firms issue contain an option. For example, a **warrant** is nothing but a long-term call option issued by the firm. **Convertible bonds** give the investor the option to buy the firm's stock in exchange for the value of the underlying bond. Unlike warrants and convertibles, which give an option to the investor, **callable bonds** give the option to the issuing firm. If interest rates decline and the value of the underlying bond rises, the firm can buy the bonds back at a specified exercise price.

QUESTIONS

QUIZ

1. **Option Payoffs.** Turn back to Table 23.2, which lists prices of various Google options. Use the data in the table to calculate the payoff and the profits for investments in each of the following September maturity options, assuming that the stock price on the expiration date is $460. *(LO1)*
   a. Call option with exercise price of $430.
   b. Put option with exercise price of $430.
   c. Call option with exercise price of $460.
   d. Put option with exercise price of $460.

FIGURE 23.7 **See Quiz Question 5.**

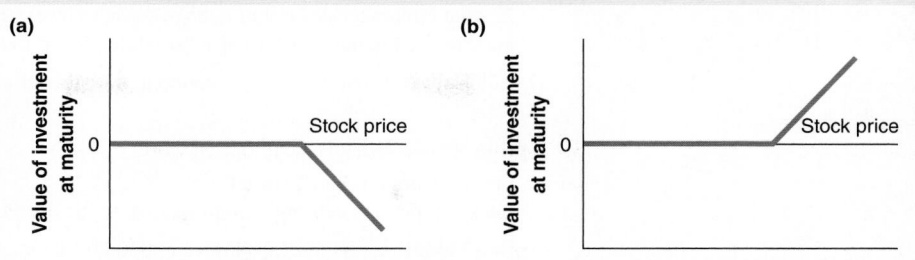

e. Call option with exercise price of $490.
f. Put option with exercise price of $490.

2. **Option Payoffs.** Redo the preceding problem assuming the stock price on the expiration date is (a) $480, (b) $440. (*LO1*)

3. **Determinants of Option Value.** Look at the data in Table 23.2. (*LO2*)

    a. What is the price of a call option with an exercise price of $460 and expiration in September 2010? What if expiration is in January 2012?
    b. Why do you think the January 2012 calls cost more than the September 2010 calls?
    c. Is the same true of put options? Why?

4. **Option Contracts.** Fill in the blanks by choosing the appropriate terms from the following list: *call, exercise, put.* (*LO1*)

    A(n) _____ option gives its owner the opportunity to buy a stock at a specific price which is generally called the _____ price. A(n) _____ option gives its owner the opportunity to sell stock at a specified _____ price.

5. **Option Payoffs.** Note Figure 23.7*a* and 23.7*b*. Match each graph with one of the following positions. (*LO1*)

    a. Call buyer
    b. Call seller
    c. Put buyer
    d. Put seller

6. **Puts versus Calls.** "The buyer of a call and the seller of a put both hope that the stock price will rise. Therefore the two positions are identical." Is the speaker correct? Illustrate with a simple example or diagram. (*LO1*)

7. **Hedging with Options.** Suppose that you hold a share of stock and a put option on that share with an exercise price of $100. What is the value of your portfolio when the option expires if

    a. the stock price is below $100? (*LO1*)
    b. the stock price is above $100? (*LO1*)

PRACTICE PROBLEMS

8. **Option Portfolios.** Mixing options and securities can often create interesting payoffs. For each of the following combinations show what the payoff would be when the option expires if (i) the stock price is below the exercise price, and (ii) the stock price is above the exercise price. Assume that each option has the same exercise price and expiration date. (*LO1*)

    a. Buy a call and invest the present value of the exercise price in a bank deposit.
    b. Buy a share and a put option on the share.
    c. Buy a share, buy a put option on the share, and sell a call option on the share.
    d. Buy a call option and a put option on the share.

9. **Option Portfolios.** Look at Figure 23.8, which shows the possible future payoffs in January 2011 from a particular package of investments. (*LO1*)

    a. What package of investments would provide you with this set of payoffs?
    b. How much would the package have cost you in July 2010? (See Table 23.2.)

c. In what circumstances might it make sense to invest in this package? Incidentally, this package of investments is known as a "straddle" by option buffs.

10. **Option Values.** What is the lower bound to the price of a call option? What is the upper bound? (*LO2*)

11. **Option Values.** What is a call option worth if
   a. the stock price is zero? (*LO2*)
   b. the stock price is extremely high relative to the exercise price? (*LO2*)

12. **Option Valuation.** Table 23.2 shows call options on Google stock with the same exercise date in January 2011 and with exercise prices $430, $460, and $490. Notice that the price of the middle call option (with exercise price $460) is less than halfway between the prices of the other two calls (with exercise prices $430 and $490). Suppose that this were not the case. For example, suppose that the price of the middle call were the average of the prices of the other two calls. Show that if you sell two of the middle calls and use the proceeds to buy one each of the other calls, your proceeds in January may be positive but cannot be negative despite the fact that your net outlay today is zero. What can you deduce from this example about option pricing? (*LO2*)

13. **Put Prices.** How does the price of a *put* option respond to the following changes, other things equal? Does the put price go up or down? (*LO2*)
   a. Stock price increases.
   b. Exercise price is increased.
   c. Risk-free interest rate increases.
   d. Expiration date of the option is extended.
   e. Volatility of the stock price falls.
   f. Time passes, so the option's expiration date comes closer.

14. **Option Values.** As manager of United Bedstead you own substantial executive stock options. These options entitle you to buy the firm's shares during the next 5 years at a price of $100 a share. The plant manager has just outlined two alternative proposals to reequip the plant. Both proposals have the same net present value but one is substantially riskier than the other. At first you are undecided which to choose, but then you remember your stock options. How might these influence your choice? (*LO2*)

15. **Real and Financial Options.** Fill in the blanks. (*LO3, LO4*)
   a. An oil company acquires mining rights to a silver deposit. It is not obliged to mine the silver, however. The company has effectively acquired a _____ option, where the exercise price is the cost of opening the mine and extracting the silver.
   b. Some preferred shareholders have the right to redeem their shares at par value after a specified date. (If they hand over their shares, the firm sends them a check equal to the shares' par value.) These shareholders have a _____ option.
   c. A firm buys a standard machine with a ready secondhand market. The secondhand market gives the firm a _____ option.

16. **Real Options.** What is the option in each of the following cases. Is it a call or a put? (*LO3*)
   a. Western Telecom commits to production of digital switching equipment specifically designed for the European market. As a stand-alone venture, the project has a negative NPV, but it is justified by the need for a strong market position in the rapidly growing, and potentially very profitable, market.
   b. Western Telecom vetoes a fully integrated automated production line for the new digital switches. It will rely on standard, less expensive equipment even though the automated

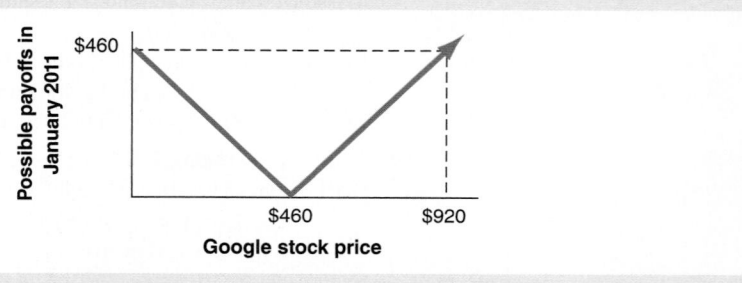

FIGURE 23.8 This strategy provides a payoff of $0 if the Google stock price remains at $460 and a payoff of $460 if Google's stock price either falls to zero or rises to $920. See Practice Problem 9.

production line would be more efficient overall using the specialized equipment, according to a discounted cash-flow calculation.

17. **Real Options.** Describe each of the following situations in the language of options. (*LO3*)

    a. Drilling rights to undeveloped heavy crude oil in southern California. Development and production of the oil now is a negative-NPV endeavor. The break-even price is $180 per barrel, versus a spot price of $140. However, the decision to develop can be put off for up to 5 years.

    b. A restaurant produces net cash flows, after all out-of-pocket expenses, of $700,000 per year. There is no upward or downward trend in the cash flows, but they fluctuate. The real estate occupied by the restaurant is owned, and it could be sold for $5 million.

18. **Real Options.** Price support systems for various agricultural products have allowed farmers to sell their crops to the government for a specified "support price." What kind of option has the government given to the farmers? What is the exercise price? (*LO3*)

19. **Hidden Options.** Some investment management contracts give the portfolio manager a bonus proportional to the amount by which a portfolio return exceeds a specified threshold. (*LO4*)

    a. In what way is this an implicit call option on the portfolio?

    b. Can you think of a way in which such contracts can lead to incentive problems? For example, what happens to the value of the prospective bonus if the manager invests in high-volatility stocks?

20. **Hidden Options.** The Rank and File Company is considering a stock issue to raise $50 million. An underwriter offers to guarantee the success of the issue by buying any unwanted stock at the $25 issue price. The underwriter's fee is $2 million. (*LO4*)

    a. What kind of option does Rank and File acquire if it accepts the underwriter's offer?

    b. What determines the value of the option?

21. **Hidden Options.** (*LO4*)

    a. Some banks have offered their customers an unusual type of time deposit. The deposit does not pay any interest if the market falls, but instead the depositor receives a proportion of any rise in the Standard & Poor's Index. What implicit option do the investors hold? How should the bank invest the money in order to protect itself against the risk of offering this deposit?

    b. You can also make a deposit with a bank that does not pay interest if the market index rises but makes an increasingly large payment as the market index *falls*. How should the bank protect itself against the risk of offering this deposit?

22. **Loan Guarantees.** The FDIC insures bank deposits. If a bank's assets are insufficient to pay off all depositors, the FDIC will contribute enough money to ensure that all depositors can be paid off in full. (We ignore the $250,000 maximum coverage on each account.) In what way is this guarantee of deposits the provision of a put option by the FDIC? (*Hint:* Write out the funds the FDIC will have to contribute when bank assets are less than deposits owed to depositors.) What is the exercise price of the put option? (*LO4*)

23. **Real Options.** After dramatic increases in oil prices in the 1970s, the U.S. government funded several projects to create synthetic oil or natural gas from abundant U.S. supplies of coal and oil shale. Although the cost of producing such synthetic fuels at the time was greater than the price of oil, it was argued that the projects still could be justified for their insurance value since the cost of synthetic fuel would be essentially fixed while the price of oil was risky. Evaluate the synthetic fuel program as an option on fuel sources. Is it a call or a put option? What is the exercise price? How would uncertainty in the future price of oil affect the amount the United States should have been willing to spend on such projects? (*LO3*)

24. **Arbitrage Opportunities.** (*LO2*)

    a. Circular File stock is selling for $25 a share. You see that call options on the stock with exercise price of $20 are selling at $3. What should you do? What will happen to the option price as investors identify this opportunity?

    b. Now you observe that put options on Circular File with exercise price $30 are selling for $4. What should you do?

25. **Convertible Bonds.** A 10-year maturity convertible bond with a 6% coupon on a company with a bond rating of Aaa is selling for $1,050. Each bond can be exchanged for 20 shares, and the stock price currently is $50 per share. Other Aaa-rated bonds with the same maturity would sell at a yield to maturity of 8%. What is the value of the bondholders' call option? Why is the bond selling for more than the value of the shares it can be converted into? (*LO4*)

CHALLENGE PROBLEMS

26. **Option Portfolios.** Repeat the three parts of Practice Problem 9 except that now the problem is to devise a package of investments with the payoffs shown in Figure 23.9. This package of investments is known as a "butterfly." (*LO1*)

27. **Option Pricing.** Look again at the Google call option that we valued in Section 23.2. Suppose that by the end of January 2011 the price of Google stock could double to $920 or halve to $230. Everything else is unchanged from our example. (*LO2*)
    a. What would be the value of the Google call in January 2011 if the stock price is $920? If it is $230?
    b. Show that a strategy of buying three calls provides exactly the same payoffs as borrowing the present value of $460 from the bank and buying two shares.
    c. What is the net cash flow in July 2010 from the policy of borrowing PV($460) and buying two shares?
    d. What does this tell you about the value of the call option?
    e. Why is the value of the call option different from the value that we calculated in Section 23.2? What does this tell you about the relationship between the value of a call and the volatility of the share price?

28. **Option Pricing.** Look once more at the Google call option that we valued in Section 23.2. Suppose (just suppose) that the interest rate on bank loans is zero. Recalculate the value of the Google call option. What does this tell you about the relationship between interest rates and the value of a call? (*LO2*)

29. **Option Pricing.** Use the Black-Scholes formula to find the value of a call option on the following stock. (You can find the spreadsheet in the chapter as well as on our Web site at **www.mhhe.com/bmm7e**). (*LO2*)

Time to expiration	1 year
Standard deviation	40% per year
Exercise price	$50
Stock price	$50
Interest rate	4% (effective annual yield)

30. **Option Pricing.** Recalculate the value of the call option in the previous problem, but use the following parameter values. Each change should be considered *independently*. Confirm that the value of the option changes in agreement with the prediction of Table 23.4. (*LO2*)
    a. Time to expiration   2 years
    b. Standard deviation   50% per year
    c. Exercise price $60
    d. Stock price $60
    e. Interest rate   6%

31. **Option Pricing.** Option prices are determined in part by volatility, and traders sometimes use the volatility estimates built into option prices to assess market conditions. The volatility estimate built into S&P 500 options may be found at Yahoo! Finance (get quotes for ticker symbol VIX). If you look at the historical plot of the VIX index, you'll see that it spikes during periods of turbulence (e.g., the recent subprime crisis or the lead-up to the invasion of Iraq), and for this reason it is often called a "fear gauge." Let's see how traders back out these estimates of

FIGURE 23.9 This strategy provides a total payoff of $30 if the stock price is $460 and a payoff of zero if the stock price is either (a) $430 or less or (b) $490 or more. See Practice Problem 26.

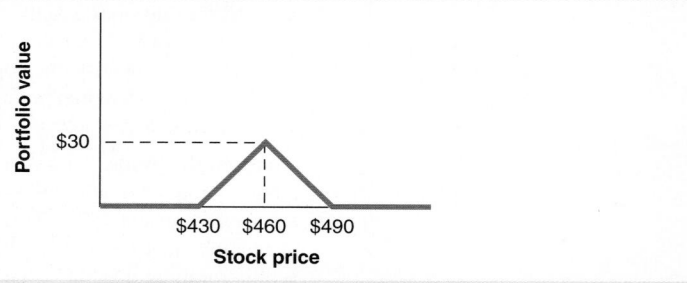

volatility from option prices. To do so, consider the option in Challenge Problem 29. Assume that option traders see the option selling at a price of $9.50 and wonder what volatility level this price implies. (*LO2*)

a. Go to the Tools menu of the Black-Scholes spreadsheet in this chapter (available at our Web site, www.mhhe.com/bmm7e), look under the *Data* tab for *What-If Analysis*, select *Goal Seek*, and a dialog box will appear. Use the dialog box to "set cell E7 to value 9.50 by changing cell B2." This directs the spreadsheet to change the value of cell B2 (the volatility estimate) to a level that makes the option price (cell E7) equal to $9.50. The resulting volatility parameter is called the option's *implied volatility*, that is, the volatility level implied by its market price. This sort of inference is the basis for the VIX index.

b. What happens to implied volatility if the option price is only $9? Why has it decreased?

WEB EXERCISES

1. You can find option prices on finance.yahoo.com. Enter the company symbol and then click on *Options*. Try looking up option prices for Dell Computer (DELL) and Pfizer (PFE). Does the price of calls increase or decrease with (a) the exercise price and (b) time to expiration? Would your answer be the same for puts? Why or why not?

2. Several Web sites contain calculators that use the Black-Scholes formula for valuing options. Try valuing a call option on Dell Computer or Amazon.com. The inputs are the same as those in our simple valuation example, except that instead of putting in the spread of possible stock prices, you must put in the standard deviation of stock returns. You can find estimates of the standard deviation of Dell and Amazon in Table 11.5. (Note that the program also asks you for the stock's dividend yield. At the time of writing neither firm pays a dividend.) How different are the values you obtain from the prices shown on finance.yahoo.com? What happens to the option value if you change the standard deviation? Can you explain?

3. Find IBM's most recent income statement. What was the value that IBM assigned to the stock options it granted its employees in the most recent year? How did IBM estimate the value?

SOLUTIONS TO SELF-TEST QUESTIONS

23.1 a. The call with exercise price $490 costs $10.10. If the stock price at the expiration date is $400, the call expires valueless and the investor loses the entire $10.10. If the stock price is $550, the value of the call at expiration is $550 − $490 = $60 and the investor's profit is $60 − $10.10 = $49.90.

b. The put with exercise price $490 costs $39.36. If the stock price at the expiration date is $400, the value of the put is $490 − $400 = $90 and the investor's profit is $90 − $39.36 = $50.64. If the stock price is $550, the put expires valueless and the investor loses the entire $39.36.

23.2 a. The call seller receives $10.10 for writing the call. If the stock price at expiration is $460, the call expires valueless and the investor keeps the entire $10.10 as a profit. If the stock price is $520, the value of the call at expiration is $520 − $490 = $30. In other words, the call seller must deliver a stock worth $520 for an exercise price of only $490. The investor's net profit is negative at $10.10 − $30 = −$18.90. The call seller makes a loss whenever the value of the call at expiration is more than the initial premium received for writing the option. In other words, he loses if the stock price is above $490 + $10.10 = $500.10

b. The put seller receives $39.36 for writing the put. If the stock price at expiration is $460, the final value of the put is $490 − $460 = $30. In other words, the put seller must pay an exercise price of $490 for a stock worth only $460. The investor's net profit is $39.36 − $30 = $9.36. If the stock price is $520, the put expires valueless and the put seller keeps the entire $39.36 as a profit. The put seller makes a loss when the value of the put at expiration is greater than the initial premium received for writing the option. In other words, he loses if the stock price is below $490 − $39.36 = $450.64.

23.3 Put-call parity states that value of stock + value of put = value of call + present value of exercise price. Therefore, in the case of Witterman

$$\$55 + \text{value of put} = \$8.05 + \frac{\$60}{1.04}$$

and value of put = $8.05 + $57.69 − $55 = $10.74.

23.4 The value of a put option is higher when the exercise price is higher. You would be willing to pay more for the right to sell a stock at a high price than the right to sell it at a low price.

23.5 First consider the payoff to the put holder in the lower volatility scenario:

Stock price	$400	$520
Put value	$60	0

In the higher volatility scenario, the value of the stock can be $340 or $580. Now the payoff to the put is

Stock price	$340	$580
Put value	$120	0

The expected value of the payoff of the put is higher in the high-volatility scenario.

23.6 The payoffs are as follows:

		Payoff in 3 Months If Stock Price Equals:	
	Cash Flow Today	$15	$60
Strategy A			
Buy three calls	?	$ 0	+$ 90
Strategy B			
Buy two shares	−$60	+ $30	+$120
Borrow PV($30)	+ 29.70	− 30	− 30
	−$30.30	$ 0	+$ 90

Note: PV($30) at an interest rate of 1% for 3 months is 30/1.01 = $29.70.

The initial net cash outflow from strategy B is $30.30. Since the three calls offer the same payoffs in the future, they must also cost $30.30. One call is worth 30.30/3 = $10.10.

23.7 a. The developer has the option to sell the potential housing development to the country club. This abandonment option is like a put that guarantees a minimum payoff from the investment.
   b. The exercise price of the option is the price at which it can be sold to the country club. The asset value is the present value of the project if maintained as a housing development. If this value is less than the value as a golf course, the project will be sold.
   c. The abandonment option increases NPV by placing a lower bound on the possible payoffs from the project.

23.8 a. Conversion value = 155.49 × $12 = $1,866.
      Conversion price = $1,000/155.49 = $6.43 (unchanged).
   b. Bond value = $52.50/1.07 + 52.50/1.07^2 + 52.50/1.07^3 + 1,052.50/1.07^4 = $940.72.

23.9 a. In 5 years, the bond will be a 15-year maturity bond. The bondholder can sell the bond back to the firm at face value. The bondholder therefore has a put option to sell a 15-year bond for face value even if interest rates have risen and the bond would otherwise sell below face value.
   b. The exercise price is the face value of the bond.
   c. The bondholder will sell the bond back to the company if interest rates increase or the company's credit deteriorates.
   d. More valuable. The bondholder now has the right, but not the obligation, to sell the bond at face value in 5 years.

SOLUTIONS TO EXCEL SPREADSHEET QUESTIONS

1.

Stock	Call	Δ Call*	Slope**
300	0.77		
325	2.03	1.27	0.051
350	4.54	2.51	0.101
375	8.86	4.32	0.173
400	15.46	6.60	0.264
425	24.65	9.20	0.368
450	36.55	11.89	0.476
475	51.03	14.48	0.579
500	67.85	16.82	0.673
525	86.67	18.82	0.753
550	107.12	20.45	0.818
575	128.84	21.73	0.869
600	151.53	22.69	0.908

*Change in value of call from previous stock price
**Slope = Δ call/25

2.

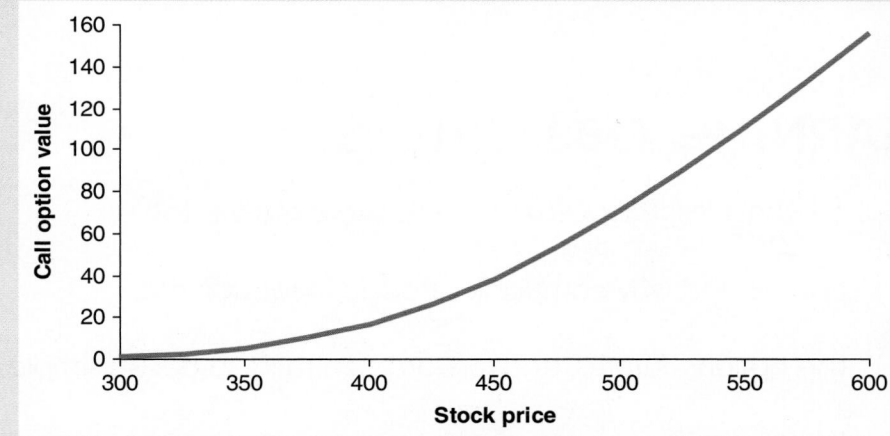

The initial slope between 300 and 325 is $(2.03 - .77)/25 = .051$. As the stock price increases, the slope approaches 1.

CHAPTER 24

Risk Management

LEARNING OBJECTIVES

After reading this chapter, you should be able to:

(1) Understand why companies hedge to reduce risk.

(2) Use options, futures, and forward contracts to devise simple hedging strategies.

(3) Explain how companies can use swaps to change the risk of securities that they have issued.

RELATED WEB SITES FOR THIS CHAPTER CAN BE FOUND AT WWW.MHHE.COM/BMM7E.

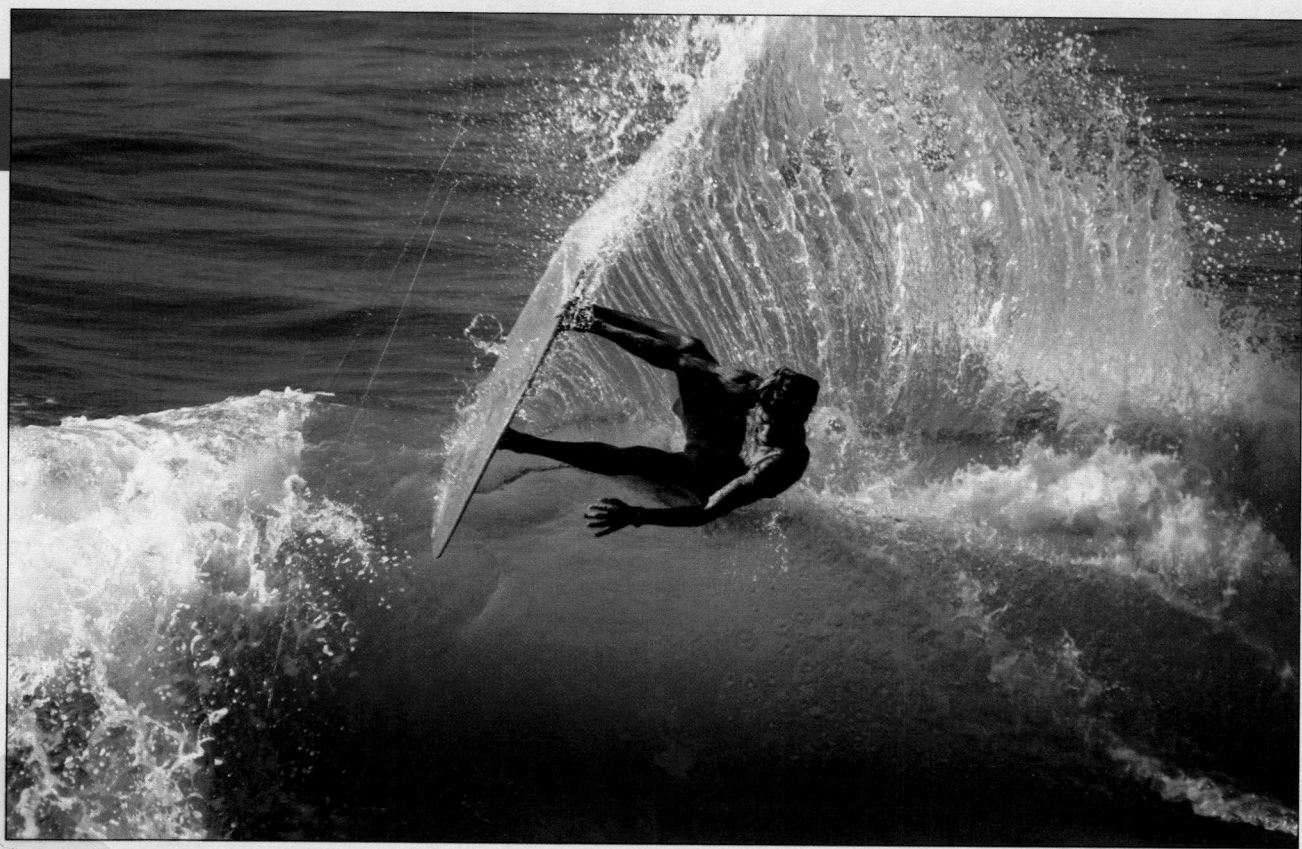

Risk management does not mean avoiding risk. It means deciding what risks to take.

We often assume that risk is beyond our control. A business is exposed to unpredictable changes in raw material costs, tax rates, technology, and a long list of other variables. There's nothing the manager can do about it.

This is not wholly true. To some extent a manager can *select* which risks to accept. For example, in the last chapter we saw that companies can consciously affect the risk of an investment by building in flexibility. A company that reduces the cost of bailing out of a project by using standardized equipment is taking less risk than a similar firm that uses specialized equipment with no alternative uses. In this case the option to resell the equipment serves as an insurance policy.

Sometimes, rather than building flexibility into the project, companies accept the risk but then use financial instruments to offset it. This practice of taking offsetting risks is known as *hedging.* In this chapter we will explain how hedging works and we will describe some of the specialized financial instruments that have been devised to help manage risk. These instruments include options, futures, forwards, and swaps. Each of these instruments provides a payoff that depends on the price of some underlying commodity or financial asset. Because their payoffs derive from the prices of other assets, they are often known collectively as *derivative instruments (or derivatives* for short).[1]

---

[1] Derivatives often conjure up an image of wicked speculators. Derivative instruments attract their share of speculators, some of whom may be wicked, but they are also used by sober and prudent businesspeople who simply want to reduce risk.

24.1 Why Hedge?

In this chapter we will explain *how* companies hedge the risks of their business. But first we should give some of the reasons *why* they do it.

Surely, the answer to this question is obvious. Isn't less risk always better than more? Well, not necessarily. Even if hedging is costless, transactions undertaken *solely* to reduce risk are unlikely to add value. There are two basic reasons for this:

- *Reason 1: Hedging is a zero-sum game.* A company that hedges a risk does not eliminate it. It simply passes the risk on to someone else. For example, suppose that a heating-oil distributor agrees with a refiner to buy all of next winter's heating-oil deliveries at a fixed price. This contract is a zero-sum game, because the refiner loses what the distributor gains and vice versa. If next winter's price of heating oil turns out to be unusually high, the distributor wins from having locked in a below-market price but the refiner is forced to sell below market. Conversely, if the price of heating oil is unusually *low*, the refiner wins because the distributor is forced to buy at the high fixed price. Of course, neither party knows next winter's price at the time that the deal is struck, but they consider the range of possible prices and negotiate terms that are fair (zero NPV) on both sides of the bargain.

- *Reason 2: Investors' do-it-yourself alternative.* Companies cannot increase the value of their shares by undertaking transactions that investors can easily do on their own. We came across this idea when we discussed whether leverage increases company value, and we met it again when we came to dividend policy. It also applies to hedging. For example, when the shareholders in our heating-oil distributor invested in the company, they were presumably aware of the risks of the business. If they did not want to be exposed to the ups and downs of energy prices, they could have protected themselves in several ways. Perhaps they own shares in both the distributor and the refiner and do not care whether one wins at the other's expense.

Of course, shareholders can adjust their exposure only when companies keep investors fully informed of the transactions that they have made. For example, when a group of European central banks announced in 1999 that they would limit their sales of gold, the gold price immediately shot up. Investors in gold-mining shares rubbed their hands at the prospect of rising profits. But when they discovered that some mining companies had protected themselves against price fluctuations and would *not* benefit from the price rise, the hand-rubbing turned to hand-wringing.

Some stockholders of these gold-mining companies wanted to make a bet on rising gold prices; others didn't. But all of them gave the same message to management. The first group said, "Don't hedge! I'm happy to bear the risk of fluctuating gold prices, because I think gold prices will increase." The second group said, "Don't hedge! I'd rather do it myself."

We have seen that although hedging reduces risk, this doesn't in itself increase firm value. So when does it make sense to hedge? Sometimes hedging is worthwhile because it makes financial planning easier and reduces the odds of an embarrassing cash shortfall. A shortfall might mean only an unexpected trip to the bank, but on other occasions the firm might have to forgo worthwhile investments, and in extreme cases the shortfall could trigger bankruptcy. Why not reduce the odds of these awkward outcomes with a hedge?

We saw in our discussion of debt policy in Chapter 16 that financial distress can result in indirect as well as direct costs to a firm. Costs of financial distress arise from disruption to normal business operations as well as from the effect that financial distress has on the firm's investment decisions. The better the risk management policies, the less chance that the firm will incur these costs of distress. As a side benefit, better risk management increases the firm's debt capacity.

In some cases hedging also makes it easier to decide whether an operating manager deserves a stern lecture or a pat on the back. Suppose that your export division shows a 50% decline in profits when the dollar unexpectedly strengthens against other currencies. How much of that decrease is due to the exchange rate shift and how much to poor management? If the company had protected itself against the effect of exchange rate changes, it's probably bad management. If it wasn't protected, you have to make a judgment with hindsight, probably by asking, "What would profits have been *if* the firm had hedged against exchange rate movements?"

Finally, hedging extraneous events can help focus the operating manager's attention. We know we shouldn't worry about events outside our control, but most of us do anyway. It's naive to expect the manager of the export division not to worry about exchange rate movements if his bottom line and bonus depend on them. The time spent worrying could be better spent if the company hedged itself against such movements.

A sensible risk strategy needs answers to the following questions:

- *What are the major risks that the company faces and what are the possible consequences?* Some risks are scarcely worth a thought, but there are others that might bankrupt the company.
- *Is the company being paid for taking these risks?* Managers are not paid to avoid all risks, but if they can reduce their exposure to risks for which there are no compensating rewards, they can afford to place larger bets when the odds are stacked in their favor.
- *Can the company take any measures to reduce the probability of a bad outcome or to limit its impact?* For example, most businesses install alarm and sprinkler systems to prevent damage from fire and invest in backup facilities in case damage does occur.
- *Can the company purchase fairly priced insurance to offset any losses?* Insurance companies have some advantages in bearing risk. In particular, they may be able to spread the risk across a portfolio of different insurers.
- *Can the company use derivatives, such as options or futures, to hedge the risk?* In the remainder of this chapter we explain when and how derivatives may be used.

The Evidence on Risk Management

There are three principal ways to manage risk. First, the firm can reduce risk by building flexibility into its operations. For example, a petrochemical plant that is designed to use either oil or natural gas as a feedstock reduces the threat of an unfavorable shift in the price of raw materials. Or think of a company that reduces the risk of a disaster by test marketing a new product before launching it nationally. Both firms are using *real options* to limit their risk. A second way to reduce risk is to buy an insurance policy against such hazards as fire, accidents, and theft. Finally, the firm may enter into specialized financial contracts that fix its costs or prices. These contracts are known collectively as **derivatives,** and they include options, futures, and swaps.

derivatives
Securities whose payoffs are determined by the values of other financial variables such as prices, exchange rates, or interest rates.

A survey of the world's 500 largest companies found that almost all the companies use derivatives in some way to manage their risk.[2] Eighty-five percent employ them to control interest rate risk. Seventy-eight percent use them to manage currency risk, and 24% to manage the risk of fluctuations in commodity prices.

Risk policies differ. For example, some natural resource companies work hard to hedge their exposure to price fluctuations; others shrug their corporate shoulders and let prices wander as they may. Explaining why some hedge and others don't is not easy. One study of oil and gas companies found that the firms hedged most if they had high debt ratios, no debt ratings, and low dividend payouts.[3] It seems that for these firms, hedging programs were designed to reduce the likelihood of financial distress and to improve the firms' access to debt finance.

---

[2] International Swap Dealers Association (ISDA), "2003 Derivatives Usage Survey," **www.isda.org.**

[3] G. D. Haushalter, "Financing Policy, Basis Risk and Corporate Hedging," *Journal of Finance* 55 (February 2000), pp. 107–152.

24.2 Reducing Risk with Options

In the last chapter we introduced you to put and call options. Managers regularly buy options on currencies, interest rates, and commodities to limit their downside risk. Many of these options are traded on options exchanges, but often they are simply private deals between the corporation and a bank.

Petrochemical Parfum, Inc., is concerned about potential increases in the price of heavy crude oil, which is one of its major inputs. To protect itself against such increases Petrochemical buys 6-month call options to purchase 1,000 barrels of crude oil at an exercise price of $90. These options might cost $3 per barrel.

If the price of crude is above the $90 exercise price when the options expire, Petrochemical will exercise the options and will receive the difference between the oil price and the exercise price. If the oil price falls below the exercise price, the options will expire worthless. The net cost of oil will therefore be:

	Oil Price (dollars per barrel)		
	$80	$90	$100
Cost of 1,000 barrels	$80,000	$90,000	$100,000
− Payoff on call options	0	0	10,000
Net cost	$80,000	$90,000	$90,000

You can see that by buying options Petrochemical protects itself against increases in the oil price while continuing to benefit from oil price decreases. If prices fall, it can discard its call option and buy its oil at the market price. If oil prices rise, however, it can exercise its call option to purchase oil for $90 a barrel. Therefore, options create an attractive asymmetry. Of course, this asymmetry comes at a price—the $3,000 cost of the options.

Consider now the problem of Onnex, Inc., which supplies Petrochemical with crude oil. Its problem is the mirror image of Petrochemical's; it loses when oil prices fall and gains when oil prices rise.

Onnex wants to lock in a minimum price of oil but still benefit from rising oil prices. It can do so by purchasing *put* options that give it the right to *sell* oil at an exercise price of $90 per barrel. If oil prices fall, it will exercise the put. If they rise, it will discard the put and sell oil at the market price:

	Oil Price (dollars per barrel)		
	$80	$90	$100
Revenue from 1,000 barrels	$80,000	$90,000	$100,000
+ Payoff on put option	10,000	0	0
Total revenues	$90,000	$90,000	$100,000

If oil prices rise, Onnex reaps the benefit. But if oil prices fall below $90 a barrel the payoff of the put option exactly offsets the revenue shortfall. As a result, Onnex realizes total revenues of at least $90 a barrel, which is the exercise price of the put option.

Once again, you don't get something for nothing. The price that Onnex pays for insurance against a fall in the price of oil is the cost of the put option. Similarly, the price that Petrochemical paid for insurance against a rise in the price of oil was the cost of the call option. Options provide protection against adverse price changes for a fee—the option premium.

Notice that both Petrochemical and Onnex use options to insure against an adverse move in oil prices. But the options do not remove all uncertainty. For example, Onnex may be able to sell oil for much more than the exercise price of the option.

Figure 24.1 illustrates the nature of Onnex's insurance strategy. Panel *a* shows the revenue derived from selling the 1,000 barrels of oil. The firm is currently exposed to oil price risk: As prices fall, so will the firm's revenue. But, as panel *b* illustrates, the payoff on a put option to sell 1,000 barrels rises as oil prices fall below $90 a barrel, and therefore it can offset the firm's exposure. Panel *c* shows the firm's total revenues after it buys the put option. For prices below $90 per barrel, revenues are $90,000. But revenues rise $1,000 for every dollar that oil prices rise above $90. The profile in panel *c* should be familiar to you: Think back to the protective put strategy we first saw in Section 23.1. In both cases, the put provides a floor on the value of the overall position.

Self-Test 24.1

Draw three graphs like those in Figure 24.1 to illustrate how Petrochemical puts a ceiling on its costs by purchasing call options on oil.

FIGURE 24.1 Onnex can buy put options to place a floor on its overall revenues.

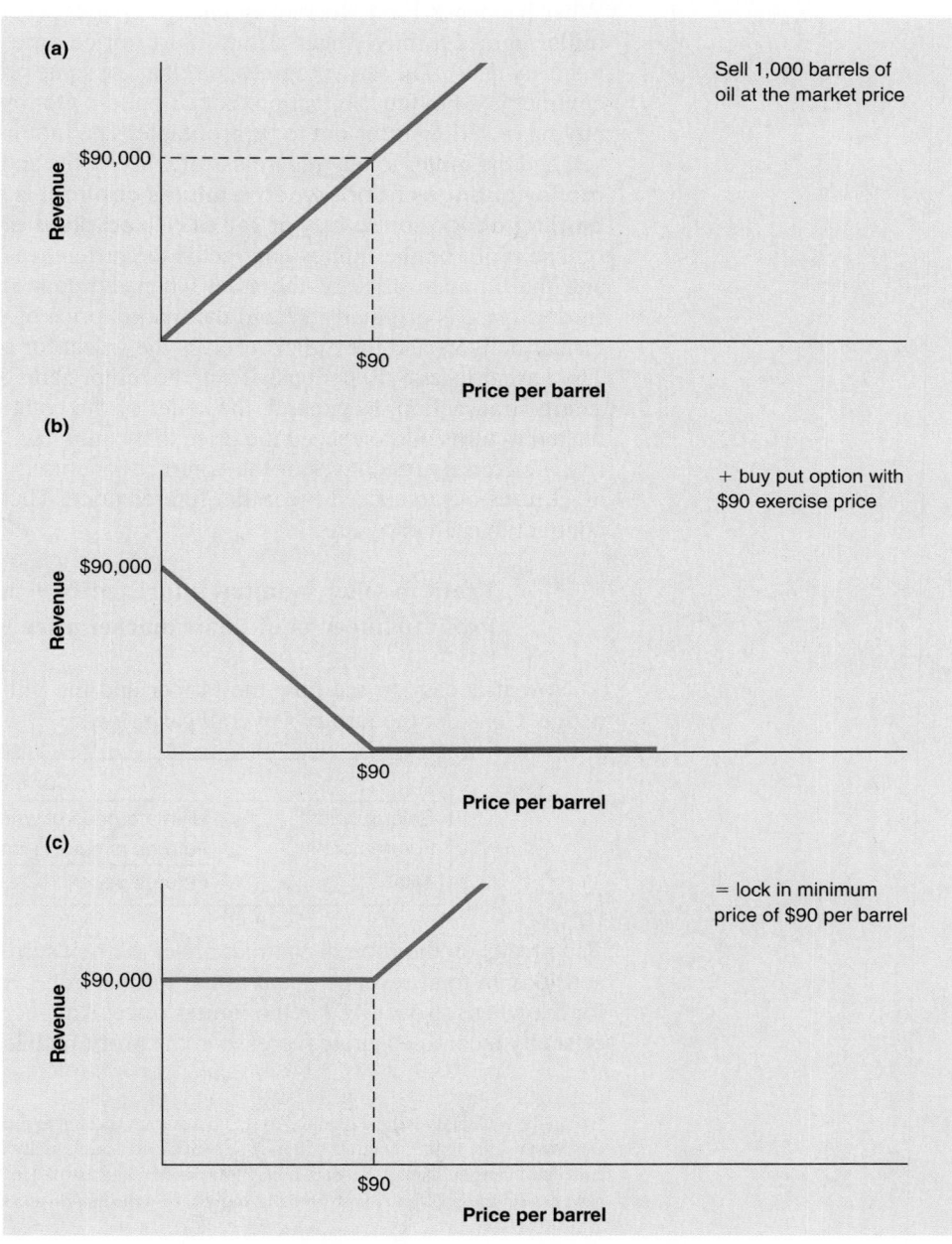

24.3 Futures Contracts

futures contract
Exchange-traded promise to buy or sell an asset in the future at a prespecified price.

Suppose you are a wheat farmer. You are optimistic about next year's wheat crop, but still you can't sleep. You are worried that when the time comes to sell the wheat, prices may have fallen through the floor. The cure for insomnia is to sell wheat *futures*. In this case, you agree to deliver so many bushels of wheat in (say) September at a price that is set today. Do not confuse this **futures contract** with an option, where the holder has a *choice* whether to make delivery; your futures contract is a firm promise to deliver wheat at a fixed selling price.

A miller is in the opposite position. She needs to *buy* wheat after the harvest. If she would like to fix the price of this wheat ahead of time, she can do so by *buying* wheat futures. In other words, she agrees to take delivery of wheat in the future at a price that is fixed today. The miller also does not have an option; if she still holds the futures contract when it matures, she is obliged to take delivery.

Let's suppose the farmer and the miller strike a deal. They enter a futures contract. What happens? First, no money changes hands when the contract is initiated.[4] The miller agrees to buy wheat at the futures price on a stated *future* date (the contract maturity date). The farmer agrees to sell at the same price and date. Second, the futures contract is a binding obligation, not an option. Options give the right to buy or sell *if* buying or selling turns out to be profitable. The futures contract *requires* the farmer to sell and the miller to buy regardless of who profits and who loses. **Just remember, no money changes hands when a futures contract is entered into. The contract is a binding obligation to buy or sell at a fixed price at contract maturity.**

The profit on the futures contract is the difference between the initial futures price and the ultimate price of the asset when the contract matures. For example, if the futures price is originally $7 and the market price of wheat turns out to be $7.50, the farmer delivers and the miller receives the wheat for a price $.50 below market value. The farmer loses $.50 per bushel and the miller gains $.50 per bushel as a result of the futures transaction. In general, the seller of the contract benefits if the price initially locked in turns out to exceed the price that could have been obtained at contract maturity. Conversely, the buyer of the contract benefits if the ultimate market price of the asset turns out to exceed the initial futures price. Therefore, the profits on the futures contract to each party are

Profit to seller = initial futures price − ultimate market price

Profit to buyer = ultimate market price − initial futures price

Now it is easy to see how the farmer and the miller can both use the contract to hedge. Consider the farmer's overall cash flows:

	Cash Flow
Sale of wheat	Ultimate price of wheat
Futures profits	Futures price − ultimate price of wheat
Total	Futures price

The profits on the futures contract offset the risk surrounding the sales price of wheat and lock in total revenue equal to the futures price. Similarly, the miller's all-in cost for the wheat also is fixed at the futures price. Any increase in the cost of wheat will be offset by a commensurate increase in the profit realized on the futures contract.

---

[4] Actually, each party will be required to set up a margin account to guarantee performance on the contract. Despite this, the futures contract still may be considered as essentially requiring no money down. First, the amount of margin is small. Second, it may be posted in interest-bearing securities, so that the parties to the trade need not suffer opportunity cost from placing assets in the margin account.

Both the farmer and the miller have less risk than before. The farmer has hedged (that is, offset) risk by selling wheat futures; the miller has hedged risk by buying wheat futures.[5]

EXAMPLE 24.1 ▶ Hedging with Futures

Suppose that the farmer originally sold 5,000 bushels of September wheat futures at a price of $7 a bushel. In September, when the futures contract matures, the price of wheat is only $6 a bushel. The farmer buys back the wheat futures at $6 just before maturity, giving him a profit of $1 a bushel on the sale and subsequent repurchase. At the same time he sells his wheat at the spot price of $6 a bushel. His total receipts are therefore $7 a bushel:

Profit on sale and repurchase of futures	$1
Sale of wheat at the September spot price	$6
Total receipts	$7

You can see that the futures contract has allowed the farmer to lock in total proceeds of $7 a bushel.

Figure 24.2 illustrates how the futures contract enabled the farmer in Example 24.1 to hedge his position. Panel *a* shows how the value of 5,000 bushels of wheat varies with the spot price of wheat. The value rises by $5,000 for every dollar increase in wheat prices. Panel *b* is the profit on a futures contract to deliver 5,000 bushels of wheat at a futures price of $7 per bushel. The profit will be zero if the ultimate price of wheat equals the original futures price, $7. The profit on the contract to deliver at $7 rises by $5,000 for every dollar the price of wheat *falls* below $7. The exposures to the price of wheat depicted in panels *a* and *b* obviously cancel out. Panel *c* shows that the total value of the 5,000 bushels plus the futures position is unaffected by the ultimate price of wheat, and equals $7 \times 5,000 = $35,000. In other words, the farmer has locked in proceeds of $7 per bushel, equal to the original futures price.

The Mechanics of Futures Trading

In practice the farmer and miller would not sign the futures contract face-to-face. Instead, each would go to an organized futures exchange such as the Chicago Board of Trade.

Table 24.1 shows the price of wheat futures at the Chicago Board of Trade in August 2010, when the price for immediate delivery was about $7 a bushel. Notice that there is a choice of possible delivery dates. If, for example, you were to sell wheat for delivery in March 2011, you would get a higher price than by selling December 2010 futures.

TABLE 24.1 The price of wheat futures at the Chicago Board of Trade on August 16, 2010

Delivery Date	Price per Bushel
December 2010	$7.30
March 2011	7.49
May 2011	7.42
July 2011	7.13
September 2011	7.15
December 2011	7.25

Source: The Chicago Board of Trade Web site, www.cmegroup.com.

---

[5] Neither has eliminated all risk. For example, the farmer still has quantity risk. He does not know for sure how many bushels of wheat he will produce.

FIGURE 24.2 The farmer
can use wheat futures to
hedge the value of the crop.
See Example 24.1.

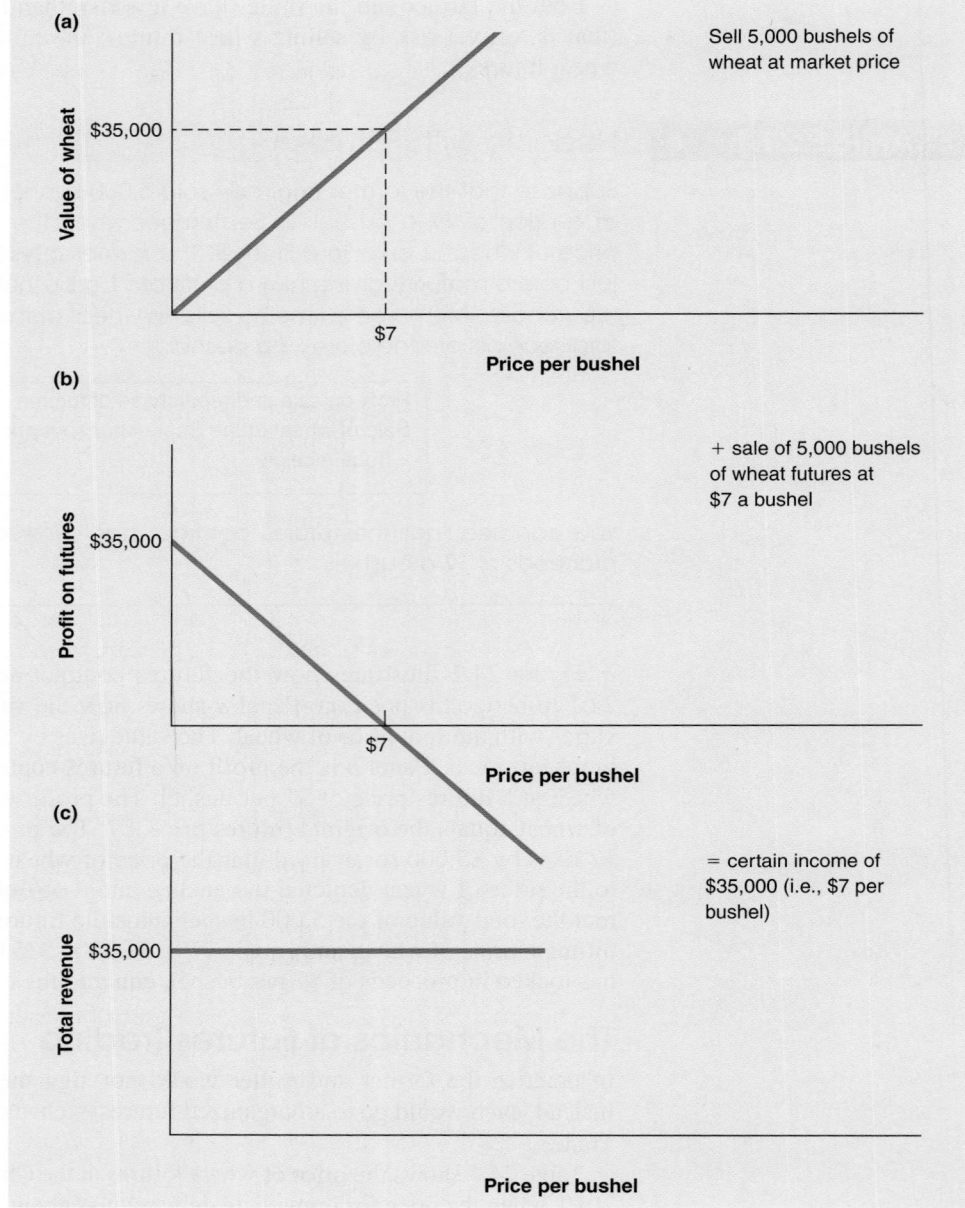

The miller would not be prepared to buy futures contracts if the farmer were free to deliver half-rotten wheat to a leaky barn at the end of a cart track. Futures trading is possible only because the contracts are highly standardized. For example, in the case of wheat futures, each contract calls for the delivery of 5,000 bushels of wheat of a specified quality at a warehouse in Chicago, Toledo, or Burns Harbor.

When you buy or sell a futures contract, the price is fixed today, but payment is not made until later. However, you will be asked to put up some cash or securities as *margin* to demonstrate that you are able to honor your side of the bargain.

In addition, futures contracts are *marked to market*. This means that each day any profits or losses on the contract are calculated; you pay the exchange any losses and receive any profits. For example, our farmer agreed to deliver 5,000 bushels of wheat at $7 a bushel. Suppose that the next day the price of wheat futures increases to $7.05 a bushel. The farmer now has a loss on his sale of 5,000 × $.05 = $250 and must pay this sum to the exchange. You can think of the farmer as buying back his futures position each day and then opening up a new position. Thus after the first day the farmer has realized a loss on his trade of $.05 a bushel and now has an obligation to deliver wheat for $7.05 a bushel.

Of course our miller is in the opposite position. The rise in the futures price leaves her with a *profit* of 5 cents a bushel. The exchange will therefore pay her this profit. In effect the miller sells her futures position at a profit and opens a new contract to take delivery at $7.05 a bushel.

spot price
Price that is paid for immediate delivery.

The price of wheat for immediate delivery is known as the **spot price.** When the farmer sells wheat futures, the price that he agrees to take for his wheat may be very different from the spot price. But the future eventually becomes the present. As the date for delivery approaches, the futures contract becomes more and more like a spot contract and the price of the futures contract snuggles up to the spot price.

The farmer may decide to wait until the futures contract matures and then deliver wheat to the buyer. But in practice such delivery is rare, for it is more convenient for the farmer to buy back the wheat futures just before maturity.[6]

Self-Test 24.2

Suppose that 2 days after taking out the futures contract the price of September wheat increases from $7.05 to $7.20 a bushel. What additional payments will be made by or to the farmer and the miller? What will be their remaining obligation at the end of this second day?

Commodity and Financial Futures

We have shown how the farmer and the miller can both use wheat futures to hedge their risk. It is also possible to trade futures in a wide variety of other commodities, such as sugar, soybean oil, pork bellies, orange juice, crude oil, and copper.

Commodity prices can bounce up and down like a bungee jumper. For example, in June 2008 copper prices hit a high of nearly $9,000 a ton. Six months later the price was less than $3,000 a ton. For a large user of copper, such as the Olin Corporation, these price fluctuations could knock the company badly off course. Olin therefore reduces its exposure to movements in the price of copper and other metals by hedging with commodity futures. A number of copper producers have also found that hedging increases their debt capacity. So, when the Canadian company Equinox needed to borrow $584 million to finance its new Zambian mine, the lenders first insisted that Equinox reduce its exposure to fluctuations in the copper price by hedging 30% of its planned output.

For many firms, the wide fluctuations in interest rates and exchange rates have become at least as important a source of risk as changes in commodity prices. You can use *financial futures* to hedge against these risks.

Financial futures are similar to commodity futures, but instead of placing an order to buy or sell a commodity at a future date, you place an order to buy or sell a financial asset at a future date. You can use financial futures to protect yourself against fluctuations in short- and long-term interest rates, exchange rates, and the level of share prices.

Figure 24.3 shows the explosive growth of worldwide futures trading. Table 24.2 lists some of the more popular financial futures contracts.

---

[6] In the case of some of the financial futures described later, you cannot deliver the asset. At maturity the buyer simply receives (or pays) the difference between the spot price and the price at which he or she has agreed to purchase the asset.

Self-Test 24.3

You plan to issue long-term bonds in 9 months but are worried that interest rates may have increased in the meantime. How could you use financial futures to protect yourself against a general rise in interest rates?

FIGURE 24.3 Worldwide turnover in futures contracts has expanded sharply.

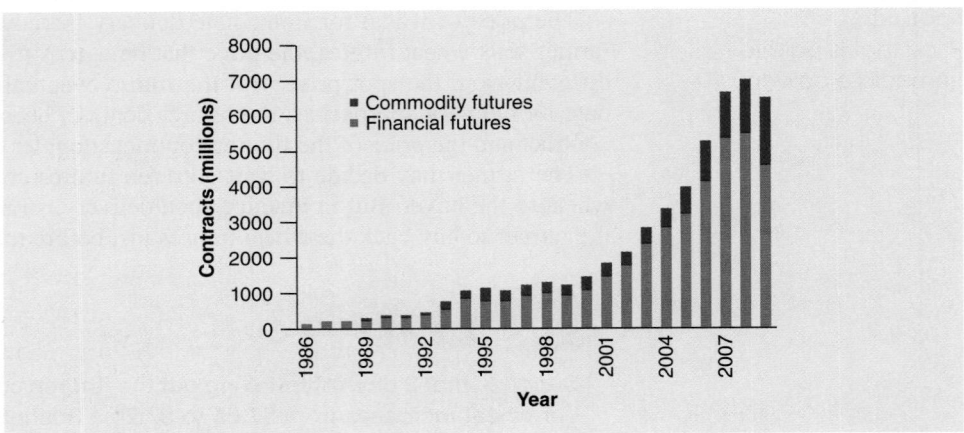

Source: Bank for International Settlements, **www.bis.org.**

TABLE 24.2 Some financial futures contracts

Contract	Principal Exchange
U.S. Treasury notes and bonds	CBT
Eurodollar deposits	CME
Standard & Poor's Index	CME
Euro	CME
Yen	CME
German government bonds (Bunds)	Eurex

Key to abbreviations:
    CBT   Chicago Board of Trade
    CME   Chicago Mercantile Exchange

24.4   Forward Contract

Each day billions of dollars of futures contracts are bought and sold. We have seen that this liquidity is possible only because futures contracts are standardized. Futures contracts mature on a limited number of dates each year (take another look at the wheat contract in Table 24.1), and the contract size is standardized. For example, a contract may call for delivery of 5,000 bushels of wheat, 100 ounces of gold, or 62,500 British pounds. If the terms of a futures contract do not suit your particular needs, you may be able to buy or sell a **forward contract.**

forward contract
Agreement to buy or sell an asset in the future at an agreed price.

Forward contracts are custom-tailored futures contracts.[7] **You can write a forward contract with any maturity date for delivery of any quantity of goods.** For example, suppose that you know that you will need to pay out yen in 3 months' time. You can fix today the price that you will pay for the yen by arranging with your bank to buy yen forward. At the end of the 3 months, you pay the agreed sum and take delivery of the yen.

---

[7] One difference between forward and futures contracts is that forward contracts are not marked to market. Thus with a forward contract you settle up any profits or losses when the contract matures.

EXAMPLE 24.2 ▶ Forward Contracts

Computer Parts Inc. has ordered memory chips from its supplier in Japan. The bill for ¥53 million must be paid on July 27. The company can arrange with its bank today to buy this number of yen forward for delivery on July 27 at a forward price of ¥110 per dollar. Therefore, on July 27, Computer Parts pays the bank $53 million/ (¥110/$) = $481,818 and receives ¥53 million, which it can use to pay its Japanese supplier. By committing forward to exchange $481,818 for ¥53 million, its dollar costs are locked in. Notice that if the firm had not used the forward contract to hedge and the dollar had depreciated over this period, the firm would have had to pay a greater amount of dollars. For example, if the dollar had depreciated to ¥100/dollar, the firm would have had to exchange $530,000 for the ¥53 million necessary to pay its bill. The firm could have used a futures contract to hedge its foreign exchange exposure, but standardization of futures would not allow for delivery of precisely ¥53 million on precisely July 27.

The most active trading in forwards is in foreign currencies, but in recent years companies have increasingly entered into forward rate agreements that allow them to fix in advance the interest rate at which they borrow or lend.

24.5 Swaps

Suppose Computer Parts from Example 24.2 decides to produce memory chips instead of purchasing them from outside suppliers. It has issued $100 million in floating-rate bonds to help finance the construction of a new plant. (Recall from Chapter 14 that floating-rate loans make interest payments that go up and down with the general level of interest rates. The coupon payments on the bonds are tied to a specific short-term interest rate.) But the financial manager is concerned that interest rates are becoming more volatile, and she would like to lock in the firm's interest expenses. One approach would be to buy back the floating-rate bonds and replace them with a new issue of fixed-rate debt. But it is costly to issue new debt to the public; in addition, buying back the outstanding bonds in the market will result in considerable trading costs.

A better approach to hedge out its interest rate exposure is for the firm to enter an interest rate **swap.** The firm will pay or "swap" a fixed payment for another payment that is tied to the level of interest rates. Thus if rates do rise, increasing the firm's interest expense on its floating-rate debt, its cash flow from the swap agreement will rise as well, offsetting its exposure.

Suppose the firm pays the LIBOR rate on its floating-rate bonds. (Recall that LIBOR, or London Interbank Offer Rate, is the interest rate at which banks borrow from each other in the eurodollar market. It is the most frequently used short-term interest rate in the swap market.) The firm's interest expense each year therefore equals the LIBOR rate times $100 million. It would like to transform this obligation into one that will not fluctuate with interest rates.

Suppose that current rates in the swaps market are "LIBOR for 5% fixed." This means that Computer Parts can enter into a swap agreement to *pay* 5% on "notional principal" of $100 million to a swap dealer and *receive* payment of the LIBOR rate on the same amount of notional principal. The dealer and the firm are called *counterparties* in the swap. The firm pays the dealer .05 × $100 million and receives LIBOR × $100 million. The firm's *net* cash payment to the dealer is therefore (.05 − LIBOR) × $100 million. (If LIBOR exceeds 5%, the firm receives money from the dealer; if it is less than 5%, the firm pays money to the dealer.) Figure 24.4 illustrates the cash flows paid by Computer Parts and the swap dealer.

swap
Arrangement by two counterparties to exchange one stream of cash flows for another.

FIGURE 24.4 Interest rate swap. Computer Parts currently pays the LIBOR rate on its outstanding bonds (the arrow on the left). If the firm enters a swap to pay a fixed rate of 5% and receive a floating rate of LIBOR, its exposure to LIBOR will cancel out and its net cash outflow will be a fixed rate of 5%.

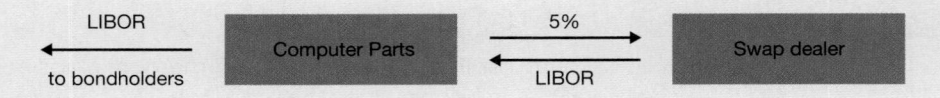

Table 24.3 shows Computer Parts's net payments for three possible interest rates. The total payment on the bond-with-swap agreement equals $5 million regardless of the interest rate. The swap has transformed the floating-rate bond into synthetic fixed-rate debt with an effective coupon rate of 5%. The firm has thus hedged away its interest rate exposure without actually having to replace its floating-rate bonds with fixed-rate bonds. Swaps offer a much cheaper way to "rearrange the balance sheet."[8]

There are many other applications of interest rate swaps. A portfolio manager who is holding a portfolio of long-term bonds but is worried that interest rates might increase, causing a capital loss on the portfolio, can enter a swap to pay a fixed rate and receive a floating rate, thereby converting the holdings into a synthetic floating-rate portfolio (see Self-Test 24.4). Or a pension fund manager might identify some money market securities that are paying excellent yields compared with other comparable-risk short-term securities. However, the manager might believe that short-term assets are inappropriate for the portfolio. The fund can receive the interest rate on these high-yielding securities and enter a swap in which it receives a fixed rate and pays a floating rate based on a lower-yielding money market security. It thus captures the benefit of the advantageous *relative* yields on its securities but still establishes a portfolio with the fixed interest rate risk characteristic of long-term bonds.

Self-Test 24.4

Consider the portfolio manager who is holding a $100 million portfolio of long-term 5% coupon bonds and wishes to reduce price risk by transforming the holdings into a synthetic floating-rate portfolio. Assume that the portfolio currently pays a 5% fixed rate and that swap dealers currently offer terms of 5% fixed for LIBOR. What swap would the manager establish? Show the total income on the fund in a table like Table 24.3, and illustrate the cash flows in a diagram like Figure 24.4.

There are many variations on the interest rate swap. For example, currency swaps allow firms to exchange a series of payments in dollars (which may be tied to a fixed or floating rate) for a series of payments in another currency (which also may be tied

TABLE 24.3 An interest rate swap can transform floating-rate bonds into synthetic fixed-rate bonds.

	LIBOR Rate		
	4.5%	5.0%	5.5%
Interest paid on floating-rate bonds (= LIBOR × $100 million)	$4,500,000	$5,000,000	$5,500,000
+ Cash payment on swap [= (.05 − LIBOR) × notional principal of $100 million]	500,000	0	−500,000
Total payment	$5,000,000	$5,000,000	$5,000,000

---

[8] You might wonder what's in this arrangement for the swap dealer. The dealer will profit by charging a bid-ask spread. Since the dealer pays LIBOR in return for 5% in this swap, it might search for another trader who wishes to receive a fixed rate and pay LIBOR. The dealer will pay a 4.9% rate to that trader in return for the LIBOR rate. So the dealer pays a fixed rate and receives floating with one trader but pays floating and receives fixed with the other. Its net cash flow is thus fixed and equal to .1% of notional principal.

to a fixed or floating rate). These swaps can therefore be used to manage exposure to exchange rate fluctuations.

EXAMPLE 24.3 ▶   Currency Swaps

Suppose that the Possum Company wishes to borrow Swiss francs (SFr) to help finance its European operations. Since Possum is better known in the United States, the financial manager believes that the company can obtain more attractive terms on a dollar loan than on a Swiss franc loan. Therefore, the company borrows $10 million for 5 years at 5% in the United States. At the same time Possum arranges with a swap dealer to trade its future dollar liability for Swiss francs. Under this arrangement the dealer agrees to pay Possum sufficient dollars to service its dollar loan, and in exchange Possum agrees to make a series of annual payments in Swiss francs to the dealer.

Possum's cash flows are set out in Table 24.4. Line 1 shows that when Possum takes out its dollar loan, it promises to pay annual interest of $.5 million and to repay the $10 million that it has borrowed. Lines 2a and 2b show the cash flows from the swap, assuming that the spot exchange rate for Swiss francs is $1 = SFr2. Possum hands over to the dealer the $10 million that it borrowed and receives in exchange 2 × $10 million = SFr20 million. In each of the next 4 years the dealer pays Possum $.5 million, which it uses to pay the annual interest on its loan. In year 5 the dealer pays Possum $10.5 million to cover both the final year's interest and the repayment of the loan. In return for these future dollar receipts, Possum agrees to pay the dealer SFr1.2 million in each of the next 4 years and SFr21.2 million in year 5.

The combined effect of Possum's two steps (line 3) is the conversion of its 5% dollar loan into a 6% Swiss franc loan. The device that makes this possible is the currency swap.

Self-Test 24.5

Suppose that the spot exchange rate had been $1 = SFr3 and that Swiss interest rates were 8%. Recalculate the Swiss franc cash flows that the dealer would agree to (line 2b of Table 24.4) and Possum's net cash flows (line 3).

24.6 Innovation in the Derivatives Market

Almost every day some new derivative contract seems to be invented. At first there may be just a few private deals between a bank and its customers, but if the contract proves popular, one of the futures exchanges may try to muscle in on the business.

Derivatives dealers try to identify the major risks that face businesses and then design a contract that will allow them to lay off these risks. For example, a major hazard for many financial institutions is the possibility that a large customer will get into difficulties and default on its debts. Credit default swaps offer a way for the lender to

TABLE 24.4 Cash flows from Possum's dollar loan and currency swap (figures in millions)

	Year 0		Years 1–4		Year 5	
	$	SFr	$	SFr	$	SFr
1. Issue dollar loan	+10		−.5		−10.5	
2. Arrange currency swap						
a. Possum receives $	−10		+.5		+10.5	
b. Possum pays SFr		+20		−1.2		−21.2
3. Net cash flow	0	+20	0	−1.2	0	−21.2

insure against such a default. The provider of the insurance promises to pay out if the borrower defaults on its debts and in return charges a premium for taking on the risk. We described credit default swaps in Chapter 6.

Iron ore prices are volatile. With fluctuating demand from China, iron ore prices roughly doubled in 2008 and halved in 2009 before surging again in early 2010. The futures exchanges reasoned that both producers and users might welcome a contract that allowed them to hedge these price movements. Therefore, in July 2010 the New York Mercantile Exchange (part of the CME Group) introduced a futures contract based on the price of iron ore landed in China.

Real estate businesses and builders worry about fluctuations in house prices. So wouldn't it be nice if they could stop worrying and hedge themselves against these fluctuations? Well, now they can do so by dealing in real estate futures or options on the Chicago Mercantile Exchange. Real estate futures were launched in 2006 and enable participants to protect themselves against changes in house prices in 10 U.S. cities.

It seems to be very difficult to predict which new contracts will succeed and which will bomb. By the time you read this, iron ore contracts may have been forgotten, and everyone will be talking about the new growth market in _____ derivatives. Perhaps you can help fill in the missing word.

24.7 Is "Derivative" a Four-Letter Word?

Our earlier examples of the farmer and the miller showed how derivatives—futures, options, or swaps, for example—can be used to reduce business risk. However, if you were to copy the farmer and sell wheat futures without an offsetting holding of wheat, you would not be *reducing* risk; you would be *speculating.*

A successful futures market needs speculators who are prepared to take on risk and provide the farmer and the miller with the protection they need. For example, if an excess of farmers wished to sell wheat futures, the price of futures would be forced down until enough speculators were tempted to buy in the hope of a profit. If there is a surplus of millers wishing to buy wheat futures, the reverse will happen. The price will be forced up until speculators are drawn in to sell.

Speculation may be necessary to a thriving derivatives market, but it can get companies into serious trouble. For example, for 10 years a Japanese trading company, Sumitomo Corporation, used the futures market to place huge bets on the price of copper; its chief trader, known in the business simply as "Mr. Copper," was lauded for his contributions to firm profits. However, in June 1996 the copper market was battered by the revelation that the man with the Midas touch had managed to hide losses amounting to about $2 billion.

Sumitomo has plenty of company. In 1995 Baring Brothers, a blue-chip British merchant bank, became insolvent. The reason: Nick Leeson, a trader in its Singapore office, had lost $1.4 billion speculating in futures on the Japanese stock market index. The same year Daiwa Bank reported that a bond trader in its New York office had managed to hide losses over 11 years of $1.1 billion. In 2008 the French bank Societé Generale joined the billion-dollar club when it reported that one of its derivatives traders had lost a record $7.2 billion on unauthorized trades.

The nearby Finance in Practice box discusses another billion-dollar debacle. In this case, Metallgesellschaft claimed to be using futures markets to hedge, but it still managed to lose well over $1 billion. Whether the firm really was hedging, however, is a matter that is subject to debate.

Do these horror stories mean that firms should ban the use of derivatives? Of course not. But they do illustrate that derivatives need to be used with care. **Speculation is foolish unless you have reason to believe that the odds are stacked in your favor. If you are not better informed than the highly paid professionals in banks and other institutions, you should use derivatives for hedging, not for speculation.**

Meltdown at Metallgesellschaft

Metallgesellschaft AG was one of Germany's most respected companies, with more than 20,000 employees and revenues of some $10 billion. Its 251 subsidiaries were engaged in engineering, mining, financial services, and commodities trading, and its major shareholders included such blue-chip German companies as Deutsche Bank, Daimler-Benz, and Allianz.

However, in 1993 Metallgesellschaft was nearly brought to its knees by losses of $1.4 billion from trading in oil futures. The problem arose in one of its U.S. subsidiaries, MGRM. MGRM offered its customers firm price guarantees for up to 10 years on any oil that they agreed to buy. These guarantees proved very popular, so by the end of 1993 the company had entered into long-term contracts to supply 160 million barrels of oil worth more than $3 billion.

There was only one problem. MGRM did not own the oil that it had promised to deliver and would therefore have to buy it from the major oil companies. If the price of oil rose above the price that customers had agreed to pay, MGRM would make a loss on every barrel of oil that it had sold. The apparent solution was for MGRM to hedge its exposure by buying oil futures. This would fix the price at which the company could buy oil when it needed to deliver it. The company would have liked to buy oil futures that matured on the same dates as it was obliged to deliver the oil, but, unfortunately, most futures trading takes place in contracts that mature within a year. MGRM's solution was to buy short-term oil futures and to replace them when they matured.

During the second half of 1993 oil prices fell by 25%, and MGRM's contracts to deliver oil at a predetermined price looked increasingly attractive. However, at the same time the company started to pile up large losses on its purchases of oil futures. This was not in itself a cause for concern. If MGRM was truly hedged, the profits on the oil contracts should have exactly offset the losses on the futures.

So what went wrong? One view is that management focused on the accumulating losses on the futures positions and failed to recognize the gains on the oil contracts. When the losses became sufficiently large, management's nerve cracked and it sold out of its futures positions at the wrong time. Moreover, because MGRM's futures positions were marked to market, the company had to find the cash each day to cover the losses on these positions. This problem of financing the hedge may have contributed to management's decision to abandon its strategy.

Other commentators are less convinced that all would have come right if only management had not panicked. They argue that the company's strategy of hedging long-term liabilities with short-term futures was fundamentally flawed. The problem was that MGRM could not predict the price at which it would be able to replace each futures contract when it matured. If the price of the new future was below that of the maturing one, MGRM would make a profit from the trade. But unfortunately for MGRM, the reverse proved to be the case, so the company incurred a loss each time it replaced the maturing futures contract with a new one.

While financial experts continued to debate the cause of MGRM's losses, the company's bankers struggled to put together a rescue package. A massive $1.9 billion loan from 150 international banks was needed to keep the company from foundering.

SUMMARY

Why do companies hedge to reduce risk? *(LO1)*

Fluctuations in commodity prices, interest rates, or exchange rates can make planning difficult and can throw companies badly off course. Financial managers therefore look for opportunities to manage these risks, and a number of specialized instruments have been invented to help them. These are collectively known as *derivative instruments*.

How can options, futures, and forward contracts be used to devise simple hedging strategies? *(LO2)*

In the last chapter we introduced you to put and call options. **Options** are often used by firms to limit their downside risk. For example, if you own an asset and have the option to sell it at the current price, then you have effectively insured yourself against loss.

Futures contracts are agreements made today to buy or sell an asset in the future. The price is fixed today, but the final payment does not occur until the delivery date. Futures contracts are highly standardized and are traded on organized exchanges. Commodity futures allow firms to fix the future price that they pay for a wide range of agricultural commodities, metals, and oil. Financial futures help firms to protect themselves against unforeseen movements in interest rates, exchange rates, and stock prices.

Forward contracts are equivalent to tailor-made futures contracts. For example, firms often enter into forward agreements with a bank to buy or sell foreign exchange or to fix the interest rate on a loan to be made in the future.

How can companies use swaps to change the risk of securities that they have issued? *(LO3)*

Swaps allow firms to exchange one series of future payments for another. For example, the firm might agree to make a series of regular payments in one currency in return for receiving a series of payments in another currency.

QUESTIONS

QUIZ

1. **Risk Management.** Large businesses spend millions of dollars annually on insurance. Why? Should they insure against all risks or does insurance make more sense for some risks than others? *(LO1)*

2. **Hedging.** *(LO2)*
   a. An investor currently holding $1 million in long-term Treasury bonds becomes concerned about increasing volatility in interest rates. She decides to hedge her risk by using Treasury bond futures contracts. Should she buy or sell such contracts?
   b. The treasurer of a corporation that will be issuing bonds in 3 months also is concerned about interest rate volatility and wants to lock in the price at which he could sell 8% coupon bonds. How would he use Treasury bond futures contracts to hedge his firm's position?

3. **Commodity Futures.** What commodity futures are traded on futures exchanges? Who do you think could usefully reduce risk by buying each of these contracts? Who do you think might wish to sell each contract? *(LO1)*

4. **Hedging.** "The farmer does not avoid risk by selling wheat futures. If wheat prices stay above $9.40 a bushel, then he will actually have lost by selling wheat futures at $9.40." Is this a fair comment? *(LO1)*

5. **Marking to Market.** Suppose that in the 5 days following a farmer's sale of September wheat futures at a futures price of $9.83 the futures price is:

Day	1	2	3	4	5
Price	$9.83	$9.89	$9.70	$9.50	$9.60

   At the end of day 5 the farmer decides to quit wheat farming and buys back his futures contract. What payments are made between the farmer and the exchange on each day? What is the total payment over the 5 days? Would the total payment be any different if the contract was not marked to market? *(LO2)*

6. **Futures versus Spot Positions.** What do you think are the advantages of holding futures rather than the underlying commodity? What do you think are the disadvantages? *(LO2)*

PRACTICE PROBLEMS

7. **Hedging with Futures versus Puts.** A gold-mining firm is concerned about short-term volatility in its revenues. Gold currently sells for $1,200 an ounce, but the price is volatile and could fall as low as $1,000 or rise as high as $1,400 in the next month. The company will bring 1,000 ounces to the market next month. *(LO2)*
   a. What will be total revenues if the firm remains unhedged for gold prices of $1,000, $1,200, and $1,400 an ounce?
   b. The futures price of gold for 1-month-ahead delivery is $1,080. What will be the firm's total revenues at each gold price if the firm enters a 1-month futures contract to deliver 1,000 ounces of gold?
   c. What will total revenues be if the firm buys a 1-month put option to sell gold for $1,080 an ounce? The puts cost $12 per ounce.

8. **Hedging with Calls.** A large dental lab plans to purchase 1,000 ounces of gold in 1 month. Assume again that gold prices can be $1,000, $1,200, or $1,400 an ounce. *(LO2)*

   a. What will total expenses be if the firm purchases call options on 1,000 ounces of gold with an exercise price of $1,080 an ounce? The options cost $15 per ounce.

   b. What will total expenses be if the firm purchases call options on 1,000 ounces of gold with an exercise price of $1,040 an ounce? These options cost $25 per ounce.

9. **Forward Contract.** Assume that the 1-year interest rate is 4% and the 2-year interest rate is 5%. You approach a bank and ask at what rate the bank will promise to make a 1-year loan in 12 months' time. The bank offers to make a forward commitment to lend to you at 10%. Would you accept the offer? Can you think of a simple, cheaper alternative? *(LO2)*

10. **Hedging Project Risk.** Your firm has just tendered for a contract in Japan. You won't know for 3 months whether you get the contract but if you do, you will receive a payment of ¥10 million 1 year from now. You are worried that if the yen declines in value, the dollar value of this payment will be less than you expect and the project could even show a loss. Discuss the possible ways that you could protect the firm against a decline in the value of the yen. Illustrate the possible outcomes if you do get the contract and if you don't. *(LO2)*

11. **Hedging with Futures.** Show how Petrochemical Parfum (see Section 24.2) can also use futures contracts to protect itself against a rise in the price of crude oil. Show how the payoffs would vary if the oil price is $80, $90, or $100 a barrel. Assume the futures price is $90 per barrel. What are the advantages and disadvantages for Petrochemical of using futures rather than options to reduce risk? Repeat the exercise for Onnex. *(LO2)*

12. **Futures Contracts.** Log onto the on-line *Wall Street Journal* **www.wsj.com** and find the prices of gold futures in the Markets Data Center. What is the date of the most distant contract? Suppose that you buy 100 ounces of gold futures for this date. When do you receive the gold? When do you pay for it? Is the futures price higher or lower than the current spot price? Can you suggest why? *(LO2)*

13. **Hedging Currency Risk.** When the euro strengthened in 2007, German luxury car manufacturers found it increasingly difficult to compete in the U.S. market. How could they have hedged themselves against this risk? Would a company that was hedged have been in a better position to compete? Explain why or why not. *(LO1)*

14. **Swaps.** What is a currency swap? An interest rate swap? Give one example of how each might be used. *(LO3)*

CHALLENGE PROBLEM

Templates can be found at
www.mhhe.com/bmm7e.

15. **Swaps.** Firms A and B face the following borrowing rates for a 5-year fixed-rate debt issue in U.S. dollars or euros: *(LO3)*

	U.S. Dollars	Euros
Firm A	8%	6%
Firm B	6	5

   Suppose that A wishes to borrow U.S. dollars and B wishes to borrow euros. Show how a swap could be used to reduce the borrowing costs of each company. Assume a spot exchange rate of 1 euro to the dollar. *(LO3)*

WEB EXERCISES

1. Log on to **www.cmegroup.com** and find the recent quotes for soybean futures. What is the longest maturity for this contract? Is there more trading in the nearer or more distant contracts? Does it cost more to buy soybeans for delivery in the next few months or for later delivery? You could also check out how successful the Nymex iron ore contract has been. Has it proved popular, or has it ceased to trade?

2.   Every 3 years the Bank for International Settlements undertakes a survey of derivatives trading which is available on its Web site, www.bis.org. Which are the most important types of derivative contract? Which have been growing most rapidly? Why? Who do you think would find them useful?

SOLUTIONS TO SELF-TEST QUESTIONS

24.1   See Figure 24.5.

FIGURE 24.5 Petrochemical places a ceiling on its costs.

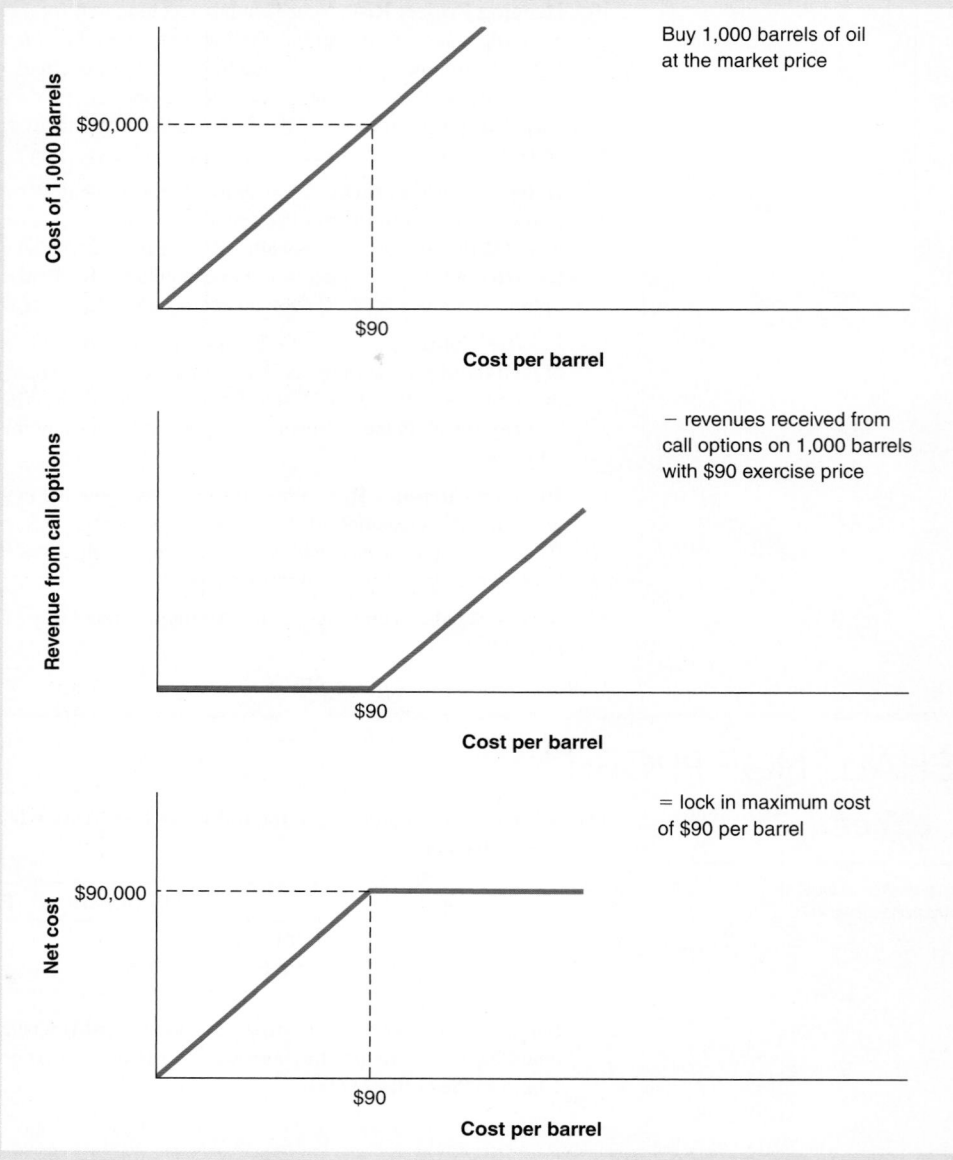

24.2   The farmer has a further loss of 15 cents a bushel ($7.20 − $7.05) and will be required to pay this amount to the exchange. The miller has a further profit of 15 cents per bushel and will receive this from the exchange. The farmer is now committed to delivering wheat in September for $7.20 per bushel, and the miller is committed to paying $7.20 per bushel.

24.3   You sell long-term bond futures with a delivery date of 9 months. Suppose, for example, that you agree to deliver long-term bonds in 9 months at a price of $100. If interest rates rise, the price of the bond futures will fall to (say) $95. (Remember that when interest rates rise, bond prices fall.) In this case the profit that you make on your bond futures offsets the lower price that the firm is likely to receive on the sale of its own bonds. Conversely, if interest rates fall, the company will make a loss on its futures position but will receive a higher price for its own bonds.

24.4 The manager should enter a swap to pay a 5% fixed rate and receive LIBOR on notional principal of $100 million. The cash flows will then rise in tandem with the LIBOR rate:

	LIBOR Rate		
	4.5%	**5.0%**	**5.5%**
Interest received on fixed-rate bonds ($= .05 \times \$100$ million)	$5,000,000	$5,000,000	$5,000,000
+ Cash flow on swap [$= (LIBOR - .05) \times$ notional principal of $100 million]	−500,000	0	+500,000
Total payment	$4,500,000	$5,000,000	$5,500,000

The diagram describing the cash flows of each party to the swap is as follows:

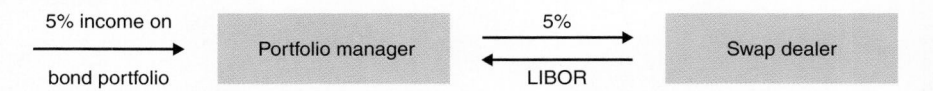

The manager nets a cash flow proportional to the LIBOR rate.

24.5 The following table shows revised cash flows from Possum's dollar loan and currency swap (figures in millions):

	Year 0		Years 1–4		Year 5	
	$	**SFr**	**$**	**SFr**	**$**	**SFr**
1. Issue dollar loan	+10		−.5		−10.5	
2. Arrange currency swap						
a. Possum receives $	−10		+.5		+10.5	
b. Possum pays SFr		+30		−2.4		−32.4
3. Net cash flow	0	+30	0	−2.4	0	−32.4

Notice that in exchange for $10 million today the dealer is now prepared to pay SFr30 million. Since the Swiss interest rate is now 8%, the dealer will expect to earn $.08 \times 30 =$ SFr2.4 million interest on its Swiss franc outlay.

CHAPTER 25

What We Do and Do Not Know about Finance

We began this book with the claim that finance is important, interesting, and challenging. We hope that you have come to agree. Now it is time to sum up. We begin this chapter with a very brief recap of the six most important ideas in finance. By now, these should be second nature to you.

Of course, there are still many puzzles that remain to be worked out. We will give you our list of the nine most important unsolved problems in finance.

We have tried to provide you with the essentials of finance, but it would be a dull subject if you could learn all that there is to know in one book. Therefore, we provide a short road map of the important topics that you may encounter in more advanced finance classes.

T. S. Eliot wrote, "To make an end is to make a beginning. The end is where we start from." We

Too bad Einstein didn't tackle the unsolved problems of finance.

hope that the end of this book is also the beginning for you of a growing study of finance.

25.1 What We Do Know: The Six Most Important Ideas in Finance

What would you say if you were asked to name the six most important ideas in finance? Here is our list.

Net Present Value (Chapter 5)

When you wish to know the value of a used car, you look at prices in the second-hand car market. Similarly, when you wish to know the value of a future cash flow, you look at prices quoted in the capital markets, where claims to future cash flows are traded (remember, those highly paid investment bankers are just secondhand cash-flow dealers). If you can buy cash flows for your shareholders at a cheaper price than they would have to pay in the capital market, you have increased the value of their investment.

This is the simple idea behind *net present value* (NPV). When we calculate a project's NPV, we are asking whether the project is worth more than it costs. We are estimating its value by calculating what its cash flows would be worth if a claim on them were offered separately to investors and traded in the capital markets.

This is why we calculate NPV by discounting future cash flows at the opportunity cost of capital—that is, at the expected rate of return offered by securities having the same degree of risk as the project. In well-functioning capital markets, all equivalent-risk assets are priced to offer the same expected return. By discounting at the opportunity cost of capital, we calculate the price at which investors in the project could expect to earn that rate of return.

Like most good ideas, the net present value rule is obvious when you think about it. But notice what an important idea it is. The NPV rule allows thousands of shareholders, who may have vastly different levels of wealth and attitudes toward risk, to participate in the same enterprise and to delegate its operation to a professional manager. They give the manager one simple instruction: "Maximize net present value."

Risk and Return (Chapters 11 and 12)

Some people say that modern finance is all about the capital asset pricing model. That's nonsense. If the capital asset pricing model had never been invented, our advice to financial managers would be essentially the same. The attraction of the model is that it gives us a manageable way of thinking about the required return on a risky investment.

Again, it is an attractively simple idea. There are two kinds of risks—those that you can diversify away and those that you can't. The only risks people care about are the ones that they can't get rid of—the nondiversifiable ones.

You can measure the *nondiversifiable,* or *market,* risk of an investment by the extent to which the value of the investment is affected by a change in the *aggregate* value of all the assets in the economy. This is called the *beta* of the investment. The required return on an asset increases in line with its beta.

Many people are worried by some of the rather strong assumptions behind the capital asset pricing model, or they are concerned about the difficulties of estimating a project's beta. They are right to be worried about these things. One day, we will have much better theories than we do now, but we are prepared to bet that these more sophisticated theories will retain the two crucial ideas behind the capital asset pricing model:

- Investors don't like risk and require a higher return to compensate.
- The risk that matters is the risk that investors cannot get rid of.

Efficient Capital Markets (Chapter 7)

The third fundamental idea is that security prices accurately reflect available information and respond rapidly to new information as soon as it becomes *available.* This *efficient-market theory* comes in three flavors, corresponding to different definitions of "available information." The weak form (or random-walk theory) says that prices reflect all the information in past prices; the semistrong form says that prices reflect all publicly available information; and the strong form holds that prices reflect all acquirable information.

Don't misunderstand the efficient-market idea. It doesn't say that there are no taxes or costs; it doesn't say that there aren't some clever people and some stupid ones. It merely implies that competition in capital markets is very tough—there are no money machines, and security prices reflect the true underlying values of assets on the basis of the best information available to investors.

The efficient-market hypothesis has been extensively tested, and the tests have revealed several pricing "anomalies," or seeming profit opportunities with simple investment strategies. We showed you just a few examples of these anomalies in Chapter 7. But the academic journals are now filled with dozens and dozens more of these puzzles. Does this mean that investors are leaving easy money on the table?

Unfortunately for all of us, this body of evidence has *not* translated into easy money. Superior returns are elusive, and only a few mutual-fund managers have been able to generate such returns with any consistency. Implementing the anomalies in real markets is apparently far more difficult than finding them on data tapes of past returns.

MM's Irrelevance Propositions (Chapters 16 and 17)

The irrelevance propositions of Modigliani and Miller (MM) imply that you can't increase value through financing policies unless these policies also increase the total cash flow available to investors. Financing decisions that simply repackage the same cash flows don't add value.

Financial managers often ask how much their company should borrow. MM's response is that as long as borrowing does not alter the *total* cash flow generated by the firm's assets, it does not affect firm value.

Miller and Modigliani used a similar argument to show that dividend policy does not affect value unless it affects the total cash flow available to present and future shareholders. A firm that pays you an increased dividend and gets the cash back by selling more shares is simply putting cash in one of your pockets and taking it out of another.

The same ideas can be run in reverse. Just as splitting up the cash flows doesn't add value, neither does combining different cash-flow streams. This implies that you can't increase value by putting two whole companies together unless you thereby increase total cash flow. Thus there are no benefits to mergers solely for diversification.

You can think of these irrelevance propositions as a form of "conservation of value." You can't increase value simply by putting two companies together, nor can you create value by splitting up total cash flow into several pieces, for example, into debt and equity claims. The whole is just the sum of the parts.

Option Theory (Chapter 23)

In everyday conversation we often use the word "option" as synonymous with "choice" or "alternative"; thus we speak of someone as *having a number of options.* In finance an *option* refers specifically to the opportunity to trade in the future on terms that are fixed today. Smart managers know that it is often worth paying today for the option to buy or sell an asset tomorrow.

We saw in Chapters 10 and 23 that companies are willing to pay extra for capital projects that give them future flexibility. Also, many securities provide the company or the investor with options. For example, a convertible bond gives the owner an option to exchange the bond for shares.

Managers spend much more time thinking about options than they used to. This is partly because they increasingly use options to help limit risk. Also, managers and economists are more aware that many assets contain disguised real options. For example, the opportunity to abandon a project and recover its salvage value is a put option.

If options are so prevalent, it is important to know how to value them. One of the great finance developments of recent years was the discovery by Black, Scholes, and Merton of a formula to value options. We reviewed briefly the determinants of option value in Chapter 23.

Agency Theory

A modern corporation is a team effort involving many players, including management, employees, shareholders, and bondholders. The members of this corporate team are bound together by a series of formal and informal contracts to ensure that they pull together.

For a long time economists assumed that all players acted for the common good. But in the last 20 years we have learned a lot about the possible conflicts of interest and how companies try to overcome such conflicts. These ideas are collectively known as *agency theory*.

Consider, for example, the relationship between the firm's shareholders and managers. The shareholders (the *principals*) want managers (their *agents*) to maximize firm value. To encourage managers to do so, firms seek to tie the managers' compensation to the value they have added. Moreover, managers who persistently neglect shareholders' interests face the threat that their firm will be taken over and they will be turfed out.

Although we didn't allocate a separate chapter to agency theory, the theory has helped us to think about such questions as these:

- How can an entrepreneur persuade venture capital investors to join in his or her enterprise? (Chapter 15)
- What are the reasons for all the fine print in bond agreements? (Chapter 16)
- Are mergers, acquisitions, and LBOs simply attempts to "rip off" other players, or do they change management's incentives to maximize company value? (Chapter 21)

Are these six ideas exciting theories or plain common sense? Call them what you will, they are basic to the financial manager's job. If after reading this book you really understand these ideas and know how to apply them, you have learned a great deal.

25.2 What We Do Not Know: Nine Unsolved Problems in Finance

Since the unknown is never exhausted, the list of what we do not know about finance could go on forever. Here are nine unsolved problems that seem ripe for productive research.

What Determines Project Risk and Present Value?

A good capital investment is one that has a positive NPV. We have talked at some length about how to calculate NPV, but we have given you very little guidance about how to find positive-NPV projects, except to say in Chapter 10 that projects have positive NPVs when the firm has some competitive advantage. But why do some companies earn superior returns while others in the same industry do not?

When are superior returns merely windfall gains, and when can they be anticipated, created, and planned for? What is their source, and how long do they persist before competition wears them away? Very little is known about any of these important questions.

Here is a related question: Why are some real assets risky and others relatively safe? In Chapter 12 we suggested a few reasons for differences in project betas—differences in operating leverage, for example, or in the extent to which a project's cash flows respond to the performance of the national economy. These are useful clues, but we have as yet no general procedure for estimating project betas. Assessing project risk is therefore still largely a seat-of-the-pants matter.

Risk and Return—Have We Missed Something?

In 1848 John Stuart Mill wrote, "Happily there is nothing in the laws of value which remains for the present or any future writer to clear up; the theory is complete." Economists today are not so sure about that. For example, the capital asset pricing model is an enormous step toward understanding the effect of risk on the value of an asset, but there are many puzzles left, some statistical and some theoretical.

The statistical problems arise because the capital asset pricing model is hard to prove or disprove conclusively. It appears that average returns from low-beta stocks are too high (that is, higher than the capital asset pricing model predicts), and those from high-beta stocks are too low. But this could be a problem with the way the tests are conducted and not with the model itself.

We also described the puzzling discovery that expected returns appear to be related to firm size and to the ratio of the book value of the stock to its market value. Of course, these findings could be just a coincidence—an accidental result that is unlikely to be repeated. But if they are not a coincidence, the capital asset pricing model cannot be the whole truth. Perhaps firm size and the book-to-market ratio are related to some other variable x that, along with beta, truly determines the expected returns demanded by investors. But we cannot yet identify variable x and prove that it matters.

Meanwhile, work is proceeding on the theoretical front to relax the simple assumptions underlying the capital asset pricing model. Here is one example: Suppose that you love fine wine. It may make sense for you to buy shares in a grand cru chateau, even if that soaks up a large fraction of your personal wealth and leaves you with a relatively undiversified portfolio. However, you are *hedged* against a rise in the price of fine wine: Your hobby will cost you more in a bull market for wine, but your stake in the chateau will make you correspondingly richer. Thus you are holding a relatively undiversified portfolio for a good reason. We would not expect you to demand a premium for bearing that portfolio's undiversifiable risk.

In general, if two people have different tastes, it may make sense for them to hold different portfolios. You may hedge your consumption needs with an investment in winemaking, whereas somebody else may do better to invest in Baskin-Robbins.[1] The capital asset pricing model isn't rich enough to deal with such a world. It assumes that all investors have similar tastes; the "hedging motive" does not enter, and therefore they hold the same portfolio of risky assets.

Merton has extended the capital asset pricing model to accommodate the hedging motive.[2] If enough investors are attempting to hedge against the same thing, this model implies a more complicated risk–return relationship. However, it is not yet clear who is hedging against what, so the model remains difficult to test. Given the rich possibilities for these extra hedging motives, there are many plausible alternative risk measures beyond beta and many potential competitors to the simple capital asset pricing model.

In the meantime, we must recognize the CAPM for what it is: an incomplete but extremely useful way of linking risk and return. Recognize too that its most basic message, that diversifiable risk doesn't matter, is accepted by nearly everyone.

---

[1] In practice, such hedging is more easily said than done. Baskin-Robbins is part of Pernod Ricard, which of course also produces fine wines.

[2] See R. Merton, "An Intertemporal Capital Asset Pricing Model," *Econometrica* 41 (1973), pp. 867–887.

Are There Important Exceptions to the Efficient-Market Theory?

The efficient-market theory is persuasive, but no theory is perfect—there must be exceptions.

Some of the apparent exceptions could simply be coincidences, for the more that researchers study stock performance, the more strange coincidences they are likely to find. For example, there is evidence that daily returns around new moons have been roughly double those around full moons.[3] It seems difficult to believe that this is anything other than a chance relationship—fun to read about but not a concern for serious investors or financial managers. But not all exceptions can be dismissed so easily. We saw that the stocks of firms that announce unexpectedly good earnings continue to perform well for a couple of months after the announcement date. Some scholars believe that this may mean that the stock market is inefficient and investors have consistently been slow to react to earnings announcements. Of course, we can't expect investors never to make mistakes. If they have been slow to react in the past, it will be interesting to see whether they learn from their mistake and price the stocks more efficiently in the future.

Some researchers believe that the efficient-market theory ignores important aspects of human behavior. For example, psychologists find that people place too much emphasis on recent events when they are predicting the future. We don't yet know how far such behavioral observations can help us to understand apparent anomalies.

During the dot-com boom of the late 1990s stock prices rose to astronomical levels. The NASDAQ Composite Index rose 580% from the beginning of 1995 to its peak in March 2000 and then fell by nearly 80%. Maybe such extreme price movements can be explained by standard valuation techniques. However, others argue that stock prices are liable to speculative bubbles, where investors are caught up in a whirl of irrational exuberance. Now it may well be true that some of us are liable to become overexcited, but why don't professional investors bail out of the overpriced stocks? Perhaps they would do so if it were their own money at stake, but maybe there is something in the way that their performance is measured and rewarded that encourages them to run with the herd.

These are important questions. Much more research is needed before we have a full understanding of why asset prices sometimes seem to get so out of line with what appears to be their discounted future payoffs.

Is Management an Off-Balance-Sheet Liability?

In Chapter 7, we argued that the market value of the firm should equal intrinsic value, the value of the firm as a going concern. But sometimes it appears that price does not equal intrinsic value. For example, closed-end funds are firms whose only asset is a portfolio of common stocks; intrinsic value should be easy to observe here, yet the stock of closed-end funds often sells for less than the value of the fund's portfolio. Other examples abound. For instance, real estate stocks often appear to sell for less than the market value of the firm's net assets. In the early 1980s, the market values of many large oil companies were less than the market values of their oil reserves. Analysts joked that you could buy oil cheaper on Wall Street than in west Texas.

These are cases where it is relatively easy to compare the market value of the firm with the value of its underlying assets. The discrepancies that sometimes arise here suggest that similar discrepancies might be widespread in other firms where value is harder to measure.

One possibility is that gaps between market value and asset value reflect the value added of management. Of course, if market value is less than the value of assets, then

---

[3] K. Yuan, L. Zheng, and Q. Zhu, "Are Investors Moonstruck? Lunar Phases and Stock Returns," *Journal of Empirical Finance*, 13 (2006), pp. 1–23.

the market seems to view managers' value added as negative. Perhaps investors are worried that managers extract too much of the firm's cash flow for their own interests or pet projects. Of course, managers commit their human capital to the firm and rightfully expect a reasonable return on their personal investment. In most firms, managers and employees coinvest with stockholders and creditors—human capital from the insiders and financial capital from outside investors. So far, we know very little about how this coinvestment works.

How Can We Explain Capital Structure?

Modigliani and Miller's article about capital structure emphasized that the value of a firm depends on real variables—the goods it produces, the prices it charges, and the costs that it incurs. Financing decisions merely affect the way that the cash flows are packaged for distribution to investors. What goes into the package is more important than the package itself.

Does it really not matter how much your firm borrows? We have come across several reasons why it *may* matter. Tax is one possibility. Debt provides a corporate tax shield, and this tax shield may more than compensate for any extra personal tax that the investor has to pay on debt interest. Perhaps managers are concerned with potential bankruptcy costs. Perhaps differences in capital structure reflect differences in the relative importance of growth opportunities. So far, none of these possibilities has been either proved relevant or definitely excluded.

The upshot of the matter is that we still don't have an accepted, coherent theory of capital structure. It is not for want of argument on the subject.

How Can We Resolve the Payout Controversy?

We spent all of Chapter 17 on dividend policy without being able to resolve the dividend controversy. Many people believe dividends are good; others believe they are bad and repurchases are good; and still others believe that as long as the firm's investment decisions are unaffected, the payout decision is largely irrelevant. If pressed, we largely take the middle view, but we can't be dogmatic about it.

Perhaps the problem is that we are asking the wrong question. Instead of inquiring whether dividends are good or bad, perhaps we should be asking *when* it makes sense to pay out high or low dividends. Investors in mature firms with few investment opportunities may welcome the financial discipline imposed by a high dividend payout, while for younger firms or firms with a large cash surplus, the tax advantage of stock repurchase may be more influential.

The way that companies distribute cash has changed over the last few decades. An increasing number of companies do not pay any dividends, while the volume of stock repurchase has mushroomed. This may partly reflect an increase in the proportion of small high-growth firms with lots of investment opportunities, but this does not appear to be the complete explanation. Understanding these shifts in payout policy may help us to understand how that policy affects firm value.

How Can We Explain Merger Waves?

There are many plausible reasons why two firms might wish to merge. If you single out a *particular* merger, it is usually possible to think up a reason why that merger could make sense. But that leaves us with a special hypothesis for each merger. What we need is a *general* hypothesis to explain merger waves. For example, nobody seemed to be merging in 2002, yet only 4 years later, mergers were back in fashion. Why?

We can think of other instances of financial fashions. For example, from time to time there are hot new-issue periods when there seems to be an endless supply of speculative new issues and an insatiable demand for them. In recent years economists have been developing new theories of speculative bubbles. Perhaps such theories will help to explain these mystifying financial fashions.

What Is the Value of Liquidity?

Unlike Treasury bills, cash pays no interest. On the other hand, cash provides more liquidity than Treasury bills. The value of this liquidity declines as you hold increasing amounts of cash. When you have only a small proportion of your assets in cash, a little extra can be extremely useful; when you have a substantial holding, any additional liquidity is not worth much. Unfortunately, we don't really understand how to value the liquidity service of cash, and therefore we can't say how much cash is enough or how readily the firm should be able to raise it. In our chapters on working capital management we largely finessed these questions by speaking vaguely of the need to ensure an "adequate" liquidity reserve.

A better knowledge of liquidity would also help us to understand how corporate bonds are priced. We already know part of the reason that corporate bonds sell for lower prices than Treasury bonds—corporate bonds are risky. However, the differences between the prices of corporate bonds and Treasury bonds are too large to be explained just by the possibility that the company will default. It seems likely that the price difference is partly due to the fact that corporate bonds are less liquid than Treasury bonds. But until we know how to price differences in liquidity, we can't really say much more than this.

Investors seem to value liquidity much more highly at some times than at others. When liquidity suddenly dries up, firms can find it very difficult to borrow. This happened in the financial crisis of 2007–2009 when investors became concerned about the rising default levels in the subprime mortgage market. Many banks that had sold these mortgages had subsequently repackaged them and traded the packages to financial institutions both in the United States and abroad. As the music began to stop, no one was quite sure who would be left holding the parcel. Dealers became increasingly reluctant to quote a price for buying or selling bonds, and banks became wary about lending to each other. Those banks that earlier in the year had been able to borrow at .1% above the Federal Reserve's target interest rate found that they now needed to pay a spread of over 4%—if they could borrow at all.

Why Are Financial Systems Prone to Crisis?

Financial markets work well most of the time, but we don't understand why they sometimes shut down or clog up, and we can offer relatively little advice to managers as to how to respond.

The crisis that started in 2007 was an unwelcome reminder of the fragility of financial systems. One moment everything seems to be going fine; the next moment markets crash and banks fail, and before long the economy is in recession. We know that systemic banking crises are often preceded by credit booms and asset price bubbles. When the bubbles burst, housing prices and stock prices fall, often precipitously, and deep recession follows.

Our understanding of these financial crises is limited. We need to know what causes them, how they can be prevented, and how they can be managed when they do occur. Crisis prevention will have to incorporate good governance systems, well-constructed compensation schemes, and efficient risk management. Understanding financial crises will occupy economists and financial regulators for many years to come. Let's hope that they figure out the last one before the next one knocks on the door.

That concludes our list of unsolved problems. We have given you the nine uppermost in our minds. If there are others that you find more interesting and challenging, by all means construct your own list and start thinking about it.

25.3 A Final Word

We titled this chapter "What We Do and Do Not Know about Finance." We should perhaps have added a third section, "What We Know about Finance but Haven't Told You." After all, this book is an introduction to finance and there are plenty of topics that we have only skimmed over. Here are some examples:

- Investment decisions always have side effects on financing—every dollar has to be raised somehow. Sometimes these side effects may be important. For instance, if the project allows the company to issue more debt, it may bring with it valuable tax shields. How can companies allow for these financing side effects when evaluating new investment projects? We touched on this issue in Chapter 13 when we showed you how to calculate the weighted-average cost of capital, but there is a huge body of knowledge about how best to allow for financing side effects in project valuation.
- We stressed in Chapter 14 the wide variety of claims that companies can sell to raise money. We described the principal ones, but there are others that we largely ignored. Leasing is an example. Companies lease assets rather than buy them because it is convenient and because in some circumstances there can be tax advantages. A lot is now known about how to value leases.
- Treasurers of large corporations worry about fluctuations in exchange rates, interest rates, and commodity prices. Various tools—including options, futures, forwards, and swaps—have been invented to help managers hedge against these risks. Many of the best brains in finance have been applied to devising and valuing these new instruments. We only touched on the problem of option valuation and said nothing at all about valuing futures. It's an exciting area and there is no shortage of books and articles to help you learn more.

QUESTIONS

QUIZ

If you have reached this far, you deserve a break. So we haven't provided any heavyweight problems at the end of this chapter. Instead we have included a quiz of the "Trivial Pursuit" variety. You don't need to know the answers to be a financial wizard, and for the most part they are not to be found in earlier chapters. However, they may help you to impress your friends at smart dinner parties.[4]

1. What do these countries' currencies have in common?
   - Australia
   - Canada
   - Hong Kong
   - New Zealand
   - Singapore
   - Taiwan
   - United States

   [Score 10]

2. What do the following countries' currencies have in common?
   - Estonia
   - Finland
   - Ireland
   - Greece
   - Portugal

   [Score 10]

---
[4] The answers are given on pages 702–703.

3. Government bonds are known by a variety of names. In which countries are the following government bonds issued?
   - Bunds
   - JGBs
   - Gilts
   - OATs
   - Tesobonos

   [Score 2 for each correct answer]

4. Each of these indexes measures stock market performance in a different country. What are the countries?
   - CAC Index
   - DAX Index
   - FTSE Index
   - Hang Seng Index
   - Nikkei Index

   [Score 2 for each correct answer]

5. Where is each of these futures markets located?
   - CME
   - Eurex
   - LME
   - NYMEX
   - TFX

   [Score 2 for each correct answer]

6. Name the company:
   a. Among the world's largest insurance companies, this firm required emergency loans of over $80 billion from the U.S. government to cover its losses on credit default swaps.
   b. In 2007, depositors in this U.K. bank formed long queues as they rushed to withdraw their money.
   c. This former investment banking giant filed for bankruptcy in September 2008, at the time the largest-ever U.S. bankruptcy.
   d. This bank failed after a 10-day bank run in September 2008, the largest bank failure in U.S. history.

   [Score 2.5 for each correct answer]

7. Match the acquiring firm with the acquired.

Acquiring Firms	Acquired Firms
Comcast	Live Nation
Ticketmaster	National Semiconductor
Texas Instruments	Marvel Entertainment
Wells Fargo	NBC Universal
Walt Disney	Wachovia

   [Score 2 for each correct answer]

8. To which country does each of the following banks belong?
   - ING
   - Banesto
   - Barclays Bank
   - Commerzbank
   - Mizuho Bank

   [Score 2 for each correct answer]

9. In which state are the major U.S. corporations commonly incorporated?
   - Alabama
   - California
   - Delaware

- Illinois
- Maryland

[Score 10]

10. Spot the "odd one out."
    - Butterfly
    - Odd lot
    - Straddle
    - Vertical spread

    [Score 10]

11. What do the following abbreviations stand for?
    - CD
    - LBO
    - MTN
    - OTC
    - SEC

    [Score 2 for each correct answer]

12. Spot the "odd one out."
    - Delta Airlines
    - United Airlines
    - Southwest Airlines
    - Eastern Airlines
    - Pan Am

    [Score 10]

13. Match up the following events and dates:
    - 1963   The first financial futures contract was traded in Chicago.
    - 1972   The first swap was arranged (between the World Bank and IBM).
    - 1973   The first eurobond was issued (by the Italian company Autostrade).
    - 1981   The first traded options market was formed in the United States.
    - 1997   The U.S. Treasury first issued indexed bonds.

    [Score 2 for each correct answer]

14. Match each of the following Asian countries with its currency:
    - China   Baht
    - South Korea   Dong
    - Mongolia   Tugrik
    - Thailand   Won
    - Vietnam   Yuan

    [Score 2 for each correct answer]

15. In which year did the U.S. stock market decline by 43%?
    - 1931
    - 1939
    - 1987

    [Score 10]

16. Brokers on the New York Stock Exchange often refer to stocks by their nicknames. To which stocks do the following nicknames refer?
    - Big Blue
    - Ketchup
    - Mickey Mouse
    - Timber

    [Score 2.5 for each correct answer]

17. Each of the following organizations made large losses from trading. Match each firm with a major cause of the loss.
    - Barings   Copper futures
    - Metallgesellschaft   Nikkei index futures

www.mhhe.com/bmm7e

- Allied Irish Bank   Oil futures
- Procter & Gamble   Currencies
- Sumitomo Corporation   Swaps

[Score 2 for each correct answer]

18. What do the following professors of finance have in common?
- Harry Markowitz
- Merton Miller
- William Sharpe
- Robert Merton
- Myron Scholes

[Score 10]

19. Match each of the following individuals with one of the quotations.
- Bernie Cornfeld   a. "Do you sincerely want to be rich?"
- Gordon Gecko   b. "Where are the customers' yachts?"
- John Maynard Keynes c. "Believing that fundamental conditions of the country are sound . . . my son and I have for some days been purchasing sound common stocks."
- John D. Rockefeller   d. The stock market "is, so to speak, a game of Snap, of Old Maid, of Musical Chairs—a pastime in which he is a victor who says Snap neither too soon nor too late, who passes the Old Maid to his neighbor before the game is over, who secures a chair for himself when the music stops."
- Fred Schwed   e. "Greed is good."

[Score 2 for each correct answer]

20. International bond issues are often known by nicknames. For example, an international bond issued in Southeast Asia is known as a "dragon bond." What is the common term for a bond issued by a foreign company in the bond market of each of the following countries?
- Japan
- Netherlands
- Spain
- United Kingdom
- United States

[Score 2 for each correct answer]

ANSWERS TO QUIZ

1. Each of their currencies is called the dollar.
2. They are all members of the European Monetary Union (EMU) and therefore all use the euro.
3. Bunds = Germany
   JGBs (Japanese Government Bonds) = Japan
   Gilts = United Kingdom
   OATs (Obligations Assimilables du Trésor) = France
   Tesobonos = Mexico
4. CAC Index = France
   DAX Index = Germany
   FTSE Index = United Kingdom
   Hang Seng Index = Hong Kong
   Nikkei Index = Japan
5. CME (Chicago Mercantile Exchange) = Chicago
   Eurex = Frankfurt
   LME (London Metal Exchange) = London
   NYMEX (New York Mercantile Exchange) = New York
   TFX (Tokyo Financial Exchange) = Tokyo

6. a. AIG
    b. Northern Rock
    c. Lehman Brothers
    d. Washington Mutual

7.

Acquiring Firms	Acquired Firms
Comcast	NBC Universal
Ticketmaster	Live Nation
Texas Instruments	National Semiconductor
Wells Fargo	Wachovia
Walt Disney	Marvel Entertainment

8. ING = Netherlands
    Banesto = Spain
    Barclays Bank = United Kingdom
    Commerzbank = Germany
    Mizuho Bank = Japan

9. Delaware

10. "Odd lot" refers to an order to buy or sell fewer than 100 shares. The other terms all refer to combinations of options.

11. CD = certificate of deposit
    LBO = leveraged buyout
    MTN = medium-term note
    OTC = over-the-counter
    SEC = Securities and Exchange Commission

12. Southwest is the only one of these airlines that has not been through Chapter 11 bankruptcy proceedings.

13. 1963   The first eurobond was issued (by the Italian company Autostrade).
    1972   The first financial futures contract was traded in Chicago.
    1973   The first traded options market was formed in the United States.
    1981   The first swap was arranged (between the World Bank and IBM).
    1997   The U.S. Treasury first issued indexed bonds.

14. China = Yuan
    South Korea = Won
    Mongolia = Tugrik
    Thailand = Baht
    Vietnam = Dong

15. 1931

16. Big Blue = IBM
    Ketchup = Heinz
    Mickey Mouse = Disney
    Timber = Weyerhaeuser

17. Barings   Nikkei index futures
    Metallgesellschaft   Oil futures
    Allied Irish Bank   Currencies
    Procter & Gamble   Swaps
    Sumitomo Corporation Copper futures

18. Each received the Nobel Prize for his contribution to financial economics.

19. Bernie Cornfeld   (head of Investors' Overseas Services in address to the fund sales force) = a
    Gordon Gecko   (in the movie *Wall Street*) = e
    John Maynard Keynes   (writing in *The General Theory of Employment, Interest and Money*, 1936) = d
    John D. Rockefeller   (at the start of the 1929 Great Crash) = c
    Fred Schwed   (in a 1940 book of that title) = b

20. Japan = Samurai bond
    Netherlands = Rembrandt bond
    Spain = Matador bond
    United Kingdom = Bulldog bond
    United States = Yankee bond

If you scored:

0–50	You weren't trying.
51–80	Not bad.
81–120	You are probably going to be an investment banker.
121–160	You are probably an investment banker *already*.
161–200	You probably cheated.

APPENDIX A
Present Value and Future Value Tables

APPENDIX TABLE A.1 Future value of $1 after t years = $(1 + r)^t$

Number of Years	1%	2%	3%	4%	5%	6%	7%	8%	9%	10%	11%	12%	13%	14%	15%
	Interest Rate per Year														
1	1.0100	1.0200	1.0300	1.0400	1.0500	1.0600	1.0700	1.0800	1.0900	1.1000	1.1100	1.1200	1.1300	1.1400	1.1500
2	1.0201	1.0404	1.0609	1.0816	1.1025	1.1236	1.1449	1.1664	1.1881	1.2100	1.2321	1.2544	1.2769	1.2996	1.3225
3	1.0303	1.0612	1.0927	1.1249	1.1576	1.1910	1.2250	1.2597	1.2950	1.3310	1.3676	1.4049	1.4429	1.4815	1.5209
4	1.0406	1.0824	1.1255	1.1699	1.2155	1.2625	1.3108	1.3605	1.4116	1.4641	1.5181	1.5735	1.6305	1.6890	1.7490
5	1.0510	1.1041	1.1593	1.2167	1.2763	1.3382	1.4026	1.4693	1.5386	1.6105	1.6851	1.7623	1.8424	1.9254	2.0114
6	1.0615	1.1262	1.1941	1.2653	1.3401	1.4185	1.5007	1.5869	1.6771	1.7716	1.8704	1.9738	2.0820	2.1950	2.3131
7	1.0721	1.1487	1.2299	1.3159	1.4071	1.5036	1.6058	1.7138	1.8280	1.9487	2.0762	2.2107	2.3526	2.5023	2.6600
8	1.0829	1.1717	1.2668	1.3686	1.4775	1.5938	1.7182	1.8509	1.9926	2.1436	2.3045	2.4760	2.6584	2.8526	3.0590
9	1.0937	1.1951	1.3048	1.4233	1.5513	1.6895	1.8385	1.9990	2.1719	2.3579	2.5580	2.7731	3.0040	3.2519	3.5179
10	1.1046	1.2190	1.3439	1.4802	1.6289	1.7908	1.9672	2.1589	2.3674	2.5937	2.8394	3.1058	3.3946	3.7072	4.0456
11	1.1157	1.2434	1.3842	1.5395	1.7103	1.8983	2.1049	2.3316	2.5804	2.8531	3.1518	3.4785	3.8359	4.2262	4.6524
12	1.1268	1.2682	1.4258	1.6010	1.7959	2.0122	2.2522	2.5182	2.8127	3.1384	3.4985	3.8960	4.3345	4.8179	5.3503
13	1.1381	1.2936	1.4685	1.6651	1.8856	2.1329	2.4098	2.7196	3.0658	3.4523	3.8833	4.3635	4.8980	5.4924	6.1528
14	1.1495	1.3195	1.5126	1.7317	1.9799	2.2609	2.5785	2.9372	3.3417	3.7975	4.3104	4.8871	5.5348	6.2613	7.0757
15	1.1610	1.3459	1.5580	1.8009	2.0789	2.3966	2.7590	3.1722	3.6425	4.1772	4.7846	5.4736	6.2543	7.1379	8.1371
16	1.1726	1.3728	1.6047	1.8730	2.1829	2.5404	2.9522	3.4259	3.9703	4.5950	5.3109	6.1304	7.0673	8.1372	9.3576
17	1.1843	1.4002	1.6528	1.9479	2.2920	2.6928	3.1588	3.7000	4.3276	5.0545	5.8951	6.8660	7.9861	9.2765	10.7613
18	1.1961	1.4282	1.7024	2.0258	2.4066	2.8543	3.3799	3.9960	4.7171	5.5599	6.5436	7.6900	9.0243	10.5752	12.3755
19	1.2081	1.4568	1.7535	2.1068	2.5270	3.0256	3.6165	4.3157	5.1417	6.1159	7.2633	8.6128	10.1974	12.0557	14.2318
20	1.2202	1.4859	1.8061	2.1911	2.6533	3.2071	3.8697	4.6610	5.6044	6.7275	8.0623	9.6463	11.5231	13.7435	16.3665

Number of Years	16%	17%	18%	19%	20%	21%	22%	23%	24%	25%	26%	27%	28%	29%	30%
	Interest Rate per Year														
1	1.1600	1.1700	1.1800	1.1900	1.2000	1.2100	1.2200	1.2300	1.2400	1.2500	1.2600	1.2700	1.2800	1.2900	1.3000
2	1.3456	1.3689	1.3924	1.4161	1.4400	1.4641	1.4884	1.5129	1.5376	1.5625	1.5876	1.6129	1.6384	1.6641	1.6900
3	1.5609	1.6016	1.6430	1.6852	1.7280	1.7716	1.8158	1.8609	1.9066	1.9531	2.0004	2.0484	2.0972	2.1467	2.1970
4	1.8106	1.8739	1.9388	2.0053	2.0736	2.1436	2.2153	2.2889	2.3642	2.4414	2.5205	2.6014	2.6844	2.7692	2.8561
5	2.1003	2.1924	2.2878	2.3864	2.4883	2.5937	2.7027	2.8153	2.9316	3.0518	3.1758	3.3038	3.4360	3.5723	3.7129
6	2.4364	2.5652	2.6996	2.8398	2.9860	3.1384	3.2973	3.4628	3.6352	3.8147	4.0015	4.1959	4.3980	4.6083	4.8268
7	2.8262	3.0012	3.1855	3.3793	3.5832	3.7975	4.0227	4.2593	4.5077	4.7684	5.0419	5.3288	5.6295	5.9447	6.2749
8	3.2784	3.5115	3.7589	4.0214	4.2998	4.5950	4.9077	5.2389	5.5895	5.9605	6.3528	6.7675	7.2058	7.6686	8.1573
9	3.8030	4.1084	4.4355	4.7854	5.1598	5.5599	5.9874	6.4439	6.9310	7.4506	8.0045	8.5948	9.2234	9.8925	10.6045
10	4.4114	4.8068	5.2338	5.6947	6.1917	6.7275	7.3046	7.9259	8.5944	9.3132	10.0857	10.9153	11.8059	12.7614	13.7858
11	5.1173	5.6240	6.1759	6.7767	7.4301	8.1403	8.9117	9.7489	10.6571	11.6415	12.7080	13.8625	15.1116	16.4622	17.9216
12	5.9360	6.5801	7.2876	8.0642	8.9161	9.8497	10.8722	11.9912	13.2148	14.5519	16.0120	17.6053	19.3428	21.2362	23.2981
13	6.8858	7.6987	8.5994	9.5964	10.6993	11.9182	13.2641	14.7491	16.3863	18.1899	20.1752	22.3588	24.7588	27.3947	30.2875
14	7.9875	9.0075	10.1472	11.4198	12.8392	14.4210	16.1822	18.1414	20.3191	22.7374	25.4207	28.3957	31.6913	35.3391	39.3738
15	9.2655	10.5387	11.9737	13.5895	15.4070	17.4494	19.7423	22.3140	25.1956	28.4217	32.0301	36.0625	40.5648	45.5875	51.1859
16	10.7480	12.3303	14.1290	16.1715	18.4884	21.1138	24.0856	27.4462	31.2426	5.5271	40.3579	45.7994	51.9230	58.8079	66.5417
17	12.4677	14.4265	16.6722	19.2441	22.1861	25.5477	29.3844	33.7588	38.7408	44.4089	50.8510	58.1652	66.4614	75.8621	86.5042
18	14.4625	16.8790	19.6733	22.9005	26.6233	30.9127	35.8490	41.5233	48.0386	55.5112	64.0722	73.8698	85.0706	97.8622	112.4554
19	16.7765	19.7484	23.2144	27.2516	31.9480	37.4043	43.7358	51.0737	59.5679	69.3889	80.7310	93.8147	108.8904	126.2422	146.1920
20	19.4608	23.1056	27.3930	32.4294	38.3376	45.2593	53.3576	62.8206	73.8641	86.7362	101.7211	119.1446	139.3797	162.8524	190.0496

APPENDIX TABLE A.2 Discount factors: Present value of $1 to be received after t years = $1/(1 + r)^t$

	Interest Rate per Year														
Number of Years	1%	2%	3%	4%	5%	6%	7%	8%	9%	10%	11%	12%	13%	14%	15%
1	0.9901	0.9804	0.9709	0.9615	0.9524	0.9434	0.9346	0.9259	0.9174	0.9091	0.9009	0.8929	0.8850	0.8772	0.8696
2	0.9803	0.9612	0.9426	0.9246	0.9070	0.8900	0.8734	0.8573	0.8417	0.8264	0.8116	0.7972	0.7831	0.7695	0.7561
3	0.9706	0.9423	0.9151	0.8890	0.8638	0.8396	0.8163	0.7938	0.7722	0.7513	0.7312	0.7118	0.6931	0.6750	0.6575
4	0.9610	0.9238	0.8885	0.8548	0.8227	0.7921	0.7629	0.7350	0.7084	0.6830	0.6587	0.6355	0.6133	0.5921	0.5718
5	0.9515	0.9057	0.8626	0.8219	0.7835	0.7473	0.7130	0.6806	0.6499	0.6209	0.5935	0.5674	0.5428	0.5194	0.4972
6	0.9420	0.8880	0.8375	0.7903	0.7462	0.7050	0.6663	0.6302	0.5963	0.5645	0.5346	0.5066	0.4803	0.4556	0.4323
7	0.9327	0.8706	0.8131	0.7599	0.7107	0.6651	0.6227	0.5835	0.5470	0.5132	0.4817	0.4523	0.4251	0.3996	0.3759
8	0.9235	0.8535	0.7894	0.7307	0.6768	0.6274	0.5820	0.5403	0.5019	0.4665	0.4339	0.4039	0.3762	0.3506	0.3269
9	0.9143	0.8368	0.7664	0.7026	0.6446	0.5919	0.5439	0.5002	0.4604	0.4241	0.3909	0.3606	0.3329	0.3075	0.2843
10	0.9053	0.8203	0.7441	0.6756	0.6139	0.5584	0.5083	0.4632	0.4224	0.3855	0.3522	0.3220	0.2946	0.2697	0.2472
11	0.8963	0.8043	0.7224	0.6496	0.5847	0.5268	0.4751	0.4289	0.3875	0.3505	0.3173	0.2875	0.2607	0.2366	0.2149
12	0.8874	0.7885	0.7014	0.6246	0.5568	0.4970	0.4440	0.3971	0.3555	0.3186	0.2858	0.2567	0.2307	0.2076	0.1869
13	0.8787	0.7730	0.6810	0.6006	0.5303	0.4688	0.4150	0.3677	0.3262	0.2897	0.2575	0.2292	0.2042	0.1821	0.1625
14	0.8700	0.7579	0.6611	0.5775	0.5051	0.4423	0.3878	0.3405	0.2992	0.2633	0.2320	0.2046	0.1807	0.1597	0.1413
15	0.8613	0.7430	0.6419	0.5553	0.4810	0.4173	0.3624	0.3152	0.2745	0.2394	0.2090	0.1827	0.1599	0.1401	0.1229
16	0.8528	0.7284	0.6232	0.5339	0.4581	0.3936	0.3387	0.2919	0.2519	0.2176	0.1883	0.1631	0.1415	0.1229	0.1069
17	0.8444	0.7142	0.6050	0.5134	0.4363	0.3714	0.3166	0.2703	0.2311	0.1978	0.1696	0.1456	0.1252	0.1078	0.0929
18	0.8360	0.7002	0.5874	0.4936	0.4155	0.3503	0.2959	0.2502	0.2120	0.1799	0.1528	0.1300	0.1108	0.0946	0.0808
19	0.8277	0.6864	0.5703	0.4746	0.3957	0.3305	0.2765	0.2317	0.1945	0.1635	0.1377	0.1161	0.0981	0.0829	0.0703
20	0.8195	0.6730	0.5537	0.4564	0.3769	0.3118	0.2584	0.2145	0.1784	0.1486	0.1240	0.1037	0.0868	0.0728	0.0611

	Interest Rate per Year														
Number of Years	16%	17%	18%	19%	20%	21%	22%	23%	24%	25%	26%	27%	28%	29%	30%
1	0.8621	0.8547	0.8475	0.8403	0.8333	0.8264	0.8197	0.8130	0.8065	0.8000	0.7937	0.7874	0.7813	0.7752	0.7692
2	0.7432	0.7305	0.7182	0.7062	0.6944	0.6830	0.6719	0.6610	0.6504	0.6400	0.6299	0.6200	0.6104	0.6009	0.5917
3	0.6407	0.6244	0.6086	0.5934	0.5787	0.5645	0.5507	0.5374	0.5245	0.5120	0.4999	0.4882	0.4768	0.4658	0.4552
4	0.5523	0.5337	0.5158	0.4987	0.4823	0.4665	0.4514	0.4369	0.4230	0.4096	0.3968	0.3844	0.3725	0.3611	0.3501
5	0.4761	0.4561	0.4371	0.4190	0.4019	0.3855	0.3700	0.3552	0.3411	0.3277	0.3149	0.3027	0.2910	0.2799	0.2693
6	0.4104	0.3898	0.3704	0.3521	0.3349	0.3186	0.3033	0.2888	0.2751	0.2621	0.2499	0.2383	0.2274	0.2170	0.2072
7	0.3538	0.3332	0.3139	0.2959	0.2791	0.2633	0.2486	0.2348	0.2218	0.2097	0.1983	0.1877	0.1776	0.1682	0.1594
8	0.3050	0.2848	0.2660	0.2487	0.2326	0.2176	0.2038	0.1909	0.1789	0.1678	0.1574	0.1478	0.1388	0.1304	0.1226
9	0.2630	0.2434	0.2255	0.2090	0.1938	0.1799	0.1670	0.1552	0.1443	0.1342	0.1249	0.1164	0.1084	0.1011	0.0943
10	0.2267	0.2080	0.1911	0.1756	0.1615	0.1486	0.1369	0.1262	0.1164	0.1074	0.0992	0.0916	0.0847	0.0784	0.0725
11	0.1954	0.1778	0.1619	0.1476	0.1346	0.1228	0.1122	0.1026	0.0938	0.0859	0.0787	0.0721	0.0662	0.0607	0.0558
12	0.1685	0.1520	0.1372	0.1240	0.1122	0.1015	0.0920	0.0834	0.0757	0.0687	0.0625	0.0568	0.0517	0.0471	0.0429
13	0.1452	0.1299	0.1163	0.1042	0.0935	0.0839	0.0754	0.0678	0.0610	0.0550	0.0496	0.0447	0.0404	0.0365	0.0330
14	0.1252	0.1110	0.0985	0.0876	0.0779	0.0693	0.0618	0.0551	0.0492	0.0440	0.0393	0.0352	0.0316	0.0283	0.0254
15	0.1079	0.0949	0.0835	0.0736	0.0649	0.0573	0.0507	0.0448	0.0397	0.0352	0.0312	0.0277	0.0247	0.0219	0.0195
16	0.0930	0.0811	0.0708	0.0618	0.0541	0.0474	0.0415	0.0364	0.0320	0.0281	0.0248	0.0218	0.0193	0.0170	0.0150
17	0.0802	0.0693	0.0600	0.0520	0.0451	0.0391	0.0340	0.0296	0.0258	0.0225	0.0197	0.0172	0.0150	0.0132	0.0116
18	0.0691	0.0592	0.0508	0.0437	0.0376	0.0323	0.0279	0.0241	0.0208	0.0180	0.0156	0.0135	0.0118	0.0102	0.0089
19	0.0596	0.0506	0.0431	0.0367	0.0313	0.0267	0.0229	0.0196	0.0168	0.0144	0.0124	0.0107	0.0092	0.0079	0.0068
20	0.0514	0.0433	0.0365	0.0308	0.0261	0.0221	0.0187	0.0159	0.0135	0.0115	0.0098	0.0084	0.0072	0.0061	0.0053

APPENDIX TABLE A.3 Annuity table: Present value of $1 per year for each of t years $= 1/r - 1/[r(1 + r)^t]$

| | Interest Rate per Year | | | | | | | | | | | | | | |
Number of Years	1%	2%	3%	4%	5%	6%	7%	8%	9%	10%	11%	12%	13%	14%	15%
1	0.9901	0.9804	0.9709	0.9615	0.9524	0.9434	0.9346	0.9259	0.9174	0.9091	0.9009	0.8929	0.8850	0.8772	0.8696
2	1.9704	1.9416	1.9135	1.8861	1.8594	1.8334	1.8080	1.7833	1.7591	1.7355	1.7125	1.6901	1.6681	1.6467	1.6257
3	2.9410	2.8839	2.8286	2.7751	2.7232	2.6730	2.6243	2.5771	2.5313	2.4869	2.4437	2.4018	2.3612	2.3216	2.2832
4	3.9020	3.8077	3.7171	3.6299	3.5460	3.4651	3.3872	3.3121	3.2397	3.1699	3.1024	3.0373	2.9745	2.9137	2.8550
5	4.8534	4.7135	4.5797	4.4518	4.3295	4.2124	4.1002	3.9927	3.8897	3.7908	3.6959	3.6048	3.5172	3.4331	3.3522
6	5.7955	5.6014	5.4172	5.2421	5.0757	4.9173	4.7665	4.6229	4.4859	4.3553	4.2305	4.1114	3.9975	3.8887	3.7845
7	6.7282	6.4720	6.2303	6.0021	5.7864	5.5824	5.3893	5.2064	5.0330	4.8684	4.7122	4.5638	4.4226	4.2883	4.1604
8	7.6517	7.3255	7.0197	6.7327	6.4632	6.2098	5.9713	5.7466	5.5348	5.3349	5.1461	4.9676	4.7988	4.6389	4.4873
9	8.5660	8.1622	7.7861	7.4353	7.1078	6.8017	6.5152	6.2469	5.9952	5.7590	5.5370	5.3282	5.1317	4.9464	4.7716
10	9.4713	8.9826	8.5302	8.1109	7.7217	7.3601	7.0236	6.7101	6.4177	6.1446	5.8892	5.6502	5.4262	5.2161	5.0188
11	10.3676	9.7868	9.2526	8.7605	8.3064	7.8869	7.4987	7.1390	6.8052	6.4951	6.2065	5.9377	5.6869	5.4527	5.2337
12	11.2551	10.5753	9.9540	9.3851	8.8633	8.3838	7.9427	7.5361	7.1607	6.8137	6.4924	6.1944	5.9176	5.6603	5.4206
13	12.1337	11.3484	10.6350	9.9856	9.3936	8.8527	8.3577	7.9038	7.4869	7.1034	6.7499	6.4235	6.1218	5.8424	5.5831
14	13.0037	12.1062	11.2961	10.5631	9.8986	9.2950	8.7455	8.2442	7.7862	7.3667	6.9819	6.6282	6.3025	6.0021	5.7245
15	13.8651	12.8493	11.9379	11.1184	10.3797	9.7122	9.1079	8.5595	8.0607	7.6061	7.1909	6.8109	6.4624	6.1422	5.8474
16	14.7179	13.5777	12.5611	11.6523	10.8378	10.1059	9.4466	8.8514	8.3126	7.8237	7.3792	6.9740	6.6039	6.2651	5.9542
17	15.5623	14.2919	13.1661	12.1657	11.2741	10.4773	9.7632	9.1216	8.5436	8.0216	7.5488	7.1196	6.7291	6.3729	6.0472
18	16.3983	14.9920	13.7535	12.6593	11.6896	10.8276	10.0591	9.3719	8.7556	8.2014	7.7016	7.2497	6.8399	6.4674	6.1280
19	17.2260	15.6785	14.3238	13.1339	12.0853	11.1581	10.3356	9.6036	8.9501	8.3649	7.8393	7.3658	6.9380	6.5504	6.1982
20	18.0456	16.3514	14.8775	13.5903	12.4622	11.4699	10.5940	9.8181	9.1285	8.5136	7.9633	7.4694	7.0248	6.6231	6.2593

| | Interest Rate per Year | | | | | | | | | | | | | | |
Number of Years	16%	17%	18%	19%	20%	21%	22%	23%	24%	25%	26%	27%	28%	29%	30%
1	0.8621	0.8547	0.8475	0.8403	0.8333	0.8264	0.8197	0.8130	0.8065	0.8000	0.7937	0.7874	0.7813	0.7752	0.7692
2	1.6052	1.5852	1.5656	1.5465	1.5278	1.5095	1.4915	1.4740	1.4568	1.4400	1.4235	1.4074	1.3916	1.3761	1.3609
3	2.2459	2.2096	2.1743	2.1399	2.1065	2.0739	2.0422	2.0114	1.9813	1.9520	1.9234	1.8956	1.8684	1.8420	1.8161
4	2.7982	2.7432	2.6901	2.6386	2.5887	2.5404	2.4936	2.4483	2.4043	2.3616	2.3202	2.2800	2.2410	2.2031	2.1662
5	3.2743	3.1993	3.1272	3.0576	2.9906	2.9260	2.8636	2.8035	2.7454	2.6893	2.6351	2.5827	2.5320	2.4830	2.4356
6	3.6847	3.5892	3.4976	3.4098	3.3255	3.2446	3.1669	3.0923	3.0205	2.9514	2.8850	2.8210	2.7594	2.7000	2.6427
7	4.0386	3.9224	3.8115	3.7057	3.6046	3.5079	3.4155	3.3270	3.2423	3.1611	3.0833	3.0087	2.9370	2.8682	2.8021
8	4.3436	4.2072	4.0776	3.9544	3.8372	3.7256	3.6193	3.5179	3.4212	3.3289	3.2407	3.1564	3.0758	2.9986	2.9247
9	4.6065	4.4506	4.3030	4.1633	4.0310	3.9054	3.7863	3.6731	3.5655	3.4631	3.3657	3.2728	3.1842	3.0997	3.0190
10	4.8332	4.6586	4.4941	4.3389	4.1925	4.0541	3.9232	3.7993	3.6819	3.5705	3.4648	3.3644	3.2689	3.1781	3.0915
11	5.0286	4.8364	4.6560	4.4865	4.3271	4.1769	4.0354	3.9018	3.7757	3.6564	3.5435	3.4365	3.3351	3.2388	3.1473
12	5.1971	4.9884	4.7932	4.6105	4.4392	4.2784	4.1274	3.9852	3.8514	3.7251	3.6059	3.4933	3.3868	3.2859	3.1903
13	5.3423	5.1183	4.9095	4.7147	4.5327	4.3624	4.2028	4.0530	3.9124	3.7801	3.6555	3.5381	3.4272	3.3224	3.2233
14	5.4675	5.2293	5.0081	4.8023	4.6106	4.4317	4.2646	4.1082	3.9616	3.8241	3.6949	3.5733	3.4587	3.3507	3.2487
15	5.5755	5.3242	5.0916	4.8759	4.6755	4.4890	4.3152	4.1530	4.0013	3.8593	3.7261	3.6010	3.4834	3.3726	3.2682
16	5.6685	5.4053	5.1624	4.9377	4.7296	4.5364	4.3567	4.1894	4.0333	3.8874	3.7509	3.6228	3.5026	3.3896	3.2832
17	5.7487	5.4746	5.2223	4.9897	4.7746	4.5755	4.3908	4.2190	4.0591	3.9099	3.7705	3.6400	3.5177	3.4028	3.2948
18	5.8178	5.5339	5.2732	5.0333	4.8122	4.6079	4.4187	4.2431	4.0799	3.9279	3.7861	3.6536	3.5294	3.4130	3.3037
19	5.8775	5.5845	5.3162	5.0700	4.8435	4.6346	4.4415	4.2627	4.0967	3.9424	3.7985	3.6642	3.5386	3.4210	3.3105
20	5.9288	5.6278	5.3527	5.1009	4.8696	4.6567	4.4603	4.2786	4.1103	3.9539	3.8083	3.6726	3.5458	3.4271	3.3158

APPENDIX TABLE A.4 Annuity table: Future value of $1 per year for each of t years = $[(1 + r)^t - 1]/r$

							Interest Rate per Year								
Number of Years	1%	2%	3%	4%	5%	6%	7%	8%	9%	10%	11%	12%	13%	14%	15%
1	1.0000	1.0000	1.0000	1.0000	1.0000	1.0000	1.0000	1.0000	1.0000	1.0000	1.0000	1.0000	1.0000	1.0000	1.0000
2	2.0100	2.0200	2.0300	2.0400	2.0500	2.0600	2.0700	2.0800	2.0900	2.1000	2.1100	2.1200	2.1300	2.1400	2.1500
3	3.0301	3.0604	3.0909	3.1216	3.1525	3.1836	3.2149	3.2464	3.2781	3.3100	3.3421	3.3744	3.4069	3.4396	3.4725
4	4.0604	4.1216	4.1836	4.2465	4.3101	4.3746	4.4399	4.5061	4.5731	4.6410	4.7097	4.7793	4.8498	4.9211	4.9934
5	5.1010	5.2040	5.3091	5.4163	5.5256	5.6371	5.7507	5.8666	5.9847	6.1051	6.2278	6.3528	6.4803	6.6101	6.7424
6	6.1520	6.3081	6.4684	6.6330	6.8019	6.9753	7.1533	7.3359	7.5233	7.7156	7.9129	8.1152	8.3227	8.5355	8.7537
7	7.2135	7.4343	7.6625	7.8983	8.1420	8.3938	8.6540	8.9228	9.2004	9.4872	9.7833	10.0890	10.4047	10.7305	11.0668
8	8.2857	8.5830	8.8923	9.2142	9.5491	9.8975	10.2598	10.6366	11.0285	11.4359	11.8594	12.2997	12.7573	13.2328	13.7268
9	9.3685	9.7546	10.1591	10.5828	11.0266	11.4913	11.9780	12.4876	13.0210	13.5795	14.1640	14.7757	15.4157	16.0853	16.7858
10	10.4622	10.9497	11.4639	12.0061	12.5779	13.1808	13.8164	14.4866	15.1929	15.9374	16.7220	17.5487	18.4197	19.3373	20.3037
11	11.5668	12.1687	12.8078	13.4864	14.2068	14.9716	15.7836	16.6455	17.5603	18.5312	19.5614	20.6546	21.8143	23.0445	24.3493
12	12.6825	13.4121	14.1920	15.0258	15.9171	16.8699	17.8885	18.9771	20.1407	21.3843	22.7132	24.1331	25.6502	27.2707	29.0017
13	13.8093	14.6803	15.6178	16.6268	17.7130	18.8821	20.1406	21.4953	22.9534	24.5227	26.2116	28.0291	29.9847	32.0887	34.3519
14	14.9474	15.9739	17.0863	18.2919	19.5986	21.0151	22.5505	24.2149	26.0192	27.9750	30.0949	32.3926	34.8827	37.5811	40.5047
15	16.0969	17.2934	18.5989	20.0236	21.5786	23.2760	25.1290	27.1521	29.3609	31.7725	34.4054	37.2797	40.4175	43.8424	47.5804
16	17.2579	18.6393	20.1569	21.8245	23.6575	25.6725	27.8881	30.3243	33.0034	35.9497	39.1899	42.7533	46.6717	50.9804	55.7175
17	18.4304	20.0121	21.7616	23.6975	25.8404	28.2129	30.8402	33.7502	36.9737	40.5447	44.5008	48.8837	53.7391	59.1176	65.0751
18	19.6147	21.4123	23.4144	25.6454	28.1324	30.9057	33.9990	37.4502	41.3013	45.5992	50.3959	55.7497	61.7251	68.3941	75.8364
19	20.8109	22.8406	25.1169	27.6712	30.5390	33.7600	37.3790	41.4463	46.0185	51.1591	56.9395	63.4397	70.7494	78.9692	88.2118
20	22.0190	24.2974	26.8704	29.7781	33.0660	36.7856	40.9955	45.7620	51.1601	57.2750	64.2028	72.0524	80.9468	91.0249	102.4436

							Interest Rate per Year								
Number of Years	16%	17%	18%	19%	20%	21%	22%	23%	24%	25%	26%	27%	28%	29%	30%
1	1.0000	1.0000	1.0000	1.0000	1.0000	1.0000	1.0000	1.0000	1.0000	1.0000	1.0000	1.0000	1.0000	1.0000	1.0000
2	2.1600	2.1700	2.1800	2.1900	2.2000	2.2100	2.2200	2.2300	2.2400	2.2500	2.2600	2.2700	2.2800	2.2900	2.3000
3	3.5056	3.5389	3.5724	3.6061	3.6400	3.6741	3.7084	3.7429	3.7776	3.8125	3.8476	3.8829	3.9184	3.9541	3.9900
4	5.0665	5.1405	5.2154	5.2913	5.3680	5.4457	5.5242	5.6038	5.6842	5.7656	5.8480	5.9313	6.0156	6.1008	6.1870
5	6.8771	7.0144	7.1542	7.2966	7.4416	7.5892	7.7396	7.8926	8.0484	8.2070	8.3684	8.5327	8.6999	8.8700	9.0431
6	8.9775	9.2068	9.4420	9.6830	9.9299	10.1830	10.4423	10.7079	10.9801	11.2588	11.5442	11.8366	12.1359	12.4423	12.7560
7	11.4139	11.7720	12.1415	12.5227	12.9159	13.3214	13.7396	14.1708	14.6153	15.0735	15.5458	16.0324	16.5339	17.0506	17.5828
8	14.2401	14.7733	15.3270	15.9020	16.4991	17.1189	17.7623	18.4300	19.1229	19.8419	20.5876	21.3612	22.1634	22.9953	23.8577
9	17.5185	18.2847	19.0859	19.9234	20.7989	21.7139	22.6700	23.6690	24.7125	25.8023	26.9404	28.1287	29.3692	30.6639	32.0150
10	21.3215	22.3931	23.5213	24.7089	25.9587	27.2738	28.6574	30.1128	31.6434	33.2529	34.9449	36.7235	38.5926	40.5564	42.6195
11	25.7329	27.1999	28.7551	30.4035	32.1504	34.0013	35.9620	38.0388	40.2379	42.5661	45.0306	47.6388	50.3985	53.3178	56.4053
12	30.8502	32.8239	34.9311	37.1802	39.5805	42.1416	44.8737	47.7877	50.8950	54.2077	57.7386	61.5013	65.5100	69.7800	74.3270
13	36.7862	39.4040	42.2187	45.2445	48.4966	51.9913	55.7459	59.7788	64.1097	68.7596	73.7506	79.1066	84.8529	91.0161	97.6250
14	43.6720	47.1027	50.8180	54.8409	59.1959	63.9095	69.0100	74.5280	80.4961	86.9495	93.9258	101.4654	109.6117	118.4108	127.9125
15	51.6595	56.1101	60.9653	66.2607	72.0351	78.3305	85.1922	92.6694	100.8151	109.6868	119.3465	129.8611	141.3029	153.7500	167.2863
16	60.9250	66.6488	72.9390	79.8502	87.4421	95.7799	104.9345	114.9834	126.0108	138.1085	151.3766	165.9236	181.8677	199.3374	218.4722
17	71.6730	78.9792	87.0680	96.0218	105.9306	116.8937	129.0201	142.4295	157.2534	173.6357	191.7345	211.7230	233.7907	258.1453	285.0139
18	84.1407	93.4056	103.7403	115.2659	128.1167	142.4413	158.4045	176.1883	195.9942	218.0446	242.5855	269.8882	300.2521	334.0074	371.5180
19	98.6032	110.2846	123.4135	138.1664	154.7400	173.3540	194.2535	217.7116	244.0328	273.5558	306.6577	343.7580	385.3227	431.8696	483.9734
20	115.3797	130.0329	146.6280	165.4180	186.6880	210.7584	237.9893	268.7853	303.6006	342.9447	387.3887	437.5726	494.2131	558.1118	630.1655

APPENDIX B
Solutions to Selected End-of-Chapter Problems

CHAPTER 1

1. Investment decisions: Purchase a new computer; conduct research to develop a new drug; shut down the factory. Financing decisions: Take out a bank loan or sell bonds; issue shares of stock to raise funds; buy or lease a new machine.

2. Unlike proprietorships, corporations are legally distinct from their owners, and so they have limited liability and pay taxes on their earnings. Shares of public corporations trade in stock markets, unlike those of private corporations.

6. a. financial
   b. financial
   c. real
   d. real
   e. real
   f. financial
   g. real
   h. financial

12. Takeover defences increase the target firm's agency problems. If management is protected against takeovers by takeover defences, it is more likely that managers will act in their own best interest, rather than in the interests of the firm and its stockholders.

22. The contingency arrangement aligns the interests of the lawyer and the client.

27. a. Find the rate of return available on other riskless investments, e.g., 1-year maturity U.S. Treasury notes.
    b. The opportunity cost is 20%. Not a worthwhile capital investment unless the expected return on the project is greater than 20%.

32. If you know that you will engage in business with another party on a repeated basis, you will be less likely to take advantage of your business partner should the opportunity to do so arise.

CHAPTER 2

4. Derivatives markets, foreign exchange markets, commodity markets, money market.

5. Buy shares in a mutual fund.

10. Look up the price of gold in commodity markets, and compare it to $2,500/6 = $416.67/ounce.

13. a. False
    b. False
    c. True
    d. False
    e. False
    f. False

18. These funds collect money from small investors and invest the money in the stock or bonds of large corporations, thus channeling funds from investors to corporations. The advantages of mutual funds for individuals are diversification, professional investment management, and record keeping.

CHAPTER 3

1.

Assets		Liabilities and Shareholders' Equity	
Cash	$ 10,000	Accounts payable	$ 17,000
Receivables	22,000	Long-term debt	170,000
Inventory	200,000		
Store and property	100,000	Shareholders' equity	145,000
Total assets	$332,000	Liabilities and share-holders' equity	$332,000

5. a. Taxes = $2,575
   Average tax rate = 12.88%
   Marginal tax rate = 15%
   b. Taxes = $8,625
   Average tax rate = 17.25%
   Marginal tax rate = 25%
   c. Taxes = $83,897
   Average tax rate = 27.97%
   Marginal tax rate = 33%
   d. Taxes = $1,027,314
   Average tax rate = 34.24%
   Marginal tax rate = 35%

12. Dividends = $600,000

13. Total taxes are reduced by $2,000.

14. a. Book value = $200,000
    Market value = $50,200,000
    b. Price per share = $25.10
    Book value per share = $0.10

15.

Sales	$10,000
Cost of goods sold	6,500
G & A expenses	1,000
Depreciation expense	1,000
EBIT	1,500
Interest expense	500
Taxable income	1,000
Taxes (35%)	350
Net income	$ 650

Cash flow = net income + depreciation = $1,650

18. Cash flow will be $3,000 less than profits.

20. a. Cash flow = $3.95 million
    Net income = $1.95 million
    b. CF increases by $0.35 million
    NI decreases by $0.65 million
    c. Positive impact. Investors should care more about cash flow than book income.
    d. Both CF and NI decrease by $0.65 million.

23. a. 2010: Equity = $890 − $650 = $240
    2011: Equity = $1,040 − $810 = $230

b. 2010: NWC = $90 − $50 = $40
   2011: NWC = $140 − $60 = $80
c. Taxable income = $330
   Taxes paid = $115.50
d. Cash flow from operations = $174.50
e. Gross investment = $450
f. Other current liabilities increased by $45.

25. Net working capital decreased by $50.

27. Earnings per share in 2010 = $1.70
    Earnings per share in 2011 = $1.52
31. Price per share = $13.70

CHAPTER 4

1. a. Long-term debt ratio = 0.42
   b. Total debt ratio = 0.65
   c. Times interest earned = 3.75
   d. Cash coverage ratio = 7.42
   e. Current ratio = 0.74
   f. Quick ratio = 0.52
   g. Operating profit margin = 12.64%
   h. Inventory turnover = 19.11
   i. Days sales in inventory = 19.10 days
   j. Average collection period = 67.39 days
   k. ROE = 13%
   l. ROA = 6%
   m. Payout ratio = 0.699918

8. a. ROE = 13.41%

$$\frac{\text{Assets}}{\text{Equity}} \times \frac{\text{sales}}{\text{assets}} \times \frac{\text{after-tax operating income}}{\text{sales}}$$
$$\times \frac{\text{net income}}{\text{after-tax operating income}}$$
$$= \frac{27{,}503}{9{,}121} \times \frac{13{,}193}{27{,}503} \times \frac{1{,}223 + 685(1 - .35)}{13{,}193}$$
$$\times \frac{1{,}223}{1{,}223 + 685(1 - .35)} = .129796 = 13\%$$

11. a. Debt-equity ratio $= \dfrac{\text{long-term debt}}{\text{equity at start of year}}$

    b. Return on equity $= \dfrac{\text{net income}}{\text{average equity}}$

    c. Operating profit margin $= \dfrac{\text{after-tax operating income}}{\text{sales}}$

    d. Inventory turnover $= \dfrac{\text{cost of goods sold}}{\text{average inventory}}$

    e. Current ratio $= \dfrac{\text{current assets}}{\text{current liabilities}}$

    f. Average collection period $= \dfrac{\text{average receivables}}{\text{average daily sales}}$

    g. Quick ratio
       $= \dfrac{\text{cash + marketable securities + accounts receivable}}{\text{current liabilities}}$

14. The current ratio is unaffected. The quick ratio falls.

16. Days' sales in inventory = 2

18. a. Times interest earned = 1.25
    b. Cash coverage ratio = 1.5
    c. Fixed payment coverage = 1.09

20. Total sales = $54,750
    Asset turnover = 0.73
    ROA = 3.65%

22. $\dfrac{\text{Book debt}}{\text{Book equity}} = 0.5$

    $\dfrac{\text{Market equity}}{\text{Book equity}} = 2$

    $\dfrac{\text{Book debt}}{\text{Market equtiy}} = \dfrac{0.5}{2} = 0.25$

24. Perhaps the firm has a lower ROA than its competitors; perhaps it pays a higher interest rate on its debt.

26. a. The shipping company
    b. United Foods
    c. The paper mill
    d. The power company

CHAPTER 5

1. a. $46.32
   b. $21.45
   c. $67.56
   d. $45.64

3. $100 \times (1.04)^{113} = \$8{,}409.45$
   $100 \times (1.08)^{113} = \$598{,}252.29$

5. PV = $548.47

9. PV = $796.56

10. a. $t = 23.36$
    b. $t = 11.91$
    c. $t = 6.17$

11. Effective annual rate
    a. 12.68%
    b. 8.24%
    c. 10.25%

13. $n = 11.9$ years

15. APR = 52%; EAR = 67.77%

20. The PV for the quarterback is $11.37 million. The PV for the receiver is $11.58 million.

24. a. EAR = 6.78%
    b. PMT = $573.14

28. APR = 19.188%; EAR = 20.97%

30. The value of the lease payments is $38,132. It is cheaper to lease the truck.

34. a. PMT = $277.41
    b. PMT = $247.69

35. $66,703.25

37. $79,079.37

46. $100 \times e^{0.10 \times 8} = $222.55
    $100 \times e^{0.08 \times 10} = $222.55

47. $n = 44.74$ months

48. The present value of your payments is $736.01. The present value of your receipts is $930.66. This is a good deal.

50. $r = 8\%$

53. a. The present value of the payoff is $1,116.79. This is a good deal.
    b. PV is $771.09. This is a bad deal.

60. $3,230.77

62. $2,964.53

66. a. Nominal rate = 3%
    b. Nominal rate = 7.12%
    c. Nominal rate = 9.18%

68. a. $79.38
    b. $91.51
    c. Real interest rate = 4.854%
    d. $91.51/(1.04854)^3 = $79.38

70. a. $228,107
    b. $13,950

71. Approximately 24 years. Purchasing Power increases by 57.84%

77. FV = $1.188; PV = $0.8418

78. $2,653.87

CHAPTER 6

1. a. Coupon rate remains unchanged.
   b. Price will fall.
   c. Yield to maturity increases.
   d. Current yield increases.

3. Bond price = $1,333.33

4. Coupon rate = 8%
   Yield to maturity = 9.119%

9. Rate of return on both bonds = 10%

10. a. Price will be $1,000.
    b. Rate of return = −1.82%
    c. Real return = −4.68%

11. a. Bondholder receives $80 per year.
    b. Price = $1,065.15
    c. The bond will sell for $1,136.03.

12. a. 8.971%
    b. 8%
    c. 7.18%

16. 20 years

18. a. Price = $641.01
    b. $r = 12.87\%$

19. a. Yield to maturity = 5.165%
    b. Rate of return = 30.61%

22. a. 9.89%
    b. 8%
    c. 6.18%

25. a. 4.902%
    b. 2.885%
    c. 0.9434%
    d. −0.926%

CHAPTER 7

3. a. $66.67
   b. $66.67
   c. Capital gains yield = 0
      Dividend yield = expected return = 12%

6. a. 14%
   b. $P_0 = $24

11. a. $DIV_1 = $1.04
       $DIV_2 = $1.0816
       $DIV_3 = $1.1249
    b. $P_0 = $13
    c. $P_3 = $14.6237
    d. Your payments are:

	Year 1	Year 2	Year 3
DIV	$1.04	$1.0816	$ 1.1249
Sales price			$14.6237
Total cash flow	$1.04	$1.0816	$15.7486
PV of cash flow	$0.9286	$0.8622	$11.2095
Sum of PV = $13			

13. a. $P_0 = $31.50
    b. $P_0 = $45

16. $P_0 = $33.33

18. a. (i)   Reinvest 0% of earnings.
              $g = 0$; $P_0 = $40
        (ii) Reinvest 40% of earnings.
              $g = 6\%$; $P_0 = $40
        (iii) Reinvest 60% of earnings.
              $g = 9\%$; $P_0 = $40
    b. (i)   Reinvest 0% of earnings.
              $g = 0$; $P_0 = $40
              PVGO = $0
        (ii) Reinvest 40% of earnings.
              $g = 8\%$; $P_0 = $51.43
              PVGO = $11.43
        (iii) Reinvest 60% of earnings.
              $g = 12\%$; $P_0 = $80
              PVGO = $40
    c. In part (a), the return on reinvested earnings was equal to the discount rate.
       In part (b), the return on reinvested earnings was greater than the discount rate.

19. a. $P_0 = $18.10
    b. $DIV_1/P_0 = 5.52\%$

21. a. 6%
    b. $35
    c. $10
    d. 11.667
    e. Price = $25; P/E = 8.333
    f. Higher growth opportunities increase price and P/E.

23. a. P/E = 33.33/4 = 8.33
    b. P/E increases to 10.

25. a. P_0 = $125
    b. Assets in place = $80
       PVGO = $45

29. a. Market-to-book ratio = $800/$200 = 4
    b. Market-to-book ratio = ½

30. $16.59

41. a. P_0 = $52.806
    b. P_1 = $57.143
    c. Return = 0.1200

43. a. Expected return = 8%
    b. PVGO = $16.67
    c. P_0 = $106.22

CHAPTER 8

1. Both projects are worth pursuing.

3. NPV_A = $23.85 and NPV_B = $24.59. Choose B.

5. No.

7. Project A has a payback period of 2.5 years.
   Project B has a payback period of 2 years.

11. 0.2680

13. IRR_A = 25.69%
    IRR_B = 20.69%
    Project A has higher IRR, but B has higher NPV.

14. NPV = −$197.7. Reject.

15. a. r = 0 implies NPV = $15,750.
       r = 50% implies NPV = $4,250.
       r = 100% implies NPV = 0.
    b. IRR = 100%

17. $NPV_{9\%}$ = $2,139.28 and $NPV_{14\%}$ = −$1,444.54. The IRR is 11.81%.

20. NPV must be negative.

22. a.

Project	Payback
A	3 years
B	2 years
C	3 years

    b. Only B
    c. All three projects
    d.

Project	NPV
A	−$1,010.52
B	$3,378.12
C	$2,404.55

    e. False

26. a. If r = 2%, choose A.
    b. If r = 12%, choose B.

27. $22,637.98

29. b. At 5% NPV = −$0.443
    c. At 20% NPV = $0.840
       At 40% NPV = −$0.634

30. a. The equivalent annual cost of owning and operating Econo-cool is $252.53. The equivalent annual cost of Luxury Air is $234.21.
    b. Luxury Air.
    c. Econo-cool equivalent annual cost is $229.14. Luxury Air equivalent annual cost is $193.72.

33. a. The equivalent cost of owning and operating the new machine is $4,465.82. The old machine costs $5,000 a year to operate. You should replace.
    b. If r = 12%, do not replace. Equivalent annual cost = $5,539.68.

CHAPTER 9

3. $2.3 million

5. Increase in net cash flow = $106 million

6.

Revenue	$160,000
Rental costs	30,000
Variable costs	50,000
Depreciation	10,000
Pretax profit	$ 70,000
Taxes (35%)	24,500
Net income	$ 45,500

8. Cash flow = $3,300

10. Cash flow = $56,250

11. a.

Year	MACRS(%)	Depreciation	Book Value (end of year)
1	20.00	$ 8,000	$32,000
2	32.00	12,800	19,200
3	19.20	7,680	11,520
4	11.52	4,608	6,912
5	11.52	4,608	2,304
6	5.76	2,304	0

    b. After-tax proceeds are $18,332.

17. Cash flow = $3.7055 million

18. a. Incremental operating CF = $1,300 in years 1 to 6
       Net cash flow at time 0 = −$4,800
    b. NPV = −$4,800 + [$1,300 annuity factor (16%, 6 years)]
       = −$9.84
    c. NPV = $137.09

21. a. Initial investment = $53,000
    b.

Year	Cash Flow ($000)
1	20.9
2	17.3
3	13.7
4	10.1

    c. NPV = − $4,377.71
    d. IRR = 7.50%

23. NPV = −$10,894.31. Don't buy.

24. Equivalent annual (net-of-tax) costs:
    Quick and Dirty: $2.074 million
    Do-It-Right: $1.891 million
    Choose Do-It-Right.

26. NPV = $-$349,773.33

30. a. $71.75 million
    b. $40.25 million per year
    c. NPV = $28.35 million; IRR = 31.33%

CHAPTER 10

2. Variable costs = $0.50 per burger
   Fixed costs = $2.5 million

5. a. $1.836 million
      $-$5.509 million
   b. $544,567
   c. Fixed costs can increase by $3 million before pretax profits are reduced to zero.

6. a. NPV = $5.61 million
   b. NPV = $2.88 million
   c. NPV = $6.75 million
   d. Price = $1.59 per jar

9. $1.50

12. Accounting break-even is unaffected. NPV break-even increases.

13. CF break-even is less than zero-profit break-even sales level.

15. a. Accounting break-even sales level is $6,400 per year. NPV break-even sales level is $7,166.
    b. Accounting break-even is unchanged. NPV break-even is $7,578.

16. a. Accounting break-even increases.
    b. NPV break-even falls.
    c. MACRS makes the project more attractive.

18. NPV will be negative.

21. DOL = 1

24. a. Average CF = $0
    b. Average CF = $60,000

27. a. NPV = $-$681,728. The firm will reject the project.
    b. NPV = $69,855. The project is now worth pursuing.

CHAPTER 11

1. Return = 15%
   Dividend yield = 5%
   Capital gains yield = 10%

3. a. Rate of return = 0
      Real rate = -3.85%
   b. Rate of return = 5%
      Real rate = 0.96%
   c. Rate of return = 10%
      Real rate = 5.77%

5.

Asset Class	Real Rate
Treasury bills	0.87%
Treasury bonds	2.04%
Common stock	8.05%

15. The bankruptcy lawyer

17. b. $r_{stock} = 13\%$
       $r_{bonds} = 8.4\%$
       Standard deviation (stocks) = 9.8%
       Standard deviation (bonds) = 3.2%

19. Our estimate of "normal" risk premiums will fall.

21. a. General Steel
    b. Club Med

23. Sassafras is *not* a risky investment to a diversified investor. Its return is better when the economy enters a recession. In contrast, the Leaning Tower of Pita has returns that are positively correlated with the rest of the economy.

CHAPTER 12

1. a. False
   b. False
   c. False
   d. True
   e. True

3. It is not well diversified.

7. Required return = $r_f + \beta(r_m - r_f) = 14.75\%$
   Expected return = 16%
   The security is underpriced.

11. a. $\beta_A = 1.2$
       $\beta_D = 0.75$
    b. $r_m = 12\%$
       $r_A = 14\%$
       $r_D = 9\%$
    c. $r = r_f + \beta(r_m - r_f)$
       $r_A = 13.6\%$
       $r_D = 10\%$
    d. Stock A

13. NPV = $-$25.29

15. $P_1 = $52.625

19. $400,000

23. $\beta = 4/7 = 0.5714$

25. a. False
    b. True
    c. False
    d. True
    e. False

26. $r = r_f + \beta(r_m - r_f) = 12\%$
    The 11% expected return is unattractive relative to its risk.

CHAPTER 13

1. 4.88%

4. 13.75%

8. The cost of equity capital is 11.2%.
   WACC = 8.74%

11. WACC = 12.42%

16.

	Dollars	Percent
Bonds	$ 9.36 million	30.3%
Preferred stock	1.50 million	4.9
Common stock	20.00 million	64.8
Total	$ 30.86 million	100.0%

17. 11.36%
18. The IRR is less than the WACC of firms in the computer industry. Reject the project.
19. a. $r = 16\%$
    b. Weighted-average beta = 0.72
    c. WACC = 10.56%
    d. Discount rate = 10.56%
    e. $r = 18\%$

CHAPTER 14

1. a. 60,000 shares issued
   b. Outstanding shares = 58,000
   c. 40,000
3. a. funded
   b. Eurobond
   c. subordinated
   d. sinking fund
   e. call
   f. prime rate
   g. floating rate
   h. private placement, public issue
   i. lease
   j. convertible
   k. warrant
6. a. 100 votes
   b. 1,000 votes
7. a. 200,001 shares
   b. 80,000 shares
9. Par value of common shares = $400,000
   Additional paid-in capital = $1,600,000
   Retained earnings = $500,000
12. Similarity: The firm promises to make specified payments. Advantage of income bonds: Interest payments are tax-deductible expenses.

CHAPTER 15

1. a. Subsequent issue
   b. Bond issue
   c. Bond issue
3. a. A large issue
   b. A bond issue
   c. Private placements
4. Less underwriter risk; less signaling effect from debt; easier to value.
7. a. 10%
   b. Average return = 3.94%
   c. I have suffered the winner's curse.
10. No
12. 12% of the value of funds raised.
14. a. Net proceeds of public issue = $9,770,000
    Net proceeds of private placement = $9,970,000

b. The public issue
c. The private placement can be custom-tailored, and its terms can be more easily renegotiated.
15. a. $12.5 million
    b. $5.80 per share
17. a. $10
    b. $18.3333
    c. $8.3333
    d. 200 rights

CHAPTER 16

4. $280 million
11. P/E = 10/1.25 = 8 (no leverage)
    P/E = 10/1.33 = 7.5 (leveraged)
14. a. Low-debt plan: $D/E = 0.25$
    High-debt plan: $D/E = 0.67$
b.

	Low-Debt Plan		High-Debt Plan	
EPS	$8.75	$13.75	$8.33	$15.00
Expected EPS	$11.25		$11.67	

c.

	Low-Debt	High-Debt
EPS	$10.00	$10.00

16. $r_{equity} = 14\%$
22. a. 11.2%
    b. The PV of the tax shield had been 0.35 × $800 = $280 million. New market-value balance sheet:

Assets	Liabilities and Equity	
$2,420	Debt	$0
	Equity	$2,420

24. Distorted investment decisions, impeded relations with other firms and creditors.
31. a. Stockholders gain; bondholders lose.
    b. Bondholders gain; stockholders lose.
    c. Bondholders lose; stockholders gain.
    d. Original stockholders lose; bondholders gain.

CHAPTER 17

1. a. May 7: Declaration date
   June 6: Last with-dividend date
   June 7: Ex-dividend date
   June 11: Record date
   July 2: Payment date
   b. The ex-dividend date, June 7.
   c. Dividend yield = 1.11%
   d. Payout ratio = 15.79%

2. a. Price = $64
    b. Price = $64
    c. Price = $80, unchanged

10. a. No effect on total wealth.
    b. No change: fewer shares, but higher price.

12. With a repurchase, shareholders will own fewer shares at a higher price. Their overall position is the same as with a dividend.

14. a. 1,250 shares. Value of equity remains at $100,000.
    b. Same effect as the stock dividend.

16. a. $50; $45
    b. $48.50

18. a. Price = $19.45
    b. Before-tax return = 13.11%
    c. Price = $20.09
    d. Before-tax return = 14.48%

19. a.

Stock	Pension	Corporation	Individual
A	10.00%	6.500%	9.00%
B	10.00	7.725	8.75
C	10.00	8.950	8.50

    b.

Stock	Price
A	$100
B	$ 81.25
C	$ 62.50

23. a. Dividend: $19 per share; repurchase: $20 per share.
    b. If the firm pays a dividend, EPS = $2. If the firm does the repurchase, EPS = $2.105.
    c. If the dividend is paid, the P/E ratio = 9.5. If the stock is repurchased, the P/E ratio = 9.5.

CHAPTER 18

1. a. False
    b. False
    c. True
    d. False
    e. True
    f. True
    g. False

6. Sales revenue will increase less than proportionally to output; costs and assets will increase roughly in proportion to output. Costs and assets will increase as a proportion of sales.

9. The balancing item is dividends. Dividends must be $200.

11. a. Internal growth rate = 10%
    b. Sustainable growth rate = 15%

13. a. Internal growth rate = 5.56%
    b. Sustainable growth rate = 8.33%

15. a.

Income Statement	20% Growth	5% Growth
Revenue	$2,400	$2,100
Cost of goods sold	2,160	1,890
EBIT	240	210
Interest expense	40	40
Earnings before taxes	200	170
State and federal taxes	80	68
Net income	120	102
Dividends	80	68
Retained earnings	$ 40	$ 34

Balance Sheet	20% Growth	5% Growth
Assets		
Net working capital	$ 240	$ 210
Fixed assets	960	840
Total assets	$1,200	$1,050
Liabilities and Shareholders' Equity		
Long-term debt	$ 400	$ 400
Shareholders' equity	640	634
Total liabilities and shareholders' equity	$1,040	$1,034
Required external financing	$ 160	$ 16

    b.

Second-Stage Pro Forma Balance Sheet	20% Growth	5% Growth
Assets		
Net working capital	$ 240	$ 210
Fixed assets	960	840
Total assets	$1,200	$1,050
Liabilities and Shareholders' Equity		
Long-term debt	$ 560	$ 416
Shareholders' equity	640	634
Total liabilities and shareholders' equity	$1,200	$1,050

17. a. g = 2.5%
    b. Issue $1,000 in new debt.
    c. 1.5%

19. a. Internal growth rate = 10%
    b. External financing = $200,000
    c. Internal growth rate = 25%
    d. External financing = $50,000

21. Payout ratio can be at most 0.444.

23. Profit margin = 10%

25. g = 12%

27. Required external financing is zero.

29. Higher

CHAPTER 19

1.

	Cash	Net Working Capital
a.	$2 million decline	$2 million decline
b.	$2,500 increase	Unchanged
c.	$5,000 decline	Unchanged
d.	Unchanged	$1 million increase
e.	Unchanged	Unchanged
f.	$5 million increase	Unchanged

2. a. Long-term financing, total capital requirement, market-able securities.
  b. Cash, cash, cash balance, marketable securities.

5. Lower inventory period and cash conversion cycle; reduce net working capital.

7. a. Cash conversion cycle falls.
  b. Cash conversion cycle increases.
  c. Cash conversion cycle falls.
  d. Cash conversion cycle increases.
  e. Cash conversion cycle falls.
  f. Cash conversion cycle increases.

16. The order is .75 times the following quarter's sales forecast:

Quarter	Order
1	$270
2	$252
3	$288
4	$288

18.

Quarter	Collections
1	$348
2	$368
3	$352
4	$352

20.

	Quarter			
	First	Second	Third	Fourth
Cash at start of period	$40	$10	$15	−$14
+ Net cash inflow (from Problem 18)	−30	+5	−29	−41
= Cash at end of period	10	15	−14	−55
Minimum operating cash balance	30	30	30	30
Cumulative financing required (minimum cash balance minus cash at end of period)	$20	$15	$44	$85

22.

	Quarter			
	First	Second	Third	Fourth
Cash requirements				
1. Cash required for operations	$50	$15	−$26	−$35
2. Interest on bank loan	0.00	0.90	0.90	0.73
3. Interest on stretched payables	0	0	0.8	0
4. Total cash required	$50.00	$15.90	−$24.30	−$34.27
Cash raised in quarter				
5. Bank loan	$45	$ 0	$ 0	$ 0
6. Stretched payables	0	15.9	0	0
7. Securities sold	5	0	0	0
8. Total cash raised	$50	$15.9	$ 0	$ 0
Repayments				
9. Of stretched payables	0	0	$15.9	0
10. Of bank loan	0.00	0.00	8.40	34.27
Bank loan				
11. Addition to cash balances	$ 5	$ 0	$ 0	$ 0
Bank loan				
12. Beginning of quarter	$ 0	$45	$45	$36.6
13. End of quarter	$45.00	$45.00	$36.60	$2.33

23.

Sources of Cash	
Sale of marketable securities	$ 2
Increase in bank loans	1
Increase in accounts payable	5
Cash from operations:	
Net income	6
Depreciation	2
Total	$16
Uses of Cash	
Increase in inventories	$ 6
Increase in accounts receivable	3
Investment in fixed assets	6
Dividend paid	1
Total	$16
Change in cash balance	0

24.

	February	March	April
Sources of cash			
Collections on current sales	$ 100	$ 110	$ 90
Collections on accounts receivable	90	100	110
Total sources of cash	$ 190	$ 210	$ 200
Uses of cash			
Payments of accounts payable	$ 30	$ 40	$ 30
Cash purchases	70	80	60
Labor and administrative expenses	30	30	30
Capital expenditures	100	0	0
Taxes, interest, and dividends	10	10	10
Total uses of cash	$ 240	$ 160	$ 130
Net cash inflow (sources − uses)	−$ 50	+$ 50	+$ 70
Cash at start of period	$ 100	$ 50	$ 100
+ Net cash inflow	−50	+50	+70
= Cash at end of period	$ 50	$ 100	$ 170
+ Minimum operating cash balance	$ 100	$ 100	$ 100
= Cumulative short-term financing required (minimum cash balance minus cash at end of period)	$ 50	$ 0	−$ 70

CHAPTER 20

1. a. $10
    b. 40 days
    c. 9.6%

4. a. Due lag and pay lag fall.
    b. Due lag and pay lag increase.
    c. Terms lag and pay lag increase.

6. Available balance with bank = $275,000

8. Extra cash available = $22,000.
    Interest = .06 × $22,000 = $1,320.

11. a. 20 days
    b. $1.096 million
    c. Average days in receivables will fall.

13. a. The expected profit from a sale is −$3. Do not extend credit.
    b. $p = 0.96$
    c. The present value of a sale is positive, $365.28.
    d. $p = 0.1935\%$

14. a. The expected profit of a sale is positive, $90.
    b. $p = 0.875$

19. a. Yes
    b. Credit should not be advanced.
    c. Net benefit from advancing credit = $50.

20. a. $30,000
    b. $6
    c. $180

22. Yes

23. Cash balances fall relative to sales.

24. PV(REV) = $1,200
    PV(COST) = $1,000
    Slow payers have a 70% probability of paying their bills. The expected profit of a sale to a slow payer is therefore 0.70($1,200 − $1,000) − 0.30($1,000) = −$160.
    Expected savings = $16. The credit check costs $5, so it is cost effective.

26. Sell only to groups 1, 2, and 3.

CHAPTER 21

1. a. Economies of scale is a valid reason.
    b. Diversification is not a valid reason.
    c. Possibly a valid reason.
    d. Merging to increase EPS is not a valid reason.

2. By merging, the firms can even out the workload over the year.

4. LBO: 5
    Poison pill: 3
    Tender offer: 4
    Shark repellent: 2
    Proxy contest: 1

6. $25 per share

8. a. $6.25 million
    b. $4 million
    c. NPV = $2.25 million

12. a. NPV = $10,000
    b. SCC will sell for $53.33; SDP will sell for $20.
    c. Price = $52.63
    d. NPV = $7,890

13. a. Total market value = $4,000,000 + $5,000,000 = $9,000,000
    Total earnings = $200,000 + $500,000 = $700,000
    Number of shares = 262,172
    Price per share = $9,000,000/262,172 = $34.33
    Price-earnings ratio = $34.33/$2.67 = 12.86
    b. 0.81 shares
    c. $567,365
    d. −$567,365

CHAPTER 22

1. a. 76.66 euros; $130.44
    b. 100.94 Swiss francs; $99
    c. Direct exchange rate will decrease and indirect exchange rate will increase.
    d. U.S. dollar is worth more.

3. a. $$\frac{1 + r_x}{1 + r_\$} = \frac{f_{x/\$}}{s_{x/\$}}$$

    b. $$\frac{f_{x/\$}}{s_{x/\$}} = \frac{E(s_{x/\$})}{s_{x/\$}}$$

    c. $$\frac{1 + i_x}{1 + i_\$} = \frac{E(s_{x/\$})}{s_{x/\$}}$$

    d. $$\frac{1 + r_x}{E(1 + i_x)} = \frac{1 + r_\$}{E(1 + i_\$)}$$

6. a

8. Borrow the present value of 1 million Australian dollars, sell them for U.S. dollars in the spot market, and invest the proceeds in an 8-year U.S. dollar loan. In 8 years, it can repay the Australian loan with the anticipated Australian dollar payment.

10. a. 4%
    b. 14%
    c. −6%

14. Canadian dollar should be depreciating relative to the U.S. dollar.

16. Net present value = $0.9629 million

18. a. Depreciation of Trinidadian dollars
    b. Borrow in Trinidad.
    c. Its exposure is mitigated.

CHAPTER 23

1.

	Payoff	Profit
a. Call option, X = 430	30	−11.20
b. Put option, X = 430	0	−11.05
c. Call option, X = 460	0	−22.50
d. Put option, X = 460	0	−22.20
e. Call option, X = 490	0	−10.10
f. Put option, X = 490	30	−9.36

5. Figure 23.7a represents a call seller; Figure 23.7b represents a call buyer.

7. a. The exercise price of the put option.
   b. The value of the stock.

10. Lower bound is either zero or the stock price minus the exercise price, whichever is greater. The upper bound is the stock price.

14. You will be more tempted to choose the high-risk proposal.

16. a. Call option to pursue a project.
    b. Put option to sell the equipment.

18. Put option with exercise price equal to support price.

20. a. Option to put (sell) the stock to the underwriter.
    b. Volatility of the stock value; the length of the period for which the underwriter guarantees the issue; the interest rate; the price at which the underwriter is obligated to buy the stock; and the market value of the stock.

22. Put option on the bank assets with exercise price equal to the deposits owed to bank customers.

24. a. Buy a call option for $3. Exercise the call to purchase stock. Pay the $20 exercise price. Sell the share for $25. Riskless profit equals $2.
    b. Buy a share and put option. Exercise the put. Riskless profit equals $1.

CHAPTER 24

1. They should insure against events that would result in financial distress and against risks that the insurance company can diversify away.

4. No

6. Advantages: liquidity, no storage costs, no spoilage. Disadvantages: no income or benefits that could accrue from holding asset in portfolio.

7.

	Gold Price		
	1000	1200	1400
a. Revenues	$1,000,000	$1,200,000	$1,400,000
Futures contract gain	80,000	−120,000	−320,000
b. Total revenues	$1,080,000	$1,080,000	$1,080,000
c. Revenues	$1,000,000	$1,200,000	$1,400,000
+ Put option payoff	80,000	0	0
− Put option cost	12,000	12,000	12,000
Total revenues	$1,068,000	$1,188,000	$1,388,000

9. Reject its offer. Instead borrow for 2 years at 7% and relend for 1 year at 6%.

11. The futures price for oil is $90 per barrel. Petrochemical will take a long position to hedge its cost of buying oil. Onnex will take a short position to hedge its revenue from selling oil.

	Oil Price ($ per barrel)		
	$80	$90	$100
Cost for Petrochemical:			
Cash flow to buy 1,000 barrels	−80,000	−90,000	−100,000
+ Cash flow on long futures position	−10,000	0	10,000
Net cost	−90,000	−90,000	−90,000
Revenue for Onnex:			
Revenue from 1,000 barrels	$80,000	$90,000	$100,000
+ Cash flow on short futures position	10,000	0	−10,000
Net revenues	$90,000	$90,000	$ 90,000

The benefit of futures is the ability to lock in a riskless position without paying any money. The benefit of the option hedge is that you benefit if prices move in one direction without losing if they move in the other direction. However, this asymmetry comes at a price: the cost of the option.

12. The futures price is greater than the spot price for gold. This reflects the fact that the futures contract ensures your receipt of the gold without tying up your money now. The difference between the spot price and the futures price reflects compensation for the time value of money. Another way to put it is that the spot price must be lower than the futures price to compensate investors who buy and store gold for the opportunity cost of their funds until the futures maturity date.

14. A currency swap is an agreement to exchange a series of payments in one currency for a given series of payments in another currency. An interest rate swap is an exchange of a series of fixed payments for a series of payments that are linked to market interest rates.

Glossary

A

ACH   See *Automated Clearing House.*

acquisition   Takeover of a firm by purchase of that firm's common stock or assets.

additional paid-in capital   Difference between issue price and par value of stock. Also called *capital surplus.*

agency problems   Managers, acting as agents for stockholders, may act in their own interests rather than maximizing value.

aging schedule   Classification of accounts receivable by time outstanding.

annual percentage rate (APR)   Interest rate that is annualized using simple interest.

annuity   Equally spaced level stream of cash flows with a finite maturity.

annuity due   Level stream of cash flows starting immediately.

annuity factor   Present value of a $1 annuity.

authorized share capital   Maximum number of shares that the company is permitted to issue.

Automated Clearing House (ACH)   An electronic network for cash transfers in the United States.

average tax rate   Total taxes owed divided by total income.

B

balance sheet   Financial statement that shows the value of the firm's assets and liabilities at a particular time.

balancing item   Variable that adjusts to maintain the consistency of a financial plan. Also called *plug.*

bankruptcy   The reorganization or liquidation of a firm that cannot pay its debts.

beta   Sensitivity of a stock's return to the return on the market portfolio.

bond   Security that obligates the issuer to make specified payments to the bondholder.

book value   Net worth of the firm according to the balance sheet.

break-even analysis   Analysis of the level of sales at which the project breaks even.

business risk   See *operating risk.*

C

call option   Right to buy an asset at a specified exercise price on or before the expiration date.

callable bond   Bond that may be repurchased by the firm before maturity at a specified call price.

capital asset pricing model (CAPM)   Theory of the relationship between risk and return which states that the expected risk premium on any security equals its beta times the market risk premium.

capital budget   List of planned investment projects.

capital budgeting decision   Decision to invest in tangible or intangible assets. Also called *capital expenditure (CAPEX) decision.*

capital expenditure (CAPEX) decision   See *capital budgeting decision.*

capital markets   Markets for long-term financing.

capital rationing   Limit set on the amount of funds available for investment.

capital structure   The mix of long-term debt and equity financing.

CAPM   See *capital asset pricing model.*

carrying costs   Costs of maintaining current assets, including opportunity cost of capital.

cash conversion cycle   Period between firm's payment for materials and collection on its sales.

cash dividend   Payment of cash by the firm to its shareholders.

CEO   Acronym for chief executive officer.

CFO   See *chief financial officer.*

chief financial officer (CFO)   Oversees the treasurer and controller and sets overall financial strategy.

collection policy   Procedures to collect and monitor receivables.

commercial paper   Short-term unsecured notes issued by firms.

common-size balance sheet   Balance sheet that presents items as a percentage of total assets.

common-size income statement   Income statement that presents items as a percentage of revenues.

common stock   Ownership shares in a publicly held corporation.

company cost of capital   Expected rate of return demanded by investors in a company, determined by the average risk of the company's securities.

compound interest   Interest earned on interest.

concentration account   System whereby customers make payments to a regional collection center which transfers funds to a principal bank.

constant-growth dividend discount model   Version of the dividend discount model in which dividends grow at a constant rate.

consumer credit   Bills awaiting payment from final customer to a company.

controller   Officer responsible for budgeting, accounting, and taxes.

convertible bond   Bond that the holder may exchange for a specified amount of another security.

corporation   Business organized as a separate legal entity owned by stockholders.

cost of capital   Minimum acceptable rate of return on capital investment.

costs of financial distress   Costs arising from bankruptcy or distorted business decisions before bankruptcy.

coupon   The interest payments paid to the bondholder.

coupon rate   Annual interest payment as a percentage of face value.

credit analysis   Procedure to determine the likelihood a customer will pay its bills.

credit policy   Standards set to determine the amount and nature of credit to extend to customers.

credit risk   See *default risk.*

cumulative voting   Voting system in which all the votes one shareholder is allowed to cast can be cast for one candidate for the board of directors.

current yield   Annual coupon payment divided by bond price.

D

decision tree   Diagram of sequential decisions and possible outcomes.

default premium   The additional yield that bond investors require for bearing credit risk.

default risk   The risk that a bond issuer may default on its bonds. Also called *credit risk.*

degree of operating leverage (DOL)   Percentage change in profits given a 1 percent change in sales.

depreciation tax shield   Reduction in taxes attributable to depreciation.

derivatives   Securities whose payoffs are determined by the values of other financial variables such as prices, exchange rates, or interest rates.

discount factor   Present value of a $1 future payment.

discount rate   Interest rate used to compute present values of future cash flows.

discounted cash flow (DCF)   Another term for the present value of a future cash flow.

diversification   Strategy designed to reduce risk by spreading the portfolio across many investments.

dividend   Periodic cash distribution to shareholders.

dividend discount model   Discounted cash-flow model which states that today's stock price equals the present value of all expected future dividends.

Dow Jones Industrial Average   Index of the investment performance of a portfolio of 30 "blue-chip" stocks.

Du Pont formula   A breakdown of ROE and ROA into component ratios.

E

economic value added (EVA)   Income that is measured after deduction of the cost of capital. Also called *residual income.*

effective annual interest rate   Interest rate that is annualized using compound interest.

efficient markets   Markets in which prices reflect all available information.

equivalent annual annuity   The cash flow per period with the same present value as the cost of buying and operating a machine.

eurobond   Bond that is marketed internationally.

eurodollars   Dollars held on deposit in a bank outside the United States.

EVA   See *economic value added.*

exchange rate   Amount of one currency needed to purchase one unit of another.

ex-dividend   Without the dividend. Buyer of a stock after the ex-dividend date does not receive the most recently declared dividend.

expectations theory of exchange rates   Theory that expected spot exchange rate equals the forward rate.

F

face value   Payment at the maturity of the bond. Also called *principal* or *par value.*

financial assets   Claims to the income generated by real assets. Also called *securities.*

financial deficit   Difference between cash the companies need and the amount generated internally.

financial institution   A bank, insurance company, or similar financial intermediary.

financial intermediary   An organization that raises money from many investors and provides financing to individuals, corporations, or other organizations.

financial leverage   Debt financing to amplify the effects of changes in operating income on the returns to stockholders.

financial markets   Markets in which securities are issued and traded.

financial risk   Risk to shareholders resulting from the use of debt.

financial slack   Ready access to cash or debt financing.

financing decision   The form and amount of financing of a firm's investments.

fixed costs   Costs that do not depend on the level of output.

fixed-income market   Market for debt securities.

floating rate preferred   Preferred stock for which the dividend rate is linked to current market interest rates

flotation costs   The costs incurred when a firm issues new securities to the public.

forex   Abbreviation for foreign exchange; also abbreviated *fx.*

forward contract   Agreement to buy or sell an asset in the future at an agreed price.

forward exchange rate   Exchange rate agreed today for a future transaction.

free cash flow   Cash available for distribution to investors after the company has paid for any new capital investment or additions to working capital.

fundamental analysts   Investors who attempt to find mispriced securities by analyzing fundamental information, such as firm performance and earnings prospects.

funded debt   Debt with more than 1 year remaining to maturity.

future value (FV)   Amount to which an investment will grow after earning interest.

futures contract   Exchange-traded promise to buy or sell an asset in the future at a prespecified price.

FV   See *future value.*

fx   Abbreviation for foreign exchange; also abbreviated *forex.*

G

GAAP   See *generally accepted accounting principles.*

general cash offer   Sale of securities open to all investors by an already-public company.

generally accepted accounting principles (GAAP) Procedures for preparing financial statements.

H

hedge fund A private investment pool, open to wealthy or institutional investors, that is only lightly regulated and therefore can pursue more speculative policies than mutual funds.

I

income statement Financial statement that shows the revenues, expenses, and net income of a firm over a period of time.

inflation Rate at which prices as a whole are increasing.

information content of dividends Dividend increases send good news about future cash flow and earnings. Dividend cuts send bad news.

initial public offering (IPO) First offering of stock to the general public.

interest rate parity Theory that forward premium equals interest rate differential.

interest rate risk The risk in bond prices due to fluctuations in interest rates.

interest tax shield Tax savings resulting from deductibility of interest payments.

internal growth rate Maximum rate of growth without external financing.

internal rate of return (IRR) Discount rate at which project NPV = 0.

internally generated funds Cash reinvested in the firm; depreciation plus earnings not paid out as dividends.

international Fisher effect Theory that real interest rates in all countries should be equal, with differences in nominal rates reflecting differences in expected inflation.

intrinsic value The present value of the cash payoffs anticipated by an investor in a security.

investment grade Bonds rated Baa or above by Moody's or BBB or above by Standard & Poor's.

IPO See *initial public offering.*

IRR See *internal rate of return.*

issued shares Shares that have been issued by the company.

J

junk bond Bond with a rating below Baa or BBB.

just-in-time approach System of inventory management that requires minimum inventories of materials and very frequent deliveries by suppliers.

L

law of one price Theory that prices of goods in all countries should be equal when translated to a common currency.

lease Long-term rental agreement.

leveraged buyout (LBO) Acquisition of a firm by a private group using substantial borrowed funds.

limited liability The owners of the corporation are not personally responsible for its obligations.

line of credit Agreement by a bank that a company may borrow at any time up to an established limit.

liquidation Sale of bankrupt firm's assets.

liquidation value Net proceeds that could be realized by selling the firm's assets and paying off its creditors.

liquidity Ability to sell an asset on short notice at close to the market price.

loan covenant Agreement between firm and lender requiring the firm to fulfill certain conditions to safeguard the loan.

lock-box system System whereby customers send payments to a post-office box and a local bank collects and processes checks.

M

majority voting Voting system in which each director is voted on separately.

management buyout (MBO) Acquisition of the firm by its own management in a leveraged buyout.

M&A Abbreviation for mergers and acquisitions.

marginal tax rate Additional taxes owed per dollar of additional income.

market capitalization Total market value of equity, equal to share price times number of shares outstanding.

market index Measure of the investment performance of the overall market.

market portfolio Portfolio of all assets in the economy. In practice a broad stock market index is used to represent the market.

market risk Economywide (macroeconomic) sources of risk that affect the overall stock market. Also called *systematic risk.*

market risk premium Risk premium of market portfolio. Difference between market return and return on risk-free Treasury bills.

market-to-book ratio Ratio of market value of equity to book value of equity

market value added The difference between the market value of firm's equity and its book value.

market-value balance sheet Financial statement that uses the market value of all assets and liabilities.

maturity premium Extra average return from investing in long-versus short-term Treasury securities.

merger Combination of two firms into one, with the acquirer assuming assets and liabilities of the target firm.

MM's dividend-irrelevance proposition Under ideal conditions the value of the firm is unaffected by dividend policy.

MM's proposition I (debt irrelevance proposition) The value of a firm is unaffected by its capital structure.

MM's proposition II The required rate of return on equity increases as the firm's debt-equity ratio increases.

modified accelerated cost recovery system (MACRS) Depreciation method that allows higher tax deductions in early years and lower deductions later.

money market Market for short-term financing (less than 1 year).

mutual fund An investment company that pools the savings of many investors and invests in a portfolio of securities.

mutually exclusive projects Two or more projects that cannot be pursued simultaneously.

N

net present value (NPV) Present value of cash flows minus investment.

net working capital Current assets minus current liabilities.

net worth Book value of common stockholders' equity plus preferred stock.

nominal interest rate Rate at which money invested grows.

NPV See *net present value.*

NPV break-even point Minimum level of sales needed to cover all costs including the cost of capital.

NYSE New York Stock Exchange.

O

open account Agreement whereby sales are made with no formal debt contract.

operating leverage Degree to which costs are fixed.

operating profit margin After-tax operating income as a percentage of sales.

operating risk Risk in firm's operating income. Also called *business risk.*

opportunity cost Benefit or cash flow forgone as a result of an action.

opportunity cost of capital Expected rate of return given up by investing in a project.

outstanding shares Shares that have been issued by the company and are held by investors.

P

par value Value of security shown in the company's accounts.

payback period Time until cash flows recover the initial investment in the project.

payout ratio Fraction of earnings paid out as dividends.

P/E ratio See *price-earnings multiple.*

pecking order theory Firms prefer to issue debt rather than equity if internal finance is insufficient.

pension fund Investment plan set up by an employer to provide for employees' retirement.

percentage of sales model Planning model in which sales forecasts are the driving variables and most other variables are proportional to sales.

perpetuity Stream of level cash payments that never ends.

planning horizon Time horizon for a financial plan.

plowback ratio Fraction of earnings retained by the firm.

poison pill Measure taken by a target firm to avoid acquisition; for example, the right for existing shareholders to buy additional shares at an attractive price if a bidder acquires a large holding.

preferred stock Stock that takes priority over common stock in regard to dividends.

present value (PV) Value today of a future cash flow.

present value of growth opportunities (PVGO) Net present value of a firm's future investments.

price-earnings multiple (P/E ratio) Ratio of stock price to earnings per share.

primary market Market for the sale of new securities by corporations.

primary offering Sale of new securities by corporations.

prime rate Benchmark interest rate charged by banks.

private placement Sale of securities to a limited number of investors without a public offering.

pro formas Projected or forecast financial statements.

profitability index Ratio of net present value to initial investment.

project cost of capital Minimum acceptable expected rate of return on a project given its risk.

prospectus Formal summary that provides information on an issue of securities.

protective covenant Restriction on a firm to protect bondholders.

proxy contest Takeover attempt in which outsiders compete with management for shareholders' votes. Also called *proxy fight.*

purchasing power parity (PPP) Theory that the cost of living in different countries is equal, and exchange rates adjust to offset inflation differentials across countries.

put option Right to sell an asset at a specified exercise price on or before the expiration date.

PV See *present value.*

R

random walk Security prices change randomly, with no predictable trends or patterns.

rate of return Total income and capital appreciation per period per dollar invested.

real assets Assets used to produce goods and services.

real interest rate Rate at which the purchasing power of an investment increases.

real options Options to invest in, modify, postpone, or dispose of a capital investment project.

reorganization Restructuring of financial claims on failing firm to allow it to keep operating.

Residual income See *economic value added.*

restructuring Process of changing the firm's capital structure without changing its assets.

retained earnings Earnings not paid out as dividends.

return on assets (ROA) After-tax operating income as a percentage of total assets.

return on capital (ROC) After-tax operating income as a percentage of long-term capital.

return on equity (ROE)   Net income as a percentage of shareholders' equity.

rights issue   Issue of securities offered only to current stockholders.

risk premium   Expected return in excess of risk-free return as compensation for risk.

ROA   See *return on assets.*

ROC   See *return on capital.*

ROE   See *return on equity.*

S

S&P 500   See *Standard & Poor's Composite Index.*

scenario analysis   Project analysis given a particular combination of assumptions.

seasoned offering   Sale of securities by a firm that is already publicly traded.

secondary market   Market in which previously issued securities are traded among investors.

secured debt   Debt that has first claim on specified collateral in the event of default.

security market line   Relationship between expected return and beta.

sensitivity analysis   Analysis of the effects on project profitability of changes in sales, costs, and so on.

shark repellent   Amendments to a company charter made to forestall takeover attempts.

shelf registration   A procedure that allows firms to file one registration statement for several issues of the same security.

shortage costs   Costs incurred from shortages in current assets.

simple interest   Interest earned only on the original investment; no interest is earned on interest.

simulation analysis   Estimation of the probabilities of different possible outcomes, e.g., from an investment project.

sinking fund   Fund established to retire debt before maturity.

specific risk   Risk factors affecting only that firm. Also called *diversifiable risk.*

spot price   Price paid for immediate delivery.

spot rate of exchange   Exchange rate for an immediate transaction.

spread   Difference between public offer price and price paid by underwriter.

stakeholder   Anyone with a financial interest in the firm.

Standard & Poor's Composite Index   Index of the investment performance of a portfolio of 500 large stocks. Also called the *S&P 500.*

standard deviation   Square root of variance. Another measure of volatility.

statement of cash flows   Financial statement that shows the firm's cash receipts and cash payments over a period of time.

stock dividends and splits   Distributions of additional shares to a firm's stockholders.

stock repurchase   Firm buys back stock from its shareholders.

straight-line depreciation   Constant depreciation for each year of the asset's accounting life.

subordinated debt   Debt that may be repaid in bankruptcy only after senior debt is paid.

sustainable growth rate   Steady rate at which a firm can grow without changing leverage; return on equity $\times$ plowback ratio.

swap   Arrangement by two counterparties to exchange one stream of cash flows for another.

T

technical analysts   Investors who attempt to identify undervalued stocks by searching for patterns in past prices.

tender offer   Takeover attempt in which outsiders directly offer to buy the stock of the firm's shareholders.

terms of sale   Credit, discount, and payment terms offered on a sale.

trade credit   Bills awaiting payment from one company to another.

trade-off theory   Debt levels are chosen to balance interest tax shields against the costs of financial distress.

treasurer   Manager responsible for financing, cash management, and relationships with banks and other financial institutions.

treasury stock   Stock that has been repurchased by the company and held in its treasury.

U

underpricing   Issuing securities at an offering price set below the true value of the security.

underwriter   Firm that buys an issue of securities from a company and resells it to the public.

V

variable costs   Costs that change as the level of output changes.

variance   Average value of squared deviations from mean. A measure of volatility.

venture capital   Money invested to finance a new firm.

W

WACC   See *weighted-average cost of capital.*

warrant   Right to buy shares from a company at a stipulated price before a set date.

weighted-average cost of capital (WACC)   Expected rate of return on a portfolio of all the firm's securities, adjusted for tax savings due to interest payments.

workout   Agreement between a company and its creditors establishing the steps the company must take to avoid bankruptcy.

Y

yield curve   Graph of the relationship between time to maturity and yield to maturity.

yield to maturity   Interest rate for which the present value of the bond's payments equals the price.

Credits

CHAPTER 1

Page 3 © The McGraw-Hill Companies, Inc./Jill Braaten, Photographer

CHAPTER 2

Page 31 © Brand X Pictures/ PunchStock

CHAPTER 3

Page 53 Ingram Publishing

CHAPTER 4

Page 79 Robert Michael/Corbis

CHAPTER 5

Page 113 AP Photo/David Zalubowski

CHAPTER 6

Page 159 Courtesy of Terry Cox

CHAPTER 7

Page 185 © Alan Schein Photography/ Corbis

CHAPTER 8

Page 227 Photodisc/Getty Images

CHAPTER 9

Page 263 Tyler Stableford/Getty Images

CHAPTER 10

Page 291 Stockbyte

CHAPTER 11

Page 317 Polka Dot Images/ Jupiterimages

CHAPTER 12

Page 345 Leif Jansson/Pica Pressfoto

CHAPTER 13

Page 371 VisionsofAmerica/ Joe Sohm/Photodisc/Getty Images

CHAPTER 14

Page 399 Getty Images

CHAPTER 15

Page 423 Getty Images

CHAPTER 16

Page 445 © Goodshoot/PunchStock

CHAPTER 17

Page 470 © Medioimages/Superstock

CHAPTER 18

Page 503 John Lund/Blend Images LLC

CHAPTER 19

Page 527 The Kobal Collection/The Picture Desk

CHAPTER 20

Page 559 AP Photo/Ross D. Franklin

CHAPTER 21

Page 591 Photodisc/Getty Images

CHAPTER 22

Page 619 © Reuters New Media Inc./ Corbis

CHAPTER 23

Page 645 Getty Images

CHAPTER 24

Page 671 © Corbis

CHAPTER 25

Page 691 © Bettmann/Corbis

Global Index

Page numbers followed by n refer to notes.

A

Airbus, 6, 227
Allianz, 685
Allied Irish Bank, 48, 702
Anglo Irish Bank, 48
Arbitrage, 621
Arcelor, 604–605
Argentine currency crisis, 622
Aristotle, 24
Asia, Federal Express operations, 306
Aston Martin, 610
Athabasca, Canada, tar sands, 658
Aufsichtsrat, 20
Australia
    corporate governance, 20
    exchange rate in 2010, 620
    interest rate in 2010, 619
    National Safety Council, 548
    Ned Kelly, 144–145, 163
    risk premium, 324
Avon Products, 7
Axa, 177

B

Banco Santander, investment and financing
    decisions, 5
Banesto, 700
Bank bailouts, 48
Banker's acceptances, 562
Bank for International Settlements, 688
Bank loans, hazardous, 548
Bank of England, 641
Bankruptcy
    law in France, 234
    outside United States, 477
Banks and Banking
    Barings Bank collapse, 25, 684
    international, 24
    limit on gold sales, 672
    London branches, 411–412
    Société Générale losses, 684
Barclays Bank, 431, 580, 700
    corporate bond indexes, 45
Barings Bank collapse, 25, 684, 701
Belgium, risk premium, 324
Benetton, 8
BHP Billiton, 546
Big Mac index, 624–625
Black, Conrad, 17
Blythe, Nils, 34
BNP Paribas, 411
Boards of directors
    in France, 20
    in Germany, 20
Bonds
    Eurobonds, 412
    international issues, 412
    semiannual coupon payments, 163

Bosch, 8
BP (British Petroleum)
    dividend suspension, 486
    Gulf oil spill of 2010, 486
Brazil
    exchange rate in 2010, 620
    interest rate in 2010, 619
Brazilian reals, 621
British Energy, 374
British pound, 621
Buying forward, 622, 630n

C

Cadbury Schweppes, 592
Canada
    corporate governance, 20
    Equinox Company, 679
    exchange rate in 2010, 620
    mutual funds, 39
    oil reserves, 658
    payment systems, 576
Capital budgeting; *see* International capital
    budgeting
Capital investment projects, 24
    Channel Tunnel, 232, 233
    by international companies, 619
Capital market equilibrium, 628
Capital markets, international, 411–412, 631
Cash flow(s)
    Channel Tunnel project, 233
    hedged, 634
    in international capital budgeting, 634
Cash management, international, 578
Channel Tunnel, 24, 232, 233, 239–240
China
    demand for iron, 684
    economic nationalism, 599
    exchange rate in 2010, 620
    Industrial and Commercial Bank, 426
    initial public offering in, 426
    mutual funds, 39
China National Offshore Oil Corporation, 599
China Telecom, 36
Christian Dior, 5
Chunga, Margaret, 34
Coca-Cola Company, international business, 619
Code of Hammurabi, 24
Commerzbank, 700
Companies
    overseas interests, 619
    secrecy vs. transparency, 486
Conditional sales, 562
Conrad, Joseph, 636n
Consols, 127–128
Corporate governance
    Australia, 20
    Canada, 20
    Europe, 20
    Germany, 20

    Japan, 20
    United Kingdom, 20
    worldwide differences, 20
Cost advantage, nuclear vs. fossil-fuel
    stations, 374
Cost of capital
    for foreign investment, 636
    in international capital budgeting, 633
Covered interest rate parity, 630
    and hedging, 631–632
Cross-border financial statement, 68
Cross rate, 621
Currencies
    Argentine crisis, 622
    Australia, 620
    Brazil, 620, 621
    British pound, 621
    Canada, 620
    China, 620
    euro, 25, 621
    European, 620
    forward contracts, 622
    futures contracts, 622–623
    Haitian gourdes, 622
    India, 620
    interest rate parity, 631
    Japanese yen, 620, 621, 680–681
    Korean won, 620, 621
    Mexican peso, 620–621
    South Africa, 620
    spot rate in Sept. 2010, 620
    Swiss franc, 622, 683
    U.S. dollar, 621
    Vietnamese dong, 622
Currency appreciation, 622
Currency depreciation, 622
    and hedging, 631–632
Currency swaps, 683

D

Daimler-Benz, 593, 685
Daiwa Bank losses, 684
Danone, 599
Dar es Salaam exchange, 186
Default on loans in foreign currency, 628n
Default risk, Greece, 174n
Denmark, risk premium, 323, 324
Derivatives
    Barings Bank collapse, 684
    BIS survey of, 688
    Daiwa Bank losses, 684
    Metallgesellschaft debacle, 684, 685
    Société Générale losses, 684
    and speculation, 684
    Sumitomo Corporation losses, 684
Deutsche Bank, 44, 411, 431, 594, 685
Deutsche Börse, 35, 36
Dimson, Elroy, 319, 320, 321, 324, 325, 327,
    328, 374

Direct quote, 620, 621
Discount rate
  fudge factors, 637
  United Kingdom, 374
Dojima Rice Market, 24
DP World, 599
Dragon bond, 702

E

East India Company, 24
Economic exposure, 632
Economic nationalism, 599
Economic risk, 632
Economist, 594
Electric utilities, United Kingdom, 374
Electronic bill presentment and payment
        system, 576
Electronic trading, 35
Eliot, T. S., 691
Enel, 426
Equinox Company, 679
Erb, C., 635n
Eurex, 680
Euro, 25, 412, 580, 621
  futures contracts, 680
Eurobonds, 412
Eurodollar deposits, 680
Eurodollar market, 24, 580
Eurodollars, 411–412
Euronext, 35, 186
Europe
  bank limit on gold sales, 672
  conditional sales, 562
  corporate governance, 20
  economic nationalism, 599
  exchange rate in 2010, 620
  Federal Express operations, 306
  mutual funds, 39
  payment systems, 575–576
  sale of RJR Nabisco operations, 608
  semiannual coupon payments, 163
  takeover activities, 604
European Central Bank, 48
European Commission, 48
  merger blocked by, 598
European Monetary Union, 25, 580
European Union
  antitrust policy, 596
  exchange rates Sept. 2010, 520
  International Financial Reporting Standards, 68
  takeover activities, 604
Eurotunnel, 232, 233
  calculating net present value, 232, 233
  restructuring, 234
Euroyen, 411, 580
Exchange rate fluctuations, 619, 621–623
  avoiding, 622–623
  economic risk, 632
  problems caused by, 622
  transaction risk, 631–632
Exchange rate risk
  hedging
      currency swaps, 683
      economic risk, 632

forward contracts, 622
  futures contracts, 622–623
  with swaps, 683
  transaction risk, 631–632
minicase, 642
Exchange rates
  Big Mac index, 624–625
  cross rate, 621
  definition, 620
  expectations theory, 629–630
  and expected inflation, 628
  expected spot rate, 629–630
  fixed, 622
  floating, 621–622
  forward rate, 622–623, 629–630
  futures market, 622–623
  and inflation, 624–625
  interest rate parity, 631
  and interest rates, 630–631
  interest rates and inflation, 626–628
  international Fisher effect, 628
  law of one price, 624
  nominal, 626, 627
  purchasing power parity, 625
  quoted against dollar, 621
  real, 626, 627
  for selected regions in 2010, 620
  spot rates, 620–622
Expectations theory of exchange rates, 629–630
Expected inflation, 628
Expropriation risk, 635

F

Federal Express
  in Asia and Europe, 306
  overseas business, 4
Fiat, 8
Fidelity Investments, overseas funds, 39
Finance, history of, 24–25
Financial crisis of 2007–2009
  and government debts, 48
  spread worldwide, 48
Financial managers
  and expectations theory of exchange rates, 620
  and interest rate parity, 631, 632
  of international businesses, 623
Financial planning failure at Vivendi, 505
Financial scandals
  Barings Bank, 25, 684
  Daiwa Bank, 684
  Metallgesellschaft, 685
  Parmalat, 25, 66–67
  Société Générale, 25
  Sumitomo Corporation, 684
Financial Times, 620
Financial Times Company, 319
Financial Times Index, 319
Financing
  examples, 5–6
  micro finance, 35
Finland, Electronic bill presentment and
        payment system, 576
Fixed exchange rate, 622
Floating exchange rates, 621–622

Ford Motor Company
  integration of overseas operations, 635
  overseas sales and production, 632
Forecasting
  exchange rates, 623
  in international capital budgeting, 633–634
Foreign exchange market, 37
  arbitrage, 621
  buying forward, 622
  case, 642
  conduct of, 620
  cross rate, 621
  daily turnover, 620
  direct quotes, 620
  exchange rate fluctuations, 621–622
  expected spot rate, 629–630
  and fixed rates, 622
  and floating rates, 621–622
  forward contracts, 622
  forward premium, 622
  forward rates, 622–623, 629–630
  futures markets, 622–623
  hedging in
      economic risk, 632
      financial hedge, 632
      operational hedge, 632
      transaction risk, 621–632
  indirect quotes, 620
  and inflation, 624–626
  and interest rates, 626–628
  international Fisher effect, 628
  quotations, 620–621
  spot exchange rates, 620–622
  spot rates Sept. 2010, 620
  theories, 623
Foreign investment
  avoiding fudge factors, 636–637
  capital budgeting, 633–637
  cost of capital, 633, 636
  expropriation risk, 635
  and forward exchange rate, 633–634
  net present value analysis, 633–634
  political risk, 635–636
Fortis, 48
Forward contracts, 622
  Japanese yen, 680–681
Forward discount, 622, 629
Forward exchange rate
  and capital budgeting, 633–634
  expectations theory, 622–623
  versus expected spot rate, 629–630
  interest rate parity, 631
  and interest rates, 630–631
  in September 2010, 620
  versus spot rate, 630–631
Forward premium, 622
France
  boards of directors, 20
  Eurotunnel and bankruptcy law, 234
  identifying corporations, 8n
  mortality bonds, 177
  nominal vs. real interest rate, 626, 627
  opposition to mergers in, 599
  payment systems, 576
  risk premium, 324
  Société Générale, 684

Frankfurt stock exchange, 186
Friedrich, John, 548
Froot, K. A., 630n
Fudge factors, 636–637
Futures contracts, 622–623
    and Barings Bank collapse, 684
    Metallgesellschaft debacle, 685
    Sumitomo Corporation losses, 684
    worldwide turnover 1966–2007, 680
Futures market, 622–623
    early Japan, 24

G

Générale des Eaux, 516
Genzyme, 592
Germany
    boards of directors, 20
    corporate governance, 20
    government bonds, 680
    hyperinflation 1922–23, 142
    identifying corporations, 8n
    limits on gold sales, 672
    Metallgesellschaft debacle, 685
    payment systems, 576
    risk premium, 324
GlaxoSmithKline, 6, 11
    investment and financing decisions, 5
Gold, 624
Gold sales limits, Germany, 672
Gorgon, 5
Governments
    bank bailouts, 48
    ownership by, 374
Greece
    debt problem, 25, 48
    fear of government default, 174n
Groupe Eurotunnel, 234

H

Hammurabi, 24
Harvey, Campbell R., 635n
HBOS, rights issue, 431, 432
Hedged cash flows, 634
Hedging
    exchange rate risk
        currency swaps, 683
        economic risk, 632
        forward contracts, 622
        futures contracts, 622–623
        minicase, 642
        transaction risk, 631–632
    financial hedge, 632
    in international capital budgeting, 634
    operational, 632
    versus speculation, 632
Hennessy, 5
Hinkley Point C nuclear power station, 374
Hollinger International, 17
Home bias, 636n
Honda Motors, 36
    investment and financing decisions, 5
Hong Kong, exchange rate in 2010, 620

HSBC Holdings, 24, 411
Hudson's Bay Company, 8
Hungary, inflation rate, 25
Hyperinflation
    Germany 1922–1923, 142
    Hungary in late 1940s, 25
    in Yugoslavia in 1993, 25
    Zimbabwe in 2008, 142
Hypo Group, 48

I

IKEA, 8
Inco, 605
Incremental cash flows at Sony, 266
Indexed bonds, real yield in United
        Kingdom, 173
India, exchange rate in 2010, 620
Indirect quote, 620
Industrial and Commercial Bank of China, 426
Inflation
    Big Mac index, 624–625
    and exchange rates, 624–625
    expected, 628
    in Hungary, 25
    and interest rates, 626–628
    international Fisher effect, 628
    law of one price, 624
    purchasing power parity, 625
    in Yugoslavia, 25
Inflation rate
    average, 629
    in Germany 1922–1923, 142
    in Zimbabwe 2008, 142
ING, 48, 700
Initial public offering
    China, 426
    by HBOS, 431
    Italy, 426
    Japan, 426
    nationalized enterprises, 426
Interest rate parity, 631
Interest rates
    country differences, 619
    covered interest rate parity, 630
    and exchange rates, 624–625
    and inflation, 626–628
    international Fisher effect, 628
    London Interbank Offered Rate, 546, 554,
        580, 681, 682n
    nominal, 626–628
    real, 626–628
International banking
    in 15th century, 24
    London Interbank Offered Rate, 546, 554,
        681, 682n
    origin of, 24
International bond issues, 702
International capital budgeting
    avoiding fudge factors, 636–637
    cost of capital, 636
    decision at Toyota, 263
    and forward exchange rate, 633–634
    net present value analysis, 633–634
    political risk, 635–636

International capital markets, 411–412, 631
International cash management, 578
International Country Risk Guide, 635, 641
International financial management
    basic relationships
        exchange rates and inflation, 624–625
        expected spot rate, 629–630
        forward rate, 629–630
        hedging exchange rate risk, 622–623,
            631–632
        inflation and interest rates, 626–629
        interest rate parity, 631
        interest rates and exchange rates,
            630–631
        law of one price, 624
        nominal exchange rate, 626, 627
        purchasing power parity, 625
        questions to consider, 623
        real exchange rate, 626, 627
    capital budgeting, 633–637
    capital investment, 619
    cost of capital, 636
    foreign exchange market, 620–623
International Financial Reporting Standards, 68
International Fisher effect, 628
International money market, 580
International Securities Exchange, 645
International Swap Dealers Association, 685
Investment decisions
    Alaska–Canada pipeline, 24
    Eurotunnel Company, 24
    examples, 5–6
Investors
    in Channel Tunnel project, 232
    effect of inflation on interest rates,
        626–628
    effect of interest rates on exchange rates,
        630–631
    home bias, 636n
    repayment option, 410–411
Ireland
    debt problem, 48
    risk premium, 324
Iron, China's demand for, 684
Italy
    Enel, 426
    initial public offering in, 426
    nominal vs. real interest rate, 626, 627
    payment systems, 576
    risk premium, 323, 324

J

Jaguar, 593
Japan
    bank mergers, 594
    corporate governance, 20
    Daiwa Bank, 684
    early futures market, 24
    exchange rate in 2010, 620
    initial public offering in, 426
    land prices, 213
    money market, 580
    mutual funds, 39
    Nikkei Index, 213, 323–324

Nippon Telegraph and Telephone, 426
  risk premium, 324
  Sumitomo Corporation, 684
Japanese yen, 621
  forward contracts, 680–681
  futures contracts, 680
Joint stock companies, 24
Just-in-time systems, 89

K

Kelly, Ned, 145–146
Keynes, John Maynard, 702

L

Land prices, Japan, 213
Land Rover, 593
Latin America, mutual funds, 9
Latin Monetary Union, 25
Law of one price, 624
Leeson, Nick, 25, 684
Lenovo, 18, 605
London
  bank branches in, 411–412
  capital markets, 411–412
  foreign exchange turnover, 620
London Interbank Offered Rate, 409, 546, 554,
    580, 681, 682n
London Stock Exchange, 35, 186
Louis Vuitton, 5
LVMH, 6, 7, 36
  investment and financing decisions, 5

M

Macquarie Bank, 35, 41
Malawi, micro loans, 34
Mergers
  blocked in European Union, 598
  Daimler-Benz and Chrysler, 593
  in emerging countries, 605
  Japanese banks, 594
  stopped by popular resentment, 599
Messier, Jean-Marie, 516, 604
Metallgesellschaft, 701
  debacle, 684, 685
Mexico
  exchange rate in 2010, 620
  peso, 620–621
MGRM, 685
Micro finance/loans, 34
Microloan Foundation, United Kingdom, 34
Mill, John Stuart, 695
Mitsubishi UFJ, 411
Mittal, 604–605
Mizuho Bank, 594, 700
Money; see Currencies; Exchange rates
Money market, international, 580
Morgan Stanley Capital International, 319
Mortality bonds, 177
Multinational corporations
  international cash management, 578
  reducing political risk, 635–636

N

NASDAQ purchase of OMX, 35
Nationalized enterprises, 426
National Safety Council, Australia, 548
Natural gas pipeline, Alaska–Canada, 24
Netherlands
  payment systems, 576
  risk premium, 324
Net present value
  of Eurotunnel, 232, 233
  in international capital budgeting, 633–634
Nikkei Index, 213, 319
Nippon Telegraph and Telephone, 426
Nissan Motors, 70, 204
Nokia, 36
Nominal exchange rates, 626, 627
Nominal interest rate, 626–628
  France, 626, 627
  Italy, 626, 627
  United Kingdom, 626, 627
  in United Kingdom 1985–2010, 174
Nomura, 41
Norway, risk premium, 324
Novartis, 36
Nuclear power stations, United Kingdom, 374
NYSE-Euronext, 35

O

Oil futures, 685
Oil reserves, Canada, 658
OMX, 35
Operational hedging, 632
Options
  in ancient world, 24
  annual volume, 645

P

Panasonic, 591, 592
P&O, 599
Parmalat, 25, 67–68
Payment systems, in Europe, 575–576
Pernod Ricard, 695n
Perpetuities, 410
  consols, 127–128
Petrobras, 36
Peugeot Citroen, 18
Phillips Petroleum, 248
Political risk
  expropriation risk, 635
  in foreign investment, 635–636
  scores for selected countries, 635
  website, 635
Porsche, 8
Potash, 546
Present value, Channel Tunnel project, 233
Price(s)
  Big Mac index, 624–625
  economic risk, 632
  effects of inflation, 624–630
  law of one price, 624
  purchasing power parity, 625
  transaction risk, 631–632

Project analysis in international capital
    budgeting, 634
PRS Group, 635
Purchasing power parity
  definition, 625
  nominal vs. real exchange rates, 626

R

Real exchange rate, 626, 627
  short term changes in, 626
Real interest rate, 626–628
  France, 626
  Italy, 626, 627
  United Kingdom, 626, 627
Repayment option, 410–411
Revenues, 5
Rights issue by HBOS, 431, 432
Rio Tinto, 227
Risk
  controlling, 25
  economic, 632
  of expropriation, 635
  factors in investment, 636
  political, 635–636
  transaction, 631–632
Risk premium, national comparisons,
    323–324
Roche, 592
Rolls-Royce, 302
Royal Bank of Scotland, 18, 48
Royal Dutch Shell, 7

S

Sanofi-Aventis, 592
Sanyo, 591, 592
Schering-Plough, 592
Seagram, 516, 604
Selling forward, 630n
Semiannual coupon payments, Europe, 163
Shanghai International Port, 49
Smith, Adam, 15
Société Générale, 25, 684
Sony Corporation, 24, 36, 266
South Africa
  exchange rate in 2010, 620
  risk premium, 324
South Korea
  currency of, 621
  exchange rate in 2010, 620
South Sea Bubble, 24
Sovereign Bank, 5
Soviet Union, and Eurodollar market, 24
Spain, risk premium, 324
Speculation, 632, 684
Spot exchange rate, 620–622
  definition, 621
  expectations theory, 629–630
  forecasting, 623, 624–625
  versus forward rate, 622–623, 629–630
  interest rate differences, 620–631
  interest rate parity, 631
  for September 2010, 620
Spot interest rate and inflation, 624

Stock exchanges
   consolidation of, 35
   Euronext, 186
   Frankfurt, 186
   London, 186
   Nikkei, 213
   Sweden, 35
   Tanzania, 186
   Tokyo, 186
Stock price decline for HBOS, 431
Stored value cards, 576
Sumitomo Corporation, 684, 702
Swatch Group, 8
Sweden
   exchange rate in 2010, 620
   payment systems, 576
   risk premium, 324
   sale of stock exchange, 35
Swiss francs, 683
Swiss Re, 18
Switzerland
   exchange rate in 2010, 620
   risk premium, 324
Sykes, T., 548

T

Tata Group, 593, 605
Tele Atlas, 592
Thales, 24
Tokyo Gas, 594

Tom Tom, 592
Toyota Motor Corporation, 36, 70–71, 81,
      83–84, 227, 573, 632
   capital budgeting decision, 263
   just-in-time systems, 89
   problems at, 80
Transaction risk, 631–632

U

UBS, 48, 411, 431
Underwriters, in United Kingdom, 431
Unilever, 36
United Kingdom
   Barings Bank collapse, 25, 684
   consols, 127–128
   corporate governance, 20
   discount rate, 374
   electric utilities, 374
   exchange rate in 2010, 620
   Financial Times Index, 319
   identifying corporations, 8n
   Microloan Foundation, 34
   nominal interest rate 1985–2010, 174
   nominal vs. real interest rate, 626, 627
   payment systems, 576
   perpetuities, 410
   real yield on indexed bonds, 173
   risk premium, 324
   underwriters, 431
   yield on nominal bonds, 173

V

Vale, 605
Versace, 18
Veuve Cliquot, 5
Viskanta, T., 635n
Vivendi, 68, 604
   collapse of, 505
Volkswagen, 7, 505, 632
Vorstand, 20

W

West Lb, 48
WuXi PharmaTech, 598

Y

Yield on nominal bonds in United Kingdom, 173
Yuan, K., 696
Yugoslavia, inflation rate, 25

Z

Zambian copper mine, 679
Zara, growth and market power, 43
Zheng, L., 696
Zhu, Q., 696
Zimbabwe, hyperinflation 2008, 142

Page numbers followed by n refer to notes.

A

Abandonment option, 307, 658
Abandonment value, 307
Accelerated depreciation, 278
Accounting
 accrual, 61–62
 cash, 61–62
 convergence of standards, 68
 gray areas
  cookie-jar reserves, 66
  mark-to-market
   accounting, 67
  off-balance-sheet assets and
   liabilities, 66–67
  revenue recognition, 66
 inflation of earnings by, 67
 at Lehman Brothers, 67
 mark-to-market, 67
 principles-based, 68
 rules-based, 68
Accounting break-even analysis,
 298–300
Accounting earnings, 66
Accounting profits
 adjusted, 272
 and cash flow, 265
Accounting rates of return
 and economic value added, 86
 problems with, 87–88
 return on assets, 87
 return on capital, 86–87
 return on equity, 87
Accounting scandals; see
  Corporate scandals
Accounting standards, 66
Accounts payable, 532
Accounts payable period
 definition, 534
 estimating, 535
Accounts receivable, 265
 on balance sheet, 54
 collection period, 569
 collections, 539–541
 credit policy, 560–571
 as current asset, 531
 level divisions, 534n
 mistake of restricting, 536–537
 payment of, 541
 types of, 559
Accounts receivable financing, 547
Accounts receivable period
 definition, 534
 estimating, 534
Accrual accounting, 61–62
 on income statement, 63
Acid-test ratio, 96
Acquisitions, 598; see also
  Mergers
Additional paid-in capital, 405
Administrative expenses, 541

Adobe Systems, 221
Affiliated Computer Services
 Inc., 660
After-tax company cost of
 capital, 377
After-tax cost of debt, 371, 377
After-tax income, 409
 dividends from, 69, 70
After-tax operating income, 85
 calculating, 87
After-tax rate of interest, 456–457
Agency costs, 603
Agency problems, 48
 and blockholders, 18
 and board of directors, 18
 and compensation plans, 18–19
 definition, 17
 legal/regulatory
  requirements, 18
 mitigation of, 19
 and shareholder pressures, 19
 specialist monitoring, 18
 and stakeholders, 17–18
 and takeovers, 19
Agency theory, 694
Agents, 17, 694
Aggressive growth plan, 504
Aggressive stocks, 346
Aging schedule, 569–570
AIG, 18, 47–48, 169
Air cargo deregulation, 4
Airline industry
 market risk, 336
 negative equity, 445n
Alaska Air Group, 46
Alcoa, 660, 661
Allegheny Corporation, 658
Allen, F., 387n, 458n
Allen, Paul, 423
Allied Crude Vegetable Oil
  Refining Company, fraud
  at, 547
Altman, Edward I., 102, 565
Altria Group, 368, 393, 492
Amazon.com, 189, 192, 205, 217,
 329, 480, 667
American call, 646n
American Electric Power, 189,
 192, 221, 524
American Stock Exchange, 35
America Online, 610
Amortization, 94n
Amortizing loans, 132–133
Andrade, G., 611
Angel investors, 425
Announcement effect, 212–213,
 486
Ann Taylor Stores, 586
Annual percentage rate
 of bonds, 163n
 definition, 138

Annuity
 versus annuity due future
  value, 137
 definition, 127
 future value, 133–135
 present value, 129–130
Annuity due
 versus annuity future value, 137
 definition, 136
 future value, 137
 present value, 136–137
Annuity factor, 129
 for Bill Gates, 131–132
 in lottery winnings, 131
Annuity table, 130
 future value, A-5
 present value, A-4
Antitrust law, 598–599
 Oracle and PeopleSoft, 605–606
Apple Inc., 34, 35
 dividends, 33
 financing decisions, 32
 founding of, 423
 and Massachusetts law, 427n
Aqua America, 198, 200, 202–203,
 204, 205
Aramark, 426
Archipelago Exchange, 35, 187
Articles of incorporation, 8
Asked yield to maturity, 161
Asquith, P., 434n, 482n
Asset-backed bonds, 414–415
Asset price bubbles, 698
Assets
 on balance sheet, 54–57, 189
 and bankruptcy costs, 461
 book vs. market value, 57–59
 at historical cost, 57
 leasing vs. buying, 699
 liquid, 54, 95–96
 mark-to-market accounting, 67
 matching maturities, 529–530
 needed by corporations, 3
 negative-risk, 332
 of pension plans in 2010, 40
 real vs. financial, 7, 38
 relative liquidity, 96, 530n
 short- vs. long-lived, 236–238
Asset turnover ratio, 88
Asset vs. portfolio risk, 330–333
Asymmetric information, 464
ATMs, 576
AT&T, 83, 84, 85
Auction, 428n
 for stock repurchase, 483
Authorized share capital, 405
Automated Clearing House
 system, 577
Average collection period, 89
Average risk, 371
Average tax rate, 70

B

Backdating scandal, 660
Baker, M., 482n
Balance sheet
 assets and liabilities on, 54–57
 assets on, 189
 book vs. market values,
  57–59, 206
 common-size, 56–57
 current market value
  excluded, 88
 definition, 54
 effect of transactions, 62–63
 Home Depot, 54–57, 82
 intangible assets on, 55
 liabilities on, 189
 main items of, 56
 market-value, 205–206
 pro forma, 508–512
 tangible assets on, 54
 window dressing, 67
Balancing item, 507–508
Bandler, J., 660
Bank accounts; see also Banks and
  Banking
 concentration accounts, 574
 demand deposits, 531
 effective interest rates, 139
 proliferation of, by
  companies, 574
 time deposits, 531
Banker's acceptance, 562
Banking crises, 698
Banking crisis of 2007–2009, 15,
 48, 329
Bank loans, 7, 33, 159
 fixed interest rate, 546
 line of credit, 545–546
 secured loans, 547–548
 self-liquidating, 546
 short- vs. long-term, 546
Bank of America, 35, 41, 44, 47,
 67, 176, 431, 546, 586, 592
Bank of America warrants, 659
Bank of New York, 594
Bank runs, 44n
Bankruptcy, 24
 in accounting scandals, 67–68
 Chapter 11, 460, 475–476
 Chapter 7, 475
 and credit scoring, 563–565
 definition, 459, 475
 duration of proceedings, 477
 Eastern Airlines, 460
 Enron, 460
 financial distress without,
  461–463
 L. A. Gear, 532
 LBOs, ending in, 609
 Lehman Brothers, 460, 549

Bankruptcy—*Cont.*
  Pacific Gas & Electric, 409
  postpetition creditors, 477
  prepackaged, 475n
  as protection from litigation, 477
  recent examples, 476
  and warrants, 659
  WorldCom, 175
Bankruptcy costs
  direct, 460
  examples, 460
  indirect, 460–461
  paid out of assets, 459–460
  and value of the firm, 460
  varying by type of assets, 461
Bankruptcy procedures
  asset liquidation, 475
  liquidation vs. reorganization,
    476–477
  reorganization, 475–476
  workout, 475
Bankruptcy Reform Act of
    1978, 475
Banks and Banking, 20, 31
  check handling and float,
    574–575
  credit checks by, 562
  dividend restrictions, 481
  holdings of corporate
    equities, 406
  interest-free reserves, 412n
  lock-box system, 574–575
  merger activity, 594
  sale of subprime mortgages, 698
  subprime mortgages, 47
  sweep programs, 573–574
  use of financial statements, 53
Bank syndicates, 546
Barnes & Noble, 586
Base period, 140
Baskin-Robbins, 695
Bear Stearns, 47, 415
Beaver, William H., 563–565
Bechtel, 426
Before-tax income, 409
Behavioral finance
  attitudes toward risk, 214
  beliefs about probabilities, 215
Behavioral psychology, 491
Berkshire Hathaway, 435, 592
Berra, Yogi, 446
Best-case plan, 504
Best efforts bases, 427
Beta(s)
  of common stocks, 346
  of cyclical businesses, 362
  definition, 346
  Dell Inc., 360
  Dow Chemical vs. Con Ed,
    348–349
  fate of, 358
  measuring, 346–348
  of portfolios, 350–352
  and required return, 692
  and risk premium, 353–354
  for selected common stocks, 350

  for selected companies, 359
  spreadsheet solutions, 347
  of Treasury bills, 353
Bid-ask spread, 187
Bid price, 160, 161
Bill and Melinda Gates
    Foundation, 131
Black, Conrad, 17
Black, Fischer, 357, 655, 694
Black-Scholes option pricing
    model, 659
Blockbuster, 598
Blockholders, 18–19
Bloomingdale strategy, 91
Blue-sky laws, 427
Board of directors, 9
  and agency problems, 18
  composition and function, 407
  election of, 407
  financial decisions, 11
  and management, 603
  and Sarbanes-Oxley Act, 18
Bob Evans Farms, 46
Boeing Company, 4, 6, 45, 306,
    329, 350, 359, 385
  investment and financing
    decisions, 5
Bondholders, 126
  with convertible bonds, 659
  effect of financial distress, 462
  losers in LBOs, 609
  Marriott Corporation, 413
  risk of call to, 410
  versus shareholders, 463
Bond market, 36
  historical performance, 319–322
  junk bonds, 608–610
  size of, 160
Bond price quotations, 160
Bond prices
  asked yield to maturity, 160, 161
  bid price, 160, 161
  calculating, 162
  changes approaching maturity,
    170
  corporate bonds, 175
  decline for Marriott
    Corporation, 413
  discount, 167
  in financial press, 160
  and interest rates, 161–166
  premium, 167
  semiannual coupon payments, 163
  of strips, 171–172
  Treasury vs. corporate
    quotations, 175
  varying with interest rates,
    163–165
  worst year for investors, 322
Bond-rating firms, 174–175
Bonds, 159; *see also* Corporate
    bonds; Treasury bonds
  asset-backed, 414–415
  callable, 410–411
  compared to stock, 36
  convertible, 36, 415–416

  coupon, 160
  definition, 160
  differences among, 160
  direct costs, 429
  expected rate of return, 382
  face value, 160
  floating-rate, 681, 682
  indexed, 173
  interest rate risk, 165–166
  interest rates, 45–46
  junk bonds, 46, 174–175, 411
  liquid, 175
  long-term, 172
  maturity date, 36
  par value, 160
  present value calculation, 162
  relative liquidity of, 698
  short-term, 172
  structured investment vehicles, 95
  yield curve, 171–174
  yield on, 142
  yield to maturity, 166–168
Bond valuation, 159
  spreadsheet solution, 170–171
Bookbuilding method, 430–431
Book rates of return, 85
Book value, 83
  and capital structure, 380–381
  and company cost of capital,
    376–377
  debt and equity, 88
  and debt ratios, 93
  definition, 57, 189
  versus market value, 57–59,
    189–191
  reliability of, 95
  for selected companies, 189
Booms, 330–332
Bootstrap game, 596–597
Borders Group, 586
Borrowing
  by Apple Inc., 33
  from banks, 545–548
  cash balance and need for, 541
  effect on value
    debt and cost of equity,
      451–454
    earnings per share, 448–450
    MM proposition I, 446–448
    restructuring, 447–448
    risk and return, 450–451
  from finance companies, 545
  pros and cons, 697
  tax disadvantages, 458
Bradshaw, Mark, 92
Brav, A., 485
Break-even analysis
  accounting break-even point,
    298–300
  in credit decision, 567
  definition, 298
  and economic value added, 301n
  example, 301–302
  at Lockheed, 302–303
  net present value, 300–303
  sales volume, 298

  Break-even sales volume, 299
Brealey, R. A., 387n, 458n
Bridge loans, 40n
Brin, Sergey, 423
Bristol Myers Squibb, 410
Brokers, in stock trading, 186–187
Bruck, C., 610n
Buckle, Inc., 586
Buffett, Warren, 15n, 435
Build-to-order production, 573
Bureau of Labor Statistics, 140n
Burlington Northern Santa Fe, 592
Burrough, B., 607n
Business organizations
  corporations, 8–9
  partnerships, 9–10
  sole proprietorships, 9
Business plans
  best-case, 504
  normal growth, 504
  retrenchment, 504
  for start-ups, 424
Business risk, 450

C

Callable bonds, 410–411, 661
Callaway Golf, 46
Call options
  and convertible bonds, 659
  definition, 646
  Google Inc., 646
  payoff diagram, 649
  price of, 646
  profit diagram, 649
  versus put options, 646–647
  for risk reduction, 674–675
  selling, 647–649
  stock price and value of,
    652–653
  value at expiration, 646
Call price, 410–411
Call provisions, 645
Campbell Soup Company, 189, 192,
    329, 350, 359, 385, 593
Capacity expansion, 392
Capacity to pay, 563
Capital, 7, 36
  and credit decision, 563
  required for start-ups, 423
Capital asset pricing model, 371
  basis of, 356
  to calculate company cost of
    capital, 374–375
  critique of, 358
  definition, 354
  expected return based on, 382
  expected vs. actual returns, 358
  and hedging, 695
  ideas behind, 692
  making sense of, 354–355
  in practice, 356–358
  prediction of risk premium, 357
  recent problems with, 357
  security market line, 355–356

small- vs. large-firm stocks, 358
value and drawbacks, 695
value stocks vs. growth stocks, 358
Capital budget, 292
Capital budgeting, 10–11, 227;
    see also Project analysis
as discounted cash flow, 263–264
focus on cash flow, 265
and incremental cash flows, 266–268
and options, 645
problems and solutions
    analyze competitive advantage, 294
    eliminating conflicts of interest, 292
    ensuring consistent forecasts, 292
    reducing forecast bias, 293–294
project authorization, 292–293
and project risk, 359–362
proposed budget, 292
in strategic planning, 504
what-if questions, 295
Capital budgeting decisions, 6
Allegheny Corporation, 658
and capital rationing, 249
case, 258–259
choosing between two projects, 234
investment timing problem, 234, 235–236
long- vs. short-lived equipment, 235, 236–238
mutually exclusive projects, 235
and payout policy, 487
real options
    definition, 657
    option to abandon, 658
    option to expand, 658
replacement problem, 235, 238–239
return and cost of capital, 240–241
steps, 263
and stock prices, 185
used in practice, 251
Capital expenditure decisions, 6
Capital expenditures, 541
in free cash flow, 65
on income statement, 63
on statement of cash flow, 64
Capital gain, 193
versus dividends in taxation, 493
Capital gains tax, 70
Capital investment, 271
Capital investment decisions
decision rule comparisons, 250
internal rate of return, 240–248
in mergers, 591
net present value analysis, 228–239
payback rule, 239–240
profitability index, 248–250

Capital investment projects, 228
decision rules
    net present value rule, 229, 241
    payback rule, 239–240, 241
    rate of return rule, 241
discounted-payback period, 240
internal rate of return
    for long-lived projects, 241–243
    pitfalls, 243–248
    mutually exclusive, 244–246
net present value rule for selecting
    long- vs. short-lived equipment, 236–238
    replacement of equipment, 238–239
    timing decision, 235–236
payback period, 239–240
Pentagon Law of Large Projects, 234
valuing long-lived projects
    new computer system, 231–232
    office block rental, 230–231
    spreadsheet solutions, 233–234
Capital market history
estimating cost of capital from history, 322–324
historical record, 319–322
market indexes, 319
Capital markets, 36
assumption in MM proposition I, 447
efficient, 692–693
pricing of assets, 692
Capital rationing, 249
Capital structure
case, 474–475
changes at Sealed Air Corporation, 466–467
changes in, 445
and corporate taxes
    debt financing advantage, 454–456
    implications, 458
    value of shareholders' equity, 456
    weighted average cost of capital, 456–458
definition, 372, 446
effect of changes on expected return, 386–387
effect of restructuring, 447–448
industry differences, 446, 464
L. A. Gear, 523
lack of coherent theory of, 697
measuring, 380–381
optimal, 445, 459
pecking order theory, 464–465
rebalancing, 456
trade-off theory, 459, 463–464
and value of the firm, 446–454
valuing entire businesses, 387–389

Capital structure decision, 7
Capital surplus, 405
CAPM; see Capital asset pricing model
Careers in finance, 20–22
Careersinfinance.com, 22
Cargill, 426
Carrying costs, 536, 571
Carve-outs, 610
Cash
advantage of holding, 530
calculating, 60–61
components, 531
corporate sources of, 400–404
as current asset, 531–532
disadvantage of surplus, 530
forecasting sources of, 539–541
forecasting uses of, 541
liquidity of, 574
management of, 531–532
mergers financed by, 599–601
retained and reinvested, 33
versus short-term securities, 573
tracing changes in., 537–539
transported across time, 43
use of surplus, 595
uses of
    accounts receivable payments, 541
    capital expenditures, 541
    labor and administrative costs, 541
    tax, interest, and dividends, 541
valuing liquidity of, 698
Cash accounting, 61–62
Cash balance, 56n, 559
calculating, 64–65
and cumulative financing requirements, 541–543
example, 541
minimum operating cash balance, 541
and need to borrow, 541
what-if questions, 543
Cash before delivery, 560
Cash budgeting
cash balance, 541–543
forecasting sources of cash, 539–541
forecasting uses of cash, 541
means of producing, 539
Cash conversion cycle, 533–536
accounts payable period, 534
accounts receivable period, 534
calculating, 535
definition, 534
estimating accounts payable period, 535
estimating accounts receivable period, 534
estimating inventory period, 534
inventory period, 534
net working capital, 533
production cycle dates, 534
for selected industries, 536

Cash coverage ratio, 94
Cash dividends, 479
advantage for firms, 486
from Apple Inc., 33
declaration date, 481
definition, 480
ex-dividend date, 481
information content, 486–487
from Microsoft, 491–492
payment date, 481
record date, 481
regular vs. special, 480
in U.S. 1980–2008, 480
Cash flow(s), 263–264; see also
    Project cash flows;
    Statement of cash flow
and accounting profits, 265
basic financial resource, 445
from bonds, 166–167
from collections, 539–541
in corporations, 11
discounted to a common date, 123
discounting
    by nominal interest rate, 143
    by real interest rate, 143
equivalent annual annuity, 236–238
expected forecasts, 362
forecasting, 387–388
identifying
    discounting cash flow, not profits, 264–265
    incremental cash flow, 266–270
    separate financing from investment decisions, 270
incremental, 266–269
and inflation, 269–270
from investment in working capital, 268
level, 127–135
midyear convention, 276n
multiple, 124–127
versus net income, 63
from new computer system, 231–232
from office block project, 230–231
and payout policy, 490–491
versus profit, 264–265
real vs. nominal, 269–270
spreadsheet solution, 233
on TIPS, 173
and value of the firm, 446
Cash flow analysis
changes in working capital, 276
investment in fixed assets, 274–275
operating cash flow, 275–276
total project cash flow, 276
Cash flow estimates, 291
Cash flow forecasts, 295
Cash flow for new investments, 63–65
Cash flow from financing, 63–65

Cash flow from operations, 63–65
Cash inflow, 61
Cash management
  centralization of, 574
  check handling and float, 574–575
  concentration accounts, 574
  electronic funds transfer, 576–578
  lock-box systems, 574–575
  reasons for holding cash, 573
  short-term securities vs. cash, 573
  sweep programs, 573–574
  three means of, 673
  types of payment systems, 575–578
Cash on delivery, 560
Cash outflows, 61, 62, 541
Cash payments
  from perpetuity, 127–128
  valuing, 143–144
Cash ratio, 96–97
Caterpillar, 368, 393
Cerberus Capital Management, 593n
Certificates of deposit, 579
Channel stuffing, 66
Chapter 11 bankruptcy, 460
  L. A. Gear, 532
  process, 475–476
  as protection from litigation, 477
Chapter 7 bankruptcy, 475
Character, and credit decision, 563
Charge card, 576
Charles River Laboratories, 598
Check Clearing for the 21st Century Act, 574
Check handling, 574–575
Chevron, 5
Chicago Board of Trade, 35, 37, 677
Chicago Board Options Exchange, 645
Chicago Mercantile Exchange, 24, 35, 684
Chicago Tribune Company, 609
Chief financial officer, 10
Chipotle Mexican Grill, 545–546
CHIPS; see Clearing House Interbank Payment System
Chordia, T., 213
Chrysler Corporation, 336, 404, 593n, 595, 609
  staving off bankruptcy, 462n
Cisco Systems, 175, 530
Citicorp, 411
Citigroup, 176, 431
Class A or B shares, 407
Clearing House Interbank Payment System, 577–578
Closed-end fund, 38n, 696
Closely held companies, 8
CME Group, 684
Coca-Cola Company, 83, 84, 85, 473

Coefficient of correlation, 207–208
Collateral, 411
  accounts receivable financing, 547
  and credit decision, 563
  inventory financing, 547–548
Collateralized debt obligations, 415
Collection policy
  aging schedule, 569–570
  definition, 569
  factors for, 570
  and sales department, 570
  statement of account, 570
Collections of accounts receivable, 539–541
Comcast, 592, 703
Comment, R., 487n
Commercial banks; see also Banks and Banking
  deposit insurance, 44n
  in financial crisis of 2007–2009, 48
  functions, 40
  holders of corporate bonds 2010, 42
  holdings of equities 2010, 42
  number of, 40
Commercial draft, 562
Commercial paper, 36, 401–402, 531
  defaults, 549
  definition, 548
  minimum maturity, 548
  in money market, 579
  recent problems with, 549
  safety of, 548–549
Commodity futures, 679–680
Commodity markets, 37–38, 44
Commodity prices, 45
Common-size balance sheet, 56–57
Common-size income statement, 60
Common stock, 185
  additional paid-in capital, 405
  Amazon vs. Con Ed, 190–191
  authorized share capital, 405
  bid-ask spread, 187
  book value, 189–191
  classes of, 407
  and company cost of capital, 374–375
  and convertible bonds, 177
  definition, 186
  dividend yield, 188
  expected rate of return
    based on CAPM 382
    based on dividend discount model, 382–383
    false precision, 383
  expected rate of return in 1981, 323
  expected return and volatility, 330
  fluctuating rates of return, 321

growth stock, 191, 202–205, 358
historical returns, 325
holders of, in 2010, 406
income stock, 191, 202–205
incremental risks, 332
initial public offerings, 423
issued and outstanding shares, 405
issued but not outstanding, 405
large vs. small firms, 358
liquidation value, 190
listing in secondary markets, 186
market value, 189–191
measuring betas, 346–349
measuring market risk, 346–352
measuring variation in returns, 327–329
most risky investment, 352
net common equity, 405–406
open auction issue, 430–431
overvalued, 434
and ownership of corporations, 406–407
par value, 405
portfolio betas, 350–352
price-earnings ratio, 188
primary offering, 426
reading market listings, 187–189
and retained earnings, 405
risk in mutual funds, 351–352
risks, 320
risk/standard deviation, 334
seasoned offering, 431–432
secondary offering, 426
shareholders, 404–405
standard deviation of returns, 328
total risk and market risk, 350
trading in secondary market, 186–187
treasury stock, 405
two parts of returns, 347
value stocks, 358
volume of trade, 186
voting procedures, 407
Common stock valuation
  case, 332–334
  by comparables, 191–192
  constant-growth dividend discount model, 197–199
  difficult and imprecise, 214
  dividend discount model, 194–197
  effect of repurchase on, 484
  efficient market hypothesis, 211–212
  estimating required rate of return, 199–200
  fundamental analysis, 210
  growth stocks, 205
  market anomalies, 212–213
  with market-value balance sheet, 205–206

no-growth dividend discount model, 197
nonconstant growth, 200–202
price and intrinsic value, 192–194
technical analysis, 206–210
Companies; see also Corporations
  countercyclical, 330
  credit scoring for, 563–565
  extent of derivatives use, 673
  fair behavior by, 17
  financial managers, 10–11
  financing decisions, 6–7
  insolvency, 404
  internal growth rate, 518
  investment decisions, 6
  investment grade, 45–46
  investments by, 113
  leasing vs. buying, 699
  line of credit, 545–546
  liquidity choice, 530
  loan covenants, 463
  long-term goals, 504
  measuring betas, 348
  mutually consistent goals, 505
  paying for investments, 113
  payout ratio, 203
  plowback ratio, 203
  proliferation of bank accounts, 574
  reasons for holding cash, 573
  sustainable growth rate, 97–98, 203–204
  transparency, 103
Company cost of capital, 359–360
  after-tax, 377
  based on market value of securities, 376–377
  calculated as weighted average, 374–377
  calculating, 371
  definition, 373
  and investors, 376
Company values, 46
Compensation plans
  for jobs in finance, 22
  linked to stock prices, 46
  for managers, 18–19
Competition in financial markets, 400
Competitive advantage
  in product markets, 400
  in project analysis, 294
Competitiveness, 6
Complementary resources, combined by merger, 595
Compound growth, 24, 117
  continuous, 139
  effective annual interest rate, 138–139
Compound interest
  definition, 114
  future value, 114–117
  present value calculation using, 118–119
  purchase price of Manhattan, 116

Concentration accounts, 574
Conditional sales, 562
Condition of business, and credit decision, 563
Conflict of interest
  eliminating, 293
  shareholders vs. bondholders, 463
Conglomerate merger
  bootstrap game, 596–597
  definition, 593
Consistency in financial planning, 505
Consolidated balance sheet, 54
Consolidated Edison, 190–191, 206, 329, 346, 348–350, 359, 368, 385, 554
Constant dollars, 141
Constant-growth dividend discount model, 383
  definition, 198
  example, 198
  formula, 198
  perpetuity formula, 198–199
  required forecasting, 197–198
Consumer credit, 531
  definition, 560
Consumer price index, 141–142
  and inflation, 140
Continental Airlines, 476
Contingency planning, 505
Contingent rent agreement, 303
Continuous compounding, 139
Controller, 10
Conversion value, 661
Convertible bonds, 36, 177, 415–416
  Alcoa, 661
  conversion value, 661
  definition, 659
  direct costs, 429
  options on, 645
  valuation, 661
Convertible preferred stock, 416
Convertible securities
  convertible bonds, 415–416
  convertible preferred stock, 416
  warrants, 415
Cookie-jar reserves, 66
Coolidge, Calvin, 321
Cornfeld, Bernie, 702
Corporate bonds
  callable, 410–411, 661
  call provisions, 645
  compared to Treasury bonds, 174
  convertible, 177, 415–416
  default premium, 174
  default risk, 174–176, 411
  floating-rate bonds, 177
  insuring against default, 176
  investment grade, 174–175
  liquid, 175
  Marriott Corporation, 413
  maturities, 410
  mortality bonds, 177
  prices vs. Treasury bonds, 698

prices/yields for selected companies, 175
  promised vs. expected yield to maturity, 177
  speculative grade, 174–175
  with warrants, 659
  yield on, 142
  yield spread vs. Treasury bonds, 176
  zero-coupon bonds, 177
Corporate control, ways of changing, 591; see also Market for corporate control
Corporate debt
  distinguishing characteristics
    callable bonds, 410–411
    country and currency differences, 411–412
    default risk, 411
    interest rates, 409
    maturities, 409–410
    protective covenants, 412
    public vs. private placement, 412
    repayment provisions, 410
    security, 411
    sinking fund, 410
    subordinated debt, 411
  and limited liability, 409–410
  Marriott Corporation, 413
  Procter & Gamble, 414
  RJR Nabisco, 412n
Corporate financing
  case, 439–440
  common stock, 404–407
  convertible securities, 415–416
  debt financing, 409–415
  general cash offers, 431–434
  initial public offerings, 426–430
  open auctions, 430–431
  patterns of
    amounts of debt, 403–404
    commercial paper, 401–402
    debt ratios, 402
    financial deficit, 401
    internally generated funds, 400
    reliance on internal funds, 403
    sources of cash, 400–403
  preferred stock, 407–408
  private placements, 434–435
  seasoned offerings, 431–432
  venture capital, 424–425
Corporate governance, 19–20
  agency costs, 603
Corporate scandals, 67–68, 427; see also Fraud
  Enron Corporation, 103, 413–414
  in United States, 25
Corporate taxes
  and capital structure
    debt advantages, 454–456
    implications of decisions, 458

and value of shareholders' equity, 456
    weighted average cost of capital, 456–458
  and changes in capital structure, 387
  expense deductions, 68–69
  interest deductions, 69
  loss carryback, 69
  rate variation, 68
Corporate venturers, 425
Corporations
  agency problems, 16–19
  all-equity financing, 464
  assets needed by, 3
  bankruptcies, 24
  blockholders, 18–19
  board of directors, 9, 407
  closely held, 8
  cost disadvantages, 9
  definition, 8
  financial accounts, 53
  financial manager's tasks, 10–11
  flow of savings to, 33–42
  goals of
    and agency problems, 16–19
    corporate governance, 120
    value maximization, 11–14
  limited liability, 8
  means of payout
    cash dividends, 480–481
    stock repurchase, 482–484
  need for financial institutions, 32–33
  net common equity, 405–406
  net worth, 407
  no-dividend group, 480
  ownership of, 406–407
  payout decisions
    cash dividend advantages, 486
    in context of dividends and repurchases, 486–487
    managerial views, 485
    target dividend, 485
    target payout ratio, 485
  privately held, 426
  public companies, 8–9
  separation of ownership and control, 9, 603
  shareholders, 8
  stock betas for, 350
  stock issues, 185
  tax disadvantage, 9
  threat of takeover, 612
  total financing in U.S., 42
  wildly dispersed ownership, 603–604
Correlation coefficient, 333n
Cost(s)
  of general cash offer, 433
  of investments, 227
  of operating corporations, 9
  of proxy contests, 603–604

Cost-cutting projects, 271–272
Cost of capital, 31; see also Company cost of capital; Opportunity cost of capital
  of cyclical businesses, 362
  debt and cost of equity, 451–454
  definition, 46
  definition and use of, 373–374
  in economic value added, 84–85
  effect of restrictions, 452
  excluded from income statement, 84
  Geothermal example, 372–373
  investment timing decision, 235
  measuring, 322–323
  nominal, 269–270
  project, 360–361
  and rate of return, 317
  and risk, 317
  for selected companies, 84
  and taxes, 371
  using historical evidence to estimate, 322–323
Cost of debt, after-tax, 377
Cost of equity, 371
  and debt, 451–452
  false precision, 383
Cost of goods sold, 62
Cost reduction, 392
Costs of financial distress, 458–463, 672
  without bankruptcy, 461–463
  bankruptcy costs, 459–461
  definition, 459
  effect on stakeholders, 462
  investor assessment, 459
  varying by type of asset, 461
Countercyclical firms, 330
Counterparties, 681
Coupon, 160, 509
Coupon rate, 165
Credit, 560
  five Cs of, 563
Credit agencies, 562–563
Credit agreements
  banker's acceptances, 562
  commercial draft, 562
  conditional sales, 562
  open account, 562
  sight draft, 562
  time draft, 562
  trade acceptance, 562
Credit analysis, 560
  based on financial ratios, 563
  definition, 562
  hazard analysis, 565
  numerical credit scoring, 563–565
  Z-score model, 565
Credit booms, 698
Credit bureaus, 563n
Credit cards, 575–576

Credit decision
  bases of
    dangerous accounts, 569
    looking beyond immediate
      order, 569
    profit maximization, 569
  credit policy for, 566
  with repeat orders, 568
  without repeat orders, 566–567
Credit-default swaps, 176,
  683–684
Credit history, 566
Credit management steps, 560
Credit operation efficiency, 89
Creditors
  and bankruptcy costs, 460
  postpetition, 477
  preference for liquidation, 477
  priority in bankruptcies, 475n
Credit policy
  aging schedule, 569–570
  collection policy, 569–571
  consumer credit, 560
  credit analysis, 562–569
  definition, 566
  open account, 562
  terms of sale, 560–562
  trade credit, 560
Credit rating agencies, 48
Credit risk, 174
Credit sales, 89n
Credit scoring
  models, 566
  for small businesses, 566
  software for, 566
Credit transfer, 576
Cross-border financial statements,
  68
Cryogenic Concepts, 14
Cumulative financing
  requirements, 541–543
Cumulative voting, 407
Currency swaps, 682–683
Current assets, 56
  accounts receivable, 531
  on balance sheet, 54
  borrowing on strength of, 547
  cash, 531–532
  components, 96
  costs and benefits, 536–537
  inventory, 531
  liquidity of, 530n
  marketable securities, 531
  for selected industries, 533
  on statement of cash flow,
    63–64
  types of, 559
Current dollar cash flow, 143
Current dollars, 141
Current liabilities
  on balance sheet, 55
  and net working capital, 96
  on statement of cash flow,
    63–64
  in working capital, 532–533

Current ratio, 96
Current yield, 167
Cutoff period, payback rule, 239
Cyclical businesses, 362

D

Dangerous accounts, 569
Davidson, S. M., 16
DeAngelo, H., 532
DeAngelo, L., 532
Debit cards, 575–576
Debt; *see also* Corporate debt;
    Financial leverage
  book value, 88
  collateral for, 411
  and cost of equity, 451–454
  explicit cost, 453
  financing without, 464
  fixed-rate, 681, 682
  implicit cost, 453
  increasing financial risk, 453
  issue costs, 433
  and sustainable growth rate, 518
  and uncertainty on stock
    return, 450
Debt-equity mix; *see also* Capital
    structure
  in calculating company cost of
    capital, 375–376
  restructuring, 447–448
Debt-equity ratio, 93
  MM proposition II, 453–454
Debt-equity trade-off, 459,
  463–464
Debt financing, 7
  bonds, 36
  commercial paper, 36,
    401–402
  and operating risk, 450
  over-reliance on, 403–404
  Procter & Gamble, 414
  and profit margin, 90
  tax advantages, 454–456
  two costs of, 385–386
Debt general cash offer, 432
Debtholders; *see also* Bondholders
  income vs. shareholders, 92
  rates of return for, 375–376
Debt investors, 7
Debt issues, 401
Debt market; *see also* Bond
    market; Money market
  asset-backed bonds, 414–415
  collateralized debt obligations,
    415
  mortgage pass-through
    certificates, 414–415
  private placement in., 434–435
Debt policy
  capital structure and taxes,
    454–458
  case, 474–475
  and cost of capital, 451–454

  costs of financial distress,
    458–463
  effect on earnings per share,
    448–450
  effect on risk and return,
    450–451
  effect on value of the firm,
    446–454
  and financing choices
    financial slack, 465–466
    pecking order theory,
      464–465
    trade-off theory, 463–464
  loan covenants, 463
  managerial views, 465–467
  MM proposition I, 446–448
  MM proposition II, 452–454
  and restructuring, 447–448
Debt ratios, 93–94
  effect of financing decisions,
    402
  increase in, 404
  nonfinancial industries, 446
  in trade-off theory, 464
Debt securities, 36
Debt-to-value ratio, 376–377
Decision making
  delegated by shareholders,
    11–12
  in financial environment, 32
Decision rules
  for assets with different lives,
    237
  comparison of, 250
  for investment timing, 236
  net present value rule, 229, 241
  payback rule, 239–240
  rate of return rule, 241
Decision tree, 306
Declaration date, 481
Default
  on commercial paper, 549
  investor fear of, 698
  in junk bond market, 608
  and subordinated debt, 411
Default premium, 174
Default risk, 102, 159, 411
  on corporate bonds, 174–176
  definition, 174
  insuring against, 176
  in money market, 580
  and project risk, 463
Defensive stocks, 346
Defined-benefit pension plans, 39n,
  40n
Defined-contribution pension
  plans, 39
Deflation, 140
Degree of operating leverage,
  304–305
Del Campo, J., 323n
Dell Inc., 191, 329, 350, 359,
  360–361, 368, 369, 385,
  573, 593, 616, 667
Delphi, 595

Delta Airlines, 336
Demand deposits, 531, 573
Department of Justice, 611
Deposit insurance, 44n
Depreciation
  accelerated, 278
  and calculation of profit,
    60–61
  and cash coverage ratio, 94
  and cash flow, 64
  and corporate tax, 68–69
  estimating, 54
  in financial plan, 512–513
  modified accelerated cost
    recovery system, 278
  nominal vs. real amount, 277
  as noncash expense, 400n
  in project cash flow, 272
  purpose of, 57
  straight-line, 275–276
Depreciation allowance, 63
Depreciation deduction, 272
Depreciation tax shield, 272,
  277–279
Deregulation of air cargo, 4
Derivatives, 671
  credit-default swaps, 683–684
  definition, 673
  futures contracts, 676–680
  identification of risks, 683–684
  innovations, 683–684
  iron ore futures, 684
  options, 674–675
  problems caused by, 684–685
  real estate futures, 684
  speculation problem, 684
  swaps, 681–683
Derivatives groups, in banks, 21
Derivatives market, 37–38
DIAMONDS, 44
Dimon, James, 487
Dimson, Elroy, 319, 320, 321, 324,
  325, 327, 328
Direct costs
  of bankruptcy, 460
  of stock issues, 429–430
Direct debit, 576
Direct deposit, 577
Direct negotiation for stock
  repurchase, 483
Direct payment, 576, 577
Discount basis interest rate
  quotes, 579
Discount bonds, 167
  price changes, 170
Discounted cash flow, 118
  by company cost of capital, 360
Discounted cash-flow analysis,
  263–264
  calculating cash flow
    capital investment, 271
    changes in working capital,
      273–274
    operating cash flow,
      271–273

case, 287–288
examples
 calculating net present value, 276
 cash-flow analysis, 274–276
 depreciation tax shield, 277–279
 forecasting working capital, 277
 salvage value, 279
 identifying cash flows, 264–268
 spreadsheet solution, 280
Discounted cash flow methods, 243
Discounted cash flow rate of return, 242
Discounted cash flows, 263
Discounted-payback period, 240
Discount factors, 119
 present value table, A-2
Discounting
 cash flow, not profits, 264–265
 incremental cash flows, 266–269
 nominal cash flows, 269–270
 opportunity cost of capital, 692
 real cash flows, 269
Discount rate, 118
 and cash flow, 143
 choosing, 373–374
 fudge factors, 362
 increase and NPV increases, 244
 and internal rate of return, 242–243
 nominal, 269
 for stock's cash flow, 192
Diversifiable risks, 334, 692
 fire insurance, 335
 wildcat oil wells, 335
Diversification, 43–44
 eliminating specific risks, 334, 345
 and macro risks, 336
 market vs. specific risks, 333–334
 as reason for merger, 596
 to reduce variability, 329–330
 unable to eliminate market risk, 346
Divestitures, 610
Dividend cuts, 486, 487
Dividend discount model
 for common stock valuation, 194–197
 constant-growth, 197–199
 definition, 194
 estimating expected rate of return, 199–200
 expected return based on, 382–383
 investors' time horizon, 194–197
 with no growth, 197
 nonconstant growth, 200–202
 required forecasting, 197–198

Dividend policy
 advantage of cash dividends, 486
 cash dividends, 480–481
 effect of taxes, 492, 493
 high payout policy, 491–492
 low payout policy, 492–493
 managerial views, 485
 Microsoft, 491–492
 MM irrelevance proposition, 488–491, 693
 in percentage of sales models, 507–508
 resolving, 697
 stock dividends, 491–492
 stock splits, 491–492
 target dividend, 485
 target payout ratio, 485
 trade-off in, 487
Dividend reinvestment plan, 479
Dividends, 541
 from after-tax income, 69, 70
 on after-tax income, 409
 cash, 480–481
 from common stock, 192–194
 compared to repurchases, 483–484
 determining rate of growth, 203–205
 double taxation of income, 70
 information content, 486–487
 limitations on, 481
 MM irrelevance proposition, 488–491
 payout ratio, 203
 on preferred stock, 378, 383–384, 408
 required forecasting of, 197–198
 stock, 481–482
 stock splits, 481
 suspended by BP, 486
 in U.S. 1980–2008, 480
Dividend yield, 188, 193, 318, 383
Dollars, nominal vs. real, 141
Dot-com boom/bubble, 213, 215, 329, 696
Double taxation, 9n, 70
Dow Chemical, 83, 84, 189, 192, 329, 346–350, 359, 385, 400–402, 410–411, 416
 common stock, 404–406
 preferred stock, 406
 weighted average cost of capital, 377–378
Dow Jones Industrial Average, 44
 history and function, 319
 low in 1932, 321
 percentage changes, 1900–2010, 328
Dow Jones Wilshire 500 index, 319
Drexel Burnham Lambert, 610
Due lag, 582
Dun & Bradstreet, 562, 586
Dunlap, "Chainsaw" Al, 66

Du Pont Corporation, 319, 368, 393
Du Pont formula, 90–91
 and return on assets, 90–91
 and return on equity, 94–95

E

Earning power, 190
Earnings
 of cyclical businesses, 362
 inflation of, 67
 plowback ratio, 203
 reinvested, 97
 scrutiny of, 66
Earnings announcement puzzle, 212, 213
Earnings before interest, taxes, depreciation, and amortization, 94n, 563
Earnings before interest and taxes, 59, 94
 in free cash flow, 65
Earnings per share, 66
 effect of borrowing on, 448–450
 effect of change in operating income, 450
 impact of merger on, 597
Earnings reinvestment, 479
Earnings variability and project risk, 351–362
Eastern Airlines bankruptcy, 460
Eastman Kodak, 393
Easy-money policy, 47
eBay, 190, 428
EBIT; see Earnings before interest and taxes
EBITDA; see Earnings before interest, taxes, depreciation, and amortization
Economic gain from mergers, 600
Economic order quantity, 572
Economics of vertical integration, 594–595
Economic value added, 537
 and accounting rates of return, 86–88
 and break-even analysis, 301n
 calculating, 84–85
 definition, 84
 as performance measure, 85
 problems with, 87–88
 for selected companies, 84
Economies of scale, gained in mergers, 594
Economists, disagreements among, 695
Economy, differing scenarios, 330–332
Effective annual interest rate
 on bank accounts, 139
 of bonds, 163n
 calculating, 138–139
 definition, 138

Efficiency measures
 asset turnover ratio, 88
 inventory turnover, 88–89
 receivables turnover, 89–90
Efficient capital markets, 400, 692–693
Efficient market, 211
Efficient market hypothesis, 693
 exceptions to, 696
 and investor performance, 211–212
 and market anomalies, 212–213
 semistrong-form, 211
 and stock market bubbles, 213–214
 strong-form, 211
 weak-form, 211
Ehrbar, A., 537n
Eight O'Clock Coffee, 593n
Einstein, Albert, 691
Eisner, Michael, 604
Electric utilities, 304n
 less than average macro risk, 336
Electronic communications networks, 186
Electronic funds transfer, 576–578
 advantages, 578
 direct deposit, 577
 direct payment, 577
 wire transfer, 577–578
Electronic trading, 35
Eli Lilly, 595
Ellison, Larry, 18–19, 659
End-of-month sales, 560
Enron Corporation, 18, 25, 66–67, 103, 427
 bankruptcy, 460, 477
 special-purpose entities, 103, 413–414
Equifax, 563n
Equipment
 required by law or policy, 292–293
 salvage value, 279
Equity, 425
 book value, 88
 debt and cost of, 451–452
 general cash offer, 432
 and internal growth rate, 517
 issue costs, 433
Equity financing, 7
 holders of, 406
 and leverage ratio, 95
Equity investors, 7
Equity issues, 401
Equity markets, 36
Equivalent annual annuity
 calculating, 236–237
 definition, 236
 examples, 237–238
 of new equipment, 238
Erie and Union Railroad, 159
Estée Lauder, 46
European call, 646n

EVA; *see* Economic value added
EVA Dimensions, 82, 88
Excess funds, 559; *see also* Idle
  cash
Exchange rate fluctuations,
  hedging, 679
Exchange traded funds, 43–44
Exchange-traded portfolios, 212
Ex-dividend date, 481
Executive stock options
  backdating scandal, 660
  calculating, 659
Exercise price, 646–647
  Google stock, 648
Expansion option, 305–307, 658
Expected cash flow forecasts,
  362
Expected profit, 567
Expected rate of return, 229,
  374–375, 692, 695
  on bonds, 382
  calculating, 354
  and changes in capital structure,
    386–387
  on common stock, 193
    based on CAPM, 382
    based on dividend discount
      model, 382–383
    false precision, 383
  on common stock 1981, 323
  company cost of capital,
    359–360
  with dividend discount model,
    199–200
  estimating, 322–323
  from investment vs. shareholder
    return, 228
  on preferred stock, 383–384
  for securities of same
    risk, 193
  for selected companies, 359
Expenses, tax-deductible, 68–69
Experian, 563n
Expiration date, 646, 647
Explicit cost of debt, 385–386,
  453
External financing, 465
  and growth rate, 515–518
  required, 515–516
ExxonMobil, 82–83, 84, 85, 86,
  329, 336–337, 350, 359,
  385, 480, 592

F

Face value, 160
  and yield to maturity, 167
Factor
  for collection policy, 570
  definition, 547
Factoring, 547
Fair, Isaac & Company, 563n,
  566
Fama, Eugene F., 482n
Fannie Mae, 18, 47, 67, 169

Federal Deposit Insurance
  Corporation, 44n, 665
Federal Express, 4, 20, 83, 84,
  186, 189, 192, 400–402,
  426, 462
  air freight expansion, 306
  financing decisions, 4–5
  founding and early financing,
    4–5
  initial public offering, 4, 186
  investment decisions, 4, 5
  limit order book, 187
  market capitalization, 188
Federal funds rate, 546n
Federal Reserve System,
  415, 699
  and Fedwire, 577–578
  and financial crisis of
    2007–2009, 47
  responsibility for financial
    crisis, 48
  tight money policy 1979, 163
Federal Trade Commission
  and Blockbuster, 598
  and Whole Foods Market, 599
Fedwire, 577–578
Fernandez, P., 323n
FICO score, 563n
Fidelity, 368
Fidelity Investments, 39
Field warehousing, 548
Finance
  careers in, 20–22
  history of, 24–25
  most important ideas in
    agency theory, 694
    efficient capital markets,
      692–693
    MM irrelevance propositions,
      693
    net present value, 692
    option theory, 693–694
    risk and return, 692
  unsolved problems
    capital structure, 697
    exceptions to efficient market
      theory, 696
    financial crises, 698
    merger waves, 697–698
    payout policy, 697
    present value determination,
      694–695
    project risk determination,
      694–695
    risk and return, 695
    value of the firm, 696–697
    valuing liquidity, 698
Finance companies, 545
Finance.yahoo.com, 187
Financial Accounting Standards
  Board, 66
  on option valuation
    models, 659
Financial analysts, 20
Financial assets, 38
  definition, 7

options on
  callable bonds, 661
  convertible bonds, 659–661
  executive stock options,
    659
  warrants, 659
  variety of, 7
Financial calculators
  annuity present value, 137
  to find internal rate of
    return, 246
  to find net present value, 246
  interest rates, 123–124
  operation of, 121
  present value calculations, 121
Financial crises, explaining, 698
Financial crisis of 2007–2009,
  403n
  and asset-backed bonds,
    414–415
  effect on airlines, 445n
  effect on bond market, 175
  and government debts, 48
  investor fear of default, 698
  and Lehman Brothers, 67
  and money market, 580
  origin of, 47
  peak of, 47–48
  responsibility for, 48
Financial deficit, 401
Financial distress; *see also* Costs of
    financial distress
  without bankruptcy, 461–463
  and capital investment
    strategies, 462
  costs of, 672
  debtholder-stockholder conflict,
    463
  definition, 458
  effect of financial leverage,
    460
  effect on stakeholders, 462
  investor assessment, 459
Financial environment, 32
Financial futures, 679–680
Financial institutions, 31
  commercial banks, 40
  definition, 40
  factors, 547
  in financial crisis of 2007–2009,
    47–48
  flow of savings to corporations,
    33–42
  functions
    diversifications, 43–44
    payment mechanism, 45
    providing liquidity, 44–45
    risk transfer, 43–44
    transporting cash across
      time, 43
  importance to companies,
    32–33
  insurance companies, 41
  investment banks, 40–41
Financial instruments for hedging;
  see Hedging

Financial intermediaries
  definition and functions, 38
  hedge funds, 39
  mutual funds, 38–39
  pension funds, 39–40
Financial investment criteria
  bonds
    default risk, 174–176
    interest rates and bond prices,
      161–166
    rates of return, 168–171
    yield curve, 171–174
    yield to maturity, 166–168
  common stock
    behavioral finance, 214–215
    efficient market hypothesis,
      211–212
    fundamental analysis, 210
    growth and income stocks,
      202–206
    technical analysis, 206–210
  flight to quality, 580
  and shareholder value, 80–81
  valuation of common stock
    by comparables, 191–192
    dividend discount model,
      194–202
    price and intrinsic value,
      192–194
Financial leverage
  cause of financial distress, 460
  definition, 92, 450
  measuring, 92–95
    cash coverage ratio, 94
    debt ratio, 93
    times interest earned ratio, 94
  and return on equity, 94–95
Financial managers, 3, 6–7, 503
  chief financial officer, 10
  controller, 10
  essential role of, 11
  investment trade-off, 13–14
  knowledge of financial markets, 31
  in large corporations, 10–11
  treasurer, 10
  use of shelf registration, 433
Financial markets, 31
  bond market, 36
  capital markets, 36
  commodities markets, 37
  competition in, 400
  definition, 35
  derivatives market, 37–38
  in financial crisis of 2007–2009,
    47–48
  fixed-income market, 36
  flow of savings to corporations,
    33–42
  foreign exchange markets, 37
  functions
    diversification, 43–44
    payment mechanism, 45
    providing liquidity, 44–45
    risk transfer, 43–44
    transporting cash across time,
      43

importance to companies, 32–33
information provided by
  on commodity prices, 45
  on company values, 46
  on cost of capital, 46–47
  on interest rates, 45–46
money market, 36
options market, 37–38
over-the-counter market, 36
stock market, 35–36
Financial plan, 503
  balancing item, 507–508
  depreciation in, 512–513
Financial planning; *see also*
      Short-term financial
      planning
  alternative business plans, 504
  to avoid surprises, 503
  big-picture focus, 504
  case, 525
  to establish goals, 504
  external financing and growth,
      515–518
  long-term focus, 504
  long-term links to short-term,
      528–531
  planning horizon, 504
  reasons for
    contingency planning, 505
    forcing consistency, 505
    options to consider, 505
  and strategic plans, 504
Financial planning models
  assumption in percentage of
      sales models, 513–514
  components
    functions, 506
    inputs, 506
    outputs, 506
  consistency between
      assumptions and plans,
      508
  danger of complexities, 515
  and growth rate changes, 512
  improved model, 508–512
  limits to, 515
  percentage of sales models,
      507–508
  pitfalls in design, 512–513
  purpose, 506
  role of, 514–515
Financial ratios
  benchmarks for performance,
      100
  case, 110–111
  comparisons with past, 100–101
  in credit analysis, 563–565
  in financial plan, 506, 507
  at Home Depot over time,
      100–101
  interpreting, 98–101
  leverage ratios, 92–94
  limitations, 79–80
  liquidity ratios, 95–97
  for major industry groups,
      98, 99

payout ratio, 97
plowback ratio, 97
profitability ratios, 86–89
role of, 101–102
  default risk, 102
  transparency, 103
  to understand value added,
      80–81
Financial risk
  definition, 450
  increased by debt, 453
Financial slack
  dark side of, 466–467
  and debt policy, 466–467
  definition, 465
  at L. A. Gear, 532
  threat of financial distress,
      466–467
  valued by managers, 465
Financial statements; *see also
      specific statements*
  cross-border, 68
  Enron, 103
  filed with SEC, 54
  for financial plan, 506
  for financial planning model,
      508–512
  pro forma, 506, 507
  users of, 53
  websites for, 56
Financial system, 33
Financing
  cash flows as basic source, 445
  company options, 33–35
  composition of, 371
  by corporations, 3
  debt vs. equity, 7
  effects of investment decisions
      on, 699
  of Federal Express, 4–5
  forms of, 33
  by Home Depot, 60
  for investment and growth, 97
  MM irrelevance propositions,
      693
  multiple sources and WACC 378
  of U.S. corporations, 42
  and value of the firm, 79
Financing decisions, 3
  Apple Inc., 32–33
  case, 439–440
  cash payments at different
      dates, 113
  common stock, 404–407
  compared to investment
      decisions, 7, 399
  convertible securities, 415–416
  corporate debt, 409–415
  definition, 6
  effect on debt ratios, 402
  examples, 5
  by Federal Express, 5
  and financial slack, 465–467
  general cash offer, 431–434
  in history, 24–25
  initial public offering, 426–431

investors, 6–7
  kinds of financing, 7
  means of, 6–7
  patterns of corporate finance,
      400–404
  and payout policy, 487
  pecking order theory, 464–465
  preferred stock, 407–408
  private placement, 434–435
  real vs. financial assets, 7
  separate from investment
      decisions, 270
  task of financial managers,
      10–11
  trade-off theory, 463–464
  value creation with, 400
  venture capital, 424–425
Financing requirements, 505
Fire insurance, 335
Firm commitment, 427
First Call, 201n
First Data Corporation, 175
First-stage financing, 424
Fisher, L., 482n
Five Cs of credit, 563
Fixed assets, 56
  on balance sheet, 54
  investment in, 274–275
Fixed costs, 295
  and operating leverage,
      303–305
  potential advantages, 303
Fixed-income market, 36
Fixed-income securities, 578–579
Fixed-rate debt, 681, 682
Flexible production facilities, 308
Flight to quality, 580
Float
  definition, 574–575
  reducing, 578
Floating interest rates, 36, 409
Floating-rate bonds, 177, 681, 682
Floating-rate portfolio, 682
Floating-rate preferred stock, 408
Flotation costs, 429–430
Food companies, macro risk, 336
Forbes, 212
Ford Motor Company, 6, 330,
      332–333, 336, 347, 350,
      359, 365, 369, 384n, 385,
      399, 402, 413, 480, 481,
      548–549, 586, 610
  investment and financing
      decisions, 5
Forecast bias, resolving, 293–294
Forecasting
  ensuring consistency in, 293
  in financial plan, 506
  operating cash flow, 387–388
  versus planning, 505
  sources of cash, 530–541
  uses of cash, 541
Forelle, C., 660
Forward contracts
  characteristics, 680–681
  definition, 680

and futures contracts, 680
  risk reduction with, 680–681
Fraud; *see also* Corporate scandals
  Allied Crude Vegetable Oil
      Refining Company, 547
  Bernard Madoff, 15
  charges for Goldman Sachs, 16
Freddie Mac, 18, 47, 66, 169
Free cash flow
  definition, 65, 387
  for Home Depot, 65
  managers with, 466
  motive for takeover, 595
  parts of, 65
  in valuing entire businesses,
      388–389
Free-cash-flow theory of
      takeovers, 609
Free credit, value of, 120–121
Frock, Roger, 462n
Fudge factors, 362
Fundamental analysis, 210
Fundamental analysts, 210
Funded debt, 409
Futures, 676
Futures contracts
  characteristics, 676–677
  commodity futures, 679–680
  definition, 676
  financial futures, 679–680
  and forward contracts, 680
  for iron ore prices, 684
  margin account, 676n
  mechanics of trading, 677–679
    margin requirement, 678
    marked to market, 678–679
    spot price, 679
  versus options, 676
  problems with, 684–685
  profits on, 676
  real estate, 684
  for risk reduction, 676–680
  standardized, 680
Futures market
  Chicago Mercantile Exchange,
      24, 35, 684
  New York Mercantile Exchange,
      37, 46, 684
  prediction markets, 37
  requirements for success, 684
Future value
  of annuity, 133–135
  of annuity due, 137
  of annuity vs. annuity due, 137
  calculating, 115–116
  and compound interest,
      114–117
  definition, 114
  of multiple cash flows, 124–125,
      128
  in present value calculations,
      117–118
  of retirement savings, 135
  spreadsheet solution, 122–123
Future value tables, 116, 135, A-2,
      A-5

G

Gantchev, Nickolay, 429n
Gasoline prices, 141
Gates, Bill, 131–132, 143–144, 423
Genentech, 426, 592
General cash offer
  costs of, 433
  definition, 432
  market reaction, 433–434
  rights issue, 432
  seasoned offering, 431–432
  and shelf registration, 432–433
General Dynamics, 4
General Electric, 179, 189, 192, 319, 598
Generally accepted accounting principles, 57, 66, 103
  and International Financial Reporting Standards, 68
General Mills, 336
General Motors, 18, 160, 179, 336, 404, 487, 548, 595
Geothermal Corporation
  cost of capital, 372–373
  WACC, 379–380
Global Crossing, 67
Goals
  from financial planning, 504
  long-term, 504
  mutually consistent, 505
Going-concern value, 190
Goldman Sachs, 10, 15, 21, 41, 175, 431
  and housing crisis, 16
  and SEC, 16
Goodwill, 55
Google Finance, 56
Google Inc., 37, 83, 84, 85, 86, 88, 205, 206, 368, 402, 480, 646, 647–648, 650–651, 656, 657, 666
  auction IPO, 431
  founding of, 423
  initial public offering of 2004, 204
Gordon, Myron, 198
Gordon growth model, 198
Government, Troubled Asset Relief Program, 487
Government bonds
  amount publicly held, 160
  rate of return vs. yield to maturity, 168–169
  sales of, 159
Gradley, Richard, 21
Graham, J. R., 66, 323n, 465n, 485, 530n
Grand Union, 476
Greenbacks, 24
Greenmail transactions, 483
Greenspan, Alan, 215n
Greenwood, R., 482n

Growth
  from external financing, 515–518
  limited by opportunities, 97
Growth company, 190
Growth rate
  and changes in financial planning, 512
  internal, 517
  sustainable, 518
Growth stocks, 191, 358
  determining dividend growth, 203–205
  reasons for buying, 202
  valuing, 205
Growth vs. no-growth company, 190–191
Gulf oil spill of 2010, 486

H

H. J. Heinz Company, 350, 359, 385
Hard rationing, 249
Harvard Industries, 476
Harvey, C. R., 66, 323n, 465n, 485, 530n
Haushalter, G. D., 673n
Healy, P., 482n, 486, 611
Hedge funds, 16
  definition and functions, 39
  vulture funds, 39
Hedging
  and CAPM, 695
  financial instruments for, 671
  with forward contracts, 680–681
  with futures contracts, 676–680
  innovations in derivatives, 683–684
  versus investor choices, 672
  with options, 674–675
  problems with derivatives, 684–685
  reasons for, 672–673
  sensible strategy for, 673
  with swaps, 681–683
  types of derivatives, 673
  value of tools for, 699
  as zero-sum game, 672
Helyar, J., 607n
Herman Miller Corporation, 537
Hewlett-Packard, 611
Hickey, Robert, 413
High-price and high-margin strategy, 91
High-yield bonds, 174–175
Histogram, 324, 325
Historical cost, 57, 190
  versus mark-to-market accounting, 67
Hollywood Videos, 598
Home Depot, 19, 81, 83, 85, 86, 87–88, 90, 91, 93, 94, 95, 96, 97, 98, 100, 101, 106, 107, 368, 393

balance sheet, 54–57
cash coverage ratio, 94
debt ratio, 97–101
economic value added, 84–85
efficiency measures, 88–90
financial statements, 54–60, 63–64
free cash flow, 65
income statement, 59–60
market capitalization, 81
market value added, 81–82
return on assets, 90–91
statement of cash flow, 63–64
summary of performance, 99
sustainable growth rate, 97–98
times interest earned ratio, 94
total capitalization, 84
Honeywell Corporation, 598
Horizontal merger, 592
Horizon value, 388–389
Hostile takeovers, 591
  examples, 604–605
  poison pills, 605–607
  shark repellent, 606
Host Marriott Corporation, 413
Households
  holdings of corporate bonds in 2010, 42
  holdings of equities 2010, 42, 406
House price fluctuations, 684
Housing crisis
  and Goldman Sachs, 16
  subprime mortgages, 25, 47
Human assets, 593
Hurdle rate, 14, 46

I

IBES, 201n
IBM, 37, 318, 329, 335, 336–337, 350, 359, 385, 480, 593, 602, 616, 667
Icahn, Carl, 19, 604
Idle cash, 574
  invested in money market, 578–580
Illiquid assets, 95
ImClone Systems, 595
Implicit annual interest rate, 561
Implicit cost of debt, 385–386, 453
Income
  subject to corporate tax, 68–69
  subject to personal tax, 69–70
Income statement
  accrual accounting, 63
  capital expenditures on, 63
  common-size, 60
  cost of capital excluded, 84
  definition, 59
  earnings on, 59–60
  effect of transactions, 62–63
  expense items, 59
  Home Depot, 69–70

profit vs. cash flow, 60–63
pro forma, 508–512
Income stocks, 191
  determining dividend growth, 203–205
  reasons for buying, 203
Incremental cash flows
  allocated overhead costs, 268
  forecasting, 266
  ignoring sunk costs, 266–267
  including opportunity cost, 267
  indirect effects, 266
  recognizing investment in working capital, 267–268
  terminal cash flow, 268
Indexed bonds
  during American Revolution, 173n
  definition, 173
  TIPS, 173
Index funds, 43
Index mutual funds, 43–44
Indirect costs of bankruptcy, 460–461
Individual investments, 113
Industries, debt ratios, 446
Inefficiencies, eliminated by mergers, 595–596
Inflation
  base period, 140
  and consumer price index, 140
  definition, 139
  effect on Bill Gates, 143–144
  effect on cash flow, 269–270
  effect on depreciation, 277
  and nominal vs. real interest rates, 172–174
  and time value of money and interest rates, 141–142
  real or nominal present value calculations, 144
  real vs. nominal cash flows, 139–141
  valuing real cash payments, 143–144
Inflation indexed debt, 25
Inflation rate
  and interest rates, 142
  in U.S. 1900–2010, 140
Information content of dividends, 486–487
Information value in sensitivity analysis, 297
Initial public offering
  Apple Inc., 35–36
  Apple IPO and Massachusetts, 427n
  arranging, 427
  bookbuilding method, 430–431
  case, 439–440
  definition, 35, 186, 423–424, 426
  direct costs, 429–430
  Federal Express, 4, 186
  financing decision, 5

flotation costs, 429–430
Google Inc., 204, 423
issue price, 427
Microsoft, 423
and open auctions, 430–431
overpricing, 429
as primary offering, 426
prospectus, 427
versus remaining privately
    owned, 426
and SEC registration, 427
underpricing, 427–429
underwriters, 427, 431
underwriters' spread, 427
Visa, 430
Innovation
    by Apple Inc., 33
    in derivatives market, 683–684
Inputs to financial plan, 506
Insolvency, 404, 481n
Installment plan, 126
Institutional investors, 18–19, 42
    proxy contests, 604
Insurance companies
    holdings of corporate bonds in
        2010, 42
    holdings of equities in 2010, 42,
        406
    long-term financing by, 41
    reinsurance, 43n
    risk reduction by, 43
Intangible assets, 3, 6
    on balance sheet, 55
    and going-concern value, 190
    investment in, 113
    lacking abandonment value, 307
Intel Corporation, 7, 57, 117, 393,
    425, 426, 530
Interest
    compound, 114–117
    versus coupon rate, 165
    simple, 114
    tax-deductible, 69
Interest coverage, 94
Interest-free reserves, 412n
Interest payments, 64n, 509, 541
    on before-tax income, 409
    floating, 36
    and interest coverage, 94
    on Treasury bonds, 160
Interest rate quotes, 138
Interest rate risk, 165–166
Interest rates
    on bank loans, 546
    and bond prices, 126
    comparing, 138
    and compound interest, 114–117
    discount basis quotes, 579
    discount rate, 118
    floating, 409
    floating-rate bonds, 177
    floating-rate preferred stock,
        408
    on government bonds, 159
    hedging fluctuations in, 679

information on, 45–46
long-term bonds, 45
long- vs. short-term bonds, 172
market vs. coupon, 164
per period, 561
present value calculation,
    123–124
prime rate, 509
real vs. nominal, 141–142, 172–
    174, 269
TED spread, 546
ten-year Treasury bonds,
    1900–2009, 164
on trade credit, 561
varying bond prices, 163–165
Interest rate swaps, 681–682
Interest tax shield, 85n, 456–457,
    609
    definition, 455
    perpetual, 455–456
    as valuable asset, 455–456
    value of shareholders' equity,
        456
    and value of the firm, 455
Internal growth rate
    definition, 518
    determinants, 518
Internally generated funds, 465
    companies relying on, 402
    definition, 400
    reliance on, 403
Internal rate of return
    and discount rate, 242–243
    financial calculator solution,
        245
    for long-lived projects, 241–243
    modified, 248, 260
    versus opportunity cost of
        capital, 243
    pitfalls
        cost of capital, 244
        multiple rates of return,
            247–248
        mutually exclusive projects,
            244–246
        mutually exclusive projects
            with different outlays,
            246–247
Internal rate of return rule,
    240–248
    agreement with net present
        value rule, 243
    for choosing between mutually
        exclusive projects,
        259–260
    definition, 241
    discount rate, 241, 242
    and opportunity cost of capital,
        240–241
    summary on, 250
Internal Revenue Service, 68, 69,
    274, 277, 612
International Monetary Fund, 48
Internet, bill payment by, 575–576
Intrinsic value

of common stock, 192–194
    definition, 192
    and fundamental analysis, 210
    and market value, 696
Inventories
    carrying costs, 536
    composition of, 571
    costs of holding, 571
    as current asset, 531
    and economic value added,
        537
    level divisions, 534n
    relative liquidity, 530n
    shortage costs, 536–537
    types of, 559
Inventory financing
    example of fraud, 547
    and field warehousing, 548
Inventory management
    carrying costs, 571
    composition of inventories, 571
    economic order quantity, 572
    essential features, 572
    just-in-time systems, 573
    and production to order, 573
    storage costs, 571
Inventory period
    definition, 534
    estimating, 534
Inventory turnover
    versus profit margin, 91
    for selected industries, 92
Inventory turnover ratio, 88–89
Investment banks, 10, 20, 22
    bridge loans, 40n
    in financial crisis of 2007–2009,
        47–48
    functions, 40–41
    investments by, 41
    largest, 41
    underwriters, 427, 431
    underwriting, 41
Investment decisions, 3; see also
        Capital budgeting
        decisions; Financial
        investment criteria
    characteristics, 6
    compared to financing
        decisions, 7
    considering options, 505
    examples, 5
    by Federal Express, 4–5
    fundamental trade-off, 13–14
    in history, 24–25
    long-term consequences, 6
    new, 503
    opportunity cost of capital, 14
    and payout policy, 487
    separate from financing
        decisions, 270
    side effects on financing, 699
    terminology for, 6
    warped, 462
Investment expenditures,
    recognizing, 265

Investment grade bonds, 174–175
Investment grade companies,
    45–46
Investment income, tax treatment,
    70
Investment management
    departments, 22
Investment risk
    and dispersion of possible
        outcomes, 324
    measures of dispersion,
        324–325
Investments
    annuities, 128–130
    compound interest, 114–117
    costs of, 227
    by dividends, 113
    flow of, 34
    future value, 190
    historical performance,
        319–322
    in intangible assets, 113
    least and most risky, 352
    limited opportunity for, 97
    liquidity of, 44–45
    need for borrowing, 159
    paying for, 113
    perpetuities, 127–128
    rates of return, 14
    relative risks, 229
    risky, 12, 14
    in tangible assets, 113
Investment strategies of hedge
    funds, 39
Investment timing decision, 234,
    235, 236
Investment trade-off
    opportunity cost of capital, 14
    and value maximization,
        13–14
Investors, 6–7
    and asymmetric information,
        464
    behavioral finance
        attitudes toward risk, 214
        beliefs about probabilities,
            215
    and blue-sky laws, 427
    in CAPM, 356–358
    choices without hedging, 672
    and company cost of capital,
        376
    concern of macro risks, 336
    deceived by Enron, 413–414
    differing time horizons,
        194–197
    diversification, 43
    early repayment demand,
        410–411
    earnings reported to, 66
    effect of dividend change,
        478–487
    fear of default, 698
    fundamental analysts, 210
    in initial public offerings, 35

Investors—*Cont.*
  irrational exuberance, 215, 696
  overconfidence, 215
  reaction to price cycles, 209
  required return, 371
  senior vs. junior, 415
  technical analysts, 206
  use of financial statements, 54
  valuing liquidity, 698
  venture capital firms, 425–426
  wide choice of securities, 319
  worst year for bonds, 322
Iowa Electronic Markets, 37
IPO; *see* Initial public offering
Iridium failure, 6
Iron ore futures, 684
Irrational exuberance, 215, 696
Issue costs, 433
Issued and outstanding shares, 405
Issued but not outstanding stock, 405
Issue price, 427

J

J. D. Edwards & Company, 605
Jarrell, G., 487n
JCPenney, 83, 84
Jensen, Michael C., 466, 482n, 609n
Jinghua Yan, 210
Jobs, Steven, 423
Johnson, J., 516, 604n
Johnson, Ross, 607–608, 609
Johnson & Johnson, 83, 84, 189, 190, 191, 192, 350, 359, 385, 425
Jorwar, A. N., 434n
JPMorgan Chase, 40, 47, 175, 176, 431, 580
  dividend cut, 486, 487
Junior investors, 415
Junk bond market
  default rates, 608
  and Drexel Burnham Lambert, 610
  and takeover business, 608
Junk bonds, 46, 174–175, 411
Just-in-time systems, 573

K

Kahn, V. M., 566
Kaplan, S., 609
Kellogg, 336
Keown, A., 210
Kinko's, 4, 401
Kohlberg Kravis Roberts, RJR Nabisco LBO, 607–608, 609–610
Kolasinski, Adam, 357
Kozlowski, Dennis, 17
Kraft Foods, 592

L

L. A. Gear, 530
  bankruptcy, 532
  capital structure, 532
Labor costs, 541
Lamont, O. A., 611
Large-firm vs. small-firm stocks, 358
Lazard, 41
LBO; *see* Leveraged buyouts
Lease, 413
Leasing, 699
Lee, Dorothy K., 413
Legal capital, 481
Legal requirements, 18
Lehman Brothers, 8, 24, 25, 47
  bankruptcy, 460, 477, 549
  default by, 580
  repo agreements, 67
Level cash flows
  future value of annuities, 133–135
  valuing annuities, 129–133
  valuing perpetuities, 127–128
Leveraged buyouts, 93
  case, 616
  cash cow company targets, 609
  compared to other acquisitions, 607
  decline and recovery, 609–610
  definition, 607
  ending in bankruptcy, 609
  free-cash-flow theory, 609
  and incentives, 609
  junk bond market, 608
  management buyouts, 607
  private equity, 607
  RJR Nabisco, 607–608, 609–610
  and stakeholders, 609
  and taxes, 608–609
Leverage ratios
  cash coverage ratio, 94
  debt equity ratio, 93
  debt ratio, 93–94
  and equity financing, 95
  function, 92
  ignoring short-term debt, 93
  times interest earned ratio, 94
Levi Strauss & Company, 426
Liabilities
  on balance sheet, 54–57, 189
  book vs. market value, 57–58
  matching maturities, 529–530
Lie, E., 660
Life insurance companies, 20
Limited liability, 8, 10
Limited liability companies, 9–10
Limited liability partnerships, 9–10
Limited partnerships, 9
  venture capitalists, 425
Limit order book, 187
Line of credit, 545–546
Liquid assets, 54, 95–96

Liquidation
  creditor preference for, 477
  definition, 475
  versus reorganization, 476–477
Liquidation value, 190, 191
Liquid bonds, 175
Liquidity
  advantages of, 530n
  of assets, 95
  of cash holdings, 574
  corporate vs. government securities, 580
  corporate vs. Treasury bonds, 698
  definition, 44, 95
  explaining value of, 698
  measures of, 95–97
  of money market, 579
  provided by financial institutions, 44–45
  of structured investment vehicles, 95
Liquidity ratios
  cash ratio, 96–97
  current ratio, 96
  less desirable characteristics, 95
  net working capital to total assets, 96
  quick ratio, 96
Litigation
  bankruptcy as protection from, 477
  malpractice suits, 10
Live Nation, 703
Loan covenants, 463
Loans, amortizing, 132–133; *see also* Bank loans
Lochhead, Scott, 429n
Lock-box system, 574–575
Lockheed Corporation, 266–267, 302–303
Long-term bonds, 172
Long-term debt, 36
Long-term debt-equity ratio, 93
Long-term debt ratio, 93
  and sustainable growth rate, 98
Long-term finance, 399; *see also* Corporate finance
Long-term financial planning
  focus of, 504
  links to short-term planning
    advantage of liquidity, 530–531
    kinds of approaches, 529
    time horizons, 528
    total capital requirements, 528–530
Long-term financial planning decisions, 527
Long-term financing, 41
Long-term liabilities, 55, 58
Long-term loans
  repayment provisions, 410–411
Long-term Treasury bonds, 320
Long- vs. short-lived equipment choice, 235, 236–238

Loss carryback, 69
Loss of degree of freedom, 328n
Lotteries, 131
Lowe's, 19, 83, 100, 106

M

Machine tool manufacturers, market risk, 336
Macro risks; *see* Market risks
Madoff, Bernard, 15
Maintenance, 392
Majority voting, 407
Makkula, Mike, 32
Malkiel, Burton G., 212n
Malpractice suits, 10
Management
  of corporations, 603
  cost of mergers to, 600–601
  means of changing
    carve-outs, 610
    divestiture, 610
    leveraged buyouts, 607–610
    proxy contests, 603–604
    spin-offs, 610
    takeovers, 604–607
  as off-balance-sheet liability, 696–697
  replacing, 595–596
Management buyouts
  definition, 607
  payoff from incentives, 609
Managers
  adding value, 79
  agency problems, 16–19
  and asymmetric information, 464
  dishonest, 103
  eliminating conflicts of interest, 293
  ethics of value maximization, 14–15
  with free cash flow, 466
  threat of takeover, 612
  use of WACC, 371
  and value maximization, 16–19
  value of financial slack for, 465
  views of debt policy, 465–467
  views on dividends, 485
Manhattan Island purchase, 116
Manufacturing, flexible production facilities, 308
Manville Corporation, 477
Margin account, 676n
Marginal tax rates, 70
Margin requirement, 678
Marked to market, 678–679
Marketable securities, 531
Market anomalies
  earnings announcement puzzle, 212, 213
  new issue puzzle, 212–213
Market capitalization, 206
  definition, 81
  Federal Express, 188
  for selected companies, 84

Market for corporate control, 591,
    602–610
  agency costs, 603
  definition, 603
  and separation of ownership and
      management, 603
  ways of changing management
    divestitures, 610
    leveraged buyouts, 607–610
    proxy contests, 603–604
    takeovers, 604–607
Market index, 319
Market order, 186–187
Market portfolio, 323
  and CAPM, 354–359
  definition, 346
  expected rate of return,
      353–354
  market risk premium, 353–354
  mutual fund risks, 351–352
  risk and return, 352–359
  and security market line,
      355–356
Market price, 229
Market risk premium
  calculating, 353–354
  definition, 352
  measuring, 382
  for past century, 352
Market risks, 43, 692
  airlines, 336
  definition, 334
  machine tool manufacturers,
      336
  as macro risks, 336
  measuring
    betas, 346–349
    portfolio betas, 350–352
    and total risk, 350
  not eliminated by
      diversification, 346
  versus specific risks, 333–334,
      345
  spreadsheet solution, 348
Market-to-book ratio, 206
  definition, 83
  examples, 83
  for selected companies,
      191–192
Market value, 229
  basis of company cost of capital,
      376–377
  versus book value, 57–59,
      189–191
  in calculating WACC,
      380–381
  company examples, 46
  and debt ratios, 93
  of equity, 404
  excluded from balance
      sheet, 88
  fluctuations, 83
  impact of merger on, 597
  and intrinsic value, 696
  measure of capital structure,
      380–381

measuring, 81–84
  for selected companies, 189
Market value added
  definition, 81
  examples, 83
  measuring, 81–84
Market-value balance sheet, 58–59,
    205–206
Market vs. coupon rate, 164
Markowitz, Harry, 702
Mark-to-market accounting, 67
Marriott Corporation, bondholder
    problems, 413
Marriott International Inc., 413
Marsh, Paul R., 319, 320, 321, 324,
    325, 327, 328
Martin, K. J., 596
Marvel Entertainment, 703
Masonite, 609
Massachusetts, and Apple IPO,
    427n
Massachusetts Bay Colony, 24
MasterCard, 576
Masulis, Ronald W., 434n, 472
Matching maturities, 529–530
Maturities, 409–410
  of commercial paper, 548
  limited in money market,
      578–579
  matching, 529–530
Maturity date, 36
Maturity premium, 320
Maximizing value; see Value
    maximization
McCain, John, 37
McConnell, J. J., 596
McDonald's, 189, 192,
    201–202, 329, 350,
    359, 385, 524
McGuire, William W., 660
McNichols, Maureen F., 563–565
Mellon Financial Corporation,
    594
Memorex, 476
Merchant banks, 40n
Merck & Company, 554, 592
Mergers
  banking, 594
  benefits and costs, 610–612
    and deregulation, 611
    wave of 1990s, 610–611
  case, 616
  conglomerate, 593
  Daimler-Chrysler, 593
  definition, 598
  versus divestitures, 610
  dubious reasons for
    bootstrap game, 596–597
    diversification, 596
  evaluation of
    cash financing, 599–601
    stock financing, 601–602
    warnings on, 602
  explaining waves of, 697–698
  horizontal, 592
  LBOs, 607–610

mechanics of
  and antitrust law, 598–599
  form of acquisition, 598
  and popular opposition,
      598–599
  tender offer, 598
  pharmaceutical industry, 595
  and price-earnings ratio, 597
  questions preceding, 599–601
    cost to management, 600–601
    cost to shareholders, 600–601
    economic gain, 600
  recent, 591, 592
  RJR Nabisco, 24–25
  sensible motives for
    combining complementary
        resources, 595
    to create synergies, 593–594
    economics of vertical
        integration, 594–595
    economies of scale, 594
    eliminating inefficiencies,
        595–596
    use of surplus funds, 595
  takeovers, 604–607
  in U.S., 1962–2009, 591, 592
  vertical, 592
Merrill Lynch, 25, 41n, 47, 431,
    592
Merton, Robert, 655, 694, 695, 702
Michaely, R., 485
Microsoft Corporation, 19, 189,
    191, 329, 350, 359, 385,
    437, 445, 446, 480, 530
  cash dividend, 491–492
  founding of, 423
MidAmerica Energy, 279
Middle-of-the-road policy for
    financing, 529
Midyear cash flow convention,
    276n
Mikkelson, W. H., 434n
Milken, Michael, 610
Miller, Merton H., 446, 488, 693,
    696, 702
Minimum operating cash balance,
    541
Minuit, Peter, 116, 117
Mitchell, M., 611n
MM debt-irrelevance proposition,
    450
MM dividend-irrelevance
    proposition
  assumptions behind, 490–491
  description, 488–490
MM proposition I, 693
  cost of equity, 452
  definition, 450
  on shareholder risk, 450–451
  simplifying assumption, 447
  and value of the firm, 446–448
MM proposition II, 693
  debt-equity ratio, 453–454
  definition, 452
Modified accelerated cost recovery
    system, 278

Modified internal rate of
    return, 248
  with multiple rates of return,
      260
Modigliani, Franco, 446, 488,
    693, 696
Money; see also Time value of
    money
  greenbacks, 24
  in 17th century America, 24
Money management, 22
Money market, 36
  certificates of deposit, 579
  commercial paper, 579
  corporate vs. government
      securities, 580
  default risk, 580
  definition, 578
  fixed-income securities,
      578–579
  interest rates, 579
  limited maturities, 578–579
  liquidity of, 579
  recent market turmoil, 580
  repurchase agreements, 579
  Treasury bills, 579
  yields, 580
Moody's Investors Service Inc.,
    174, 411, 413, 563, 579
Moore, Gordon, 117
Morgan Stanley, 10, 21
Morrison, A. D., 16
Mortgage amortization, 132–133
Mortgage-backed securities, 47
  toxic, 48
Mortgage pass-through certificates,
    414–415
Mortgages, present value analysis,
    132–133
Motorola, 604
Mullins, D. W., 434n
Multiple cash flows
  future value, 124–125
  present value, 126–127
  spreadsheet solution, 128
Multiple discriminant
    analysis, 565
Multiple internal rate of returns,
    260
Multiple rates of return, 247–248
Municipal bonds, 174n
Murphy, T., 573n
Mutual funds, 22
  closed end, 38n, 696
  consistently successful, 212
  versus exchange traded
      funds, 44
  functions, 38–39
  holders of corporate bonds in
      2010, 42
  holdings of corporate equities,
      406
  holdings of equities in 2010, 42
  number of, 39
  open end, 38n
  risks, 351–352

Mutually exclusive projects,
    244–246
  with different outlays, 246
  internal rate of return rule for,
    259–260
Myers, S. C., 387n, 434n, 458n

N

Najluf, N. S., 434n
Nardelli, Robert, 19
NASDAQ, 35, 36, 186
  number of stocks traded, 319
NASDAQ Composite Index, 696
NASDAQ 100 index, 44
NASDAQ stock index, rise and
    decline of, 213
National Association of Security
    Dealers Automated
    Quotation system, 186n
National Semiconductor, 703
NBC Universal, 592, 703
Negative-risk assets, 332
Neiman Marcus, 106
Net asset value, 38n
Net common equity, 405–406
Net current assets, 55
Net income
  versus cash flow, 63
  and internal growth rate, 517
Net present value, 228, 377
  break-even point, 300
  calculating, 229, 276, 692
  definition, 229
  examples, 228–229
  financial calculator solution, 245
  to measure worth of project, 263
  negative, 265
  negative in accounting
      break-even analysis, 300
  new computer system, 232
  office block project, 230–231
  and opportunity cost of capital,
    229
  in profitability index, 248
  recognizing investment
      expenditures, 265
  and sensitivity analysis, 296
  steps in calculating, 232
  timing option, 307–308
Net present value break-even
    analysis, 300–301
Net present value profile, 241
  and IRR, 242–243
Net present value rule
  agreement with internal rate of
      return rule, 243
  to choose among projects
    investment timing decision,
      235–236
    long- vs. short-lived
        equipment, 236–238
    replacement of old
        equipment, 238–29

to choose between two projects,
    234
  definition, 229
  vs. payback rule, 239
  and rate of return rule, 241
  summary on, 250
  value of, 692
  valuing long-lived projects,
    230–234
Net working capital, 55, 65;
    see also Working capital
    entries
  definition, 96, 267, 533
  function of sales, 513–514
Net worth, 407
New issue puzzle, 212–213
Newmont Mining, 329, 332–333,
    350, 351, 359, 365, 385
New products
  development of, 6
  effect on existing products, 266
  investment in, 293
Newspage Corporation, 175
New York Mercantile Exchange,
    37, 45, 684
New York Stock Exchange, 8–9,
    11, 36, 185, 186
  changes since 2007, 35
  formation of, 24
  number of stocks traded, 319
  trading volume, 620
New York Stock Exchange
    Composite Index, 206–207
New York Stock Exchange stocks,
    357
No-dividend companies, 480
No-growth dividend discount
    model, 197
No-growth perpetuity, 197
Nominal cash flows, 139–141,
    269–270
Nominal cost of capital, 269–270
Nominal dollars, 141
Nominal interest rate, 141–142,
    172–174, 269
Nominal rate of return, 318
Nonconstant growth stocks
  estimating McDonald's value,
    201–202
  investment horizon, 201–202
  terminal value, 201
  valuation errors, 202
  value of dividends, 200–202
Nondiversifiable risks, 692
Non-profit organizations
  holdings of corporate equities,
    406
Normal growth, 330–332
Normal growth plan, 504
NPV; see Net present value entries
Numerical credit scoring
  FICO score, 563n
  financial ratios for, 563–565
  five Cs of credit, 563
  Z-score model, 565

O

Obama, Barack, 37
Off-balance-sheet assets and
    liabilities, 66–67
Olin Corporation, 679
One-at-a-time sensitivity analysis,
    297
Open account, 562
Open auction issue, 430–431
Open-end fund, 38n
Open-market repurchase, 482–483
Operating cash balance, 541
Operating cash flow, 275–276
  of cost-cutting projects,
    271–272
  dealing with depreciation, 272
  example, 273
  forecasting, 387–388
  formula, 271
Operating income
  after-tax, 85
  calculating, 87
  effect on earnings per share, 450
  in management buyouts, 609
  for selected companies, 84
Operating leverage, 303–305, 451n
  and project risk, 361
Operating profit margin, 90
Operating risk
  definition, 450
  effect of debt, 450–451
Opportunity cost
  in accounting break-even
      analysis, 300
  definition, 267
  of holding cash, 573
Opportunity cost of capital, 14, 31,
    46–47, 84, 229, 322, 359,
    692; see also Cost of
    capital
  additional, 515
  to discount future cash flows,
    263
  effect on shareholders, 373–374
  estimating, 263
  ignored by Lockheed, 302
  versus internal rate of return,
    243
  and project risk, 317
  relation to return, 240–241
Optimal capital structure,
    445, 459
Option(s)
  to abandon, 307
  considered in financial planning,
    505
  to expand
    decision tree, 306
    example, 305–306
Option ARM loan, 47n
Option premium, 646, 648
Options
  annual volume, 645
  backdating scandal, 660

calls and puts, 646–649
  on convertible bonds, 645
  on financial assets
    callable bonds, 661
    convertible bonds, 659–661
    executive stock options, 659
    warrants, 659
  payoff and profit, 650–651
  versus payoff from holding
      stock, 652
  protective put, 650
  put-call parity, 651
  on real assets, 657–658
  and risk characteristics of
      portfolio, 650
  for risk reduction, 674–675
  types traded, 645
Options market, 37–38
Option theory, 693–694
Option to abandon, 307, 658
Option to expand, 305–306, 658
Option-valuation models
  Black-Scholes model, 655, 657,
    659
  simple model, 656
Option values
  determinants, 652–655
  models for, 655–657
  upper and lower limits, 652
Oracle Corporation, 18–19, 480,
    659
  bid for PeopleSoft, 605–607
Orange, M., 516, 604n
Ordinary income, 70
Ordinary least squares regression,
    349n
Outputs of financial plan, 506
Outside directors, 407
Outsourcing vs. vertical
    integration, 595
Overconfidence, 215
Overhead costs, 268
Overpricing, 429
Over-the-counter market, 36
Overvalued stocks, 434

P

Pacific Capital Bancorp, 186
Pacific Gas & Electric, 409, 549
Page, Parry, 423
Palepu, K., 482n, 486, 611
Palm, 611
Pandora, Inc., 438
Partch, M. M., 434n
Partnership
  definition, 9
  types of, 9–10
  unlimited liability, 9
Par value
  of bonds, 160
  of common stock, 405
  of outstanding shares, 481
Paulson, John, 39n

Payback period, 239–240
  discounted, 239
  summary on, 250
Payback rule, 228
  advantage of simplicity, 240
  cutoff period, 239
  definition, 239
  length of payback periods,
      239–240
  problems with, 239
  reasons for using, 240
Pay lag, 582
Payment date, 481
Payment mechanism, 45
Payment systems
  checks, 574–575
  electronic funds transfer,
      576–578
  United States, 576
Payoff
  on hedging instruments, 671
  on options, 649, 650–561
Payoff diagram, 649
Payout policy, 479
  and capital budgeting, 487
  case, 499–500
  controversy
    assumptions behind MM
        proposition, 490–491
    effects of changes, 487–488
    MM dividend-irrelevance
        proposition, 488–490
  decisions on, 485–487
  and financing decisions, 487
  high vs. low, 491–493
  implication of tax rates, 493
  and investment decisions, 487
  managerial views, 485
  means used
    cash dividends, 480–481
    stock dividends, 481–482
    stock repurchase, 482–484
    stock splits, 482
  and overall cash flow, 490–491
  reasons for dividend value
      decrease, 492–493
  reasons for dividend value
      increase, 491–492
Payout ratio, 97
  definition, 203
Pecking order theory of capital
    structure
  asymmetric information, 464
  definition, 465
  external financing, 465
  internal financing, 465
Peets Coffee & Tea, 586
Penn Central Railroad, 24
Pension Benefit Guarantee
    Corporation, 475n
Pension funds
  definition and function,
      39–40
  holdings of corporate bonds in
      2010, 42

holdings of equities in 2010,
    42, 406
  monitors of company
      performance, 18
  not taxed, 70
Pension plans
  assets in 2010, 40
  defined-benefit, 39n, 40n
  defined-contribution, 39
Pensions, 413
Pentagon Law of Large Projects, 234
PeopleSoft, 605–607
PepsiCo, 189, 192, 473, 599
Percentage capital gain, 318
Percentage of sales models
  assumptions in, 513–514
  balancing item, 507–508
  complications, 513–514
  definition, 507
Percentage return, 318
Percentages squared, 326
Performance measures, 85
Permanent working capital
    requirement, 530n
Perpetuities
  definition, 127
  no-growth, 197
  preferred stock dividends as, 378
  present value, 198
  valuing, 127–128
Perpetuity formula, 383–384,
    455–456
Personal tax
  average rate, 70
  on capital gains, 70
  on dividend income, 70
  marginal rates, 70
  on ordinary income, 70
Petersen, M. A., 571n
Pfizer Inc., 7, 329, 350, 359, 369,
    385, 473, 592, 667
Pharmaceutical industry mergers,
    595
Pinkerton, J., 210
Pinkowitz, L., 530–531
Planet Hollywood, 476
Planning horizon, 504
Plowback ratio, 97, 518
  definition, 203
Plug; see Balancing item
Poison pill, 605–607
Ponzi, Charles, 15n
Ponzi scheme, 15
Portfolio betas, 350–352
Portfolio risk
  and economic scenarios,
      330–332
  example, 332–333
  macro risks, 336
Portfolios
  diversification, 329–330
  floating-rate, 682
  performance of, 320–322
  risk characteristics and options,
      650

Positive-NPV projects, 694–695
  and discount rate, 306
  plausibility, 294
  what-if questions, 294–295
Postpetition creditors, 477
Postretirment benefits, 413
Powerball lottery, 131, 137
Power Computing Corporation, 32
Prediction markets, 37
Preferred stock, 378
  convertible, 416
  definition, 407
  dividends, 408
  expected rate of return, 383–384
  floating-rate, 408
  lack of voting privileges, 408
  and net worth, 407
  tax advantage, 408
Premium bond, 167
  price changes, 170
Prepackaged bankruptcies, 475n
Present value
  of annuity, 129–130, 136–137
  calculating, 117–123
  of cash flow, 264
  of cost of machinery, 236
  definition, 117
  determination questions,
      694–695
  discounted cash flow
      calculation, 118
  discount factor, 119
  effect of interest rates, 165
  examples, 120–121
  financial calculator solution,
      121
  finding interest rates, 123–124
  formula, 118
  and future value, 117–118
  in future value of annuity, 134
  as intrinsic value, 192
  investment timing decision, 235
  of lottery winnings, 131
  mortgage payments, 132–133
  of multiple cash flows, 126–127,
      128
  new computer system, 232
  office block project, 230–231
  of perpetuities, 127–128, 198
  projected cash flows, 300–301
  of real cash payments, 143
  and risk, 229
  spreadsheet solution, 122–123,
      233
  of stream of future cash,
      126–127
  of Treasury bonds, 162, 163
  using compound interest, 118
Present value of growth
    opportunities, 204–205
  on market-value balance sheet,
      206
Present value tables, 119, A-3, A-4
Present value tax shield, 455
Presidential futures prices, 37

Price(s)
  of assets, 692
  of commodities, 679
  corporate vs. Treasury bonds, 698
  of gasoline, 141
  with inflation, 139–141
Price-earnings multiple, 188
Price-earnings ratio, 188
  and company prospects, 205
  and mergers, 597
  for selected companies,
      191–192
Primary issue, 35–36
Primary market, 35–36
  definition, 186
Primary offerings, 186, 426
Prime rate, 509
Principal (par value), 160
Principals, 694
Principles-based accounting, 68
Private equity financing, 425
Privately owned businesses, 426
Private placement, 412
  advantage, 434–435
  definition, 434
  and Rule 144a (SED), 434
Probabilities, beliefs about, 215
Probability theory, 215
Procter & Gamble, 204
  debt issue, 414
Production cycle, 534
Production to order, 573
Product life cycle, 98
Product markets, competitive
    advantages in, 400
Products, sales of new vs. existing,
    266
Professional corporations, 10
Profit
  versus cash flow, 60–63,
      264–265
  cash vs. accrual accounting,
      61–62
  from channel stuffing, 66
  and depreciation, 60–61
  determining factors, 190
  economic value added, 84
  expected, 567
  from options, 650–651
  taxation of, 69
Profitability, 79
Profitability index, 228, 248–250
  with capital rationing, 249
  definition, 248
  and hard rationing, 249
  pitfalls, 249
  positive net present value, 248
  and soft rationing, 249
  summary on, 250
Profitability ratios
  asset turnover ratio, 88
  inventory turnover, 88–89
  receivables turnover, 89–90
  return on assets, 87
  return on equity, 87

Profit diagram, 649
Profit margin, 90
   versus inventory turnover, 91
   low vs. high, 90–91
   for selected industries, 92
Profit maximization
   and credit decision, 569
   not well-defined, 12–13
Profit per dollar of assets, 85
Pro forma balance sheet, 507, 508
Pro forma income statement, 507
Pro formas, 506
   second-stage, 509–510
Project analysis
   break-even analysis
      accounting, 298–300
      net present value, 300–303
      operating leverage, 303–305
   case, 315
   investment process
      analyzing competitive
         advantage, 294
      capital budget, 292
      consistent forecasts, 293
      eliminating conflicts of
         interest, 293
      project authorization,
         292–293
      reducing forecast bias,
         293–294
   real options
      flexible production facilities,
         308
      option to abandon, 307
      option to expand, 305–307
      timing, 307–308
   what-if questions, 291, 294–298
      scenario analysis, 297–298
      sensitivity analysis, 295–297
Project authorization information
   capacity expansion, 293
   maintenance cost reduction, 293
   new product investments, 293
   outlays required, 292–293
Project betas, 694–695
Project cash flows, 263
   calculating net present value,
      276
   capital investment, 271
   cash flow analysis, 274–276
   changes in working capital,
      273–274
   dealing with depreciation, 272,
      277–279
   and financing, 270
   forecasting working capital, 277
   identifying, 264–268
      allocated overhead costs, 268
      incremental cash flows,
         266–268
      terminal cash flow, 268
   mistakes in forecasting, 268
   operating cash flow, 271–273
   salvage value, 279
   spreadsheet solution, 280
   with zero net present value, 380

Project cost of capital
   estimating, 360–361
   and project risk, 360
Project risk
   and capital budgeting,
      359–362
      versus company risk,
         359–360
      project cost of capital,
         360–362
   common perceptions of, 362
   and company cost of capital,
      359–360
   contemplating
      big risks as diversifiable,
         335
      market risks as macro risks,
         336
      risks as measurable, 336–337
   determinants
      earnings variability,
         361–362
      operating leverage, 361
   determination questions,
      694–695
   and diversification
      assets vs. portfolio risk,
         329–330
      market vs. specific risk,
         333–334
   estimating cost of capital,
      322–323
   with fear of default, 463
   fudge factors in discount rate,
      362
   measuring
      benchmarks, 324
      calculating variance, 327
      standard deviation, 324–327
      variance, 324–327
      variation in stock returns,
         327–329
   opportunity cost of capital, 317
   and security market line, 361
Property, plant, and equipment, 54
Prospectus
   definition, 427
   example, 440–443
Protective covenants
   definition, 412
   and Marriott Corporation, 413
Protective put, 650
Proxy access, 604
Proxy contest/fight, 407
   costs of, 603–604
   definition, 603
   at PeopleSoft, 606
Public companies, 8–9
Public Company Accounting
      Oversight Board, 68, 103
Public placement, 412
Puerto Rico, 120
Put-call parity, 651
Put options
   definition, 647
   payoff diagram, 649

profit diagram, 649
protective put, 650
for risk reduction, 674–675
selling, 647–649
Puttable bonds, 661

Q

QQQs, 44
QUBES, 44
Quick ratio, 96
Qwest Communications, 67

R

Rajan, R. G., 571n
Rajgopel, S., 66
Random walk theory, 208–209,
   693
Rate of return rule, 241
Rates of return, 14; *see also*
      Accounting rates of return;
      Expected rate of return
   for bonds, 168–171
   calculated for bonds, 166–168
   in capital market history,
      319–322
   common stock, 1900–2010, 321
   common stock fluctuations, 321
   and cost of capital, 46–47, 317
   and current yield, 167
   with debt-equity mix, 375–376
   definition, 169
   differing, 371
   estimating, 322–323
   estimating cost of capital from
      history, 322–323
   Ford Motor Company, 365
   Geothermal example, 372
   government bonds, 1900–2010,
      321
   histogram, 324, 325
   on market portfolio, 346–352
   maturity premium, 320
   multiple, 247–248
   Newmont Mining, 365
   nominal, 318
   and opportunity cost of capital,
      47
   percentage return, 318
   real, 318
   relation to opportunity cost of
      capital, 240–241
   specific vs. market risk, 345
   Treasury bills, 1900–2010, 321
   Treasury bills in 1981,
      323–323
   Treasury bills in 2011, 323
   variable, 330
   Walt Disney Company, 365
   versus yield to maturity,
      167–169
Raw materials, dependence on
      single source, 308

Real assets, 38
   definition, 7
   risky vs. safe, 694–695
Real cash flows, 139–141
Real dollars, 141
Real estate bubble, 213
Real estate futures, 684
Real interest rate, 142, 172–174,
   269
Real options
   Allegheny Corporation, 658
   definition, 307, 657
   flexible production facilities,
      308
   option to abandon, 307, 658
   option to expand, 305–307,
      658
   for risk management, 673
   timing, 307–308
Real rate of return, 318
Real-time, gross settlement system,
   577n
Rebalancing capital structure, 456
Receivables, 89
   aging schedule, 569–570
   liquidity of, 530n
Receivables turnover ratio, 89–90
Recession, 330–332
Recession of 2007–2009, 48
Record date, 481
Registration statement, 427
Regression line, 349n
Regular dividends, 480
Regulatory requirements, 18
Reinhardt, U. E., 303n
Reinsurance, 43n
Reinvestment, 33
Relaxed approach to financing,
   529, 530
Rent, contingent, 303
Reorganization
   definition, 475
   versus liquidation, 476–477
   procedures, 475–476
Repayment provisions, 410–411
Replacement problem, 235,
   238–239
Repurchase agreements
   Lehman Brothers, 67
   in money market, 579
Reputation, and financial
      transactions, 15
Required external financing,
   515–516
Required return, 371, 692
   calculating, 374–375
Reserve accounts, misuse of, 66
Residual income, 84, 537
Resources, complementary, 595
Restrictive financing policy, 529
Restructuring
   and cost of capital, 452
   effect on capital structure,
      447–448
   by Marriott Corporation, 413
   and operating income, 450

Retained earnings, 56n, 60
    definition, 405
Retirement savings, 135
Retrenchment plan, 504
Return
    actual vs. expected, 358
    effect of debt, 450
    on Treasury bonds, 161–162
Return on assets
    and credit scoring, 563
    definition, 87
    Du Pont formula, 90–91
    at Home Depot, 87
    Home Depot vs. Lowe's,
        100–101
    profit margin, 90
    for selected industries, 92
Return on capital
    calculating, 85
    definition, 85
    for Home Depot, 85–86
    for selected companies, 84
Return on equity, 517, 518
    definition, 87
    and financial leverage, 94–95
    for Home Depot, 87
    for software firms, 98
Revenue recognition, 66
Revenues, examples of, 5
Rhie, Jung-Wu, 563–565
RHI Entertainment, 186
Rich, Jeffrey, 660
Rieker, M., 487
Rights issue, 431n, 432
Risk(s)
    asset vs. portfolio, 330–333
    attitudes toward, 214
    in cost of capital, 317
    diversifiable, 335, 692
    hedging, 671
    incremental, 332
    market, 692
    market vs. specific, 333–334
    measurable, 336–337
    of New York Stock Exchange
        stocks, 334
    not eliminated by hedging, 672
    and operating leverage, 305
    ordinary meaning of, 362
    and present value, 229
    selection of, 671
    of various securities, 371
Risk and return
    CAPM, 354–359, 692, 695
    effect of borrowing on,
        450–451
    least and most risky
        investments, 352
    market risk premium, 352–354
    security market line, 355–356
    statistical problems, 695
Risk-averse, 12
Risk-free rate, 354
    measuring, 382
Risk-free return on Treasury bills,
    353

Risk management
    derivatives, 673
    evidence on, 673
    with forward contracts,
        680–681
    with futures contracts, 676–680
    innovations in derivatives,
        683–684
    with options, 674–675
    problems from derivatives,
        684–685
    reasons for hedging, 672–673
    with swaps, 681–683
    value of tools for, 699
Risk premium
    and beta, 353–354
    in CAPM, 356–357
    CAPM prediction, 357
    on equally weighted index,
        357n
    future, 323
    and security market line, 356
    United States, 323, 324
Risk reduction; see also Risk
        management
    with options, 674–675
    versus speculation, 684
Risk-return trade-off, 330
Risk tolerant, 12
Risk transfer, 43–44
Ritter, Jay, 212n, 428n, 429n
Ritz-Carlton Hotel, 593
RJR Nabisco LBO, 24–25, 413,
    607–608, 609–610, 612
Road shows, 427
Rockefeller, John D., 702
Rodriguez, Albert, 21
Roll, R., 482n
Ruback, R., 611
Rules-based accounting, 68

S

Safeway, 593
Sales
    conditional, 562
    credit agreements, 562
    of new vs. existing products,
        266
    on open accounts, 562
Sales department vs. collection
        department, 570
Sales-to-assets ratio, 88
Sales volume, 298
    break-even, 299
    break-even point, 300
Salvage value, 274, 279
Sarbanes-Oxley Act, 18, 103, 427,
    610
    cost and burden of, 68
Savings
    flow in commercial banks, 40
    pooled in hedge funds, 39
    pooled in mutual funds, 38–39
    pooled in pension funds, 39–40

Savings banks, 40n
Scenario analysis, 505
    definition, 297
    example, 298
    and simulation analysis,
        297–298
Schiller, Robert, 215n
Scholes, Myron, 655, 694, 702
Schrefflen, R., 573n
Schwartz, S. L., 213
Schwed, Fred, 702
Sealed Air Corporation, 445
    capital structure changes,
        466–467
Seasoned offering, 431–432
    direct costs, 429
Secondary market, 36
    definition, 186
Secondary offering, 426
Secondary transactions, 36
Second-stage financing, 425
Second-stage pro formas, 509–510
Secured debt, 411
Secured loans
    accounts receivable financing,
        547
    definition, 547
    hazards of, 548
    inventory financing, 547–548
Securities, 7; see also Bonds;
        Common stock; Corporate
        bonds; Preferred stock
    commercial paper, 36
    electronic trading, 35
    fixed-income, 578–579
    mortgage-backed, 47
    private placement, 434–435
    relative safety or risk, 320
    shelf registration, 433
    short-term, 36
    at true value, 400
    valuation difficulties, 214
    wide choice for investors, 319
Securities and Exchange
        Commission, 16, 18, 548
    financial statements filed with,
        654
    and International Financial
        Reporting Standards, 68
    on private placement, 434
    and proxy access, 604
    registration statements, 427
    Rule 144a, 434
Security market line
    definition, 355–356
    and project acceptance, 361
Security prices, 692–693
Self-liquidating loans, 546
Selling, Thomas I., 92
Semistrong-form efficiency, 211,
    693
Senior investors, 415
Sensitivity analysis
    definition, 295
    fixed costs, 295
    limitations, 297

net present value, 296
    one-at-a-time, 297
    for project analysis, 295–296
    unknown unknowns, 296
    value of information, 297
    variable costs, 295
Separation of ownership and
        control
    and agency problems, 16–19
    and agency theory, 694
    definition, 9
    downside of, 9
Shareholder risk, 450–451
Shareholders, 7, 8, 404–405
    and agency theory, 694
    and bankruptcy, 477
    blockholders, 18–19
    versus bondholders, 463
    and control of firms, 603
    cost of mergers to, 600–601
    delegation of decision making,
        11–12
    dividend reinvestment plan,
        479
    effect of financial distress, 462
    effect of leverage, 451
    effect of opportunity cost of
        capital, 373–374
    and ethics of value
        maximization, 14–16
    income vs. debtholders, 92
    investments in Home Depot,
        81–83
    large number of, 9
    no-growth stock, 197
    ownership of corporations,
        406–407
    in PeopleSoft proxy fight,
        605–606
    pressures on managers, 19
    proxy contests, 603–604
    rates of return for, 375–376
    return on equity, 87
    rights issues, 432
    risk-averse, 12
    risk tolerant, 12
    and stock dividends, 481–482
    and stock splits, 482
    use of financial statements, 53
    value maximization goal,
        11–14
    voting procedures
        majority or cumulative
            voting, 407
        proxy contests, 407
Shareholders' equity
    on balance sheet, 55–56
    book vs. market value, 58
    and interest tax shield, 456
Shareholder value
    created at Home Depot, 86
    and financing decisions, 80–81
    and investment decisions, 80–81
    maximizing, 79
Shark repellent, 606
Sharpe, William F., 345, 702

Shearson Lehman Hutton, 607
Shelf registration
    advantages, 433
    definition, 433
    financial manager use of, 433
Shivakumar, L., 213
Shortage costs, 536–537
Short sellers, 39
Short-term bonds, 172
Short-term debt, 93
Short-term financial planning, 504
    case, 556–557
    cash budgeting, 539–543
    decisions, 527
    links to long-term planning
        amount of liquidity, 530–531
        time horizons, 528
        total capital requirements,
            528–530
    sources of financing
        bank loans, 545–548
        commercial paper, 548–549
    tracing changes in cash and
        working capital, 537–539
    working capital, 531–537
Short-term financing
    line of credit, 545–546
    sources
        commercial paper, 548–549
        regular bank loans, 545–546
        secured loans, 547–548
Short-term financing plan
    evaluation, 544–545
    example, 543–545
Short-term securities, 36, 559
    versus cash, 573
Sidel, R., 487
Sight draft, 562
Simple interest, 114
Simulation analysis, 297–298
Sinking fund, 410
Skinner, Douglas, 485n
Small Business Administration,
    475n
Small businesses, credit scoring,
    566
Small-firm vs. large-firm stocks,
    358
Smith, Fred, 462
Soft rationing, 249
Sole proprietorships, 9
Solera, Sherry, 21
Southern California Edison, 549
Special dividends, 480
Specialist in stock trading, 186
Specialist monitoring, 18
Special-purpose entities, Enron,
    103, 413–414
Specific risk, 334
    versus market risk, 333–334,
        345
Speculation, 684
Speculative bubbles, 696, 698
Speculative grade bonds, 174–175
Spinning, 431

Spin-offs, 610
    by 3Com, 611
Spot price, 679
Spread, 160, 176, 427
Spreadsheets
    annuity present value, 137
    Black-Scholes option pricing
        model, 657
    bond valuation, 170–171
    for calculating risk, 347
    cash budget, 540
    for financial planning, 511
    future value calculation,
        122–123
    interest rates, 124
    multiple cash flows, 128
    present value calculation,
        122–123
    present value of cash flows, 233
    short-term financing plan,
        542–544
Squared deviations, 326
Stafford, E., 611n
Stakeholders
    definition, 17
    effect of financial distress, 462
    in LBOs, 609
    relation to companies, 17–18
Standard and Poor's, 174–175,
    329, 411, 563, 579
Standard and Poor's
    Composite/500 Index,
    43–44, 319, 346, 348,
    351–352
Standard and Poor's Depository
    Receipts, 43–44
Standard deviation, 334
    calculating, 326
    Consolidated Edison, 346
    definition, 325
    Dow Chemical, 346
    of returns, 332
    selected common stocks, 329
Standard deviation of returns, 328
Starbucks, 18, 330, 350, 359, 385
Start-ups
    business plan, 424
    capital requirements, 423
    Federal Express, 4
    first-stage financing, 424
    initial public offerings,
        426–430
    second-stage financing, 425
    venture capital for, 424–425
State laws
    blue-sky laws, 427
    dividend restrictions, 481
Statement of account, 570
Statement of cash flow
    definition, 63
    free cash flow, 65
    of Home Depot, 63–64
    items on, 63–65
Statement of shareholders' equity,
    54n

Staunton, Mike, 320, 321, 324,
    325, 327, 328
Stern Stewart & Company, 84, 537
Stertz, Bradley A., 593n
Stewart, G. Bennett, III, 537n
Stickney, Clyde P., 92
Stock, 7; see also Common stock;
        Preferred stock
    aggressive, 346
    amount traded in exchanges,
        319
    blockholders, 18–19
    defensive, 346
    exercise price, 646–647
    factors affecting returns, 346
    measuring variations in returns,
        327–329
    mergers financed by, 601–602
    payoff from holding, 652
    primary issue, 35–36
    primary offerings, 186
    in secondary market, 186
    secondary transactions, 36
    total market value, 42n
Stockbroking firms, 22
Stock dividends, 481–482
Stock exchanges
    electronic communications
        networks, 186
    limit order book, 187
    NASDAQ, 186
    New York Stock Exchange, 186
    number of stocks traded, 319
Stockholders, 8; see also
        Shareholder entries
Stock market, 31
    consolidation, 33
    crash of 1929, 24, 329
    crash of 2007–2009, 24, 322
    decline in 2002, 322
    decline in 2008, 14
    effects of macro uncertainties,
        336–337
    efficient market hypothesis,
        211–212
    as equity market, 36
    functions, 35–36
    fundamental analysts, 210
    historical performance, 319–322
    market anomalies
        earnings announcement
            puzzle, 212, 213
        new issue puzzle, 212–213
    and market risk, 43
    primary, 186
    primary market, 35–36
    reaction to stock issues,
        433–434
    secondary, 186
    secondary market, 36
    technical analysts, 206
    volatility in 1900–2010, 328
Stock market bubbles, 213–214
Stock market listings, 187–189
Stock options, 426, 660

Stock price(s)
    Amazon vs. Con Ed, 190–191
    announcement effect, 486
    Apple Inc., 423
    and asymmetric information,
        464
    and behavioral finance,
        214–215
    bid-ask spread, 187
    book vs. market value, 189–191
    and call options, 646
    and company values, 46
    effect of acquisition news, 611
    effect of new issues, 433–434
    effect of repurchase on, 484
    efficient market hypothesis,
        211–212
    ex-dividend, 481
    fundamental analysis, 210
    Google Inc., 423
    Home Depot, 81
    and intrinsic value, 192–194
    liquidation value, 190
    Microsoft, 423
    and option valuation models,
        655–657
    overpricing, 429
    par value, 405
    and put options, 647
    random walk, 208–209
    reactions to news, 210
    reasons for knowing, 185
    and rights issues, 432
    in selling calls or puts, 647–649
    speculative bubbles, 696
    technical analysis, 206–210
    trading range, 482n
    underpricing, 427–429
    and value of call option,
        652–653
    yardstick for performance, 426
Stock price quotations, 187–189
Stock repurchase, 405
    by Apple Inc., 33
    compared to dividends,
        483–484
    definition, 482
    examples, 480
    information content, 486–487
    means of
        auction, 483
        direct negotiation, 483
        greenmail transactions, 483
        open-market repurchase,
            482–483
        tender offer, 483
    and share valuation, 484
    in U.S. 1980–2008, 480
Stock splits, 482
Storage costs, 571
Straight-line depreciation,
    275–276
Strategic plans
    and capital budgeting, 504
    purpose, 504

Strategy matched with capital budget, 292
Stream of cash flows, 124
Strips
    definition, 171–172
    measure of yield curve, 171–172
    yield in May 2010, 172
Strong-form efficiency, 211, 693
Structured investment vehicles, 95
Stuyvesant, Peter, 24
Subordinated debt, 411
Subprime mortgage market, 698
Subprime mortgages, 25, 47, 66, 415
    mark-to-market accounting, 67
Sunbeam Corporation, 66
Sunk costs, ignoring, 266–267
Sun Life Financial, 592
Sun Microsystems, 480
Surplus funds, merger as use for, 595
Sustainable growth rate, 203–204, 518
    calculating, 97
    definition, 97–98
    variability in, 98
Swaps
    counterparties, 681
    credit-default, 683–684
    currency swaps, 682–683
    definition, 681
    interest rate swaps, 681–682
    for risk reduction, 681–683
Sweep programs, 573–574
Synergies
    elusive, 594
    mergers to create, 593–594
Systematic risk, 334

T

Takeovers, 19
    case, 616
    effect of threat on managers, 612
    free-cash-flow theory, 609
    hostile, 604–607
    Oracle and PeopleSoft, 605–607
    poison pills, 605–607
    by proxy contests, 603–604
    shark repellent, 606
    tender offer, 604
    unsuccessful, 604
Tangible assets, 3, 6
    on balance sheet, 54
    easy to sell, 307
    heavy investment in, 227
    investment in, 113
Target dividend, 485
Target payout ratio, 485
Target Stores, 536, 624
Taxable income, 70

Taxation
    advantage for partnerships, 9
    capital gains, 70, 493
    capital structure and, 454–458
    and changes in capital structure, 386–387
    corporate tax, 68–69
    and cost of capital, 371
    depreciation deduction, 272
    depreciation tax shield, 277–279
    disadvantage for corporations, 9
    disadvantages in borrowing, 458
    and dividend policy, 492, 493
    double taxation, 9n
    on individual income, 70
    interest tax shield, 455–456
    and LBOs, 608–609
    and municipal bonds, 174n
    personal tax, 69–70
    and preferred stock dividends, 408
    and WACC, 377
Tax payments, 541
Tax rates
    on corporations, 68
    personal taxes, 70
Tax shield, 85n; *see also* Depreciation tax shield; Interest tax shield
Technical analysis, 206–210
Technical analysts, 206
TED spread, 546
Tender offer, 483, 604
    definition, 598
10K reports, 54
10Q reports, 54
Terminal cash flow vs. incremental cash flow, 268
Terminal value, 201
Terms lag, 582
Terms of sale
    cash before delivery, 560
    cash on delivery, 560
    credit sales, 560–561
    definition, 560
    due lag, 582
    end-of-month sales, 561
    implicit annual interest rate, 561
    pay lag, 582
    terms lag, 582
    trade credit interest rates, 561
Tesla Motors, 440n
Texas Instruments, 703
Thaler, R. H., 611
3 Com, 611
Ticketmaster, 703
Tiffany & Company, 536
Tight money policy, 163
Time deposits, 531
Time draft, 562

Time horizon
    of investors, 194–197
    long-term financial planning, 504
    long- vs. short-term financial planning, 528
Time line for future value, 125
Times interest earned ratio, 94
Time value of money
    annuity due, 136–137
    definition, 117
    effective annual interest rate, 138–139
    future value of annuity, 133–135
    future values, 114–117
    and inflation
        and interest rates, 141–142
        real vs. nominal calculations, 144
        real vs. nominal cash flows, 139–141
        valuing real cash payments, 143–144
    level cash flows, 127–135
    multiple cash flows, 124–126, 128
    present values, 114–124
Time Warner, Inc., 175, 610
Timing option, 307–308
TIPS; *see* Treasury Inflation Protected Securities
Total capitalization, 84
    for selected companies, 84
Total capital requirements
    finding best level of
        advantages of liquidity, 530
        matching maturities, 529–530
        permanent working capital requirement, 530
    for long- vs. short-term financing, 528–530
    seasonal variations, 528
Total project cash flow, 276
Total return
    on bonds, 167
    yield to maturity as measure of, 168
Total risk and market risk, 350
Trade acceptance, 562
Trade credit, 531
    credit scoring for, 563–565
    definition, 560
    source of funds, 570
Trade-off theory of capital structure, 459, 463–464
Trading range, 482n
Transaction costs, 573
Transactions
    effect on balance sheet, 62–63
    effect on income statement, 62–63
Transparency, 103
Trans Union, 563n
Trans World Airlines (TWA), 476

Treasurer, 10
Treasury bills, 531
    historical returns, 325
    least risky investment, 352
    in money market, 579
    performance since 1900, 320–322
    rate of return 1981, 322–323
    rate of return 2011, 323
    safety of, 320
    standard deviation of returns, 328
Treasury bonds, 159
    auction in 2003, 160
    auction sales, 431
    compared to corporate bonds, 174
    historical returns, 325
    interest rates, 161–166
    performance since 1900, 320–322
    price fluctuations, 320
    prices vs. corporate bonds, 698
    rate of return vs. yield to maturity, 168–169
    real interest rate, 172–173
    standard deviation of returns, 328
    strips, 171–172
    trading of, 126
    yield to maturity, 167
Treasury Department, purchase of toxic mortgage-backed securities, 48
Treasury Inflation Protected Securities, 25, 173
Treasury stock, 405
Triple-A bonds, 411
Tropicana, 609
Troubled Asset Relief Program, 487
True value, 400
Trust, in financial transactions, 15
Truth-in-lending laws, 138n
Tyco International, 17

U

Underpricing, 430
    definition, 427
    disadvantage, 428
    and investor returns, 429
    reasons for, 427–428
Underwriters
    best efforts basis, 427
    and costs of general cash offer, 433
    definition, 427
    firm commitment, 427
    largest in U.S., 431
    road shows, 427
    services performed by, 431
    spinning by, 431
    warrants for, 659

Underwriters' spread, 427, 430
Unfunded debt, 409
Union Pacific, 6, 13–14
    dividend dates, 481
    dividend reinvestment plan, 479
    investment and financing
        decisions, 5
    stock repurchase, 482
UnitedHealth Group Inc., 660
United States
    dividends/stock repurchase
        1980–2008, 480
    dot-com bubble, 213
    inflation rate 1900–2010, 140
    labeling corporations, 8n
    mergers 1962–2009, 591, 592
    payment systems, 576
    real estate bubble, 213
    risk premium, 323, 324
    tax system, 9n
Universal Studios, 516, 604
Unlimited liability, 9
Unocal, 599
US Airways Group Inc., 8n
U.S. Robotics, 611

V

VA Linux, 431
Valuation by comparables,
    191–192, 202
Valuation errors, 202
Value; see also Future value;
        Present value
    of call option at expiration, 646
    created with financing decisions,
        400
    of entire businesses, 387–389
    of no-growth stock, 197
    of put option at expiration, 647
    of real cash payments,
        143–144
Value added
    and cost of capital, 84
    financial ratios to understand,
        80–81
    by managers, 79
    from real options, 306
Value Line Investment Survey, 98n
Value maximization, 3
    ethics of, 14–16
    goal of shareholders, 11–14
    and investment trade-off, 13–14
    and managers
        agency problems, 16–19
        and blockholders, 18
        and board of directors, 18
        and compensation plans,
            18–19
        legal/regulatory requirements,
            18
        shareholder pressure, 19
        specialist monitoring, 18
        and stakeholders, 17–18
        takeovers, 19

opportunity cost of capital, 14
    and profit maximization, 12–13
Value of the firm
    bases of, 465–466
    and capital structure, 446–454,
        697
    components, 93
    definition, 79
    destroying, 79
    and human assets, 593
    impact of payout decisions,
        489
    and liquidation value, 190
    market capitalization, 81–84
    market-to-book ratio, 83
    market vs. asset values,
        696–697
    MM proposition I, 446–448
Value stocks, 358
Vanguard Explorer Fund, 38, 351
Vanguard 500 Index, 43
Vanguard Index fund, 354
Vanguard Index Trust 500, 352
Vanguard Total Stock Market
        index, 44
Van Kampen Merritt, 413
Variable costs, 295
    linked to sales, 303
    and operating leverage,
        303–305
Variables
    in scenario analysis, 297–298
    in sensitivity analysis, 297
    trade-off between, 303
Variance, 324–327
    calculating, 327
    definition, 325
Venture capital, 33
    and business plan, 424
    definition, 424
    first-stage financing, 424
    second-stage financing, 425
Venture capital firms, 423,
    425–426
Venture capitalists, 4, 5
Verizon Communications, 227,
    504, 505
Vertical integration
    economics of, 594–595
    versus outsourcing, 595
Vertical merger, 592
Visa International initial public
        offering, 430
Vlasic, Bill, 593n
Voting procedures
    with common stock, 407
    lacking with preferred stock,
        408
Vulture funds, 39

W

WACC; see Weighted average cost
        of capital
Wachovia, 25, 592, 703

Wall Street Journal, 160, 185, 199,
    202, 204, 660
    stock market listings, 187
Wall Street Walk, 19
Walmart, 6, 11, 83, 84, 85, 189,
    192, 329, 350, 359, 385,
    456, 480, 573, 624
    investment and financing
        decisions, 5
Walmart strategy, 91
Walt Disney Company, 329,
    350, 359, 365, 385, 604,
    703
Warrants, 415, 659
Washington Mutual, 404
Weak-form efficiency, 211, 693
Webb, Susan, 21
Weighted average cost of capital,
    84n, 85n, 373–380
    accuracy of, 379–380
    calculating
        expected returns on bonds,
            382
        expected returns on common
            stock, 382–383
        expected returns on preferred
            stock, 383–384
        summary, 384
        using market value,
            380–381
    calculating company cost of
        capital, 374–377
    case, 394–396
    corporate tax and debt policy,
        456–458
    definition, 377
    Dow Chemical, 377–378
    Ford Motor Company, 384n
    formula, 377
    Geothermal Corporation,
        379–380
    interpreting
        common mistakes, 385–386
        corporate taxes, 387
        effect on returns with capital
            structure changes,
            386–387
        when unusable, 384–385
    managerial use of, 371
    measuring capital structure,
        380–381
    multiple sources of capital,
        378
    with preferred stock, 378
    real-company, 384
    for selected companies, 385
    and taxes, 377–378
    valuing entire businesses,
        387–389
Weiss, L. A., 460n
Wells-Fargo, 586, 592, 703
Wendy's International, 524
What-if questions, 291, 505
    on cash balances, 543
    crucial to capital budgeting,
        295

function of, 294
    scenario analysis, 297–298
    sensitivity analysis,
        295–297
Whole Foods Market, 599
Wickes Furniture, 609
Wildcat oil wells, 335
Wild Oats Markets, 599
Wilhelm, W. J., Jr., 16
Williams Act of 1968, 605n
Williamson, R., 530–531
Wilshire 5000 Market Index,
    211
Window dressing, 67
Wind power project, 279
Winner's curse, 428
Wire transfer, 577–578
Working capital, 559
    additional investment in,
        268
    and cash conversion cycle,
        533–536
    cash flow from changes in,
        273–274
    changes in, 276
    components
        changing with cycle of
            operations, 533–534
        current assets, 531–532
        current liabilities, 532–533
    forecasting, 277
    mistakes in forecasting, 268
    permanent requirements,
        530n
    recognizing investment in,
        267–268
    tracing changes in, 537–539
Working capital management,
    536
    accounts receivable credit
        policy, 560–571
    case, 588
    cash management, 573–578
    inventory management,
        571–573
    investing idle cash, 578–580
    and money market, 578–580
Working capital trade-off
    carrying costs, 536
    costs and benefits of investment
        in, 536–537
    shortage costs, 536–537
Workout, 475
WorldCom, 18, 67, 175, 427
Wozniak, Steven, 423
Wruck, K. H., 466, 532
Wurgler, J., 482n
Wyeth, 592
Wynn Resorts, 586

X

Xerox Corporation, 66, 82,
    83, 84
XTO Energy, 592

Y

Yahoo!, 19, 187
Yahoo! Finance, 56
Yield
 on corporate bonds, 142, 175
 on money market investments
  corporate vs. government
   securities, 580
  default risk, 580
  in recent market turmoil, 580

short- vs. long-term bonds, 172
on TIPS in 2010, 173
Yield curve
 definition, 171
 nominal vs. real interest rate,
  172–174
 upward-sloping, 172
Yield spread, Treasury vs.
  corporate bonds, 175–176
Yield to maturity, 160, 161
 and current yield, 167

definition, 167
measure of total return
 interest rate fluctuations,
  168
 trial and error calculation,
  168
promised vs. expected, 177
versus rate of return,
  168–169
selected corporate bonds, 175
for Treasury bonds, 167

Z

Zack's, 201n
Zero-coupon bond, 120n, 177
Zero net present value, 242, 247
 and project cash flows, 380
Zero-stage investment, 424
Zero-sum game, hedging as, 672
Zhao Quanshui, 429n
Ziemba, W. T., 213
Z-score model, 565